This book is to be returned on or before
the last date stamped below.

23. NOV 79	22. NOV '80	STORE
06. FEB 80	30. SEP 81	02. AUG 84
22. FEB 80	19 JAN 82	**01.** MAR 85
	23. MAR 82	14. JUN 85
15. OCT '80	14. JUL 82	11. JUL 85
		Sutton 30/07
01. NOV '80	04. SEP 82	10 SEP 1985
	21. DEC 82	20. JUN 86
	01. FEB 84	
	22. FEB 84	10. APR 87

The Law of Social Security

The Law of
Social
Security

by A. I. Ogus, B.C.L., M.A.
Senior Research Fellow,
Centre for Socio-Legal Studies, Oxford;
Rowntree Research Fellow,
Wolfson College, Oxford

and E. M. Barendt, B.C.L., M.A.
of Gray's Inn, Barrister;
Fellow of St. Catherine's College, Oxford

With a Foreword by
the Rt. Hon. Lord Scarman, O.B.E.
Lord of Appeal in Ordinary

London
Butterworths
1978

England	Butterworth & Co (Publishers) Ltd
London	88 Kingsway WC2B 6AB
Australia	Butterworths Pty Ltd
Sydney	586 Pacific Highway, Chatswood, NSW 2067
	Also at Melbourne, Brisbane, Adelaide and Perth
Canada	Butterworth & Co (Canada) Ltd
Toronto	2265 Midland Avenue, Scarborough M1P 4S1
New Zealand	Butterworths of New Zealand Ltd
Wellington	77–85 Customhouse Quay
South Africa	Butterworth & Co (South Africa) (Pty) Ltd
Durban	152/154 Gale Street
USA	Butterworth (Publishers) Inc
Boston	19 Cummings Park, Woburn, Mass 01801

ISBN—Casebound   0 406 63355 x
Limp   0 406 63356 8   WAZ

Printed by J. W. Arrowsmith Ltd, Bristol.

Foreword
by the Rt. Hon. Lord Scarman, OBE, Lord of Appeal in Ordinary

Social security is now the subject of rights and duties. Inevitably, therefore, it is a legal subject. Anthony Ogus and Eric Barendt by this work have committed themselves, without compromise or condition, to this basic proposition: and I commend their work to all who understand the need of a legal approach to a legal subject. But they do not – nor I for that matter – under-rate the value of the contributions other disciplines make to the development of a coherent and well-grounded national system of social security; and, of course, no lawyer can understand, or help forward, the law unless he is capable of an inter-disciplinary approach.

I expect this book to become one of the indispensable text-books of the law. Certainly an authoritative, and independent, work is needed. At present, tribunals and practitioners have to rely heavily on the material produced, but not invariably published, by the Department of Health and Social Security. The department does a fine job: but it is not, and never has been, the office of a government department to declare or interpret the law. If law is to be administered justly, the independence, as well as the skills, of the lawyer must be mobilised. *Ogus and Barendt* will become, I hope, a name as familiar to the lawyer as Chitty, Salmond, Buckley, and Simon.

Finally, this work gives us an opportunity of measuring the extent to which our social security law satisfies the obligations accepted by the United Kingdom as a signatory of the European Social Charter 1961 and the International Covenant on Economic, Social, and Cultural Rights 1966. If any doubt should continue to be entertained that social security has to be part and parcel of English law, our international obligations are the answer.

I commend this book to lawyers primarily – but also to members of the other disciplines concerned with the behaviour of man in society; to politicians; and to all who are concerned to ensure that humanity and compassion are secured by law as well as by generosity.

Scarman

Preface

The growth of interest in social security law, both of teachers and practitioners, has been rapid in the last few years. The process has not been free from controversy: opinions differ both as to the academic merit of the subject and to the preferred method of presentation. Some contend that the social security system has not sufficient intellectual weight for the serious student of law; others view the educational objective more in terms of fostering the arithmetic ability to calculate the entitlement of a given individual to benefit rather than of providing any analysis of the principles of the system as a whole. A third approach stresses the desirability of covering, within one university course, broad and diverse areas of the welfare system including not only social security but also housing, education and legal services. We do not adopt these perspectives. The book has been written from a conviction that social security should take its place alongside other, more traditional, legal subjects as fully worthy of critical study, and its unity and technical character make it, in our view, more suitable for this purpose than the necessarily vague outlines of 'welfare' or 'poverty' law.

Legal education has tended in the past to concentrate on law as a method of determining relationships between individuals. While public law – the relationship between the state and the individual – has not been neglected, attention has been focussed for the most part on the formal or constitutional nature of the relationship rather than on its substance. The emphasis has been on the individual's ability to invoke judicial controls over unlawful executive activity rather than on the content of the rights conferred on the individual by the state within the proper exercise of its powers. While social security law raises problems of the constitutional limits of executive powers, it also lays down in considerable detail rules which materially affect the lives of all members of the community. As a body of law, it consists of a complex network of primary and subordinate legislation and case-law (notably Commissioners' decisions, though in some areas judicial rulings are not unimportant), the scrutiny of which provides an excellent training in the handling of a variety of legal instruments. As a reflection of competing social and economic policies, it reveals the way in which a very important branch of state activity has evolved, and how general objectives and strategies are translated into particular principles and rules of law.

In contrast to their counterparts in most other countries, the British universities have accepted 'social administration' as an intellectual discipline in its own right, though necessarily it has relied on other disciplines such as economics, history and sociology for its tools of analysis. Social security, in the context of general social policy, has featured prominently in its publications. This work does not attempt to compete with such studies. Quite apart from the limits to our own competence, we have not the space here both to expound a complex area of law and to subject the policies on which it is based to rigorous interdisciplinary analysis. At the same time, we have sought to explain the law in terms of its policy background and the insights offered by other disciplines, as we believe that the functioning of a social security system cannot be understood without reference to the objectives and values which it incorporates.

This goal has, with other factors, created the problem of preserving a satisfactory balance between historical and policy background, general principle and technical rules. In writing this book we have had in mind not only law students but also practitioners and other professional groups with an interest in this area. To accomplish these various objectives, we have adopted a compromise solution. We have inset not only, as is customary in legal texts, quotations and case summaries, but also technical rules which do not raise issues of legal principle.

As we explain in the opening chapter, the term 'social security' is open to several interpretations, and the scope of this book proceeds from no precise and unchallengeable definition. We have decided to confine ourselves to an account of those financial benefits which are administered by the Department of Health and Social Security. This means that, on the one hand, we do not treat the National Health Service, the various housing allowances, or redundancy payments, but on the other hand we do include the war pensions and industrial injury schemes.

Social security is an area of law which is notoriously subject to frequent and major changes. In the preparation of this text we have been relatively fortunate. The major reconstruction of the system which took place during the period 1973 to 1975 has now been completed. Nevertheless, inevitably there has been a regular flow of new regulations and decisions, as well as committee reports and policy statements. Of those occurring since the manuscript went to press, we have been able to incorporate some in the text, while more important developments have been summarised in the Appendix. We state the law as we understand it to be on 6 April 1978. The rates of benefits and contributions which we mention are those in force on that date.

The original drafts of chapters 1–4, 6 (Parts One and Three), 8, 16 and most of 10 were prepared by A. I. Ogus, and those of 5, 6 (Part Two), 7, 9, 10 (Parts Three and Eight) and 11–15 by E. M. Barendt. The work is a joint product in the sense that both authors accept responsibility for the whole.

We wish to thank Lord Scarman for generously agreeing to write the foreword and the many who offered us their expert advice and assistance. We are particularly grateful to the officials of the Department of Health and Social Security who painstakingly and often forthrightly criticised our manuscript and saved us from countless errors; they, of course, in no way are responsible for the views expressed in the book. We are also indebted to Tony French who assisted in research on chapter 11; Helen Beynon who checked references to certain Parliamentary papers; David Bentley, Tony Bradley, Peter Corfield, Stephen Cretney, Tony Lynes, Mavis Maclean, Walter Merricks, Martin Partington and David Yardley who read and commented on various sections; the staff of Butterworths who compiled the Tables and Index; and finally Audrey Hiscock, Vera Kastner, Angela Palmer, Lorna Pollock and others who courageously and cheerfully typed the manuscript in its various stages. The Centre for Socio-Legal Studies, Oxford and the Max-Planck Projektgruppe für Sozialrecht, Munich provided inspiration from, respectively, an interdisciplinary and comparative standpoint.

A.I.O.
E.M.B.

Oxford
April 1978

Contents

Abbreviations

Statutes

CBA	Child Benefit Act
FAA	Family Allowances Act
FANIA	Family Allowances and National Insurance Act
FISA	Family Income Supplements Act
IIDA	Industrial Injuries and Diseases (Old Cases) Act
NAA	National Assistance Act
NHIA	National Health Insurance Act
NIA	National Insurance Act
NI(II)A	National Insurance (Industrial Injuries) Act
NISBA	National Insurance and Supplement Benefit Act
SBA	Supplementary Benefits Act
SSA	Social Security Act
SSBA	Social Security Benefits Act
SS(MP)A	Social Security (Miscellaneous Provisions) Act
SSPA	Social Security Pensions Act
UIA	Unemployment Insurance Act
WCA	Workmen's Compensation Act

Books

Atiyah	*Accidents, Compensation and the Law* (2nd edn)
Calvert	*Social Security Law* (2nd edn)
Dupeyroux	*Droit de la Sécurité Sociale* (6th edn)
George	*Social Security: Beveridge and After* (1968)
Handbook	Supplementary Benefits Commission, *Supplementary Benefits Handbook* (1977)
Harris	*William Beveridge* (1977)
Kaim-Caudle	*Comparative Social Policy and Social Security* (1973)
Lynes	*The Penguin Guide to Supplementary Benefits* (3rd edn)
Micklethwait	*The National Insurance Commissioners* (1976)
Walley	*Social Security: Another British Failure?* (1972)

Reports and Papers

Beveridge	Social Insurance and Allied Services (1942), Cmd. 6404.
Finer	Report of the Committee on One-Parent Families (1974), Cmnd. 5629.
Fisher	Report of the Committee on Abuse of Social Security Benefits (1973), Cmnd. 5228.
McCarthy	Report of the Royal Commission of Inquiry: Social Security in New Zealand (1972).
Pearson	Report of the Royal Commission on Civil Liability and Compensation for Personal Injury, vol. I, (1978), Cmnd. 7054-I.
Social Insurance, Part I	White Paper: Social Insurance, Part I (1944), Cmd. 6550.
Social Insurance, Part II	White Paper: Social Insurance, Part II, Workmen's Compensation (1944), Cmd. 6551.

Chronological Table of Statutes

References in this Table to "Statutes" are to Halsbury's Statutes of England (Third Edition) showing the volume and page at which the annotated text of the Act will be found.

Chronological Table of Statutory Instruments

List of Cases

Note on citation of National Insurance Commissioner Decisions

Reported decisions of the National Insurance Commissioners provide a most important source of social security law. There has been a standard method for citing these decisions since 1951. It starts with the prefix 'R', indicating that the case is reported. There then follows in parenthesis the series initial, denoting the particular social security benefit involved in the case. Hitherto there have been eight series:

- (A) Attendance allowance
- (F) Family allowances and child benefit
- (G) General – miscellaneous benefits (maternity benefit, widow's benefit, guardian's allowance, child's special allowance, invalid care allowance and death grant)
- (I) Industrial injuries benefits
- (M) Mobility allowance
- (P) Retirement pensions
- (S) Sickness and invalidity benefits
- (U) Unemployment benefit

After the series initial, the number and (after an oblique stroke) the year of the case follow. For example, $R(P)$ $9/55$ refers to the ninth reported retirement pensions case in 1955, and $R(I)$ $12/75$ refers to the twelfth reported decision on industrial injuries benefits in 1975. The decisions are published individually by HMSO, and then bound every four years. Industrial injuries cases are bound in separate volumes.

Numbered decisions of the Commissioners are not published, but may be read at the Commissioners' offices (see page 631). A few of these decisions are discussed in this book. They are identified by reference to two letters ('C' standing for 'Commissioner', and the relevant series letter), followed by the appropriate number and year. Thus, CG $17/69$ refers to the seventeenth numbered case in 1969 concerning one of the miscellaneous benefits, e.g., maternity, widow's benefit.

Before 1951 a reported case was referred to simply by its number and series initial, with the addition of the suffix 'K' or 'KL'. For both numbered decisions, and reported decisions up to the end of 1950, the letter 'S' or 'W' is added after the 'C' to denote a Scottish or a Welsh case. For example, CS $11/49$ (KL) refers to the eleventh English decision of the Commissioner on sickness benefit during 1949, a case which has been reported; *CSU 14/48* (*KL*) refers to the fourteenth Scottish case on unemployment benefit in 1948 – and a decision which has been reported. Now a reported decision merely indicates in the heading whether it is a Scottish or a Welsh case.

Some reference is made in this book to decisions of the Northern Ireland Commissioners. Such decisions are cited in much the same way as British cases, though the number and year precede the series initial. These initials also differ from those used in citing British decisions. They are –

(AA)	Attendance allowance
(DG)	Death grant
(FA)	Family allowances
(II)	Industrial injuries benefits
(IVB)	Invalidity benefits
(MB)	Maternity benefit
(NCIP)	Non-contributory invalidity pension
(P)	Retirement pensions, widow's benefit, guardian's allowance, child's special allowance
(SB)	Sickness benefit
(UB)	Unemployment benefit

Thus, *R 1/71* (*FA*) refers to the first reported Northern Ireland decision during 1971 on family allowances. Before 1960 the letter 'R' was omitted.

Table of Decisions

Decisions of the National Insurance Commissioner

Decisions of the Northern Ireland National Insurance Commissioner

1 Social Security and Social Policy

Part one. Objectives of Social Security

A. General

For Beveridge, the aim of social security was the fulfilment of need:

> 'to abolish want by ensuring that every citizen willing to serve according to his powers has at all times an income sufficient to meet his responsibilities.'[1]

Others have laid stress on the redistributive function:

> 'to decrease inequalities in the distribution of incomes and command-over-resources-over-life set by the economic system.'[2]

A third perspective emphasises social integration. The New Zealand Royal Commission on Social Security recognised that an important goal of the system should be to

> 'ensure . . . that everyone is able to enjoy a standard of living much like that of the rest of the community, and thus is able to feel a sense of participation in and belonging to the community.'[3]

It is apparent from these statements that it is impossible to divorce the objectives of social security from political ideologies and values, and the starting point for an account of the policy issues involved in the system must be an outline of such ideologies and values as have had an influence on its development.

B. Ideologies

There are, of course, risks inherent in over-simplifying political creeds and inevitably any one current system of social security reflects a multitude of influences. Yet the isolation of three fundamentally different ideologies and the attitude of each to social welfare should help to clarify the choice of objectives in social security as well as the historical and political background of the British system.

---

1. Para. 444.
2. Titmuss *Commitment to Welfare* (2nd edn), p. 65.

3. *McCarthy*, p. 65.

i) Repressive individualism

In the period of emergent industrialism and capitalism, welfare was to be achieved through personal effort.[4] Each individual was considered free to maximise his own expectations through activities and transactions unfettered by state intervention. There was thought to be work available for anyone who wanted it, and destitution was therefore seen as resulting not from social or economic forces but rather from personal failings, a view bolstered by the Puritan ethic of work.[5] Moreover, poverty constituted not only a deviation from moral discipline, but also a threat to civil order, as it was typically associated with crime and political unrest.[6] In this context relief of the poor was necessarily repressive and punitive: a generous system of welfare would have encouraged more idleness and therefore more social chaos. The poor law perfectly reflected this ideology,[7] and it is nowhere better epitomised than in the workhouse system, established on a widespread basis in the 18th century, and administered nationally from 1834.[8] Relief was granted to able-bodied persons only if they were willing to subject themselves to the rigours of the workhouse, where life was intentionally made harsh and repellant. The guiding principle was the so-called doctrine of 'less eligibility'. In the words of the Poor Law Commissioners,

> 'the first and most essential of all conditions is that the situation of the individual relieved shall not be made really or apparently so eligible as the situation of the independent labourer of the lowest class.'[9]

Some mitigation of the doctrine was granted only where it was patent that the individual's plight arose from accident rather than from personal inaptitude, thus for the blind, the crippled and the aged.[10]

ii) Liberal individualism

The second ideology may have grown out of a similar industrial system but the political climate had changed. There had arisen new humanitarian ideals, associated first with the philanthropist movement, and subsequently more generally with the middle classes who had benefited most from the industrial and commercial expansion.[11] However, as the economy became more than ever dependent on an efficient labour force, it became appreciated that social welfare conferred on the working population might improve rather than hinder productivity.[12] Both movements inspired the

4. Tawney *Religion and the Rise of Capitalism* (1921), pp. 253–273.
5. Ibid., at pp. 218–249.
6. Fraser *Evolution of the British Welfare State* (1973), pp. 28–31.
7. The classic study is Webb and Webb *History of English Local Government* (1927), vol. 7. See also Marshall *The Old Poor Law*, 1795–1834 (1968), and Rose *The English Poor Law*, 1780–1930 (1971).
8. *Webb and Webb*, ante n.7, at pp. 215–264.
9. Report of Royal Commission on Poor Law (1834), Cd. 2728, para. 228.
10. The so-called system of 'out-relief': see Bruce *The Coming of the Welfare State* (4th edn), pp. 117–128.
11. Gilbert *The Evolution of National Insurance in Great Britain* (1966), pp. 22–27.
12. Rimlinger *Welfare Policy and Industrialization in Europe, America and Russia* (1971), pp. 36–38.

massive welfare measures taken in the 19th century to improve health and environmental conditions.[13] Such improvements, however, in no way provided direct financial help to the poorer sections of the community. The advent of the labour movement as a political force stimulated progress in this direction. The trade unions were able to press for higher wages and, more significantly for our purposes, the friendly societies and industrial assurance societies offered some collective insurance protection against hazards to the breadwinner, notably those of premature death and funeral expenses.[14] This system of alleviating need accorded well with the laissez-faire doctrine of welfare through individual initiative: it maintained the traditional virtues of thrift and foresight; and its cost did not impede economic progress.[15] The limitations of this method of social welfare were obvious: it did not cover the large variety of hazards to which the earner was subject, and the lowest wage-earners were unable to afford contributions.[16]

The ideology which emerged of liberal individualism, or welfare capitalism, reaffirmed faith in the competitive market system as the moral and just way to prosperity: it aimed to reward endeavour with material gain and continued to rest primarily on the responsibility of the individual freely to determine his own style and level of living.[17] But at the same time it was recognised that there would be some who would fall victims to the free play of market forces. In the first place, the industrial processes themselves created dangers and thereby imposed costs on workers. For such directly caused losses as injuries or death resulting from employment risks, private law was the suitable instrument for compensation, and though at the time the law of tort was hindered in its remedial capacity by the doctrine of common employment and the need affirmatively to prove fault,[18] the solution was found in the quasi-tortious Workmen's Compensation Act 1897,[19] which based liability on a no-fault principle. To reconcile the scheme with the need for continuous economic expansion and the fact that the employer might be morally innocent, it nevertheless limited compensation to generally no more than one half of the workman's lost earnings.[20] Outside this relatively narrow area the principle according to which the burden was to be assumed by the activity creating the risk was inoperative: other social hazards could not be so directly connected with particular enterprises. Thus for a second group whose state of need could not be attributed to personal failings, typically the unemployed and the sick, another solution had to be found. The natural resort was the insurance

13. See generally, *Bruce*, ante n.10, at pp. 128–153.
14. See generally, Gosden *The Friendly Societies in England 1815–1875* (1961): and *Self Help: Voluntary Associations in the Nineteenth Century* (1973).
15. George *Social Security and Society* (1973), pp. 17–18; Pinker *Social Theory and Social Policy* (1971), pp. 90–91.
16. See Majority Report of the Royal Commission on the Poor Law (1909), Cd. 4499, p. 536.
17. The classic modern restatements are Friedman *Capitalism and Freedom* (1962), and Hayek *The Constitution of Liberty* (1960). See generally George and Wilding *Ideology and Social Welfare* (1976), chap. 2.
18. *Atiyah*, pp. 316–317; Hanes *The First British Workmen's Compensation Act* (1968).
19. Post, pp. 266–267.
20. Post, p. 266.

principle which would engender the traditional virtue of individual responsibility and investment of personal resources, and would not be far removed from the typical market economy device of the 'exchange' transaction.[1] The notion that such risks were something which the community as a whole should bear received partial recognition by the sharing of insurance costs between the employer (who would pass it on in the form of prices) and the employee; but in order that individual initiative should not be stifled and to discourage idleness, benefit would be paid at only a survival level.[2] This was the scheme adopted for unemployment and sickness under the National Insurance Act 1911. It was also applied by analogy in 1925 to those risks against which individuals might be expected to provide – old age or premature death – but which, in the case of low-earners, typically went unprotected.[3] In such cases, the compulsory insurance of manual workers and low-paid non-manual workers could be justified within the liberal philosophy on grounds of paternalism.

There was left a hard core of poverty cases outside these two categories, either because the individual's contribution record was inadequate, or because the duration of the interruption of employment was excessive. The cases might be undeserving and in 1909 the Majority of the Royal Commission on the Poor Law could still argue that it was necessary to treat them as a distinct group of society whose predicament was, in some way, attributable to defects in moral character.[4] But humanitarian sentiments were allowed to prevail. A means-tested financial benefit had already in 1908 been introduced to protect the aged from the poor law,[5] and a similar device, in the form of unemployment assistance, was adopted for the vast numbers of unemployed who during the inter-war period had exhausted their right to insurance benefit.[6]

The pattern established by the end of the 1930s – social insurance covering the major causes of income loss and conferring benefit at a flat-rate survival level, combined with a scheme of residual means-tested assistance for those remaining – was in its essence left unaltered by the programme instituted in 1946–47 and inspired by the Beveridge Report. His primary aims were to make the insurance scheme more comprehensive (it was extended to groups hitherto excluded, and the coverage of work accidents and diseases was transferred from the individual employer's responsibility), to substitute 'subsistence' for 'survival' as the minimum level, to unify its administration, but, most important of all, to rationalise it in terms of the liberal ideology. He was eager to recognise the freedom of the individual to pursue his own welfare above the subsistence level.

'Social security must be achieved by cooperation between the State and the individual. . . . The State in organising security should not stifle incentive, opportunity, responsibility; in establishing a national minimum, it should leave room and

1. *Pinker*, ante n.15, at pp. 135–144.
2. *Bruce*, ante n.10, at pp. 198–199.
3. Widows', Orphans' and Old Age Contributory Pensions Act, 1925.
4. Ante n.16, at p. 643.
5. Old Age Pensions Act 1908: post, p. 190.
6. The major measure was the Unemployment Insurance Act 1934. See post, pp. 80 and 477

encouragement for voluntary action by each individual to provide more than that minimum for himself and his family.'[7]

As will be seen, the specific programme sponsored by Beveridge failed, but the ideology inherent in it continues to exert a considerable influence on contemporary social policy. This is illustrated in material terms by an enormous growth in occupational coverage of sickness and retirement.[8] In political terms, it is matched by a vocal group from the right which sees our present 'economic and spiritual malaise' as the result of irresponsibility and waste engendered by the welfare state, and which argues for less state intervention and a return to the Victorian virtues of duty, order and efficiency.[9]

iii) Collectivism
The third ideology takes as its starting point a rejection of the market system as the method of achieving a just distribution of social welfare.[10] The notion that the state should provide merely a minimum amount sufficient for subsistence purposes through some residual institutional machinery is discredited. The social services, and social security in particular, should be concerned to remedy inequities resulting from the market economy; they should therefore incorporate as a primary objective the redistribution of resources from the rich to the poor.[11] While 'need' remains the typical criterion for determining to whom this programme is to be directed, it is given a broader perspective. No longer is it to be confined to describe those who are 'poor' in the sense that their resources are insufficient to maintain themselves according to some objective standard of minimum subsistence. Need is, instead, seen as something which is relative to the general prosperity and level of earnings, and therefore reflects the grosser inequalities in a society at any given time.[12] Welfare is to be 'universalist' in that it is to be conferred on all those within broadly based social categories (the aged, the sick, the disabled, large families) without the socially divisive and stigma-producing means test.[13] Indeed, some exponents of the ideology look beyond the more immediate aim of income support to the remoter and necessarily vaguer goal of social integration, enabling all persons fully to participate in and belong to the community.[14]

While this last aspect has remained at best a tacit element in British social policy since the Second World War, the collectivist objectives as a whole are fully evident in the family allowances scheme[15] introduced in

7. Para. 9.
8. E.g. the number of male workers in the private sector covered by such schemes grew from 4.33 million in 1956 to 8.1 million in 1967: Government Actuary, Occupational Pension Schemes, First and Third Surveys.
9. E.g. ed. Boyson Down With the Poor (1971).
10. Tawney The Acquisitive Society (1931), chaps. 4–5; Titmuss Commitment to Welfare (2nd edn), chaps. 12–13.
11. Titmuss, ibid., chap. 16.
12. See post, p. 22 and the references cited there.
13. Titmuss, ante n.10, chap. 10; Townsend Sociology and Social Policy (1975), pp. 149–153.
14. E.g. Townsend, ibid., chap. 2; McCarthy, p. 65.
15. See, generally, Hall, Land, Parker and Webb Change, Choice and Conflict in Social Policy (1975).

1945, and, outside the social security field, in the National Health Service and the education programme. Even so, the universalist and redistributional features were to become ambivalent. The real value of family allowances was allowed to decline, and it was only in the late 1960s and 1970s that there was renewed pressure for a significant degree of state family endowment.[16] Within the health and educational fields, there continues to be great scope for privately financed facilities. For the purposes of the present book, the conflict between the individualist and the collectivist approach to welfare has taken its sharpest form over the relative roles of state and occupational schemes in the provision for retirement. The huge growth in group and other forms of private coverage, itself a result of the low level of benefit offered by the flat-rate (and even later the graduated) national insurance scheme, was regarded as socially divisive by many arguing from a collectivist perspective.[17] Many of the occupational schemes did not correspond to Beveridge's model of voluntary and individual initiative based on freedom of choice, since they were often compulsory and offered few alternatives.[18] At the same time, they tended to discriminate against bad risks, who might be unable to obtain appropriate coverage, and against manual workers who, unlike their clerical and managerial counterparts, would probably achieve their optimal earning level at an early stage in their working life, and who would thereby suffer if, as was typically the case, the basis of the earnings-related pension was the earnings-level immediately before retirement.[19] The Conservative plan of integrating the occupational with the state approach by allowing the latter to play only a residual role[20] was unacceptable to the Wilson government of 1974, and when the new earnings-related scheme was introduced a year later, it offered a more equal form of partnership between the two: the state pension, when fully operative, would include a substantial earnings-related element, but individuals were given the ability to opt instead for an occupational scheme which satisfied certain conditions.[1]

Collectivist influences may be seen at work in the new non-contributory and non-means tested benefits for the disabled (introduced in the period 1975–77)[2] but in this field too there is considerable interplay and overlap between public and private provision. Of particular significance are the relationships between sickness benefit and occupational sick-pay[3] and between industrial and non-industrial disability benefits and common law damages.[4]

The relative lack of discussion of the social integration objective has been attributed by some to what is regarded as a developing political and ideological consensus.[5] The phenomenon, it is argued, is common to affluent industrial societies and is an inevitable consequence of working

16. E.g. ed. Bull *Family Poverty* (2nd edn), and post, p. 448.
17. Titmuss *Social Policy* (1974), chap. 7; *Townsend*, ante n.13, chap. 19.
18. *Titmuss*, ante n.17, at p. 94.
19. Ibid., at p. 98.
20. White Paper *Strategy for Pensions*

(1971), Cmnd. 4755; post, p. 194.
1. Post, pp. 223–227.
2. Post, pp. 167–187.
3. Post, p. 148.
4. Post, p. 270.
5. George *Social Security and Society* (1973), pp. 29–32.

class and trade union satisfaction with a capitalist system from which they have derived a proportionately increasing share of its resources. On the other hand, the intellectual left continues to stress that social security, as presently constituted, does little more than remove the worst excesses of the capitalist system, and has no impact on the fundamental inequalities which exist within our society.[6]

c. Values

i) General
Some of the most important social, political and economic values, such as freedom and individual responsibility or equality and community responsibility, are closely associated with the ideologies described above. There are, however, others which are not necessarily identifiable with any particular ideology and yet which exert to a greater or lesser extent an influence on social security legislation.

ii) Demographic aims
There are two distinct objectives which may be referred to as demographic and with which a social security system may be concerned. The first relates to the size of the population. Of course, one of the effects of adequate financial provision for the aged is to increase the longevity of life and thus the population as a whole.[7] The welfare of the aged is so obviously a *sine qua non* of social security, that the problem does not call for discussion. In some countries the level of family endowment is thought to have a significant impact on the birth rate and in this sense social security has been regarded as an instrument of demographic policy.[8] Undeniably it played an important role in the introduction of family allowances in Britain.[9] In the recent discussions of family endowment, however, demographic issues have been relatively neglected.[10]

The second demographic notion, that of the mobility of labour, has featured more prominently in recent British social policy.[11] On the one hand, the legislation has been concerned to encourage persons to acquire new occupational techniques when they become redundant either because of natural labour wastage or because of their own physical disabilities. An individual's contribution record is maintained and his right to benefit preserved during periods of retraining or rehabilitation,[12] and perhaps the chief motivation for the introduction in 1966 of earnings-related supple-

6. E.g., Kincaid *Poverty and Equality in Britain* (1973); Jordan *Poor Parents* (1974).
7. *Dupeyroux*, pp. 191–198.
8. *Kaim-Caudle*, pp. 18–21; Wynn *Family Policy* (1972), pp. 291, 312. For the relatively higher allowances granted in most other EEC countries see Commission of the European Communities, *Comparative Tables of the Social Security Systems* (9th edn), Table X-1.
9. Hall, Land, Parker and Webb *Change, Choice and Conflict in Social Policy* (1975), pp. 170–174.
10. But see *Walley* at pp. 183–187, and *Wynn*, ante n.8, loc. cit.
11. See generally ed. Bartholomew *Manpower Planning* (1976).
12. Post, pp. 72–73.

ment to unemployment benefit was the perceived need to soften the blow of unemployment and thus to encourage labour mobility.[13] On the other hand, a recipient of unemployment benefit may be disqualified if after a substantial period, usually six months, he refuses an offer of a suitable position in another district.[14] Much of the international provision in the social security field has been designed to encourage the mobility of labour from one state to another. The prime example is the legislation emanating from the European Economic Communities.[15]

iii) The family

On a superficial analysis it may appear as if the social security system serves to undermine the integrity of the family unit. In an historical sense, it is true that originally support by other family members was the first and sometimes the only refuge from destitution,[16] and that this function has to a considerable extent been superseded by state financial provision. But while dependence on remoter family relationships may, to some extent, have diminished in importance,[17] the legal interdependence of the inner family unit has in fact increased and is in no way overridden by the social security system which intervenes to replace maintenance obligations only when they remain unfulfilled.[18] The other argument turns on the extent of support for natural, as opposed to legal, family relationships. It is said that recognition of 'illicit' relationships acts as an incentive to marital break-down.[19] It must be conceded that for some, but by no means all, purposes, social security has regard to the consequences of such a relationship rather than the legal family as the basic unit. This occurs, for example, in the case of the means-tested benefits,[20] child benefits[1] and dependants' increases to personal benefits,[2] but in other instances *de facto* relationships are ignored: a woman living with a man has no title to widow's benefit should he die, and cannot rely on his contributions to her own retirement pension; she will be the object of a dependant's increase to his benefit only if she is caring for a child.[3]

There is little evidence to suggest that such state support as exists for *de facto* families acts as an incentive to marriage breakdown.[4] Even if it does, the consequent evil has to be weighed against the competing desire to protect the welfare of children by not forcing couples to continue to cohabit when a marriage has already disintegrated, and by recognising new obligations that may arise from alternative, if illicit, relationships.[5] Whether for the purposes of social security, the 'family' is that recognised by the law generally or a broader concept, it is indisputable that its

13. Post, p. 425.
14. Post, pp. 116–119.
15. Post, chap. 16.
16. Eekelaar *Family Security and Family Breakdown* (1971), pp. 15–19.
17. Schweinitz *England's Road to Social Security* (1943), pp. 223–225.
18. See generally *Finer*, Part 4, and post, pp. 539–547.
19. The argument is stated and repudiated in Friedmann *Law in a Changing Society* (2nd edn), pp. 287–289. See

also *Finer*, para. 2.7.
20. Post, pp. 487–559.
1. Post, p. 460.
2. Post, p. 388.
3. Post, p. 388.
4. Cf., *Finer*, pp. 6–18.
5. The issue has been very fully discussed in the context of divorce legislation: see Cretney *Principles of Family Law* (2nd edn), pp. 79–83, and the references there cited.

economic welfare constitutes one of the primary objectives of the system. This is evident not only from the attempts to make child benefit and family income supplement underwrite intra-family maintenance, but also from the way in which, in sharp contrast to that of some other countries, British law has traditionally concentrated its income maintenance programme on family needs rather than earnings replacement.[6]

iv) Sexual equality

Social security law has been deliberately excluded from the operation of the sex discrimination legislation and it remains an area where there are significant differences between the treatment of men and women.[7] As regards single women, the pre-war discrimination based on the assumption that they were 'poor risks' was abolished in 1945[8] and the only major difference remaining is that the retirement age for women is five years earlier than that for men.[9] The different treatment of married women stems in part from the practice, described in the last paragraph, of treating the family as a single financial unit. The model which has traditionally dominated, and to a lesser extent still dominates, social policy thinking is that of the wife doing the housework and caring for the children while the husband is the breadwinner.[10] The consequence is that where, for the purpose of the means-tested benefits, the family is regarded as a single financial unit, only the husband is generally allowed to claim.[11] Another is that under the new invalid care allowance, the husband but not the wife may claim for loss of earnings involved in looking after an invalid[12] – the role is, it is assumed, one which a wife is normally expected to undertake without reward. In order, too, that marriage should not result in financial detriment, a woman living with a man 'as his wife' is treated for these purposes as if she were lawfully married to him.[13]

Even if a wife were to contribute to the family income, account was to be taken of the fact that the employment was liable to interruption for childbirth and, in the words of Beveridge, her earnings were 'a means not of subsistence but of a standard of living above subsistence', and thus in the case of unemployment or sickness she could fall back on her husband's support.[14] The position of the married woman earner within the insurance system was thus regarded as subsidiary, and a complex set of rules was formulated to deal with it, including notably the ability to opt out of the insurance scheme.[15] With the changing social attitudes, and the increasing participation of married women in the labour market,[16] this option was

6. Cf., post, pp. 25 and 384.
7. See generally Land in ed. Barker and Allen *Sexual Divisions and Society* (1976), pp. 108–132. Townsend *Sociology and Social Policy* (1975), chap. 17; ed. Tomandl *Die Frau in der Sozialversicherung* (1976); ISSA Studies and Research no. 5, *Women and Social Security* (1973).
8. Post, p. 64.
9. Post, pp. 196–199.
10. *Walley*, pp. 75–76, 156–161, 206–207, 240–241; Clarke and Ogus, 5 B. Jo.

Law and Society, p. 7.
11. Post, p. 486.
12. Post, pp. 181–182.
13. Post, pp. 404–408.
14. Para. 108.
15. Post, p. oo.
16. Beveridge relied on the fact that before the Second World War only about $12\frac{1}{2}\%$ of married women were gainfully employed (para. 108). In 1975 the figure was over 45%: General Household Survey 1975, Table 5.1.

abolished for those marrying after 5 April 1977.[17]

A housewife not engaged in paid employment had no place in the insurance scheme, except insofar as she could have regard to her husband's contributions for the purposes of maternity, retirement and widow's benefit. It was assumed that all other needs could be fulfilled through the social services.[18] In the case of disability this was by no means assured and in 1977 she became entitled to the non-contributory invalidity pension in her own right.[19] Even more disturbing have been the financial consequences of breakdown of marriage. This was a contingency which Beveridge had foreseen, but his proposal of a temporary 'separation' benefit[20] was not accepted. Hence the deserted or divorced mother had to rely on national assistance (later supplementary benefit) and the Finer Committee's call for a non-contributory guaranteed maintenance allowance for single parent families[1] has so far gone unheeded.

The acceptance of the subordinate status of a married woman has also resulted in discrimination against male insured persons. A widow receives substantial benefit, and thus is not expected to maintain herself by earnings if she has dependent children, or is aged over 50.[2] But a husband receives no benefit on the death of his wife.[3] The assumption is, presumably, that he may easily find a replacement child carer or housekeeper, whereas the widow is not expected to take such a positive approach to remarriage.[4]

v) Work and productivity

All social security systems incorporate values connected with work and productivity.[5] Social insurance normally centres on the employment relationship and earnings are often reflected in the level of benefits. Moreover, certain income support programmes, particularly those for unemployment, sickness or invalidity, are based on the inability to work arising from external circumstances rather than on the individual's own preference for leisure over work. These approaches may be related to a number of different aims or values. First, there is the economic argument that a change in the ratio between the productive and unproductive members of society results in a reduction of the nation's resources and thus in a net loss in social welfare.[6] It must not, however, be assumed that labour is in all circumstances and for all persons more socially beneficial than leisure: there is, for any given society at any given time, an optimal level of employment, and social costs are incurred only when the number active falls below this level.[7] Secondly, there is the view advanced by some members of the medical profession that work is psychologically beneficial

17. Post, p. 67.
18. Post, p. 65.
19. Post, p. 169.
20. Para. 347, and see *Finer*, vol. 2, pp. 136–149; *Harris*, pp. 403–405.
 1. *Finer*, vol. 1, pp. 276–314.
 2. Post, pp. 234–235.
 3. Post, p. 232, cp., p. 346.
 4. Cf. Clarke and Ogus, ante, n.10.
 5. Stein, *Work and Welfare in Britain and the USA* (1975).
 6. *Dupeyroux*, at p. 91.
 7. Atkinson *Poverty in Britain and the Reform of Social Security* (1969), p. 104.

to the individual.[8] The work ethic, often associated with the Protestant or Puritan tradition,[9] is deeply embedded in social attitudes[10] and is inevitably reflected in social welfare provisions. There is a fear that, however small the actual proportion of 'work-shy' claimants may be, the contagion will spread if the system is not seen to check abuses.[11] It is felt inequitable that those who by their own endeavours are able to maintain themselves and their families should support others who are able but unwilling to work.[12]

These values are incorporated into the social security system through direct controls against voluntary unemployment and through indirect work incentives. The former include the medical tests for incapacity to work,[13] the condition for unemployment benefit of availability for work,[14] and the disqualification for voluntarily leaving employment.[15] The indirect methods are based on the assumption that if a person is financially better off with benefit than in work, he will normally prefer to remain idle. Whether or not the assumption is justified – and it has been challenged by some sociologists[16] – it has had a continuous influence on the level of benefit throughout the history of social welfare. The poor law, it will be recalled, explicitly adopted the principle that recipients of welfare should be worse off than those in the lowest paid employment.[17] The national assistance and supplementary benefit schemes for many years contained the 'wage stop' rule, according to which claimants were not to receive more by way of benefit than they would have earned in their normal employment, notwithstanding that the amount in question was below the officially recognised subsistence level.[18] Earnings-related benefits fall short of 100% indemnity and the level of flate-rate benefit is generally well below the average wage. In fact, if work incentives are the primary motivations for these rules, the system is remarkably inefficient in ensuring that no claimants are better off with benefit than in employment. The much discussed 'poverty trap' exists for many who lose entitlement to a considerable range of means-tested benefits when their income exceeds a certain point;[19] and the combination of earnings-related benefits (free of tax) and increases for dependants means that some of those with large families profit from being out of work.[20]

8. Stevenson *Claimant or Client* (1973), p. 81.
9. Tawney *Religion and the Rise of Capitalism* (1921), pp. 228–249.
10. *Stevenson*, ante n.8, loc. cit., and Romanyshyn *Social Welfare* (1968), pp. 184–194 and the works there cited.
11. *Stevenson*, ante n.8 at p. 80; *Fisher*, para. 37.
12. Ibid.
13. Post, pp. 152–155.
14. Post, pp. 104–108.
15. Post, pp. 113–115.
16. E.g. Townsend, who argues that controls over work are more social than economic: *Social Services for All* (1970), Fabian Pamphlet, chap. 10.
17. Ante, p. 2.
18. Post, p. 526.
19. Post, p. 557.
20. Post, pp. 25 and 384.

Part two. Strategies

A. Introduction

In Part One we considered the range of objectives that a social security system might adopt. In this part we discuss the different strategies available to meet these objectives. Social security, as we define it for the purpose of this book,[1] is a system of cash benefits conferred on individuals satisfying conditions of entitlement. In section B, we consider how recipients may be selected and classified according to their needs. Section C is concerned with the principles for assessing benefits, and section D with the methods of financing them. Finally, in section E we contrast the cash benefit system with two other types of social welfare: benefits in kind, and fiscal relief.

B. Selection and classification of need

i) General

The primary question arising under a system of cash benefits relates to the circumstances in which and the persons to whom benefits are paid. To postulate that a social welfare system must be 'selective' is merely to state the obvious. The same benefits cannot be enjoyed to the same degree by all members of society. Even the most 'universal' of schemes, such as the social dividend proposal (described later in this chapter[2]) which purports to grant benefit to all, nevertheless effectively takes it back from many through the medium of taxation. The debate on 'universality versus selectivity'[3] is thus concerned not with a choice between two extreme alternatives but rather on the nature and extent of the selectivity process. At a very broad level, two fundamentally different approaches should be distinguished. In the first, generally referred to as the means test method, the target is poverty as such, and the primary condition of entitlement is a level of resources below a stipulated amount. The second attempts to focus on presumed needs (often but not exclusively involving income deprivation) arising from certain circumstances, e.g. unemployment, disability, old age, the maintenance of children. The one approach is not necessarily coterminous with the other – it is possible that entitlement to a particular benefit may depend on conditions both of non-financial circumstances and of income[4] – but the relative weight to be given to each strategy raises an important issue of social policy.

ii) Means-tested benefits

The primary assumption behind the means test approach is that deprivation of income and other resources constitutes the greatest need on which the social security system should concentrate. It is typically combined

1. Cf., post, p. 40.
2. Post, p. 38.
3. See esp. *McCarthy*, chap. 14; Titmuss *Commitment to Welfare* (2nd edn), chap. 10; Townsend *Sociology and Social Policy* (1975), chap. 9; Reddin in ed. Robson and Crick *The Future of the Social Services* (1970), chap. 2.
4. See Collard in ed. Bull *Family Poverty* (2nd edn), chap. 2.

with concern that welfare expenditure (which involves a substantial degree of redistribution) should be limited to cases of *demonstrated* need and that the conditions for receipt should be kept within carefully observed limits.[5] The process has, however, been attacked by a battery of arguments.[6] Means tests are regarded as socially divisive not the least because those who are subject to them are conscious of the continuity of a tradition dating back to the poor law.[7] They imply strong control functions by governments and bureaucrats whose attitudes may be coloured by their own moral judgments of poverty.[8] Perhaps most important of all, it is claimed that means tests are stigmatising and for that, and other reasons, result in a lower than desirable take-up rate.[9] The stigma issue is a complex one and the evidence on which the argument is made tends to be impressionistic rather than scientific.[10] The notion that self-declarations of poverty are of their nature degrading is commonly held, but, as has been observed,[11] the humiliation may result not so much from the process of claiming relief as from the poverty itself which is revealing of personal failure, particularly when it is associated with circumstances of living which are commonly regarded as morally unacceptable, e.g. unemployment or fatherless families.[12] The evidence for the take-up problem is more tangible. The estimates of take-up rates – the proportion of those eligible for a given benefit who actually receive it – are of course unreliable in that there is never a certain way of discovering how many people in fact satisfy eligibility conditions at any one time.[13] Nevertheless, surveys, both governmental and independent, have revealed a situation which few would regard as satisfactory.[14] In 1973 it was estimated that only about one half of those entitled to family income supplement had actually applied for it,[15] and local surveys of take-up of rent rebates found variations of between 48% and 64%.[16] One commentator has claimed that for 1973 the amount of unclaimed benefit was worth about £416 million.[17] Some of the low response is undoubtedly due to ignorance:[18] the means test approach places a high premium on publicity and communication, and the National Consumer Council has argued that there is room for much improvement in the methods of distributing information.[19]

5. Cf., *Beveridge*, para. 369; *Townsend*, ante n.3, at pp. 136–137; Rejda *Social Insurance and Economic Security* (1976), pp. 405–408.
6. See National Consumer Council Paper *Means-Tested Benefits* (1976) and the references cited in n.3 ante.
7. *Townsend*, ante n.3, at pp. 149–153; NCC Paper, ante n.6, at pp. 15–17.
8. See generally Stevenson *Claimant or Client* (1973).
9. On stigma generally see Goffman *Stigma: Notes on the Management of Spoiled Identity* (1963); *Stevenson*, ante n.8, chap. 1; *Titmuss*, ante n.3, chap. 3; Pinker *Social Theory and Social Policy* (1971), chap. 4.
10. See *Kay* in ed. Bull, ante n.4, chap. 3, and the reasons for low take-up found

in some small surveys, reported in Lister *Take-Up of Means-Tested Benefits* (1974), Povery Pamphlet No. 18, pp. 16–19.
11. *Pinker*, ante n.9, at pp. 141–144.
12. *Stevenson*, ante n.8, at pp. 16–17.
13. NCC Paper, ante n.6, at pp. 25–26.
14. See, particularly, ibid., at pp. 27–36 and *Lister*, ante n.10.
15. Written Answer, 871 HC Deb. col. 158.
16. *Lister*, ante n.10, at pp. 15–17.
17. Field *New Society*, 27 March 1975.
18. In a study made in Islington it was found that 72% of non-take up of six benefits examined was due to ignorance: *Lister*, ante n.10, at p. 17.
19. See NCC Paper, ante n.6, chap. 4; and the studies on the effects of publicity there reported.

The selectivity process involved in means tests by implication aims at locating those in greatest need at lowest cost. However, in practice they emerge as an expensive form of welfare. In 1975 the administration of supplementary benefits cost some 13% of benefit expenditure,[20] compared with 5% for the contributory benefits.[1] Undoubtedly one reason for this is the complexity of the means-testing process,[2] and the problem is intensified by the proliferation of different tests for different benefits: in Britain today, if local authority grants are included, there are about 45 different means-tested benefits, and though entitlement to some will follow automatically from entitlement to others (the 'passport principle') this is not generally the case.[3] Indeed, it has been argued that, at least as presently administered, means tests inequitably shift many of the costs of selection (e.g., those resulting from problems in dealing with bureaucracy, waiting, frustration, travelling) from the public purse to the individual who, *ex hypothesi*, is not in a position to bear them.[4]

General considerations of the merits of means tests leave open the question as to the form such tests might take. The McCarthy Royal Commission in New Zealand was quick to assert what appeared to it to be a fundamental distinction between 'means tests' and 'income tests': the former but not the latter take into account the claimant's capital resources.[5] The income test was less stigmatising as the claimant's total circumstances need not be opened to public scrutiny; it also avoided any incentive to dissipate capital resources to gain entitlement. In Britain, while the level of capital resources disregarded under the present supplementary benefit scheme is reasonably generous,[6] the tradition has always been to take them into account presumably on the ground that to disregard them creates inequities between claimants. This same problem is inherent in the difficult choice between simplicity and comprehensiveness:[7] to do justice to each recipient involves a rigorous scrutiny of all his circumstances which is both expensive and disagreeable. If the objective is to be achieved by rules conferring rights, there is a danger of creating a complex and unwieldy body of law which those directly concerned would be unlikely fully to understand. If the more flexible alternative of a wide discretion is preferred, this creates the risk of bureaucratic power and apparent arbitrariness.

There has been no consistent development in British social policy either towards or against means tests. The early forms of welfare were, of course, almost wholly dependent on this method: it was adopted in the poor law – its 'workhouse test'[8] – and under the Speenhamland system.[9] While the

20. SBC Annual Report 1975, p. 97.
1. Social Security Statistics 1975, Table 44.02.
2. Cf., Donnison, 5 Jnl. Soc. Pol. 337, 352–354.
3. See generally NCC Paper, ante n.6, at pp. 53–62.
4. *Collard*, ante n.4, at p. 42.
5. *McCarthy*, p. 139.
6. See post, pp. 506–507.
7. *Stevenson*, ante n.8, chap. 2; Marshall in ed. Timms and Watson *Talking About Welfare* (1976), chap. 1; Wilding in ed. Alder and Bradley *Justice, Discretion and Poverty* (1976), chap. 4; Titmuss, 42 Political Q.113; and post, p. 474.
8. See generally Taylor in ed. Martin *Comparative Development in Social Welfare* (1972), chap. 3.
9. See generally, *Neuman*, ibid, chap. 4.

creation of national insurance in the early years of this century was clearly directed towards eliminating reliance on the poor law, it proved to be inadequate to cope with the massive unemployment between the wars, and through unemployment assistance the means test again became a regular feature of the welfare system.[10] Beveridge's aim was to reduce means-tested welfare to a minimum: he foresaw a gradual reduction in the numbers reliant on national assistance as resulting from the more comprehensive national insurance network.[11] His hopes were not to be realised both because national insurance benefits were stubbornly kept below the typical subsistence level and because the scheme failed to cope adequately with two social hazards, marital breakdown and long-term disability.[12] While expressing disquiet at the number of individuals in receipt of national assistance, or supplementary benefit as it subsequently became, governments of the period 1960 to 1974 continued to tolerate and even to extend the means-tested approach, through, for example, the introduction of family income supplement,[13] exemption from prescription charges,[14] rate and rent rebates.[15] The Labour administration of 1974–75 committed itself to a policy which if successful would reduce the numbers in receipt of supplementary benefit.[16] The measures taken included earnings-related retirement and invalidity pensions,[17] more generous family benefits[18] and new non-contributory benefits for the disabled.[19] The proposal of the Finer Committee[20] for a new allowance to assist single parent families was not, however, implemented.

iii) Criterion of assumed needs

The alternative strategy of selecting circumstances or individuals whose needs are assumed rather than demonstrated is more widely favoured. Inevitably it raises the fundamental question, to which reference has already been made,[1] of what is comprehended by 'needs' and of whether their satisfaction is properly the subject of state intervention as opposed to individual initiative. If the hypothesis is accepted that the objective of a social security system is to make provision for economic insecurity, then it appears possible to list the typical causes of such insecurity, and to summarise, within an historical perspective, the forms of benefit developed in our system.

a) CAUSES OF ECONOMIC INSECURITY. There have been several attempts to categorise the causes of insecurity,[2] perhaps the best known

10. Bruce *The Coming of the Welfare State* (4th edn), pp. 262–272.
11. Para. 23.
12. Post, pp. 471–472.
13. Post, chap. 13.
14. S.I. 1971/340, made under Health Services and Public Health Act 1968. See now S.I. 1975/1688.
15. Housing Finance Act 1972 and S.I. 1974/421 (as amended).
16. White Paper, Better Pensions (1974), Cmnd. 5713, paras. 3–4; Report on

Social Security Provision for Chronically Sick and Disabled People, 1973–74, HC 276, para. 58.
17. Post, pp. 165 and 224.
18. Post, chap. 11.
19. Post, pp. 167–187.
20. *Finer*, vol. 1, pp. 284–314.
1. Ante, p. 5.
2. E.g., Turnbull, Williams and Cheit, *Economic and Social Security* (4th edn), pp. 3–4; Krause, 18 Zeitschrift für Sozialreform 385, 509.

being that of Beveridge.[3] The variety of circumstances causing financial hardship is infinite. While some are regarded uncontroversially as properly the subject of individual initiative, for example, property loss through fire, theft or vandalism,[4] and others are endemic in a society of mixed cultures and values, for example, lack of ambition, idleness, personal extravagance,[5] there is a broad category of hazards which in most industrially developed societies are regarded as appropriate for state intervention. They may be divided into three groups.

1. EARNINGS LOSS. According to Beveridge,[6] about 75% of cases of financial need arose from interruption or loss of earning power: the main instances being personal disability, maternity, old age and unemployment.

2. LOSS OF MAINTENANCE. Impairment of the breadwinner's income necessarily results in the problems of maintaining those who are dependent on him, but the same need can arise from the wage-earner's death, or the breakdown of the family through separation or divorce.

3. SPECIAL EXPENSES. In addition there are a number of special needs which may arise independently of the individual's employment history: they include the support of children, hospital and other medical needs, funeral expenses, education and housing costs.

b) BRITISH METHODS OF PROVIDING FOR ECONOMIC INSECURITY. It may be found helpful to give at this stage a brief guide to the British development of cash benefits for each of the above causes of economic insecurity. Full treatment is reserved for the chapter devoted to the benefits in question.

1. EARNINGS LOSS
Industrial accidents and diseases.[7] The first to benefit from special treatment were those injured or contracting diseases as a result of their employment. The Workmen's Compensation Act 1897 originally imposed responsibility on the employer. In 1946, the state assumed control, and benefits became payable under a national insurance scheme.

War pensions.[8] Provision for those injured while active in the armed forces was developed in the 19th century by various procedures. During the First World War responsibility was assumed by a new Ministry of Pensions. The benefits available for lost earnings are mostly analogous to those available for industrial injuries, and though Royal Warrant and Orders in Council rather

3. Paras. 311–312.
4. Ibid., at para. 312.
5. Rejda *Social Insurance and Economic Security* (1976), pp. 8–9.
6. Para. 11.
7. Post, chap. 8.
8. Post, chap. 9.

than legislation govern entitlement the system is now administered by the Department of Health and Social Security.

Unemployment.[9] State unemployment insurance was introduced for certain industries in 1911, and was, during the interwar years extended to other employments. The 1946 Act completed the process.

Sickness and invalidity.[10] Compulsory sickness insurance was also introduced in 1911. Sickness benefit was payable for the first six months, and disablement benefit (at a lower rate) thereafter. The scheme was administered by the Approved Societies. These were abolished in 1946, as was the distinction between short-term and long-term benefits. In 1970, however, a new invalidity allowance was created to assist those incapable of work for more than six months, and in 1975 a pension was introduced for those in the same group who were unable to satisfy the contribution requirements.

Maternity.[11] Maternity allowance, to provide compensation for lost earnings during confinement, was introduced in 1946.

Invalid care.[12] In 1975 an invalid care allowance was created for relatives and others (though not wives) who would, but for the decision to look after an invalid, have been in paid employment.

Old age.[13] A means-tested, non-contributory, pension was introduced in 1908 for those over 70 years. Contributory pensions became payable under the Widows', Orphans' and Old Age Contributory Pensions Act 1925 to insured persons between the ages of 65 and 70 (after which they passed to the non-contributory scheme). Under the 1946 Act, the system was replaced by a contributory retirement pension payable on *retirement* to a man over 65 and a woman over 60, and to a man aged 70 and a woman aged 65 irrespective of whether he/she was still at work. A non-contributory pension for those aged 80 and over was introduced in 1971.

2. LOSS OF MAINTENANCE
Loss of earnings of breadwinner.[14] Increases to the benefits listed above to assist in the maintenance of dependants were introduced unsystematically. They were added as an emergency measure to the unemployment insurance scheme in 1921, but soon thereafter became permanent. For workmen's compensation the principle was admitted as late as 1940, and no provision at all was made in the pre-war sickness and old-age schemes. Under the 1946 Acts dependency increases became payable as an addition to all earnings-replacement benefits.

9. Post, chap. 3.
10. Post, chap. 4.
11. Post, pp. 252–256.
12. Post, pp. 179–183.
13. Post, chap. 5.
14. Post, pp. 383–398.

Death of breadwinner. Survivor benefits for widows and children of the deceased existed from the beginning in the war pensions[15] and workmen's compensation[16] schemes. The history of provision for other widows is complicated.[17] The 1925 Act introduced a contributory scheme under which all widows of insured persons received a pension. The scheme was restructured in 1946 so that after the initial widow's allowance, payable to all for six months, benefit continued at a substantial rate only if the woman had dependent children (widowed mother's allowance) or was aged 40 or over (widow's pension). Following further modifications in 1957 and 1970, widows between 40 and 50, without dependent children, received at a reduced rate. Where both parents of a child had died, an orphan's pension became, under the 1925 Act, payable to his guardian,[18] and in 1946 the benefit was renamed guardian's allowance. In 1957 there was introduced the child's special allowance to compensate a divorced woman whose former husband had been contributing to the maintenance of the child.[19] Outside the industrial injuries[20] and war pension[1] schemes there is no provision for widowers or other adult dependants.

Breakdown of marriage. Beveridge's tentative suggestion that on the breakdown of a marriage, the woman should receive a temporary separation benefit[2] was not implemented, and apart from the child's special allowance mentioned above, there has never been a benefit specifically directed to cover this need. In 1974 the Finer Committee recommended the creation of a guaranteed maintenance allowance for single parent families[3] but the government has not yet committed itself to the principle, and hitherto the only advantage conferred on this group has been the more rapid introduction of a child benefit to cover the first child.[4]

3. SPECIAL EXPENSES

Family support.[5] Family allowances were introduced in 1945, but were payable only to families with two or more children. In 1975 they were superseded by the child benefit which became payable to all families with children.

Maternity.[6] The maternity grant, a lump sum intended to assist with the expenses incurred from confinement, first became payable under the health insurance scheme of 1911. The 1946 Act in addition provided for an attendance allowance to cover the costs of domestic help. The two benefits were effectively merged in

15. Post, pp. 376–379.
16. Post, p. 341.
17. Post, pp. 230–236.
18. Post, pp. 256–263.
19. Post, pp. 239–242.
20. Post, pp. 346–349.

1. Post, p. 378.
2. Para. 347.
3. Vol. I, pp. 284–314.
4. Post, p. 449.
5. Post, chap. 11.
6. Post, pp. 249–252.

1953, and by the same legislation a new home confinement grant was introduced, on the assumption that home births were more expensive. The assumption proved to be unreal and this grant was abolished in 1964.

Funeral expenses.[7] The need to avoid the humiliation of a pauper's funeral had for a long time stimulated the private insurance market, but the national insurance death grant was created only in 1946. At first there were complex rules to determine the persons entitled to receive the benefit. Since 1957 it became payable into the estate of the deceased person and in practice is therefore claimed by his personal representatives.

Disabled. The need to provide additional resources for the severely disabled over and above the standard benefit was acknowledged first in the area of war pensions[8] and subsequently adopted in the industrial injuries scheme.[9] In both schemes there are allowances payable for constant attendance and for exceptionally severe disablement. Other disabled persons had to wait much longer for analogous provision. The attendance allowance, introduced in 1970, is payable to persons so severely disabled that they require frequent attention or constant supervision.[10] A mobility allowance was established in 1975 for those unable, or virtually unable, to walk.[11]

Others. There are a large number of other cash benefits, conferred either nationally or locally, and concerned with such diverse needs as health, education and housing. These are not regarded as 'social security benefits' and do not come within the scope of this book.[12]

C. Levels of cash benefit

i) Flat-rate or earnings-related

Having determined the circumstances in which a cash benefit will be payable, the social security system must then decide on what principle that benefit will be calculated. Where it is intended as some replacement for the interruption or loss of earnings, the fundamental issue arises whether the benefit should be flat-rate or earnings-related. The main theoretical argument in favour of the latter approach is that based on free-enterprise incentives, a predictably popular creed in the United States of America:

'a free-enterprise society which stresses the rewards of individual initiative should also embody incentive principles: that the higher

7. Post, pp. 243–247.
8. Post, pp. 374–376.
9. Post, pp. 317–335.
10. Post, pp. 171–178.
11. Post, pp. 183–187.

12. Reference should be made to e.g. Smith and Hoath *Law and the Underprivileged* (1975), chaps. 7 and 11, and ed. Pollard *Social Welfare Law* (1977).

income secured by the higher-paid worker should be reflected in high social security benefits when he cannot work."[13]

Allied to this is the notion, popular with some trade unions, that benefit is merely a 'deferred wage' and therefore should reflect the collective bargaining process which determined the amount of that wage.[14] The argument is a compelling one in a wholly state-controlled economy where the state is both the employer and the provider of benefits, on the assumption that the initial wage level accords with the distributional dictates of its conception of social justice.[15] For this very reason it is opposed by those who argue that an earnings-related scheme reinforces differentials, on the whole dictated by market forces, and which may therefore be inequitable.[16] As the New Zealand Royal Commission has observed, 'differentials in market earnings are based on ability to take advantage of the market rather than on conditions of equity'.[17] This viewpoint is linked to the principle that the social welfare system should operate as a mechanism for redistribution rather than merely as a compensation for losses incurred through social risks.[18]

The debate may involve fundamental issues of social philosophy but typically the matter is decided by more pragmatic, political considerations. Increasing affluence, as manifest in post-war industrial societies, reinforces concern for the preservation of differentials.[19] As recent history on wages policy has confirmed, there is no great popular desire for more equality.[20] This goes a long way to explain the gradual movement in British social policy away from Beveridge's flat-rate principle of subsistence to the earnings-related approach. Beveridge regarded protection of resources above the subsistence level as a matter for individual initiative.[1] In fact, national insurance benefits were for a long time regarded as inadequate, and there emerged a glaring disparity between those who were able and willing to augment state provision by occupational schemes, and those who were not. This image of 'two nations' was the inspiration for the Labour party's national superannuation programme of earnings-related provision, an approach which, while arguably ideologically inconsistent with the socialist objective of egalitarianism, nevertheless found a convenient justification in the notion that the privileges of the minority would be passed to the majority.[2]

The Conservative government's answer was the scheme of graduated pensions,[3] a solution which at the time appeared to be attractive but which

13. Burns *Social Security and Public Policy* (1956), p. 40. See also Richardson *Economic and Financial Aspects of Social Security* (1960), p. 42, and *Walley*, p. 145.
14. *Burns*, ante n.13, at p. 41; *George*, p. 36.
15. *McCarthy*, p. 173.
16. George *Social Security and Society* (1973), pp. 32–33, 51; Lister *Social Security: The Case for Reform* (1975), Poverty Pamphlet no. 22, pp. 39–40;

Kincaid *Poverty and Equality in Britain* (1973), pp. 236–237.
17. *McCarthy*, p. 170.
18. Cf. ante, pp. 5–7.
19. *George*, p. 36, and see the Swedish Report *Social Policy and How It Works* (1969).
20. See generally *George*, ante n.16, at pp. 73–79.
1. Para. 302.
2. Labour Party Pamphlet *National Superannuation* (1957).
3. Post, pp. 222–223.

turned out in practice to be a method more for replenishing the depleted National Insurance Fund than for providing an adequate income for old age.[4] The Labour party, returned to power in 1964 with national superannuation playing a prominent part in its election manifesto, nevertheless postponed full implementation of the programme in order that the matter be subjected to further study. As an interim measure, earnings-related supplements were introduced in 1966 for the short-term unemployment and sickness benefits.[5] In 1969 the full programme emerged as a Bill but was lost at the dissolution of Parliament. The new Conservative administration adopted the principle of earnings-related benefits but with a much more prominent role given to occupational schemes.[6] Finally in 1975, the Labour party, once more in power, instituted its new earnings-related scheme, applicable to retirement, widow's and invalidity pensions.[7] By these means, the British social insurance scheme had created a bridge between the two traditions:[8] the flat-rate system inspired by Beveridge and maintained in only a few industrially developed countries (notably New Zealand), and the earnings-related system, historically dating from Bismarck's German schemes in the 19th century, and now adopted by the great majority.

ii) Determination of benefits according to need
Despite the major move towards the earnings-related principle described in the last paragraph, there remains a substantial area of benefits which do not vary according to the previous earnings of the recipients. These include not only the flat-rate components in the standard income-replacement benefits for sickness, unemployment and retirement, but also those designed to accommodate special expenses or needs and those which are means-tested. For all within this category, decisions must be taken on the approprite level of financial support. There has been a considerable amount of literature devoted to this question, much of it concerned with theoretical problems of assessing need and defining poverty. Less well treated are the political and other pressures which in practice operate on governmental decision-makers in this area.

a) ASSESSING NEEDS. The Beveridge objective, it will be recalled, was that of a minimum level of 'subsistence' on the basis of 'normal needs'. How were such needs to be assessed? Already earlier in the century some scientific measurement had been attempted, notably by Rowntree. He drew up a list of 'consumption necessities', e.g., food, clothing and housing expenditure.[9] The method was adopted by Beveridge as a guide;[10] he applied a variable of age and also added a margin for inefficiency in

4. It provided a modest return for contributions and offered no protection against inflation: see *George*, pp. 52–53; White Paper on National Superannuation and Social Insurance (1969), Cmnd. 3883, para. 20; Lynes *Pensions Rights and Wrongs* (1963), Fabian Pamphlet.

5. Post, pp. 424–426.
6. Post, p. 194.
7. Post, pp. 165, 224, 237.
8. Cf., *Dupeyroux*, pp. 114–121.
9. *Poverty–A Study of Town Life* (1901); *Human Needs of Labour* (1937).
10. Paras. 217–232; cf., *Harris*, pp. 396–399.

spending. In another respect, however, his criteria were more stringent than those proposed by Rowntree who had allowed a small amount for 'personal sundries', e.g., trade union subscriptions, newspapers, radio, beer, tobacco.[11] Of course, as determinants for individual needs, these models were deficient, in that they had to be based on perceived averages.[12] Any shortfall was therefore to be remedied by supplementary schemes based on detailed means tests. This handicap was only one of a number of aspects which were vigorously criticised by commentators in the 1950s and 1960s. The most comprehensive and widely publicised was that of Townsend.[13] He rejected any absolute objective notion of poverty based on subsistence requirements: he regarded it instead as a relative concept to be measured only by reference to the living standards of a particular society at a particular time. Others have stressed that poverty is a psychological state dependent on an individual's own expectations:[14] this may be conditioned by his own or his neighbour's previous level of earnings or standard of living. Finally there is the perspective which has regard to the effect of deprivation on the lives of individuals within the community – a state of 'virtual non-participation'.[15] It is beyond dispute that when all these various ideas are taken on board,[16] at least for the practical purpose of fixing levels of benefit, the ship becomes unseaworthy. Yet such a conclusion should not be used as an excuse for rejecting all forms of sociological data and for relying instead on guesswork or tradition.[17] Political values and strategies may be debatable but the results of research can provide the factual framework within which the appropriate decisions may be made.[18] Indeed, there is now a wealth of information available on the needs of families,[19] the disabled,[20] and the aged.[1]

b) FIXING SCALES OF BENEFIT. Undoubtedly these studies influence to a certain extent governmental decisions on the level of benefits, but it is important to appreciate that there are other factors which may play an equal if not primary role. Regard has typically been had not only to the level of prices but also to the general level of earnings: a system in which benefits are significantly above the incomes of the lower paid is likely to be politically unacceptable, if for no other reason than it is thought to have an

11. *Human Needs of Labour* (1937), p. 61.
12. The problem of variations in rent Beveridge felt to be particularly acute but after some hesitation decided that to make a separate award for household needs would be impracticable: paras. 193–216.
13. (1954) Br. Jo. of Sociology 330 and (1962) ibid., 210. See also the collection of essays: ed. Townsend *The Concept of Poverty* (1970).
14. E.g. Runciman *Relative Deprivation and Social Justice* (1966).
15. See Economic Council of Canada, *The Challenge of Growth and Change* (1968). The definition won the approval of the NZ Royal Commission:

McCarthy, pp. 104–105. See also Goldthorpe in ed. Wedderburn *Poverty, Inequality and Class Structure* (1974), chap. 11.
16. Cf. the ambitious study by Baratz and Grigsby, 1 Jnl. Soc. Pol. 119–134.
17. Wynn *Family Policy* (1970), p. 36.
18. Lynes in ed. Young *Forecasting in the Social Sciences* (1968), p. 147; George *Social Security and Society* (1973), p. 50.
19. E.g. *Wynn*, ante n.17, chaps. 2–6.
20. E.g. ed. Boswell and Wingate *The Handicapped Person in the Community* (1974).
1. E.g., Townsend and Wedderburn *The Aged in the Welfare State* (1965).

effect on work incentives.[2] Similarly there are considerations of equity as between different categories of social security beneficiaries: this has led, for example, to differences between the contributory and non-contributory invalidity pensions,[3] even though these benefits may be directed towards identical needs. Account must also be taken of the funds which are available: the considerations here include the levels of contribution and of taxation, and also the relationship between cash benefits and other welfare services such as housing, education and health. Such factors operate quite legitimately within a rational framework of social policy. Not always so appealing, though of immense importance in practice, is the way in which decisions are reached on purely political grounds: for example, the raising of benefits to a generous level in the year before a general election is by no means unknown. The influence too of political pressure groups may be seen on such decisions as the level of war pensions[4] and industrial injury benefits[5] and those paid to the disabled.[6] Even more typical is the practice of adopting the structure of benefits inherited from previous administrations and merely raising them by a certain percentage to take account of inflation.

c) THE PROBLEM OF INFLATION. Inflation has such an immediate impact on the level of benefits that some special discussion is called for.[7] That the value of social security benefits should be maintained in line with inflationary trends is almost self evident. The only possible argument to the contrary, that adjustment exerts an inflationary pressure on the rest of the national economy, is easily countered by the notion of social justice, that those already worse off should not make further sacrifices for general welfare.[8] Much more controversial is the choice of method for adjusting to inflation. In the first place, there is the question whether the determining criterion should be wage or price rises. To a certain extent this raises the same issues as those already described in relation to flat-rate or earnings-related benefit.[9] In periods of industrial growth, it is arguable that social security recipients should benefit from increased prosperity as reflected in earnings levels;[10] on the other hand, when rising prices outstrip earnings, for example during a wage freeze, there is a danger that those beneficiaries at the very bottom of the income scale will suffer the most.[11] There is considerable diversity of approach to these questions in the various social security systems:[12] in Britain some flexibility is achieved by requiring the Secretary of State to ensure that the real value of some benefits is main-

2. *McCarthy*, chap. 19; *Fisher*, paras. 35–36; Burns *Social Security and Public Policy* (1956), chap. 4. The argument has been attacked by e.g. Kincaid *Poverty and Equality in Britain* (1973), chap. 12 and Jordan *Poor Parents* (1974), chap. 4.
3. Post, p. 167.
4. Post, p. 354.
5. Post, p. 265.
6. Post, p. 140.
7. For general discussions see Dupeyroux, (1975) Droit Social 141; Pechman, Aaron, Taussig *Social Security: Perspectives for Reform* (1968); pp. 96–104; ed. Wilson *Pensions, Inflation and Growth* (1974).
8. *George*, p. 35.
9. *Ante*, p. 20.
10. Trinder in ed. Young *Poverty Report 1975*, p. 58.
11. Trinder in ed. Willmott *Sharing Inflation?* (1976), chaps. 2–4.
12. Ed. *Wilson*, ante n.7, at pp. 374–378.

tained with reference to the general level of either prices or earnings, whichever is more advantageous to the beneficiary.[13]

Secondly, it must be decided whether benefits are to be adjusted automatically through the application of some prices- or earnings-index. The main argument for indexing is that of certainty and the reduction of time-lag between the inflationary changes and modifications to the benefits scale.[14] The objection to the method is that is deprives government policy of flexibility – it may be desirable on grounds of social or economic justice to show preference for a particular group of individuals.[15] Opinions will differ as to whether this is an advantage or a disadvantage, but, more tacitly than openly, the ability to adjust to inflation in different proportions has played an enormously important role in British social policy since the Second World War. For political reasons, rights to benefit once created are difficult to remove, but if change is felt to be desirable it may be achieved by the indirect method of allowing the real value of benefits to be eroded through inflation. Two examples should suffice to illustrate the process. The differentials between industrial injury and non-industrial sickness benefit were, after much discussion, accepted in 1946.[16] Today the principle of discrimination is not so easily defended and successive governments have undermined it by maintaining the arithmetic differential rather than the proportional differential between the two schemes. The death grant was formerly regarded as important. Now priorities seem to have changed and the lump sum payable has remained the same since 1967.[17]

Thirdly, if legislation does not provide for the automatic adjustment of benefits, the question remains how frequently should up-rating take place and with reference to what period of time. The problem is not an easy one to solve for, on the one hand, it involves balancing the high administrative costs of frequent adjustments against social costs resulting from delayed up-rating; and, on the other hand, attempts to base adjustments on predictions of future rates of inflation are notoriously haphazard.[18]

iii) Determination of earnings-related benefits

Some of the problems inherent in relating benefits to a claimant's previous earnings are of a practical nature; for example, the type of earnings of which account may be taken and the nature of proof required.[19] Others raise delicate questions of social policy. To achieve equity as between those, typically manual workers, whose optimal earnings are reached at an early age and those, typically white-collar workers, who reach their earnings peak later in life, it may be necessary to have regard to widely divergent periods as the basis for the calculation.[20] In the British system

13. SSA 1975, s.125, as amended by SSPA 1975, Sch. 4, para. 51. Not all benefits are, however, covered: see post, pp. 433–434.
14. *Trinder*, ante n.10, at p. 54.
15. *Dupeyroux*, ante n.7, at p. 147; *Pechman, Aaron, Taussig*, ante n.7, at pp. 101–102.
16. Post, p. 269.
17. Post, p. 246.
18. For an account of the relevant principles under SSA 1975, see post, pp. 433–436.
19. Post, pp. 426–432.
20. Cf., White Paper Better Pensions (1974), Cmnd. 5713, p. iii.

there is an important difference between the earnings-related supplements to short-term benefits which are assessed according to the earnings in the year preceding that in which benefit is awarded,[1] and the long-term benefits which (when fully operative) will be based on the twenty 'best years' of working life.[2] Neither of these approaches copes adequately with the case where an individual is rendered unemployable. It is rare indeed for a social security system (in contrast to the common law method of awarding damages for future lost earnings[3]) to base the earnings award on future hypothetical income, though the New Zealand Accident Compensation scheme has, to a certain extent, incorporated the principle.[4]

Between what limits of earnings should the base for the calculation be set? Of course, all schemes must set an upper limit: to allow a millionaire to claim as sickness benefit a proportion of all his lost earnings would offend notions of social justice. Typically, where contributions are earnings-related a ceiling is imposed to limit the liability of high salary-earners and at least on analogy with the principles of insurance (though not in accordance with redistributive objectives),[5] there should be a correlation between liability and entitlement. Imposing a lower earnings limit is not an invariable practice, but in terms of administrative costs it makes little sense to have regard to earnings below the subsistence level where the earnings-related benefit constitutes a supplement to a flat-rate benefit designed to provide maintenance at that level.[6]

The question of what proportion of lost earnings should be recoverable is not susceptible to a precise answer as it depends on several factors. First, there is the ubiquitous issue of work incentives: most systems regard 100% indemnities as inadvisable on this ground. Secondly, regard must be had to the circumstances of the typical beneficiary: most people expect to tolerate some drop in living standards when no longer earning. On the other hand, the needs of some, particularly those disabled, may well increase. Thirdly, the matter is complicated by tax considerations – earnings are taxable, benefit is often not.[7] Finally, confusion may be created by overlap between components of benefit designed to compensate for lost earnings and those designed to compensate needs. Our flat-rate system took account of family needs through the award of dependants' increases.[8] The method remained unaffected by the introduction of earnings-related benefits. The flat-rate system may not have been sufficient to guarantee the level of subsistence for which it was intended; the earnings-related benefits (particularly those granted for short-term benefits) may appear to be ungenerous;[9] but since the family man is entitled to both, the relationship between his previous income, when working, and his financial situation on

1. Post, pp. 425–426.
2. Post, p. 224.
3. Cf., Ogus *Law of Damages* (1973), pp. 184–192.
4. Accident Compensation Act 1972, ss. 117–118.
5. Cf. ante, p. 20.
6. There is, however, a danger of regressive distribution if the threshold is set too high, as may have been the case when in 1966 the supplement became payable on earnings only above £9: Kincaid *Poverty and Equality in Britain* (1973), pp. 99–101.
7. Cf. post, p. 35.
8. Post, pp. 383–398.
9. *Kincaid*, ante n.6, loc. cit.

benefit involves highly complex calculations which will vary greatly between individuals.[10] When account is also taken of fiscal considerations it will emerge that some are significantly better off on benefit than when working, while others are significantly worse off. A generous interpretation of this state of affairs would suggest that this compromise between divergent policy objectives creates a satisfactory redistributive effect in that those with large families stand to gain most and inequitable earnings differentials are corrected. A more cynical interpretation suggests that there is now no rational framework underlying the level of income support offered by our social security system, that different, half-hearted strategies have been instigated to respond to different political demands, and that the end result is an uncoordinated conglomeration of financial handouts.

D. Financing of benefits

There are two main methods of financing social security benefits: by a fund the resources of which are earmarked exclusively for the purpose, and by general taxation. The first approach is often, though as will emerge largely misleadingly, referred to as the 'insurance' method. It may itself involve either flat-rate or earnings-related contributions.

i) The insurance concept

At the centre of the British system is the contributory scheme. Until 1973 this was referred to as 'national insurance'. Following recodification, the concept has been replaced by the blanket term 'social security' which includes both contributory and non-contributory (but confusingly not means-tested) benefits.[11] Though the change may create ambiguities and will take some time to pass into general public use, it does have the merit of diverting attention from the notion of insurance which has for so long dogged our system. The preoccupation can be explained on historical grounds.[12] Private insurance to cover what are today regarded as social risks, e.g., retirement and premature death, was widespread in the 19th century[13] and greatly influenced the German and British developments in social welfare. The notion was consistent with the then prevailing liberal and individualistic philosophy.[14] Under the National Insurance Act 1911 benefit was seen to rest on past economic performance rather than need per se, and bad risks, those employed in certain industries, women and children, were excluded. The scheme was popular with the middle classes for it seemed to encourage thrift and also with the working classes because it created, for the first time, a framework of legal rights to welfare.[15] As was

10. Cf., *Walley*, pp. 205–209.
11. See *Micklethwait*, chap. 3, and post, p. 40.
12. *McCarthy*, pp. 154–155; Burns *Social Security and Public Policy* (1956), chap. 2, Titmuss *Social Policy* (1974), chap. 7.
13. Gosden *Self-Help: Voluntary Associations in the 19th Century* (1973).
14. Cf. ante, pp. 3–4.
15. Pinker *Social Theory and Social Policy* (1971), p. 90.

pointed out by Beveridge,[16] and has since been stated by many others,[17] the analogy between the contributory schemes and private insurance is an inappropriate one. In a private insurance scheme premiums are based on the risk attendant on the particular circumstances of the insured person (age, sex, health, occupation, family commitments). Provided that the risk-rating is sufficiently precise, there can properly be no redistribution between insured individuals except in the very limited sense that those for whom the risk does not materialise will support those who become subject to it. The trend in social security legislation has been almost wholly against relating contributions to the degree of risk. Thus at an early stage unemployment insurance and workmen's compensation were extended to industries particularly sensitive to the hazards in question, without varying the rates of contribution.[18] The separate categorisation of married women has been ended by the 1975 legislation, at least for those marrying after 5 April 1977,[19] so that apart from minor exceptions,[20] all that remains is the very broad division between the employed, the self-employed and the non-employed.[1] There is, it should be noted, an argument that, at least as regards certain hazards which might be avoided by more careful management, employers' contributions should be 'experience-rated'.[2] But in Britain, in sharp contrast to some other systems,[3] the incentive or prevention objectives of social welfare have been kept distinct from the financing provisions.

The second important respect in which contributory schemes differ from private insurance relates to the actuarial basis of their administration. The latter must be actuarially sound in the sense that the benefits payable must be closely related to contributions already paid. A social security fund, on the other hand, may adopt the 'pay as you go' approach so that benefits payable at a particular time are related not to previous accumulations of contributions but to the finances made available from current contributions.[4] As a result there may be redistribution as between generations of insured persons. The history of the British scheme is revealing in this respect. Since the 1911 Act contributions have theoretically been 'actuarially related' to benefits:[5] this meant that contributions would be sufficient to meet the expected demand for benefit. But it rested on two assumptions:[6] that all insured persons would enter the scheme at the age of 16; and that there would be no increases in the rate of benefit. Both were, and continued to be, patently false. Beveridge's proposal that payment of the full rate of retirement pension should be gradually reached only after

16. Paras., 24–25.
17. E.g., *McCarthy*, pp. 145–146; Richardson *Economic and Financial Aspects of Social Security* (1960), pp. 145–146; *George*, pp. 45–46; Rejda *Social Insurance and Economic Security* (1976), pp. 36–39; *Pearson*, para. 271.
18. Post, pp. 42 and 266.
19. Post, pp. 66–68.
20. Post, pp. 68–69.
 1. Post, p. 46.
 2. *Burns*, ante n.12, at pp. 165–171;

Rejda, ante n.17, at pp. 383–390; *Atiyah*, pp. 517–521 and post, pp. 267–268.
 3. *Kaim-Caudle*, pp. 100–101, 231–232, 294–295.
 4. See generally *Burns*, ante n.12, chap. 10; *Richardson*, ante n.17, chap. 5; Wilson *Pensions, Inflation and Growth* (1974), pp. 35–42; *Rejda*, ante n.17, chap. 7.
 5. See e.g., NIA 1946, s. 19(1)(a).
 6. *George*, pp. 50–51.

twenty years of contributions[7] was unacceptable to the post-war govern-ment,[8] and the need for constant revision of benefit to keep pace with rising prices rendered further inoperative the 'actuarial principle'. This is not to imply that it is devoid of influence on the present social security system. The new earnings-related component in the retirement and invalidity pensions, payable from 1978, would impose a politically unac-ceptable burden on present contributors if it were to be fully paid at once. It has therefore been decided to implement the programme only gradually as the earnings-related contributions create the necessary pool of resources.[9]

ii) Types of contribution

The first question arising under a contributory scheme is whether both employers and employees should participate. Some would argue that the problem is an unreal one for whichever group pays the net effect is, in the long run, the same: an employer paying the contributions will pay less in the form of wages.[10] Most economists, however, regard the problem as a complex one:[11] the proportions in which the cost will be distributed between consumer (through higher prices), investor (through lower profits) and employee (through lower wages) will vary according to such factors as the elasticity of demand for the goods or services in question, the bargaining power of the wage-earners and the level of unemployment. To the extent that the burden falls on consumers, the distributional effect is likely to be regressive since lower-income groups spend proportionately more on consumption. Conversely, Beveridge contended that social security provision was one of the costs of production which should be reflected in the price of the product if competition was not to be dis-torted.[12] The other arguments he deployed for employers' contributions were of a more amorphous character: it is in the interest of the employer that his employees' health and welfare should be protected; he should feel 'concerned for the lives of those who work under (his) control, should think of them not as instruments in production but as human beings';[13] finally it was desirable that employers should have a basis for participation in the administration and strategies of the scheme. Whatever weight be given to these various factors, there is, it is submitted, one overriding consideration: a tax on employers is an easy source of revenue and one that tends to be politically popular.[14]

Should contributions be flat-rate or related to the ability to pay? The principle of the flat-rate contributions was as central to Beveridge's philosophy as that of flat-rate benefit: taxation according to capacity

7. Paras. 240–243.
8. Social Insurance, Part I, paras. 84–86.
9. Post, p. 224.
10. E.g., *Richardson*, ante n.17, at p. 62; Kincaid *Poverty and Equality in Britain* (1973), pp. 89–90.
11. Eckstein in ed. Bowen, Harbison, Lester, Samuels *The American System*

of Social Insurance (1968), chap. 3; Pechman, Aaron, Taussig *Social Security – Perspectives for Reform* (1968), chap. 8; *George*, pp. 47–48.
12. Para. 276.
13. Ibid.
14. *George*, p. 48.

'involves a departure from existing practice, for which there is neither need nor justification and which conflicts with the wishes and feelings of the British democracy.... Contribution means that in their capacity as possible recipients of benefits the poorer man and the richer man are treated alike.'[15]

The rhetoric in this passage should not be allowed to cloud the real issue: the extent of redistribution to be admitted as a central objective of the system. Beveridge's commitment to the 'insurance' principle led him to forswear a substantial degree of redistribution which would have resulted from financing by progressive taxation methods, but the alleged dichotomy between on the one hand an 'insurance fund' and on the other hand earnings-related contributions is a false one. There is no reason, in principle, why the 'fund' or 'earmarked taxes' approach, even if used to finance flat-rate benefits, should not be combined with earnings-related contributions.[16] Beveridge's dogmatic preference for flat-rate contributions was indeed one of the reasons why his plan eventually failed. The burden on the lower paid of contributions sufficient to support an adequate level of benefits was too great. In the result a shift to a system of earnings-related contributions was inevitable. As has already been suggested,[17] the introduction of the graduated pension scheme in 1959 may be seen less as an attempt to provide a satisfactory degree of income maintenance for beneficiaries than a necessary boosting of the National Insurance Fund through earnings-related contributions. Once, however, the principle of earnings-related benefits had become widely accepted, adoption of an earnings-related method of contribution became mandatory and automatic: continuance of a flat-rate method would, of course, have resulted in redistribution in the wrong direction. The extension of contributions liability to individuals deriving profits from business undertakings, not only to those wholly self-employed but also to those combining salaried employment with self-employment,[18] brought the contribution assessment close to income tax, but several important differences remain: contributions are not payable on income unconnected with earnings or profitable undertakings; liability is imposed only up to a prescribed upper limit; the rate of contributions is uniform throughout the scale of income, whereas for tax it is progressive.

One consequence of this new system of assessing contributions has been a very substantial increase in the liability of self-employed persons.[19] So sharp has been the reaction of this group to the change that a petition has been addressed to the Commission of Human Rights alleging that the United Kingdom government has infringed the Convention by a discriminatory expropriation of property.[20] The question whether the liabil-

15. Para. 273.
16. Cf. Lister *Social Security: The Case for Reform* (1975), Poverty Pamphlet no. 22, pp. 39–41.
17. Ante, p. 21.
18. Post, pp. 58–63.
19. Post, p. 63, and see National Federation of Self Employed Policy

Strategy and Tactics Committee Research Paper 3 (1977).
20. The alleged infringement is of art. 14 of the Convention and art. 1 of Protocol No. 1. Cp. decision of the Commission on Application No. 4130/69.

ity is excessive in relation to entitlement to benefit under the scheme is a difficult one to resolve. If the appropriate comparison is between the contributions of the self-employed and the *aggregate* of contributions for employed persons (i.e., from both employer and employee) the argument is not so easy to maintain. It is generally accepted that on this basis, under the flat-rate system prevailing before 1973, other contributors were in fact subsidising contributions from the self-employed, and the reform has merely abolished this form of subsidy.[1] On the other hand, it can be argued that the comparison is not an appropriate one since many self-employed persons in fact run small businesses with employees of their own. This means that they must pay in addition to their own contributions those for their employees without, at the same time, having the facility to distribute the cost through increased prices to the extent that is possible for larger enterprises.[2] The argument rests on the status of the small trader within the economy as a whole and on the combined effect of social security contributions and general taxation: for that reason it is hard to assess. If anomalies do arise, it is primarily because there is a great variety of situations which the concept of 'self-employed' encompasses. The contention of the National Federation of Self-Employed that as *individuals*, their contributions to the scheme should be no greater than those of other individuals[3] does seem to be inappropriate.

iii) General taxation

Under Beveridge's plan and consistently thereafter, a place in the contributory scheme was alloted to general taxation but it was a small one (between 10% and 20%).[4] It was thought desirable not on redistributional principles but because it was clear that contributions recovered by the flat-rate method would otherwise be insufficient. In contrast, and, by definition, non-contributory benefits were to be financed from general taxation. In the post-war rationalisation, the scope for this approach was intended to be limited. True, family allowances constituted a major device for redistribution but Beveridge at least was equivocal on whether they should be financed from general taxation or from the national insurance fund, and in the end recommended the former on the pragmatic ground that the rate of contributions was already as high as the lower paid could afford.[5] Moreover, the other non-contributory scheme, national assistance, was regarded as a safety net, resort to which would gradually disappear. Paradoxically, while national assistance, and its successor supplementary benefit, increased in importance as more and more became dependent on it, the extent of redistribution through the family allowances scheme declined as the level of benefit did not keep pace with rising prices. The

1. See Standing Committe B Debates on Social Security Amendment Bill 1974, cols. 36–61.
2. Research Paper, ante n.19, at paras. 36 and 39.
3. Ibid., at para. 35.
4. *Beveridge*, para. 282. In 1975 the Exchequer contributed £817 million,

about 18% of the total: *Social Security Statistics 1975*, Table 44.02.
5. Para. 415. For the background to FAA 1945 generally see the excellent study by Land in Hall, Land, Parker, and Webb *Change, Choice and Conflict in Social Policy* (1975), chap. 9. See also *Harris*, pp. 343–344.

period 1970 to 1975, however, saw a very marked shift towards benefits financed from general taxation: family income supplement, payable to low wage-earners, the attendance allowance and the non-contributory invalidity pension, invalidity care allowance, mobility allowance. Some had argued for an even more extensive use of the technique in relation to those with family commitments through a new, generous, level of child endowment and a guaranteed maintenance allowance for single parent families.[6] They were to be mostly disappointed: the child benefit scheme fell short of expectations in both respects.

There has been much discussion, particularly by economists,[7] on the respective merits of contributory schemes and general taxation as methods for funding social security benefits. The arguments are difficult to unravel because not only do the contributory schemes themselves contain several different strategies (employer or employee, flat-rate or earnings-related), but also because the effect of the methods on industrial growth and level of earnings is still highly controversial. The general consensus of opinion is, however, as one might expect, that the taxation approach is more redistributional, and therefore preferable on grounds of social justice, while the contribution approach tends to greater economic efficiency and therefore increased overall welfare. As important as these theoretical studies are, they do not feature much in the discussions within the political arena. Instead, we tend to be confronted with broad vague sentiments based on what the public allegedly wants. Thus Beveridge felt able to report that

'benefit in return for contributions, rather than free allowances from the State, is what the people of Britain desire'.[8]

and the mood was echoed in the government White Paper which followed it.[9] The Crossman Paper on National Superannuation discredited arguments for a move to general taxation methods:

'people do not want to be *given* rights to pensions and benefits; they want to *earn* them by their contributions'.[10]

The vacuity of these statements may be self-evident, but their very existence provides the key to understanding why in the British and other systems the contributory approach remains the primary strategy for social security provision: the popularity of the method rests on its psychological appeal.[11] People are prepared to subscribe more by way of contributions, which they see as offering returns in the form of personal and family security, than they would be willing to pay by taxation, which might be

6. Post, p. 37.
7. Burns *Social Security and Public Policy* (1956), chap. 9; *Eckstein*, ante n.11; *Pechman, Aaron, Taussig*, ante n.11; Culyer *The Economics of Social Policy* (1975), pp. 202–204; Rejda *Social Insurance and Economic Security* (1976), pp. 162–172; *Dupeyroux*, pp. 169–178; *McCarthy*, chap. 16.

8. Para. 21.
9. Social Insurance, Part I, para. 6.
10. White Paper, National Superannuation and Social Insurance (1969), Cmnd. 3883, para. 25.
11. *McCarthy*, p. 158; *Eckstein*, ante n.11, at p. 51; Wilson *Pensions, Inflation and Growth* (1974), p. 28.

diverted to a wide variety of uses.[12] They are led to believe that because of
their contributions to the scheme they are participating in its administration and may thus exercise closer political control on its development.[13]
As has been observed, however, the same degree of public scrutiny should
operate through the parliamentary supervision of public spending
generally, if our political system is functioning properly.[14] Indeed, the
Royal Commission in New Zealand regarded as an important reason for
preferring the taxation approach the flexibility inherent in a system which
does not tie funds down to a particular form of social welfare but rather
allows different political administrations to take different views on social
priorities.[15] One undeniably genuine and important factor is that of
stigma. Sociologists have shown that we have been conditioned to bestow
greater esteem on systems built on exchanges (benefits in *return* for
contributions) than those incorporating unilateral transfers.[16] Nevertheless,
one may question whether this is an attitude which our social security
system should foster, and whether it is appropriate to perpetuate beliefs in
what are, in most respects, unreal differences between general and earmarked taxation. In the words of one commentator, the main effect of our
'contributory system' is 'to create confusion among the contributors/tax
payers and fiscal illusion'.[17]

E. Other forms of welfare provision

The policy-maker concerned to confer welfare on different groups within
society has three broad strategies available to him. He may arrange for
cash payments to be made (what we refer to as 'social security'), he may
provide for benefits in kind (typically known as 'social services'), or he may
exploit possibilities created by the fiscal systems, through e.g., tax reliefs.
In this section we explore the relationship between social security and the
other forms of welfare, and discuss some of the issues involved in the
choice between the various strategies.

i) Benefits in cash or in kind
Social welfare, as broadly construed, embraces a wide range of benefits in
kind, among many others those for health, education and housing.[18] On a
simple view, these services may be regarded as complementary to, and
independent from, the cash benefits which form the subject-matter of this
book: cash benefits, it might be said, are designed for income maintenance,
whereas the services are designed to fulfil other objectives of social policy.
However, the relationship between the two is both more complex and yet,
paradoxically, relatively neglected in the literature and governmental

12. National Superannuation, ante n.10, at
    para. 25.
13. Beveridge, para. 274.
14. *Culyer*, ante n.7, at p. 203.
15. *McCarthy*, p. 158.
16. Pinker *Social Theory and Social Policy*

(1971), chap. 4; Pruger, 2 Jnl. Soc.
Pol. 289.
17. *Culyer*, ante n.7, at p. 204.
18. See generally Baugh *Introduction to the
    Social Services* (2nd edn).

policy statements.[19] Three different approaches emerge from the three ideologies described in Part One of this chapter.

During the first period of public welfare, as represented by the poor law, attention was directed to poverty as a threat to order and stability.[20] As a remedial measure, the transfer of money was regarded as inappropriate since it neither guaranteed the protection of society nor did it constitute a sufficient incentive to avoid poverty. Moreover it was assumed that, almost as a matter of definition, people who were poor could not be trusted to use the money wisely.[1] The result was a combination of setting the poor to work and providing them with the minimum necessities of life in kind, the impotent through the system of 'poorhouses', the able-bodied through the workhouse, and the uncontrollable through penal institutions. Under the second, liberal individualist, approach, welfare is to be achieved through the operation of market forces and free enterprise.[2] Those substantially disadvantaged by poverty from participating fully in the system must be compensated by a degree of financial support. How that money is to be spent remains a matter of individual liberty and responsibility. Benefits in kind are thus reserved for those who are incapable of exercising that responsibility: the senile and the mentally handicapped.[3] This particular philosophy continues to exert a strong influence on our welfare system, and, in particular, may be used to explain why the Supplementary Benefits Commission is given power in specified circumstances to confer benefits in kind rather than cash.[4] Indeed, if the tenets of individualism are accepted, there is no reason why it should not be extended more widely to cover health services (as in most Western European systems[5]) and even education, through the provision of 'education vouchers'.[6]

The third collectivist approach is characterised by increased attempts at social integration and a very broad provision of social services.[7] While not opposed to income redistribution as such, the protagonists of this view place much greater reliance than the individualists on the extensive use of benefits in kind. The emphasis results from certain criticisms of the individualist philosophy. First, certain types of good, for example, health or education, are not proper subjects for the operation of market forces either because the social costs of mistaken decisions are too great or because, adopting a paternalist stance, it is not to be assumed that in such areas individuals always act as rational maximisers of their own welfare.[8]

19. Cf. International Social Security Association Studies and Research no. 6, *The Role of Social Services in Social Security* (1974); DHSS Report on Social Security Provision for Chronically Sick and Disabled People 1973–74 H.C. 276, paras, 26–28.
20. Cf. ante, p. 2.
 1. Report of Royal Commission on Poor Law (1834), Cd. 2728, pp. 276–277.
 2. Cf. ante, p. 3.
 3. Richardson *Economic and Financial Aspects of Social Security* (1960), pp. 51–52; Steiner, *The State of Welfare*

(1971), pp. 17–20.
 4. Post, p. 609.
 5. See Roemer *The Organisation of Medical Care under Social Security* (1969), ILO Studies and Reports no. 73, and ed. Martin *Comparative Developments in Social Welfare* (1972), chap. 8.
 6. See *Culyer*, ante n.7, at pp. 211–214, and the references there cited.
 7. Cf. ante, p. 5.
 8. Titmuss *Commitment to Welfare* (1968), pp. 147–150; Culyer, *The Economics of Social Policy* (1975), chap. 6.

Secondly, the model ignores the causes of poverty; by the careful use of services to prevent as well as to react to social hazards, the problem of inadequate income may, in some cases, be avoided.[9] Thirdly, the income redistribution technique is less sensitive to specific needs and less personal in its administration – the individual guidance implicit in the social service model may both respond in a humane way to individual circumstances and at the same time encourage greater social activity and participation.[10]

Certain consequences of adopting the benefits in kind approach should, however, be noted: it is inevitably much more costly to administer than the simple provision of cash benefit; it distorts the price structure in that it induces greater consumption of certain goods;[11] and it creates problems for legal enforcement. An individual deprived of a cash benefit may without undue difficulty appeal to a tribunal, whereas his counterpart inadequately met by the social services may find that either the authority concerned was under no duty to provide the service, or if it was, that a court will not be prepared to enforce it.[12]

ii) Social security and taxation

The relationship between the social security and taxation systems constitutes an important feature of the policy issues arising under social legislation.[13] There are three independent but related matters which call for discussion: first, the manner in which the tax system may, through its granting of reliefs, itself operate as a direct instrument of income support; secondly, the extent to which social security benefits are taxable, and the implications which this has on the degree of redistribution; thirdly, the desirability or otherwise of integrating taxation with social security.

a) TAX AS AN INSTRUMENT FOR INCOME SUPPORT. Since the introduction of progressive taxation in 1907 there has been what Titmuss has described as 'a remarkable development of social policy operating through the medium of the fiscal system'.[14] Most significantly this has taken the form of family support, through the granting of children's and other dependants' allowances[15] – the amount of income permitted to be accumulated before tax is imposed. If applied consistently throughout the tax structure, the system of reliefs has a retrogressive effect, for the value of the relief increases as the rate of tax increases. This fact added weight to the movement to introduce family allowances[16] – a benefit of equal value to

9. DHSS Report, ante n.19, at para. 27; Crosland *The Future of Socialism* (1961), pp. 145–146; Lebel in ISSA Studies and Research no. 6, ante n.19, at pp. 126–127.

10. *Lebel*, ibid., at p. 125; DHSS Report, ante n.19, at para. 26; *Crosland*, ante n.9, at p. 148; *Titmuss*, ante n.8, at p. 150.

11. *Dupeyroux*, pp. 213–219.

12. *Lebel*, ante n.9, at p. 125. For an example of the problems of obtaining a mandamus order where a duty does lie see *R v Bristol Corpn, ex parte*

Hendy [1974] 1 All ER 1047, [1974] 1 WLR 498, CA.

13. See in general Atkinson, 1 Jnl. Soc. Pol. 135–148, and Field, Pond and Meacher *To Him Who Hath* (1977).

14. *Essays on the Welfare State* (2nd edn), p. 45.

15. There are also minor forms of tax relief for the blind and disabled; see Whiteman and Wheatcroft *Income Tax* (2nd edn), pp. 919, 945.

16. See Hall, et al, *Change, Choice and Conflict in Social Policy* (1975), pp. 199–202, and post, p. 445.

all families. But, in 1945, it was not regarded as a sufficient reason for replacing tax relief by family benefits. It was felt that there was a difference of principle between the two systems. The Chancellor of the Exchequer had argued that while the family allowance was 'intended to reduce financial hardship arising from the maintenance of children . . . tax relief given in respect of children represents a recognition of the fact that the possession of children reduces the capacity to pay'.[17] The difficulty with the argument is that it confuses two different questions of equity: as between those with family commitments and those without, it is of course proper that the burden on the former should be reduced; but as between those with higher incomes and those less well endowed it is wrong that the former should gain a disproportionate advantage. It was this consideration which led in 1968 to a new, compromise, solution: the so-called 'claw-back'.[18] The amount by which family allowances were increased in that year was in effect deducted from the individual's tax relief, so that the benefit of the increase was used as the basis for a more extensive integration between the social security and taxation systems. One subsidiary difference between tax relief and monetary benefit should, however, be noted. While the former increases the take-home pay of the breadwinner (usually the father), the latter is normally paid directly to the mother.[19] As the Labour government was to discover in 1976,[20] this raises a delicate problem of distribution *within* the family.

b) TAX LIABILITY OF BENEFICIARIES. It has already been seen that the value of tax reliefs increases regressively in proportion to the taxable income of an individual. The same is true of such social security benefits as are not made taxable. Despite the problem of equity thereby created, the taxation of benefits has, at least until recently, been a neglected issue of social policy.[1] Not surprisingly, in the light of the decision in 1945 to maintain tax reliefs alongside the new family allowances, the latter were made subject to tax. The post-war government decided, logically, that all income-maintenance benefits (thus unemployment and sickness benefit, maternity allowance and retirement pension[2]) should also be taxed. As regards the short-term benefits, the policy was reversed in 1949, as it proved to be impracticable.[3] Beneficiaries could not be incorporated into the PAYE scheme and taxes had thus to be collected retrospectively. The recovery of millions of small debts by the Revenue was uneconomic.[4] Given the circumstances then prevailing, the decision was not unreasonable. Since 1949, however, the situation has changed dramatically. On the one hand, benefits have become earnings-related, so that they are more

17. White Paper on Family Allowances: Memorandum by the Chancellor of the Exchequer (1942). Cmd. 6134, p. 5. See also *Beveridge*, para. 422.
18. See generally Lynes in 'ed. Bull *Family Poverty* (2nd edn), chap. 10.
19. Post, p. 462.
20. Post, p. 449.
1. Cf. *Walley*, pp. 207–208 and Houghton

Paying for the Social Services (1968), IEA Occasional Paper 16, pp. 28–29.
2. Though anomalously not industrial injury benefit.
3. Finance Act 1949.
4. *Houghton*, ante n.1, at p. 28 and see Report of the Committee on the Taxation of Pensions for Retirement (1954), Cmd. 9063, paras. 271–294.

than ever before a true income substitute, and the amounts involved are no longer negligible. On the other hand, the administration of tax and social security is more clearly integrated than it was – indeed, the records of taxpayers are now kept under their national insurance numbers. Quite apart from the primary consideration that benefits should not be regressive, there are two other compelling reasons for reinstating the earlier policy. The typically low tax thresholds which currently exist together with non-taxed earnings-related benefit means that the beneficiaries are often better off out of work than when employed, which raises problems of work incentives.[5] These are exacerbated if, as is often the case with white-collar workers who would otherwise be liable for a significant amount of tax, support is forthcoming also from occupational schemes.[6] Secondly, the existence of a progressive system of taxation collected by the PAYE method means that during spells of unemployment or sickness an employee may be entitled to weekly refunds of tax paid on previous earning, thus creating a kind of 'parallel system of . . . benefits . . . calculated on the mythical basis that the worker, during his unemployment or sickness, had no social security income at all'.[7] It is difficult to find valid objections to these arguments, but to put them into effect creates political obstacles: it may seem to the uninitiated observer as if the Chancellor is 'taxing the sick', a charge which has more rhetorical than rational appeal[8] but which in the political arena is not so easily repudiated.

c) INTEGRATION OF TAX AND SOCIAL SECURITY. The perceived need both to rationalise the existing relationship between taxation and social security and to remove anomalies created by untaxed benefits was joined by a third force which saw in an integrated tax-welfare scheme the way to abolish poverty altogether. The movement has developed from and been inspired by three different sources. The first is ideological and emanates mainly from the United States of America, particularly from Friedman's conviction that welfare is best achieved through competitive capitalism and by reducing state intervention.[9] Poverty, as inhibiting freedom or full participation in the economy, is to be eliminated, and the most efficient way of achieving this is to extend the tax system downwards so that those below the poverty level should receive instead of contribute – the negative income tax.[10] The system was more fully worked out by other American writers,[11] and a moderate version was adopted by the Nixon administration, though it failed to pass through Congress.[12] The second source comprised commentators on this side of the Atlantic. Less influenced, perhaps, by the ideological factors than by the methods proposed, they regarded as cumbersome and inefficient the coexistence of various benefit schemes, particularly when the tax system provided in effect a means-

5. *Walley*, p. 208.
6. *Houghton*, ante n.1, at p. 29.
7. *Walley*, p. 207.
8. Cf., *Atiyah*, p. 371 and *Houghton*, ante n.1, at p. 18.
9. *Capitalism and Freedom* (1962).
10. Ibid., at pp. 190–192.

11. See, especially, Green *Negative Taxes and the Poverty Problem* (1967) and ed. Theobald *The Guaranteed Income* (1967).
12. See generally Moynihan *The Politics of a Guaranteed Income* (1973).

tested approach without stigma. The Labour party at one time dallied with
the idea of using tax returns for national assistance claims.[13] Others
proposed to adopt the American model of negative income tax.[14] A slightly
less ambitious, but arguably more practical, plan to cover employed
persons and national insurance beneficiaries was advanced by the Conservative government in 1972.[15] The Tax Credit scheme, as it was called,
though in general endorsed by a Parliamentary Select Committee[16] never
reached the stage of draft legislation and it remains to be seen whether a
future Conservative administration will resurrect the idea.

The third stream of influence extends back to 1943 when, as an alternative to the Beveridge plan, Lady Rhys Williams urged the adoption of a
'social dividend', the payment to all members of society of weekly amounts
necessary for the ordinary needs of living.[17] This notion has been
elaborated and modified by others,[18] and is associated with less dramatic
versions of the same theme which would concentrate on universal and
generous child or family endowment.[19] While the Child Benefit Act 1975
was publicised as directed towards this end, and will eventually supersede
family support through the tax system, its critics allege that it still falls far
short of the level of endowment which they regard as desirable or necessary.[20]

There is not the space here to consider the details of the many different
schemes proposed.[1] Instead, an attempt will be made to describe their
common themes and to present some of the policy issues they raise. In
their essentials, the models of both schemes are easily comprehended. The
negative income tax (NIT) involves an extension of existing tax schedules
below a certain exemption level. If an individual's income falls above that
level, he is taxed in the normal way; if it falls below, he receives a payment
representing some proportion of the difference between his income and
the exemption level. The level itself would be fixed according to socially
acceptable variables, but on most proposals these would be confined to the
size of the family and possibly the age of its members. The exclusion of
other than economic criteria would mean that the traditional categories of
the contributory benefit schemes (e.g. unemployment, sickness, retire-

13. Election Manifesto 1964.
14. Notably Lees, Lloyds Bank Rev., Oct.
    1967, pp. 1–15 and a study group
    sponsored by the Institute of
    Economic Affairs, *Policy for Poverty*
    (1970), Research Monograph 20.
15. Green Paper, Proposals for a Tax-
    Credit System, Cmnd. 5116.
16. 1972–73 HC 341.
17. Rhys Williams *Something to Look
    Forward To* (1943).
18. Notably Brown and Dawson *Personal
    Taxation, Incentives and Tax Reform*
    (1969).
19. The most influential have been those
    of *Walley*, pp. 191–202 (see also ed.
    Bull *Family Poverty* (2nd edn), chap.
    9), and of the Child Poverty Action

Group: see Field and Townsend *A
    Social Contract for Families* (1975).
20. See post, pp. 448–449.
 1. The literature of the subject is
    immense. In addition to the works
    already cited see Hayhoe *Must the
    Children Suffer?* (1968); Conservative
    Political Centre; Atkinson *Poverty in
    Britain and the Reform of Social
    Security* (1969), chap. 9; Townsend
    Social Services for All (1970), Fabian
    Essays, chap. 10; Barker in ed. Bull,
    ante n.19, chap. 5; Atkinson *Tax
    Credit System and the Redistribution of
    Income* (1973), Institute of Fiscal
    Studies; Lynes in ed. Young *Poverty
    Report 1974*, pp. 92–99.

ment etc.) would be abandoned. The scheme would be administered principally by tax returns. If intended to be fully comprehensive, it would therefore be necessary to extend the system of income statements to those at present outside the tax structure, and would also involve the creation of additional machinery to cope with sudden changes in earnings and family circumstances. Especially with regard to these latter factors, the social dividend proposal (SD) is fundamentally different. It would offer an automatic payment, according to the assessed level of needs, to all citizens. Those already possessing sufficient resources would of course not benefit, as their dividend would, along with other funds be ploughed back through a proportionate tax on income.

The first advantage asserted by the proponents of both types of scheme is that they avoid the problems inherent in means-tested benefits of stigma and low take-up.[2] The stigma argument is indisputable, but that on take-up applies with greater force to SD than to NIT, for the latter would still require a complex means-test to be completed, for which purpose the present form of income tax return would prove insufficient.[3] The second claim is that by abolishing all the various categories involved in the typical social security scheme the system would become at once more comprehensive and simpler: it would also focus on those in greatest need.[4] Again the proposition seems to be well founded, but it nevertheless raises the question whether the abolition of special treatment for different categories is a desirable objective. It is not so obvious, for example, that a man retired at 55 should be paid the same as someone considerably older, or that the disabled should be treated no differently from the unemployed.[5] Moreover, no system of standard computerised assessment would be able to deal adequately with special circumstances which occur suddenly and which require immediate assistance, so that inevitably some form of discretionary aid (akin to the present payments for exceptional needs under the Supplementary Benefits Act[6]) would have to complement the general scheme.[7] Indeed in respect of NIT, there is a problem created by the period of assessment. In accordance with PAYE methods, this would typically fall in line with the normal periods of employment pay, but it is difficult to see how this could apply satisfactorily to the self-employed; and for others with considerable variations in earnings, difficulties would be caused by the fact that the assessment for the welfare payment would be based on the previous rather than the current period.[8] In this respect, the SD approach of guaranteeing a minimum income *in advance* (leaving it to the tax mechanism to draw on differentials retrospectively) would be preferable.[9]

Widely differing views have been expressed on the difficult issue of work incentives. Advocates of the proposals typically lay great stress on this

2. *Lees*, ante n.14, at pp. 9–10; *Hayhoe*, ante n.1, at p. 10. These problems are discussed ante, p. 13.
3. *Walley*, p. 280.
4. *Lees*, ante n.14, at pp. 7–9, IEA Study, ante n.14, at pp. 35–36.
5. *McCarthy*, pp. 162–163.
6. See post, pp. 519–525.
7. Green Paper, ante n.15, at para. 1; *Walley*, p. 280.
8. *Lynes*, ante n.1, at pp. 25–26.
9. Culyer *The Economics of Social Policy* (1975), pp. 103–104.

objective.[10] Unfortunately, there is far too little evidence on how welfare payments and tax rates affect working patterns[11] and in any event much would depend on the exact details of the scheme in question. There are, however, two independent problems of incentive to be solved. The first relates to those below the break-even point, and thus in receipt of benefit. Under the NIT scheme, it would be possible to reduce the proportion payable on the difference between the break-even point and the claimant's pre-benefit income to take account of the problem, though some authors argue that with such scanty evidence on how incentives work in practice, it has yet to be proved that such a step would be either effective or necessary.[12] More serious perhaps is the problem for those above the exemption level. It has been estimated that the marginal tax rate for these would be high, if the benefits of the scheme are to be sufficiently generous, and it is feared that quite apart from the problem of political acceptability, this would act as a serious disincentive on output.[13]

Consideration of the cost of the various schemes and their likely effects in terms of distribution lies beyond the scope of this work, though as one might expect, there is a broad conflict of opinion on such matters ranging from those who are convinced that poverty would thereby be abolished to those who foresee as a result only the rationalisation of the existing systems of social security and taxation, leaving untouched the basic problems of inequality. One reason why it is impossible to reconcile these various attitudes is that they rest on different ideological bases.[14] Most of those arguing for integration between the tax and social security systems tend to see poverty as the difference between those below and those above a certain level of income and they therefore seek to guarantee to all members of society a standard of living at that particular level. Their opponents see poverty as a reflection of economic and social inequalities generally and fear that such a concentrated effort on the income question alone would deflect attention from the more important objective of social and economic integration.

Part three. Scope and Structure of Book

A. Scope

The term 'social security' in legal and non-legal contexts carries a variety of meanings which must be carefully distinguished if ambiguity is to be avoided.[15] First, as one area of social policy it is used both in British and international sources to connote the measures necessary to secure the

10. E.g. *Green*, ante n.11, chap. 8; *Lees*, ante n.14, at pp. 10–11, Green Paper, ante n.15, at para. 103.

11. Cf., *Culyer*, ante n.9, at pp. 103–104, and the references cited at p. 110.

12. *Townsend*, ante n.1, at pp. 59–61.

13. Atkinson *Poverty in Britain etc.*, ante n.1, at pp. 167–168; *Culyer*, ante n.9, at pp. 102–104.

14. Cf., *Barker*, ante n.1, at pp. 65–69.

15. See, in general, *Micklethwait*, chap. 3; *George*, chap. 1; Rejda *Social Insurance and Economic Security* (1976), p. 9; Doublet *Sécurité Sociale* (5th edn), pp. 11–19; Kaufmann, *Sicherheit als Soziologisches und Sozialpolitisches Problem* (1970), chap. 3.

political and economic objective of freedom from want. It was in this sense
that it was adopted by Beveridge,[16] and subsequently, under his influence,
passed into international currency[17] within the auspices of such institutions as the International Labour Organisation[18] and the Council of
Europe.[19] Secondly, as a legal term of art, it was admitted relatively late
into British legislation and as such remains a source of some confusion.[20]
In institutional terms, the Ministry of Social Security[1] later superseded by
the Department of Health and Social Security,[2] was concerned with the
national schemes of income maintenance: national insurance, family
allowances, supplementary benefits and war pensions. But as used in the
Social Security Acts of 1973 and 1975, and the subordinate instruments
made under those Acts, the term is applied to those benefits which were
formerly payable under the national insurance schemes (industrial and
non-industrial) and which are now referred to as 'contributory benefits'[3]
together with the non-contributory benefits for the aged, the disabled and
guardians.[4] 'Social security' in this narrow legal sense does not include
child benefit or the means-tested family income supplement and supplementary benefit. Thirdly, and paradoxically in the light of this development, in popular current usage it is often intended to refer solely to the
means-tested supplementary benefit scheme.[5]

For the purpose of determining the scope of this book, we have adopted
the institutional meaning. We are concerned to describe the law governing
entitlement to such financial benefits as are administered by the Department of Health and Social Security, arising primarily from the following
instruments:

Social Security Act 1975 (as amended by Social Security Pensions
    Act 1975);
Supplementary Benefits Act 1976;
Family Income Supplements Act 1970;
Child Benefit Act 1975;
Royal Warrant of 1964 (for war pensions).

16. Paras. 11–13, and 300.
17. There is, however, little uniformity on
    whether the expression, as used in
    international instruments, includes
    medical care and social assistance.
18. See, Declaration of Philadelphia
    (1944), art. 3(f) and Convention no.
    102 on Minimum Standards of Social
    Security (1952). See, further, post p.
    000.
19. E.g., European Code of Social Security
    (1964). See, further, post, p. 000.
20. *Micklethwait*, chap. 3.

1. Created by Ministry of Social Security
   Act 1966. To add to the confusion the
   Act whose primary purpose was the
   replacement of national assistance by
   the supplementary benefit scheme was
   subsequently renamed the
   Supplementary Benefit Act 1966 by
   SSA 1973, s.99(18).
2. S.I. 1968/1699. For the history of the
   administrative changes see post, chap.
   14.
3. SSA 1975, Part II, chap. I.
4. Ibid, chap. II.
5. *Micklethwait*, p. 26.

B. Structure

In the first part of the book (chapters 2 to 10) we deal with those benefits which are governed principally by the Social Security Act 1975. However, because of the close relationship between the industrial injury and war pension shemes, we have inserted our account of the latter within this part, notwithstanding that it is governed by Royal Warrant and Orders in Council, so that the two chapters (8 and 9 respectively) may be read consecutively. The rest of this part is concerned with the system of contributions (chapter 2) and those benefits entitlement to which depends on the fulfilment of contribution conditions,

> viz., unemployment benefit (chapter 3), invalidity and sickness benefits (chapter 4), retirement pensions (chapter 5), widow's benefit, child's special allowance and death grant (chapter 6) and maternity benefits (chapter 7).

It also contains accounts of the non-contributory benefits payable under the Social Security Act 1975 (placed near those contributory benefits to which they most closely relate):

> non-contributory invalidity pension, attendance, invalid care and mobility allowances (chapter 4), old age pension (chapter 5), widow's pension (chapter 6) and guardian's allowance (chapter 7).

Finally, in chapter 10 there is a discussion of certain concepts which are common to several or most of the above benefits:

> increases for dependants; marriage; cohabitation; residence and presence; hospital in-patients; imprisonment and detention in legal custody; earnings-related supplements; the calculation of earnings; the uprating of benefits; overlapping benefits.

The next part treats the three schemes which are independent of the Social Security Act 1975, viz., child benefit (chapter 11) and the means-tested supplementary benefits (chapter 12) and family income supplement (chapter 13).

The book concludes with matters arising in connection with all the above-mentioned schemes: the administration of benefits (chapter 14), adjudication (chapter 15), and the impact on the British system of certain international legal obligations, notably those emanating from the European Economic Communities (chapter 16).

2 Contributions

Part one. Introduction

In chapter 1 the various methods of financing social security benefits were considered, and it was seen how British policy has continued to favour the contributory approach. In this chapter we describe the liability to pay contributions and the general principles governing the fulfilment of contribution conditions. The basic concepts are derived from the insurance schemes existing before the Second World War but their character has since changed in several fundamental respects.

A. Risk-related insurance

As has already been explained,[1] private insurance influenced the development of national insurance, and this is particularly evident in the early efforts of the state schemes to relate liability to the risks attached to particular categories of individuals or employments. The first unemployment insurance of 1911 covered only those trades in which the employment pattern was thought to be reasonably stable.[2] Moreover, employers of men who by the age of 60 had paid more by way of contribution than they had received by way of benefit were entitled to a refund.[3] This right lasted only until 1920, at which time also insurance coverage was extended to all manual workers engaged under a contract of service, and non-manual workers of a similar description whose income was below a certain level.[4] However, the principle of differentiation was not totally abandoned, for industries with particularly low unemployment might adopt their own special scheme and, with the approval of the Minister, opt out of national insurance,[5] an arrangement permitted for the finance and banking industries until 1946.[6] Unemployment insurance was extended to agriculture only in 1936 and then at special rates of benefit and contribution.[7] Other forms of insurance did not call for the same degree of differentiation but the health scheme was administered by Approved Societies, who could offer by way of benefit in return for the nationally

1. Ante, p. 26.
2. Post, p. 79.
3. NIA 1911, s.94.
4. UIA 1920.

5. Ibid., s.18.
6. See S. R. & O. 1938, Nos. 589 and 656.
7. UI(Agriculture) Act 1936.

determined rate of contributions whatever they wished above the national minimum.[8] Finally, mention should be made of the low rates of contribution paid, and the even lower benefits received, by women on the ground that they were 'poor risks'.[9]

B. Comprehensive insurance

One of the primary objectives of the Beveridge plan, and the legislation which implemented it, was to abolish such vestiges of the risk-related approach which remained, and to establish a fully comprehensive system in which all would share in supporting the burden of those subjected to the prescribed social risks:

> 'The term "social insurance" . . . implies both that it is compulsory and that men stand together with their fellows'.[10]

The policy gave rise to four important modifications of the pre-war schemes. First, compulsory insurance was extended to those previously above the income limits. Secondly, it included those substantially free from one or more of the social risks (e.g., civil servants in relation to unemployment) or with sufficient protection under their terms of employment (e.g., the police in relation to sickness and old age – though members of HM Forces in a somewhat analogous position were allowed to pay a lower rate of contributions[11]). Thirdly, the Approved Societies were no longer to administer health insurance, and the special arrangements for agriculture, banking and finance were also abolished. Finally, the self-employed were covered for all purposes except unemployment and industrial injury. The special status of women as such was also eradicated; instead, the legislation singled out for special treatment those who were married. They could opt out of insurance in their own right, and, if they elected to stay in, would pay lower contributions and receive lower benefits.[12] The comprehensive coverage was completed by the compulsory insurance of all remaining persons over sixteen who were not gainfully employed: in return for their weekly contribution, they qualified for all benefits except those for unemployment, sickness and industrial injury.[13] Contributions could not, of course, be extracted from those on very low incomes and the problem was met by, on the one hand, exempting from liability (and also therefore from entitlement to all benefits) those whose income did not exceed £2 a week,[14] and, on the other hand, excusing from the payment of contributions, but nevertheless crediting for certain purposes, those unemployed or incapable of work or undergoing education or training.[15] While Beveridge's assumption was that many would participate in occupational schemes to lift their income above the standard subsistence rate of benefit, there was no question of using this as an

---

8. Post, p. 139.
9. Post, p. 64.
10. *Beveridge*, para. 26.
11. Post, p. 68.

12. Post, p. 65.
13. NIA 1946, s.4(2)(c).
14. Ibid., s.5(1)(a)(iii).
15. Ibid., s.5(1)(a)(i)–(ii).

argument to justify exemption from the national scheme. Different considerations were, however, to prevail when earnings-related pensions were introduced, first with the limited graduated scheme of 1959,[16] and subsequently with the more comprehensive approach of 1975.[17] In both cases, contributions to the state earnings-related element was voluntary in the sense that those with sufficient coverage elsewhere might opt out.

c. Liability according to capacity

The policy issues raised by the nature of the contributions payable have already been discussed in chapter 1.[18] Here it is necessary merely to relate how the insurance system gradually evolved towards a principle of liability according to capacity to pay. Under the early schemes, flat-rate contributions of the worker were matched by those of his employer, generally on an equal basis,[19] and the fund was augmented by a grant from the Exchequer. Certain concessions were, however, granted to low-wage earners who paid a reduced contribution.[20] The principles were maintained under the 1946 reconstruction, except that the liability of the employer was somewhat lower than that of the employee.[1] The flat-rate approach, of which Beveridge was such an enthusiastic advocate, proved insufficient to finance benefits at the desired level and a shift to an earnings-related method became inevitable. Under the graduated pensions scheme, those contributing paid $4\frac{1}{2}\%$ of their earnings between £9 and £15, the employer being liable for a similar amount.[2] The hybrid system for those in employment of flat-rate and graduated contributions was replaced in 1973–75 by a single system of contributions paid on earnings between a much wider band.[3] The assimilation to an income tax method of financing was taken even further by imposing on the self-employed, in addition to a flat-rate liability, a charge on profits and gains,[4] notwithstanding that the earnings-related supplements for sickness, maternity and widow's benefits continued to be unavailable to this group. In times when pay restraint was an important economic objective, it was politically easier to impose increased contributions not only on the self-employed but also on employers. So, in contrast to the position prevailing after 1946, the liability of the latter was set at a rate higher than that of employees.[5]

d. Unity of administration

Before the co-ordinating legislation of 1946 there were in effect three independent insurance schemes: those for unemployment and for health

16. Post, pp. 193–194.
17. Post, pp. 225–227.
18. Ante, pp. 28–30.
19. Though not under the original national health scheme to which the employer paid 3d a week and the male employee 4d: NIA 1911, Sch. 2.
20. See, e.g., NHIA 1924, Sch. 2.
1. The ratio was approximately 55–45: NIA 1946, Sch. 1.
2. NIA 1959, s.1(1).
3. Post, p. 56.
4. Post, p. 63.
5. Post, p. 58.

both dating from 1911,[6] and that for widows', orphans' and old age pensions established in 1925.[7] But the financing of the health and pensions schemes was amalgamated so that in practice each insured person had to maintain two insurance records, in the form of cards to which stamps representing weekly contributions were affixed. In 1946 the three schemes were replaced by a single national insurance system, with the weekly contribution stamp serving for all the contributory benefits. The independent industrial injuries scheme superseded the workmen's compensation legislation, which had imposed liability for compensation on the individual employer, but the contributions to this insurance fund were added automatically to those payable for employed persons under the main scheme. In 1973 the separate industrial injuries fund was abolished and henceforth benefits were financed by the ordinary National Insurance Fund. The introduction of earnings-related contributions necessarily made their calculation and collection more complicated and under the legislation of 1973–75 administration was simplified by combining the process with that of income tax assessment, notably for employed persons through the PAYE system.[8] The affixing of stamps to an insurance card remained only for the flat-rate contributions by the self-employed, and even they could be paid by direct debit from the contributor's bank or by National Giro.[9]

E. Outline of system

The monies collected from social security contributions are neither used exclusively for the financing of social security benefits nor do they provide the funds necessary for all such benefits.

1. SOCIAL SECURITY BENEFITS FINANCED BY CONTRIBUTIONS. All contributory benefits (formerly national insurance benefits), viz., those for unemployment, sickness, invalidity, maternity, widowhood, retirement (Categories A and B), child's special allowance, and death grant, and benefits for industrial injuries (including old workmen's compensation cases), are so derived.

2. SOCIAL SECURITY BENEFITS FINANCED BY GENERAL TAXATION. All remaining social security benefits are financed from the Exchequer, thus child benefit, family income supplement, supplementary benefits, war pensions and the non-contributory benefits under the Social Security Act 1975, viz., attendance allowance, non-contributory invalidity pension, invalid care allowance, mobility allowance, guardian's allowance, and Category C or D retirement pensions.

3. OTHER PURPOSES FINANCED BY CONTRIBUTIONS. The social security contributions are used partly to finance the National

6. NIA 1911.
7. Widows', Orphans' and Old Age Contributory Pensions Act 1925.
8. See, generally, S.I. 1975/492, Part V.
9. Ibid., Reg. 46(3).

Health Service, the Redundancy Fund and the Maternity Pay Fund.[10]

The funds collected under the Social Security Act 1975 are derived from three sources: insured persons, employers and the Exchequer. The Exchequer contributes each year 18% of the amount of all other contributions used for contributory benefits (i.e., excluding the sums payable for the National Health Service, the Redundancy and Maternity Pay Funds[11]). Contributions from insured persons and employers are divided into four categories:

> *Class 1*. Primary contributions from 'employed earners' and secondary contributions from 'employers and other persons paying earnings', both being earnings-related.
> *Class 2*. Flat-rate contributions from self-employed earners;
> *Class 3*. Voluntary flat-rate contributions from earners and others;
> *Class 4*. Contributions payable on the basis of profits or gains arising from a trade, profession or vocation.

Part Two describes the principles of categorisation, the methods of assessing liability and also the grounds on which persons may be exempt from contributions. In Part Three we consider the position of married women, widows and other special categories of contributors. Finally, Part Four is concerned with the contribution conditions which must be satisfied for entitlement to benefit and the rules to assist those otherwise unable to qualify.

Part two. Classification of Contributions

A. General

This Part is devoted to the principles governing liability to pay contributions of Classes 1, 2 and 4 and entitlement to pay those in Classes 2 and 3. Under the pre-1973 legislation insured *persons* were categorised accordingly.[12] Under the new scheme, the classification is of *contributions*. The important reason for this change of terminology is that an insured person may now be liable to pay contributions both as an employed (Class 1), and as a self-employed, person (Classes 2 and 4). The law defining the various categories remains, however, substantially unchanged. In particular, regard must be had to the complex case-law distinguishing between employed and self-employed persons. In this connection, it is worth observing that adjudication of disputes as to classification and the fulfilment of contribution conditions is within the jurisdiction not of the normal statutory authorities, viz., insurance officer, local tribunals and Commissioner, but of the Secretary of State.[13] A question of law arising

---

10. See SSA 1975, ss.1(1) and 134, as amended by Employment Protection Act 1975, s.40.

11. SSA 1975, s.1(5).

12. NIA 1965, s.1(2).

13. SSA 1975, s.93: cf., post, p. 621.

from any such decision may be referred for final determination to the High Court (or in Scotland the Court of Session) either by the Secretary of State if he thinks fit or by a person aggrieved by the decision.[14] Many of the High Court decisions are of course published in the ordinary law reports, and for the period 1950–60, HMSO published selected decisions of the Minister on classification questions.[15]

B. Primary Class 1 contributions

Class 1 contributions may confer title to any contributory benefit. The primary contributions of this class are payable by 'employed earners'.[16] An 'employed earner' is defined as

> 'a person who is gainfully employed in Great Britain either under a contract of service, *or* in an office (including elective office) with emoluments chargeable to income tax under Schedule E'.[17]

The second alternative was added in 1973,[18] the intention being to correlate Class 1 contributors with Schedule E tax payers and thus to facilitate the collection of contributions through the PAYE system.

i) Gainfully employed

For both alternative formulations, the contributor must be 'gainfully employed'. This replaces the phrase 'gainfully occupied' used in the earlier legislation.[19] The significance of the modification is unclear. A body of case-law had been built around the interpretation of 'gainfully occupied' for the purposes not only of the classification of contributors but also in relation to retirement pensions[20] and increases for dependants.[1] One possible view is that, in the light of different policy considerations, it was thought desirable to keep distinct the interpretation of the phrase in its various contexts. If so, this would justify the authorities approaching the changed statutory formula *de novo*. A more likely explanation is that the notion of 'occupation' was thought to be too restrictive when applied to the new category of 'office with emoluments'. If this is correct, it should follow that the interpretation of the concept has remained substantially unchanged. The basic idea is that the contributor

> 'receives from his master under the contract of employment something by way of remuneration for the services which he is contractually bound to render to the master under the contract of service'.[2]

Under the former legislation, it was important to determine what was to be

14. SSA 1975, s.94.
15. The 'M' Decisions. It is not clear why publication ceased in 1960.
16. SSA 1975, s.1(2).
17. Ibid., s.2(1)(a).
18. SSA 1973, s.1(7).

19. NIA 1965, s.1(2).
20. Ibid., s.30(2), cf., post pp. 202–210.
1. Ibid., s.43(1)(b); cf., post p. 387.
2. Per Slade J, *Vandyk v Minister of Pensions and National Insurance* [1955] 1 QB 29 at 38.

regarded as 'remuneration'.[3] Under the new system the problem no longer arises because contributions are earnings-related and there is a body of rules, described below,[4] governing the nature and calculation of 'earnings' for this purpose.

ii) Contract of service

The classification of individuals into employed and self-employed persons, as characterised by the distinction between a 'contract of service' and a 'contract for services', has been a regular legal conundrum and not only in social security law. The Social Security Act 1975 makes only a marginal effort to alleviate the problems by prescribing that 'contract of service' means

> 'any contract of service or apprenticeship, whether written or oral and whether expressed or implied'.[5]

Resort must therefore be had to the case-law.[6] As implied above, decisions on the matter are not limited to social security law: many other legal consequences flow from the existence of a contract of service, for example, the right to a redundancy payment and the imposition of vicarious liability on the employer. The first question thus arises whether decisions on such other areas may legitimately throw light on the problem under discussion. On one view, the different legal consequences give rise to different policy issues, and it is therefore dangerous to cross legal boundaries.[7] It may be conceded that the policy considerations applicable in the present context are, for the most part, peculiar to social security law. They are, first, that the employee is financially more dependent on his employer, thus justifying a system of joint contributions and, secondly, that his occupation is such that insurance against unemployment, exclusive to Class 1 contributors, is regarded as appropriate. But the better view appears to be that there are uniform answers to the problem.[8] When Parliament uses the term 'contract of service', it must be assumed to have in mind the traditional judicial interpretation of the phrase, and it would create great confusion and administrative inconvenience if an individual was an 'employee' for some purposes but not for others.

A second preliminary question is whether the distinction between a contract of service and a contract for services is one of law or of fact. This is important because the jurisdiction of the High Court (or Court of Session) is limited to determinations of issues of law.[9] Earlier dicta suggested that regard should primarily be had to the terms of the contract, and that their proper construction was a question of law.[10] According to

---

3. See, by way of analogy, the decisions on retirement pensions and dependants' increases: post, pp. 426–432.
4. P. 56.
5. Sch. 20.
6. There are particularly valuable descriptions in Atiyah *Vicarious Liability* (1967) pp. 35–95, and Rideout *Principles of Labour Law* (2nd edn), pp. 1–12.

7. *Rideout*, ante n.6, at p. 9.
8. Cf. *Atiyah*, ante n.6, at pp. 32–33.
9. See generally post, p. 623.
10. Per Lord Parker CJ, *Morren v Swinton and Pendlebury Borough Council* [1965] 2 All ER 349 at 352, DC; per Megaw J, *Amalgamated Engineering Union v Minister of Pensions and National Insurance* [1963] 1 All ER 864 at 869.

more recently expressed opinions, however, account must also be taken of the conduct of the parties and other evidence external to the contract.[11] The process of balancing these various factors is a matter which the Secretary of State is alone entitled to perform and his decision will be reviewed by the courts only if it contains a false proposition of law on its face, if it was supported by no evidence, or if the facts were found such that no person acting judicially and properly instructed on the law could have come to that decision.[12]

What then are the principles of law as to which the finder of facts should be instructed? Judicial views on the theoretical nature of the distinction have undergone serious transformation. The classical nineteenth-century test was one of supervision and control: 'a servant is a person subject to the command of his master as to the manner in which he shall do his work'.[13] The first High Court decisions under the National Insurance Act 1946 placed great reliance on this criterion,[14] but its limitations in the modern technological and commercial world soon provoked a more critical attitude. It was obvious in the first place that there could be little or no direct control over the work of a professional or skilled employee, such as a doctor working in a hospital,[15] a theatrical or circus artist[16] or a political columnist,[17] nor where the employer was a corporate entity and the employee was of a high status, e.g., a company director.[18] Secondly, it is imprecise. The 'employer' of an independent contractor, for example, may reserve to himself the right to direct not only what is to be done, but in broad outlines how it is to be done.[19]

Dissatisfaction with the control test prompted Denning LJ (as he then was) to formulate a new criterion, whether the alleged employee was 'part and parcel of the organisation',[20] whether he was 'employed as part of the business, and his work is done as an integral part of the business'.[1]

11. Per Megaw J, *Willy Scheidegger Swiss Typewriting School (London) Ltd v Minister of Social Security* (1968) 5 KIR 65 at 69; per Cooke J, *Construction Industry Training Board v Labour Forces* [1970] 3 All ER 220 at 224, DC; per Bridge J, *Rennison & Son v Minister of Social Security* (1970) 10 KIR 65 at 69.
12. Per Lord Widgery CJ, *Global Plant v Secretary of State for Health and Social Security* [1971] 3 All ER 385 at 393. The view is supported by May J in *Graham v Brunswick* (1971) 16 KIR 158 at 163.
13. Per Bramwell B, *Yewens v Noakes* (1880) 6 QBD 530 at 532–533.
14. *Gould v Minister of National Insurance* [1951] 1 KB 731, [1951] 1 All ER 368; *Stagecraft v Minister of National Insurance* 1952 SC 288. That the 'control' theory still has considerable influence on the DHSS administration may be inferred from its use in the leaflets which are issued to members of

the public. See, e.g., NI 46 (Non-NHS nurses and midwives): 'in general, if you can be told what to do and how to do it you are an employee'.
15. *Cassidy v Minister of Health* [1951] 2 KB 243, [1951] 1 All ER 574, CA.
16. *Whittaker v Minister of Pensions and National Insurance* [1967] 1 QB 156, [1966] 3 All ER 531.
17. *Beloff v Pressdram* [1973] 1 All ER 241.
18. *Lee v Lee's Air Farming* [1961] AC 12, [1960] 3 All ER 420, PC; NB. by virtue of his 'office', such a person is now a Class 1 contributor; post, p. 53.
19. E.g., *Construction Training Board* case, ante, n.11 (contract construction labourer); M25 (tailoring outworker); M48 (BBC interviewer).
20. *Bank voor Handel en Scheepvaart v Slatford* [1953] 1 QB 248 at 295.
1. *Stevenson, Jordan and Harrison v Macdonald and Evans* [1952] 1 TLR 101 at 111, CA.

This approach, and an analogous test of 'economic reality' emanating from the United States Supreme Court,[2] have attracted some support.[3] They have the advantage of directing attention to the admittedly important issue of whose assets are involved in the undertaking and who stands to profit or lose on its outcome, but it can be objected that, though these are factors to be taken into account, they are no more decisive than was (or is) the control element. It has indeed become obvious, and is readily acknowledged in almost all recent cases on the subject,[4] that it is a question of having regard to a number of factors, any number or combination of which might be relevant in a given case. The mere reference to such factors does not, of course, indicate how they are to be deployed, or what weight is to be given to each. For the most part, judges have refused to be drawn on this issue, contenting themselves with the general proposition that the relative importance of the various factors will vary from case to case.[5]

Some of the more important factors, to which the Secretary of State should attribute such weight as in his discretion seems appropriate, may be described as follows.

1. SUPERVISION OF WORK. Though the control test has rightly been repudiated as the sole or decisive criterion, close and regular supervision of the work process clearly remains an important factor, especially for less skilled occupations.[6]

2. POWERS OF APPOINTMENT AND DISMISSAL. This factor is often mentioned,[7] but if it refers to the appointment and dismissal of the person whose classification is in question it is generally helpful only in indicating to which of two 'employers' he is contractually engaged.[8] More important for the present purpose is whether the 'employee' has the power to employ a substitute to assist him or to whom his duties may be delegated[9]

3. FORM OF REMUNERATION. The typical contract of service provides for regular remuneration in the form of a salary or wages, while the typical contract for services prescribes a fixed

---

2. *US v Silk*, 331 US 704 (1946). See also a dictum of Lord Wright in *Montreal Locomotive Works v Montreal and A-G* [1947] 1 DLR 161 at 164, PC.

3. Notably in *Market Investigations v Minister of Social Security* [1969] 2 QB 173, [1968] 3 All ER 732; and *Beloff v Pressdam*, ante, n.17.

4. *Ready Mixed Concrete South East Ltd v Minister of Pensions and National Insurance* [1968] 2 QB 497, [1968], 1 All ER 433; *Willy Scheidegger* case, ante, n.11; *Construction Training Board* case, ante, n.11; *Rennison's* case, ante, n.11; *Challinor v Taylor*, [1972] ICR 129, NIRC; *Ferguson v John Dawson & Partners (Contractors)* [1976] 3 All ER 817, CA.

5. E.g., Cooke J, in *Construction Training Board* case, ante n.11, at 224; Bridge J, in *Rennison's* case, ante n.11, at 68.

6 *AEU* case, ante n.10; *Construction Traning Board* case, ante n.11; and compare, e.g., two decisions on timber fellers, M34 and M40.

7. E.g., by Lord Thankerton in one of the first judicial attempts to enumerate the relevant factors; *Short v Henderson* (1946) 62 TLR 427 at 429, HL.

8. E.g., *Mersey Docks and Harbour Board v Coggins and Griffith (Liverpool) Ltd* [1947] AC 1, [1946] 2 All ER 345, HL; M5; M14; M35; and see post, p. 57.

9. *Ready Mixed Concrete* case, ante n.4; M23; M25; M34; M48.

sum for the job. The distinction accords well with the 'economic reality' theory. In the words of Lord Widgery CJ, 'if a man agrees to perform an operation for a fixed sum and thus stands to lose if the work is delayed, and to profit if it is done quickly, that is the man who on the face of it appears to be an independent contractor working under a contract for services'.[10] While the method of payment may thus provide some guideline,[11] it is not a very reliable criterion. There have been cases where an individual paid on the basis of time has been held to be self-employed.[12] Conversely, the courts have not shown great reluctance to find a contract of service where the employee is paid a fixed rate for the job[13] or where both parties have sought artificially to transform the nature of the contract by converting wages into a different form of payment, e.g., the so-called 'lump'.[14]

4. DURATION OF CONTRACT. Again, there is a tendency for the duration of contracts for services to be determined according to a specific undertaking, or at least a specific (and often short) time period, whereas a contract of service will often be of an indefinite period. The factor has been adverted to in some cases,[15] but it can at best play a subordinate role. There are many occupations where the pattern is reversed.[16]

5. EQUIPMENT. The question whether the 'employee' is bound to use his own plant or equipment is perhaps of greater assistance. It too is related to the 'economic reality' idea. A worker who uses his own equipment is investing his own resources in the undertaking. But the criterion carries force only where such an investment is on a large scale.[17] In many occupations it is customary for an employee under a contract of service to provide his own tools.[18]

6. PLACE OF WORK. If the work is undertaken at the individual's own premises he is more likely to be regarded as self-employed. If, on the other hand, the occupation is peripatetic (e.g., a sales representative) the question is usually resolved by the degree of supervision exercised by the 'employer'.[19]

10. *Global Plant* case, ante n.12, at p. 391.
11. E.g., *Gould's* case, ante n.14; *Construction Training Board* case, ante n.11; *Challinor v Taylor*, ante n.4.
12. E.g., *Ready Mixed Concrete* case, ante n.4.
13. E.g., *Market Investigations* case, ante n.3.
14. *Ferguson v John Dawson*, ante n.4; and see further post, p. 52.
15. E.g., *Argent v Minister of Social Security* [1968] 3 All ER 208, [1968] 1 WLR 1749; M48.
16. E.g., *Stagecraft v Minister of National Insurance* 1952 SC 288; *Construction Training Board v Labour Forces* [1970]

3 All ER 220, DC; *Ready Mixed Concrete* case, ante n.4; *Willy Scheidegger Swiss Typewriting School (London) Ltd v Minister of Social Security* (1968) 5 KIR 65.
17. E.g., *Inglefield v Macey* (1967) 2 KIR 146; *Ready Mixed Concrete* case, ante n.4.
18. E.g., M14.
19. E.g., *Ready Mixed Concrete* case, ante n.4; *Willy Scheidegger* case, ante n.16; *Market Investigations* case, ante n.3; *Global Plant v Secretary of State for Social Services* [1972] 1 QB 139, [1971] 3 All ER 385; M22; M33.

7. OBLIGATION TO WORK. Under some contracts, it is left to the person 'employed' to decide how much, if at all, he is to work. If so, it is very persuasive evidence that he is self-employed.[20] The case must be contrasted with that in which the individual is given an option whether or not to work for a specific period (e.g., a day) and in which, if he so agrees, he is under an obligation to perform specific tasks during that period. Such a contract will often be one of service.[1]

8. DISCRETION ON HOURS OF WORK. A related idea is that the more discretion an individual has as to when he performs his duties, the more likely he is to be classified as self-employed.[2] But the criterion is in no way decisive, and there are instances of contracts of service being held to confer such a broad discretion.[3]

The question remains as to the weight, if any, to be given to any attempts by the parties themselves conclusively to determine the issue by a declaration in the contract. It is a question which has assumed, in recent years, increased importance, in the light of efforts, particularly in the construction industry, to avoid the financial burdens of the employment relationship arising from both fiscal and social security legislation.[4] The approach taken by the judiciary has, with one notable exception,[5] been uniform. While regard must be had to the obligations arising from the explicit terms of the contract to see whether they are more consistent with a contract of service or a contract for services, the exact terminology in fact used may be of no legal significance.[6] Two alternative justifications have been advanced for this approach. Some judges purport to search for the true 'intentions' of the parties which, they argue, are to be found in the obligations arising under the contract rather than from the exact terminology employed. The problem with this argument is that in many cases the terminology will indeed represent the intentions of the parties.[7] To overcome this objection other judges have relied overtly on public policy considerations. 'I think that it would be contrary to the public interest if . . . the parties, by their own whim, by the use of a verbal formula, unrelated to the reality of the relationship, could influence the

20. E.g., *Willy Scheidegger* case, ante n.16; M9; M11; M17; M47; M51; M65.
1. E.g., *Market Investigations* case, ante n.3.
2. E.g., *Willy Scheidegger* case, ante n.16; M9; M11; M13; M17; M25; M44.
3. E.g., *Market Investigations* case, ante n.3; *Global Plant* case, ante n.19; M40; M60.
4. See the Report of The Committee of Inquiry under Professor Phelps Brown into Certain Matters Concerning Labour (1968), Cmnd. 3714; Wedderburn *The Worker and the Law* (2nd edn), pp. 61–67 and de Clark, 30 MLR 6. The social security implications of the problem were fully

discussed in the House of Commons Standing Committee E Debates on the Social Security Bill 1973, cols. 83–122.
5. Lawton LJ in *Ferguson v John Dawson* [1976] 3 All ER 817 at pp. 827–829, CA.
6. *Inglefield v Macey*, ante n.17; *Ready Mixed Concrete v Minister of Pensions and National Insurance* [1968] 2 QB 497, [1968] 1 All ER 433; *Construction Training Board* case, ante n.16; *Rennison v Minister of Social Security* (1970) 10 KIR 65; *Ferguson v John Dawson* (majority judgments), ante n.5.
7. See Lawton LJ, in *Ferguson v John Dawson*, ante n.6, at 828.

decision . . .'.[8] If there is such a principle of public policy, it is one which is both obscure in its origins[9] and vague in its scope. The efforts of the judiciary to distinguish between genuine and bogus self-employment have been matched by a variety of responses from the legislature. On the one hand, the increased burden of contributions under Classes 2 and 4 resulting from the 1973–75 legislation has made the status of self-employment less attractive.[10] On the other hand, the Secretary of State has been given power to make regulations for securing that the liability to pay Class 1 contributions is not avoided by 'abnormal practice' in relation to the payment of earnings.[11]

iii) Office with emoluments
The second category of primary Class 1 contributions was introduced to ensure that Class 1 was co-extensive with tax liability under Schedule E. An 'office-holder' is a traditional common law term which has never been rigorously defined, but which is used to denote someone who works under the general auspices and direction of an institution (often a public service) without there being a contract of employment.[12] Usually it connotes 'a subsisting, permanent, substantive position, which had an existence independent of the person who filled it, and which went on and was filled in succession by successive holders'.[13] There are, of course, many honorary office-holders, but if emoluments – statutorily defined as including 'salaries, fees, wages, perquisites and profits'[14] – are payable, they are chargeable to income tax under Schedule E and thus give rise to liability for Class 1 contributions. For more details reference should be made to the standard texts on taxation;[15] it will be sufficient here to offer a few examples of office-holders: company directors (where there is no contract of service),[16] trustees and executors,[17] consultants under the National Health Service,[18] accountants acting as company auditors,[19] solicitors acting as company registrars.[20]

iv) Classification by the Secretary of State
As has already been indicated, decisions on the classification of individual cases are in the first instance made by the Secretary of State. Quite independently of this jurisdiction, he has reserved to him two further powers, the exercise of which affects the classification of an individual or

8. Per Megaw LJ, in *Ferguson v John Daswon*, ante n.6, at 825.
9. Some authority may be found in the landlord/tenant case of *Addiscombe Garden Estates v Crabbe* [1958] 1 QB 513, [1957] 3 All ER 563, CA.
10. See post, pp. 62–64.
11. SSA 1975, Sch. 1, para. 4(c)–(d).
12. Per Parker J, *Re National Insurance Act 1911 Re Employment of Church of England Curates* [1912] 2 Ch. 563 at 568–569; and see Rideout *Principles of Labour Law* (2nd edn), pp. 12–13.
13. Per Rowlatt J, *Great Western Rly Co v Bater* [1920] 3 KB 266 at 274,
approved by Lord Atkin in *McMillan v Guest* [1942] AC 561 at 564, HL.
14. Income and Corporation Taxes Act 1970, s.183(1).
15. E.g., Whiteman and Wheatcroft *Income Tax* (2nd edn), chap. 14.
16. *McMillan v Guest* ante n.13.
17. *Dale v IRC* [1954] AC 11, [1953] 2 All ER 671, HL.
18. *Mitchell and Edon v Ross* [1962] AC 814, [1961] 3 All ER 49, HL.
19. *Ellis v Lucas* [1967] Ch. 856, [1966] 2 All ER 935.
20. *IRC v Brander and Cruickshank* [1971] 1 All ER 36, [1971] 1 WLR 212, HL.

an occupation. Under the first, intended to counter the practice of 'lump' payments by means of which employers and employees collaborate in an attempt to avoid Class 1 contributions, he may

> 'where he is satisfied as to the existence of any practice in respect of the payment of earnings whereby the incidence of earnings-related contributions is avoided or reduced by means of irregular or unequal payments, give directions for securing that such contributions are payable as if that practice were not followed'.[1]

A rather unhappy feature of this provision is that it appears to confer an absolute discretion, there being no right of appeal to the High Court or other authorities. The second, of a more traditional nature, confers on him the power to shift earners in prescribed occupations from one class to another.[2] In some cases, the power will be exercised where there is genuine doubt as to the appropriate classification of a given occupation. In others, it will be a conscious act of policy to extend or reduce insurance cover where this is deemed appropriate in the light of the social needs and circumstances of the occupation in question.[3] Perhaps the most important issue is whether an occupation, otherwise to be categorised as Class 1, should be excluded from unemployment benefit, and, conversely, an occupation, otherwise characterised as Class 2 should be so included. One advantage accruing from the 1973 alignment of Class 1 with Schedule E tax liability is that the number of occupations transferred from one class to another has been substantially reduced.[4] The prevailing Categorisation of Earners Regulations fall into two groups.

   1. EMPLOYMENTS TREATED AS CLASS 1.[5] These contain four occupations – a) office cleaners, b) certain part-time lecturers, teachers and instructors,[6] c) ministers of religion receiving a stipend or salary, d) employment by a spouse for the purposes of that spouse's employment, – and the general group of those working under an agreement with an agency where the agency is paid by the 'employer' (excluding cases where the employee works at the employer's house or on other premises supervised by him and where he works as an entertainer or as a model).

   2. EMPLOYMENTS DISREGARDED.[7] The second group comprises employments which are excluded from both Classes 1 and 2, viz., employment by a member of the family in a private home occupied by both the employer and employee which is not employment for the purposes of the trade or business of that employer;

1. S.I. 1975/492, Reg. 19.
2. SSA 1975, s.2(2).
3. The principle has been made explicit by the National Insurance Advisory Committee in its various pronouncements on classification issues: see, e.g., its Report of Share Fishermen 1947–48 HC 137, and on Actors, Artistes and Entertainers

(1952) Cmd. 8549.
4. For the pre-1973 Regulations, see S.I. 1972/555.
5. S.I. 1975/528, Sch. 1, Part I, as amended by inter alia S.I. 1977/1015 and S.I. 1977/1987.
6. For details see S.I. 1977/1915 or Leaflet NI. 222.
7. S.I. 1975/528, Sch. 1, Part III.

and work as a self-employed person where the individual is not ordinarily so employed.

There is another set of Regulations which extend and restrict the concept of employed earner's employment for the purposes of the industrial injury scheme.[8] This is considered below in chapter 8.[9]

v) Residence or presence

The Act refers to gainful employment in Great Britain.[10] The more detailed conditions as to residence and presence are contained in the Contributions Regulations.[11] In a subsequent chapter, the meaning of such concepts as 'resident' and 'ordinarily resident' which are common to other areas of the law is considered.[12] Here it will be sufficient to state the rules for primary Class 1 contributions.[13]

1. The major condition is that at the time of employment the earner is resident or present in GB – temporary absences being disregarded – or is then ordinarily resident in GB.

2. If, however, he is not normally resident or employed in the UK, but, in pursuance of employment which is mainly abroad for an employer whose place of business is also outside the UK, he works for a time in GB, contributions are payable only when he has been continuously resident in GB for fifty-two contributions weeks. The same proviso applies also to other non-residents who, on vacation from full-time studies abroad, are in GB on temporary employment in some way connected with their studies and to those working in GB as apprentices for foreign masters.

3. Even if an employee is working abroad, he may still be liable to contribute if he is ordinarily resident in GB, was resident there before the commencement of the employment and (most important of all) his employer has a place of business in GB. The liability exists only for the first fifty-two contribution weeks of the foreign employment.

vi) Age

To be liable, the earner must be over sixteen[14] and under pensionable age (sixty-five for men, sixty for women).[15]

vii) Low earners

Liability to contribute arises only where the earnings of the employee equal or exceed the 'lower earnings limit'.[16] This is an arbitrary figure fixed by the Secretary of State (in 1978–79 £17–50 per week[17]). What is

8. S.I. 1975/467.
9. Post, p. 271.
10. SSA 1975, s.2(1).
11. S.I. 1975/492.
12. Post, pp. 413–416.
13. S.I. 1975/492, Regs. 113–114.

14. SSA 1975, s.4(2)(a).
15. SSPA 1975, s.4(1), though secondary contributions are payable in respect of employment above the relevant ages.
16. SSA 1975, s.4(2)(b).
17. S.I. 1977/1953.

to be regarded as earnings for the purpose of this rule depends primarily on the provisions described in the next paragraph.

viii) Calculation of contributions

The person liable for primary Class 1 contributions pays a specified percentage (in 1978–79 6·5%[18]) of his earnings up to the upper earnings limit (in 1978–79[19] £120 per week).[20] Those opting out of the new pensions scheme pay less (in 1978–79, 4%) on earnings between the lower and upper limits.[1] The earnings on which the calculation is based are the individual's gross earnings from his employment or employments[2] but certain payments are disregarded:[3]

> (1) Payments on account of a person's earnings, comprising sums on which contributions have already been made; (2) holiday payments either from a fund to which more than one secondary contributor (i.e., employer) contributes and the management and control of which are not vested in such contributors, or where the party making the payment is entitled to reimbursement; (3) gratuities not paid directly or indirectly by the secondary contributor; (4) payments in kind; (5) payments to or from trustees; (6) payments by way of pensions including those under recognised occupational pensions schemes; (7) payments for goods or services supplied by the earner and on which VAT is chargeable; (8) payments by way of a pension; (9) redundancy payments; (10) reimbursement of expenses.

If husband and wife are jointly engaged in employment and the earnings therefrom are paid jointly, the amounts of earnings upon which the calculation of contributions is based are the same as that employed by the Inland Revenue for the purposes of income tax.[4]

c. Secondary Class 1 contributions

i) Designation of contributors

Secondary Class 1 contributions are payable by 'employers and other persons paying earnings'.[5] The statutory definition of the contributor depends on the status of the earner: if he works under a contract of service, the secondary contributor is his employer;[6] if he is engaged in an office

---

18. S.I. 1977/2180.
19. S.I. 1977/1953.
20. SSA 1975, s.4(6). In fact, the employer who is in general responsible for deducting the contributions from the wages or salary may calculate the contributions either by applying the prescribed percentages himself, or by adopting the scale figures set out in Sch. 1 of the Contributions Regulations: S.I. 1975/492, as amended.

1. SSPA 1975, s. 27(2).
2. SSA 1975, Sch. 1, para. 1, and S.I. 1975/492, Reg. 16.
3. Ibid., Reg. 17, as amended by S.I. 1976/88, Reg. 2.
4. S.I. 1975/492 and see Whiteman and Wheatcroft *Income Tax* (2nd edn), pp. 926–930.
5. SSA 1975, s.1(2).
6. Ibid., s.4(4)(a).

with emoluments, it is either

'such person as may be prescribed in relation to that office',

or if no such person is prescribed

'the government department, public authority or body of persons responsible for paying the emoluments of the office'.[7]

There is little to add to the provisions concerning an office-holder. As regards employment under a contract of service, the principles elaborated under that head should assist in determining not only the existence of such a contract, but also the parties to it. Where it is clear that an earner is employed under a contract of service, but unclear with which of two parties the contract was made, the issue should be resolved by answering such questions as: who supervised the work? who paid the employee? who had the right to appoint and dismiss him?[8] Cases of doubt, and cases where the party legally categorised as an employer under a contract of service is regarded as an inappropriate secondary contributor, may be subjected to the Secretary of State's power to transfer liability to another prescribed person.[9] So far he has exercised this power in only a few instances:[10]

1. An office cleaner is employed by the person for whom the work is done, unless he/she is supplied and paid by an agency, in which case the agency is the employer.

2. In other cases, where an employee renders personal services under an agreement with an agency, the agency is treated as the employer.

3. Where the earner is employed in a company which has gone into voluntary liquidation but which carries on business under a liquidator, the person holding the office of liquidator at the time of the employment is treated as the employer.

4. A barrister's clerk is treated as being employed by the head of his chambers.

5. In respect of Anglican ministers of religion, the secondary contributions are payable by the Church Commissioners; for other ministers, by the administrators of the fund from which the minister's remuneration is paid.

Where an earner is employed under two or more independent contracts of service, and is paid by each employer an amount equal to or exceeding the lower earnings limit both will be liable to contribute. However, if the earnings in one or more of the employments are lower than that limit, and

7. SSA 1975 s.4(4)(b).
8. Atiyah *Vicarious Liability* (1966), pp. 160–161; and see Lord Porter in *Mersey Docks and Harbour Board v Coggins and Griffith (Liverpool) Ltd.* [1947] AC 1 at 17. Two reported decisions of the Minister, M14 and M35, by implication, apply these criteria.
9. SSA 1975, s.4(5)(b).
10. S.I. 1975/528, Sch. 3, as amended by S.I. 1977/1987.

the relevant employer carries on business in association with another employer, the earnings may be aggregated to achieve the necessary liability and the contributions are then payable by each of those employers on a proportionate basis.[11]

ii) Residence

Liability for secondary contributions arises only where the party otherwise liable is resident or present in Great Britain or has a place of business there.[12] The same Regulation optimistically adds that even if these conditions are not met an employer may pay the contributions 'if he so wishes'.

iii) Amount

The secondary contributor is liable, in 1978–79, for 12% of earnings, but in relation to employments contracted-out of the new pensions scheme the amount on earnings between the lower and upper limits is $7\frac{1}{2}\%$.[13]

D. Class 2 contributions

Contributions under Class 2 may confer title to any contributory benefit except unemployment benefit, and the earnings-related supplements to short-term benefits.[14] They are payable by self-employed earners[15] and differ from Class 1 contributions in three important respects: since *ex hypothesi* there is no contract of service, there is for each employment only one contributor; the contribution is payable on a flat-rate basis; a self-employed person where not liable to contribute because, for example, his earnings are too small or he does not satisfy the residence conditions may pay voluntarily.

i) Persons liable

A self-employed person is defined as

> 'a person who is gainfully employed in Great Britain otherwise than in employed earner's employment (whether or not he is also employed in such employment)'.[16]

a) COMBINATIONS OF EMPLOYMENTS. The negative and rather confusing formulation means that if a person is in a gainful employment for which Class 1 contributions are not payable he is necessarily self-employed[17] even though he may concurrently and independently be employed in a Class 1 employment. The liability to pay under the two Classes (and as we shall see also under Class 4) was a major innovation of the Social Security Act 1973. The justification for the new approach is not immediately apparent but may readily be inferred from general policy considerations.

11. S.I. 1975/492, Reg. 10.
12. Ibid., Reg. 113(1)(b).
13. S.I. 1977/2180, and liability under NI Surcharge Act 1976.

14. SSA 1975, s.13(1).
15. Ibid., s.1(2).
16. Ibid., s.2(1)(b).
17. Unless disregarded, ante, p. 54.

The acceptance of an earnings-related principle for contributions naturally led to the conclusion that a proportionate part of a self-employed person's profits should be payable whether or not he was also employed under a contract of service: hence Class 4. But as will be seen, it was thought too expensive administratively to impose such a charge on profits below a certain figure. The flat-rate contributions under Class 2 may thus be seen as an arbitrary amount intended to represent a charge on those profits made up to the level in question.

b) GAINFUL EMPLOYMENT. The shift in terminology from 'gainfully occupied in employment' to 'gainfully employed' has already been the subject of comment in relation to Class 1 contributions.[18] As was suggested there, the authorities on the interpretation of the earlier formulation should be used as guidelines for the term currently employed. In the present context, the matter is of more than academic interest, for while there is no liability to pay where earnings are below a certain level, the self-employed earner if 'gainfully employed' may in such circumstance voluntarily contribute. Thus an individual undertaking a new enterprise will be *entitled* to pay Class 2 contributions as soon as he is 'gainfully employed', notwithstanding that his current failure to make substantial profits exempts him from *liability* to pay. 'Gainfully occupied' under the former legislation was held not necessarily to imply the making of a net profit on an enterprise.[19] Thus in relation to self-employment, it was said that

> 'the question is not to be posed at any particular time, has he in fact received some net profit from his activities ... but does he hold himself out as being anxious to become employed for purpose of gain'.[20]

The answer to this latter question is a matter of fact for the determining authority. But assistance may be derived from decisions on analogous issues within other areas of social security law, notably in relation to retirement pensions.[1]

c) CONTINUING EMPLOYMENT. The boundaries of self-employment are not always easy to determine. To a certain extent, the answer will be supplied by the 'gainfully employed' criterion discussed in the last paragraph. To reinforce the notion that regard should be had to an individual's endeavours over a substantial period rather than to short-term and spasmodic profit/loss accounting, the Regulations prescribe that where a person is a self-employed earner (or is treated as such)

> 'the employment shall . . . be treated as continuing unless and until he is no longer ordinarily employed in that employment'.[2]

18. Ante, p. 47.
19. *Vandyk v Minister of Pensions and National Insurance* [1955] 1 QB 29.
20. Per Slade J, ibid., at 38.
1. Post, pp. 202–209.

2. S.I. 1975/528, Sch. 2.
3. S.I. 1975/492, Reg. 113(1)(d). For 'resident' and 'ordinarily resident' see post, pp. 414–416.

d) RESIDENCE. A self-employed earner is liable to pay contributions only
if he is either ordinarily resident in Great Britain or was resident there for a
period of at least twenty-six of the immediately preceding fifty-two
contribution weeks.[3] Where he not liable under these rules an earner may
nevertheless voluntarily contribute.[4]

e) AGE. The contributor must be over sixteen years[5] and under pensionable age (men sixty-five, women sixty).[6]

ii) Exceptions

There are two grounds on which a self-employed person may be excepted
from liability to pay contributions: inability to earn, and low earnings. As
regards the first, he must show that throughout the week for which the
exception is claimed (excluding Sunday or an equivalent rest day), he/she
received sickness, invalidity, industrial injury benefit, unemployability
supplement or maternity allowance, or was in prison or detained in legal
custody.[7] An exception for low earnings has existed ever since self-
employed persons were compulsorily insured in 1946,[8] the justifications
being to exclude occasional profit makers and to reduce administrative
expenditure. The minimum earnings figure (for 1978–79) is (£950) a year.[9]
Earnings, for this purpose, mean 'net earnings' from the employment,[10] and
is effectively such income as is chargeable to income tax under Schedule
D:[11] thus from gross earnings may be deducted expenses necessarily
incurred in connection with the employment.[12] In furtherance of this policy
of integrating contributions and tax liability, the Regulations adopt the
Inland Revenue rule of allowing assessments to be based on earnings from a
preceding tax year.[13] Earnings for a particular year are treated as less than
the threshold if, in the preceding year, the individual's earnings were less
than that amount and there had since been no material change of circumstances, or if the year for which exception is claimed the earnings are
expected to be less than that amount.[14] The onus is on the self-employed
earner to claim exception, and if he is successful he will be granted a
certificate of exception.[15] When an exception is granted on either of the two
grounds specified in this paragraph, the self-employed person may voluntarily pay contributions (either of Class 2 or of Class 3).[16]

4. But only if he is either present in GB, in the week in question, or if abroad, had been resident there and had paid Class 1 or 2 contributions for 3 years immediately preceding his departure: ibid., Regs. 113(1)(c) and 115.
5. SSA 1975, s.7(1), as amended by Education (School-leaving Dates) Act 1976, s.2(4).
6. SSPA 1975, s.4(2).
7. S.I. 1975/492, Reg. 20, as amended by S.I. 1976/88.
8. See, in general, NIAC Report on Liability for Contributions of Pensions with Small Incomes (1955), Cmd. 9432.
9. S.I. 1977/2180.
10. S.I. 1975/492, Reg. 22(2).
11. See Whiteman and Wheatcroft *Income Tax* (2nd edn), chaps. 5–8.
12. Ibid., chap. 8.
13. Ibid., at pp. 312–324.
14. S.I. 1975/492, Reg. 22(1)(b).
15. Ibid., Regs. 21 and 23.
16. Ibid., Regs. 20(3) and 23(b).

iii) Amount

Whether contributions are mandatory or voluntary, the amount is the same: the flat-rate payment in 1978–79 of £1·90 per week.[17] There may, however, be introduced under regulations a special, higher, rate to cover exceptional cases where individuals are treated as self-employed earners but are not liable to pay Class 4 contributions.[18] At the time of writing, no such regulation has been introduced.

E. Class 3 contributions

Beveridge's conception of social insurance was a comprehensive one – all of working age were to be included. Under his scheme, as implemented in the 1946 legislation, there was to be a third class of *compulsory* contributions, for those who would need provision for medical treatment, retirement and funeral expenses, and who were not in a gainful occupation but were of working age.[19] Typically included were students, unmarried women engaged in unremunerated domestic work, those retiring early under an occupational pension scheme, and persons in receipt of private income. Of course they must have had resources to pay contributions, and so there were exemptions for those below a minimum income level.[20] This class of contributions, so defined, was abolished by the 1973 Act. The new Class 3 allows only for *voluntary* contributions, and these may be paid either by non-employed persons or those contributing in Classes 1 or 2, but with deficiencies in their contribution record. They may enable a person to qualify only for maternity grant, widow's benefit, retirement pensions (Categories A and B), child's special allowance and death grant.[1] The amount of such contribution is the flat-rate sum, in 1978–79, of £1·80.[2]

i) Persons entitled to contribute

The contributor must be over sixteen[3] and under pensionable age (sixty-five for men, sixty for women),[4] and with some exceptions resident in Great Britain during the year for which he makes his contribution.[5]

ii) Making up a reckonable year

The 1975 Act prescribes that:

> 'payment of Class 3 contributions shall be allowed only with a view to enabling the contributor to satisfy contribution conditions of entitlement to benefit'.[6]

17. S.I. 1977/2180.
18. SSA 1975, s.7(4).
19. Paras. 310 and 317.
20. See NIA 1946, s.5(1)(a)(iii).
1. SSA 1975, s.13(1).
2. S.I. 1977/2180.
3. SSA 1975, s.8(1).
4. S.I. 1975/492, Reg. 24A(1)(e), inserted

by S.I. 1977/1755.
5. S.I. 1975/492, Reg. 113(1)(e). Those abroad can contribute on the same conditions as are prescribed in relation to Class 2 voluntary contributions: ante n.4, p. 60. For 'residence' see post, pp. 414–415.
6. SSA 1975, s.8(2).

As will be seen, for those benefits for which Class 3 payments may count, a year of contributions will only qualify towards entitlement if a minimum number of contributions has been made. At the end of each contribution year a Class 1 contributor is sent a statement of his account indicating any shortage, and how many Class 3 contributions will be necessary to make up a reckonable year. Class 2 contributors with an incomplete record may, as already indicated, voluntarily pay additional contributions of that class, but if they wish to secure entitlement only to the more limited benefits available to Class 3 contributors, they may in the alternative make up the number with additional payments of the latter class. There are rules to prevent an individual making unnecessary contributions, e.g., where his record is complete for a given year, or where he will be credited with contributions for that year.[7] If such payments have nevertheless been made, the contributor is entitled to a refund,[8] though he may, if he prefers, have the extra contributions appropriated to satisfy conditions for another tax year.[9]

F. Class 4 contributions

It was evident that if the self-employed were to make earnings-related contributions to the National Insurance Fund, this in practice could be achieved only by integrating assessment and administration with the fiscal system.[10] A fourth category of contributions was therefore created which would effectively coincide with tax liability under Schedule D of the Income Tax Acts. Entitlement to benefit, however, is established by reference only to contributions of Classes 1, 2 or 3; Class 4 is simply the most convenient means of securing earnings-related contributions from those paying Class 2 contributions. The principle of coincidence with tax liability is stated in the Social Security Act thus:

> 'Class 4 contributions shall be payable in respect of all annual profits or gains immediately derived from the carrying on or exercise of one or more trades, professions or vocations, being profits or gains chargeable to income tax under Case I or Case II of Schedule D . . . and the contributions shall be payable (a) in the same manner as any income tax . . . and (b) by the person on whom the income tax is (or would be) charged, in accordance with assessments made from time to time under the Income Tax Acts'.[11]

For the nature and extent of this liability, then, reference should be made to the standard texts on taxation.[12] What follows is an account of those aspects of the assessment which are peculiar to Class 4 contributions.

---

7. SSPA 1975, s.5(1), and S.I. 1975/492, Reg. 24A, inserted by S.I. 1977/1755.
8. S.I. 1975/492, Regs. 28–30, as amended by S.I. 1977/1755.
9. SSA 1975, s.8(2)(a) and S.I. 1975/492, Reg. 26.
10. For the policy considerations relevant to the liability of the self-employed, see ante, pp. 29–30.
11. SSA 1975, s.9(1).
12. E.g., Whiteman and Wheatcroft *Income Tax* (2nd edn), chaps. 5–8.

i) Persons liable

The condition of residence in the United Kingdom is that applied under the Income Tax Acts,[13] but in contrast to that legislation, liability for contributions does not extend to earners who are under sixteen or over pensionable age.[14] As with income tax, a husband and wife may either aggregate their income or be assessed separately. In the case of the latter, the wife's separate assessment will be treated as the base for her contributions.[15] If income is, however, aggregated, as under tax law, the husband will be liable to pay contributions on his wife's profits and gains, though they will nevertheless be regarded as her contributions.[16] In the case of partnerships, as under tax law, each partner is liable according to his share of the profits,[17] but contributions are not payable by those liable to tax as trustees, administrators, executors and other nominal holders of property.[18]

A person charged for income tax under both Schedule E and Schedule D, because he is both employed under a contract of service and derives profits from a trade or business, for that reason will also be liable to pay contributions of both Classes 1 and 4, provided that in either case his earnings or profits exceed the relevant lower limit. Some difficulty is caused where tax and social security liability do not correspond in this way. Thus, while actors, musicians and those working for agencies pay Class 1 contributions, their earnings or profits are nevertheless chargeable to tax under Schedule D. The solution provided by the regulations is to deduct from the profits and gains chargeable to Schedule D, the amount of earnings on the basis of which the Class 1 contributions were assessed, so that liability for Class 4 will be attracted only if the remainder exceeds the threshold.[19] Conversely, a person paying Class 2 contributions but whose earnings are chargeable to tax under Schedule E, will be liable for Class 4 at the same rate as other self-employed persons, though in his case liability is deferred until the end of the relevant tax year and any payments will thereafter be recovered by the DHSS and not the Inland Revenue.[20]

ii) Amount of liability

In 1978–79, the amount payable is 5·00% of profits and gains between £2,000 and £6,250 per year chargeable under Schedule D.[1] Account must therefore be taken of such deductions and reliefs as are there provided,[2] but the following tax reliefs do not apply for the purposes of Class 4 contributions:[3] personal allowances;[4] payments under annuity contracts

---

13. Ibid., chap. 2.
14. SSA 1975, s.9(8) as amended by SSPA 1975, Sch. 5.
15. SSA 1975, Sch. 2, para. 4(1).
16. Ibid., para. 4(3).
17. Ibid., para. 5.
18. Ibid., para. 6.
19. S.I. 1975/492, Reg. 52, as amended by S.I. 1975/1855, Reg. 7, and S.I. 1977/755, Reg. 12.

20. SSA 1975, s.10, and S.I. 1975/492, Regs. 61–68.
1. S.I. 1977/2180.
2. See Whiteman and Wheatcroft, ante n.12, chap. 8.
3. SSA 1975, Sch. 2, para. 3(2).
4. Under Income and Corporation Taxes Act 1970, Part 1, chap. II.

and trust schemes;[5] the carrying forward of losses;[6] the payment of interest.[7]

Part three. Special Categories

A. Married women and widows: General

The policy issues relevant to social security discrimination between men and women were described in chapter 1.[8] Here we trace the history of the role of women within the contributory scheme, and describe such special rules as currently exist governing their liability (or entitlement) to contribute. Treatment of the special rules on the fulfilment of contribution conditions is reserved until the general discussion of that subject in Part Four.

Before the Second World War, women insured under the unemployment and health schemes, whether married or single, both paid less by way of contributions and received less by way of benefit. But the amount paid was disproportionately large in comparison with the amount received, apparently because women were regarded as poor risks.[9] Why a similar approach was not taken to poor-risk male workers is not clear. As regards single women, Beveridge recommended removal of the anomaly: in terms of risk, it was no longer appropriate to treat them as a separate category, and, in terms of subsistence needs, the average cost of feeding them was only 1s. a week less than that of men.[10] Indeed, to achieve the same level of benefit, they were to pay less;[11] it being assumed that many would marry and would eventually claim retirement benefit on the basis of the husband's contributions.

The position of a married woman was, however, very different: 'all women by marriage acquire a new economic and social status, with risks and rights different from those of the unmarried'.[12] They gain a legal right to maintenance, at the same time agreeing to perform a vital, but unpaid, service. The underlying notion is that of the family as a single economic unit, the wife doing the housework for the husband, who in return maintains her. According to the figures then available,[13] over 80% of married women of working age regarded marriage as their sole occupation. Even if a wife was an earner, she was different from a single woman in that employment was liable to interruption for childbirth, and, more significantly, her earnings were 'a means, not of subsistence but of a standard of living above subsistence'.[14] It followed that in sickness or

5. ICTA 1970, ss.226–227.
6. Ibid., s.173.
7. Ibid., s.175 and Finance Act 1972, s.75.
8. Ante, pp. 9–10.
9. Land in ed. Barker and Allen *Sexual Divisions and Society* (1976), p. 109.
10. Para. 123; cf. *Harris*, pp. 403–405.
11. Under NIA 1946, Sch. 1, the standard weekly rate of contributions by employed persons was 4s 9d (males) and 3s 9d (females).
12. *Beveridge*, para. 108.
13. Beveridge relied on the 1931 census. He regarded the much higher figures for wartime work (see Thomas *Women at Work: Wartime Social Survey* (1944)) as a temporary phenomenon.
14. *Beveridge*, para. 108.

unemployment she did not need compensation on the same scale as the primary breadwinner: she could fall back on her husband's income, or his benefit if his earnings were interrupted. It was therefore proposed that a married woman who was an earner could choose either to opt out of the scheme, and thus become wholly dependent on her husband's contributions for retirement pension and maternity grant, or else to contribute in her own right.[15] In the case of the latter she would receive only two-thirds of the standard rate for unemployment and sickness benefit. To meet any criticisms of equity, and to provide a substantial benefit for a need which was particularly applicable to married women contributors, it was also proposed that maternity allowance would be 50% higher than the standard short-term benefit.[16] These proposals were implemented in full by the 1946 legislation,[17] and remained in force until 1975. The only two significant modifications occurring between those dates both curtailed some of the advantages of the married woman's special status: in 1953, the level of maternity allowance was reduced to that of the other short-term benefits,[18] and in 1959 contributions to and benefits from the graduated retirement pension scheme were to be paid in full.[19]

The status thus attributed to married women had other implications for the contributory scheme. In the first place, it meant that any contributions paid before marriage by a woman who subsequently decided to opt out were ignored. Secondly, it meant that there was a problem in maintaining a contribution record, particularly for retirement pension purposes, should the marriage end by death or dissolution before pensionable age was reached. To meet this problem certain concessions were made: the contribution conditions for the various benefits were eased, special credits were available, and (after 1970[20]) the woman might rely on her former husband's insurance record, both before and during the marriage, even if he had since remarried.

By the 1970s, the social and economic climate had changed considerably. Now 42% of married women of working age were in paid employment.[1] The movement against sexual discrimination had intensified, and the social security position of married women was a prime target.[2] The main criticisms were that in contemporary economic conditions her earnings had become an essential element in the family's income, no longer the subordinate accessory which Beveridge had assumed and that full reliance on the husband's insurance record rendered the wife's position vulnerable, not only on termination of the marriage but also during its currency – she

15. As a non-earner, she might similarly opt between contributions under Class IV and relying on her husband's contributions.
16. *Beveridge*, para. 113, and see post, p. 248.
17. NIA 1946, s.59 and S.I. 1948/1470.
18. NIA 1953, s.6. See also post, p. 253.
19. NIA 1959, s.1; the argument was that the 'graduated' element, being designed to provide a level of benefit above

subsistence, was appropriate for contributors without discrimination according to sex or marital status: White Paper, Pensions for Old Age (1958), Cmnd. 538, para. 37.
20. NIA 1970, s.3.
1. British Labour Statistics Year Book (1974).
2. See, e.g., report of Labour Party Study Group, *Towards Equality: Women and Social Security* (1969).

had no means of ensuring that contributions were being paid.[3] The shift to a universal earnings-related contribution scheme in the Social Security Act 1973 provided an obvious opportunity to make fundamental changes to the married woman's option, but the Conservative government resisted pressure from the opposition for such action, chiefly on the ground that since under the existing arrangements only one quarter of married women earners had chosen to contribute independently, they must be assumed to have known what was best for them and that compulsory insurance would impose on them an inequitable burden, for they would not receive a sufficient return for their contributions.[4]

The new Labour government proposed to abolish the married woman's option as part of its new approach to retirement pensions. The ability, for the purpose of the woman's pension entitlement, to take into consideration such years during which she was 'precluded from regular employment by responsibilities at home'[5] was regarded as the key provision which would ensure a fair return for her contributions, and it was complemented by other measures. The new scheme would dispense with the rule hitherto in force that a married woman was entitled to a pension on her own contributions only if she had paid contributions or received credits for at least a half of the weeks between marriage and her reaching pensionable age.[6] Most widows would inherit the whole of the earnings-related component which their husbands had earned. Finally, a retired widow would be able to base her entitlement to such a component on her own earnings as well as those of her husband.

The abolition of the power to opt out was not, however, applied to all married women. In order that existing family financial arrangements should not be unduly prejudiced, those already married or widowed when the new provisions came into force were allowed to choose between 'full' and 'reduced' liability. It is this new form of option which must now be described.

B. Reduced liability under 1975 Pensions Act[7]

i) Nature of option

For those who are entitled to elect for the reduced status, the effect is not, as before the 1975 Act, to relieve them from liability for all contributions. Exercise of the option confers on them immunity from liability to pay any Class 2 contributions[8] and disentitles them from paying Class 3 contributions.[9] But the obligation to pay those of Class 4 remains unaffected, and, as regards Class 1, the liability is reduced to 2% rather than excluded

3. See in particular the contributions of Mr M. Meacher in the Standing Committee E Debates on the Social Security Bill 1973, cols. 228–231.
4. Ibid., at cols. 217–224, (Mr P. Dean, Under-Secretary of State).
5. SSPA 1975, s.19(3): see Appendix.
6. Cf., post, p. 213.

7. The rules are to be found in S.I. 1975/492, Regs. 91–99, as amended by S.I. 1975/1855 and S.I. 1977/544. The references which follow are to the relevant Regulations as amended.
8. S.I. 1975/492, Reg. 91(3).
9. Ibid., Reg. 96.

altogether.[10] A married woman or widow who opts for this reduced liability will be unable to claim maternity allowance, unemployment, sickness or invalidity benefit and, in the case of retirement pension, may qualify only on the basis of her husband's contributions.[11]

ii) Women entitled to elect for reduced liability

a) MARRIED WOMEN. The election is restricted to those already married before 6 April 1977.[12] Two categories must be distinguished.

1. A woman married before that date but on or after 6 April 1975 may, provided that the marriage is still subsisting, opt for reduced liability, but for this purpose she must have made the election in the appropriate form by 11 May 1975,[13] and if no such election was made, she remains liable for full contributions, provided that the ordinary conditions for liability are satisfied.

2. The position is slightly different for a woman already married on 6 April 1975. She too may elect for reduced liability, and if under the former insurance arrangements she was paying full contributions (i.e., she had not exercised the married woman's option) she must have registered her election by 11 May 1977[14] – otherwise she is liable for full contributions. If, however, under the previous arrangements she had opted out she is automatically treated as having elected for reduced liability under the new scheme,[15] though, of course, she is entitled to revoke and opt instead for full liability.

b) WIDOWS. The equivalent power to elect for reduced liability is conferred on women who were widowed before 6 April 1978 and who at the time of the election were entitled to widow's benefit under the industrial, non-industrial or war pension schemes.[16]

1. For those already widowed on 5 April 1975 and who have not remarried since the position is similar to that of married women, viz., those who had at the time opted out of liability under the previous scheme are automatically treated as having elected for reduced liability, while those who were paying full contributions must have registered their claim by 11 May 1977, if they wish to opt for reduced liability under the new scheme.[17]

2. For those widowed between April 1975 and April 1978, the contribution liability is automatically reduced for an initial period following the husband's death: until the end of the tax year in which he died, if he died before 1 October; or until the end of the following year if he died after that day.[18] At the end of that

---

10. Ibid., Reg. 95.
11. Cf., post, pp. 214–215.
12. S.I. 1975/492, Reg. 91(1). For the meaning of marriage, see post, pp. 398–404.
13. Ibid., Reg. 98.
14. Ibid., Reg. 91(4).
15. Ibid., Reg. 93.
16. Ibid., Reg. 91(8).
17. Ante, n.14 and 15.
18. S.I. 1975/492, Reg. 94.

period, the reduced liability will continue only if the widow registers an election in the appropriate form, or if at the date of his death she had already elected for reduced liability as a married woman under the new scheme.[19]

iii) Election and revocation

For an election under the conditions described above to be valid it must be made in the prescribed form.[20] It will then be treated as continuing for each complete tax year, unless or until it is revoked/or, in the case of married women, the marriage is terminated, and, in the case of a widow, she remarries or lives with a man as his wife.[1] The election will then cease to have effect for the tax year immediately following that in which revocation was made or the other event referred to occurs.

c. Other special cases

Certain categories of occupation are selected for special treatment either because provision is not necessary for some hazards (e.g., unemployment) or because there are difficulties in fulfilling the normal conditions for contributions.

i) HM Forces

One of the consequences of the Beveridge principle of universality was to extend insurance to Crown employees, who had previously been excluded from the national schemes. The principle, affirmed in the Social Security Act 1975, is that the provisions apply 'to persons employed by or under the Crown in like manner as if they were employed by a private person'.[2] However, members of HM forces are in a special position.

> Apart from maternity grant and allowance,[3] they have no need for provision (and are not entitled to benefit) for unemployment, sickness or disability.[4] In their case, the aim is merely to ensure that they will be sufficiently covered, in terms of contributions, for needs arising after they have returned to civilian life. Class 1 contributions are therefore payable, but the rate is reduced by 0·8% (primary) and 1·35% (secondary).[5] For the purposes of satisfying the residence conditions for contributions, a serving member of the forces[6] is treated as 'present in Great Britain'.[7]

ii) Employment on the Continental Shelf

The problem here is simply that of satisfying the residence requirements. Regulations therefore prescribe that

19. S.I. 1975/492, Reg. 94(4).
20. Ibid., Regs. 91(5) and 91(7). A certificate of election is then issued: ibid., Reg. 97.
1. Ibid., Reg. 92.
2. SSA 1975, s.127(1).
3. Post, chap. 7.
4. For war pensions see post, chap. 9.
5. S.I. 1975/492, Reg. 109, as amended by S.I. 1977/1755.
6. For the definition of 'serving member of the forces' see S.I. 1975/492, Reg. 1(2) and Sch. 5, Part II.
7. Ibid., Reg. 108.

an employment in an area designated under the Continental Shelf Act 1964 in connection with the exploitation of resources, or the exploration, of the sea bed and subsoil, is deemed to be employed within GB.[8]

iii) Airmen

Similar considerations apply to airmen.

> Provided that the employer has a place of business in GB, if the aircraft is British, or the principal place of business is in GB, in the case of other aircraft, the airman is treated as present in GB,[9] though if he is neither domiciled nor has a place of residence there, no contributions are payable.[10]

iv) Mariners

> For a person employed as a mariner,[11] the normal residence requirements for contributions are replaced by the simple condition that he is domiciled or resident in GB.[12] Certain mariners are excluded from the operation of the Redundancy Payments scheme,[13] and the contributions of those within this category are reduced by 0.2%.[14] If the employment is wholly or partly on a 'foreign-going ship',[15] it is reduced by 0.7%.[16] There are also special methods of calculating earnings for the purpose of earnings-related contributions.[17]

Part four. Contribution Conditions

Under the system in force before 1975, contributions were predominantly flat-rate. It was therefore convenient to express the conditions of contributions for the various benefits in terms of the number of weekly contributions paid (or credited) during a specified period (often a 'contribution year'). With the adoption of the earnings-related system and the interdependence with tax liability, such concepts were no longer feasible, and so they have been replaced by 'earnings factors' (representing the amount of earnings on which liability to contribute is based) and the 'tax year' (6 April–5 April) as the usual contributory period. Apart from the provision necessary for the new earnings-related additional component to long-term benefits, the principles governing the contribution conditions and the modes of satisfying them remain substantially unaltered.

---

8. Ibid., Reg. 76.
9. Ibid., Reg. 73(1). For the definition of 'airmen' and 'British aircraft' see ibid., Reg. 72.
10. Ibid., Reg. 73(2).
11. For definition, see ibid., Reg. 77.
12. Ibid., Reg. 78.
13. See S.I. 1973/1281, art. 3.
14. S.I. 1975/492, Reg. 80(1).
15. For definition see ibid., Reg. 77.
16. Ibid., Reg. 80(2).
17. Ibid., Regs. 82–86, as amended by S.I. 1975/1855 and S.I. 1977/1755.

A. Earnings factors

Contributions to Class 1 are earnings-related, those of Class 2 and Class 3 are flat-rate. In any one tax year, an individual might combine contributions of one class with those of either or both of the other classes. It was therefore necessary to create some common denominator whereby equivalent conditions could be exacted from those paying different types of contributions. The device chosen was the 'earnings factor': this is a sum expressed in pounds representing the aggregate of contributions made by an individual in each tax year in each class.[18] For Class 1 contributions, the factor is the earnings between the lower and upper earnings limit on which the contributions are calculated.[19] For Class 2 or 3 contributions (which are flat-rate) it is the lower earnings limit for Class 1 contributions multiplied by the number of contributions made in the relevant tax year.[20] The same earnings factors are attributed to contributions which have been credited,[1] though these are calculated separately from factors derived from contributions actually paid.[2]

The Social Security Act 1975 envisaged that the earnings factors, as described above, would be used not only to indicate the minimum amount of contributions necessary to qualify for the various contributory benefits but also to provide the basis for the calculation of the earnings-related supplements to the short-term benefits.[3] The Social Security Pensions Act 1975 imposed on it a similar function in connection with the new earnings-related 'additional component' for the long-term benefits.[4] Because of the substantial gap in time between the receipt of the relevant earnings and the payment of the benefit it became necessary to 'revalue' the earnings factors to keep pace with inflation. Under the Pensions Act, therefore, the Secretary of State is directed to review in each tax year the general level of earnings obtaining in Great Britain, and if he concludes that the earnings factors for any previous tax year have not maintained their value in relation to the general level of earnings, he must lay before Parliament an order directing that the earnings factors shall be increased by such percentages as he thinks necessary to restore their values.[5]

B. Conditions for benefit

In the section of the book devoted to the individual contributory benefits, the contribution conditions of each will be specified. At this stage, it will be convenient to review the general pattern of rules. The aim of these rules has been to preserve a fair balance between the average contributor and

18. SSA 1975, s.13(5).
19. Ibid., s.13(5)(a). Technically it is
    $$\frac{100(P + S)}{R}$$ where P = the amount of contribution paid, S = the smallest sum required to make $P + S$ a multiple of 10p, and R = the percentage of earnings of which the contributions are calculated: S.I.

1975/468, Reg. 2. For the current limits see ante, pp. 55–56; cp. Appendix.
20. SSA 1975, s.13(5)(b) and S.I. 1975/468, Regs. 7–8.
1. Ibid., Regs. 5 and 7.
2. SSA 1975, s.13(5).
3. Post, p. 426.
4. Post, pp. 224–225.
5. SSPA 1975, s.21(2), (3).

the average beneficiary.[6] This objective of equity has given rise to two fundamental principles. The first is that the claimant's record of contributions should be sufficient in terms both of initial establishment in the scheme and of consistency over a period of time. The second is that there should be a difference according to whether he is claiming a short-term or a long-term benefit. In the case of the latter, where he will draw heavily on the fund's resources, it is appropriate that the tests should be more stringent. There is, in fact, also a third category of benefits where for political and other reasons it is though sufficient that a minimal degree of contributions has taken place (e.g., death grant and child's special allowance). These latter benefits excepted, the contributions conform to a neat pattern.

i) Initial condition

The first test, based on the idea of initial establishment in the scheme, can be satisfied only by contributions actually paid, i.e., credits do not qualify. In the case of short-term benefits (unemployment and sickness benefit, maternity and widow's allowance, and maternity grant) it is that during any one tax year since the age of sixteen the claimant has paid contributions, the earnings factors from which is at least twenty-five times the lower earnings limit for that year.[7] For those contributors at the lower end of the income scale (or making flat-rate Class 2 contributions) this will mean approximately six months' contributions. For the long-term benefits (retirement pensions, Categories A and B, and the remaining widow's benefits – but not invalidity benefit, entitlement to which depends on fulfilling the conditions for sickness benefit) the qualifying earnings factor is fifty-two times the lower earnings limit (equivalent to one year's contributions at the lowest end of the scale[8]).

ii) Continuing condition

For the second qualifying condition, credits are equivalent to paid contributions, but the difference between the short-term and long-term benefits becomes considerable. For the former, the earnings factor derived from contributions paid or credited during the tax year immediately preceding the year during which the entitlement to benefit falls must have been at least fifty (for maternity grant twenty-five) times the lower earnings limit.[9] For the latter, the position is more complicated as the contributions determine entitlement not merely to the basic component in the benefit, but also to the earnings-related additional component. To qualify for the basic component, for each of not less than 90% of the tax years of his working life (viz., between sixteen and pensionable age) the claimant must have paid, or been credited with, contributions the earnings factor of which was fifty-two times the lower earnings limit.[10] An alternative mode

---

6. See NIAC Report on the Question of Contribution Conditions and Credits Provisions (1956), Cmnd. 9854, para. 36.
7. SSA 1975, Sch. 3, paras. 1–4.
8. Ibid., para. 5, as amended by SSPA 1975, s.19(2).
9. SSA 1975, Sch. 3, paras. 1–3.
10. Ibid., para. 5, as amended by SSPA 1975, s.19(2).

of satisfying the condition is to have achieved the relevant earnings factor for at least twenty years (or, in the case of widowed mother's allowance and widow's pension for 50% of the working life if that is less than twenty years) and to establish that during each of the remaining years the contributor was 'precluded from regular employment by responsibilities at home'.[11] The additional component is based on the surplus of earnings factors above the minimum qualifying factor for each tax year.[12] The contributor is entitled to select and aggregate such surpluses from his twenty most profitable years.[13]

c. Credits

The system of crediting contributions is designed to assist those who are already established in the scheme but, for reasons beyond their control, have been unable to continue to make the requisite payments, sufficient to satisfy the second condition. To the extent that crediting is permitted, the beneficiaries are being subsidised by other contributors and for that reason there must be, in the words of the National Insurance Advisory Committee, 'real and substantial justification'[14] for each case. There are four main categories of contributors who may so benefit: those unemployed or otherwise incapable of work; those engaged in full-time education or training; new entrants; and women whose marriages have been terminated.

i) Unemployed or incapable of work
The first, most obvious, category is that in which a contributor has been prevented by unemployment or sickness from working.

> 'For the purposes of entitlement to any benefit by virtue of the person's contributions he shall be entitled to a Class 1 credit in respect of each week of unemployment or incapacity . . .'[15]

The condition is fulfilled if he is in receipt of an unemployability supplement under the industrial injury scheme or such an allowance in equivalent schemes.[16] Otherwise it is necessary that each of the six days from Monday to Saturday was a day of unemployment or incapacity for work.[17]

> A 'day of unemployment' is one which counted for unemployment benefit, or would have been so counted if a claim had been made in time.[18] Employment on a particular day may, however, be dis-

11. SSPA 1975, s. 19(3); cf., Appendix.
12. Ibid., s.6(4).
13. Ibid., s. 6(2), and see post, p. 224.
14. Report on Credits for Approved Training Courses (1953), Cmd. 8860, paras. 17–18. See also Report on Contribution Conditions and Credits, ante n.6.
15. S.I. 1975/556, Reg. 9(1).
16. Ibid., Reg. 9(2)(b), and see SSA 1975, Sch. 5.

17. S.I. 1975/556, Reg. 9(2)(a), though he may on religious grounds substitute Sunday for another day in the week: ibid.
18. Ibid., Reg. 9(3), and see post, pp. 90–92. Where unemployment benefit was not paid contributors must have made a declaration of availability for employment at the employment exchange or analogous institution: ibid., reg. 9(7).

regarded if *either* the employment in question was for a total of not more than eight hours in the week, and it was not in the contributor's main occupation, and it was consistent with his availability for full-time employment[19] *or* he was engaged in the employment for only one day in the week and the earnings derived therefrom did not exceed the lower earnings limit then in force.[20] A 'day of incapacity for work' is one which counts for sickness, maternity or invalidity benefit, or would have so counted if the claim had been made in time.[1]

ii) Starting credits

Individuals begin contributing to the scheme at different ages, according to their circumstances. Many will commence employment on reaching the school-leaving age of sixteen; others will remain in full-time education for several more years. At whatever time the entry is made, it will rarely coincide with the tax year (the base period for contribution conditions) and unless concessions are made a substantial number of payments will have no insurance significance. The system of credits goes some way to maintaining equity between these various categories of entrant. The rules may be classified according to the type of benefit for which credit is claimed.

1. For retirement pensions and widow's benefits, only a small concession is made. A person is entitled to the number of Class 3 credits necessary to bring the relevant earnings factor up to a reckonable year for the first three years of possible employment, viz. the tax year during which he reached the age of sixteen and the two following tax years.[2]

2. For unemployment and sickness benefits and maternity allowance, Class 1 credits are granted for the 'relevant past year' (the base of the contribution conditions for these benefits) if it was a year in which the contributor reached seventeen, or any previous years.[3]

3. Credits may be claimed for maternity grant on the basis of either (1) or (2).[4]

iii) Education and training

The third set of rules makes concessions for those who start contributing late, or interrupt their contribution record, because they are engaged in education or training. It is not, however, thought appropriate that all persons engaged in education or training courses at whatever age and for whatever purpose should be subsidised by the fund.[5]

---

19. Ibid., Reg. 9(4)(a).
20. Ibid., Reg. 9(4)(b).
1. Ibid., Reg. 9(5), and see post, pp. 151–158. If no benefit was in fact paid, the contributor must within a prescribed time write to the DHSS stating the grounds on which he claims to be

entitled to the credit: ibid., Reg. 9(8).
2. Ibid., Reg. 4(1).
3. Ibid., Reg. 5(1).
4. Ibid., Reg. 6.
5. See NIAC Report on Credits for Approved Training Courses, ante n.14.

a) COURSE BEGUN BEFORE AGE TWENTY-ONE. In this case, the policy is an ungenerous one: it is simply to grant credits for the year in which full-time education, apprenticeship or a training course approved by the Secretary of State ended, so that the year may be constituted a reckonable year for the purposes of entitlement to unemployment benefit, sickness benefit or maternity allowance.[6]

b) INTERRUPTIONS FOR APPROVED TRAINING COURSES. Clearly it is felt desirable to encourage individuals to improve their capacity for a job or equip themselves with the necessary skills for a new one. This form of vocational training, it may be argued, is in the national interest, and therefore justifies some form of subsidisation by the National Insurance Fund.[7] Thus the Regulations prescribe that[8] a contributor shall be granted credits for each week during any part of which he was engaged in a course of full-time training approved by the Secretary of State, provided that all of the following conditions are satisfied:

1. The course was not in pursuance of his employment;
2. He had reached eighteen before the beginning of the tax year during which the week in question began;
3. The course was not intended to last more than one year;[9] and
4. For at least one of the last three tax years before the course began, he had paid or had been credited with contributions amounting to at least fifty times the lower earnings limit for that year.[10]

iv) Termination of marriage

A woman may obtain employment for the first time where a marriage has been terminated by death or dissolution or when children cease to require full-time attention. The position of such a woman is analogous to that of new entrants and similar credit facilities are available.

1. For the purpose of satisfying the 'continuing' condition of unemployment benefit, sickness benefit, and maternity allowance, a woman whose marriage has been terminated may be credited with the necessary number of Class 1 contributions for any year during the whole or any part of which the marriage was subsisting. During one year which was either the last year before the marriage terminated or any subsequent year, she must, however, have paid Class 1 or Class 2 contributions, the earnings factor derived from which was at least twenty-five times the lower earnings limit for that year.[11]

---

6. S.I. 1975/556, Reg. 8.
7. NIAC Report, ante n.14, at paras. 20–21.
8. S.I. 1975/556, Reg. 7.
9. Though if it was training of a disabled person under the Employment and Training Act 1973, it may be

permitted for 'such longer period as is reasonable in the circumstances': S.I. 1975/556, Reg. 7(2)(b).
10. This condition may be waived if 'in the circumstances of the case there is reasonable ground': ibid., Reg. 7(2)(a).
11. S.I. 1974/2010, Reg. 2.

2. For the same purpose, a widow who ceases to be entitled to widow's allowance or widowed mother's allowance (in the latter case because she has no longer dependent children of the relevant age to care for[12]) will be credited with the requisite number of Class 1 contributions for every year up to and including that in which she ceased to be entitled to the widow's benefit referred to.[13]

3. For the purposes of entitlement to maternity grant, death grant, and until 6 April 1979 retirement pension (Categories A or B), a widow is credited with such Class 3 contributions as are necessary to enable her to acquire the requisite earnings factor for the tax year in which she was widowed and any other year during which she was entitled to a widow's benefit (other than the age-related widow's pension, or, if she was widowed before 6 April 1975, the widow's basic pension).[14] From 6 April 1979, a new system for protection of entitlement to retirement pension will be introduced.[15]

D. Other assistance in satisfying contribution conditions

i) Aggregate of contributions by new entrants

The credit facilities available to new entrants serve to assist them only in satisfying the second of the two contribution conditions. The fortuitous timing of their entry in relation to the relevant tax years may constitute an obstacle to the fulfilment of the first condition. The legislation, therefore, makes a further concession for entitlement to the short-term benefits (viz. unemployment, sickness and maternity benefits and widow's allowance).

> Where the last complete tax year, before the beginning of the year in which occurred the event for which benefit is claimed, was either the year in which the claimant first became liable for contributions of Classes 1 or 2, or the year preceding that year, he may for the purposes of satisfying the first contribution condition for the short-term benefits, aggregate the contributions which he has actually paid, and that aggregate is then treated as having been paid in the last complete year.[16]

ii) Widows deemed to satisfy first condition

Widows joining, or rejoining, the scheme once their entitlement to widow's allowance or widowed mother's allowance has expired are faced with a similar problem, and for the purposes of entitlement to

---

12. See post, pp. 234–236.
13. S.I. 1974/2010, Reg. 3(1)(b).
14. Ibid., Reg. 6; cp. Appendix.
15. Post, p. 213.
16. SSA 1975, Sch. 3, para. 8. He is deemed to satisfy this condition if he has been able successfully to apply the aggregation principle to a previous claim for another short-term benefit (except widow's allowance) and the contributions in question were of the appropriate class: ibid., paras. 9–13.

unemployment and sickness benefit or maternity allowance, they are deemed to have satisfied the first contribution condition.[17]

iii) Spouse's contributions and retirement pensions

As will be revealed in chapter 5, a woman who is, or has been, married may rely on her husband's contributions for the purposes of a Category B retirement pension and, if the marriage has been terminated, also for a Category A pension: from 6 April 1979 an equivalent facility will be granted to widowers.[18]

E. Partial satisfaction of contribution conditions

To avoid an 'all or nothing' solution, the legislation has always provided for a reduced benefit where the second contribution condition has been only partially satisfied. For short-term benefits (unemployment and sickness benefits and maternity allowance) 75% of the standard rate is payable if the earnings factor derived from the claimant's contributions is between twenty-five and thirty-seven and a half times that limit.[19] The same percentages are applied to increases for adult dependants, but increases for child dependants are payable in full whether or not the second condition is satisfied.[20] For retirement pensions (Categories A and B), widowed mother's allowance and widow's pensions, the percentage of benefit payable is calculated according to the proportion of reckonable years (i.e., years in which the qualifying earnings factor has been achieved) to the number of reckonable years of working life prescribed for the benefit in question.[1] No benefit is, however, payable at less than 25% of the standard rate.[2] As with the short-term benefits, increases for adult dependants are subject to the same reduction and increases for child dependants are payable in full.[3] To assist entitlement to unemployment, sickness and maternity benefits (but not the earnings-related supplement), there are provisions for filling gaps in the contribution record resulting from employment abroad.[4]

17. S.I. 1974/2010, Reg. 3(1)(a).
18. Post, p. 215.
19. S.I. 1975/564, Reg. 14; S.I. 1975/553, Reg. 8.
20. S.I. 1975/564, Reg. 14(3); S.I. 1975/553, Reg. 8(3).

1. S.I. 1974/2059, Reg. 5(3).
2. Ibid., Reg. 5(1).
3. Ibid., Reg. 5(2).
4. S.I. 1975/492, Reg. 18, and S.I. 1975/553, Reg. 11, both as amended by S.I. 1977/1509, Reg. 3.

3 Unemployment Benefit

Part one. Introduction

A. General

Unemployment, as a major cause of earnings loss and financial hardship, has from the beginning been an object for protection under social security legislation. Yet it differs from other social hazards similarly so protected in one important respect: unlike the natural phenomena of sickness, old age, birth and death, it results in a large degree from the interplay of economic forces. As such, the level of unemployment to be tolerated, the means of combating it and the extent of financial support granted to victims, can be influenced by a government as part of its overall economic policy.[1] By its control of investment, rates of interest, taxation, pay and prices, it may stimulate demand for goods and services which will induce a high level of employment.[2] Where, in contrast, unemployment results from an excessive supply of labour in the wrong location or with inappropriate skills, the government may encourage the mobility of industries and workers through its regional policies, and the adaptation of the labour force to new industrial processes and techniques through training schemes.[3] Finally, by means of its various employment agencies, it may provide a service whereby unemployed persons are given guidance and information as to the nature and location of vacant situations.[4]

It has always been assumed that the level and form of financial assistance available to the unemployed influence decisions by individuals whether to accept redundancies or to acquire new skills by retraining.[5]

1. The literature on the subject is immense. Lawyers should find particularly helpful e.g., Lester *Economics of Unemployment Compensation* (1962); Haber and Murray *Unemployment Insurance in the American Economy* (1966); Hauser and Burrows *The Economics of Unemployment Insurance* (1969).
2. The policy originated in Keynes *The General Theory of Employment, Interest and Money* (1936).
3. For a comparative survey see Zarka 95 Int. Lab. Rev. 509. On training, the most important British measures have been the Industrial Training Act 1964 and the Employment and Training Act 1973.
4. See ibid., s.1, which established the Manpower Services Commission and the Employment Service Agency. Under the auspices of the latter, Unemployment Benefit Offices and Employment Offices have replaced the employment exchanges. See Dept. of Employment *People and Jobs: A Modern Employment Service* (1973), and Showler *Onto a Comprehensive Employment Service* (1973), Fabian Pamphlet.
5. This was the explicit assumption on which the introduction of earnings-related supplements was based: post, p. 425. See generally Hill in ed. Worswick *The Concept and Measurement of Involuntary Unemployment* (1976), chap. 9.

Thus the subject matter of this chapter had considerable implications for the mobility of labour. The same applies where it is the policy of an administration, explicit or implicit, to maintain less than 'full' employment, where this is thought necessary to reduce demand and thus to decelerate inflation.[6] Such an aim will be tolerated politically only where those rendered unemployed as a result can sustain a reasonable standard of living. Two direct methods of assisting the workless have been developed within the British system. The first is unemployment benefit which forms part of the contributory scheme of social security and with which we are here concerned. The second, the redundancy payments system, introduced in 1965, confers a lump sum award on redundant workers who have been with the same employer for at least two years prior to the redundancy.[7] The rationale of the scheme is not primarily welfare or income-maintenance but more the recognition that the employee has some form of 'proprietary interest' in his job for the deprivation of which he should be compensated. This, and the fact that it is not administered by the DHSS, means that it does not come within the scope of this book.[8]

B. History[9]

Prior to the twentieth century, relief from the consequences of unemployment took one of two forms: private schemes of insurance administered by trade unions and friendly societies, or resort to the antiquated and degrading poor law. Once it become widely recognised that unemployment was not, in the great majority of cases, the result of personal moral failing but rather the product of economic forces, there was an obvious case for some form of state protection outside the poor law. The Royal Commission of the Poor Law, reporting in 1909,[10] placed great reliance on the system of labour exchanges (established on a national basis some four years previously[11]), and the redeployment of labour and industry. The Majority recommended the extension of unemployment insurance but felt that it should continue to exist on a voluntary basis and should be administered independently for each trade group.[12]

The most penetrating analysis of unemployment in the early years of this century came from Beveridge.[13] For him, the creation of labour exchanges was only part of a broader approach to unemployment which though influenced by economic policy required residual support in an

6. George *Social Security and Society* (1973), pp. 85–92.
7. Redundancy Payments Act 1965, as amended inter alia by Employment Protection Act 1975.
8. Accounts of the scheme will be found in the standard works on labour law and in Grunfeld *Law of Redundancy* (1971).
9. Tillyard *Unemployment Insurance in Great Britain 1911–1948* (1949); Cohen *Unemployment Insurance & Assistance in*

Britain (1938), chaps. 1–3; Harris *Unemployment and Politics, 1886–1914* (1972).
10. Cd. 4499.
11. Unemployed Workmen Act 1905.
12. Ante n.10, at para. 604. The Minority Report reached similar conclusions (p. 1200) but concluded that compulsory insurance in some industries was practicable.
13. *Unemployment: A Problem of Industry* (1909). See also *Harris*, chap. 6.

insurance scheme: the unemployed must be able 'to subsist without demoralisation till they can be reabsorbed again after industrial transformations'.[14] The philosophy attracted widespread attention but a more direct influence on Churchill and Lloyd George, the political pioneers of the National Insurance Act 1911, was the system then operating in Germany. Like the German model, the Act established a compulsory scheme involving a three-way levy, the employee, the employer and the state contributing in equal proportions. For each of five contributions paid, an insured person during unemployment might receive a weekly benefit of 7s to a maximum of 15 weeks a year. The experimental nature of the first essay in state unemployment insurance must not be overlooked. It was restricted to certain industries (notably building and shipbuilding) whose records were sufficiently detailed for actuarial calculations to be made with fair precision, and which in total included only $2\frac{1}{4}$ million of a 10 million working population. Existing private schemes were maintained and even encouraged. Finally, the benefits payable were not very generous. The scheme was not regarded as providing a substitute for wages but rather a supplement to personal savings to avoid resort to charity or the poor law. In short, it was conceived of as a temporary lifebelt.[15]

The First World War was responsible for certain important changes. On the one hand, an Act of 1916 extended the scheme to all persons working on munitions.[16] On the other hand, soldiers returning to civilian life but unable to find employment were not insured, and were granted a donation or 'dole'.[17] This led to the feeling that those unemployed through no fault of their own were entitled to relief as of right, which, in turn, induced the government to promise a universal insurance scheme. A reform of 1920 went a long way in fulfilling the promise.[18] The scheme now covered all workers except those in agriculture, domestic service and the civil service; the numbers insured rising from 4 to 11 millions. The ex-serviceman's donation had also made special provision for dependants. There was a growing awareness that unemployment was a family rather than an individual problem, and it had become manifestly clear that an unemployed married man with children was often unable to maintain the family without resort to the poor law. The result was the introduction of dependants' allowances.[19] The reform was a fundamental one: it meant that the insurance fund was now the primary source for maintaining the majority of the unemployed.[20]

Unfortunately the burden placed on the scheme became, in times of great economic depression, too heavy to bear. The actuaries in computing the level of contributions and benefits had assumed an unemployment level of 5·32%. Between 1920 and 1940 the figure never fell below 10%, and during some periods was much higher. The result was a debt of

14. Ibid., at p. 236.
15. Royal Commission on Unemployment Insurance, Final Report (1932), Cmd. 4185, para. 198.
16. NI (Part II)(Munition Workers) Act 1916.
17. Paid under powers conferred on the Board of Trade by ibid., s.3(1).
18. UIA 1920.
19. Under the U Workers' Dependants (Temporary Provisions) Act, 1921, made permanent by UIA 1922, s.1.
20. *Tillyard*, ante n.9, at p. 69.

£59 million in the insurance fund, and as a concession to extreme political and economic pressure both at home and abroad, in 1932 the government made its notorious cut in benefit of 10%.[1] But there was a second problem, even graver. In the 1920s it became evident that a large proportion of unemployment in Britain was confined to certain industries which were situated in narrow geographical areas. In consequence, in these areas there was chronic and long-term unemployment, against which the scheme gave no protection, for benefit was given only for a limited period. The only method of saving the persons affected from the poor law was to establish an uncovenanted benefit scheme which would run alongside standard insurance. Throughout the interwar years some such system continued to operate, though under different guises. Under the 1920 Act, for example, benefit might be paid in advance of contributions on the assumption that in the long run such contributions would be made.[2] An 'uncovenanted benefit' was introduced in 1921[3] (later known as 'extended' or 'transitional' benefit). This was payable at the discretion of the Minister[4] in the exercise of which he might investigate the personal and financial circumstances of the claimant, a practice of course impossible under the standard insurance scheme. The Blanesburgh Committee, reporting in 1927,[5] found this dual system to be unsatisfactory and recommended that all benefits should be paid as of right. The proposal was enacted[6] but the onset of extreme economic difficulties meant that the aim of abolishing uncovenanted benefit was never realised. The 'transitional arrangements' which were intended to be superseded were several times extended. Indeed in 1933 the number of claimants in receipt of transitional benefit exceeded those on insurance benefit.

A major review of the system was undertaken by the Royal Commission on Unemployment Insurance in 1930–32.[7] As implemented by the Unemployment Insurance Act of 1934, its recommendations established a pattern which, subject to certain modifications, has remained ever since. The basis was a distinction, hitherto only partially recognised, between insurance and relief. The former should continue (and indeed be extended to certain industries as yet excluded, notably agriculture) along traditional lines of covenanted benefit, limited in duration. When the right to benefit had been exhausted special assistance, based on a means test, would be provided and administered by the Unemployment Assistance Board. The latter was, of course, the precursor of the Supplementary Benefits Commission, and details of its subsequent history will be found in a later chapter.[8]

Under Beveridge's plan and the subsequent legislation, unemployment was integrated into the general scheme of social insurance and was made compulsory for all employed earners. It was, in fact, Beveridge's intention

1. S.R. & O. 1932/814. See Gilbert *British Social Policy 1914–39* (1972), pp. 162–175.
2. UIA 1920, s.8(4).
3. UIA 1921, s.3.
4. For a short period in 1924–25 the claimant had a right to such benefit (UIA (No. 2) 1924, s.1(1)) but this was soon repealed by UIA 1925, s.1.
5. Published by Ministry of Labour.
6. UIA 1927.
7. Interim Report (1931), Cmd. 3872; Final Report (1932), Cmd. 4185.
8. Post, pp. 477–478.

that the benefit should be of unlimited duration.[9] But the recommendation was not found acceptable: there were fears that it would be an inducement to abuse, and his suggested safeguard – a requirement that an individual undergo training after six months unemployment – was regarded as impracticable.[10] The only major modification to the scheme subsequent to 1946 was the introduction of the earnings-related supplement in 1966.[11]

c. Scope and structure

The law governing entitlement to unemployment benefit is complex. The difficulties result partly from the need to adapt the system to changing industrial practices (particularly the shift from six-day to five-day working) and partly from the relationship between social security and the law governing contracts of employment. The problems have been exacerbated by a reluctance in the DHSS to reformulate traditional concepts, some of which are outmoded, and a tendency instead to prefer patchwork solutions, occasionally implemented by poorly drafted regulations.[12]

Viewed from a very broad level of generality, however, the structure of the system is not difficult to comprehend. Apart from the contribution conditions (Part Two), entitlement rests on two fundamental notions. The first is that the claimant should be unemployed (Part Three). The complexities in this area of the law arise primarily from the fact that benefit may be payable notwithstanding that the contract of employment between the claimant and his employer is still subsisting, viz., for periods of lay-off or short-time. The second idea is that the unemployment should be involuntary, that is, must result from external economic factors rather than from the claimant's own conduct or physical condition. If he is physically or psychologically incapable of work he must satisfy the relevant criteria for the disability benefits. The involuntary nature of the unemployment is judged first by the requirement (Part Four) that he be 'available' for work and subsequently by the sanctions of disqualification imposed where the claimant voluntarily leaves his employment, is dismissed for misconduct, or refuses a suitable offer of employment (Part Five). On one view, the notion may also account for the disqualification of those involved in a trade dispute (Part Six). The remainder of the chapter is largely devoted to an account of the rules governing special categories of employment, notably seasonal workers (Part Seven), and the duration and amount of benefit (Part Eight).

Part two. Contribution Conditions

Only persons who have paid Class 1 contributions can qualify for unemployment benefit.[13] The exclusion of the self-employed has not been

9. Paras. 129–130.
10. Social Insurance, Part I, para. 67.
11. Post, p. 425.

12. Cf., Ogus, 4 ILJ 12.
13. SSA 1975, s.13(1): the one exception is share fishermen, post, p. 131.

controversial: it has generally been regarded as too difficult to ascertain when they are not gainfully occupied. In the words of Beveridge, 'the income of a farmer, a shopkeeper or a business manager may come at any time; how busy or how active he is on a particular day is largely within his own control. It is not practicable to have a general system of maintaining earnings of persons gainfully occupied otherwise than by way of employment, by benefits conditional upon not working or appearing to work on a particular day.'[4]

The contribution conditions for class 1 contributors are:

1. The claimant must have paid contributions of that class for any one year before the date of claim, and the earnings factor derived from such contributions must be not less than that year's lower earnings limit multiplied by twenty-five.

2. In the last complete year before the year in which falls the beginning of the period of interruption of employment, the claimant must have paid, or been credited with, contributions of that class, the earnings factor from which must be not less than that year's lower earnings limit multiplied by fifty.[15]

Part three. Unemployment

A. General

Benefit is payable in respect of 'any day of unemployment which forms part of a period of interruption of employment'.[16] This proposition contains a number of diverse elements. For the purposes of exposition they will be classified as follows. In the case of a claimant who has severed his connection with his employer the primary question is whether he is 'unemployed' in the sense that he is not following a gainful occupation (section B). It is then necessary to show that the day of unemployment in respect of which the claim is made is a day which the law treats as forming part of a period of interruption of employment (section C). In the case where the contract with the employer is still subsisting but the employee has been laid off, there are additional requirements to be satisfied (section D), in particular that the day of unemployment is one on which the claimant would normally have worked.

B. Whether unemployed

The legislature has not attempted to define 'unemployed'.[17] There are obvious dangers in seeking to explain its meaning by reference to the

14. Para. 122.
15. SSA 1975, Sch. 3, para. 1. For the concepts involved see ante, chap. 2.
16. Ibid., s.14(1)(a).
17. For statutory definitions in the USA, see, e.g., California Unemployment Insurance Code, § 1252, and Michigan, Employment Security Act, § 421.48.

concept of 'employment' as it is used in other areas of the law. For many purposes,[18] it means being party to a contract of service, but this is clearly unhelpful here for an independent contractor or a self-employed person is not 'unemployed'. A more helpful analogy is the concept of 'gainfully employed' which is used for the purposes of contributions to distinguish employed and self-employed persons from those not so employed.[19] The general principle is that a claimant is unemployed if he is not following an occupation from which he intends to derive remuneration.

i) Remuneration and profits

The profitable nature of the occupation has been given a broad interpretation. The remuneration may be in kind rather than money,[20] and need not have been actually paid to the claimant on the day or days in question.[1] So a person working according to an unexpired contract is employed, notwithstanding that his employer defaults on payment.[2] Conversely, if the claimant has started a business he may have to wait for returns on his capital outlay.[3] If he has changed his employment, he may have to work for a certain period (e.g., a 'waiting-week') before receiving wages, or he may have to perform certain duties in necessary preparation for employment.[4] In such cases, provided that the obligation arises from the employment, he is not unemployed. In this connection, problems have arisen regarding training courses for employment. Even though the course may be run by the alleged employer, he may not, at this stage, have entered into a contract of employment with the claimant. The standard approach taken under the Unemployment Insurance Acts by the Umpire was to determine on the evidence available whether, explicitly or implicitly, the employer had undertaken to employ the claimant on his successful completion of the course. If so, whether or not he received remuneration, the claimant was gainfully employed.[5] A presumption that there was a tacit understanding to this effect regularly arose where the training was a condition precedent to the employment,[6] and (perhaps unjustifiably) this was not rebutted by the fact that the trainee might have to wait for a vacancy.[7] These principles have been applied to the modern legislation.[8] But in the most recent reported decision,[9] the Commissioner

18. E.g., vicarious liability in the law of tort.
19. SSA 1975, s.2(1) and see *R(U) 3/67*. See also the question, relevant to retirement pension, whether a claimant is engaged in an occupation inconsistent with retirement: post, pp. 202–204. Under Reg. 6(1)(h) of the 1948 Unemployment Regulations (S.I. 1948/1277) the claimant was not unemployed if he was 'following any gainful occupation ...'. The word 'gainful' was removed by a 1949 amendment (S.I. 1949/1984 Reg. 2) but it has been accepted since *R(U) 34/53* that the change of wording was of no significance. See also *R(U) 2/67*.

20. *CWU 42/50*. If the alleged employment is a contract of service this will infringe the Truck Acts, but a claimant seeking unemployment benefit is estopped from relying on the illegality of a contract: *UD 1404/27*. (Umpire's decision under old Unemployment Insurance Acts).
1. *R(U) 16/64*.
2. *R(U) 5/75*.
3. *R(U) 12/55*.
4. *UD 7979*.
5. *UD 4903*.
6. E.g., *UD 2605/28*.
7. *UD 8839/24*.
8. *CU 162/50*; *R(U) 30/51*; *R(U) 4/59*.
9. *R(U) 3/67*, H. Magnus, Dep. Comr.

took a quite different stance. He argued that under the National Insurance legislation, then in force, a person was employed if he was gainfully occupied in employment, and not employed if he was not so gainfully occupied. Attendance at a training course was neither an 'occupation' nor was it 'gainful'. It is submitted that the former approach is preferable. It is consistent with the generally held view that the immediate receipt of monetary benefit is not crucial to a finding of gainful employment.[10]

Other problems arise where the claimant is engaged, or allegedly engaged, in his own business. Must the business be profitable? Must he spend a substantial proportion of his time working for the business? It is clear that the mere fact that the claimant is the proprietor is not sufficient by itself to render him 'gainfully employed'.[11] Although it appears that there is a presumption that a partner assumes certain responsibilities in managing the firm[12] this may be rebutted if it is clear that he was not *personally* active.[13] There are two factors to be considered. On the one hand there is the subjective intention of the claimant. As the Commissioner has said, 'a gainful occupation is one in which a person is engaged with the desire, hope and intention of obtaining for himself, directly and personally, remuneration or profit in return for his services and efforts.'[14] On the other hand, there are the objective factors of the number of hours spent on the business seen in the light of the amount of work which might reasonably be done, and this might vary with the season.[15]

Subject to the special regulations on subsidiary occupations,[16] it does not generally assist the claimant to show that the amount paid by way of remuneration was small. In *R(U) 4/64*

> C attended an occupational centre where disabled persons were employed on light simple work for what the local tribunal described as a 'nominal wage'. He was held to be following a gainful occupation: 'he attended during normal working hours to do certain set industrial work for a prescribed payment.'[17]

But the payment may be so small as to indicate that it was not intended as remuneration. To be contrasted with the above decision is *R(U) 2/67*.

> C attended a training centre for mentally disabled persons. Light work was undertaken by patients and the products were sold. But the object was therapeutic not commercial and the weekly payments of £1 were not regarded as remuneration but 'more in the nature of pocket money given as an incident of rehabilitation treatment.'[18]

10. See *British Guiana Credit v Da Silva* [1965] 1 WLR 248 at 253, PC, per Lord Donovan. (*RU*) 3/67 does, however, receive some support from *R(I) 2/75* in which J. S. Watson, Comr., regarded as conclusive a finding by the Secretary of State that a student trainee was not an 'employed earner' for the purposes of the industrial injury scheme.
11. *R(U) 11/57*.
12. *R(U) 22/64*.
13. *R(U) 11/57* and see *UD 4072/28*.
14. *CU 30/49*, para. 5, and see the cases on retirement pension considered post, p. 204, and on earnings, post, p. 427.
15. *CU 235/50*; *R(U) 8/55*; cp. *R(U) 1/67*.
16. Post, p. 89.
17. *R(U) 4/64*, para. 7.
18. Per R.G. Micklethwait, Chief Comr, at para. 11.

ii) Work undertaken

The fact that on a particular day or period of days an employee is given no work by his employer does not necessarily mean that he is unemployed. The question in every case is whether, under the contract of employment, on its proper construction, he was bound to make his services available to the employer.[19] Some contracts for part-time work are so broad in this respect that harsh consequences may arise. A typical contract for a part-time professional footballer contains a clause that in return for the payment of a small weekly sum the player is bound to attend for training whenever the club so requires. Unless the authorities are able to find that such a term has been modified or waived in practice,[20] they must inevitably reach the conclusion that the player was following an occupation with the club for the whole of the week.[1]

iii) Duration of occupation

A claimant may concede that he has followed a gainful occupation but allege that the occupation had not begun or had ceased on the day (or period) for which benefit is claimed. If the alleged occupation is self-employment, the authorities must assess, on the evidence available, the period of time during which it might reasonably be concluded that he was personally active in the business.[2] The fact that no receipts were taken during the period is not conclusive,[3] but it may show that there was no work which the claimant might profitably undertake.[4] Where the alleged occupation is under a contract of employment the task should be much simpler. Prima facie he is gainfully occupied from the date of his appointment to the date of his discharge.[5] But there are several important qualifications to this principle.

a) CONTRACTS FOR PARTICULAR WORK. If the employment is for a specific job of work and does not oblige the employee to make himself available to the employer throughout the period of the contract, he may be gainfully occupied only for so long as he is actually engaged on the job in question. In *R(U) 1/73*

> A census enumerator was appointed in March 1971. He was paid a lump sum for the execution of certain specific duties which were to begin on 1 April 1971. R. S. Lazarus, Commissioner, held that he was gainfully occupied only from this latter date.

The decision contrasts with several in which it was held that a census *officer* was employed throughout the period of appointment.[6] In the 1973 case, the Commissioner, though critical of these earlier decisions, felt able to distinguish them on the ground that census officers were given different instructions: they had to attend a training session before the duties com-

19. *R(U) 5/58* and see the decisions on guarantee agreements, post, p. 103.
20. *R(U) 8/59.*
1. *R(U) 24/53; R(U) 10/57; R(U) 23/57.*
2. *R(U) 11/57.*
3. *R(U) 12/55.*
4. *R(U) 8/55.*
5. *R(U) 3/72,* R.J.A. Temple, Comr.
6. Those reported are *R(U) 16/61* and *R(U) 3/72.*

menced.[7] But this fact was not regarded as significant in the earlier decisions and *R(U) 1/73* seems to depart from the view apparently held previously that the duration of the occupation is conclusively established by the contract of employment. The departure does, indeed, seem a proper one. In the words of the Commissioner, 'I find it hard to see the logic of holding that a person follows the occupation of census enumerator on a day on which his employer does not require him to, and he does not, do any part of the specified job for which he is employed.'[8]

b) WHETHER CONTRACT TERMINATED. In some cases it is by no means easy to decide whether or not the contract of employment has been terminated. If the contract was for a fixed term, it will end by lapse of time,[9] but if, as in most cases, it was of indefinite duration, it is terminable by due notice.[10] The problem arises where both parties anticipate and intend that the employment relationship will be resumed after the expiration of a short period. The employee may have been given his 'cards', told that he may seek other temporary employment, but that in consideration of a retainer fee he will be expected to return. Has the contract been terminated or merely suspended?[11] The decisions of the Commissioner reveal two different approaches.

1. In the first, the receipt of payment was regarded as evidence of a contractual obligation to return to the employment, and hence of a subsisting contract of employment.[12] But if there was no retainer fee, or if the sum was so small that it could be regarded as a 'gratuity', the inference of a subsisting contract was unlikely to be drawn.[13]

2. A new approach was taken by the Commissioner in 1968.[14] Regard was had to the extent of the claimant's obligations during the interim period. If the payment was made in order that the claimant should be at the disposal of the employer when required, he was properly to be regarded as gainfully occupied. But if the payment was only an inducement to get him to return once the period had elapsed, and he was free to do whatever he liked throughout the period, he was not gainfully employed.

Approach (1) was popular at a time when the concept of 'termination' was given a special meaning in unemployment insurance law. The doctrine (originating in the Umpires' decisions under the old Unemployment Insurance Acts) was that a contract was not 'terminated' if

7. *R(U) 1/73*, para. 10, R.S. Lazarus, Comr.
8. Ibid., at para. 14.
9. *Semble* the old rule that where a contract did not specify a termination date there was a presumption that it was a yearly hiring is no longer valid: *Richardson v Koeford* [1969] 3 All ER 1264, [1969] 1 WLR 1812, CA.
10. The law on the appropriate notice is governed by the Contracts of Employment Act 1972, as amended by Employment Protection Act 1975. See, generally, Hepple and O'Higgins, *Individual Employment Law* (2nd edn),

chap. 12.
11. The problem is not peculiar to the law of unemployment insurance. See Kahn-Freund, 10 Rev. Dir. Inter & Comp. Lav. 3.
12. *CU 28/48*; *CU 62/48*; *R(U) 8/54*. In *R(U) 38/52*, the claimant was not bound to return but because of past practice was 'expected' to return. It is difficult, on any ground, to support the decision that she was gainfully occupied.
13. *R(U) 20/51*.
14. *R(U) 6/68*, H. Magnus, Comr. See also *R(U) 8/68* (Tribunal decision).

it was intended that the relationship of employment should be resumed at the next available opportunity. As will be seen,[15] the doctrine no longer applies. This alone should justify the general adoption of (2) which, in any event, would seem to be more realistic.[16] It is artificial to regard a claimant who remains idle until the end of the period in question as gainfully occupied. The payment, if substantial, may disentitle the claimant on the quite different ground that it was a payment in lieu of wages, the principle next to be considered.

c) PAYMENT IN LIEU. If a person is paid money by his employer in substitution of wages for a period *after* the termination of the contract, it is sound policy that for such a period he should not be entitled to unemployment benefit. The principle has been recognised since 1924[17] but its formulation has caused some difficulties. In modern industrial practice it has become increasingly common to combine wages in lieu of notice with 'golden handshakes' or other severance payments and the problem is to what extent these should be covered by the principle and, if so, for what period they should disentitle the recipient. Prior to 1966 a claimant was ineligible for benefit if he continued to receive wages or received compensation which was substantially equivalent to the wages lost.[18] This proved to be too restrictive an approach and in 1966 was replaced by the concept of payment in lieu either of notice to terminate or, if the contract was for a term certain, of the remuneration which would have been paid if the contract had not been terminated.[19] This too was thought to be insufficiently broad – in particular it could not apply to employees (e.g., civil servants) whose contract was not for a term certain and who were legally not entitled to notice. The current Regulation, introduced in 1971,[20] provides that

> 'a day shall not be treated as a day of unemployment if it is a day in respect of which a person receives a payment (whether or not a payment made in pursuance of a legally enforceable obligation) in lieu either of notice or of the remuneration which he would have received for that day had his employment not been terminated. . .'[1]

1. *Nature of payment.* The only payments covered by this Regulation are those made in lieu either of notice or of the remuneration which the employee would have received if the contract had not been terminated. Damages for wrongful dismissal[2] and compensation for unfair dismissal[3]

15. Post, p. 98.
16. Cf., *R(U) 7/54.*
17. See UIA (No. 2) 1924, s.1(4).
18. S.I. 1948/1277, Reg. 6(1)(d). By S.I. 1954/117, Reg. 3(2), 'substantially equivalent' compensation was limited to a sum which exceeded 2/3 of the remuneration which would have been paid (if the contract had not been terminated) less the standard rate of unemployment benefit.

19. S.I. 1966/1049, Reg. 7(1).
20. S.I. 1971/807, Reg. 2.
1. S.I. 1975/564, Reg. 7(1)(d).
2. *R(U) 4/56.*
3. *R(U) 5/74,* criticised by J. Reid, 4 ILJ 54. The same principle is applied by S.I. 1975/564, Reg. 7(1)(i) to complementary remedies under the Employment Protection Act 1975, ss.71, 72, 78, 80, 101 and 103.

are included as in both cases the award contains a major element representing loss of remuneration; and the principle necessarily extends to settlements made in pursuance of such claims.[4] Prior to 1971 purely gratuitous payments were ignored,[5] and this remains true under the new Regulation, for the reference in parentheses to the absence of a legally enforceable obligation does not alter the character of the payment which must be made in lieu of notice or as a substitute for remuneration.[6] The character of the payment will thus depend on the intention of the parties: the description given to it by them may be some evidence of its character but is by no means conclusive.[7] A payment may be intended to include elements both of remuneration and of bounty. In such cases, a Tribunal of Commissioners has held that regard must be had to its overriding characteristic – it would be wrong to sever the payment into its constitutive elements.[8] The fact that it thereby constitutes a greater sum than would have been paid to the claimant if the contract had not been terminated is regarded as irrelevant.[9]

2. *Duration of disentitlement.* The most controversial question arising under the Regulation is as to the period of disentitlement. The position prior to 1971 was that where the relevant contract was one for a term certain the 'remuneration' would be treated as covering the unexpired period of the contract,[10] and where it was a payment in lieu of notice it would be attributed to the length of notice required under the contract (or failing that the general law of employment) whether or not the sum was intended to be limited to that period.[11] Arguably this was too generous; an employee might be paid the equivalent of a salary for say six months when the period of notice required was only three months. The 1971 reform modified the law in three major respects: it omitted the reference to contracts for a term certain; by the passage in parentheses, payments in lieu of notice were to be covered 'whether or not . . . made in pursuance of a legally enforceable obligation'; and the period of disentitlement was limited to a maximum of one year. In a series of cases in 1973 the Chief Commissioner supported the view of the Department that these amendments had drastically altered the law.[12] He held that the passage in parentheses allowed payments which the employer was not legally obliged to make to be allocated to days of unemployment beyond the period of legal notice. This view was not shared by H. Magnus, Commissioner, who held that, as under the previous law, the claimant was disentitled only for the period of legal notice.[13] The decision was upheld, and that of the Chief Commissioner was repudiated, by a Tribunal majority.[14] In their view the limited objective of the passage in parentheses was to cover cases, such as

4. *R(U) 17/52*; *R(U) 4/56*; *R(U) 10/58*; *R(U) 5/74.*
5. *CU 639/48.*
6. *R(U) 7/73,* para. 45 (Tribunal majority).
7. Ibid., and see *R(U) 29/55*; *R(U) 4/56*; *R(U) 10/58*; *R(U) 8/73.*
8. *R(U) 7/73,* paras. 35–37; and see *R(U) 9/73.*
9. *R(U) 7/73,* para. 35; *R(U) 9/73.*
10. *R(U) 3/68.*
11. See esp. *R(U) 37/53.*
12. *R(U) 7/73*; *R(U) 8/73*; *R(U) 9/73* (dissenting opinions).
13. *R(U) 5/73*; *R(U) 6/73.*
14. *R(U) 7/73*; *R(U) 8/73*; *R(U) 9/73* (majority opinions).

civil servants, who had no right to a period of notice.[15] The present position is, then, that where the contract is for a fixed term (i.e., there is no requirement as to notice), the claimant in receipt of a relevant payment will be disentitled for the rest of that term. In all other cases, he is barred for the period of notice and this is to be determined according to the contract of employment or under the general law of employment.[16] This interpretation of the Regulation is supported by a Report of the National Insurance Advisory Committee,[17] but may nevertheless be criticised as being overgenerous.[18]

d) SUSPENSION. Finally it should be noted that though in general the termination of a contract will establish title to benefit, the converse proposition that its subsistence will defeat a claim does not follow. Benefit may be paid where a contract is merely *suspended*. A full account is given below.[19]

iv) Exclusion of subsidiary occupations

It is regarded as inappropriate to disentitle the claimant on the ground that he is following a subsidiary occupation if it is only marginally profitable and it is consistent with him being available for full-time employment. For the occupation to be disregarded, the onus is on the claimant[20] to satisfy four conditions.[1]

a) EARNINGS NOT TO EXCEED 75p PER DAY. The policy of exempting part-time work from consideration is subject to the important qualification that it must not be too profitable. The fear of abuse and of work disincentives explains the current harsh limit of 75p per day.[2] The method of calculating the earnings for the purpose of the rule is described in chapter 10.[3]

b) AVAILABLE FOR FULL-TIME EMPLOYMENT. The claimant must be available for full-time employment in an employed earner's employment. This repeats a condition which must in any event be satisfied by anyone claiming unemployment benefit and which is fully considered below.[4]

c) SUBSIDIARY OCCUPATION CONSISTENT WITH FULL-TIME EMPLOYMENT. The Commissioner has discredited the view that 'consistency' is tautologous with 'availability'. While availability is partially dependent on the claimant's attitude – whether he is willing to take on full-time employment compatible with the subsidiary occupation – 'consistency'

15. *R(U) 8/73.*
16. See references cited ante n.10, p. 86.
17. Report on Draft Amendment Regulations, 1970–71 HC 394, para. 4.
18. Cf., Reid, 4 ILJ 53.
19. Post, pp. 92–104.
20. *R(U) 16/64*; *R(U) 2/67.*
1. S.I. 1975/564 Reg. 7(1)(h). There is an interesting analogy in the law of the

Federal German Republic: Arbeitsförderungsgesetz 1969, art. 101.
2. The amount remained at 3s 4d (17p) from 1948 to 1953, and at 6s 8d (34p) from that date until 1972 when it was raised to its present level.
3. Post, pp. 426–432.
4. Post, pp. 104–108.

involves looking at the circumstances of the occupation at the time of the claim and assessing the prospects of obtaining full-time employment consistent with it.[5] Thus in *R(U) 12/59*.

> C, who was unemployed, found part-time work as a relief park keeper. His duties began at 4 p.m. Although he was *available* for full-time employment as a factory machinist, he had no reasonable prospects of finding such employment ending before 4 p.m. He could not rearrange his hours of work in the park, and the subsidiary occupation was thus inconsistent with the full-time employment for which he was available.

It follows, of course, that where the contract for the subsidiary occupation prescribes that the employee be at the disposal of the employer whenever required it cannot be consistent with full-time employment.[6] On the other hand, if the working hours can be rearranged or fewer demands are made on the claimant's time, 'consistency' may be established.[7]

d) SUBSIDIARY OCCUPATION NOT USUAL MAIN OCCUPATION. A fourth condition was added in 1955: the subsidiary occupation had to be 'different in nature from' the full-time occupation.[8] The object of the provision was clearly to prevent collusion: an employer dismissing the claimant and then re-engaging him at a nominal wage. But by concentrating on the *nature* of the occupation, the Regulation cast its net too wide. In one instance it was applied to disentitle a man who was registered for employment as a general farmworker but who, outside his normal working hours, cultivated his own small holding.[9] A 1960 amendment narrowed the rule.[10] The present position is that the claimant will be ineligible for benefit only if he follows the subsidiary occupation under a contract of service and if it is 'not his usual main occupation'.[11]

C. Periods of unemployment

It will be recalled that title to benefit rests on proof of a 'day of unemployment which forms part of a period of interruption of employment'.[12] It is now necessary to consider the meaning of 'day' and 'period'.

i) Day of unemployment

The minimum unit of time recognised for benefit purposes is a day: a claimant cannot be unemployed on part only of a day. If he is employed for more than a token amount[13] on a particular day, it will not constitute a day of unemployment. If this principle were employed universally it

5. *R(U) 4/64*; *R(U) 2/67*.
6. *R(U) 24/53*.
7. *R(U) 31/53*; *R(U) 4/64*; *R(U) 4/77*.
8. S.I. 1955/143, Reg. 2.
9. *R(U) 26/58*. See also *R(U) 12/57*.
10. S.I. 1960/781, Reg. 2.
11. S.I. 1975/564 Reg. 7(1)(h). For

'contract of service' see ante pp. 47–53.
12. SSA 1975, s.14(1)(a).
13. For analogous purposes under the industrial injury scheme an hour has been regarded as sufficient: CI 263/49; cf. *CS 37/53* where 15 minutes was disregarded.

would cause hardship to night-workers who might lose a shift but still work for more than a token amount on each calendar day.[14] The Regulations, therefore, allow for an exception to the general rule: where a person works through midnight he is deemed to be employed on that day on which the greater part of his shift falls.[15] For the exception to apply, however, the shift must begin within twenty-four hours of one calendar day and end within twenty-four hours of the following day; the general principle applies to longer periods of unemployment. Thus in *R(U) 18/56*

> C was employed as a deckhand on a trawler from 18.00 hours on Monday to 02.00 hours on Wednesday. He claimed benefit for Monday on the ground that the greater part of his shift fell on Tuesday and Wednesday. But it was held that the Night Regulations did not apply.

ii) Days of rest

Benefit is payable on the basis of a six-day week. Thus the daily rate is one-sixth of the appropriate weekly rate.[16] It follows that the seventh and rest day of the week is not a day of unemployment.[17] Six-day workers who normally[18] work on Sunday but not on another day may, if unemployed, claim for Sunday but not for that other day.[19] Even if a claimant does not normally work on Sunday, nevertheless if he is available for work on that day and objects on religious grounds to working on another day, that other day is substituted for Sunday.[20]

iii) Waiting-days

In some systems of unemployment insurance, the claimant is eligible for benefit on the first day of unemployment,[1] but the British scheme in common with the majority, has always insisted that a waiting-period be served. During the time of greatest unemployment between the wars the period was a week,[2] but in 1937[3] the current rule was adopted that benefit is not available for the first three days of a period of interruption of employment.[4] All the evidence shows that the administrative costs of paying benefit for one or two days is disproportionately large.[5] There is a widespread assumption that an individual is generally able to absorb a few days of earnings loss, and if he is not he may be entitled to supplementary benefit.[6] Further, in many cases the employer, through a guarantee agreement or otherwise, indemnifies his employees against short spells of

---

14. See *CS 363/49*, decided when the anomaly existed for sickness benefit.
15. S.I. 1975/564, Reg. 5(2): where the shifts are of equal duration he is deemed to be employed on the second day. Where he works through Saturday/Sunday midnight the same rules apply to determine the week in which the shift falls: *R(U) 37/56*.
16. SSA 1975, s.14(8).
17. Ibid., s.17(1)(e).
18. For the meaning of 'normally' see post, pp. 94 and 96.
19. S.I. 1975/564, Reg. 4(1).
20. Ibid., Reg. 4(3).
1. E.g., in W. Germany and in the USA: Connecticut, Maryland, Delaware and Nevada.
2. UIA (No. 2) 1921, s.3(3).
3. S.R. & O. 1937 No. 194, Reg. 2(b).
4. SSA 1975, s.14(3).
5. See NIAC Report on Very Short Spells of Unemployment (1955), Cmd. 9609.
6. Post, chap. 12.

unemployment and, under the Employment Protection Act 1975, he is bound to provide a limited form of such coverage.[7] These factors were also used to justify the decision in 1971 to abolish the right hitherto enjoyed by those unemployed for two weeks or more retrospectively to claim for the three days.[8]

iv) Periods of interruption of employment

Where a claimant is subject to intermittent periods of unemployment (e.g., where he is on short-time) it would clearly be impossibly severe to impose the three waiting-days for each such period. By means of the so-called 'continuity' and 'linking' rules, the legislation therefore enables him to aggregate spells of unemployment, so that he will be disentitled for only the first three days of the aggregate 'period of interruption of employment'. The 'continuity' rule prescribes that a 'period of interruption of employment' exists where he is unemployed for any two days (consecutive or not) within six consecutive days.[9]

> e.g., C is unemployed on Monday and Friday within the same week. These two days constitute a single period of interruption of unemployment.

The 'linking' rule then provides that any two such periods not separated by more than thirteen weeks are treated as one period of interruption of employment.[10]

> If, in the above example, C is unemployed again on the Monday and Friday of the following week, the two periods of interruption of employment are linked so that he will be entitled to benefit for the Friday of week 2 (the waiting-days being the Monday and Friday of week 1 and the Monday of week 2). Subject to the rules to be described in the next section, he will continue to be entitled for each subsequent day of unemployment forming part of a period of interruption of employment (i.e. satisfying the two-in-six continuity rule) which is not separated from the previous such period by more than thirteen weeks.

D. Benefit during suspension, lay-off or short-time

i) General

Notwithstanding that the contract of employment is subsisting an employee may be 'unemployed' in the sense that the employer is unable to provide him with work.[11] He may be 'laid-off' (i.e., the contract of employment is suspended until work is once more available[12]) or he may be put on 'short-time', (i.e., his regular hours of work and therefore

---

7. See post, p. 103.
8. SSA 1971, s.7(1) and see Sir K. Joseph, Secretary of State, introducing the Second Reading of the Bill, 816 HC Deb., cols. 61–63.
9. SSA 1975, s.17(1)(d).
10. Ibid.

11. See generally Income Data Services Handbook *Lay-offs and Short-time* (1976).
12. For a statutory definition see Redundancy Payments Act 1965, s.5(1).

generally also his wages are reduced by a certain amount every week[13]). These forms of unemployment raise a fundamental policy question as to the extent to which the costs of this form of unemployment should be borne by, respectively, the employee, the employer and other contributors to the Fund.[14] From an economic standpoint, it might seem undesirable that contributors should subsidise those industries which regularly have to lay off workers.[15] Coverage by the social security system also involves a wastage of its manpower: as has been mentioned, the administrative costs of paying benefits for short periods are high, and the employment services are not suited to dealing with persons who already have an employer but who must make themselves available for other work.[16] The force of these arguments has been increasingly recognised within recent years and during the 1960s it began to be realised that it would be more efficient for employers to assume responsibility by agreements guaranteeing a minimum amount of wages or of work. On the assumption that they could pass on the cost in the form of increased prices, it would be the consumer who would pay for the uncertainties involved in the particular industry. In the hope that guarantee agreements would become universal, the Labour government in 1966 sought to discharge the fund from liability for benefit for periods of unemployment of less than a week. The policy was put into effect immediately as regards earnings-related supplement,[17] but for the flat-rate benefit was postponed for three years while employers and unions made the appropriate arrangements.[18] At the end of that period, however, it was clear that there was nothing like universal readiness on the part of employers and employees to enter into such agreements and the implementation of the reform was postponed indefinitely. The Employment Protection Act 1975 introduced a compulsory guarantee agreement but only for a maximum of five 'workless' days within a period of three months, and subject to an overall limit of £30 for that period.[19] The social security legislation continues to offer a more generous level of financial support, and so the provision of benefit for short-term unemployment has been adapted to the new arrangements rather than replaced altogether.[20]

These policy considerations do not explain, much less justify, the extreme complexity of the law now to be examined. It has been argued elsewhere that there is a great need to revise a combination of rules which are, to a large extent, based on industrial conditions which no longer prevail, and which are expressed in language which is verbose and often unnecessarily circuitous in construction.[1] Those claiming benefit where the contract of employment has not been terminated are subject to four special rules. The subject is divided accordingly.

---

13. Cf., Redundancy Payments Act 1965, s.5(2).
14. Ogus 4 ILJ 12, from which the following discussion is substantially derived.
15. Miss M. Herbison, Minister of Pensions and NI, 724 HC Deb., col. 43, and see the First Report of the Royal Commission on Unemployment

Insurance (1931), Cmd. 3872.
16. Miss M. Herbison, ante n.15, loc. cit.
17. NIA 1966, s.2.
18. Ibid., s.3(1).
19. Ss. 22–28. See Hepple, Partington and Simpson 6 ILJ 54.
20. Post, p. 103.
 1. Ogus, ante n.14.

ii) 'Full extent normal' rule

Clearly if a man on short-time is to convince the authorities that he is unemployed on one or more days a week he must be able to prove that in the week in question he is working fewer days than normally. The principle is simple but the form of the Regulation implementing it is most unsatisfactory.

> '[A] day shall not be treated as a day of unemployment if on that day a person does no work and is a person who does not ordinarily work on every day in a week (exclusive of Sunday or the day substituted [therefor] but who is, in the week in which the said day occurs, employed to the full extent normal in his case . . .'[2]

It is not entirely clear what must be proved or by whom.[3] The Commissioner has treated it as imposing on the insurance officer the onus to prove both (1) that the claimant does not ordinarily work six days a week, *and* (2) that in the week in question he was employed to the full extent normal.[4] The reason for (1) is obscure for if the insurance officer fails to satisfy that test because the claimant ordinarily works six days a week, he will in any event fail to satisfy (2) because a six-day worker claiming benefit for one of those six days cannot be employed to the full extent normal.[5] Conversely, if (1) is satisfied, the insurance officer must, for the purposes of (2), still go on to prove that in the week in question the claimant was employed to the full extent normal.

Significantly the Commissioner has applied similar principles to the two conditions. Both involve an objective test: in determining whether the claimant ordinarily worked six days a week (for (1)) or what was normal for him (for (2)), the authorities are not concerned with his intentions or desires. It is always a question of fact to be ascertained on the basis of his employment record.[6] Further, his actual record prevails over his duties and expectations under the contract of employment.[7] Thus, if he is obliged to work five days a week but there is not enough work to keep him occupied for more than four days, four days is his 'normal' week.[8] The evidence to which reference may be made has caused some difficulty. In the years following the introduction of the Regulation the Commissioner tended to look at the claimant's record during the period of twelve months immediately previous to the date of claim.[9] The adoption of this period soon crystallised into a rule of law. But this proved to be too rigid an approach, and it became necessary to create exceptions to the rule so that the authorities could look beyond the twelve-months period when in the circumstances it was not the appropriate test for 'normality'.

The first and most important such circumstance was when the claimant's record of employment has been affected by adverse industrial condi-

2. S.I. 1975/564, Reg. 7(1)(e).
3. Ogus, ante n.14, at p. 16.
4. *R(U) 13/59.*
5. There is no difference in meaning between 'normal' and 'ordinarily': *R(U) 14/60*, para. 10 (Tribunal decision).
6. *CU 518/49*; *R(U) 2/52*; *R(U) 13/60*; *R(U) 3/74.*
7. *R(U) 19/58.*
8. *R(U) 13/56.*
9. *CU 518/49.*

tions. In applying the 'full extent normal' rule

> 'no account shall be taken, in determining either the number of days in a week on which he ordinarily works or the full extent of employment in a week which is normal in his case, of any period of short-time working due to adverse industrial conditions.'[10]

But the phrase 'adverse industrial conditions' has not been broadly interpreted: to justify looking beyond the twelve-months period the conditions must have been temporary or sporadic.[11] There must be a reduction below the standard level of employment: for the purposes of the Regulation a dropping of overtime is not 'short-time'.[12]

The second express exception to the twelve-months rule arises where the claimant's pattern of employment was irregular or casual. Indeed in these circumstances, the 'full extent normal' rule cannot function at all[13] and the Regulations now provide that the rule shall not apply to a person unless

> '(a) there is a recognized or customary working week in connection with his employment; *or*
>
> (b) he regularly works for the same number of days in a week for the same employer or group of employers.'[14]

Even with such exceptions, the twelve-months rule cannot be universally applied. If the claimant's pattern of work has changed significantly within the last year (e.g., he may have changed his job or the terms of his employment), it is obvious that regard must be had to the newly established pattern even though it has not existed for a year.[15] Indeed, more recently, the Commissioner, influenced by decisions on analogous points arising under the 'normal idle day' rule[16] has begun to favour a generally more flexible approach. The twelve-months rule is but one method of determining on the facts what, at the time of the claim, was normal for the claimant.[17]

The existence of a holiday[18] within the week of the claim will reduce what is normal for that week[19] but the fact that there is a holiday on a day on which the claimant does not normally work will not affect his claim.[20]

iii) 'Normal idle day' rule
The principle of the 'full extent normal' rule was clear and acceptable, but its application, when combined with the 'continuity' rule, produced unfortunate anomalies. A six-day worker losing one day every week could not normally claim as he would not satisfy the two-in-six continuity rule.

C who normally works Monday to Saturday is laid off on Saturday.

---

10. S.I. 1975/564, Reg. 7(1)(e).
11. *R(U) 13/60.*
12. *R(U) 2/73*, H.A. Shewan, Comr.
13. *R(U) 32/51* ; *R(U) 37/56.*
14. S.I. 1975/564, Reg. 7(2).
15. *R(U) 1/72*, H.A. Shewan, Comr.
16. Post, pp. 96–97.
17. *R(U) 1/72.*
18. For the general provisions on holidays see post pp. 99–102.
19. *R(U) 16/55.*
20. *R(U) 5/57*, Tribunal decision, overruling *R(U) 9/54.*

Unless he is laid off the following week on a day *other* than Saturday he is not unemployed on two-in-six consecutive days.

A five-day worker losing a single day would not only satisfy the continuity rule, but he might also claim for the day on which he would not normally work.

D who normally works Monday to Friday is laid off on Friday. He is thus unemployed on two-in-six consecutive days, and is entitled to benefit for both Friday and Saturday.

The matter was fully considered by the National Insurance Advisory Committee and it put forward three possible solutions to solve the anomaly.[1] The one adopted by the government was thought to be the least inconvenient administratively: a claimant should not be entitled to benefit for a day on which he would not normally work, unless he is unemployed on all the other days (excluding Sundays or its substitute) of the week. Unhappily, the indigestible statutory provision which followed[2] has given rise to difficulties even greater than those encountered with the 'full extent normal' rule. As reenacted in 1975 it prescribes that

'where a person is an employed earner and his employment as such has not been terminated, then in any week a day on which in the normal course that person would not work in that employment or in any other employed earner's employment shall not be treated as a day of unemployment unless each other day in that week [other than Sunday or a substitute therefor] on which in the normal course he would so work is a day of interruption of employment.'[3]

a) WHAT IS NORMAL. The onus is on the insurance officer to prove that the week of the claim included a day (other than Sunday or its substitute) on which the claimant would not normally work. In deciding what is 'normal', the authorities have by and large followed the pattern established for the 'full extent normal' rule. They have experienced similar difficulties and have sought to apply similar (if sometimes more clumsy) solutions. Regard is had to the claimant's employment record and not to his mental attitude,[4] or to the rights and obligations arising under the contract of employment.[5] The twelve-months rule was adapted to meet the requirements of the new condition: during the period of twelve months immediately preceding the claim, but ignoring holidays and sickness, had the claimant worked on the day in question more often than he had not?[6]

But the rule was no more successful at coping with the varying situations to which it was applied. First, short-time working due to adverse industrial conditions was to be excluded, a principle later recognised in

1. See NIAC Report on Very Short Spells of Unemployment (1955), Cmd. 9609, and Ogus 4 ILJ 12 at 16–17.
2. NIA 1957, s.4(1).
3. SSA 1975, s.17(1)(b).
4. R(U) 22/58.
5. R(U) 19/58.
6. R(U) 14/59.

an extraordinarily complex form by the Regulations,[7] though given the same interpretation as the parallel provision governing the 'full extent normal' rule.[8] Secondly, the rule could not be applied to casual employment, and this had to be specifically excluded by an Amendment Regulation.[9] Thirdly, care had to be taken in accommodating the rule to a claimant working a rota system. What is 'normal' in such circumstances must of course depend on the shift which he would have worked on the day (or week) in question, and on what was the working pattern of that shift.[10] Finally, the rule is clearly inappropriate where an employee has moved to a new situation or is governed by a new agreement, and whether working on a particular day is 'normal' for him must be judged in the light of the changed circumstances rather than on his record during the last year.[11]

What emerges from this analysis of the twelve-months rule as applied to both the 'full extent normal' rule and the 'normal idle day' rule, is that it should be replaced by a test at the same time simpler and more flexible. One possibility is that the authorities should ascertain in the light of the claimant's working record and the circumstances of his present employment the hours and days which he would ordinarily expect to work in the week in question.

b) WHETHER CONTRACT TERMINATED. The rule applies only where the claimant's 'employment as such has not been terminated.' For practical purposes there may be little difference between 'termination' and 'suspension' but for legal purposes the distinction is crucial,[12] and it has given rise to considerable difficulties. To determine whether the contract of employment has in fact been terminated, the Commissioner has been faced with a choice between applying the ordinary contractual meaning of termination (viz., that the rights and obligations of the parties have ceased[13]) and adopting the special meaning attributed to 'termination' by the Umpire under the old Unemployment Insurance Acts. On the latter view, the contract was not to be regarded as terminated unless the claimant had been 'finally discharged without any intention of resuming the rela-

---

7. S.I. 1975/564, Reg. 16(3) provides that in any week of short-time due to adverse industrial conditions, the employment is to be treated as if 'terminated' immediately after its commencement, thus excluding from operation the 'normal idle day' rule. But Reg. 16(4) then stipulates by an equally circumlocutory formula that it shall nevertheless not be treated as a day of unemployment, if quite apart from the short-time, it would still have been a normal idle day. See, in general, *R(U) 17/60*.

8. Thus the conditions must involve some temporary reductions in the working hours general in the relevant industry (*R(U) 13/60*), thus excluding conditions peculiar to the claimant

(*R(U) 14/60*) and general recessions in trade (*R(U) 1/64*).

9. S.I. 1966/1049, Reg. 13, now (in a modified form) S.I. 1975/564, Reg. 16(3).

10. *R(U) 1/61*; *R(U) 5/62*.

11. *R(U) 18/62*; *R(U) 14/60*; *R(U) 1/72*.

12. *Sneddon v Ivorycrete (Builders) Ltd.* (1966) 1 ITR 538 at 540. The distinction also plays a significant role in calculating an employee's period of 'continuous employment' under the Contracts of Employment Act 1972, Sch. 1., para. 4 of which applies to cases of suspension and para. 5 to cases of termination.

13. See, e.g., *Bunt v Fishlow Products Ltd* (1970) 5 ITR 127.

tionship of employer and employee on the next available opportunity."[14] For a long time, the special meaning prevailed,[15] notwithstanding 'a stream of indignant appellants who could not understand how their employment could be said not to have terminated when their contract of employment no longer subsisted.'[16] The line of decisions upholding this second approach was questioned by a single Commissioner in 1967[17] and effectively overruled by a Tribunal of Commissioners in 1967.[18] The Umpire had employed the doctrine not as an interpretation of the word 'termination' as used in *legislation*, but as used in a rule devised by him or his predecessors to decide whether or not a claimant had been 'continuously unemployed'. In contrast, in the modern legislation the word 'termination' is explicitly employed in contradistinction to 'suspension' – and there is nothing to suggest that the legislature intended to give it anything but its ordinary meaning. Hence the general law of contract applies.

c) WHETHER CONTRACT TREATED AS TERMINATED. If on these principles the contract has been terminated, the 'normal idle day' rule does not apply. But the same result is reached if the case comes within one of the five situations in which the Regulations treat the contract as having been terminated.

1. If the employment has been indefinitely suspended.[19] The 'normal idle day' rule is concerned with partial or short-term unemployment and is not applied to lay-offs longer than a week. Hence a distinction is drawn between ordinary suspension and indefinite suspension, which means lasting for at least six continuous days.

2. There is not a recognised or customary week in connection with the employment *or* the claimant does not regularly work for the same number of days in a week for the same employer or group of employers.[20] Reference has already been made to this proviso introduced in 1966 which seeks to exclude from the 'normal idle day' rule those in irregular employment.[1] The onus of proof is on the insurance officer to show that the claimant does not come within the regulation.

14. *UD 16930/31.* There is an interesting parallel to this doctrine in the law of redundancy. Where after termination of contract, an employee is reinstated, the employment will nevertheless be treated as having been continuous provided that the termination resulted from one of the following: (i) sickness or injury, (ii) temporary cessation of work', (iii) special arrangement or custom, (iv) National service, (v) employment outside Great Britain, (vi) strikes and lock-outs, (vii) pregnancy or confinement: Contracts of Employment Act 1972, Sch. 1, paras. 5–8, as amended by Employment Protection Act 1975, Sch. 16, Part II, para. 15.

16. E.g., *R(U) 16/59*; *R(U) 11/61*. In N. Ireland one decision went so far as to hold that where in one week C was regularly employed by a different employer, (i) the 'employment' was the totality of all employments, and therefore (ii) the termination of contract with one employer did not terminate the 'employment' as a whole: *16/59 (UB).*

16. *R(U) 7/68*, para. 26 (Tribunal decision).

17. *R(U) 4/67*, J.S. Watson, Comr. It was not necessary to decide which approach was right, as on either view the claimant succeeded.

18. *R(U) 7/68.*

19. S.I. 1975/564, Reg. 16(2).

20. Ibid., Reg. 16(6).

1. Ante, p. 95.

3. If the claimant is in casual employment.[2] This provision predates[3] and has probably been superseded by exception (2). Here the task of the claimant is harder. The burden of proof is on him, and in applying the provision the Commissioner has not been liberal in his interpretation of 'casual'.[4]

4. If the employer for whom he is working in the week in question is not his usual employer.[5] This must be read in conjunction with an additional Regulation which provides, in effect, that if in his usual employment the claimant normally works on the day in question, it will not fail to be treated as a day of unemployment under the 'normal idle day' rule merely because, as a result of a lay-off, he is not working on that day in his addition and abnormal employment.[6] This clumsy and unwieldy provision does little more than state the obvious, for the 'normal idle day' rule cannot operate to exclude benefit for a day which is not subject to the claimant's usual or normal employment.

5. If, in determining the claimant's normal course of work under s.17(1)(b) of the Social Security Act 1975, account is taken of short-time working due to adverse industrial conditions.[7] This rule has already been discussed.[8]

iv) The 'holiday' rule

a) GENERAL. The questions whether, and to what extent, a holiday should affect entitlement to benefit may be viewed from two different perspectives. On the broader perspective, payment during a holiday should in principle be excluded. A holiday is in its nature relief provided by the employer so that the employee may 'enjoy rest, recreation or amusement.'[9] The employee is thus estopped from claiming that circumstances have prevented him from pursuing his gainful occupation. But this view cannot be maintained without substantial qualifications. On the one hand, it can hardly be applied to someone whose contract of employment has been terminated. It would be speculative and impracticable for the authorities to make inquiries whether, if he had been employed in his normal occupation, the claimant would have been on holiday on a certain day or week. At the most, then, the principle can only apply where the contract of employment has been merely suspended. On the other hand, the principle draws no distinction between holidays with pay and holidays without pay, and yet the distinction must be crucial. It is only the employee on holiday *without* pay that has any legitimate claim, and yet on the general principle

2. S.I. 1975/564, Reg. 16(3)(a).
3. It was introduced by S.I. 1957/1319, Reg. 4.
4. See, especially, *R(U) 16/59* and *R(U) 11/61*. In both decisions, 'casual' was given a special meaning. The question was whether at the end of each spell of employment, the claimant might reasonably expect to be re-employed almost immediately. This interpretation was intended to render the test consistent with the special meaning at the time attributed to 'termination' but since overruled (ante, p. 98).
5. S.I. 1975/564, Reg. 16(3)(b).
6. Ibid., Reg. 16(4).
7. Ibid., Reg. 16(3)(d).
8. Ante, p. 96.
9. Per H. Magnus, Dep. Comr., *R(U) 1/66*, para. 22.

he is bracketed with another who continues to receive his ordinary wage. This last consideration lies at the heart of the *narrower* perspective. On this view, there is no need for a general principle governing holidays. The legislation should simply be concerned to protect those who are *involuntarily* on holiday *without pay*. Such persons may be ascertained by applying the ordinary rules which refuse to characterise as days of unemployment days for which remuneration is received[10] and disqualify from benefit where employment is left voluntarily.[11] On either view, there is the independent question whether a claimant, who is admittedly unemployed, but who is absent on holiday from his normal place of residence, nevertheless satisfies the ordinary requirement of being 'available' for suitable employment.[12]

On the general question of entitlement during periods of holiday, the history of the British system has been far from consistent. Originally, there were no special provisions,[13] but the Umpire of his own initiative decided that a claimant on holiday was not 'continuously unemployed'.[14] This then hardened into a rule of law[15] and was applied irrespective of whether or not the claimant had received any holiday pay. The modern law has in general maintained this position: if the employment has not been terminated or indefinitely suspended, a day of 'recognised or customary holiday in connection with that employment' is not to be treated as a day of unemployment.[16] The broader perspective was thus explicitly admitted into the system, and with it came all its attendant difficulties: problems in deciding what are customary holidays, distinctions between termination and suspension, and still the need to provide for the man who is forced to take a holiday without pay – a need which was only partially met by a typically complex measure in 1966. By adopting the narrower perspective many systems[17] not only find a more complete solution to this problem, but at the same time avoid the subtle and complex difficulties to which the British approach so unnecessarily gives rise.

b) RECOGNISED AND CUSTOMARY HOLIDAYS. The first question to be decided is whether the day in question is 'a recognised or customary holiday in connection with that employment'. There must be an agreement, express or implied, between the employer and the employee that on the day in question the employee is relieved from his working duties for the purposes of rest, recreation or amusement.[18] A mere agreement not to work is insufficient. If it is envisaged that the employee

10. Ante, pp. 83–84.
11. Post, pp. 113–115.
12. Post, p. 106.
13. UIA 1939, s.1 made statutory provision for the exclusion of holidays from unemployment benefit but owing to the outbreak of war the section never came into force.
14. *UD 228/12.*
15. *UD 7712* and see the 'codifying decision' *UD 18284/32.*
16. S.I. 1975/564, Reg. 7(1)(i).

17. Including most of those in the USA. Thus, e.g., the Illinois Unemployment Compensation Act does not in principle exclude holidays from the ambit of the fund. A simple provision (§ 440) assimilates 'vacation pay' to 'wages', and a claimant entitled to such 'wages' is ineligible for benefits for any week in which the sums equal or exceed the weekly benefit amount.
18. *R(U) 1/66* (Tribunal decision).

will take a break from his ordinary employment and take work elsewhere he is not 'on holiday'.[19] The existence of an agreement is to be determined according to the facts, regard being had in particular to the length of time during which the alleged holiday was habitually observed,[20] and whether extra payments are made for such work.[1] Although the holiday must be recognised or customary 'in connection with that employment', it need not, it seems, refer to the claimant's individual employment as distinct from the general conditions applying at his factory or place of work. This somewhat surprising proposition results from *R(U) 3/53*.

> For the purposes of their trade cycle, C's employers wished to change the dates of the factory's annual holiday. The large majority of employees agreed and the employers allowed those who wished to abide by the original agreement to take their holiday at the earlier date. It was held, however, that they were not entitled to benefit during the period when the majority took their holiday (and when the factory consequently closed). The minority were subject to the wishes of the majority. A claimant may be on holiday even if he does not wish to be so.

A similar principle operates to disentitle those on casual employment. If a man habitually works in a certain place and that place closes for an agreed holiday, the casual employee is prima facie bound by that agreement unless he can show that it does not apply to him because, for example, he had another source of employment outside the place of work in question.[2] But the existence of an alternative occupation or source of employment creates problems which are not easy to solve. In *R(U) 7/63*

> A professional musician worked partly as a school-teacher and partly as a performer. In his former capacity he generally worked four days a week. During the school's Easter vacation he did not work on these four days and received no holiday pay. It was held that he was entitled to benefit. He was not 'on holiday' from his employment as a whole which included his other occupation as a performing musician.

The same approach was taken by a Tribunal of Commissioners in a later decision.[3] They concluded that it would have been too artificial and impracticable to hold that a person could be on holiday for part only of a week. It is submitted, with respect, that this is only because the holiday rule is itself artificial and impracticable. The same result in *R(U) 7/63* could have been reached by the simpler route: (i) was the claimant unemployed on the day in question? (ii) did he receive remuneration for that day?

The existence of a special holiday rule is also responsible for another difficulty. Some 'agreed holidays' have their origin in a slack period of

19. *R(U) 8/64*.
20. *R(U) 39/53*; *R(U) 27/58*. Cp. *R(U) 11/53* which is hard to reconcile with these decisions. *Semble*, it places too much weight on the requirement of an agreement.
1. *R(U) 11/53*.
2. *R(U) 18/54*; *R(U) 31/56*.
3. *R(U) 18/64*.

trade. It is established law that if there is an agreement that there should be a holiday, the actual reasons for its institution are irrelevant.[4] This means that there will be an awkward transitional stage between 'short-time working' when benefit will be payable, and an implied 'holiday' when it will not. But the crucial question should surely be not whether there was a 'holiday' but whether the employees were paid when they were not working.

c) SUSPENSION OF CONTRACT. If the contract has been either 'terminated' or 'indefinitely suspended', the holiday rule will not apply. As elsewhere,[5] the special meaning attributed to 'termination' by the Umpire under the old Unemployment Insurance Acts was for a long time applied.[6] Following a similar change to the 'normal idle day' rule, a Tribunal of Commissioners in 1968 departed from a long line of authority and held that the ordinary contractual meaning of 'termination' should henceforth prevail.[7] For the purposes of this rule, 'indefinite suspension' is equated with termination and this is construed in accordance with the 1966 provisions on short-time unemployment.[8]

d) HOLIDAYS WITHOUT PAY. It has been seen that one of the defects of the British system is that it draws no general distinction between holidays with and without pay. With this handicap it was faced with an anomaly:[9] a man who changed his employment may not have qualified for holiday pay, and yet he may be unable to work because at the place of employment there is a general holiday shutdown. A simple solution would have been to exclude from the operation of the holiday rule holidays involuntarily taken without pay,[10] but as will have emerged from earlier remarks, such a step would effectively have robbed the holiday rule of any function. A compromise but complex solution was therefore adopted. The Regulations effectively provide that if in the same period of twelve months (beginning for this purpose on 1 March) as the holiday in question, the claimant has already been on holiday (under a contract of employment) equalling or exceeding the period of the present holiday in question, the holiday rule shall not apply to disentitle the claimant from benefit for this latter period.[11]

v) Guarantee agreements

The final question arising under this section is how entitlement to benefit for short-term unemployment may be affected by guarantee agreements.

4. *UD 18284/32*; *R(U) 4/52*.
5. Ante, pp. 87 and 98.
6. E.g., *R(U) 12/54*; *R(U) 19/54*; *R(U) 1/62*; *R(U) 18/64*; *R(U) 1/66*.
7. *R(U) 8/68*.
8. Ante, p. 98.
9. See NIAC Report on Very Short Spells of Unemployment (1955), Cmd. 9609, at paras. 63–65.
10. Thus the Massachusetts Employment Security Law § 1(r)(2): 'an individual who is not entitled to vacation pay from his employer shall be deemed to be in total unemployment during the entire period of any general closing of his employer's place of business for vacation purposes, notwithstanding his prior assent, direct or indirect, to the establishment of such vacation period by his employer.' For a summary of the US law on this point see Anno. 30 ALR 2d. 366. See also 64 Mich. LR 1100.
11. S.I. 1975/564, Reg. 7(1)(i).

These may take several forms, but in general the employer guarantees to provide the employee with a minimum amount of work, or of remuneration should the work not be available. Under the Employment Protection Act 1975 he is *bound* to pay the employee for five 'workless days' within a period of three months, but only to a maximum of £30 for that period.[12] Regulations then provide that a day on which a sum is payable under the Act is not to be treated as a day of unemployment.[13] The same applies for agreements which have been made the subject of an exemption order by an appropriate Minister.[14] For agreements which come within neither of these categories, the general principles as developed by the Commissioner apply. One crucial question is whether the agreement is construed to confer remuneration on the employee on the day or days when he does not work. The earlier decisions tended to draw a distinction between two classes of agreement: those in which the employer guaranteed a weekly *wage*; and those in which he guaranteed a certain amount of *work*. In the former case it was inferred that the intention was to pay the sum for the *whole* of the week, and that therefore the employee could not be 'unemployed' for any part of that week.[15] The same inference could not be drawn for the 'work' guarantees[16] and not unnaturally, in order that short-time workers should have access to the Fund, many employment contracts were modified so that they might be characterised as belonging to this latter type.

In *R(U) 21/56,* however, a Tribunal of Commissioners held that a mere change of wording of an agreement made solely for the purposes of unemployment benefit, and which had no effect industrially, and which did not modify the rights and obligations of the parties could not by itself confer a title to benefit. The emphasis was shifted from the question of what the employer guaranteed to what the employee undertook in consideration of the guarantee. The new approach focussed on whether or not, under the agreement, the employee was bound to make himself available to the employer on the days of the alleged unemployment.[17] This involves examining the *legal* consequences of the agreement: the fact that the employer is in practice prepared to regard the employee as available for other employment is irrelevant.[18]

That entitlement to benefit may confer advantages not only on the short-time worker (the benefit may be more valuable than the guaranteed sum[19]) but also on the employer (who may be relieved from paying

---

12. Ss. 22, 24–25: and see Hepple, Partington and Simpson 6 ILJ 54.
13. S.I. 1975/564, Reg. 7(1)(i), inserted by S.I. 1976/328. If benefit is paid pending an award under the Act, it may be recouped from the employer: S.I. 1977/622. The suggestion by Hepple et al., ante n.12, at p. 56, that entitlement to unemployment benefit pending payment under the agreement is unaffected seems to be wrong. Reg. 7(1)(i) refers to a day when such a sum is 'payable' not where it is 'paid'.
14. Under Employment Protection Act 1975, s.28.
15. *R(U) 27/51.*
16. *CWU 49/50*; *R(U) 13/51*; *R(U) 23/55.*
17. See further *R(U) 2/58* and *R(U) 15/61.*
18. *R(U) 1/76,* H.A. Shewan, Comr.
19. See Hepple et al., ante n.12, who comment on the substantial gap between the level of unemployment benefit and the guaranteed amounts under the Employment Protection Act 1975.

anything above the limit imposed by the Employment Protection Act) has led to joint efforts to undermine the validity of the guarantee agreement. This was particularly evident in some industries during the period of three-day working rendered necessary by the miner's strike in 1972. While an agreement can, subject to the Employment Protection Act, be varied or abrogated, this must be done by mutual agreement: a unilateral decision to this effect or the mere rearrangement of the work timetable will be in-effective.[20] The Commissioner has also held that an agreement cannot be revoked retrospectively.[1]

Part four. Availability

A. General

The unemployment must be involuntary. The notion is incorporated in the law first by the requirement that the claimant be 'available' for suitable employment,[2] and reinforced by the various grounds on which he may be disqualified from benefit.[3] The difficulty has been to formulate a test which provides sufficiently precise guidelines for those administering it and yet is flexible enough to allow for consideration of all the relevant factors, including the claimant's age, qualifications, working capacity and intentions, as well as the general level of unemployment and charac-teristics of the labour market particular to the locality.[4] Under the National Insurance Act 1911, the claimant had to prove that he was 'capable of work but unable to obtain suitable employment'.[5] Faced with a sudden and dangerous rise in unemployment in 1920–1921, the govern-ment decided that the conditions of eligibility had to be strengthened and introduced the notorious requirement that the claimant must prove that he was 'genuinely seeking whole-time employment but unable to obtain such employment'.[6] Although regarded by employers as an essential feature of unemployment insurance,[7] it had a serious impact on the workings of the scheme,[8] and was bitterly attacked by the trade union movement.[9] As it was interpreted, the new condition seemed to require that a claimant look around for work where there might be none available. An adverse decision left a stigma which was difficult to remove. On the recommendations of a committee,[10] the condition was repealed in 1930.[11]

20. *R(U) 10/73* (Tribunal decision); *R(U) 1/75.*
1. *R(U) 1/76.*
2. See generally Altman *Availability for Work: A Study in Unemployment Compensation* (1950).
3. Post, pp. 108–122.
4. *Fisher*, para. 237, and for economic considerations see ed. Worswick *The Concept and Measurement of Involuntary Unemployment* (1976).
5. s.86(3).
6. UIA 1921, s.3(3)(b). A substantial proportion of US systems adopted the test (or an equivalent): see Freeman 10 Ohio SLJ 181.
7. Report of the Committee on the Procedure and Evidence for the Determination of Claims for Unemployment Insurance Benefit (1929), Cmd. 3415 (the Morris Report), para. 37.
8. In 1928–29 of approx. 10 million claims, 340,000 were denied benefit for not genuinely seeking work: ibid., at para. 36.
9. Ibid., at para. 38.
10. Ibid., at para. 43.
11. UIA 1930, s.6.

Under the 1946 Act, the question was simply whether the claimant was 'available for employment'[12], and this was construed to mean whether there was a reasonable prospect of his obtaining the work for which he *held* himself available.[13] This resulted in the anomaly that some claimants might place such restrictions on their availability that for all practical purposes they were not available. On the recommendations of the National Insurance Advisory Committee,[14] a regulation was therefore introduced which limited the restrictions which an unemployed person might place on his availability.[15]

B. Statutory test

The Social Security Act 1975 provides that a day shall not be treated as a day of unemployment unless on that day the claimant

> 'is capable of work and he is, or is deemed in accordance with regulations to be, available to be employed in employed earner's employment.'[16]

The onus is on the claimant to satisfy the condition.[17] The requirement of capacity excludes cases where sickness or invalidity benefit is appropriate.[18] The limitation to 'employed earner's employment' means that availability for self-employed or other uninsured work is irrelevant.[19] The Regulations referred to treat the condition as satisfied while the claimant is engaged in manning a lifeboat or serving part-time in a fire brigade.[20] Subject to these qualifications he must prove both (i) that there is a reasonable prospect of his obtaining the relevant employment; and (ii) that he is willing and able at once to accept a suitable offer.

i) Reasonable prospect

In determining whether there are reasonable prospects of employing the claimant on his stated terms of availability, the authorities have regard to such factors as his employment history (in particular, whether in the past he has succeeded in obtaining employment on these terms),[1] and the attitude of employers.[2] The requirement is not a difficult one to satisfy, for it is not limited to the locality in which the claimant is registered, and even in times of recession, there is likely to be a reasonable prospect of his finding work somewhere.[3]

ii) Willingness and ability to accept

The general rule is that claimants must be 'prepared to accept at once any

12. s.11(2)(a)(i).
13. See esp. *R(U) 12/52* (Tribunal decision).
14. Report on the Availability Question (1953), Cmd. 8894.
15. S.I. 1955/143.
16. s.17(1)(a).
17. *R(U) 12/52*; *R(U) 34/53*.
18. See *R(U) 24/51*, and post, chap. 4.
19. *R(U) 14/51*. For the meaning of 'employed earner's employment' see ante, pp. 47–53.
20. S.I. 1975/564, Reg. 9.
1. *CU 10/49*; *R(U) 44/53*.
2. *R(U) 6/72*, D. Neligan, Comr.
3. *Calvert*, pp. 109–110.

offers of suitable employment brought to their notice.'[4] The authorities will normally assume that the claimant is prepared to accept such offers,[5] but the rule may be invoked to disentitle him where his 'statements or actings' suggest the contrary,[6] most obviously where he actually refuses a suitable offer.[7] In some cases, the question turns on whether he is *able* to accept. He cannot be available if, during the relevant period, he is contractually bound to be at the disposal of another employer.[8] On the other hand, participation in training courses has been generously construed, so that if the claimant can be readily contacted and can take up an offer immediately he will be regarded as available.[9] A similar principle operates with regard to absences for a holiday. Under the former legislation, the Umpire laid down three conditions which in such circumstances are to be satisfied,[10] and these were subsequently adopted by the Commissioner:[11]

1. the claimant must be ready and willing immediately to return and accept an offer of suitable employment;

2. he must have taken reasonable and satisfactory steps to ensure that any such offer would be brought to his notice without delay.[12]

3. there was nothing connected with his absence which would have prevented him accepting at once any such offer.

C. Reasonable restrictions test

The additional test imposed by the Regulations applies where

'a person places restrictions on the nature, hours, rate of remuneration or locality or other conditions of employment which he is prepared to accept and as a consequence of those restrictions has no reasonable prospects of securing employment . . .'[13]

The essence of the matter is that the lack of reasonable prospects should result from restrictions which the claimant himself *places* on his availability. If the restrictions result from such natural characteristics as age or sex, the Regulation does not apply. The important point was decided in 1971 in relation to a claimant aged sixty-four.[14] While clearly right in principle,

4. R(U) 1/53, para. 7, adopting *UD* 6986/30.
5. R(U) 2/57.
6. R(U) 3/65, para. 11, H.A. Shewan, Dep. Comr.
7. R(U) 4/53; R(U) 15/58.
8. R(U) 11/51; R(U) 1/53; R(U) 1/69, and see ante, p. 85.
9. CWU 47/49; CU 162/50.
10. UD 7550/35.
11. R(U) 3/65 and R(U) 4/66, though in the latter case O. George, Dep. Comr.,

thought that the conditions might be regarded as more appropriate for the exceptional employment circumstances prevailing at the time they were devised.
12. If he moves from place to place there is a presumption that he cannot satisfy this condition: R(U) 2/57.
13. S.I. 1975/564, Reg. 7(1)(a).
14. CU 3/71, cited in Mesher *Compensation for Unemployment* (1976), p. 45.

the decision drew attention to the widespread practice whereby men aged between sixty and sixty-five retired from their normal employment, became entitled to an occupational pension and then claimed unemployment benefit, often with the expectation that no suitable employment would be available for them. The National Insurance Advisory Committee had considered the problem[15] and had concluded that to modify the availability principle would be neither acceptable nor workable,[16] but, with one dissenting opinion, it did recommend that claimants in such circumstances should be subject to a special condition, and that the benefit payable should, to a certain extent, take account of the receipt of occupational pension.[17] Both Conservative and Labour governments have attempted to implement the proposal but in either case it was defeated by a combination of opposition and backbenchers.[18]

If the Regulation does apply, the claim for unemployment will fail unless one of three conditions is satisfied.

i) Adverse but temporary industrial conditions

Under the first the claimant must prove that

> 'he is prevented from having reasonable prospects of securing
> employment consistent with those restrictions only as a result of
> adverse industrial conditions in the locality or localities concerned
> which may reasonably be regarded as temporary, and having
> regard to all the circumstances, personal and other, the
> restrictions which he imposes are reasonable.'[19]

The concept of 'adverse industrial conditions' has already been the subject of discussion.[20] The limitation to such conditions as are 'temporary' has been interpreted to connote the idea of abnormality: ordinary seasonal fluctuations, such as those typically prevailing in seaside resorts, are not included.[1] The second limb contains a requirement analogous to that applicable under condition (iii), and may be conveniently considered under that head.

ii) Physical condition

Alternatively, the claimant may show that 'the restrictions are nevertheless reasonable in view of his physical condition.'[2] The provision is illustrated by $R(U)$ 6/72:

> A technical manager, suffering from a heart condition, on medical
> advice retired at the age of sixty-two. He claimed benefit but
> restricted his availability to offers of employment at a minimum

15. Report on the Question of Conditions for Unemployment Benefit and Contribution Conditions for Occupational Pensioners (1968), Cmnd. 3545. See also its report on the draft Regulations, 1969–70 HC 211.
16. Ante n.15, at paras. 31–40.
17. Ibid., part IV.
18. See Standing Committee G Debates on NI Bill 1971, cols. 165–195, and Standing Committee A Debates on Social Security (Miscellaneous Provisions) Bill 1977, cols. 186–224; cf. Appendix, on the position of students.
19. S.I. 1975/564, Reg. 7(1)(a)(i).
20. Ante, p. 95.
1. $R(U)$ 3/59.
2. S.I. 1975/564, Reg. 7(1)(a)(ii).

salary of £5,500 a year in his home town or its close environs. There was no reasonable prospect of finding such employment and it was held that in the light of his physical condition, the restriction to the locality (but not that as to remuneration) was reasonable.

iii) Generally reasonable

The third alternative is the broadest and confers a necessary degree of flexibility on the authorities. The claimant must prove that

> 'the restrictions are nevertheless reasonable having regard both to the nature of his usual occupation and also to the time which has elapsed since he became unemployed.'[3]

The consideration of 'usual occupation' is designed to protect job skills, and the general standard of remuneration to which the claimant is accustomed. On the other hand, the protection cannot last indefinitely, so that after a reasonable time has expired he must be prepared to accept an offer of a less appropriate kind.[4] The restrictions may, in any event, only be 'reasonable' if they relate to the nature of the claimant's occupation. Thus an actor who held himself available only on certain days when he was not required by the BBC was disentitled: the restrictions arose not from his occupation as an actor but from the particular arrangement with the BBC.[5] In other respects, the authorities have a broad discretion in determining reasonableness[6] so that account may be taken of the claimant's general intentions,[7] the way he defines his 'occupation',[8] his domestic circumstances[9] and the state of the labour market in the locality.[10]

Part five. Disqualification for Voluntary Unemployment

The idea that unemployment must be involuntary may be seen as justifying not only the condition that a claimant be 'available' for employment, but also the circumstances in which he may be disqualified from benefit for a maximum period of six weeks. These may be conveniently grouped under three headings:

A. losing employment through misconduct;

B. voluntarily leaving employment without just cause;

C. without good cause, refusing or failing to take, a reasonable opportunity to secure employment.

3. S.I. 1975/564, Reg. 7(1)(a)(iii).
4. R(U) 3/59 and see the analogous principle in the disqualification provisions, post, p. 117.
5. R(U) 1/69, E.R. Bowen, Comr.
6. Some American jurisdictions have adopted more detailed criteria which, however, tend to be more severe on the claimant: see, e.g., Illinois Unemployment Compensation Act, § 420.6.
7. R(U) 33/58.
8. R(U) 3/59; R(U) 1/69.
9. R(U) 14/57; R(U) 17/57; R(U) 6/59.
10. R(U) 17/57; R(U) 6/72.

Part Five concludes with an account of the principles determining the period of disqualification.

A. Misconduct

The first ground for disqualification arises where the claimant has 'lost his employment as an employed earner through his misconduct'.[11] The rule was to be found in the National Insurance Act of 1911,[12] and has existed effectively in the same form ever since. However, the exact policy considerations on which it is based have never been made entirely explicit, and as a result its interpretation and evolution have not been wholly consistent. Three alternative theories may be invoked to support the disqualification.

    1. PUNISHMENT. From a moral or social point of view, a worker who has been dismissed for misconduct is unworthy of the support of the fund: he has transgressed the ethical standards of the community.

    2. SUITABILITY. The claimant should be disqualified where his own actions reveal him as unsuitable for the job. The fund is intended to cover only those who lose employment through external circumstances, and not those whose lack of skill results in dismissal.

    3. VOLUNTARY UNEMPLOYMENT. The purpose of the disqualification is to protect the fund against voluntary unemployment. Benefit is therefore to be denied to a claimant who knew or should have known that his conduct was reasonably likely to incur dismissal.

The first theory has been most explicitly rejected in the United Kingdom.[13] The third theory is more consistent with the general purpose of the legislation, and its influence can be seen in certain decisions,[14] but like most doctrines dependent on mental states, it creates grave problems of proof.[15] The suitability theory, though less attractive on policy grounds, can account for most of the law on this subject. The authorities seek to apply an objective standard of conduct to each worker. In general, they seem not to be concerned whether he appreciated, or might reasonably have appreciated, that his conduct was likely to lead to dismissal.

i) Dismissal caused by misconduct

In principle, the insurance officer must prove that the claimant was

11. SSA 1975, s.20(1)(a).
12. NIA 1911, s.87(2).
13. *CU 190/50*; *R(U) 27/52*; *R(U) 8/74* (Tribunal decision). Some American jurisdictions prescribe a *further* period of disqualification for those convicted of a criminal offence connected with the employment, while some impose special disqualifications for 'gross misconduct': Packard, 17 Villa. LR 635.
14. *CU 190/50*; *R(U) 35/53*; *R(U) 24/55*.
15. In the US jurisdictions where this theory is favoured, the courts allow a presumption of knowledge in many situations: Packard, ante n.13.

dismissed for an act or omission which constituted 'misconduct'.[16] But the
requirement of 'dismissal' and its causal relationship with the alleged
misconduct has been broadly construed. The contract of employment
need not have been terminated by the employer: it will suffice if, as a result
of the misconduct, both parties regard the employment as ended.[17] Nor
need the 'dismissal' follow as an immediate consequence of the misconduct. In one case, a bus driver was convicted of a driving offence. He was
disqualified even though the immediate cause of his dismissal was the loss
of his licence rather than the commission of the offence.[18]

ii) Misconduct connected with employment

If a man were to be disqualified for misconduct committed in any circumstance, in effect the system would be regarding the employer's attitude to
the misconduct as conclusive, and would be adopting a punitive approach
to the claimant's entitlement. If, however, it requires that the misconduct
be related to the employment, it may still question whether the dismissal
warrants disqualification, as viewed from the policy dictate of protecting
the insurance fund. The Commissioner has adopted this latter stance and
ruled that the conduct must be 'causally but not necessarily directly
connected with the employment.'[19] The test is whether the misconduct,
whenever and wherever it occurred, was such that it would induce a
reasonable employer to dispense with the services of the claimant on the
ground that he was not fit to hold the particular situation.[20] Of course, this
will generally depend on the nature both of the misconduct and of the
employment. What a man does outside his working hours may be totally
irrelevant to his work or his employer's interests. A railway fireman who
was dismissed for fighting in a railway carriage on his return from work
was not disqualified.[1] But the misconduct may so closely affect his suitability for the job that it will justify disqualification no matter where and
when it occurs. Such was the case where a park keeper was convicted of
gross indecency with another man.[2]

iii) Types of conduct

The use of the unqualified term 'misconduct' is unhelpful in determining
the standard of conduct which is to be applied. Indeed, in the early years
of the scheme it caused some embarrassment as it had to be explained to
many women claimants that it was not intended to refer to their moral
behaviour.[3] A Royal Commission, reporting in 1932, felt that the choice of
language was unfortunate but was unable to suggest any positive
improvement.[4] According to the Commissioner, the conduct must be such

16. *R(U)* 2/77, R.J.A. Temple, Chief
    Comr.
17. *R(U)* 17/64; *R(U)* 2/76.
18. *R(U)* 7/57.
19. *R(U)* 2/77, para. 15, R.J.A. Temple,
    Chief Comr. See also *R(U)* 1/71.
20. *R(U)* 2/77.
 1. *UD* 4120.
 2. *R(U)* 1/71, R.G. Micklethwait, Chief
    Comr.

3. Tillyard *Unemployment Insurance in
   Great Britain 1911–48* (1949), pp. 24–
   25.
4. Final Report (1932) Cmd. 4185, para.
   443. To meet the objection, the ground
   for disqualification has in practice
   frequently been called 'industrial
   misconduct': see, esp. *R(U)* 24/55 and
   R(U) 1/71.

that it renders the claimant an unfit person to hold the job[5] and will include

> 'industrial shortcomings, disobedience, faulty workmanship, idleness, unauthorised absence, some types of carelessness, and conduct . . . connected with the employment adversely affecting the claimant's proper discharge of his duties.'[6]

But the refusal to leave[7] or to join a trade union[8] does not constitute misconduct.

iv) Blameworthiness

It is generally said that there must be blameworthiness,[9] but exactly what must be proved in terms of mental attitude is far from clear. On occasions, the Commissioner has tended towards a test appropriate to the 'voluntary unemployment' theory and spoken of the necessity of showing 'deliberate' or 'wilful negligence'.[10] The view most popularly held, however, is that a wilful or reckless breach of the appropriate standard is not required. A valuable illustration is provided by *R(U) 8/57*.

> C, the manager of a branch pharmacy, was dismissed when cash was found to be missing in the shop. He was prosecuted for but acquitted of embezzlement.[11] It was held that this was not sufficient to bar disqualification. 'Serious carelessness' only was required, and this might legitimately be inferred from the evidence.

The Commissioner observed, more generally,

> 'Misconduct . . . may be constituted by mere carelessness; but in considering whether a person has been guilty of misconduct it is necessary to discriminate between that type and degree of carelessness which may have to be put up with in human affairs, and the more deliberate or more serious type of carelessness which justifies withholding unemployment benefit because the employee has lost his employment through his own avoidable fault.'[12]

v) Relevance of other legal proceedings

The situation in which an employee is dismissed for misconduct may have important repercussions in other areas of law. The conduct may constitute a criminal offence. The employee may allege that he was wrongfully dismissed (i.e., his employer acted in breach of contract), or that he was entitled to the statutory remedy for unfair dismissal. The dispute may have been the subject of a court hearing or of an adjudication by an

---

5. *R(U) 24/55*; *R(U) 7/57*.
6. *R(U) 2/77*, para. 15, R.J.A. Temple, Chief Comr.
7. *UD 1528/26*.
8. *R(U) 2/77*.
9. E.g., ibid., at para. 15.
10. *R(U) 34/52*, cp. 'culpable negligence' (*R(U) 35/53*). Some schemes have

attempted to introduce such language into the statutory definition: e.g., the West German Arbeitsförderungsgesetz § 119(1)(i) and the Massachusetts Employment Law, § 25(3)(2).
11. On the significance of other proceedings generally see, post, p. 112.
12. *R(U) 8/57*, para. 6.

industrial or disciplinary tribunal. In all such situations, the question arises as to the significance for the disqualification issue of the findings of such court or tribunal.

It is evident that in many instances the concept of 'misconduct' will be wider than a criminal offence with which the claimant was charged. In such a case an acquittal by a criminal court will in no sense be conclusive of the disqualification point. The authorities must make up their own mind.[13] As regards criminal *conviction*, there is no question of double jeopardy since the object of the disqualification is not to punish the claimant,[14] and so in one case, the Commissioner said that it would be 'cogent' evidence of misconduct.[15] In another he was prepared to regard it as 'conclusive proof', provided that the charge arose on an identical issue.[16] The position is far from clear as regards the decisions of disciplinary bodies. It would seem to depend on how 'judicial' in character is the tribunal and the nature of the information emanating from its findings. It is on these two grounds that one may reconcile two apparently conflicting decisions of the Commissioner.

> In *R(U) 7/61*, the dismissal of a nurse for sleeping on duty and for failing to do her rounds was confirmed by a Hospital Management Committee. But 'misconduct' was not proved as the insurance officer had no details of the incidents on the basis of which the claimant had been dismissed, and he gained no assistance from the decision of the Committee.

> In *R(U) 10/67*, a police disciplinary committee had found a police constable guilty of a drinking offence. Here the disciplinary proceedings were more formal (a 'quasi-judicial' trial) and though not regarded as 'absolutely conclusive' for social security purposes they were nevertheless treated as 'very cogent evidence'. The claimant was disqualified.

One would have thought that a finding by an industrial tribunal that an employee was entitled to compensation for an unfair dismissal would be almost conclusive that the same employee was not guilty of such misconduct as to be disqualified from unemployment benefit. Certainly such a finding is regarded as cogent evidence on which the authorities can act, not the least because at an industrial tribunal both the employer and employee are necessarily parties to the proceedings, and it is therefore more likely that the facts will be fully investigated than in proceedings under the social security legislation where the employer is not a party.[17] But it was held in *R(U) 2/74* that the finding of an industrial tribunal was not conclusive. It involved a different question of law: whether a person had been unfairly dismissed in the main depended on the conduct of the *employer*, whereas for unemployment benefit the main emphasis is on the behaviour of the

13. *R(U) 10/54*; *R(U) 8/57*.
14. *CU 190/50*; *R(U) 27/52*; *R(U) 7/75*.
15. *R(U) 10/54*.
16. *R(U) 24/55*.

17. *R(U) 2/74*, para. 15. R.G. Micklethwait, Chief Comr., and see Lewis, 5 ILJ 119–122.

employee.[18] Different rules of evidence also applied. Statements which were not admissible before the industrial tribunal could be relied on in the insurance tribunal.[19]

B. Voluntarily leaving without just cause

The second ground for disqualification is that the claimant

'has voluntarily left such employment [as an employed earner] without just cause.'[20]

Such a provision is a typical feature of all unemployment insurance schemes, and has remained in a virtually unchanged form since the creation of the British system in 1911.[1] On the traditional theory, it may be justified on the ground that here unemployment is caused not by external circumstances but by the claimant himself.[2] For disqualification to be imposed, three conditions must be satisfied:

   (i) the claimant *left* the employment;
  (ii) the leaving was *voluntary*;
 (iii) it was *without just cause*.

i) Leaving

The onus is on the insurance officer to show that the claimant left his employment.[3] 'Leaving' is not confined to terminating the contract of employment, but includes any temporary severing of the employment relationship, including absenteeism.[4]

ii) Voluntary

The onus is also on the insurance officer to show that such leaving was voluntary.[5] It is this condition which distinguishes the case from dismissal for misconduct,[6] but in some cases it will be of no great significance which of the two is adopted,[7] and the word 'voluntarily' has been broadly construed so that it might extend to cases of termination by the employer which are instigated by the employee but which do not amount to misconduct.[8] In *R(U) 16/52*

C was engaged as a canteen assistant subject to passing a medical examination. She refused to undergo an X-ray test and was dismissed. She was disqualified for leaving her employment voluntarily without just cause. 'It is an established principle of unemployment insurance', said the Commissioner, 'that, if a person deliberately and

18. *R(U) 2/74*, para. 14.
19. Ibid., at para. f5.
20. SSA 1975, s.20(1)(a).
 1. NIA 1911, s.87(2).
 2. Cf. *R(U) 20/64*, para. 8 (Tribunal decision).
 3. Ibid., and see Kempfer, 55 Yale LJ 147.
 4. *R(U) 20/64*, para. 7.
 5. *UD 10841/30*.
 6. *R(U) 9/59*.
 7. Cf., ante, p. 110.
 8. *R(U) 5/71*, but see *R(U) 2/77*, para. 26, where R.J.A. Temple, Chief Comr., suggests that as the principle is not to be found in the Act itself it should be applied with restraint.

knowingly acts in a way which makes it necessary for the employer to dismiss him, he may be regarded as leaving his employment voluntarily.'[9]

But if the dismissal is not the 'natural consequence' of his actions, the leaving will not be voluntary. This in *R(U) 9/59*,

> C was dismissed when he refused to join the employer's superannuation scheme. He did not know at the time he entered the contract that he would be expected to join, and therefore his contract did not 'invite' dismissal.[10]

Difficulties have been caused by cases of quitting certain occupations (notably the police force) where early retirement is not only permitted but actually encouraged by an employer who may, for example, provide financial incentives to leave. In two important decisions,[11] the Commissioner has held that the leaving here is still voluntary. The material disadvantage in staying is one factor, but only one, in deciding the question of just cause.

iii) Without just cause

Once it has been established that the claimant voluntarily left his employment, the onus passes to him to show that he did so for 'just cause'.[12] The phrase is broad and flexible. Legislation provides no guidance on how it is to be interpreted and the Commissioner has warned against laying down any hard and fast rules.[13] There is a wide variety of situations which may constitute just cause.

> Examples are: reduction in wages,[14] non-compliance by the employer with the contract of employment,[15] lack of confidence in mental or physical ability to perform duties,[16] pressing domestic or personal circumstances,[17] difficulty of travel to work,[18] reluctance to join a trade union,[19] general grievances about working conditions:[20]

But though such circumstances may constitute a good reason for leaving the employment, they may not be sufficient in themselves to avoid disqualification. It is a general principle that a dissatisfied employee

---

9. *R(U) 16/52*, para. 8.
10. See also *R(U) 2/77* (refusal to join trade union).
11. *R(U) 20/64*; *R(U) 4/70*.
12. *R(U) 20/64*, para. 7.
13. *R(U) 14/52*, para. 5, cited with approval by a Tribunal of Commissioners in *R(U) 20/64*, para. 9.
14. *R(U) 15/53*.
15. *CU 248/49*.
16. *R(U) 3/73*.
17. *R(U) 31/59*.
18. *R(U) 20/69*.
19. *R(U) 38/53*.
20. *R(U) 33/51*. There may be an overlap here with the criteria applied in

deciding whether the claimant had unreasonably refused an offer of suitable employment, post. Though there is no authority on this, British law on the point might well follow the New York Unemployment Insurance Law which expressly provides (§ 593(1)(a)) that 'in addition to other circumstances that may be found to consistitute good cause, voluntary separation from employment shall not itself disqualify a claimant if circumstances have developed in the case of such employment that would have justified the claimant in refusing such employment in the first instance.'

should look for an alternative situation before leaving his present job.[1] He need not actually have secured a vacant post,[2] but the prospects of his finding one must be good.[3] The principle has not been rigidly applied. For example, it was not invoked where a wife left her job to join her husband who had been posted elsewhere,[4] nor to a spouse who was not the principal breadwinner and who was left to look after a child who would otherwise have remained unattended.[5] Nor was it applied where the current employment did not provide any opportunities for looking for another job,[6] or where the relations between the claimant and his employer or his fellow employees had become so strained that it was in the interest of all that he should quit immediately.[7] As regards grievances about working conditions and other disputes with an employer, there is another general principle, which is again subject to the undue friction exception, that before tendering his notice, a claimant should seek to redress the grievances by making representations to the employer through the proper channels, usually with the assistance of his trade union.[8]

C. Unreasonable refusal of suitable offer

The third ground for disqualification directed against voluntary unemployment comprises a number of variations on the same theme: the claimant unreasonably refuses an offer or fails to take the appropriate steps to obtain employment which is suitable for him. Originally, there was no explicit legislative provision to cover these contingencies: they were treated merely as conclusive evidence of the claimant's failure to satisfy the condition that he be available for suitable work. This led to an anomaly. A man who was held to be unavailable for work would never qualify for benefit whereas one who voluntarily left or who was dismissed for misconduct would be qualified only for a maximum of six weeks. Sensibly the insurance officer in such circumstances exercised his discretion[9] to review entitlement to benefit after six weeks of unemployment.[10] In 1930, refusal of, or failure to apply for, suitable employment became an independent ground for disqualification,[11] and with minor amendments

1. *CU 96/48*; *R(U) 14/55*; *R(U) 20/64*.
2. *R(U) 4/73*.
3. *R(U) 20/64*; *R(U) 4/70*.
4. *R(U) 19/52*: the decision must be read in the light of S.I. 1974/2010, Reg. 8, which provides that for the purposes of the disqualification provisions the test for married women 'shall be determined on the same basis as that applicable to a single woman, but not so as to exclude such consideration of the responsibilities arising from her marriage as is reasonable in the circumstances of the case.'
5. *R(U) 6/59*.
6. *R(U) 25/52*.
7. *UD 5287*.
8. *R(U) 33/51*; *R 3/65 (UB)*. Contrast

R(U) 18/57: the Commissioner held that such steps were not necessary where the *employer* issued an ultimatum to do additional work, or withdraw.
9. Under UIA (No. 2) 1921, s.10, the insurance officer was bound to review every six weeks if the claimant renewed his application.
10. See, e.g., Emerson and Lascelles, *Guide to the Unemployment Insurance Acts* (1928), p. 101.
11. UIA 1930, s.4, implementing a recommendation of the Committee on Procedure and Evidence for Determination of Claims for Unemployment Insurance Benefit (1929), Cmd. 3415, paras. 43–44.

has remained unchanged since. Of course, the claimant must continue to show that he is available for suitable employment,[12] and there is inevitably some overlap between the two areas of law[13] – most obviously on the question whether the restrictions the claimant places on his availability are reasonable.[14] But there is an important difference. The availability test is a *general* one: it is concerned with the claimant's attitude to the labour market. The grounds for disqualification to be considered in this section are concerned with the claimant's refusal or failure to follow a *particular* course of conduct, or to accept a *particular* offer of employment.

There are, in fact, four different grounds of disqualification which fall under the general heading of refusal of suitable employment:

(i) refusal or failure to apply for a suitable situation, or refusal to accept that situation when offered;

(ii) neglect to take advantage of a reasonable opportunity of suitable employment;

(iii) refusal or failure to carry out official recommendations;

(iv) refusal or failure to take advantage of a reasonable opportunity of training approved by the Secretary of State.

i) Refusal of suitable employment

The most widely used, and most frequently contested, of the four grounds arises where

'after a situation in any suitable employment has been properly notified to him as vacant or about to become vacant, he has without good cause refused or failed to apply for that situation or refused to accept that situation when offered to him'[15]

a) ONUS OF PROOF. The burden is first on the insurance officer to show that a situation, which is prima facie suitable, has been offered or notified to the claimant. It is then for the latter to prove either that employment was not suitable or that he had good cause for refusing it, or failing to apply for it.[16]

b) NOTIFICATION AND REFUSAL. 'Properly notified' in the subsection includes communications not only from offices administered by the Employment Service Agency, but also from a local education authority, any other recognised agency, or indeed from an employer seeking to fill a vacancy.[17] The claimant cannot complain that the information provided was insufficiently detailed. So long as the broad nature of the situation is clear, it is his duty to find out further particulars.[18] 'Refusal', too, has been widely construed. An explicit rejection of the offer is unnecessary: it is sufficient if the claimant's conduct was such as positively to discourage the

12. Ante, pp. 104–108.
13. See, e.g., *R(U) 2/59*.
14. Ante, p. 108.
15. SSA 1975, s.20(1)(b).
16. *R(U) 26/52*.
17. SSA 1975, s.20(5)(a).
18. *R(U) 32/52*.

employer from offering him the situation.[19]

c) SUITABILITY OF EMPLOYMENT. The real problem in this area is to decide what employment is 'suitable'. The Act does not define the concept, but some guidance is supplied by section 20(4), which provides that

> 'employment shall not be deemed to be employment suitable in the case of any person if it is either—
>
> (a) employment in a situation vacant in consequence of a stoppage of work due to a trade dispute; or
>
> (b) employment in his usual occupation in the district where he was last ordinarily employed at a rate of remuneration lower, or on conditions less favourable, than those which he might reasonably have expected to obtain having regard to those which he habitually obtained in his usual occupation in that district, or would have obtained had he continued to be so employed; or
>
> (c) employment in his usual occupation in any other district at a rate of remuneration lower, or on conditions less favourable, than those generally observed in that district by agreement between associations of employers and of employees or, failing any such agreement, than those generally recognised in that district by good employers;
>
> but, after the lapse of such an interval from the date on which he becomes unemployed as in the circumstances of the case is reasonable, employment shall not be deemed to be unsuitable by reason only that it is employment of a kind other than employment in his usual occupation if it is employment at a rate of remuneration not lower, and on conditions not less favourable, than those generally observed by agreement between associations of employers and of employees or, failing any such agreement, than those generally recognised by good employers.'

The provision in section 20(4)(a) was designed to prevent employers from using the threat of disqualification to force individuals to be employed as 'blacking labour'. It has not caused any difficulty, and consistently with its purpose it has been held not to extend to a situation in which a man, himself laid off as a result of a trade dispute, is offered work by another employer.[20] As regards the remainder of the subsection, the intention of the draftsman seems to have been to prescribe two different standards of 'suitability'. During the first period of unemployment, the claimant should be entitled to refuse employment which was not in his usual occupation, and on terms less favourable than he would have enjoyed if he had continued in his former job, or, if in another district, than were generally recognised in the trade. But after the lapse of a reasonable time, he should

19. *R(U) 28/55* (claimant presented himself for interview with the prospective employer in a dirty and unshaven state).

20. *R(U) 1/52*.

be less optimistic in his search for work and be prepared to accept work in a different occupation, though on conditions generally prevailing in that trade.

If the parliamentary spokesmen are to be believed,[1] this was indeed the general intention, but the specific provisions are more cautiously worded. Conditions (b) and (c) only apply if the claimant is offered employment in his *usual* occupation, and the import of the subsection is that if the terms offered are less favourable than he might reasonably expect, the situation is not necessarily to be regarded as suitable. This falls short of the apparent intention of the provision in two major respects: first, it has no bearing on the suitability of an offer of employment in a different occupation; secondly, offers on terms less favourable may still, if regard is had to concomitant circumstances, be regarded as suitable. Because the subsection involves a *negative* proposition, that the 'employment shall not be deemed to be . . . suitable' if conditions (a), (b) or (c) are satisfied, it leaves open the possibility that notwithstanding the fulfilment of any one of those conditions, an employment *may* be found to be suitable if regard is had to other circumstances. However, the Chief Commissioner has construed the subsection as if it commenced 'employment *shall* be deemed to be *unsuitable* . . .'.[2] He has thus concluded that if the claimant succeeds in bringing his case within (b) or (c) the authorities cannot (whatever the concomitant circumstances) characterize the employment as suitable. This interpretation is consistent both with common sense and with the apparent object of the provision, but is not justified by its wording.

The proviso for the subsection (beginning 'but after the lapse of such an interval . . .') does accord with the stated intention of prescribing a less exacting standard of suitability than that enshrined in the first half of section 20(4). Literally construed, it provides that after a reasonable lapse of time, an employment will not necessarily be unsuitable merely because it involves a different occupation, though it may be so treated on consideration of other circumstances. This would seem to be both workable and just, but the Chief Commissioner, to achieve consistency with his unorthodox interpretation of the first part of subsection 20(4) has been forced to give it a strange and restricted meaning. Notwithstanding the disjunctive 'but', he construes it as providing a solution for a different factual hypothesis, rather than qualifying the first half of Section 20(4).[3] If the *only* reason for holding the employment to be unsuitable is that it is different from the claimant's usual occupation, the authorities, if the other conditions are satisfied, are precluded from finding that it is unsuitable. Such a hypothetical situation would be rare indeed, and on the Chief Commissioner's own admission practically robs the provision of any effect. Again his reading involves a misconstruction of the words actually used. This time he has read 'shall not be deemed to be unsuitable' as being 'shall

1. Mr S. Buxton, Pres. Bd. of Trade, introducing the Amendment to NI Bill 1911, cl. 62, on which the current provision is based: 31 HC Deb., cols. 1074–1077.
2. *R(U) 5/68*, R.G. Micklethwait.
3. Ibid., at para. 13.

be deemed to be suitable'. There is an obvious need for statutory clarification of the ambiguities raised by section 20(4).

It remains to consider the practical questions arising from the subsection. What is a man's 'usual occupation' is of course, a question of fact. On the one hand, he must have followed it for some substantial time.[4] On the other hand, what was his usual occupation may have lapsed through continuous unemployment, disability or a change of locality.[5] To determine whether the rate of remuneration or the conditions of employment are 'habitually observed' or 'generally observed in that district' regard is to be had to such collective agreements as have been made. These may however be inconclusive. So in one case, it was held that the claimant was not entitled to refuse an offer on the ground that no tea-break was provided, when some employers in the area permitted a tea-break and others did not.[6] However, in Northern Ireland, a Tribunal of Commissioners faced with an analogous dichotomy (two rates of pay) focussed on the reference in the subsection to 'good' employers, and held that the claimant was entitled to hold out for the higher rate.[7]

Subject to the Chief Commissioner's doubtful ruling that in some circumstances the authorities are *bound* to hold an offer suitable or unsuitable, the statutory provisions are not conclusive on the suitability question and regard must be had to other factors. For example, it would be unfair to regard as conclusive the fact that the terms on which the claimant was offered employment in his usual occupation were as favourable as those he enjoyed in his former employment, if the long-term prospects in the situation offered were particularly dim.[8] Further, a claimant may sometimes legitimately claim that to accept an offer of employment of a lower status than that to which he was accustomed would prejudice his future chances of returning to his former occupation.[9] Of course, it will always be sufficient for him to show that the employment offered was beyond his abilities.[10] A typical ground for refusal is that the situation offered was incompatible with the claimant's domestic responsibilities.[11] Mere inconvenience for the family is not sufficient: a claimant must be prepared to make reasonable adjustments to his or her personal circumstances.[12] But the case is different where there are children or other dependent relatives whose needs must be catered for.[13]

4. *UD 7678*, suggests that this should normally be three years, but there is no reported decision on the point under modern legislation, and apparently the DHSS have regard to periods of shorter duration: cf., the cases on equivalent points under the industrial injury scheme: post, p. 319.
5. *R(U) 15/62.*
6. *R(U) 9/64.*
7. *R 16/60 (UB).*
8. Thus a claimant on short-time is justified in refusing an offer of full-time work in a similar occupation with another firm, if the long-term prospects in that other firm are no better: *R(U) 34/56.* See also *R(U) 10/61.*
9. Accepted in *R 21/60 (UB)*, but not in *R(U) 35/52* where the offer was only for 2 weeks employment.
10. *R(U) 26/52*; *R(U) 32/52.*
11. For married women, see the rule cited ante, n.4, p. 115.
12. *12/52 (UB).*
13. E.g., *R(U) 20/60.* NB. the existence of such circumstances may render the claimant's prospects of finding employment remote and therefore exclude him from benefit on the ground of unavailability: ante, p. 108.

d) WITHOUT GOOD CAUSE. The claimant may escape disqualification if the refusal or failure was with 'good cause'. In fact, this adds little to the substantive requirements of the subsection, for if there is good cause to refuse an offer of employment, it will not be an offer of 'suitable employment'. 'Suitability' and 'without good cause' are alternative formulations of the same principle, and the Commissioner has not distinguished between them.[14]

ii) Neglect to avail himself of reasonable opportunity of suitable employment

The ground for disqualification considered above arises only when the claimant has failed to apply for a situation, or has refused an offer which was made to him. Of the remaining grounds, the first two are also based on the concept of 'suitable employment' but are not limited to any specific vacancy and therefore are broader in scope. A person may be disqualified if

'he has neglected to avail himself of a reasonable opportunity of suitable employment'[15]

Notwithstanding (or perhaps because of) the breadth of this provision, it is apparently seldom invoked by the authorities[16] and as a result there is little by way of guidance on its meaning.[17] It has been employed in the exceptional situation when a claimant so behaves at or before an interview that he effectively deters a prospective employer from offering him a vacancy.[18] Unlike the other grounds for disqualification under section 20(1) there is here no defence of just (or good) cause. But this is not significant. As seen above, there is, in principle, no distinction between a defence based on just cause, and another claiming that the employment in question was 'unsuitable'. So here the factors which would have been relevant to the finding of good cause are the same as those considered in determining whether the employment was 'suitable' or the opportunity not taken was 'reasonable'.[19]

iii) Failure to carry out official recommendations

The claimant will be disqualified if

'he has without good cause refused or failed to carry out any official recommendations given to him with a view to assisting him to find suitable employment, being recommendations which were reasonable having regard to his circumstances and to the means of obtaining that employment usually adopted in the district in which he resides.'[20]

'Official recommendations' for this purpose are defined as 'recommendations in writing made by an officer of the Employment Service Agency, a local education authority, or the Secretary of State'.[1]

14. See, e.g., R(U) 20/60.
15. SSA 1975, s.20(8)(c).
16. Private communication from DHSS.
17. For its use under the UIAs, see esp. UD 11734/34.
18. R(U) 28/55.
19. R(U) 5/71, H.A. Shewan, Comr.
20. SSA 1975, s.20(1)(d).
1. Ibid., s.20(5)(b).

iv) Failure to avail himself of reasonable opportunity of training

Finally, the Act disqualifies a claimant who

> 'has without good cause refused or failed to avail himself of a reasonable opportunity of receiving training approved by the Secretary of State in his case for the purpose of becoming or keeping fit for entry into, or return to, regular employment.'[2]

This used to be treated as merely one instance of a failure to carry out written directions[3] but since 1946 has constituted a separate provision. The reason for the change of emphasis is the increasing interest in retraining and rehabilitative schemes.[4] The training scheme in question does not have to be admistered by the Department of Employment, but it has to be approved by the Secretary of State for the particular claimant. His determination that the training is suitable is conclusive and cannot be reviewed by the statutory authorities.[5] But it is still open to the claimant to contend that he had good cause for the refusal or failure;[6] or that the opportunity given to him was not, in the circumstances, 'reasonable'.

D. Period of disqualification

Under the 1911 Act there was a mandatory period of disqualification of six weeks.[7] Since 1920,[8] a shorter period may be imposed, the matter being determined by the statutory authorities, viz., the insurance officer, insurance tribunal or Commissioner.[9] This involves a discretion but it is one which must be exercised judicially, taking into account all the relevant circumstances.[10] In 1954 a Commissioner ruled that normally the maximum period should be imposed, and that there was a 'heavy burden' on the claimant to show that this would not be justifiable because of the special circumstances of his case.[11] The principle was not universally followed, and in 1974 was repudiated by a Tribunal of Commissioners.[12] The discretion conferred by the legislation was not to be fettered in this way:

> 'the correct approach is to adhere firmly to the statutory language, regarding each case as one in which a sensible discretion has to be exercised in such manner as the justice of the case requires.'[13]

The implication is that previous decisions of the Commissioner under the 1954 principle are no longer authoritative, but it might be useful to list some of the circumstances which in the past have been used to justify a period of less than the maximum:

2. Ibid., s.20(1)(e).
3. E.g., *UD 6424/36*.
4. Cf., ante, p. 77.
5. *2/57 (UB)*.
6. See, e.g., *R 10/60 (UB)*.
7. NIA 1911, s.87(2).
8. UIA 1920, s.8(2); and see UIA 1935, s. 8(2).

9. SSA 1975, s.20(1).
10. *R(U) 27/52*; *R(U) 8/74*.
11. *R(U) 17/54*.
12. *R(U) 8/74*.
13. Ibid., at para. 20, adopting a dictum of R.S. Lazarus, Comr., in *CU 273/73*, para. 7.

1. where the maximum will cause hardship, because of the claimant's domestic circumstances[14] or because he has already been subject to a serious sanction.[15]

2. where he has come close to justifying his loss of employment (through just or good cause) but has just failed[16];

3. where the Insurance Fund is already sufficiently protected (e.g., because the claimant is no longer unemployed.[17]

Where the ground for disqualification was misconduct or leaving voluntarily the period will run, in general, from the date of discharge:[18] in other cases it will commence on the date when the claimant refused an offer, or failed to take an appropriate step.

Part six. Trade Disputes Disqualification

A. Introduction

With the remaining ground for disqualification, we enter into a highly controversial area. The scheme must here grapple with problems of industrial relations,[19] and, needless to say, political opinions are well to the fore in discussions of the substantive law. The general position is that unemployment resulting directly from trade dispute in which the claimant was 'involved' should not give him a title to benefit. There is a widespread assumption that such a limitation must exist, and the principle finds a place in almost every system of unemployment insurance.[20] But the theoretical or policy justifications of the principle are not so obvious as may appear and require some consideration.[1]

In the first place, it is said that this is but another instance of *voluntary* unemployment (like misconduct, leaving, refusal, etc.), and, as such, does not come within the risk of unemployment for which the insurance fund was established. However, at least by itself, this is not a complete justification, for if applied consistently, it would compel the law to distinguish between *strikes* and *lockouts*, and this it fails to do. Moreover, the other grounds of disqualification based on voluntary unemployment recognise that in certain circumstances the leaving or refusal of employment may be excused on grounds of 'just' or 'good cause'. Here there are no such qualifications. There is, indeed, a fundamental rule that the authorities should not enter into the merits of the dispute.

14. *R(U) 27/52.*
15. *R(U) 1/71.*
16. *R(U) 35/52*; *R(U) 20/64.*
17. E.g., *R(U) 20/64.*
18. *CU 155/50.* If, however, the claimant continues to receive remuneration (e.g., by payment in lieu of notice) it will run from the date when it is no longer payable: *R(U) 35/52.*
19. This was the one area of unemployment insurance law to be considered in detail by the Royal Commission on Trade Unions and Employers Associations (the Donovan Commission). See its Report (1968), Cmnd. 3623, paras. 953–993.
20. Schindler, 38 Col. LR 858.
1. Cf., Lesser, 55 Yale LJ 167; Shamir, 17 U of Chi. LR 294; 2nd Memo. of Ministry of Social Security to Royal Commission, Minutes of Evidence, pp. 2310–2318.

Secondly, resort is had to the idea of industrial neutrality:

> 'the National Insurance Fund, to which both employers and employees contribute, should not become involved in industrial disputes . . . the scheme should not be open to the criticism that it is supporting one side or the other.'[2]

While this is, on the face of it, an appealing argument, it leaves open the question as to what constitutes 'neutrality'. It may not be neutral for payments to be made to strikers (and, as will be seen, the same may be said of supplementary benefits which are paid to the families of strikers[3]), but it is arguable that it is equally not neutral if workers with a legitimate grievance are deterred from taking industrial action because of the refusal to pay benefit.

The neutrality argument appears often to be a gloss on the less compromising stance taken by others, that on economic and political grounds, contributors to the Fund should not financially support those who withdraw their labour. There are some who would find unattractive a further alteration in the balance of power between employers and trade unions;[4] there are others whose concern would be not to encourage industrial stoppages, and therefore losses in productivity.[5] Finally, removal of the disqualification would arouse the hostility of those contributors who are not able to effectively express their grievances by withdrawing their labour.[6] Whether or not such arguments are found acceptable, depends, in the last resort, on political attitudes.

B. General rule

The Social Security Act 1975, section 19(1), provides that a

> 'person who has lost employment as an employed earner by reason of a stoppage of work which was due to a trade dispute at his place of employment shall be disqualified for receiving unemployment benefit so long as the stoppage continues.'

The onus is on the insurance officer[7] to prove that (i) there was a trade dispute; (ii) it was at the claimant's place of employment; (iii) it resulted in a stoppage; (iv) the claimant lost employment as a result of that stoppage.

i) Trade dispute
This is statutorily defined as

> 'any dispute between employers and employees, or between employees and employees, which is connected with the employment or non-employment or the terms of employment or

2. Ibid., at p. 2310.
3. Post, p. 526.
4. Mr. L. Brittan, Standing Committee F Debates on Employment Protection Bill 1975, col. 1527.
5. Mr. H. Lawson during debates on the equivalent provision in the NI Bill 1911: 31 HC Deb., 1733.
6. Mr. L. Brittan, ante, n.4, at col. 1529.
7. R(U) 17/52.

the conditions of employment of any persons, whether employees in the employment of the employer with whom the dispute arises, or not.'[8]

This is an interesting example of a statutory definition being lifted from another context in which it served a completely different purpose. It was based on that in the Trade Disputes Act 1906[9] whose object was to create an *immunity* from certain actions in tort.[10] It is not surprising, therefore, that the definition has given rise to some strange decisions. No one would question the application of the term 'trade dispute' to strikes (official or unofficial),[11] lockouts,[12] and demarcation disputes,[13] at least where the dispute arose between a group of employees and their employer or another group of employees.[14] But in *R(U) 1/74*

> in pursuance of a national pay claim, building labourers withdrew their labour on a number of building sites. The site on which C worked was unaffected until pickets from a nearby site came and pursuaded C and his fellow employees not to work. R. S. Lazarus, Commissioner, relying on certain decisions concerned with common law immunities,[15] held that there was a trade dispute between C's employer and the pickets who arrived from other sites, notwithstanding that he was not *their* employer.

Even more doubtful was the decision in *R(U) 2/53*.

> C was prevented from working by the unlawful acts of pickets who threatened him with violence. It was held that C lost his employment as a result of the trade dispute between himself and the pickets!

The necessary connection between the dispute and 'the employment or non-employment or the terms of employment or the conditions of employment' has caused some difficulty. In *R(U) 26/59* it was held that a dispute as to whether an employee was entitled to an income tax rebate under his contract of employment was not a trade dispute, since it was concerned with the existence of a term, not with whether there *should* be such a term. The distinction is an elusive one and was ignored by the Commissioner in a later case.[16]

It is of the essence of the British system that no attempt should be made to adjudicate on the merits of the dispute.[17] This applies even where the claimant alleges that he withdrew his labour for just cause because, for

---

8. SSA 1975, s.19(2)(b). Cp. Trade Union and Labour Relations Act 1974, s.29(1).
9. S.5(3).
10. See the historical survey in *R(U) 1/74*, paras. 12–15, R.S. Lazarus, Comr.
11. *R(U) 5/59.*
12. *R(U) 17/52.*
13. *R(U) 14/64.*

14. The claimant need not himself be a party to the dispute: *R(U) 3/69.*
15. E.g., *Huntley v Thornton* [1957] 1 All ER 234, [1957] 1 WLR 321.
16. *R(U) 3/71*, J.S. Watson, Comr., and see *Calvert*, p. 157.
17. See Sir J. Simon, Sol. Gen., introducing the equivalent provision in the 1911 Bill: 31 HC Deb., col. 1729. See also *R(U) 5/77.*

example, his employer was in breach of contract.[18] There is an obvious justification for this view. It would be very difficult for departmental officers to reach an objective decision on the merits of a particular dispute, and it would be very costly in terms of time and money. But it does mean that the concept of 'trade dispute' has to be stretched sometimes unnaturally wide. In one case it was held to cover the discharge of employees who had objected to a reduction in wages.[19]

It is not entirely clear when a difference of opinion becomes a dispute but 'a question . . . must reach a certain stage of contention before it may properly be termed a dispute.'[20] While it will usually end by some form of agreement, it will no longer operate to disqualify from benefit if it results in one party totally severing relations with the other.[1]

ii) Place of employment

The general rule does not require that the claimant himself be involved in the trade dispute. Subject to the exceptions on non-participation and lack of direct interest considered below,[2] it is sufficient if the dispute was located at his place of employment. The traditional justification for what is effectively a presumption of participation or interest in the dispute is that there is 'a common bond of mutual interest and loyalty . . . between workers at one place of employment which enables them to be distinguished from other workers.'[3] In the days of the small family firm this rationalisation may have been attractive, but in the industrial conditions prevailing today, its appeal is less obvious.

If, in theory, the identification of the dispute with the place of employment is not easy to justify, in practice the application of the test is even more elusive. Section 19(2)(a) of the Social Security Act 1975 defines a claimant's place of employment as 'the factory, workshop, farm or other premises or place at which he was employed . . .'. This still leaves open what is to be considered as 'other premises or place'. It is clear that each case must be decided on its facts, and that some fairly arbitrary lines must be drawn. In one case, it was held that 'the place of employment' of someone loading ships was the whole of the docks,[4] while in another the place of employment of a man working in an engineering shop attached to a group of collieries, but physically separated from them, was not the colliery.[5] To cope with this Section 19(2)(a) continues:

'where separate branches of work which are commonly carried on as separate businesses in separate premises or at separate places

18. Donovan Commission ante n.19, at paras. 993–994; cp. the principle recognised in *UD 306/29* and the Northern Ireland decision *R 20/60 (UB)* that there is no 'dispute' where an employer or employee fails to carry out a legally binding obligation. See also *Calvert*, p. 155.
19. *R(U) 27/56.*
20. *R(U) 21/59*, para. 6.
 1. *R(U) 17/52.*

 2. Post, pp. 129–130.
 3. Memo. of Ministry of Social Security, to Royal Commission, Minutes of Evidence, p. 2312.
 4. *R(U) 4/58*; cf., *UD 5568* where it was held that a person employed on a barge was not employed in the same place as the dockers at the dock where the barge happened to be.
 5. *UD 5145/26.*

> are in any case carried on in separate departments on the same
> premises or at the same place, each of these departments shall . . .
> be deemed to be a separate factory or workshop or farm or
> separate premises or a separate place, as the case may be.'

The onus of proving that certain premises are the claimant's place of
employment (the first part of section 19(2)(a)) is on the insurance officer.
The onus of proving that they constitute a separate business (the second
part of section 19(2)(a)) is on the claimant.[6] It is a formidable obstacle, for
he must satisfy the authorities that there are *separate* branches carrying on
separate businesses in *separate* departments. If the various branches are
concerned to produce components for the same end product (e.g., a motor
car), they are unlikely to be treated as separate businesses.[7] The fact that
the process on which the claimant is employed is often, in other situations,
treated as a separate business is irrelevant.[8] The case-law reveals that the
question whether the claimant does work in a separate business depends
on circumstances which are haphazard and which may be totally unrelated
to the policy behind the rule which is based on the alleged material interest
and loyalty of those working on the same enterprise. This is, perhaps, not
surprising in the light of the fact that the concepts of 'branches', 'businesses' and 'departments' are none of them terms of art, and all involve
questions of degree. Suggestions to modify the provision have, however, as
yet gone unheeded.[9]

iii) Stoppage due to trade dispute

There may be disqualification only where there has been a cessation of
work by a significant number of employees[10] arising from an unwillingness
on their part to work or from a refusal by the employer to provide work
until the dispute is settled.[11] The stoppage must constitute a move, by
either side, in the contest, the intention of both parties being eventually to
resume normal working.[12] If an employer or the whole group of employees
decide categorically that they do not wish the employment relationship to
continue on *any* terms, the cessation of work no longer forms part of the
trade dispute.[13] The question is then whether persons unemployed as a
result should be disqualified on the grounds either of voluntarily leaving or
of misconduct. To determine whether an allegedly absolute discharge or
withdrawal was intended to be taken seriously may obviously create an
acute problem of interpretation for the authorities. A series of Commissioner's decisions shows that many such statements, though formulated in the most categorical terms, are not to be taken at their face value.[14]

---

6. *R(U) 1/70*, R.G. Micklethwait, Chief
   Comr.
7. Ibid., at para. 16.
8. *R(U) 4/62*.
9. The Donovan Commission rejected, on
   the 'community of interest' argument,
   the proposal of the CBI that the
   definition of 'place of employment'
   should be extended; and, on the
   grounds that it would encourage

selective strikes, that of the TUC that
it should be narrowed: ante n.19, p.
122, at paras. 970–972.
10. *R(U) 7/58*.
11. *R(U) 19/51*.
12. *R(U) 17/52*; *R(U) 11/63*.
13. *R(U) 1/65*.
14. *R(U) 17/52*; *R(U) 19/53*; *R(U) 36/53*;
    R(U) 27/56; *R(U) 11/63*; *R(U) 1/65*.

iv) Loss of employment by reason of stoppage

The claimant must have lost his employment 'by reason of the stoppage'. It might reasonably have been assumed that this is simply a question of fact, with the onus of proving the causal link between the loss of employment and the stoppage on the insurance officer. In practice, however, the authorities appear to have been influenced by a fear that if too much is expected of the insurance officer certain unworthy claimants would succeed. This may be seen in three different situations.

In the first, the claimant loses his employment before the stoppage begins. The temporal factor is not regarded as an insuperable obstacle to disqualification. In *R(U) 30/55*,

> C left his employment without giving any reasons. A trade dispute was then in progress but a stoppage which would have affected C and his fellow employees did not start until four days later. C was disqualified for the duration of the stoppage. The Commissioner was prepared to assume that C anticipated what was going to happen and was not prepared to run the risk of being implicated in the stoppage, thus losing his benefit.

This may seem to be a harsh decision – the claimant could in any event have been disqualified for six weeks for voluntarily leaving without just cause – but it is not atypical. Indeed, in dealing with cases where the employer discharges or suspends the claimant immediately before the stoppage the authorities have traditionally invoked the so-called '12-day rule'. If the discharge occurred within twelve working days of the stoppage there was a presumption that the employment was lost by reason of the stoppage[15] and that if there had been no stoppage the claimant would have resumed the employment.[16] While the presumption was rebuttable, the rule might nevertheless operate harshly and, with the insistence on twelve days, was certainly rigid and artificial.[17] In one recent decision, the Commissioner has reserved his opinion as to the validity and applicability of the rule in present-day circumstances,[18] and in practice the rule is now very rarely invoked.[19]

Secondly, it has been consistently held that the disqualification cannot be avoided by an allegation that a claimant, losing his employment during a trade dispute, would *in any event* have been unemployed for part or all of that period for reasons of redundancy or short-time.[20] These rulings seem contrary to principle, but they have been justified on the ground that any other view would lead to extreme administrative difficulties, it being necessary to prophesy, for example, the identity of workers who would

---

15. *R(U) 20/57*. The rule was originally formulated by the Umpire (*UD 1890I/31*). A Tribunal of Commissioners reasoned that because the wording of the disqualification provision remained the same under the National Insurance Acts, the legislature intended that the rule should be retained.

16. *R(U) 31/57.*

17. Per H.A. Shewan, Comr., *R(U) 6/71*, para. 8.

18. Ibid.

19. Private communication from DHSS.

20. *R(U) 11/52*; *R(U) 32/55*; *R(U) 17/56*; *R(U) 29/59*; *R(U) 12/61* all affirmed in *R(U) 12/72*, Tribunal decision, which overruled the single inconsistent decision in *CSU 3/68.*

have been made redundant or the days when they would have been laid off.[1]

Thirdly, the authorities do not take the reference to 'loss' of employment entirely literally. The claimant need not have been employed on the day immediately prior to the date of unemployment in question.[2] The effect of the stoppage may have been to obstruct an employer's intention to re-engage a workman who had been off work for a period.[3]

v) Other Employment

The disqualification does not apply to a claimant who

> 'during the stoppage . . . has become bona fide employed
> elsewhere in the occupation which he usually follows or has
> become regularly engaged in some other occupation.'[4]

The grounds for disqualification, whatever they may be, cannot apply where the claimant has genuinely removed himself from the ambit of the dispute. But this will not be the case if he takes a temporary job for a very short time solely to requalify for benefit. The onus, then, is on the claimant to show that the new employment was 'bona fide'.[5] This means both that the employment was a genuine one and that it was taken up for an honest motive.[6] The mere fact that the employment was of short duration does not, by itself, justify an inference that the employment was not bona fide.[7] But such an inference may be drawn where it is clear from the evidence that the claimant did not intend permanently to sever relations with his original employer.[8]

C. The exceptions

The breadth of the general rule is evident. There may be a stoppage at the claimant's place of employment with which his connection is remote and yet his benefit is lost. Such a situation in fact occurred in the moulders' strike of 1920 and the unfairness of the general rule, standing alone, was fully revealed.[9] After much discussion, hesitation and amendment,[10] the Unemployment Insurance (No. 2) Act of 1924 was introduced to provide relief for those who could prove that they were neither participating in, financing, or directly interested in the dispute, nor belonged to a grade or class the members of which were participating in, financing or directly interested in the dispute. Doubts were still felt as to the equity of this amendment. In the general strike of 1926 members of a class of colliery workers throughout the country were disqualified because other members of the same class in one *particular* district belonged to a union which was

1. *R(U) 12/72*, para. 12.
2. Ibid., at para. 12 and *R(U) 13/72*.
3. E.g., *R(U) 19/56*.
4. SSA 1975, s.19(1).
5. *R(U) 39/56*.
6. *R(U) 6/74*, H.A. Shewan, Comr.
7. Ibid., at para. 10.

8. Ibid.
9. See 131 H.C. Deb., cols. 935–936.
10. For the history see 1st Memo. of Ministry of Social Security to Donovan Royal Commission: ante n.19, p. 122, Minutes of Evidence, pp. 2298–2304.

financing the dispute. The Blanesborough Committee reporting in 1927 doubted whether an entirely satisfactory form of wording could ever be found but recommended that the 'grade or class' should be specifically linked to the claimant's place of employment.[11] This was implemented in 1927,[12] but for many years thereafter the TUC continued to express dissatisfaction, and eventually in 1965 the matter was specifically referred to the Royal Commission on Trade Unions and Employers' Associations.[13] The Commission was highly critical of the law then prevailing. In the first place, it rejected the principle that an individual should be 'involved' in a dispute merely because he was 'financing' it, which had consistently been held to include membership of a union or association which was financially supporting those involved in the dispute.[14] Apart from common membership, the individual might have no other interest in the dispute.[15] Secondly, it recommended abolition of the rule which served to disqualify a claimant belonging to 'a grade or class of workers of which ... there were members employed at his place of employment any of whom are participating in or financing or directly interested in the dispute.'[16] It regarded as unreliable the traditional justification that there was a 'community of interest' between such workers.[17] The proposals of the Commission lay dormant until 1975 when they were implemented by the Employment Protection Act.[18] The present position is, then, that a claimant may escape disqualification if he can prove

> 'that he is not participating in or directly interested in the trade dispute which caused the stoppage of work.'[19]

i) Participating
The Commissioner has regarded it as both 'dangerous and unnecessary to seek to define' the meaning of 'participating'[20] but it connotes the idea of knowingly doing something or refraining from doing something which contributes to the continuance of the dispute.[1] It should involve active support of one of the parties: a man who merely abstains from *voting* against strike action has been held not to 'participate.'[2] On the other hand, it does not seem to require very positive action. In one case, attendance at a meeting called to find a solution to the dispute was regarded as exemplifying 'participation'.[3]

ii) Directly interested
In general this means that resolution of the dispute will have an immediate effect on the claimant's remuneration or conditions or work. For a long

11. Committee on Unemployment Insurance (1927), para. 137.
12. UIA 1927, s.6.
13. Ante n.19, p. 122.
14. See, e.g., *R(U) 15/55*; *R(U) 1/70*; *R(U) 12/71*.
15. See the Report of the Royal Commission on Trade Unions and Employers Associations (1968) (the Donovan Commission), Cmnd. 3623,

at para. 985.
16. NIA 1965, s.22(1) proviso (b).
17. Ante n.15, at paras. 975–976.
18. S.111(1).
19. SSA 1975, s.19(1)(a), as amended ibid.
20. Per H. Magnus, Comr., *R(U) 5/66*, para. 9.
1. *Calvert*, p. 165.
2. *R(U) 5/66*. See also *R 3/68 (UB)*.
3. *R(U) 6/61*.

time, the Commissioner applied the provision as if the word 'directly' did not appear,[4] that is, he was prepared to impose disqualification where the dispute concerned the pay or working conditions of another grade or class of employees but the settlement of which was thought likely to lead to changes in the claimant's pay or working conditions.[5] A typical case decided that

> C, a surface worker at a mine laid off when underground workers stopped work over a dispute about bonus payments, should be disqualified since the question of rights to bonus payments must affect all those working at the mine.[6]

On a similar principle, it has been held that when a stoppage results from a demarcation dispute disqualification should be imposed not only on those who withdrew their labour but also on those who stood to lose should the claim succeed.[7] Such an interpretation can lead to absurd results. In days when relativity of remuneration and pay differentials are highly prized, and when the terms of collective bargains are given wide publicity, it is obvious that a single collective bargain may affect a very large number of workers many of whom will be employed either in a different industry or in a different place.[8] It is not surprising, therefore, that in recent decisions the Commissioner has sought to restrain the broad interpretation previously placed on the 'directly interested' criterion. In *R(U) 13/71* H. A. Shewan, Commissioner, said:

> 'without attempting to define precisely what is meant by "direct interest", I think that a claimant should not be regarded as having a direct interest in another person's dispute . . . unless there is a close association between the two occupations concerned, and the outcome of the dispute is likely to affect the claimant, not at a number of removes, but virtually automatically, without further intervening contingencies.'[9]

In *R(U) 8/72* the new approach was welcomed by another Commissioner. For him, the most important factor was the causal connection between the dispute and the possible modification to the claimant's terms of employment.

> '(The) interest will not be direct if some act or event must be interposed between the outcome of the dispute and the occurrence of the change.'[10]

4. Hepple and O'Higgins *Individual Employment Law* (2nd edn), para. 1–476.
5. *R(U) 3/56*; *R(U) 25/56*; *R(U) 1/60*; *R(U) 4/62*; *R(U) 4/65*.
6. *R(U) 25/56*.
7. *Punton v Minister of Pensions and National Insurance* (No. 2) [1963] 2 All ER 693, [1963] 1 WLR 1176 affd [1964] 1 All ER 450, [1964] 1 WLR 226, CA.
8. See the critical submissions of the TUC to the Donovan Commission, ante n.15, Minutes of Evidence. The Commission itself recognised the problem but was unable to suggest a more appropriate criterion: para. 992.
9. *R(U) 13/71*, para. 8.
10. *R(U) 8/72*, para. 16, R.S. Lazarus, Comr.

D. Period of disqualification

Unlike the disqualifications for voluntary unemployment, no maximum period is stipulated for trade disputes. It is to last 'so long as the stoppage continues'.[11] This is a question of fact for determination by the authorities[12] but the onus is on the claimant to prove that the stoppage has come to an end.[13] The dispute need not have been settled,[14] but a substantial proportion of those who withdrew their labour as a result of the dispute must have returned to work.[15] Even if a settlement has been reached, it may be impracticable to restart work immediately, and in such cases the stoppage will continue 'for such time as it is necessary to remedy disrepair naturally resulting from the stoppage of work'.[16]

Part seven. Special Provisions

A. General

The nature of certain occupations makes it difficult to accommodate them within the framework of the ordinary law of unemployment benefit. For such cases, specific provision has been made. Thus a member of the armed forces may not receive benefit while serving.[17] He does become entitled on leaving, and will not be disqualified under the 'voluntary leaving' rule[18] if he does so at his own request,[19] though a six-week disqualification will be incurred if he is dismissed for disciplinary reasons.[20]

A share fisherman holds a somewhat anomalous position under the social security system. His remuneration takes the form of a share in the profits of the fishing boat and he is not employed under a contract of service.[1] As such he pays Class 2 contributions and yet for the purposes of entitlement to unemployment benefit they are treated as Class 1 contributions.[2] These circumstances necessitate two special conditions.

A condition is added to the ordinary rule of availability[3] requiring the *claimant* to prove that on the alleged day of unemployment he had not neglected to avail himself of a reasonable opportunity of employment as a fisherman.[4] Secondly, if the claimant is the master or member of the crew of a fishing boat, and either the master or member of the crew of that boat (though not necessarily the claimant himself)[5] is owner or part-owner, he must show that the failure to fish on that day resulted from either (1) the state of the weather; or

---

11. SSA 1975, s.19(1).
12. *R(U) 11/63.*
13. *R(U) 20/57.*
14. *R(U) 11/63.*
15. *R(U) 20/57.* In *R(U) 7/58* it was held that the return of 26 out of 40 workers was a sufficiently high proportion.
16. *R(U) 19/51,* para. 11.
17. S.I. 1975/493, Reg. 2.

18. Ante, p. 113–115.
19. S.I. 1975/493, Reg. 3(2).
20. Ibid., Reg. 3(1).
 1. See the definition in S.I. 1975/529, Reg. 1(2).
 2. Ibid., Reg. 8(1).
 3. Ante, p. 105.
 4. S.I. 1975/529, Reg. 8(5).
 5. *R(U) 6/63.*

(2) repairs or maintenance of the boat; or (3) absence of fish in the normal fishing grounds; or (4) 'any other good cause'.[6]

B. Seasonal workers: policy

The most important of the special rules apply to seasonal workers. This is a form of labour which is inefficient in that it gives rise to high overhead costs and low productivity, and creates shortages and surpluses of labour at different periods of the year.[7] Better organisation of the labour market and the advance of technology has reduced the amount of seasonal work in industries which are not, in their essence, seasonal (e.g., the building trade[8]). But there are still some occupations which are almost wholly seasonal (e.g., working in holiday resorts), and the problem arises how such special circumstances are to be accommodated within the framework of unemployment benefit law. There would seem to be three main solutions. One might simply apply the ordinary principles of eligibility, and impose such restraint on the granting of benefit as might seem desirable by means of the requirement that the claimant must be 'available' for employment. This is the general position in the United States,[9] and prevailed in Britain until 1931.[10] The objection was that workers whose occupation was only seasonal were only nominally 'available': they were not really attached to the labour market during their off-season. A second view was that a special insurance fund should be established, but this was rejected on the grounds of administrative inconvenience, and that the fund would not have sufficient income to pay benefits at an acceptable level.[11] The third method was that favoured by the Royal Commission on Unemployment Insurance[12] and implemented by regulations made in 1931.[13] These were found to accomplish their object only imperfectly, and were refashioned several times. Continuing concern for the operation of this area of the law induced the Secretary of State in 1975 to refer the Regulations to the National Insurance Advisory Committee for reconsideration. Its findings are summarised in the Appendix.

The current Regulations prescribe that a seasonal worker claiming benefit during his off-season should satisfy two special conditions. For the purposes of exposition it is first necessary to explain the meaning of 'seasonal worker' and 'off-season'.

6. S.I. 1975/529, Reg. 8(6). For the interpretation of 'good cause' see, e.g., *R(U) 7/55; R(U) 17/55; R(U) 3/64*.
7. Smith in ed. Ross *Employment Policy and the Labour Market* (1965), chap. 6.
8. See Wittrock, *Reducing Seasonal Unemployment in the Construction Industry* (1967), esp. chap. 6 and pp. 209–222.
9. Corp. Juris: Secundum, vol. 81, pp. 411–412.
10. See, e.g., *UD 4720*.
11. See Report of the National Insurance Advisory Committee on Seasonal Workers, 1948–49 HC 202, paras. 18–21.
12. First Report (1931), Cmd. 3872, para. 125.
13. S.R. & O. 1931 No. 818.

c. Definition of seasonal worker

In terms of policy there seems to be a choice between a narrow and a broad concept of a seasonal worker. On the narrow view the rules should only apply to those persons whose employment is truly 'seasonal', that is their work (e.g., in agriculture or tourism) varies according to climatic conditions. This seems to have been the original view taken. Under an amendment in 1935 a seasonal worker must have been employed 'in an occupation or occupations of a seasonal nature'.[14] On a broader view, it extends more generally to persons who are regularly employed for certain portions of the year (e.g., a school-meals attendant). This seems to be the position taken under the Regulations now in force.[15] A 'seasonal' worker is defined as:

> 'a person whose normal employment is for a part of parts only of a year in an occupation or occupations of which the availability or extent varies at approximately the same time or times in successive years; or any other person who normally restricts his employment to the same, or substantially the same, part or parts only of the year.'[16]

The onus of proving that the claimant is a seasonal worker is on the insurance officer,[17] though once this has been established it shifts to the claimant to show that the pattern of seasonal work has come to an end.[18] The seasonal nature of the work need not be voluntary: a disabled man may be forced by his handicap to take on only this kind of work.[19] Several more specific points under the statutory definition now arise for discussion.

i) Part(s) of a year

The shift of emphasis from the narrower to the broader meaning of seasonal workers can be seen most clearly in the pattern of employment which must be established. The Commissioners originally construed 'part or parts of the year' in accordance with the climatic theory of 'seasonal' to include only those who were substantially unemployed for a period of three months.[20] This was felt to be too lax and, following an amendment to the Regulations in 1952,[1] 'part or parts of a year' may now be of any duration, and made be aggregated, so that, however, the total period of unemployment during the year is not less than seven weeks.[2] There is no *lower* limit to the amount of *employment* necessary to qualify as seasonal, so that a man whose only work during the year was to assist the GPO over Christmas was properly to be regarded as coming within the Regulation.[3] The minimum of seven weeks of unemployment may be spread over the

---

14. S.R. & O. 1935 No. 804, Reg. 2.
15. See NIAC Report on Seasonal Workers (1952), Cmd. 8558.
16. S.I. 1975/564, Reg. 19(2).
17. R(U) 23/53.
18. R(U) 14/53; R(U) 19/54.
19. R(U) 43/52; R(U) 4/64.

20. R(U) 5/51; R(U) 7/51 (Tribunal decision).
1. S.I. 1952/1466, Reg. 2(3), following a recommendation of NIAC, ante n.15.
2. S.I. 1975/564, Reg. 19(2).
3. R(U) 3/61.

whole year.[4] The only concession to the more traditional concept of 'seasonal' is that the periods of employment must recur at approximately the same times of the year; and this has been given a flexible interpretation. In one case, a variation in the starting dates of employment of ten weeks and in the finishing dates of nine weeks was not regarded as too great.[5]

ii) Normal employment

In establishing the pattern, regard is to be had only to the claimant's 'normal employment'. This is a question of fact and is determined in a way similar to that of the analogous issue of a claimant's normal working week.[6] To decide whether or not the normal employment is for part or parts only of the year, the authorities are instructed to concentrate on

'factors inherent in the nature or conditions of the occupation'

rather than

'factors abnormal to that occupation . . . notwithstanding that those factors persist for a prolonged period.'[7]

There is a well established convention that three years of work governed by this provision raise a presumption that the claimant is a seasonal worker.[8] But it is not a rigid rule: it may be rebutted where sickness renders it difficult to discern a pattern,[9] or where the claimant has moved to a new district.[10]

D. Duration of off-season

Once it has been established that the claimant is a seasonal worker it is necessary to calculate the duration of his off-season, for the special conditions only apply to a claim during that period. The Regulation, not surprisingly, defines the 'off-season' as the part of the year (or aggregate of parts) when the claimant is normally not employed, but then excludes from consideration any period shorter than seven days.[11] The prevailing practice is to take the average periods of non-employment over the last three years, discounting abnormally short periods of work which were irrelevant to the claimant's usual occupation.[12]

E. Special conditions for seasonal workers

Claims for benefit during the seasonal worker's off-season are subject to two special conditions.

4. R(U) 5/64.
5. R(U) 8/62.
5. Ante, pp. 94–97.
7. S.I. 1975/564, Reg. 19(2).
8. R(U) 3/51, and see R(U) 6/64.

9. R(U) 36/51.
10. R(U) 14/53.
11. S.I. 1975/564, Reg. 19(2).
12. R(U) 29/51.

i) Registration

He must have been registered for employment with the Employment Service Agency or local authority for the last two years or from the time he became a seasonal worker whichever is the later.[13] But three different periods are exempted from this requirement:

1. 'Any period during which he was employed or was incapable of work.'[14]

2. 'Any considerable period.'[15]

3. 'Any temporary period throughout which he was not available to be employed by reason only of domestic necessity or compulsion of law, or by reason of any other circumstances of an exceptional character.'[16]

ii) Substantial employment

In addition he must prove *either*

1. that 'in his current off-season he has had a substantial amount of employment' before the date of claim; *or*
2. that (having regard to all the circumstances of his case, including the nature and extent of his employment (if any) in any past off-seasons and the industrial or other relevant conditions normally obtaining in the district or districts in which he is available to be employed) he can or could reasonably expect to obtain, after that day in his current off-season, employment which, together with his employment (if any) before that day in that off-season, constitutes a substantial amount of employment.'[7]

'Substantial amount of employment' is defined in the Regulations as

'employment which is equal in duration to not less than one-fourth (or such other fractional part as may, in the circumstances of the particular case, be reasonable) of the current off-season.'[18]

The primary calculation, therefore, involves ascertaining the duration of the off-season and seeing whether the amount of employment actually obtained or likely in all the circumstances to be obtained exceeds one-fourth. Under (2), there is inevitably an element of speculation. But resort may be had to the claimant's past employment record, and for this purpose the authorities will adopt much the same approach as was appropriate to

13. S.I. 1975/564, Reg. 19(3)(a).
14. On which see ante, pp. 82–90, and post, pp. 149–158.
15. E.g., 9 days in 2 years (R(U) 13/56) but not 22 days in 2 years (R(U) 26/55).
16. 'Circumstances of an exceptional

nature' have been held to include a full-time educational course (R(U) 19/64) but not mere distance to the employment exchange or other inconvenience (R(U) 7/52).
17. S.I. 1975/564, Reg. 19(3)(b).
18. Ibid., Reg. 19(2).

determine whether or not the claimant was a 'seasonal worker'.[19]

Even if the claimant fails the one-fourth test, he may yet persuade the authorities to exercise their discretion to accept a smaller amount of employment, though the reported decisions reveal a noticeable reluctance to do this.[20]

Part eight. Duration and Amount of Benefit

A. Duration

Unemployment benefit is payable for a maximum of 312 days (not counting Sunday or a substitute rest-day) in any one period of interruption of employment.[1] After the 312 days, to requalify the claimant must be in employment as an employed earner[2] for thirteen weeks, and in each of those weeks must be so employed for at least sixteen hours.[3]

B. Amount

The standard rate of unemployment benefit is the weekly amount, in 1977–78, of £14·70.[4] The Social Security Pensions Act 1975 abrogated the long-standing rule whereby a lower rate was normally payable to a married woman.[5] To the flat-rate may be added increases for dependants[6] and, from the thirteenth day of a period of interruption of employment for an aggregate maximum of 156 days within the same period, an earnings-related supplement.[7]

---

19. Ante p. 134, and see *R(U) 21/55*; *R(U) 14/61*; and *R(U) 2/63*.
20. *R(U) 14/61*; cp. *R(U) 5/55*.
 1. SSA 1975, s.18(1). For 'period of interruption of employment' see ante, p. 92.
 2. See ante, pp. 90–92.
 3. SSA 1975, s.18(2), as amended by SS(MP)A 1977, s.17(1).
 4. S.I. 1977/1325.
 5. s.18(1). To claim the standard rate

under the previous rules, the woman has to be either entitled to an increase for a husband incapable of self-support, or residing with her husband who was then entitled to an invalidity or retirement pension, or not residing with and not being maintained by her husband: SSA 1975, s.14(5).
 6. Post, pp. 383–390.
 7. SSA 1975, s.14(7): see post, pp. 424–426.

4 Benefits for Sickness and Disability

Part one. General

A. Classification

In order that the scope and order of this chapter might be properly understood it is necessary to begin by classifying the subject-matter.

i) Benefits in money or in kind

Apart from the systems of income maintenance, the sick and disabled benefit from a wide variety of facilities provided by, for example, the National Health Service and under the Chronically Sick and Disabled Persons Act 1970. Although clearly a feature of the 'welfare system' such services do not form part of the 'law of social security' as the expression has been interpreted for the purposes of this book.[1]

ii) Cause of disability

For historical and policy reasons,[2] those disabled as the result of industrial accident or diseases or of service in the armed forces are governed by different and generally more generous schemes. These will be described in chapters 8 and 9 respectively.

iii) Contributory or non-contributory

The remaining benefits are discussed in this chapter. While entitlement to the sickness and invalidity benefits (Parts Two and Three) depends on the claimant's contribution record, there are four benefits, all introduced in the 1970s, which are non-contributory: non-contributory invalidity pension, attendance allowance, invalid care allowance and mobility allowance (Parts Four to Seven).

iv) Short-term and long-term

Along with most other social security systems, the British legislation distinguishes between short-term and long-term incapacity. Sickness benefit is paid for the first six months of incapacity, invalidity benefit thereafter. Attendance allowance and invalid care allowance are not payable unless the need has lasted for six months, and though mobility

---

1. Cf. ante, p. 40. For a general description of health services, see ed. Forder *Penelope Hall's Social Services* *of England and Wales* (9th edn), chap. 6.

2. Post, pp. 264–351.

allowance is payable immediately the conditions are satisfied, these include a twelve months prognosis.

B. History[3]

The origins of the provisions for sickness benefit in the National Insurance Act 1911 may be found in two different sources. Support for the sick had been one of the chief preoccupations of the friendly societies. These had existed for several centuries, but with industrialism had come into their own in the 19th century[4] as providing assistance, both economic and social, for the more prosperous workman or artisan who wished to protect himself and his family from the squalor of the poor law. In 1905, their total membership amounted to no less that six million.[5] It was not, therefore, surprising that when the inadequacies of the poor law to cope with the sick and disabled were most clearly manifested[6] – and when the need for a compulsory insurance scheme had become fully evident[7] (in fact over one-half of the working population had no form of sickness insurance[8]) – it was thought appropriate to build on the foundations of the friendly societies. The other main influence was the system of sickness insurance already operating in Germany which had come to the attention of Lloyd George during his researches into old age pensions.[9] The political battles fought on the exact nature of the scheme to be introduced were fierce. The friendly societies, the insurance companies and particularly the medical profession all campaigned vigorously to preserve their vested interests.[10] The result was a compromise. The provision of medical services was administered by specially created bodies, the Insurance Committees, on which insured persons, medical practitioners, local authorities and central Government were represented. But the administration of cash benefits was in the hands of 'Approved Societies', such friendly societies, trade unions, insurance and collecting societies as satisfied two conditions: they were not carried on for profit and they were subject to the absolute control of their members.[11] The individual would enrol with the society of his choice but, within certain statutory limits, the society had power to make rules and regulations governing the payment of benefit,[12] and might decline to accept a person as member (except on the ground of age).[13] The scheme covered initially all manual workers, and non-manual workers earning less

3. Harris National Health Insurance 1911–1946 (1946); Levy National Health Insurance, a Critical Study (1944); Report on Social Security Provision for Chronically Sick and Disabled People, 1973–74, HC 276.
4. Gosden The Friendly Societies in England, 1815–1875 (1961), and Self-Help: Voluntary Associations in the 19th Century (1973).
5. Bruce The Coming of the Welfare State (4th edn), p. 112.
6. Report of Royal Commission on Poor Laws and Relief of Distress (1909), Cd. 4499.
7. Ibid., at pp. 107–110.
8. Mr D. Lloyd-George, 25 HC Deb., col. 610.
9. In 1911 the government issued a Memorandum on Sickness and Invalidity Insurance in Germany, Cd. 5678.
10. See, esp. Gilbert The Evolution of National Insurance in Great Britain (1966), chaps. 6–7.
11. NIA 1911, s.23.
12. Ibid., s.27.
13. Ibid., s.13.

than £160 per annum.[14] In return for weekly contributions (4d for men, 3d for women[15]) the insured person would, on proof of incapacity for work, be entitled to 10s per week (7s 6d for women) from the fourth day of incapacity for a maximum of twenty-six weeks.[16] After that period had elapsed, 'disablement benefit' was payable so long as he remained incapable of work, thought the amounts in question were half those for sickness benefit.[17] Further, to qualify the claimant must have been insured and paid contributions for twenty-six weeks in the case of sickness benefit, and 104 weeks in the case of disablement benefit.[18] The individual society could, however, pay additional benefits at its discretion and in the manner it thought fit from any surplus in its funds. The result was that benefits varied widely according to the membership and geographical location of the society. No doubt the intention was to preserve the 'private' nature of friendly society insurance, but it seemed hardly to be compatible with a compulsory scheme.[19]

In contrast to unemployment insurance which underwent many changes between 1911 and 1946, the structure of health insurance, at least as regards sickness and disablement benefits, remained more or less intact unil the wholesale revision at the end of the Second World War. The number of persons insured was gradually increased.[20] Contribution and benefit rates were increased in 1920[1] and, in the light of the economic conditions of the time, contribution requirements were relaxed[2] and Treasury subsidies reduced.[3] The Royal Commission on Health Insurance, reporting in 1926,[4] recommended certain minor changes on contribution requirements and these were effected two years later.[5] Its most substantial criticisms, however, went largely unheeded until Beveridge's Report in 1942. The scheme, it was said, was too little concerned with health improvement – 'sickness insurance' would have been a more appropriate title than 'health insurance'. The intended democratic nature of the Approved Societies had become a fiction – they were ordinary commercial undertakings in a different guise.[6] Perhaps most important of all, benefit was inadequate in that, unlike unemployment benefit, it did not provide for dependants' allowances. The 1926 Report, then, in some ways looked forward to the substantial reforms proposed by Beveridge and implemented by the government after the Second World War.

The fundamental achievement of this period was, of course, the establishment of the National Health Service.[7] The provision of medical

14. NIA 1911, ss.1, 2.
15. Ibid., s.30 (to which were added 3d from the employer and 2d from the Treasury).
16. Ibid., s.8(1)(c).
17. Ibid., s.8(1)(d).
18. Ibid., s.8(8).
19. *Harris*, ante n.3, pp. 88–93.
20. By NHIA 1928 compulsory insurance was extended to e.g., sub-contractors in the building and other trades.
 1. E.g., sickness benefit of 15s per week for men: NHIA 1920, s.2.

 2. By the Prolongation of Insurance Act 1926, and similar subsequent measures.
 3. Notably the Economy (Miscellaneous Provisions) Act 1926 reduced the State contribution from 2s 9d to 1s 7d.
 4. Cmd. 2591.
 5. NHIA 1928.
 6. The minority recommended the abolition of the Approved Societies and the transfer of their functions to local authorities.
 7. National Health Service Act 1946, implementing proposals in the White Paper (1944), Cmd. 6502.

services and of medicaments was extricated from the insurance scheme
and they were made freely available to all. Sickness benefit was brought
more into line with unemployment benefit: the rates were assimilated and
for the first time sick claimants were paid an allowance for dependants. At
the same time, though remaining ineligible for unemployment benefit, the
self-employed became entitled to sickness benefit. This was, however, a
controversial measure. At first it was thought to be too impracticable to
administer and in the original 1946 Bill there was a waiting-period of
twenty-four days for such persons. This was eventually removed[8] but the
price to be paid was an increase of 3d in the contributions demanded of the
self-employed. The Approved Societies were abolished and their functions
transferred to the newly created Ministry of National Insurance. Disablement benefit also disappeared and sickness benefit became payable for an
unlimited duration provided that the contribution requirements had been
satisfied. But the distinction between short-term and long-term incapacity
was not entirely eradicated: the contribution conditions became much
more stringent after a year's entitlement to benefit.[9] Indeed, the distinction was broadened in 1966 when earnings-related supplement was
introduced only for the first twenty-six weeks of incapacity.[10] This
important advance left unaffected those who had been incapable of work
for a longer period. The Labour administration of the late 1960s proposed,
as part of its National Superannuation scheme, an earnings-related
pension for such persons,[11] but the Bill lapsed. The succeeding Conservative government adopted an alternative strategy: the invalidity benefit
introduced in 1971[12] was in effect the standard flat-rate sickness benefit
plus a small allowance which varied according to the claimant's age at the
onset of incapacity and which was based on the assumed greater loss of
those giving up work at an earlier stage in their working life. The emphasis
on satisfying needs rather than providing earnings replacements was taken
further by certain complementary measures which rendered the conditions of invalidity benefit more favourable to the claimant than those of
sickness benefit: there was no reduction for contribution deficiencies;
higher increases were paid for dependent children;[13] and there was an
easier criterion of dependency for a working wife.[14]

During the 1960s the political background to provision for the disabled
had altered significantly. On the one hand, there had emerged some
powerful pressure groups,[15] concerned to bring to public attention the
plight of the disabled, to conduct inquiries and publish their findings, and
to campaign actively for reform. On the other hand, the 'rediscovery' of

8. See, esp. 423 HC Deb., cols. 350–364.
9. NIA 1946, s.12(2).
10. NIA 1966, s.2.
11. See White Paper, National
Superannuation and Social Insurance
(1969), Cmnd. 3883, para. 88, and the
Bill of the same name, cl. 12.
12. NIA 1971, s.3: post, pp. 163–167.
13. Post, p. 385.
14. Post, p. 387.

15. The most influential has probably been
the Disablement Income Group
formed in 1965. There is now a co-
ordinating organisation, the Disability
Alliance, which lists about 30
associations concerned with the welfare
of the disabled. See, generally, on
these movements Walker in ed. Jones
*Yearbook of Social Policy in Britain
1975*, pp. 204–207.

poverty in the 1960s had brought to light that disability featured prominently among the causes of deprivation and financial hardship.[16] Under the influence of these movements, the government sponsored in 1968–69 a massive survey of handicapped and impaired persons in Great Britain (OPCS Survey).[17] The findings largely confirmed the conjectures of those campaigning for more generous financial support. It was estimated that there were about three million 'impaired' persons, that is those lacking part or all of a limb, or having a defective organ or mechanism of the body, and that about 1,100,000 were 'handicapped' in the sense that they had difficulty in carrying out the normal functions of daily living.[18] A disturbingly high proportion (35–40%) of the 'handicapped' were in receipt of supplementary benefit, including 225,000 under pensionable age but incapable of work for more than six months, of whom 135,000 were not entitled to a contributory benefit.[19] Indeed it was estimated that a further 50,000 were entitled to, but did not, claim supplementary benefit.[20]

The first priority was to make better provision for the severely disabled.[1] Successive governments have so far remained unimpressed by the arguments[2] for a comprehensive income maintenance scheme according to the degree of disablement. Quite apart from economic considerations it is said that such a broad approach is oversimplified.

'No clear picture emerges of the "problem of disablement". There are, in fact, a number of different interlocking problems rather than one single problem. No simple analysis can be made and no single simple solution is appropriate. . . . There must be priorities. The greatest needs must be identified and met first on the basis of a sound programme of cash benefits and services which takes account both of the practical limitations of detailed assessments of need and of the choices expressed by disabled people themselves'.[3]

Efforts have therefore been directed at isolating specific needs and attempting to satisfy them with non-contributory benefits. One of the most significant findings of the OPCS Survey was the large number of persons 'handicapped' in the sense that they required assistance to cope with the normal functions of living.[4] The Labour administration had proposed to compensate the more severe cases within this group with their 'attendance allowance', included in the National Superannuation Bill of

16. See particularly Abel-Smith and Townsend *The Poor and the Poorest* (1965), p. 62.
17. The Report of the Survey by the Office of Population Censuses and Surveys was published in 3 volumes: Part One, Harris *Handicapped and Impaired in Great Britain* (1971); Part Two, Buckle *Work and Housing of Impaired Persons in Great Britain* (1971); Part Three, Harris, Smith and Head *Income and Entitlement to Supplementary Benefit of Impaired People in Great Britain* (1972).
18. *Harris*, ante n.17, at p. 18.
19. Report on Social Security Provision for Chronically Sick and Disabled People, 1973–74, HC, 276, at paras. 8 and 41.
20. *Harris, Smith and Head*, ante, n.17, at pp. 42–43.
1. Report on Social Security Provision, ante, n.19, at para. 54.
2. See particularly Disablement Income Group *Realising a Comprehensive Disability Income* (1975) and Disability Alliance *Poverty and Disability* (1975).
3. Report on Social Security Provision, ante n.19, at paras. 52–53.
4. *Harris*, ante n.17, at pp. 16–20.

1969,[5] and the succeeding Conservative government adopted this part of the programme. An allowance was introduced in 1970[6] for those requiring attention or supervision both during the day and at night, and two years later a lower-rate allowance was added to cover cases where the requisite attendance was required either during the day or at night.[7] The numbers claiming the higher rate exceeded expectations, but the response to the second of the two measures, though growing, has been somewhat less. The government has concluded from this that:

> 'There is no solid basis for a further extension of the allowance, designed, as it is, as an attendance-needs benefit. Further extension would produce a benefit for "disablement" as such rather than for attendance needs'.[8]

The argument is not altogether convincing. Low take-up can be explained on quite different grounds, not the least important of which may be the difficulties encountered in satisfying the statutory criterion.[9] What remained indisputable, however, was the need to assist those who sacrificed their own work opportunities to care for persons in receipt of attendance allowance. Quite apart from the justice of compensating a group who performed an unattractive and unpaid task, there was the economic consideration that by so doing they relieved the social services of additional burdens.[10] The resulting non-contributory invalid care allowance became payable in 1977.[11]

The dependence on supplementary benefit of many disabled persons resulted, of course, from their inability to satisfy the conditions for the contributory benefits: the majority of these had been disabled from birth, but there was also a substantial number who had not worked sufficiently to pay the requisite number of contributions.[12] In 1975 the non-contributory invalidity pension was introduced to cater for their group.[13] It became payable in circumstances similar to those of the contributory invalidity pension but without contribution conditions and (to achieve equity as compared with those who had contributed to the National Insurance Fund) at a lower rate.[14] At this level, it is not clear that the pension has fully achieved the desired objective of obviating recourse to the means-tested supplementary benefit, and there is a suspicion that those who had not been dependent on the latter profited most from the additional resources made available.[15]

5. National Superannuation and Social Insurance Bill 1969, cl. 17.
6. NI (Old persons' and widows and attendance allowance) Act 1970, renamed NIA 1970 by NIA 1972, s.8(4).
7. NIA 1970, s.2. See generally post, pp. 171–178.
8. Report on Social Security Provision, ante n.19, at para. 37.
9. See post, pp. 173–176; Carson 26

NILQ 291 and Baldwin in ed. *Jones*, ante n.15, at pp. 171, 184–191.
10. Report on Social Security Provision, ante n.19, at para. 54.
11. It was introduced by SSBA 1975, s.7. See generally post, pp. 179–183.
12. Report on Social Security Provision, ante n.19, at para. 24.
13. SSBA 1975, s.6.
14. Post, pp. 167–171.
15. *Walker*, ante n.15, at p. 201.

There were three other categories of disabled persons which attracted attention: the immobile, housewives, and children. Those unable to walk but able to drive had for some time been entitled to invalid carriages or, if they owned a car, to a private car allowance; but the disabled passenger was not assisted and the safety and reliability of the carriage had been subjected to considerable doubt.[16] Rather than switch entitlement to a small car, which would have involved a considerable increase in expenditure, the government decided to introduce, as an alternative to the invalid carriage, a cash allowance payable to adults of working age and children aged five and above who were unable, or virtually unable, to walk.[17] In 1976 the doubts regarding the safety of the carriage were confirmed and it was decided to phase it out of production.[18] The mobility allowance thus remains as the main form of assistance conferred on immobile persons.

Consideration of the disabled housewife featured prominently in the campaign conducted by the pressure groups.[19] The OPCS Survey revealed that there were some 225,000 housewives prevented by their disability from doing the household chores,[20] though of these only about one fifth were under pensionable age without entitlement to any personal benefit.[1] Married women not engaged in remunerative employment and those who had exercised the option to contract out[2] were not, of course, entitled to sickness or invalidity benefit. Although the married woman's option was prospectively abolished in 1975,[3] this still left many to whom the former rules still applied or who were not employed, and entitlement in any event depended on incapacity for paid employment. The need to provide financial assistance for those incapable of performing household duties was recognised but in 1974 the government declared that the problem had to be 'studied further' before it could be properly resolved.[4] Its hand was, however, forced by a defeat during the Committee stage of the Social Security Benefits Bill 1975:[5] women 'incapable of performing normal household duties' were to benefit from the new non-contributory invalidity pension.[6] Implementation of the extension was nevertheless delayed until the end of 1977.[7]

The chief difficulty posed by disabled children was that the extent of the problem was largely unknown. The OPCS Survey did not cover persons under sixteen, and such estimates as have been made of the number handicapped range from 80,000 to 350,000.[8] Moreover, as with the immobile, it was not clear whether the main effort should be directed at

16. See the government-sponsored Report by Lady Sharp, Mobility of Physically Disabled People (1974).
17. Introduced by SSPA 1975, s.22. See generally post, pp. 183–187.
18. Post, p. 184.
19. E.g., Disablement Income Group Creating a National Disability Income (1972), pp. 19–20.
20. Harris, see n.17 on p. 141, at pp. 63–91.
1. Report on Social Security Provision for Chronically Sick and Disabled People, 1973–74, HC, 276, at para. 43.
2. Cf. ante, p. 65.
3. Ante, p. 66.
4. Report on Social Security Provision, ante n.1, at para. 44.
5. Post, p. 167.
6. SSBA 1975, s.6.
7. Introduced by S.I. 1977/1311.
8. See Disability Alliance Poverty and Disability (1975), pp. 4–5; and Pearson, pp. 316–317.

improving facilities or granting cash allowances.[9] Attendance allowances had been payable for children aged two or more,[10] and those aged five and over were to become entitled to the mobility allowance. But it was the plight of the thalidomide children which prompted immediate government action. In 1973 a Family Fund established on a non-statutory basis[11] and administered by the Rowntree Memorial Trust was to confer benefits on severely disabled children. The government, which initially contributed £3 million, and has since continued to finance the scheme, indicated however that this was not intended as compensation for disablement, but rather to complement services already provided by statutory and voluntary bodies.[12]

The final measure in the series of reforms intended to ease the financial burden of the disabled was the long-delayed extension of the earnings-related addition to the contributory invalidity pension. This formed part of the new pensions scheme, the disabled person being, from 1 April 1979, entitled to an additional component calculated on the same basis as that payable under the new Category A retirement pension.[13]

In comparison with the system hitherto prevailing, these reforms of the 1970s might seem an impressive array of measures. The 1974 Report of the Secretary of State for Social Services, reviewing social security provision for chronically sick and disabled persons,[14] while not complacent about the nature of the problem, nevertheless regards the reforms described above as constituting a substantial step forward.[15] In general, this sentiment may be endorsed, particularly in relation to the long-term disabled, but there remain three fundamental features which should not escape criticism. In the first place, it continues to foster a number of alternative approaches – contributory, non-contributory, industrial injuries and war pensions – the differentials being easier to justify on historical and political grounds than in terms of a rational social policy.[16] The second criticism is not unconnected with the first. In the 1974 Report, the Secretary of State declared that there was a need 'to develop a comprehensive long-term strategy and coherent philosophy for meeting the needs of disabled people'.[17] It may be argued that this is exactly what is lacking in the present approach which vacillates between earnings-replacement, special needs and the degree of disablement as the criteria for the level of financial support. The answer to this may be that the legislation attempts to reflect the varying circumstances which affect disabled persons, but a more convincing explanation is that the system has developed piecemeal in response to particular political pressures and has

9. Report on Social Security Provision, ante n.1, at para. 45.
10. Post, pp. 177–178.
11. See the statement of Sir K. Joseph, Secretary of State, 847 HC Deb., cols. 446–447.
12. Written Answer, 848 HC Deb., cols. 241–242. The Family Fund does not come within the scope of this book. For an account of its workings, see Waddilove, in ed. Jones *Yearbook of Social Policy in Britain 1973*, pp. 203–220.
13. SSPA 1975, s.14, and post, p. 165.
14. Report on Social Security Provision, ante n.1.
15. Ibid., at para. 6.
16. Cf. *Pearson*, pp. 65–66.
17. Report on Social Security Provision, ante n.1, at para. 3.

been unwilling to uproot traditional and often outdated methods. Finally, despite the recent reforms, there is the continuous and almost exclusive concentration on total incapacity for work as the criterion for income-replacement. Quite apart from those who are not in regular paid employment – the recent admission of housewives to the non-contributory invalidity pension is a welcome step – there is a large group of disabled individuals who manage to work full-time or part-time but who, as a result of their condition, suffer substantial losses to their earning capacity. Britain is one of the few member states of the EEC offering no assistance for permanent partial incapacity which does not result from an industrial accident or disease.[18]

C. Definitions of disability

To a large extent the law governing entitlement to the various benefits, contributory and non-contributory, for sickness and disability is con-cerned with definitions. It might, therefore, be convenient to precede the analysis of the relevant provisions with a short account of the problems involved in assessing and defining disability.

The first is simply a question of terminology. There is, as yet, no consistency in the use of terms in this area. For the sake of clarity it is proposed in this work primarily to accept the current usage of the DHSS.[19]

'Disability' – a blanket term used to describe any form of physical and mental impairment.

'Disablement' – such physical or mental impairment as entails measureable repercussions.

'Invalidity' – chronic sickness or, more particularly, an incapacity for work lasting more than six months.

'Incapacity' – a term used in specific contexts to refer to the indivi-dual's inability to perform certain functions. Most typically these will be in connection with remunerative employment.

'Impairment' – a condition in which the individual lacks part or all of a limb or has a defective organ or mechanism of the body, whether or not the condition involves functional consequences.

'Handicap' – the disadvantage or restriction of activity caused by impairment serious enough to limit functional ability.

18. *Kaim-Caudle*, pp. 192–193; Disablement Income Group *Social Security and Disability* (1971); Commission of the European Communities *Comparative Tables of the Social Security Systems* (9th edn), Table VI. See also *Pearson*, pp. 177–178.

19. Report on Social Security Provision, ante n.1, at para. 7. The usage to a large extent reflects that employed in the OPCS Survey, see n.17 on p. 141.

Broadly speaking, the legislation adopts five different criteria of disability:

1. 'Incapacity for work'[20] – used for the purposes of sickness, invalidity (contributory or non-contributory) and industrial injury benefits.

2. 'Incapable of performing normal household duties'[1] – the new form of non-contributory invalidity pension introduced for disabled housewives in 1977.

3. Requiring 'attention' and 'supervision' from another person[2] – a test devised for attendance allowance.

4. 'Inability or virtual inability to walk'[3] – for the purposes of mobility allowance.

5. 'Degree of disablement'[4] – the extent of impairment, typically based on prescribed physical conditions, for the purposes of the industrial disablement pension.

The problem of finding appropriate criteria for disability is one that has, in recent years, been of great concern to sociologists and others attempting to establish the extent of need within the community, and the appropriate methods of coping with it.[5] A glance at the criteria listed above reveals that, with the exception of the anatomical/clinical test used for the purposes of the industrial disablement pension, they are primarily *functional*, that is, they are concerned not with the physical degree of disablement but rather its effect on the life (particularly working life) of the person in question. This is, indeed, in line with much of the current theory on this subject. Any attempt to define disability by a clinical comparison to the ideal healthy man, or the reasonably healthy man on the Clapham omnibus, is doomed to failure.[6] Nevertheless attention may be drawn to some limitations inherent in the criteria as adopted by our social security system. First, (and this is only to repeat a point made in the last section) there is very great emphasis on the incapacity to undertake remunerative employment. This is because inability to earn remains the most substantial and most typical form of financial loss. But in terms of social costs it might not always be the most decisive or appropriate criterion. It is argued that regard should be had not only to such activities as self-care, mobility, and performing household duties (to a lesser or greater extent recently adopted within the system) but also to establishing and maintaining relationships both within and outside the family.[7] Secondly, there is the degree of functional disability. Most of the definitions adopted assume an either/or dichotomy – the claimant is either

20. Post, pp. 149–156.
1. Post, p. 169.
2. Post, pp. 173–176.
3. Post, p. 185.
4. Post, pp. 308–314.
5. See, particularly: Townsend *The Disabled in Society* (1967); Blaxter *The Meaning of Disability* (1967); Sainsbury *Registered as Disabled* (1970); Nagi *Disability and the Severely Disabled: Concepts and Prevalence* (1975).
6. Forder *Concepts in Social Administration* (1974), pp. 42–43.
7. *Blaxter*, ante n.5, chap. 8; *Sainsbury*, ante n.5, at pp. 26–27.

able to perform the function in question, or he is not. It is important to recognise that generally there is a scale of difficulty with which the function can be undertaken – from being able to perform it only with very great difficulty through to performance with only moderate difficulty – and the condition may be progressive or fluctuating.[8] This point assumes some significance once it is appreciated that pain, as such, is not a quantifiable matter, and its existence must to a certain extent depend on self perception.[9] This has implications both for the method of establishing incapacity,[10] and for the delicate question of avoiding disincentives to work.[11] Thirdly, there is the problem of assessment and adjudication. Though the precise impact of medical evidence and opinions varies according to the benefit in question,[12] it is clear that in practice and for most purposes the views of the medical profession, either in the form of medical statements by general practitioners, or of examination by Medical Officers, Medical Boards or Medical Appeal Tribunals, are regarded as decisive, if not conclusive. The difficulty with this is that it assumes that medical practitioners are in a better qualified position to decide not only clinical questions relating to the degree of impairment, but also on the effects which that impairment has on the life of the individual. This has prompted some to argue for a more flexible method of determining incapacity, for example, by the participation of social workers.[13] The present position doubtless reflects existing opinions about the 'reliability' and 'status' of the medical as opposed to the social work professions. A move from the objective 'medical' to the subjective 'social' definition of disability would clearly require a major readjustment not only of the legislation itself but also of the method of adjudication. It would also necessarily confer a much wider degree of discretion than exists at present (with a consequent increase of administrative costs), and this might, in turn, provoke feelings of injustice and resentment which those arguing for reform are keen to eliminate. The conferring of a broad discretion on social workers within the field of child care[14] has created a considerable amount of controversy.[15]

Part two. Sickness Benefit

A. General

The income maintenance of those who are unable to work because they are sick remains one of the cardinal purposes of a social security system. Its importance may be gauged from the fact that in 1974–75 there were over

8. *Sainsbury*, ibid., at pp. 37–41.
9. Nagi, 38 Ind. Medicine and Surgery 27; *Blaxter*, ante n.5, at pp. 11–13.
10. Post, pp. 152–155.
11. Post, p. 148 and see Nagi and Hadley, 25 Ind. Lab. Relations Rev. 223.
12. See generally post, pp. 152–155 and 306–308.

13. *Townsend*, ante n.5, at pp. 5–6 and *Blaxter*, ante n.5, at pp. 6–7.
14. Especially under the Children Act 1975, s.2.
15. Cf. *Re T (A.J.J.) (An Infant)* [1970] Ch. 688, [1970] 2 All ER 865, CA, noted by Cretney, 33 MLR 696.

300 million recorded days of incapacity in connection with claims to benefit.[16]

It might have been assumed that the improvement in medical facilities and techniques over past decades, in particular that resulting from the introduction of the National Health Service, would have led to an overall improvement in the health of the community and consequently to a diminishing reliance on sickness benefit.[17] In fact, the contrary has occurred. Absence for sickness has shown a steady increase over a number of years.[18] The inference has been drawn that payment of sickness benefit (with its earnings-related supplement) has encouraged 'absenteeism'.[19] But this is an over-simplification. Correlation between the value of benefit and the level of incapacity is at best very imprecise. Of course, it is to some extent natural that when the rate of sickness benefit is increased the rate of absence should also rise, because a person who on grounds on health *should* have stayed at home, but could not afford to, may now do so.[20] It has been suggested that recent increases in the sickness rate may be accounted for by growing problems of job dissatisfaction,[1] but some small part might be attributable to changing attitudes in the medical profession.[2] Minor ill-health, including psychological disorder, may no longer be ignored in the way it was.[3]

Indeed, the primary legal problem arising in connection with sickness benefit is that concerned with the medical control and administration of claims. On the one hand, there are the principles for determining what amounts to 'incapable of work' which combine difficult questions of theory and medical practice.[4] On the other hand, there is the system of medical certification which has undergone several important changes in recent years.[5] To a certain extent these reflect the growing awareness that ill-health and incapacity are difficult to define and are not always susceptible to objective verification: willingness to work must in the last resort depend on a claimant's own personal decision.[6]

There is another aspect of the system which has not received the attention it deserves[7] and which may well affect work-incentive or the lack of it. In principle, an employee who satisfies the various conditions of entitlement may receive benefit whether or not he receives sick pay from

16. Social Security Statistics 1976, Table 3.70; and the number of total days lost must be considerably higher since the statistics do not record the sickness of those uninsured, nor periods of absence of less than 4 days.
17. This formed the basis of one of the arguments used for a National Health Service: Ross *The National Health Service in Great Britain* (1952), p. 15.
18. *George*, pp. 115–117, though more recently there has been a levelling-off: ante n.16, Table 3.71.
19. CBI *Absenteeism* (1970).
20. *Kaim-Caudle*, p. 105; ed. Reid and Robertson *Fringe Benefits, Labour Costs and Social Security* (1965), pp. 224–226.

1. Taylor, 25 Brit. Jo. of Ind. Medicine 106.
2. This had been foreseen by the Government Actuary in 1946: Report on the Financial Provisions of the NI Bill 1946, Cmd. 6730, Appendix, para. 15.
3. Office of Health Economics *Work Lost Through Sickness* (1975), p. 27.
4. Post, pp. 150–152.
5. Post, pp. 152–156.
6. *Kaim-Caudle*, p. 106.
7. Cf. *Reid and Robertson*, ante n.20, and Office of Health Economics *Off Sick* (1971), p. 15.

his employer.[8] Title to benefit depends on physical or mental incapacity and, though benefit may be refused if the claimant does work, his financial position is ignored even to the extent of disregarding the continued receipt of wages while he is not working. Now the coverage of sick-pay schemes is wide indeed – in 1971 it was estimated that 72% of male employees and 67% of female employees were parties to such schemes.[9] It is true that there is a wide diversity of arrangements, and the receipt of benefit is taken into account in many cases. It is, for example, common for the employer to make it up to a stated percentage of the employee's normal earnings.[10] But this is by no means universally true: it is not unknown for full wages to be paid without deduction for sickness benefit, and in any event the benefit itself is not taxable. No doubt, taking into account lost bonuses and overtime, this achieved a sort of rough justice, especially at a time when sickness benefit was flat-rate only.[11] But there is now a very strong case for a reappraisal of the interrelationship between private and public benefit, as has been done in recent years with retirement pensions.[12] The present position contrasts very strangely with unemployment benefit where the continued receipt of wages disentitles the claimant.[13] One solution, therefore, would be to adopt the principle prevailing there, that title to benefit should depend on the non-receipt of remuneration. Another would be the more radical step of compulsorily shifting the burden of insurance for short periods of sickness completely to the employer. This is the German system: employers are required to pay full wages during a period of incapacity of up to six weeks.[14]

To qualify for benefit, the claimant must show that he has satisfied the contribution requirements (section B), that the days for which the claim was made were days of 'incapacity for work' (section C). Conversely, there are grounds on which he may be disqualified from benefit (section D).

B. Contribution conditions

The contribution conditions for sickness benefit are the same as those for unemployment benefit,[15] with one major exception: Class 2 contributions qualify.[16]

C. Incapable for work

Sickness benefit is payable in respect of 'a day of incapacity for work'.[17]

8. Post, p. 158.
9. [1971] Dept. of Employment Gazette, 690.
10. *Reid and Robertson*, ante, n.20, at p. 217; *Pearson*, para. 166.
11. Ibid., at pp. 228–229.
12. Post, pp. 194–195.
13. Ante, p. 87.
14. *Gesetz über die Fortzahlung des Arbeitengelts in Krankheitsfälle, 1969,* art. 1. See also *Reid and Robertson,* ante n.20, at p. 238.
15. Ante, p. 82.
16. SSA 1975, s.13(1).
17. SSA 1975, s.14(1)(b). For the rules determining which days qualify, see post, pp. 156–158.

A day is not so regarded unless

> 'on that day (the claimant) is, or is deemed ... to be, incapable of
> work by reason of some specific disease or bodily or mental
> disablement'.[18]

This definition of incapacity is a long-standing one in social security law.[19]
It places the onus of proof on the claimant.[20]

i) Some specific disease or bodily or mental disablement

Whether the claimant comes within the statutory definition of incapacity is
a question of fact[1] for which resort must be had to expect medical opinion.
While it is impossible to state a general scientific criterion which will
resolve the problem in all cases, certain fundamental guidelines do emerge
from the reported decisions. A disease has been defined as 'a departure
from health capable of identification by its signs and symptoms, an
abnormality of some sort'.[2] Incapacity resulting from pregnancy has
caused some difficulty. Pregancy itself does not come within the above
definition, and the legislation makes provision for this condition through
maternity benefit.[3] Under earlier legislation, a woman entitled to the latter
could not draw sickness benefit for the first four weeks following her
confinement.[4] This provision was repealed in 1966,[5] but without indicating under what conditions a woman in such circumstances might qualify.
Certainly she should be entitled on proof of a physical or mental disablement resulting from, but going beyond the ordinary incidents of, pregnancy.[6]

As medical science has shown greater awareness of different types of
psychological disorder, so there has been a natural tendency to extend the
certification for 'mental disablement'.[7] Any condition which incapacitates
a claimant from work and which is accepted as such in a doctor's statement
should be sufficient.[8] But the legislation must necessarily assume some
principle of moral responsibility, or 'work-shy' persons might claim to be
mentally disabled. Of course, the distinction between a 'disease' and a
'defect of character' is sometimes very difficult to draw. In *R(S) 6/59*

> C manifested the symptoms of Munchausen's syndrome, a condition
> under which a person habitually presents himself at hospital for the
> treatment of an apparently acute illness, giving particulars of a
> physical disability, which does not in fact exist.[9] The Commissioner
> decided that he was not incapable on the grounds, first that the
> condition did not itself affect his capacity to work – a surprising view
> to take – and, secondly, that it was in any case a defect of character

18. SSA 1975, s.17(1)(a)(ii).
19. See e.g., NIA 1911, s.8(1)(c).
20. R(S) 13/52.
1. R(S) 7/53.
2. CS 221/49, para. 3.
3. Post, chap. 7.
4. NIA 1965, s.19(7).
5. NIA 1966, s.3(3).
6. CS 221/49.
7. Cf. ante, p. 148.
8. R(S) 4/56.
9. Dorland *Medical Dictionary* (24th edn), p. 1490.

rather than a disease – a plausible view but one necessarily involving some value judgment as to responsibility.

The disability must be the substantial cause of the incapacity for work. Factors extraneous to the physical or mental condition, such as the personal or domestic circumstances of the claimant, are thus irrelevant.[10] A person with limited mobility who, as a result of the weather, cannot get to his normal place of work may not draw benefit.[11]

ii) Incapable of work

The disease or disablement must render the claimant incapable of work. If taken absolutely literally this would exclude a large proportion of claims, for there are many conditions of disablement in which a person is nevertheless capable of doing *some* kind of remunerative work. The difficulty was appreciated as long ago as 1914[12] and it was, presumably, only that the relevant authorities did not construe the provision literally that delayed amendment until 1973. In that year, the type of work of which the claimant must be incapable was limited to 'work which (he) can reasonably be expected to do'.[13] Nevertheless, the amendment was intended only to restate the traditional interpretation of the statutory test.[14] It is not sufficient for the claimant to show that he is no longer capable of his normal occupation, unless in the circumstances this is the only work which it is reasonable for him to undertake. In determining this question regard is had to the claimant's age, education, training, state of health and other personal factors.[15] A man may not normally be expected to embark on a new career if he is suffering from only a temporary disablement, but if it is likely to be prolonged he might reasonably acquire the techniques for other kinds of work.[16] In practice, during the first six months of indisposition the Department will generally demand no more than that the claimant is incapable of following his usual occupation. Once that period has elapsed inquiries will be made as to his fitness for any kind of work.[17] It is, moreover, in principle irrelevant that there is no work for which the claimant is admittedly capable available in the locality or that the prospects of finding such work are poor.[18] This may clearly operate harshly, but it is limited only by a ruling that if *no* prospects for the work in question exist this may itself render that type of work unreasonable for the claimant.[19] The particular work may be only part-time, provided always that it is 'remunerative work . . . for which an employer would be willing to

---

10. *R(S) 13/54.*
11. *R(S) 8/53*; 2/58 (SB).
12. Report of the Departmental Committee on Sickness Benefit Claims under the National Insurance Act (1914), Cd. 7687, paras. 110–113.
13. NISBA 1973, s.5(1), (3), now incorporated in SSA 1975, s.17(1)(a).
14. It was felt to be necessary as a result of the confusion created by a more liberal interpretation given by Bean J in *Chesterfield Football Club v Secretary*

of State for Social Services [1973] QB 583, [1973] 1 All ER 679 to an analogous question arising under the contribution provisions. See Sir K. Joseph, Secretary of State, introducing the 2nd reading of the 1973 Bill, 855 HC Deb., col. 811.
15. *CS 320/50.*
16. *R(S) 7/60.*
17. *Fisher*, Appendix 7, paras. 6–7.
18. *R(S) 21/51*; *R(S) 24/51*.
19. *R(S) 17/51*; *R(S) 10/54*.

pay, or work as a self-employed person in some gainful occupation'.[20]

These principles have been applied to two factual situations which have provoked some difficulties. A housewife may have given up her normal job as a result of illness but she may have continued to do the housework at home. A Tribunal of Commissioners has held that if she does the work of a normal household this is prima facie evidence that she is capable of doing the same work for remuneration and thus is excluded from benefit.[1] However, it may be rebutted if the only duties she performs are 'light', e.g., the purchase and preparation of food.[2] More problematic are the cases of self-employed persons who are capable of doing some form of management or supervision of their own business. A large number of reported decisions have been concerned with this issue,[3] and it is obviously difficult to draw the line between an active manager and a mere onlooker. Perhaps the greatest assistance is to be had from the approach suggested by a Northern Ireland Commissioner.[4] According to him, the question is whether the work which the claimant is capable of doing is of such substance or extent as either (1) would be likely to command remuneration if it was carried out for an outside employer, or (2) materially affected the day-to-day carrying on of the business. To determine these points regard may be had to, e.g., the size and ownership of the business, the nature of accounting and drawing of profits, and whether there was a change of personnel consequent on the claimant's disability.

iii) Evidence of incapacity

The Medical Evidence Regulations provide that evidence of incapacity shall be furnished by the claimant either

> 'by such other means as may be sufficient in the circumstances of given by a doctor'

in the manner prescribed by the Regulations, or

> 'by such other means as may be sufficient in the circumstance of any particular case'.[5]

The alternative, unprescribed method is designed to cater for those, particularly Christian Scientists, who on grounds of conscience prefer not to attend for medical treatment,[6] but it is far from clear what sort of evidence will in such circumstances satisfy the authorities. In one case an acknowledgement by an employer of the claimant's incapacity was regarded as insufficient.[7] On the other hand, the fact of hospitalization will raise a presumption of incapacity and this remains true even where after investigation the claimant is found not to be suffering from the suspected disease.[8]

20. R(S) 11/51, para. 5 (Tribunal decision).
1. R(S) 11/51.
2. R 3/60 (SB).
3. See, inter alia, R(S) 5/51; R(S) 22/51; 4/52 (SB); 8/52 (SB); R(S) 2/61. See also the cases considered post, pp. 202-204.

4. 5/57 (SB), para. 3.
5. S.I. 1976/615, Reg. 2(1).
6. See Report of the National Insurance Advisory Committee on the draft regulations 1975-76, HC 349, para. 32.
7. R(S) 13/51.
8. R(S) 1/58.

The normal method, the prescribed form of certification by the claimant's general practitioner, has undergone several changes since its formulation in 1948,[9] the most important being in 1976 as a result of representations made by the British Medical Association and recommendations of the Fisher Committee on Abuse of Social Security.[10] The previous practice according to which the doctor 'certified' that in his opinion the patient was incapable of work at the time of examination[11] has been replaced by a statement that he advises the patient to refrain from work.[12] The National Insurance Advisory Committee has doubted whether the change will be of much practical significance[13] but the medical profession regards the new formulation as a more accurate reflection of the clinical responsibility towards the patient.[14] The other rules may be summarised briefly.

> The statement must contain a diagnosis of the claimant's disorder justifying the advice to refrain from work.[15] Where the doctor is of the opinion that work may be resumed within a period of two weeks, he is to issue a 'closed' statement, that is, one specifying the date when the claimant should be fit to resume.[16] In other cases it will be an 'open' statement, the doctor merely indicating the minimum period during which the patient should abstain from work.[17] This should not be a period greater than six months, unless (for the purposes of invalidity benefit) the claimant has already, on the advice of the doctor, refrained from work for six months.[18] In such a case, if it is his opinion that work should not be resumed for the foreseeable future, the doctor will simply enter 'until further notice'.[19] Where a claimant has been the subject of an 'open' statement but nevertheless becomes fit to resume work, the doctor should issue a 'closed' statement to that effect.[20] In such cases, where there are no longer any clinical signs of the previously disabling disorder, the doctor need not specify a diagnosis.[1]

Normally medical statements in the above form will be regarded by the Department as sufficient proof of incapacity. But in certain situations, for example, where the period of incapacity has been longer than originally anticipated, or where repeated short-term claims have been received, and where the claimant has been on holiday or on strike,[2] the Department is likely to take steps to verify the claimant's condition, either by a reference to its own Regional Medical Officer, or by an officer visiting the claimant

9. See S.I. 1948/1175.
10. *Fisher*, paras 201, 213–216.
11. See S.I. 1967/520 as amended by S.I. 1974/416.
12. S.I. 1976/615, Sch. 1, Part III.
13. Ante n.6, at para. 9.
14. Ibid., para. 6 and see *Fisher*, para. 187.
15. S.I. 1976/615, Sch. 1, Rule 6, though where disclosure would be prejudicial to the patient's well-being the diagnosis may be specified less precisely: ibid., Rule 7.
16. Ibid., Rule 10.
17. Ibid., Rule 11.
18. Ibid., Rule 12, extending the previous maximum period of 13 weeks: see NIAC Report, ante n.6, at paras 22–26.
19. S.I. 1976/615, Sch. 1, Rule 13.
20. Ibid., Rule 10.
1. Ibid., Rule 8.
2. *Fisher*, Appendix 7.

in his home.[3] The usual practice[4] in the former case is to advise the claimant to see his own doctor for an examination, and then to present himself for a further examination by the Medical Officer. The latter's opinion is then communicated to the claimant's doctor who thus has an opportunity to disagree, stating his own views. Should a conflict of opinion remain unresolved, it is the duty of the determining authorities to examine all the evidence and form their own view. They are in no sense bound to prefer the Medical Officer's opinion. Indeed, in several cases, the Commissioner has rejected his evidence.[5] Conversely, the medical statement by the claimant's own doctor is in no sense conclusive, and it may be over-ridden even where the conflicting evidence is of a non-medical character, such as the cases where a claimant allegedly disabled by influenza could not be found at home[6] or another supposed to be suffering from a sprained ligament was seen cycling.[7] If the authorities are dissatisfied as to the evidence produced by either side they may, if they think it advisable, order a further examination, perhaps by a specialist.[8]

In adverting to all relevant information available, the authorities may take into account the claimant's past medical and employment record. This may reveal a pattern which gives rise to a suspicion of malingering. In several cases, for example, the claimant's record has shown a number of claims for short periods near public holidays.[9] This by itself is not neces-sarily prejudicial to his case, but if it is supported by other factors which cast doubt on his doctor's statement, it may serve to disentitle him from benefit.[10] Of course, it would be quite wrong to use a long-term record of bad health as evidence *against* the claimant. Unless, therefore, there are additional facts which render the evidence suspect, it may help him to prove that he is incapable of work, especially if there is a seasonal cycle in his record of illness.[11]

The processes involved in validating incapacity for work are complex and have inevitably given rise to criticisms.[12] It is evident that notwith-standing the recent reforms to accommodate its objections, the medical profession is unenthusiastic about its role as supervisor of claims.[13] It is regarded as a time-wasting activity, and one that interferes with the doctor–patient relationship, particularly where the alleged illness is not accompanied by physical manifestations and where the medical statement is little more that 'the written expression of the doctor's opinion on his patient's veracity'.[14] That reference to Regional Medical Officers is an essential complement to the system may perhaps be demonstrated by the fact that about 24% of those invited to attend for examination do not keep

3. *Fisher*, Appendix 7. There is a power to disqualify the claimant should he fail to co-operate: post, p. 161.
4. See *R(S) 7/53*.
5. E.g., *R(S) 15/54* ; *30/58 (SB)*.
6. *R(S) 16/54*.
7. *3/59 (SB)*.
8. This is particularly true of psychiatric illnesses: e.g., *R(S) 4/56*.
9. *R(S) 16/54* ; *R(S) 5/60* ; *R(S) 1/67* ; *R(S) 15/55*.
10. *R(S) 4/60*.
11. *4/59 (SB)* ; *R(S) 1/67*.
12. Sainsbury *Measuring Disability* (1973), *pp.* 14–15, *Fisher*, paras. 185–194.
13. Ibid., at paras. 186–188.
14. Ibid., at para. 187.

their appointment.[15] But, as the Fisher Committee concluded, the proposal that control of sickness claims should take place wholly within the administration of the DHSS was an unrealistic one, particularly in the light of the scarcity of manpower and the difficulty of attracting suitably qualified persons to what would be a rather tedious occupation.[16] Nor was it impressed by the system adopted in Sweden[17] whereby the claimant certified himself as incapable for a limited period: this had apparently led to an increase in the number of claims for short periods of illness; and it was doubtful if it would be politically acceptable in this country.[18]

iv) Deemed incapable

A person may not be 'incapable of work' within the principles described above, and yet medical opinion may consider it advisable for him to stay at home on the grounds of the risk either to his own personal health, or to that of his fellow employees. There is special provision to resolve this problem, but the conditions which the claimant must satisfy to qualify for benefit are tightly drawn. He must prove *either* (a)

'(i) he is under medical care in respect of a disease or disablement . . . (and)

(ii) it is certified by a registered medical practitioner that by reason of such disease or disablement he should abstain from work, and

(iii) he does no work.'

or (b)

'he is excluded from work on the certificate of a Medical Officer for Environmental Health and is under medical observation by reason of his being a carrier, or having been in contact with a case, of infectious disease'.[19]

Alternative (b) covers the case where the claimant represents a risk to others working at his place of employment. But the mere advice of a doctor is insufficient. A certificate of exclusion has to be issued by a Medical Officer for Environmental Health.[20] Alternative (a) is drafted in broader terms and leaves much more to the judgment of the claimant's doctor as to whether he should abstain from work. It does not appear that the doctor has to give any reasons for a decision he takes. On one view, the Regulation is limited to assisting those who already suffer from a disease or disable-

15. Social Security Statistics 1976, Table 3.24. Another 9% were considered by the RMO not to be incapable of work.
16. *Fisher*, para. 198.
17. Ibid., at para. 197. Details of the system are given in Appendix 9.
18. *Fisher*, para. 200. On self-certification generally, see Taylor, [1969] British Medical Jo. 144.
19. S.I. 1975/564, Reg. 3(1).
20. The facts in *R(S) 1/72* indicate that this may not readily be granted. In that case, the medical officer of the local authority (the predecessor of the Medical Officer for Environmental Health) was advised that he might not give the certificate unless the infectious disease in question was a 'notifiable' disease, e.g., smallpox. D. Neligan, Comr., doubted this narrow interpretation of the regulation: ibid., at para. 14.

ment. In *R(S) 24/54* the Commissioner held that in consequence a pregnant woman who was advised by her doctor not to attend her place of work because she would come into contact there with an outbreak of measles could not succeed. This interpretation has not been followed in subsequent cases. It is argued that to be 'under medical care in respect of a disease', it is unnecessary for the patient actually to have contracted the disease, provided he was receiving medical treatment for it. In *R(S) 8/61* and *R(S) 1/72* the respective claimants had been in contact with the disease though it was not yet clear whether they had contracted it. It was held that they were entitled to benefit. 'Under medical care', moreover, does not imply the receipt of daily medical treatment – a possible but harsh interpretation. It is to be given the wider meaning of 'being treated by a doctor and seen by him at intervals'.[1]

v) Exclusion of certain days of incapacity

Benefit is payable for any day of incapacity which forms part of a period of interruption of employment[2] but this is subject to certain exceptions. For the most part, they correspond almost exactly with the equivalent provisions on unemployment benefit to which reference should be made.[3] Here it is intended to concentrate on those rules which are peculiar to sickness benefit.

a) NOT FIRST THREE DAYS. As with unemployment, benefit is not payable for the first three days,[4] and the policy considerations are similar: the rule discourages malingering; the administrative costs of paying benefit for such short periods are disproportionately high; it is difficult to verify the validity of claims; generally the sick person will have sufficient means to tide himself over three days of lost wages.[5] Even if such arguments are not regarded as conclusive, there is a strong case for shifting the onus of maintaining the income of those off sick for three days or less onto the employer rather than the National Insurance Fund, an obligation in fact incorporated in many contracts of employment but not yet compulsory.[6] Again as with unemployment benefit, the problem of coping with waiting-periods when the claimant is subject to intermittent periods of sickness is overcome by the continuity and linking rules. The waiting-period of three days must be served only at the beginning of a 'period of interruption of employment'. Such a period exists when the claimant is disabled for any two days (consecutive or not) within a period of six consecutive days, and any two such periods not separated by a period of more than thirteen weeks is treated as one period of interruption of employment.[7]

b) NOT AFTER 168 DAYS. Sickness benefit for any *one* period of inter-

1. *R(S) 8/61*, para. 17.
2. SSA 1975, s.14(1)(b).
3. Ante, pp. 90–92.
4. SSA 1975, s.14(3).
5. *Kaim-Caudle*, p. 113. A waiting period of between 2 and 6 days exists in most sickness insurance schemes (though not in Germany). The ILO Convention on

Medical Care and Sickness Benefit 1969, art. 26, prescribes a maximum period of 3 days. Prior to 1971 those incapable for more than 12 days could retrospectively claim for the waiting-days. See ante, p. 92.
6. Cf. ante, p. 149.
7. SSA 1975, s.17(1)(d).

ruption of employment cannot exceed 168 days.[8] Once this period has elapsed the claimant who continues to be incapable of work qualifies automatically for invalidity benefit.[9]

c) NOT SUNDAY (OR ITS SUBSTITUTE) OR PART OF A DAY. Benefit cannot be claimed for Sunday, or a rest day normally substituted for Sunday.[10] Nor is it payable where incapacity deprives the claimant of only part of a working day.[11] The position is the same as for unemployment benefit.[12] If, in accordance with the night-workers' Regulation,[13] a person working through midnight is deemed to work only on the second of the two days concerned, and if he is sick on the day *immediately preceding* the first of those two days, he may nevertheless claim benefit for the first of the two days.[14]

d) NOT A DAY WHEN CLAIMANT DOES ANY WORK. A claimant who, though regarded as 'incapable of work', nevertheless does some work will not, with certain exceptions, qualify for benefit.[15] Of course, the work must be something more than trivial and of a kind which would normally earn remuneration.[16] On these questions the Commissioner has adopted an approach identical to that applied to the question whether the fact that a claimant has been doing work negatives his being 'incapable of work', the primary test of entitlement.[17] Indeed, there has been such an overlap between the two issues that it may be, and has been, argued that it is no longer necessary to distinguish between them:[18] if it has been held that a man is 'incapable of work', he cannot *a fortiori* do 'any work' so as to disentitle him from benefit. But this fails to account for the possibility that a claimant may do work which he was not reasonably expected to do. In such circumstances there is no good reason why he should retain his right to benefit.[19]

There is a proviso to the rule. The authorities are to disregard *either*

> 'work which is undertaken under medical supervision as part of his treatment while he is a patient in or of a hospital or similar institution'

or

> 'work which is not so undertaken and which he has good cause for doing'

and

> 'from which, in the case of work of either description, his earnings, if any, are ordinarily not more than £10·00 a week'.[20]

8. SAA 1975, s.15(1).
9. Post, p. 165.
10. SSA 1975, s.17(1)(e).
11. See, e.g., R(S) 7/52.
12. Ante, p. 90.
13. Ante, p. 91.
14. S.I. 1975/564, Reg. 5(3).
15. Ibid., Reg. 7(1)(g).
16. R(S)25/52 and see ante, p. 84 and

post, pp. 427–430.
17. Ante, pp. 151–152, and CS 499/50; R(S) 24/52; R(S) 34/52; R(S) 37/52; R(S) 10/67.
18. R(S) 5/57.
19. R(S) 5/53.
20. S.I. 1975/564, Reg. 7(1)(g), as amended by S.I. 1977/1362, Reg. 3.

The first category of excepted work is not broad. It was introduced in 1948 as an incentive to rehabilitation, but the proposal to extend it to cover all therapeutic work undertaken under medical advice[1] was rejected. The claimant must be a patient of the institution in question, though he need not be a resident. Thus in *R(S) 3/52*,

> C, suffering from tuberculosis, was engaged for two and a half days a week in a factory specially operated for the rehabilitation of tuberculosis victims. He attended hospital as an out-patient once every two months. It was held that he was a patient 'of' (though not 'in') a hospital.

The rule on hospitalization, at least as interpreted, is a very artificial one. If, in the last case, the claimant had been under the supervision of a specialist rather than of a hospital he would not have succeeded.[2]

The second and alternative category of excusable work is much vaguer. It used to apply only to work undertaken as a 'non-employed' person,[3] but this limitation no longer obtains. Nor need the claimant show that the work was undertaken under medical supervision, but 'good cause' for doing the work must be proved. The decisions offer no guidance on how the phrase is to be interpreted in this context, but the intention was that the claimant must show not only that, in the light of medical evidence, the work was beneficial to him, but also, having regard to such factors as the nature, duration and intensity of the work, that it was reasonable for him to undertake it.[4] In truth, it appears to be a typical residuary clause which allows the authorities to ignore certain 'odd jobs' which in terms of remuneration are insignificant and which have medical approval as serving to rehabilitate the claimant.

What if there is evidence that the claimant did some work which was not excepted but the precise days of work cannot be ascertained? The Commissioner has held that in such circumstances the authorities must estimate the number of days for which the claimant is excluded from benefit as best they can.[5] However, it is very important to appreciate that the ground for disentitlement is not the number of days for which the claimant received wages, or other form of remuneration, but the number of days on which he worked. In sharp contrast to unemployment benefit, no account is taken of sick pay or wages payable to an employee during a period of incapacity.[6]

---

1. See the Report of the National Insurance Advisory Committee on the Draft Unemployment and Sickness Benefit Regulations, 1947–48, HC 141.
2. See, e.g., *R(S) 5/52*.
3. Cf. S.I. 1967/330, Reg. 7(h).
4. Report of the National Insurance Advisory Committee on the Question of Long-Term Hospital Patients (1960), Cmd. 964.
5. *R(S) 9/53*.
6. Though if, under an occupational scheme, the sick pay is reduced by the amount received by way of benefit, an arrangement may be made whereby the employee is given the sick pay unabated and the occupational fund is reimbursed by the National Insurance Fund: SSA 1975, s.92.

D. Disqualification

As with unemployment, there are certain grounds on which the claimant may be disqualified from benefit for a maximum period of six weeks. The underlying purposes of these provisions are threefold: to protect the Fund against fraudulent claims; to exclude from benefit those who are incapacitated or remain incapacitated as a result of their own deliberate conduct; and to reinforce the machinery for the control and administration of the system.

i) Misconduct

The first ground is where the claimant has 'become incapable of work through his own misconduct'.[7] Under the old National Health Insurance Acts,[8] an Approved Society might, in accordance with its own rules and subject to the approval of the Minister, suspend an insured person from benefit for misconduct.[9] The principle was derived from and analogous to[10] the defence of 'serious and wilful misconduct' under the Workmen's Compensation Act.[11] The rules of some societies spelt out in greater detail the types of misconduct which would entitle them to disqualify the sick person. Thus, according to one,[12] benefit might be refused if the condition was 'wilfully incurred' by 'fighting, wrestling, using weapons (except in self-defence), drunkenness, indecent or disorderly conduct, venereal disease.' The modern provision does not limit the misconduct to 'serious' or 'wilful', and it is possible to argue that it extends to reckless disregard of precautions ordered or recommended by, for example, an employer or a doctor.[13] The only reported decision, however, carries the implication that the conduct must be wilful.[14] The incapacity was due to alcoholism and it was held that the claimant could only rebut the inference of misconduct if he could show that his will-power had been so impaired that he was unable to moderate his drinking. There are two explicit situations in which disqualification is not to be imposed: where the incapacity is due to venereal disease or to pregnancy.[15]

ii) Examination

Disqualification may be incurred if the claimant

> 'fails without good cause to comply with a notice in writing given by or on behalf of the Secretary of State requiring him to attend for and submit himself to medical or other examination on a date not earlier than the third day after the day on which the notice was sent and at a time and place specified in that notice. . . .'[16]

---

7. SSA 1975, s.20(2)(a): S.I. 1975/564, Reg. 12(1)(a).
8. E.g., NHIA 1936, s.64(1).
9. See the Model Rules issued by the Ministry, esp. No. 13(1).
10. See Reported Decision on Appeals and Applications under NHIA 1936, s.163, No. CIII.
11. WCA 1897, s.1(2)(c). The same notion of 'wilful misconduct' is incorporated in art. 648(4) of the International Labour Code, 1951.
12. Ante, n.10, Decision XIII.
13. Potter and Stansfield *National Insurance* (2nd edn), p. 111.
14. *R(S) 2/53.*
15. S.I. 1975/564, Reg. 12(1)(a).
16. Ibid., Reg. 12(1)(b).

It will be recalled that the Department may wish to verify a claimant's alleged disability by requiring him to submit to an examination by the Regional Medical Officer. Not surprisingly, the requirement is reinforced by a sanction, hence the above regulation.[17] Of course illness or physical disability preventing the claimant attending for examination will constitute good cause.[18] What of those who on grounds of religious conviction or otherwise object to medical examination? The question was considered in *R(S) 9/51*. It was held that a Christian Scientist who satisfied the authorities on the conviction of her beliefs should not be disqualified. The onus of proof was on her, and it was not sufficient to show that she was a member of a church whose tenets forbad her submission to treatment or examination. The crux of the matter was her *personal* attitude, and this must be based on a firm conviction that her religious beliefs required her to refuse.

iii) Treatment

The third ground of disqualification arises where the claimant

> 'fails without good cause to attend for, or to submit himself to, medical or other treatment'.[19]

The rationale here is similar to that justifying the misconduct rule. The incapacity must not be voluntarily incurred. Consequently the claimant must take reasonable steps to regain his capacity to work. As regards 'good cause', there is little to add to what was said under 'examination'. But difficult questions arise as to the steps in recovery which might reasonably be required of an individual. Should he be compelled to undergo an operation for which he has a morbid fear? The matter was very fully discussed at the Committee stage of the 1911 Bill.[20] On the one hand, it was argued that to compel a person to be vaccinated or to undergo an operation interfered with a fundamental liberty, and in many cases would involve a risk greater than that inherent in avoiding the treatment.[1] The opposing view was that the contributors to the Fund ought not to support for a number of years a man who refused to undergo on wholly inadequate grounds an operation which was necessary for his health and which could not possibly endanger his life.[2] A compromise solution was reached, and the amendment so formulated has been incorporated in the legislation ever since. In its present form it provides that the

> 'disqualification shall not apply to any failure to attend for or to submit to vaccination or inoculation of any kind or to a surgical operation, unless the failure is a failure to attend for or submit to a surgical operation of a minor character, and is unreasonable.'[3]

---

17. The present form of the regulation requiring 3 days notice is a simplified version of the original (see S.I. 1948/1277, Reg. 10(b)) introduced by S.I. 1964/1112.
18. But the test is an objective one: it will be insufficient if the claimant merely 'thinks' that he is not well enough to attend: ante n.10, Decision XXXVIII.
19. S.I. 1975/564, Reg. 12(1)(c).
20. 29 HC Deb., cols. 330–342.
1. See, e.g., Mr D. Lloyd-George ibid., at col. 333.
2. See, e.g., Mr A. Chamberlain, ibid., at cols. 334–335.
3. S.I. 1975/564, Reg. 12(1)(c).

As with the other grounds of disqualification, little guidance is to be found in the Commissioners' decisions on what might be regarded as 'unreasonable' failure, and how a distinction is to be drawn between 'major' and 'minor' operations. On the latter point, however, both the policy inherent in the provision, and the currency of medical usage,[4] suggest that a 'minor' operation is one which, in ordinary circumstances, does not involve a risk to life.

iv) Rules of behaviour

Under the old National Health Insurance Acts an Approved Society might, subject to the approval of the Minister, make rules governing the behaviour of the insured person during sickness or disability.[5] The Model Rules prepared by the Minister, and in practice adopted by most societies,[6] prescribed certain standards of conduct. After 1946 these were incorporated in the draft Unemployment and Sickness Benefit Regulations, but, following recommendations of the National Insurance Advisory Committee,[7] were significantly amended before they were brought into effect. The requirements that the claimant should 'obey the instructions' of his doctor and answer 'any reasonable enquiries . . . as to the instructions given by the doctor' were regarded as otiose. As conditions of benefit, they were considered to be oppressive, and in so far as they were thought necessary to ensure that the claimant was taking sufficient steps to facilitate his recovery this objective was met by the independent requirement that he should refrain from conduct calculated to retard his recovery. Under the Regulations now in force, disqualification may be imposed if the claimant fails without good cause to observe any one of three rules.

> 1. 'to refrain from behaviour calculated to retard his recovery, and to answer any reasonable enquiries . . . by the Secretary of State or his officers directed to ascertaining whether he is doing so'.[8]

This, together with the 'misconduct' provision, constitute the statutory safeguards against voluntary disability. The latter ground governs cases where the voluntary conduct causes the incapacity; the behaviour provision applies throughout the period of disability.[9] The word 'calculated' is not to be taken too literally. The test is an objective one: was the behaviour likely to retard recovery?[10] On the other hand, there has been a limited interpretation of the 'recovery' which has been retarded. It must be from a disease or disablement: it cannot be invoked against a claimant who declines to continue rehabilitative treatment which was having no effect on his physical condition.[11] There are few reported instances of this ground for disqualification. In *R(S) 21/52* it was held to have been rightly

---

4. See Dorland *Medical Dictionary* (24th edn), at p. 1050.
5. NHIA 1936, s.64.
6. The 1938 version of the Rules are set out in Lesser *The Law of National Health Insurance* (1939), pp. 1108–1109.
7. 1947–48, HC 162, para. 26.
8. S.I. 1975/564, Reg. 12(1)(1)(d)(i).
9. There is an almost identical provision under the industrial injuries scheme: SSA 1975, s.90(1).
10. *R(S) 21/52.*
11. *R(S) 3/57.*

imposed on a claimant who, suffering from influenzal bronchitis, nevertheless undertook a motoring expedition sixty miles away and was there taken ill.

The requirement as to the answering of inquiries is regarded as an essential part of the control mechanism of sickness benefit, but the provision expressly excludes 'enquiries relating to medical examination, treatment or advice'.[12] This resulted from the National Insurance Advisory Committee's dislike of the Approved Society rules of which it was one.[13] It was thought to be too much of an intrusion into the privacy of the relationship between the medical practitioner and his patient.

> 2. 'Not to be absent from his place of residence without leaving word where he may be found.'[14]

The purpose of this rule is to provide a safeguard against deliberate and persistent avoidance of the Department's visiting officers. The pre-war rules tended to be more rigorous, not only stipulating certain times when the claimant must be at home, but also restraining him from leaving his locality at any time without either just cause or the consent of the Society. The present form of the rule has been considered unnecessarily restrictive by some,[15] but in practice it will not be invoked by the Department unless visits by officers have already proved to be ineffective[16] and it is, in any case, subject to the defence of good cause.[17]

> 3. 'To do no work for which remuneration is, or would ordinarily be, payable . . .'.[18]

It will be appreciated that there are three different grounds on which work or the ability to work may disentitle a claimant. (A) It may negative the assertion that the benefit is claimed for a 'day of incapacity' (SSA 1975, s.14),[19] in that the claimant was not incapable of work. (B) It may bring into play Regulation 7(1)(g) of the Unemployment and Sickness Benefit Regulations which prescribes that a day shall not be *treated* as a day of incapacity if a person does any work on that day.[20] (C) It may be a ground for disqualification in accordance with rule 3 cited above. The important difference between, on the one hand (A) and on the other hand (B) and (C) is that the former is concerned with the claimant's theoretical or potential work capacity, while the latter have regard to work which he has *actually* done. (B) will, of course, only operate when the claimant has succeeded on (A), i.e., it was a day of incapacity in that the claimant was not capable of doing work which was regarded as suitable, even though he may have done some work. The justification, if any, for the separate existence of (C) is that (B) will disentitle the claimant only for the day in question, whereas under (C) he may be disqualified for up to six weeks. It is arguable, then, that the specific object of (C) is to deal with those cases where the claimant

12. S.I. 1975/564, Reg. 12(1)(d)(i).
13. Ante, n.7.
14. S.I. 1975/564, Reg. 12(1)(d)(ii).
15. See the Report of the National Insurance Advisory Committee, ante, n.7.
16. *Fisher*, para. 181.
17. *R(S) 6/55.*
18. S.I. 1975/564, Reg. 12(1)(d)(iii).
19. Ante, p. 151.
20. Ante, p. 157.

has shown by his conduct that he should be disentitled for a period longer than a day. It may be urged that this is the very reason for (A) – it is a question of working capacity. But the scope of (A) is narrower: it is concerned only with 'work which the person can reasonably be expected to do'.[1] One is therefore forced to conclude that the 'non-working' rule of behaviour in (C) is based on the undesirability of work, quite independently of working as evidence of the claimant's capacity. Whether legitimate policy grounds may be found for this conclusion is at best uncertain. What remains beyond doubt is that the test to be applied under (C) is exactly the same as under (B). Indeed, the Regulation under (B) excluding from consideration certain types of work is expressly incorporated into (C).[2]

v) Good cause

The claimant may avoid disqualification if he is able to show 'good cause'. Mere ignorance of rules of conduct will not suffice.[3] The following of medical advice, if unambiguous and specific, that the claimant should do a little work,[4] or should absent himself from his residence for a few days, has been held to constitute good cause.[5]

vi) Period of disqualification

The maximum period of disqualification under the Act is six weeks. As with unemployment benefit,[6] the authorities have an unfettered discretion and the factors considered in that context apply equally here.[7]

E. Amount

The amount payable is calculated as for unemployment benefit. The claimant is thus entitled to the weekly flat-rate sum, in 1977–78, of £14·70, plus increases for dependants, and, from the thirteenth day of a period of interruption of employment, an earnings-related supplement.[8]

Part three. Invalidity Benefit

A. General

The level of benefit payable to the long-term sick or disabled under the contributory scheme has been the subject of conflicting policy and legislative changes. The Government White Paper of 1944 proposed that the full flat-rate benefit should be payable only for a maximum of three years, the disabled person being entitled thereafter to 'invalidity pension' equivalent

1. SSA 1975, s.17(1)(a).
2. S.I. 1975/564, Reg. 12(1)(d)(iii).
3. R(S) 21/52.
4. R(S) 10/60.
5. R(S) 6/55.
6. Ante, pp. 121–122.
7. See, esp., R(U) 8/74.
8. Ante, p. 136.

to the lower rate of retirement pension.[9] It was recognised that there was a need for more generous provision, but it was felt that 'sickness benefit of unlimited duration would be psychologically unwise and would tend to encourage those subject to recurrent periods of sickness to lapse into chronic invalidity'.[10] This position was politically unacceptable and the 1946 Act reverted to what had substantially been Beveridge's recommendation:[11] a benefit payable until retirement age, but subject to a more stringent contribution condition after receipt of the benefit for fifty-two weeks – the claimant had to have paid contributions for three years since entering the scheme.[12] The introduction in 1966 of earnings-related supplements for the first six months of sickness benefit[13] added further emphasis to the view that the long-term disabled were being unduly neglected.[14] It was not surprising, therefore, that a long-term earnings-related pension was included as part of the Labour government's National Superannuation scheme of 1969.[15] The Bill lapsed at the 1970 election, and the proposal was not adopted by the incoming Conservative government. Its continued adherence to the principle of flat-rate benefit led to the introduction of a compromise solution described by one commentator as 'a complete novelty and a marked departure from previous thinking about social insurance in this or (so far as I know) any other country'.[16] The new idea was that after six months the standard flat-rate benefit (which would then be called 'invalidity pension') would be supplemented by an allowance graded according to the age at which the claimant became incapable of work, the younger he was at the time of disablement, the higher rate he would receive.[17] The explanation for this differential was not only that the younger disabled person would typically have greater financial commitments but also, according to the government of the day,[18] that during his normal working life an earner should be able to put something aside for his days of retirement and that a disabled person should be compensated for his inability to do this. The emphasis on family need was reinforced by conferring on pensioners a higher increase for dependent children than those paid with sickness benefit[19] and a more generous test of dependency for a working wife.[20] All these elements were retained by the Labour administration and, under its programme for

9. Social Insurance, Part I, para. 65.
10. Ibid., at para. 67.
11. Para. 330.
12. NIA 1946, s.12(2).
13. NIA 1966, s.2(2).
14. See the parliamentary debates on the NI Bill 1959, 606 HC Deb., col. 836 and the NI Bill 1966, ibid., vol. 724, cols. 75–77.
15. See the White Papers on National Superannuation and Social Insurance (1969), Cmnd. 3883, para. 88 and Social Insurance: Proposals for Earnings-Related Short-Term and Invalidity Benefits (1969), Cmnd. 4125, paras. 25–27. The proposal to introduce an invalidity pension at 60% of the claimant's earnings to a

maximum of one and a half times the national average was incorporated in the National Superannuation and Social Insurance Bill as cl. 12.
16. Walley, p. 238.
17. The proposal was implemented by NIA 1971, s.3.
18. Sir K. Joseph, Secretary of State, introducing the NI Bill 1971: 816 HC Deb., col. 1015. The assumption has been challenged. See Walley, p. 234, Sainsbury Registered as Disabled (1970), chap. 4 and Mrs S. Williams in the debate on the 1971 Bill: 816 HC Deb., cols. 1035–1036.
19. Post, p. 385.
20. Post, p. 387.

'Better Pensions',[1] were combined with an earnings-related invalidity pension, to be calculated in the same way as the Category A retirement pension and to come into effect in 1979.[2] One other alleged weakness of the traditional scheme was partially met at the same time. It has for a long time been argued that social insurance takes insufficient heed of the financial dependency of husbands, particularly when disabled, on their wives. The contributory invalidity pension has taken a minor step away from sexual discrimination in this area by allowing a widower, incapable of work when his wife dies, to base his pension on her earnings record if it is better than his own.[3] It remains to state the principles governing entitlement to invalidity benefit as a result of these changes. It will be noted that the requirements are so closely linked to those of sickness benefit, that most of the relevant concepts will have already been the subject of discussion.

B. The pension

The pension is payable for any day of incapacity for work[4] in a period of interruption of employment during which the claimant has been entitled to sickness benefit for 168 days.[5] The rules used in connection with employment and sickness benefits for determining the existence and length of a period of interruption of employment[6] apply: in particular, any two or more days when the claimant is incapable of work or unemployed may be connected, provided that they are not separated by more than thirteen weeks.[7] The 168 days include days for which a maternity allowance was payable and any 'waiting days'.[8] The pension is payable until a man is seventy,or a woman is sixty-five. If the claimant is over pensionable age (sixty-five for men, sixty for women) he must not have retired from regular employment[9] but must have satisfied the contribution requirements for a Category A or B retirement pension.[10] Apart from this special rule there are no contribution conditions as such for invalidity pension, though of course the claimant must have satisfied the appropriate conditions for the 168 days receipt of sickness benefit. The amount payable is the flat-rate sum (1977–78) of £17·50 per week,[11] together with any increases for dependants,[12] but in the case of a person over pensionable age is at the same rate as the retirement pension to which he would otherwise have been entitled.[13] From 6 April 1979, the invalidity pension payable to claimants under pensionable age will be calculated in the same way as the Category A retirement pension,[14] that is with a flat-rate basic component, and an additional component based on the earnings factor derived from

1. (1974), Cmnd. 5713, paras 30–32.
2. SSPA 1975, s.14.
3. Ibid., s.16.
4. For the meaning of this, see ante, pp. 150–152.
5. SSA 1975, s.15(2).
6. Ante, pp. 90–92.
7. SSA 1975, s.17(1)(d).
8. Ibid., s.15(1).
9. Ibid., s.15(1)(b)(ii), and see post, pp. 201–211.
10. SSA 1975, s.15(2), as amended by SSPA 1975, Sch. 4, para. 4.
11. S.I. 1977/1325.
12. Post, pp. 385–390.
13. SSA 1975, s.15(4).
14. SSPA 1975, s.14.

the twenty 'best years' of the claimant's working life.[15] The only difference in the calculation will arise from the facts that the earnings referrred to will be those up to and including the last tax year before the invalidity pension became payable (instead of the year in which the claimant reached pensionable age),[16] and that the invalidity pensioner will also be entitled to the flat-rate invalidity allowance.

Widows and widowers will benefit from new arrangements, also to come into effect on 6 April 1979. If incapable of work for 168 days of a period of interruption of employment[17] and the contribution conditions for *widow's pension*[18] are satisfied, she will qualify for invalidity pension when her entitlement to the short-term widow's allowance[19] expires.[20] Outside the industrial injuries[1] and war pension[2] schemes there are no benefits for widowers as such. The Social Security Pensions Act 1975 has now introduced a measure to assist those who are invalids. A widower incapable of work at the time of his wife's death (or within a period thereafter yet to be prescribed), and so incapable for the standard period of 168 days of a period of interruption of employment, will from 6 April 1979 be entitled to an invalidity pension of which the earnings-related component will be based on the deceased wife's earnings record if better than his own.[3]

C. The allowance

The allowance is payable from the first day of incapacity for which the claimant is entitled to the pension. As has already been indicated, the rate is variable according to the age of the claimant on the first day of incapacity within the period of interruption of employment in question.[4] Regulations provide that for this purpose a day may be treated as one of incapacity for work even though the claimant was not, because of special rules applicable to him, eligible for sickness or invalidity benefit on that day.[5] Thus the age of a member of the forces, or of an employee not drawing benefit because of the provision of sick pay under his contract of employment,[6] or of a recipient of widow's allowance will be taken as at the first date on which, but for the special rules, he or she would have been entitled to sickness benefit.[7] Until 5 April 1979 the relevant age groups are: for the higher rate (in 1977–78 £3·50 per week[8]) those under thirty-five on the date when the period of incapacity began (or where the latter was before 5 July 1948); for the middle rate (in 1977–78 £2·30 per week[9]) those under forty-five on the relevant date; for the lower rate (in 1977–78 £1·15 per week[10]) men under sixty and women under fifty-five on the

15. Post, p. 224.
16. SSPA 1975, s.14.
17. Ibid., s.15(1), (2).
18. Post, p. 237.
19. Post, p. 233.
20. SSPA, s.15(2). The invalidity pension will be payable at the rate of widow's pension: ibid., s.15(3).
1. Post, p. 346.
2. Post, p. 378.

3. SSPA 1975, s.16.
4. SSA 1975, s.16(1).
5. S.I. 1975/564, Reg. 8(1).
6. In accordance with the arrangements authorised by SSA 1975, s.92: see n.6 on p. 158.
7. Ibid., Reg. 8(2).
8. S.I. 1977/1325.
9. Ibid.
10. Ibid.

relevant date.[11] With the introduction of earnings-related invalidity pensions from 1979, this allowance becomes less important and from 6 April of that year the age limits for the higher and middle rates are changed to forty and fifty respectively.[12] Unlike the pension, the invalidity allowance is paid so long as the incapacity lasts, so that when the claimant moves from invalidity pension to retirement pension his allowance is automatically added to the latter.

D. Disqualification and other rules governing claims

In all other respects the rules governing invalidity benefit are identical to those of sickness benefit. This applies to the method of proving incapacity,[13] the rules of behaviour and disqualifications,[14] and the effect of residence in hospital or abroad.[15] Reference should therefore be made to the relevant discussions elsewhere in this work.

Part four. Non-contributory Invalidity Pension

A. General

The OPCS survey of 1968–69 revealed that 40% of the 'very seriously handicapped', 37% of the 'severely handicapped' and 35% of the 'appreciably handicapped' were in receipt of supplementary benefit.[16] This was an embarrassment to a system of social insurance which had purported to provide adequate coverage for the sick and disabled. One of the problems was, of course, that the congenitally disabled were unable to satisfy the then existing contribution conditions for long-term sickness benefit. In 1975, as the first step in its four-stage plan to help those unable to benefit from the contributory scheme, the Labour government introduced the non-contributory invalidity pension (NCIP), similar in scope to the contributory pension, but payable at approximately two-thirds of the rate and with no entitlement to the additional allowance.[17] The government had recognised the need to provide a benefit for disabled housewives but the difficulties of formulating a new criterion of incapacity appropriate for those who were not ordinarily engaged in remunerative employment compelled them to postpone legislation. The Bill therefore originally excluded housewives from its scope, but at the Committee stage the government was defeated by a back-bench revolt and an amendment was carried entitling a married woman to the pension where she was incapable of performing normal household duties.[18] It was but a Pyrrhic victory for

11. SSA 1975, s.16(2). The higher rate is also payable to those for whom the first day of incapacity antedated 5 July 1948.
12. SSPA 1975, s.17.
13. Ante, pp. 152–155.
14. Ante, pp. 159–163.
15. Post, pp. 408–421.

16. Harris, Smith and Head *Income and Entitlement to Supplementary Benefit of Impaired People in Great Britain* (1972).
17. SSBA 1975, s.6, re-enacted as SSA 1975, s.36.
18. See Standing Committee B Debates on the Social Security Benefits Bill 1975, cols. 254–290.

there ensued a long delay before the measure was brought into effect. In the event, the new benefit became payable from 17 November 1977.[19]

B. Entitlement

The principles of entitlement to NCIP to a large extent coincide with those of the contributory invalidity pension (IP) so that the description can be kept relatively brief.

i) Incapacity for 196 days

The benefit is payable for any day on which the claimant is 'incapable of work',[20] provided that

> 'he has been so incapable for a period of not less than 196 consecutive days ending immediately before that day'.[1]

The period of 196 days is in effect the same as the 168 days required for the IP – the latter, being based on entitlement to sickness benefit, necessarily excludes Sundays (or their substitutes)[2] – but there is an important difference. For IP purposes, the claimant may aggregate short spells of incapacity within one period of interruption of employment (i.e., two or more days not separated by more than thirteen weeks).[3] For NCIP, on the other hand, the test is 196 *consecutive* days of incapacity.[4] However, once this initial requirement has been fulfilled, continuous entitlement is based on a less strict criterion. The condition of 196 days is deemed to have been met for those persons already entitled to NCIP as regards any subsequent days of incapacity within the same period of interruption of employment.[5] The 'period of interruption of employment' is construed according to the rules already described for unemployment and sickness benefit,[6] so it means that the 196 consecutive waiting days will have to be served again only if the claimant is regarded as capable of work for a period of thirteen weeks or more.

ii) Exclusions

Those under sixteen or receiving full-time education are excluded from the scheme.[7] However, under the relevant Regulations, a claimant is not to be treated as receiving full-time education if he is over nineteen, or, (if aged sixteen to nineteen) unless the Secretary of State certifies that he is receiving such education at an establishment recognised by the Secretary as being, or comparable to, university, college or school.[8]

---

19. S.I. 1977/1311.
20. Cf. ante, pp. 150–152.
1. SSA 1975, s.36(1).
2. Ante, p. 157.
3. Ante, p. 156.
4. Days when the claimant has been absent from GB, or undergoing imprisonment or detention in legal custody may not count as days of

incapacity for this purpose: S.I. 1975/1058, Reg. 4(2); cf., Appendix.
5. Ibid., Reg. 6.
6. Ante, pp. 90–92.
7. SSA 1975, s.36(2).
8. S.I. 1975/1058, Reg. 5(1). In determining the duration of the education, temporary interruptions are to be disregarded: ibid., Reg. 5(2).

iii) Housewives

When originally introduced, NCIP was confined to a person who would but for the disability have been the breadwinner of the family. It therefore did not extend to a woman substantially dependent on a man, viz., if

> '(a) she is married and either (i) she is residing with her husband, or (ii) he is contributing to her maintenance at a weekly rate not less than the weekly rate of such a pension; or
>
> (b) she is living with a man as his wife'.[9]

The new form of pension payable from 17 November 1977[10] to persons within this group, and often referred to as 'housewives' NCIP'[11] requires the claimant to satisfy the normal conditions for NCIP that she is incapable of work, but also to prove that she is 'incapable of performing normal household duties' and that both incapacities have existed for a period of 196 consecutive days.[12] With the length of time taken to formulate the criterion for this new benefit,[13] it is surprising to find that the rules laid down in the Regulations[14] are so vague, but the Department, in its representations to the National Insurance Advisory Committee,[15] argued that leaving to the statutory authorities the interpretation of 'incapacity' for the analogous purpose of sickness and invalidity benefit had worked well. It had enabled consistency to be achieved through the development of case-law while at the same time providing a degree of flexibility for justice to be done in individual circumstances.

A woman is to be treated as incapable of performing normal household duties where, as a result 'of some specific disease or bodily or mental disablement'[16] she is

> 'unable to perform to any substantial extent, or cannot reasonably be expected to perform to any substiantial extent, normal household duties'[17]

or where she fails to satisfy this condition only because she obtains 'substantial assistance from or supervision by another person'.[18] The requirement of a causal link with a disease or disablement is common to all the disability benefits.[19] In determining the question of incapacity for

9. SSA 1975, s.36(2). For the meaning of 'married' see post, pp. 398–404, of 'residing with', post, pp. 390–393, of 'contributing to . . . maintenance', post, pp. 393–397 and of 'living with a man as his wife', post, pp. 406–408.
10. S.I. 1977/1311.
11. See DHSS Leaflet NI.214.
12. SSA 1975, s. 36(1), (2).
13. During the debates on the 1975 Bill, government spokesmen stressed the difficulty of formulating a new criterion of disability and that the extension to housewives would take some considerable time to implement: see e.g. Mrs B. Castle, Secretary of State, 885 HC Deb., col. 541.

14. S.I. 1977/1312, amending S.I. 1975/1058.
15. Report on the Draft Regulations (1977), Cmnd. 6900, para. 10. The Committee itself thought it 'likely that the adjudication difficulties with the new benefit will be greater than with other incapacity benefits', but was 'not persuaded that those difficulties would be reduced if the regulations were to attempt to provide a more detailed definition': ibid., at para. 12.
16. S.I. 1975/1058, Reg. 13A(1).
17. Ibid., Reg. 13A(2)(a).
18. Ibid., Reg. 13A(2)(b).
19. Cf. ante, p. 150.

normal household duties the authorities should have regard to three main considerations: the nature and severity of the claimant's handicap, the size and composition of her family, and the physical environment in which those duties would need to be performed, including the facilities available.[20] 'Normal household duties' are not defined, but it seems that they are to be understood as referring to what the woman might reasonably be expected to do in the circumstances of the household in which she is living. This follows from the further provision that a woman satisfying the condition quoted above is not disentitled by the fact that she would not have been regarded as incapable 'in substantially different household circumstances',[1] and by the converse provision that a claimant who is not incapable of normal household duties in her actual circumstances cannot qualify if she would have been incapable in different circumstances.[2] In the typical household, the normal duties will include cooking, cleaning, shopping, washing and ironing.[3] The claimant's condition need incapacitate her from performing these duties only 'to a substantial extent'. This rather loose concept will doubtless create some difficulties for the determining authorities, but it is a welcome reaffirmation of the idea, already adopted for mobility allowance,[4] that the functional test of incapacity should not discriminate between those totally unable to perform a function, and those able to do so only with great difficulty, much pain, or extreme slowness.[5]

Incapacity is established by the claimant completing a comprehensive claim form which sets out questions relating to the household circumstances, and her ability to cope with various tasks.[6] It is normally supplemented by a full medical report, based on an examination by her doctor at the claimant's home.[7] The insurance officer then decides the question of incapacity by reference both to the form and the medical report.[8]

iv) Residence and presence

In the ordinary case, the claimant must satisfy three conditions:[9]

> (I) he must be present in GB on the day for which the claim is made;
> (II) he must have been so present for an aggregate of twenty-six weeks in the twelve months immediately preceding that day; and
> (III) he must have been resident in GB for an aggregate of ten years in the twenty years immediately preceding that date, or, if he is under twenty years of age, for an aggregate of ten years since birth. Once these conditions have been satisfied, they are deemed to have been satisfied for all subsequent days of incapacity during the same period of interruption of employment.[10] There are disregards for the

20. NIAC Report, ante n.16, at para. 22.
1. S.I. 1975/1058, Reg. 13A(3)(a).
2. Ibid., Reg. 13A(3)(b).
3. These functions are listed in the claim form (BF 450) which the claimant must complete.
4. See post, p. 185.
5. Cf. NIAC Report, ante n.16, at para. 16.
6. Ante, n.3.
7. NIAC Report, ante n.16, at para.11.
8. Ibid.
9. S.I. 1975/1058, Reg. 3(1). For the meaning of 'present' and 'resident' see post, pp. 413–416.
10. S.I. 1975/1058, Reg. 3(3).

absence of merchant seamen, and members of the forces (or their families).[11]

v) Persons of pensionable and retiring age

The pension is payable to a person who has reached pensionable age (i.e., sixty-five for men, sixty for women) only if he was entitled to it (or would have been entitled to it if not barred by the rules on overlapping benefits[12]) immediately before reaching that age.[13] He must, of course, continue to satisfy the condition as to incapacity for work. Once, however, he has reached 'retiring' age (i.e., seventy for men, sixty-five for women) this no longer applies and he may continue to receive the pension provided that he was receiving it immediately before attaining the retiring age in question.[14]

c. Disqualification and other rules governing claims

The remaining rules all follow the pattern established for the contributory sickness and invalidity benefits. This includes the issue of medical statements,[15] the disqualifications for misconduct, failure to attend for examination or treatment, or working,[16] and the special rules governing hospital in-patients, and persons abroad.[17]

D. Amount

NCIP is a flat-rate benefit at two-thirds that of IP (thus in 1977–78 £10·50 per week[18]). Increases for dependants, however, are payable at the same rate and under the same circumstances as those for IP.[19]

Part five. Attendance Allowance

A. General

The new concern for the disabled manifested in the 1960s was directed in particular to a major group insufficiently protected under existing schemes, comprising those who needed substantial personal assistance from another in matters of self care. The attendance allowance – not to be confused with the 'constant attendance allowance' payable under the industrial injury scheme since 1948[20] – was proposed in 1969 as part of the

---

11. S.I. 1975/1058, Reg. 3(2).
12. S.I. 1975/1058, Reg. 7.
13. SSA 1975, s.36(4).
14. Ibid., s.36(5) and S.I. 1975/1058, Reg. 8.
15. Ante, pp. 152–155.
16. S I. 1975/1058, Reg. 12: see ante, pp. 159–163.
17. Post, pp. 409–421.
18. S.I. 1977/1325.

19. S.I. 1975/1058, Reg. 10: see post, pp. 385–390.
20. Post, pp. 333–335. Confusion between the two has unfortunately been common. See, e.g., Mr R. Crossman, Secretary of State, in the debate on the National Superannuation and Social Insurance Bill 1970, 794 HC Deb., col. 1039, and Topliss *Provision for the Disabled* (1975), pp. 108–109.

Labour government's National Superannuation plan,[1] and was adopted by the Conservative government immediately on assuming power in 1970.[2] Provision was made for a single flat-rate benefit payable to a person requiring either 'frequent attention throughout the day and prolonged or repeated attention during the night; or ... continual supervision from another person in order to avoid substantial danger to himself or others'.[3] The joint test on the first of the alternative conditions excluded many potential claimants, and in 1973 a lower rate of allowance became payable to those who required the necessary attendance either during the day or during the night.[4] To adjudicate on the medical requirements an Attendance Allowance Board was created.[5] Application for leave to appeal against a review decision of the Board may be made to the National Insurance Commissioners, but only on a question of law.[6] The first years of entitlement to this benefit have been by no means troublefree.[7] The general concepts on which entitlement is based were left vague and undefined by the legislature, and the Board has been criticised both for its restrictive interpretation of the conditions and for the inadequacies of its procedures.[8]

B. Degree of disability

The OPCS Survey used very detailed criteria to determine the number of persons who required substantial personal assistance from others in matters of self-care.[9] For the purposes of the attendance allowance it was decided not to adopt such precise tools, but rather to allow the decision-making authority (in this case the Attendance Allowance Board) considerable discretion. A Northern Ireland Commissioner remarked in the first reported case on this benefit, that the principles of entitlement were deliberately stated in somewhat vague terms so that 'common sense' might prevail.[10] The account of the case-law which follows raises some doubts as to whether 'common sense' is a sufficiently reliable guideline.

The Social Security Act 1975 lays down two conditions both of which must be satisfied for the higher rate of allowance (in 1977–78 £14·00 per

1. See White Paper, National Superannuation and Social Insurance (1969), Cmnd. 3883, paras. 90–91 and the 1969 Bill, cl. 17.
2. NI (Old persons', and widows' and attendance allowance) Act 1970, s.4, renamed as NIA 1970 by NIA 1972, s.8(4).
3. NIA 1970, s.4(2).
4. NIA 1972, s.2(1).
5. See generally, post, p. 641.
6. See generally, post, pp. 641–642.
7. In 1973 267 out of 287 appeals to the Commissioner were successful, though in the same year leave to appeal was refused in another 187 cases: DHSS Annual Report 1973, Cmnd. 5700,

para. 11.8.
8. See esp. Carson, 26 NILQ 291, to whose analysis the following discussion is much indebted. See also *Micklethwait*, pp. 134–137.
9. These are set out in Appendix D of Harris *Handicapped and Impaired in Great Britain* (1971).
10. R 1/72 (AA). The view is reinforced by a statement of the Secretary of State (Sir K. Joseph) in the 2nd reading of the 1970 NI Bill, that the basis of the allowance was not related to any specific criterion: 803 HC Deb., col. 1007.

week[11]), but the fulfilment of either is sufficient for the lower rate (in 1977–78 £9·30 per week[12]). The 'day' condition is that the claimant

> 'is so severely disabled physically or mentally that, by day, he requires from another person either – (i) frequent attention throughout the day in connection with his bodily functions, or (ii) continual supervision throughout the day in order to avoid substantial danger to himself or others'.[13]

The 'night' condition is that:

> 'he is so severely disabled physically or mentally that, at night, he requires from another person either – (i) prolonged or repeated attention during the night in connection with his bodily functions, or (ii) continual supervision throughout the night in order to avoid substantial danger to himself or others'.[14]

i) Nature of tests

The first issue that arises under this provision is whether the two tests raise questions of law, and thereby come within the jurisdiction of the Commissioners (and eventually the ordinary courts), or are rather questions of fact on which the decisions of the Attendance Allowance Board are final. The issue is part of the general nature of decision-making and is treated as such in another chapter.[15] It is necessary here to see what implications the general principles have for entitlement to this specific benefit. On the one hand, the tendency has been for the courts to treat the question as to whether 'the words of the statute do or do not as a matter of ordinary usage of the English language cover or apply to the facts which have been proved' as a question not of law but of fact.[16] It follows that the fulfilment of the above conditions is regarded primarily as a medical question to be decided by the Board.[17] On the other hand, where a word is capable of different shades of meaning, decisions as to the correct shade of meaning in a given statute are a matter of construction and therefore of law.[18] This is the relevant principle in determining whether the Board's decision contains a false proposition of law ex facie, one of the grounds on which the Commissioner may entertain an appeal against such a decision.[19]

ii) Severely disabled

The invalid must be 'severely disabled physically or mentally'. There is no reported decision in which a claimant has failed to satisfy this criterion,

11. S.I. 1977/1325.
12. Ibid.
13. SSA 1975, s.35(1)(a).
14. Ibid., s.35(1)(b).
15. Post, pp. 641-642.
16. Per Lord Reid, *Brutus v Cozens* [1973] AC 854 at 861: applied by the Divisional Court in *R v National Insurance Comr, ex parte Secretary of State for Social Services* [1974] 3 All ER 522 at 526 and by R.G. Micklethwait, Chief Comr. in *R(A) 3/74*.
17. Per R. G. Micklethwait, Chief Comr., *R(A) 1/73*, para. 13.
18. Per Lord Widgery CJ, *R v National Insurance Comr*, ante n.16, at p. 526.
19. For this and other grounds, see post, pp. 641-642.

though the Chief Commissioner has raised the question (without answering it) whether disability attributable solely to age would be covered.[20]

iii) Requires

It is important to observe that the attention or supervision referred to in the statutory conditions must be 'required' rather than 'provided'. In other words, the test is based on the objective existence of the need rather than on the actual provision of a service.[1]

iv) Night and day

The first condition applies to day time attention; the second to night time. The distinction is crucial, since the claimant seeking a higher rate of benefit must satisfy both conditions; but 'night' is not defined in the Act, and its meaning has produced considerable discussion and disagreement. The first Commissioner to consider the point adopted the very traditional 'sunset to sunrise' common law definition.[2] This is obviously open to the objection that entitlement would thereby vary both according to the season of the year, and as between different parts of the country.[3] The Commissioner in Northern Ireland refused to follow this: according to him, the word had been left deliberately vague so that decisions could vary according to the seasons of the year, the age of the claimant, time spent in bed and household customs.[4] If the first approach was artificial, this was arguably too vague to be helpful. A third, and more satisfactory[5] view, originating also in Northern Ireland,[6] was adopted by the Divisional Court in *R v National Insurance Comr., ex parte Secretary of State for Social Services.*[7] It was clearly the intention of the legislature to treat as more onerous on members of the household attention provided during the night as opposed to during the day: this will occur if the attendant has to interrupt his normal period of repose to deal with the invalid. Lord Widgery CJ thus concluded that night for the purposes of the section was

> 'that period of inactivity, or that principal period of inactivity through which each household goes in the dark hours, and the . . . beginning of the night (could be measured) from the time at which the household, as it were, closed down for the night'.[8]

v) Attention and supervision

The greatest difficulties have been caused by efforts to give precise meanings to 'attention' and 'supervision'.

20. *CA 8/72*, para. 17, cited by Carson, ante, n.8, at p. 310, who himself asserts that a negative response would be contrary to a fundamental assessment principle embodied in ministerial statements.
1. *R(A) 1/72*; *R(A) 1/73*; *R(A) 3/74* (criticising the forms used by doctors); *R(A) 1/75*.
2. *CA 9/72*; cf. Blackstone *Commentaries* (16th edn), vol. 4, p. 224 and other authorities cited by Carson, ante n.8,

pp. 306–307.
3. Per R.G. Micklethwait, Chief Comr., *R(A) 1/73*, para. 32; per D. Neligan, Comr., *R(A) 4/74*, para. 21.
4. *R 1/72 (AA)*, T.A. Blair, Chief Comr.
5. See, however, the views of Carson, ante n.8, at pp. 307–309.
6. *R 11/72 (AA)* (unreported), cited by Carso, ante n.8, at p. 307.
7. [1974] 3 All ER 522.
8. Ibid., at p. 527.

Day condition 1 ('Frequent attention throughout the day in connection with his bodily functions'). Assistance with bodily functions which include washing, dressing, toilet needs and turning in bed[9] is necessarily an active personal service[10] which occurs on a regular basis during the invalid's normal waking hours.[11]

Day condition 2 ('Continual supervision throughout the day in order to avoid substantial danger to himself or others'). It is important here to concentrate on the concept of 'substantial danger'. It has been suggested that the phrase, though incapable of precise definition, should not be narrowly construed – the risk of harm could result not only from a fall but also from exposure, neglect 'and a good many other things'.[12] The supervision required against these hazards is precautionary and anticipatory rather than necessarily active. It is also, in this instance, against a hazard which may occur during the day, and so 'continual' imports the idea of being 'on hand' to protect the invalid, in the same way as a child minder is available to protect young children.[13]

Night condition 1 ('Prolonged or repeated attention during the night in connection with his bodily functions'). In the light of the interpretation given to 'night' by the Divisional Court,[14] this must import the idea of the attendant actively assisting with the bodily functions during the normal hours of rest. 'Prolonged' does not simply mean 'longer than normal' because if the norm were nil this would amount to any attention at all.[15] It means lasting for some length of time.[16] If the attention is prolonged in this sense it need only occur once during the night; otherwise it must be 'repeated'. Now this word, if taken literally, could mean merely occurring for a second time, but a Commissioner while not prepared to quantify the matter precisely has intimated that the attention must be given more than twice.[17] As has been observed, there is a danger that he is thereby substituting 'repeatedly' for 'repeated'.[18] The phrase 'during the night' does not indicate whether the attention must recur every night. In *R(A) 2/74* the claimant required the use of a kidney dialysis machine on three nights of every week. The Board in accordance with its usual practice had inserted the word 'ordinarily' before 'requires' and in consequence had considered themselves bound by an arithmetical test, whether on the majority of nights the attention was required. The Chief Commissioner held this to be erroneous in law.[19] The Board's general approach had the merit of viewing

9. Cf. Mr D. Ennals, Minister of State, during Standing Committee F Debates on the National Superannuation Bill, col. 548.
10. Per R. S. Lazarus, Comr., *CA 6/72* para. 10, approved in *R(A) 3/74*, para. 11.
11. *R 1/72 (AA)*.
12. Per R. G. Micklethwait, Chief Comr., *R(A) 1/73*, para. 17.
13. Per R.J.A. Temple, Comr., *R(A) 2/75*, para. 9, doubting a stricter view expressed by J.S. Watson, Comr., in *CA 11/73*, para. 13. 'Continual' is to be distinguished from 'continuous' which implies that there must be no

interruptions: D. Neligan, Comr., in *CA 5/72*, para. 8, approved by R.G. Micklethwait, Chief Comr., in *R(A) 1/73*, para. 15.
14. *R v National Insurance Comr*, ante n.7.
15. Per T.A. Blair, Chief Comr., *R 1/72 (AA)*, para. 22.
16. Ibid.
17. J.S. Watson, Comr., in *CA 9/72*, para. 15, cited by Carson 26 NILQ 291 at p. 316.
18. Carson, ibid., at p. 317.
19. *R(A) 2/74*, para. 24, and see the other unreported decisions to the same effect cited by Carson, ante n.17, at p. 317, n.42.

the matter over a period of time but should not be applied arithmetically or invariably. A broad view should be taken of the question over a substantial period. Though he was not prepared to commit himself to any precise test, Sir Robert Micklethwait did indicate that the condition would be satisfied if more than 10 hours of attention were needed on more than 150 nights in every year.[20]

Night condition 2 ('Continual supervision throughout the night in order to avoid substantial danger to himself or others'). The wording of this condition is mutatis mutandis the same as that of the equivalent day condition. But the change from day to night might carry some significance for its interpretation. The hazards to which the invalid may be subject during the night may be of a different character; if so, the nature of the 'continual supervision' required may differ. While it is generally accepted that the attendant must be passively available to deal with emergencies, there is much disagreement on how close to the invalid he must be. In Northern Ireland, the extreme view is taken that it 'requires some person to be awake "keeping an eye on him", or at least listening for him . . .';[1] in one group of British decisions it is deemed sufficient if the assistant is sleeping in the same, or perhaps an adjacent, room and is ready to intervene if necessary;[2] another group, while concentrating on this passive readiness, nevertheless excludes the case where the invalid is able of his own accord to summon assistance by the use of his voice or a bell.[3]

C. Period

The Attendance Allowance Board must be satisfied that the conditions of entitlement have been, or are likely to be, fulfilled for a period of six months.[4] Benefit is payable for such time as the Board considers that the invalid is likely to continue to fulfil these conditions.[5]

D. Residence

The invalid must be ordinarily resident in GB, present in GB on every day for which the attendance allowance is claimed, and have been present in GB for an aggregate of not less that twenty-six weeks in the year immediately preceding the date of the claim.[6] For the purpose of the latter two conditions, however, absence is treated as presence if (i) he is a merchant seaman, a member of the forces or is living with a member of the forces as a member's spouse, son, daughter, father, father-in-law, mother, mother-in-law; or (ii) if his

20. *R(A) 2/74*, para. 35.
 1. E.g., F. Reid, Comr., in *R 10/72 (AA)* (unrep.), cited by Carson, ante n.17, at p. 311.
 2. *R(A) 3/74*, approving *CA 6/72*.
 3. *R(A) 4/74* (quashed on other grounds by the Divisional Court in *R v*

National Insurance Comr, ante n.7) approving *CA 7/73*.
 4. SSA 1975, s.35(2)(b).
 5. Ibid, s.35(2)(c).
 6. S.I. 1975/598, Reg. 2(1)(a)–(c). For the meaning of the terms 'resident' and 'present' see post, pp. 413–416.

absence is for a temporary purpose and has not lasted for more than six months; or (iii) where the absence is temporary and for the specific purpose of being treated for an incapacity from which he suffered before he left GB, and he has not been absent for a period exceeding that which the Secretary of State regards as reasonable in the circumstances.[7] There are more stringent tests for those whose connection with GB is less direct; a person who is a British subject but who was born outside the UK, or a British protected person,[8] must have been present in GB for an aggregate period of fifty-two weeks in the preceding two years; and for persons who are neither British subjects nor protected persons, the qualifying period is 156 weeks in the preceding four years.[9]

E. Exclusions

The Act stipulates that 'a person' is entitled to attendance allowance.[10] In *R(A) 3/75*, Dr. Barnardo's, the well known charity, a body corporate, sought to argue that the phrase included legal as well as natural persons. The claim was rightly rejected. The conditions to be satisfied for the benefit can hardly be applied to someone other than the individual himself, let alone an institution. Explicit exclusions apply to those who are already in receipt of state subsidy for their accommodation.[11]

> More precisely the Regulations provide that it shall be a condition for receipt of the allowance that a person aged sixteen or over is not maintained free of charge while undergoing medical treatment as an in-patient either in a hospital or similar institution maintained or administered by the National Health Service or in other hospitals or similar institutions in pursuance of an arrangement with the Secretary of State for Social Services.[12] The exclusion also applies where the claimant is living in accommodation provided for him, or in which the cost of accommodation is borne wholly or partly out of public or local funds, in pursuance of a number of enactments listed in the Schedule to the Regulations.[13] However, a claimant already in receipt of allowance remains entitled to it for the first four weeks of the treatment or accommodation referred to.[14]

There are also special rules for children (i.e., those under sixteen years). Allowances are not paid to those under two years,[15] and in other cases the attention or supervision required must be 'substantially in excess of that

---

7. S.I. 1975/598, Reg. 2(2), as amended by S.I. 1977/342, Reg. 15.
8. See British Nationality Act 1948.
9. S.I. 1975/598, Reg. 2(1)(d)–(e). The disregard of absences of merchant seamen, members of the forces and their families applies also to this group of claimants: ibid., Reg. 2(3)(a).
10. SSA 1975, s.35(1).
11. Ibid., s.35(6).

12. S.I. 1975/598, Reg. 3: a person is only to be regarded as 'not being maintained' free of charge if he pays charges which are intended to cover the whole cost of accommodation and services (excluding the cost of treatment): ibid., and see *R(A) 3/75*.
13. S.I. 1975/598, Reg. 4.
14. S.I. 1975/598, Reg. 5.
15. Ibid., Reg. 6(2)(a).

normally required by a child of the same age and sex'.[16] The person entitled to receive the allowance on behalf of the child is determined according to rules of priority:

> First, a mother living with a child; failing that, a father living with the child; failing that any other person living with the child, or a mother, father, grandparent, brother or sister not living with the child but contributing to the cost of providing for him.[17] Of course, only one person is entitled to an allowance in respect of one child for any one period of time, and if more than one person satisfies the rules it is payable to the individual nominated under the discretion conferred on the Secretary of State.[18]

There are exclusions analogous to those regarding adults in hospital and analogous accommodation, but in this instance the Regulations are broader in impact.

> First, allowance is not payable in any case where the child is not accommodated in a private household unless the person who would otherwise be entitled to receive it is contributing to the cost of providing for the child[19] at a weekly rate of at least the amount of the attendance allowance (over and above any contribution required for entitlement to child benefit or increases to a contributory benefit).[20] Secondly, it is excluded where the child is undergoing medical treatment or other treatment as an in-patient in a hospital or similar institution,[1] except[2] where the maintenance is not free of charge, and the person claiming benefit is contributing to the cost of providing for the child at the rate stated above.[3] The 'four weeks' rule governing the entitlement of adults in such institutions also applies to children.[4] Finally, the exclusion also applies where the child is living in accommodation provided for him or financed wholly or partly from public or local funds in pursuance of the scheduled enactments,[5] but not where he is living in a private dwelling house with a parent or foster-parent.[6]

16. S.I. 1975/598, Reg. 6(2)(c)–(d).
17. Ibid., Reg. 6(4), and see S.I. 1977/1361, Reg. 4.
18. Ibid., Reg. 6(5) as amended by S.I. 1977/1361, Reg. 4. If according to these rules a woman is entitled, payment may nevertheless be made to her husband living with her.
19. For general problems arising under this notion of maintenance see post, pp. 393–397.
20. S.I. 1975/598, Reg. 7(1)(a), as amended by S.I. 1977/342, Reg. 15(3) and S.I. 1977/417, Reg. 2(6). On entitlement to child benefit and dependants' increases see post, pp. 452–468 and pp. 385–386 respectively.
1. S.I. 1975/598, Reg. 7(1)(c). The

Regulation defines 'hospital or similar institution' as 'any premises for the reception and treatment of persons suffering from any illness, including any mental disorder, or of persons suffering from physical disability, and any premises used for providing treatment during convalescence or for medical rehabilitation'.
2. Ibid., Reg. 7(3).
3. Ante, at n.20.
4. S.I. 1975/598, Reg. 7(2) and ante at n.14.
5. S.I. 1975/598, Reg. 7(1)(b), and ante, at n.13.
6. S.I. 1975/598, Reg. 7(1)(b), as amended by S.I. 1977/1341, Reg. 5.

Part six. Invalid Care Allowance

A. General

A household in which a severely disabled person requires attendance may suffer from financial hardship not only directly through the needs of the invalid, but also from the sacrifices made by other members of the household in looking after him. In a study carried out by Sainsbury,[7] it emerged that about two-thirds of disabled persons requiring care received it from relatives, and frequently this would involve a complete or partial interference with the relative's own earnings potential. Quite apart from the social justice of compensating such persons, the granting of state financial support also made economic sense. In many cases, the care supplied voluntarily by the individual involved a saving on public facilities which would otherwise have been necessary. In addition, an estimated 11,500 persons were in receipt of supplementary benefit substantially because they had forsaken gainful employment to care for an elderly or disabled relative,[8] and, as with NCIP, there was pressure to transfer such persons to a non-means tested benefit. The arguments apply not only to the care of severely disabled persons but also to that of small children, those temporarily sick and elderly persons. The government was not, however, prepared to introduce a general 'home care' allowance.[9] The priority was to help relatives involved in invalid care, and so they proposed to exclude not only other forms of care but also married women who were not generally breadwinners. It was conceded that the limitation of benefit to the prescribed category of relatives would involve some arbitrary distinctions being made and a promise has been given that 'the deserving cases of non-relatives will be brought into the invalid care allowance arrangements once we have got over the initial and major hurdle of paying the allowance to relatives'.[10] The non-contributory invalid care allowance (ICA) was introduced by the Social Security Benefits Act 1975[11] and re-enacted as section 37 of the Social Security Act 1975.[12]

B. Persons for the care of whom ICA is payable

As indicated above, the category of persons for the care of whom the allowance was made payable was not intended to be wide. The Act limits it to 'a severely disabled person',[13] and this is defined[14] as a person in receipt of attendance allowance[15] or the industrial injuries constant attendance allowance[16] (or its equivalent under the war pensions scheme[17]). Entitlement to these benefits has not been free from difficulty[18] but during the

7. *Registered as Disabled* (1970), p. 135.
8. Report on Security Provision for Chronically Sick and Disabled Persons 1973–74, HC 276, para. 61.
9. Ibid., at para. 60.
10. Cited in NIAC Report on the Draft Invalid Care Allowance Regulations 1975–76, HC 271, paras. 7–11.
11. S.7.

12. It became payable from 5 July 1976: S.I. 1976/408.
13. SSA 1975, s.37(1).
14. S.I. 1976/409, Reg. 3.
15. SSA 1975, s.37(2), and see ante, pp. 171–178.
16. Post, pp. 333–335.
17. Post, p. 374.
18. Ante, p. 172 and post, p. 334.

passage of the Bill through Parliament the government resisted a proposal that a broader concept of disability should be adopted.[19]

c. Persons entitled to ICA

There are three substantive conditions which the claimant must satisfy:

'(a) he is regularly and substantially engaged in caring for that person; and (b) he is not gainfully employed; and (c) the severely disabled person is either such a relative of his as may be prescribed or a person of any such other description as may be prescribed.'[20]

i) Nature of care

The linking of the ICA with attendance allowance is sufficient in itself to establish that the severely disabled person is in substantial need of care,[1] but it was still necessary to provide more guidelines for the requirement of 'regularly and substantially engaged in caring . . .'. It was decided that the best approach was to set a minimum number of hours' care which was consistent with the notion of it being a full-time occupation for the claimant, but yet which was not 'so high as to cause the claimant to have to examine in detail what among her activities constituted "caring" and whether the minimum had been met'.[2] The result was the creation of the 'thirty-five hours' rule formulated in the following Regulation:

'a person shall be treated as engaged and as regularly and substantially engaged in caring for a severely disabled person on every day in a week if, and shall not be treated as engaged or regularly and substantially engaged in caring for a severely disabled person on any day in a week unless, as at that week he is, or is likely to be, engaged and regularly engaged for at least 35 hours a week in caring for that severely disabled person'.[3]

The reason for the rather circuitous form of this provision is that the base period of the claim is for 'any day' of care, but the thirty-five hour criterion of course applies to a calendar week. It is not, however, clear that the rule as formulated will achieve the stated objective of relieving the authorities of deciding what constitutes 'caring', or how 'regular' it is to be. Is it to be assumed that the mere presence of the claimant in the premises of the disabled person will be sufficient, or is some more active role required? No doubt these questions will be answered when some decisions on the allowance are reported.

The care provided by the relative may be temporarily interrupted by, for example, his own absence or the invalid's need to enter hospital. To achieve flexibility, and to reduce the administrative expenses of frequent

19. See the remarks of Sir G. Young in Standing Committee B Debates on the Social Security Benefits Bill 1975, cols. 341–342.

20. SSA 1975, s.37(1).
1. NIAC Report, ante n.10, at para. 12.
2. Ibid.
3. S.I. 1976/409, Reg. 4(1).

investigation, the 'thirty-five hours' rule is relaxed in certain circumstances. The Regulations provide that the rule is deemed to have been
satisfied if

> (1) the claimant has only temporarily ceased to satisfy the
> conditions; and (2) he has satisfied them for an aggregate period
> of fourteen or more weeks in the immediately preceding six
> months; and (3) he would have satisfied them for at least twenty-
> two weeks in such a period but for the fact that he or the disabled
> person was undergoing treatment as an in-patient in a hospital or
> similar institution.[4]

ii) Gainful employment

The intention being to confer benefit only on those engaged full-time in
the care of the invalid, it was thought appropriate to have some form of
earnings rule, Indeed, the Department appears at one stage to have considered the argument that in principle all earnings should be taken into
account.[5] However, the fact that the majority of persons benefiting from
the new allowance would already have been in receipt of supplementary
benefit, to which the earnings disregard of £4 (£6 in the case of single
parents) applied, induced the proposal that a similar disregard of £4
should apply to the ICA. The National Insurance Advisory Committee
while accepting the fundamental argument that the nature of the
allowance would be inconsistent with a generous earnings rule nevertheless felt that £4 was too low a figure and its recommendation of £6[6] was
accepted by the government. As implemented by the Regulations, it has
the effect of excluding a claimant from the allowance on the ground of
gainful employment only where in the week immediately preceding that
for which the allowance is claimed his earnings exceeded £6.[7] The
ordinary rules for the computation of earnings apply to this provision,[8] but
the claimant is entitled to have disregarded any earnings during a week in
which he temporarily ceases to satisfy the 'caring' provisions, or during a
week in which he was, with the authority of his employer, absent from
employment.[9]

iii) Prescribed relative

The Opposition both at the Committee and at the Report Stage of the Bill
attempted to remove this condition which limits entitlement to those
having a prescribed relationship with the invalid.[10] They failed and though
the provision as it stands is broad enough to allow a wider category of
persons, the government, as yet, has limited its scope to:

> a lineal descendant or ascendant in direct line; a husband, wife,
> step-father, step-mother, step-son, step-daughter, brother, sister,

4. S.I. 1976/409, Reg. 4(2).
5. See NIAC Report, ante n.10, at para. 18.
6. Ibid., at paras. 20–23.
7. S.I. 1976/409, Reg. 8(3).
8. Post, pp. 427–432.
9. S.I. 1976/409, Reg. 8(2).
10. See Standing Committee B Debates on Social Security Benefits Bill, cols. 329–344 and (for the Report stage) 885 HC Deb., cols. 582–586.

half-brother, half-sister, step-brother, step-sister, aunt, uncle, nephew, niece; or a father-in-law, mother-in-law, brother-in-law, sister-in-law, son-in-law, daughter-in-law.[11]

Of course, not more than one such relative can claim the allowance for the same period,[12] and two or more persons who satisfy the conditions may elect, by sending an appropriate notice to the Secretary of State, which is to benefit; in default of such election, entitlement is determined at the discretion of the Secretary of State.[13]

D. Exclusions

The benefit is intended to help those who would, but for the invalid care, have been in full time employment. A woman, residing with her husband or being maintained by him or living with a man as his wife is, therefore excluded; so also are persons under sixteen or receiving full-time education.[14]

E. Persons of pensionable and retiring age

Mutatis mutandis the NCIP rules governing the entitlement of persons above pensionable and retiring age[15] apply. The claimant may accumulate ICA with a retirement pension, but only if he was entitled to the former immediately before attaining pensionable age.[16] After retiring age, he will continue to be entitled even if he no longer satisfies the conditions, provided that he was entitled immediately before reaching that age.[17]

F. Residence and presence

There are three requirements to be satisfied.

On the date for which the allowance is claimed, the claimant must be (i) ordinarily resident in GB and (ii) present in GB; and (iii) must have been present in GB for an aggregate of twenty-six weeks in the twelve months immediately preceding that date.[18] For the purposes of (ii) and (iii) a temporary absence is disregarded if it did not exceed a continuous period of four weeks or if it was specifically for the purpose of caring for the invalid who was also absent from GB (provided that at the time the latter did not lose his entitlement to attendance allowance or its equivalent.)[19] The usual disregards of absence for merchant seamen, members of the forces and their families, also apply.[20]

11. S.I. 1976/409, Reg. 6, treating anyone born illegitimate as if he had been born legitimate.
12. SSA 1975, s.37(7).
13. S.I. 1976/409, Reg. 7.
14. SSA 1975, s.37(3).
15. Ante, p. 171.
16. SSA 1975, s.37(5).
17. Ibid., s.37(6).
18. S.I. 1976/409, Reg. 9(1).
19. Ibid., Reg. 9(2).
20. Ibid., Reg. 9(3): see ante, p. 176.

G. Amount

ICA is a flat-rate benefit equivalent in amount to the NCIP (in 1977–78 £10·50 per week[1]), and the increases for dependants also follow that benefit.[2]

Part seven. Mobility Allowance

A. General

The new policy towards the disabled of isolating particular needs and providing income on a flat-rate, non-contributory basis, inevitably became directed to the question of mobility. This was not an easy subject to treat, because help in this area had existed for a considerable period of time primarily in the form of kind rather than money.[3] Since 1921 invalid vehicles have been supplied to war pensioners, first under a scheme administered by the British Red Cross Society and subsequently by the government under the Royal Warrant.[4] This generally took the form of the single-seat three-wheeler. After the Second World War, however, those receiving a war pension at 20% or more might opt instead for a small car, which might be driven by a 'nominated' driver if the pensioner so preferred.[5] The provision for other disabled persons was not so generous. In exercise of his powers under the National Health Service[6] the Minister of Health (now the Secretary of State for Social Services) made the three-wheeler available to a severely disabled person who came within one of the following categories:[7] (i) loss of both legs, one being amputated above or through the knee; (ii) defects in the locomotor system, or a severe chronic lung or heart condition so that, to all intents and purposes, he was unable to walk; (iii) a slightly less severe disability but which still seriously limited walking ability, and as a result he needed personal transport to get to and from work.[8] The three-wheeler had of course to be driven by the invalid himself. In 1964 the government decided to extend to a small category of persons the facility of a small car, as already granted to war pensioners. The category of benefit was selected according to social rather than physical circumstances: the claimant had either to be living with a relative, who was himself eligible for a three-wheeler or was blind, or to be for a

---

1. S.I. 1977/1325.
2. S.I. 1976/409, Regs. 12, 13. See post, pp. 385–390.
3. See the government-sponsored report by Lady Sharp, Mobility of Physically Disabled People (1974).
4. See ibid., at para. 11.
5. Sharp, ibid.
6. The National Health Service Act 1946, s.3(1) conferred a general power to provide 'medical, nursing and other services required at or for the purposes of hospitals'. Under the Health Services and Public Health Act 1968,

s.33, it became more specific: to 'provide invalid carriages for persons appearing to him to be suffering from severe physical defect or disability . . .'.
7. The criteria were set out in a DHSS circular. See Sharp, ante n.3, Appendix D, para. 1.
8. Work here means full-time or almost full-time paid employment, but a person who is looking after a home and needs a vehicle for, e.g., shopping, might also qualify: Sharp, ibid., at para. 1(3).

substantial part of the day in sole charge of a young child.[9] In 1972 haemophiliacs were added to this group, but in all cases the claimant had to be capable of driving himself, and no one else was allowed to drive the car. Alongside these provisions, certain cash allowances were made available. Those entitled to the three-wheeler or car were exempt from road vehicle excise duty; and, in response to the mounting pressure for the issue of cars rather than three-wheelers, from 1972 those qualifying for a three-wheeler might be allowed, as an alternative, a tax free sum of £100 per annum to help them run and maintain their own car.[10] The latter was seen as a temporary holding measure, while the whole structure of mobility benefits was examined. The appropriate report, on a study undertaken by Lady Sharp, was published in 1974,[11] and its findings were critical of the prevailing system. First, existing facilities were distributed inequitably – in particular, they were limited to invalids who themselves were able to drive. Secondly, the three-wheeler itself was unsatisfactory – it was dangerous, noisy, uncomfortable, liable to break down, and could not carry a passenger. The recommendation was that it should be replaced by a small car as soon as this became economically feasible, but with a narrower range of individuals retaining the right to elect instead for a cash allowance to help maintain and run the car.

The provision of cars would indeed have been too expensive, and the new Labour government resisted Lady Sharp's proposal as it would have reduced the range of disabled persons entitled to assistance. Instead it was decided to provide as an alternative to the three-wheeler a flat-rate, non-contributory mobility allowance. The measure was introduced as section 22 of the Social Security Pensions Act 1975[12] and became payable (initially for those between fifteen and fifty) on 1 April 1976.[13] The story did not, however, end there. Concern for the safety of the three-wheeler has provoked further investigation by the Department and on 23 July 1976 the Secretary of State, Mr. David Ennals, announced that the government was no longer satisfied with this vehicle and it would eventually be phased out of production.[14] The 1977 Social Security (Miscellaneous Provisions) Act then provided that those in possession of an invalid carriage awarded under the pre-1976 scheme would automatically be transferred to the mobility allowance, as and when they gave up use of it.

The position reached at the end of these legislative changes is not a wholly satisfactory one. Not all members of the immobile group, even though extended under the cash benefit scheme, profit from the new arrangement. The popularity of the former private car allowance suggests that those with additional resources sufficient to afford this form of transport obtain the help they need, and various arrangements for the favourable purchase or hire of vehicles have been made.[15] But for those

9. Sharp, ante n.3, Appendix D, para. 5.
10. Ibid., at para. 7.
11. Ante n.3.
12. The provision has been inserted in the SSA 1975, as s.37A.
13. S.I. 1975/2079.
14. 915 HC Deb., cols. 2229–2231, though in 1977 it was decided that production should continue until 1983; Mr D. Ennals, Secretary of State, 930 HC Deb., col. 1062.
15. See the speech of Mr D. Ennals, ibid., at col. 1064.

financially unable to take advantage of these arrangements, the cash benefit is not sufficient to provide the necessary means of locomotion. Moreover, it is not payable to those above pensionable age, and so when this age is reached there is a sharp cut off in financial assistance.

B. Entitlement

i) Inability to walk

The basic statutory test of entitlement is that the claimant is 'suffering from physical disablement such that he is either unable to walk or virtually unable to walk'.[16] This vague criterion is modelled on that previously used by the DHSS to determine entitlement to the three-wheeler. The Regulations offer a little more guidance but still leave much to the discretion of the dermining authorities.[17]

> 'A person shall only be treated . . . as unable to walk or virtually unable to do so, if his physical condition as a whole is such that, without having regard to circumstances peculiar to that person as to place of residence or as to place of, or nature of,
> employment, – (a) he is unable or virtually unable, to walk; or (b) the exertion required to walk would constitute a danger to his life or would be likely to lead to a serious deterioration in his health.'[18]

If the claimant is able to walk with a prosthesis or other artificial aid he does not qualify.[19] It will be evident from these provisions that the allowance is payable only to persons with locomotion difficulties which are causally linked to a disabling physical condition. A mental handicap (e.g., agoraphobia or mongolism) arising independently of such a condition is not, as yet, covered.[20]

ii) Ability to benefit from locomotion facilities

The allowance is not a general benefit to all severely disabled persons unable to walk. It is granted only where the invalid's condition is 'such as permits him from time to time to benefit from enhanced facilities for locomotion'.[1] This too creates some difficulties in interpretation. It is obviously intended to exclude those who are unconscious or are totally bed-ridden.[2] But it is arguable that there will be many, even in this last category, who will receive some benefit from an occasional sortie, and it is not easy to draw a line between the deserving and the undeserving except on some arbitrary basis.

16. SSA 1975, s.37A(1).
17. The insurance officer, the medical authorities and, on a point of law, the Commissioner: post, pp. 637 and 640.
18. S.I. 1975/1573, Reg. 3(1).

19. Ibid., Reg. 3(2).
20. Cf. *R(M) 2/78* in Appendix.
1. SSA 1975, s.37A(2)(d).
2. Cf. 893 HC Deb., col. 468.

iii) Prior entitlement to mobility assistance

As indicated above, the government has decided to phase out the supply of three-wheelers, and private car cash allowances are no longer payable. Transitional arrangements have been made for existing beneficiaries under either scheme. As will be revealed in the next paragraph, they may not receive mobility allowance in addition to these other facilities, but may elect either to continue under the former schemes or to transfer to the new allowance. A person opting for the latter is issued with a certificate which confers on him automatic entitlement to mobility allowance, whether or not he satisfies the conditions specified in i) and ii).[3]

iv) Exclusions

The 1975 Act empowers the Secretary of State to exclude from entitlement to the allowance those having the use of 'an invalid carriage or other vehicle' provided under section 33 of the 1968 Act or 'of any prescribed description of appliance supplied under the enactments relating to the National Health Service being such an appliance as is primarily designed to afford a means of personal and independent locomotion out of doors'.[4] The Regulations implement this exclusion, but with the proviso that if a person in possession of a vehicle informs the Secretary of State that he no longer wishes to use it and signs a declaration to that effect, he nevertheless remains entitled to the allowance.[5] In addition, in exercise of a power conferred under the overlapping benefits provisions,[6] the Secretary of State has excluded wholly or partly those receiving a grant, or receiving any payment by way of grant under section 33 towards the cost of running a private car, or any payment out of public funds which he regards as analogous thereto.[7] The Regulation apportions the payments over the various weeks of entitlement, and the weekly amounts so apportioned are deducted from the claimant's mobility allowance.

v) Period

The allowance is payable for any period throughout which the claimant satisfies the criteria stated above, but it must also be established that the 'inability or virtual inability to walk is likely to persist for at least twelve months from the time when a claim for the allowance is received by the Secretary of State'.[8]

c. Age

Under the 1975 Act, the allowance was not payable to persons over pensionable age.[9] The exclusion results not from any assumptions about the reduced mobility needs of pensioners – they do not have to forfeit possession of an invalid carriage – but rather from financial constraints.

---

3. SS(MP)A 1977, s.13(1) and S.I. 1977/1229.
4. SSA 1975, s.37A(6).
5. S.I. 1975/1573, Reg. 8(a).
6. SSA 1975, s.85(2).
7. S.I. 1975/1573, Reg. 8(b).
8. SSA, s.37A(2)(a).
9. Ibid., s.37A(5)(a).

With the eventual transfer of those entitled to the three-wheeler to mobility allowance, the bar could obviously not be extended to that group, and so Regulations made under new legislation[10] exempt from the exclusion provision those previously entitled to invalid carriages, etc., at pensionable age.[11] No child under five may receive the allowance.[12] In the case of other children (aged five to fifteen inclusive) the benefit is payable to an adult, appointed according to typical rules of priority to receive the allowance.[13] This is an interesting provision, for it appears to be the fiirst time that a benefit intended to assist a child 'follows' that child wherever he may be living, whether, for example, with a foster parent, in hospital, or in residential care. It is to this end that the Regulation insists that the recipient of the allowance must give an undertaking to use it for the child's benefit,[14] but, as indicated above, in some cases it will not be clear how the money may be directly employed to aid mobility where facilities of transport are not already available.

D. Residence and presence

In the ordinary case three conditions must be satisfied.[15]

> During the period for which benefit is claimed the invalid must be (i) ordinarily resident in GB; (ii) present in GB; and (iii) he must have been present there for an aggregate of fifty-two weeks in the eighteen months immediately preceding that period. Temporary absences not lasting for more than a continuous period of twenty-six weeks, and those for the special purposes of treating the incapacity, are disregarded.[16] There are the usual special provisions for merchant seamen, and members of the forces and their families.[17]

E. Disqualifications and other rules relating to claims

Broadly speaking, the benefit is administered in the same way as the sickness and invalidity benefits, so that the 'rules of behaviour' and the disqualifications for misconduct, failing to attend for examination or treatment formulated for those benefits, apply also here.[18]

F. Amount

The allowance is a flat-rate sum (from 5 July 1978 £10 per week[19]). Unlike the invalidity benefits, it is not deductible from supplementary benefit.[20]

10. SS(MP)A 1977, s.13(2).
11. S.I. 1977/1229.
12. SSA 1975, s.37A(5)(a); cp. *Pearson*, p. 319.
13. Viz. mother or father living with the child, or failing that, such person as the Secretary of State may determine: S.I. 1975/1573, Reg. 21.
14. Ibid., Reg. 21(3).

15. Ibid., Reg. 2. For the meaning of 'ordinarily resident' and 'present', see post, pp. 413–416.
16. Ibid., Reg. 2(3)(b)–(c).
17. Ibid., Reg. 2(3)(a): see ante, p. 176.
18. S.I. 1975/1573, Reg. 7: see ante, pp. 159/163.
19. S.I. 1978/475.
20. SSA 1975, s.37A(8).

5 Retirement Pensions

Part one. Introduction

A. General

In terms both of the number of recipients and of total expenditure, retirement pensions are undoubtedly the most important benefit provided by the British social security system. In 1976 well over 8 million people were in receipt of them. The expenditure on pensions was over £6 thousand million, about five eighths of the total budget for social security payments.[1] This proportion is typical of developed countries.[2] With continuing increases in the number of old people, both absolutely and in proportion to the rest of the population, the significance of retirement pensions is likely to increase.[3] In a democratic country the old are an element of the electorate which governments cannot easily ignore: both for this political reason and out of considerations of social justice, it is likely that expenditure on pensions will continue to rise.

Nevertheless the state does not have a monopoly in making provision for the aged. Many of them regard it as their own business to provide for themselves and their families in old age through savings and insurance policies. The years since the last war have seen a rapid growth in occupational pensions, which are generally earnings-related, often affording their recipients an appreciable addition to the state retirement pension.[4] By 1971 it seems that about half the working population was covered by such schemes.[5] However, often the benefits afforded by occupational pensions are relatively meagre, and there are various other drawbacks, in particular the absence of inflation-proofing. For these reasons, quite apart from the fact that many people are still not covered by a scheme, it has not been possible for governments simply to rely on occupational pensions to remedy the deficiencies of state provision.

---

1. DHSS Annual Report 1976, Cmnd. 6931, Table 4.
2. *Kaim-Caudle*, p. 131.
3. The proportion of people in Great Britain of pensionable age (65 for men, 60 for women) in 1851 was 4·0%, in 1948 it was 13·2% and in 1971 16·1%. By 1975 it had risen to 23·0%: DHSS Memorandum *Pension Age* (1976), para. 2.
4. Among the leading works on

occupational pension schemes are: Hosking *Pension Schemes and Retirement Pensions* (4th edn.); Pilch and Wood *New trends in Pensions* (1964). More recent information may now be found in the reports of the Occupational Pensions Board: post, p. 225.
5. See the White Paper, Better Pensions, (1974), Cmnd. 5713.

When the present system of flat-rate retirement pensions was introduced in 1946, subsequent to the Beveridge Report,[6] it was envisaged that the pension would eventually be adequate for subsistence needs without supplementation from other sources. However, despite the fact that pensions have more than kept pace with the rises in prices and average earnings,[7] it is clear that the level at which they have been paid has not been high enough to remove the dependence of large numbers of pensioners on means-tested assistance.[8] About 23% of pensioners are now in receipt of supplementary benefit.[9] The fact is that the state pension by itself has not been enough to ensure a standard of living above the official poverty line – measured by the scale rates for supplementary benefit plus the rent addition.[10]

The apparent inadequacy of the flat-rate insurance benefit, together with the problems posed by the relationship between state and private occupational schemes, have been the two issues which have dominated recent discussion about retirement pensions. Moreover, the differing approaches of Labour and Conservative governments to the right balance between state and private provision have made the subject of pensions reform highly controversial. It is anticipated (and to be hoped) that now that the Conservatives have accepted the Social Security Pensions Act 1975, with its structure of state earnings-related pensions and contracting-out for approved occupational schemes, the debate will subside and stability will be restored. In fact, neither the abortive Conservative scheme embodied in the Social Security Act 1973,[11] nor the structure which came into effect in April 1978, has affected the principal conditions of eligibility for a retirement pension. The questions which have given rise to most legal difficulty, in particular the meaning of 'retirement' and the assessment of earnings for the purposes of the 'earnings rule', are the same now as they were after the passing of the National Insurance Act 1946. That is why only a small part of this chapter is devoted to the complexities of the scheme established by the Social Security Pensions Act 1975.

The main part involves a critical analysis of the rules and policies concerning the standard *contributory* retirement pensions, now known as Category A and Category B retirement pensions.[12] There is then a short discussion of graduated retirement benefit, followed by an exposition of the scheme established by the 1975 legislation. The chapter concludes

6. Paras. 233 ff.
7. Thus the standard rate of retirement pension increased by 1,077% from 1948–76, compared with an increase of 430% in prices and 895% in earnings over the same period: Social Security Statistics 1976, Table 46.01.
8. See chap. 12, post.
9. See the Annual Report of SBC 1976, Cmnd. 6910, para 2.9.
10. An additional payment for rent is payable as part of the means-tested benefit. The Beveridge Report rejected the suggestion that a rent payment should be added to the insurance benefits, including retirement pensions.
11. The proposed scheme, which never took effect because of its immediate repeal by the Social Security (Consequential Provisions) Act 1975, is briefly discussed post, p. 194.
12. The categorisation was introduced by SSA 1973 and has been retained by the legislation now in force, SSA 1975, ss. 28, 29: see post, pp. 211–216.

with an account of the two non-contributory pensions, Category C and Category D retirement pensions.[13]

B. History

i) The Old Age Pensions Act 1908[14]

Pressure for the introduction of state old age pensions began in the 1870s. The pamphlets of an Anglican clergyman, the Rev. William Blackley, and of Charles Booth first drew attention to the acute poverty of many old people and the inadequacy of the poor law to deal with it. The call for the introduction of some state provision was taken up by the trades union movement and the new Labour party. It also attracted a few Liberals, prominent among them being Joseph Chamberlain.[15] It was resisted, however, by the Charity Organization Society, which constantly emphasised the unique virtues of self-help, and by the Friendly Societies, worried that any contributory scheme, such as that introduced in Bismarck's Germany in 1889, would hamper their own recruitment of funds.

The introduction in 1899 of a non-contributory pensions scheme in New Zealand increased interest in proposals for a state pension. The following year a Parliamentary Select Committee recommended the introduction of a means-tested scheme. Even the Friendly Societies were gradually won over to support non-contributory pensions to be financed by taxation; and in 1906 Asquith, then Chancellor of the Exchequer, promised to introduce old age pensions on this basis as soon as there was a budget surplus. The Old Age Pensions Act 1908 provided for a means-tested pension at a maximum of five shillings a week.[16] This was payable to anyone aged seventy on an annual income of less than £21, with a reduced pension on a sliding scale to persons with less than £31 a year. Persons who had been in receipt of poor relief for the previous two years were not entitled, nor were those who had recently been in prison or who had failed to maintain themselves and their dependants. At a time when it was more common than it is now to draw a distinction between the deserving and undeserving poor, these qualifications did not seem surprising. Payment was made, as it still is, through local post offices, but the administration was in the hands of local authority committees, assisted, where investigation of facts was necessary, by the Board of Customs and Excise.[17] Although many aspects of the scheme now appear quaint, at

13. Category C retirement pensions were introduced by the NI Old persons' and widows' pensions and attendance allowance) Act, 1970, renamed as NIA 1970 by NIA 1972, s.8(4): see post, p. 227. Category D retirement pensions were introduced by NIA 1971: see post, p. 228.

14. See, in particular, the very full account in Gilbert *The Evolution of National Insurance in Great Britain* (1966), Ch. IV. Also, see Bruce *The Coming of the Welfare State* (4th edn), pp. 173–181; Fraser *The Evolution of the British*

Welfare State (1975), pp. 139–143.

15. In 1895, Chamberlain joined the Conservative government; his interest in pensions waned over the years, but he continued to support a voluntary, contributory scheme.

16. Ss. 1–3, and Schedule. See *Harris*, pp. 99–103.

17. The Board retained their functions with regard to the administration of non-contributory pensions until 1947: see *Bruce*, ante n.14, at p. 181. For administration of benefits, see chap. 14, post, p. 571.

least the principle was established that in certain circumstances anyone over seventy was entitled to support from the state.

ii) The establishment of contributory pensions[18]

The Old Age Pensions Act 1919 relaxed the means test a little and, more importantly, enabled a person on poor law relief to receive a pension.[19] But it was not long before there was more radical reform. The increasing number of pensioners imposed a large burden on the Treasury at a time when the government wished to reduce taxation.[20] Another factor which induced change was the more widespread acceptance of the contributory principle after its successful use in the health and unemployment insurance schemes.

The Widows', Orphans' and Old Age Contributory Pensions Act 1925,[1] for which Neville Chamberlain, then Minister of Health, was largely responsible, introduced contributory pensions for those between sixty-five and seventy who were covered by the health insurance scheme.[2] The additional contributions were shared equally between employer and employee. The old age pension was payable irrespective of means and the other restrictive conditions existing under the 1908 Act. At the age of seventy the pensioner received his pension under the old non-contributory scheme, without the application of a means test, which, therefore, only applied to those already in receipt of the non-contributory pension. Criticism from the Labour benches focussed on the low level of the Exchequer contribution to the insurance fund.[3] But, generally, the reform was welcomed as completing the structure of insurance benefits which had been started by the pre-war Liberal government.

iii) Pensions reform and the Beveridge report

Under the 1925 Act pensions were only payable at the married couple rate when *both* spouses were over sixty-five. Husbands with dependent wives under sixty-five only received a single person's pension. This created an anomaly if, immediately before he reached sixty-five, the husband had been in receipt of unemployment benefit, because then he would also have received an additional payment for his dependent wife. The couple would thus become worse off when the husband reached pensionable age unless his wife was also sixty-five. In response, therefore, to considerable pressure, particularly from women's organisations, the Old Age and Widows' Pensions Act 1940 reduced the pensionable age for women from sixty-five to sixty.[4] This applied whether the claim was brought by an insured woman in her own right or as the wife of an insured pensioner. The change was in accordance with the position in a number of the Dominions, such as Australia and New Zealand,[5] and it increased from 28% to 63% the proportion of cases in which the married couple pension rate was payable

18. *Bruce* ibid., at pp. 246–254; Gilbert *British Social Policy 1914–1939* (1970), pp. 235–254; *Fraser*, ante n.14, at pp. 189–190.
19. S.3(1).
20. See *Bruce*, ante, n.14, at p. 246.

1. Ss.1(1)(c) and 7, 8.
2. This had been introduced by NIA 1911: see chap. 4, ante, p. 138.
3. See *Bruce*, ante n.14, at pp. 252–253.
4. S.1(1).
5. 357 HC Deb., col. 2148.

on the husband attaining pensionable age.[6] The only criticism of the measure was that it did not go far enough. Some MPs argued with the National Spinsters' Association that the pensionable age for women should be reduced to fifty-five.[7] However, the discrepancy between the relevant ages for men and women has recently given rise to controversy; it is arguable that in a laudable attempt to remove one anomaly, the 1940 Act created more problems.

The other change during the Second World War which should be mentioned here is the availability from 1940 of supplementary pensions administered by the Assistance Board.[8] Pensioners whose means did not equal their basic requirements could supplement their pensions from the Assistance Board's funds rather than have recourse as previously to the poor law authorities. The numbers of people who applied for the new form of assistance showed how inadequate their pensions were.[9]

But the most important aspect of this period was the discussion in the Beveridge Report and the adoption (for the most part) of its recommendations in the National Insurance Act 1946. The Report drew attention to the reasons why old age pensions present particular difficulties: first, old age far exceeds in importance all other causes of inability to earn and to maintain a reasonable standard of living; secondly, the economic and social consequences of old age vary considerably from person to person.[10] Thus, although the frequent recourse to supplementary pensions showed that for many the pension was inadequate, the fact that, at the start of the war, about one-third of all persons over sixty-five did not receive either a state pension or any form of public assistance revealed that some were able to manage on their own resources.

Beveridge argued that it would be prohibitively expensive for the state to pay everyone on reaching sixty-five (or sixty) a subsistence income sufficient to remove the necessity to apply for assistance.[11] For this reason, he recommended that the payment of pensions should be made conditional on the claimant's retirement from regular employment. The Report made it clear that the purpose of this condition was not to encourage early retirement from work, but to reduce the cost of the state pensions scheme. Those able to remain at work were to be encouraged to do so by the promise of an increment to the pension to be paid on their eventual retirement. It was envisaged that more people over sixty-five would remain at work, though this expectation has not been fulfilled.[12] Beveridge also proposed that full pensions should not be payable immediately, but should be phased in gradually over a twenty-year period to allow the National Insurance Fund to accumulate.[13] For obvious political reasons, the new Labour government decided to introduce the full rate immediately, a step which dramatically increased the cost and led to the reforms of the late 1950s.[14]

6. 357 HC Deb., col. 1198.
7. Ibid., cols. 1269 and 2142.
8. See chap. 12 post, p. 478, for a discussion of this aspect of the history of supplementary benefits.
9. *Bruce*, ante n.14, at p. 294.
10. Paras. 233–235.
11. Para. 244. *Harris*, pp. 394, 412.
12. Para. 255; see post, p. 220.
13. Para. 241. *Harris*, pp. 411–412.
14. Shenfield *Social Policies for Old Age* (1957), p. 98.

The National Insurance Act 1946 adopted the Beveridge scheme of retirement pensions and increments for postponed retirement, supported by an earnings rule designed to prevent evasion of the retirement condition.[15] The Labour party had earlier proposed that pensions should be payable to all who retired at sixty, but this was found to be potentially too expensive. There were two respects in which the Act was more generous than both the previous law and Beveridge's proposals. First, a pensioner with a wife under sixty was now entitled to claim a dependant's allowance for her; this had the effect of equating his pension to that payable to a married couple, both of whom were of pensionable age. This change removed one of the arguments put forward for the lowering of the pensionable age for women in 1940.[16] Secondly, the Beveridge retirement condition was not to be applied to men over seventy or women over sixty-five, who were thus entitled to full pension no matter to what extent they worked, a modification urged by a number of small traders.[17]

iv) The move towards earnings-related pensions

Under the Beveridge proposals, retirement pensions, like the other contributory benefits, were to be flat-rate. This principle was maintained rigorously until the late 1950s. In 1958 the government proposed a graduated pensions scheme, under which earnings-related contributions and benefits would be paid in addition to the flat-rate provisions.[18] The principal purpose of the scheme was to supplement through graduated contributions the National Insurance Fund which was seriously in deficit and, for this reason, the additional benefits were not generous.[19] Contracting-out was permitted on condition that the contracted-out employee enjoyed rights under his occupational scheme at least as good as those available under the state graduated scheme. In practice only the higher paid earners, who were members of the more generous occupational schemes, contracted out.[20] A major disadvantage of the new scheme was that the earnings-related addition was not inflation-proof; any attempt at this would have had serious repercussions on the occupational schemes because the contracting-out provisions would in effect have required them also to protect their members against inflation.

The Labour party has often disliked contracting-out on the ground that it may permit the higher-paid to bear a disproportionately small burden of the costs of national insurance. In any case when earnings-related supplements to short-term benefits were introduced in

---

15. The reasons for these particular rules are considered in more detail at the relevant parts of the chapter: see post, pp. 199 and 216.
16. Ante, p. 191.
17. Mr J. Griffiths, Minister of Pensions and N.I., 418 HC Deb., cols. 1733 ff.
18. Provision for Old Age: The Future Development of the National Insurance Scheme (1958), Cmnd. 638: see ante, pp. 42–45 for the history of contributions.
19. For a discussion of graduated pensions, see post, pp. 222–223.
20. For a criticism of the graduated pensions scheme, see *Walley*, Chap. XI, *passim*.

1966, no contracting-out was allowed. Everyone had to pay the supplementary graduated contributions used to finance *both* the short-term benefits *and* the addition to the existing graduated pension.[1] Three years later, the Labour government published proposals for radical reform, in particular the introduction of earnings-related pensions at 42½% of male average earnings.[2] Lower paid employees' pensions would be more generous, so the proposals involved a substantial element of redistribution. Most importantly, the scheme based pensions on average lifetime earnings, revalued in line with changes in national earnings, so that the pension was in effect not only inflation-proof but geared to rising living standards. Contracting-out from part of the superannuation scheme was to be permitted. However, before the Bill became law, the government was defeated at the 1970 election, and it became the Conservatives' turn to attempt reform of retirement pensions.

Their proposals at least reached the statute book, but were never implemented. The distinctive characteristic of this scheme, embodied in the Social Security Act 1973, was the emphasis on the role of occupational pension schemes in supplementing the basic state pension.[3] The basic pension was to be financed by earnings-related contributions from employee (collected through PAYE) and employer, the latter being required to pay more than the former.[4] The Exchequer contribution was to remain at about 18% of the total employee and employer contributions. In most other respects, the provision for a basic retirement pension did not differ from that which has been made since 1946. Occupational pension schemes had to satisfy a new administrative body, the Occupational Pensions Board, on various matters. The main conditions related to the level of benefits – a weekly pension of not less than 1% of total earnings in each year of pensionable employment and some protection of its value against inflation.[5] Employees who did not belong to a recognised occupational scheme were to be required, with their employers, to contribute to the state reserve scheme, which was to be organised by an independent Board of Management. Pensions under this scheme were not to be made conditional on retirement nor subject to an earnings rule. These two interdependent features are not generally to be found in occupational schemes, and were, therefore, thought inappropriate for a state reserve scheme modelled on such arrangements.[6]

The Conservative government's preference for occupational schemes was shown by the fact that, while tax relief for contributions to occupational schemes continued, those to the state reserve scheme were not to be tax deductible.[7] To a large extent it was envisaged that eventually the

1. NIA 1966, ss.1–4.
2. White Paper, National Superannuation and Social Insurance: Proposals for Earnings-Related Social Security (1969), Cmnd. 3883. The proposals are summarised in *Kaim-Caudle*, p. 171.
3. See the White Paper, Strategy for Pensions (1971), Cmnd. 4755, esp., paras. 23–28.

4. The employer's contribution was 7·25% of the employee's PAYE earnings, the employee's contribution being 5·25%.
5. See Cmnd. 4755, paras. 57–62, for the conditions of recognition by the Occupational Pensions Board.
6. Ibid., at para. 73.
7. Ibid., at paras. 70 and 72.

reserve scheme would cater only for those who worked in lower paid employment, (where the employers could not satisfy the conditions laid down by the Pensions Board), and for those temporarily waiting to become members of an occupational scheme.[8] Some critics, however, thought the reserve scheme might be sufficiently attractive to discourage younger people from joining occupational schemes.[9] On the other hand, older contributors would have fared poorly in the state reserve scheme, as there was, unusually for British schemes, no element of subsidy from the younger to the older generations. It was partly for this reason and partly because of the absence of guaranteed inflation-proofing that the Labour government, which took office in 1974, decided not to use the Conservatives' state reserve scheme as the basis for its own plans for an earnings-related pension.

The Labour scheme, which replaced the provisions embodied in the Social Security Act 1973,[10] was introduced in the White Paper, 'Better Pensions'.[11] This reversed the relationship between the state and occupational schemes in the previous government's legislation. Now occupational schemes must follow for the most part the standards set by the state scheme for contracting-out to be allowed. Indeed, the government considered an arrangement, common in European countries, under which private pensions merely 'topped up' the state provisions, instead of permitting contracting-out.[12] But recent improvements in private pension schemes made this drastic step unnecessary. The details of the new state scheme are considered later in this chapter.[13]

Part two. Entitlement to a Retirement Pension

In this Part of the chapter the conditions of entitlement to a retirement pension, as laid down in the Social Security Act 1975, are set out. Generally, they have not been altered by the recent reform of the pensions system except for the contribution requirements where major changes have been made, in particular in their application to married women.[14]

A. Claims

A claim for a retirement pension must be made within three months from the date on which, apart from this condition of claiming, the applicant

---

8. Ibid., at para. 77.
9. *Walley*, pp. 168–176; for a more critical view of the Conservative proposals, see Titmuss *Social Policy* (1974), pp. 102–120.
10 The relevant provisions of the 1973 Act were repealed by the Social Security (Consequential Provisions) Act 1971, s.3.

11. (1974), Cmnd. 5713.
12. Ibid., para. 56. See *Kaim-Caudle*, chap. VI, for a survey of some European systems.
13. Post, pp. 223–227.
14. See post, pp. 213–215.

would be entitled to the pension.[15] Where a claim is made more than three months after this date, it is only payable for the last three months; for the period before that the claimant is disqualified. The requirement should be distinguished from the separate rule stipulating the giving of notice of retirement, which is discussed later.[16]

B. Pensionable age

i) Policy

The second condition of eligibility for a retirement pension (Category A or Category B)[17] is that the claimant has attained pensionable age.[18] 'Pensionable age' is sixty-five for men and sixty for women.[19] The lower age for women dates from 1940, when the war-time government made the change under pressure from women's organisations. The principal object was to enable the typical married couple, where the husband was sixty-five and the wife a few years younger, to draw the full married couple's pension.[20] However, this reason can no longer support the distinction, since a dependant's allowance for a wife of any age has been paid to a retired husband over sixty-five since the National Insurance Act 1946. The allowance raises the husband's total pension to the sum payable to a married couple both of whom are over pensionable age.[1]

In the last twenty years the difference between the pensionable ages for men and women has become increasingly controversial. Even if they were the same, women would draw pensions on average for considerably longer than men, because of their greater life expectancy.[2] The recent moves towards sexual equality as expressed in the Equal Pay Act 1970 and the Sex Discrimination Act 1975 reinforce dissatisfaction with the difference. The question was first considered by the Committee on the Economic and Financial Problems of the Provision for Old Age in 1954.[3] It concluded that though in principle there was much to be said for the restoration of the age parity which had existed before 1940, the savings achieved by a raising of the pensionable age for women would be small. Moreover, because of the introduction of the dependant's allowance by the 1946 legislation, any increase would for the most part only affect unmarried women.[4] The only dissent from this view was expressed by Dr. (now Dame) Janet Vaughan – the only woman member of the Committee – who thought the change should be made for reasons of principle. More recently, the various courses by which equality of pensionable age might

15. S.I. 1975/560, Reg. 13, and Sch.1, para. 5. The requirement also applies to claims for a graduated pension: *R(P) 1/74*. For the general rules concerning claims, see post, pp. 587–597.
16. Post, p. 211.
17. The categories of retirement pensions are discussed post, pp. 211–216.
18. SSA 1975, ss. 28, 29.

19. Ibid., s.27(1).
20. See ante, p. 191.
1. The amounts payable for Category A and B retirement pensions are set out, post, p. 215.
2. See the figures given in the DHSS Memorandum, *Pension Age* (1976), para. 1.
3. Cmd. 9333 (the 'Phillips Committee').
4. Ibid., at para. 193.

be achieved have been considered by the Equal Opportunities Commission (EOC), the body set up under the Sex Discrimination Act 1975.[5] Although it did not come to any firm conclusions on any of the alternative approaches, it thought that, with suitable transitional arrangements to protect the expectations of existing women contributors, it would not be politically impossible to raise the female pensionable age to sixty-five.[6]

Other proposals to equalise the pensionable ages have included the suggestion that that for men should be reduced to sixty; a Private Member's Bill to this effect was introduced in 1976.[7] It was strongly resisted by the government on the ground of the extra costs it would entail – about £1,700 million a year.[8] Against this it could be contended that the withdrawal of men between sixty and sixty-five from the labour market would ease unemployment, and that there would be consequent savings in sickness and unemployment benefit. It has been estimated that this might reduce the cost of the reform by about a third to £1,000 million.[9] A third approach, also considered by the EOC in its discussion paper, would be to reduce the pensionable age for men to sixty-four and a half and raise that for women to sixty and a half and then gradually work to the position where everyone would draw a retirement pension at sixty-two and a half.[10] But this would also lead to an increase in expenditure, and, of course, there is the political point that the reform would be unpopular with women.[11]

It does seem hard to defend the distinction in pensionable ages on other than political grounds. Many countries do not draw it, e.g., France, Germany, the Netherlands, Ireland, Canada and the United States, though some do, e.g., Austria, Italy, Belgium and Australia.[12] Sometimes the special position of single women is recognised: in Denmark, a pension is payable in this case at sixty-two, as compared with a pensionable age of sixty-seven for men and married women,[13] while in New Zealand, the age pension may be payable to a single woman of fifty-five who is unable to work because of her ill-health.[14] A comparison with other countries, therefore, shows that there is no insuperable objection in principle to the payment of pensions at a common pensionable age, but it may, of course, be more difficult to make the change to this position when women have been accustomed to more favourable treatment. Nevertheless, it is hoped that parity will gradually be achieved, even though the economic arguments make immediate reform unlikely.

5. *Sex Equality and the Pension Age* (1976).
6. Ibid., at pp. 18–20. Jersey has done this successfully.
7. The Bill was introduced by Mr G. Janner, 906 HC Deb., col. 1321.
8. See the Memorandum submitted by the DHSS to the EOC, ante n.2, at para. 22.
9. Ibid., at para. 26.
10. Ante n.5, at pp. 20–21. The DHSS Memorandum, ante n.2, at paras. 36–37 points out that the cost of an immediate common pensionable age of 62½ would be about £700 million – this is because there are relatively few women who receive pensions on their own contributions record, and consequently there would be little saving in raising their pensionable age to 62½.
11. Ante n.5, at p. 21.
12. *Kaim-Caudle*, pp. 191–192. For France, see Lynes *French Pensions*, Occasional Papers on Social Administration (1967), and *Dupeyroux*, p. 401.
13. *Kaim-Caudle*, p. 148.
14. New Zealand Social Security Act 1964, s.16.

The second principal question of policy is whether the pensionable age of sixty-five (or sixty) is too high or low, though this issue has not been canvassed so often as the difference between the ages for men and women. Clearly any fixed age is to some extent arbitrary; it is impossible to determine accurately for everyone when the ability to work declines so that it is appropriate to pay a pension – whether actually conditional on retirement, as in the United Kingdom, or not.[15] In certain occupations, the ability to work and earn a living remains generally unimpaired until well after the persons concerned are sixty-five. In other occupations, particularly manual and industrial work, it is common for working ability to decline before the age of sixty-five. The Phillips Committee found that sixty-five was the standard pensionable age in most countries with a developed pensions system, but on the basis of the medical evidence recommended that the minimum retirement age should be raised to sixty-eight for men and sixty-three for women; this should be done one year at a time at intervals if not less than five years.[16] The recommendation has not been implemented and seems unlikely to be taken up again.

Indeed, it is likely that now the pressure will be more to reduce the pensionable age for men, at least to equate it with that for women. The trend in other countries has on the whole been to reduce the ages at which pensions are payable. Thus, Canada has from 1970[17] made pensions payable at sixty-five instead of seventy, and in the same year Ireland introduced retirement pensions at sixty-five, in addition to the previous old-age pension payable to men and women alike at seventy.[18] In France where a reduced pension may be claimed at sixty, recent reforms have increased the proportion of the full pension payable to those claiming before sixty-five.[19] It seems that only in Denmark has the pensionable age been increased: first, from sixty to sixty-five and then in 1957, it was raised again to sixty-seven for men and married women.[20]

The raising of the pensionable age would, it is suggested, be contrary to the general policy applied in the pensions field. It is not usual now to look at pensions as primarily compensation for a total inability to earn. Rather it is thought right that people who have passed their best working years should be entitled to retire on a reasonable standard of living.[1] Early retirement is more popular, despite Beveridge's expectations. Although there is something to be said for the proposition that people should be encouraged to work when they are able to do so, it would generally be thought a reactionary step to raise the minimum pensionable age. Moreover, any increase would be resisted by the TUC on the grounds that older people would be a source of cheap labour, thereby depressing the

15. See Shenfield *Social Policies for Old Age* (1957), at p. 121; *George*, pp. 152–153. This difficulty has led to suggestions for a flexible retirement age with reduced pensions payable to those who retired before, say, 65. The problems associated with this proposal are discussed by the EOC in its paper, ante n.5, at pp. 21–22.

16. Ante n.3, paras. 182 ff.
17. *Kaim-Caudle*, pp. 176–177.
18. Ibid., at p. 175.
19. *Dupeyroux*, p. 401.
20. *Kaim-Caudle*, p. 148.
 1. See George *Social Security and Society* (1973), pp. 109–114.

market, and that inevitably a certain amount of unemployment amongst younger people must result.[2]

ii) The law

The legal difficulties concerning the age condition are relatively few. Generally the claimant will prove his age by reference to his birth certificate, though a population census has been accepted as providing satisfactory evidence, and in a particular case better than the entry on a discharge certificate from the Royal Marines.[3] In an important recent case in which the applicant was a Pakistani immigrant from a district where there had been at the relevant time no register of births, it was held that documentary evidence is not the only method of proof to establish the claimant's age; medical evidence is admissible, its weight depending on the thoroughness of the examination and the degree of certainty with which the opinion is given.[4] The Commissioner pointed out that sometimes in this situation unsatisfactory documentary evidence is tendered out of a desire to improve the case or to please the authorities, and that this should not prejudice the applicant's argument where there is other good evidence that it is well-founded.

It might seem that a retirement pension should be payable from the exact date the claimant reaches sixty-five (or sixty), (assuming the retirement condition is satisfied), and the Social Security Act 1975 certainly states that a claimant is entitled to retirement pension on reaching pensionable age.[5] But the Claims and Payments Regulations provide that benefit is only to commence from a Thursday.[6] The result is that entitlement to pension starts on the Thursday following the claimant's birthday, rather than on the day when the claimant reaches pensionable age. In *R(P) 2/73* it was held that it would be far-fetched to argue that the Regulation was unreasonable and, therefore, ultra vires in that it 'discriminated' against certain claimants in respect of the date of their birth.[7]

c. The retirement condition

i) Policy

The third condition for entitlement to a pension is the feature which is the most characteristic of the British pensions system – the retirement condition, introduced by the 1946 legislation after the recommendation in the Beveridge Report.[8] In order for a man to obtain a pension between sixty-five and seventy, or for a woman to obtain one between sixty and sixty-five, he (or she) must show that he (or she) has retired from regular employment. As has been explained earlier, the object of the requirement

---

2. Indeed, the TUC has supported the proposal for reducing the pensionable age for men to 60: see *Sex Equality and the Pension Age* (1976), p. 8.
3. *CP 11/49.*
4. *R(P) 1/75*, R.G.A. Temple, Comr.
5. SSA 1975, ss. 28, 29.

6. S.I. 1975/560, Reg. 15(9). This point is more fully discussed in the chapter on Administration of benefits, post, p. 607.
7. Per H.A. Shewan, Comr. See also *R(P) 16/52.*
8. Ante, p. 192.

is to reduce pensions expenditure by making provision only for those who are not working. Those who are able to carry on working are encouraged to do so by the prospect of an increment to their pension when it is eventually payable – in any case not later than seventy (or sixty-five in the case of a woman), when the retirement condition is no longer applicable.[9] It must, therefore, be seen in conjunction with the provision for increments to pensions for deferred retirement and also together with the earnings rule. This latter rule is designed to prevent the evasion of the retirement condition which would otherwise be possible if the claimant left employment on attaining pensionable age, and then resumed full-time work shortly after obtaining his pension.

Britain is almost alone in imposing a retirement condition on claimants below a certain age. None of the continental European countries does so, nor does Australia or New Zealand.[10] The earnings-related scheme in Canada, introduced in 1965, does impose a retirement condition, but the basic provision under the earlier Old Age Security Acts does not.[11] In the United States, the principal scheme under the Social Security Acts assumes a retirement condition,[12] and it does this indirectly by the imposition of a very low earnings limit, which makes retirement in fact, if not in law, a necessary condition for making a claim.

Rather surprisingly the retirement condition has attracted comparatively little criticism, though, as will be seen, the earnings rule which complements it has often been challenged.[13] The Phillips Committee in 1954 did not find support for the abolition of the retirement condition.[14] The reasons for this general acceptance of the change from old-age pensions to retirement pensions are hard to state accurately. It may be suggested, however, that one explanation lies in the general move towards earlier retirement; fewer and fewer people remain at work after reaching the age of sixty-five (or sixty, in the case of women).[15] This, of course, may itself be influenced by the retirement condition, but the trend is probably partly attributable to cultural and social factors, and partly to the expansion of occupational schemes providing benefits on the person's retirement. A second explanation for the absence of strong criticism may be that the condition has been very liberally interpreted by the Commissioners, so that it is possible to do a substantial amount of part-time work without losing entitlement to the state pension. The position has become even more favourable since the addition in 1960 of the alternative rule that an applicant may be treated as retired if his earnings are not expected to exceed those stated in the earnings rule.[16]

Nevertheless it may still be argued that to some extent the retirement condition does discourage people able and willing to do so from working.

9. SSA 1975, s.27(5).
10. *Kaim-Caudle*, chap. VI *passim*.
11. Ibid., at pp. 175–183.
12. See Appendix VI to the Phillips Committee Report, Cmd. 9333, and the discussion by Shenfield, ante n.15, at pp. 111–113.
13. See post, pp. 216–218.
14. Ante n.12, at para. 195.
15. George *Social Security and Society* (1973), pp. 109–114. Figures supporting this observation are given in the DHSS Memorandum to the EOC, *Pension Age* (1976), at para. 16.
16. The change was made by the NIA 1960, s.3: see post, pp. 210–211.

The alternative of part-time work, particularly in industry, may be virtually impossible to secure. It can also be added that occupational and civil
service pensions do not generally impose a condition of retirement from all
work, and in this way the rule discriminates against those wholly reliant on
their state pension.[17] Recently the government has indicated that it may be
prepared to contemplate the abolition of the retirement condition (and the
earnings rule) at a time when financial circumstances permit.[18] It is
doubtful, however, whether there will be any immediate moves in this
direction.

ii) The law: general provision

The legal requirement of 'retirement' is exacted by sections 28(1) and 29 of
the Social Security Act 1975; it is that the person concerned 'has retired
from regular employment'.[19] The term 'retirement' is not defined as such
in the legislation, but section 27(3) sets out certain circumstances in which
a person is to be *treated* as retired from regular employment; in practice it
is the construction and interpretation of this subsection (and its predecessors) which have occupied the attention of the Commissioners. It is worth
setting out the principal terms of this subsection:

> '. . . a person may . . . be treated as having retired from regular
> employment at any time after he has attained pensionable age –
> (a) whether or not he has previously been an earner;
> (b) notwithstanding that he is, or intends to be, an earner, if –
> (i) he is or intends to be so only occasionally or to an
>   inconsiderable extent, or otherwise in circumstances not
>   inconsistent with retirement, or
> (ii) his earnings can be expected not to exceed, or only
>   occasionally to exceed, the amount any excess over which
>   would, under section 30(1) below (earnings rule), involve
>   a reduction of the weekly rate of his pension; . . . .'

It will be seen that a person may be treated as retired, despite the fact
that he is earning or intends to be earning in employment, if one of four
conditions is satisfied.[20] Most of the reported decisions on retirement
pensions have concerned the satisfaction of these conditions. However,
before these provisions are considered, some general remarks should be
made about the meaning of 'retirement'.

a) THERE IS NO NECESSITY THAT THE PERSON HAS BEEN EMPLOYED AT
SOME TIME. The notion of 'retirement' strongly suggests that the claimant
must have been employed and then have given up his work. This will
almost always be the case. But section 27(3)(a) makes it clear that this need

17. See Shenfield *Social Policies for Old
   Age* (1957), at p. 105.
18. Mr D. Ennals, Secretary of State, 921
   HC Deb., col. 1175.
19. SSA 1975, ss.28(1) and 29. See
   Micklethwait, p. 116, where it is argued
   that the formulation should be: 'is

retired'. The point is discussed post, p.
204.
20. See *Micklethwait*, p. 116, where it is
   contended that it would be a drafting
   improvement to enumerate the four
   conditions, instead of dealing with
   them in just two subparagraphs.

not be so, although, of course, a person who has not been working may not have paid contributions for entitlement to a Category A retirement pension.[1] But a woman may be eligible for a Category B pension on the basis of her husband's contributions, and she may well not have worked before her 'retirement'.

b) THERE IS NO NECESSITY FOR THE PERSON TO HAVE RETIRED IN CONSEQUENCE OF REACHING PENSIONABLE AGE. In order to claim a retirement pension (Categories A and B) the claimant must show that he or she has retired and has reached pensionable age. But the two events need not be connected. Thus, in *CP 70/50* the claimant, the owner of a ladies hairdressers, gave up regular work in this business when she was fifty-two; since then she had only worked about two and a half to three and a half hours a week. The profits from the business were very small. When she reached sixty, she claimed a pension, and it was held that she was entitled to it, although she had not retired in consequence of attaining pensionable age.

c) THE MEANING OF 'EMPLOYMENT'. The claimant must show that he has retired from 'regular employment'. In Schedule 20 to the 1975 Act, 'employment' is defined to include 'any trade, business, profession, office or vocation'.[2] This confirms the wide meaning given to the notion of 'employment' by the Commissioner. In *CP 7/49*

> A convent Sister was compelled by persistent arthritis to give up full-time work, and did only very light work such as writing letters and arranging flowers for one or two hours a day.

It was held that the Sister was in 'employment', as this concept covered a vocation, including a religious vocation.[3] The fact that the claimant was not rewarded in cash, but by way of free board and lodging did not matter, since payment in kind constitutes remuneration for work and, therefore, an indication that the claimant is 'engaged in a gainful occupation', (the term used in the 1946 Act), or as the present Act formulates it in section 27(3)(b), 'is, or intends to be, an earner'. Further, in *R(P) 2/76*, R. J. A. Temple, the Chief Commissioner, held that a city councillor in receipt of attendance allowances was pursuing a gainful occupation and, therefore, had not retired. It did not matter that he was not 'employed' in the narrow sense of being under a contract of service or for services.[4]

'Employment' includes employment under a contract for services, so that a claimant who continued after pensionable age to live with an old friend as a paid companion was held not to have retired.[5] It was said in this case that it might have been different if the claimant were living with a

---

1. For contribution conditions for Category A and B retirement pensions, see post, pp. 211–213.
2. See on this ante, pp. 47–53.
3. *Cp.*, *R(P) 7/54*, where it was held that membership of a purely devotional religious community did not constitute 'employment'. See post, p. 206. for a further discussion of *CP 7/49*.
4. For further discussion of this case, see post, pp. 208 and 427.
5. *CP 21/49*.

near relative, and the money was paid as a gratuity out of affection. However in *R(P) 3/52*, the claimant gave up full-time work in order to look after her brother-in-law and his mentally deficient daughter in return for free board and lodging. The Commissioner awarded her a pension, but only on the ground that her employment was 'in circumstances not inconsistent with retirement'. It would appear, therefore, that the suggestion in the earlier case that work for a close relative would not constitute 'employment' is wrong.

It is not exactly clear how relevant the fact that the claimant continues to earn is to the question whether he has retired from regular employment. The provision (section 27(3)(b)) that a person may be treated as retired in certain circumstances, notwithstanding that he continues to earn, implies that normally the receipt of such earnings is incompatible with retirement. In some cases, the Commissioner appears to have drawn this inference: thus, in *R(P) 7/52*, the claimant who continued to work his farm, albeit on a reduced scale, for the purposes of making a living (rather than as a pure hobby) was held not to have retired.[6] Moreover, the fact that the earnings or profits are very low does not mean that the claimant is not continuing in employment.[7]

But in a few cases the Commissioner does not appear to have put so much weight on the fact of continued earnings, and has looked more at the nature and amount of the work done by the claimant after the alleged retirement in order to determine whether he has in fact retired. This was the approach adopted in a case where a former coal-dealer let out four properties at a substantial rent; as he performed no work in connection with this, his income did not preclude a holding that he had retired.[8] This is surely correct in that it could not be said the the claimant was 'engaged in a gainful occupation', though his income from letting out his property was much the same as it would have been had he been engaged in running a property business. However, in *R(P) 19/56*, where the claimant was a partner with his son in a dairy business, but performed only very light duties after reaching pensionable age, it was held that he could not be treated as retired. The Commissioner said:

> 'In determining whether the claimant was at the relevant time retired, I therefore take into account not only the evidence as to his activities, but also the circumstance that he was a partner, and the circumstance that his financial return from the venture in which he was a partner was a substantial one.'[9]

It appears that the extent of the financial return and the nature of the work

6. It was, moreover, held that his work was inconsistent with retirement, so he could not take advantage of the third condition in s.27(3)(b)(i); *cp.*, *R(P) 6/53.*

7. Though it may mean that the 'earnings' condition is applicable: see post, p. 210.

8. *CP 129/50*, and see *R(P) 16/56* for the same approach, though with a different result.

9 It was said that the result would have been different if the claimant had been merely a shareholder in a farming enterprise. (See also *R(P) 9/56.*)

done by the claimant are both relevant in determining whether or not he has retired.[10]

d) THE CLAIMANT'S INTENTIONS FOR THE FUTURE. The mere fact that the claimant is not working at the time of his alleged retirement is not by itself enough to show that he has retired from regular employment. The retirement must be final and intended to be permanent.[11] From the Act itself it would appear that the absence of any intention to earn in the future is enough;[12] but it may be that the insurance officer requires the claimant to show a positive intention not to work,[13] and the cases are not inconsistent with this view. An illusory intention to resume work will not, however, preclude a finding of retirement: thus, when a miner entertained hopes of working again, though this was impossible because of his injuries, it was held that he had retired from employment.[14] The opposite decision was reached when a claimant had a reasonable expectation of resuming work.[15] It is quite irrelevant for this purpose that at the time concerned the claimant is actually doing little or no work.[16]

It is arguable that the requirement that the applicant does not intend to earn in the future (however interpreted) is virtually impossible to apply, and that the only relevant criterion should be whether he is working at the time when he claims a retirement pension. This might be the appropriate test if the law required only that the person *is* retired.[17] But the legislation demands that the claimant *has* retired. The requirement would be too easy to evade – by a temporary cessation of work at sixty-five (or sixty) – if the claimant's future intentions were ignored altogether. The present position, however, does lead to the odd result that a person, who has abandoned work at sixty-five and subsequently changes his mind and resumes work is entitled to receive a retirement pension,[18] while a person out of work at sixty-five, but open-minded about the possibility of taking on work later, is not so entitled.[19] It seems unfortunate that this anomaly has not been corrected in any of the many recent pensions reforms.

iii) The law – 'Treated as retired'

The most frequent source of legal difficulty has been whether to *treat* a claimant who is working, and intends to continue to work, part-time as retired. Section 27(3)(b) of the 1975 Act (set out on page 201) provides that a claimant may be treated as retired if one of four alternative condi-

10. 'Earnings' are defined by SSA 1975, s.3, as including any remuneration or profit derived from an employment. This is perfectly compatible with the submission in the text. Similar questions arise with regard to the computation of earnings: post, pp. 426–432.
11. See *141/49 (P)* where there is a full treatment of this point by the Northern Ireland Commissioner.
12. S.27(3)(b).
13. *Calvert*, p. 271.
14. *CP 49/49*.
15. *R(P) 8/51* and see *R(P) 8/52*.
16. *R(P) 10/53*.
17. This has been suggested as more desirable by *Micklethwait*, p. 116.
18. His pension may, of course, be reduced or extinguished by the earnings rule: post, pp. 216–219.
19. The anomaly is substantially lessened by the introduction of the earnings proviso, now SSA 1975, s.27(3)(b)(ii): see post, p. 210. Moreover, if he is genuinely seeking work, he may be entitled to unemployment benefit at the retirement pension rate: SSA 1975, s.14(6).

tions is satisfied. The first three of these have existed unamended since the 1946 legislation. The fourth – the 'earnings' condition, as it is generally known – was added by the National Insurance Act 1960. In practice it is this fourth condition which is the most easily satisfied by claimants: provided it can be shown that his earnings from part-time work are not expected generally to exceed the amount permitted by the earnings rule (now £40),[20] the person concerned will be treated as retired.[1] The other three conditions will, therefore, only be relevant if the applicant cannot satisfy this requirement, because his earnings are unusually high. They are as a result relatively unimportant, as is evidenced by the fact that the number of reported decisions on these provisions has sharply declined since 1960. However, the case-law on the interpretation of the three conditions in section 27(3)(b)(i) is extremely interesting and, as it may still be significant in some situations,[2] it would seem to merit relatively extensive treatment before the 'earnings' condition is discussed.

It might have been thought that these three conditions – earning 'only occasionally or to an inconsiderable extent, or otherwise in circumstances not inconsistent with retirement' – would bear distinct meanings. But in fact they have been so construed that there is considerable overlap between them. The number of hours worked a week would appear from the cases to be relevant to all three conditions, particularly the second and third. As a result of the Tribunal decision in *R(P) 8/54*, a claimant may work for too many hours to be regarded as earning 'to an inconsiderable extent', but the part-time nature of the work as so revealed may be found, in conjunction with other factors, to lead to the conclusion that the work is 'in circumstances not inconsistent with retirement'.

a) AN EARNER 'ONLY OCCASIONALLY'. There does not appear to be any recent reported case in which this condition has been applied. Indeed, it is arguable that it is otiose in that occasional work is merely the opposite of 'regular employment'; someone who works 'only occasionally' has, it might be submitted, left regular employment and, therefore, satisfied the retirement condition. The Commissioner's approach seems consistent with this. In *CP 33/49* it was held that a schools meals attendant, employed for twelve and a half hours a week during term-time, was not working 'only occasionally'; her employment was regular. Similarly, someone employed as a chair collector in the holiday months was not considered to be working only occasionally.[3] The seasonal nature of the work was discounted. Perhaps the most marginal case was *R(P) 16/55*. There a shop assistant working two full days (and a total of sixteen hours) a week did not satisfy this condition.[4] The Commissioner said that a claimant is not working 'only occasionally' when he 'works regularly at fixed recurring weekly periods, and not merely now and then or as occasion requires'. Clearly, the work of a self-employed person cannot easily be

20. S.I. 1977/1325, Reg. 4.
1. For the earnings rule, see post, pp. 216–219.
2. As in *R(P) 2/76*: post, p. 208.

3. *R(P) 8/52.*
4. But the third condition was applied, so the applicant was treated as retired.

described as occasional, since his office or premises will usually be open during normal business hours and he will deal with customers when required.[5] In the most recent case concerning the first condition, the Commissioner decided that an author was not engaged in his occupation only occasionally, as he proposed to rely on his writing as one source of income.[6]

b) AN EARNER 'TO AN INCONSIDERABLE EXTENT'. This exception also is now of very little importance. The leading modern authority is *CP 33/49*, where a schools meals attendant worked twelve and a half hours a week after reaching pensionable age. The Commissioner upheld the 'twelve-hour rule', formulated by the Umpire in construing the identical provision in the earlier Contributory Pensions Regulations of 1946.[7] This stated that the claimant was engaged in a gainful occupation to an inconsiderable extent if he was working for not more than twelve hours a week, or (if more) less than one quarter of the normal working hours of a week for the relevant occupation. It was further decided that the hours have to be considered in relation to the normal working months of the trade in question: it was, therefore, wrong for the claimant to contend that, averaged out over the whole year, her working week was less than twelve hours. She was accordingly not treated as retired. The application of the rule can be illustrated by reference to two cases in the same year: in the first,[8] a convent Sister whose light duties came to no more than one or two hours a day was treated as retired under this condition, while in the second,[9] a paid companion whose duties took up at least twenty-four hours a week was held not to be in a gainful occupation to an inconsiderable extent.

It might be thought that the Commissioner would take account of the actual work done by the claimant, rather than his attendance at the place of work in determining whether he is engaged in a gainful occupation to an inconsiderable extent.[10] But in *CP 126/49*, where a woman was put on three and a half hours a day light work after straining her heart, it was decided that the fact that she was not required to work for all these hours was irrelevant. Nor are low earnings indicative of employment to an inconsiderable extent.[11] Now that the earnings condition has been introduced, the point is an academic one, but it is suggested that as the second condition has been drafted since 1965 in terms of an *earner* to an inconsiderable extent, the amount of the claimant's earnings might well be considered relevant.

c) AN EARNER 'OTHERWISE IN CIRCUMSTANCES NOT INCONSISTENT WITH RETIREMENT'. This third condition produced a large number of

5. *R(P) 2/53*.
6. *R(P) 1/60*.
7. Reported Decision UP 4/47, construing S. R. & O. 1946, No. 1508, Reg. 10(1).
8. *CP 7/49*.
9. *CP 21/49*.

10. The formulation, 'engaged in a gainful occupation to an inconsiderable extent', was employed in the legislation until NIA 1965, when the present requirement in terms of 'an earner' was introduced.
11. *R(P) 1/52*.

cases until the early 1960s when the earnings condition was introduced. It is arguable that the use of the word '*otherwise*', following the first and second conditions, suggests that the frequency of, and the hours worked in, the claimant's part-time employment are irrelevant to the third condition.[12] But the Commissioners' view is that the frequency and regularity of the work are material, though not conclusive, factors in determining whether this condition is satisfied. The result is that in many cases claimants working for well over the number of hours, which would entitled them to be treated as retired under the first or second condition, have been treated as retired under the third condition. It is, in fact, often difficult to see exactly what factors have persuaded Commissioners to come to the conclusion that the person is working 'in circumstances not inconsistent with retirement'.

The leading case is the Tribunal decision in *R(P) 8/54* :

> The claimant who had been employed in the school meals service since 1943, gave notice of retirement, but stated that she intended to continue in the same employment, working twelve and a half hours a week. The Tribunal held that this would not be inconsistent with retirement, as it was the type of work which someone who had retired from regular employment might well perform.

There are two points which may be emphasised. First, although the hours of work and level of earnings were not conclusive, they were both relevant factors in determining whether the third condition was satisfied. In this case it was satisfied, though the hours exceeded the number (twelve) relevant to the second condition.[13] Secondly, it was decided that a claimant need not show some specific circumstance causing a change of occupation, or an alteration in the terms of his employment, for the work to be consistent with retirement.[14]

Although it is unnecessary to show a change of circumstances to satisfy the condition, such a change may influence the Commissioner in treating the claimant as retired.

> In *R(P) 6/54*, a railway station porter intended to retire from his regular employment and immediately to start part-time work for twenty hours a week as an outside porter. He was to work for tips, and not regular wages. The Commissioner ruled that the change in the nature of his employment enabled him to be treated as retired; it was unlikely that he would in fact work for the full twenty hours, though he would be in attendance for that time.

It, therefore, seems that for this condition, unlike the second one, actual work may be more relevant than the hours of attendance.[15] But, in another case, it was emphasised that it is the present scale of the claimant's activity,

---

12. See *Calvert*, p. 276.
13. See ante, p. 206; *CP 33/49*, where the third condition was not even considered, would now be decided differently.

14. On this point the Tribunal overruled *R(P) 15/52*.
15. It is not clear that this is the case for self-employed people: see post, p. 209.

rather than whether there has been a reduction in his working hours, which is important.[16]

Although the number of hours worked may be low enough to enable the claimant to succeed on this third condition (though more than the upper limit of twelve imposed for the second one), it seems that the Commissioners will also draw an upper limit on the hours worked beyond which it is virtually impossible to contend that the work is not inconsistent with retirement. (It could be argued that this too is an incorrect view of the scope of the third condition and that, in principle, there should be no upper limit.) Apart from *R(P) 6/54* (the railway station porter case), there have been very few cases where more than eighteen hours work a week has been held not inconsistent with retirement.[17]

> Thus, in *R(P) 5/57*, the claimant was employed as a bank guard four hours a day for six days a week. Despite the fact that his duties were very light – for most of the time, he read his newspaper and did crossword puzzles – the regularity and the number of hours precluded him from being treated as retired.

In a number of cases it has been emphasised that there must be some feature of the part-time work which is particularly characteristic of occupations followed by elderly people who have given up their regular employment.

> Thus, in *R(P) 11/55*,[18] where the claimant had given up her smallholding and had taken on a school-cleaner's job for twenty-five hours a week, it was decided that in the absence of any such special feature she should not be treated as retired.

It is not enough to argue that the work is part-time. The nature of the work, the freedom which the claimant has to choose his hours, the pressure under which he works (or lack of it), and whether it is done as a hobby or is still pursued as a substantial source of livelihood are all relevant factors in determining whether it presents features characteristic of a post-retirement occupation. In an interesting recent case, the Chief Commissioner, R. J. A. Temple, rejected the argument that the work of a city councillor presented special features which were characteristic of the occupations followed by retired people; in view of the number of hours (generally thirty) which the claimant spent weekly on council business, it could not be said that his work was not inconsistent with retirement.[19]

16. *R(P) 8/56*. Also see *R(P) 1/54* (reduction from 45 to 20 hours a week was not enough for the claimant to be treated as retired).

17. *R(P) 10/55* and *R(P) 2/59* are two such cases. In rather more cases 18 hours' work has been held inconsistent with retirement: *R(P) 4/57*; *R(P) 6/55*; *R(P) 11/55*; *R 1/60 (P)*; *R(P) 2/76*.

18. The Commissioner followed *R(P) 6/55* (20 hours' research work inconsistent with retirement), and distinguished *R(P) 6/54*.

19. *R(P) 2/76*. The case incidentally shows that the third condition may be important despite the introduction of the earnings condition. The attendance allowances claimed by the applicant precluded any reliance on that condition.

In *R(P) 11/55*, it was suggested that the claimant must point to a special feature characteristic of post-retirement occupation. However, in *R(P) 13/55*, the test was formulated in a slightly different way:[20]

> A Methodist minister retired from his full-time charge and was placed on the list of retired ministers. He later took up duties as a part-time supernumerary minister, with a salary of £260 a year and a free house. The Commissioner decided that he was entitled to be treated as retired.

The Commissioner's approach in this case was summarised as follows:[1]

> 'Having regard to the rather inconclusive nature of the inferences falling to be drawn, in this case, from the size of congregation, hours of work involved, and amount of remuneration, I am not prepared to say that there is any feature in the occupation which would render it unreasonable to speak of a person engaged in it as having retired from regular employment.'

This formulation would appear more favourable to the claimant, but it seems from the cases to make comparatively little difference, and the Commissioner does not appear to be wedded to one version of the test rather than the other.[2]

The position of self-employed persons may present particular difficulties.

> In *R(P) 12/55*, the woman gave up employment as a school meals attendant on reaching pensionable age, and then kept a small sweet shop in her house, open for thirteen hours a day. Although this occupation was found to be characteristic of those pursued by retired people, it was held that she could not be treated as retired because the number of hours for which the shop was open made the manner of its pursuit inconsistent with retirement.[3]

A claimant, however, who worked twenty hours a week in his own off-licence business, where trade was light, was held to have retired.[4] The freedom which he enjoyed to organise his own hours was emphasised as a crucial factor. But it was not decisive in *R(P) 1/60* where a writer was not treated as retired under this condition because he set no specific limit to the number of hours devoted to his writing. It must be said that it is not always clear from these cases whether the number of hours actually worked, or rather the number of hours which the self-employed person is

---

20. The Commissioner followed *R(P) 9/54* (Baptist Minister with similar duties) and did not follow *R(P) 11/52*, where the Methodist minister's duties seem to have been lighter than those in *R(P) 13/55*; *R(P) 11/52* may now be regarded as wrongly decided.
1. *R(P) 13/55*, para. 9.
2. E.g., in *R(P) 4/57*, the test in *R(P) 11/55* was applied, while in *R(P) 5/57*, the test in *R(P) 13/55* was followed, but in both cases the result was that the claimant was not treated as retired.
3. The Commissioner followed *R(P) 12/53* (sub-postmistress keeping office open for 44 hours a week was not treated as retired, even though the business was very slight).
4. *R(P) 2/59*.

prepared to work (if occasion warrants) is decisive. The latter would, it is submitted, be the more appropriate; the actual number of hours worked does not necessarily provide clear guidance whether the claimant can really be said to have retired from his previous business.

In summary, the Commissioners appear concerned in applying this condition to see whether there is some feature of the work undertaken by the claimant which is characteristic of the work generally done by elderly people, and in determining this the hours of work are extremely relevant. But the level of the claimant's earnings is not generally of much significance.[5] Some of the decisions are hard to reconcile, as is perhaps inevitable where the Commissioners are asked to interpret such a vague and imprecise requirement.

d) THE EARNINGS CONDITION. It has already been pointed out that the retirement condition creates the apparent anomaly that a person is not entitled to claim a pension if he intends to work after pensionable age (subject to the qualifications as to part-time work, etc., just discussed), while if he has retired, he may then resume work and keep his pension, subject to the earnings rule.[6] This anomaly was mitigated to some extent by the relatively liberal interpretation of the first three conditions for being treated as retired. But, as has been said, for the most part the level of the claimant's earnings was not relevant in determining whether they were satisfied. This was particularly hard on lower-paid workers such as women in textile factories,[7] who worked long hours and were, therefore, unable to satisfy the three conditions. For this reason, the earnings condition was introduced by the National Insurance Act 1960. The effect of the change was well summarised by Mr. Douglas Houghton, the opposition spokesman, during the uncontentious committee stage:[8]

> 'It will mean that they can go to the limit of the earnings rule irrespective of the number of hours worked without finding themselves questioned as to whether what they are doing is inconsistent with retirement.'

Under the earnings condition, the claimant will be treated as retired if his earnings are expected not to exceed, or only occasionally to exceed, the amount above which a deduction from the pension would be made under the earnings rule. For 1977–78 this amount is £40.[9] Thus, if the claimant's anticipated weekly earnings from part-time work are only £35, he will be treated as retired under this fourth condition, while if his earnings are likely to be £50, he must satisfy one of the first three conditions already discussed. The calculation of earnings for the purposes of this condition raises problems which are common to many benefits under the Social Security Act 1975, and, as such, is dealt with in chapter 10.[10]

5. R(P) 16/56.
6. See ante, p. 204.
7. 630 HC Deb., col. 220.
8. Ibid., col. 1096.
9. S.I. 1977/1325, Reg. 4.
10. Post, pp. 426–432.

iv) Notice of retirement

Under the Act, the claimant must give notice of retirement in order to be treated as retired.[11] This requirement must be distinguished from that of a claim for a pension, which has already been mentioned.[12] The Claims and Payments Regulations require that the notice be given in writing to the Secretary of State, specifying the date of retirement. This date must, of course, not be earlier than that of the relevant pensionable age, and not later than four months after the giving of the notice.[13] The date of retirement specified may antedate that of the notice for up to three months; this period may be extended up to twelve months, if there was good cause for the delay in giving the retirement notice.[14] The requirement does not apply to a man over seventy or woman over sixty-five, as they are deemed to retire on reaching that age.[15]

There is some case-law on what constitutes a valid notice of retirement. A recorded note of a conversation with a claimant taken by an insurance officer may amount to such notice,[16] as may a notice of appeal.[17] In one case, a British subject gave notice of his retirement to the Sécurité Sociale in Paris on his sixty-fifth birthday.[18] The Commissioner held that the Sécurité Sociale, under the reciprocal arrangements in force between the United Kingdom and France for the payment of pensions, could be regarded as agents of the Ministry of Pensions and, therefore, the notice was valid.

Granted that the retirement condition must be met to the satisfaction of the authorities, there does not appear to be any reason why this requires special notice, and cannot be treated like any other disputed matter when a claim is made. But it does not seem, on the other hand, that the requirement gives rise to any difficulty, particularly since notice may be given in normal circumstances up to three months after the date of retirement.[19]

D. Contributions

The fourth requirement of entitlement to a Category A or B retirement pension is that the claimant has satisfied the contribution conditions. This is in practice much more important than the retirement condition, since failure to satisfy that will only prevent the award of a pension for the five years until the person is deemed to have retired,[20] while the omission to pay contributions may render him ineligible for these categories of pension.[1] A person may claim a Category A pension on the basis of his (or her) *own* contributions, or a Category B pension on the basis of a hus-

---

11. SSA 1975, s.27(4).
12. *R(P) 3/59*: see ante, p. 195, and see post, pp. 587–597.
13. S.I. 1975/560, Sch. 2, para. 4(2).
14. Ibid., Sch. 2, para. 4(3). For the meaning of 'good cause for delay', see post, pp. 601–606.
15. SSA 1975, s.27(5).
16. *R(P) 4/53*.

17. *R(P) 8/51*.
18. *R(P) 14/55*.
19. For further treatment of the administration of retirement pension, see post, p. 597.
20. SSA 1975, s.27(5); ante, p. 200.
1. The claimant may be eligible for a non-contributory retirement pension: post, pp. 227–228.

band's (or under the Social Security Pensions Act 1975[2] a wife's) contributions.[3] (The rates of these pensions are set out at the end of this Part of
the chapter.[4]) Exposition of the contributions requirements is particularly
difficult, first, because of the special rules applying to married women and
widows, and secondly, because of the changes made by the Social Security
Pensions Act 1975 (hereinafter referred to as 'the Pensions Act'). The
position of married women, is, therefore, discussed in the next section.
Here we are concerned with the general contribution requirements for
both Category A and Category B retirement pensions.

These are set out in paragraph 5 of Schedule 3 to the Social Security Act
1975, as amended by section 19 of the Pensions Act 1975. The amended
conditions apply from 6 April 1979, and are:

> (i) the claimant must have paid in at least one year contributions
> of the relevant class equal to a sum fifty-two times the lower
> earnings limit;[5]

and

> (ii) the claimant must have paid or been credited with contributions
> equivalent to that sum for nine-tenths of his working life.[6]

The effect of this second contribution condition is that where the
claimant's working life has been more than forty years, up to five years'
payment of contributions may be missed. These conditions are further
modified by section 19(3) of the Pensions Act 1975 under which it is
enough for contributions to have been paid or credited for twenty years,
provided that:

> 'In each of the other years, the contributor concerned was, within
> the meaning of regulations, precluded from regular employment
> by responsibilities at home'.[7]

Clearly this provision is primarily for the benefit of women, who have
spent a number of years out of the employment field,[8] but it might equally
enure for the benefit of men.

Under the Regulations it is provided that a retirement pension (either
Category A or B) may be paid at a reduced rate to a person who does not
fully satisfy the second contributions requirement.[9] This rate is the proportion of those years of contributions liability (that is nine-tenths of the
years of the claimant's working life), in which contributions amounting to
the sums prescribed have in fact been paid or credited. But no benefit is
payable at all unless this proportion is at least 25%.

2. S.8: post, p. 215.
3. A person may not be awarded both
   pensions (SSA 1975, s.27(6)), but if
   because of deficient contributions he
   (or she) is not entitled to the whole of
   a Category A retirement pension, part
   of a Category B pension may be used
   to supplement the deficiency (SSPA
   1975, s.9).
4. Post, p. 215.
5. Before 6 April 1979, the requirement
   was the payment of contributions equal
   to a sum 50 times the lower earnings
   limit.
6. For details, see SSA 1975, Sch. 3,
   para. 5(4).
7. For the regulation defining the
   circumstances when this provision
   applies, see Appendix.
8. Cf. ante, p. 66.
9. S.I. 1974/2059, Reg. 5, as amended by
   S.I. 1978/392, Reg. 6.

The Social Security Act 1975 relaxed the contribution conditions for a Category A retirement pension where the claimant is a widow.[10] The contributions of her late husband may be substituted for her own if they are insufficient to satisfy the second contributions condition.[11] Under the Pensions Act 1975 this privilege has been replaced by a broader provision enabling any claimant to make use of his or her former spouse's contributions for the purpose of securing a Category A pension, whether the marriage was terminated by death or divorce.[12]

E. Married women

The pensions position of a woman who is, or has been, married is sufficiently complex to justify separate treatment. It has become even more complex as a result of the Pensions Act. She may be entitled to claim a Category A pension on the basis of her own contributions. Alternatively she may be entitled to a Category B pension on the basis of her husband's, or former husband's, contributions. She may not, of course, receive both pensions, but is to secure the one more favourable to her.[13] The Pensions Act provides that, from 6 April 1979, she[14] may supplement a Category A pension, which owing to deficient contributions is less than the full amount, with that part of the Category B pension to which she is also entitled, so as to bring the former pension up to the prescribed sum.[15]

i) Claim by married women on their own contributions (Category A pension)

The Social Security Act 1975[16] provided that a married woman was not entitled to a Category A pension unless (in addition to the usual requirements) she showed either that her marriage occurred after she was fifty-five, or alternatively, she satisfied the second contributions requirement for at least half the number of tax years between the date of her marriage and the date when she reached sixty.[17] However, the law has been changed by the Pensions Act 1975, which repeals this provision of the consolidation Act, and, therefore, removes these additional requirements for those women who reach pensionable age on or after 6 April 1979. The position of married women has been further improved by the provision enabling the second contributions condition to be satisfied if they are paid or credited for twenty years where the contributor was not at work because of domestic responsibilities.[18]

10. SSA 1975, s.28(3).
11. A divorced woman might similarly use her former husband's contributions up to the year when the marriage ended S.I. 1974/2010, Reg. 4.
12. SSPA 1975, s.20: this provision comes into force on 6 April 1979: S.I. 1975/1689. Also see S.I. 1978/392, Reg. 7.
13. SSA 1975, s. 27(6).
14. This also applies to widowers: see

post, p. 215.
15. This ability to 'combine' the two pensions applies both to the basic component and the new earnings-related component: post, pp. 224–225.
16. S.28(2).
17. Fuller information on this requirement may be obtained from the DHSS leaflet NI. 15, para. 6.
18. SSPA, s.20: ante, p. 212.

ii) Claim on a husband's contributions (Category B pension)

A woman who is, or *has been*, married may in certain circumstances be entitled to a Category B retirement pension by virtue of her husband's contributions. These are set out in section 29 of the Social Security Act 1975. They are unaffected by the Pensions Act 1975, though this legislation has extended Category B pensions to widowers.[19] Two preliminary points should be mentioned before the conditions of entitlement are examined in detail.

First, where the woman's husband is still alive (and has himself reached pensionable age and retired), it does not generally make any difference that his wife is entitled to a Category B pension, since in most circumstances (whether she is under or over pensionable age) a dependant's allowance will be paid to her husband in respect of her.[20] This allowance is the same as the lower rate of Category B retirement pension paid to a woman whose husband is still alive.[1] A Category B pension is, however, payable at a higher rate when the wife becomes a widow, and partly for this reason entitlement to the pension may be important. Moreover, the dependency allowance is an increase to the *husband's* pension, and, therefore, may be reduced because of his earnings as well as hers. The Category B pension, paid directly to the wife, is only subject to a reduction if *her* earnings exceed the prescribed limit under the earnings rule.[2]

Secondly, the United Kingdom system, under which a pension may be payable to a wife on the basis of her husband's contributions, or a dependant's allowance may be paid in respect of her whatever her age, is generous compared with most other systems. In some countries, e.g., Austria, Germany and the USA, a pension is only payable to a woman either if she is a widow, or alternatively she has paid contributions for her own pension.[3]

The circumstances in which a married woman or widow may claim a Category B retirement pension when she has attained pensionable age (sixty) are as follows:

1. Where a woman is married at the time she reaches pensionable age, she may claim such a pension at the lower rate if both she and her husband have retired, and he is sixty-five and has satisfied the contribution conditions for a Category A retirement pension.[4]

2. She may also claim a Category B pension at the lower rate if she marries her husband after she is sixty, subject otherwise to the same conditions as in (1).[5]

19. Post, p. 215.
20. For dependants' allowances, see post, pp. 383–398. They are only payable in certain circumstances set out by SSA 1975, ss. 45, 46, so there may be cases where a husband is not entitled to an increase for his wife, though she is entitled to a Category B pension on the basis of his contributions.

1. For the two rates at which a Category B retirement pension is payable, see post, pp. 215–216.
2. For the earnings rule, see post, pp. 216–219.
3. *Kaim-Caudle*, p. 192.
4. SSA 1975, s.29(2). The contribution conditions are discussed ante, p. 212.
5. Ibid., s.29(3).

3. A widow may claim a Category B pension at the higher rate if her husband died after she reached pensionable age, provided that before his death he had satisfied the contributions conditions. In this case there is no need for the woman to have retired. The reason is that if the woman were under pensionable age, she would be entitled under the same conditions to a widow's pension, eligibility for which is not dependent on retirement.[6]

4. Where the woman's husband has died before she reaches sixty, she may claim a Category B pension, *if she has retired* and was entitled, immediately before she became sixty, to a widow's pension in consequence of his death. In this case there is no separate contributions requirement for entitlement to the retirement pension; but she would only have been entitled to the widow's pension if the contributions conditions for that benefit had been satisfied. The Category B pension is paid at the same rate as the widow's benefit.[7] The effect here of the imposition of the retirement condition is that the claimant may opt either to receive the retirement pension (retirement condition exacted before she is sixty-five) or to continue with her widow's pension (no retirement condition exacted): it does not generally seem to matter which benefit is chosen, though, of course, the former benefit may be reduced because of the earnings rule.[8]

F. Widowers

The Pensions Act 1975 has extended entitlement to a Category B pension to widowers. Section 8 provides that a retired man may claim it if his wife died when they were both over pensionable age, and she was then either entitled to a Category A pension or would have been so entitled if she had retired by that date. The rate of this pension is the same as that for a Category A pension.[9] This reform would appear to cover the relatively unusual case where the wife's contributions record is superior to her husband's.

G. Amounts of contributory retirement pensions

The rates of the two contributory retirement pensions are for 1977–78 as follows: Category A retirement pension, £17.50; Category B pension,

---

6. Ibid., s.29(4). For widow's pension, see chap. 6, post, pp. 236–237.
7. SSA 1975, s.29(5): for the rates of widow's pensions, see post, p. 237.
8. Post, pp. 216–219, for the earnings rule. In certain circumstances it will be advantageous for the widow to claim retirement pension, e.g., if her husband was over 65 when he died and

had deferred his retirement, thereby earning an increment to his pension (post, p. 220). For further details, see DHSS leaflet NI. 15A.
9. SSPA 1975, s.8(2). When this part of the Act comes into force (6 April 1979: S.I. 1975/1689), the rate will consist of the basic component plus an earnings-related component: post, pp. 223–225.

£17·50 (the higher rate) and £10·50 (the lower rate).[10] After 6 April 1979 these retirement pensions will consist of a basic component, equivalent to the standard flat-rate pension, and an additional earnings-related component. The method by which this additional component is calculated is discussed in Part Five.[11] Further, graduated retirement benefit may be payable, for the calculation of which see Part Four.[12]

Part three. Consequences of the Retirement Condition

We have emphasised already the importance of the retirement condition. In this Part of the chapter a number of aspects of the pensions system dependent on it are considered. Foremost among these is the controversial earnings rule. The other topics discussed here are the increments to the pension which may be earned if retirement is postponed beyond pensionable age, and the process of deretirement – when a retired person chooses to end his retirement and resume full-time work.

A. The earnings rule

i) Policy

The Beveridge Report advocated an earnings rule to support the retirement condition.[13] The government accepted this, and the National Insurance Act 1946 contained the rule. An amendment was moved during the Committee stage of the Bill to delete it, but it was successfully resisted.[14] If the rule did not exist, it would be too easy for a person of pensionable age to obtain a pension on cessation of work, and then resume full-time employment afterwards without loss of income. The earnings rule prevents this by providing for a reduction or extinction of the pension if a certain earnings limit is exceeded. Although frequently criticised, both in principle and on its detail, the rule has consistently been defended (at least until recently) by governments and expert committees.[15]

The arguments against the earnings rule are first, that it is unfair to people who have paid contributions all their working life for a pension, part or all of which may be forfeited if they choose to continue working after reaching pensionable age; and secondly, it provides a disincentive to those who are able to work and might thereby make a useful contribution to the economy. There is a misconception that the rule prohibits the earning of more than a certain wage. It does not do so; it merely provides for a reduction or extinction of the pension if earnings exceed the amount prescribed by the legislation. The first argument may be countered by the contention that people are not contributing towards an *old-age* pension,

10. S.I. 1977/1325.
11. Post, pp. 224–225.
12. Post, p. 222.
13. Para. 248.
14. 423 HC Deb., cols. 677–692.

15. The Phillips Committee Report, Cmd. 9333, para. 194; Report of the National Insurance Advisory Committee on the Earnings Limit for Retirement Pensions (1966), Cmnd. 3197, para. 13.

but to a *retirement* pension with an earnings limit. If this were understood, it could not be contended that the earnings rule disappoints reasonable expectations. There is more in the second argument: the earnings rule may well deter some people from working, or from working as much as they might like to. But the number of pensioners affected is much smaller than is popularly believed. The National Insurance Advisory Committee in 1966 found that 88·3% of male pensioners (between the ages of sixty-five and sixty-nine, when the earnings rule applies[16]) with *earnings* were entirely unaffected by the rule, and that of all pensioners, less than five years above pensionable age, only 1½% had their pensions extinguished or reduced.[17] Of course, earnings may be artificially depressed because of the rule, but it seems improbable that large numbers of pensioners are affected. Moreover, it is possible that if the earnings rule were abolished, or the limit substantially raised, some of those who now defer retirement would retire and only work part-time; so perhaps the earnings rule keeps some people in full-time work![18]

Nevertheless, it continues to be unpopular and controversial, and some have called for its abolition.[19] (It was abolished for widows' pensions in 1964).[20] Above the higher limit, at which pension is withdrawn commensurately with the pensioner's earnings, there is in effect a tax rate of 100%. It may be argued that this is one aspect of the poverty trap – pensioners are prevented from increasing their standard of living because of the rules of the welfare system itself.[1] It is, however, debatable whether this implies that the earnings rule should be abolished, or that more generous retirement pensions should be paid, the latter course obviating the necessity for those over pensionable age to work.

When it was introduced in 1946, the earnings rule provided only for extinguishment of that part of the retirement pension equivalent to the excess earned over the stipulated limit – thus, for each £1 earned over the limit, £1 would be deducted from the pension. The National Insurance Advisory Committee Report of 1956 recommended that there should be a band within which only half the excess earnings should be deducted (the 'proportionate band'), and this was implemented by the National Insurance Act 1956.[2] The effect of this reform is to some extent to reduce the deterrent effect of the earnings rule, and to encourage more pensioners to work. At the moment the proportionate band is £4.[3] It is arguable that this is too narrow, in view of the increase in average earnings and the recent substantial raising of the earnings limit (from £9·50 in 1974/5 to £40 in 1977).[4]

16. The earnings rule, like the retirement condition, does not apply to persons over 70 (men) or 65 (women): SSA 1975, s.30(1).
17. Ante n.15, at para. 16.
18. Ibid., at paras. 19–28.
19. See *An End to the Earnings Rule?*, (1976) Conservative Political Centre.
20. NIA 1964, s.1(5).
1. The low disregards of part-time earnings may have a similar effect for recipients of supplementary benefits: post, pp. 509–510.
2. NIA 1956, s.1, implementing the proposals in the NIAC Report, Cmd. 9752.
3. SSA 1975, s.30(1)(a).
4. Between 1974 and 1977 the earnings limit was raised successively to £13, £20, £35, and £40.

Indeed at the Report stage of the Social Security Benefits Bill 1975, the opposition and some Labour back-benchers combined to raise the earnings limit for 1977 to £50.[5] The government reversed this defeat in the Social Security (Miscellaneous Provisions) Act 1977, leaving the limit at £35:[6] this was subsequently raised to £40 for the year 1977–78.[7] Two important concessions were made during the passage of the 1977 Act. First, the earnings limit is now to be reviewed annually under section 125 of the Social Security Act 1975, and, if appropriate, increased in line with the general level of earnings.[8] Secondly, the whole operation of the earnings rule and the costs of its abolition are to be reviewed, 'including the extent to which it acts as a disincentive to work', and a report published by the end of October 1978.[9] Indeed, at several stages during the discussion of the 1977 Bill, government spokesmen emphasised that they did not defend the earnings rule in principle, but considered it too expensive at the moment to abolish it.[10]

We have left to the end what is perhaps the most difficult and fundamental question of all, though it is one which has been surprisingly little debated. The law provides for a reduction of pension if the pensioner is in receipt of 'earnings'. It is often hard to decide what this term means for the purposes of the rule;[11] in particular, narrow lines have to be drawn between profits from a business on the one hand, and shares or gratuitous payments on the other. However, in the context of the pensioner's needs, it is not obvious why he should suffer a deduction from his pension in the former case and not in the latter. In other words, what is the justification for the present *earnings* rule as opposed to a rule which provides for a reduction of pension in the light of the pensioner's means? The answer, of course, lies in the history of provision for old age, and the close connection of the earnings rule with the retirement condition. In defence of the present position, it may be said that it is right for the state not to pay a pension (or to pay a reduced one) to someone who is willing to support himself by regular employment; on the other hand it would be wrong not to allow someone to supplement his state pension by an occupational pension or the proceeds of insurance policies, annuities, and shares, probably provided for out of his income when he was in regular employment. Although the distinction between earnings and other income may sometimes be a fine one, its erosion would lead to the replacement of the present system by a means-tested retirement pension, presumably financed by general taxation. This would be a complete departure from the Beveridge structure and the fundamental principles of the welfare state. Compared with this, change in the opposite direction through the abolition of the earnings rule itself would be relatively minor.

5. 885 HC Deb., cols. 463–530.
6. S.5(1).
7. S.I. 1977/1325, Reg. 4.
8. For review of benefits under the SSA 1975, see post, pp. 433–436.
9. SS(MP)A 1977, s.6.
10. E.g., see Mr D. Ennals, Secretary of State, 921 HC Deb., cols. 1175–1176; Mr E. Deakins, Under-Secretary of State, 926 HC Deb., col. 106.
11. Post, pp. 426–430.

ii) Application of the rule

Section 30 of the Social Security Act 1975 provides that:

> where the earnings of a person (less than five years over pensionable age) exceed the earnings limit for the week before that for which he is entitled to the pension, it is to be reduced by half the excess up to £4 (the proportionate band) and for the whole of the excess after this £4.

The earnings rule applies separately to a wife's earnings, so that the dependant's increase for her (but not his pension) may be reduced by her earnings.[12] It may also be reduced by his earnings, as the increase of benefit forms part of his pension.[13] The 'week' for the purposes of the estimating the claimant's earnings is the calendar week, ending on the Saturday before the week for which he is entitled to his pension.[14] A proviso to section 30(1) makes it clear that the subsection does not affect the pension payable for the first week of retirement – in other words, the fact that his earnings for his last week of employment exceed the earnings limit will not affect the first pension payment.[15]

There is a considerable amount of case-law, in addition to the Computation of Earnings Regulations,[16] concerning what income is to be regarded as 'earnings' and how it is to be assessed. The rules are relevant to a number of benefits, apart from retirement pensions, and are, therefore, discussed in chapter 10 (General Provisions).[17]

iii) The rule under the Social Security Pensions Act 1975

Section 11 of the Pensions Act, as amended by section 5(2) of the Social Security (Miscellaneous Provisions) Act 1977, provides that the earnings rule is only to apply to the basic component (for 1977–78, £17·50[18]) of the new earnings-related pension to be payable from 6 April 1979. It will not apply to reduce or extinguish the earnings-related part (the 'additional component'), nor any increase of pension for deferred retirement which is attributable to this additional component, nor any graduated retirement benefit. (Until April 1979, the earnings rule does apply to this benefit[19]).

B. Increments for deferred retirement

Although the retirement condition inevitably encouraged people to give up work on reaching pensionable age, Beveridge hoped and expected that those able to continue work beyond the age of sixty-five (or sixty) would do so.[20] They were to be induced by the prospect of increments to their

12. SSA 1975, s.48.
13. In this respect a married couple will be more favourably placed if the wife is entitled to a Category B retirement pension: this is her pension and is unaffected by her husband's earnings: see ante, p. 214.
14. SSA 1975, Sch. 20: see post, p. 607,

for payment of retirement pensions.
15. See *R(P) 2/56*.
16. S.I. 1974/2008.
17. Post, pp. 426–432.
18. S.I. 1977/1325, Reg. 5.
19. S.I. 1978/393: post, p 222.
20. Paras. 244 ff.

pensions, either on retirement, or on reaching seventy (or sixty-five in the case of women) when the retirement condition would no longer be applicable. The increments to the standard rate would give the persons concerned some, if not all, of the savings consequent on their postponed retirement.

In fact it has been doubtful whether this aspect of the Beveridge scheme has worked. The Phillips Committee in 1953 found there was no evidence that the prospect of increments encouraged people to stay on at work after reaching pensionable age: 'a small prospective increase in the pension later on, though welcome when it comes, can seldom affect the decision'.[1] On balance, however, it thought there would be unfavourable public reaction to the abolition of increments, and no change was recommended. The increments themselves have been too low and the social forces inducing early retirement too strong to allow the success of this feature of the retirement pensions scheme.[2] There has been a continuing decline in the number of pensions awarded each year with increments, and it seems that there would have to be a radical increase in the rewards for postponed retirement for this picture to change.

Under section 28 of the Social Security Act 1975, the weekly rate of a Category A retirement pension may be increased by one-eighth per cent for every period of six days (between sixty-five and seventy or earlier retirement) which are treated as days of increment,[3] that is, days on which the claimant would have been in receipt of a pension had he retired and on which he was not in receipt of unemployment, sickness or other prescribed form of social security benefit. A widow entitled to a Category A pension will receive an increase of one-sixteenth per cent if her husband before his death was in receipt of, or would have been in receipt of, if he had retired before his death, a pension with increments. Where a married woman is entitled to a Category B retirement pension, her pension rate is increased while he is alive by one-sixteenth per cent of his pension on the basis of his deferred retirement while he is alive, and by one-eighth per cent after his death.[4] Here, of course, she is claiming on his contributions, and she is, therefore, entitled to the full increment on his death.

The Social Security Pensions Act 1975 makes a number of changes to pension increments which take effect on 6 April 1979.[5] The most important are the provisions that a woman may receive the whole of her husband's increment on his death (instead of half, as under the Social Security Act 1975), and also that a husband may benefit on his wife's death from the increments to which she was entitled on the basis of her deferred retirement.[6] Further, the increment to a Category B pension is to be related to the Category B rate of pension, and not, as under the previous legislation, to that of the husband's Category A pension.[7]

A further change has been made by the Social Security (Miscellaneous

1. The Phillips Committee Report, Cmd. 9333, at paras. 200–201.
2. See *George*, p. 159.
3. See S.I. 1978–392, Reg. 4 for the definition of 'days of increment'.
4. SSA 1975, s.29(10).
5. S.I. 1975/1689.
6. SSPA 1975, Sch. 1, para. 4.
7. Ibid., at para. 5.

Provisions) Act 1977. The amount of the increment has been increased to one-seventh per cent of the weekly rate of the relevant pension for any incremental period of six days.[8] As under the prevailing rules there must be a minimum increment of one per cent of the standard pension rate,[9] it follows that the effective minimum is now forty-two qualifying days of deferred retirement (forty-two days at one-seventh per cent equals one per cent).

c. Deretirement

The National Insurance Act 1957, section 1 introduced the procedure by which a retirement pensioner under seventy (or sixty-five) might elect to deretire. The former pensioner may accordingly resume full-time work, thus earning increments to his pension when he eventually retires or becomes seventy (or sixty-five). The option does not appear to have been often used. The National Insurance Advisory Committee in 1966 found that only about 2,500 pensioners a year had elected to deretire.[10] It adduced two reasons for this. First, the decision entailed at that time payment of contributions and loss of pension with any addition for dependants, so that the pensioner must be confident of a relatively good income to afford the election; secondly, deretirement results in a loss of flexibility, in that the person concerned must give up his work to regain his pension, while if he has not deretired, all he needs do to obtain a full pension is to reduce his earnings. The latter reason does not appear very convincing since, as we have seen, retirement need not involve a total cessation of work. Largely because there did not seem to be any widespread demand for it, the Committee did not recommend that it should be possible for those over pensionable age to move frequently into and out of retirement. The position is still that a person may elect *only once* to deretire.[11]

The Regulations provide that a woman entitled to a Category B pension may not deretire while her husband is alive, and also that a husband who is entitled to a Category A pension may not so elect unless his wife, if entitled to a Category B pension on his contributions, consents to his election or unless 'that consent is unreasonably withheld'.[12] The only reported case on this provision comes from Northern Ireland. In *R 6/60 (P)*,

> A man, whose wife refused her consent to his deretirement, contended that she had a substantial private income and, therefore, her withholding of consent was unreasonable. The Commissioner held that in fact her resources were slighter than the husband thought, and that to refuse consent because of the substantial financial detriment which would be occasioned by the loss of her pension was not to withhold it unreasonably.

8. s.3(1)(b). This change also comes into effect on 6 April 1979.
9. SSPA 1975, Sch. 1, para. 1.
10. Report of the National Insurance Advisory Committee on the Earnings Limit for Retirement Pensions (1966), Cmnd. 3197, at paras. 57–62.
11. S.I. 1974/2059, Reg. 2(2)(a).
12. Ibid., Reg. 2(2)(b).

The Commissioner said that it was for the husband to show that the wife had acted unreasonably, and that examples of such unreasonable behaviour would be pique, spite or a desire just to stand in his way.[13]

Because of its consequences – loss of entitlement to pension and any dependants' increases – deretirement is regarded as a serious step. For this reason, notice of an election to deretire must be made in writing, and a document should not be construed as good notice, unless it is clearly intended to be one.[14] Unlike a retirement notice, it may not take effect before the date on which it is given.[15]

Though there is no evidence that the present position with regard to deretirement creates substantial problems, it is difficult to conclude that it is wholly satisfactory. With a liberally construed retirement condition and a generous earnings limit, there seems comparatively little scope for the deretirement procedure. And if there is a case for it, it appears odd that the election can only be made once. The real difficulty is perhaps attributable to the nature of the retirement condition itself, that it focusses on a past state ('has retired'), rather than imposes, as has been suggested,[16] a continuing condition ('is retired'). Of course, there would be practical difficulties in the latter alternative, but its adoption would avoid the artificialities of the deretirement procedure.

Part four. Graduated Retirement Benefit

Graduated retirement benefit[17] was introduced by the National Insurance Act 1959, this legislation marking the first departure from the principle of flat-rate contributions and benefits laid down in the Beveridge Report.[18] Under the National Insurance Act 1965[19] (the relevant provision of which is still in force) the benefit is an addition to the weekly rate of retirement pension payable to a person over pensionable age who has retired from regular employment: the supplement is calculated as 2½p for each unit of graduated contributions paid by the claimant.[20] A unit is £7·50 in the case of a man, and £9·00 for a woman; any contributions totalling a half or more of a unit are treated as a complete unit.[1] So, for example, a man who paid £177 in graduated contributions is entitled to 60p a week graduated pension, and a woman who paid £135 will receive 38p a week.[2]

13. The Commissioner followed with approval the approach taken in cases where consent is refused to the assignment of a lease: *Shanly v Ward* (1913), 29 TLR 714, CA. Compare the objective approach now taken in the consent to adoption cases: Cretney *Principles of Family Law*, (2nd edn), pp. 397–399.
14. *R(P) 1/61*.
15. S.I. 1974/2059, Reg. 2(4).
16. See ante, p. 204.
17. The legislation uses the term 'benefit', though the DHSS leaflets refer to graduated pension, and the two words are used interchangeably here.
18. Ante, p. 44, for graduated contributions.
19. Ss.36, 37 (the sections are now kept in force by S.I. 1978/393, made under the Social Security (Consequential Provisions) Act 1975).
20. NIA 1965, s.36(1).
1. Ibid., s.36(2), (3).
2. DHSS Leaflet NI.15, para. 12.

This additional benefit can be paid to a person who is not entitled to a standard retirement pension because he does not satisfy the contributions conditions for the latter.[3] But the requirements that the claimant has attained pensionable age and has retired are exacted.[4] A married woman may be entitled to this benefit on the basis of her own graduated contributions, and may draw it even if she is not able to claim her Category B pension because her husband has not yet retired. A widow is entitled to the graduated pension earned on her own contributions *and* half that earned by her husband.[5] If a person entitled to graduated benefit does not retire on reaching pensionable age, half the sum to which he was entitled at that time counts as additional graduated contributions; an extra graduated pension is then payable when he eventually retires or reaches seventy (or sixty-five).[6]

The graduated pensions scheme was widely thought inadequate as an attempt at an earnings-related provision.[7] One weakness in particular was that the benefit was not proof against inflation. With the introduction of fully earnings-related pensions under the Pensions Act 1975, there is no place for the older scheme. Graduated contributions have not been payable since April 1975, though the additional benefit will continue to be paid to those who had acquired a right (actual or prospective) to it at that time.[8] Moreover, under the Pensions Act the amount of the graduated pension may be increased under the up-rating provisions of the Social Security Act.[9]

Part five. The Social Security Pensions Act 1975[10]

In this Part an outline is given of the new scheme established by the Pensions Act 1975. Some aspects have already been mentioned: the alterations in contributions requirements,[11] the changes effected in the position of married women, widows and widowers,[12] and the scope of the earnings rule under the new regime.[13] Here attention is concentrated first, on the state earnings-related pension and secondly, on its relationship with occupational schemes.

A. General

The Labour government which took office in 1974 was dissatisfied with the Conservatives' Social Security Act 1973 on the grounds of the priority

3. Ante, pp. 211–213.
4. NIA 1965, s.36(1). The earnings rule does not apply after April, 1979.
5. Ibid., s.37.
6. S.I. 1978/393, Sch. 2. This applies even if the deferred retirement occurs after April 1975, when payment of graduated contributions ended.
7. Ante, p. 193.

8. S.I. 1978/393, Reg. 3.
9. SSPA 1975, s.24(1) implemented by S.I. 1978/393: for up-rating of benefits generally, see post, pp. 433–436.
10. See Mesher, 39 MLR 321 for an admirable summary of the Act.
11. See ante, p. 212.
12. Ante, p. 213.
13. Ante, p. 219.

it gave to occupational pensions and the inadequate provision in the state reserve scheme for those who were shortly to retire.[14] The new plan as originally outlined in the White Paper *Better Pensions*[15] provides for a state earnings-related element in the weekly pension ('the additional component') which is to be paid to anyone whose employer has not contracted-out and made satisfactory arrangements for occupational pensions for his employees. The scheme enables some earnings-related pension to be paid to those who are near retirement when it is introduced – though maximum benefits will not be paid until after the pensioner has contributed for twenty years. To some extent, therefore, the plan in its early years is redistributive between generations, an aspect of the provisions which has worried many Conservatives.[16] The earnings-related pension is to be inflation proof and, as will be seen,[17] the state will take over responsibility for the inflation proofing of that part of the contracted-out occupational pensions which is equivalent to the additional component, once it is in payment.

B. Earnings-related pensions

Section 6 of the Pensions Act provides that the weekly rate of a Category A retirement pension is to consist of a basic component (for 1977–78 £17·50) and an additional earnings-related component.[18] This will provide after twenty years 25% of a person's average earnings in a band between the 'lower earnings limit'[19] and a ceiling of seven times that level. The earnings-related pension builds up annually at a rate of $1\frac{1}{4}\%$, thereby reaching 25% after twenty years. If there have been earnings above the lower limit for more than that period, the 'best' twenty years are taken.[20] This formula is more satisfactory for manual workers than the assessment of pension with regard to the final year's earnings or the average of the last few years, which is a common feature of occupational pension schemes.

In order to keep pace with inflation and rising living standards, the claimant's earnings-factor, on the basis of which the additional component is calculated, is to be revalued 'in relation to the general level of earnings obtaining in Great Britain'.[1] The Secretary of State is directed to review this level in each tax year and then to increase the earnings factor by such percentage as is necessary to restore its relative value.[2] The rate at which the pension is paid is to be reviewed annually under the general provisions to that effect in the Social Security Act 1975.[3] The Pensions Act provides that the basic component is to be revised in the light of rises in earnings or

14. The Conservative scheme embodied in the 1973 Act is briefly discussed ante, p. 194.
15. (1974), Cmnd. 5713.
16. Sir G. Young, 888 HC Deb., col. 1538, and Mr K. Clarke, ibid., at col. 1560.
17. Post, p. 226.
18. S.7 makes similar provision for widow's Category B retirement

pensions and s.8 for widower's Category B pensions.
19. For this concept, see ante, p. 70.
20. SSPA 1975, s.6(2).
1. Ibid., s.21(1).
2. Ibid., s.21(3).
3. SSA 1975, ss.124–126: post, pp. 433–436.

prices, whichever is the more advantageous to the claimant, while the additional component is only to be increased in line with prices.[4]

These provisions do not, from an international perspective, break new ground.[5] The principle of earnings-related pensions has long been accepted in this country, and the only real dispute has been whether the state or employers should be the senior partner in the enterprise. The government's proposals were, therefore, not attacked in general, though at the Committee stage a Conservative attempted to increase the basic component, and to reduce the earnings-related component to much smaller proportions $-\frac{1}{4}\%$ each year, culminating after twenty years in only a 5% earnings-related addition.[6] The major drawback of the new provisions is that it will be very difficult for a prospective pensioner to calculate his future pension: he will have to estimate his best twenty years' earnings, keep a note of the revisions of his earnings factor, and then ascertain his pension with regard to these figures and the basic component.

c. Occupational pensions and contracting-out[7]

Much the most complicated part of the 1975 Pensions Act is that regulating occupational pension schemes and their relationship with the state earnings-related provision. There can be no contracting-out, of course, from the basic component. But sections 26–29 permit partial contracting-out from the full earnings-related contributions and benefits, where the occupational scheme provides the pensions required by the Act, and where the appropriate consents have been given by the Occupational Pensions Board.[8] When these conditions are met, the employee pays 2·5% less in contributions, and the employer's contribution is reduced by 4·5%.[9] The claimant then receives his state pension (calculated according to the formula described in the preceding section) minus the additional component or 'the guaranteed minimum pension' (GMP), whichever is less.[10]

The GMP is calculated in much the same way as the state additional component. In effect it is a weekly amount calculated as a percentage of the person's total earnings for the years (since the Pensions Act) of his working life.[11] If the person concerned (in 1975) is less than twenty years under pensionable age, then the percentage is $1\frac{1}{4}\%$ of earnings over the remaining years of his working life; otherwise it is 25% of his earnings for

4. SSPA 1975, s.23(4).
5. *Kaim-Caudle*, pp. 135–137 (Germany) and 177–182 (Canada).
6. Mr R. Boscawen, Standing Committee A Debates on Social Security Pensions Bill, col. 155 ff. The amendment was withdrawn after it became clear that it did not even obtain the support of all the Conservative members of the Committee!
7. Much useful information on contracting-out for occupational pension schemes is to be found in DHSS leaflets NP. 23 and 29.
8. SSPA 1975, s.30. The Board was set up by the SSA 1973 to regulate occupational schemes and is one of the few survivals of that legislation.
9. Ibid., s.27(2).
10. Ibid., s.29(1).
11. Ibid., s.35: see DHSS leaflet, NP 23, para. 6.

the years in his working life after the provisions come into force.[12] However, there is no provision for taking into account the 'best' twenty years of the person's working life, as there is for the calculation of the state earnings-related component. The earnings on the basis of which GMP is calculated are revised to allow for earnings increases in line with the statutory procedure.[13] Every approved occupational scheme must at the least provide this minimum pension.[14] In determining the amount of state pension to which the pensioner in a contracted-out scheme is entitled, the GMP (if less than the additional component) is deducted. It follows from this that the government is in effect providing the *subsequent* inflation-proofing when a pensioner is in receipt of an approved occupational pension, by continuing to pay the difference between the full state pension (basic plus additional component, revised annually to allow for inflation) and the guaranteed minimum pension (calculated at the pensioner's retirement) which must be provided by the occupational scheme.

Although the state guarantees the equivalent of the additional component against inflation, occupational pensions schemes must provide security against changes in the value of earnings *during the person's working life*. They must grant a pension of not less than $1\frac{1}{4}\%$ of either his average annual salary throughout his service in contracted-out employment or his final salary, in either case multiplied by his years of service up to forty.[15] Moreover, where they assess pension by reference to average salary, this must be revalued as with earnings factors for the state additional component.[16] Occupational schemes are left a certain amount of freedom with regard to the assessment of the salary by reference to which the person's pension is calculated;[17] they may also provide for a minimum period of service before the person qualifies for benefits in excess of the GMP.[18]

Generally, occupational benefits will be more generous than the GMP, and in some cases a pension up to half the annual average salary, or much more typically, the final salary will be provided. But this will not be the case where the minimum period of service is not completed, or the person leaves his employment well before he reaches pensionable age. Here, the pensioner may only receive the GMP. There are special provisions when an earner's employment is terminated before he reaches the scheme's normal pension age, involving in some cases the payment of a 'limited revaluation premium' by the employer to the state to cover the cost of annual revision in the light of inflation.[19] The protection of 'early leavers', as they are called, and the transfer of occupational pension rights have also

---

12. The exact formula in the second case is $25/N\%$ of the total earnings factors for the tax years in the person's working life from 1978–79, N being the number of years of working life since section 36 came into effect, viz. November 1975: S.I. 1975/1689.
13. SSPA 1975, s.35(5). For the statutory procedure, see SSPA 1975, s.21 and ante, p. 224.
14. Ibid., s.33(1)(b).
15. Ibid., s.34(2).
16. Ibid., s.34(2). These schemes are comparatively rare.
17. Ibid., s.34(5).
18. Ibid., s.34(3).
19. Ibid., ss.35(5) and 45. See DHSS leaflet NP 29, paras. 37–44.

entailed some very complicated provisions in the 1975 Act, but an exposition of these would be outside the scope of this book.[20]

Part six. Non-contributory Pensions

A. Category C retirement pensions

This pension was introduced by the National Insurance (Old persons' and widows' pensions and attendance allowance) Act 1970,[1] primarily to provide for those who were uninsured under the pre-1948 schemes and who were over pensionable age when the 1946 Act came into effect. They never had the chance to establish eligibility to a pension under this legislation. For a number of years backbenchers of both parties had attempted to help this group, but the Labour government had consistently rejected moves to provide them with pensions on the grounds that such a step would violate the contributory principle and not necessarily assist those most in need.[2] The 1970 Act was the first measure of the new Conservative government. However, it was pointed out that it did not provide any assistance for people who had been able to qualify for a pension under the 1946 Act, but for some reason – probably deficient contributions – had failed to do so. Moreover, the rate of this new pension was lower than the equivalents at that time of the full Category A or higher rate Category B retirement pension; it was considered inappropriate to pay the same amount as that receivable by persons who had contributed fully to the National Insurance Fund.[3]

The Category C pension is payable to a person who was over pensionable age on 5 July 1948, has been resident in Great Britain for a period of at least ten years between that date and 1 November 1970 and was ordinarily resident there on 2 November 1970 or on the date of the claim.[4] A woman, married to a man in receipt of this pension, is also entitled to it, provided she is over pensionable age and has retired.[5] Further, the Regulations provide for its payment in certain conditions to the widow of a man who was over pensionable age on 5 July 1948.[6] These requirements are broadly as follows:

    (i) she is over pensionable age, has retired, and was over forty when her husband died;

and (ii) *either* (a) her husband was entitled to a Category C pension, *or* (b) he died before 2 November 1970 and she satisfied specified residence conditions.

---

20. Ibid., paras. 47–51.
1. S.I. The Act was renamed NIA 1970, by NIA 1972, s.8(4).
2. Mr D. Houghton, 803 HC Deb., col. 1017.
3. Mr P. Dean, Under-Secretary of State, ibid., at col. 1551.

4. SSA 1975, s.39(1), and S.I. 1974/2059, Reg. 6. For the concepts of 'residence' and 'ordinary residence', see post, pp. 414–416.
5. SSA 1975, s.39(1)(b).
6. S.I. 1974/2059, Reg. 8.

Analogous conditions are imposed for the payment of a Category C pension to a woman whose marriage to a husband (over pensionable age on 5 July 1948) was terminated by divorce.[7] It will be noted that in some circumstances the pension is conditional on the claimant's retirement, though this will generally not be required. However, rather oddly, both Category C and D pensions are known in the legislation as retirement pensions.

The Category C pension is paid at two rates: a lower rate (for 1977–78, £6·30), where the claimant is, and has been since she became entitled, a married woman, and a higher rate in all other cases (for 1977–78, £10·50).[8]

B. Category D retirement pensions

A year after Category C pensions were introduced, the same government provided for non-contributory pensions to all persons over eighty.[9] Any person over eighty, not entitled to any other category of pension and who satisfies the residence conditions is entitled to a Category D retirement pension.[10] It is not entirely clear why this measure so closely followed the introduction of Category C pensions; probably the government became convinced that the needs of all those over eighty should be met, irrespective of the circumstance whether they had ever had the chance to join the 1946 Act scheme.[11] In any case, the numbers of people covered by this new pension were estimated to be only about 50,000. The amount of the Category D pension is £10·50 except where the pensioner is, and has been since she became entitled to it, a married woman, when it is paid at the lower rate of £6·30.[12]

It appears that virtually everyone entitled to a Category C retirement pension would be entitled to a Category D pension if he were not able to claim the former. The major exceptions are wives (or widows) of husbands who were over pensionable age on 5 July 1948; they are entitled to a Category C pension, but will not (if under eighty) be entitled to a Category D retirement pension. This group will decline in numbers over the next few years and it will then be appropriate to consider whether it is necessary to retain the separate Category C retirement pension.[13] The number of recipients of Category D pensions may also be expected to decline, as those who did not exercise the option to pay contributions afforded them by the 1946 legislation die. But there will always be some people whose contribution record is deficient, in particular those immigrants and British citizens returning from abroad who have not been obliged to pay contributions for their working life; it will be necessary to keep the Category D retirement pension as a residual provision for them.

7. S.I. 1974/2059, Reg. 9.
8. S.I. 1977/1325.
9. NIA 1971, s.5.
10. SSA 1975, s.39(1)(c): the residence conditions are set out in S.I. 1974/2059, Reg. 7.
11. Sir K. Joseph, Secretary of State, 816

HC Deb., cols. 1013–1014.
12. S.I. 1977/1325.
13. The Social Security statistics for 1976 show that about 3,000 women under 80 benefit from the Category C pension: Table 13.35.

c. The age addition

The National Insurance Act 1971 also introduced an additional payment of 25p (known as the 'age addition') for pensioners of all categories over eighty.[14] As Sir Keith Joseph said during the Second Reading in the House of Commons, 'this age addition recognises, albeit in a small way, the special claims of very elderly people, who on the whole need help rather more than others'.[15] In fact the measure now appears as an insignificant gesture since its value has not been increased since its introduction. A person in receipt of certain other prescribed benefits, and who would be entitled to a retirement pension if he were to claim it rather than continue in receipt of the alternative benefit, is also entitled to the age addition.[16] No claim is required for the addition: it is paid automatically.[17]

14. The provision is now in SSA 1975, s.40(1).
15. 816 HC Deb., col. 1019.
16. SSA 1975, s.40(2): see S.I. 1974/2059, Reg. 15, which prescribes these other benefits. For the age addition to supplementary benefit, see post, p. 493.
17. S.I. 1975/560, Reg. 3(c): see post, p. 588 (claims and payments).

6 Benefits on Death

It is convenient to consider together, in one chapter, three benefits payable on the death of a contributor. These are widow's benefit (Part One), child's special allowance, payable when the deceased was maintaining a child of a former marriage (Part Two), and death grant, a sum paid for partial indemnity of funeral expenses (Part Three).

Part one. Widow's Benefit

A. General

It has been written of the history of British provision for widowhood that 'no part of our social security has shown such a consistent pattern of political failure as this'.[1] The problems have arisen for a variety of reasons: there have been differing views concerning the extent to which widows should be regarded as part of the potential labour force, and the extent to which benefit should be regarded as an unqualified return on the husband's contributions or rather a limited entitlement based on need. At the same time, it has been necessary to take account of the public sympathy aroused by widowhood and the tendency to distinguish it from other circumstances where a family is deprived of a breadwinner (e.g., divorce).

Lloyd George had planned to extend his programme of national insurance to cover widowed mothers and orphans. His failure to do so resulted not from any unwillingness on the part of the Liberal government but from a massive political lobby organised by the industrial assurance companies, which saw in the proposal a threat to their business and to the livelihood of their employees.[2] After the First World War, political pressure, particularly from women's associations, for some form of mother's pension had grown,[3] and the hostility of the industrial assurance companies had abated. The notion of a comprehensive scheme for all unsupported mothers was firmly resisted – it would be inappropriate and impracticable to make provision for deserted or divorced wives on a

1. *Walley*, p. 249.
2. Gilbert *The Evolution of National Insurance in Great Britain* (1966), pp.
326–343.
3. *Finer*, Appendix 2, paras. 77–88.

contributory insurance basis[4] – but there was an acknowledged powerful case for a widowed mother's pension. Yet what emerged in the Baldwin government's proposal was the surprising notion of a pension of ten shillings per week payable for life or until remarriage to *all* widows, regardless of means or family commitments. Payment to childless widows was by no means a popular move[5] but Churchill, influenced by the administrative difficulties of providing a more selective scheme and by the naive assumption that if the husband had paid his contributions, the insurance principle would require that benefit could not be refused to the widow,[6] steered the measure through Parliament as part of the Widows', Orphans' and Old Age Contributory Pensions Act 1925.

The rashness of this decision had long-term harmful effects on the future of widows' benefits. The flat-rate universal scheme meant that widows with families suffered economic hardship while childless recipients were relatively well off. The hostility of Beveridge to the scheme is evident from the incisive terms in which he criticised it:

'there is no reason why a childless widow should get a pension for life; if she is able to work, she should work'.[7]

Under his plan, the abolition of long-term entitlement for childless widows or those able to work was to be accompanied by more generous treatment of widows with children. He proposed a short-term benefit payable to all widows for thirteen weeks, to allow them to adjust to the new circumstances, and a pension payable only for so long as there were dependent children.[8] The government, while accepting these two basic principles, was also impressed by an argument which he had rejected, that a pension equal to a retirement pension should be paid to a widow who, at her husband's death or when her youngest child ceased to be dependent upon her, had reached an age at which she would find it hard to take up paid work.[9] It also considered it unfair to deprive childless widows of rights already conferred on them by their husband's contributions, so the 'ten shillings pension' would still be paid when the husband had died before 1948.

The embodiment of these proposals in the National Insurance Act 1946 may have implemented this new policy,[10] but the formulation of particular rules consistent with that policy exercised the minds of successive governments and necessitated some important changes in the period after 1950. These included the abolition of an earnings rule, the introduction of an earnings-related supplement, and the revising of the methods of determining when it would be unreasonable to expect the widow to work.

4. Second Interim Report of the Committee on Insurance and Other Social Services (Anderson Committee) (1923), available at the Public Record Office. See *Finer*, loc. cit., and Gilbert *British Social Policy 1914–1939* (1970), pp. 242–244.
5. Opposition was expressed by the trade unions and indeed by some members of the government itself: *Walley*, pp. 63–64.
6. Ibid., p. 64.
7. Para. 153.
8. Para. 346.
9. Social Insurance, Part I, para. 121.
10. It was reiterated by the National Insurance Advisory Committee in its Report on the Question of Widow's Benefits (1956), Cmd. 9684, para. 27.

These will be described at relevant stages in the discussion of the various benefits available, and Part One will conclude with a critique of the present law.

B. Widowhood

A claimant must, of course, prove that she 'has been widowed'. This involves two elements: she was lawfully married to a man, and while so married he died. The first will be considered in detail in chapter 10;[11] the second calls for treatment here. The primary method of proof is by a certificate issued by the Registrar General,[12] but other less formal means will suffice, it being necessary to satisfy the statutory authorities on the balance of probabilities that the husband is dead.[13] The real problem arises where he has been absent for some years and nothing has been heard of him. In many areas of law, legislation has intervened to create a presumption of death if a person has been absent for a continuous period of seven years, and there is no reason to believe that he has been living within that time.[14] No such statutory provisions exist in social security law, and the question arises whether an equivalent presumption may be invoked as part of the common law. The reported decisions of the Commissioner on the point appear to reject the possibility. In *R(G) 1/62* it was held that at common law a man is presumed to live his normal span, and that the onus is on the claimant to rebut the presumption by evidence that, for example, he was last seen setting out on a dangerous mission, or was known to be at the site of a calamity. Such evidence had been available in an earlier case when a claim succeeded ten months after the hat and jacket of the missing spouse had been found at the landing stage of a port.[15] In the 1962 case no equivalent circumstances could be invoked and, despite the fact that nothing had been heard of the husband for twenty-five years, the claim failed. It may be, however, that the latter decision is not conclusive on the point. It purported only to apply the law of Scotland and the English decision of *Chard v Chard*[16] was not cited. In that case Sachs J, having carefully reviewed the relevant authorities, advanced a proposition to cover the situation where legislation had not intervened, and where there was no acceptable affirmative evidence that the missing person was alive at sometime during a continuous period of seven years or more. It was to the effect that,

> 'if it can be proved first, that there are persons who would be likely to have heard of him over that period, secondly that those persons have not heard of him, and thirdly that all due inquiries have been made appropriate to the circumstances',

11. Post, pp. 398–404.
12. Under a special arrangement with the DHSS. See SSA 1975, s.160. The certificate, formerly issued free of charge, now costs 75p: S.I. 1975/1291.
13. *R(G) 4/57*
14. See, e.g., Offences against the Person Act 1861, s.57 (as a defence to bigamy); Matrimonial Causes Act 1973, s.19(3) (dissolution of marriage); and generally Treitel, 17 MLR 530.
15. *R(G) 4/57*.
16. [1956] P. 259.

the missing persion will be presumed to have died at some time within that period.[17] Whether this dictum should be applied to social security law remains an open question. *Chard v Chard* was concerned with the validity of a subsequent marriage. The policy considerations relevant to a benefit intended as a replacement for the husband's maintenance which, ex hypothesi, is not paid in cases of prolonged absence, may point to a different conclusion.

C. Remarriage and cohabitation

All widow's benefits cease on remarriage and payment is suspended during a period in which she is living with a man as his wife[18] (the latter concept is discussed in chapter 10[19]). Under the industrial scheme,[20] and in some foreign systems,[1] a lump-sum is payable to a widow on remarriage, presumably as an incentive to her to relieve the public fund of her support. Whether it has such an effect is highly speculative, but in any event, there is no obvious reason for the different treatment of industrial and non-industrial widows.

D. Widow's allowance

The initial benefit is paid to enable the widow to readjust to her new circumstances of life, and is the most generous flat-rate personal benefit available under our social security system (in 1977–78, £24·50 per week[2]). It also confers entitlement to an addition based on the average earnings of the deceased husband,[3] and to an increase for dependent children.[4] Irrespective of her family circumstances, the allowance is payable to a widow under pensionable age at the death of the husband, (or over if he was not then entitled to a Category A retirement pension) provided that the husband had satisfied the contribution conditions,[5] viz.,

> in any one year ending before the date on which he attained pensionable age or died, he must have actually paid Class 1, 2 or 3 contributions, and the earnings factor derived from such contributions must be not less than that year's lower earnings limit multiplied by twenty-five.[6]

Under the 1946 Act, the allowance was payable only for thirteen weeks,[7] but in 1966 the period was extended to twenty-six weeks.[8] Entitlement begins on the date of death.[9]

---

17. Ibid., at p. 272.
18. SSA 1975, ss.24(2), 25(3) and 26(3).
19. Post, pp. 404–408.
20. Post, p. 345.
1. *Finer*, Appendix 3, para. 70.
2. S.I. 1977/1325.
3. Introduced by NIA 1966, s.4(1) and re-enacted as SSA 1975, s.24(3). For details of the addition, see post, pp.

424–426.
4. SSA 1975, s.41, post, pp. 385–386.
5. SSA 1975, s.24(1).
6. Ibid., Sch. 3, para. 4; for earnings factors etc., see ante, chap. 2.
7. NIA 1946, s.17(2)(a).
8. NIA 1966, s.4(3), re-enacted as SSA 1975, s.24(2).
9. *R(G) 3/52.*

E. Widowed mother's allowance

For Beveridge, care of a family constituted the principal reason for making long-term provision for widows.[10] To determine the circumstances in which such care might be presumed, the legislation imposes conditions similar to those employed where an increase to a personal benefit for child dependants is claimed.[11] It may, however, be questioned whether the two situations are truly analogous: the widowed mother's allowance (WMA) is based on the idea that family responsibilities prevent a widow working, which implies that the child or children should be living with the widow; the increases to personal benefit are meant to assist the claimant with *financial* obligations.[12]

The necessary relationship between the widow and child or children is, for the most part, governed by the principles of child benefit.[13] The claimant must prove either that she is pregnant by her late husband or that she is entitled to child benefit in respect of a child who is either

'(a) a son or daughter of the woman and her late husband; *or* (b) a child in respect of whom her late husband was immediately before his death entitled to child benefit;[14] *or* (c) if the woman and her late husband were residing together immediately before his death, a child in respect of whom she was then entitled to child benefit'.[15]

As will be seen, child benefit is generally not payable for children aged sixteen to nineteen or those absent from Great Britain.[16] The traditional test of dependency for WMA was not so limited and so to preserve the broader base for the allowance, those 'entitled to child benefit' in the rules cited above are 'deemed' to include those who would have been entitled to child benefit if the child in question had been under sixteen or present in Great Britain.[17]

The contribution conditions are different from those applicable to the widow's allowance, resembling instead those imposed for retirement pensions. They are:[18]

1. in any year ending before that in which the husband died or reached pensionable age, he must actually have paid contribu-

---

10. Para. 153, where he used the term 'guardian's allowance'.
11. Cf. post, pp. 385–386.
12. In 1956 NIAC had drawn attention to the anomaly (Report on the Question of Widow's Benefits (1956), Cmd. 9684, paras. 76–78) but its recommendation to exclude benefit in cases of non-residence has not been implemented.
13. Post, chap. 11.
14. This is deemed to include a child of the widow's previous marriage if the husband of *that* marriage was immediately before *his* death entitled

to child benefit for that child and the woman was entitled to child benefit at the time of the death giving rise to the present entitlement to WMA: S.I. 1974/2059, Reg. 13A(2), inserted by S.I. 1977/342, Reg. 4.
15. SSA 1975, s.25(1), (2), as amended by CBA 1975, Sch. 4, para. 9.
16. Post, pp. 453 and 465.
17. S.I. 1974/2059, Reg. 13A(1), inserted by S.I. 1977/342, Reg. 4.
18. SSA 1975, Sch. 3, para. 5 as amended by SSPA 1975, s.19(1), (2). On the concepts involved see ante, chap. 2.

tions of Classes 1, 2 or 3 and the earnings factor derived therefrom must be not less than the qualifying earnings factor for that
year. The condition is deemed to be satisfied if he was entitled to
invalidity pension at any time during the year in which he
attained pensionable age or died, or the year immediately preceding that year.

2. for each year of his working life, less one year for each ten years'
working life, he must have paid or been credited with contributions of Classes 1, 2 or 3, and the earnings factor derived therefrom must be not less than the qualifying earning factor for the
year in question. This condition is deemed to have been fulfilled
if the husband had satisfied the criterion for at least half the
number of years (or twenty of them, if that is less than half) and
in the remaining years he was precluded from regular employment by responsibilities at home.

The emphasis placed by Beveridge and post-war governments on the
WMA, as fulfilling the needs of widows with family commitments, was
not always fully reflected in the amounts payable. Under the 1946 Act[19]
the widow was paid a flat-rate weekly sum less than that of the widow's
allowance, and equal to that of the widow's pension, and in addition
received for each of the qualifying children the standard rates of increase
to personal benefit for dependent children. In 1956 the inadequacy of
this provision was revealed by the fact that about 30% of WMA recipients
were also in receipt of a national assistance grant, a proportion higher than
that for any other category of national insurance beneficiary.[20] The family
needs of a long-term beneficiary were evidently greater than those of
someone whose earnings were only temporarily interrupted, and the
National Insurance Advisory Committee recommended that the children's
element in the benefit should be raised to a higher level. The proposal was
implemented[1] and to supplement her flat-rate benefit (in 1977–78 £17·50[2])
the widow is entitled to an addition for each child about twice that
available as an increase to short-term personal benefits.[3] Under the original scheme, there was a reduction for earnings, similar to that applicable
to retirement pensions.[4] The rule was an extremely unpopular one, and
there was continuous pressure for its removal.[5] After a number of concessions had been made, the rule was finally abolished as one of the first
measures enacted by the Wilson government in 1964.[6]

19. NIA 1946, Sch. 2, Part I.
20. NIAC Report, ante n. 12, at para. 38.
1. FANIA 1956, s.2(1).
2. S.I. 1977/1328.
3. Post, pp. 385–386.
4. Cf., ante, pp. 216–219.
5. The NIAC, while remaining
committed to the principle underlying
the earnings rule, had found great

difficulties in its application: see
Report on the Earnings Rule (1955),
Cmd. 9752. A proposal for its abolition
for several years played a leading role
in the Labour Party Manifesto. See the
parliamentary debate on the National
Insurance Bill 1964, 702 HC Deb., col.
1297ff.
6. NIA 1964, s.1(5).

F. Widow's pension

The continuance of provision for a widow after her last child reaches an age of non-dependency has been the subject of greatest dispute and the most important changes since the 1946 Act. Beveridge saw no reason to distinguish between widows and single women and concluded that, apart from a 'training' allowance, nothing beyond the ordinary benefits for unemployment and sickness should be conferred on the childless widow until pensionable age.[7] The post-war government felt that this would create hardships for elderly widows who had little or no working experience, and quite independently of its decision to maintain the 'ten shillings pension' for those childless widows already qualified under the old scheme, introduced a new, long-term pension payable to those aged fifty or over when the husband died, or forty or over when entitlement to WMA ceased.[8] In both cases, it was felt necessary to establish evidence of prolonged absence from the labour market by requiring proof that the claimant had been married for a period of at least ten years,[9] though if the widow was incapable of self-support, the pension was payable irrespective of the duration of the marriage or her age at her husband's death or when WMA ceased.[10] In 1956 this concession was revoked,[11] but at the same time the duration of marriage test for all widows was reduced to three years[12] and subsequently, in 1970 abolished altogether.[13]

As regards the age condition, the distinction between those who had, and those who had not been, entitled to WMA was an eleventh hour political concession made before the 1946 Bill was passed, and was difficult to justify except on sentimental grounds. In 1956, following the National Insurance Advisory Committee's recommendations,[14] the preferential treatment for widowed mothers was removed and henceforth the 'fifty year' age test was to apply to all, except, of course, those already benefiting from the earlier concession.[15] This second instance of the rare practice of actually narrowing entitlement to social welfare was not to remain effective for long. The main objection was the all-or-nothing distinction which depended on the widow's exact age when her husband died or when her entitlement to WMA ceased. Accordingly, as part of its National Superannuation plan, the Labour government proposed to introduce a sliding scale of pensions for those aged between forty and fifty at the relevant date. The proposal was resurrected by the succeeding Conservative government and was implemented in 1970.[16]

---

7. Para. 156.
8. NIA 1946, ss.17(1)(c) and 18(1)(a).
9. Ibid., ss.17(1)(c) and 18(1)(b).
10. NIA 1946, s.18(3).
11. Except for those already entitled to it: FANIA 1956 s.2(6).
12. Ibid., s.2(2), following a NIAC recommendation: ante n.12.
13. NIA 1970, s.3, which, however conferred a power by regulations to exclude or reduce pension where the husband had attained pensionable age before marriage and had died within a year. The power was never exercised and was itself abolished by SSA 1973, Sch. 28.
14. NIAC Report on the Question of Widow's Benefits (1956), Cmd. 9684, para. 45.
15. FANIA 1956, s.2(5).
16. NI (Old persons' and widows' pensions and attendance allowance) Act 1970, s.2, (renamed NIA 1970 by NIA 1972).

As a result of these various modifications, the present rule for entitlement is that the widow must have been over forty years of age[17] at the date of the husband's death or when she ceased to be entitled to WMA.[18] If at that date, she was under fifty years of age, the weekly rate of pension (in 1977–78, £17·50[19]) is reduced by 7% for each year of age less than fifty (any fractions of a year counting as one whole year).[20]

> Thus a benefit payable to a widow aged forty-seven years at her husband's death is reduced by 21%, and if aged forty-one years by 63%.

The contribution conditions are the same as those for WMA,[1] and as with that benefit, no earnings rule applies.

G. Old cases

In order to protect those with vested interests under the old legislation, equivalents to WMA and the pension are payable to widows of persons over pensionable age on 5 June 1948.[2]

H. Social Security Pensions Act 1975

As part of the new pensions arrangements, the widow's pension and widowed mother's allowance will, from 1 April 1979, contain an additional earnings-related component.[3] The husband must have satisfied the contribution conditions for a Category A retirement pension, and the amount of the additional component will be calculated as for that benefit.[4]

J. Critique

The history of widows' pensions has been a struggle between two conflicting principles: that of providing universal income maintenance for a widow irrespective of age and family circumstances, and that of guaranteeing an income to a widow only when she is deemed to be unlikely to obtain the necessary income support for herself. The result of the struggle has been a compromise solution conditioned as much by political sentiment as by any clear objective and sociological perspective.[5] The phenomenon has not been peculiar to Britain. The writer of a comparative survey has observed that,

17. For guidance on how age is to be determined see ante, p. 199.
18. SSA 1975, s.26(1).
19. S.I. 1977/1325.
20. SSA 1975, s.26(2).
1. Ibid., Sch. 3, para. 5; ante, p. 234.

2. S.I. 1970/1280, Regs. 3–5.
3. SSPA 1975, s. 13.
4. Ante, pp. 211–213 and 224–225.
5. Cf. Marris *Widows and their Families* (1958), chap. 7.

'the variety of responses [to the problems of widowhood] is due to historical circumstances and the unequal strength of the pressure groups influencing public opinion and the public authorities. It seldom follows any logical pattern'.[6]

There are, perhaps, four major criticisms that can be made of the existing provisions. First, the system divides widows into certain categories which are based on assumptions of their needs as individuals in certain situations of life,[7] whereas it is arguable that the need for security belongs to the family rather than the widow, who may not herself suffer any financial loss. Secondly, it does not take sufficient heed of the changing pattern of women's participation in industry. The rules on widow's benefits, particularly following the abolition of the earnings rule, are based on the stereotype of the woman looking after the family, with paid employment being regarded as an exceptional activity. This no longer reflects social reality: in 1975 over half the married women over thirty-five were employed in full-time or part-time work.[8] Thirdly, entitlement is based entirely on a man's contributions. This too is based on the model of the husband being the sole, or at least primary, breadwinner. There is much to be said for integrating survivor benefits with retirement pensions.[9] Just as occupational pension schemes generally provide for both retirement and death, so a state scheme might allow a husband or wife to commute the retirement entitlement of the deceased spouse to a pension payable at his (or her) premature death.[10] This would also deal with the argument which has often been deployed for the more favourable treatment of widows, that the husband's death robs him of the return on his insurance contributions which a retirement pension would have brought him.[11] Finally, and following from the last point, there is the objection based on sex discrimination in favour of women. Outside the industrial injury and war pension schemes,[12] there is no benefit for widowers.[13] While the Social Security Pensions Act 1975 has made a modest attempt to mitigate the inequality by enabling a husband in certain circumstances to benefit from his deceased wife's contributions[14] it leaves unaffected the basic principle. The lack of provision to cover lost household services may rest on the questionable assumption that it is easier for the widower than for the widow to find a replacement spouse.[15] Quite apart from this, it fails to take account of the working wife's contributions to the family income. In the United States, such questions have been elevated to a constitutional plane.

6. Laroque, 106 Int. Lab. Rev. 1, 7. See also Tamburi, in ISSA Studies and Research No. 5 *Women and Social Security* (1973), pp. 128ff.
7. *Marris*, ante n.5, at p. 91.
8. HMSO General Household Survey 1975, Table 5.2.
9. *Walley*, pp. 254–255.
10. Laroque, ante n.6, at pp. 8–9.
11. Cf. the Norwegian system described by *Tamburi*, ante n.6, at p. 152.
12. Post, pp. 346 and 378, respectively.
13. For the availability of widower's benefits in other systems see *Tamburi*, ante n.6, at pp. 149–150. *Finer* (pp. 349–350) recommends its introduction to Britain.
14. Ante, p. 215.
15. Cf. Clarke and Ogus 5 B. Jo. Law and Society 1.

In *Weinberger v Wiesenfeld*,[16] the Supreme Court held that a social security statute conferring death benefits only on the widow violated the Equal Protection clause.

Part two. Child's Special Allowance

A. General

There was one group of women with dependent children who might suffer hardship on the death of the children's father because they would not be eligible for widowed mother's allowance. These were women whose marriage had been terminated by divorce and who since then had received some provision from the former husband for the children of the marriage (or other children). Although this provision might cease, they would not then become entitled to any benefit on the husband's death for the simple reason that they were not widows. The Royal Commission on Marriage and Divorce drew attention to the gap and recommended that such a woman should be entitled to draw an allowance under the national insurance system for children living with her if the death of her former husband resulted in the loss of the money he had been contributing towards their maintenance.[17] The National Insurance Advisory Committee adopted this recommendation, subject to the modification that the benefit should be payable to a divorced woman, whether she had been the 'guilty' party or not.[18] The proposal was implemented by section 5 of the National Insurance Act 1957.

Four years later, some changes were made to the structure of the benefit, the most important of which was that the value of the child's special allowance (CSA), was no longer to be limited by reference to the amount contributed for the maintenance of the child (or children) by the former husband before his death.[19] From April 1978 £6·10 is payable for all children, the same amount as is paid by way of increase to a widow's benefit for dependent children.[1] Nothing is paid for the ex-wife herself; in this respect her position is still worse than that of a widow. The number of recipients of a child's special allowance has been relatively small though it has been slowly rising. In 1976, 677 women received it (as against 198 in 1960).[2]

---

16. 95 S.Ct. 1225 (1975), noted in 44 Ford LR 170. See, more generally, West, 49 Ind. LJ 181.

17. (1956), Cmd. 9678, paras. 714–716. The former husband might, of course, have made some financial provision for the children after his death, but this does not affect the entitlement to the allowance. In this respect the current provision goes beyond the Royal Commission's proposal.

18. Report on Question of Dependency Provisions (1956), Cmd. 9855, paras. 72–73.

19. FANIA 1961, s.7(2)(b).

20. S.I. 1977/1325.

1. Post, p. 385.

2. DHSS Social Security Statistics 1976, Table 9.35.

B. Entitlement

Section 31 of the Social Security Act 1975 (as amended by the Child Benefit Act)[3] sets out the conditions for entitlement to CSA. There are broadly three requirements, in addition to the rule which limits the benefit to a woman whose marriage has been terminated by divorce, or, under the Regulations, whose voidable marriage has been annulled.[4] A woman who entered into a bigamous marriage in all good faith is not entitled to a CSA on the death of her former 'husband', because a bigamous marriage is void.[5] The distinction in this context between a void and voidable marriage seems difficult to defend, as the financial loss to the woman's children on the man's death may not differ.[6] The allowance is not payable if the woman remarries or lives with a man as his wife.[7]

i) Death and contribution conditions
The first requirement is that the woman's former husband must have died[8] and must have satisfied the contribution conditions.[9] These are that:

> in any one year ending before the date on which the husband attained pensionable age or died, he must have actually paid Class 1, 2 or 3 contributions, and the earning factor derived from such contributions must be not less than that year's lower earnings limit multiplied by fifty.[10]

ii) The relationship between woman and child
As with WMA the necessary relationship between the woman and the child falls into line with the child benefit scheme. She must be entitled to child benefit in respect of the child at the time of the claim and, *either* she *or* her former husband must have been so entitled immediately before his death.[11] The alternative condition based on the husband's entitlement is treated as satisfied if the child in question is a child of the marriage terminated by divorce, and for that purpose also any absence of the child from Great Britain is ignored.[12] The child need not be a son or daughter of the marriage which has ended in the divorce.

iii) The husband must have been paying a contribution, etc.
It is the third requirement which has raised the only points of difficulty for the Commissioner. Section 31(c) of the 1975 Act requires

3. Sch. 4, para. 10.
4. S.I. 1975/497, Reg. 3.
5. *R(G) 3/59.*
6. In family law, the financial provisions on the termination of a void marriage are the same as those which obtain at the end of a voidable one. On the other hand, social security law generally does not accord any significance to a void marriage: post, p. 400.
7. SSA 1975, s.31 proviso, as amended by SS(MP)A 1977, s.22(2). See generally on this post, pp. 404–408.
8. Cf., ante, p. 232.
9. SSA 1975, Sch. 3, Part I, para. 6.
10. For the concepts involved see ante, chap. 2.
11. SSA 1945, s.31(b), as amended by CBA 1975, Sch. 4, para. 10. For entitlement to child benefit, see post, chap. 11. There is a minor category of persons so entitled who are treated as not so entitled: see S.I. 1977/342, Reg. 3.
12. S.I. 1975/497, Reg. 4, inserted by S.I. 1977/342, Reg. 6(3).

'either:

> (i) that husband had before his death been contributing at not less than the prescribed weekly rate to the cost of providing for that child, or

> (ii) at the date of the husband's death she was entitled, under an order of a court, trust or agreement which she has taken reasonable steps to enforce, to receive (whether from that husband or from another person) payments in respect of that child at not less than that rate provided or procured by that husband'

Limb (ii) of this provision was introduced in 1967 as an alternative to the requirement of the actual providing of money by the former husband.[13] It enables CSA to be claimed where the woman has unsuccessfully attempted to enforce a maintenance or financial provision order against him. The case law interpreting the first limb of section 31(c) must, therefore, now be read in the light of the possibility that the claimant might succeed under this alternative head. The prescribed rate under the Regulation is 25p a week;[14] and has not been increased since the allowance was introduced in 1957. The combination of this and the fact that the allowance has not since 1961 been limited to the amount actually paid by the former husband,[15] underlines the lack of real significance of the former husband's contributions as a qualifying requirement. The allowance cannot now, as it was originally, be justified as providing 'compensation' for the loss of the husband's support, but may rather be seen simply as a substitute for the widowed mother's additional allowance for her children. It is arguable that the requirement that the husband has been contributing to the cost of providing for the child now serves so little purpose that it could be abolished.

The notion of 'contributing . . . to the cost of providing for the child' in the first limb of section 31(c) is common to other areas of social security law, notably that governing entitlement to increases to personal benefit for child dependants. Guidance on its interpretation may therefore be had from discussions in that context.[16] There are, however, points of special interest to the CSA which must be considered here. The first arises from the fact that, for the purposes of the allowance, the husband must have been contributing 'before his death', even though the payments need not be *received* by that time.[17]

In *R(G) 5/59*, where the husband had made only three or four payments under a court order in the four years before his death, the Commissioner ruled that the phrase, 'had before his death been contributing', meant 'had *immediately* before his death been contributing'. Otherwise the words 'before death' would have no significance at all. A second reason for this

---

13. NIA 1967, s. 1(2) and Sch. 4, para. 4.
14. S.I. 1975/497, Reg. 2.
15. Ante, p. 239.
16. Post, pp. 393–397.
17. See *R(G) 17/59*, where the husband died before the sale of a house, half the proceeds of which were to be paid to the former wife, could be completed and a deed of covenant signed.

interpretation was that the purpose of the allowance was to confer a benefit on a woman who suffered financial loss on her former husband's death, and this would only be the case if he had been contributing immediately before that time. For the reasons given in the previous paragraph this second argument is perhaps now of less weight, but the Commissioner's interpretation of the provision and his disallowance of the claim on the facts was obviously correct.[18]

On the other hand, the fact that payments were irregular will not be a decisive obstacle to entitlement. As with the analogous test governing entitlement to dependants' increases, the Commissioner has been prepared to average payments over a substantial period (e.g., a year),[19] and because the prescribed rate of contributions is so low (25p a week) even infrequent payments made during such a period will probably satisfy the requirement.

Involuntary and temporary cessations in the payment of contributions are also generously treated. For the purposes of the CSA, this is important because of the proximity of the husband's death. Thus the Commissioner has held that a period in hospital when the husband was suffering from a terminal illness might be ignored,[20] but such an illness does not cover 'a long period of incapacity which ultimately terminates in death': it means a period when the person is dying.[1] In other circumstances, entitlement turns on whether an interruption was temporary or permanent. In deciding this issue, regard will be had to the reason for the interruption, the husband's general contributions record and his attitude to the children during the period. In *R(G) 15/59*

> the claimant's former husband contributed regularly to the maintenance of her two children until he became unemployed just over four months before he died. Although he was a sick man for this period, he did secure employment for about eight weeks, and then he entered hospital for the six weeks before his death. The Commissioner ruled (1) that the period in hospital when the husband was suffering from a terminal illness should be ignored, and (2) that the earlier cessation of payments when he became unemployed was temporary and involuntary. An allowance was therefore awarded.

It was not until the husband entered hospital that it became clear he would not recover, so that before that time there was every prospect that payments would be resumed, and throughout he had taken an interest in the children. These factors were not present in *R(G) 3/60*, where the husband stopped paying maintenance shortly after he had left his work because of infirmity, and there was never any chance that he would be able to resume payments in the eighteen months before his death. The Commissioner held that the cessation of payments, though involuntary, was not temporary.

18. See also *R(G) 6/59*. In *R(G) 5/59*, the claimant had tried to enforce the maintenance order, and therefore her claim would now probably succeed on

the basis of limb (ii).
19. *R(G) 15/59* and post, p. 394.
20. *R(G) 15/59*.
1. *R(G) 3/60*.

Part three. Death Grant

A. General

Although the payment of a state lump sum benefit on death dates only from 1946, the need to provide for a decent burial has played an important part in the history of social policy. The desire to avoid imposing on relatives the humiliation of a pauper's funeral was an important cultural phenomenon of the industrial revolution and accounts in part for the rapid expansion of friendly and burial societies, but particularly industrial assurance companies, in the nineteenth century.[2] Indeed, by 1874, one company alone, the Prudential, had over one million policy holders.[3] The large commercial interest in the funeral expenses insurance resulted in stalwart opposition to any attempt to transfer the insurance to state management.[4] Fierce competition between the companies resulted in allegations of sharp practice and exploitation. A series of committees investigated the matter,[5] and their recommendations as implemented by legislation,[6] did much to strengthen the law. But when Beveridge again surveyed the problem during the Second World War, he found that there was a very strong case for further drastic reform.[7] First, the administrative costs of insurance were very high, averaging over 37% of premiums paid. Secondly, there was a high proportion of abortive insurance, i.e., policies which lapsed before they could mature.[8] Thirdly, the cost of insurance constituted a substantial drain on the resources of the lower-income groups: 'hundreds of thousands of families with less than enough to live on contribute substantial proportions of their incomes to industrial assurance.'[9]

Beveridge therefore proposed to incorporate 'funeral grants' into his social insurance scheme. A lump sum, varying according to age, would be payable on the death of a contributor, or a member of his family.[10] The proposal was adopted by the government,[11] and was included in the 1946 Act. However, the method of conferring payment proved to be almost wholly misconceived. The grant could be claimed by any person who had 'reasonably incurred or reasonably intends to incur ... any expenses of an

2. An extensive history of the matter is to be found in Wilson and Levy *Industrial Assurance* (1937).
3. Bruce *The Coming of the Welfare State* (4th edn) p. 112.
4. See, Gilbert *Evolution of National Insurance in Great Britain* (1966), pp. 328–332.
5. Royal Commission to inquire into Friendly and Building Societies (Northcote Commission) (1872–74), First Report, C. 452, Second Report C. 514, Third Report C. 842, Fourth Report C. 961; Report of Departmental Committee on the Business of Industrial Assurance Companies and Collecting Societies (Parmoor Committee) (1920), Cmd.

6414; Committee on Industrial Assurance and Assurance on the Lives of Children under Ten Years of Age (Cohen Committee) (1933), Cmd. 4376.
6. Notably the Assurance Companies Acts 1909 and 1923.
7. Paras. 157–160 and Appendix D.
8. The evidence revealed that the number of policies so failing in any one year was about two-thirds of the number issued: ibid., Appendix D., para. 79.
9. The estimated figure was 3–5% of income: ibid., at para. 80.
10. Paras. 159–160 and 350.
11. Social Insurance, Part I, paras. 132–138.

appreciable amount, in connection with the funeral of the deceased,"[12] but this was not to include a body corporate or an unincorporated association.[13] The rule created very substantial difficulties in the administration of the grant.[14] More than one person might come within the statutory provision, and though the Minister had power to determine priority as between claimants, and to suspend payment, this did not wholly solve the problem.[15] The bar on legal entities caused grave difficulties where a solicitor, a friendly society, a trade union or an employer had paid the bill.[16] Entitlement on mere proof of intention to incur the expenditure meant that individuals could benefit without paying out some or all of the money received. Finally, delicate questions of fact arose from the interpretation of what was 'reasonably' incurred, what was an 'appreciable' amount, and what were expenses 'in connection with the funeral.'[17] To meet the difficulties, the National Insurance Advisory Committee proposed a radical revision of the rules of entitlement:[18] the grant would constitute an asset of the deceased which would form part of his estate on death (as with arrears of other national insurance benefits). It would therefore be for his personal representatives to claim, and the sum payable would be fixed, irrespective of the amount actually spent on the funeral and concomitant purposes. The new principle was introduced in 1957,[19] and with some modifications, has been in force ever since.

B. Persons whose death is covered

The deceased must be within one of the statutory categories.[20] They are as follows.

    (i) The deceased was himself a contributor.[1]

    (ii) The deceased was at death the husband, wife, widow or widower[2] of the contributor or a child in respect of whom the contributor was entitled to child benefit.[3]

    (iii) The deceased was under 16 years and either (I) was predeceased by a contributor who at his death was entitled in respect of him to child benefit or (II) was the posthumous son or daughter of the contributor.[4] Alternatively, it will be sufficient if one of the child's parents is or was a contributor, or a

---

12. NIA 1946, s.22(1), (2). The expenses were deemed to include those incurred by the attendance of the claimant or other persons at the funeral, the purchase of mourning, and any loss of remuneration: ibid., s.22(2).
13. Ibid., s.22(4).
14. See the NIAC Report on the Death Grant Question (1956), Cmnd. 33.
15. See, e.g., CG 115/50, and R(G) 6/55.
16. See, e.g., R(G) 2/52 (bank); CG 192/50 (solicitor); R(G) 8/52 (employer).

17. E.g., CG 65/50; CG 66/50; CG 145/50; R(G) 21/52.
18. Ante, n.14.
19. NIA 1957, s.7.
20. SSA 1975, s.32(1).
1. Ibid., s.32(2)(a).
2. For questions of proof of marriage see post, pp. 398–404.
3. SSA 1975, s.32(2)(b), as amended by CBA 1975, Sch. 4, para. 11. For entitlement to child benefit, see post chap. 11.
4. SSA 1975, s.32(2)(c), as amended by CBA 1975, Sch. 4, para. 11.

contributor was immediately before the child's death entitled to a dependant's increase for that child.[5]

The remaining two categories were designed to assist those who for some legitimate reason might not have made any or sufficient contributions before their death.

> (iv) the deceased (1) was a child during the tax year in which he died or the preceding tax year, or at his death was aged sixteen to nineteen years and was at that time incapacitated for regular employment,[6] *and* (2) would have satisfied the conditions of category (iii) if he had still been a child at his death.[7]

> (v) the deceased was (1) over nineteen years at his death; (2) continuously since reaching that age had been incapacitated for regular employment;[8] and (3) was at death residing[9] (or would, if not living in an institution[10] have been residing) with a near relative,[11] who was either a contributor or the wife or widow of a contributor.[12]

C. Persons excluded

It has been held, both in Britain[13] and in Northern Ireland,[14] that a still-born child is not a 'person' for the purpose of this benefit, a view which has been criticised as not necessarily following from the language of the Act, and as flouting the intention of the legislature.[15] The child must, therefore, be living at the time of birth, and this means breathing.[16] Persons who had reached pensionable age on 5 July 1948 are excluded,[17] on the ground that they had not contributed to the scheme. Persons who die abroad are also excluded[18] unless the case comes within the prescribed exceptions established by the Regulations:

> viz, members of the forces, airmen, mariners, workers on the Continental Shelf, persons entitled (or who would have been

5. S.I. 1975/565, Reg. 2(1) as amended by S.I. 1977/342. For increases for child dependants see post, pp. 385–386.
6. 'Incapacitated' means incapacitated by reason of illness or disablement of the mind of body: SSA 1975, s.32(3)(a); cf., ante, p. 150.
7. S.I. 1975/565, Reg. 3.
8. Cf., ante, n.6.
9. See post, pp. 390–393.
10. 'A school, hospital or establishment accepted by the Secretary of State as providing residential accommodation for disabled persons': SSA 1975, s.32(3)(b).
11. A person 'of whom the deceased was the son or daughter or remoter issue; or . . . who was the deceased's son or daughter or remoter issue; or . . . who was the deceased's step-father, step-mother or step-child, or brother, sister, half-brother, or half-sister, step-brother or step-sister' (and includes any relationship which would have subsisted if a person born illegitimate had been born legitimate): ibid., s.32(3)(c).
12. Ibid., s.32(2)(d).
13. R(G)3/51.
14. R 1/68 (DG).
15. Calvert, 20 NILQ 52.
16. R(G) 3/51, in which the Commissioner preferred the evidence of a post-mortem examination to that of the midwife who had contended that the child had lived for five minutes.
17. SSA 1975, s.32(5).
18. Ibid.

entitled if the relevant conditions had been satisfied) to other contributory benefits, and, most important of all, persons normally resident in GB who die within thirteen weeks of leaving GB.[19]

D. Contributions

It was always the intention of the creators of the scheme that the contribution requirements for the death grant should be easily met[20] and this is certainly the case.

> The 'contributor' referred to in paragraph B must in any one year before that in which the deceased died, or in which the contributor reached pensionable age or himself died, have actually paid contributions of Classes 1, 2 or 3, the earnings factor derived from which is not less than twenty-five times that year's lower earnings limit.[1]

E. Amount

The standard sum payable is £30·00 but is reduced for young persons (under three, £9·00; three to six, £15·00; six to nineteen, £22·50), and for men who had reached fifty-five and women who had reached fifty on 5 July 1948 (£15·00) on the basis that their contributions to the scheme had not been substantial.[2] It is sad to report that these figures have remained unchanged since 1967 and are only 50% higher than those payable in 1948. They now cover only a fraction of the cost of a simple funeral.[3] In the circumstances, it is difficult to resist the conclusion that successive governments no longer attach to funeral expenses the importance which they certainly possessed in the first half of this century. This may be because cultural attitudes to local authority funerals (the modern equivalent of paupers' funerals) have changed, or because there are generally sufficient assets at death. A more likely explanation is that following the 1957 shift in entitlement from those incurring expenditure to the deceased person's estate, the benefit has lost such connection as it once had with actual funeral expenses, and has become no more than a subsidy by social security contributors to the estates of deceased persons, thus undermining the original objective of the scheme.[4]

F. Payment

As indicated above, the primary feature of the 1957 reform was to transfer entitlement from individuals incurring expenditure to the estate of the deceased person himself, on analogy with arrears of personal benefit which are payable after the beneficiary's death. The Claims and Payments

19. S.I. 1975/563, Reg. 7.
20. Social Insurance, Part I, para. 135.
   1. SSA 1975, Sch. 3, para. 7. For 'earnings factor' and 'earnings limit' see

ante, chap. 2.
2. SSA 1975, Sch. 4, Part II, para. 2.
3. *Lynes*, p. 104.
4. *Calvert*, p. 248.

Regulations provide that, as regards any benefit payable on death, the Secretary of State may 'appoint such person as he may think fit to proceed with or to make a claim for the benefit',[5] but also, in case of death grant, postulate that claims may be made by persons aged sixteen or more who are the personal representatives, legatees, next of kin or creditors of the deceased.[6] It is not inconceivable that in a given case either no such person exists or no such claim is made. Consequently the Secretary of State has power to pay the grant to 'any person who gives an undertaking in writing to pay the whole or part of the deceased's funeral expenses', on condition, however, that if the person fails to carry out the undertaking the grant is repayable.[7] It is presumably under this Regulation that a local authority, exercising its duty to dispose of the body of a deceased person when no other suitable arrangements have been made,[8] and also probably any other legal entity, may be paid the death grant. The Secretary of State is given power to distribute benefit among the possible beneficiaries, but in the normal case it will be paid to the executors or administrators. If none has been appointed then the sum will be paid to the next of kin, if he or she has incurred the expenditure.[9] But to meet exceptional circumstances, the discretion is drawn in even wider terms. First, 'the Secretary of State may dispense with strict proof of the title of any person' claiming under the Regulations;[10] secondly, 'under arrangements made by the Secretary of State with the consent of the Treasury' in cases of emergency (probably local or national disasters), the grant may be paid pending the determination of a claim, without proof of satisfaction of the relevant conditions.[11] Payment is suspended where a person qualified to receive death grant is imprisoned or detained in legal custody,[12] but in this case payment may be made to a person appointed by the Secretary of State to receive and deal with it on behalf of the beneficiary.[13]

5. S.I. 1975/560, Reg. 27(1).
6. Ibid., Reg. 27(2). 'Personal representatives' are confined to executors and administrators. See R(G) 3/65 where it was held that the grant was not payable to a hospital almoner who intended to transfer it to a charity nominated by the deceased.
7. S.I. 1975/560, Reg. 27(4).
8. NAA 1948, s. 50(1). The authority may recover from the deceased's estate the expenses incurred, less what has been received by way of death grant: ibid., s. 50(4), as amended by Social Security (Consequential Provisions) Act 1975, Sch. 2, para. 5.
9. DHSS Leaflet, NI 49, para. 4.
10. S.I. 1975/560, Reg. 27(7).
11. S.I. 1975/565, Reg. 6.
12. Ibid., Reg. 5(1), and post, pp. 421–424.
13. Ibid., Reg. 5(2).

7 Miscellaneous Benefits

Part one. Maternity Benefits

A. General

There are now two maternity benefits payable to a mother before or after her confinement. They provide some assistance in both the major respects in which the mother and her family may have additional needs at this time. First, there is a lump sum maternity grant to cover some of the additional costs which arise on the birth of a child. Secondly, at some stage before this the mother will probably have given up work with a consequent loss of income. The resulting need has been met since 1946 by the payment of a weekly maternity allowance.

The grant was first paid under the National Insurance Act 1911 as one of the benefits in Lloyd George's health insurance scheme.[1] In substance it remained unchanged during the inter-war years. The Beveridge Report mentioned it briefly, making the important point that the benefit is not designed to cover the entire costs of maternity, 'which has a resonable and natural claim upon the husband's earnings'.[2] It recommended the introduction of the maternity allowance in order to encourage women to give up work well before child birth. It was to be paid at a higher rate than unemployment and sickness benefit, and could be awarded whether or not the woman had claimed exemption from paying contributions.[3] This proposal was accepted by the government; the 1946 legislation also provided a third type of benefit, an attendance allowance which could be claimed by a mother, not entitled to the maternity allowance, for the four weeks after birth.[4] It was a useful contribution towards the additional costs of domestic help during this period.

The benefits went through a number of changes in the 1950s and 1960s before the present position was reached. The attendance allowance was abolished in 1953, but partly to offset this, the maternity grant was increased from £4 to £9.[5] A special home confinement grant was paid to

---

1. For the history of maternity benefits, see *George* p. 129, and the Report of the National Insurance Advisory Committee on Maternity Benefits (1952), Cmd. 8446, paras. 6–13.
2. Para. 341.
3. For this exemption, see chap. 2, ante, p. 65.
4. This allowance is not to be confused with the non-contributory attendance allowance or the constant attendance allowance, ante, p. 171, and post, p. 333.
5. NIA 1953, ss. 1, 2.

mothers giving birth at home to cover the additional costs not incurred by those confined in hospital.[6]

This grant was abolished in 1964,[7] as mothers were discharged from hospital more rapidly after confinement than had previously been the case and so there was little difference in the costs of a home and a hospital birth.[8] From then on there have been payable only the two benefits mentioned in the first paragraph.

The rules and policy considerations relevant to the two benefits are discussed in section B (maternity grant) and section C (maternity allowance). Some provisions relevant to both, in particular the meaning of 'confinement', are discussed in section B.

B. Maternity grant

Broadly, there are two principal conditions for entitlement to the grant. First, either the woman 'has been confined'[9] *or* she must, when she claims, be pregnant at a stage not more than eleven weeks before the expected week of confinement.[10] Secondly, she, or her husband, must satisfy the relevant contribution conditions. The only other important legal point concerns the grants which may be paid where there is a multiple birth.

i) Confinement

a) 'HAS BEEN CONFINED'. 'Confinement' means 'labour resulting in the issue of a living child, or labour after twenty-eight weeks of pregnancy resulting in the issue of a child whether alive or dead'.[11] Thus, a woman whose 6 months' pregnancy terminated without the issue of a live child is not entitled,[12] nor is a woman who delivers a 'hydatidiform mole'.[13] Where labour begins on one day and the birth takes place the following day, the latter is the day of confinement.[14]

The only difficulties appear to arise in cases where the woman has a miscarriage after a number of weeks' pregnancy, and it-has to be calculated whether that period has amounted to twenty-eight weeks in order to establish entitlement. In *R(G) 4/56*, the Commissioner estimated the period by counting back from the expected date of confinement – on the assumption that the gestation period was the 273 days stated in a medical dictionary. In another case, the Commissioner accepted the evidence of a gynaecological registrar, who had examined the foetus, in reaching the conclusion that the woman had not been pregnant for more than twenty-three to twenty-five weeks.[15]

The term 'pregnancy' is not defined in the legislation. This omission enabled a Commissioner in Northern Ireland to hold that a woman was

6. NIA 1953, s.4. This grant was introduced following the recommendations of NIAC, ante n.1, at paras. 22–35.
7. NIA 1964, s.1(4).
8. Miss M. Herbison, Minister of Pensions & N.I., 702 HC Deb., cols. 1305–1306.
9. SSA 1975, s.21(1).
10. S.I. 1975/553, Reg. 3, made under SSA 1975, s.21(5).
11. Ibid., s.23(1)(a).
12. *CWG* 1/49.
13. *CG* 3/49: for this condition, see Dorland's *Medical Dictionary* (24th edn), p. 937.
14. SSA 1975, s.23(1)(b).
15. *R(G)* 12/59.

'confined', when she produced, only two months before the expected date of confinement, a foetus which had ceased developing three months after conception.[16] The claimant was, therefore, held entitled to a maternity allowance, and presumably would have been entitled to a grant.

b) WOMAN PREGNANT AT A STAGE NOT MORE THAN ELEVEN WEEKS BEFORE EXPECTED WEEK OF CONFINEMENT. Under the first condition discussed in the previous paragraphs, title to the grant only arises after the confinement (or birth of the child, to use non-technical language). But, of course, substantial expenditure may be incurred before the birth, e.g., on buying a cot or clothes. For this reason, if the claimant wishes, she may be paid the grant when 'she is pregnant and has reached a stage in her pregnancy which is not more than eleven weeks before the expected week of confinement.'[17] The National Insurance Advisory Committee thought there was some danger that a woman receiving the grant eleven weeks before an anticipated birth might not spend it wisely, and recommended that the period should be reduced to eight weeks.[18] It was reduced in 1954 to nine weeks,[19] but it has since returned to eleven weeks. The reference point for contribution conditions is appropriately modified when the woman claims the grant on this basis.[20]

ii) The contribution conditions
Either the woman or her husband:

1. in any one year before the confinement (or before the start of the week of expected confinement, where the claim is made on the basis of (i) (b) above) must have paid Class 1, 2 or 3 contributions, and the earnings factor derived from those contributions must be not less than that year's lower earnings limit multiplied by twenty-five;

2. in respect of the last complete year before the benefit year in which the confinement (or the expected week of confinement) occurs must have paid or been credited with Class 1, 2 or 3 contributions, and the earnings factor derived from those contributions must be not less than that year's lower earnings limit multiplied by twenty-five.[1]

Often the woman will not herself have paid sufficient contributions and must rely on her husband's record. She cannot rely on the contributions of a man, not her husband, with whom she has been living, even if he is the father of the child in question.[2] If the grant is claimed *after* confinement the contribution requirement is not satisfied if the man in question was not the claimant's husband at the time of the confinement, even though he subsequently married her.[3] In *R(G) 2/68*, the Commissioner explained

16. R 1/64 (MB).
17. S.I. 1975/553, Reg. 3.
18. Ante n.1, at paras. 98–99.
19. S.I. 1954/189, Reg. 3.
20. See S.I. 1975/553, Reg. 3(b).

1. SSA 1975, Sch. 3, para. 2, and S.I. 1975/553, Reg. 3. For the concepts involved, see chap. 2, ante, pp. 70–72.
2. CG 3/49; and see further, post, p. 251.
3. R(G) 1/52; R(G) 2/68.

this rule on the ground that there is a presumption that, when a benefit is payable on a certain event (here, confinement) subject to the satisfaction of certain conditions, they must be satisfied *at the time of that event*.[4] In that case, therefore, the woman was not entitled to a grant, as she had been divorced from her first husband some time before her confinement, and only married the second husband a month after it. But the Act provides that a woman may rely on the contributions of her deceased husband, if she has given birth to his posthumous child.[5]

The legal position is even more complicated when the claim is made on the alternative basis that the woman is pregnant, and it is not more than eleven weeks before the expected week of confinement.[6] In *R(G) 1/67*, R. G. Micklethwait, the Chief Commissioner, ruled that a claimant was entitled to a grant on this basis, when she had a husband (who satisfied the contribution condition) at some stage during the period before confinement when title to the grant arose. It did not matter that the man had ceased to be her husband, on the grant of the decree absolute of divorce, the day *before* the grant was claimed, and that she was not married at the actual time of the confinement.[7] If the decree had been made absolute earlier than the beginning of the eleven weeks period before the expected week of confinement, the claim would have failed. It seems odd that entitlement should depend on the timing of a decree absolute, particularly as the former husband will, in all probability, not be the father of the child in question!

As an alternative to satisfying these requirements, the claimant will be entitled to a grant if she satisfies the contribution conditions for maternity allowance at the full, or a reduced rate.[8] Generally, it will be harder to satisfy these conditions than those already discussed.

In the normal case, however, the contribution conditions are very easy to satisfy, and the overwhelming majority of births entitle the mother to receive a maternity grant.[9] But there are some groups of mothers who are unlikely to be entitled, because of failure to satisfy these requirements: student wives of student husbands, single women who have not been at work, wives of long-term prisoners.[10] It has been argued that maternity grants, like family allowances and the new child benefit, should be non-contributory and paid automatically. This was recommended by the Finer Committee.[11]

A more modest reform would be to enable a woman to claim on the contributions of the child's putative father. This proposal was considered by the National Insurance Advisory Committee in 1952, but was rejected, as it would entail prying into the relationship of the persons concerned.[12]

---

4. *R(G) 2/68*, D. Reith, Comr., para. 8.
5. SSA 1975, s.21(2).
6. See ante, p. 250.
7. The Chief Commissioner disapproved of the headnote in *R(G) 1/65* (where the facts were similar to those in *R(G) 1/67*) in so far as it suggested that it was material that the claimant had a husband *at the date of her claim*.

8. SSA 1975, s.21(1)(b); post, p. 254.
9. See *Finer*, para. 5.290.
10. Ibid., and see *George*, p 132, and *Walley*, p. 222.
11. *Finer*, para. 5.293.
12. Report of the National Insurance Advisory Committee on Maternity Benefits (1952), Cmd. 8446, paras. 119–121.

This particular objection would not apply if paternity had been admitted or established in a court; but the proposal would not assist a woman pregnant by a man with no contributions record, and does not in principle appear to have much to commend it.

iii) Multiple births

More than one maternity grant may be paid in the event of a multiple birth.[13] There is, of course, a risk that one or more of a number of twins, triplets, etc., will not long survive child birth and, therefore, an excessive amount could be paid by way of maternity grants. This contingency led to a change in the Regulations in 1954; since then a mother is only to be entitled 'for each child who has lived for at least twelve hours after being born'.[14] The reform was accepted by the majority of the National Insurance Advisory Committee, but Titmuss dissented on the grounds that the necessity to prove survival caused embarrassment for the mother and difficult administrative work for the hospital staff.[15] It is submitted that if both twins die within the twelve hours, one grant would be payable under the general rules, but it is possible that a literal construction of the Regulation dictates that no grant is payable in this circumstance! That would be a wholly unjustifiable result of what is in any case arguably a harsh rule.

iv) Amount

The maternity grant is £25.[16] It has only been increased once since 1965, and has not, therefore, kept pace with inflation.[17]

C. Maternity allowance

i) General

The maternity allowance was introduced by the National Insurance Act 1946 to compensate a mother for the loss of income occasioned by giving up employment, and indeed to encourage her to cease work before the expected birth.[18] In fact it is not known whether this second aim has succeeded; the evidence heard by the National Insurance Advisory Committee in 1952 was that the majority of women would leave work in any case a few weeks before confinement.[19] After some hesitation the Committee thought the allowance should be retained, as it was particularly useful for separated and divorced women, who were entirely dependent on their work for financial support and might be reluctant to leave it unless the benefit was paid.[20] It was recommended, however, that those women who exercised the married woman's option not to pay contributions[1] should no longer be eligible; they were inclined to give up work in any case

13. SSA 1975, s.21(4).
14. S.I. 1975/553, Reg. 2.
15. NIAC Report, 1953–54, HC 97.
16. SSA 1975, Sch. 4, Part II, para. 1.
17. The up-rating provisions do not apply

to lump-sum benefits: post, p. 434.
18. Ante, p. 248.
19. Ante, n.12, at paras. 56–59.
20. Ibid., at para, 66.
1. See chap. 2, ante, p. 65.

well before the expected date of birth and were less in need of the allowance than other women.[2] Since the implementation of this recommendation in the National Insurance Act 1953,[3] entitlement to the allowance has been dependent on the woman *herself* satisfying the contribution conditions.

A woman is eligible immediately before and after confinement for sickness benefit as an alternative to maternity allowance.[4] She is treated as automatically entitled to the benefit for the six weeks before and the two weeks after confinement, though she might be entitled for a longer period if she suffers from some disablement apart from her pregnancy.[5] In fact maternity allowance has been payable at a higher rate than the sickness benefit usually payable for a married woman, so the alternative entitlement to the latter has for the most part been irrelevant.[6] Following the Social Security Pensions Act 1975 married women are to be paid sickness benefit at the same rate as other claimants, and there will be no difference between that rate and the amount of the maternity allowance.[7]

ii) Entitlement

a) MATERNITY ALLOWANCE IN RESPECT OF EXPECTATION OF CONFINEMENT. In the normal circumstances an allowance will be claimed before confinement when the woman gives up work. She is entitled if she is pregnant and 'has reached a stage in her pregnancy which is not more than' fourteen weeks before the expected week of confinement.[8] The period for which it is awarded ('the maternity allowance period') is eighteen weeks, starting with the eleventh week before the expected week of confinement.[9] A woman ceases to be entitled if her pregnancy is terminated, otherwise than by confinement, before the start of the maternity allowance period.[10]

Where an allowance is awarded on this basis, it is generally the 'expected week of confinement' which is relevant for determining the maternity allowance period, and not the actual date of confinement. This is the case even if after the original award it becomes clear that the birth took place outside the expected week. Thus is *R(G) 8/55*,

> the midwife, who completed the certificate of expected confinement, wrongly stated the the birth was expected on 2 August, when the doctor expected it a month later. The confinement had taken place before the insurance officer became aware of this clerical mistake. The Commissioner held that, 'the review of the decision should be

2. Ante n.12, at para. 68.
3. s.6(4).
4. She is not, of course, entitled to both at the same time: post, p. 437.
5. See the discussion in the NIAC Report, ante n.12, at paras. 15–16, and see ante, p. 150.
6. However, before earnings-related maternity allowances were introduced in 1973, an earnings-related supplement was paid, assessed at the difference between the flat-rate

allowance and what would have been payable to the woman as earnings-related sickness benefit. See post, p. 255.
7. S.18: for the amount of maternity allowance, see post, p. 255.
8. SSA 1975, s.22(1)(a), and S.I. 1975/553, Reg. 4(1).
9. SSA 1975, s.22(2).
10. S.I. 1975/553, Reg. 4(2): see *R(G) 4/56*. For the meaning of 'confinement', see ante, p. 249.

based on what the "expected week of confinement" really was'. The actual date of the confinement was wholly irrelevant for determining the maternity allowance period.[11]

Two qualifications must be made. First, if the woman is confined before the usual maternity allowance period, i.e., more than eleven weeks before the expected week of confinement, then the period for which the allowance is payable becomes the eighteen weeks from the week in which the confinement take place.[12] Secondly, if the woman has not been confined by the end of the expected week of confinement, the maternity allowance period may be extended.[13]

b) MATERNITY ALLOWANCE BY VIRTUE OF FACT OF CONFINEMENT. A woman may alternatively claim a maternity allowance when she has actually been confined. In that case it is generally payable for a seven week maternity allowance period, beginning with the week of confinement.[14] In some cases it may be paid for more than this period. Where the woman was in fact confined more than eleven weeks before her expected date of confinement, then she may receive the allowance for the eighteen weeks beginning with the week of confinement.[15] Secondly, where she shows that she did not work for the period up to eleven weeks before the week of confinement *and* had good cause throughout this time for her failure to make a claim on the basis of her expectation, then she will be entitled to an allowance from the start of this period until six weeks after the week of confinement.[16]

iii) The contribution conditions
These are that the claimant must

1. in any one year before the beginning of the maternity allowance period have paid Class 1 or 2 contributions, and the earnings factor derived from those contributions must be not less than that year's lower earnings limit multiplied by twenty-five;

2. in respect of the last complete year before the year containing the period of the interruption of employment which includes the beginning of the maternity allowance period have paid or been credited with Class 1 or 2 contributions, and the earnings factor derived from those contributions must be not less than that year's lower earnings limit multiplied by fifty.[17]

It was mentioned earlier that a woman will be entitled to a maternity grant if she satisfies the contributions conditions for an allowance, whether or not she satisfies the generally more relaxed conditions for the

---

11. See also *R(G) 2/61*.
12. S.I. 1975/553, Reg. 5(1).
13. Ibid., Reg. 5(2), (3).
14. Ibid., Reg. 6(1).
15. Ibid., Reg. 6(2).
16. Ibid., Reg. 6(3): see chap. 14, post, pp.
601–606, for the meaning of 'good cause'.
17. SSA 1975, Sch. 3, para. 3. For the term 'period of interruption of employment', see SSA 1975, s.17(1)(d), chap. 3, ante, pp. 92–93.

grant.[18] The circumstances in which this happens must be rare, but it can occur because the years in which the contributions must have been paid or credited for the two benefits may be different; the grant conditions are assessed by reference to the benefit year in which the *confinement occurs* or is expected to occur, while the allowance conditions generally refer to the benefit year in which the *allowance period begins*. A single woman who gives up work some time before her expected confinement might, therefore, satisfy the allowance contribution conditions more easily than she does the specific conditions for the grant. It was in the light of this type of case that the National Insurance Advisory Committee recommended in 1952 that entitlement to the allowance should carry with it entitlement to the maternity grant.[19]

iv) Disqualification from receiving maternity allowances

A woman who has been awarded the allowance may become disqualified from receiving it in certain circumstances.[20]

1. A woman doing any work in employment, whether as employee or self-employed, during the maternity allowance period is to be disqualified for such part of that period (not less than the number of days worked) as is reasonable.

The force of the phrase, 'does any work in employment', is to make it clear that a woman who does housework cannot be disqualified. In contrast to sickness benefit, the claimant cannot contend here that she has failed to observe the requirement for 'good cause', and the disqualification is for a reasonable period, rather than a maximum of six weeks.[1]

2. If during the maternity allowance period, the claimant fails without good cause to take due care of her health and answer reasonable inquiries concerning it, she may similarly be disqualified for a reasonable period.

3. If she fails without good cause to attend a medical examination, she will be disqualified for a reasonable period.[2] But if the confinement occurs after the failure to attend, she is not disqualified from the allowance for the days of, and after, the confinement.

v) Amount

For 1977–78 the weekly amount of the flat-rate maternity allowance is £14·70.[3] Increases for child dependants, and in some cases for the claimant's husband, may also be payable;[4] an allowance may be increased in respect of the child for whose birth the claimant is confined.[5] An earnings-related supplement to maternity allowance was introduced by the

18. Ante, p. 251.
19. Report of the National Insurance Advisory Committee on Maternity Benefits (1952), Cmd. 8446, para. 55.
20. S.I. 1975/553, Reg. 9.
1. For sickness benefit disqualifications, see chap. 4, ante, pp. 159–163.

2. See ante, p. 159, for the similar disqualification from receipt of sickness benefit.
3. S.I. 1977/1325.
4. See post, p. 385–390.
5. SSA 1975, s.41(3).

Social Security Act 1973;[6] the rules concerning its payment are discussed in chapter 10.[7]

vi) Maternity pay

The Employment Protection Act 1975 confers a right to maternity pay from the employer in certain circumstances: the woman must have been continuously employed for two years by him and must continue in employment up to eleven weeks before the expected week of confinement.[8] The pay is to continue for six weeks after the eleventh week before the expected confinement, and is to be nine-tenths of a week's pay less the flat-rate maternity allowance.[9] This allowance is to be deducted whether it is in fact paid or not. Presumably the figure of nine-tenths of weekly earnings was arrived at on the assumption that the other one-tenth would be paid to the woman by way of the earnings-related supplement to the allowance.

Part two. Guardian's Allowance

A. Introduction

Guardian's allowance (GA) is a non-contributory benefit, which is broadly payable to a person looking after a child, both of whose parents are dead. The allowance was introduced in 1946, replacing the orphan's pension which had been payable since the Widows', Orphans' and Old Age Contributory Pensions Act 1925. This had provided a weekly pension payable to 'the guardian or the other person having the charge of the child', in respect of any orphan, defined as a child both of whose parents were dead.[10] The National Insurance Act 1946, unlike the 1925 legislation, enabled an allowance to be paid, where one of the child's parents was dead and the other could not be traced.[11]

The fact that in certain circumstances GA may be paid in respect of a child, whose parents are not both dead, raises the difficult question: what is the rationale or principle justifying the payment of this benefit? Is it primarily designed to 'compensate' the child for the loss of his parents *or*, on the other hand, to provide some state assistance to encourage a person to look after a child who for some reason lacks parental support? The rationale for the pension paid under the 1925 Act would appear to have been the former, since entitlement was dependent on the child having the status of an orphan.[12] Now that the requirements for entitlement have

6. S.17(4). Before then, a mother in receipt of the allowance also might receive an earnings-related sickness benefit: ante, p. 253, n.6.
7. Ante, pp. 424–426.
8. S. 35.
9. Employment Protection Act 1975, s.37.
10. S.4. N.B.: orphan's pension was not, and the guardian's allowance is not, restricted to the 'guardians' of a child

in the sense in which that term is used in family law: see Cretney *Principles of Family Law*, (2nd edn), pp. 320–323.
11. NIA 1946, s.19(1), proviso (ii); see now the comparable provision in SSA 1975, s. 38(2)(b).
12. Widows', Orphans' and Old Age Contributory Pensions Act 1925, s.44; and see the views of the Commissioners in *R(G) 10/52*.

been relaxed, the question is less easy to answer. The policy seems to be to pay an allowance where one parent is dead and the other can for practical purposes be treated as non-existent so that the child is virtually an orphan, but not to pay an allowance merely because the surviving parent neglects his responsibilities to the child.[13] Whatever the merits of this distinction, the formulation of the policy in the legal requirements for entitlement has produced difficulties for the Commissioners. Thus, in *R(G) 10/52*, a Tribunal ventured the opinion that GA is payable either when the child concerned has the status of an orphan or 'the relationship normally uniting parents with each other or with their child no longer obtains.' But the Northern Ireland Commissioners in two recent cases[14] have adopted an even broader approach, and have suggested in effect that it is the absence of a parent (or parents) able to assume financial responsibilities for the child, which now justifies the award of the allowance.[15] This uncertainty about the principle underlying the GA is largely responsible for the complex law discussed in the next section.[16]

There would appear to be two alternative paths of reform, both of which would be in a sense more logical than the present complicated position. First, entitlement to GA could be extended to cover anyone looking after a child who is without financial support from a parent, whether this is because both parents are dead, or the surviving parent cannot be found or, if found, cannot be induced to contribute towards his maintenance. Indeed, on this basis, there would be no justification for insisting on the present requirement that at least one parent is dead. Alternatively it may be questioned whether there is any justification for paying guardians a special allowance. The second course, therefore, would be to abolish it altogether. It can be argued to this end that the former orphan's pension was introduced before family allowances were payable, and that its successor, the guardian's allowance, should now be reconsidered in the light of the introduction of the (eventually) more generous child benefit scheme.[17] It is not clear that a guardian should receive assistance in respect of a child living with him beyond the provision afforded anyone else (including a parent) discharging the same responsibilities. But until child benefit rates approach that of the allowance,[18] GA is unlikely to be abolished.

B. Entitlement

i) General

Entitlement to a guardian's allowance is now governed by section 38 of the Social Security Act 1975,[19] and the Regulations made under it.[20] First, the

13. See the Report of the National Insurance Advisory Committee 1948, HC 165, paras. 8–13.
14. *R 3/74 (P); R 3/75 (P)*, Tribunal decision.
15. Ibid., at paras. 9–10: see post, p. 261. This is clearly opposed to the view of NIAC in 1948: ante n.13.
16. See esp., pp. 259–261.
17. See chap. 11, esp. post, pp. 449–452.
18. Post, p. 263, for the amount of the allowance.
19. As amended by CBA 1975, Sch. 4, para. 12.
20. S.I. 1975/515.

claimant must be entitled to child benefit (or treated under Regulations as so entitled)[1] in respect of the particular child on behalf of whom the allowance is claimed.[2] The other principal conditions are then set out in subsection (2). These are:

> '(a) that both of the child's parents are dead; or
>
> (b) that one of the child's parents is dead and the person claiming a guardian's allowance shows that he was at the date of the death unaware of, and has failed after all reasonable efforts to discover, the whereabouts of the other parent; or
>
> (c) that one of the child's parents is dead and the other is in prison.'

Thus, the usual requirement is that both the child's parents are dead, but, in the circumstances described in paragraphs (b) and (c), the condition that the child has the status of orphanhood, which obtained under the 1925 legislation, has been substantially modified.

The term 'parent' does not now include a step-parent, so the fact that one step-parent is still alive would not debar the person looking after the child from being entitled to the allowance.[3] A step-parent himself might be entitled, since the disqualification in section 38(6), (a parent is not to be entitled to a guardian's allowance is respect of his child), would not apply to him. It is somewhat less clear whether 'parent' includes a 'natural father'; this question is discussed later in the context of the rules concerning illegitimate children.[4]

Under section 38(3) it is provided that at least one of the child's parents must satisfy various prescribed conditions, 'as to nationality, residence, place of birth or other matters'.[5]

> The Regulation now requires either that one parent was born in the UK, or that by the date of the death of the parent whose death gives rise to the claim for GA, one of them has been present in Britain for at least fifty-two weeks in any period of two years after the child became sixteen.[6]

In effect one of the parents must have had some link with Britain, though this may be relatively slight. There are no conditions, however, with regard to the residence of the claimant.

---

1. See S.I. 1977/342, Regs. 2 and 3, and post, p. 386.
2. CBA 1975, Sch. 4, para. 12(a), amending SSA 1975, s.38(1). For the conditions of entitlement to this benefit, see chap. 11, post, pp. 456–465.
3. Until the NIA 1957, s.6, a step-parent was regarded as a 'parent' for the purposes of the legislation: see R(G) 6/52.
4. See post, p. 262.
5. See Calvert, pp. 248–249, for a discussion of this provision.
6. S.I. 1977/342, Reg. 9(3), replacing S.I. 1975/515, Reg. 6.

ii) One parent dead, and the claimant unaware of, or unable to discover, the whereabouts of the other parent

It should be noted that the claimant must show that *one* of the child's parents is dead by the normal means of proof.[7] He will not succeed if he can merely show that he is unaware of, (or has failed after all reasonable efforts to discover), the whereabouts of both parents. To allow a claim to succeed on these facts would be finally to abandon the principle that the child must be an orphan, or be in a position very similar to this. But it can be argued that the normal parent-child relationship is as much absent if both parents are 'missing', as it is if one is dead and the other's whereabouts cannot be discovered.[8]

Under the 1946 Act the rule was that an allowance could be paid if one parent was dead, and the other 'cannot be traced'.[9] A Tribunal of Commissioners interpreted this as requiring the claimant to demonstrate that there was no evidence indicating whether the second parent was alive or dead.[10] On this objective test it was not enough for him to show that he was unable himself by reasonable efforts to discover the parent; his claim would be defeated if there was *any* evidence to suggest that the other parent was still alive. On the recommendation of the National Insurance Advisory Committee, the rule was changed to the present formulation, now contained in section 38(2)(b).[11] The meaning of this is not, however, entirely plain. In particular, it is not clear if the requirement is satisfied when there is evidence that the second parent is still alive, but the claimant cannot find out after reasonable efforts where he is living. The views of the British and the Northern Ireland Commissioners would appear to differ on this question.

The principles relevant to a determination whether a claimant 'has failed after all reasonable efforts to discover the whereabouts' of the second parent were stated in *R 2/61 (P)* by the Northern Ireland Commissioner. The test is subjective in the sense that the claimant must have made those inquiries of the parent's 'whereabouts' which could reasonably have been expected of him: '. . . the onus lies upon the person claiming the allowance to show that he has made such efforts to the best of his particular ability'.[12] Where there are no profitable lines of inquiry, only very slight efforts will be expected; but a claimant who made no attempt to find the father, because she did not think it would be in the child's best interests to do so, was refused an allowance.[13] Efforts made before the death of the other parent may be taken into account, but in general it seems that the claimant

7. See the discussion ante, p. 232 in the context of widows' pensions. In *R(G) 11/52*, a Tribunal of Commissioners indicated that the presumption of death after seven years' absence could be relied on in guardian's allowance cases.
8. See the statement of principle in *R(G) 10/52*, set out ante, p. 257.
9. NIA 1946, s.19(1).
10. *R(G) 11/52*.
11. Ante, p. 258. See the NIAC report on Question of Dependency Provisions (1956), Cmd. 9855, para. 88.
12. *R 2/61 (P)*, para. 15. There is no reason to think that the British Commissioner would not agree with this statement of principle.
13. *R(G) 4/59*.

must make an attempt to discover the whereabouts of the missing parent *after* the other's death.[14]

A claim will fail if the whereabouts of the missing parent are discovered otherwise than by the efforts of the claimant. This was decided in *R(G) 3/68*:

> In April 1967 an allowance was claimed in respect of a child whose father had died in February, and the whereabouts of whose mother were unknown. Later that month, and again in May and June, the child received letters from his mother from an address in the Soviet Union; but she did not reply to letters sent to her concerning wardship proceedings taken by the claimant. The Commissioner, R. S. Lazarus, held that the mother's whereabouts had been discovered, and that GA was not payable.

The decision is important on four points, on the last two of which the Northern Ireland Commissioners have recently taken a different attitude. a) The Commissioner ruled that the insurance officer and local tribunal should not disregard facts which have come to light since the date of the claim. In the case it became clear that the mother was still alive only after it was made, but this was enough to defeat it. In the converse case where the claimant was aware of the parent's whereabouts at the date of death, but since then the parent has disappeared and the claimant has not discovered his whereabouts, both the British and the Northern Ireland Commissioners take the view that an allowance is not payable.[15] b) In *R(G) 3/68* the mother's whereabouts were not discovered *by reason of* the claimant's efforts. The Commissioner ruled that this did not matter; an allowance could not be paid if the whereabouts were discovered by any means by the time the case was decided. This has met with the approval of F. A. Reid, a Northern Ireland Commissioner,[16] and seems clearly right. c) The address given by the mother in *R(G) 3/68* indicated a town, from which it could at most be inferred that the letters were written. But the Commissioner ruled that 'whereabouts' and 'residence' were not synonymous, and that, therefore, the fact that the claimant did not know exactly where the mother lived was irrelevant: he did know the mother's *whereabouts*. But the Northern Ireland Commissioner in *R 3/74 (P)* took a stricter view. In an urban environment, ' "whereabouts" must be taken to mean a place identifiable with some particularity'.[17] Knowledge of a village where the parent lived would be adequate, but usually the name of a city or large town would be too imprecise. This point is integrally connected with the fourth one. d) The Commissioner in *R(G) 3/68* supported his interpretation with some observations on the principles underlying the availability of a guardian's allowance. He said that entitlement did not merely depend on the

14. *R 1/73 (P)*, T.A. Blair, Comr.; on this point, *R(G) 10/55*, decided on the pre-1957 formulation, still appears relevant.
15. See *R 3/75 (P)*, where the British Commissioner's views in CG 1/75 are discussed.
16. *R 3/74 (P)*.
17. Ibid., at para. 7, per F.A. Reid, Comr.

absence of a person under an enforceable legal duty to maintain the child, but on the entire non-existence of the parent-child relationship.[18] In effect, he concluded that the claimant could not take advantage of the relaxation of the rule that both parents were dead, if it was clear that the second parent was alive. As the letters from the Soviet Union indicated here that the mother was alive, the claim failed.

This view of the meaning of section 38(2)(b) has been rejected by the Northern Ireland Commissioner in *R 3/74 (P)* and by a Tribunal in *R 3/75 (P)*. In both cases, it was said that the section might enable a claimant to succeed if he could not discover the whereabouts of the second parent, i.e., precisely where he is living, even though there is good evidence that he (or she) is alive. The continued existence of the parent-child relationship did not preclude the award of GA. In the later case, the Tribunal said that if the British Commissioner were right, the provision would have been drafted: '. . . to discover whether he is still alive'.

The difference between the two approaches may be illustrated simply by reference to an example given in *R 3/75 (P)*:[19]

> C claims an allowance in respect of a child, one of whose parents is dead and the other is missing. About the time of the claim, C receives a letter from the second parent without an address or legible postmark. It seems that the British Commissioner would refuse to award GA in this case – he certainly would if it was clear which town the letter came from – while in Northern Ireland, the Commissioners would award GA, unless the claimant was able to discover where the parent lived.

It is submitted that the interpretation placed upon the provision by the Northern Ireland Commissioners is to be preferred. The other view seems to reduce the significance of the legislative change referred to earlier to a mere reformulation of the requirement.[20] On the other hand, the Report of the National Insurance Advisory Committee which recommended that change does seem to bear out the more restrictive view taken in *R(G) 3/68*.

iii) One parent dead, and the other in prison

The second modification to the general requirement that both parents are dead can be discussed more briefly. A parent is to be treated as being in prison if

> 'he is serving a sentence of imprisonment of not less than five years or of imprisonment for life, or is in legal custody as a person sentenced or ordered to be kept in custody during Her Majesty's pleasure or until the directions of Her Majesty are known'.[1]

In assessing the five years for this purpose, no account is taken, inter alia, of any period of the sentence served before the first parent's death.[2] There

18. He quoted with approval the Commissioners in *R(G) 10/52*: see ante, p. 257.

19. At para. 9.

20. Ante, p. 258.

1. S.I. 1975/515, Reg. 5: see *R(G) 4/65* for a case interpreting this provision.

2. S.I. 1975/515, Reg. 5(2)(a).

is one interesting provision: the amount of GA is to be reduced by the amount of any contribution made by the parent in prison or custody to the cost of providing for the child.[3] This suggests that, in this case at least, the rationale for payment of the allowance is not 'compensation' for loss of the normal parent-child relationship, but for the loss of the financial support usually provided by parents.[4]

iv) Adopted children

Where a valid adoption order has been made in favour of two spouses jointly, they, (and not the natural parents), are to be treated as the child's parents for the purposes of section 38(2).[5] Therefore for GA to be awarded, either both adopting parents must be dead, or one of them must be dead and the other's whereabouts cannot be discovered, etc. Where a child has been adopted by one person, GA may be payable on his death.

v) Illegitimate children

Regulation 3(1) of the Guardian's Allowance Regulations provides as follows:

> 'Where a child . . . is illegitimate and:
>
> (a) a person has been found by a court of competent jurisdiction to be the father of the child, or
>
> (b) there is no such finding but in the opinion of the determining authority the paternity of the child has been admitted or established,
>
> section 38(2) of the Act shall be modified so as to have effect as if the mother and father of the child were the child's parents within the meaning of that subsection.'

For GA to be payable, therefore, *either* both the natural father and mother must have died, *or* one of them must be dead and the other must be missing, within the terms of section 38(2)(b),[6] or in prison. This provision does not apply, however, if the child in question has previously been adopted, for then it is the death of the adoptive parents which is necessary as a precondition for the availability of GA. Nor does it apply when the conditions in regulation 3(1)(a) or (b) have not been satisfied: in that case, the mother's death alone suffices, and it is wholly immaterial whether the natural father is alive or not.[7] It has been decided that the paternity of a child is admitted, and prima facie established, by the entry of the father's name on the birth certificate.[8]

A difficult question is whether the term 'parent' in the relevant provision of the legislation includes the *natural* father of the child. This is important because section 38(6) provides that the allowance is not payable to a parent of the child. 'Parent' is not now, and never has been, defined in the social security legislation, but a Tribunal of Commissioners in *R(G) 12/55* ruled

---

3. S.I. 1975/515, Reg. 5(6).
4. Contrast the Commissioners' views in *R(G) 10/52* and *R(G) 3/68*, ante, pp. 257 and 261.
5. S.I. 1975/515, Reg. 2.
6. Ante, p. 258.
7. S.I. 1975/515, Reg. 3(2).
8. See *R(G) 15/52*; *R(G) 4/59*.

that a natural father is a 'parent' for the purposes of entitlement to guardian's allowance. Therefore, he was not entitled when he looked after the child subsequent to the death of its adoptive parents.[9] This ruling has been criticised as a matter of interpretation, as generally the word 'parent' in a statute does not include the natural father.[10] Moreover, it is arguable that the specific provision in Regulation 3(1) that, for the purposes of section 38(2) of the Act, the natural father is to be treated as a parent in certain circumstances implies that generally he should not be so treated. On the other hand, if the natural father were eligible to receive GA in the rare circumstances which obtained in this case, it seems that in theory the natural mother should similarly be entitled if she looked after her child on the death of its adoptive parents, though it would be odd to hold that she was not a 'parent'. On balance, therefore, the ruling by the Tribunal seems correct.

vi) Children of divorced spouses

Regulation 4(1) covers the case where the child's parents are divorced.[11] If, on the death of one parent, 'the child was not in the custody of, or being maintained by, the other parent *and* there was no order of a court granting custody of the child to that other parent or imposing any liability on him for the child's maintenance', then the requirement in section 38 is satisfied by the death of the first parent. In this case the parent-child relationship has already been severed with the other parent, so there is every justification for modifying the usual requirement for both parents to have died before GA is awarded. However, the mere fact that a court order has been made against the surviving spouse means that the parent-child relationship has not been destroyed and the allowance is not payable; it does not matter that no money has been paid under the order.[12]

vii) Husband and wife residing together and entitled to GA

Under section 38(5) of the Social Security Act 1975, as amended,[13] it is provided that where a husband and wife are residing together[14] and are both otherwise eligible for a guardian's allowance, it is the latter who is entitled. But payment may be made to either, unless she elects that it is not to be made to her husband.[15]

viii) Amount

The weekly amount of the allowance after 3 April 1978, when the new rate of child benefit (£2·30 for all children) came into force,[16] is £6·10 for all children.[17]

9. This appears to be the only situation where a natural father could claim GA with any plausibility; in other cases he would have to be dead before the payment of the allowance could arise!

10. See *Calvert*, p. 250. He criticises the Tribunal for not giving enough weight to the decision of the Court of Appeal in *Re M.* [1955] 2 QB 479, [1955] 2 All ER 911.

11. The regulation also applies on the annulment of a voidable marriage: S.I. 1975/515, Reg. 4(3).

12. See *R(G) 10/52*.

13. CBA 1975, Sch. 4, para. 12(c).

14. On this, see post, pp. 390–393.

15. See S.I. 1977/342, Reg. 9(4).

16. See chap. 11, post, p. 449.

17. S.I. 1977/1328, Reg. 3.

8 Industrial Injury

Part one. Introduction

Provision for the consequences of industrial accidents and diseases has always taken a prominent position among social welfare systems. Typically it manifests four characteristics:

> 'It is the oldest branch of social security, it provides the most generous benefits, it is a pace-setter for other social security provisions and it is administered as a separate entity'.[1]

The surge of legislation at the end of the nineteenth century in the industrialised countries was quite remarkable in its coincidence.[2] The movement may be attributed to a number of causes:[3] the increasing power of the trades unions; the inadequacies of the tort system as a means of compensation; social concern at the high accident rate in industry; the need for an incentive to industrial safety and the rehabilitation of disabled members of the labour force. Granted that historically there were special reasons why compensation for employment injury should be in the vanguard, it is more difficult to justify its continued, though indirectly diminishing,[4] precedence over other disability schemes as regards both administration and the level of benefits. Such a justification was, however, attempted by Beveridge in a famous passage of his Report.[5] Having conceded that,

> 'a complete solution is to be found only in a completely unified scheme for disability without demarcation by the cause of disability',

he nevertheless submitted three arguments for maintaining a differential.

> 'First, many industries vital to the community are also specially dangerous. It is essential that men should enter them and desirable, therefore, that they should be able to do so with the

1. *Kaim-Caudle*, p. 65.
2. 1883, Italy; 1884, Germany; 1894, Norway; 1897, UK; 1898, France and Denmark.
3. Cf. *Atiyah*, pp. 316–318; *Dupeyroux*, pp. 42–48; Wilson and Levy

Workmen's Compensation (1939), vol. 1, chap. 1; Friedman and Ladinsky, 67 Col. LR 50.
4. Post, pp. 269 and 349.
5. Paras. 80–86. See also Appendix for *Pearson*.

assurance of special provision against their risks . . . . Second, a
man disabled during the course of his employment has been
disabled while working under orders. This is not true generally of
other accidents or of sickness. Third, only if special provision is
made for the results of industrial accident and disease, irrespective
of negligence, would it appear possible . . . to limit the employer's
liability at Common Law to the results of actions for which he is
responsible morally and in fact, not simply by virtue of some
principle of legal liability'.

The main difficulty with the first argument is that it confuses the source
of the injury – the environmental condition of working – with its
consequences. The fact that an individual may be subjected to a greater
hazard at work than elsewhere does not mean that his need will be greater
if the risks materialise.[6] If there is a case for discrimination between
various groups of disabled persons it must surely be made according to the
gravity of the consequences to the individual and his family rather than to
the cause of the injury.[7] The loss of a breadwinner's income may create the
greatest potential hardship and it will arise whether an employee is injured
at work or elsewhere. The argument based on the need to pay more
compensation to those encountering higher risks in special occupations
also logically leads to the probably unacceptable proposition that workers
in low-risk industries should receive less than steeplejacks or bricklayers.[8]
Beveridge himself conceded that the second and third arguments were less
convincing than the first, and the notion of working 'under orders' is
certainly an artificial and arbitrary one.[9] Can it be said that an individual
crossing the street, or using a dangerous product at home, is incurring a
risk any more 'voluntarily' than an employee at work? The third argument
has been superseded, somewhat ironically, by later events. Notwithstanding the more generous social security provision, common law liability for
industrial injuries has been extended rather than, as Beveridge had hoped,
reduced.[10] What remains is the political fact that those initially privileged
were unwilling to sacrifice their more generous treatment in favour of a
broader based scheme.[11] Nor must it be forgotten that the differentiation
of certain sources of injury and illness is itself expensive to operate. The
categorisation of accidents into industrial and non-industrial, based on the
familiar but notorious formula 'out of and in the course of employment' is,
as this chapter will reveal,[12] a fruitful source of dispute and necessarily

6. Report of the Royal Commission of Inquiry on Compensation for Personal Injury in New Zealand (The Woodhouse Report) (1967), para. 52.
7. Aiken and Reid *Employment Welfare and Safety at Work* (1971), p. 208.
8. Woodhouse Report, ante n.6, loc, cit; Young *Industrial Injuries Insurance* (1964), p. 91.
9. *Atiyah*, p. 324; *Young*, ante n.8, at p. 92; Woodhouse Report, ante n.6, at para. 53.
10. *Atiyah*, p. 324, and post, p. 270.
11. The history was recently repeated in Australia when the National Compensation Bill encountered strong opposition from the trade unions on the ground that it would abolish advantages hitherto enjoyed under the workmen's compensation schemes.
12. Post, pp. 276–293.

frequent adjudication.[13]

The history of special provision for industrial accidents and diseases has been the subject of intensive study[14] and need not be expounded in detail here. The Workmen's Compensation Act 1897, in certain respects, bore traces of the traditional common law liability, but in more important respects foreshadowed a system of social insurance. Liability was imposed on the employer himself, but compensation was payable for all accidents 'arising out of and in the course of employment', irrespective of proof of negligence.[15] Loss was effectively shared between employer and the employee, for the latter might claim at most only one half of his average earnings,[16] and that subject to a statutory maximum.[17] Short-term claims were excluded by a waiting period of three weeks.[18] The principle of individual employer's liability led naturally to an adversarial method of adjudicating claims, and though provision might be made for less formal arbitration proceedings would typically be taken in the county courts and often, on appeal, to the higher courts.[19] Apart from cases of death, for which a lump sum of three years' annual earnings, to a maximum of £300, was payable to dependants,[20] compensation would normally take the form of weekly payments. However, the concept of a 'private right' was used to support the idea that an individual might compromise his claim for a lump sum settlement. Indeed, after six months of payments, an employer had the *right* to redeem the continuing obligation by a lump sum, provided only that it was registered with, and obtained the approval of, a county court judge.[1]

Originally the Act was confined in its scope to certain dangerous trades.[2] In 1906, it was extended to cover all manual occupations, and those non-manual workers earning less than £250 a year.[3] Employment-related illnesses had been a major source of hardship, and in the same year, compensation became payable to those suffering from certain specified diseases which were attributable to the nature of the employment.[4] The only other substantial reform before the scheme was abolished in 1946 was the introduction of increases for dependants. It was regularly urged that payment according to earnings (and only partial compensation at that) did not provide sufficient security for those with large family responsibilities.

13. The Royal Commission on Civil Liability and Compensation for Personal Injuries estimated that the cost of administering the industrial injury scheme was about 12% of the total paid in benefits. The equivalent figure for the non-industrial sickness benefit was about 8½%: *Pearson*, para. 121.
14. *Wilson and Levy*, ante n.3; *Young*, ante n.8.
15. In 1897 £1 per week (WCA 1897, Sch. 1, para. 1(b)). The WCA 1923, s.4(1) raised the maximum to £1·50.
16. WCA 1897, s.1(1).
17. *Ibid.*, Sch. 1, para. 1(b). Under WCA 1923, s.4(2), for workmen earning less than £2·50 per week, the proportion was fixed on a scale varying from 50%–75%.
18. WCA 1897, s.1(2)(a), reduced to one week by WCA 1906, s. 1(2)(a) and three days by WCA 1923, s.5.
19. See *Wilson and Levy*, ante n.3, vol. 2, at pp. 255–262; *Young*, ante n.8, at pp. 79–81.
20. WCA 1897, Sch. 1, para. 1(a)(i), post, p. 341.
1. WCA 1897, s.1(3)–(4).
2. These are listed ibid., s.7.
3. WCA 1906, s.13.
4. Ibid., s.8.

As regards death cases, the point was conceded in 1923, after which child dependants' allowances might supplement the lump sum to the widow,[5] but despite a firm recommendation for similar provision for living claimants,[6] it was not until 1940 that the proposal was implemented.[7]

The brevity of this account should not be allowed to disguise the complexity of the scheme's operation, the frequency of government reviews and legislative changes, and the general contention and dissatisfaction which it engendered. The criticism reached its height in the late 1930s with the publication by Wilson and Levy of their massive sociological and comparative treatise on the subject.[8] A Royal Commission established in 1938 curtailed its inquiries on the outbreak of war and its task was assumed by Beveridge as part of his overall survey of social security. His own dislike of the scheme is immediately apparent: 'the pioneer system of social security in Britain was based on a wrong principle and has been dominated by a wrong outlook'.[9] From his exposition of the weaknesses of workmen's compensation the following may be highlighted: the adversarial nature of adjudication which was disruptive of good industrial relations and which created problems of adequate representation for the workman;[10] the lack of any obligation on employers to insure against liability with the consequent lack of security for accident victims;[11] the ability to compromise a claim for a lump sum settlement, which presupposed equality of bargaining power and under which a claimant was tempted to accept less than his due;[12] the high administrative costs of the scheme, resulting in part from the inefficiencies of the private insurance market[13] and in part from the excessive resort to litigation.[14]

The question whether each industry should continue to bear its own accident costs or whether all risks should be pooled, as in unemployment and health insurance, was more debatable, and has continued to be a controversial issue.[15] There are two main arguments for relating the financial responsibility of the industry or firm to the risks created by its activities, as evidenced by the number of injury claims. The first is that it

5. WCA 1923, s.2.
6. Report of Committee on Workmen's Compensation (Holman Gregory Report) (1920), Cmd. 816, para. 62.
7. WC (Supplementary Allowances) Act 1940, s.1(1).
8. Wilson and Levy Workmen's Compensation (1939).
9. Para. 80.
10. Para. 79(1)–(ii); Wilson and Levy, ante n.8, vol. 2, chap. 15. The point was also stressed in Social Insurance, Part II, para. 23.
11. Para. 79(iii). If the defendant was insured, the worker's position was more secure. The Employers' Liability Insurance Companies Act 1907 (later incorporated into the Assurance Companies Act 1909) required a deposit of £20,000 with the Board of Trade.
12. Para. 79(iv); Wilson and Levy, ante n.8, vol. 2, chap. 7.
13. Para. 79(vii). Appendix E of the Report revealed that the proportion of administrative costs to premiums paid was, for some insurance companies, 46%.
14. In 1938 alone 75 appeals had gone to the Court of Appeal: Potter and Stansfield National Insurance (Industrial Injuries) (2nd edn), p. 8.
15. Report of the Royal Commission of Inquiry on Compensation for Personal Injury in New Zealand (The Woodhouse Report) (1967), at paras. 328–336; Report of the Committee on Safety and Health at Work (1972), Cmnd. 5034 (Robens Report), paras. 428–430; Atiyah, 4 ILJ 1, 89; Phillips, 5 ILJ 148; Pearson, paras. 898–904.

acts as an incentive to safety and the prevention of injuries.[16] Secondly, it avoids the price distortion which results from a low-risk industry subsidising a high-risk industry: for example, the accident record of the mining industry is very high, and it has been calculated that if the industrial injury scheme were risk-related, the 'fair' price of coal (in 1969) would have been higher by 15p per ton.[17] Such distortion, it is argued, leads to over-employment in dangerous industries and insufficient expenditure on accident prevention.[18] Opponents of the differential approach doubt the force of the incentive argument. A system of risk-rating, or premium-loading, can hardly be based on culpability; it discriminates unfairly between large and small enterprises; and such evidence as is available suggests that it has no significant effects on safety.[19] The price-distortion argument is countered by the principle of social interdependence. No industry works in isolation from others. Coal, for example, is used in the production of many other goods.[20] Further, price-distortion may indeed be appropriate. In 1944 the government noted that hazardous employments included certain important industries like mining and shipping which had to face foreign competition.[1] Finally, even if the differential approach may be more equitable it is certainly much more expensive to administer.[2] In the light of such considerations, Beveridge formulated a compromise solution: a general pooling of responsibility with a special charge on certain high-risk industries.[3] The proposal did not win the approval of the government[4] and the National Insurance (Industrial Injuries) Act 1946 created a fund based on flat-rate contributions (five-twelfths each from the employer and employee, the remaining one-sixth being paid by the Exchequer). Despite a recommendation by the Robens Committee on Safety and Health at Work to reopen the matter,[5] and greater readiness abroad to maintain variable premium rates,[6] the principle of uniform contributions has remained unchanged.

In most other respect, Beveridge's plan to unify responsibility and administration of industrial injuries compensation under a national insurance scheme, and at the same time to afford more generous benefits than those available for unemployment and sickness,[7] and without contribution requirements, was accepted. The exact form and level of benefits remained, however, a matter for considerable dispute. The proposal to pay a rate of benefit, which would, only after a period of thirteen weeks' incapacity, be higher than that for sickness,[8] was rejected: preferential treatment was to be provided throughout.[9] Conversely, the government was not prepared to depart from the general principle of flat-rate benefits

16. Calabresi *The Cost of Accidents* (1970); Ison *The Forensic Lottery* (1967), chap. 5.
17. *Kaim-Caudle*, p. 71.
18. Phillips, ante n.15, at pp. 150–151.
19. Woodhouse Report, ante n.15, at para. 336; Atiyah, ante n.15, at pp. 90–102; cp. Phillips, ante n.15, at pp. 157–160.
20. Woodhouse, ante n. 15, at para. 335.
1. Social Insurance, Part II, para. 23(iii).

2. See, e.g., the very complex French system of differentials: *Dupeyroux*, pp. 689–696.
3. Paras. 88–92.
4. Social Insurance, Part II, para. 31.
5. Ante n.15, at para. 447.
6. *Kaim-Caudle*, pp. 69–75.
7. Paras. 97–105.
8. Para. 332.
9. Social Insurance, Part II, paras. 26–27.

in favour of an earnings-related pension,[10] as Beveridge had recommended.[11] It proposed, for long-term cases, the tariff method of compensation, derived from the war pensions scheme and based on the degree of disablement.[12] This idea of basing benefits on need rather than earnings-potential proved to be unacceptable politically, and there ensued an unsatisfactory compromise combining the tariff benefit with the so-called 'special hardship allowance' which compensated for impaired earning capacity. This, and the direct application of earnings-related supplements to short-term cases, are fully described at a later stage in this chapter.[13]

Two other developments subsequent to 1946 deserve mention here. While the policy of discriminating between the industrial and non-industrial disabled has not been openly challenged by successive governments (though it has been repudiated in some foreign systems[14]), the value of the differential has been allowed to erode through the process of inflation. In 1946 the industrial injury benefit was 73% higher than sickness benefit;[15] in 1978 the equivalent figure is 12%.[16] The financing of the industrial injuries scheme and its administration were closely (though not completely) analogous to those of the national insurance scheme, and since 1946 there has been a continuous process of integrating the two. In 1973–75, the high point of the process was reached by the incorporation of both schemes into the Social Security Acts and the abolition of the separate Industrial Injuries Fund.[17] In part, the decision was attributable to the fact that the latter, in sharp contrast to the non-industrial fund,[18] was showing a healthy surplus (in 1972 some £400 million[19]). A more principled argument for amalgamation was based on the increasing dislike of discrimination between the industrially injured and the non-industrially injured and the administrative convenience of combining two funds into one, which was henceforth to be financed on an earnings-related basis.[20]

The second issue, that of overlap with other systems of compensation, particularly that of the common law action, was raised by Beveridge but not solved by him. He asumed, as a matter of principle, that

> 'an injured person should not have the same need met twice over. He should get benefit at once without prejudice to any alternative remedy, but if the alternative remedy proves in fact to be available, he should not in the end get more from the two sources together than he would have got from one alone'.[1]

The principle gave rise to some difficult legal issues and the government

10. Ibid., at paras. 28–29.
11. Para. 332.
12. Social Insurance, Part II, para. 29; and see post, pp. 308–314 and 371.
13. Post, pp. 302 and 318–332.
14. The distinction has been abolished in Holland (Incapacity Insurance Act 1966) and New Zealand (Accidents Compensation Act 1972).
15. NIA 1946, Sch. 2, and NI(II)A 1946, s.11(3).
16. S.I. 1977/1325. See also on death benefit, post p. 349.
17. SSA 1973, s.94.
18. See DHSS Annual Report 1972, Cmnd. 5352, paras. 11.10 and 11.12.
19. DHSS Annual Report 1971, Cmnd. 5019, para. 357.
20. See Standing Committee E Debates on Social Security Bill 1973, cols. 1609–1611. For contributions to the National Insurance Fund see ante, chap. 2.
1. Para. 260.

appointed a committee to examine them.[2] The majority finding to a large extent supported Beveridge's diagnosis: entitlement to social security benefits should not depend on the availability of a common law claim, but that since both forms of compensation were intended to satisfy the same need, duplication should be avoided, and the net value of the benefit should be deducted from the common law award of damages.[3] The Labour government was politically embarrassed by this recommendation, and, under considerable trade union pressure reached the compromise solution of deducting one half of the sickness, injury or disablement benefit payable for a period of five years from the common law compensation.[4] The alleged justification that the employee had himself paid for half the cost of the benefit (through his five-twelfths contribution) has been heavily criticised.[5] The problem is germane more to the concept of compensation within the law of damages than to social security, to which its impact is only incidental, and for full discussion reference should be made to the standard works on the former subject.[6]

Claims for all categories of benefit under the industrial injuries scheme must satisfy two conditions:

> (i) that the person injured or killed was an employed earner (Part Two); *and*
>
> (ii) that the injury or death was caused by 'accident arising out of and in the course of his employment' (Part Three) or resulted from a disease prescribed in relation to that employment (Part Four).

Injury benefit (Part Five) is paid for the first six months of incapacity for work. After that period disablement benefit (Part Six) is paid for loss of physical or mental faculty and may be supplemented by certain increases and additions (Part Seven). The chapter concludes with a discussion of certain miscellaneous matters (Part Eight) and death benefit (Part Nine).

Part two. Persons Covered

The Workmen's Compensation Act 1897 covered only specified dangerous employments,[7] but in 1906 was extended to all persons working under a contract of service or apprenticeship, with a few exceptions, the most

2. See Final Report of the Committee on Alternative Remedies (Monckton Report) (1946), Cmd. 6860.
3. Ibid., at paras. 48, 92, 96, 98, notwithstanding the objection that tortfeasors would thereby be subsidised by contributors to the National Insurance Fund. The Committee rejected the idea of subrogating the victim's common law claim to the fund: ibid., at para. 41.
4. Law Reform (Personal Injuries) Act 1948, s.2(1).
5. E.g., Atiyah, pp. 407–411; Williams, 37 MLR 28.
6. Ogus Law of Damages (1973), pp. 222–230; Street Principles of the Law of Damages (1962), chap. 4; Fleming International Encyclopedia of Comparative Law, vol. XI, chap. 11; Luntz Assessment of Damages for Personal Injuries and Death (1974), chap. 5; Pearson, chap. 13.
7. WCA 1897, s.7.

important of which were non-manual workers earning more than £250 (subsequently £420) a year.[8] The 1946 state scheme covered the same categories, but included also all non-manual employees irrespective of income, and did not permit contracting-out which had been possible under workmen's compensation. In general, the categories of insured persons were the same as those regarded as 'employed persons' for the purposes of the non-industrial national insurance schemes. However, there were reasons for creating distinctions between the scope of the two schemes: first, 'employment' in the non-industrial scheme was confined to those working a minimum number of hours a week, a limitation which had not existed under the Workmen's Compensation Act and which was therefore considered inappropriate for the industrial scheme; secondly, the non-industrial benefits were, in general, payable only on the fulfiment of certain contribution conditions, whereas under the industiral scheme, as with its predecessor, the employee was covered as from the first day of employment, irrespective of contributions. For these reasons the scope of the two schemes had to be distinguished precisely and this was achieved in the Schedules to the 1946 Acts.

The amalgamation of the two schemes in 1975 resulted in a change of terminology from 'insured persons' to 'employed earners', the expression used to denote class 1 contributors to the non-industrial scheme.[9] The effect has been to extend industrial injuries benefits to some who had been self-employed before 1975, notably 'office-holders' (e.g., directors of limited companies).[10] The present position is, then, that the scheme covers those who are 'employed earners', as the term is interpreted for the contribution provisions of the Social Security Act 1975.[11] This is subject to the power of the Secretary of State to extend or exclude, by regulation, categories of such earners for the purposes of the industrial benefits.[12] The more important categories so regulated may be summarised as follows.

1. Included are apprentices, members of fire brigades and other rescue services, mine inspectors, special constables.[13]

2. Excluded is employment by a relative in the house of that relative and not for the purpose of trade or business, or by a spouse (unless, in the case of the latter, it is for the purpose of the spouse's business and the earnings therefrom exceed the current lower earnings limit for non-industrial class 1 contributions).[14]

3. The employment must be in Great Britain,[15] but workers on the Continental Shelf,[16] and mariners and airmen employed on, respectively, a British ship or aircraft[17] are included.

As with analogous questions arising under the non-industrial schemes,

8. WCA 1906, ss.1, 13.
9. SSA 1973, s.94(2), as amended by NIA 1974, s.6(5) and Sch. 4, para. 27(b).
10. See ante, p. 53.
11. SSA 1975, ss.2(1)(a) and 50(1). See, generally, ante, pp. 47–53.
12. Ibid., s.51(1)–(2) and S.I. 1975/467.
13. Ibid., Sch. 1, Part I.
14. Ibid., Part II. For the earnings limit, see ante, p. 55.
15. SSA 1975, s.2(1)(a).
16. S.I. 1975/467, Sch. 1, Part I, para. 7.
17. Ibid., Sch. 2; cf. ante, p. 69.

disputes as to classification are determined not by the statutory authorities but by the Secretary of State.[18] He is also given power to direct that where a contract of service is rendered void or unlawful as a result of non-compliance with any statutory requirement passed for the protection of employed persons, the employment is nevertheless, for the purposes of industrial injury benefits, to be treated as an employed earner's employment.[19]

Part three. Industrial Injury

Entitlement to the various industrial benefits is fundamentally based on proof that the 'employed earner suffers personal injury caused ... by accident arising out of and in the course of his employment'.[20] This contains three different elements:[1]

    A. a personal injury,
    B. caused by an accident,
    C. arising out of and in the course of employment.

The discussion will be divided accordingly.

A. Personal injury

This means a 'hurt to body or mind'.[2] Thus it includes a nervous disorder or nervous shock.[3] Even a trivial hurt which is ephemeral, like the watering of an eye,[4] will qualify, though, as will be seen,[5] to recover injury or disablement benefit, the claimant must proceed to establish incapacity for work or loss of faculty respectively. Damage to property is not included. Consequently, compensation is not available for loss arising from damage to an artificial limb or clothing.[6] In this respect, the British system compares unfavourably with certain foreign schemes under which a person so affected may recover at least the cost of repair and sometimes also any consequent loss of earnings.[7]

B. Accident

The personal injury must be caused 'by accident' which, with some exceptions, occurred within Great Britain.[8] On the orthodox view, the requirement of an 'accident' has a twofold object: to exclude

18. SSA 1975, s.93(1)(d) and R(I) 2/75. See, generally, post, pp. 621–624.
19. SSA 1975, s.156.
20. SSA 1975, s.50(1).
1. Cf. Lord Denning MR in Re Dowling [1967] 1 QB 202, at 217.
2. Per Lord Simon, Jones v Secretary of State for Social Services [1972] AC 944 at 1020.

3. R(I) 49/52; R(I) 22/59.
4. R 5/60 (II).
5. Post, pp. 300 and 306.
6. R(I) 7/56.
7. E.g., W. Germany, Reichsversicherungsordnung, § 548; New Zealand, Accident Compensation Act 1972, s.110.
8. SSA 1975, s.50(5).

sickness,[9] and to facilitate proof that the injury was work-caused.[10] But it has given rise to considerable difficulty and has been removed in several jurisdictions.[11] In Britain, judicial interpretation and legislative intervention have greatly reduced the rigours of the original test and it remains to be seen whether it succeeds in fulfilling the declared objectives.

i) Meaning of 'accident'

The starting point must be Lord Macnaghten's famous dictum in 1903:[12]

> 'The expression "accident" is used in the popular and ordinary sense of the word as denoting an unlooked-for mishap or an untoward event which is not expected or designed'.

But 'popular' meanings are notoriously unreliable and, as critics have pointed out,[13] nowhere more so than in this context. It soon became clear that Lord Macnaghten's definition was neither accurate nor sufficient. In the first place, while it was construed to exclude deliberate acts by the injured party himself, it has been held to include a deliberate, even unlawful, act of a third party. The point was decided in *Trim Joint District School v Kelly*,[14] in which pupils assaulted and killed a schoolmaster responsible for discipline. Secondly, the phrase 'not expected' could not be taken seriously. An event need not be unforeseeable or exceptional to constitute an 'accident'.[15] To take a frequently encountered example, a man incapacitating himself by heavy exertions does not have to prove that the strain was violent or exceptional for his job.[16]

There has been considerable debate on the question whether, by its very nature, the accident must be 'external' to the claimant: that is, whether the accident is always independent of the 'injury' or whether what constitutes the 'injury' may also constitute the 'accident'. A situation may arise where due to a strain, an internal physiological change occurs, resulting in eventual disability to the claimant. On one view (now, it seems, the prevailing view), in such a case 'accident' and 'injury' are interchangeable terms: they cannot be independently defined.[17] On another view,[18] the

9. Report of Departmental Committee on Workmen's Compensation (1904), Cd. 2208. para. 103; Canadian Commission of Inquiry into Workmen's Compensation (1966) (Tysoe Commission), p. 178.

10. Report of Departmental Committee on Disease Provisions of National Insurance (Industrial Injuries) Act (Beney Committee) (1955), Cmd. 9548, para. 55.

11. In the USA: California, Iowa and Massachusets (Horovitz 12 Law Soc. Jo. 465, 493). See also the Model Workmen's Compensation Act prepared by the Council of State Legislation in 1963. In Australia: New South Wales and Victoria (Luntz 40 ALJ 179).

12. *Fenton v J. Thorley & Co Ltd* [1903] AC 443 at 448.

13. See *Trim Joint District School Board of Management v Kelly* [1914] AC 667 at 681, per Lord Loreburn; *Re Dowling* [1967] 1 AC 725 at 759, per Lord Wilberforce; *Jones v Secretary of State for Social Services* [1972] AC 944 at 1009, per Lord Diplock. See also Bohlen 25 Harv. LR 378.

14. Ante, n.13. See also *CI 51/49* and *R(I) 30/58*.

15. *Clover Clayton v Hughes* [1910] AC 242; *CWI 6/49*; but the 'abnormality' of an event may be relevant in proving the causal link between the injury and the accident: post, p. 275.

16. *CI 5/49*.

17. *Re Dowling*, ante n.13; *Jones's* case, ante n.13.

18. *Jones's* case, ante n.13; per Viscount Dilhorne at p. 987, per Lord Diplock at pp. 1009–1010.

distinction is between a 'causative incident' (the accident), something external which has a physiological effect on part of the claimant's anatomy, or a phsychological effect on his mind, *and* the adverse physical or medical consequences of that condition (the injury). In the case of incapacity caused by heavy exertion, the distinction is difficult to draw but nevertheless must exist: the 'accident' is the physical exertion and the 'injury' is the consequent physiological change. Within the context of the present discussion, the matter is entirely linguistic. No practical consequences flow from the difference of views. In either case, there is a 'personal injury by accident'. The debate is relevant only to the issue, arising under claims for disablement benefit, of the relative competence of the statutory and medical authorities in determining the aetiology of the disability.[19]

The essence of the 'accident' requirement, and the focal point of much of the case-law, is the difficult question whether the claimant's condition was caused by an 'event' as opposed to a 'process'. It is, of course, a method of distinguishing between an accident insurance scheme and a health insurance scheme. This is not to say that industrial illness or diseases are excluded from the scheme but, as will be seen, there is separate provision for them.[20] The notion of 'accident' in the words of Lord Porter,[1] and subsequently adopted by a Tribunal of Commissioners,[2] does not include the growth of incapacity by a continuous process. The claimant must be able to point to 'an incident or series of incidents ... which caused or contributed to the origin or progress of the disease'.[3] Inevitably the inquiry is an elusive one, and many decisions are difficult to reconcile. A few will illustrate the difficulty and give some indication of the present tendency of Commissioners' decisions.

> Strain to chest muscles caused by the daily lifting of heavy weights is not covered,[4] but a claimant, who, when lifting heavy equipment on a particular day, felt severe pains in the chest and subsequently suffered from coronary thrombosis, was entitled to succeed. He had experienced a physiological change at that particular time.[5]

> A worker who developed a psychoneurotic condition having worked near a machine which produced explosive reports at irregular intervals recovered. Each explosion was 'an accident' and thus the condition was the result of a 'series of accidents'. The interval between each such explosion was not so short that the series was to be regarded as a single continuous process.[6] On the other hand, a claimant who became sick on inhaling gas which leaked from the vehicle he used from time to time did not succeed: the illness was caused by the taking of breath on an infinite number of occasions, and these did not constitute separate incidents.[7]

Apart from the somewhat arbitrary nature of some of these distinctions,

19. Post, pp. 306–308.
20. Post, pp. 293–297.
  1. *Roberts v Dorothea Slate Quarries* [1948] 2 All ER 201, at 205–206, HL.
  2. *CI 257/49.*

3. Ibid., at para. 11.
4. *R(I) 42/51.*
5. *R(I) 54/53.*
6. *R(I) 43/55.*
7. *R(I) 32/60.*

it is apparent from other decisions that certain illogicalities may ensue. A claimant will be fortunate if the condition, though developing gradually, manifests itself on a particular occasion. Thus in *R(I) 18/54* the claimant had been using a pad for three months, the buckle of which rubbed against a nerve. One day, he felt a numbness in his leg, and he was allowed to recover on the basis that this constituted a particular incident.[8] Even more anomalously, a person who encounters an employment risk only once will be in a better position than one who is exposed to it regularly. Hence, a nurse who had come into contact with, and was infected by, a child with poliomyelitis succeeded,[9] but a doctor who was attending a large number of patients infected with tuberculosis and subsequently contracted the disease was refused benefit. It was assumed that he must have been infected by the regular penetration of bacteria into his system.[10] It must be noted, however, that once the claimant has succeeded in establishing, on the balance of probabilities, that the injury resulted from an event or a series of events,[11] his claim will not be jeopardised by his failure to identify the specific occasion when the condition began or was aggravated: for procedural purposes the earliest probable date will be taken.[12]

ii) Causal link between accident and injury

The claimant must also prove, on the balance of probabilities, that the accident 'caused' the injury.[13] This does not mean that it has to be the sole cause of the injury; it is sufficient if it is a contributory cause, in combination with, for example, a condition from which the claimant already suffered.[14] It is irrelevant that the previous condition rendered the claimant more susceptible to the later event.[15] But, at the same time, the accident must have been 'an efficient cause (*causa causans*) and not a mere condition (*causa sine qua non*)' in which the earlier cause operated.[16] Thus in *R(I) 4/58*,

> The claimant suffered from burns when his clothing, which had been soaked in inflammable liquid in a work accident, caught fire when coming into contact with a cigarette which he was lighting at home. It was held that the *causa causans* of the injury was the lighting of the cigarette, and not the accidental soaking.

iii) Critique

It will be apparent from the analysis above that the requirement of an 'accident' has produced severe difficulties and it may be seriously questioned whether there are not preferable alternatives. The traditional justification for the requirement is that it preserves the distinction between

---

8. The case should be compared with *R(I) 11/74* in which the claimant was unable to advert to a specific date.
9. *CI 159/50.*
10. *CI 83/50.*
11. See, *R(I) 8/66.*
12. *CI 49/49*; *CI 196/50.*
13. In contrast to the war pension scheme,

where the burden of proof of the causal link between service and the disability generally favours the claimant; post, p. 365.
14. *R(I) 19/63.*
15. *CI 147/50.*
16. *R(I) 14/51*, para. 6. See also *R(I) 12/58*, para. 5.

a scheme concerned to compensate injuries and one providing relief for sickness. In the usual case it does indeed have this effect, but the distinction itself is not wholly conclusive in determining the scope of the British scheme. On the one hand, a claimant will succeed if he can show that an illness (not an injury) was attributable to an event rather than to a process. On the other hand, as will be seen, he is entitled to benefit if he suffers from a prescribed disease, provided that it was contracted in the appropriate prescribed employment. One alternative, then, would be to link the two concepts and allow recovery for any injury or disease which was work-caused. The list of prescribed diseases could function simply as an aid in proving the causal connection between the condition and the employment: if the claimant's condition was prescribed, the onus of disproving the connection would pass to the insurance officer. The suggestion was made in 1948 by a committee reviewing the policy of scheduling industrial diseases,[17] but repudiated by another committee some seven years later on the ground that proof of the connection between employment and an unprescribed disease would be too difficult.[18] However, such a system operates in the Federal Republic of Germany[19] and an EEC Recommendation of 1962 has urged its adoption on member states.[20]

Another less radical alternative is that proposed by Sir Owen Woodhouse as part of his recommendations for new schemes in both New Zealand[1] and Australia.[2] The idea is to incorporate in legislation a list of all possible forms of accident to be made the subject of compensation, and for such a purpose it might be possible to adopt a classification of injuries and external causes of injury prepared by the World Health Organisation.[3] Of course, like all attempts at exhaustive listing, this could not be a perfect solution and would have to be supplemented by some residual general clause. But it might serve to remove some of the doubt and uncertainty which the case law on the more traditional approach reveals.

C. Employment risk

i) General

It is of the essence of an industrial injuries insurance scheme that the accident must be connected with the employment. In 1897, the Workmen's Compensation Act contained a test which was adopted by English

---

17. Report of Departmental Committee on Industrial Diseases (Dale Committee), Cmd. 7557, para. 26.
18. Report of Departmental Committee on Disease Provisions of National Insurance (Industrial Injuries) Act (Beney Committee) (1955), Cmd. 9548, at para. 88.
19. Reichsversicherungsordnung, § 551.
20. No. 2188/62. See *Journal Officiel* of 31 August 1962. Cf. *Pearson*, p. 188.

1. Report of Royal Commission of Inquiry into Compensation for Personal Injuries in New Zealand (1967), para. 289(c).
2. Report of National Committee of Inquiry into Compensation and Rehabilitation in Australia (1974), para. 350.
3. The relevant parts are conveniently published in a Schedule to the draft Bill at the end of the Australian report.

speaking jurisdictions throughout the world, and remains the basis of the current scheme: personal injury by accident 'arising out of and in the course of employment'.[4] This classic formulation, perhaps the most notorious in the whole of social security law, has been responsible for vast amounts of disputed claims and complex litigation. In 1920, a judge in the House of Lords was moved to remark that:

> 'The language of the Act and the decisions upon it are such that I have long since abandoned the hope of deciding any case upon the words "out of and in the course of" upon grounds satisfactory to myself or convincing to others';[5]

and two years later a Departmental Committee reported that:

> 'No other form of words has ever given rise to such a body of litigation'.[6]

The original Act sought to delimit the connection with the employment more precisely by requiring that the accident should occur, 'on, in or about' the employer's premises,[7] but this condition was soon abandoned.[8] Most obviously it discrimininated against employees whose work took them away from the employer's premises. Other common law jurisdictions have attempted to mitigate the rigours of the statutory test by amending the formula. Thus, in some systems, the workman need only show that the accident arose '*in* the course of employment',[9] while in others he is given the alternative of proving that it happened 'out of *or* in the course of employment'.[10] But no formula adopted (and this includes non-English speaking jurisdictions[11]) has managed to alleviate problems involved in establishing the connection between the work and the accident. As Atiyah has observed:

> 'The difficulty is inherent in the system; it has nothing to do with the "meaning" of ... words .... The difficulty is inherent in the concept of insurance against special "employment" risks.'[12]

The most significant reforms, therefore, both in Britain and elsewhere, have not been through a modification of the basic formula, but rather by specific extensions of the scheme to cover contingencies which might not otherwise have been regarded as employment risks. As will be seen, the most important developments in this respect have been the coverage of certain accidents occurring on a journey to or from work,[13] or caused by a natural event or the conduct of a third party.[14]

4. WCA 1897, s.1.
5. Per Lord Wrenbury, *Armstrong, Whitworth & Co. v Redford* [1920] AC 757 at 780, HL.
6. Departmental Committee Report on Workmen's Compensation (Holman Gregory Report) (1920), Cmd. 816, para. 29.
7. WCA 1897, s.7(1).
8. WCA 1906, s.1(1).
9. E.g., in the USA: N. Dakota, Pennyslvania, Texas and Washington.
10. E.g., in Australia, New South Wales.
11. See, e.g., *Dupeyroux*, pp. 446–455.
12. P. 328.
13. Post, pp. 283–284.
14. Post, p. 290.

ii) The statutory test

It has long been a subject of debate whether the formula 'out of and in the course of employment' involves two different principles or only a single test. It has sometimes been said that the authorities should treat the phrase as a combined whole.[15] The more generally accepted view is that the 'in the course of' criterion delimits the time, place and activity of the work, while the 'out of' criterion concerns itself with the cause or connection between the accident and the work.[16] In the simple case, the distinction is obvious. A man working at his bench inadvertently spikes himself with a pin which he had earlier put in his trouser pocket. The accident arises 'in the course of' his employment but not 'out of' it. But there are other situations where there is an inevitable overlap between the two tests. If, for example, an employee injuries himself through horseplay on his employer's premises and during the normal hours of duty, it might be said either that the accident did not arise out of the employment because the risk was not caused by his work, or that it did not arise in the course of employment, because the claimant's activity at the time interfered with and diverged from his ordinary working duties. For the sake of clarity of exposition, the traditional distinction has been followed in this work, and the overlap recognised at appropriate points in the discussion.

iii) In the course of employment

a) GENERAL PRINCIPLES. According to the classic formulation of Lord Loreburn,

> 'An accident befalls a man "in the course of" his employment if it occurs while he is doing what a man so employed may reasonably do within a time during which he is employed, and at a place where he may reasonably be during that time to do that thing'.[17]

From this, it will be seen that the limits to the course of employment are determined by three different criteria: place, time and activity. A claimant will set up a prima facie case if he is able to show that the accident occurred at his normal *place* of work during his normal *hours* of work. His *activity* at the time of the accident may be relevant in two different respects. It may serve to defeat a prima facie case by showing that the claimant interrupted the time element in the work or deviated from the spatial element for reasons unconnected with his employment. Or it may serve to extend the 'course of employment' to cover hours or places not normally considered as within its ambit. The discussion will proceed accordingly.

It must also be observed that the notion of employment covers functions and objectives which are regarded as reasonably incidental to the actual

---

15. See, e.g., *CSI 63/49*; *R(I) 62/51*.
16. E.g., per Lord Wright, *Dover Navigation v Craig* [1940] AC 190 at

199, HL; *R(I) 10/52*; *R(I) 2/63*.
17. *Moore v Manchester Liners Ltd* [1910] AC 498 at 500–501.

work process.[18] The contract of employment is rarely relevant or helpful in determining what is to be so regarded. Obviously this varies enormously according to the nature of the work and the status of the claimant, and the courts and the Commissioner have been reluctant to lay down general principles. But during the course of the analysis which follows it will be seen that resort is usually had to two different but related notions. Under the first (supervision test) the adjudicating authority considers whether the accident happened while the claimant was under the authority, supervision or control of his employer.[19] The alternative and complementary criterion (public zone test) is concerned to ascertain whether the activities of the claimant at the time of the accident were such as to distinguish him from an ordinary member of the public.[20]

b) FIXED PLACE AND HOURS OF WORK. Most employees have fixed places and hours of work. The task, here, is to determine what, for the purposes of benefit, are to be regarded as the limits of the employment. The law allows the claimant a certain amount of time and space to 'prepare himself for, or to disengage himself from', his employment.[1] As regards time, the course of employment includes a reasonable period at either end of his official hours of duty. What this amounts to may depend on the nature of the job and the character of the claimant. Thus, a sixty-two year old worker who preferred to take a leisurely bath rather than be involved in the crush for buses home was covered.[2] Arriving early the more properly to equip oneself for work will be generously treated,[3] but not if the intention is instead to fit in a game of billiards.[4]

As regards place, the exact area is difficult to locate. It generally includes the premises in which the claimant is about to work, or has just worked, and the access to them.[5] The 'public zone' test will usually be conclusive in determining the necessary limits. The claimant must be within an area excluded from public access,[6] but this is to be decided according to

18. *Armstrong, Whitworth & Co v Redford,* ante n.5 at pp. 777, 779, 780; *R v Industrial Injuries Comr, ex parte Amalgamated Engineering Union* [1966] 2 QB 31 at pp. 48, 50, 51. In the recent decision *R v National Insurance Comr, ex parte Michael* [1977] 2 All ER 420 at 423–424, 427, the Court of Appeal has stressed that the words 'reasonably incidental' were not intended, and should not be used, as a substitute for the test of 'in the course of employment'. They essentially govern the type of activities covered when the claimant is at his place of work during the normal hours of employment.

19. See particularly *R(I) 84/51.* The test is traditionally used to establish circumstances in which an employer is vicariously liable for the acts of his employee: Atiyah *Vicarious Liability* (1967), chap. 5, and is also favoured by the French industrial injuries scheme (*Dupeyroux,* pp. 451–453).

20. See particularly *R(I) 61/51.*

1. *Gane v Norton Hill Colliery* [1909] 2 KB 539, CA; *R(I) 61/51; R(I) 3/72.*

2. *R(I) 22/51.*

3. *R v National Insurance Comr, ex parte East* [1976] ICR 206.

4. *R(I) 1/59.*

5. *R(I) 7/52; R(I) 5/67.*

6. Even if the claimant's duties sometimes take him into the 'public zone': *R(I) 72/51; R(I) 7/62.* See also *R(I) 7/52; R(I) 23/55; R(I) 70/57.* 'Access' here means qua member of the public – not, of course, for business purposes: *R(I) 41/57.*

existing practice rather than legal rights.[7] The question is whether the members of the public make substantial use of that part of the land.[8] Equally, the mere fact that the land on which the accident occurs is owned by the employer is rarely conclusive.[9] British Railways and the National Coal Board own vast areas of land, and the claimant may be on a part of it miles from his place of work.[10] Conversely, a social worker injured while descending a staircase common to several households may recover, though her business took her to only one.[11] The authorities must determine the part of the land in which the claimant normally works, and this may be particularly difficult in agricultural cases.[12] It is not possible to reconcile all the decisions.[13] In some cases the authorities are apparently prepared to show some indulgence, and avoid nice distinctions which would have the effect of depriving the claimant of benefit. They may then admit a claim on the vague basis that the claimant had 'so nearly approached the means of access as to make it reasonable to hold that he had returned to the sphere in which his employment operated'.[14]

c) EXTENSIONS FOR AUTHORISED OR INCIDENTAL PURPOSES. The spatial and temporal boundaries may be extended for purposes which are reasonably necessary for, or incidental to, the employment. Obviously this covers, primarily, situations where the employer directly or indirectly authorises the employee to perform his duties outside normal hours, or his usual locality, e.g., where a bus conductor was required by her employer to make a cup of tea for herself and the driver at the end of each journey.[15] But it seems that 'employer' in this context must be strictly construed. An unauthorised request from an immediate superior will not bring the resulting activity within the scheme.[16] This may operate harshly, for the employee may find it difficult to refuse the request and feel that his prospects of promotion will otherwise suffer. But the test should be a subjective one: if *he* has reasonable grounds to think that the request has the implied authority of the employer, he should succeed.[17] Where the claimant is under no obligation to carry out the activity, but is merely permitted to, the case is more difficult. Obviously mere knowledge of, or acquiescence by, the employer is insufficient. The issue becomes whether or not the activity in question is sufficiently connected with the employment. There are obvious cases like working overtime,[18] collecting equipment or clothing necessary for work,[19] or taking a bath after duty in a mine.[20] The receipt of wages comes within the scope of employment but

7. R(I) 43/51; R(I) 1/68.
8. Per Lord Macmillan, *Northumbrian Shipping Co Ltd v McCullum* (1932) 25 BWCC 284, HL.
9. CI 65/49; R(I) 67/52; R(I) 43/51.
10. CI 69/49; R(I) 67/52.
11. R(I) 3/72.
12. See R(I) 7/52 and R(I) 42/56.
13. Cf. R(I) 42/56, para. 11.
14. R(I) 3/53, para. 4.
15. R(I) 21/53. See also the cases where the employee is obliged to participate

in physical education, competition or other 'outside' activities e.g., CI 228/50; R(I) 4/51; R(I) 80/52; R(I) 66/53; R(I) 39/56.
16. R(I) 36/55; R(I) 8/61.
17. In R(I) 36/55, paras. 7, 8, the Commissioner speaks of acting under the 'ostensible' authority of the employer.
18. R(I) 52/52.
19. R(I) 72/54; R(I) 20/58.
20. CI 22/49.

not the cashing of a money order representing them: the processes of employment are complete when the money order is received by the employee.[1] Participants in a trade union meeting are also covered, provided that it is directly concerned with the terms and conditions of employment with the particular employer.[2]

The status of recreational activities is problematic. In *R v National Insurance Comr, ex parte Michael*,[3] the Court of Appeal regarded as wrong the dictum of a Commissioner[4] that such activities can never come within the course of employment.[5] But at the same time it held that a police constable injured when playing football for his force was not covered by the statutory formula. The court was not impressed by the argument, which had succeeded before some Commissioners,[6] that such activity improved the fitness and morale of the force and therefore was in pursuance of the employment.[7] It is to be doubted, however, whether the ruling has affected the authority of earlier decisions in favour of the claimant where he was injured while participating in physical exercises which were a compulsory part of a training or educational course considered desirable by the employer,[8] or in games which were regarded as therapeutically valuable to patients at the hospital where he was employed.[9]

The meeting of an emergency is deemed to have the employer's authorisation.[10] Thus an accident is covered if it happens while the claimant is 'taking steps, on an actual or supposed emergency' at his place of work, 'to rescue, succour or protect persons who are, or are thought to be or possibly to be, injured or imperilled, or to avert or minimise serious damage to property'.[11]

d) ACCIDENTS WHILE TRAVELLING. Accidents to the claimant while travelling have always posed special problems for industrial injury schemes, and they have been the subject of much dispute both general and specific. For the purposes of discussion it is necessary to distinguish between three types of case.[12]

1. The employee is required to make a journey for purposes necessary or incidental to his employment.

2. The employee's work is peripatetic: that is, the employment consists of travelling from place to place.

3. The employee merely travels to and from his work.

1. *R(I) 34/53.* In W. Germany the legislation expressly extends the protection to cover such activity: Reichsversicherungsordnung § 548(1).
2. *R(I) 63/55; R(I) 9/57; R(I) 46/59.* See also *CI 526/75* noted at 6 ILJ 123.
3. [1977] 2 All ER 420.
4. J.S. Watson, Comr., *R(I) 5/75,* para. 21.
5. Per Roskill LJ ante n.3, at p. 426; per Lawton LJ, ibid., at p. 431.
6. *R(I) 13/66; CI 7/73.*
7. Per Lord Denning MR, ante n.3, at p. 423; per Roskill LJ, ibid., at p. 429.
8. *R(I) 31/53; R(I) 66/53; R(I) 2/68,* and see *R v National Insurance Comr ex parte Michael,* ante n.3, per Lawton LJ at pp. 430–431.
9. *R(I) 3/57.*
10. *R(I) 11/56; R(I) 63/54* (Tribunal decision).
11. SSA 1975, s.54.
12. Cf. Ogus 4 ILJ 188.

1. This is merely an instance of the situation discussed in the preceding section. The employee's place and hours of work are defined but he is required by his employer, expressly or impliedly, to make a journey for purposes connected with the employment.[13] Thus, an employee instructed to proceed at a specified time from one working place to another is protected.[14] Travel from home to work does not, in general, come within this category even if the claimant is paid for travelling time or for expenses incurred.[15] The distinction is between a journey *to* duty and a journey *on* duty.[16] But there are exceptions all of which may be justified on the supervision principle: an employee obliged by his employer to travel to work by a specific mode of transport;[17] an employee called out from home by his employer for a specific purpose (e.g., an emergency) and under a duty, expressly or impliedly, to arrive by the shortest practical route and as quickly as possible.[18] The suggestion has also been made that the exclusion of journeys to and from work should be confined to cases involving 'reasonable daily travelling distance or commuter distance', and that different considerations apply where the journey involves longer distances.[19] But the suggestion was rejected by a Commissioner who decided that a civil servant injured during the journey from his home to a temporary place of employment some one hundred miles away was not entitled.[20] Nor does it make any difference if the employee is carrying with him tools or essential equipment for his work:[1] to succeed he must show that he had to make some special and required journey to deliver or collect such equipment.[2] The question whether an employee injured while staying away from home during the course of his travels may succeed is resolved along similar lines. If the employee is required by his employer to stay at a particular place,[3] or is in some way supervised by his employer there,[4] benefit is payable. If he is free to stay where he likes, he is not covered during the passage to the chosen accommodation.[5]

2. Certain types of employment are peripatetic: they necessarily involve frequent journeys. Obvious examples of such situations are sales representatives,[6] insurance agents,[7] journalists[8] and home helps.[9] In such cases, benefit is payable for accidents occurring during travel for the purposes of the work. But in defining the limits of the course of the employment, an important distinction has to be drawn.[10] A person who has no fixed hours and no precisely definable place of work may be

13. See, generally, *R v National Industrial Injury Benefits Tribunal, ex parte Fieldhouse* (1974), 17 KIR 63, DC, *Vandyke v Fender* [1970] 2 QB 292, [1970] 2 All ER 335, CA, and *R(I) 5/77*.
14. *R(I) 11/57*; *R(I) 4/59*; *R(I) 39/59*.
15. *R(I) 9/51*; *R(I) 34/57*; *R(I) 3/71*.
16. *R(I) 45/52*, para. 3.
17. *R(I) 8/51*; *R(I) 17/51*; *3/58 (II)*.
18. *R(I) 21/51*; *R(I) 27/56*: the mere fact that the employee is required to report for duty earlier than normal is not sufficient – his employer is not

concerned with the mode or speed of his journey.
19. *CI 21/68*.
20. *R(I) 3/71*, J.S. Watson, Comr.
 1. *R(I) 48/52*; *R(I) 78/53*; *R(I) 16/58*.
 2. *R(I) 34/59*.
 3. *R(I) 30/57*.
 4. *CI 347/50*.
 5. *R(I) 22/54*.
 6. *R(I) 38/53*.
 7. *CSI 63/49*.
 8. *R(I) 55/53*.
 9. *R(I) 2/67*.
10. Ibid., at para. 10.

protected against injuries occurring on his way home.[11] Conversely, a person whose work requires him to be at particular places at particular times is treated no differently from other employees who have fixed places of work. His employment does not begin until he arrives at his first call, unless his employer specifies a particular route or mode of transport.[12] To decide into which of the two categories a particular case falls involves considerations of the circumstances of the job. But there has been a noticeable tendency in recent Commissioners' decisions to take a more restricted view of peripatetic occupations. A decision of 1967[13] in which a home help unsuccessfully claimed benefit for an injury inflicted while travelling from her home to her first call – she worked on her own and was not required to report for information at any office – may be contrasted with one of 1954[14] in which a chief fire officer succeeded when injured travelling from his home to the annual dinner of the local fire brigade.

3. If the journey comes within neither category described above, it is difficult to regard it as creating an 'employment risk'. Arguably, on the 'public zone' principle, the employee travelling to and from work is in a position no different from other members of the public, and yet there has been considerable political pressure to extend industrial injury schemes to cover such journeys. It was apparent that there was little hope of reconciling the inclusion of these cases with the general principles on 'course of employment'. Specific legislative extension was necessary. In some systems, this has been forthcoming: special provision is made for journeys to and from work. Typical is the French legislation:

> 'An accident occurring on a journey between (the employee's) principal dwelling, a secondary dwelling characterised by a definite degree of stability or any other place which the employee habitually uses for family purposes, and the place of work, is also deemed to be a work accident'.[15]

The British system has never been so generous. Under the Workmen's Compensation Acts, no concessions were made. The present position is a compromise between that strict view and the more generous foreign examples. It first appeared in an unsuccessful Workmen's Compensation Bill in 1936, sponsored by the Trade Unions Congress,[16] but was not adopted until the 1946 Act.[17] Section 53(1) of the Social Security Act 1975 provides that:

> 'An accident happening while an employed earner is, with the express or implied permission of his employer, travelling as a passenger by any vehicle to or from his place of work shall, notwithstanding that he is under no obligation to his employer to travel by that vehicle, be deemed to arise out of and in the course

11. E.g., R(I) 4/70.
12. R(I) 19/57; R(I) 2/67; R(I) 12/75.
13. R(I) 2/67. See also R(I) 12/75.
14. R(I) 64/54.
15. Codes des Sécurités Sociales, art. 415(1). See also Appendix for

recommendations of the Pearson Commission.
16. See Wilson and Levy Workmen's Compensation (1939), Vol. 2, pp. 59–61.
17. S.9.

of his employment if –

(a) the accident would have been deemed so to have arisen had he been under such an obligation; and

(b) at the time of the accident, the vehicle –
   (i) is being operated by or on behalf of his employer or some other person by whom it is provided in pursuance of arrangements made with his employer; and
   (ii) is not being operated in the ordinary course of a public transport service.'

The crucial limiting feature of this provision is condition (b). It may be justified in terms of the 'supervision' principle – which also emerges clearly in the case-law on what constitutes 'arrangements', for the purposes of the provision. The employer need not initiate the arrangement, and need not himself own or provide the vehicle,[18] but there must be something more than a mere undertaking by a third party to provide a vehicle for the use of the employees. The employer must be involved in some way in the running of the service.[19] The 'public zone' principle features in the exclusion of vehicles 'operating in the ordinary course of a public transport service'. But the words do not imply that the vehicle must be provided by a private company. The question is whether members of the public may and do habitually use the service.[20] On this point, the authorities have regard to such factors as whether the service is advertised in the ordinary time-table, whether it connects directly with the employer's premises, whether it ceases during closure of the factory.[1] A claimant cannot be a 'passenger' if he is also driving the vehicle.[2] A 'vehicle' includes 'a ship, vessel, hover-craft, aircraft'[3] and, perhaps surprisingly, need not be designed to carry a passenger (e.g., a tractor).[4] The accident must happen while the claimant is 'travelling as a passenger', so that walking to meet the vehicle, or between two vehicles, is not included.[5]

e) INTERRUPTIONS AND DEVIATIONS. The 'course of employment' includes not only the objective elements of time and space but also the subjective one of the claimant's activity.[6] The traditional criterion is that of performing a duty for the employer,[7] but the tendency has been to mitigate the rigours of this notion and to concentrate instead on what is 'reasonably incidental to' the employment: 'if the man is doing something for his own purposes which is reasonably incidental to his employment, he is still acting in the course of his employment'.[8] Only *material* inter-

18. R(I) 49/53.
19. R(I) 5/60.
20. R(I) 67/51: a claim does not fail merely because the public is entitled to use the service (though ordinarily this will be the case) if there is evidence that it rarely does so.
1. R(I) 15/57.
2. CI 49/49; R(I) 9/59.
3. SSA 1975, s.53(2).
4. R(I) 42/56.

5. R(I) 67/52; R(I) 48/54.
6. See especially Lord Finley LC in Davidson & Co v M'Robb [1918] AC 304 at 314–315.
7. See, e.g., St. Helens Colliery Co Ltd v Hewitson [1924] AC 59, HL.
8. Per Salmon LJ R v Industrial Injuries Comr, ex parte Amalgamated Engineering Union [1966] 2 QB 31 at 51, CA. See also R(I) 1/77 (putting up Xmas decorations).

ruptions of the working pattern destroy the connection with the employment:[9] trifling or inadvertent departures are disregarded.[10] Of course, what is reasonably incidental to a man's employment is a question very much for individual judgment, but the case-law has established a pattern of activities and events which are normally to be regarded as coming within or outside the course of employment.

1. *Deviation from journey.* Most obviously, an employee who deviates from a journey for purposes unconnected with his work, e.g., to visit a public house, will not succeed.[11] But stopping to take a meal en route is covered.[12] The position of an employee whose duties are peripatetic will, of course, be more flexible, as, ex hypothesi, he has no fixed hours or places of work. Thus a salesman returning home after entertaining a business associate succeeded.[13] But a point may be reached in his travels where he steps beyond the boundaries of his employment. Generally the employee will have discretion where he stays overnight so the course of employment will be broken from the point at which his journey ends.[14] An apparent deviation may, however, be covered where the employee had no reasonable alternative. Thus in one case,[15] the widow of an employee succeeded when her husband, a passenger in his employer's van, had departed from the prescribed route to enable a fellow employee to visit a doctor: it would have been unreasonable to expect the deceased to have left the van during the deviation.

2. *Breaks between spells of duty.* There is a large number of cases involving accidents to employees in breaks between spells of duty, and it is impossible to reconcile all of them. Certainly, as one Commissioner remarked,[16] some fine distinctions are necessary (though undesirable) if decisions are to be based on logical principles. But the 'logical principle' involved is a vague one of the supervision and control of the employer, which does not make the prediction of decisions easy. Lunch and tea breaks, if spent on the employer's premises, are usually protected,[17] but not if the employee is off the premises and free to do what he likes,[18] nor, or course, if he exceeds the time allocated.[19] Quite apart from formal breaks, many occupations involve lulls in the working effort. A distinction is drawn between voluntary idleness which will interrupt the course of employment,[20] and a lull imposed by the pattern of work. If, in the latter case, an employee, to fill in

---

9. *R(I) 4/73*, per H.A. Shewan, Comr., at para. 5.
10. Per Salmon LJ, *R v Industrial Injuries Comr, ex parte Amalgamated Engineering Union*, ante n.8, loc. cit.
11. *R(I) 40/55.*
12. *C(I) 148/49.*
13. *R(I) 38/53.*
14. *R(I) 22/51; R(I) 51/61; R(I) 22/54;* cp. where the employee is bound, in practice if not by the terms of his employment, to stay at a particular place: *CI 374/50; R(I) 30/57.*
15. *R(I) 40/56.*

16. *R(I) 11/55*, para. 5.
17. *R(I) 11/53*, but not at the beginning or end of a day's work *(CI 120/49; R(I) 11/54)* unless the meal or refreshment is regarded as part of the employee's remuneration *(R(I) 15/55).*
18. *R(I) 84/52; R(I) 24/53.* But cp. the case where during the break he continues to perform an employment duty, e.g., keeping an eye on a bus while drinking tea: *R(I) 20/61.*
19. *R(I) 49/57; ex parte AEU*, ante n.8.
20. *Ex parte AEU*, ibid.

time, does something not unreasonable, not prohibited by his employer, and which does not interrupt someone else's work, he will succeed.[1] But this will not be so if he removes himself completely from his sphere of operations so that he is no longer under the supervision of his employer.[2]

3. *Non-working activities.* Even though a claimant may have been at his place of work during his normal working hours, what he was doing at the time of the accident may have been so far removed from his duties that he is regarded as having been outside the course of employment. The widow of an employee killed while taking a nap during night duty could not recover.[3] The interruption of work to achieve something entirely for personal purposes is similarly treated: a level-crossing keeper fetching milk from the garden;[4] a factory worker leaving work without permission to accompany a fellow employee to the work stores.[5] As regards physical activities not reasonably incidental to work, e.g., smoking, retrieving a lost object, or saying something to a fellow employee, there has been a significant change of attitude within recent years. The former approach was to refuse benefit if the claimant was voluntarily so engaged[6], but to allow it where he was responding in a natural or instinctive way to a situation initiated by another.[7] Such an approach led to invidious inquiries into mental attitudes and was hardly practicable. The new attitude was led by the Court of Appeal in *R v Industrial Injuries Comr, ex parte Amalgamated Engineering Union.*[8] Lord Denning MR said:

> 'In the ordinary way, if a man while at his place of work,
> during his hours of work, is injured by a risk incidental to his
> employment, then the right conclusion usually is that it is an
> injury which arises out of and in the course of the employment,
> even though he may not be doing his actual work but chatting to
> a friend or smoking or doing something of that kind.'[9]

Although these remarks were obiter, they have been taken as affecting the authority of prior decisions. The course of employment is not broken merely because, at the time, the employee was doing something for his own purposes. The question is, first, whether the interruption was a natural one and, secondly, whether it was a reasonable use of the employee's time. A recent decision reveals the impact of the new approach.

In *R(I) 4/73,*[10] a factory worker was acting as agent for a football pools firm. While being handed a coupon by a fellow employee he was injured. It was held that though strictly speaking he was not, at the time, doing something he was employed to do, nevertheless it did not involve a *material* interruption of his employment.

---

1. *R(I) 46/53*; *R(I) 13/66*; *R(I) 13/68.*
2. *R(I) 1/58.*
3. *R(I) 68/54*; cp. where sleeping is involuntary: *R(I) 36/59.*
4. *R(I) 9/59.*
5. *R(I) 1/58.*
6. *R(I) 68/52*; *R(I) 78/52*; *R(I) 32/55*; *R(I) 41/56.*
7. *R(I) 57/54*; *R(I) 21/60.*
8. [1966] 2 QB 31.
9. Ibid., at p. 49.
10. See also *R 3/74 (II).*

iv) Out of the employment

a) GENERAL CAUSAL TEST. The second element in the statutory test requires that the accident arises 'out of (the) . . . employment'.[11] It is not sufficient that the accident happens within the temporal and spatial limits of the employment: it must be causally linked to it.[12] For example, a man may suffer from a heart attack while he is working, but benefit is not payable unless, in some way, the condition resulted from his work. The courts and tribunals have been wary of precise formulations on this point.[13] Some have generalised in terms of employment being the 'proximate' cause of the accident;[14] others have stipulated that it be the *causa causans*, rather than the *causa sine qua non*, of the accident.[15] In its most recent pronouncement, a Tribunal of Commissioners has attempted to be more specific.[16] Basing their view on some prominent House of Lords decisions under the Workmen's Compensation Acts,[17] the Commissioners argued that the crucial question is whether the claimant's own act (or by implication an 'external cause') creates a risk which is different from that created by the employment. Once the *sine qua non* test is satisfied, i.e., it is established that the accident would not have happened but for the employment, then it will generally be held to have arisen out of that employment, unless the claimant (or another) added or created 'a different risk . . . and this different risk was the real cause of the accident'.[18] But like all similar tests of causation, it is of limited utility. The authorities will always have to form their own decision on the facts of a given case,[19] guided only by the general orientation of the test, which in this instance implies that the requirement of a causal link should be liberally construed.

b) STATUTORY PRESUMPTION. Under the Workmen's Compensation Act, the onus of proving that the accident arose both out of and in the course of employment lay on the claimant. In 1946, it was felt that some of the difficulties of establishing the causal link might be mitigated if the burden was on the authorities to prove that the accident did *not* arise out of the employment. The statutory presumption in its present form provides that:

> 'an accident arising in the course of an employed earner's employment shall be deemed, in the absence of evidence to the contrary, also to have arisen out of that employment'.[20]

Its introduction was greeted by some as a revolutionary measure which

11. SSA, 1975, s.50(1).
12. *Dover Navigation Co Ltd v Craig* [1940] AC 190, [1939] 4 All ER 558; *R(I) 16/61*; *R(I) 2/63*.
13. See, e.g., *Dover Navigation* case, ante n. 12, per Viscount Maugham at p. 193 and Lord Wright at p. 199; *R(I) 2/63*, para. 20.
14. E.g., *R(I) 8/54*; *R(I) 75/54*; *R(I) 27/60*.
15. E.g., *R(I) 13/65*; *R(I) 26/59*.

16. *R(I) 2/63*.
17. Notably *Thom v Sinclair* [1917] AC 127; *Upton v Great Central Rly Co* [1924] AC 302; *Harris v Associated Portland Cement Manufactures Ltd* [1939] AC 71; and *Cadzow Coal Co Ltd v Price* [1934], 1 All ER 54.
18. *R(I) 2/63*, para. 26.
19. Ibid., at para. 16.
20. SSA 1975, s.50(3).

would lead to a great improvement in the claimant's position.[1] They were to be disappointed. No major change did result and it is not difficult to see why. For the presumption to apply, not only must the claimant prove that the accident occurred in the course of the employment,[2] but also there must be no 'evidence to the contrary'. In fact, in almost every disputed case, there is *some* evidence to the contrary. The approach taken by the Commissioners is that the presumption applies only if there is *nothing* in the known circumstances from which it might reasonably be inferred that the accident did not arise out of the employment.[3] Thus an epileptic found injured at the foot of a staircase could not invoke the principle: the fact of his epilepsy was 'evidence to the contrary'.[4] The first sign of a more generous interpretation of the provision came in 1964.[5]

> C, a post office engineer, was repairing a fault in a phone booth when a young man opened the door apparently to make a call. C remembered nothing more until he arrived home bleeding from a head wound. The Commissioner discounted the possibility that C might have provoked an assault as being too 'speculative' and thus not constituting contrary evidence. The presumption therefore applied and C was awarded benefit.

c) PRE-EXISTING CONDITIONS. A major problem that arises in applying the general causation principles concerns the effect of pre-existing conditions. An employee may have a latent physical disability (e.g., a heart condition) unconnected with his work. Should the disability manifest itself during the course of the employment, the authorities must decide whether the accident arose 'out of' that employment. The problem is resolved on principles analogous to those already described concerning the causal link between the 'accident' and the 'injury'.[6] If the employment provides merely the background or setting for the event, the claimant will not succeed.[7] The work must contribute in a material degree to the risk.[8] Once that is established, the fact that the prior condition rendered him more liable to sustain an accident will be irrelevant.

> A lavatory attendant, as a result of a disability, had to wear shoes with calipers. He slipped while opening a lavatory door. The fact that the shoes were particularly smooth and slippery was ignored. The movement at work contributed in a material degree to the accident.[9]

d) COMMON RISKS. The causation test implicit in the requirement that the accident arise out of the employment carries with it the assumption

---

1. See Mr R. Prentice, Standing Committee B Debates on the Family Allowances and National Insurance Bill 1961, cols 51–52.
2. *CI 47/49.*
3. *CI 3/49,* approved in *R v National Insurance (Industrial Injuries) Comr, ex parte Richardson* [1958] 2 All ER 689, [1958] 1 WLR 851, DC. See also *R(I)*

41/55 and *R(I) 30/60.*
4. *CI 68/49.*
5. *R(I) 1/64.*
6. Ante, p. 275. Cp. the rules governing war pension claims: post, pp. 360–365.
7. *R(I) 12/52.*
8. *R(I) 73/51.*
9. *CI 82/49.*

that the employment creates a risk for the claimant which is greater than, or at least different from, that to which he would have been subject as a member of the public. Should the assumption not be justified, the employment may not be the substantial cause of the accident. In principle, then, an employee struck by lightning,[10] or bitten by an animal,[11] while working should not succeed. The employment has not exposed him to a risk greater than that to which an ordinary member of the public is subject. On the other hand, if the 'accident has occurred to the workman by reason of the employment bringing about his presence at the particular spot and so exposing him to a danger . . .', he will be entitled.[12] So a seaman suffering from heat exhaustion while working aboard a vessel in the Arabian sea was clearly covered, and it was irrelevant that other persons living in tropical climates are exposed to the same risk.[13] Here the employment took the claimant to a locality to which he would otherwise not have gone. While the theoretical distinction between these cases may be clearly recognised, there is a large shady area between them which cannot easily be divided according to any precise criterion. As a consequence, the authorities tended to approach the problem causistically, declining to justify their decisions in terms of principle. The resulting unpredictability may be gauged from comparing two, unhappily typical, cases:

> A foreign body struck the eye of a lorry driver while on the road. He was not entitled: 'I do not think that a person driving a lorry is thereby exposed to any greater risk of getting something in his eye than anyone else'.[14]

> A piece of grit entered the eye of a police motorcyclist when on patrol duty. He succeeded: 'a man who is employed to drive a motor-bicycle about the streets of a city is exposed by his employment to a greater risk of getting something in his eye than a person not so employed'.[15]

The confusion created by such decisions led to dissatisfaction with the statutory formula. The reaction of some Commissioners was to aid the injured person by broadening the category of 'locality risks'. They were prepared to hold, more often than was perhaps justifiable, that the employment had taken the claimant to the particular spot where he encountered the hazard. It was so decided in the case of a bus driver stung by a wasp[16] and that of an agricultural worker struck by lightning.[17] Another device was to find an intermediate agent which intervened between the original hazard and the injury and so to regard it, rather than the original hazard, as the 'proximate cause' of the injury. Thus when an

10. *R(I) 7/60.*
11. *CI 101/50; R(I) 89/52.*
12. Per Russell LJ, *Lawrence v George Matthews (1924) Ltd* [1929] 1 KB 1, 20, CA.
13. *R(I) 4/61,* following *Dover Navigation Co Ltd v Craig* [1940] AC 190,

[1939] 4 All ER 558.
14. *R(I) 62/53,* para. 3.
15. *R(I) 67/53,* para. 5. See also *R(I) 71/53.*
16. *R(I) 5/56.*
17. *R(I) 23/58.*

employee, riding a bicycle on her employer's business, was blown off by a freak gust of wind, the Commissioner felt able to decide in her favour on the somewhat artificial ground that 'the proximate cause was that she fell from her bicycle while travelling on duty, and it does not seem to me to be necessary to consider any remoter cause'.[18]

Such generous approaches were by no means universal. In 1958, the Divisional Court held that a bus conductor, attacked while on duty by a gang of youths, could not succeed because his position was no different from that of any other person on the bus.[19] The decision created consternation among the trade unions, and there was immediate pressure for legislative reform.[20] It was forthcoming in 1961, the method chosen being to extend the coverage of the scheme to certain specified risks.[1] The provision, as re-enacted in 1975, is that:

> 'an accident shall be treated . . . as arising out of an employed earner's employment if –
>
> a) the accident arises in the course of the employment; and
> b) the accident either is caused by another person's misconduct, skylarking or negligence, or by steps taken in consequence of any such misconduct, skylarking or negligence, or by the behaviour or presence of an animal (including a bird, fish or insect), or is caused by or consists in the employed earner being struck by any object or by lightning; and
> c) the employed earner did not directly or indirectly induce or contribute to the happening of the accident by his conduct outside the employment or by any act not incidental to the employment'.[2]

The risks selected for special protection manifestly reflect particular situations in which claimants had previously encountered difficulty in recovering benefit, and there is no obvious common principle to which they all relate.[3] The cumulative effect of this provision, and the Commissioners' decisions previously referred to, reduces the significance of the 'out' requirement, provoking one commentator to the conclusion that

> 'we appear to have got very close to the stage when an accident arising in the course of employment will almost inevitably fall within the system'.[4]

But, so far at least, successive governments have refused to abandon the 'out' requirement. To do so, it is argued, would make nonsense of the existence of the special scheme for work-caused accidents.[5] The argument is

18. R(I) 27/60, following a similar idea in R(I) 46/54.
19. Ex parte Richardson, ante n.3.
20. See General Council Report of the TUC (1960).
1. FANIA 1961, s.2.
2. SSA 1975, s.55(1). It applies only to accidents occurring after 19 December

1961: ibid., s.55(2).
3. See the Standing Committee B Debates on the 1961 Bill.
4. Atiyah, p. 330.
5. Mr J. Boyd Carpenter, Minister of Pensions and N.I., in the Standing Committee B Debates on the 1961 Bill, cols. 59–60.

obviously sound, but it seems hard to reconcile with the policy behind the 1961 reform.

e) CLAIMANT'S CONDUCT. One of the limitations of the 1961 provision is that the claimant should not

'directly or indirectly induce or contribute to the happening of the accident by his conduct outside the employment or by any act not incidental to the employment'.[6]

This is a restatement of the principle already existing in the case-law prior to the enactment and falls now for consideration. It is clear, in the first place, that the mere negligence or carelessness of the claimant is not by itself sufficient to bar entitlement to benefit:[7] the legislation has not incorporated the common law doctrine of contributory negligence. For some time, under the Workmen's Compensation Acts, the courts did flirt with the notion of so-called 'added risk'. According to this doctrine, 'a peril voluntarily super-induced on what arose out of the employment, to which the workman was neither required nor had authority to expose himself',[8] would deprive him of a remedy. The doctrine has been discredited,[9] and held not to apply to the social security scheme.[10] It has been supplanted by another principle of causation more favourable to the claimant: the conduct of an employee will defeat his claim only if (1) he 'added or created a different risk' to or from that arising from the employment and (2) 'this different risk was the real cause of the accident'.[11] In the case in which this test was propounded,

C, attempting to light a cigarette, as permitted by his employer, ignited gas which was escaping from an unlit blow-pipe. He was awarded benefit. C's act converted a potential risk into an actual explosion. 'It did not make it a different danger or create a fresh one'.[12]

In contrast in another case,

In an effort to warm himself, C poured petrol onto a fire and was burned by the conflagration. Fires were prohibited on the site, but in terms of causation C's act had added or created a different risk from that inherent in the circumstances of the employment.[13]

It is convenient here to consider the relevance of the fact that the claimant's conduct was prohibited by his employer or by the law generally. In the early years of the Workmen's Compensation Act, employers were

6. SSA 1975, s.55(1)(c).
7. Harris v Associated Portland Cement Manufactures Ltd [1939] AC 71; R(I) 36/59.
8. Per Viscount Haldane, Lancashire and Yorkshire Rly Co v Highley [1917] AC 352, 361. See also Barnes v Nunnery Colliery Co Ltd [1912] AC 44 and Plumb v Cobden Flour Mills Co Ltd

[1914] AC 62.
9. Thomas v Ocean Coal [1933] AC 100; Noble v Southern Rly Co [1940] AC 583, [1940] 2 All ER 383.
10. R(I) 2/63; R 4/70 (II).
11. R(I) 2/63; R(I) 3/63.
12. R(I) 2/63, para. 29.
13. R(I) 24/51.

frequently able to rely on the existence of such a prohibition as a defence.[14] The position was altered in 1923,[15] when the legislature provided that an act would be

> 'deemed to have arisen out of and in the course of employment, notwithstanding that the workman ... acting in contravention of any safety or any other regulation ... or of any orders given by or on behalf of his employer, or that he was acting without instructions from his employer, if such act was done by the workman for the purposes of and in connection with his employer's trade or business'.

It was optimistically argued by some that this effectively overruled the 'out' requirement. Such an interpretation, though perhaps feasible on a literal view of the phrase 'acting without instructions', was obviously unintended: it would place disobedient employees in a better position than obedient ones. The argument was quickly denounced by the House of Lords.[16] 'Acting without instructions' was equated with an implied prohibition. More importantly, the provision left open the possibility that the employee was, in any event, acting outside the scope of his employment. If so, he failed. The effect of the 1923 reform was merely to prevent a certain class of evidence being sufficient of itself to oust the right to compensation.[17] It did not operate to extend the scope of the employment. The point was confirmed by legislative amendment when the provision was incorporated into the national insurance scheme.[18] A new condition was added. For the fiction to apply, the claimant must now show that:

> 'a) the accident would have been deemed so to have arisen had the act not been done in contravention of any such regulations or orders, or without such instructions as the case may be; and
> b) the act is done for the purposes of and in connection with the employer's trade or business'.[19]

On condition (a), the claimant must show that apart from the contravention the accident arose out of and in the course of employment. Thus, if he is doing something quite different from that which he was employed to do, he cannot benefit from the provision.[20] For example, in *R v D'Albuqerque, ex parte Bresnahan*[1]

> D, a dock labourer engaged in loading a ship, attempted to move an obstacle with a fork lift truck which had been left unattended by its driver. He fell into the dock with it and was drowned. His widow failed. It was not within the scope of his employment to use a fork lift truck and therefore condition (a) was not satisfied.

14. See, e.g., *Lowe v Pearson* [1899] 1 QB 261, CA.
15. WCA 1923, s.7.
16. *Kerr v James Dunlop & Co* [1926] AC 377.
17. Per Viscount Dunedin, ibid., at p. 386.
18. NI(II)A 1946, s.8.
19. SSA 1975, s.52.
20. CI 11/49; R(I) 77/54; R(I) 7/55; R(I) 41/56; R(I) 12/61.
1. [1966] 1 Lloyds Rep. 69, DC.

Whether the act is 'done for the purposes of and in connection with the employer's trade or business' has been given a generous interpretation in the recent cases. Thus, it was held to be in the interests of both the employer and the employee (though prohibited by the former) that a locomotive driver should take a short cut on his way from the railway shed to a station.[2]

Part four. Industrial Diseases

A. General

Soon after the passing of the first Workmen's Compensation Act, it became clear that the 'personal injury by accident' formula was inadequate to cope with sickness or disease resulting from employment. It has already been seen[3] that in principle an incapacity resulting from a 'process' as opposed to an 'event' is not caught by the general provisions. Granted that protection should be afforded in these cases, there would appear to be two basic possibilities:[4] (1) to provide a general definition of occupational disease as an alternative to the 'accident' formula, the claimant having to satisfy the authorities (with or without the aid of a presumption) that the disease was contracted as a result of his employment; (2) to create a list of specified diseases which experience and medical expertise have shown to be typical risks for certain specified categories of employment. Generally with the aid of a presumption, the claimant would then have to show that he contracted a prescribed disease as a result of working in the prescribed occupation. Persuasive arguments can be made out for either approach.[5] (1) has the great advantage that its scope is wider (those suffering from non-prescribed diseases in (2) are without remedy) and it is more flexible: legislatures, it is claimed, cannot keep pace with new and changing industrial risks. The advantages claimed for (2) tend to be more incidental to the policy of providing compensation for those suffering from industrial diseases. Thus it is said that the requirement of prescription encourages more detailed and intensive study of the problems, which in turn contributes to safety and rehabilitation systems. The more general coverage in (1) creates difficulties of proof (particularly of causation) and thereby greater uncertainty and, it is claimed, is thereby more costly and more conducive to false claims and abuse. There is no international uniformity on the point. The majority of American jurisdictions have adopted the 'blanket approach' in (1).[6] An EEC recommendation of 1962[7] urged the adoption of a combination of the two approaches: the claimant to have a presumption in his favour for scheduled diseases, but against him for

2. R(I) 5/67.
3. Ante, pp. 272–275.
4. Cf. Riesenfeld, 52 Calif. LR 531, 542–543.
5. Sears & Groves, 31 Rocky Mountain LR 462; Angerstein, ibid., vol. 18, p. 240.
6. Riesenfeld, ante n.4.
7. No. 2188/62. Journal Officiel, 31 August 1962; cf., Pearson, p. 188.

non-scheduled diseases. It has, as yet, been implemented only in Germany.[8]

The British system has always adopted the 'schedule approach'. In 1906 the Workmen's Compensation scheme was extended to cover a limited number of specified diseases.[9] A Departmental Committee set up shortly after the passing of the Act felt that a new disease should be included only if it were so specific to the prescribed employment that in individual cases the causal link with the employment could be established without difficulty, or, in other words, that the claimant would be unlikely to contract it outside his work.[10] Thus bronchitis was not added since 'it would attract endless litigation, as no one knows whether the sufferer has contracted it from dust irritation, or would have contracted it anyway, as hundreds of other people in the locality do'.[11] This pragmatic approach was bitterly attacked by the trade unionists who argued that all diseases attributable to a workman's ordinary occupation should be covered. But two committees reviewing the law between the wars resisted change.[12] Though hardship and injustice were conceded, it was felt that a broader test would involve greater difficulties of proof and would place too heavy a burden on employers who, of course, paid the benefit at that time. The principle of inclusion was reiterated in the National Insurance (Industrial Injuries) Act 1946,[13] and is still law, section 76(2) of the Social Security Act 1975 providing that:

'(a) it ought to be treated, having regard to its causes and incidence and any other relevant considerations, as a risk of their occupations and not as a risk common to all persons; and

(b) it is such that, in the absence of special circumstances, the attribution of particular cases to the nature of the employment can be established or presumed with reasonable certainty'.

Although the principle has remained unaltered, it is clear that the practice has shifted significantly.[14] In the early days, the emphasis was on showing that the disease was peculiar to the specified employment, and not to others. Later, the crux became whether the employment created a vulnerability to the disease greater than that of the general public, even though other employments were equally susceptible. While proviso (b) remains a serious obstacle to the admission of some diseases, there is apparent a tendency to attach less importance to it. So in 1974 occupational deafness was added,[15] notwithstanding the finding of the Industrial

8. Reichsversicherungsordnung, § 551.
9. WCA 1906, s.8, following the recommendations of a Departmental Committee (1904), Cd. 2208.
10. Report of the Departmental Committee on Compensation for Industrial Diseases (Gladstone Committee) (1907), Cd. 3495.
11. Ibid., at para. 25.
12. Report of the Departmental

Committee on Compensation for Industrial Diseases (Holman Gregory Committee) (1920), Cmd. 816; Report of the Departmental Committee on Compensation for Industrial Diseases (1932).
13. S.55(2); cp. Appendix for *Pearson.*
14. Young *Industrial Injuries Insurance* (1964), p. 26.
15. S.I. 1974/1414.

Injuries Advisory Council that loss of hearing is a common affliction and has 'a number of different causes'.[16]

B. Proof of prescribed disease

Proof that the claimant is suffering from a prescribed disease or injury 'due to the nature of (his) employment' is an alternative basis of entitlement to that provided by 'a personal injury caused by accident arising out of and in the course of employment'.[17] Inconvenient overlaps between the two criteria are prevented by the provision that

'a person shall not be entitled to benefit in respect of a disease as being an injury by accident arising out of and in the course of any employment if at the time of the accident the disease is in relation to him a prescribed disease by virtue of . . . that employment'.[18]

To establish entitlement on the basis of a prescribed disease the claimant must satisfy three conditions:

(i) he suffers from a prescribed disease;

(ii) that disease is prescribed in relation to his occupation;

(iii) the disease developed as a result of employment in that occupation.

i) Suffering from prescribed disease
A Schedule to the Prescribed Diseases Regulations lists descriptions of conditions covered by the scheme.[19] The claimant must prove that he is suffering from or has suffered from one such condition which resulted in the incapacity for work or loss of faculty, on which title to injury and disablement benefits are respectively based.[20] Evidence is normally supplied through doctors specialising in the relevant diseases.[1] A decision is then made by the insurance officer in the light of that evidence. He may refer the question, or an appeal may be brought against his decision, to a Medical Board, and from that body to a Medical Appeal Tribunal.[2] Because of the expertise required for pneumoconiosis and bysiniosis claims, there are special boards constituted to diagnose these diseases,[3] and the right of appeal to a Medical Appeal Tribunal is more limited.[4]

ii) Disease prescribed for claimant's occupation
Against the description of each disease, there is listed in the Schedule the

16. Report on Occupational Deafness (1973), Cmnd. 5461, para. 45.
17. SSA 1975, s.76(1).
18. Ibid., s.76(5).
19. S.I. 1975/1537, Sch. 1, Part I.
20. Though NB: those suffering from pneumoconiosis or byssinosis are not entitled to injury benefit: ibid., Reg. 34.

1. DHSS Leaflet NI.2. Details of likely symptoms and after effects of prescribed diseases are given in the DHSS Booklet, *Notes on the Diagnosis of Occupational Diseases* (1972).
2. S.I. 1975/1537, Part V. On these bodies see generally post, pp. 635–641.
3. S.I. 1975/1537, Regs. 49–51.
4. Ibid., Reg. 49(4).

occupation or occupations for which the disease is prescribed. The claimant's task is to prove that he has been employed in the relevant occupation on or after 5 July 1948.[5] It is important to appreciate that the scheduled description is not a legal categorisation of the type of occupation but a factual account of work actually undertaken,[6] very often of a vague character. Moreover, it necessarily requires that the authorities make quantitative and qualitative judgments on the nature of the claimant's work. Thus, the prescribed occupation for tuberculosis must involve 'close and frequent contact with a source or sources of tuberculosis infection . . .'.[7] What amounts to 'close and frequent contact' has given rise to some hotly disputed cases.[8] Happily the disease has become less prevalent. Though the claimant's employment may embrace the prescribed activity, the actual involvement in the activity may be trivial or non-existent. Under the *de minimis* principle, he will not be entitled to benefit.[9] In one case[10]

> A watchman at an ammunition dump claimed to have developed silicosis from having worked in an occupation 'involving exposure to dust'.[11] When not patrolling the site, he used a hut with an earth floor. Dust rose from the floor when he walked on it. His claim for benefit was rejected. The amount of dust raised was trivial, and was not in excess of that met with in the ordinary course of life.

In other words, applying the 'public zone' test,[12] it was not an employment risk.

iii) Causal link between occupation and disease

Finally the claimant must establish the causal link between employment in the prescribed occupation and the prescribed disease. In the ordinary case, there is a presumption that the disease was due to the nature of the relevant occupation if he was employed in it at any time within one month preceding the date of the development of the disease.[13] But in three special cases, the presumption operates in different circumstances.

> 1. Tuberculosis – he must have been first employed in the relevant occupation at least six weeks before the date of development, and have been last so employed not more than two years before that date.[14]

5. S.I. 1975/1537, Reg. 2(a). For older cases see post, p. 340. In the cases of pneumoconiosis, byssinosis and occupational deafness, there are further conditions to be satisfied: see S.I. 1975/1537, Reg. 2(b)–(d).

6. Therefore it is not sufficient for the claimant to establish that he was contractually bound to undertake such work. The question is whether he actually *did* the work: *CI 59/49.*

7. S.I. 1975/1537, Sch. 1, Prescribed Disease No. 38.

8. See the cases summarised in Jenkins *Digest of Commissioners' Decisions* (1964) under the heading 'Tuberculosis'.

9. See, e.g. *CI 265/49.*

10. *R(I) 40/57.*

11. S.I. 1975/1537, Sch. 1, Part II, para. 1.

12. Cf., ante, p. 279.

13. S.I. 1975/1537. Reg. 4(1).

14. Ibid., Reg. 4(2).

2. Occupational deafness – he must have been employed for an aggregate of at least twenty years in a relevant occupation, and to have been last so employed not more than one year before the date of claim.[15]

3. Pneumoconiosis and byssinosis – it is sufficient if, on aggregate, he has been employed for two years or five years respectively in a relevant occupation.[16]

The 'date of development' varies according to the benefit claimed. For injury benefit, it is the first day on which the claimant was incapable of work as a result of the disease, or if later, the date from which benefit is payable; for disablement benefit, the day on which he first suffered the relevant loss of faculty or the date from which benefit is payable; for death benefit, the date of death.[17]

To rebut the presumption, where it exists, the insurance officer must prove on the balance of probabilities that the disease was not due to the nature of the relevant occupation.[18] In some cases, he will seek to show that it was caused by employment in an occupation not prescribed.[19] In others, the disease may allegedly arise from activities or contacts outside his employment[20] or from a condition pre-existing in the claimant before the commencement of the occupation.[1] In all cases, the question is not whether the employment was the sole cause of the disease: it is sufficient if it was the real and substantial cause.[2]

C. Recrudescence and fresh attacks

If a claimant has already been awarded benefit for a particular disease and has recovered wholly or partly, but then suffers a further attack, the consequences will vary according to the time when the attack occurs and whether it is regarded as a recrudescence or rather a fresh attack. If it occurs during an injury benefit period or during a period taken into account by an assessment of disablement relating to the earlier attack, there are two possibilities. If it is treated as a recrudescence of the earlier attack it cannot give rise to a new claim but may be taken into account as a basis for reviewing the previous assessment of disablement.[3] If it is found to be a fresh attack, the normal rules apply and the claimant is treated as if no previous claim had been made.[4] If the further attack occurs outside the periods mentioned, it is treated as being contracted afresh and the claim is unaffected by the earlier receipt of benefit.[5] Decisions as between recrudescence and fresh attack are made by those bodies which determine diagnosis questions.[6]

15. S.I. 1975/1537, Regs. 2(d) and 4(5).
16. Ibid., Regs. 2(b)–(c) and 4(3)–(4).
17. Ibid., Reg. 6.
18. R(I) 37/52.
19. E.g., R(I) 9/53.
20. E.g., R(I) 20/52.

1. E.g., R(I) 37/52; R(I) 38/52.
2. R(I) 10/53.
3. S.I. 1975/1537, Reg. 7(4).
4. Ibid., Reg. 7(3) and see R(I) 10/53.
5. S.I. 1975/1537, Reg. 7(1)(b).
6. Ante, p. 295.

Part five. Injury Benefit

A. General

Most state systems of compensation distinguish between temporary and permanent disablement. For non-industrial cases, as has been seen, different provision is available for sickness benefit, payable for the first six months, and invalidity benefit, payable thereafter.[7] For industrial disablement, the historical arguments for such a distinction were less compelling. Under the Workmen's Compensation Acts compensation was payable for a proportion of the employee's lost wages, whatever the duration of the disability, though after six months, the employer liable could insist on the commutation of the weekly payment into a lump sum.[8] Beveridge's recognition, based on both theoretical and political grounds, of the need to maintain a differential between industrial and non-industrial cases,[9] prompted the recommendation that for the first thirteen weeks the injured employee should rely on sickness benefit; thereafter he might be awarded a pension based on two-thirds of his lost earnings (to a statutory maximum).[10] The need for the distinction was felt to be acute only for those industrial accidents which resulted in prolonged disability. The post-war government, in its White Paper, rejected the proposal.[11] It recognised the need for a differential but felt justified in extending it to short-term as well as long-term cases. For the initial period, then, the claimant was to be paid a flat-rate benefit, but on a scale higher than that to be awarded for sickness or unemployment. Thirteen weeks was also thought to be an inappropriately short and inflexible period. The transfer from the flat-rate benefit to the disablement pension should take place 'at a date appropriate to the circumstances of the individual case' when the consequences of the accident had 'settled'.[12] Entitlement to short-term benefit, like sickness benefit, would require proof of *total* incapacity for work, whereas the long-term benefit would be based not on lost earning capacity but on the degree of disablement, which might be partial or total. This latter concept underwent significant modifications in implementation; in particular, as will be seen,[13] Parliament resiled from a system of compensation wholly unrelated to earning capacity.

The earnings-related supplement was added to the short-term 'injury benefit' in 1966,[14] but this reinforced rather than detracted from the principle of differentiation between the temporarily and the permanently disabled. Whatever form of compensation is considered appropriate for the latter, the distinction may be justified on grounds of both expediency and principle. For those temporarily but totally disabled from work there is a need for the determination of title to benefit to be simple and rapid.[15] But

---

7. Ante, chap. 4.
8. See generally Willis *Workmen's Compensation* (37th edn), pp. 406–414.
9. Para. 85.
10. Para. 100.
11. Social Insurance, Part II, para. 26.
12. Ibid., at para. 27.
13. Post, p. 304.

14. Post, p. 302.
15. See, in particular, the remarks of Lord Diplock in *Jones v Secretary of State for Social Services* [1972] AC 944 at 1006, and those of Mr Dean, Under Secretary of State, in Standing Committee D Debates on the National Insurance Bill 1972, cols. 391–392.

where benefit is to be paid over a substantial period, and for degrees of
disablement which fall short of total incapacity for work, the investigation of
the claim, the prognosis of the claimant's condition, and the remedying of
particular needs require more sophisticated rules and a more elaborate
machinery of administration. The basic condition of entitlement to injury
benefit is thus a simple one. Section 56(1) of the Social Security Act 1975
provides that:

> 'an employed earner shall be entitled to injury benefit in respect
> of any day during the injury benefit on which, as the result
> of the relevant injury, he is incapable of work'.

B. Incapacity for work

The claimant must first prove incapacity for work on the days for which
benefit is claimed. The requirement is exactly the same as that for the
sickness and invalidity benefits, and the authorities have applied identical
principles. These have been discussed in some detail in chapter 4.[16]

C. Causal link between injury and incapacity

Secondly, the claimant must establish that the incapacity resulted from the
'personal injury caused by . . . accident arising out of and in the course of
his employment' or the 'personal disease or injury due to the nature' of the
employment.[17] In general, it can be said that the employment injury must
be the 'effective cause' (*causa causans*) of the incapacity but need not be its
sole cause.[18] This means that though the incapacity would not have
occurred but for a condition afflicting the claimant prior to the accident, he
may still recover,[19] provided he can show that the accident rendered him
more prone to the consequences of the earlier condition, or, to put it
another way, aggravated that condition.[20] In other cases, the employment
injury occurs first and the question is whether a subsequent incapacity is
still linked to it. Courts interpreting the workmen's compensation legislation tended to use the common law test of whether a *novus actus interviens*
broke the chain of causation.[1] In *R(I) 3/56*, a Tribunal of Commissioners
attempted to reformulate the guiding principles: if the immediate cause of
the incapacity is injury by a non-industrial accident, the claimant may still
succeed if he can prove that an injury previously arising from an industrial

16. Ante, pp. 151–158.
17. Though those suffering from
pneumoconiosis or byssinosis are not
entitled to injury benefit: S.I.
1975/1537, Reg. 34.
18. *Dunham v Clare* [1902] 2 KB 292, CA,
(a case on the analogous provision
under the WCA, and rejecting the view
that the incapacity must be the 'natural
and probable consequence' of the
injury – the test then prevailing in the

law of tort). See also *R(I) 3/56*.
19. *Laverick v W. Gray & Co Ltd* (1919)
12 BWCC 176, CA; *CI 50/50*; *R(I)
3/56*.
20. *CI 4/49*; *CI 147/50*; cp., *CI 168/49*;
CI 413/50; *R(I) 33/51*.
 1. *Dunham v Clare*, ante n.18; *Hogan v
Bentick West Hartley Collieries
(Owners) Ltd* [1949] 1 All ER 588,
CA.

accident was the 'effective cause' of the non-industrial accident;[2] if, as a result of a non-industrial accident, the condition arising from an industrial accident is aggravated, or the period of incapacity prolonged, he will be entitled so long as the industrial injury condition continues to be the 'effective cause' of the incapacity, even though the industrial accident was not in any other way linked to the non-industrial accident.[3] Though the wording of these rules may be difficult, the principles emerging are typical of those applied to causal questions throughout the law, and the question is always one of fact, the authorities, with the aid of medical evidence, judging the matter from a common sense point of view.[4] Cases where the causal link has been allegedly broken by the negligence of a third party (e.g., a doctor) gave rise to some difficulty under the Workmen's Compensation Acts. Though the point has not been the subject of a reported decision under social security legislation, the principle must hold good that if the incapacity resulted substantially from the third party's act and the employment injury was only the condition of, or setting for, the act, resort must be had to a remedy against the third party rather than to the insurance fund.[7] Alternatively, it may be argued that the incapacity resulted from the claimant's own reluctance to undergo an operation rather than from the original employment injury. In theory, no doubt, such a finding is possible,[6] but the unreasonableness of the claimant's decision must be certain beyond any doubt for the authorities to refuse benefit on this basis,[7] and, as will be seen, there are statutory grounds to disentitle a claimant for behaving 'in a manner calculated to retard his recovery' or for wilful obstruction of medical treatment.[8]

D. Benefit period

i) Days of incapacity

The basis of entitlement to injury benefit being incapacity for work, it naturally falls into line with the other social security benefits which are payable where employment ceases. Thus the day for which benefit is claimed must, consistently with the rules on unemployment and sickness benefits, form part of a 'period of interruption of employment'.[9] Three waiting-days must be served,[10] though as with unemployment and sickness

2. See *R(I) 9/52*; cp. *CI 114/49*.
3. *Brown v George Kent Ltd* [1913] 3 KB 624, CA.
4. The reports of the Commissioners' decisions contain a number of cases to guide the authorities on the aetiology of certain regularly occurring types of incapacity.
5. *Rocca v Stanley Jones & Co Ltd* (1914) 7 BWCC 101, CA; *Hogan v Bentick West Hartley Collieries (Owners) Ltd*, ante n.1; and see the cases on criminal law: *R v Jordan* (1956), 40 Cr. App. Rep. 152 (CCA); *R v Smith* [1959] 2

QB 35, [1959] 2 All ER 193 (Cts. Martial App. Ct.).
6. *Warncken v Moreland* [1909] 1 KB 184, CA; cf. on special hardship allowance post p. 327; on the criminal law, *R v Blaue* [1975] 3 All ER 466, [1975] 1 WLR 144, CA; and on the law of damages, Ogus *Law of Damages* (1973), pp. 181–182.
7. *Tutton v Owner of the Majestic* [1909] 2 KB 54, CA.
8. Post, p. 338.
9. SSA 1975, s.56(5)(a): cf. ante, p. 92.
10. SSA 1975, s. 56(5)(b).

benefit the continuity and linking rules operate so that: any two days of interruption of employment (consecutive or not) within a period of six consecutive days constitute a period of interruption of employment, and any two such periods not separated by a period of more than thirteen calendar weeks are treated as one period of interruption of employment.[11] The other rules governing the days for which benefit is payable apply equally here, so that:

1. Sunday (or its substitute) is not treated as a day of incapacity;[12]

2. Where the claimant is a night worker, the night-shift is attributed to the second of the two days unless the greater portion falls in the first day.[13]

All these rules have already been examined in the chapter on unemployment benefit and require no further comment here.

ii) Duration of benefit

Injury benefit is payable for a maximum of 156 days (excluding Sundays) beginning with the day of the accident giving rise to the employment injury.[14] After the expiration of that period, the claimant may, of course, be entitled to disablement benefit.

iii) Unavailability of disablement benefit

The transition from injury to disablement benefit may take place before the period of 156 days has expired, if the claimant is no longer incapable of work,[15] and so, in the alternative, the injury benefit period is defined as the part of the 156 days for which 'disablement benefit in respect of the accident is not available'.[16] Clearly, double recovery is to be avoided, but the position becomes complicated where during the period of 156 days the injured person claims for disablement benefit, because he is capable of returning to work, but then is subjected to a further period of incapacity resulting from the original accident. In such circumstances, the legislation impliedly confers on him a right to elect between the two benefits. It does so in a circumlocutory way by providing that:

> 'where he makes a claim for disablement benefit in respect of the accident before the end of that period and does not withdraw it before it is finally determined, then if on any day of that period not earlier than the making of the claim he is not so incapable of work, the fact that he is or may be so incapable on a subsequent day of the period shall be disregarded. . .'[17]

Disablement benefit is not 'available' if the claimant withdraws his claim 'before it is finally determined' and hence injury benefit will be payable.[18]

11. Ibid., s.17(1)(d), ante, p. 92.
12. SSA 1975, s.17(1)(e), ante, p. 91.
13. S.I. 1975/564, Reg. 5, ante p. 91, and see R(I) 31/55.
14. SSA 1975, s. 56(4).
15. Ibid., s.57(4).
16. Ibid., s.56(4).
17. Ibid., s.57(4).
18. R(I) 15/63.

The subsection gives no clue as to when this condition will be satisfied. On one extreme view, the claim might be regarded as finally determined when the insurance officer makes his initial decision on the disablement benefit application. The other extreme interpretation is that withdrawal is possible until the time has elapsed for all possible appeals to the medical authorities, to the statutory authorities and perhaps even to the ordinary courts. Neither view is plausible. The latter interpretation is obviously highly impracticable, and the former would considerably undermine the policy of election which obviously inspired the provision. After lengthy consideration of the matter the Commissioner in 1963[19] reached a sensible compromise solution:[20] the *normal* time for appeal to the medical authorities on the assessment of disability must have expired.[1] The possibility of the claimant being given leave to appeal out of time is ignored.[2] The course of action most favourable to a claimant will depend on whether the aggregate of entitlement to disablement benefit and the various additions will exceed the amount payable for injury benefit.

E. Amount

Injury benefit is a flat-rate weekly sum (in 1977–78 £17·45[3]), to which may be added increases for dependants.[4] There are, however, lower rates for beneficiaries under eighteen years.

1. For those under sixteen years not in full-time or substantially full-time employment (in 1977–78 £6·10[5]).

2. For those under sixteen years in full-time, or substantially full-time employment,[6] and for those under eighteen years not entitled to a dependant's increase[7] (in 1977–78 £14·70[8]).

Those under eighteen entitled to a dependant's increase are paid at the normal rate.[9] Earnings-related supplement is also payable from the thirteenth day of a period of interruption of employment[10] but as this is, strictly speaking, part of the non-industrial contributory scheme, the claimant must satisfy the relevant contribution conditions for sickness benefit.[11]

---

19. *R(I) 14/63.*
20. Following a Northern Ireland decision to the same effect: *R 59/61 (II).*
  1. On this see post, p. 638. Where the assessment is a provisional one, the appeal procedure referred to relates to that award rather than the final determination: *R(I) 14/63,* para. 30.
  2. The Commissioner left open the question whether a right of appeal to the Commissioner himself from the

Medical Appeal Tribunal falls within the appropriate concept of proceedings.
  3. S.I. 1977/1325.
  4. Post, pp. 383–398.
  5. S.I. 1975/559, Reg. 3(2)(b) and S.I. 1977/1325.
  6. S.I. 1975/559, Reg. 3(2)(a).
  7. SSA 1975, Sch. 4, Part V, para. 1(b).
  8. S.I. 1977/1325.
  9. SSA 1975, Sch. 4, Part V, para 1(a).
  10. See generally, post, pp. 424–426.
  11. Ante, p. 149.

Part six. Disablement Benefit

A. General

Once the need to distinguish between short-term and long-term accident victims had been recognised,[12] the question arose as to the method of awarding compensation for the latter. In the first place, it was clear that in contrast to injury benefit, provision should be made for those who were only partially disabled, that is, whose earning capacity had been reduced rather than eliminated altogether. Such persons had been covered by the workmen's compensation legislation, and the principle of compensation applicable there, both to totally and to partially disabled, had been that of 50% (and for lower paid workers 75%) of lost earnings, though subject to a statutory maximum.[13] Beveridge preferred to retain this mode of compensation, but on the level of two-thirds of lost earnings, to bring the scheme in line with the more generous protection offered by European and American systems.[14] The post-war government was not, however, prepared to accept this recommendation. It was seen as conflicting with the then generally held dogma of social insurance that any differential in benefit should be based on need, typically according to the extent of family responsibility, rather than on earnings.[15] Further, it was felt that one of the main weaknesses of the workmen's compensation scheme had been the difficulty of calculating the earnings-based award: predictions had to be made not only on the future earnings of the claimant in the light of his reduced capacity, but also on those which he would have received if he had not been injured. The government proposed what was described as 'an entirely new approach' (though it had formed the basis of the war pensions scheme for some time[16]): benefit payable according to the degree of disablement, irrespective of actual earnings loss. The rates would be assessed on the claimant's assumed needs, and therefore might include increases for family responsibilities and for any additional care and attention necessary. The refusal to take account of earnings would act as a general incentive to rehabilitation and work generally. The philosophy at first gained considerable support: even Beveridge appeared to have been convinced by it.[17] But when its implications were gradually digested, it became increasingly clear that the total disregard of the earnings factor was not viable, and in the face of growing opposition (particularly from the trade unions), the government was forced to make compromise after compromise, so that what eventually emerged was very different in both substance and form from the original proposals.

First, at an early stage, it was realised that provision had to be made for those who were rendered totally unemployable as a result of the accident. The work incentive argument could not be applied to them, and they

12. Ante, p. 298.
13. WCA 1925, s.9(2). In 1940 child allowances, analogous to those payable with unemployment benefit were introduced: WC (Supplementary Allowances) Act 1940.
14. Paras. 99–100.
15. Social Insurance, Pt. II, paras. 28–29.
16. Cf. post, p. 371.
17. See his contributions to the Commons debate on Social Insurance, Part II: 404 HC Deb., vol. 1436.

would naturally feel aggrieved if they were to receive the same benefit as others who were still able to earn: hence the unemployability supplement.[18] There was a second category of injured persons who would also have fared better under the workmen's compensation scheme. The courts there had developed a special doctrine to cover so-called 'odd-lot' cases, where the injury had rendered the worker incapable of work normally available on the market, but not of special employment which in practice, because of his lack of training or geographical or social circumstances, might not have been available.[19] On the Second Reading of the 1946 Bill, the government introduced an amendment which would enable the authorities to add 25% to the assessment of disablement (though not so as to exceed 100%) if the claimant were able to show that he was no longer capable of following his previous occupation, and could not be so retrained as to enable him to follow one of an equivalent standard.[20] At the Committee stage this was felt to be an unattractive rule as it would have operated unfairly for those assessed at between 75% and 100%, and a flat-rate addition of 11s 3d was substituted.[1] Between the passing of the 1946 Act and its coming into effect, however, even this solution was found to be wanting. It was too inflexible a method of treating those whose earnings had been only partially affected: it was considered too low for some workers, and yet inappropriate for those, e.g., juveniles, who had not yet established a clear employment pattern. At the eleventh hour, the government therefore introduced a new Bill which would enable the authorities to award a sum for lost earnings up to a limit of 15s 0d – a special hardship allowance.[2]

Though there have been amendments to the rate of benefit and the introduction of an allowance for the exceptionally severely disabled,[3] the structure of disablement benefit has remained unaltered. What emerges is a jumble of benefit and allowance, some parts directed towards need, others towards income replacement. Yet the system as a whole is consistent with neither objective and seems to have no overall rational structure. The 'needs' approach has obviously been undermined by the unemployability and special hardship allowances, and for the purposes of the latter the authorities must continue to make the difficult calculations necessary under the Workmen's Compensation Acts and which the original proposals were designed to obviate. Nor is the income replacement objective consistently satisfied. The unemployability and special hardship allowances go only a certain way in that direction, and arguably cannot be taken further as otherwise, with the basic disablement pension and the other allowances (none of which is incidentally taxable), the claimant may be placed in a better financial position than he was in before the accident.[4] If the view is now that, on the whole, the system strives to compensate for lost earning potential, then the basic disablement benefit must be rational-

18. Post, p. 317.
19. See Willis *Workmen's Compensation* (37th edn), pp. 308–313.
20. 414 HC Deb., col. 276.
1. See Standing Committee A Debates on the Bill, cols. 514–528.
2. NI(II)A 1946, s.1 and see post, pp. 318–332.
3. Post, p. 335.
4. *Atiyah*, pp. 344–347.

ised as payable for the non-material consequences of accidents, in the way that non-pecuniary damages are available under the common law.[5] Nor is it to be forgotten that a social security beneficiary may to a substantial extent accumulate entitlement with any damages awarded in a common law action against the person responsible for the accident.[6]

The typical European scheme combines a scale of disablement with the claimant's earning potential, so that for 100% disablement there is an effective indemnity of his full earning capacity, and for lesser degrees of incapacity the figure is reduced on a proportionate basis (e.g., for 30% disablement, he will receive a pension based on 30% of his pre-accident earnings),[7] though in all cases there is a maximum above which earnings will not be taken into account. The typical American scheme (still based on the workmen's compensation model) continues to compensate for a proportion (two-thirds to three-quarters) of actual lost earnings, generally combined with a small family allowance,[8] and this approach, based on actual earnings loss, is also incorporated in the New Zealand accident compensation scheme (which is not confined to employment injuries).[9] The interesting proposals for accident compensation in Australia combined this traditional method for the totally incapacitated, with the scale method of assessment applied to 60% of the *national average earnings* for those only partially disabled.[10]

For the analysis of the prevailing principles under the British industrial injuries scheme it is proposed to deal in this Part with the basic disablement, and in Part Seven with increases and allowances which might be added.

B. Loss of faculty

Under the original 1946 Act, title to disablement benefit was based on proof that the claimant had, as a result of the industrial accident, sustained a loss of faculty which was likely to be permanent or substantial.[11] The requirement posed a severe obstacle for a large range of employees who sustained only minor injuries – in 1953 it was estimated that 10% of all claimants had been refused benefit on this ground.[12] In that year, Parliament replaced the formula by the simple requirement that the employee

5. Ogus *Law of Damages* (1973), pp. 194–218; cf., *Pearson*, para. 490.
6. Ante, p. 270.
7. See *Kaim-Caudle*, pp. 91–93. The French system incorporates a bias in favour of the more seriously disabled on the assumption that the loss of earning potential increases at a greater rate as the degree of disablement becomes more severe: see *Dupeyroux*, pp. 485–488.
8. See the Report of the National Commission on State Workmen's Compensation Laws (1972), pp. 63–70.
9. Accident Compensation Act 1972, s.113, and see Harris, 37 MLR 361, 369–372.
10. See Report of the Australian Commission of Inquiry into Compensation and Rehabilitation (1974), paras. 389–401.
11. NI(II)A 1946, s.12(1)(a). 'Substantial' meant a disablement of 20% or more: ibid., s.12(1)(a)(ii).
12. Mr O. Peake, Minister of NI, introducing the second reading of the NI(II) Bill (No. 2) 1953; 516 HC Deb., col. 2109.

'suffers as a result of the relevant accident from loss of physical or mental faculty such that the assessed extent of the resulting disablement amounts to not less than 1 per cent.'[13]

'Loss of faculty' is not defined in the legislation. It is one link in the statutory chain of causation: accident – injury – loss of faculty – disablement, and its meaning, therefore, must be understood in the light of those other elements.[14] Whereas 'injury' covers all the adverse physical or mental consequences of the accident,[15] 'loss of faculty' connotes 'impairment of the proper functioning of part of the body or mind',[16] and this is 'a cause of disabilities to do things which in sum constitute the disablement' which is the subject of the assessment.[17] If this seems to be very complicated, its practical importance is small. In some cases, the medical authorities have mistaken their proper function by failing to recognise a loss of faculty where the existence of such loss was patent, (e.g., a condition which rendered a hand sensitive) but which did not entail a significant degree of disablement. As the Commissioner pointed out,[18] the proper ground for refusing benefit in such a case was that the extent of disablement was less than 1%, rather than that there was no loss of faculty at all.[19] However, it seems in a case like this that the medical authorities are not bound to make an assessment; for the Act provides that 'there shall be deemed not to be any relevant loss of faculty with the extent of the resulting disablement, if so assessed, would not amount to 1 per cent'.[20]

What amounts to an 'impairment of the proper functioning' may sometimes cause difficulties. In one case, the malfunctioning of one kidney was regarded as a loss of faculty, even though the claimant could survive by using the other kidney.[1] For some time there was doubt as to whether disfigurement constituted a loss of faculty, on the ground that a person does not put his appearance to any use. The traditional view that it was covered has now been confirmed by the Social Security Act 1975 which provides that 'references to loss of physical faculty include disfigurement, whether or not accompanied by any actual loss of faculty'.[2] This oddly-worded subsection does imply, however, by using the contradistinction of 'actual' loss of faculty, that were it not for the Act, disfigurement would not be regarded as a loss of faculty.[3]

C. Causal link with relevant accident

The next task is to establish that the loss of faculty resulted from the industrial accident or prescribed disease. The onus of proof is on the

13. NI(II)A 1953, s.3, now SSA 1975, s.57(1).
14. *Jones v Secretary of State for Social Services* [1972] AC 944, per Lord Diplock at pp. 1009–1010 and Lord Simon at p. 1019.
15. Per Lord Diplock, ibid., at p. 1010; 'hurt to body or mind': Lord Simon, ibid., at p. 1020.
16. Per Lord Simon, ibid., cf. 'loss of

power or function of an organ of the body': Lord Diplock, ibid., at p. 1010.
17. Per Lord Diplock, ibid.
18. *R(I) 6/61*.
19. The same point emerges in *R(I) 7/63* and *R(I) 14/66*.
20. SSA 1975, s.57(3).
1. *R(I) 14/66*.
2. SSA 1975, s.57(2).
3. But see *R(I) 39/60*.

claimant and the standard is the balance of probabilities.[4] The ordinary principles of causation apply,[5] so the claimant need not show that the accident was the sole or even *the* effective cause – it is sufficient if it was *a* real and effective cause.[6] The major problem here has been the question of competence to make a binding decision on the point. One of the disablement questions to be resolved by the medical authorities is 'whether the relevant accident has resulted in a loss of faculty'.[7] But disablement benefit generally follows an award of injury benefit, and for this purpose the *statutory* authorities (viz., insurance officer, local insurance tribunal, and Commissioner) will have made a decision that the claimant had sustained an injury by accident arising out of and in the course of employment. Section 38(3) of the National Insurance (Industrial Injuries) Act 1965 provided that such a decision should be 'final'. The Act was ambiguous on what aspects of that decision were to be regarded as 'final', and 'final' for what purposes. It was, of course, clear that the medical authorities could not challenge a decision that an accident had arisen out of and in the course of employment[8] but could they reopen the question whether the physical condition of the claimant *resulted from* the accident? For a long time it was assumed that they could. On the one hand, it was argued that there were two different statutory chains of entitlement: for an injury benefit (accident – injury) and for a disablement benefit (accident – loss of faculty – disablement); and on the other hand, the policy arguments seemed strongly to favour this interpretation. Injury benefit was for a short-term disability and it was desirable to make a speedy decision. Conversely, where benefit was payable for a substantial number of years, it was necessary to examine the nature of the claimant's condition and its aetiology more carefully by referring the question to the medical authorities, and the latter should be able to depart from the earlier, less expert decision taken by the statutory authorities.[9] The view was challenged in 1966 and for the next six years there was a prolonged and complex debate on the matter which was twice taken to the House of Lords.

In *Re Dowling,*[10] the House of Lords held, with Lord Wilberforce dissenting, that the demarcation of jurisdiction hitherto accepted was wrong. A finding in that case by the insurance officer that the claimant had suffered an injury by accident was held to be binding on the medical authorities. Such determination was regarded as the starting point of their jurisdiction (or as Lord Hodson put it, 'a ticket of admission'[11]). In the case in question, the 'injury', a cardiac condition caused by exertion at work, was, in a sense, also 'the accident' (the problem has already been discussed[12]), and the speech of at least one judge[13] could be read as limiting the decision to such a case. The argument was that the medical authorities had no jurisdiction to decide whether there had been an 'accident' and in

4. *R(I) 12/62.*
5. Cf. ante, pp. 299–300, and 275.
6. *R(I) 3/66* (Tribunal decision).
7. SSA 1975, s.108(1)(a).
8. NI(II)A 1965, s.49(4), re-enacted as SSA 1975, s.107(4).
9. See esp. the speech of Lord Diplock in

Jones' case, ante n.14, at p. 1007.
10. *Minister of Social Security v Amalgamated Engineering Union* [1967] 1 AC 725.
11. Ibid., at p. 749.
12. Ante, p. 273.
13. Lord Hodson, ante n.10, at p. 751.

this type of case such a finding necessarily meant that there had also been an 'injury'. It was on this ground that the Commissioner sought in several subsequent cases to distinguish the *Dowling* decision, holding that it did not apply where the 'accident' was clearly external to, and separate from, the 'injury'.[14] The matter was taken again to the House of Lords in 1971, when two cases were heard *en banc*.[15] Their Lordships, by a majority,[16] again decided that the statutory authorities' finding that there had been an 'injury by accident' was binding on the medical tribunal, and that *Dowling* should not be overruled. Nor were they prepared to distinguish the former decision on the ground that it was an 'accident/injury' case.[17]

The government of the day sought to reverse the effect of the ruling as soon as possible, but the matter provoked a bitterly fought debate in a Standing Committee of the House of Commons. The opposition viewed the measure as a deliberate and direct attack on workers' rights. Mrs. Barbara Castle, for example, concluded that it was 'designed to establish the victory of unimaginative bureaucracy'.[18] But it was passed[19] and, in its re-enacted form, prescribes that a decision by the statutory authorities that a claimant sustained an injury by an industrial accident is to be regarded as determining only that the accident arose out of and in the course of employment, that it was an insured employment, and that benefit was not precluded because the accident happened outside Great Britain,[20] but

> 'neither any such decision nor the reference to a medical board or medical appeal tribunal . . . in connection with any claim to or award of disablement benefit is to be taken as importing a decision as to the origin of any injury or disability suffered by the claimant, whether or not there is an event identifiable as an accident apart from any injury that may have been received'.[1]

It is now clear beyond doubt that the pre-1966 position has been restored, and that the medical authorities have an unfettered power to decide that the loss of faculty did not result from the relevant accident.[2]

D. Assessment of disablement

i) General

The final link in the chain is the degree of disablement on which the award of benefit is based. It will be recalled that entitlement to injury benefit

14. See, e.g., *R(I) 10/68*.
15. *Jones v Secretary of State for Social Services*; *Hudson v same* [1972] AC 944.
16. Viscount Dilhorne, Lords Wilberforce and Diplock dissenting.
17. See especially Lord Simon ante n.15, at pp. 1022–1023. On this point, the views of the other members of the majority are, however, less explicit.
18. Standing Committee D Debates on the National Insurance Bill 1972, col. 373.
19. NIA 1972, s.5.

20. On this see ante, p. 272.
1. SSA 1975, s.117(3).
2. The statutory authorities have an indirect power to review a decision on the point if satisfied that it was given in ignorance of, or was based on a mistake as to, some material fact; or that there has been a relevant change of circumstances since the decision was given; SSA 1975, s.104(1). This applies to all decisions under the Social Security Act and is dealt with post, pp. 642–644.

depends on incapacity for work. The aim of the long-term benefit is very different. Although the unemployability supplement and special hardship allowance are based on loss of earning capacity, disablement benefit itself is assessed solely by reference to the physical or mental capacities of the claimant, whether or not these result in any loss of earnings.[3] The benefit is payable for the hardships caused by the injuries per se, and the ability to earn, or indeed to claim unemployment or sickness benefit on the grounds appropriate to them, does not affect entitlement. The general principle of assessment is to take into account all disabilities incurred as a result of the loss of faculty

> 'to which the claimant may be expected, having regard to his physical and mental condition at the date of the assessment, to be subject during the period taken into account by the assessment as compared with a person of the same age and sex whose physical and mental condition is normal'.[4]

With the exception of the factors mentioned in this provision, measurement is objective: 'the assessment shall be made without reference to the particular circumstances of the claimant other than age, sex and physical and mental condition'.[5] It follows that not only is the effect of the disability on the claimant's earning capacity irrelevant,[6] but personal and social circumstances are also ignored.[7] On its review of the principles of assessment in 1965, a Departmental Committee found no good reason for departing from this objective approach.[8] The finding has been criticised by many, particularly sociologists,[9] who feel that insufficient regard has been paid to the considerable amount of research which has taken place in the last twenty years on the functional, social and psychological effects of disability.[10] Resentment and conflict, it has been argued, are bound to result from a method of assessment in which the criteria used are so particularistic about the disability itself and so vague about its actual social consequences for the patient, and empirical work has shown that claimants of industrial injury benefit feel the system of compensation to be unjust and incomprehensible.[11] The problem of definition is common to all disabilities and, as such, it has already been considered in chapter 4.[12]

Whatever the merits and demerits of the clinical criteria adopted in this context, it must be admitted that the formulation of the legal rules has

3. See the Report of the Inter-Departmental Committee on Assessment of Disablement due to Specified Injuries (1947), Cmd. 7076, paras. 5–7.
4. SSA 1975, Sch. 8, para. 1(a).
5. Ibid., para. 1(c).
6. R(I) 3/61.
7. In R(I) 6/75 C sought to have his assesment of disability reduced from 20% to 19% on the ground that the consequent award of a lump sum gratuity instead of a pension would enable him to purchase a small

business. The reduction was quashed by the Commissioner.
8. Report of the Committee on the Assessment of Disablement (McCorquodale Committee), Cmnd. 2847.
9. See esp. Townsend The Disabled in Society (1967).
10. See the references cited in Townsend, ibid., and Blaxter The Meaning of Disability (1976).
11. Blaxter, ibid., at pp. 187–189.
12. Ante, pp. 145–147.

given rise to great complexity and confusion. In 1967 Lord Denning MR was moved to remark:

> 'the judges have been at their wits' end to know what some of the provisions mean . . . . If the judges find this difficult, I can imagine how impossible it must be for those who have to apply them. These are, for the most part, not lawyers, but medical men and civil servants. No wonder they have developed their own particular terms . . . which they may understand but no one else does'.[13]

And in the same case Willmer LJ said:

> 'I regard it as deplorable that, in a matter which so vitally affects the lives and welfare of working men and women, there should be so much obscurity and so much room for doubt'.[14]

ii) Assessment for prescribed conditions

Schedule 2 of the Industrial Injuries (Benefit) Regulations[15] contains a tariff of the prescribed degrees of disablement. The first column sets out descriptions of the injury and the second column the degree of disablement, expressed as a percentage of total disablement (e.g., loss of a hand and a foot, 100%; loss of thumb, 30% etc.). For each specified condition, then, the prima facie assessment is the prescribed degree of disablement, but the medical authorities are not tied to this figure: it is subject

> 'to such increase or reduction . . . as may be reasonable in the circumstances of the case where, having regard to the [statutory provisions and regulations] . . . that degree of disablement does not provide a reasonable assessment of the extent of disablement resulting from the relevant loss of faculty'.[16]

The conditions specified in the tariff must, it seems, be construed literally. Thus, for example, reference to the loss of the phalanx of a finger does not cover loss of *part* of the phalanx of a finger.[17] Although the Act specifically entitles the Secretary of State to make special provision for the difference between injuries to the hand and arm of right and left-handed persons,[18] he has not yet done so, though it may be a suitable case for the medical authorities to increase or reduce assessment in the exercise of their discretion referred to above.

Suppose that a claimant, as a result of a relevant accident, suffers from two of the conditions specified in the tariff, may the prescribed degrees of disablement be aggregated? For a long time the problem created a great deal of uncertainty.[19] The position has been clarified by legislation changes.[20] The prima facie application of the prescribed degree occurs

---

13. *R v Industrial Injuries Comr, ex parte Cable* [1968] 1 QB 729 at 737.
14. Ibid., at p. 740.
15. S.I. 1975/559.
16. Ibid., Reg.2(6).
17. *R(I) 22/63*.

18. SSA 1975, Sch. 8. para. 1(d).
19. See *CSI 74/50*; *R(I) 39/61*; *R v Industrial Injuries Comr ex parte Cable*, ante, n.13.
20. NIA 1969, s.7(1)(a) and S.I. 1970/1551.

only where the condition in question is 'the sole injury which a claimant suffers as a result of the relevant accident . . . whether or not such injury incorporates one or more other injuries' as specified.[1] In other words, if one injury is incorporated into another, the assessment should be made according to the prescribed degree of the more serious disability. Where the accident results in two separate injuries, there is no automatic assessment under the tariff, and the principles next to be described apply.

iii) Assessment for non-prescribed conditions

For conditions not specified in the Schedule, assessment is at large. It is a question of fact, and the decision of the medical authorities will generally be regarded as conclusive, though they 'may have such regard as may be appropriate to the prescribed degrees of disablement' of the injuries specified in the Schedule.[2] The prescribed degrees of disablement, then, provide a guideline for the appropriate assessment, but no more. In one case,[3] the claimant suffering from a condition of the finger which was more severe than one prescribed finger condition but less severe than another prescribed finger condition sought to argue that as a matter of *law* medical authorities were bound to assess at a figure between the two prescribed degrees of disablement. The argument was rejected. The discretion of the medical authorities was not to be fettered by thus enlarging the Schedule. In cases where the claimant has sustained multiple (and separate) injuries, and there is no composite disability for which the Schedule prescribes an assessment, the medical authorities must form their own judgment on the total disablement resulting from the various injuries.[4] They may compare this total condition with those giving rise to the prescribed degrees of disablement and select an appropriate figure.[5]

iv) Reductions for disability resulting from extraneous cases

The fact that the claimant's condition results in part from an extraneous cause, that is, one not arising from an industrial accident, in principle justifies a reduction in the assessment of the disability. It is felt that the Fund should not be charged with the burden of such disabilities as the claimant would have suffered if he had not been injured in the industrial accident. The policy is a simple one to understand, but the provisions implementing it have caused great difficulties. The chief concern has been to see that generous treatment should be given to an employee who sustains two disabilities, only one of which is caused by an industrial accident, but which are in some way connected, so that the total disability resulting is greater than the sum of the two disabilities taken separately. A simple example will illustrate the point.

> Under the tariff, the loss of vision in one eye, the other being normal, is 30%, but the loss of sight 'to such an extent as to render the claimant unable to perform any work for which eyesight is

1. S.I. 1975/559, Reg.2(6).
2. Ibid., Reg.2(7).
3. *R(I) 23/63*.
4. *R v Industrial Injuries Comr, ex parte Cable*, ante n.13.
5. Ibid.

essential' is assessed at 100%.[6] Thus a claimant, already blind in one eye, who loses the sight of the other eye in an industrial accident under the ordinary principle unmodified would be entitled to only 30%, but the effect of the accident has been to increase disablement from 30% to 100%.

The solution originally adopted was the so-called 'paired-organs' rule. Where the claimant sustained an injury to one of a pair of similar organs, whose functions were interchangeable or complementary, and the other had already been incapacitated – in an industrial accident or otherwise – the total disablement was treated as resulting from an industrial injury.[7] Application of the doctrine, however, produced difficulties and anomalies,[8] and in 1969–70 it was replaced by a new set of rules.[9]

a) TOTAL DISABLEMENT. The medical authorities should first assess the total disablement resulting from the relevant loss of faculty, whether or not it was derived in part from another cause.[10] In so doing, they should not merely arbitrate between two opposing views (those of the claimant and those of the Department) but rather obtain all the information which they regard as relevant, and assess the disablement resulting from the relevant loss of faculty on the balance of probabilities.[11] They may then, for the purpose of making a reduction from the first assessment, only take account of causes other than the relevant accident to the extent allowed by the Industrial Injuries (Benefit) Regulations 2(3) and 2(4).[12]

b) OTHER EFFECTIVE CAUSE PRECEDES INDUSTRIAL ACCIDENT. The first of these Regulations provides that where the other effective cause is a condition or injury which precedes the industrial accident the medical authorities must assess what would have been the disablement resulting from the earlier disability if the industrial accident had not occurred.

E.g., C has suffered an amputation to one foot. In the industrial accident he suffers an amputation to the other foot. Total disablement is 90%. If there had been no industrial accident he would have been disabled to the extent of 30%. Benefit is then payable on an assessment of 90% − 30% = 60%.

c) INDUSTRIAL ACCIDENT PRECEDES OTHER EFFECTIVE CAUSE. In the converse case where the industrial accident precedes the other effective cause, the solution is not so simple. On the ordinary principles of causation, it is arguable that no account should be taken of the fact that the

6. S.I. 1975/559, Sch. 2, items 32 and 4 respectively.
7. S.I. 1964/504, Reg. 2(4).
8. See R v Medical Appeal Tribunal, ex parte Bulpitt [1957] 2 QB 384; see also Report of the Industrial Injuries Advisory Council on the Rules Governing the Assessment of Disablement (1956), Cmd. 9827; and

Micklethwait 37 Medico-Legal Jo. 172, 185.
9. NIA 1969 s.7(1)(a); S.I. 1970/1551.
10. S.I. 1975/559, Reg.2(2).
11. R v Industrial Injuries Comr, ex parte Cable, ante n.13; R v National Insurance Comr, ex parte Viscusi [1974] 2 All ER 724, [1974] 1 WLR 646, CA.
12. S.I. 1975/559.

other cause has exacerbated the claimant's condition, since the later 'unconnected event' has superseded the effect of the industrial accident. This was indeed the position prevailing before the 1970 reform, and yet it creates an apparent inequality of treatment according to the sequence of events.[13] The Committee which reviewed the issue in 1956[14] was divided on the issue. The minority opinion was that the assessment should take account of the greater incapacity caused by the non-industrial accident (as in Regulation 2(3)), but the majority found no justification for such a 'radical' departure from the ordinary rules of causation. Aware, presumably, of the political repercussions of strict adherence to the ordinary rules, however, they suggested the compromise solution of taking into account 50% of the increase in disability. A compromise solution was in fact adopted by the Department in 1970, but not that proposed by the Committee. It was decided to take into account the *whole* of the increase for those more seriously injured, but to ignore it altogether for those less seriously injured.[15] The dividing line was arbitrarily made at an 11% disablement. Regulation 2(4), which now incorporates the solution, lays down two rules.

1. The authorities should only take into account the disablement which would have resulted if the non-industrial accident had not occurred.

> E.g., C loses the whole of a ring finger in an industrial accident. As a result of a later non-industrial accident, the hand containing that finger is rendered useless. Benefit is payable only for the disability of the ring finger = 7%.

2. Where the assessment made under the first rule is 11% or more, a solution analogous to that in Regulation 2(3) is adopted. From the assessment of total disablement is deducted the degree of disablement resulting solely from the non-industrial accident (i.e., if the industrial accident had not occurred).

> E.g., in an industrial accident, C is amputated through the left foot. He is subsequently amputated through the right foot. Amputation of a foot is 30%, thus the second rule applies. Total disablement is 90% from which is deducted 30% for the right foot. Benefit is payable for 60%.

d) WHERE 100% DISABLEMENT. A special rule operates where the total assessment of disabilities is 100%. In such circumstances the medical authorities are given power *not* to reduce for the fact that some of the disablement has been caused by a non-industrial event, if they are satisfied that, 'in the circumstances of the case, 100% is a reasonable assessment of the extent of disablement resulting from the loss of faculty'.[16] This is designed to cover cases where the disability caused by the industrial accident itself, without the addition of disability arising from an

13. The common law has had to cope with similar problems. See *Baker v Willoughby* [1970] AC 467, [1969] 3 All ER 1528; Ogus *Law of Damages* (1973), pp. 64-66.
14. Ante n.8.
15. S.I. 1970/46.
16. S.I. 1975/559, Reg. 2(6).

extraneous event, would amount to 100%. It would obviously be unjust to make a deduction merely because the non-industrial event has made the claimant's condition even worse. The anomaly arose because the tariff knew no degree of assessment higher than 100%. The practice adopted under the former legislation was to aggregate the disabilities even where they in total exceeded 100% and then to make the appropriate deduction. The Regulation quoted above does not compel the authorities to take this course, but it would seem to be a reasonable exercise of their power to follow the earlier practice.

e) PERIOD OF ASSESSMENT. The assessment is made for the period 'during which the claimant has suffered and may be expected to continue to suffer from the relevant loss of faculty', but beginning not earlier than the end of the injury benefit period[17] (on which see above[18]). It will in any event terminate on the claimant's death,[19] but it may be limited to an earlier day, on the ground either that the disability is expected to end by that date or because the assessment is a provisional one. A provisional assessment is to be made where 'the condition of the claimant is not such, having regard to the possibility of changes therein (whether predictable or not), as to allow of a final assessment'.[20] If the assessment is final, it may be modified only by a review – to be considered in the next paragraph. If it is provisional the claimant's condition must be examined again at the end of the period for which the assessment was made, and the new assessment (either provisional or final) will apply from that time.[1] A provisional assessment is in no sense binding on a subsequent assessment, and the medical authorities determining the latter may come to a different view on whether a condition which was also the subject of the previous assessment resulted from the relevant accident.[2] On the other hand, a subsequent assessment cannot modify the benefit for the earlier period.[3]

E. Review

The insurance officer or the local tribunal has a general power to review its decision under the Social Security Act where either is satisfied that the decision was given in ignorance of, or was based on a mistake as to, some material fact, or that there has been a relevant change of circumstances since the decision was given.[4] This power is considered in chapter 15.[5] But quite independently of this, the *medical* authorities are given specific powers of reviewing decisions on entitlement to disablement benefit. The first condition is that there must be 'fresh evidence'.[6] The term is relevant also to a Commissioner's general power of review and has

17. SSA 1975, Sch. 8, para. 4.
18. Ante, p. 301.
19. SSA 1975, Sch. 8, para. 4.
20. Ibid.
 1. Ibid.
 2. *R v Industrial Injuries Comr, ex parte Howarth* (1968) 4 KIR 621, CA; *R v*

National Insurance Comr, ex parte Viscusi [1974] All ER 724, [1974] 1 WLR 646, CA.
 3. *R(I) 8/69.*
 4. SSA 1975, s.104.
 5. Post, pp. 642–644.
 6. SSA 1975, s.110(1).

been interpreted to mean facts coming to light after the hearing, or evidence available at that time, but which the claimant could not reasonably have been expected to adduce at the hearing.[7] Secondly, the fresh evidence must reveal that the earlier decision

'was given in consequence of the non-disclosure or misrepresentation by the claimant or any other person of a material fact (whether the non-disclosure or misrepresentation was or was not fraudulent)'.[8]

'Non-disclosure' has been construed as meaning the 'failure to disclose a fact known to a person [at the time of the hearing], but who does not disclose it'.[9] The cumulative effect of the two conditions is, therefore, to confine the power of review quite narrowly. It does not extend to evidence available only after the first hearing, and the failure to disclose the material must be based on reasonable grounds. The intention was to exclude the possibility of a claimant (or indeed the Department) dissatisfied with a decision being able to perpetuate proceedings indefinitely by seeking out new opinions from doctors or other sources.[10]

There was clearly a need for special provision to cover deteriorations in the claimant's condition arising since the time of the original hearing. Consistent with the general policy of finality, however, the relevant measure in the 1946 Act was very restrictive. The claimant had to show that there had been an unforeseen aggravation to his condition which was *substantial*, and even then the medical authorities would have power to review only if to refuse him a revision would create 'substantial injustice'.[11] These harsh limitations provoked strong criticism, and they were revised in 1953.[12] Since that date, it has been sufficient if the medical board is satisfied

'that since the making of the assessment there has been an unforeseen aggravation of the results of the relevant injury'[13],

though if the original assessment was made, confirmed or varied by a medical appeal tribunal, then the leave of that body must be obtained.[14] The aggravation must be 'unforeseen' in the sense that it was not taken into account in the earlier assessment, and, of course, it must have been substantially caused by the relevant injury – the principles of causation applied are the same as those governing the injury/loss of faculty connection.[15] The power of revision is in no way inhibited by the earlier assessment, and as *R(I) 7/65* shows the final assessment might not favour the claimant.

7. See post, p. 644, and the references there cited.
8. SSA 1975, s.110(1).
9. Per Diplock J, *R v Medical Appeal Tribunal (North Midland Region)*, *ex parte Hubble* [1958] 2 QB 228 at 242, approved by the Court of Appeal, [1959] 2 QB at 408.
10. Per Diplock J, ante n.9, loc. cit.
11. NI(II)A 1946, s.40(2).
12. NI(II)A 1953, Sch. 1.
13. SSA 1975, s.110(2).
14. Ibid., s.110(5). The granting of leave is discretionary and the statutory authorities have no jurisdiction to overturn it: *R(I) 15/68*.
15. *R(I) 18/62* and ante, p. 306.

Following an operation to his injured elbow, C sought a review, on the ground of unforeseen aggravation, of a 5% life assessment previously made. On review, the medical board made a provisional reassessment of 10% for six months, followed by subsequent assessments at 7%, 3% and finally 2% for life. The Commissioner held that the final assessment of 2% did not constitute an error of law, notwithstanding that it was less than the 5% life assessment originally made.

The 1953 reform also plugged another gap. Where unforeseen aggravation is shown, the medical authorities may now alter a previous finding that no loss of faculty had resulted from the relevant accident.[16]

Where the authorities have exercised their general power of revision based on non-disclosure or misrepresentation of a material fact, the revised benefit may be payable from the date of application for review or from such earlier date as it may consider 'reasonable in the circumstances', provided that it is not earlier than the date of the original award.[17] For a review on the ground of unforeseen aggravation, on the other hand, they may not backdate payment for more than three months before the date of application.[18]

F. Benefit

Where the extent of disablement is assessed at less than 20%, benefit is payable in the form of a gratuity.[19] A maximum amount is prescribed for a 19% disability (in 1977–78 £1,900) and for each lesser degree of disablement there is a corresponding figure proportional to that amount.[20] If the award is for life,[1] or for seven years or more, that sum is payable.[2] If the period is less, the claimant receives such a proportion of the sum as the period in question bears to seven years (e.g., for one year, one-seventh of the stipulated amount).[3] The award of a gratuity is non-recurring – it is a once-for-all entitlement – and in general is payable in a lump sum,[4] but Regulations empower the authorities to pay it by way of instalments 'at such times as appear reasonable in the circumstances of the case' if (1) the claimant is under 18 or (2) the amount exceeds £52 and the claimant requests that the payment be made by way of instalment.[5] For amounts of 20% or over, a pension of a legislatively prescribed amount (proportional to the degree of disablement) is payable on a weekly basis for the period

16. Now SSA 1975, s.110(3).
17. S.I. 1975/558, Reg. 32.
18. Ibid., Reg. 35.
19. SSA 1975, s.57(5).
20. S.I. 1975/559, Sch. 2, as amended by S.I. 1977/1325.
 1. If the award is for 'life', and the claimant dies before the commencement of the period for which it is payable, his personal representative is not entitled: R(I) 23/52 (cp. R(I) 59/54 where C died

before examination of the medical board which subsequently – and perhaps surprisingly – assessed at 14% 'for life'. It was held that the gratuity was payable to his estate).
 2. S.I. 1975/559, Reg. 6(a).
 3. Ibid., Reg. 6(b).
 4. S.I. 1975/560, Reg. 18(2).
 5. Ibid., Reg. 18(3). The decision on the form of assessment is not susceptible of appeal: ibid., Reg. 18(4).

stipulated in the award.[6] For example, in 1977–78, the relevant rates for 100% and 50% are £28·60 and £14·30 respectively.[7]

Part seven. Increases and Additions

A. General

The decision to base disablement benefit on functional disability and assumed need rather than on loss of earnings, meant that special provision had to be made for persons disadvantaged by physical or social circumstances, hence the constant attendance, hospital attendance and exceptionally severe disablement allowances. The original disinclination to take account of earning capacity led quite logically to the notion that a claimant might accumulate his disablement benefit with the 'ordinary' national insurance benefits for unemployment, sickness or retirement. The claimant might, however, fail to satisfy the contribution conditions for these benefits and thus for those totally incapacitated the unemployability supplement was made available. As has already been described,[8] political and other motives forced the post-war Labour government to resile from the strict position of no compensation for reduced earning capacity, and for this contingency the special hardship allowance was introduced.

B. Unemployability supplement

The Act provides for an increase to disablement pension (but not gratuity) if

> 'as the result of the relevant loss of faculty the beneficiary is incapable of work and likely to remain so permanently'.[9]

The criterion of incapacity is that used elsewhere in social security law (notably for the sickness and invalidity benefits[10]). In the words of the Commissioner, the claimant must prove that:

> 'Having regard to his age, education, experience, state of health and other personal factors, there is no work or type of work which he can reasonably be expected to do.'[11]

The difficulty of obtaining such employment because of the labour market conditions generally, or those pertaining in the claimant's locality, is regarded as irrelevant.[12] The criterion, so elaborated, is one of fact for the statutory authorities to decide, and though the opinion of the medical authorities will be taken into account, along with other relevant evidence, it is not conclusive.[13] The fact that the claimant has been able to work will,

6. SSA 1975, s.57(6).
7. S.I. 1977/1325. There is a lower rate for beneficiaries under eighteen not entitled to a dependant's increase.
8. Ante, p. 303.

9. SSA 1975, s.58(1).
10. Ante, pp. 151–158.
11. CI 99/49, para. 10.
12. Ibid., and R(I) 43/54.
13. CI 44/49; R(I) 10/61.

of course, in general disentitle him. To encourage some activity, and rehabilitation, the Act provides that for the purpose of entitlement to unemployability supplement such work is to be ignored if the earnings therefrom do not exceed a prescribed amount,[14] in 1977–78 £520 a year.[15]

The incapacity must 'result from' the relevant loss of faculty. The ordinary principles of causation apply,[16] so that the loss need be only a material or substantial, not the sole, cause of the disability. Further, the authorities have been prepared to extend the so-called 'last straw' doctrine to unemployability supplement. In deciding the causation issue, they are entitled to look at the claimant's aggregate disablement, even though part of his condition results from extraneous causes or constitutional conditions. If he can prove that a small degree of disablement resulting from the loss of faculty, when added to his constitutional condition, changed him from a person 'capable' of work to a person 'incapable', he will succeed.[17]

The supplement is a flat-rate weekly sum (in 1977–78 £17·50[18]) payable for a period determined by the insurance officer, but renewable from time to time.[19] To this amount may be added two different forms of increase. First, there are those payable for child and adult dependants.[20] Secondly, to bring the supplement in line with the non-industrial invalidity allowance (introduced in 1971),[1] there is payable an increase variable according to the age of the claimant at the first day of incapacity or the beginning of the first week for which the supplement is payable.[2] The 1977–78 rates for the relevant age groups are: under thirty-five, £3·50 per week; between thirty-five and forty-five, £2·30 per week; between forty-five and fifty-five (women) or sixty (men), £1·15 per week.[3] From 6 April 1979, the age limits for the higher and middle rates are changed to forty and fifty respectively.[4] The reasoning behind these increases and the modification to the age groups has already been examined.[5]

C. Special hardship allowance

i) General

The history of how the allowance for partial, as opposed to total, loss of earnings was belatedly introduced into the industrial injuries scheme has already been related.[6] The essence of the matter is a comparison between the claimant's position before the accident and that consequent on his physical disabilities. For the purposes of exposition, however, we distinguish between the conditions for entitlement, and the methods of quantifying the allowance payable. Title to the allowance requires proof that 'as the result of the relevant loss of faculty', the claimant *either*

14. SSA 1975, s.58(3).
15. S.I. 1977/1362.
16. Cf., ante, pp. 299 and 307.
17. R(I) 10/61.
18. S.I. 1977/1325.
19. SSA 1975, s.58(4).
20. Post, pp. 385–390.

1. Ante, pp. 166–167.
2. SSA 1975, s.59.
3. S.I. 1977/1325.
4. SSPA 1975, s.17.
5. Ante, pp. 164–167.
6. Ante, p. 304.

'(a) is incapable, and likely to remain permanently incapable, of following his regular occupation; *and*

(b) is incapable of following employment of an equivalent standard which is suitable in his case . . . '

or

'is, and has at all times since the end of the injury benefit period been, incapable of following that occupation or any such employment'.[7]

ii) Regular occupation

The first element in the comparison between the claimant's pre-accident and post-accident situation is his 'regular occupation' at the time of the accident. One might have expected that the term would be endowed with a highly specific and technical meaning. Happily this has not been the case. It will be recalled[8] that for the purpose of the Prescribed Diseases provisions the authorities, in attributing a 'prescribed occupation' to the claimant, are concerned less with the name given to his category of employment than with its nature. So here, the Commissioner has shown on a number of occasions that the claimant's 'regular occupation' is to be regarded as a question of fact, determinable on consideration of all the relevant evidence: the label given to the employment by the employer, or employees and employers generally, or trade union rules and agreements, is not thought to be particularly helpful.[9] Consistently with this, though surprising in the light of the overall policy of the legislation, a Tribunal of Commissioners has held that the regular occupation need not be in an 'employed earner's employment' (i.e., one covered by the industrial scheme)[10]. There is thus no magic in the finding of a specific category of work. The object is rather to establish a pattern of earnings on the basis of which the subsequent comparison can be made. If the claimant fails to establish such a pattern, the increases will not be payable;[11] but the authorities have shown great readiness to find a regularity although the duration of the employment is very limited. In one case,[12]

C had been employed for ten weeks as a trainee impressioner. The normal period of training was four to eight weeks, and it appeared most unlikely that C would eventually have qualified. It was held that C's 'regular occupation' was 'trainee impressioner', notwith-

7. SSA 1975, s. 60(1).
8. Ante, p. 296.
9. *R(I) 28/51*; *R(I) 66/51*; *R(I) 11/65*; *R(I) 6/75*.
10. *R(I) 15/56* (Tribunal decision). The Act expressly requires that 'employment of an equivalent standard' for the purposes of the post-accident occupation shall include only employed earners' employment but makes no corresponding limitation as regards the pre-accident regular occupation. The

Commissioners inferred that the omission was deliberate: the number who would be insured for the purpose of disablement benefit but whose *regular* occupation was not in an insurable employment would necessarily be small, and it was not thought fair or worthwhile to exclude them from the SHA.
11. *R(I) 3/60*; *R(I) 18/60*.
12. *R(I) 1/63*.

standing the fact that the training period, *in any event*, would have come to an end in another four weeks.

The date when the regular occupation must be considered is that of the accident, or, in the case of a prescribed disease, the formally attributed date of development.[13] A rigid application of the latter rule may cause hardship. The date of development selected by the medical authorities may be arbitrary, and frequently is later than that of the appearance of the first symptoms.[14] Should the claimant, as a result of these symptons, have abandoned or retired from his employment before the selected date he will have no 'regular occupation' on which to ground his claim. In the early cases, the Commissioner was prepared to 'ignore' the rule where the abandonment resulted from an incapacity which was clearly related to work in the regular occupation.[15] Fortunately, a more formal basis for the just solution was provided by the introduction of a new regulation. If the claimant has been awarded a disablement benefit in respect of a prescribed disease after he had been insured against the disease but before the date of development, for the purposes of entitlement to special hardship allowance

> 'Any occupation he has so abandoned may be treated as his regular occupation . . . if it would have been so treated had the date of development . . . fallen immediately before he so abandoned it'.[16]

In deciding whether or not the claimant had established any regular occupation, therefore, the authorities have been disposed to treat his claim generously. Greater difficulties may be encountered where, though in regular employment in the period before the accident, the claimant has moved from one type of employment to another, with consequent changes in his pattern of earnings. The general principle applied is that the authorities should have regard to the whole employment history rather than to an isolated period before, or at the time of, the accident (or date of development).[17] They will be primarily concerned with the claimant's own intentions. If he voluntarily transfers from one type of employment to another he may rapidly establish the new 'regular occupation'.[18] But if the change was necessitated by his state of health, and he hoped eventually to return to his former occupation, the latter may still be treated as his 'regular occupation'.[19] If, at the time of the accident, he has been engaged in an occupation for a substantial period of time, there is a presumption that that has now become the relevant occupation,[20] though this may still be rebutted, as in *R(I) 44/52*.

> C changed from bus-driving to store-keeping to earn more money. At the time of the accident he was not yet earning more. It was held

13. CI 440/50.
14. Cf. ante, p. 297.
15. CWI 8/50; R(I) 34/51.
16. S.I. 1975/1537, Reg. 19. The causal connection between the abandonment and the relevant disease may, however, be difficult to prove. See R(I) 8/58; R(I) 13/58; and R(I) 31/58.
17. CI 80/49; R(I) 5/52.
18. R(I) 65/54.
19. CI 80/49; R(I) 5/52.
20. R(I) 22/52: three years.

that bus-driving was still his regular occupation, as he would have returned to it if he were unable to secure the hoped-for increase of earnings.

The non-technical interpretation of 'regular occupation' has also led to the conclusion that more than one occupation can be included, so that the earnings therefrom can be aggregated.[1] However, the Act explicitly provides that 'reference to a person's regular occupation is to be taken as not including any subsidiary occupation of his'.[2] It seems evident that the draftsman of the original provision had not contemplated the varieties of activities and earnings which claimants would argue came within their 'regular occupation'. The efforts of the Commissioner to exclude casual work and yet include normal overtime pay, to exclude subsidiary occupations, and yet include co-equal occupations, has challenged his ingenuity and created some nice and perhaps arbitrary distinctions. Voluntary work done for the employer outside the normal activities (e.g., the work's Fire Brigade[3]) is 'subsidiary', but work which is, in some way, contemplated by the contract of employment, without being obligatory under it, may be included (e.g., a colliery repairer working regular weekends on overtime as a shaftsman[4]). A combination of two or more activities, with the same employer or for different employers will be covered,[5] but not if one of those activities is clearly subordinate to the other(s), typically where a full-time employee engages in private contract or other work in his spare time.[6] The dividing line between these various distinctions is obscure and some of the decisions are impossible to reconcile.[7] In principle it is difficult to see why regular overtime payments should be included but regular subsidiary work for an external source excluded. At the Committee stage of the Family Allowances and National Insurance Bill 1961, an amendment to remove the 'subordinate occupation' provision was introduced but subsequently withdrawn, its mover expressing the hope that the National Insurance Commissioner would 'take the hint' and give 'a more liberal interpretation' in the future.[8]

Is account to be taken of promotion or the prospect of advancing to a different, better-paid, occupation? The original legislation drew a sharp distinction between the prospects of advancement, and therefore of a higher standard of remuneration, *within* a particular occupation, and the prospects of promotion to a different occupation or grade. Only the former were to be considered by the authorities.[9] This was subject to the obvious objection that decisions would turn on verbal distinctions – between 'grades' and 'occupations' – which were inconsistent with the growing

1. R(I) 43/52; R(I) 33/58; R(I) 6/75.
2. SSA 1975, s.60(2)(a).
3. R(I) 58/54 and see R(I) 13/62.
4. R(I) 24/55 and see R(I) 10/65.
5. R(I) 43/52; R(I) 16/54; R(I) 11/65; R(I) 6/75 (same employer); R(I) 33/58 (different employers).
6. CWI 30/50; R(I) 54/54; R(I) 9/61. The fact that C receives payment from

an external source for work carried out primarily for his employer will not disentitle him: R(I) 60/52.
7. E.g., R(I) 24/55 and R(I) 2/70.
8. Mr R. Prentice, Standing Committee B Debates, col. 84.
9. NI(II)A 1946, s.14(2), now SSA 1975, s. 60(2).

tendency of the Commissioner to adopt a more flexible and less technical approach to 'regular occupation'. The drawing of these distinctions fell harshly on trainees and others who had every reason to expect that qualification or promotion would normally ensue.[10] After consultations with the TUC, the government in 1961[11] extended the concept of regular occupation to include

'employment in the capacities to which the persons in that occupation (or a class or description of them to which he belonged at the time of the relevant accident) are in the normal course advanced, and to which, if he had continued to follow that occupation without having suffered the relevant loss of faculty, he would have had at least the normal prospects of advancement'.[12]

To succeed under this provision, the claimant must satisfy two conditions:[13] first, objectively, he must show that advancement to the alleged occupation or grade was normal for persons in his occupation; and secondly, subjectively, that he possessed the personal qualities and employment record to justify advancement according to this normal pattern. The existence of the first, objective, test will debar the abnormally gifted or industrious worker from reaping the benefits of these qualities,[14] and to that extent still leaves room for improvement.

iii) The 'permanent' condition

The first of the two alternative conditions requires the claimant to prove that he '(a) is incapable, and likely to remain permanently incapable, of following his regular occupation; and (b) is incapable of following employment of an equivalent standard which is suitable in his case'.[15]

a) WHETHER POST-ACCIDENT WORK IS REGULAR OCCUPATION. After the accident the claimant may have returned to his pre-accident employment, and yet his capacity for the work may have been adversely affected. The question thus arises whether for the purpose of limb (a) of the first condition he is thereby rendered incapable of following his regular occupation. According to a Tribunal of Commissioners, the test is whether 'he is unable to fulfil all the ordinary requirements of employers in that field of labour'.[16] The mere fact that the claimant has been unable to earn as much as before is (as will be seen) a necessary condition, but taken by itself is not sufficient. However, 'if a person obtains employment in his old job only through charity or because he has an exceptional employer, he should be regarded as incapable of following his regular occupation'.[17] As for the analogous purpose of determining what was his regular occupation, not much significance is to be attributed to labels attached to the work: regard

10. See CI 442/50; R(I) 44/51; R(I) 53/52; R(I) 29/55; R(I) 3/60.
11. FANIA 1961, s.3(1).
12. Now SSA 1975, s.60(3).
13. R(I) 8/67.
14. See R(I) 8/73 where the claimant was held to have satisfied the second, but not the first condition.
15. SSA 1975, s.60(1).
16. CI 443/50, para. 11.
17. Ibid., para. 12.

must be had to the nature of the activity.[18] An employee unable to perform the normal incidents of his regular occupation (e.g., a miner compelled to work in dust-free conditions[19] or a stevedore incapable of lifting heavy cargo,[20]) will satisfy the condition. An ability to work only part-time instead of full-time will qualify[1] but failure to work overtime is insufficient,[2] unless the claimant can show that, as evidenced by practice over many years, such working was normal for him.[3] A mere reduction in productivity will not suffice,[4] but if it is so far below the norm that the claimant is fortunate to be employed, he will succeed;[5] the same applies where he has to rely substantially on his workmates to maintain the previous output.[6]

b) WHETHER POST-ACCIDENT WORK IS EQUIVALENT. The second limb requires the claimant to prove that he is incapable of following a suitable employment which is of an equivalent standard. For some time, the Commissioners in interpreting this condition of entitlement (section 60(1)) applied the same test as they used for the purpose of assessing the amount of the allowance, as prescribed by section 60(6), viz., the difference between the claimant's probable standard of remuneration in his regular occupation and that of the employment which he is capable of following after the accident.[7] Thus, for both purposes the question was whether the claimant's actual earnings, i.e., his take home pay, were equivalent to those which he would have received if he had continued in his regular occupation.[8] So if he was earning the same he would fail even though he had to work longer hours because the *rate* of pay was lower.[9] Conversely, if the rate of pay was the same but his actual earnings reduced as a result of his impaired ability, he would succeed.[10] In subsequent decisions, the Commissioner sought to clarify the relationship between section 60(1) and section 60(6). The former provision governed *entitlement*, and logically that issue preceded the process of *quantification* prescribed by the latter.[11] For the question of entitlement, it was necessary to take a longer view: whether, in general, over a period of say twelve months, the level of earnings[12] had become equivalent to that available in the regular occupation – short-term differences were relevant to section 60(6) but not to section 60(1).[13] The matter was taken further by the Court of Appeal in *ex parte Humphreys*.[14] It was stressed that the 'standard of remuneration'

18. *R(I) 28/51.*
19. *R v Industrial Injuries Comr, ex parte Langley* [1976] ICR 36, DC; *R(I) 4/76.*
20. *R(I) 28/51.* See also *CI 201/50* and *R(I) 39/55.*
1. *CI 444/50.*
2. *CI 443/50; CWI 30/50.*
3. *R(I) 10/65.*
4. *CI 447/50; CI 448/50.*
5. *CWI 30/50; R(I) 6/66.*
6. *R(I) 39/52; R(I) 5/55;* cp. *R(I) 29/52.*
7. Post, p. 329.
8. *CI 89/50.*
9. *R(I) 40/51; R(I) 78/51.* So also if the assistance of workmates was necessary

to maintain the required output: *R(I) 29/52.*
10. *CI 205/50.*
11. *R(I) 31/59.*
12. 'Earnings' here means 'the amount of money (or its equivalent) which a person receives in return for his services' *(R(I) 60/52)*, thus will not include payments to idemnify expenses *(R(I) 1/54)* or for the provision of uniform *(R(I) 33/52)*. See, further, post, pp. 427–432.
13. *R(I) 31/59; R(I) 5/62.*
14. *R v Deputy Industrial Injuries Comr, ex parte Humphreys* [1966] 2 QB 1, [1965] 3 All ER 885.

relevant to section 60(1) was an objective one: the normal earnings of persons employed in that occupation.[15] In 1968, a Tribunal of Commissioners took the opportunity of restating the law.[16] The same evidence might be relevant for both subsections yet for essentially different purposes. Section 60(1) was concerned with title to benefit and involved a comparison of the objective standards of remuneration between the two occupations. It was an impersonal standard, viz., the normal earnings of persons working in the occupations. It did not depend on what the claimant had earned or indeed could earn. Such matters were only relevant to the assessment question under section 60(6)[17]. More recently, the Court of Appeal, in yet another review of the provisions, has refined its interpretation of section 60(6).[18] As will be seen, this seems to have had the effect of bringing that subsection closer to the objective comparison required under section 60(1).[19] The meaning of the latter, however, appears to be unaffected.[20]

The employment which is of an 'equivalent standard' must be one covered by the industrial scheme, i.e., 'an employed earner's employment'.[1] In addition it must be 'suitable in his case'. This, like the 'equivalent' requirement, has caused some difficulty. At first, the Commissioner was prepared to confer on it the meaning given to analogous provisions in unemployment benefit law.[2] An employment would not be unsuitable merely because of family or personal circumstances, but such factors as location, means of transport, and the length of time necessary to find alternative employment were regarded as relevant considerations.[3] In *ex parte Humphreys*,[4] the Court of Appeal rejected this approach, holding that the requirement refers to 'employment which is suitable having regard to his personal qualifications, including his mental and physical capacity'.[5] The question is, therefore, given the claimant's physical and psychological condition, his training, experience and general aptitude, was he capable of that kind of employment, wherever it might be situated? Insofar as the test is concerned with physical capacity, it merely repeats a requirement already present in the legislative provision.[6] The additional and crucial element is the mental and intellectual capacity.

It is unnecessary that the claimant should have worked, continually or otherwise, in the employment which is held to be both suitable and of an equivalent standard.[7] The fact that he has done so, for even a short period, will be persuasive evidence that he is capable of following that employ-

15. See further, post, p. 329.
16. *R(I) 6/68.*
17. See e.g., *R(I) 7/68* where the fact that C was working only part-time was regarded by a Tribunal of Commissioners as irrelevant for s.60(1).
18. *R v National Insurance Comr, ex parte Mellors* [1971] 2 QB 401, [1970] 1 All ER 740.
19. Post, p. 331.
20. See *R(I) 1/72*, and *R(I) 4/77*.
1. SSA 1975, s.60(2)(b), in contrast to 'regular occupation', ante, p. 319. For the meaning of 'employer earners' employment' see ante, pp. 47–55.
2. Ante, pp. 117–119.
3. *R(I) 24/57.*
4. Ante n.14.
5. Ibid., at pp. 18–19; and see *R(I) 4/76.*
6. It was for this reason that the Commissioner had rejected such a test in *R(I) 29/52.*
7. *R(I) 48/53*; *R v Deputy Industrial Injuries Comr, ex parte Humphreys*, ante n.14.

ment. If he loses the job for reasons unconnected with the disability resulting from the employment injury (e.g., redundancy as a result of trade recession) his capacity for the employment for the purposes of section 60(1) remains unaffected.[8] The same may apply where he has not yet been able to secure such employment, because, for example, there was no vacancy in his area.[9]

c) PERMANENT INCAPACITY. The incapacity to follow the regular occupation (first limb) but not the incapacity to follow employment of an equivalent standard (second limb) must be shown to be permanent. This poses a severe obstacle for a claimant who, though at present unable to work in his regular occupation, nevertheless cannot prove that this is likely to continue for the indefinite future. The onus of proof is on him[10] and it is not sufficient to show that the loss of faculty, as opposed to incapacity for work, is likely to be permanent.[11] Even more critically, the rule penalises a claimant who, in an effort to rehabilitate himself, returns to his regular occupation and tries to cope, perhaps only for a trial period. Prior to 1953 the difficulty was alleviated only for victims of pneumoconiosis. A Regulation creates a rebuttable presumption that such a person satisfies the 'permanent' condition if he has received advice from the Pneumoconiosis Medical Board that he should not follow his regular occupation except under special conditions (e.g., that the environment is dust-free).[12] It also provides that, for the purposes of the condition, any work in the regular occupation or in a suitable employment of equivalent standard which he carried out 'between the date of development of the disease and the date of the current assessment of his disablement, or for a reasonable period of trial thereafter, shall be disregarded'.[13]

iv) 'The continuing condition'

The limited assistance given to pneumoconiosis victims did little to help the large number of other industrially disabled persons who, having courageously gone back to their regular occupations after the accident, found that they were for ever barred from the special hardship allowance. In 1953 Parliament was prompted to remedy the defect by providing an alternative test which the claimant might satisfy:[14] that he 'is, and has at all times since the end of the injury benefit period been, incapable' of following his regular occupation or suitable employment of an equivalent stan-

---

8. *R(I) 27/57*; *R(I) 42/61*.
9. *R(I) 29/53*.
10. *R(I) 7/53* where C had agreed to undergo an operation which if successful (though this was far from certain) would have enabled him to return to his regular occupation.
11. *R(I) 86/52*.
12. Now S.I. 1975/1537, Reg. 38(a) and see *R(I) 34/60*; *R(I) 35/60*; *R(I) 4/76*. The fact that at the time the 'advice' was received the claimant was already

working under the approved conditions does not prevent his relying on the Regulation. The provision is based on his 'receiving' the advice, not following it: *R(I) 69/54*.
13. S.I. 1975/1537, Reg. 38(b). For the 'date of development' see ante, p. 297; for the 'date of current assessment' see esp. *R(I) 74/54*; and for 'reasonable period of trial' see *R(I) 44/54* and *R(I) 74/54*.
14. NI(II)A 1953, s.4.

dard.[15] The new provision considerably eased the claimant's burden. If, since the time of the accident or development of the disease, he has continuously been incapable of the relevant occupation or suitable employment, there is no longer a need to make predictions as to whether the condition will persist indefinitely. He must, of course, show that throughout the period in question he was in receipt of a disablement pension. If the pension had been limited in duration to a specific date and payment had ceased, the 'continuing' condition is not satisfied even if subsequently the claimant renewed his claim, or on review his entitlement to disablement benefit was reinstated: the gap in entitlement is decisive.[16] More significantly, taken by itself, the 'continuing' condition is not able to remedy the plight of a claimant who, unwisely or otherwise, returns to work in the hope that he is fit to carry out his duties but eventually succumbs to the effects of his indisposition. The Act therefore supplements the provision by empowering the Secretary of State to make regulations that working in the relevant occupation or employment 'during a period of trial or for purposes of rehabilitation or training or in other prescribed circumstances' shall not prevent the claimant satisfying the condition.[17] In the exercise of this power, the Secretary of State has provided for the disregard of work in the regular occupation or suitable employment of equivalent standard in two different circumstances.

a) The first arises where he has worked in the relevant occupation or employment 'for the purpose of rehabilitation or training or of ascertaining whether he had recovered from the effects of the relevant injury'.[18] There has been some disagreement as to how broadly this Regulation is to be construed. Obviously it covers cases where there is some uncertainty as to the effect of the disability on the claimant's capacity and he returns to the employment to see whether he has in fact recovered sufficiently to enable him successfully to carry out the normal working activities.[19] But it frequently happens that, with or without medical advice, the injured employee returns to work under the belief that he is fit to do so, though perhaps subject to certain restrictions (e.g., avoiding the heavier aspects of his normal duties). After a period of such working, it then transpires that he cannot cope, and he withdraws. In an early case, the Commissioner decided that on such facts, the claimant should not succeed.[20] The work in question was not *for the purpose* of rehabilitation, training or ascertaining whether he had recovered. This approach has been disavowed in later cases.[1] The very object of the Regulation was to encourage injured persons to return to work without prejudicing their chance of obtaining special hardship allowance, should the attempt prove to be unsuccessful. A nar-

15. SSA 1975, s.60(4).
16. R(I) 25/57; R(I) 29/58; R(I) 33/59.
    But not where the only reason for the gap is the inability of the medical authorities (under the Determination of Claims and Questions Regulations, S.I. 1975/558, Reg. 35) to antedate a revised assessment for more than three

months: R(I) 9/66, D. Neligan, Dep. Comr.
17. SSA 1975, s.60(4).
18. S.I. 1975/559, Reg. 9(1)(a).
19. R(I) 1/69, R.G. Micklethwait, Chief Comr.
20. R(I) 81/53.
 1. R(I) 13/61; R(I) 1/69.

row construction would exclude a large number of persons whom it was clearly intended to benefit.[2] Although, therefore, in theory the authorities should consider what was in the mind of the claimant and his doctor during the period of work, there is no dogmatic insistence that the *primary* objective must have been rehabilitation. The period to be disregarded under this Regulation is *any* period during which he so works with the approval of the Secretary of State or on the advice of a medical practitioner, and any other period up to six months without such approval or advice.[3]

b) Alternatively the authorities should disregard work in the relevant occupation or employment 'before obtaining surgical treatment for the effects' of the injury,[4] that is

> 'any period during which he worked thereat and throughout which it is shown that having obtained the advice of a medical practitioner to submit himself to such surgical treatment he was waiting to undergo the said treatment in accordance therewith, *and* any other period during which he worked thereat and throughout which it is shown that he was in process of obtaining such advice'.[5]

'Surgical treatment' in this context does not necessarily include the use of the surgeon's knife – 'manipulative' treatment will suffice[6] – but it is important that throughout the period for which the disregard is claimed, he should be waiting to obtain the treatment. A doctor should have given a definite opinion that surgical treatment was desirable and that it should be carried out as soon as could conveniently be arranged. The claimant must have accepted the advice and intended to give up work as soon as the arrangement has been made.[7] A substantial period of waiting will raise the presumption that the claimant did not use reasonable zeal and expedition in trying to secure the necessary surgical treatment, and will disentitle him.[8]

v) Incapacity

Both of the conditions in section 60(1) are based on proof of an incapacity which results from the relevant loss of faculty. The onus of proving this causal connection is on the claimant,[9] though, in certain circumstances pneumoconiosis victims benefit from a presumption to that effect.[10] On the general causation issue there is little to add to the now familiar principle that the loss of faculty need not be the sole or even primary cause

2. Ibid., at para. 11, per R.G. Micklethwait, Chief Comr.
3. S.I. 1975/554, Reg. 9(2)(a).
4. Ibid., Reg. 9(1)(b).
5. Ibid., Reg. 9(2)(b).
6. *R(I) 13/56*.
7. *R(I) 81/53*.
8. *R(I) 35/57*, where the period was four and a half years.

9. *R(I) 56/51*.
10. The same circumstances in which the presumption described ante, p. 325, operates: S.I. 1975/1357, Reg. 38(a). For the effect of the presumption, see e.g., *R(I) 35/50* and *R v Industrial Injuries Comr, ex parte Langley* [1976] ICR 36, DC.

of the incapacity: it is sufficient if it is a substantial cause.[11] The test has been applied typically where the claimant has left the relevant occupation or employment and it is alleged that the incapacity was caused by his age,[12] or by a pre-existing disability,[13] rather than by the loss of faculty resulting from the industrial accident.

Greater difficulties have arisen where objectively the claimant is regarded as fit for his work, but his apprehensions for the consequences of another accident have led to a refusal to continue. Initially the authorities adopted a strict approach. They were only prepared to make special concessions for a worker who had lost the sight of one eye and who feared that another accident would result in total blindness.[14] 'No form of disablement', it was said, 'is more generally dreaded than total blindness, and few are more disastrous in their effect on earning power'.[15] But the exception could be rationalised on a more general basis. The 'incapacity' in question was not the physical condition but the neurosis which prevented the claimant from working. So, in his most recent pronouncement, the Commissioner has not limited the principle to cases of total blindness.[16] The question is whether on all the evidence the 'apprehensions' amount to an incapacity, and where, given the nature of the claimant's disability, the general conditions of work were such that there existed a reasonable basis for the inference that it would be dangerous to continue, he is entitled to succeed. These causation issues, then, turn primarily on medical evidence. For some time, the Commissioner held that a decision of the medical authorities on the point was conclusive,[17] but the view was eventually rejected by the Divisional Court.[18] The finding of a loss of faculty necessary for entitlement to disablement benefit, and from which the incapacity results, comes wholly within their jurisdiction and cannot be reviewed by other bodies. But the entitlement to special hardship allowance raises another issue – the physical consequences of that loss of faculty – and any view on this expressed by the medical authorities is of evidentiary value but is not binding on the statutory authorities, who must reach their own decision. In particular, they are entitled to have regard to the opinion of the claimant's own doctor, or of other medical experts.

vi) Amount and duration of allowance

The special hardship allowance is 'payable for such period as may be determined at the time it is granted, but may be renewed from time to time'.[19] Although the authorities have, in consequence, a discretion as to the duration of the allowance, it has been suggested that it should generally be for a substantial period (e.g., twelve months) unless there are special circumstances, most importantly where changes are anticipated in

11. R(I) 17/59.
12. R(I) 29/51; R(I) 37/51; R(I) 67/53.
13. R(I) 64/52; R(I) 49/54.
14. R(I) 61/52; R(I) 44/54. Cp. R(I) 85/52; R(I) 8/56; R(I) 6/59.
15. R(I) 85/52, para. 5.
16. R(I) 15/74.
17. See e.g., R(I) 26/60.
18. R v Industrial Injuries Comr, ex parte Ward [1965] 2 QB 112, [1964] 3 All ER 907, adopting the view expressed by O. George, Dep. Comr., in R(I) 2/65.
19. SSA 1975, s.60(6).

the standard of remuneration either in the claimant's regular occupation or in his post-accident occupation.[20] In the latter case, however, it is undesirable to select a period of less than three months.[1] When the stipulated period comes to an end, the claimant must reapply. A Tribunal of Commissioners, by a majority, has decided that the provision that it 'may be renewed from time to time' is not sufficient to impose a duty on the insurance officer of his own initiative to renew the award.[2]

The amount of the allowance is to be determined,

> 'by reference to the beneficiary's probable standard of remuneration during the period for which it is granted in the employed earner's employments, if any, which are suitable in his case and which he is likely to be capable of following as compared with that in his regular occupation'.[3]

The working of this subsection is very similar to that of section 60(1), in particular the reference to 'standard of remuneration'. As has already been indicated,[4] the relationship between the two provisions has been the subject of considerable debate, and even at the present time must remain somewhat conjectural. On the *traditional* analysis,[5] universally accepted before 1969, section 60(1), dealing with the question of entitlement, requires a comparison of the normal earnings of persons in the claimant's regular occupation and in the employment of which he is now admittedly capable, judged objectively.[6] Section 60(6), on the other hand, which only comes into play when section 60(1) has been satisfied, bases the amount of the allowance on a comparison of the personal standard of earnings of the claimant in his regular occupation and in the relevant post-accident employment respectively.[7] Thus in calculating the difference for the latter purpose, the authorities should have regard to the claimant's ability (as evidenced by regular practice[8]) to earn overtime[9] or bonus payments,[10] to any history of absenteeism[11] or to the fact that he was a seasonal worker[12] – whether these incidents of work attached to his pre-accident or to his post-accident employment. At the same time, it must be remembered that the comparison is not based on actual earnings either before or after the accident. It is concerned with probable standards of remuneration and thus may be entirely hypothetical.[13] So, as regards the regular occupation, the authorities must speculate on what would have been the claimant's standard of earnings if he had not been injured and had continued to follow that employment.[14] This means that they must obtain the relevant information on any increases in the basic earnings of persons in that type

20. *CI 81/49.*
 1. *CI 330/50.*
 2. *R(I) 6/62.* See also post, p. 588.
 3. SSA 1975, s.60(6).
 4. Ante, p. 323.
 5. See particularly *R(I) 6/68* (Tribunal decision).
 6. *R v Deputy Industrial Injuries Comr, ex parte Humphreys* [1966] 2 QB 1, [1965] 2 All ER 903, CA.

 7. *CWI 17/49; R(I) 10/55; R(I) 6/68.*
 8. Thus not where earned only spasmodically: *CI 81/49; R(I) 54/54.*
 9. *CI 81/49; R(I) 27/57.*
10. *R(I) 66/51; R(I) 47/54.*
11. *R(I) 23/51; R(I) 61/52.*
12. *R(I) 76/52; R(I) 5/53; R(I) 56/53.*
13. *R(I) 11/65; R(I) 1/68.*
14. *R(I) 14/57; R(I) 1/63.*

of employment.[15] No doubt, for the purposes of this probable and hypothetical standard, the authorities may turn at the outset to the claimant's
actual earnings,[16]•but there is an underlying principle that they should
compare 'like with like'. In *ex parte Humphreys*[17]

> C, unable to continue his regular occupation as a collier at Wrexham,
> moved to Doncaster where he secured employment as a welder-
> burner. For domestic and other reasons, he was forced to return to
> Wrexham. The standard of earnings of a welder-burner was inferior
> to that of a collier both in Wrexham and in Doncaster. But a
> welder-burner in Doncaster earned as much as a collier in Wrexham.
> The Court of Appeal quashed a decision disentitling him to the
> special hardship allowance.

For the purposes of section 60(1), he had succeeded in showing that the
standard of remuneration for a welder-burner was not equivalent to that of
a collier, whether in Wrexham or in Doncaster. To calculate the amounts
of his increase while in Wrexham, it was necessary to compare what he
would earn as a welder-burner *there* as compared with what he would have
earned if he had continued as a collier. Hence also, where a housewife was
working only part-time in her regular occupation, and could only work
part-time in the employment subsequent to the accident, it was held quite
improper to compare her pre-accident part-time earnings with what she
could have earned in her new employment if she had worked full-time.[18]

Hitherto we have used the expression 'standard of remuneration' as
though it were self-explanatory. But in fact it raises serious problems of
interpretation. We have seen that for the purposes of section 60(1), it was
construed to mean the *amount* rather than the *rate* of earnings, so that if
the claimant had to work longer hours for the same amount of money, he
would fail to establish a title to the increase.[19] In 1971, for the purpose of
calculating the amount of increase under section 60(6), the same issue was
taken to the Court of Appeal.[20]

> In his regular occupation as a coal miner, C would have earned
> £28 1s 9d for working 36¼ hours, no overtime being available. In
> his post-accident employment as a lorry driver, for a considerably
> longer period of working (which included overtime), his average
> earnings were £27 6s 2d.

On the traditional approach he would only have been entitled to the
difference between these amounts viz., 15s 7d per week. The approach had

15. *R(I) 43/52*; *R(I) 88/52*; *R(I) 11/65*. In
theory the onus of proving these
increases is on the claimant but it
would seem from the general
sentiments expressed by the
Commissioner in *R(I) 8/67* that the
analogy with civil law suits will not be
pushed very far: the insurance officer
is under an obligation (moral?) to assist
in collecting and presenting the
relevant facts.

16. See e.g., *R(I) 2/70*, and post, pp. 426–
432.

17. [1966] 2 QB 1.

18. *R(I) 7/68*, overruling *R(I) 10/66*.

19. Ante, p. 323.

20. *R v National Insurance Comr, ex parte
Mellors* [1971] 2 QB 401, [1971] 1 All
ER 740.

been challenged by the Chief Commissioner in two unreported decisions.[1]
He had taken one hour's working as the basis for the comparison. The
difference between the average earning value of each hour's work was
multiplied by the number of hours worked in the regular occupation. This
more refined approach won only the support of a dissenting judgment in
the Divisional Court[2] and was repudiated by the Court of Appeal. If taken
to its logical conclusion this form of calculation would involve comparing
not only the duration of work in the two relevant occupations but also the
domestic advantages or disadvantages, the amount of leisure within the
working period, and the relative hazards, strains and inconveniences of the
work. Not only were such matters outside the competence of the determining authorities and highly impracticable, but they were also irrelevant
to the purpose of the special hardship allowance which was concerned to
compensate *financial* losses resulting from the reduced working capacity.
The right approach was to compare the level of remuneration which would
have probably been received in a normal working week in the regular
occupation with the level of remuneration which the *claimant* was capable
of receiving in a normal week's work. Insofar as the decision reaffirms the
traditional approach, it is to be welcomed. The difficulty it creates is that,
in endeavouring to exclude from consideration the nature of the working
conditions, the judges of the Court of Appeal used language which recalled the more objective, impersonal test generally applied to the
entitlement issue under section 60(1). Thus Sachs LJ referred to 'what
would be earned each week in the employment if the claimant was
working the number of hours or shifts which are normally worked by
men employed in that grade in the place of employment'.[3] The apparently
clear distinction between the objective and subjective standards hitherto
applied to the entitlement and quantum issues respectively now seems to
have been undermined, and means that little heed is to be taken of the
claimant's own working pattern. That this will cause problems was
impliedly recognised by the Court of Appeal itself, for it was thought that
some special exception would have to be made for part-time workers.[4] If
special consideration is to be given to such workers, what of seasonal
workers, those regularly earning bonus payments, or those absenting
themselves for private contract work outside? It is respectfully submitted
that the orthodox approach prevailing before 1971, whereby the post-
accident earning capacity was assessed on a subjective basis, is to be
preferred.[5]

There is a statutory maximum to the amount payable by way of special
hardship allowance. This is, in 1977–78, £11·44, or the amount by which
the weekly rate of the claimant's disablement pension (excluding any
allowances for dependants, constant attendance or exceptionally severe
disablement) falls short of that payable for a 100% assessment.[6]

1. *CI 18/68* and *CI 29/68*, R.G.
   Micklethwait, Chief Comr.
2. Donaldson J, [1971] 2 QB 401, 413–
   415.
3. Ibid., at p. 423.
4. Ibid., per Lord Denning MR at p.
421, per Sachs LJ at p. 424, per
Buckley LJ at p. 426.
5. Cf. *Micklethwait*, p. 108.
6. SSA 1975, Sch. 4, Part V, para. 6 and
   S.I. 1977/1325.

vii) Critique

As a compromise to cope with the demand for some form of compensation
for lost earnings, the allowance, with its rather inappropriate reference to
'special hardship', and its formulation in terms of different *standards* of
remuneration in categories of occupation or employment, has proved to be
far from ideal. There is the continued uncertainty as to whether it is a
personal loss of earnings which must be established, or rather some
objective standard based on level of earnings normally to be found in the
categories of employment in question. Further, unusually in social security
law, the type of evidence on which title to the allowance and its computation are decided can rarely be secured by the claimant unassisted. So
acute has been the problem, that the Commissioners have been loathe to
regard questions of onus of proof as decisive. One has been induced,
without any statutory authorisation, to recognise some obligation in the
insurance officer to collect and present the information relevant to the
issue,[7] without making it clear how the obligation is to be enforced.
Finally, the very complexity of the law, as revealed by the length of
analysis in this work, suggests that some major review of its provisions
is desirable.[8] While not being an ideal solution, there is much to be
said for the practice in some foreign jurisdictions of basing compensation for lost earnings on an entirely hypothetical impairment of capacity:
the claimant's pre-accident earnings multiplied by his degree of disablement.[9]

D. Hospital treatment allowance

If the basic disablement benefit can be rationalised in terms of compensation for the non-material consequences of disability, expressed broadly
as the loss of enjoyment of life, the in-patient at a hospital or analogous
institution suffers that loss whether his disablement is assessed at 5% or at
100%. For this reason, the 1946 Act introduced an allowance for disablement pensioners in such circumstances: their disablement was treated as if
it had been assessed at 100%.[10] There was no logical reason for excluding
those in receipt of a gratuity and in 1953 the allowance was extended to
them.[11] The 1975 Act now provides that:

> 'where a person is awarded disablement benefit but the extent of
> his disablement is assessed for the period taken into account by
> the assessment at less than 100%, it shall be treated as assessed at
> 100% for any part of that period, whether before or after the
> making of the assessment for the award of benefit, during which

7. See esp., *R(I) 8/67*, H. Magnus, Comr.
8. Cf. *Micklethwait*, p. 110, and *Pearson*,
   para. 817.
9. See, e.g., for France, *Dupeyroux*, pp.
   485–486.
10. NI(II)A 1946, s.16. Cf. war pensions,
    post, p. 375. Hospital treatment under
    the NHS is of course free so that the

allowance cannot be regarded as a
partial indemnity of medical expenses.
Under the original Bill there was
provision for a reduction of 10s a week
from the allowance if the treatment
was 'free of charge', but this was
removed at the Committee stage.
11. NI(II)A 1953, s.3(3).

he receives, as an in-patient in a hospital or similar institution, medical treatment for the relevant injury or loss of faculty'.[12]

Originally the hospital treatment had to be of a kind approved by the Minister.[13] This requirement has since been removed, and the limitation to a 'hospital or similar institution' has been broadly construed so that, for example, rehabilitation centres are included.[14] Since the purpose of the allowance is to benefit those who are forced by their condition to remain within the institution, any degree of attendance which falls short of total residence will disqualify the claimant from being an 'in-patient'.[15] 'Medical treatment' is defined in the Act as 'medical, surgical or rehabilitative treatment (including any course of diet or other regimen)'.[16] It must be 'for the relevant injury or loss of faculty'. If the claimant is in hospital for a completely unconnected purpose he is not entitled unless in addition he receives treatment for the industrially-caused condition which is more than incidental. Thus, a claimant who was in receipt of disablement benefit for head injuries received in an industrial accident, but who was being treated in hospital for tuberculosis, could not succeed merely because he was given the occasional aspirin to relieve headaches resulting from the earlier injuries.[17]

The allowance is payable for any period of treatment as an in-patient which coincides with any part of the period taken into account by the assessment of disablement.[18] Short gaps between periods of treatment can be disregarded under a 'linking rule' which provides that 'a person who receives medical treatment as an in-patient for two or more distinct periods separated by an interval of less than a week in each case shall be treated as receiving such treatment continuously from the beginning of the first period until the end of the last'.[19] The effect of an award of the allowance will be to entitle the claimant to a 100% disablement pension for the relevant period. If the assessment was less than 20% and as a result he has been awarded a disablement gratuity wholly or partly for the period for which the allowance is payable, the weekly value of the gratuity so paid will be deducted from the pension.[20]

E. Constant attendance allowance

The remaining two allowances have in common a peculiar characteristic: entitlement, duration and quantum questions are all determined not by the statutory authorities, viz., insurance officer, local insurance tribunal, Commissioner, but by the Secretary of State.[1] The result is that in terms

12. SSA 1975, s.62(1).
13. NI(II)A 1946, s.16.
14. R(I) 14/56.
15. So where C stayed the night at home, but was in all other respects treated as an in-patient, he failed: R(I) 27/54.
16. SSA 1975, Sch. 20.
17. R(I) 68/53.
18. SSA 1975, s.62(1) re-enacting NI(II)A 1953, s.3(3) which had replaced the

earlier unsatisfactory requirement that he should have been entitled to disablement benefit when he entered the hospital: NI(II)A 1946, s.16. For the difficulties caused by the earlier rule, see CI 129/49; CI 14/50; R(I) 50/52; and R(I) 51/52.
19. SI 1975/559, Reg. 14.
20. SSA 1975, s.62(2).
1. SSA 1975, s.95(1)(b).

of legal principle much concerning this area of the social security system is shrouded in secrecy.[2] Apparently, internal guidelines for interpretation are circulated within the Department, but their contents have been jealously guarded.[3] Nor is it at all obvious why the two allowances in question should be selected for such treatment. The constant attendance allowance resembles, in policy objectives if not in detailed provisions, the non-industrial attendance allowance which is not reserved for adminis-trative decision, and, as has been seen, the statutory authorities have in that context played a fundamental role in interpreting the rules.[4]

The Act provides that where disablement pension is payable at 100%, and as a result of the relevant loss of faculty the claimant 'requires constant attendance', the pension is to be increased by an amount determinable in accordance with regulations and not exceeding the legislatively prescribed amount.[5] The Regulations effectively lay down four different standards by which the need for attendance is to be judged and for which different rates of increase are to be payable.[6]

1. Where the claimant is 'to a substantial extent dependent on [constant] attendance for the necessities of life and is likely to remain so dependent for a prolonged period', the lower of the two fixed rates is payable (in 1977–78 £11·40 per week[7]).

2. If, however, the attendance required for (1) is 'part-time only' then 'such sum as may be reasonable in the circumstances' is payable.

3. Alternatively, when 'the extent of such attendance is greater by reason of the beneficiary's exceptionally severe disablement', a sum up to 150% of the fixed rate in (1) is payable.

4. The higher of the two fixed rates (in 1977–78 £22·80 per week[8]) is payable where the claimant is 'so exceptionally severely disabled as to be entirely, or almost entirely, dependent on such attendance for the necessities of life, and is likely to remain so dependent for a prolonged period and the attendance so required is whole-time'.

It is obvious that the vagueness of these principles confers great scope on the decision-maker who, as has been seen, in this case is not challengeable. How are such phrases as 'substantial extent', 'entirely or almost entirely dependent', 'prolonged', 'exceptionally severely disabled', to be construed? No answers can be given. All that can be offered by way of commentary is based on what emerged during the Parliamentary debates and on what follows logically from the language of the Act, and the small number of regulations operating in this field. The attendance in question may be provided by anyone; it is not necessary to prove that he came in from

2. See the pertinent criticism of Carson, 126 NLJ 59, and the Appendix for Pearson.
3. Ibid., at p. 60.
4. Ante, pp. 172–176.

5. SSA 1975, s.61.
6. S.I. 1975/559, Reg. 11.
7. S.I. 1977/1325.
8. Ibid.

outside.[9] But if the claimant is a hospital in-patient, he is entitled only if the treatment he receives there is not provided free.[10] It is unnecessary to show that the claimant actually *receives* the attendance; the statutory criterion is based on need.[11] The highest standard (4. ante) was introduced at the Report stage of the Bill to bring the scheme into line with war pensions,[12] and in the words of the Minister 'will take a considerable amount of attendance and nursing to qualify'.[13]

F Exceptionally severe disablement allowance

The exceptionally severe disablement allowance was introduced in 1966[14] following the recommendations of the McCorquodale Committee on the Assessment of Disablement.[15] It felt that the system then prevailing gave insufficient assistance to some of those in receipt of 100% disablement pension. The 100% assessment contained a wide range of physical conditions, and recipients differed considerably, from those who were completely helpless to others substantially short of that condition. The Committee was disinclined to modify the tariff, either by creating differentials between 90% and 100%, or by extending it to 200%–300%, as had been suggested. Nor did it find appealing the proposal that in cases of severe multiple injuries, the authorities should be allowed to aggregate separate conditions instead of assessing the total disablement. It fell back upon what was the simplest solution: adding yet one more flat-rate addition to the existing pension and allowances.

Under the Social Security Act, the flat-rate increase (in 1977–78 £11·40 per week[16]) is payable to a claimant who is in receipt of 100% disablement pension together with a constant attendance allowance under categories (3) and (4) above, and 'his need for constant attendance of an extent and nature qualifying him for such an increase' of those standards 'is likely to be permanent'.[17] Entitlement to this allowance is, therefore, geared very closely to that of the constant attendance allowance and depends on the interpretation made by the Secretary of State, but not unfortunately available.

9. Mr J. Griffiths, Minister of NI, introducing the 2nd Reading of the 1946 Bill in the House of Commons, 414 HC Deb., col. 278.
10. S.I. 1975/559, Reg. 13(1), though if he was entitled to disablement pension in the period immediately before the date he entered the hospital for treatment, the requirement does not apply for the first four weeks: ibid., Reg. 13(2).
11. Potter and Stansfield *National Insurance (Industrial Injuries)* (2nd edn), p. 95.
12. On war pensions, see post, p. 374.
13. 419 HC Deb., col. 870. The word 'exceptionally' was added to the regulation by S.I. 1966/338.
14. NIA 1966, s.6.
15. (1965), Cmnd. 2847.
16. S.I. 1977/1325.
17. SSA 1975, s.63(1).

Part eight. Miscellaneous Provisions

It is appropriate now to consider three miscellaneous matters related to claims for industrial injury and disablement benefits. The first concerns persons whose disablement results from successive accidents; the second involves rules governing the behaviour of claimants; and the third describes the position of those whose claim originally arose under the workmen's compensation legislation.

A. Successive accidents

Where a claimant's disablement results from two conditions, (injury or disease), and both are covered by the industrial injury scheme, benefit is assessed for the total disablement resulting from both. Problems will arise where a separate assessment has been made for the disability resulting from the first accident, and benefit on that basis is already payable. The fundamental principle applied to this situation is that no claimant should receive, in aggregate, more than is payable on a 100% disablement pension.[18] The principle provoked some criticisms during the Committee stage of the 1946 Bill in that it compared unfavourably with the workmen's compensation legislation under which an injured employee was not barred from successive actions.[19] The criticism, however, failed to recognise the difference between the old scheme, based on loss of earnings, and the new scheme (derived from the war pension model) based primarily on loss of faculty.[20] A disablement of more than 100% is a contradiction in terms. The principle is not to be circumvented by entitlement to a lump sum gratuity. Where, then, a claimant is in receipt of disablement pension for life and he suffers a further loss of faculty for which a disablement gratuity would otherwise be payable, the Regulations provide that:

> if the aggregate disablement exceeds that resulting from the first accident, the claimant may elect for a pension in lieu of the gratuity at a rate representing the difference between the aggregate disablement and the rate of his existing pension.[1] The aggregate pension must not, however, exceed 100%,[2] and if a maximum 100% pension is already payable for the first accident, no further gratuity or pension is payable for the consequences of the second accident.[3]

Of course, the principle so formulated takes no account of the possibility that as a result of either accident, the claimant may be entitled to increases for loss of earnings or constant attendance. The Regulations, accordingly, modify the principle.

    1. C is in receipt of disablement pension. As a result of a second accident he suffers a further loss of faculty for which a gratuity

---

18. SSA 1975, s.91(1)(a).
19. Standing Committee A Debates, cols. 350–364.
20. Ibid., at cols. 353–354.

1. S.I. 1975/559, Reg. 34(1).
2. Ibid., Reg. 34(2)(b).
3. Ibid., Reg. 34(2)(a).

would normally be payable and he is rendered permanently incapable of work. He may add the unemployability supplement to his disablement pension, as if the permanent incapacity had resulted from the first accident.[4]

2. If the aggregate of disablement resulting from the two accidents is 100%, he is entitled to a constant attendance allowance, notwithstanding that neither loss of faculty, taken by itself, would have so entitled him.[7]

3. He will not, of course, be entitled to more than one increase for unemployability, constant attendance allowance or dependants.[6]

B. Conduct of the claimant

The legislation lays down rules governing the conduct of a claimant for two independent purposes. First, as a direct instrument of social policy, it attempts to encourage greater personal safety by refusing benefit should the disability have been incurred in certain circumstances, e.g., through the exclusive fault of the injured person. Secondly, to prevent fraud and abuse, it requires the claimant to satisfy certain standards of conduct after the disability has been incurred.

i) Conduct at time of accident

Compensation systems have varied considerably in their willingness to treat certain forms of conduct as a ground for disentitling a claimant from benefit. Under the Workmen's Compensation Acts, the employer would escape liability if the injury was caused by the employee's 'serious and wilful default'.[7] After 1906, however, the doctrine was excluded in cases of serious and permanent disablement.[8] In France, benefit may be reduced for the 'inexcusable fault' of the accident victim.[9] In Germany, it may be reduced or withheld altogether for injuries caused by criminal acts.[10] In most systems there are exclusions for intentional self-injuries.[11] In Britain, there is no explicit rule comparable to these provisions, but, as has been seen, an intentionally inflicted injury will generally not be regarded as an 'accident'.[12] The lack of sanction for other degrees of faulty conduct has not been controversial. The general opinion is that the prospect of a reduced benefit is unlikely to operate as an effective deterrent.[13]

4. Ibid., Reg. 35(1).
5. Ibid., Reg. 35(3).
6. Ibid., Reg. 35(4).
7. WCA 1897, s.1(2)(c).
8. WCA 1906, s.1(2)(c).
9. *Dupeyroux*, pp. 495–503.
10. Reichsversicherungsordnung, § 554(1).
11. E.g., New Zealand Accident Compensation Act 1972, s.137; France, Codes des Sécurités Sociales, art. 467;

Germany, ante, n.10, § 503. Cp. Report of the National Committee of Inquiry into Compensation and Rehabilitation in Australia (1974), which regarded deliberate self-injury as manifesting mental illness and should not therefore lead to disqualification from benefit (para. 351(b)).
12. Ante, p. 275, cf. suicide, post, p. 343.
13. *Atiyah*, pp. 512–514.

ii) Post-accident conduct

The forms of abuse to which the industrial injuries scheme is susceptible were enumerated by the DHSS in its memorandum to the Fisher Committee:[14] the attribution of non-work accidents to the course of employment; the attribution of unrelated physical conditions to the effect of an industrial accident or disease; the prolongation of incapacity (malingering); the misrepresentation of potential earning capacity (to establish title to special hardship allowance). Most of these risks of abuse are met by the system of medical certification and, in the case of disablement benefit, determination by the medical authorities. These procedures are described elsewhere.[15] In addition, the Social Security Act and regulations made under it impose certain obligations, coupled with sanctions in the event of non-compliance.

1. 'It shall be the duty of any person claiming or entitled to injury benefit in respect of any injury not to behave in any manner calculated to retard his recovery'.[16] It has been held that in this context 'calculated' does not connote a subjective intention but rather the objective likelihood of the behaviour retarding recovery.[17] However, if the claimant is unsure whether his conduct may have this effect he may plead in defence that he failed to comply with the duty 'for reasonable cause'.

2. He must, on receipt of the appropriate notice,[18] subject himself for medical examination or treatment[19] (though this qualification cannot be imposed for a refusal to undergo a 'non-minor' surgical operation[20]).

3. The victim of an industrial accident must give notice of the accident 'as soon as is practicable after the happening thereof' to his employer.[1]

In the event of non-compliance without reasonable cause with any of these obligations, or if there has been 'wilful obstruction of, or misconduct in connection with' medical examination or treatment, the statutory authorities may disqualify the claimant from benefit for a period up to a maximum of six weeks.[2]

c. Workmen's compensation cases

The industrial injuries scheme applies only to accidents occuring or diseases developing on or after 5 July 1948.[3] Earlier cases were governed by

14. Para. 222.
15. Ante, pp. 152–155, and 308–316.
16. SSA 1975, s.90(1).
17. *R(I) 26/51.*
18. For the requirements as to what constitutes valid notice see S.I. 1975/560, Reg. 24(2).
19. SSA 1975, s.89 and S.I. 1975/560,

Reg. 24(1).
20. S.I. 1975/559, Reg. 40(6); cf. ante, p. 161.
1. SSA 1975, s.88(a) and S.I. 1975/560, Reg. 22.
2. SSA 1975, s.90; S.I. 1975/559, Reg. 40; and see *CI 242/50.*
3. SSA, 1975, ss.50(1) and 76(1).

the Workmen's Compensation Acts. In order, however, to maintain approximate equality between beneficiaries under the two schemes, state benefits are available to those with rights of compensation under the old legislation. The numbers involved are small, and, of course, are declining.[4] It is proposed therefore to give a simplified outline of the law now governed principally by the Industrial Injuries and Diseases (Old Cases) Act 1975.[5]

1. BASIC ALLOWANCE. Under the workmen's compensation legislation, those injured after 1923 were more favourably treated.[6] It was therefore felt desirable to provide a more generous supplement for earlier invalids. For such persons, a basic allowance is payable if on or after 21 March 1951 a claimant is entitled to weekly payments of compensation under the WCAs;[7] and he is totally or partially incapacitated for work.[8] In cases of total incapacity the sum payable is such as to bring the compensation up to £2·00 per week.[9] In cases of partial incapacity it is such amount as will bring the compensation up to two-thirds of the estimated loss of earnings resulting from the accident, to a maximum of £2·00 per week.[10]

2. MAJOR INCAPACITY ALLOWANCE. To quality for this allowance the claimant must be entitled, at any time since 5 July 1956, to the basic allowance or to weekly payments of compensation under WCAs for accidents or diseases occurring after 1923. In addition, as a result of the accident or disease, the claimant must be totally incapable of work and likely to remain so for at least thirteen weeks.[11] The amount payable is equivalent to the weekly industrial disablement pension for those assessed at 100% less the weekly amount of any WCA compensation and the basic allowance (if any).[12]

3. LESSER INCAPACITY ALLOWANCE. This is payable to those who are not entitled to a major incapacity allowance but who are partially or totally incapacitated and who, since 1 March 1966, have been entitled to weekly payments of compensation under WCA for lost earnings.[13] The amount payable is a proportionate

4. In 1976, supplementary allowances were being paid to 5,721 persons for accidents occurring since 1924 and to 445 persons entitled to compensation before that date: DHSS Social Security Statistics 1976, Table 23.30.
5. For the relevant regulations see (as amended) S.I. 1966/165.
6. In particular, the Act raised the maximum weekly payment from £1 to £1·50: WCA 1923, s.4(1).
7. So those who settled for a lump sum after that date may also benefit.
8. IIDA 1975, ss.2(1), 2(3)(a) and 2(3), (7).

9. Ibid., s.2(6)(a).
10. Ibid. The assessment of the normal earnings in an occupation carried on by the claimant before the accident may of course be problematic. Cases of partial incapacity are treated as total incapacity if the claimant is in fact unemployed (though not receiving unemployment benefit) and the failure to obtain work is mainly the result of the accident: IIDA 1975, s.3(3).
11. Ibid., ss.2(1), 2(3)(b), 2(7), 14(4)(a).
12. Ibid., s.2(6)(b).
13. Ibid., s.2(4).

part of the lost earnings to a maximum of £8·00 on a scale prescribed in Regulations.[14] The allowance may be accumulated with any WCA compensation up to £2·00 per week. Anything in excess of that amount is deducted from the allowance.[15]

4. ADDITIONAL PAYMENTS. The major incapacity allowance only brings WCA recipients up to the level of disablement pensions. Additional measures were therefore necessary to confer on them the highly important additions and allowances available under the industrial injuries scheme. The Social Security Act 1975, section 159, combined with the appropriate Regulations[16] treats those entitled to WCA payments on or after 5 July 1948, and who are, as a result of the relevant injury or disease, incapable of work and likely to remain permanently so incapable[17] as if they came within the general scheme for the purposes of entitlement to unemployability supplement, and the allowances for dependants, constant attendance and exceptionally severe disablement.[18]

5. DISEASES RESULTING FROM PRE-1948 EMPLOYMENT. Special provision is also made for those who subsequently became disabled through an industrial disease, but were employed in the prescribed occupation only before 1948.[19] However, the provisions do not extend to all prescribed diseases, but are restricted to those which generally take some considerable time to manifest themselves.[20] The benefits payable are similar to the major and lesser incapacity allowances,[1] to which may be added, in appropriate cases, the supplements and allowances referred to in the previous paragraph.[2]

6. ADMINISTRATION. Up to and including 30 June 1977, all claims were determined by the Workmen's Compensation Supplementation and the Pneumoconiosis, Byssinosis and Miscellaneous Diseases Benefit Boards and these bodies were wholly independent of the DHSS machinery.[3] From 1 July 1977, however, these administrative Boards were wound up and their functions transferred variously to the Secretary of State and to the statutory authorities.[4] From that date any claimant who is dissatisfied with a decision on his claim has rights of appeal similar to those of other claimants under the industrial injuries scheme.

14. S.I. 1975/1138.
15. Ibid., art. 2.
16. S.I. 1975/559, Regs. 43, 44.
17. The criteria applied are those of SSA 1975, s.13, ante, pp. 322–325.
18. Cf. ante, pp. 317, 333 and 335.

19. IIDA 1975, s.5.
20. Ibid., s.5(2), (3).
1. Ibid., s.7(2).
2. Ibid., s.7(3).
3. IIDA 1975, ss.4, 8.
4. SS(MP)A 1977, s.10.

Part nine. Death

A. Introduction

At first glance, it might appear that the position of a family whose breadwinner has been killed is not far removed from that in which he is totally incapacitated for work. In both cases, the family has lost the benefit of his earnings. But quite apart from the obvious difference that there is no longer a need to support or care for the injured person himself, there are more difficult and subtle problems which the social security system has to resolve. An injury compensation programme is not concerned with the ultimate destiny of the benefit: the earnings indemnity, and any increase for dependants, is paid to the accident victim himself. In case of death, on the other hand, benefit is payable directly to the dependant (unless he is a child) and it must be determined as a matter of policy which categories of dependency are to be recognised and for what period of time such dependency is to be presumed. In particular, guidance is required on whether the dependants are to be expected to find alternative support, for example by remarriage or by going out to work.

The Workmen's Compensation Act 1897 made provision for those wholly or partly dependent on the deceased. In the former case, the dependant received a lump sum representing the deceased's earnings over the last three years before his death or £150, whichever was the larger, but not exceeding a maximum of £300.[5] If there was no one wholly dependent on him, those partially dependent would receive a proportionate part of the stipulated amount.[6] The notion that compensation should be based wholly on the deceased's earning record without regard to the number of dependants came under sharp criticism in the ensuing years.[7] The Holman Gregory Committee, reporting in 1920,[8] was divided on the question as to whether compensation should be based on lost earnings or on need. The former was found to have created hardship in cases of large families, and yet the latter would depart from a fundamental tenet of the workmen's compensation legislation. The 1923 Act adopted a compromise solution. The lump sum payment, based on the earnings record, was retained, but this might be supplemented by a new children's allowance. Where the widow and the children were, at the death, wholly dependent on the deceased, there might be payable for each child a sum representing 15% of the average weekly earnings.[9] For those only partially dependent, a proportionate part might be claimed.[10] The total paid by way of death benefit was not to exceed £600.[11]

The replacement of workmen's compensation by the industrial injury scheme which was not, at least as originally conceived, based on earnings, meant that the method had to be abolished. Beveridge proposed to replace

5. WCA 1897, Sch. 1, para. 1 (a)(a).
6. Ibid.
7. E.g., Departmental Committee Report on Workmen's Compensation (1904), Cd. 2208.
8. Departmental Committee Report on Workmen's Compensation, Cmd, 816.
9. WCA 1923, s.2(a).
10. Ibid., s.2(b).
11. Ibid., s.2, proviso.

it by a lump sum 'industrial grant' which would supplement a widow's ordinary, non-industrial, benefit (thus maintaining the differential between the industrial and non-industrial schemes) and which would extend to other dependants.[12] The government accepted that special provision should be made for fatal cases resulting from industrial accidents or diseases but was not attracted by the idea of a lump sum.[13] It therefore proposed, and subsequently introduced, a pension, analogous to that payable to non-industrial widows:[14] an initial high flat-rate benefit (earnings-related supplements being added in 1966) for the first six months, which would fall to one level if the widow had children to care for or was otherwise deemed incapable of joining the labour market, and another if she did not come within either of these categories. Differentials between the industrial and non-industrial schemes were preserved not only by somewhat higher payments to the industrial widow but also by the much broader provision for other adult dependants, including the widower. The concept of dependency implicit in these provisions compares favourably with their equivalents in foreign systems,[15] but the amount payable is usually less generous, and for certain categories of dependants has been much eroded by inflation. In France a widow's pension is generally 30% of the deceased's average earnings,[16] while in New Zealand it is 50% of what would have been paid by way of earnings-related compensation to the deceased if he had been totally disabled, plus a lump sum of $1000.[17] To analyse the British system, it is proposed first to described the general conditions of entitlement, then to consider separately the various benefits available.

B. Death caused by industrial accident or disease

Industrial death benefit is payable if 'the earner dies as a result of the injury',[18] which of course must have been caused 'by accident arising out of and in the course of his employment' or a prescribed disease. The claimant must first satisfy the ordinary test of an employment accident (or prescribed disease) on principles already described. The problem arising for particular attention here is that of causation.

i) Instantaneous death

Although the Act envisages a chain of causation, accident – injury – death, the death may be instantaneous. In other words, the accident will be

12. Para. 334.
13. Social Insurance, Part II, para. 30.
14. Ante, pp. 230–239.
15. In general foreign systems cover a narrower range of relatives and do not include the 'housekeeper'. For France, see Dupeyroux, pp. 440–443; for Germany, Reichsversicherungsordnung, §§ 614–615. Predictably the coverage under

the New Zealand scheme is very broad, extending to 'each person ... who was totally or partially dependent on the deceased' at the time of the accident: Accident Compensation Act 1972, s.123(1)(c).
16. Dupeyroux, p. 492.
17. Accident Compensation Act 1972, ss.123(1)(a)(i) and 124(a)(i).
18. SSA 1975, s.50(2)(c).

constituted by the death. In such circumstances, it must be established that it was the condition of the employment which substantially caused the death rather than a pre-existing condition.[19] If the deceased committed suicide, that will be sufficient to take the death outside the employment risk,[20] but, adopting a principle from workmen's compensation law,[1] the Commissioners apply a presumption against suicide. The onus is on the insurance officer to rebut the presumption by 'convincing evidence' that the circumstances of death could be satisfactorily explained only by suicide.[2]

ii) Non-instantaneous death

Where the death is not coincidental in time with the accident, the problem becomes solely one of causation. The onus is on the claimant to show, on the balance of probabilities, that the industrial injury 'plays a material part in bringing about death; it may cause death or contribute to or precipitate death or materially accelerate it'.[3] The injury must be the *causa causans* rather than a *causa sine qua non* of death;[4] but need not be the direct cause. In *CI 142/49*,

> D, suffering from dermatitis, a prescribed disease, attended a hospital for treatment of the condition. He subsequently died, inter alia, from pneumonia. It was held that the dermatitis had caused a general lowering of D's resistance to pneumonia which may have been attributable to stripping for examination as part of the treatment for dermatitis in the hospital.

Of course, the chain of causation will be broken if some new cause intervenes and supersedes the effects of the industrial accident or disease.[5] One unfortunate instance of this may be suicide. The 'voluntary' quality of this act will be sufficient to constitute a *novus actus interveniens*, but the dependant may nevertheless succeed if he is able to establish that the state of mind conducive to the suicidal act was itself the result of the industrial accident.[6] This may occur, for example, where the accident causes brain damage, changes the mental disposition of the deceased, intensifies a pre-existing nervous condition or brings about an immediate change in the employee's psychological state which develops into insanity.[7]

The question whether the death resulted from the injury is one of fact. In deciding the issue, the statutory authorities are not bound to follow the opinions of medical boards or any independent witness but must form their own independent judgment on all the evidence available. For guidance, there exists a large number of reported Commissioner's decisions which analyse the relationship between death and certain

19. See, e.g., *R(I) 13/54* and *R(I) 16/56*.
20. *R(I) 42/59*.
1. E.g., *Southall v Cheshire County News* (1912) 5 BWCC 251, CA.
2 *CSI 23/50* and *CI 113/50*.
3. Per J.S. Watson, Comr, *R(I) 9/67*,

para. 13, and see *R(I) 54/52*.
4. *R(I) 14/51*.
5. *R(I) 54/52*.
6. *CI 172/50*; *R(I) 2/57*.
7. See the WCA cases cited in *R(I) 38/51*.

industrially caused conditions (especially pneumoconiosis[8]); but these, unlike decisions on law, are not treated as binding on the statutory authorities, as medical opinion may change in the course of time.[9]

The difficulties of proof are not to be underestimated, and in two sets of circumstances Parliament has intervened to alleviate the problem.

(a) *Seriously disabled.* If a person dies at a time when he was receiving constant attendance allowance, he is treated as if he died as a result of the injury for which the disablement pension was payable.[10]

(b) *Victims of pulmonary disease.* If (after 30 March 1977) a person dies as a result of a pulmonary disease and this occurred during a period of entitlement to disablement pension (assessed at not less than 50%) in respect of pneumoconiosis or byssinosis, the death is treated as if it were caused by the disease in question.[11]

c. Widow's benefits

i) Entitlement
A widow must first establish that she was, at the time of death, lawfully married to the deceased. This requirement is shared by the non-industrial scheme, and will be discussed in chapter 10.[12] To claim industrial benefit she must in addition establish the necessary degree of dependency on the deceased, that on the death

'either (a) she was residing with him, or (b) she was receiving or entitled to receive, or would but for the relevant accident have been receiving or entitled to receive from him periodical payments for her maintenance of not less than the prescribed amount'.[13]

Why these conditions are thought necessary for the industrial scheme but not for the non-industrial scheme is not obvious. It may be that for the purposes of the latter satisfying the contribution conditions is considered sufficiently onerous. Whatever the reasons for the difference, a widow will not find it difficult to prove maintenance, since the prescribed amount is an average weekly rate of 25p or more.[14] This, and the alternative residence condition, follow the pattern established where an increase to personal benefit is claimed for a dependant. This will be considered fully

8. These decisions are listed in Jenkins *Digest of Commissioners' Decisions* (1964), under 'Death Benefit' and analysed in Bell *How to Get Industrial Injuries Benefits* (1966), pp. 162–185.

9. *R(I) 9/67*; *R v Deputy Industrial Injuries Comr, ex parte Moore*, [1965] 1 QB 465, [1965] 1 All ER 81, CA, and see *Micklethwait*, pp. 74–75.

10. SSA 1975, s.75(1), reenacting NIA 1971, s.8(2).

11. SS(MP)A 1977, s.9(1).

12. Post, pp. 398–404.

13. SSA 1975, s.67(1).

14. S.I. 1975/559, Reg. 15. The amount has remained unchanged since 1946.

in chapter 10.[15] Such differences as exist are verbal rather than substantive.[16]

ii) Form and duration of benefit

The form of the various benefits and their duration also follow the non-
industrial model, though with some significant differences. The initial rate
of widow's pension for the first twenty-six weeks[17] after death is equivalent
to the (non-industrial) widow's allowance (in 1977–78 £24·50 per week[18]).
There is, however, no separate provision in the industrial scheme for an
earnings-related supplement, so for the industrial widow to obtain this
addition, her deceased husband must have satisfied the relevant contribution conditions for the non-industrial supplementary allowance.[19] The two
rates for the permanent pension payable at the end of the six months perio
again parallel those payable under the non-industrial scheme. T
higher rate (£18·05 per week[20]) is paid where the widow is:[1]

> *either* (1) entitled to receive allowance for a child of the decea
> family;[2] *or* (2) was over fifty at the deceased's death or was ove
> at the end of the period for which the child's allowance was p   ;
> *or* (3) was permanently incapable of self-support at the de   's
> death;[3] *or* (4) is pregnant by the deceased.

However, unlike the non-industrial scheme, there are no scaled h   ates
for those widowed between the ages of forty and fifty.[4] In cases   vered
by the higher rate, the pension is payable at £5·25 per week.[5]   chever
rate, it terminates on death, or remarriage,[6] but in the event   latter a
lump-sum gratuity is paid of fifty-two times the weekly ra   nsion to
which the widow was then entitled.[7] Payment is also suspe   uring any
period in which the beneficiary is 'living as husband and w   a man not
her huband,[8] though if she remarries following any such   he remains
entitled to the gratuity.[9]

---

15. Post, pp. 390–397.
16. The reference to maintenance by
    'periodical payments' is peculiar to
    industrial death benefit since the words
    import nothing which is not already
    implied in the general maintenance
    provisions: see e.g., *R(I) 37/54*. The
    same applies to the explanatory s.67(3)
    which provides that '(a) references to a
    widow receiving or being entitled to
    receive payments from the deceased
    are only to her receiving or being
    entitled to receive (whether from him
    or from another) payments provided or
    procured by the deceased; and (b)
    "entitled" means, in relation to such
    payments, entitled under any order of
    a court, trust or agreement which the
    widow has taken reasonable steps to
    enforce.'

17. SSA 1975,
18. S.I. 1977/
19. Ante, p.
20. S.I. 197
 1. SSA 19   ).
 2. See pe   .
 3. See p   7.
 4. Ant   and see *Pearson*, paras.
    835
 5. SS   68(3) and S.I. 1977/1325.
 6. S   s.67(2).
 7. Ibid., s.67(2)(b).
 8. Ibid., s.67(2) proviso, as amended by
    SS(MP)A 1977, s.22(4).
 9. S.I. 1975/559, Reg. 17.

D. Widower's benefit

The benefit payable to a widower has no parallel in the non-industrial scheme, and even in the case of industrial death it is not widely available, for the claimant must prove that at the time of the wife's death he was both

'being wholly or mainly maintained by her or would but for the relevant accident have been so maintained';

and

'was permanently incapable of self-support'.[10]

For the meaning of 'wholly or mainly maintained' and 'permanently incapable of self-support' reference should be made to discussions elsewhere.[11] The sex discrimination implicit in the provision is consistent with a notion, deeply embedded in social security law, and arguably anachronistic,[12] that the roles of husband and wife are not interchangeable: the husband's role is to earn, the wife's to care for the children. In Germany, the prevailing rule is more equitable, such that it satisfied the Federal Administrative Court that it did not conflict with the Sex Equality Law.[13] The widower is there entitled to a pension if he satisfies the authorities that the wife shared in the maintenance of the family.[14] In New Zealand, no distinction at all is drawn between the widow and widower: in both cases it is only necessary to prove 'dependence'.[15] The rate of widower's pension in Britain is the same as that of a widow who is not expected to work (in 1977–78 £18·05 a week[16]), but it is not terminable on remarriage or suspended on cohabitation, thus producing further evidence of discrimination.

E. Children

Two conditions must be satisfied for claims made on behalf of children of the deceased. The first is equivalent to that imposed for the purpose of an increase to personal benefit.[17] At the time of his death, the deceased must have been residing with the child, or have been making contributions at the requisite rate to the cost of providing for him.[18] The second draws on the principles governing entitlement to child benefit. At the time of death, the deceased must have been entitled to child benefit in respect of the child (or be treated by regulations as having been so entitled).[19] The death benefit is then payable to any person who after the death becomes so

10. SSA 1975, s.69(1).
11. Post, pp. 393–397 and 397. respectively.
12. Cf., *Walley*, pp. 206–207, 241.
13. BVerfG, 24 July 1963, I BVL 11/61.
14. Reichsversicherungsordnung, § 593.
15. Accidents Compensation Act 1972, s.123(1)(a).
16. SSA 1975, s.69(1) and S.I. 1977/1325.
17. Post, pp. 385–386.

18. SSA 1975, s.70(4), incorporating s.65(1), on which see post pp. 393–397.
19. SSA 1975, s.70(1) as amended by CBA 1975, Sch. 4, para. 25. The 'deeming' Regulation (S.I. 1975/559. Reg. 16(2) as amended by S.I. 1977/342, Reg. 7(4)) includes children aged 16–19 otherwise not so qualifying. For entitlement to child benefit, see post, chap. 11.

entitled (or is treated as being so entitled).[20] Where there is more than one
such person, priority is given to the surviving spouse.[1] The needs of a
widow are likely to be greater than those of other claimants, and should
she be entitled to receive benefit for the child,[2] it is payable at a higher rate
(from 3 April 1978 for each child £6·10 per week); for other cases, there is
a lower rate (from 3 April 1978 for each child £2·20 per week).[3]

F. Parents and other relatives

The harmonisation of provisions for dependants in social security legislation has never been made complete. There are several important
differences between the rules governing the entitlement of parents and
other relatives to industrial death benefit and those conferring increases
for such persons on claimants to personal benefit. In particular, the former
introduce a degree of dependency which is less than that required elsewhere. As will be seen, parents and certain relatives are generally entitled
to a gratuity if they were being maintained 'to a substantial extent' by the
deceased. Moreover, the range of dependants who may claim in the event
of an industrial death is far wider than under other circumstances. The
remarkable feature of the provisions under discussion is that the sums
payable have remained static since 1946. This would appear to be one of
those instances where an overt policy of harmonisation would have
deprived existing beneficiaries of their rights and where the government
has seen fit to whittle away the differences by allowing inflation to erode
the value of the relevant benefits.[4] Whatever be the justification for the
policy, its effect has been to leave the rules in a state of great complexity, as
well as to render them unreal in their assumed fulfilment of certain needs.
The 1975 Act, to a large extent, classifies parents and relatives separately.
In fact there is a sufficient overlap of provisions to justify treating them
together. Such differences as do exist will be described as and when they
arise.

i) Persons entitled

A step-parent is included in the notion of 'parent',[5] and according to the
Act 'in a case where the deceased was illegitimate' it also includes his
mother.[6] The position of the natural father is obscure. He is not explicitly
excluded by this provision, which does not purport to define exhaustively
who may be considered a parent, but there is a common law principle that
a 'parent' does not include the natural or putative father of an illegitimate
child.[7] However, should he fail to qualify as a 'parent', such a person may

20. SSA 1975, s.70(1), as amended by
CBA 1975, Sch. 4, para. 25.
1. SSA 1975, para. 1(c). Other priorities
can be determined according to S.I.
1975/559, Sch..7.
2. The rate also applies where the widow
is entitled to death benefit, and has not
ceased to reside with the child, but the
claim is made by another person: S.I.

1975/559, Reg. 23A (inserted by S.I.
1977/342, Reg. 7(6)).
3. S.I. 1977/1328.
4. Cf., *Pearson*, p. 183.
5. SSA 1975, s.71.
6. Ibid.
7. *Butler v Gregory* (1902) 18 TLR 370,
DC; *Re M* [1955] 2 QB 479, [1955] 2
All ER 911, CA.

yet be entitled as a 'relative'. For the purposes of this latter concept, the categories of relationship permitted for an increase of personal benefit (listed in chapter 10[8]) are applied to industrial death benefit, and include a person who is such a relative by adoption or would have been such a relative if 'some person being illegitimate had been born legitimate'.[9] Of course, the classifications of spouse, parent or relative are mutually exclusive, so that an individual can claim under only one of these heads.[10] A person who was a child at the time of death (or was a posthumous child of the deceased[11]) may nevertheless qualify in his own right as a 'relative', but only from the time when he ceases to be a child[12] and can prove that he was at the time of death, and when he ceased to be a child, permanently incapable of self-support.[13]

ii) Pensions

If at the death, the parent or relative was being wholly or mainly maintained by the deceased, or would but for the accident from which the death resulted have been so maintained,[14] he is, subject to qualifications which will follow, entitled to a pension.[15] 'Wholly or mainly' here means contributing 50%–100% of the actual cost of maintaining the person in question.[16] An impression of generosity may have been given in the last paragraph by the range of persons entitled to claim, but this is rapidly contradicted by two major qualifications. In the first place, there is, tucked away in a Schedule to the Act, a rule that not more than one relative can claim a pension[17] and even he will not qualify if a pension is currently being paid in respect of the same death to a widow, widower or parent.[18] In any such case, as will be seen, a dependant who otherwise satisfies the conditions may be awarded a gratuity. Secondly, the amount of the pension (£1·00 per week,[19] or if two parents living together £0·75 each[20]) has remained constant since the introduction of the scheme in 1946. Even these sums are maxima. There is a statutory qualification that the pension shall not exceed the rate of weekly contributions which the deceased was in fact making to the claimant's maintenance.[1] The absurdity of this provision requires little elaboration. In what circumstances 50%–100% of

---

8. Post, p. 390.
9. S.I. 1975/559, Reg. 18.
10. SSA 1975, s.72(6).
11. Ibid., s.72(8), though in this case the conditions for entitlement are somewhat modified: see S.I. 1975/559, Reg. 19.
12. As defined by CBA 1975, viz., under sixteen or aged sixteen to nineteen and undergoing full-time education: cf., post, chap. 11.
13. SSA 1975, s.72(7) (the double condition is the probable meaning of an obscurely-worded provision). For the interpretation of 'permanently incapable of self-support' see post, p. 397.
14. Effectively the claimant must establish

the fact of maintenance at the time of the accident. The reference to hypothetical maintenance does not cover cases of future possible (but not actual) dependency: CI 38/50; 6/50 (II). It is therefore less generous than the tort action under the Fatal Accidents Act 1976 (cf. Ogus Law of Damages (1973) pp. 265–266).
15. SSA 1975, ss.71(2) and 72(2).
16. S.I. 1975/559, Reg. 33(1), (2). For the rules on calculating maintenance see post, pp. 393–397.
17. SSA 1975, Sch. 9, para. 2.
18. Ibid., para. 3.
19. Ibid., s.72(2).
20. Ibid., s.71(5)(a).
1. Ibid., s.74(1)(a).

maintaining an individual will today cost less than £1·00 per week may best be left to the imagination!

iii) Gratuity

Fulfilment of the alternative, lesser, degree of dependency may entitle the claimant to a lump sum gratuity. It must be established that at the time of death, or the accident leading to it, the parent or relative was 'being to a substantial extent maintained by the deceased'.[2] The latter phrase is defined by the Regulations as being not less than 25p a week.[3] If it is surprising to learn that substantial maintenance can be constituted by so derisory an amount, the answer is that the rate in question was that originally prescribed in 1948. The sum of £52 payable by way of gratuity has also remained constant.[4] As was seen in the last paragraph, there are many who may satisfy the 'wholly or mainly maintained' criterion but who are not entitled to a pension. If the reason is that the relative was ousted by the prior claim of a widow, parent or other relative, a gratuity of £104 is nevertheless payable.[5] In other cases a weekly allowance of £1·80 is payable for a maximum of thirteen weeks.[6] Analogous to the rules on pensions, the Regulations ensure that the gratuity does not exceed a prescribed number of weekly contributions by the deceased to the maintenance of the dependant. For gratuities payable in lieu of pensions the maximum is 156 times the weekly rate of contributions;[7] for all other gratuities the multiplier is 104.[8]

G. Women having care of children

A woman having care of a child or children in respect of whom the deceased was entitled (or treated as entitled) to child benefit may also claim.[9] She must prove that at the date of death she was both residing with and was being wholly or mainly maintained by him.[10] Benefit is in the form of a weekly allowance payable as long as the care of the children continues, but ceasing on marriage or remarriage and suspended during a period of cohabitation.[11] It is sad to report that here, as with parents' and relatives' benefits, the sum payable (£1·00 per week[12]) has remained constant since 1946. Again it can only be assumed that the more favourable position of an industrial 'housekeeper' has been deliberately allowed to erode through the process of inflation.

2. SSA 1975, ss.71(1), 72(1)(b).
3. S.I. 1975/559, Reg. 33(3).
4. SSA 1975, ss.71(5)(b), 72(5)(a).
5. Ibid., Sch. 9, para. 4(2).
6. Ibid., s.72(5)(b).
7. S.I. 1975/559, Sch. 5, para. 1.
8. Ibid., para. 2. There are also maxima for the aggregate of gratuities payable for any one person's death: parent's gratuities must not exceed £78 and for relatives £52, or £104 if a pension is not payable: SSA 1975, Sch. 9, para. 6(1)–(2).
9. On the position of such a woman under social security law generally, see post, pp. 388–389.
10. SSA 1975, s.73(1). For 'residence' and 'maintenance' see post, pp. 390–393 and 393–397.
11. SSA 1975, s.73(3).
12. Ibid.

9 War Pensions

Part one. Introduction

A. General

War pensions are almost certainly the most ancient type of state benefit. It is said that they existed in classical Greek times,[1] and in Britain their history has been traced back to the days of King Alfred.[2] The first statutory provisions, for payment of benefit to soldiers and sailors from the local rates, can be found in measures at the end of the sixteenth century.[3] Even if attention is confined to the origins of the present system of disability pensions, the story must be started during the nineteenth rather than the twentieth century. The explanation for this rich heritage is not hard to discover: it has generally been thought right to make special provision for those injured, and also for the relatives of those killed, in the service of their country. War pensions are as old as patriotism itself.

Although there has recently been some reaction to the special position and privileges of war pensioners,[4] for the most part the tendency in the last hundred years has been to improve their position; this was particularly marked in the two World Wars, when Parliament frequently discussed the subject and urged the government to make more generous provisions. It may be that the comparative absence of armed conflict in the last thirty years, and the consequent reduction in the number of claimants, will be responsible for a gradual decline in the special position of war pensioners. While in the year 1947 to 1948, 1,112,908 pensions were in payment, at the end of 1976 there were only 413,000 pensions being paid.[5] However, despite the reduction in numbers, expenditure on war pensions in the five financial years 1971–72 to 1975–76 nearly doubled.[6] This represents a higher annual cost than the payment of industrial injuries benefits.[7] It may, therefore, be concluded that, notwithstanding changing attitudes to

---

1. See the reference to Solon's observation in Plutarch's *Lives* made by Mr J. Manders, 401 HC Deb., col. 1519.
2. Halsbury *Laws of England* 3rd edn., Vol. 39, p. 153, n.(d).
3. E.g., 35 Eliz. 1, c.4 (1592–93); 39 Eliz. 1 c.21 (1597–98); 43 Eliz. 1 c.3 (1601).
4. See the discussion in Standing Committee B Debates on the Social Security Benefits Bill 1975, col. 149.
5. The figures are taken from the 23rd Annual Report on War Pensioners, 1948, HC 10 (covering the period 1 April 1939 to 31 March 1948), and the Report for 1976, HC 472.
6. Annual Report for 1976, Table 2.
7. See DHSS Annual Report 1975, Cmnd. 6565, para. 7.9

war pensions – inevitable thirty years after the last world war – this benefit
will remain of significance for some years.

In this introductory part of the chapter, there is an outline of the
modern history of war pensions and an examination of the reasons for their
special position in the social security system. There is also a very brief
treatment of their administration; this discussion will illustrate some of the
peculiar features of these pensions which distinguish them from other
benefits. Parts Two and Three are respectively concerned with the rules
regarding entitlement to, and the assessment of, war pensions. Part Four
deals with those payable on the death of a member of the forces, and Part
Five with some miscellaneous rules. Part Six discusses very shortly other
comparable schemes providing pensions for persons outside the regular
forces.

B. History

During the early nineteenth century, the Commissioners of the Chelsea
Hospital were responsible for the award of disability pensions to soldiers
wounded in combat. Admission to the Hospital entailed forfeiture of the
pension, but the Commissioners had discretion under statute to reaward it
on discharge.[8] From 1846 payment of pensions was made by the Secretary
of State for War. There was no provision at this time for widows and
children; the first move in this direction was the institution of the Patriotic
Fund by voluntary subscription in 1854, under which small pensions
might be paid to them.[9] During the later part of the century entitlement to
pensions was put on a more legal footing; since then awards have been
regulated by the terms of the Royal Warrants in the case of soldiers, and by
Orders in Council in the case of navy personnel and marines.[10] The Boer
War was responsible for a further development: for the first time, disease
attributable to war service was compensated in the same way as physical
injury.[11]

War pensions became a crucial problem in the course of the First World
War. They were frequently debated in Parliament; the political parties
vied with each other to initiate measures to improve the lot of the war
wounded and bereaved, so much so that alarm was expressed that the
subject might be dominated by party considerations, and so lend itself to
corruption.[12] Many changes were made in the rules concerning entitlement to pensions, and also, and perhaps more importantly, with regard to
their administration. In this latter respect these changes have for the most

8. Chelsea and Kilmainham Hospitals
   Act 1826, ss.10, 24.
9. The Patriotic Fund was put on a
   statutory basis by the Patriotic Fund
   Reorganisation Act 1903.
10. Orders in Council regulating navy
    personnel disability pensions are
    passed under the Naval and Marine
    Pay and Pensions Act 1865; for army
    soldiers, pensions are paid under the

Pensions Pay and Yeomanry Act 1884.
Air force disability pensions are paid
by orders made under the Air Force
(Constitution) Act 1917, s.2.
11. Compare the more cautious treatment
    of disease in the industrial injuries
    system, ante, pp. 293–297.
12. See the motion introduced by Sir M.
    Barlow, 108 HC Deb., col. 333 ff.

part survived the last fifty years, so that despite the improvements to the system during the Second World War, the years 1914–18 were perhaps the most influential in the development of war pensions.

In 1914, pensions were administered by four authorities: the Chelsea Commissioners, the War Office, the Admiralty Commissioners (for navy pensions) and the Royal Patriotic Fund Corporation.[13] Considerable disquiet was expressed at this dispersal of authority; in particular, the Chelsea Commissioners, who were responsible for the award of army pensions under the terms of the Royal Warrants, were subjected to criticism.[14] It was irksome to MPs that decisions on entitlement were not subject to any appeal and that no Minister was answerable for them. The mischief suggested its own remedy. Responsibility was transferred to a new Ministry of Pensions.[15] From that time, decisions were taken in the name of the Minister, and shortly afterwards an appeal tribunal was formally constituted.[16] The latter development did much to dispel anxiety concerning the concentration of power in the hands of the Minister. Legislation passed at the end of the First World War established a legal right to receive a war pension, once it had been awarded by the Minister.[17] Before this payments had been discretionary. (It has, however, never been clear whether there is a legal right to the pension, prior to the Minister's decision.) With regard to the conditions of entitlement, the major changes were: a disability aggravated by war service (as distinct from one attributable to service), attracted a full pension instead of the previous four-fifths award; a claim could be made by a widow in respect of the death of her husband which was not in itself attributable to war service, provided that he was then in receipt of a pension.[18] The principal alteration in the rules of assessment made during the same period was that pensions were from then on to be assessed with regard to the degree of *physical disability itself* rather than the loss of earning capacity. This remains the basis of their assessment.[19] Alternative pensions, as they were then known, could be awarded to compensate for the claimant's loss of earning capacity.

Claims for a disability pension in respect of service after 30 September, 1921, were transferred back to the Chelsea Commissioners and the other authorities which had administered them in 1914.[20] Now all claims with regard to service between that date and 3 September, 1939 (the outbreak

13. At this time the Patriotic Fund enjoyed Royal patronage and title, a fact which emphasised the importance of war pensions in popular feeling.
14. They were even termed, 'some kind of mystery board or secret society', 80 HC Deb., col. 1989.
15. Ministry of Pensions Act 1916, s.2; further powers were given to the new Ministry by the Naval and Military War Pensions, &c. (Transfer of Powers) Act 1917. See post, pp. 512–513, on the history of the Ministry.
16. War Pensions (Administrative Provisions) Act 1919, s.8.
17. War Pensions (Administrative Provisions) Act 1919, s.7; War Pensions Act 1920, s.8. See also Pensions Appeal Tribunals Act 1943, s.11.
18. The changes were introduced by the Royal Warrant 1917. See the 1st Annual Report of the Minister of Pensions, 1918, Cmd. 14.
19. See post, pp. 370–376, on rules of assessment.
20. War Pensions Act 1920, s.1.

of the Second World War) are handled by the Ministry of Defence.[1] The inter-war years saw, not surprisingly, a decline in the importance of these pensions. The appeal tribunals set up in 1919 did not have jurisdiction over claims brought after September 1921 and, in an attempt to achieve finality, it was provided that awards under the 1919 Royal Warrant were final and unreviewable.[2]

The outbreak of the Second World War, and the consequent increase in claims, necessitated the retransfer of administration to the Ministry of Pensions, which with its departmental successors has ever since then remained responsible for war pensions.[3] From 1939 criticism of the entitlement rules mounted and several changes were made in response. By far the most important was the imposition in some cases of the burden of proof on the Ministry to show that the disablement was neither attributable to, nor aggravated by, service.[4] The claimant was given the benefit of any doubt on this question. It is interesting that a similar relaxation of the law occurred at much the same time in the United States of America.[5] This strong presumption in favour of the claimant is without parallel in the British social security system.[6] Another change enabled claims to be made more than seven years after the termination of the service, though here the claimant has to satisfy an initial evidential burden.[7]

The Royal Warrants issued during this war limited entitlement to injuries due to *war* service. By the Warrant of 1949[8] pensions could be awarded for disablement occasioned in peace-time service, and, with some qualifications, service in the Territorial and Reserve Forces.[9] The other principal development since 1945 has been the provision of additional benefits for seriously injured servicemen and their dependants, often to cover loss of earning capacity. These have generally been the same as the increases to disablement benefit for industrial injuries.[10]

One of the constant features of the war pensions' schemes has been that the provisions regarding entitlement and assessment are to be found not in statutes, but in Royal Warrants and Orders. This has been criticised, largely on the ground that it prevents MPs from moving amendments to the schemes.[11] But traditionally it has been part of the Royal Prerogative to make dispositions and arrangements for the armed forces, and attempts to

---

1. One odd consequence of this is that the Parliamentary Commissioner for Administration has no jurisdiction to investigate complaints of maladministration with regard to the award of pensions for this period: see Parliamentary Commissioner Act 1967, Sch. 3, para. 10(a), and 1st Report of the PCA for 1967–68, HC 6, para. 28.
2. War Pensions Act 1921. However, the Commissioners could, and the DHSS still can, make a discretionary award under the terms of the Dispensing Warrant of 1884.
3. See post, pp. 571–574, for the history of the Ministry and the DHSS.
4. The law on the burden of proof is fully discussed, post, pp. 365–369.
5. See Fitzgibbons, 31 Iowa L. Rev. 1, pp. 13–16.
6. For the weaker presumptions in the claimant's favour in industrial injuries cases, see ante, p. 287 discussing SSA 1975, s.50(3)), and p. 296 (discussing SSA 1975, s.77(3)).
7. Royal Warrant (RW) 1964 Cmnd. 2467, Art. 5: see post, p. 368.
8. RW 1949, Cmd. 6499.
9. See now RW 1964 Art. 4(4).
10. Ante, pp. 317–335.
11. See e.g., Mr W. Dobbie, 391 HC Deb., col. 731.

regulate war pensions by statute – beyond the necessary administrative and tribunal provisions – have always failed.[12] However, section 12 of the Social Security (Miscellaneous Provisions) Act 1977 now provides that war pensions may be governed by Orders in Council, and that these Orders are to be issued as statutory instruments and laid before Parliament. This procedure should ensure more scrutiny of the content of the pensions schemes, and perhaps prefaces a consolidation of the present instruments regulating the benefits for the three services.[13]

c. Policy

Mention has been made of the privileged position of war pensioners. Not only is there the strong presumption in certain cases that a serviceman suffering from a disability is entitled to a pension, but the level and range of awards is wider than that afforded by other benefits for people suffering from similar disabilities. The most obvious analogy is industrial disablement benefit, which also compensates for a mere disability, not necessarily related to loss of earning capacity.[14] War pensions compare favourably with this benefit, however, in the matters of burden of proof, the absence of any requirement that the injury be attributable to an 'accident' as distinct from a continuous process of events,[15] the concept of 'war' or 'service risk' wider than that of 'course of employment',[16] and the range of allowances which supplement the basic disablement benefit in the two cases. It is only relatively recently that the popular appeal of this privileged position has been doubted; in a recent poll it was found that 82% of those interviewed thought that all disabled people should be given the same benefits irrespective of the cause of their handicap.[17]

Two explanations may be adduced for the traditional preferences given to war pensioners. In the first place, the force of popular sentiment cannot be overestimated. It is this which was responsible for the frequency of Parliamentary debates and questions in both wars. In the First World War the facts that the numbers involved were so large, and that frequently the wounded or killed would be conscripts, reinforced the general feeling that those disabled and their families should be generously treated.[18] This political factor has been reinforced by the pressure exerted by the British Legion (now the Royal British Legion) and other ex-servicemen's organisations.

---

12. See the Service Disability Pensions Bill of 4 December 1962, introduced by Opposition backbenchers, and the similar Bill of 16 December 1964, introduced by Labour backbenchers.
13. RW 1964 (army); Order in Council of 25 September 1964 (navy); Order by HM 1964, Cmnd. 2472 (air force). These are all printed in 1964 Statutory Instruments published by HMSO.
14. Ante, pp. 305–307.
15. Cp., for industrial injuries, ante, pp. 273–275.
16. Cp., ante, pp. 276–286.
17. See Mr D. Price, in Standing Committee B Debates on the Social Security Benefits Bill 1975, col. 149.
18. Nothing else would have been compatible with Lloyd George's pledge in 1918 to make 'a fit country for heroes to live in'.

Secondly, it is argued[19] that many of those who are injured in, for example, an industrial accident will have a right of action in tort against the person responsible for the injuries. This certainly accounts for many of those injured in factory and traffic accidents. But a serviceman has generally no right of action in respect of injuries suffered while in combat or in training. Section 10 of the Crown Proceedings Act 1947 provides that neither a member of the armed forces on duty nor the Crown shall be liable for injuries suffered by another member of the forces, if the latter is on duty and the Crown certifies that the injury (or death) will be treated as attributable to service for entitlement to a pension.[20] This argument is analogous to those which were used to justify the special provision for those injured in industrial accidents. The introduction of workmen's compensation in 1897 was partly justified because of the then limitations on common law claims, in particular the defences of volenti non fit iniuria and common employment.[1]

Although this second argument cannot be entirely ignored, it does not seem convincing. Firstly, it is not obvious why greater state provision should be made for those whose common law rights of action are excluded by special defences, whether statutory or common law, than for those who never have any right at all. If the emphasis is placed on the criterion of need, as it arguably should be, there seems little reason for putting those injured in service in any special position with regard to state benefits. Moreover, this second argument is wholly irrelevant to the justification for another legal privilege of some war pensioners, the exemption from estate duty, and now capital transfer tax, of the estates of those who have died from wounds inflicted on active service.[2] This suggests that the matter is really one of the popular sentiment that those who have been wounded or die in the service of their country are entitled to some special measure of compensation from the state.

D. Administration

The special position of war pensions has hitherto been discussed in terms of the rules of entitlement, but it is also reflected to some extent in aspects of their administration, now the responsibility of the Department of Health and Social Security.[3] First, the Secretary of State is assisted by a

---

19. See the letter by the National Chairman of the Royal British Legion to *The Times*, 4 February 1975.
20. This does not mean, however, that an injured soldier, or the family of a dead soldier, is assured of a pension or tort damages. In *Adams v War Office* [1955] 3 All ER 245, [1955] 1 WLR 1116, it was held by Glyn-Jones J that the issue of a certificate only enabled a claim to be made on the basis of attributability; it did not entitle the claimant to a pension, and he would

fail if the other conditions imposed by the Royal Warrant were not satisfied.
1. See *Atiyah*, pp. 316–317.
2. The estate duty exemption which dates from 1894 is discussed by Dymond *Death Duties* (15th edn), pp. 1172–1185. For capital transfer tax, see Finance Act 1975, Sch. 7, para. 1.
3. For the changes in the government departments responsible for war pensions, see chap. 14, post, pp. 572–573.

Central Advisory Committee on War Pensions, and by local war pensions committees,[4] the composition and work of which are discussed in the general chapter on administration of benefits.[5] Here it may be emphasised that part of the function of the local committees is to supplement the work carried out by the war pensioners' welfare service, which was established within the Ministry of Pensions in 1948. The Department's welfare officers help pensioners with problems, and ensure they receive all the benefits and other assistance to which they are entitled.[6] This assistance, together with that of the pensions committees and ex-servicemen's organisations, probably secures a higher degree of take-up of war pensions than of any other social security benefit.[7]

Secondly, there are no prescribed claim forms or procedures, though a document is usually completed and sent to the DHSS central office at Blackpool, where claims are now handled.[8] Difficult legal problems arise when the claimant applies to an official or department which has no authority to issue certificates or make statements with regard to entitlement: if this official or department does issue a certificate of entitlement, in what circumstances, if any, is the department which does have authority bound by it? This was the issue in the famous case, *Robertson v Minister of Pensions*.[9]

> C, an army officer, wrote in 1941 to the War Office concerning his disability. A month later he received a reply to the effect that it was accepted as attributable to war service. The War Office had consulted all its branches, but not the Minister of Pensions, to whom responsibility for the award of pensions had been transferred from 3 September, 1939. Relying on the War Office's letter, C refrained from obtaining an independent medical opinion on his disability, and destroyed some relevant X-ray plates and documents. The Minister of Pensions later held that C was not entitled to a pension as his injury was not attributable to war service, and this was upheld by the pensions appeal tribunal.

On appeal from the tribunal,[10] Denning J held that the Crown was bound by the War Office's representation on which Robertson had reasonably relied and, therefore, the Minister, as another officer of the Crown, was bound by this assurance. The decisive fact here would seem to have been that between October 1921 and September 1939 the War Office had dealt

---

4. These were instituted by the War Pensions Act 1921.
5. Post, pp. 585–586.
6. Their work is discussed in detail in the Annual Reports on War Pensioners, published separately since the merger of the Ministries of Pensions and National Insurance in 1953: post, p. 513.
7. For the problem of take-up generally, see ante, p. 13.
8. Where a man dies in or is discharged from service because of an injury or disease, the papers are sent automatically to the Department for consideration of a war pension: see the Ministerial statement in 1945, 401 HC Deb., col. 970. For the claims procedure generally, see post, pp. 587–593.
9. [1949] 1 KB 227, [1948] 2 All ER 767.
10. For the appeal system, see post, p. 662.

with war pension claims, so that an applicant reasonably understood it to be the relevant department for handling them. Whatever the limits of the principle stated in this case, it at least affords some measure of protection to the citizen, bewildered by administrative re-organisation, which here the departments themselves did not appear to understand properly![11]

In practice, the decision on a claim is taken in the Blackpool central office. Where the matter involves a medical question, the decision must be taken in accordance with the certificate of a medical officer or board of officers appointed by the Secretary of State.[12] However, even here the decision is that of the Secretary of State, and not the medical officer, for the question of 'attributability' or 'aggravation' by service is not a purely medical one.[13] The particular service concerned must give the DHSS all the evidence relating to the claim, including documents concerning the claimant's medical history.[14]

There is an appeal from the Secretary of State's decision to an independent appeal tribunal, the Pensions Appeal Tribunal, which hears the case de novo. There is then a further right of appeal on law only to a nominated High Court judge, whose decisions have played an important part in the development of the rules regarding entitlement to a war pension, analysed in Part Two of the chapter.[15]

Part two. Entitlement

A. General

The fundamental principle is that a war pension may only be awarded when the disablement or death of the member of the forces is due to service.[16] There must, therefore, be some causal connection between the service and the injury or death; it is not enough that either occurred *during* service.[17] Although, as will be seen, this principle has been applied liberally for the benefit of the serviceman and his dependants, it has often been attacked as unnecessarily restrictive, particularly during the Second World War. It was contended that a war pension should be awarded in respect of any serviceman who died or suffered injury or disease while serving in the forces, irrespective of the cause of the disablement. The need to show some causal connection between service and the disability

---

11. The decision is an important and controversial one in the area of estoppel and public authorities. Denning J's approach was criticised by Viscount Simonds in *Howell v Falmouth Boat Construction Co.* [1951] AC 837 at 845. For further discussion, see Treitel, [1957] P.L. 321, 325–329, and Hartley and Griffith *Government and Law* (1975), pp. 295–297.
12. RW 1964, Art. 2(4).
13. See Denning J in *Starr v Minister of Pensions* [1946] 1 KB 345, 350–351.

14. Ibid., at p. 350.
15. Post, pp. 660–663, for the procedure before the appeal tribunal, and the right of further appeal to the nominated judge.
16. RW 1964, Art. 3. References to the Royal Warrant should be taken as including references to the same rules in the Order in Council (Royal Navy) and the Order by Her Majesty (RAF).
17. This principle is similar to that prevailing in the industrial injuries scheme: see chap. 8, ante, p. 278.

was arguably productive of too many difficult border line decisions. Manpower and time were wasted in arriving at these, and, it was said, inevitably some deserving claims were rejected.[18] The maxim, 'fit for service, fit for pension', however, never attracted the government. The White Paper of July 1943[19] rejected it partly on the ground that a disablement entirely unrelated to service should be covered by general social security provisions. Another reason was that to treat indiscriminately all disablement arising during service would be to do less than justice to those whose injury or illness was genuinely due to the dangers and risks of service. Since 1945 the fundamental entitlement principle has rarely been criticised; this is perhaps largely attributable to the more generous criteria of eligibility which were introduced towards the end of the war by the relevant Warrant and statutory orders,[20] and their subsequent treatment by the nominated judge on appeals from the tribunals.

The provisions of the Royal Warrant of 1964, now in force, distinguish between entitlement to a pension in respect of a claim made for disablement, or a death which occurs (whenever the claim is made), within seven years of the end of service, and entitlement when the claim for disablement is made, or the death occurs, more than seven years after the termination of service. The principal difference is that in the latter cases the initial burden of proof is on the serviceman, while in the former it is for the Secretary of State to show that the disablement or death was not due to service.[1]

Article 4(1) of the 1964 Royal Warrant sets out the basic conditions for entitlement to a pension on a claim in respect of disablement brought within seven years of the end of the member's service; or when the death of a member occurs within that period, whenever the claim is brought:

> 'Where, not later than 7 years after the termination of the
> service of a member of the military forces, a claim is made in
> respect of a disablement of that member, or the death occurs of
> that member and a claim is made (at any time) in respect of that
> death, such disablement or death, as the case may be, shall be
> accepted as due to service ... provided it is certified that –
>
> (a) the disablement is due to an injury which –
>   (i) is attributable to service; or
>   (ii) existed before or arose during service and has been and
>   remains aggravated thereby; or
>
> (b) the death was due to or hastened by –
>   (i) an injury which was attributable to service; or
>   (ii) the aggravation by service of an injury which existed
>   before or arose during service.'

Article 5 is concerned with entitlement when the claim for disablement

---

18. See 391 HC Deb., cols. 716 ff., esp.
    col. 827.
19. Changes in War Pensions, Cmd. 6459.
20. RW 1943, Cmd. 6489 (army); S.R. &

O. 1944, No. 99 (navy); HM Order,
1943–44 HC 7 (air force).
1. See post, pp. 365–369, for discussion
   of the burden of proof.

is brought, or the death occurs, more than seven years after the termination of service. It provides for the issue of a certificate on the same grounds as Article 4(1), except that Article 5(1)(b) prescribes that it must be certified that 'the death was due to or *substantially* hastened by' an injury attributable to or aggravated by service.[2] Another distinction is that Article 4 only covers claims made in respect of service after 2 September 1939, but Article 5 provides that a claim may be made in respect of *death* more than seven years after the end of service, irrespective of the date of that service.[3]

Under both Articles a war pension will only be awarded if it is certified, (1) there is a disablement due to, or death due to or hastened by, an injury, which is (2) attributable to, *or* (3) aggravated by service. After these conditions for entitlement have been analysed, the complex question of the burden of proof under Articles 4 and 5 is fully discussed. The last section of this Part is devoted to a short treatment of the case-law on Article 6, which provides that a pension may be reduced or withheld if the injury or death of the serving-member of the forces 'was caused or contributed to by [his] serious negligence or misconduct'.

B. Disablement

'Disablement' means physical or mental injury or damage, or the loss of physical or mental capacity.[4] A successful claim may, therefore, be made for acute hysteria or neurosis, provided, of course, that it is attributable to, or aggravated by, service.[5] 'Injury' is defined as including 'wound or disease'.[6] There is virtually no limit, therefore, to the quality or type of impairment which may entitle the claimant to a war pension, though many difficult cases naturally concern claims in respect of illness and disease where the causation issue is complex. As a consequence of the alternative definition of 'disablement', it has been held that a claimant may be entitled in respect of his injury, even though he has not suffered any loss of capacity for work or the enjoyment of life.[7] In this case, however, a nil assessment will be made until the time when the injury causes a loss of flexibility or movement in the injured limb, or some other handicap.[8]

2. Post, pp. 376–379 (death benefits).
3. Article 71(7) provides that Article 5 will only have effect with regard to deaths (claimed to be due to service in the 1914 World War) which occur after 1 October 1964. Claims for disablement in the 1914–18 war, of which there are very few, are brought under the RW 1919, Cmd. 457 and RW 1920, Cmd. 811.
4. RW 1964, Art. 1(10). The industrial injuries scheme also covers nervous shock: ante, p. 272.
5. See post, pp. 360–365, for the discussion of these conditions. Cp., the more restrictive position under the

civilians' scheme, where recovery is limited to personal injuries, post, p. 382.
6. RW 1964, Art. 1(15), cp., the provision for disease in industrial injuries, ante, pp. 293–297.
7. *Harris v Minister of Pensions* [1948] 1 KB 222, [1948] 1 All ER 191.
8. For the rules with regard to the assessment of disabilities see post, pp. 370–376. An incapacity *for work* is not a necessary condition for an award as it is for industrial injury, though not disablement, benefit: ante, pp. 299, 309.

Occasionally the question arises whether a particular disease is a separate phenomenon from another injury or illness for which a claim has already been made.[9] If an acute anxiety state is brought about by worry over a disease, in respect of which a pension is already being paid, the appropriate course is to apply for an increase in the assessment for the first disease, not to make an entirely new claim.[10] The test would appear to be whether the further condition is a separate disease rather than part of the accepted illness or injury.

c. 'Attributable to service'

i) General principles

A war pension will be awarded if it is certified that the disablement or death is due to an injury attributable to service. Before the changes introduced by the Royal Warrant of December 1943, the injury had to be '*directly* attributable to service'; the removal of the qualifying adverb was one of the relaxations introduced by the coalition government to ease the conditions for entitlement under the war pensions schemes.[11] The question whether the injury is attributable to service is one of fact, but the nominated judge will allow an appeal by either claimant or the Secretary of State if the appeal tribunal has applied the wrong principles of law in arriving at its decision.[12] A tribunal, therefore, makes a mistake of law if it holds that a particular injury or type of disease cannot be attributable to war service merely because a previous decision of the judge in another case was to the effect that that injury or disease was not then attributable to service.[13] In each case the Secretary of State (or medical board) and, on appeal the tribunal, must consider all the circumstances, and must not be bound by previous decisions regarding the same type of injury.[14]

The court's attitude on questions of attributability has been shown clearly in the 'pre-existing disposition' cases. The particular issue there was whether it should be held that a disease or neurosis was atrributable to service when the soldier's pre-existing temperament or disposition made him especially vulnerable to it. The court has consistently held that where service brought on a disease, which did not exist before, it was attributable to the service; only if the soldier's condition before service actually amounted to the illness in question, albeit a latent illness, could it be held

9. E.g., *Secretary of State for Social Services v Yates* (1969) 5 WPAR 765. (The War Pensions Appeal Reports (WPAR) are available for consultation at the DHSS, though they are not published.)

10. *Goodman JA v Minister of Pensions* (1951) 5 WPAR 13. See 5th Report of the PCA, 1972–73 HC 406, Case No. C.33/T.

11. See the White Paper, ante n. 19, and the Debate in the House of Commons introduced by Sir J. Anderson, Lord President of the Council, 391 HC Deb., cols. 716–722.

12. *Horsfall v Minister of Pensions* (1944) 1 WPAR 7.

13. See *Freeman v Minister of Pensions and National Insurance* [1966] 2 All ER 40 [1966] 1 WLR (suicide); *Kincaid v Minister of Pensions* (1948) 3 WPAR 1423 (leukaemia).

14. The same principle is followed by the Commissioner, and the medical authorities, in industrial injuries cases: ante, p. 306.

that the service merely aggravated the injury.[15] Denning J stated the principle to be as follows:

'The task of the Minister and of the tribunal is to ascertain what are the causes of the arising of the disease, not to assess their relative potency. If one of the causes is war service the disease is attributable to war service, even though there may be other causes and, it may be, more powerful causes, operating, and to which it is also attributable.'[16]

The court's refusal to evaluate the relative weight of service and other factors in bringing about the disablement, coupled with the fact that the onus of proof is on the Secretary of State in those cases where the claim is brought, or the death occurs, within seven years of the end of service, has meant that in practice the criteria for entitlement are generous. On the other hand, the court has been aware that the law does not embody the maxim, 'fit for service, fit for pension', so that in a number of circumstances a pension has been refused although the disability arose during the claimant's period of service. Three types of cases have proved particularly difficult.

ii) Anxiety states
In the first, the question has been whether an acute anxiety state was attributable to service. In one decision it was held that the strain of hard training, followed by the worry induced by orders for foreign service, might well be the precipitating cause of the claimant's acute neurosis, although there was medical evidence to the effect that he had an unstable personality.[17] On the other hand, in two cases, the nominated judge, Denning J, held that the claimant's worry about his wife's relations with other men while he was in the army, leading in both cases to acute neurosis, could not be held attributable on the facts to service.[18] The husband's enforced separation from his wife was not the cause, but only the circumstance in which the real cause of the illness, the wife's conduct, operated. It is not easy to reconcile these cases, and the latter two decisions may be thought wrongly decided in the light of Denning J's principle set out earlier.

iii) Suicide, etc.
The second difficult question is whether suicide can ever be said to be caused by service in the forces. In *X.Y. v Minister of Pensions*,[19]

15. E.g., *Baird v Minister of Pensions* (1946) 1 WPAR 169; *O'Neill v Minister of Pensions* (1947) 1 WPAR 839. Similar principles have been employed in industrial injuries cases in determining whether an accident caused an injury, to which the claimant's previous condition rendered him more susceptible, ante, p. 275.
16. *Marshall v Minister of Pensions* [1948] 1 KB 106 at 109.
17. *Hollorn v Minister of Pensions* [1947] 1 All ER 124.
18. *W v Minister of Pensions* [1946] 2 All ER 501; *R. J. v Minister of Pensions* (1947) 1 WPAR 351.
19. [1947] 1 All ER 38. The decision was followed by *Miers v Minister of Pensions and NI* (1964) 5 WPAR 673, where the deceased shot himself after worries about his army career and promotion prospects. See ante, p. 343, for the problem in industrial death benefit cases.

the deceased's fiancée attempted to persuade him to marry her while he was on embarkation leave. He refused, and shortly after his return to service, she wrote calling off the engagement; he then shot himself. Denning J held that the tribunal was right not to attribute the death to service.

However, in a more recent decision,[20] it was held that the suicide was so attributable; the deceased took his life because of the pain and anxiety resulting from a disability which was itself due to service. Edmund Davies J emphasised that each case should be decided on its own facts, and that there is no rule of law prohibiting a suicide's dependants claiming a war pension. A similar problem arises when the deceased accidently takes his own life through the administration of an overdose.

A surgeon lieutenant, who suffered from sleeplessness, took an overdose of chloral hydrate, thus straining a weak heart and thereby killing himself. Denning J held that his death was the result of an act exclusively in the deceased's personal sphere, and was not attributable to service.[1]

iv) Claimant on leave, etc.

The third line of cases where causation presents particular problems occurs when the serviceman is injured or killed when on leave, or temporarily away from camp.[2] This has been the topic of political debate as well as legal argument. The 1943 White Paper[3] stated that the Ministry of Pensions would relax its attitude to claims in respect of accidents occasioned outside the serviceman's place of duty; it would in future treat accidents sustained in the soldier's spare time, or while he was travelling to and from home on short leave, or when he was travelling between his place of duty and privately arranged accommodation (if he were allowed to live out) as attributable to war service. But an injury or illness arising during a period of full leave would not be treated as so attributable. The nominated judge, however, has pointed out that the question of attributability must be decided solely on the facts in the light of the provisions in the Royal Warrant. Thus, a bicycling accident suffered on the claimant's day-off,[4] and an accident at the claimant's home where, owing to a lack of room in the barracks, he was billetted,[5] have both been held not to be attributable to service. On the other hand, in two cases the judge held that an injury

20. *Freeman v Minister of Pensions* [1966] 2 All ER 40, [1966] 1 WLR 456.

1. *Wedderspoon v Minister of Pensions* [1947] KB 662, followed by *Monaghan v Minister of Pensions* (1947) 1 WPAR 971, (where the deceased choked after drinking bottle of raw spirit found during the Allied advance into Belgium). But cp, *Jones v Minister of Pensions* [1946] 1 All ER 312, where it was held that the mere fact that the claimant adopted a course of action

within his own control – failure to report sick – did not mean that service was not a cause of his illness.

2. There are analogous problems in the industrial injuries scheme, when the accident occurs while the employee is travelling, ante, pp. 281–284.

3. Changes in War Pensions, Cmd. 6459.

4. *Standen v Minister of Pensions* (1947) 1 WPAR 905.

5. *Ridley v Minister of Pensions* [1947] 2 All ER 437.

while on full leave was so attributable. In the first,[6] Denning J held that the injury suffered by a soldier who shot himself in the left foot while cleaning his rifle on embarkation leave was attributable to war service; in the second,[7] Ormerod J decided that the appellant shot in the back with a blank cartridge by some cadets on shooting practice was entitled to a pension, although the incident occurred while he was on leave; the decisive fact was that he was required to wear uniform which may have created the impression in the cadets' minds that he was involved in their exercise!

v) Miscellaneous cases

The court has had less difficulty in other situations. Injuries occasioned by playing a game for the serviceman's own amusement are not attributable to service,[8] nor are injuries resulting from private fights between soldiers[9] or from assaults by third parties entirely unrelated to the military character of the victim.[10] But even if the initial injury is not attributable to service, negligent treatment in hospital will enable the claimant to be considered for a pension, if he went to that particular hospital because he was a serviceman, rather than merely because it was the nearest available.[11]

vi) Critique

It is difficult to detect any clear principle or policy running through these decisions, despite the attempt by the nominated judges, particularly Denning J, to formulate one. On the one hand, they have been concerned to award a pension when the service has any real causal connection with the injury or disease, but on the other hand, they have carefully refrained from holding a claimant entitled merely because the service was a cause (*causa sine qua non*) of the disablement. The case-law sometimes resembles in its apparent inconsistency the decisions of the Commissioners interpreting the 'out of and in the course of employment' test for entitlement to industrial injuries benefit.[12] The absence of such a two-limbed test in the war pensions provisions makes the reasoning less complex than in the Commissioner's rulings, but the results are often as hard to understand. For example, it is difficult to see why a claimant cleaning his rifle on leave should succeed,[13] while a claimant suffering neurosis about his absent wife when he was actually in service failed.[14] In the last resort the decision will depend on the court's judgment how closely related the injury is to the incidents of service life.

6. *Williams H. v Minister of Pensions* [1947] 2 All ER 564.
7. *Giles v Minister of Pensions* (1955) 5 WPAR 445.
8. *Horsfall v Minister of Pensions* ante n. 12; cf., on industrial injuries, ante, p. 281.
9. *Richards v Minister of Pensions* (1956) 5 WPAR 631.
10. *Gaffney v Minister of Pensions* (1952) 5 WPAR 97.
11. *Minister of Pensions v Horsey* [1949] 2 KB 526, [1949] 2 All ER 314. See also *Buxton v Minister of Pensions* (1948) 1 WPAR 1121.
12. See chap. 8, ante, pp. 276–293.
13. *Williams H. v Minister of Pensions*, ante n.6.
14. *W. v Minister of Pensions*, ante n.18.

D. Aggravated by service

The issue whether the claimant is entitled to a pension because service has aggravated an injury, which is primarily attributable to other causes, only arises if it is first found that his injury was not attributable to service conditions.[15] The difference between an award on the basis of attributability and an award on the basis of aggravation is that in the former case the pension is paid as long as the disability continues, while in the latter, it is payable only so long as the disability remains aggravated by the service conditions.[16]

It must be certified that the disablement is due to an injury which 'has been *and remains aggravated*' by service.[17] The construction of this part of Article 4 was considered in the leading case, *Shipp v Minister of Pensions*.[18] Denning J held that it did not mean that the disablement must be found to be aggravated by service at the time the claim was made, or at the date of the Minister's decision. Such a construction would penalise those who made late claims or whose claims were handled slowly by the Ministry; the words must be read as meaning, 'and remains aggravated or remained aggravated during the period of disablement'.[19] A claim may, therefore, be made in respect of a past disablement. However, where a claim in respect of a disablement is brought under Article 5 more than seven years after the end of service, the aggravation must remain at the time the claim is made, though it need not subsist after that date.[20] In this case it is reasonable to require the aggravation to remain at this time in view of the long period which has passed since discharge from service. In all cases the tribunal is entitled to consider whether the aggravation remains at the date of the hearing before it, provided the claimant has been told that the question will be raised.[1]

The judge has held that the Secretary of State and tribunal should be reluctant to conclude that the injury is no longer aggravated by service unless the evidence is quite clear.[2] The reason is that once an award on this basis has been terminated, it cannot be revived. The award should only be terminated if the claimant is in no worse a condition than he was in before the service, or if the disease has progressed to the same extent as it would have done if the man had not been in service.[3] The tribunal may take into account the fact that the claimant is working full-time in coming to its conclusion whether the injury remains aggravated by service.[4]

Rather oddly, aggravation by service may occur before the onset of a disease. Thus, where the serving-man was so weakened by his period of service that he was unable to resist typhoid contracted on leave, his widow was awarded a pension.[5] The reasoning is that the disease, though not

15. E.g., *Baird v Minister of Pensions* (1946) 1 WPAR 1121.
16. See Denning J in *Marshall v Minister of Pensions*, ante n.16, at p. 108.
17. RW 1964, Art 4(1)(a)(ii).
18. [1946] 1 KB 386, [1946] 1 All ER 417.
19. Ibid., at p. 390.
20. RW 1964, Art. 5(3).
  1. *Ansell v Minister of Pensions* (1948) 3 WPAR 2237.
  2. *Sanders v Minister of Pensions* (1948) 4 WPAR 31.
  3. *Whitt v Minister of Pensions* (1947) 1 WPAR 343.
  4. *Collicott v Minister of Pensions* (1948) 3 WPAR 1715.
  5. *Bridge v Minister of Pensions* (1946) 1 WPAR 139.

attributable to service, was more acute because of his weakened condition. A difficult question arose in the recent case, *Sullivan v Secretary of State for Social Services*:[6]

> C was discharged in 1962 on the ground of a gastric ulcer attributable to service in respect of which he was awarded a pension. Six years later he claimed a further award on the ground of his anxiety state which arose when he gave up the French horn because of the ulcer. The Secretary of State and tribunal rejected this claim. Willis J concluded it could reasonably be held that C's anxiety state was not attributable to service; but on the alternative argument based on aggravation, the tribunal was wrong to hold that the service factors must cause a deterioration of a condition *before discharge* for an aggravation claim to be made. The aggravation, as in this case, could arise subsequently to the discharge.

As in attributability cases, the problem sometimes arises whether the serviceman's own responsibility for the course of action which leads to the disablement or death precludes a finding that service aggravated the injury.[7] In *Jones v Minister of Pensions*,[8] a hardworking officer with a strong sense of duty refused to report sick. About eighteen months later he died from cancer. Denning J held that the officer's conduct was a reasonable response to the pressures of war service, which was, therefore, responsible for aggravating the disease and so hastening his death.

E. Burden of proof

Before 1943 the burden of proof was on the serviceman. The imposition of the burden on the Minister in those cases governed by Article 4, where the claim is brought within seven years of the end of service, so that it is for him to show the absence of any connection between service and the injury, was the most important of the reforms made in that year.[9] However, under Article 5 an initial burden of proof is on the applicant, so this provision must be considered separately. One point, however, is common to both Articles: it is for the applicant to prove that there is a disablement.[10] It is only after this is shown that the cause of the disablement must be considered.

i) Claims under Article 4

The relevant provisions of Article 4 are:

> '(2) ... in no case shall there be an onus on any claimant under this Article to prove the fulfilment of the conditions set out in paragraph (1)[11] of this Article and the benefit of any reasonable doubt shall be given to the claimant.'

6. (1971), 5 WPAR 799.
7. Ante, p. 361.
8. *Jones v Minister of Pensions*, ante p. 362, n. 1.
9. See ante, p. 353, for the reforms made

in the Second World War.
10. *Royston v Minister of Pensions* [1948] 1 All ER 778.
11. See ante, p. 358.

'(3) ... where an injury which has led to a member's discharge or death during service was not noted in a medical report made on that member on the commencement of his service, a certificate under paragraph (1) of this Article shall be given unless the evidence shows that the conditions set out in that paragraph are not fulfilled.'

a) ARTICLE 4(2). The judical interpretation of this Article has undergone several vicissitudes in the last thirty years. The question is whether it imposes on the Secretary of State the general civil burden of proof – to make out his case on the balance of probabilities – or whether it imposes the stricter criminal burden of proof – to show beyond reasonable doubt that the injury was not attributable to, nor aggravated by, service. On a literal construction the latter seems the correct answer, but, as the court has observed,[12] the problem has been complicated by the connected question of the relationship between Article 4(2) and Article 4(3).

At first both the High Court in England[13] and the Court of Session in Scotland[14] took the view that the burden of proof under Article 4(2) was the criminal one. The one difference between Article 4(2) and 4(3) was said to be that under the former the issue was to be decided by weighing the evidence adduced by the Minister and the applicant, while under the latter the applicant could rely merely on the presumption.[15] But in *Miller v Minister of Pensions*[16] Denning J held that the burden imposed by Article 4(2) was only the ordinary civil one, that is, the Minister had to show on a balance of probabilities that injury was not caused by service conditions. So, although there was medical evidence in the case that it was impossible to show beyond reasonable doubt that war conditions could play no part in causing cancer of the gullet, it was ruled that the relative incidence of the disease in servicemen (approximately seven cases a year out of an average annual total of 1,700) made it clear on a balance of probabilities that the cancer was not attributable to service. In contrast, the judge said that Article 4(3) imposed the criminal burden of proof.

The previous position, however, was restored by Edmund Davies J in *Judd v Minister of Pensions*.[17]

During an exercise in the course of army service, the claimant fell from a strong rope and sustained back injuries. He continued to complain of lumbar pains which were assessed at 30% of a full disability pension. Twenty years later cervical spondylosis was diagnosed, but the Minister and the tribunal rejected any connection between this and the claimant's service, the tribunal stating that it was shown on the balance of probabilities that service had not

12. See Edmund Davies J in *Judd v Minister of Pensions*, [1966] 2 QB 580 at 591, [1965] 3 All ER 642.
13. *Starr v Minister of Pensions* [1946] 1 KB 345, [1946] 1 All ER 400; *Rowing v Minister of Pensions* [1946] 1 All ER 664.
14. *Irving v Minister of Pensions* 1945 SC 21.
15. Denning J, in *Starr v Minister of Pensions*, ante n.13, at p. 350.
16. [1947] 2 All ER 372.
17. Ante, n.12.

caused or worsened the disability. Edmund Davies J decided this was the wrong test and, on the facts, made an award.[18]

The judge stated that the opening words of Article 4(2) imposed at least the ordinary civil burden on the Minister, and that the concluding words of the paragraph would be redundant if the burden were no higher than that.

A perennial problem has been the application of the principles of proof where the aetiology of the disease concerned is unknown, and surmises about the part played by service conditions are necessarily conjectural. During the Second World War the Ministry had a list of diseases which, according to the weight of medical opinion, could not be held attributable to war service.[19] It was revised from time to time, and was used as a guide rather than as a determinant of particular applications.[20] Nevertheless, its use was criticised in Parliament, and certainly its employment was outside the provisions of the Warrant. The nominated judge has consistently ruled that the evidence must show that it is improbable that the service played any part.[1] The leading authority now is *Coe v Minister of Pensions and National Insurance*.[2]

> C claimed a pension when symptoms of Behcet's syndrome (a disease causing blindness) appeared fourteen months after he had left the Navy. The claim was rejected by the Minister as the aetiology of the disease was not known, and it seemed improbable that any service factors could have been responsible. The appeal tribunal dismissed C's appeal, but Edmund Davies J allowed it on the ground that the approach adopted by the Ministry and tribunal imposed an onus on the applicant.

Three rules were laid down to assist the Minister and tribunals in determining such claims.

> Rule 1: if the medical evidence is that nothing at all is known about the aetiology of the disease, then neither the presumption in Art. 4(2), nor that in Art. 4(3), is rebutted.

> Rule 2: if there is evidence before the tribunal to the effect that the disease is one which arises and progresses independently of service factors, then the presumption is rebuttable even if the precise origins are not known.

> Rule 3: it is not enough for the Ministry to argue that there is no evidence suggesting any connection between the onset of the disease and service conditions.

18. The usual course is for the nominated judge to remit the case to the tribunal to reconsider, but in some cases the judge himself is prepared to make an award: See *Moxon v Minister of Pensions* [1945] KB 490, [1945] 2 All ER 124. See post, p. 662, for the nominated judge's powers.

19. Sir W. Wormersley, Minister of Pensions, 391 HC Deb., cols. 796–798.

20. Sir W. Wormersley, Minister of Pensions, 402 HC Deb., col. 1644.

1. *Smith AS v Minister of Pensions* (1947) 1 WPAR 495; *Donovan v Minister of Pensions* (1947) 1 WPAR 609.

2. [1967] 1 QB 238, [1966] 3 All ER 172.

As attributability is a question of fact,[3] there is nothing to prevent tribunals coming to different conclusions on the attributability to service of a particular disease of unknown origin; but they must apply the correct test with regard to the onus of proof.[4]

b) 'THE COMPELLING PRESUMPTION' UNDER ARTICLE 4(3). The presumption applies whenever the serviceman is discharged, or dies, because of an injury not noted in the medical report which was made on him at the start of his service. Its effect is that the pension will be awarded, unless it is shown beyond reasonable doubt that the injury was not attributable to, or aggravated by, service.[5] The serviceman who is invalided has the advantage that his case is automatically considered by the Department.[6] There is no need for him (or his dependants if he is killed) formally to apply for a pension. In cases under Article 4(3) the nominated judge has held that the tribunal should look at all the facts[7] and it is not bound to accept that the diagnosis which led to the man's discharge was correct.[8]

ii) Claims under Article 5

Paragraph (2) of this Article provides that where a claim is brought, or the death occurs, more than seven years after the end of service, the disablement or death shall only be certified as due to, or substantially hastened by, service if 'it is shown that the conditions' set out in the Article are fulfilled. Paragraph (4) states that where on reliable evidence a reasonable doubt exists whether they are fulfilled, the benefit of that doubt should be given to the claimant. The leading case is *Dickinson v Minister of Pensions*[9] construing the identical provisions in the 1949 Royal Warrant:[10]

> A widow claimed that her husband's death from a coronary was substantially hastened by worry brought on by neurasthenia which in its turn had been aggravated by war service. The Ministry and tribunal dismissed her claim as she had not produced sufficient reliable evidence in its support. Ormerod J upheld the tribunal's approach.

The clear words of Article 5(2) supported the general principle that it is for an applicant to make out his claim. Only when a tribunal has found that enough reliable evidence has been adduced in support of the application, is it bound under Article 5(4) to give the benefit of any reasonable doubt to the claimant. This decision has been followed in England by the nominated judge in a case[11] arising under the equivalent provisions in the Personal Injuries (Civilians) Scheme 1964,[12] and in a case on the Royal

3. Ante, p. 360.
4. Edmund Davies J in *Coe v Minister of Pensions*, ante n.2, at p. 243.
5. *Birchenough v Minister of Pensions* (1949) 4 WPAR 635.
6. See Ministerial Statement, 401 HC Deb., col. 970.
7. *Troughear v Minister of Pensions* (1947) 1 WPAR 569.
8. *Hayden v Minister of Pensions* (1947) 1WPAR 775.
9. *Dickinson v Minister of Pensions* [1953] 1 QB 228, [1952] 2 All ER 1031.
10. RW 1949, Cmd. 7699.
11. *Cadney v Minister of Pensions and National Insurance* [1965] 3 All ER 809, [1966] 1 WLR 80.
12. See post, p. 382.

Warrant in Scotland.[13] The *Dickinson* case seems correct as a matter of interpretation of the provisions in the Warrant. It is also, it is submitted, right that where a claim is brought (or the death occurs) as long as seven years after the termination of the service, the claimant should be required to adduce some evidence that the disablement or death was connected with service in the forces.

iii) Critique

Attention has been drawn in Part One of this chapter to the uniquely favourable position of the claimant for a war pension with regard to the burden of proof.[14] The generous provision in the Royal Warrant has been liberally construed by the nominated judges, particularly in the *Judd*[15] and *Coe*[16] decisions. The result in effect is that a claimant bringing an application within seven years of the end of service need not produce any evidence to succeed; it is for the Secretary of State to rebut the presumed connection between service and injury (or disease) beyond reasonable doubt. It is difficult to see any difference here between Article 4(2) and 4(3). On the other hand, under Article 5 the claimant must adduce some reliable evidence before he can enjoy the benefit of any reasonable doubt. It is probably because of this second category of claim that the proportion of successful applications for a war pension has not been higher: on average, about 50% of claims succeed.[17]

F. Serious negligence or misconduct

Article 6 provides that the Secretary of State may withhold, cancel or reduce an award on the ground that the injury or death 'was caused or contributed to, by the serious negligence or misconduct' of the serviceman. There is surprisingly little case-law on this provision, nor is there any indication how the responsible minister has applied his discretionary power. The two leading cases are both decisions of Ormerod J. In the first,[18] 'serious negligence' was defined 'as negligence of a quality that would certainly call for some criminal action if it were done in civil life'. However, shortly afterwards the judge said this remark was only obiter, and should be related to the particular facts of this case, in which the alleged 'serious negligence or misconduct' consisted in the careless riding of a motor-cycle. In the second case,[19] he, therefore, allowed the

---

13. *Minister of Social Security v Connolly* 1967 SLT 121.
14. Ante, p. 353.
15. See Edmund Davies J in *Judd v Minister of Pensions* [1966] 2 QB 580 at 591.
16. Ante, n.2.
17. Thus, in 1973, 3,265 out of 6,477 claims were successful (Report on War Pensioners for 1973, HC 12, p. 4); in 1976, only 2,760 out of 5,789 succeeded (Report for 1976, HC 472, p. 3).

18. *Robertson v Minister of Pensions* (1952) 5 WPAR 245, 266.
19. *Minister of Pensions v Griscti* (1955) 5 WPAR 457. This approach is consonant with that of Denning J in *Williams H. v Minister of Pensions*, [1947] 2 All ER 564, where the case was sent back to the tribunal to consider whether the applicant, in shooting himself in the foot, had been guilty of serious negligence or misconduct.

Minister's appeal and ruled that the applicant was guilty of serious negligence or misconduct in disobeying an order not to handle enemy ammunition.

It is possible to infer from the comparative dearth of reported decisions that Article 6 has rarely been invoked; this may be because the view is taken that it should only apply in extreme circumstances. As in the industrial injuries system,[20] it is clear that the common law test of contributory negligence has no place in the war pensions scheme. But the latter differs from industrial injuries in providing that 'serious negligence or misconduct' may as such debar recovery.[1] In both systems wrongful conduct may lead to a ruling that the injury was not due to the employment or service.[2] Outside the situation where there is deliberate disobedience to orders (as in the *Griscti* case) it is hard to think of circumstances where the judge would hold an inquiry attributable to service, but nevertheless caused or contributed to by the applicant's negligence or misconduct. As a broad view is taken of questions of attributability, it seems to follow that, apart from these cases, there is relatively little room for the application of Article 6.

Part three. Assessment of Awards

This Part is concened with the awards which may be made for a disabled ex-serviceman and his dependants. The pensions which may be paid on death to his widow, children and other relatives are discussed in Part Four. War pensions consist of a basic disability award, assessed according to the degree of disablement in the particular case, supplemented by a variety of further allowances, mainly to assist the more severely disabled pensioners, including payments in respect of their dependants. Small additions to the basic award, though not these supplementary allowances, are paid to officers depending on their precise rank.[3] Pensions for officers are expressed in annual sums and paid either monthly or quarterly, those for other ranks are expressed and paid weekly. It seems difficult now to justify this 'class' differentiation, which appears to be without parallel in the social security system.

A. The basic award

i) Principles of assessment
These principles are for all practical purposes identical to those adopted by the industrial scheme. For a full account of such principles and for the difficulties to which they have given rise, reference should be made to chapter 8.[4] The rules are set out in Article 9 of the Warrant. The degree of

20. Ante, p. 291.
 1. Ante, p. 369.
 2. Ante, pp. 292, 362.
 3. The complex rules for determining the relevant rank of a member of the forces for war pensions purposes are set out in RW 1964, Art. 7.
 4. Ante, pp. 308–314.

disablement is to be assessed by comparing the condition of the disabled person with 'the conditions of a normal healthy person of the same age and sex, without taking into account the earning capacity of the member in his disabled condition in his own or any other specific trade or occupation', and without regard to any other individual factors. The assessment of incapacity for the basic award entirely ignores loss of earning ability resulting from the disablement, and any special factors which might make the loss of a limb particularly hard for the claimant, e.g., the loss of a finger by a pianist or sportsman. The Royal British Legion has in the past urged that the basic pension should be divided into two elements: first, a flat-rate disability benefit for the injury itself and, secondly, a sum for loss of earning capacity.[5] But the government has preferred to meet cases of reduced earning ability by the introduction of supplementary allowances.[6]

The degree of disablement assessed on this principle is to be expressed as a percentage, total disablement being represented by 100%. 'The maximum 100% assessment, while representing total disablement for pension purposes does not necessarily denote complete helplessness but more often than not a condition which although a major handicap is considerably short of this.'[7] A weekly pension for lesser degrees of disablement is paid at the appropriate percentage of disablement in multiples of 10 down to 20%. Awards for disablement of less than 20% are paid as lump sum gratuities.[8] Schedules to the Royal Warrant set out assessments for some particular injuries in the same form as is adopted for the industrial injuries scheme;[9] in other cases, the appropriate percentage is for the judgment of the Secretary of State.

ii) Review and appeal

The degree of disablement is generally assessed on an interim basis until the serviceman's condition permits a permanent assessment.[10] The Secretary of State may review an interim award when there is any change in the degree of disablement. But a final assessment may only be revised either if there has been a *substantial* increase in the degree of disablement, or the decision was made in consequence of *either* ignorance of, or a mistake as to, a material fact, *or* of a mistake of law.[11]

Appeal from either an interim or final assessment lies to an assessment tribunal, the composition of which is discussed elsewhere.[12] It is empowered to re-assess the disablement.[13]

iii) Amounts

The maximum basic disablement pension, expressed in terms of an annual payment for officers is for 1977–78 £1,796·00, and for other ranks ex-

5. See e.g., 391 HC Deb., cols. 786 ff (1943), and 401 HC Deb., cols. 1500–1502, 1505, 1515 (1944).
6. See post, pp. 373–374.
7. Committee on the Assessment of Disablement (1965), Cmnd. 2647, para. 9.
8. RW 1964, Art. 11, as amended by RW 1967, Cmnd. 3385.
9. Ante, p. 310.
10. RW 1964, Art. 9(2)(c).
11. Ibid., Art. 67. cp., the different grounds for review in industrial injuries cases, ante, pp. 314–316. There is no need there for the applicant to show a *substantial* change in the degree of his disablement.
12. Post, p. 660.
13. Pensions Appeal Tribunals Act 1943, Sch., para. 3.

pressed in terms of a weekly payment is for 1977–78 £29·44.[14] More complete figures for the payments, which vary a little according to the precise rank of the claimant, may be found in the Schedules to the up-rating Regulations, now made by statutory instrument for all three forces.[15]

B. Increases and additions

As under the industrial injuries scheme, there are a variety of supplementary allowances which may be paid to a war pensioner.[16] Although the usual formulation of eligibility is that 'a member of the military forces . . . *may be* awarded' the further allowance, it is not entirely clear that they should be regarded as discretionary. When it is clearly intended to confer a discretion on the Secretary of State, this is expressly spelt out in the Warrant.[17]

For the purpose of clarity of exposition the allowances are discussed under three broad heads: first, those paid for the maintenance of members of the claimant's family; secondly, those intended to provide compensation for unemployment, or the lowered standard of occupation pursued by the claimant; and thirdly, those intended to meet his special needs in the case of particularly severe disablement. In many cases these allowances are equivalent to those provided in the industrial injuries scheme, and are not, therefore, discussed in detail here.

i) Allowances for member of the claimant's family

a) GENERAL ALLOWANCE FOR DEPENDANTS. Under Article 12 an allowance may be awarded for the claimant's wife and children. Further it may also be paid in respect of an unmarried dependant living with him as his wife, if she has in her care a child for whom an allowance may be made.[18] Where the claimant is a woman, a supplement may be given for her husband if he has been supported by her for not less than six months before the end of her service, and is incapable of self-support.[19] Normally, an award for a child is not made beyond sixteen, but there is a discretionary power to continue to make an award for a child who is a student or apprentice, or who is incapable of supporting himself owing to an infirmity which arose before he reached that age.[20]

These allowances are without equivalent for the long-term industrial disablement pension, to which may be added a dependant's increase only if a claimant is in receipt of the unemployability supplement.[1] Clearly governments take the view that these allowances in the war pensions

14. S.I. 1977/1630.
15. The instrument is made under the SS(MP)A 1977, s.12: ante, p. 354.
16. Ante, pp. 317–335.
17. E.g., see RW 1964, Art. 12(3): 'The award, continuance and amount of any allowance in respect of a wife, husband or child who is living apart from the

member shall be at the discretion . . .'
18. Ibid., Art. 12(5). See Art. 1(33) for a restrictive definition of 'an unmarried dependant living as a wife'.
19. Ibid., Art. 12(4).
20. Ibid., Art. 12(8).
 1. Ante, p. 318.

scheme are anomalous, for their rate has not been increased since 1964. The maximum allowance of 50p is paid for the wife of a pensioner with a 100% disablement, and the maximum payment for a child is 37½p.[2] The supplement for the wife and children of a pensioner with a lesser disablement is calculated as a percentage of that figure (50p and 37½p) in the same way as the basic pension is.

b) EDUCATION ALLOWANCE. This may be paid under Article 13 in certain prescribed circumstances. These are principally that the child must be at least five, that the circumstances of the family must be such as to require the extra payment, and that the Secretary of State is satisfied that the type of education concerned is suitable. The amount of the supplement is determined by him, subject to a maximum (for 1977–78, £120 per annum).[3] There is no equivalent allowance in the industrial injuries scheme.

ii) Reduced earning capacity allowances

This second group of supplementary payments is designed to compensate the war pensioner for the reduced opportunities for earning which he suffers owing to his disabilities. To some extent, they counterbalance the inflexibility of the basic award, which, as has been said,[4] does not take into account loss of, or reduced, earning capacity.[5]

a) UNEMPLOYABILITY ALLOWANCE. This allowance, payable under Article 17 of the Warrant, is often known, like its equivalent in the industrial injuries scheme,[6] as the 'unemployability supplement'. It similarly takes the form of an additional allowance for the claimant himself, and in certain circumstances for the dependants in respect of whom an allowance may be paid under Article 12.[7] As with the industrial injuries supplement, a war pensioner may be deemed unemployable even though he has annual earnings up to a prescribed amount, for 1977–78, £520.[8] The rate for the personal allowance for 1977–78 is £18·60; for adult dependants; £10·50, and for child depends £6·10.

b) INVALIDITY ALLOWANCE. This further payment was introduced in 1971.[10] It is payable to an ex-serviceman in receipt of the unemployability allowance, who is or was under sixty (fifty-five in the case of a woman pensioner), when that allowance was first paid.[11] The rate varies according

2. RW 1964, Art. 12, Table.
3. S.I. 1977/1630.
4. Ante, p. 371.
5. For a further discussion of this point, see ante, pp. 303–305, in the context of industrial injuries.
6. Ante, p. 317.
7. RW 1964, Art. 17(4) set out these circumstances.
8. S.I. 1977/1630, Reg. 3.
9. S.I. 1977/1630 as amended by S.I.

1978/278. The figures for officers are £969·80, £547·50 and £318·10.
10. See the RW 1971, Cmnd. 4742, Part III, adding Art. 17A to the 1964 RW. For the comparable invalidity allowance introduced by NIA 1971 for the long-term sick and disabled, see ante, pp. 166–167; and for the industrial injury unemployability supplement, ante, p. 318.
11. RW 1964, Art. 17A(1).

to the claimant's age at that time: thus, if he was under thirty-five when
unemployability allowance was first paid, the invalidity allowance rate is
£3·70, if he was under forty-five then, it is £2·30, and in any other case it is
£1·15.[12] Neither the unemployability allowance nor the invalidity
allowance is payable to a pensioner in receipt of a retirement pension.[13]

c) ALLOWANCE FOR LOWERED STANDARD OF OCCUPATION. This
allowance, which used to be known as the 'special hardship allowance'
until 1949, is comparable with the allowance of that name payable under
the industrial injuries scheme.[14] The grounds of entitlement are virtually
identical and, therefore, reference should be made to the long discussion in
chapter 8. Like the industrial injuries provision, a war pensioner's basic
disablement pension, together with his allowance for his lowered standard
of occupation, may not exceed the maximum pension payable if the
disablement is 100%.[15] The rate for this allowance is subject in any event
to a maximum (for 1977–78, £596·50 for officers, £11·44 weekly for other
ranks),[16] but otherwise there is no formula in the Warrant for its calculation.[17]

iii) Serious disablement allowances
This third group comprises a variety of further allowances which may be
made in cases of serious disablement.

a) CONSTANT ATTENDANCE ALLOWANCE. This may be awarded in
respect of a pensioned disablement, the degree of which is not less than
80%, if it is shown to the Secretary of State's satisfaction that constant
attendance is necessary because of the disablement.[18] In an exceptional
case of severe disablement, the usual maximum amount payable (in 1977–
78, £594·40 for officers, £11·40 for other ranks)[19] may be increased subject
to a limit (in 1977–78, £1,118·80 for officers, £22·80 for other ranks).[20]
There are thus two maxima at which the allowance may be paid, compared
with four in the similar provision in the industrial injuries scheme.[1]

b) SEVERE DISABLEMENT OCCUPATIONAL ALLOWANCE. Article 15 provides that a pensioner in receipt of a constant attendance allowance, which
has been increased because of his severe disablement, may also receive this
further allowance, 'for any period during which he is ... ordinarily
employed in a gainful occupation'. The object of this provision appears to
be to compensate the exceptionally severely disabled pensioner who
nevertheless is able to pursue an occupation. There is no parallel benefit in
the industrial injuries system. It is paid at a flat-rate, in 1977–78, £297·20
for officers, and £5·70 weekly for other ranks.[2]

12. S.I. 1977/1630.
13. RW 1964, Art. 17(3), 17A(6).
14. Ante, pp. 318–332. See Appendix.
15. RW 1964, Art. 19(3).
16. S.I. 1977/1630.
17. Cp., SSA 1975, s.60(6), discussed ante,
pp. 329–331.
18. RW 1964, Art. 14.
19. S.I. 1977/1630.
20. Ibid.
1. Ante, pp. 333–334.
2. S.I. 1977/1630.

c) EXCEPTIONALLY SEVERE DISABLEMENT ALLOWANCE. This was introduced, as was the equivalent provision in the industrial injuries system,[3] following the recommendations of the McCorquodale Committee on Assessment of Disablement.[4] It will be paid when the disablement is, and is in the Secretary of State's view likely to remain, one for which the constant attendance allowance is payable, or would be if the serviceman were not in a hospital or other institution. As with the industrial injuries supplement, entitlement is, therefore, geared to eligibility for the constant attendance allowance; however, it does not appear to depend on the pensioner's receipt of a 100% disablement benefit.[5] The amount is (for 1977–78) a flat-rate £594·40 for officers, £11·40 for other ranks.[6]

d) TREATMENT ALLOWANCES. As in the industrial injuries system,[7] a pensioner receiving medical treatment is entitled to an allowance equal to the 100% disablement pension, with the maximum additional allowances (50p and 37½p respectively) for his wife and children. But it is not confined to treatment in hospital.[8] 'Treatment' is defined as 'a course of medical, surgical or rehabilitative treatment', which the Secretary of State is satisfied the pensioner should receive.[9] It excludes treatment which involves only an occasional interruption in the pensioner's normal work. In this situation, a part-time treatment allowance is payable,[10] subject to a maximum (from April 1978) of £10·75 per day, for both officers and other ranks.[11] In certain cases additional treatment allowances may be payable.[12] Under Article 22 the treatment allowance may be paid where the pensioner has to abstain from work following a course of treatment.

e) COMFORTS ALLOWANCE. This supplement, like the following two, is without any equivalent in the industrial injuries scheme. It may be awarded where the claimant is in receipt of a constant attendance allowance, and *either* an unemployability allowance *or* a 100% basic award from multiple injuries which, in the Secretary of State's view, are so serious as to justify the award of a comforts allowance.[13] The rate for 1977–78 is £255·50 for officers, £4·90 weekly for other ranks.[14] A lower rate of comforts allowance (for 1977–78, £127·70 for officers, £2·45 for other ranks) is payable to a pensioner who is in receipt of either the constant attendance allowance or the unemployability allowance.[15]

f) ALLOWANCE FOR WEAR AND TEAR OF CLOTHING. This is generally awarded to a pensioner who regularly wears an artificial limb.[16] Where one

3. Ante, p. 335.
4. Committee on the Assessment of Disablement (1965), Cmnd. 2647, para. 9. The purpose of this allowance is discussed, ante, p. 335.
5. Cp., the position in industrial injuries, ante, p. 335.
6. S.I. 1977/1630.
7. Ante, pp. 332–333.
8. Cp. ante, p. 333.

9. RW 1964, Art. 21(8).
10. Ibid., Art. 23.
11. S.I. 1978/278.
12. For further details, see DHSS leaflet MPL 149, pp. 8–9.
13. RW 1964, Art. 18(1)(a).
14. S.I. 1977/1630.
15. RW 1964, Art. 18(1)(b).
16. Ibid., Art. 16(1)(a).

artificial limb is worn, the allowance is paid at a lower rate, in 1977–78 £25·00 per annum for both officers and other ranks.[17] A higher rate, £40·00 per annum, is payable where more than one such limb is worn, or the Secretary of State is satisfied that the wear and tear on the pensioner's clothing as a result of the disablement is exceptional.

g) AGE ALLOWANCE. A supplement is paid to pensioners over sixty-five with a disablement assessed at 40% or over.[18] This is paid at four different rates depending on whether the degree of pensioned disablement is 40%–50% (£104·30 for officers, £2·60 for other ranks), 50%–70% (£161·60 and £3·10), 70%–90% (£229·40, £4·40), or over 90% (£323·30, £6·20).[19]

Part four. Awards in Respect of Death
A. General

Awards may be made in respect of a death of a member of the forces which is due to service.[20] As with claims by disabled members of the forces, the conditions of entitlement depend on the date of the material event; in this case, however, they vary according to whether the *death* (rather than the claim in respect of that death) occurs less or more than seven years after the termination of service. If the death occurs not later than seven years after this, the death is to be accepted as due to service, provided it is certified that it was 'due to or hastened by *either* an injury attributable to service, *or* the aggravation by service of an injury which existed before or arose during service'.[1] Where the death occurs more than seven years after service, it must be certified that it was due to, or *substantially* hastened by, an injury attributable to, or aggravated by, service.[2]

The general condition that death must be due to service is more restrictive than the approach which obtained in the First World War. Then a widow might receive what was termed a 'modified pension' (half the husband's pension) if he was in receipt of a war pension at the date of his death, even though the death itself was not caused by his war service. This provision seems to have been unique to the British war pensions scheme.[3] Awards of this type were not made after 1921. But there have been two modifications to the general position, though in the first case only for the benefit of widows, and not for all dependants. Article 33 of the Royal Warrant 1964 provides a temporary allowance, now payable for twenty-six weeks,[4] for the widow, or unmarried dependant who has lived as the wife of a severely disabled pensioner, whatever the cause of his death. It is payable whenever the member of the forces was in receipt of a constant

17. S.I. 1977/1630.
18. RW 1964, Art. 20.
19. S.I. 1977/1630.
20. RW 1964, Art. 25.
  1. Ibid., Art. 4(2). See ante, pp. 360–365. for 'attributable to' and 'aggravated by'

service.
2. Ibid., Art. 5(1)(b).
3. See *Comparative Tables of War Pension Rates in Allied Countries and Germany during Great War* (1920), Cmd. 474.
4. RW 1966, Cmnd. 3023, Art. 1.

attendance or an unemployability allowance, or in a case where though eligible for the latter, he was in fact in receipt of the lowered standard of occupation allowance.[5] Additional allowances may be paid for this period for the serviceman's children. The second change provides that from 1971 the death of a member of the forces in receipt of a constant attendance allowance at the normal maximum rate (or one who would have been in receipt of this allowance if he had not been in hospital) is to be treated as due to service for the purposes of awards on his death.[6]

B. Widows' benefits

There are two rates at which war widows' pension is paid; a higher rate (for 1977–78, £22·95)[7] is paid if the widow is over forty, or is in receipt of an allowance for a child of the deceased, or is incapable of self-support.[8] In other cases, a lower rate (for 1977–78, £5·50)[9] is paid. A widow was formerly only entitled if she was living with the deceased at the date of his death or if the Secretary of State took the view that the separation was attributable to the soldier's mental instability. But this restriction was removed by the Royal Warrant of 1974.[10] A frequent source of controversy during the Second World War was the question whether pensions should only be paid to widows who had married the deceased before his disability arose. It was not until 1946 that the present position was reached that the date of marriage is irrelevant.[11]

An unmarried dependant who has been living as a wife of the member of the forces[12] may be awarded a pension on his death, as long as she has in her charge his child and is in receipt of a child allowance.[13] The amount of this pension is at the discretion of the Secretary of State, subject to a maximum, for 1977–78, £1,149·80 in the case of officers, and £21·60 for other ranks.[14] A supplementary rent allowance may be paid to a widow, or an unmarried dependant, who has lived as a wife, provided the household includes a child. It is not, for 1977–78, to exceed £8·60 but is otherwise subject to the Secretary of State's discretion.[15] Although this provision may not appear generous, it is yet another respect in which the war pensions scheme is unusual. There is no other social security benefit (apart from supplementary benefits) where an allowance is paid for rent.

5. A person in receipt of the allowance for lowered standard of occupation may prefer not to apply for the unemployability allowance because of the loss of concurrent social security benefits – see RW 1968, Cmnd. 3728. It was, therefore, reasonable to make this temporary allowance available for widows, etc., of soldiers in receipt of the lowered standard of occupation allowance who had been eligible for the unemployability allowance.
6. RW 1971, Cmnd. 4742. See ante, p. 344, industrial death benefit.
7. S.I. 1977/1630. For officers' widows a higher pension is payable up to a maximum of £1,794.
8. RW 1964, Art. 27.
9. S.I. 1977/1630. For officers' widows a pension is payable up to a maximum of £420 for a major. Beyond that rank, the higher rate is paid.
10. Cmnd. 5670, Art. 4.
11. RW 1946, Cmd. 6799.
12. See Art. 1(33) for the definition of an 'unmarried dependent living as a wife'.
13. RW 1964, Art. 30.
14. S.I. 1977/1630.
15. RW 1964, Art. 31.

A further allowance is paid to some widows of sixty-five, and then at a higher level when they reach seventy.[16]

These benefits cease on the remarriage or cohabitation of the widow (or other recipient).[17] Rather oddly, the position on remarriage differs substantially according to whether the widow had been married to a soldier or an officer. In the former case the Secretary of State may award a gratuity equal to one year's pension. There is no such provision for officers' widows, but they may be more favourably placed in that on the death of the husband of the remarriage, the Secretary may at his discretion restore the lost pension. There is no apparent justification for this difference. The Secretary of State has discretion to restore the widow's pension on termination of a period of cohabitation.[18]

c. Widowers

A widower may be awarded a pension, where he was dependent on a female member of the armed forces, and is in pecuniary need and incapable of self-support.[19] The rate is at the discretion of the Secretary of State, subject to a maximum payment, for 1977–78, of £1,187·60 per annum for the widower of an officer, and £22·70 weekly for the widower of a soldier.[20]

d. Children

The child of a deceased member of the forces is entitled to receive a pension on similar conditions to those which are applicable for the payment of an allowance for him when the father is alive and in receipt of a disablement pension.[1] The amount of the allowance is from April 1978 £408.50 for the child of an officer, and £7.70 for the child of a soldier.[2] Further, an education allowance may be payable in the same circumstances, and subject to the same maximum (£120 per annum), as those which obtain when a disabled serviceman claims this benefit.[3]

e. Parents and other relatives

Despite constant pressure in the House of Commons for its reintroduction, the automatic allowance for the parents of a deceased

16. RW 1964, Art. 32, as amended by RW 1971.
17. RW 1964, Art. 42.
18. Ibid., Art. 42(b). Widows' benefits under the Social Security Act 1975 are automatically paid on the termination of cohabitation, for they are only suspended when this begins: ante, p. 233.
19. Ibid., Art. 34: see ante, p. 346, for the similar conditions for a widower's death benefit in industrial injuries.
20. S.I. 1977/1630.
1. RW 1964, Arts. 35–37: see ante, p. 372 for child allowances supplementing a disablement pension.
2. S.I. 1978/278.
3. RW 1964, Art. 38; see ante, p. 372.

serving-man, which had been payable in the First World War, was not provided in the Warrants issued during the Second war and afterwards.[4] Article 40 provides that a parent may be awarded a pension only 'if he is in pecuniary need by reason of having reached the age of not less than sixty-five years in the case of a man, or sixty years in the case of a woman, or infirmity or other adverse condition which is not merely of a temporary character'.[5] The Secretary of State must take into account in determining need, the extent to which the deceased member before and during his service supported the parent, and the extent to which he was likely to continue doing so if he had not died. A pension cannot be awarded at all if a widow is in receipt of a pension in respect of the deceased serviceman, unless the parent was actually dependent on him. There is a considerable discretion as to the rate of benefit awarded to parents. There is a maximum and minimum rate (in 1977–78, £1·00 and £0·25 a week for soldiers, £75·00 and £15·00 for officers). These rates have not been increased since 1949.[6] Where both parents claim, it is for the Secretary of State to select which parent may receive the award.[7]

Any other person may be awarded a pension if he was dependent on the deceased and is in pecuniary need and incapable of self-support.[8] Not more than one such person may claim, except in the case of juvenile dependants, i.e. a brother, sister, grandchild of less than sixteen. The Secretary of State's decision as to which of two or more eligible dependants is to benefit is final. The maximum amount payable to an adult dependant is, for 1977–78, £54·00 in respect of officers, and £1·00 a week for other ranks, and for juvenile dependants £26·00 and £0·30 a week respectively.[9] But the total sum awarded to one parent and another dependant is not to exceed the maximum which may be awarded in exceptional circumstances where there are two eligible parents.[10]

Part five. General Miscellaneous Provisions

A. Overlap provisions

The object of these provisions is to prevent overcompensation from public funds or from a combination of these funds and a damages award. Article 56 provides that the Secretary of State may take into account any other compensation which is, or may be, awarded a claimant and may withhold or reduce the pension or gratuity accordingly. Compensation which might have been obtained but for the unreasonable act or omission of the claimant may also be taken into account for this purpose. 'Compensation' means any periodical or lump sum payment in respect of death or dis-

---

4. 387 HC Deb., col. 1511; 391 HC Deb., col. 764; 433 HC Deb., col. 159. See 1st Report of the PCA for 1975–76, HC 37, Case No. C.291/V.

5. See ante, p. 347, for the equivalent provision in industrial injuries, which employs a similar test for eligibility.

6. See the comparable failure to increase parent's death benefit in industrial injuries scheme, ante, p. 347.

7. RW 1964, Art. 40(8).

8. Ibid., Art. 41.

9. S.I. 1977/1630.

10. RW 1964, Art. 41(4).

ability for which provision is made under any statute, ordinance, regulation or scheme,[11] or any sum recoverable as damages at common law.[12] A similar rule applies to children who are provided for from public funds.[13] Another overlap measure enables a deduction to be made from a pension or gratuity where the claimant is being cared for in an institution which is supported by public funds, though this does not apply where he has entered it for the purpose of receiving medical or surgical treatment.[14] The pensions of servicemen entering Chelsea Hospital are terminated, but may be restored on departure from it.[15]

B. Forfeiture provisions

The Secretary of State may withhold, or direct the forfeiture of, a pension on the ground that the person to, or in respect of whom, it has been awarded is serving a term of imprisonment or detention after a court order, or is deported from or required to leave the United Kingdom.[16] A forfeited pension may be restored upon terms imposed by the Secretary of State. The rule discussed in Part Four under which a widow's pension may be terminated on remarriage or cohabitation is, of course, tantamount to a forfeiture provision.[17]

There are two other provisions analogous to forfeiture rules. Under the first, the Secretary of State may reduce a pension by not more than half, if the claimant refuses unreasonably to undergo medical, surgical or rehabilitative treatment.[18] Secondly, an award may be cancelled if a pension is not drawn for a continuous period of a year or more.[19]

C. Commencing date of awards

A point of difficulty concerns the date from which a war pension is payable. Article 65 of the 1964 Royal Warrant provides that, except where the Secretary of State otherwise directs with regard to an individual case or class of cases, pensions shall be paid from the date of application or appeal as a result of which the claim is accepted. In other words, there is no general provision for back-dating awards. The Parliamentary Commissioner for Administration has frequently been asked to investigate complaints of maladministration when the Department of Health and Social Security has refused to depart from the general rule. It is the Department's policy only to make back payments when there is substantial evidence that the applicant was prevented from claiming earlier because of physical or mental disability, or it is clear that there has been some error in

---

11. This might include the Criminal Injuries Compensation schemes under which awards have been made to soldiers and their families in respect of the Northern Ireland troubles.
12. RW 1964, Art. 56(3).
13. Ibid., Art. 59.
14. For the position where the pensioner is

receiving medical treatment, see ante, p. 375.
15. RW 1964, Art. 58.
16. Ibid., Art. 62; cf.; under SSA 1975, post, pp. 421–424.
17. See ante, p. 378.
18. RW 1964, Art. 63: cf., ante, p. 338.
19. Ibid., Art. 64.

processing the claim. The justification for this informal 'rule' is that it is necessary as a corollary to the ex-serviceman's ability to bring his claim any time after the disability occurs. The Parliamentary Commissioner has accepted the 'rule' as reasonable and refused to infer maladministration from its application.[20]

In one situation, consequent upon a special report by the Parliamentary Commissioner, the DHSS made a direction back-dating awards in a class of cases not covered by the general rule. After the *Judd* decision,[1] the Department decided it would review any claim which had previously been rejected on the basis of the earlier rules with regard to the burden of proof. The DHSS accepted the Parliamentary Commissioner's recommendation that where a claim was accepted, payments should be made from 4 October, 1965 (the date of the *Judd* judgment) rather than from the date when the revision was made.[2] Otherwise, the date of payment would have depended arbitrarily on the order in which the DHSS reviewed the claims.

Part six. Other War Pension and Civilian Schemes

There are a number of schemes similar to the war pensions scheme providing pensions for those outside the regular armed forces who are injured in war service. The conditions of entitlement are on the whole more restrictive in these schemes, due to the fact that for members of the forces pensionable disablement can be due to any aspect of service, whereas for civilians the disablement must be related specifically to the effects of war. They have been less liberally construed by the nominated judge than the equivalent requirements in the Royal Warrant. One reason for this was that often the effect of allowing a claim by a merchant mariner or civilian for a pension was to debar him from pursuing his remedy under the workmen's compensation legislation or at common law.[3] In other respects, for example, on the questions of causation and burden of proof, authorities on the construction of these schemes have followed cases on the Royal Warrant provisions[4] and in their turn they have been cited in war pensions cases.[5] There are two principal types of scheme, neither of which is of much practical importance now.

i) Schemes for mariners and other seafaring persons
Under the Pensions (Navy, Army, Air Force and Mercantile Marine) Act 1939, as amended by the Pensions (Mercantile Marine) Act 1942, the

20. 2nd Annual Report of the PCA for 1968, 1968–69 HC, 129, para. 20; Annual Report for 1970, 1970–71 HC, 261, Case No. C536/L. See Appendix.
1. Ante, p. 366.
2. 2nd Report of the PCA for 1970, 1970–71 HC, 507 (Report on Captain Horsley's Claim).
3. See Tucker J in *Re Kemp* [1945] 1 All ER 571, discussing Personal Injuries

(Emergency Provisions) Act 1939, s.3.
4. E.g., *Cadney v Minister of Pensions and National Insurance* [1965] 3 All ER 809, [1966] 1 WLR 80; see ante, p. 368.
5. *Minister of Pensions v Chennell* [1947] KB 250 has been an influential authority on problems of causation in the war pensions area.

Secretary of State may make schemes for the benefit of merchant marines and other seafaring persons who have suffered war injuries, war risk injuries, or have incurred disabilities by certain other specified causes. There are a number of such schemes,[6] administered in much the same way as war pensions; there is a right of appeal from the initial decision in the DHSS to the Pensions Appeal Tribunal.[7] The concepts of 'war injury' and 'war risk injury' have been more narrowly developed than the notion of 'injury attributable to service' in the Royal Warrant: for example, a merchant mariner injured by equipment which was not normally kept on board ship during peace-time was held not to have incurred a 'war risk injury'.[8]

ii) Civilian Injuries' Scheme

Under the Personal Injuries (Civilians) Scheme 1976,[9] made under the Personal Injuries (Emergency Provisions) Act 1939, a civilian may receive a pension for disablement or incapacity due to a 'war injury', or in the case of a civil defence volunteer a 'war service injury', in both cases sustained between 3 September 1939 and 19 March 1946. 'War service injury' and 'war injury' are both defined in the 1939 Act, the latter being accorded the same definition as in the Pensions (Navy, Army, Air Force and Mercantile Marine) Act of 1939. An appeal lies from the Secretary of State's decision to a Pensions Appeal Tribunal.[10] The nominated judge seems to have adopted a restrictive approach when the claimant has suffered mental shock or hysteria at the sight of war damage. The definitions in the 1939 Act of both 'war injury' and 'war service injury' refer to *physical* injury', and Tucker J has held that this excludes mental shock, in contradistinction to the position under the Royal Warrant where 'disablement' is defined to mean 'physical or mental injury or damage'.[11]

A 'war service injury' must have arisen out of and in the course of the performance by the volunteer of his civil defence duties and, therefore, an injury sustained while bicycling to his place of duty did not entitle a defence worker to recover a pension.[12] In an important ruling, often followed in cases construing the Royal Warrant, it was held that a 'war injury' was caused by the discharge of a missile, even though it was a few days before it was carelessly picked up and tampered with by a small boy, resulting in injury to the claimant.[13] The discharge of the missile was not too remote for it to be regarded as the cause of the injury and so a pension was awarded.

6. E.g., the War Pensions (Naval Auxiliary Personnel) Scheme 1964, S.I. 1964/1985; the War Pensions (Mercantile Marine) Scheme 1964, S.I. 1964/2058.
7. See Pensions Appeal Tribunals Act 1943, s.2.
8. *Douglass v Minister of Pensions* (1952) 5 WPAR 85; also see *Cook v Minister of Pensions* (1948), 1 WPAR 1223.
9. S.I. 1976/585.
10. Pensions Appeal Tribunals Act 1943, s.3.

11. *Youn v Minister of Pensions* [1944] 2 All ER 308 ('war injury'); *ex parte Haines* [1945] KB 183, [1945] 1 All ER 349, and *Re Drake* [1945] 1 All ER 576 ('war service injury'): see ante p. 359.
12. *Davis v Minister of Pensions* [1951] 2 All ER 318. For the similar position with regard to such accidents in industrial injuries, see ante, p. 362.
13. *Minister of Pensions v Chennell* [1947] KB 250, [1946] 2 All ER 719.

10 General Provisions

In this chapter we consider a number of issues and concepts which are common to several or all of the benefits payable under the Social Security Act 1975 (viz., those discussed in chapters 3 to 8). The principles to be described are themselves primarily governed by that Act and, as a matter of law, are not binding on the authorities administering war pensions, child benefits, family income supplements or supplementary benefits unless, and to the extent that, they are specifically adopted in the legislation concerned with the latter schemes. In practice, however, where there is no reason to adopt a different interpretation, the provisions of the Social Security Act, as developed by the Commissioners' decisions, may properly act as guidelines for the administration of those areas of social security law which are not governed by that Act. This applies particularly to the meaning attributed to such concepts as 'marriage', 'living as man and wife', 'residence', 'presence', 'imprisonment' and 'detention in legal custody'.

Part one. Increases for Dependants

A. General

The principle that special allowance should be made for persons dependent on the claimant was, of course, recognised from the beginning as regards benefits which were means-tested. Family support is without doubt the most significant differential in assessing an individual's need. For those benefits governed wholly or partly by the contributory principle such provision is not so obvious but is readily acceptable. If the benefit is intended to provide a minimum standard of living for the claimant, then regard should be had to his family needs, even though, in the absence of a family-weighted contribution, this will mean that those without family obligations will be subsidising those with them. With the general shift of the contributory benefits towards the earnings-related principle, the continuation of dependants' allowances becomes more questionable:[1] There would appear to be only two possible rationalisations for their

1. Cf., ante, p. 25.

existence: they might be regarded simply as a means of redistributing resources to individuals with family responsibilities; alternatively, and perhaps more realistically, they may reflect the facts that the earnings-related additions represent only a proportion of the lost income and that there is a recognised need to raise the value of the flat-rate benefit to a socially acceptable level. As some foreign systems clearly show, a fully effective programme of earnings indemnity is incompatible with the payment of dependants' allowances.[2] Moreover, when regard is also had to the fact that social security benefits are not normally taxable, the present compromise between the family-needs approach and the earnings-related principle can produce some odd results. A low wage-earner with a large family is often in the position where his flat-rate benefit, plus earnings-related supplement and dependants' allowances (all untaxed) exceed his average net earnings.[3] To preserve a work incentive the legislation, therefore, imposes the rather arbitrary ceiling of 85% of average gross earnings on the benefit payable.[4]

Significantly, in England, there has never been a thoroughgoing rationalisation of these increases. Before the Second World War, the principle was applied to the various benefit schemes only gradually and somewhat haphazardly, It was added to the unemployment insurance scheme in 1921 on a temporary basis to relieve 'winter hardships',[5] but in the next year was made permanent.[6] Remarkably, additions for dependants were never included in the national health insurance scheme, and the reasons for the distinction remain far from obvious. They were belatedly added to workmen's compensation in 1940,[7] as a result of continuous complaints that the ceiling to earnings-related compensation was too low for those with heavy family responsibilities. Beveridge in his restatement of the social insurance principle, based as it was on a system of flat-rate benefit, was content to see the increase payable to all recipients of insurance benefit.[8] The contemporaneous introduction of family allowances necessitated a technical modification of the rules, though in no fundamental way interfered with them. By the time earnings-related supplements were introduced for short term benefits in 1966, the principle of increase for dependants was already firmly entrenched, and there was no serious attempt to argue that it should be discontinued.[9] But the reform prompted the decision to pay the increases on a higher scale to long-term beneficiaries who were not entitled to the supplement.[10] The replacement in 1975 of family allowances by the child benefit, which became payable for the first or only child of a family,[11] necessitated further technical

2. E.g., in W. Germany, Denmark and Netherlands the benefit payable for short-term employment injury bears such a high proportion to lost earnings that no dependants' allowances are payable: *Kaim-Caudle*, p. 88. See also *Dupeyroux*, pp. 114–121 and *McCarthy*, pp. 169–171.
3. Cf., *Walley*, pp. 205–206.
4. Post, p. 426.

5. Unemployed Workers Dependants' (Temporary Provisions) Act 1921.
6. UIA 1922.
7. WC (Supplementary Allowances) Act 1940.
8. Paras. 311 and 325.
9. Cf., *Walley*, p. 206.
10. Post, p. 385.
11. Post, chap. 11.

changes, and at the same time the opportunity was taken to restructure the law so that, in general, the definition of dependent children would be shared by both schemes.

The Social Security Act 1975 makes, with certain exceptions, common provision for all the non-industrial benefits payable under it, but deals with the industrial benefits separately. However, the principles are so similar that they will be considered together, the differences being treated as and when they emerge. There are, moreover, certain key concepts, such as 'maintenance', 'residence' and 'incapacity for self-support' which are common to two or more of the increases which may be claimed. These will be discussed after the rules for each category of dependency have been described.

B. Persons for whom increase payable

i) Children

Increases for child dependants may be added to those benefits payable under the Act which, broadly speaking, are intended to compensate for loss of full-time earnings. These benefits may be divided into two groups.

1. Unemployment or sickness benefit (where the beneficiary is under pensionable age), maternity allowance and industrial injury benefit.[12]

2. Unemployment or sickness benefit (where the beneficiary is over pensionable age); invalidity and Category A, B or C retirement pensions; widow's, widowed mother's, child's special and invalid care allowances; non-contributory invalidity pension; and industrial disablement pension (if accompanied by unemployability supplement).[13]

A higher rate of weekly increase (from 3 April 1978 £6·10 per child[14]) is paid for benefits within group 2 either because it is assumed that the family needs of the beneficiary are greater, or because there is no entitlement to the earnings-related supplements which are generally available to those within group 1. The lower rate of weekly increase payable to the latter (from 3 April 1978) is £2·20 for each child.[15] To qualify for the increase the beneficiary must satisfy two conditions, the first referring to his relationship with the child and the second to the state of the latter's dependence on him.

a) SUFFICIENT RELATIONSHIP. Until 1977 there were complex provisions for determining the children for whom the addition might be claimed. The introduction in that year of child benefit payable to all families with children meant that the rules specifying the nature of the relationship with the child could be largely integrated. The general rule for the increase

---

12. SSA 1975, ss.41(2) and 64(1).
13. Ibid., and S.I. 1977/343, Reg. 1(3).

14. S.I. 1977/1325, as amended by S.I. 1977/1328.
15. Ibid.

simply incorporates the law on child benefit: it is payable where the beneficiary is 'entitled to child benefit in respect of a child or children'.[16] On this test, therefore, reference should be made to the discussion in chapter 11.

In certain respects, however, the pre-1977 rules on increases covered a wider range of relationships than those acknowledged under the new child benefit scheme. To ensure that the entitlement of this broader group is preserved, a Regulation enumerates situations in which for the purpose of the increase a person is treated as if he were entitled to child benefit.

1. The beneficiary is *either* a parent of the child *or* is wholly or mainly maintaining him, *and* is residing with a parent of the child, *and* that parent is living with the child and receives child benefit for him.[17]

2. The beneficiary is a parent of the child and is contributing to the cost of providing for him at a rate of not less than the amount of increase payable to group 1 beneficiaries, *and* the child benefit is payable to the beneficiary's wife or former wife who is also a parent of the child.[18]

3. The beneficiary is entitled to a family benefit in respect of that child payable by the government of a country outside the UK.[19]

Conversely, there is a situation where child benefit is payable but the increase is excluded.

A parent of the child (not being the claimant of the increase) is treated as responsible for the child under CBA 1975, s.3(1)(a).[20] (The exclusion does not, however apply to a beneficiary who under the same provision is treated as responsible for the child and who is wholly or mainly maintaining him[1]).

b) DEPENDENCE. The second condition is that the beneficiary must prove *either* that the child in question is living with him *or* that he is contributing to the cost of providing for the child at a weekly rate of not less than the amount of the increase, over and above the amount (if any) received by way of child benefit.[2] If the beneficiary is a married woman residing with her husband, she must in addition prove that he is incapable of self-support.[3]

ii) Wife
An increase for a wife may be claimed to supplement those benefits

16. SSA 1975, ss.41 and 64(1), as amended by CBA 1975, Sch. 4, para. 13(a) and 21(a).
17. S.I. 1977/343, Reg. 6(1).
18. Ibid., Reg. 6(2), though increases to invalid care allowance are not governed by this provision.
19. Ibid., Reg. 6(4).
20. Ibid., Reg. 7(1). For CBA 1975, s.3(1)(a) see post, p. 456.
1. S.I. 1977/343, Reg. 7(2).
2. SSA 1975, ss.43(1), (2) and 65(1), (2), as amended by CBA 1975, Sch. 4, paras. 15 and 22.
3. SSA 1975, ss.41(6) and 65(4).

mentioned in the last section to which a man may be entitled:

> Unemployment and sickness benefits, invalidity and category A or C retirement pensions, non-contributory invalidity pension and invalid care allowance, industrial injury and disablement pension (if accompanied by an unemployability supplement).[4]

The marriage must be recognised by English law and sufficiently proved.[5] The usual test of dependancy applies: the beneficiary must either be residing with this wife[6] or contributing to her maintenance at not less than the amount of the increase.[7]

An interesting policy question is raised if the wife is herself an earner. If the object of the increase is to satisfy the need for support, a self-supporting wife should be excluded. If, on the other hand, it is to provide compensation for the loss of actual support, then at least up to certain limits it should continue to be payable. Quite apart from this, there is the incentive issue: should the wife, assuming she is capable of doing so, be encouraged to work? The stance adopted by the various statutory provisions is not a uniform one.[8] In the case of short-term benefits (viz., those for unemployment, sickness and industrial injury), the 'needs' approach is uncompromisingly adopted: the increases is not payable if the wife's weekly earnings exceed the amount of that increase.[9] The same also applies for long-term benefits (retirement, invalidity and disablement pensions) where the wife is not residing with the husband, i.e., where she has to satisfy the alternative maintenance test.[10] In the case of a wife residing with a long-term beneficiary, a different, more liberal, approach was introduced in 1971 to encourage her to supplement the household income.[11] Entitlement to the increase is not affected up to a stipulated amount (in 1977–78 £35·00 per week[12]) but beyond that there is a reduction in the increase of 50% for any excess up to £4·00, and of 100% for any greater excess.[13]

Just as the earnings rule differs according to the nature of the benefit, so also does the amount of increase which is payable for adult dependants. There are in fact three rates: the highest (in 1977–78, £10·50 per week) is payable to the long-term beneficiaries; the second rate (in 1977–78, £9·10 per week) is payable to short-term beneficiaries; and the lowest rate (in 1977–78, £6·30 per week) to recipients of non-contributory benefits.[14]

4. SSA 1975, ss.44(1), 45 and 66(1); S.I. 1975/1058, Reg. 9; S.I. 1976/409, Reg. 13(2).
5. Post, pp. 398–404.
6. Post, pp. 390–393.
7. SSA 1975, ss.44(1)(a), 45(2) and 66(1)(a). But NB., for the invalid care allowance the claimant *must* prove residence – there is no maintenance alternative: S.I. 1976/409, Reg. 13(2).
8. For the analogous rule on retirement pensions see ante, pp. 216–219.
9. SSA 1975, s.44(1)(b); S.I. 1977/343, Reg. 8(1).

10. SSA 1975, s.45(2)(b).
11. NIA 1971, s.4.
12. SS(MP)A 1977, s.5(1). The monetary limit is subject to the up-rating procedure (post, p. 433) and the Secretary of State is under a duty to review the operation of the earnings rule and to lay a report before Parliament by 31 October 1978: ibid., ss.6, 7.
13. SSA 1975, ss.45(3), (4), and 66(4), (5).
14. S.I. 1977/1325.

iii) Husbands

Our social security system proceeds on the conventional but challengeable assumption that the husband is the breadwinner and the wife remains at home to care for the children. Except to the extent that the wife may supplement the family income by her own earnings, there is no recognition of the possiblity of the roles being interchanged.[15] The result is that a married woman may claim for her husband an increase to unemployment, sickness and industrial injury benefits, maternity allowance, invalidity and disablement pensions[16] only if she proves, in addition to the standard residence or maintenance alternative requirements for wife's and childrens' increases[17] that her husband is incapable of self-support.[18] The amount of the increase is that payable for adult dependants for the benefit in question.[19]

iv) Women with care of children

Another fundamental characteristic of the social security system has been its realistic view of so-called 'common-law' marriages. The relationship is treated as if the parties were married for the purposes of the means-tested benefits,[20] but their position with regard to those benefits payable under the Social Security Act is less favourable.[1] Except for a short period of 'entitlement' under the Unemployment Insurance Acts,[2] an increase for the cohabitee has been granted only if she has care of the beneficiary's children, or more precisely, under current legislation, child or children in respect of whom the beneficiary is entitled to both child benefit[3] and a child's increase to personal benefit.[4] The Commissioner has held that the necessary care will be shown if the woman, traditionally referred to as a 'housekeeper', 'to a substantial extent performs those duties for a child, with which a child needs assistance because he or she is a child, or exercises that supervision over a child which is one of the needs of childhood'.[5] It does not connote exclusive care[6] or even a greater amount of care than that provided by the claimant himself.[7] But the mere distant supervision of a child's needs while he is at boarding school does not qualify.[8]

This firm emphasis on the care of a child carries no necessary implication of a sexual relationship with the beneficiary. The woman need not

---

15. Cf. ante, pp. 9 and 238. The Family Expenditure Survey 1975, Table 35, does reveal that the number of households where 'role-reversal' does take place is still small, but the principle remains important.
16. Nb., but not to a retirement pension, nor to a short-term benefit payable to a woman over the pensionable age: SSA 1975, s.44(5).
17. Ante, pp. 386 and 387.
18. SSA 1975, ss.44(3)(a), 47(1)(a) and 66(1)(b).
19. Ante, p. 387.

20. Post, chaps. 12 and 13.
1. Cf., ante, pp. 8–9.
2. UIA 1922, s.1(1), repealed by UIA 1927, s.4(2).
3. SSA 1975, ss.44(3)(c), 46(2) and 66(1)(d) as amended by CBA 1975, Sch. 4, paras. 16, 18 and 23.
4. S.I. 1977/343, Reg. 10(2)(a) (or would have been so entitled but for overlapping provisions).
5. CS 726/49, para. 11.
6. UD 10914/31.
7. CS 726/49, paras. 9, 10.
8. R(S) 17/54.

be residing with the beneficiary;[9] indeed, in such a case the increase may be paid even where he is residing with his wife, provided that the latter is in full-time work and does not herself primarily care for the children.[10] It follows too that a female beneficiary in full-time work may claim an increase under this head. The short-term benefits for which the increase may be claimed thus include maternity allowance as well as those for sickness, unemployment and industrial injury.[11] The long-term benefits are Category A and C retirement and invalidity pensions, the non-contributory invalidity pension and invalid care allowance, and the industrial disablement pension (with unemployability supplement).[12]

To qualify for any of these increases the woman must either be residing with the beneficiary or being maintained by him at not less than the standard rate of the increase, or employed by him for consideration of not less than that amount.[13] The earnings rules applicable to wives[14] operate also with regard to these women, but with some necessary modifications. The exclusion of those earning more than the amount of the increase is effective for the short-term benefits, but the amounts (if any) which the beneficiary pays her are, of course, ignored, and the exclusion does not apply at all to those women employed by the beneficiary and not residing with him.[15] As regards the long-term benefits, the standard earning deduction rules apply to women who are residing with the beneficiary, though here also earnings payable by the latter are ignored.[16] There are, moreover, some further limitations which do not apply to wives.

The woman must not be imprisoned or detained in legal custody[17] (though it is a little difficult to see how she may be so and yet still caring for the children), or absent from GB.[18] Finally, an increase to disablement or invalidity pension is not payable if the beneficiary has a wife who is entitled to a Category B or C retirement pension.[19]

v) Relatives

When reviewing the provision for dependants in 1956, the National Insurance Advisory Committee conceded that the rule governing payments for adult dependants other than the wife and the 'housekeeper' were based more on the historical antecedents of the scheme than on any logical development of a principle of social insurance.[20] At the same time, the coverage of all dependants would involve far-reaching changes to the

9. *CS 726/49*, unless an increase is claimed for an invalid care allowance: ante n. 7 on p. 387. A non-residing female must, however, be maintained by the beneficiary, post, p. 393.
10. *R(S) 20/54*.
11. SSA 1975, ss.44(2),(3) and 66(1)(d).
12. Ibid., ss.46(1) and 66(1)(d); S.I. 1977/343, Reg. 1(3).
13. Ibid., Reg. 10(2)(b). For the invalid care allowance, residence must be proved, ante n.7 on p. 387.
14. Ante, p. 387.
15. S.I. 1977/343, Reg. 10(2)(e).
16. Ibid., Reg. 10(4).
17. Ibid., Reg. 10(2)(d).
18. Unless she is residing with him and he is not disqualified: ibid., Reg. 10(2)(c) and (3).
19. SSA 1975, s.46(3), presumably because this is analogous to an increase for a wife, and a beneficiary may not claim increases for both a wife and a resident 'housekeeper'.
20. Cmd. 9855.

scheme, and add to the burden on contributors. The result is something of a patchwork. The increase may supplement the usual short-term benefits (for unemployment, sickness, maternity and industrial injury[1]) and long-term disability benefits (invalidity and industrial disablement pensions[2]) but not retirement pensions[3] or the invalid care allowance. The relative must come within a prescribed class:

> all direct lineal ascendants or descendants, and siblings, whether of whole- or half-blood[4] or parents-in-law; also any such who are related by adoption[5] or would have been related if somebody born illegitimate had been born legitimate[6].

Further, there must be the necessary degree of dependency. Unlike the rule for other categories of dependant, the claimant must for this purpose prove that the relative is both residing with, and being wholly or mainly maintained by, him.[7] There are the usual 'sex-discrimination' limitations, so that a male relative must be incapable of self-support and a female relative must not be earning more than the amount of the increase.[8] In addition, if the latter is married (not, of course, to the claimant) she will succeed only if either her husband is incapable of self-support or she is not residing with him and is unable to obtain financial assistance from him.[9] The increase is not payable if the relative is imprisoned or detained in legal custody or (with certain exceptions for sickness and other disability benefits[10]) absent abroad.[11]

C. 'Residing with' or 'living with' the beneficiary

The principle that a beneficiary should be either maintaining the dependant or residing (or living) with him is not difficult to rationalise. If the beneficiary shares a home with another, and is an earner, it is a reasonable assumption that he is contributing to that other's maintenance. The different formulation for adult dependants ('residing with') and children ('living with') is deliberate. The latter concept was that used in the family allowances, and subsequently the child benefit, legislation and was explicitly incorporated into the national insurance scheme in 1957.[2] As will be seen in chapter 11 it carries a broader meaning than 'residing with'[13] and it is submitted that, notwithstanding a Commissioner's decision to the contrary,[14] it is that meaning which was intended by Parliament to apply

1. SSA 1975, ss.44(2) and 66(1)(a).
2. Ibid., ss.47 and s.66(1)(d); S.I. 1977/343, Reg. 1(3).
3. Or where the non-industrial benefits already mentioned are payable to a person over pensionable age: SSA 1975, ss.44(5) and 47(2).
4. Though in the latter case, not extending beyond one degree of ascent or descent.
5. An adoption need not have conformed with the prescribed legal methods: CI

266/50.
6. S.I. 1977/343, Sch. 1.
7. SSA 1975, ss.44(3)(b), 47(1)(b) and 66(1)(c).
8. S.I. 1977/343, Reg. 9(2)(a)–(b).
9. Ibid., Reg. 9(2)(c).
10. See post, p. 410.
11. S.I. 1977/343, Reg. 9(2)(d).
12. NIA 1957, s.6(4).
13. Post, pp. 457–459.
14. R(I) 11/62, where it was held to have the same meaning as 'residing with'.

for the purposes of children's increases to personal benefit.[15] It thus remains to consider the concept of 'residing with' which qualifies the relationship with adult dependants.

The term is not defined in the Social Security Act and guidance is to be had only from the case-law.[16] The basic idea is that the two people concerned should be living under the same roof.[17] This does not mean either that one of them should be the owner or tenant of the property[18] or that, in the case of spouses, they are sleeping in the same bed or otherwise maintaining the normal relationship of husband and wife.[19] But there must be an element of continuity and permanence in the co-residence.[20] In some cases, it will be necessary for the claimant to prove that he has acquired a new 'co-resident'. It will be more difficult to establish that living in a hotel, lodgings or the home of relatives constitutes co-residence than the entering into a tenancy agreement or setting up home with a woman as his wife.[1] More often, the question is whether an admitted co-residence has in fact ceased. On this the legislation is more helpful. Regulations made under the Social Security (Miscellaneous Provisions) Act 1977 lay down three rules.

i) Temporary absence
Under the first rule

> 'two persons shall not be treated as having ceased to reside together by reason of any temporary absence the one from the other'.[2]

This reinforces the notion that 'residing with' implies a permanent rather than a temporary condition, but it is naturally difficult to draw the line between the two. Some authorities, applying an equivalent rule under regulations previously in force, held that the test depends primarily on the parties' state of mind: did they intend to resume co-residence when the period of separation had ceased? Or has the separation been so long that, on reasonable inference, it was likely to be permanent?[3] On this view, the purpose of the absence becomes important. Thus the acquisition of accommodation removed from the family but near the claimant's employment will not generally be regarded as indicative of 'temporary' absence,[4] but it may be so categorised if the claimant is merely looking for work and intends that the family should join him when he finds it,[5] or

---

15. The argument is reinforced by the fact that under the CBA 1975, the term qualifying the relationship between two *adults* has been altered from 'living with': post, p. 460. It was clearly intended to harmonise the two schemes.
16. The expression is also used in the Rent Acts (see, e.g., *Morgan v Murch* [1970] 2 All ER 100, [1970] 1 WLR 778, CA) and in the law of family maintenance (see, e.g., *Curtin v Curtin* [1952] 2 QB 552, DC).

17. Per Lord Goddard CJ, ibid., at p. 556; *R(P) 15/56*.
18. *CU 201/50*.
19. *Curtin v Curtin* ante n.16; *R(S) 14/52*.
20. *CS 3/48*. See also S.I. 1977/956, Reg. 2(3), post, p. 392.
1. *R(P) 4/54*; *R(F) 1/62*.
2. S.I. 1977/956, Reg. 2(4).
3. See, e.g., *CS 3/48*; *CS 6/48*; *R(S) 1/51*.
4. *UD 4053/28*; *UD 5131/29*; *R(S) 1/51*; *R(S) 10/55*; *R(I) 37/55*.
5. *R(S) 14/58*.

lodges near the work but returns home at weekends and for holidays.[6] Other authorities have regarded the intention of the claimant as too elusive a criterion and have concentrated more on the duration of the absence. In the early 1950s the Commissioner devised a rule of thumb that:

'a period of absence which has lasted for more than a year, and of which there is no reasonable prospect of its coming to an end, cannot ... be spoken of as "temporary" '.[7]

This was then combined with another rule of thumb that the 'reasonable prospect of its coming to an end' should be judged within a period of six months from the date of application.[8] The two tests were regularly applied[9] but they were not regarded as hard and fast rules, and might be ousted by special circumstances.[10] In 1962, a Tribunal of Commissioners reported on a tendency to take a 'much shorter term view of residence', and implied that it would be better to regard the matter as one of degree in each case, rather than argue it in terms of legal presumption.[11]

ii) Widows

In relation to widow's benefit the position of persons under nineteen who may be engaged in full-time education or training away from home has caused some difficulties.[12] The Regulations thus prescribe that

'in the case of a woman who has been widowed, she shall not be treated as having ceased to reside with a child or person under the age of nineteen by reason of any absence the one from the other which is not likely to be permanent'.[13]

iii) Hospital in-patients

The application of the 'residing with' criterion to cases where the beneficiary or the dependant is in hospital has been equally problematical. The National Insurance Advisory Committee reviewed the matter in 1955 and concluded that special provision should be made for spouses.[14] Under the current rule,

'two spouses shall not be treated as having ceased to reside together by reason only of the fact that either of them is, or they both are, undergoing medical or other treatment as an in-patient in a hospital or similar institution, whether such absence is temporary or not'.[15]

Where the treatment of a dependant is free under the National Health Service, the need of the beneficiary to support him or her is obviously

---

6. *UD 6702/29*; *UD 15405/32*.
7. *CP 84/50* unreported, but cited in *R(P) 7/53*, para. 8.
8. *R(P) 7/53*.
9. See, e.g., *R(U) 15/54*; *R(S) 7/55*; *R(U) 14/58*.
10. See, e.g., *R(S) 14/55*.
11. *R(U) 11/62*.

12. Cf., *Fox v Stirk and Bristol Electoral Registration Officer* [1970] 2 QB 467, [1970] 3 All ER 7, CA, (on franchise qualifications).
13. S.I. 1977/956, Reg. 2(3).
14. Report on the Question of Dependency Provisions, Cmd. 9855.
15. S.I. 1977/956, Reg. 2(2)(b).

reduced. For this reason, as will be seen later in this chapter, there are rules for adjusting the rates of the increases.[16] In that context, too, the meaning of 'medical or other treatment as an in-patient in a hospital or similar institution' will be considered.

D. Maintenance by beneficiary

In some cases, the beneficiary may prove as an alternative to 'residence' that he was 'maintaining' the dependant. In others, he must prove both 'residence' and 'maintenance'. The required degree of maintenance varies according to the category of the alleged dependant. The beneficiary must contribute to the cost of providing for a child at a weekly rate of not less than the amount of the increase claimed;[17] he must 'contribute to the maintenance' of a spouse or 'housekeeper' to a similar extent.[18] In the case of adult relatives, the criterion is that of 'wholly or mainly maintaining' the person in question.[19] This latter can only be established if first, when in employment, the beneficiary was contributing more than one half of the cost of maintaining the relative, and secondly, such contributions during the period for which the increase is claimed, are also not less than the amount of that increase.[20]

i) Mode and time of payments

The maintenance question is one of fact and not of legal liability. The mere existence of an obligation to maintain, even if the result of a court order, will not be sufficient to establish title to the increase.[1] The claimant must therefore prove that he has actually been making the appropriate payments during the relevant period[2] but he does not have to go further and show that the sums were actually received or consumed by the person in question; for example, the money might be held by the clerk of a court[3] or diverted to the DHSS.[4] The fact that the prescribed amount of maintenance required is expressed in terms of weekly payments does not, of

16. Post, pp. 416–421.
17. SSA 1975, ss.43(1), (2) and 65(1), (2).
18. Ibid., ss.44(1), 45(2), 47(1) and 66(1); S.I. 1977/343, Reg. 10(2).
19. SSA 1975, ss.44(3)(b), 47(1)(b) and 66(1)(c).
20. S.I. 1977/343, Reg. 2(1).
 1. *R(U) 25/59*; *R(U) 1/77*.
 2. There is one qualification to this where an increase for a child is claimed. For this purpose, as has been seen (ante, p. 386), the beneficiary may qualify because he was entitled to child benefit in respect of that child. That entitlement may itself depend on the claimant making contributions to the cost of providing for the child (post, pp. 459–461). It was established law under the family allowances scheme that such contributions had to be made in the week preceding the week of the

claim (see *R(F) 8/61*). To obviate the difficulty which will result if that rule is applied to child benefit (cf. *R(U) 11/62*, Tribunal decision), the Regulations provide that the maintenance condition is deemed to be satisfied if the beneficiary (a) 'gives an undertaking in writing to make such contributions; and (b) on receiving the amount of the ... increase in question, he in fact makes such contributions': S.I. 1977/343, Reg. 5(1). See further on this provision *R(U) 1/77*, and NIAC Report on Amended Regulations (1966), Cmnd. 2959.
 3. *CS 638/49*.
 4. Cf., post, pp. 543–544. There is no reported case on the point but the proposition in the text should be accepted as a matter of principle.

course, mean that the actual payments must be made weekly. On the other hand, they must be regular payments which on average equal or exceed the prescribed rate. Thus a payment of an occasional lump sum cannot be treated as regular maintenance and apportioned to weekly payments.[5] Interruptions in payments cannot be ignored,[6] so that if the claimant falls in arrears, he may not count against current payments any payments made to clear arrears.[7] Thus in *R(U) 25/58*.

> C was bound, under a court order, to pay his separated wife £1·15 per week. For about forty weeks prior to his claim for the increase, he was paying her on average £1·30, but of this 15p was arrears. He was therefore unable to show that he was currently contributing at the then prescribed rate of £1·25 per week. As the Commissioner observed, any other ruling would unduly benefit husbands who accumulated arrears.[8]

ii) Payment in kind

It has long been recognised that maintance need not necessarily take the form of a monetary payment. Account may be taken of the regular provision of food, clothing, fuel and other items necessary for sustenance and welfare.[9] So also if the claimant conveys to the dependant his beneficial interest in the matrimonial home.[10] The calculation of maintenance will then proceed on the basis of the rateable value, or interest on the capital value, of the property transferred.[11] In another case, the same principle was applied to the transfer of a business share: the interest obtained on the purchase-money of the share sold was deemed to be a regular contribution to maintenance.[12]

iii) Joint maintenors

A Regulation deals with the situation, presumably not of frequent occurrence, where a dependant is being maintained by two or more beneficiaries. If the aggregate amount of such maintenance equals or exceeds the rate necessary for any one of them to claim the increase, such increase is payable notwithstanding that no one individual himself is able to satisfy the criterion.[13] The recipient will be the person who makes the largest contribution, or, if there is no such person, then either the eldest member of the group or one designated by the majority in a written notice sent to the Secretary of State.[14]

5. *R(U) 14/62*.
6. Compare child benefit, post, p. 460, where the rule is perhaps more generous.
7. *R(U) 11/62*.
8. *R(U) 25/58*, para. 7. In *R(S) 3/74* R.G. Micklethwait, Chief Comr., refused to apply the 'allocation' Regulation (post, p. 395) to assist in cases of regular but inadequate payments.
9. *CI 111/50*; *R(I) 10/51*.

10. *R(U) 3/66*, though J.S. Watson, Dep. Comr., reserved his opinion on whether the position would have been the same if the dependant had sold or let the property in question. In *R(S) 6/52* it was held that such a sale would not affect the claimant's rights.
11. *R(U) 3/66*.
12. *R(I) 37/54*.
13. S.I. 1977/343, Reg. 2(2).
14. Ibid., Reg. 2(2)(b).

iv) Allocation principle

Sometimes maintenance payments are explicitly allocated as between wife (or ex-wife) and children; sometimes they are not. It would be invidious if the exact classification of the payments were to be decisive in determining whether one or other dependant would qualify for the increase. So long as a marriage is subsisting,[15] the system assumes a principle of non-discrimination between a beneficiary's wife and his children. Where a payment is made to a wife or children or both, the authorities are given discretion to apportion the maintenance in such a way as will entitle the claimant to the largest payment by way of increase.[16] A typical exercise of this power would be as follows.

> C, in receipt of unemployment benefit, is paying by way of maintenance every week £9·00 for his wife and £2·00 for each of two children. If the apparent apportionment were to be binding, C could claim no increase since the prescribed amount of maintenance is for an adult dependant £9·10, and for a child £2·20. By notionally apportioning the aggregate of £13·00 into £9·10 for the wife, £2·20 for the first child and £1·70 for the second child, the authorities will be able to confer on C title to an increase for the wife and for the first child.

v) Family fund[17]

The technique used for calculating individual dependency in the typical situation where money from various sources is used to support a number of individuals is a judicial creation and owes nothing to legislative prescription. It was originally conceived by judges deciding dependency issues under the Workmen's Compensation Acts,[18] and subsequently adopted by the Umpire adjudicating unemployment insurance claims.[19] There being nothing in the post-war legislation to discourage its continued application, it was in 1949 accepted as part of national insurance law[20], a decision reaffirmed by Tribunals of Commissioners in later cases.[1]

The fundamental principle is that the authorities should have regard to the normal phenomena of family support rather than to strict legal obligations to maintain.[2] Thus if a woman is in fact supported by her brother, a cousin or a son, it is irrelevant that she is in law wholly dependent on her husband. The modification of the intra-family maintenance obligations resulting from the abolition of the poor law in 1948[3] did not therefore affect the matter.[4] The technique proceeds by calculating the 'unit cost' of each family member. For this, the total family income is divided by the number of individuals (counting two children as one adult).

15. Cf., R(S) 9/61.
16. S.I. 1977/343, Reg. 3.
17. See, generally, Kahn-Freund, 16 MLR 148, 164–173.
18. See, esp., Main Colliery Co v Davies [1900] AC 358, HL, and Hodgson v West Stanley Colliery [1910] AC 229, HL.

19. See, esp., UD 18381/31.
20. CSI 50/49.
1. R(I) 1/57 and R(I) 20/60.
2. See particularly the speech of Lord Loreburn LC in Hodgson v West Stanley Colliery, ante n.18, at p. 232.
3. NAA 1948, ss.1 and 42.
4. CSI 50/49.

In a family group of three adults (H, the husband, W, his wife and B, his brother) and two children (K and L) there will be 4 units. If the total family income is £120·00 (H contributing £70·00, W £10·00 and B £40·00) per week, the unit cost of one adult is $£\frac{120}{4} = £30\cdot00$ and of one child £15·00.

Each individual then has a surplus or deficit of contribution over cost.

H has a surplus of £40·00, B a surplus of £10·00, W a deficit of £20·00, and K and L each a deficit of £15·00.

To assess the degree of dependency of an individual with a deficit on an individual with a surplus, one divides the amount of the deficit proportionally between those providing a surplus.

H is providing $\frac{4}{5}$ of the total surplus and B $\frac{1}{5}$. Thus the extent of W's dependency on H is $\frac{4}{5} \times 20 = £16\cdot00$, and the extent of K's (or L's) dependency on H is $\frac{4}{5} \times 15 = £12\cdot00$.

The calculation is to be applied to the family circumstances existing at the time immediately prior to the event (e.g., sickness, unemployment, retirement) for which the benefit is payable: subsequent changes in the composition of the group or financial contributions are to be ignored,[5] and the average or normal contributions of individuals are to be assessed as at that date.[6]

If the method is one of simple arithmetic, it nevertheless raises some delicate issues when applied to actual family situations. It is sometimes argued that the method does not accord with the reality of how a particular family organises its household budget. The answer to this is that it is a convenient and less expensive method of calculating typical expenditure. Complete accuracy is neither obtainable nor (presumably) desirable. The method should be departed from only where there is clear evidence that it substantially conflicts with the actual circumstances.[7] It may be that an individual member consumes more or less than the attributed 'unit cost', e.g., because he is aged or disabled, but it has always been held that no account is to be taken of the actual way in which money is spent.[8] Contributions raise greater difficulties: doubt may be cast on whether a particular sum should constitute a contribution to the household budget, or whether it should be attributed to one person rather than another. It has been held that sums required for personal liabilities or for special needs should be excluded from the calculations.[9] Such needs are, of course, not easy to define but the cases provide some useful examples: life insurance premiums,[10] special clothing for an invalid,[11] a scholarship grant for a child.[12] On the other hand, social security benefits are normally integrated into the household fund.[13] A contributory benefit is regarded as a resource

5. CS 52/50.
6. R(I) 10/51.
7. R(I) 46/52; R(U) 37/52; R(I) 20/60.
8. CS 52/50; R(I) 1/57; R(I) 20/60.
9. R(I) 1/57.
10. CI 111/50; CI 266/50.
11. CS 221/50 (unreported).
12. UD 16621/32.
13. CP 96/50; CI 266/50; R(S) 6/53; R(I) 8/65.

provided by the person on whose contributions the benefit is payable.[14] Non-contributory benefits are attributed to the individual or individuals for whom they are paid. Thus in the case of supplementary benefit, the sum will be apportioned between the claimant and the dependants whose requirements are aggregated with his.[15] A Tribunal of Commissioners has suggested that if a constant attendance allowance were used to pay an outsider to come in and provide the requisite service, the benefit might be excluded from the fund.[16] If that is right the same would apply where a non-industrial attendance allowance is used for the same purpose.

E. Incapable of self-support

Claims for male dependants and female relatives are conditional on proof that the person concerned is 'incapable of self-support'.[17] The Act defines this as

> 'incapable of supporting himself by reason of physical or mental infirmity and is likely to remain so incapable for a prolonged period'.[18]

'A prolonged period' has been interpreted by the Commissioner as being not less than six months,[19] but the estimate is taken not at the time of the claim but from when the period of incapacity began.[20] The test is not the same of that of 'incapacity for work',[1] the requirement generally employed to establish title to the disability benefits[2]. One import of the difference is that, for the present purpose, the person's capacity over the whole of the period is considered rather than for particular days: 'the term "self-support" implies a state of affairs which is reasonably stable, settled and continuous'.[3] Thus a person only intermittently incapacitated may still qualify[4] and the authorities are not to assume that the dependant will always work to the maximum of his assessed capacity.[5] Short periods of working may be ignored,[6] so also those during which an individual has worked contrary to the advice of a doctor who considers him unfit.[7]

Nor is ability to work equivalent to 'self-support'. The test is a more complex one. The statutory formula may be elaborated into five subordinate elements:[8]

> (1) the dependant must be suffering from a physical or mental infirmity; (2) he would, but for this infirmity, have worked; (3) the

14. *CP 96/50*.
15. *R(I) 8/65*.
16. *R(I) 1/57*, para. 19, declining to evaluate the merits of *UD 17142/31*.
17. Ante, pp. 388–390. The same test applies to male dependants (esp. widowers) claiming industrial death benefit, ante, pp. 346 and 368. But they must be '*permanently* incapable of self-support', which means 'likely to remain so incapable for the remainder of his life': SSA 1975, Sch. 20.

18. Ibid.
19. *CS 288/50*.
20. *CS 343/49*; *CS 288/50*; *R(S) 2/56*.
1. *CG 4/48*; *CG 5/48*; *R(G) 3/56*.
2. Ante, pp. 151–152.
3. *R(G) 3/56*, para. 6.
4. Ibid.
5. *R(G) 3/57*.
6. *CG 30/49*.
7. *R(G) 16/52*.
8. *CG 4/48*, para. 7.

usual remuneration for this work would have been enough to support him; (4) he would have been able to do the work under the conditions on which it is usually available; (5) he would have been able to do the work sufficiently well to earn at the requisite rate.

Condition 1, which is entirely a medical question,[9] means that someone in full-time education cannot qualify on that ground alone.[10] Of the remaining issues, 4 and 5 depend partly on medical, partly on other, considerations, and the authorities must base their decision on all relevant evidence available.[11] The work which the dependant might otherwise have done may include domestic work, so that a woman able to look after herself and her children at home may find herself treated as able to earn sufficiently from such an occupation.[12] At the same time, the work must be readily available and the person so qualified as to be reasonably acceptable to an employer.[13] Perhaps the most important feature which distinguishes the test from 'incapacity for work' is that the earnings from the work of which the dependant is capable would have enabled him to be maintained at 'a reasonable standard of living'. In the first reported case on the point, the Commissioner decided that the appropriate level was higher than the grant which would have been paid to a person in the dependant's circumstances by way of national assistance (subsequently replaced by supplementary benefit).[14] While maintaining this principle, a Commissioner in 1957 selected an arbitrary figure of £3·00 per week.[15] Assuming that this was correctly decided and that the level should bear the same relationship to the current level of supplementary benefits, the present figure (in 1977–78) would be about £19·00. In assessing whether or not the actual or potential earnings of the dependant exceed the figure, unearned income and capital resources are to be ignored,[16] but expenses reasonably and necessarily incurred in earning the sum are to be deducted.[17]

Part two. Marriage

A. General

While it may be the case that a significant proportion of social welfare provision is concerned with remedying the lack of the traditional family structure, nevertheless much of the social security legislation, particularly that part concerned with contributory benefits, focusses on the unit of the family as defined by the general law.[18] References in the legislation to 'marriage', 'wife', 'husband', 'widow' and 'widower' have all been con-

9. *CG 4/48*, at para. 9.
10. *CS 41/49*. See also *CS 788/49* where the Commissioner rejected the argument that a male aged seventeen was not a 'man' and that he should thus be exempt from the condition.
11. *CG 4/48*, para. 10.
12. E.g., *R(G) 4/51*.
13. *CG 4/48*; *CG 5/48*.
14. *CG 3/48*.
15. *R(G) 2/57*. In 1958 it became £3·15: *R(G) 2/58*.
16. *R(G) 2/57*.
17. Thus where the claimant employs another person to do the housework: *R(G) 2/58*.
18. See, generally, ante, pp. 8–9.

strued to require the existence of a marriage which is recognised in the United Kingdom,[19] and which was subsisting at the time of the claim or the event which gave rise to entitlement.[20] What is legally recognised as a valid marriage is determined according to the general law of England (or Scotland), including as it does the principles of private international law when, for example, the validity of foreign marriages, or divorces, is in question. There is no space here to describe such rules in detail.[1] Instead a brief outline will be provided, together with such principles as have been developed within the framework of the social security legislation.

B. Marriages celebrated in the United Kingdom

A marriage celebrated in England and Wales must have satisfied the rules regarding formalities, which include the necessary preliminaries as well as due solemnisation, whether by civil or religious proceedings.[2] Production of the marriage certificate[3] will constitute prima facie evidence that the marriage has been duly celebrated,[4] but the absence of such a certificate will not be fatal. Provided that the parties can establish with sufficient reliability that a ceremoney in due form took place[5] and that it was followed by prolonged cohabitation as husband and wife, a valid marriage will be presumed.[6] The presumption will be rebutted by proof as to the invalidity of the marriage[7] but the standard of proof required is uncertain. One authority suggests that 'clear proof' will be sufficient,[8] but perhaps the better view is that the invalidity must be proved beyond reasonable doubt.[9] Scottish law, in contrast to English law, recognises a marriage 'by habit and repute', but the doctrine is narrowly confined:[10] there must have been a substantial period of cohabitation,[11] the bulk of which was in Scotland,[12] and the parties must have been free to marry[13] and consented, as between themselves, to a state of marriage.[14]

19. *CG 3/49*; *R(S) 4/59*. Thus under Scots law if the claim is made in Scotland.
20. *R(G) 1/52*; *R(P) 14/56*; *R(G) 2/73*. For the special problems arising with regard to maternity benefit see ante, pp. 250–251.
1. For the English family law see Bromley *Family Law* (5th edn), chap. 2, and Cretney *Principles of Family Law* (2nd edn), chaps. 2–3; for Scots family law see Clive and Wilson *Law of Husband and Wife in Scotland* (1974), chaps. 3–4 and for the relevant principles of private international law, Dicey and Morris *The Conflict of Laws* (9th edn), chap. 15.
2. *Bromley*, ante n.1, at pp. 33–52; *Cretney*, ante n.1, at pp. 5–25.
3. SSA 1975, s.160 makes provision for the obtaining of copies of the certificate for this purpose.
4. *CG 203/49*.
5. See *38/49 (P)*; *R(P) 4/60*; *R(G) 2/70*.
6. *CG 53/50*.
7. *R(G) 1/51*.
8. Per Harman LJ, *Re Taylor* [1961] 1 All ER 55 at 63.
9. Per Sir Jocelyn Simon P, *Mahadervan v Mahadervan* [1964] P. 233 at 244–246, adopted (obiter) by R.J.A. Temple, Comr., in *R(G) 2/70*, para. 17.
10. See *Low v Gorman* 1970 SLT 356, and generally *Clive and Wilson* ante n.1, at pp. 116–122. The law appears not to have been affected by the Marriage (Scotland) Act 1977.
11. 'Years' rather than 'months'; *R(G) 8/56*, para. 11.
12. *R(G) 1/71*.
13. *R(P) 1/51*; *R(I) 37/61*; cp., *R(G) 7/56* which regarded an impediment to marry as fatal only if known to the parties.
14. *R(G) 8/56*; *R(P) 1/58*; *R(G) 1/71*.

C. Marriages celebrated abroad

In general a foreign marriage will be recognised as valid by English and Scots law if it satisfied the formalities of the law of that jurisdiction where the marriage took place,[15] and if each party had capacity according to his domicile at the time of the alleged marriage.[16] The large number of immigrants, particularly from India and Pakistan, has caused considerable difficulties here. The problem is that sometimes expert evidence on the foreign law in question is required but it will not always be readily available to an insurance officer or local tribunal.[17] Decisions on the domicile of an individual at different stages of his life are also fraught with difficulties, depending as they do on a considerable amount of background information on family circumstances at some remote time or place.[18]

D. Effects of marriages void or voidable or terminated by divorce

A marriage which is void[19] because, for example, it is bigamous[20] or within the prohibited degrees[1] has no effect at law and cannot be relied on for the purposes of entitlement to benefit. On the other hand, the fact that a marriage is void may revive an entitlement to widow's benefit from a 'previous' marriage if it had ceased to be payable on the alleged remarriage.[2] The widow may not, of course, claim for any period during which she was cohabiting with the second 'husband' and she will in any event be subject to the rules on time-limits.[3] A marriage which is terminated by divorce is treated as valid until the decree is made absolute, but from that date it is no longer effective to ground entitlement. Though there is no direct decision on the point, it is assumed that a previous entitlement to widow's benefit is not revived by dissolution of a subsequent marriage[4] – in this respect it is different from a marriage held to be void. The problems to which divorced marriages give rise are concerned mainly with whether a foreign decree should be recognised: this is determined by the rules of private international law.[5]

15. *R(U) 1/68* and see *Dicey and Morris*, ante n.1, at pp. 234–258.
16. *R(G) 3/75* and see *Dicey and Morris*, ante n.1, at pp. 258–275.
17. See the remarks of R.S. Lazarus, Comr., in *R(G) 2/71*, paras. 4 and 8.
18. See e.g., *R(P) 1/57*; *R(G) 2/71* and *R(G) 3/75*.
19. See generally *Bromley*, ante n.1, at pp. 74–82.
20. *R(G) 2/63*.
 1. *R(G) 10/53*.
 2. *CG 28/53*, cited in *R(G) 1/73*.
 3. Post, p. 597.
 4. See *R(G) 1/73*, para. 14 (Tribunal majority).
 5. Much of the law on recognition of foreign divorces is governed by the Recognition of Judicial Divorces and Legal Separations Act 1971, as modified by the Domicile and Matrimonial Proceedings Act 1973. See, in general, Dicey and Morris *The Conflict of Laws* (9th edn), pp. 315–330. The Commissioner has in several instances been faced with the problem of customary divorces by 'talaq'. In *R(G) 2/71* and *R(G) 4/74* such a divorce was recognised because, on the expert evidence available, it was found that on the balance of probabilities the divorce would have been recognised by the law of domicile even though there was no direct judicial authority in the particular jurisdiction (cp., *R(G) 1/70*), though it was important to ascertain whether the correct procedure had been adopted (see *R(G) 5/74*). The

Between void marriages and those terminated by divorce comes the third and problematic category of voidable marriages,[6] (e.g., those which have not been consummated). Prior to 1971, for most legal purposes, such a marriage was regarded as valid and subsisting until the time of the decree of nullity, but the securing of such a decree would operate to invalidate the marriage retrospectively.[7] Under a legislative reform of 1956,[8] power was given to the Minister to provide by regulations that, for specified purposes, a voidable marriage was to be treated as a marriage terminated by divorce. This power was exercised as regards questions of entitlement arising under guardian's and child's special allowances.[9] The principles governing other benefits under social security legislation were unclear. In particular, there were conflicting decisions on whether a widow who lost benefit on entering a voidable marriage was entitled to claim for all periods except those during which she was cohabiting with the second 'husband'.[10] The process of retrospectively invalidating a marriage caused grave problems in other areas of the law and in 1971, following the recommendations of the Law Commission,[11] the Nullity of Marriage Act was passed, section 5 of which provides that

> 'a decree of nullity granted . . . on the ground that a marriage is voidable shall operate to annul the marriage only as respects any time after the decree had been made absolute, and the marriage shall, notwithstanding the decree, be treated as if it had existed up to that time'.

Some consequences of this provision are undisputed. For the purpose of claiming benefit based on the marriage, it is, during its subsistence to the time of the decree of nullity, to be regarded as valid. It is also clear that a widow cannot claim benefit on a previous marriage for any period before the decree.[12] The problem is, however, whether such a claim is valid for the period *after* the decree: in other words, is the woman's status as a widow revived by the annulment of the second marriage? The arguments are evenly balanced. If attention is focussed on the first part of section 5 (down to the words 'after the decree had been made absolute'), it might be said that, for the period after the decree, the marriage is annulled and therefore to be regarded as if it had never existed. If, conversely, attention is focussed on the last limb of section 5 ('and the marriage shall, notwithstanding the decree, be treated as if it had existed up to that time'), it might be said that even for purposes subsequent to the decree, the marriage is to be treated as having existed at some time, and thus the woman's

Domicile and Matrimonial Proceedings Act 1973, s.16 provides that from 1 January 1974 and subject to certain exceptions, such divorces will no longer be recognised. Divorces obtained before that date are unaffected by the new provision.

6. See generally Bromley *Family Law* (5th edn), pp. 82–99.

7. Ibid., at p. 97.

8. NIA 1957, s.9(1)(c).

9. S.I. 1957/1392. See now S.I. 1975/497, Reg. 3 and S.I. 1975/515, Reg. 4(3).

10. In *R(G) 3/72*, following unreported decisions in *CG 2/70*, *CG 1/71* and *CG 2/71*, J.S. Watson, Comr., held that a widow was not so entitled. In *R(G) 1/53* it had been held that she was entitled.

11. Report No. 33, 1970–71, HC 164.

12. *R(G) 1/73*, para. 14.

status as a widow is forever lost. A Tribunal of Commissioners, having taken into account the Law Commission's report on which proposals the measure was passed, preferred the second interpretation.[13]

E. Polygamous marriages

The extent to which the courts should recognise as valid a polygamous marriage has always been a delicate issue,[14] and entitlement to social security benefits features not least among the problems to which it has given rise. In simple terms, is it to be regarded as fair that contributors with one wife should subsidise those with two? When the matter first arose for decision by the Commissioner, a harsh stance was adopted. It was held that the use of the terms 'wife', 'husband', and 'widow' in the National Insurance Act was intended to incorporate the notion familiar to English law of 'the voluntary union for life of one man and one woman to the exclusion of all others'.[15] The approach had the effect of treating as invalid for social security purposes not only actual polygamous marriages[16] but also any marriage celebrated under a law which permitted polygamy, whether or not it had at all times been in fact monogamous.[17] The only recourse of a person married under such circumstances was to show that the law of the place where the marriage was celebrated had converted it into a monogamous marriage,[18] or that the same result had been achieved by the parties changing their domicile to a jurisdiction which recognised only monogamous marriages.[19] These two avenues were not always open and statutory reform was obviously called for.

Following the National Insurance Advisory Committee's proposals,[20] it was forthcoming in 1956. Henceforth, a marriage which had in fact at all times been monogamous was to be recognised as valid, even where it had been entered into under a law which permitted polygamy.[1] Though this was certainly an improvement on the previously existing law, it was by no means a totally satisfactory solution:[2] it did not cover marriages which were at one time polygamous but which were no longer so; and it did not apply where at the time benefit was claimed the marriage was polygamous but only one wife was resident in Great Britain. The policy argument for extending benefit may be stronger for the first group than for the second, but in either case refusal would seem unfair to a husband who has duly

13. R(G) 1/73, at paras. 18–20 and 25. R(G) 2/73. Cf., the discussions in *Bromley*, ante n.6, at pp. 97–98 and Cretney *Principles of Family Law* (2nd edn), pp. 71–72.
14. See Law Commission Report No. 42, 1970–71 HC 227; *Dicey and Morris*, ante n.5, at pp. 279–299, and the literature cited there at n.27.
15. Per Lord Penzance, *Hyde v Hyde and Woodmansee* (1866) LR 1 P & D. 130, 133, quoted in R(G) 18/52, para. 19.
16. R(G) 6/51.

17. R(G) 18/52 (Tribunal decision). See also R(G) 11/53, R(G) 3/55, R(G) 7/55 and the critical survey of the case law by Webb, 19 MLR 687.
18. As by the Indian Hindu Marriage Act 1955: see R(G) 12/56.
19. Under the doctrine of *Ali v Ali* [1968] P. 564, [1966] 1 All ER 664; see R(G) 5/75.
20. Report on the Question of Widows Benefit (1955), Cmd. 9684.
1. FANIA 1956, s.3.
2. See Law Commission Report, ante n.14, at paras. 125–134.

been paying his contributions. Moreover, supplementary benefit is certainly payable[3] and in *Iman Din v National Assistance Board*,[4] it was held that a polygamously married man could be compelled to reimburse the Board for national assistance (the precursor of supplementary benefit) paid to one of his wives. The gaps were partly filled by reform in 1971.[5] In its present version the measure provides that

> 'a polygamous marriage shall . . . be treated as having the same consequences as a monogamous marriage for any day, but only for any day, throughout which the polygamous marriage is in fact monogamous'.[6]

There are also special rules governing entitlement to retirement pensions of women who are parties to a polygamous marriage.[7] The broad effect is that such a woman may claim retirement pension on her husband's contributions as from any date on which the marriage was in fact monogamous, and in such cases the rate of pension payable is that which would have been payable in the case of a monogamous marriage whether or not, prior to the date in question, the marriage had been polygamous.

It will be apparent that nothing has yet been done to confer entitlement on persons who at the time of the claim (or in the case of widow's benefit at the time of the contributor's death) are actually polygamously married. The Law Commission had studied the problem in some detail but felt unable to recommend on grounds of administrative feasibility or acceptability by the general public, adoption of any of the following six proposals.[8]

1. A man having more than one wife to pay increased contributions and each of the wives to be entitled to benefit. The necessity of discovering which contributors had more than one wife would create administrative inconvenience both to the DHSS and to employers.

2. As in (1) but without increased contributions. In policy terms this would involve a subsidy by other contributors. This objection is not a major one because the numbers involved would be small, and in any event unmarried contributors already subsidise married contributors. But it would create a temptation to claim for spurious wives, and would probably be unacceptable to public opinion.

---

3. Cf., post, p. 487.
4. [1967] 2 QB 213, [1967] 1 All ER 750, DC.
5. NIA 1971, s.16(3) and S.I. 1972/1150.
6. S.I. 1975/561. Reg. 2(1): for the purposes of this provision a 'polygamous marriage' is one 'celebrated under a law which, as it applies to the particular ceremony and to the parties thereto, permits polygamy' (ibid., Reg. 1(2)): a 'monogamous marriage' is one

'celebrated under a law which does not permit polygamy' (ibid.); a marriage is 'in fact monogamous' 'when neither party to it has any spouse additional to the other' (ibid., Reg. 2(2)). For equivalent provisions under CBA 1975, see S.I. 1976/965, Reg. 12.
7. S.I. 1975/561, Reg. 3.
8. Law Commission Published Working Paper No. 21, paras. 61–66. The Report which followed (No. 42) took the matter no further: ante n.2.

3. As in (2) but benefits to be divided equally between all the wives. The amount so payable might consequently be small, and would therefore not achieve the objective of avoiding recourse to supplementary benefit.

4. Only wives living in Britain to be entitled. This was rejected on grounds of equity.

5. The DHSS to have discretionary power to select the wife for full benefit. This would be a very difficult discretion to exercise.

6. The contributor to be given a power to nominate a wife for full benefit. This would encourage discrimination and would be difficult to administer: the problem in (4) would arise if no election was made; power to vary would have to be conferred; and finally all social security contributors would have to be notified of the rule, which might bring the system into disrepute.

In the result, no further modifications to the rules have been made, though it is at least arguable that the equity objection to (4) is not a major one. For several other purposes, the social security legislation discriminates against those who are resident abroad. Further it would involve little danger of exploitation since the number of men with two wives living in Britain is apparently very small.[9]

Part three. Living Together as Husband and Wife

A. General

For certain purposes social security legislation treats a woman living with a man (not her husband) in the same way as a married woman. Thus a woman loses entitlement to widow's benefit[10] (and its equivalents in the industrial injuries and war pension schemes[11]), child's special allowance,[12] non-contributory invalidity pension[13] and invalid care allowance[14]

'for any period during which she and a man to whom she is not married are living together as husband and wife'.[15]

Such a woman is treated in the same way as a married woman in both the supplementary benefits[16] and family income supplements[17] schemes, and her requirements and resources will be assessed with the man's if he claims benefits.

9. See the remarks of Mr D. Ennals (Under-Secretary of State) in 707 HC Deb., col. 1603.
10. SSA 1975, ss.24(2), 25(3) and 26(3).
11. Ibid., ss.67(2), 71(3)(b), 72(4)(a) and 73(3) and R.W. 1964, Cmnd. 2467, art. 42.
12. SSA 1975, s.31.
13. Ibid., s.36(2)(b).
14. Ibid., s.37(3)(b).
15. SS(MP)A 1977, ss.14(7) and 22(2) and (4), amending the relevant provisions of SSA 1975.
16. SBA 1976, Sch. 1, para. 3(1)(b); and see post, pp. 487–488 on the aggregation principles.
17. FISA 1970, s.1(1)(b).

The 'cohabitation rule', as it is often referred to, was included in the national insurance widow's scheme introduced in 1925[18] but, perhaps surprisingly, was not expressly contained in the National Assistance Act 1948. If a woman cohabiting with a man claimed assistance, the National Assistance Board was compelled to use its discretionary powers to refuse an award.[19] In 1966, when supplementary benefits replaced national assistance, the rule was embodied in the legislation,[20] and, subject to a recent change in its formulation, has remained a constant, if controversial, feature of both the contributory and the means-tested schemes.

Though the arguments are equally applicable to both schemes, criticisms of the rule, which became particularly forthright in the late 1960s and 1970s,[1] tended to focus on its effect on supplementary benefit entitlement, and the Supplementary Benefits Commission has produced two special reports defending the rule, though instituting changes in its administration.[2]

The main justification advanced by the Commission, and accepted by the Finer Committee on One-Parent Families,[3] is that –

> '. . . it would be wrong in principle to treat the women who have the support of a partner both as if they had not such support and better than if they were married. It would not be right, and we believe public opinion would not accept, that the unmarried "wife" should be able to claim benefit denied to a married woman'.[4]

Although the rule's existence is regretted, it is, therefore, thought necessary to ensure equity between married and unmarried women. Two main arguments against the rule may be identified. The first is that an unmarried woman is not legally entitled to support for herself or her children (if not his own) from the man with whom she is living.[5] The distinction as regards rights to maintenance between married and unmarried women was regarded as crucial by the Supreme Court of the United States when it held invalid an Alabama regulation disqualifying a family from receiving assistance if, inter alia, a man lived in or visited the mother's house for the purposes of cohabitation.[6] The Commission's answer to this argument is that in general the men concerned do support the woman (and her children) with whom they are living, and that only a small minority refuse to accept responsibility.[7] The risk of hardship for some women does not justify, in its view, abrogation of the rule and the consequent unfairness to

18. Widows', Orphans' and Old Age Contributory Pensions Act 1925, s.21(1).
19. SBC Report, *Living Together as Husband and Wife* (1976), para. 8.
20. SBA 1966, Sch. 2, para. 3(1).
1. See esp., Lister *As Man and Wife* (1970), Poverty Pamphlet.
2. *Cohabitation* (1971) and *Living Together as Husband and Wife*, ante n.19.
3. Para. 5.269.

4. *Cohabitation*, para. 7.
5. *Living Together as Husband and Wife*, para. 22. It should be noted, however, that the obligation to maintain cannot be enforced in the magistrates' court while the spouses are living together: Cretney *Principles of Family Law* (2nd edn), p. 221.
6. *Smith v King* 88 S.Ct. 2128 (1968). See La France et al., *Law of the Poor* (1973), pp. 338 ff.
7. Ante n.19, at para. 22.

those who are married. This argument would appear to be acceptable, provided the Commission is right in its assessment that relatively few cases of hardship result from the rule's application. The Commission's own evidence suggests that some relationships between the claimant and the man concerned terminate soon after the cessation of benefit payments, and this often leads to a further application for assistance.[8] To some extent this might be thought to cast doubt on the argument for the rule.

The second principal argument is that whatever the rule's merits in theory, its application leads to such intrusion into privacy and consequent anxiety on the part of claimants that its maintenance cannot on balance be justified.[9] There is no obvious answer to this contention, and it is interesting that in its recent report the Commission does not even attempt one. To some extent the solution lies in a more sensitive administration of the rule, and the Commission has made a number of changes in its practice which should go some way to meeting the criticism.[10]

B. The meaning of 'living together'

The term 'cohabiting' was never defined in the social security legislation. This was criticised by the Fisher Committee Report on Abuse of Social Security Benefits,[11] but the Commission has always maintained the view that precise statutory definition was impossible.[12] In the only case on the rule to reach the courts, Lord Widgery CJ, said that the phrase 'cohabiting as man and wife', then in force, was 'so well known that nothing I could say about it could possibly assist in its interpretation'.[13] Recently, however, the Social Security (Miscellaneous Provisions) Act 1977 replaced the term 'cohabiting' by 'living together',[14] largely on the ground that the former had acquired a perjorative meaning,[15] but it does not seem that any different interpretation is intended.[16] Nor has it ever been suggested that the interpretation should differ according to whether it is a contributory or a means-tested benefit which is in question.[17] It is therefore proposed to consider together such guidelines on the meaning as emerge from the National Insurance Commissioner's decisions and the Supplementary Benefits Commission's policy statements contained in its handbook. As was stressed by the Chief Commissioner in the most recently reported decision on the matter, it is necessary for the determining authorities to

8. Ante, n.19, at paras. 30, 34 and 35–48.
9. Ibid., at para. 18.
10. For a short discussion of these reforms, see post, pp. 487–488.
11. Para. 330(b).
12. Ante n.19, at paras. 49–51.
13. *R v South West London Supplementary Benefits Appeals Tribunal, ex parte Barnett*, DC, (unreported).
14. Ss. 14(7) and 22(2)–(4).
15. Ante n.19, at para. 52.
16. Originally the change was put forward in the consolidation Supplementary Benefits Bill 1976, but it was rejected by the Joint Committee on Consolidation Bills (HL 199, HC 449), and reintroduced as a legislative change by the 1977 Bill. There was, however, no suggestion in the debates that the new phrase had a different meaning from the previous formulation.
17. When a claimant suspected of cohabitation is in receipt of both types of benefit, it seems that the SBC will always follow the decision on the contributory benefit.

have regard to a number of factors, none of which is by itself conclusive.[18]

i) Members of same household

It is a necessary condition for the application of the rule to the means-tested benefits,[19] and an obvious assumption for its application to the contributory benefits,[20] that the man and woman should be members of the same household, i.e., residing together under the same roof.[1] If, for example, he spends much of his time at another house, it will be difficult to infer that the two parties are living together.[2]

ii) Duration

The duration and stability of the cohabitation is clearly an important factor.[3] Where there is no evidence as to continuity of co-residence or where its existence remains uncertain, benefit should not be refused. The suggestion that a couple should be allowed to live together for a number of months without entitlement being affected has, however, been rejected.[4]

iii) Financial support

Both the Commissioner and the SBC have rejected the argument that the man can only be held to be living with the woman if he is supporting her financially. In one case the Commissioner said that:

> 'It is certainly not the law that where there is no common household fund there can be no cohabitation'.[5]

In *R(G) 3/71* the Commissioner, H.A. Shewan, pointed out that regularity of financial contributions might tend to show that the payer was a lodger rather than someone living with the claimant as her husband. The SBC's view is that it would be unrealistic to place primary emphasis on the level and consistency of financial contributions: this would encourage the man not to support the claimant in order to improve her chance of receiving benefit.[6] Moreover, the assessment of the contributions would present practical difficulties.[7] Where, however, there *is* evidence that the man and woman do pool their resources, this will be taken into account in determining whether they live together.[8]

iv) Sexual relationship

The existence or absence of a sexual relationship is never conclusive of the relationship of the persons concerned.[9] In some cases, however, it may be

18. *R(G) 2/72*, R.G. Micklethwait.
19. FISA 1970, s.1; SBA 1976, Sch. 1, para. 3(1).
20. See, e.g., *R(G) 11/55*.
1. On 'residing together', see ante, pp. 390–393.
2. Handbook, para. 21(a).
3. Ibid., at para. 21(b); cf., *R(P) 6/52*.
4. SBC Report, *Living Together as Husband and Wife* (1976), para. 55(2).
5. *R(G) 2/64*, commenting on *CG 214/50*.
6. Ante n.4, at para. 55(3). Cp., Lister *As*

Man and Wife (1970), Poverty Pamphlet, pp. 41–42 where it is suggested that more weight should be given to the financial aspects of the relationship.
7. *Cohabitation*, para. 8; *Living Together as Husband and Wife*, para. 55(3).
8. *R(G) 2/72*; Handbook, para. 21(c).
9. See *Thomas v Thomas* [1948] 2 KB 294, DC, discussing the meaning of 'cohabitation' in the context of matrimonial legislation.

of great weight, particularly when it is also established that they have children and intend to marry.[10] This is naturally a sensitive area, and the SBC is anxious to emphasise that it is not concerned with the sexual morals of the claimant. Its staff is instructed not to question claimants about their sexual relationship and not to inspect the sleeping arrangements.[11]

v) Children
There will be a strong presumption that a man and woman are living together as husband and wife if they are looking after their own children.[12]

vi) Public acknowledgment
A public acknowledgment by a woman that she is living with someone as his wife by taking his surname is compelling evidence of cohabitation.[13] On the other hand, little significance is to be attached to a refusal to acknowledge the relationship in public.[14]

Part four. Residence and Presence

A. General

The geographical boundaries of the social security system may not seem to raise policy issues of the dimension encountered elsewhere but it has long been an area the difficulties of which have provided a fruitful supply of problems for lawyers. Under the poor law perhaps the question giving rise to most litigation was that concerned with the 'settlement' of paupers, the condition of residence on which the responsibility of parishes was based.[15] Happily, the centralisation of social security obviated the need to distinguish between parts of the country, but the increased facilities for foreign travel, the growth of multinational enterprises and the emergence of the 'migrant worker' underline the continued importance and difficulty of the topic. To some extent the problems have been solved by reciprocal agreements with other national systems and by the 'co-ordinating' Regulations of the European Economic Communities. These instruments are described in chapter 16. The discussion in the present chapter is concerned with the limits imposed by the British social security legislation independently of the facilities available under the instruments. The rules emerging will thus indicate the circumstances in which an individual must resort to the additional facilities described in chapter 16.

10. *R(G) 2/64*; *R(G) 3/71*.
11. Ante n.4, at para. 55(4).
12. *CG 214/50*; *R(G) 3/64*; *R(G) 3/71*; *R(G) 2/72*.
13. *R(G) 5/68* and see *CG 7/75*, reported *LAG Bulletin*, Sept. 1975, p. 246.
14. *CP 97/49, R(P) 6/52*.

15. Blackstone, *Commentaries*, vol. 1, p. 362 refers to the 'infinity of expensive law-suits between contending neighbourhoods'. See, generally, Holdsworth, *History of English Law* (1938), vol. X, pp. 257–269. See also post, p. 480.

B. The framework

In general, the relationship with Great Britain, as expressed in such concepts as 'residence', 'presence', or (in a very few instances) 'nationality', is relevant for four different purposes.

i) Participation in the contributory scheme

There are rules to determine who is compelled (or in the case of non-employed persons and certain self-employed persons who is entitled) to contribute to the scheme. These have been set out in chapter 2.[16]

ii) Alternatives to contribution conditions

For those benefits the entitlement to which depends on the fulfilment of contribution conditions there is no *positive* requirement as to residence. Participation in the scheme for the requisite number of years is prima facie sufficient to justify the conferring of benefit. Indeed, to a limited extent, the system is prepared to make concessions to those whose work abroad has prevented them from making the requisite contributions. The rules designed to implement this policy were also mentioned in chapter 2.[17]

iii) Disqualifications for absence

The Social Security Act 1975 lays down as a general ground for disqualification for contributory benefits absence (whether of the claimant himself or a dependant for whom an increase is claimed) from Great Britain.[18] This principle, as elaborated and modified in the Regulations, is described in this Part.

iv) Requirements for non-contributory benefits

For benefits entitlement to which does not depend on fulfilment of contribution conditions, the need to impose limits on the scheme, according to an individual's connection with Great Britain, is more obvious and important. For each such benefit there is, therefore, a combination of rules generally requiring 'residence', 'ordinary residence', or at least 'presence' in Great Britain. The rules are stated in the appropriate chapters; here it will be necessary only to given an account of the interpretation of the general concepts employed.

C. Absence as a ground of disqualification from contributory benefits

The principles applicable proceed according to consistent but sometimes controversial policy dictates. There is no relief for absent persons claiming unemployment benefit, it being felt desirable to maintain unequivocally the claimant's attachment to the labour market in this country. Those entitled by reason of their incapacity or confinement are given some

---

16. Ante, pp. 55, 58, 60 and 63.   18. SSA 1975, s.82(5)(a).
17. Ante, p. 76.

concessions, notably for temporary absences. The most generous provision is for those whose entitlement in no way rests on their inability to work, because, for example, they have reached pensionable age or are caring for dependent children. Here the disqualification is often removed altogether. The general rule is then that a person is disqualified from receiving benefit (or an increase in benefit for a dependant) during a period during which the person (or the dependant) is absent from Great Britain.[19] The modifications to the rule are as follows.

i) Benefits for incapacity

For the purposes of sickness benefit, invalidity benefit, unemployability supplement, and maternity allowance a temporary absence is disregarded if

(a) the Secretary of State has certified that it is consistent with the proper administration of the Act that the disqualification should not apply *and*

either

(b) the absence is for the specific purpose of being treated for incapacity which commenced before he left Great Britain

or

(c) when the absence began he was, and had for six months continuously been, incapable of work and when benefit is claimed he has remained continuously so incapable since the absence began.[20]

The claimant must first establish that the absence is only temporary. No guidance is given for the interpretation of this, but the Commissioner has held that a seasonal worker, absent for the period of his off-season, cannot escape disqualification.[1] In other cases, it depends on the specificity of the intent to return. If there is only a vague hope to return sometime in the future, or when the claimant's health improves, the absence will not be temporary.[2] If there is an unequivocal intention to return when the claimant is fit to do so, the issue turns on the duration of the absence. A practical test, enunciated by the Commissioner, is that at the end of a twelve-month period there should be a reasonable prospect of the residence abroad coming to an end within the next six months.[3]

Condition (a) was originally introduced in 1975 to solve some of the difficulties, described below, arising from the other two conditions. It conferred a discretion on the Secretary of State to determine what was 'reasonable in all the circumstances of the case, having regard in particular . . . to the nature of the person's incapacity and to his location'.[4]

19. Ibid. Absence means not physically present (*R(U) 18/60*; *R(S) 16/62*). For the meaning of 'Great Britain' and for other points arising under the rule, see post, pp. 413–416.
20. S.I. 1975/563, Reg. 2(1), as amended by S.I. 1977/1679. For the analogous but not completely identical rule for industrial injury benefit see S.I. 1975/563, Reg. 9(1).
1. *R(I) 14/51*; *R(I) 73/54*.
2. *R(S) 3/58*; *R(S) 5/59*; *R(S) 9/59*.
3. *R(S) 9/55*.
4. S.I. 1975/563, Reg. 2(1).

In 1976 the Commissioner held that the Regulation was ultra vires.[5] An amendment of 1977 therefore introduced the concept of consistency with the proper administration of the Act.[6] It is to be anticipated, however, that the Secretary of State will continue to have regard to the considerations mentioned under the 1975 Regulation.

Under condition (b), it is necessary to show, first, that the claimant was suffering from the incapacity at the time of departure from Great Britain.[7] 'Incapacity' has been given the meaning attributed to it for the purpose of entitlement to benefit:[8] viz., an incapacity for work[9] constituted by a specific disease or bodily or mental disablement.[10] The ordinary condition of pregnancy is not sufficient,[11] and the incapacity must have been diagnosed (or capable of being diagnosed) before the absence began.[12] The requirement that the absence must be for the *specific purpose* of being treated has been generously (perhaps too generously) construed. The treatment need not be the sole objective of the absence – it may rank alongside other social or pleasureable purposes.[13] It need not be unavailable in Britain;[14] nor, apparently, need it be actually received by the claimant – it is sufficient if the purpose of the visit was to obtain it.[15] More surprisingly, and arguably wrongly, the specific purpose need not be formulated before the claimant leaves the country.[16] Greater difficulty has arisen from the meaning of 'being treated'. There is general agreement that some activity by a person other than the claimant must be involved,[17] but there is little uniformity on what form is envisaged. Some decisions imply that medical supervision or care is required;[18] others do not regard this as necessary.[19] In cases of mental illness, the authorities scrutinise the nature of the 'treatment' with particular care,[20] but in one case a claimant with psychological problems avoided disqualification when he was assisted in the solving of his spiritual problems by a Doctor of Divinity.[1] On one major issue there is, however, no disagreement: it has repeatedly been held that to go abroad merely to convalesce, for a change of environment, air or food, or to obtain freedom from anxiety, even if undertaken according to medical advice, does not amount to 'being treated'.[2] Indeed, in the only case which has been taken to the Divisional Court in this area the decision was limited to this simple proposition.[3] It is to be regretted that no further guidance was offered on what is a most confusing area of case-law.

The alternative condition (c) was introduced in 1967[4] to assist the long-term incapacitated. In these cases, proximity to the labour market is

5. *CS 5/75*, and see NIAL Report, Cmnd. 6967.
6. S.I. 1977/1679.
7. See, e.g., *R(S) 35/52*, *R(S) 19/54* and *R(S) 8/59*.
8. Cf., ante, pp. 150–156.
9. *R(S) 9/59*.
10. *R(S) 1/75*.
11. *R(G) 5/53*; *R(S) 1/75*.
12. *R(S) 1/75*.
13. *CSS 71/49*; *R(S) 6/61*.
14. *R(S) 3/54*.
15. *R(S) 6/61*.
16. *CS 317/49*; *R(S) 1/57*; *R(S) 1/75*.
17. *CSS 71/49*; *CS 474/50*; *R(S) 10/51*.
18. *R(S) 16/51*; *R(S) 5/61*; *R(S) 2/69*.
19. *R(S) 10/51*; *R(S) 2/51*.
20. See *R(S) 5/61*.
1. *R(S) 1/65*.
2. *R(S) 16/51*; *R(S) 10/52*; *R(S) 25/52*; *R(S) 5/61*; *R(S) 3/68*; *R(S) 1/69*; *R(S) 2/69*.
3. *R v National Insurance Comr, ex parte McMenemey* (1966), reported as Appendix to *R(S) 2/69*.
4. S.I. 1967/828.

obviously of less importance. On the other hand, the absence must still be temporary, and therefore the number likely to succeed on this ground must be relatively small.

ii) Long-term benefits immune from disqualification

When the benefit in question is paid irrespective of the working capacity of the claimant, supervision of the claim is less important and, arguably, he should receive the return on the contributions paid irrespective of where he chooses to live. The disqualification does not, therefore, apply to retirement pensions, child's special allowance, widow's benefit,[5] industrial disablement and death benefit.[6] There is, nevertheless, an important qualification to be made. Those claiming widow's benefit, child's special allowance or retirement pension may not be entitled to an increase resulting from an up-rating of benefit[7] unless they satisfy certain residence conditions.[8] The disqualification is not, however, automatic and it is for the Secretary of State to determine, when issuing the up-rating order, whether or not these special conditions are to apply.[9] The policy is a traditional one: in the 1950s and 1960s when increases were made to the standard rate of pension those resident abroad were not allowed to benefit.[10] In insurance terms it was argued that the contributions on which the pension was based were not actuarially related to the increases and that it would be inequitable for the other contributors to the fund, effectively paying for the increases, to assist those living abroad.[11] Alternatively, it could be said that the funds available for up-rating benefits were limited, and priority was to be given to those living, and paying taxes, in Britain.[12]

iii) Lump-sum benefits

A person, e.g., the administrator of the deceased's estate may be paid the death grant notwithstanding his absence from Great Britain.[13] A maternity grant is payable to a woman abroad if *either*

    1. during the tax year before the confinement she, or the person on whose contributions she relies, had paid, or been credited with,

5. In the case of widow's allowance, however, the woman or her late husband must have been in GB at the time of the death or the contribution conditions for widowed mother's allowance or widow's pension must have been satisfied: S.I. 1975/563, Reg. 4(2).
6. Ibid., Regs. 4(1), 9(3) and 9(6).
7. Under SSA 1975, s.124.
8. Normally 'ordinary residence' in GB. See S.I. 1975/563, Reg. 5.
9. Ibid., Reg. 5(1).
10. See, e.g., FANIA 1952, s.5 and S.I. 1952/2144; NIA 1960, s.2 and S.I. 1960/2422; NIA 1963, s.1, and S.I. 1963/394.

11. See the remarks of Mr P. Dean, Under-Secretary of State, in Standing Committee E Debates on Social Security Bill 1973, col. 783.
12. In 1973, there were about 150,000 National Insurance beneficiaries living abroad. The majority would benefit under reciprocal arrangements with the country in question. It was thought that hardship was likely only regarding those resident in other countries (e.g., at that time Portugal and Spain); ibid., at cols. 784–786.
13. S.I. 1975/563, Reg. 7(2). For the rules governing the absence of the deceased himself see ante, p. 245.

contributions the earnings factor from which was at least fifty times that year's lower earnings limit; *or*

2. at the date of confinement her husband was a serving member of the forces.[14]

iv) Spouses

It is part of the general rule that a claimant may not receive an increase for an absent dependant. In some cases, this caused hardship, for a person resident in Great Britain might, while abroad, have married a person who had never set foot in this country. The foreign spouse would not, as a result of the marriage, 'acquire' the residence of the claimant (as for example under the old rules whereby a woman on marriage acquired the domicile of her husband) and the increase would not be payable.[15] There has, therefore, been introduced a modification to the rule so that

'a husband or wife shall not be disqualified for receiving any increase (where payable) of benefit in respect of his or her spouse by reason of the spouse's being absent from Great Britain, provided that the spouse is residing with the husband or wife, as the case may be'.[16]

D. Some common concepts

It remains to provide an account of the meaning of concepts which are common to the various rules on residence and absence.

i) 'United Kingdom' and 'Great Britain'

For some purposes the geographical unit is the 'United Kingdom', but for the majority it is 'Great Britain'. The former means 'Great Britain and Northern Ireland',[17] the latter, England, Wales and Scotland.[18] Notwithstanding the fact that British courts may exercise criminal jurisdiction over British ships, aircraft and embassies, they are not regarded as part of the territory for purposes of the residence requirements.[19] The same is true of the Continental Shelf but special provisions render persons employed there immune from disqualification.[20]

ii) Presence and absence

The two concepts are mutually exclusive.[1] To be 'absent' from Great Britain does not necessarily imply that the person concerned must have

14. Ibid., Reg. 3.
15. See, e.g., *CG 32/49* and *55/50 (MB)*.
16. S.I. 1975/563, Reg. 13 (previously S.I. 1958/1084).
17. Royal and Parliamentary Titles Act 1927, s.2(2).
18. Union with Scotland Act 1706, preamble, art.1; and Wales and Berwick Act 1746, s.3. Northern

Ireland, the Isle of Man and the Channel Islands are thus excluded. However, as a result of the relevant reciprocal agreements, the various schemes are almost wholly integrated.
19. *CSG 2/48*; *CP 93/49*; *R(S) 8/59*; *R(I) 44/61*; *R(P) 8/61*.
20. S.I. 1975/563, Reg. 11.
1. *R(U) 18/60*.

been present at some time in the past – it simply means not present.[2] Both presence and absence are questions of fact dependent on physical circumstances and concerned in no way with intention, or external events. Thus in a case where a claimant would have arrived in England but for technical problems in the mode of transport, it was to no avail for her to argue that she would but for another's fault have been present in Great Britain.[3]

iii) 'Residence'

This is the term most widely used to represent the necessary connection with Great Britain. Its use has not of course been confined to social security legislation. There are many other areas, notably taxation,[4] bankruptcy[5] and matrimonial causes,[6] where it features prominently. Although the Commissioner has pointed out the danger of relying on decisions made in quite a different context,[7] nevertheless he has drawn freely from them for ideas in elucidating the term.[8]

The burden of proof is normally on the claimant to show that he is 'resident' in Great Britain at the relevant time.[9] The question is one of fact and degree[10] and does not lend itself easily to definition but reference has been made to the word's ordinary meaning, formulated in the Oxford English Dictionary as 'to dwell permanently or for a considerable time, to have one's settled or usual abode'.[11] Though the claimant need not be physically present at any one particular time, there must be a sufficient amount of physical presence in the place on which the residence may be grounded: a theory of 'constructive residence' is not recognised.[12] Conversely, the degree of permanence necessary need not be such as to render the place in question the claimant's domicile;[13] he may, consequently, be resident in more than one place or country at any one time.[14]

Within these broad outlines there are a number of factors to be taken into account. Perhaps the most important is the intention of the claimant himself. If he intends to settle in one place, he is likely to reside there.[15] In *R(P) 6/58*,

2. *R(U) 16/62*.
3. *R(S) 8/59*.
4. E.g., Income and Corporation Taxes Act 1970, ss.49–51; and see *Simon's Taxes* (3rd edn) E5–104.
5. E.g., Bankruptcy Act 1914, s.1(2)(b) and see Williams *Bankruptcy* (18th edn), pp. 58–59.
6. E.g., Matrimonial Proceedings (Magistrates' Courts) Act 1960, s.1(3) and see Bromley *Family Law* (5th edn), pp. 6–8.
7. E.g., *R(G) 2/51*; *R(P) 4/54*; *R(P) 1/72*.
8. A prime example is the Tribunal decision of *R(F) 1/62*.
9. *R(G) 2/51* (Tribunal decision).
10. *R 5/62 (UB)*; *R(P) 2/67*. See also *Levene v IRC* [1928] AC 217 at 222, HL and *IRC v Lysaght* [1928] AC 234 at 241, 243, HL.
11. Quoted in *Levene v IRC* ante n.10, at p. 222, *Fox v Stirk and Bristol*

Electoral Registration Officer [1970] 2 QB 463 at 475, 477, CA, and *CG 32/49*.
12. *CG 32/49*; *55/50 (MB)*; *R 5/62 (UB)*; *R(P) 1/72*. For the theory as applied to the poor law see *R v Glossop* (1866) LR 1 QB 227 and *West Ham Union v Cardiff Union* [1895] 1 QB 766.
13. *R(F) 1/62*; *R 1/71 (P)*. For the concept of domicile generally, see Dicey and Morris *Conflict of Laws* (9th edn), chap. 8.
14. *R(G) 2/51*; *R(P) 2/67*. See also *Re Norris, ex parte Reynolds* (1888) 4 TLR 452, *Levene v IRC*, ante n.10, *IRC v Lysaght*, ante n.10, and *Fox v Stirk and Bristol Electoral Registration Officer*, ante n.14.
15. See esp., the dictum of Somervell LJ in *Macrae v Macrae* [1949] P. 397 at 403.

C returned from Rhodesia where he had been living for nine years in the hope that he would benefit under the will of a relative. Eleven months later, when his expectations were not fully realised, he went back to Rhodesia. It was held that during these eleven months he was 'resident' in GB, as it had been, at the time, his intention permanently to stay there.

Conversely, a person taking a job abroad may still be resident in Britain if he intends to return immediately on its completion.[16] But in this situation the authorities are likely to have regard to the nature of the employment: if it is of a finite nature, e.g., a fixed term contract, the intention to return will prevail;[17] if, however, it is of indeterminate length, the mere expression of hope to return at sometime in the future will generally be insufficient.[18] Of course, the amount of time actually spent in Britain (or abroad) may be significant – in *Fox v Stirk*[19] Lord Denning MR, spoke of a stay amounting to residence when it involves 'a considerable degree of permanence' – but if the intention is unequivocal, even a short time may be sufficient.[20] Another very important factor in practice is the nature of arrangements made for living while the individual is in Britain. It is not necessary that he should own or rent his own accommodation, but if he stays throughout in a hotel or with relatives, he must be able to show that he made his 'home' there.[1] If he leaves furniture and other personal effects in one place, this will help to show that he is still resident there even if he has lived for a considerable period elsewhere.[2] In any event, it is easier to prove a continued residence in one place than a change to another country.[3]

iv) 'Ordinarily resident'

In tax law both 'resident' and 'ordinarily resident' are employed, but the weight of judicial opinion holds that there is little difference in meaning between the two.[4] Social security law too sometimes adopts one, sometimes the other formulation. The Commissioners clearly regard the distinction as significant,[5] but they have been very reticent on the nature of the difference. Discussions of the principles elaborated in the last paragraph have not discriminated between the two: in particular, it has

16. *CG 204/49.*
17. *R(G) 2/51.*
18. *CG 165/50*; *R(G) 5/52.* See also *Lewis v Lewis* [1956] 1 All ER 375, [1956] 1 WLR 200.
19. [1970] 2 QB 463, 475.
20. *R(F) 1/62* and see *Macrae v Macrae*, ante n.15.
 1. *R(P) 4/54*; *R(F) 1/62*; *R(P) 1/72*; and see: *Re Norris, ex parte Reynolds*, ante n.14; *Re Erskine, ex parte Erskine* (1893) 10 TLR 32 and *Levene v IRC*, ante n.10.
 2. *R(G) 2/51*; *R(F) 1/62*; *R(P) 2/67.* See also *Hopkins v Hopkins* [1951] P. 116, [1950] 2 All ER 1035; *Stransky v Stransky* [1954] P. 428 and *Lewis v*

Lewis, ante n.18.
 3. *R(F) 1/62*; *Macrae v Macrae*, ante n.15.
 4. In *Levene v IRC*, ante n.10, at p. 225 Viscount Cave LC thought that there was little difference in meaning. In a divorce case, *Hopkins v Hopkins* ante n.2, at p. 121 Pilcher J was unable to find any difference in the interpretation offered by the tax cases, but in *Stransky v Stransky*, ante n.2, at p. 437 Karminski J intimated that the word 'ordinary' added a degree of permanency to the concept of residence.
 5. See *R(P) 2/67* and *R(P) 1/72.*

been said that a person may have two 'ordinary residences', just as he may have two 'residences'.[6] It is therefore difficult to offer more by way of generalisation than that 'ordinary residence' requires a greater degree of permanence than mere 'residence'.

v) Days of residence and absence

Where part of a day is spent in this country and part abroad, the question arises whether it will count as a day of residence or of absence.

> The policy has always been not to have regard to fractions of a day. A decision in 1948 held that it was convenient to assume that the state of things which first occurred on a day prevailed throughout that day, so that if a claimant is absent at the beginning of a day he will remain absent until midnight.[7] This view no longer pertains. The current interpretation is that a person bearing the burden of proving that he was resident, or absent, on a day or period, must establish that he was resident or absent *throughout* that day or period.[8]

Part five. Hospital In-patients

A. General

Where the claimant, or a dependant for whom he is entitled to an increase, is a long-term hospital in-patient, enjoying free maintenance there under the National Health Service, the amount payable is reduced. The policy is an obvious one, and may be seen as part of the provisions for overlapping benefits:[9] to the extent that a person's primary living needs are being supplied by services financed by public funds full benefit is inappropriate.[10] The rules governing personal benefit and dependant's increases are classified according to the length of stay in hospital.

B. Adjustments to personal benefit

No adjustment is made for the first eight weeks of free in-patient treatment. It is assumed that expenditure will continue to be incurred during short stays: in particular, it is unlikely that a person will discontinue his occupation of premises, and thus he will remain liable for rent or mortgage repayments. Once, however, this period has elapsed, it is assumed that his living expenses will be significantly reduced, though if he has dependants the family home will still have to be maintained. The rules are classified,

6. *R(G) 2/51*, para. 7 (Tribunal majority).
7. *CU 54/48*.
8. *R(S) 1/66*; *R 1/68 (SB)*.
9. Cf., post pp. 437–443.
10. See NIAC Reports on Draft Hospital In-Patient Regulations 1948–49 HC 241 and on the Question of Long-Term Hospital Patients (1960), Cmnd. 464.

therefore, according to the length of stay in hospital, and the existence or non-existence of dependants.

1. *From 9–52 weeks*

   If the claimant has a dependant for whom an increase is, or would but for the rules to be described in the next paragraph be, payable, benefit is reduced by 20% of the standard rate; if he has no such dependant it is reduced by 40%; but the reduction in any case is not to leave him with less than 20% of the standard rate.[11]

2. *From 53–104 weeks*

   After a year, the principle is modified so that the claimant himself, while in receipt of treatment, never receives more than 20%[12] – often referred to as 'pocket-money' benefit.[13] The next 20% is not payable, but if he has a dependant, and has made an appropriate application to the Secretary of State,[14] any excess remaining is paid to that dependant.[15] A spouse who has also received free in-patient treatment for a year or more is not regarded as a dependant for this purpose.[16] If the claimant has no dependant or the appropriate application has not been made, the next 40% is not payable, and any excess will be paid to him by way of 'resettlement' benefit only when he is discharged from hospital.[17]

3. *After 104 weeks*

   After the two year period has elapsed, a claimant without dependants, is entitled to nothing beyond the 20% 'pocket-money'.[18] If he has dependants (and has made the appropriate application) the adjustment in (2) is made, except that the following may not count as dependants:[19] (a) a husband, where the wife claimant is in receipt of retirement pension (Categories A or B), contributory or non-contributory invalidity pension or unemployability supplement (unless she is receiving an increase of one of these benefits other than retirement pension for him); (b) a wife entitled to Category A retirement pension where the husband claimant is in receipt of sickness benefit, contributory or non-contributory invalidity pension, retirement pension or unemployability supplement;[20] (c) a spouse in receipt of free in-patient treatment for more than 52 weeks.

---

11. S.I. 1975/555, Reg. 5. For the meaning of 'dependant' see ibid., reg. 2(3).
12. Ibid., Reg. 6.
13. See NIAC Reports, ante n.10.
14. See S.I. 1975/555, Reg. 6(5).
15. Ibid., Reg. 6(1). The excess may, alternatively, be paid to another person who satisfies the Secretary of State that he will apply the sum for the benefit of the dependant: ibid., Reg. 6(5).
16. Ibid., Reg. 6(3), as amended by S.I. 1977/1693.
17. S.I. 1975/555, Reg. 6(2). On the 'resettlement' benefit, see further, post, p. 418.
18. S.I. 1975/555, Reg. 7(2).
19. Ibid., Reg. 7(3), as amended by S.I. 1977/1693.
20. Though in this case a different rate is payable: S.I. 1975/555, Reg. 7(4), as amended by S.I. 1977/1693.

C. Adjustment to increases for dependants

There are analogous rules governing the adjustment of increases for dependants. They may be summarised as follows.

1. *Dependent spouse in-patient*

   Where a dependent spouse has been an in-patient for a period of eight weeks, the rate of increase payable for that person is reduced by 20%, though not so as to reduce it to less than 20% of the standard rate.[1] After 104 weeks, if the dependent in-patient is a wife and is still regarded as 'residing with' the beneficiary husband,[2] the reduced increase is not payable at all unless he is regularly incurring expenditure, or causing some payments to be made, on her behalf.[3]

2. *Both beneficiary and dependent spouse in-patients*

   Where for a period of fifty-two weeks both have been in-patients, the rate of increase is reduced by 20% (though not so as to reduce it to less than 20% of the standard rate), the next 20% is not payable, and any part of the remaining increase exceeding 40% of the standard rate is payable for the benefit of a child of the beneficiary's family to some other person undertaking to use it for that purpose or to the dependant (if he/she leaves hospital).[4] If no arrangements to this effect have been authorised, no dependency increase is payable.[5]

3. *Child dependant in-patient*

   Where a child dependant has been an in-patient for a period of twelve weeks the increase is payable only if the beneficiary is regularly incurring expenditure on his behalf, or causing some such payment to be made for his benefit.[6]

D. Resettlement benefit

As indicated above,[7] money payable during the second year of the treatment may be accumulated and paid to the beneficiary if and when he is discharged. The arrangement is, however, subject to further regulation.

It is not payable unless the discharge is effected with the approval of the relevant (usually medical) authority[8] – the policy being to discourage persons leaving hospital before they are ready to do so, thereby avoiding further financial burden on the National Health Service[9] – or if he is continuing to receive free in-patient treatment in another NHS institution, or is residing in any prescribed

1. S.I. 1975/555, Reg. 11(1), as amended by S.I. 1977/1693.
2. Cf., ante, pp. 390–393.
3. S.I. 1975/555, Reg. 11(2), as amended.
4. Ibid., Regs. 11(3) and 12, as amended.
5. Ibid., Reg. 10, as amended.
6. Ibid., Reg. 13.
7. Ante, p. 417.
8. S.I. 1975/555, Reg. 15(1)(a).
9. *R(S)* 1/54, para. 7.

accommodation.[10] Resettlement benefit is payable in weekly instalments during the beneficiary's lifetime but not normally exceeding
160% of the standard rate.[11] If the patient resumes the treatment or
residence, it is suspended until his next discharge;[12] if the resump-
tion occurs after an interval of more than twenty-eight days, any
amount still outstanding is deducted from any future resettlement
benefit.[13]

E. Incapacity to enjoy proceeds

The condition of some long-term patients is such that there is little use to
which the money can be put, and their chances of discharge, and therefore
of resettlement benefit, are remote. Prior to 1960 the practice was to
accumulate the 'pocket-money' benefit and pay it to the beneficiary's estate
on his death. The National Insurance Advisory Committee regarded this
as a waste of resources,[14] and as a result a new regulation was introduced.
Where a single claimant has been an in-patient for over a year and a
medical officer treating him issues a certificate to the effect that no sum, or
only a specified weekly sum (less than that to which he would otherwise be
entitled) can be applied for the 'personal comfort or enjoyment' of the
patient, his weekly entitlement is reduced to that sum (if any).[15] However,
this procedure will only be permitted if the beneficiary is himself unable to
act,[16] and should he eventually be discharged he will be entitled to
additional resettlement benefit equal to the further reduction made during
the first fifty-two weeks.[17]

F. Free in-patient treatment

Adjustments are made only for periods of 'free in-patient treatment'. The
Regulations provide that

> 'a person shall be regarded as receiving or having received free
> in-patient treatment for any period for which he is or has been
> maintained free of charge while undergoing medical or other treat-
> ment as an in-patient' in a 'hospital or similar institution' maintained
> or administered under the National Health Service or by the
> Secretary of State (or Defence Council) or in such an institution
> 'pursuant to arrangements made by the Secretary of State or by
> anybody in exercise of functions' on his behalf.[18]

10. S.I. 1975/555, Reg. 15(1)(b). For
    'prescribed accommodation', see post,
    p. 420.
11. S.I. 1975/555, Reg. 15(2): the
    Secretary of State has a discretion to
    modify this regulation in particular
    cases.
12. Ibid., Reg. 15(3)(a).
13. Ibid., Reg. 15(3)(b).
14. Report on the Question of Long-Term
    Hospital Patients (1960), Cmnd. 964,
    paras. 48–51.
15. S.I. 1975/555, Reg. 16(2).
16. Ibid., Reg. 16(4).
17. Ibid., Reg. 16(5).
18. Ibid., Reg. 2(2). For the institutions
    covered, see *R(S) 4/53* and *R(S) 2/54*.

It is clear, in the first place, that the word 'treatment' is a misnomer. The object of these Regulations is to avoid overpayments to persons being maintained free of charge in hospitals and similar state-financed institutions, and the nature of the treatment offered there is not crucial. Hence the Chief Commissioner has ruled that the phrase should not be the subject of refined distinctions: the mere fact that a person is an in-patient in a hospital is strong prima facie evidence that he is undergoing 'medical or other treatment'.[19] In any event, the receipt of nursing services will be sufficient.[20] In the light of these policy objectives, the finding that he is an 'in-patient' is obviously very important; and the phrase has been consistently interpreted to mean 'housed overnight' at the relevant institution.[1] Thus a person living at home because there are not sufficient beds available at the hospital, even though in all other respects he is treated as an in-patient, is not an 'in-patient' for the purposes of these Regulations.[2] The patient must be maintained free of charge and the Regulations provide that he shall not be so regarded

> 'if he is paying or has paid, in respect of his maintenance, charges which are designed to cover the whole cost of the accommodation or services (other than services by way of treatment) provided for him in the hospital or similar institution'.[3]

The onus is on the patient to satisfy this condition,[4] and, if necessary, the authorities will inspect the hospital's accounts to verify the proportion of costs paid by him.[5] The 'board and lodging' costs may be borne by the patient himself or by a third party, but none must be financed from public funds.[6]

G. Calculation of periods

The periods of in-patient treatment referred to must in principle be continuous, but this is modified by the Regulations to take account of the possibilities both of time spent in other accommodation maintained at public expense, and of short interruptions to the free treatment.

i) Residence in other accommodation

The period of in-patient treatment is deemed to include any period of prior residence in 'prescribed accommodation'.[7] This is defined as

> 'any hospital accommodation or similar accommodation in which that person is residing or has resided either as a patient or inmate

---

19. *R(P) 1/67*, para. 14 (R.G. Micklethwait).
20. Ibid., at para. 13, and see *Minister of Health v General Committee of Royal Midland Counties Home for Incurables at Leamington Spa* [1954] Ch. 530, at 541, 547, 549–550, CA.
 1. *CS 65/49*; *R(S) 8/51*; *R(I) 14/56*.
 2. *R(I) 27/59*.
 3. S.I. 1975/555, Reg. 2(2).
 4. *CS 59/49*.
 5. *R(P) 13/52*. See also *R(S) 2/52*, which took into account the fact that the claimant was an NHS employee from whose salary a deduction was made.
 6. *R(S) 4/53*.
 7. S.I. 1975/555, Reg. 17(2)(a).

or as a person in need of care and attention and wholly or partly
at the cost of a local authority, the Secretary of State
or, . . . (under the National Health Service Acts) anybody in
exercise of functions on behalf of the Secretary of State' or 'any
residential accommodation provided for that person under Part
III of the National Assistance Act'.[8]

In deciding whether an individual is caught by this provision regard is to
be had to the nature of the services made available to him at the institution, rather than to the objective characterisation of the institution itself.[9]
If it has been decided by the appropriate authority that the residence is not
temporary, it is deemed, for purposes of the rules on adjustment, to have
lasted for fifty-two weeks.[10]

ii) Linking of periods

Any two or more periods of free in-patient treatment (or residence in
prescribed accommodation) separated by intervals not exceeding twenty-
eight days may be linked,[11] though the aggregate period thus taken into
account does not include the intervals themselves.[12]

H. Amount of adjustments

The amount of adjustment is represented as a percentage of the 'standard
rate' of Category A retirement pension.[13] The benefit to be reduced is,
with one exception,[14] that which is payable after the Overlapping Regulations have taken effect.[15] The age addition[16] is not affected, however,
unless the beneficiary has been an in-patient for more than fifty-two weeks
and he has no wife or child 'residing' with him.[17]

Part six. Imprisonment and Detention in Legal Custody

A. General

The disqualification from benefit (or a dependant's increase) during
periods when a person is 'undergoing imprisonment or detention in legal
custody'[18] has always existed in social security law,[19] and yet its policy

8. Ibid., Reg. 15(4). But if the
accommodation is maintained by a
voluntary organisation or is a
registered disabled persons' home or
old persons' home under the Public
Health Act 1936 or National Assistance
Act 1948, the rule is not to apply
unless he has received free in-patient
treatment there for at least eight
weeks: ibid., Reg. 17(3).
9. Compare R(S) 15/55 with R(S) 26/54
and R(S) 6/58.
10. S.I. 1975/555, Reg. 17(2)(b). For the
meaning of 'residence' see R(P) 17/55;

R(P) 1/67 and ante, pp. 414–415.
11. S.I. 1975/555, Reg. 17(4).
12. See R(S) 8/51. On parts of a day see
CS 131/49; R(S) 8/51 and R(S) 9/52.
13. S.I. 1975/555, Reg. 2(1).
14. See, ibid., Reg. 18(2).
15. Ibid., Reg. 18.
16. Ante, p. 229.
17. S.I. 1975/555, Reg. 19. For the
meaning of 'residing with', see ante,
pp. 390–393.
18. SSA 1975, s.82(5).
19. Cf. NIA 1911, s.87(3).

basis remains ambiguous. It may be seen simply as a penal provision to apply to persons who have forfeited their natural rights as citizens.[20] If this were so, it would be appropriate to confine the disqualification to those imprisoned or detained in connection with a criminal offence. As will appear, this is in practice how the provision has been interpreted, though its wording is not so limited. The alternative policy basis is identical to that encountered in relation to hospital in-patients: the detainee is being maintained at public expense and thus has no need of income support.[1] This may indeed be the case but it is to be observed that in comparison with the hospital in-patients rules, those on detention are much stricter: there is no period of eight weeks to adapt to new circumstances; and there is no provision for either 'pocket-money' or 'resettlement' benefit.

B. Scope of disqualification

> 'A person shall be disqualified for receiving any benefit, and an increase of benefit shall not be payable in respect of any person as the beneficiary's wife or husband, for any period during which that person is undergoing imprisonment or detention in legal custody'.[2]

This Regulation applies to all benefits except guardian's allowance,[3] but 'imprisonment or detention in legal custody' is nowhere defined. On a strict reading it would cover all cases where a court would legitimately refuse an order of habeas corpus.[4] Subject to exceptions described below, it therefore covers in theory not only imprisonment following conviction in a criminal court but also the detention of those awaiting trial, mentally disordered persons, children in need of care and protection, and those committed for contempt of court. The historical evolution of the Regulation reveals, however, that the scope is not intended to be so broad. Prior to 1960 grave confusion was caused by the operation of the provision in relation to mental hospital detention orders. While the majority of Commissioners' decisions required that the order be connected with criminal proceedings or a criminal act,[5] the Divisional Court held that the detention need not have a punitive or corrective purpose: it applied whenever the person was 'detained by reason of a legal proceeding or as the result of a court proceeding'.[6] The National Insurance Advisory Committee was critical of this approach: it saw no reason why those detained in a mental hospital should not be treated like other hospital in-patients.[7] The one case

---

20. Per Widgery, arguendo, *R v National Insurance Comr, ex parte Timmis* [1955] 1 QB 139 at 145, DC.
1. Cf. ante, p. 416.
2. S.I. 1974/2079, Reg. 11(1).
3. Ibid., Reg. 11(2). The allowance is payable to a person appointed by the Secretary of State to receive and deal with it on behalf of the beneficiary: ibid., Reg. 12(3).
4. Per Lord Goddard CJ, *R v National Insurance Comr, ex parte Timmis*, ante n.20, at p. 149.
5. *R(S) 20/53; R(S) 21/52; R(P) 10/54; R(S) 3/55; R(S) 4/55; 1/55 (SB)*.
6. *R v National Insurance Comr, ex parte Timmis*, ante n.20, at p. 148.
7. Report on the Question of Long-Term Hospital Patients (1960), Cmnd. 964.

where it was thought that the 'detention' disqualification should continue to apply was understandably that in which an individual was transferred from a prison (or an analogous institution) to a mental hospital during the currency of his sentence.[8]

The amending Regulations,[9] brought into force in 1960, were clearly intended (and thought by the Committee itself[10]) to implement these recommendations. The obvious aim was to limit the disqualification provision to periods of detention consequent on, or closely connected with, criminal convictions. The Regulations do not, however, explicitly so provide. They apply only to criminal proceedings; other proceedings are not mentioned. Thus it is provided that there will be no disqualification for a period of imprisonment or detention in legal custody

> 'in connection with a charge brought or intended to be brought against him in criminal proceedings or pursuant to any sentence or order for detention made by a court in such proceedings unless, in relation to him, a penalty is imposed at the conclusion of those proceedings or, in the case of default of payment of a sum adjudged to be paid on conviction, a penalty is imposed in respect of such default'.[11]

The Regulation thus indicates that where someone is, for example, remanded in custody in respect of a criminal charge from which he is later acquitted, his title to benefit remains unaffected. In this connection, it has been held that a suspended sentence is a 'penalty . . . imposed at the conclusion of . . . proceedings'.[12]

As regards mentally abnormal offenders, there is a Regulation covering the one situation thought by the National Insurance Advisory Committee to be appropriate for disqualification:

> 'the said provisions shall not operate to disqualify a person for receiving any benefit . . . , or to make an increase of benefit not payable in respect of a person, for any period during which that person is undergoing detention in legal custody after the conclusion of criminal proceedings[13] if it is a period during which he is liable to be detained in a hospital or a similar institution[14] in Great Britain as a person suffering from mental disorder[15] unless –

8. Ibid., at para. 19.
9. S.I. 1960/1283.
10. See its report on the draft regulations, 1959–60 HC 276.
11. S.I. 1974/2079, Reg. 11(3).
12. R(S) 1/71. ' "Penalty" means a sentence of imprisonment, borstal training, or detention (under Children and Young Persons Act) . . . or an order for detention in a detention centre': S.I. 1974/2079, Reg. 11(6)(c).
13. 'Criminal proceedings against any person shall be deemed to be concluded upon his being found insane

in those proceedings so that he cannot be tried or his trial cannot proceed'; ibid., Reg. 11(6)(g).
14. This means any place (other than prison or analogous institution) in which 'persons suffering from mental disorder are or may be received for care or treatment'; ibid., Reg. 11(6)(b). For 'mental disorder' see post, n.15.
15. The reference to 'mental disorder' is to be construed as including references to any mental disorder within the meaning of the Mental Health Act 1959: S.I. 1974/2079, Reg. 11(6)(f).

(a) pursuant to any sentence or order for detention made by the court at the conclusion of those proceedings, he has undergone detention by way of penalty in a prison, a detention centre, a borstal institution or a young offenders institution; *and*

(b) he was removed to the hospital or similar institution while liable to be detained as a result of that sentence or order, and, in the case of a person who is liable to be detained (under the Mental Health Act 1959) . . . a direction restricting his discharge has been given'.[16]

Thus, a person transferred from a prison, detention centre, borstal or young offenders' institution may be disqualified but only for the period of his original sentence,[17] and for this purpose the Home Secretary, or Secretary of State for Scotland, will issue a certificate stating the earliest date on which the person would have been expected to be discharged.[18] Of course, any other period of detention may well be subject to the rule on hospital in-patients.[19] Persons not the subject of criminal proceedings are outside the scope of these two Regulations, and, in the absence of reported decisions on the point, one can only assume that administratively the Department (whatever its statutory powers) does not disqualify persons detained in other circumstances.

c. Suspension of benefit

It follows from the discussion in the last paragraph that there are circumstances in which persons undergoing imprisonment or detention in legal custody are not disqualified from benefit. Those transferred to mental hospitals are entitled to receive the benefit themselves:[20] in other cases payment is suspended until their release.[1]

Part seven. Earnings-related Supplements

A. General

The shift in the theoretical basis of contributory benefits from the flat-rate subsistence, advocated by Beveridge, to a partial replacement of lost earnings was gradual. The policy issues involved were discussed in chapter 1,[2] and elsewhere there are descriptions of the rules governing long-term benefits (retirement, widow's invalidity and industrial disablement pensions).[3] We are concerned here with the earnings-related supplements which are payable with certain short-term benefits. As regards

16. S.I. 1974/2079, Reg. 11(4).
17. See, e.g., *R(P) 2/57*.
18. S.I. 1974/2079, Reg. 11(5).
19. Ante, pp. 416–421.
20. S.I. 1974/2079, Reg. 12(2).

1. Ibid., Reg. 12(1); for guardian's allowance, however, see ante n.3.
2. Ante, pp. 19–21.
3. Ante, pp. 165–166, 224–225, 237, and 318–332.

unemployment benefit, the impetus came in the early 1960s from the National Economic Development Council which felt that some of the hardships had to be removed from unemployment if mobility of labour was to be encouraged.[4] Its proposal for an earnings-related addition was approved in principle by the two major political parties. The TUC, however, felt that it would be improper to differentiate between unemployment and the other short-term benefits: in all cases there was a need to safeguard those out of work from drastic falls in income.[5] The National Insurance Act 1966 thus introduced a supplement payable with widow's allowance, and unemployment and sickness benefit.[6] Those in receipt of maternity allowance and industrial injury benefit were also entitled provided that they were able to satisfy the conditions for sickness benefit. Since 1975, however, the supplement has been payable with maternity allowance in its own right.[7]

B. Circumstances in which payable

A woman entitled to a widow's allowance may claim the earnings-related addition, based on her deceased husband's earnings, for each week of the period for which the allowance is payable.[8] As regards sickness and unemployment benefit and the maternity allowance, the supplement is payable only from the thirteenth day of the period of interruption of employment, and for a maximum of 156 days within any one such period.[9] The justification for the waiting-period, substantially longer than the normal three days, is the disproportionately heavy administrative costs of calculating and paying the supplement for very short periods.[10] Only those qualifying for benefit on the basis of Class 1 contributions are entitled,[11] and persons over pensionable age are also excluded.[12]

C. Amount payable

The beneficiary entitled to the supplement receives one third of the

4. Report on Conditions Favourable to Foster Growth (1963), esp. paras. 50–52.

5. See White Paper on Earnings-Related Short-Term Benefits (1966), Cmnd. 2887. The Conservative opposition was not so convinced of the desirability of the uniform approach. In particular, there were widespread occupational schemes for short-term sickness. See, e.g., Mr P. Dean on the 2nd Reading of the National Insurance Bill 1966, 724 HC Deb., cols. 97–101.

6. NIA 1966, s.2.

7. SSA 1975, s.22(4).

8. Ibid., s.24(3).

9. Ibid., ss.14(7) and 22(4). For the meaning of 'periods of interruption of employment', see ante, p. 92.

10. Miss M. Herbison, Minister of Pensions and NI, introducing the 2nd Reading of the 1966 National Insurance Bill, 724 HC Deb., col. 40. The argument does not, of course, apply with the same force to maternity allowance (the period of interruption of employment will inevitably be longer) but in this case it was found more convenient to adopt a similar rule. See the Standing Committee E Debates on the Social Security Bill 1973, cols. 632–636.

11. SSA 1975, s.13(3).

12. Ibid., s.14(7)(a); though of course retirement pensioners may be entitled to the earnings-related component or the graduated pension.

difference between the lower earnings limit for the relevant year and his 'reckonable weekly earnings' not exceeding £30, plus 15% of so much of those earnings as exceed £30 but do not exceed the upper limit.[13] However, the aggregate of the benefit and supplement payable must not exceed 85% of those earnings.[14] The 'relevant year' for this calculation is the tax year (i.e., April to April) ending before the benefit year (i.e., January to January) in which falls the first day of the period of interruption of employment or, in the case of widow's allowance, the date of the husband's death.[15] The 'reckonable weekly earnings' refer to the earnings factor derived only from contributions[16] actually paid by the claimant or late husband during the 'relevant year' divided by fifty.[17] The general policy of not enabling a claimant to receive more by way of benefit than his normal earnings in full-time work is used to justify the 85% ceiling:[18] the deficit of 15% is explicable on the ground that the earnings factor is based on the claimant's gross earnings (before tax) and tax is not payable on the benefit or the earnings-related supplement.[19] On the other hand, it is important to note that the gap between the relevant tax year and the period of receipt of the supplement is substantial – between nine and twenty-one months – and in times of rapid inflation the difference between the claimant's normal earnings and the amount of benefit received might be substantial.

Part eight. Earnings

A. General

There are a number of rules arising under the Social Security Act 1975 in connection with entitlement to, or assessment of, benefit which refer to the weekly earnings of a person either before benefit was payable or during a period of entitlement. They are for the following purposes:

1. to calculate the special hardship allowance added to industrial disablement benefit,[20]

2. to disregard casual or subsidiary work, the earnings from which are below a specified level, where entitlement to benefit is based on incapacity for work, unemployment or retirement – such rules apply to sickness and invalidity benefits,[1] industrial injury

---

13. Ante, p. 55–56.
14. SSA 1975, Sch. 6, para. 3.
15. Ibid., para. 1(2). The rule, according to which two periods of interruption of employment not separated by more than thirteen weeks are linked (ante, p. 92) applies for this purpose so that the 'first day' will be the first day of the first period so linked: *R(U) 4/68* and *R(S) 1/70*.
16. Cf., ante, p. 70.

17. SSA 1975, Sch. 6, para. 2.
18. See the speech of Miss Herbison, ante n.10, at cols. 38–39.
19. Ibid., col. 39. The opposition nevertheless thought that in comparison with other countries 85% was too high: Sir K. Joseph, ibid., at col. 58.
20. Ante, pp. 318–332.
1. Ante, p. 157.

benefit,[2] non-contributory invalidity pension[3] and invalid care allowance,[4] unemployment benefit[5] and retirement pension,[6]

3. to determine whether the earnings of a wife, housekeeper or female relative disentitle a claimant to a dependant's increase for such a person,[7]

4. to assess the amount to be deducted from retirement pension for earnings received during the period of entitlement.[8]

The law governing the calculation of earnings for these purposes is primarily to be found in the Computation of Earnings Regulations[9] and the Commissioners' decisions. As such it is significantly different from the methods used to assess and classify contribution liabilities (and also the 'reckonable earnings' for the purpose of the earnings-related supplement) which bear striking resemblances to income tax law.[10]

B. What are 'earnings'?

The Social Security Act 1975 provides that ' "earnings" includes any remuneration or profit derived from any employment', the latter term being defined to include 'any trade, business, profession, office or vocation'.[11] These definitions show that a line is to be drawn between earnings, including profits, which are derived from an occupation, and payments which vest in the recipient in some other capacity, e.g., shareholder. The Regulations state more narrowly that ' "earnings" means earnings derived from a gainful employment'.[12] It is clear, however, that the term is not confined to the salary or profits drawn from employment or business, and may include, for example, an allowance paid to the holder of an office.[13]

The leading decision is that of the Tribunal of Commissioners in *R(P) 7/61* :

> C claimed an increase of pension for his wife for a period during which she was absent from work through sickness and was in receipt of payments from her employer under a sick pay scheme. This provided that the payments could be withdrawn at any time and the scheme wound up. C contended that for the period in question his wife was not engaged in a gainful occupation, and that the payments did not constitute earnings. Both contentions were rejected.

It was held first, that the wife was still gainfully occupied,[14] as the contract

2. Ante, p. 300.
3. Ante, p. 171.
4. Ante, p. 181.
5. Ante, p. 89.
6. Ante, p. 210.
7. Ante, p. 387.
8. Ante, pp. 216–219.
9. S.I. 1974/2008.
10. Ante, pp. 56, and 63–64.
11. SSA 1975, s.3(1), and Sch. 20.
12. S.I. 1974/2008, Reg. 1(2).

13. See *R(P) 2/76* (a city councillor in receipt of an allowance for attendance held to be gainfully occupied: ante, p. 202).
14. This was the term used in NIA 1965, s.30: it does not appear that the change in wording made by the SSA 1975 has any significance; see *R(P) 2/76*, paras. 22–23, per R.J.A. Temple, Chief Comr.

of employment subsisted; it did not matter that she was not actually working during the relevant period.[15] Secondly, the payments were earnings since she received them *as an employee*. Again, the fact that they were described as ex gratia payments was immaterial. A similar broad approach is evidenced by *R(P) 1/65*, where a member of the City Livery Company (a pensioner) was paid a fee each time he attended a meeting of the Company's court. Attendance was voluntary, and it was clear that the claimant would have attended whether a fee was payable or not. It was held that the fees constituted earnings from employment; it was important that the claimant actually received money for his work, and immaterial that his motive was not one of financial gain.[16]

A difficult case on the other side of the line is *R(P) 4/67*:

> C, a former partner in a firm of accountants, was paid £1,000 at the end of his first year of retirement for advisory services rendered to the firm. At no time during this year when the claimant gave advice was it suggested that a payment would be made.

The Commissioner, H. Magnus, held that the payment did not constitute earnings, as there was no contractual obligation on either party, and the claimant never expected or even hoped to be paid. It was suggested, however, that any further payment for advisory services would be so construed. The suggestion was borne out by the later case *R(P) 1/69*, where a similar payment made the following year to this claimant was held to constitute 'earnings'.[17] The Commissioner, D. Neligan, laid particular emphasis on the fact that the claimant had been awarded earned income tax relief on the £1,000.[18] Other situations where it may be difficult to determine whether payments constitute 'earnings' can now conveniently be discussed under a number of specific headings.

i) Director's fees and partnership profits

A director's fees will constitute earnings from employment, even though the duties – attendance at an annual general meeting – are very slight.[19] The fact that he has considerable financial power is enough to make a directorship a gainful employment.[20] In a Northern Ireland case, it was held that a woman who owned a farm (worked by her son) and enjoyed the profits from it was in an analogous position to a director; therefore, the income was treated as earnings, and not as interest on an investment.[1]

---

15. See *R(U) 4/60* (C's wife gainfully occupied for the whole of the week, even though she only worked for three days); cp., *R(U) 8/60*, where the wife was not working at all.
16. The Dep. Comr., G. Glover, followed Salmon J in *Benjamin v Minister of Pensions and National Insurance* [1960] 2 QB 519, [1960] 2 All ER 851, and not the narrower approach of the Comr. in *CP 7/49*; see also *R(P) 2/76*.

17. See also *R(G) 1/60*.
18. The attitude of the tax authorities is relevant, but not decisive: see *R(P) 1/65*, para. 10, (G. Glover, Dep. Comr.).
19. *R(P) 9/55*; *R(G) 14/56*.
20. *2/57 (P)*.
1. Compare the cases on the 'retirement condition', where there appears to be more emphasis on the work done by the claimant: ante, pp. 205–206.

Partnership profits are clearly earnings for social security purposes, while dividends from a limited liability company are not.[2] Nor is trust income.[3]

ii) Payments for assisting in spouse's business
Some nice questions arise when one spouse assists in a business, typically a retail shop, owned and conducted by the other. The approach taken by the Commissioner is that if, say, the wife does appreciable work and brings money into the business, she is to treated as gainfully employed, and a proportion of the profits will be regarded as her earnings.[4] This principle will not be applied if the amount of work is trivial, or if the wife organises her husband's business while he is temporarily unable to work.[5] On the other hand, the fact that no money passes between the spouses does not preclude a finding that one spouse draws 'earnings' from the other's business.[6]

iii) Payments in kind and other miscellaneous payments
The law with regard to payments in kind and other miscellaneous payments is considerably clarified by the Computation of Earnings Regulations.[7] Under Regulation 3, the following do not count as earnings:

    (a) the value of luncheon vouchers (up to 15p a day);
    (b) the value of meals provided at the place of work;
    (c) the value of accommodation in which the employee is required to live as a condition of his employment;[8]
    (d) the value of food or produce provided for his needs and those of his household;
    (e) sums (or remuneration in kind) provided by the employer in December as a Christmas bonus, up to £10.

The implication of this last rule is that other bonuses are to be taken into account.[9] Other remuneration in kind, e.g., board and lodging (not disregarded under the Regulations), is to be included and its value is the actual worth of the services, not the amount the claimant has saved by receiving them.[10]

iv) Payments assigned or not received by the claimant
The fact that the claimant immediately assigns his or her salary to a third party has been held by a Northern Ireland Commissioner to be irrelevant.[11] So also is the fact that the earnings are not actually received in the week in question.[12] This ruling has been followed with striking effect:

> C claimed an increase of pension for his wife, thinking that the profits from her business in Italy did not amount to earnings,

2. R(P) 9/56; R(U) 22/64.
3. R(G) 9/55.
4. R(P) 7/51; R(S) 17/52.
5. R(S) 8/56; R(U) 11/57.
6. R(P) 6/57, para. 3.
7. S.I. 1974/2008. Many of the provisions were the result of the recommendations of NIAC (1966), Cmnd. 3179.
8. See R 2/72 (P).
9. See R(G) 7/59.
10. CP 1/48; R 5/61 (P).
11. 2/59 (P).
12. R(P) 5/53.

because they were not transmitted to this country. But the earnings rule was applied and the increase refused.[13]

The Commissioner, H. A. Shewan, held that a man earns what he is entitled to receive in return for his work or services, irrespective of whether he is actually paid.

v) Payments under the Employment Protection Act

Regulations may be made under the Social Security (Miscellaneous Provisions) Act 1977 to provide that certain payments governed by the Employment Protection Act 1975 are to be treated as earnings.[14] They will include sums payable

    (a)　by way of maternity pay;
    (b)　in respect of arrrears of pay;
    (c)　by way of pay in pursuance of an order for the continuation of the contract of employment;
    (d)　by way of remuneration in pursuance of a protective award under the EPA 1975.

C.　Earnings which cannot be immediately ascertained

Special problems are posed by earners whose employment, generally self-employment, produces earnings which 'are not immediately ascertainable'.[15] The various rules on earnings normally refer to a weekly or daily amount and the problems arise, typically in connection with self-employment, where money is not received on this basis. For the purpose of dealing with such cases, the Regulations distinguish between two categories of claim.

The first arises where the earner is a retirement pensioner or an adult dependant of a retirement or invalidity pensioner. If a statement of the earner's profits or gains has been or will be delivered to the Inland Revenue, the earnings are to be calculated by dividing the profits or gains by the number of weeks in the relevant assessment period during which he was employed.[16] This is the current income tax year,[17] or, in the case of self-employed claimants, the accounting period, whether or not this is a full year.[18] Pending the delivery of such a statement, the Secretary of State may suspend payment of the pension or dependant's increase and make an interim award instead. When the assessment is finally determined, any excessive interim payments may be recovered from the beneficiary.[19] In this case, unlike the normal rule governing recovery for overpayment of

---

13.　R(P) 1/70.
14.　SS(MP)A 1977, s.18.
15.　The phrase is used in S.I. 1974/2008, Regs. 2(3) and 5(1)(b). Similar problems arise where a claimant for unemployment benefit is pursuing a subsidiary occupation, the earnings from which must not exceed 75p a

day, if he is to remain eligible for benefit: these are discussed, ante, pp. 89–90.
16.　S.I. 1974/2008, Reg. 5.
17.　R(P) 1/73, para. 33, per R.G. Micklethwait, Chief Comr.
18.　R 2/75 (P).
19.　S.I. 1974/2008, Reg. 6(3).

benefit,[20] the claimant cannot argue that recovery should not be made because he used due care and diligence.[1] Here the overpayment is attributable not to a mistake which has subsquently been reviewed but to a deliberate decision regarding the level of an interim payment.

In all other cases, Regulations direct the authorities to calculate the earnings 'as best they may', taking into account available information and 'the probabilities of the case'.[2] By implication this vindicates the practice, previously authorised by the Commissioner,[3] of averaging the claimant's receipts over the period of employment. But the problem of deciding when the claimant was employed is not easy to solve.[4] Unless there is clear evidence of the occupation being seasonal, it should be averaged over a period of twelve months.[5]

D. Deductions from earnings

The question next arises as to what deduction may be made from gross profits, wages or salary. The frequency with which retirement pensioners (or the adult dependants of retirement or invalidity pensioners) take in boarders or lodgers made it convenient to formulate a special rule for these cases. Where full board and lodgings is provided, half the amount paid in excess of £6·00 per week is treated as earnings;[6] where less is provided, the authorities should have regard to half the amount of such smaller sum as they consider to be reasonable in the circumstances.[7] In all other cases, the Regulations provide an exhaustive list of such deductions as may be made.[8]

    (a) social security contributions;

    (b) 'expenses reasonably incurred ... without reimbursement in respect of –'

        (i) travel between home and work, and in connection with and for the purpose of work;

        (ii) premises, tools and equipment for the claimant's work;

        (iii) protective clothing;

        (iv) trade union or professional association subscriptions;

        (v) reasonable provision for the care of another member of the claimant's household, because of his necessary absence from home;

        (vi) the cost (up to 15p) of a meal during hours of work, for which no voucher is given.

    (c) 'any other expenses (not being sums the deduction of which from wages or salary is authorised by or under any enactment) reasonably incurred by him without reimbursement in connection with and for the purposes of that employment.'

20. For this, see chap. 14, post, pp. 612–614.
1. R(P) 1/73, cp. R(P) 2/74.
2. S.I. 1974/2008, Reg. 2(3).
3. R(P) 2/51.
4. R(U) 1/67, and NIAC Report, ante, n.7, at paras. 52–56.
5. See e.g., R(P) 4/56 and R(P) 1/62.
6. S.I. 1974/2008, Reg. 7(a).
7. S.I. 1974/2008, Reg. 7(b).
8. Ibid., Reg. 4.

Income tax, whether paid through PAYE or after assessment, is not deductible;[9] nor are contributions payable to occupational pension schemes.[10]

The major legal difficulty arises from the inconsistent interpretation by the Commissioners of the phrase 'in connection with that employment'. In some older cases, this was construed to mean 'in consequence of' the employment; on that approach the expense would be deducted if it was incurred as a result of the work done by the claimant.[11] In at least three more recent reported decisions, the Commissioner has taken the view that this is a gloss on the ordinary meaning of the phrase, and that the expenses must be reasonably connected with the employment.[12] It does not appear, however, that this change in approach would affect previous rulings disallowing deductions for insurance premiums,[13] household rent,[14] subscriptions to a sick fund,[15] and the costs of sending a child to boarding-school when this was the very reason why the claimant went to work.[16]

Whether an expense is reasonable for the purpose of the deduction provisions is to be determined by reference to the level of the claimant's earnings and the particular facts of the case.[17] Among the miscellaneous expenses held to have been reasonably incurred in connection with the claimant's employment have been: the costs of domestic assistance in the home;[18] commission paid to an employment agency;[19] and 15% of the cost of new fixtures and installations for a business, and of the legal expenses incurred in acquiring them.[20] In a Northern Ireland case, the Commissioner ruled that the expenses (in the case, travelling expenses to a holiday camp) should be averaged over the whole of the earning period during which they were incurred.[1]

In conclusion, it is interesting to observe that the allowable expenses for determining earnings compare favourably with those allowed for income tax purposes.[2] Tax legislation, for example, does not authorise deduction of the cost of meals, expenses of looking after a relative, and the Inland Revenue is reluctant to allow for travelling expenses.[3] On the other hand, the allowances are comparable with those under the Supplementary Benefit General Regulations in assessing a claimant's net earnings, though there income tax may also be deducted.[4]

---

9. S.I. 1974/2008, Reg. 4(c), abrogating the previous position whereby PAYE payments were deducted: *R(P) 3/56*; *R(P) 3/62*. The change followed a recommendation of NIAC, (1966), Cmnd. 3179, paras. 41–47. For the different approach to supplementary benefits see post, p. 510.
10. *R(P) 2/75*.
11. *CG 114/49*; *R(P) 2/54*.
12. *R(P) 2/56*; *R(P) 1/64*; *R(P) 1/66*.
13. *R(G) 7/52*.
14. *CP 2/48*.
15. *R(G) 7/52*.
16. *R(G) 7/53*; cp. *R(G) 9/51*.
17. *R(G) 1/56*; *R(G) 7/62*.
18. *R(G) 7/62*.
19. *R(G) 6/54*.
20. *R(P) 3/57* (but no sum could be deducted for 'depreciated' goodwill).
1. *R 2/72 (P)*.
2. See the remarks to this effect by NIAC, ante, n.9, at para. 81.
3. See Whiteman and Wheatcroft *Income Tax* (2nd edn), paras. 14.42–14.56.
4. Post, p. 510.

Part nine. Up-rating of Benefits

A. General

The problem of maintaining the value of benefits in relation to rising prices and wages and the various solutions available were considered in chapter 1.[5] It remains here to describe the methods currently adopted under the social security legislation. Prior to 1973, for all benefits except those awarded under the national assistance (subsequently supplementary benefits), war pensions, and family income supplement schemes[6] modifications to the amount payable could be made only by Act of Parliament. Moreover, the government was is no instance bound to ensure that benefits kept pace with inflation, and the real value of some, notably family allowances, declined considerably.[7] The sharp increase in the rates of inflation in the early 1970s and the desire to confer on contributors the security that benefits would retain their value prompted the Conservative government to introduce in 1973, for the most important contributory benefits a mechanism for annual 'up-rating'[8] – a word which one judge has described as 'a recruit to the English language which does not notably enrich it'.[9] This both imposed on the Secretary of State a duty to ensure that such benefits retained their value in relation to the general level of prices and enabled him to adjust the amounts payable by order laid before Parliament. As a result of subsequent amendments, the annual review of long-term benefits was to take account of rises in prices *or* earnings whichever would be more advantageous to beneficiaries.[10] To analyse the current principles, it is necessary to distinguish between the Secretary of State's *power* to up-rate certain benefits and his *duty* to up-rate others.

B. Power to up-rate

Under section 124 of the Social Security Act 1975, the Secretary of State has power by order to increase any of the following:

> Benefits, grants and increases for dependants payable under the Act; earnings-related supplements; limits for the earnings rules; and certain allowances payable under the Old Cases Act.

Any such order must be laid be laid in draft before Parliament, together with a report of the Government Actuary giving his opinion on the likely effect on the National Insurance Fund of making the order, and that draft must then be approved by a resolution of each House.[11] Apart from the procedural requirement, the power is without conditions or restrictions:

---

5. Ante, pp. 23–24.
6. War Pensions Act 1921, s.4; NAA 1948, s.5(2); SBA 1966, s.5(2); FISA 1970, s.3(4).
7. Cf., post, p. 446.
8. SSA 1973, ss.7, 8.

9. Per Megarry VC, *Metzger v Department of Health and Social Security* [1977] 3 All ER 444, at 445.
10. NIA 1974, s.5; SSBA 1975, ss.3, 4.
11. SSA 1975, s.124(2), (3).

'for whatever reason he thinks fit, and at whatever time he thinks fit, the Secretary of State may make whatever increase he thinks fit'.[12]

C. Duty to up-rate

Section 125 contains provisions of a very different nature: it imposes on the Secretary of State a duty both to review the level of current payments and, as a result of that review, to lay before Parliament an up-rating order. The former imposes on him an obligation to review in each tax year 'for the purpose of determining whether [they] have retained their value in relation to the general level of earnings or prices obtaining in Great Britain' the sums payable under the Act for all contributory, non-contributory and industrial benefits, including increases for dependants, but excluding death grant, maternity grant and the age-addition.[13] For the purposes of such a review

'the Secretary of State shall estimate the general level of earnings and prices in such manner as he thinks fit and shall have regard either to earnings or prices according to which he considers more advantageous to beneficiaries, except that he shall have regard only to prices' as regards the sums payable for unemployment, sickness and industrial injury benefit, maternity allowance and the lower rate allowance paid under the industrial scheme for the deceased's children.[14]

The Social Security (Miscellaneous Provisions) Act 1977 imposed a similar duty to review the financial limits above which earnings affect the amount of, or entitlement to, retirement pension (Categories A and B), and increases for a wife payable with a retirement pension (Categories A and C) and invalidity and industrial disablement pensions.[15] In these cases, the Secretary of State is to have regard only to the general level of earnings.[16]

He is not bound to review at yearly intervals; he is only required to do so in each tax year. Thus, in theory there may be a gap between reviews of anything between a month and nearly two years,[17] but the practice hitherto has been to review every April.[18] There is no direction on how the general level of earnings or prices is to be estimated or with regard to what period. In particular the Secretary of State is not obliged to review the whole of the period since the last review took place: he is concerned simply to consider the sums payable at the moment of review and, looking to the past, determine whether they have or have not retained their value.[19]

12. Per Megarry VC, *Metzger* case, ante n.9, at p. 446.
13. SSA 1975, s.125(1). Regulations made under SSPA 1975, s.24(1)(a) have now extended the provision to graduated retirement benefits: S.I. 1978/393.
14. SSA 1975, s.125(2).
15. S.7(1).
16. S.7(2).
17. *Metzger* case, ante n.9 at p. 448.
18. Ibid., at p. 447; and see Lustgarten and Elliott, 126 NLJ 756, 757.
19. Per Megarry VC, *Metzger* case, ante n.9, at pp. 448, 450.

It has been argued that this process may create an anomaly.[20] If, as the result of a review in (say) April, it has been found that the value of benefits has fallen by a certain amount and it is decided to up-rate benefits by that amount in November of the same year, this will not take into account any further inflation between April and November. For the review in the following April, the Act does not compel the Secretary of State to do more than ascertain that the value of benefit in relation to prices (or earnings) *as at the previous November* has been maintained, and the rate of inflation prior to that date might therefore be ignored. A similar problem could arise if, in exercise of his power under section 124, the Secretary of State authorised a small increase to one or more of the benefits which was unrelated to the review or any inflationary change. In that case too he would be obliged under the review procedure only to ascertain that the value of the benefit with its small increase (which had itself not taken into account any previous inflation) had retained its value since the increase was introduced.[1] In *Metzger v Department of Health and Social Security*[2] Megarry VC rejected the argument that the possibility of such anomalies necessitated construing section 125 as imposing the duty to review in relation to the changes in prices (or earnings) which have occurred since the end of the period to which the Secretary of State had regard in his last review:

> 'I cannot see how this could possibly be said to require a notional redrafting of this part of the Act to thrust a process of comparison . . . into a statutory provision which lays down neither this nor any other process in determining what the Secretary of State "thinks necessary"'.[3]

The duty to issue an up-rating order arises where as a result of the review the Secretary of State concludes that the benefits under scrutiny have not retained their value. He is then obliged to

> 'prepare and lay before each House of Parliament the draft of an up-rating order increasing those sums at least to such extent as he thinks necessary to restore their value'.[4]

The duty is excluded where 'it appears to him that the amount of the increase would be inconsiderable'.[5] Although in practice, he is likely to rely primarily on the review to select an appropriate increase, he need not confine himself to such information, for the Act does not prescribe any method of determining what he 'thinks necessary'. In the *Metzger* case, however, Megarry VC expressed the view that to be consistent with the statutory language the order should be intended to restore the value as at the date when it comes into effect rather than at some earlier date (e.g.,

20. Lustgarten and Elliott, ante n.18.
1. *Metzger* case, ante n.9, at p. 450.
2. Ante, n.9; upheld by the CA. See Appendix.
3. Ante, n.9 at p. 450.
4. SSA 1975, s.125(3). Like the

equivalent procedure under s.124 this is subject to an affirmative resolution and is to be accompanied by a report of the Government Actuary: ibid., ss.125(4) and 126(2).
5. Ibid., s.126(3).

when the review was made).[6] If this is right then under existing practice an order based on an April review, and laid before Parliament in July, must attempt to predict the increases of prices and earnings which will take place by November when the order will come into effect.[7] The first of the alleged anomalies under the review procedure will therefore be avoided unless this prediction underestimates the extent of the inflation in the seven months from April to November.

In providing for the increases the Secretary of State is expressly permitted to

> 'adjust the amount of the increase so as to secure that the sums specified for any particular benefits continue to differ from each other by the same amount . . .'.[8]

This is clear legislative authority for the practice whereby the real value of differentials (e.g., between sickness and industrial injury benefit) which were once regarded as important but which are no longer so easy to justify may be allowed to erode through the process of inflation.[9] The effect of the provision is that where the Secretary of State is concerned to maintain the same amount between two particular benefits, he will increase one of them (e.g., sickness benefit) by the percentage regarded as appropriate for benefits generally, but limit the increase of the other (e.g., injury benefit) so that the monetary difference between the amounts payable remains what it was before the up-rating order.

D. Other social security benefits

The up-rating procedure of the Social Security Act 1975 applies only to the benefits specifically governed by section 125. The Secretary of State has an unfettered discretion as regards increases to other benefits under that Act and to war pensions,[10] family income supplement[11] and supplementary benefit.[12] The Child Benefit Act 1975 imposes on him a duty in each year following the introduction of the scheme to

> 'consider whether the rate or any of the rates then in
> force . . . should be increased having regard to the national
> economic situation as a whole, the general standard of living and
> such other matters as he thinks relevant'[13]

but does not prescribe any course of action when that duty to consider has been fulfilled.

6. Ante n.9, at p. 449. The view coincides with a statement made by Mr. P. Dean, Under-Secretary of State, in Standing Committee E Debates on Social Security Bill 1973, col. 769.

7. *Metzger* case, ante n.9, at p. 449.

8. SSA 1975, s.126(4).

9. See the discussion, ante, p. 24.

10. See, e.g., War Pensions Act 1921, s.4(1).

11. FISA 1970, s.2(2).

12. SBA 1976, s.2(3) (though the amounts payable cannot be *reduced* by regulations).

13. CBA 1975, s.5(5): cf., post, p. 451.

Part ten. Overlapping Benefits

A. General

Any broadly based system of social welfare encounters the problem arising from the availability of two or more benefits to cover the same, or an essentially similar, risk. The problem has two dimensions. The first is concerned with those overlaps in the social welfare system itself; an obvious example is sickness benefit and industrial injury benefit. The general principle to be applied has never been in doubt: 'double provision should not be made for the same contingency'.[14] The principle may be stated thus easily but its implementation is more difficult as it begs the question of what benefits are intended to cover the same contingency: for example, does a war pension deal with the same risk as sickness benefit? Moreover, even where it is conceded that two benefits are concerned with the same risk, the intention may be to allow the beneficiary to accumulate them: one obvious example is child benefit and increases to a personal benefit for dependent children. Finally there is the problem of deciding what are the limits of the social welfare system for the purpose of applying the principle: are local authority benefits included? Most of these questions receive a solution, explicit or implicit, within the social security legislation itself. An account of these rules forms the subject matter of Sections B to E. The second dimension poses even greater difficulties. In many cases there is an overlap between public welfare benefits and private provision, e.g., occupational schemes. There is no consistent policy on this issue, partly because there has never been an overall view of the relationship between the public and private sector, partly because the policy issues themselves are so difficult. They include deciding whether benefits are payable 'as of right' as under a private insurance contract, or are payable rather 'according to need'. In section F a brief summary will be given of the various measures taken, most of them discussed in detail in other parts of the book.

B. Recipients of benefits payable under SSA 1975

i) Income-replacement benefits

The principle that double payments should not be made for the same contingency finds its first and most obvious application with regard to benefit intended as a partial replacement of lost earnings. Thus adjustment is made to those in receipt of two or more of the following, non-industrial, personal benefits:[15] unemployment, sickness and invalidity benefit, retirement pension, maternity allowance, widow's benefit, non-contributory invalidity pension, invalid care allowance. Entitlement to benefits not intended as income-replacement, viz., death grant, maternity grant,

14. NIAC Report on Draft Overlapping Regulations 1948–49 HC 36, para. 9. The principle had been stated both by Beveridge, para. 321 and in Social Insurance, Part I, para. 147.

15. S.I. 1975/554, Reg. 3(1).

attendance and mobility allowance, is not affected.[16] For the purposes of adjustment, an earnings-related supplement is regarded as part of the benefit to which it is added,[17] but an age addition is affected only insofar as the same addition is made to another benefit.[18] The adjustment is made according to the following rules:[19]

1. A non-contributory benefit is deducted from a contributory benefit.

2. Unless an alternative arrangement has been made, a proportionate part of a benefit paid weekly is deducted from one paid on a daily basis.

3. In all other cases, the claimant receives the higher or highest of the benefits to which he is entitled.

The relationship between non-industrial benefits and industrial injury benefits or war pensions is necessarily more complicated, and perhaps more controversial. For the purposes of these rules, the original plan was to equate war pensions with industrial injury benefits.[20] However, at the end of the Second World War there was a strong feeling that war pensions should be regarded as 'compensation' for injuries suffered during service in the national cause and and were thus different from other benefits intended to 'relieve hardship'.[1] In the result, there may be an accumulation of unemployment, sickness, invalidity benefit or maternity allowance with a war disablement pension. As regards industrial injury benefits, there was an obvious case for adjusting an overlap of a personal benefit for income-replacement with injury benefit or the unemployability supplement to a disablement pension,[2] but not with the disablement pension itself, as this was compensation for the injury. Widow's benefit is in a category of its own, since by its nature it is more akin to a dependant's benefit than to a personal benefit, so adjustment is made to prevent overlap, not only with the industrial injury benefit and unemployability supplement, but also with the industrial death benefit and (in the light of the policy discussed below) the war pension death benefit.[3] Finally there is a provision to deduct from personal benefit anything received by way of 'training allowance', (i.e., an allowance payable out of public funds[4] by a government department or by or on behalf of the Manpower Services Commission for maintenance during a period of training).[5]

16. S.I. 1975/554, Reg. 3(2).
17. Ibid., Reg. 4(1), and see Appendix.
18. Ibid., Reg. 3(3)(i): so also for the invalidity allowance (ante, p. 166) where the claimant is also entitled to an age increase to a Category A retirement pension: ibid., Reg. 3(3)(ii).
19. Ibid., Reg. 3(4).
20. See Social Insurance, Part I, paras. 148–149.
1. See statement of Mr H.A. Marquand, Minister of Pensions, to House of Commons, 454 HC Deb., col. 1660 and NIAC Report ante n.14, at para. 20.
2. S.I. 1975/554, Sch, paras. 1–5: in general the industrial benefit is deductible from the non-industrial benefit.
3. Ibid., para. 3, and see Appendix.
4. The fund must be a British fund (R(P) 5/56) and controlled by the Government (R(P) 13/56).
5. S.I. 1975/554, Sch. Grants for full-time education and teacher training are, however, excluded: ibid., Reg. 2(1) and see R(U) 38/56 and R 1/68 (P).

ii) Benefits for special needs

The case for adjusting benefits intended to remedy specific needs arises only as regards overlap between the different schemes for disability. Thus the attendance allowance, invalidity allowance, the mobility allowance and the hospital treatment increase may not be accumulated with their equivalents in other schemes, viz., respectively, constant attendance allowance, the invalidity addition, the mobility addition and the treatment allowance.[6]

iii) Dependency benefits

Dependency benefits (meaning not only increases to personal benefits for children or adults, but also child's special allowance, and child's allowance under the war pension scheme[7]), for the same dependant for the same period may not be accumulated.[8] Unlike the rule for personal benefits, the regulations on dependants included the war pension scheme: for no obvious reason,[9] the argument based on compensation for loss sustained in a national cause was not extended generally to members of a serviceman's family.[10] There are two exceptions to this: both a war pension allowance for a child's education and a dependency benefit which is part of a war disablement pension (not being payable as an increase to unemployability supplement) are disregarded.[11] The former may be rationalised on the ground that it covers a special need, and the latter in that it is really part of the 'compensation' for the injury.

C. Child benefit

Child benefit is payable to all families and may be regarded as a general redistributional device. It is therefore distinguishable from child dependency benefits which are primarily intended to cope with the additional financial problems arising when the main source of income is lost and from family income supplement which is concerned to boost *earned* income. These benefits may, then, be aggregated. However, child benefit is taken into account as a resource for the purposes of supplementary benefits.[12]

D. Means-tested benefits

Both of the means-tested benefits are concerned to raise income and other resources to a specified level, but there is a difference of emphasis between the two. With a few exceptions, the family income supplement takes into account the receipt of all social security benefits, though since the amount

6. S.I. 1975/554, Sch, paras. 6, 7, 10.
7. Ibid., Reg. 2(1).
8. Ibid., Regs. 5–7, as amended by S.I. 1977/342 and S.I. 1978/433.
9. Cf., NIAC Report ante, n.14, at para. 23, where it was argued that the dependant's benefit was not

'compensation' for the injury sustained.
10. The additions payable are, however, very small (averaging only 15p a week): ante, p. 373.
11. S.I. 1975/554, Regs. 6(3) and 7(4).
12. Post, p. 510.

payable is not modified for a period of a year, entitlement to short-term benefits during that period will effectively be disregarded.[13] While it is a general principle of the supplementary benefit scheme to have regard to all forms of income, it also aims at differentiating between claimants according to their special needs. Insofar as social security benefits are directed towards such needs, the legislation allows them to be partly or wholly disregarded in the calculation of resources. The detailed rules are fully discussed below.[14]

Where, under either scheme, a social security benefit is treated (in whole or in part) as a resource, it nevertheless remains payable in full but the amount paid by way of family income supplement or supplementary benefit is reduced. However, in the case of the latter there is a special rule to cover the contingency where the supplementary benefit was not reduced on account of entitlement to another social security benefit payable for the same period. This situation frequently arises because the other benefit is often paid later than the supplementary benefit. Where this occurs, the authority administering the other benefit is given power to deduct from it the amount overpaid by way of supplementary benefit.[15]

E. Recipients of National Health Service facilities

To the extent that a social security beneficiary is being maintained free of charge at a hospital or other institution his need for financial support is reduced, and if the maintenance is financed from public funds, there is a strong argument for reducing the amount of benefit. There are special rules governing this subject which have been fully discussed in Part Five of this chapter.

F. Social security benefits and private rights

In many situations, a person subject to a hazard covered by the contributory or non-contributory schemes will be entitled to benefit from another source directed towards the same hazard but arising by way of private law, for example through an occupational scheme. Indeed, in the Beveridge scheme such arrangements were to form an important part of the general welfare system: while the state was to provide the minimum security for each kind of hazard, 'it should leave room and encouragement for voluntary action by each individual to provide more than that minimum for himself and his family'.[16] The argument logically leads to a principle that a person prudent enough to avail himself of facilities elsewhere should be entitled to reap the reward of his prescience and aggregate the public with the private benefit. Unfortunately, the matter is much more complex. In the first place, it is no longer the policy that the state benefit should provide merely the minimum. The unreality of the Beveridge laissez-faire

---

13. Post, p. 569.
14. Pp. 508–511.

15. SBA 1976, s.12.
16. Para. 9.

thesis has emerged through the hugh reliance on national assistance and supplementary benefit, and gradual introduction of earnings-related benefits. Secondly, the insurance basis of the social security scheme has become increasingly undermined as evident in the shift to earnings-related contributions and the introduction of non-contributory benefits.[17] Thirdly, in those fields where occupational schemes are widespread, e.g., sick pay and retirement, it is illusory to regard them as resulting from the 'voluntary' action of individuals. Most frequently they result from collective bargains between trade unions and employers and are compulsory. Indeed, the argument is now that for certain risks, e.g., short-term illness or unemployment, it is a more efficient use of resources for the public system to be superseded by private arrangements between employer and employee.[18]

In the light of these considerations, we may briefly survey the position reached in the most important areas of overlap betwen public and private provision. Because no general principle exists, different rules prevail in different areas, and these have generally been described in the sections of the book devoted to the specific benefits in question. The purpose here is to provide, by way of summary, an outline of the various approaches adopted.

i) Private insurance
Life insurance is very common; accident or sickness insurance is comparatively rare and, for practical purposes, private insurance against unemployment (as opposed to redundancy schemes) is non-existent. Where private insurance does exist, it fits neatly into Beveridge's prototype and it has never been doubted that the income so obtained might be fully accumulated with the non-means tested benefits.

ii) Redundancy payments
Although there might appear to be an overlap between unemployment benefit and redundancy payments, they are intended to be complementary rather than alternative schemes for dealing with unemployment. The redundancy payments scheme is intended to provide compensation for the loss of a job, the employee having been deprived of his proprietary interest in the employment;[19] the social security benefit is intended as a partial replacement of income lost as the result of the redundancy. Entitlement to one benefit is not affected by receipt of another.

iii) Guarantee agreements
Insofar as an employer agrees, or is bound to maintain a certain degree of remuneration for periods when an employee is laid-off or put on short-time, the employee is to that extent not regarded as unemployed. The guarantee payments are treated as wages and will disentitle him from benefit.[20]

17. Ante, p. 27.
18. Cf. ante, pp. 93 and 149.

19. Cf., ante, p. 78.
20. Ante, pp. 102–104.

iv) Sick pay agreements

The position is very different in the case of sick pay. Notwithstanding the obvious overlap between the private and public sector, or the rule pertaining to guarantee agreements, entitlement to sickness, invalidity and the industrial injury benefits remains unaffected by the receipt of sick pay.[1] It is left to the private sector to adapt to the social security system either by reducing the amount of sick pay or by claiming a reimbursement of the amounts received from the public source.[2]

v) Maternity pay

The rules governing overlap between maternity allowance and maternity pay come midway betwee those described in (iii) and (iv). An employer who confers maternity pay in fulfilment of his obligations under the Employment Protection Act 1975 is entitled to make a deduction for maternity allowance.[3] Any payments which exceed the statutory obligations are treated in the same way as sick pay.

vi) Occupational retirement pension schemes

The desire to maintain an appropriate standard of living in old age, has inevitably been responsible for a degree of private provision which has had the greatest impact on the public sector. It is clearly not feasible to raise revenue in the public sector to such extent that the retirement pension will be fixed at a level regarded as reasonable for all members of society. The effort has been directed more at integrating the private with the public sector, so that under the new pensions arrangements those unlikely to invest in private schemes, or unable to do so, will be able to rely on a genuinely adequate pension, related to their pre-retirement income, while those sufficiently covered by a private scheme will be able to opt out of the earnings-related component in the public scheme.[4]

In the last decade unsuccessful efforts have been made by successive governments to use the receipt of an occupational scheme as a ground for limiting entitlement to unemployment benefit. The phenomenon which has been giving rise to the concern was the substantial number of people who had retired on an occupational pension before the age at which social security pensions are payable and who were able to draw unemployment benefit because there were few vacancies for persons of that age. The National Insurance Advisory Committee, with one member dissenting, regarded it as a case of 'non-employment' rather than 'unemployment', in that it was far from clear that individuals retiring from their usual occupation really intended to find alternative employment.[5] Less persuasively, the majority also argued that the combination of occupational pension and unemployment benefit resulted in an overlap of compensation for the same loss of earnings.[6] It recommended both a new condition for unemploy-

1. Ante, p. 158.
2. Ante, p. 149.
3. Ante, p. 256.
4. Ante, p. 225.
5. Report on the Question of Conditions
for Unemployment Benefit and Contribution Conditions for Occupational Pensioners (1968), Cmnd. 3545, para. 41.
6. Ibid., at para. 50.

ment benefit and a sliding scale of benefit. The proposals met with a storm of opposition;[7] and when Conservative and Labour governments sought in turn to implement the recommendations at least in part, each was defeated by a combination of the opposition and some of its own backbenchers.[8]

vii) Common law actions

Equally perplexing has been the accumulation of social security benefits with common law rights.[9] This occurs most notably where the recipient of sickness, invalidity or industrial benefit has a personal injury claim, or a beneficiary of widow's benefit has a right under the Fatal Accidents Act 1976. Beveridge had assumed that some adjustment was necessary.[10] The Monckton Committee, examining the question in 1946, agreed but sensibly concluded that it would be wrong to disturb full entitlement to the social security benefit.[11] The latter was payable almost immediately and was not subject to problems of proof of fault, or quantum of damages. It recommended instead that the damages award should take account of the benefit paid or payable,[12] a proposal which in its entirety proved to be politically unacceptable, and resulted in an unsatisfactory compromise: a deduction of one half of any sums paid or payable within five years from the time when the cause of action accrued for sickness or invalidity, industrial injury and disablement benefit and non-contributory invalidity pension.[13]

The Pearson Royal Commission on Civil Liability and Compensation for Personal Injuries has made proposals for substantial reform on these matters. If implemented, they would result in a much closer integration of social security and the common law (see further the Appendix).

7. See NIAC Report on the Draft Regulations, 1969–70 HC 211, para. 4.
8. Ante, p. 107.
9. See, generally: *Pearson*, chap. 13; *Atiyah*, chap. 18.
10. Para. 260.
11. Final Report of Departmental Committee on Alternative Remedies (1946), Cmd. 6860, paras. 41–43.
12. Ibid., at paras. 48, 92, 96, 98.
13. Law Reform (Personal Injuries) Act 1948 s.2(1), as amended by NIA 1971, Sch. 5, para. 1 and Social Security (Consequential Provisions) Act 1975, Sch. 2, para. 8. For details and the case-law see Ogus *Law of Damages* (1973), pp. 224–225.

11 Child Benefit

Part one. Introduction

A. General

Until recently, family provision has been treated as the poor relation (or Cinderella[1]) of the social security system. Family allowances were not introduced until 1945, and then in the 1950s and 1960s were neglected: they were rarely uprated in line with rising living standards, and did not appear to be regarded as significant benefits. The result was that Britain's provision for children has been less generous than that of most other European and some Commonwealth countries.[2] In particular, the allowances were not payable for the first child of the family, though in this respect the British system was not unique.[3] Although in 1975–76 more people were in receipt of them than any other social security benefit (with the exception of retirement pensions), the total amount spent on family allowances was only £534,000,000, rather less than that on unemployment and on supplementary benefit.[4] In contrast, income tax allowances for children have been much more valuable and have often been increased by the annual Finance Act. They do not, however, benefit families who have a low income and do not pay tax. The primary object of the change to child benefit made by the Child Benefit Act 1975 was, therefore, to pay appreciably more to all persons looking after children than was afforded by family allowances, and gradually to withdraw income tax allowances which have been of more benefit to the higher income groups.

In this Part of the chapter, there is first, a short outline of the history of family allowances, and then an examination of the reasons which led to their replacement by child benefit. The third section contains a discussion of some of the policy questions arising under the new scheme – in particular, the question whether the rate of benefit should be varied according to the child's age or other factors. In Part Two of the chapter, the legal conditions for entitlement to child benefit are analysed. Part Three contains a short discussion of the rules regarding claims to, and payment of, benefit.

---

1. The term is used by *Kaim-Caudle*, p. 264.
2. See the figures given in *Poverty* (1966) No. 1, p. 15, and Wynn *Family Policy* (1970), Appendix 3.
3. See *Kaim-Caudle*, p. 271 (Netherlands) and p. 273 (West Germany). Germany introduced family allowances for the first child in 1975: see *Poverty* (1974) No. 30, p. 27 (M. and A. Wynn).
4. See the figures in the Annual Report of the DHSS 1975, Cmnd. 6565, paras. 7.9.

B. The history of family allowances[5]

The first proposal to introduce a special allowance for the benefit of children was made in 1796 by William Pitt, then Chancellor of the Exchequer. His enlightened attitude is exemplified by his peroration, often quoted in modern debates: 'Let us make relief, in cases where there are a number of children, a matter of right and an honour, instead of a ground for opprobrium and contempt.'[6] But the Bill never became law, because of the pressure of other business; Pitt was more successful, as will be seen,[7] when he introduced income tax allowances for children. It seems that the issue was not discussed widely again until after the First World War, when Eleanor Rathbone founded the Family Endowment Society, an important pressure group in the inter-war years. In her book, *The Disinherited Family*, published in 1924, she argued that it was in the interest of society as a whole to ensure that children were well clothed and fed, and that a state allowance should be paid to make this possible. The case for such a payment took on additional strength from the fact that in 1921 and 1922 dependants' allowances were introduced for the unemployed.[8] The absence of any comparable provision when the man was in work might have been viewed as a disincentive to employment. But, unlike other European countries, there was no move at this time to introduce family allowances in Britain.[9]

The introduction of the Family Allowances Bill in 1945, during the last months of the war-time Coalition government, was largely influenced by the Beveridge Report. This adduced three principal arguments for the payment of family allowances. First, the only way of guaranteeing a reasonable subsistence income for all families, whether the head of the family was in work or not, was to pay an allowance for children: this object could not be secured by wages, as they did not take account of the size of a man's family.[10] Secondly, 'it is dangerous to allow benefit during unemployment or disability to equal or exceed earnings during work. But, without allowances for children, during earning and not earning alike, this danger cannot be avoided.'[11] The third argument seems surprising these days: the provision of family allowances was thought conducive to a higher birth rate.[12] The Beveridge Report further argued that payments should be financed by general taxation, so that the whole community should share in the task of maintaining children. But parents were not to be relieved of their entire responsibility, and for this reason it was recommended that

5. See *Walley*, pp. 16–20, 54–55, 70–73; Land in *Poverty* (1966) No. 2, p. 13; Hall, Land, Parker and Webb *Change, Choice and Conflict in Social Policy* (1975), chap. 9. *Harris*, pp. 341–346.
6. Quoted by Sir W. Jowitt, introducing the debate on Social Insurance, Part I 404 HC Deb., col. 988.
7. See post, p. 447.
8. See ante, p. 384.
9. In the inter-war years family allowances were introduced in France, Germany and the Netherlands. New Zealand had been the first country to introduce such a scheme – in 1926.
10. Para. 411.
11. Para. 412.
12. Paras. 15 and 413. Churchill gave particular emphasis to this point when he announced the Coalition government's acceptance of Beveridge's proposals in a broadcast in 1943.

nothing should be paid for the first child in a family.[13] Lastly, the Report rejected the argument that the allowance for each child should be reduced as the size of the family increased; there were no real economies of scale when this occurred. A flat rate payment of 8s (40p) was proposed, though Beveridge indicated that at some future time consideration should be given to grading allowances according to the children's age.[14]

The government modified the scheme proposed by Beveridge in some minor respects. The most important change was that a substantial part of the allowance was to be paid in kind through the provision of free school meals and milk. This reduced the cash payment to 5s (25p) a week, which the government proposed should belong to the father. But on a free vote Miss Rathbone's amendment to make allowances the property of the mother was passed.[15] As the title of the Act and the name of the benefit suggested, the allowance was to be paid to families 'for the benefit of the family as a whole.'[16] The claimant was required to show that the family contained at least two children. The legislative provisions defining a 'family' for the purposes of the allowance were complex and gave rise to a number of cases before the Commissioners in which the question was whether a particular child was a member of one or other of two families.[17] (Under the Child Benefit Act these difficulties have largely disappeared.[18])

The rate of payment was not increased until 1952, and was then raised again for third and subsequent children in 1956. After that there was no change until 1968. The introduction by an Act of 1956 of an extra 2s (10p) for third and subsequent children meant that relatively older children attracted larger allowances, though it is difficult to see this development as fulfilling Beveridge's suggestion that they might be graduated according to age.[19] The 1956 Act also made the allowance payable in respect of children receiving full-time education, or in an apprenticeship, until they reached the age of eighteen; previously the general age limit had been sixteen.[20] The 1964 Act further raised the limit for these groups of children to 19.[1]

There is no obvious reason why family allowances were so neglected throughout this period. It has been suggested that to some extent they suffered because they were the first benefit introduced after the Beveridge Report: the 1945 Act was passed before the Attlee Labour government assumed office and, therefore, the role of family allowances in combating poverty was not discussed during the late 1940s.[2] A second reason is perhaps that the demographic argument for their payment was no longer taken seriously; indeed, there was some anxiety that the country might be

13. Para. 417. See *Harris*, p. 412.
14. Para. 421. The argument on the appropriate rates for paying benefit still continues: see post, pp. 450–451.
15. For the similar controversy concerning the allocation of tax credits and child benefit, see post, p. 448.
16. FAA 1945, s.1, repeated in FAA 1965, s.1.
17. See e.g., *R(F) 3/63*; *R(F) 8/64*; *R(F) 1/74*, interpreting FAA 1945, s.3, or

the same section of the FAA 1965. The Commissioners assumed jurisdiction to determine these issues in 1959; post, p. 620.
18. Post, pp. 457–458.
19. Cp., *George*, p. 191.
20. FAA 1945, s.2.
1. FANIA 1964, s.1. The 1945 Act, the 1964 Act and other statutes were consolidated in the FAA 1965.
2. The point is made by *Walley*, p. 182.

overpopulated by the end of the century.[3] In fact, there seems very little evidence that the availability of family provision affects population trends.[4] But the belief that it does may have been partly responsible for government reluctance to increase the level of payments. Thirdly, it appears that the allowances were among the least 'popular' of the welfare benefits.[5] Certainly, there has rarely been the same widespread demand for more generous provision for families as there has for pensioners, and it may be for this political reason that governments decided to economise on family allowances.

The last major development before the change to the new system occurred in 1968. There were two increases, the first of 7s (35p) and the second of 3s (15p) within twelve months. The Labour government's intention was that these should benefit the poorer families who did not earn enough to pay income tax. In order to prevent taxpayers benefiting from the increases, an equivalent sum was 'clawed back' from them by a reduction in the value of the children's income tax allowance. The 'claw back' remained a feature of the family allowances system until it was replaced by child benefit under the 1975 Act.[6] The device had first been suggested in the Beveridge Report. The rule was that the amount of the child tax allowance available was to be reduced by the increase in the annual value of the family allowances since 1968 (in 1976, £52), when the person concerned was entitled to and did actually claim the latter.[7] This was the first time family and tax allowances had been considered together; it signalled the advent of the approach which led to the Child Benefit Act 1975.

C. The change to child benefit

Before the 1975 legislation is discussed, something should be said about child income tax allowances, because their abolition is a crucial aspect of the new scheme. They were first introduced by William Pitt two years after his unsuccessful attempt to provide a family benefit. But they were abolished in 1806, and were not reintroduced until 1909. Since 1957 their value has been graduated according to the child's age, a significant difference from family allowances. In 1976–77 the value of the child tax allowance (CTA) was as follows: for a child under eleven, £300; for a child from eleven to sixteen, £335; and for a child over sixteen, £365.[8] If he was receiving full-time instruction at any school, university or other educational establishment,[9] there was no age limit.[10] Unlike family

3. Ibid., at pp. 186–187, and see the same author in ed. Bull *Family Poverty* (1972), p. 109.
4. See Schorr in *Poverty* (1967) No. 2, p. 8.
5. See Bull, n.3, at pp. 167–168.
6. There are discussions of the 'claw back' by Kincaid *Poverty and Equality in Great Britain* (1973), pp. 69–73, and by Lynes, ante n.3, at p. 118.
7. Income and Corporation Taxes Act

(ICTA) 1970, s.24(1).
8. Finance Act 1976, s.29(2).
9. This includes training for a trade, profession or vocation in circumstances where the child is expected to devote all his time to it for at least two years: ICTA 1970, s.10(4).
10. In both family allowances and child benefit (see post, p. 453) there is an upper age limit of nineteen.

allowances, CTA may be claimed in respect of the first child. Although it is only recently that it has become common to look at tax allowances as a type of family endowment, their value to the taxpayer with children has obviously been considerable. Two further points may be made. First, CTA may benefit high earners proportionately more than those on an average income, because it reduces the recipient's taxable income, and so enables the former to pay tax at a lower rate. Secondly, since tax is normally deduced by PAYE at source, CTA typically benefits the male wage-earner rather than the child's mother.

Towards the end of the 1960s a number of schemes were suggested for integrating family allowances and tax allowances.[11] The Labour party put forward proposals in 1969; then the Conservative government, which took office the following year, recommended their integration as part of a tax credit system.[12] Although the 1974 Labour government was not in favour of this radical reform, it did support a child endowment scheme which had much in common with the tax credit proposal so far as it applied to children. Thus the Child Benefit Bill, introduced in May 1975, enjoyed all party support, and the opposition was only concerned to amend the measure in detail. Its purpose was well summarised by Mrs. Castle, the Secretary of State for Social Services:

> 'It achieves a long overdue merger between child tax allowances and family allowances into a new universal, non-means tested, tax-free cash benefit for all children, including the first, payable to the mother. In this way it ensures that the nation's provision for family support is concentrated first and foremost where it is needed most – on the poorest families; and that it goes to the person responsible for caring for the children and managing the budget for their food, clothing and other necessities.'[13]

The scheme has two major advantages over family allowances. First, the benefit of tax allowances was to be extended to those poorer families who had not been able to take advantage of CTA because their income was too low to pay tax – this was to be achieved through the more generous level of child benefits. Secondly, the new benefit was to be payable for the first child. In these respects the measure followed the tax credit proposals.

However, child benefit differs from the original tax credit scheme outlined in the Conservative government's Green Paper.[14] First, the benefit is tax-free; under the Conservatives' proposals, the tax credit (equivalent to the child benefit) would be treated as part of the recipient's income for the purposes of tax, as were family allowances. Secondly, it is paid to the mother, while the original proposal was that credits should be payable to the father. But the Select Committee on Tax Credits had recommended that child credit should be paid to the mother, and this

---

11. See *George*, pp. 196–197; *Walley*, pp. 193–194.
12. *Ante*, p. 37.
13. 892 HC Deb., col. 330.
14. (1971), Cmnd. 5116.

approach was followed in the Child Benefit Bill. Mrs. Castle referred warmly to the support given by the TUC for this proposal, even though its implementation entailed a reduction in the take-home pay of union members.

The government made it clear that it did not intend to bring the Act into effect until April 1977, though it was pressed by the Conservatives in both Committee and at the Report stage[15] to pay the benefit from April 1976. Instead, an interim child benefit for all children of unmarried or separated parents was paid from that date to deal with the special problems faced by single-parent families.[16] For a short period in 1976 it was suggested that the implementation of the new scheme for other families should be further postponed. The official reason was that the government did not want take-home pay to be reduced, as it would be on the lowering of the child tax allowances, at a time when it was naturally anxious for its pay policy not to be jeopardised.[17] In fact, there is some suspicion that it was more concerned about the possible public expenditure implications of the change to child benefit when the time came to fix its rates.[18] The government's provisional proposal to postpone the scheme, and in its place extend family allowances to the first child, was heavily criticised.[19] Eventually in September 1976 it accepted the recommendation of a joint Labour party-TUC working group to introduce child benefit in phases.[20]

The compromise is that from April 1977, CTA for children under eleven will be phased out over three years, and the higher tax allowances for older children will be reduced. They will be abolished later when it becomes practicable. Child benefit is tax-free, as originally proposed, and there is to be no 'claw-back' from the (reduced) tax allowances.[1] The tax changes were made by the Finance Act 1977.[2] For the tax year 1977–78 the effect of this was that the tax allowances were reduced by £104 for the first child and by £130 for second and subsequent children. Child benefit for this year was paid at the rates of £1 for the first child (£1.50 for one-parent families) and £1·50 for each subsequent child.[3] From April 1978, the rate has been increased to £2·30 for all children, with an additional £1 for the first child in a one-parent family.[4] Apart from these families, there is no distinction drawn between the benefit payable for first and subsequent children. To finance these improvements, an additional £300 million has been allocated for child benefits.[5]

15. Standing Committee A Debates on the Child Benefit Bill 1975, cols. 266 ff.; 896 HC Deb., col. 179.
16. CBA 1975, s.16. The interim benefit ceased when child benefit became payable in April 1977. A single parent family, however, receives from April 1978 £1 more benefit than other families.
17. The immediate abolition of CTA for children under eleven would have reduced take-home pay by over £3 a week for a two child family.
18. See *New Society*, 17 June and 24 June, 1976, containing reports of the Cabinet discussions on the introduction of the child benefit scheme.
19. 912 HC Deb., cols. 284 ff.
20. 918 HC Deb., cols. 112–114.
1. For 'claw-back', see ante, p. 447.
2. Ss.24–26.
3. S.I. 1976/1267, Reg. 2.
4. S.I. 1977/1328, Reg. 2.
5. See Mr D. Healey, Chancellor of the Exchequer, 935 HC Deb., cols. 991–992.

D. Two policy questions

For the reasons already given the child benefit scheme represents a considerable advance over the previous system of family and tax allowances. But there remain some difficulties, and until these are resolved, it will be hard to come to a final verdict on the success of the change.[6] In particular, there are two questions of policy on which the attitude of the government has yet clearly to be determined. The first is the very important question whether the benefit should be paid at a flat rate or varied according to the child's age and any other relevant factor; the second concerns the approach to up-rating it in the light of inflation.

i) Should the benefit be flat-rate or graduated according to age/other factors?

There is a considerable body of evidence which suggests that the expense of providing for a child varies with its age.[7] An adolescent child attending school may cost more than an adult to feed and clothe, while younger children will require much less expenditure. This was recognised by the Beveridge Report.[8] Family allowances had, however, been flat-rate, though after 1956 a higher payment was made for third and subsequent children in one family.[9] The Child Benefit Act 1975 does contemplate that benefit may be paid eventually at different rates. Section 5(2) and (3) provide as follows:

'(2) Different rates may be prescribed in relation to different cases, whether by reference to the age of the child in respect of whom the benefit is payable or otherwise.

(3) The power to prescribe different rates under subsection (2) above shall be exercised so as to bring different rates into force on such day as the Secretary of State may by order specify.'

It does not seem at all clear on a literal construction of these provisions whether the government is under a duty to prescribe different rates or has a discretion whether to do so: the latter would appear to be indicated by subsection (2), but subsection (3) could be interpreted as imposing a duty. The debates in Parliament, even if admissible in a court of law,[10] do not provide any guidance on this point.

The government resisted a number of amendments to introduce graduated rates of benefit. The principal opposition proposal was to pay it at three different rates, depending on whether the child fell into the age groups, up to five, six to fifteen, sixteen and over.[11] Quite apart from the evidence of the higher costs of providing for adolescents, it was pointed out that the supplementary benefit scales provide for payment at five

6. For a general critique of the scheme, see Trinder *Poverty Report 1976*, p. 71. Also see Field, Meacher and Pond *To Him Who Hath* (1977), pp. 222–224.
7. Wynn *Family Policy* (1970), Appendix 3; M. & A. Wynn *Poverty* (1975–76) No. 33, p. 4.
8. Para. 421.
9. See ante, p. 446.
10. See Cross *Statutory Interpretation* (1976), pp. 134–136.
11. Standing Committee A Debates, cols. 73 ff.; 895 HC Deb., col. 223.

different rates for children under eighteen depending on their age,[12] and that the child tax allowances to be replaced by child benefit were also graduated.[13] But, although approving of differential rates in principle, the government took the view that more research should be done before this could be implemented. In particular, not enough was known, it was said, about the economic costs of the first child (when the family has to buy clothes, a pram, etc., which may be used for subsequent children) and whether marginal costs are affected by the total number of children in a family.[14] Moreover, the payment of a higher child benefit for older children would either entail awarding less for younger ones, which would be politically difficult, or spending more on the total scheme at a time when public expenditure was being reduced.

It is suggested that the case for paying higher rates for older children has now been established, and that the government should introduce the necessary regulations as soon as practicable. The time when the higher tax allowances are phased out will afford an ideal moment to increase the benefit for them. On the other hand, it must be conceded that the general practice of other countries is to pay higher allowances according to the child's rank (i.e., more for the second or third child, etc.) and not according to his age.[15] It is, of course, possible to vary payments according to both factors: for example, an increase could be paid for a child when it became, say, eleven, if it were the second or third child, but not if it were the first.[16]

ii) How often should benefit be up-rated?[17]

It has been mentioned how rarely family allowances were increased, and how as a result their contribution to the average family budget became virtually negligible.[18] There was, therefore, some anxiety during the debates on the 1975 Bill that child benefit would similarly lag behind rises in the cost of living. But amendments during the Committee stage to link the benefit with price movements (and in a Labour back-bench amendment to link it with prices or earnings, whichever were the more favourable) were rejected.[19] The government did not regard child benefit as similar to other social security benefits for this purpose and, therefore, rejected automatic annual review. The reason given by Mrs. Castle was that it was not a subsistence benefit, but a supplement to what is normally a full wage and, therefore, the considerations relevant to other benefits, such as retirement pensions, did not apply.[20]

12. SBA 1976, Sch. 1, para. 7(c): post, pp. 490–491.
13. See ante, p. 447.
14. Standing Committee A Debates, cols. 99–100. The Beveridge Report (para. 417) and a recent DHSS report by McClements (unpublished) both suggest that there is no evidence for economies of scale as the family size increases: Standing Committee A Debates, col. 81.
15. See Kaim-Caudle, p. 285, and see p. 253 for the reasons given by the Royal Commission on Social Security (1972) in New Zealand for rejecting age-related benefits.
16. The French system has this complicated structure: see Poverty (1975) No. 31, p. 40.
17. For up-rating of social security benefits, see ante, pp. 433–436.
18. See ante, p. 446.
19. Standing Committee A Debates, col. 146.
20. Ibid., at col. 161.

However, at the Report stage a government amendment was moved to insert what is now section 5(5):

> 'In the year beginning with the appointed day[1] and in each subsequent year beginning with the anniversary of that day, the Secretary of State shall consider whether the rate or any of the rates then in force under this section should be increased having regard to the national economic situation as a whole, the general standard of living and such other matters as he thinks relevant.'

It should be noted that this does not impose more than a duty to *consider* whether there should be an increase in benefit in the light of all the relevant factors, which might, of course, include the desirability of reducing (or at least, not increasing) public expenditure. And the duty to consider does not arise every twelve months; it may be discharged at any time during the year in question, which may be nearly two years after the previous review.[2] Although Mrs. Castle was right to point out that there was no obligation even to consider an increase in family allowances or tax allowances,[3] the significance of this new legal requirement is hard to determine. It is not yet known whether there will be regular up-ratings though there has been an increase in benefit for the tax year 1978–79. This increase would appear to be largely attributable, however, to the gradual introduction of higher benefits as the tax allowances are reduced, rather than to an up-rating in the light of inflation.[4]

Part two. Entitlement to Child Benefit

Under section 1 of the Child Benefit Act 1975,

> 'a person who is responsible for one or more children in any week ... shall be entitled to a benefit ... for that week in respect of the child or each of the children for whom he is responsible'.

There are two major issues in the determination of entitlement to child benefit: first, whether the child is one in respect of whom benefit is payable, and secondly, whether the claimant is to be treated 'as responsible for a child'. Since two or more persons may concurrently be responsible for the same child, difficult questions as to priority of title to the benefit may arise if there is more than one claim; these are discussed at the end of the second section. The third section is concerned with the residence qualifications which have to be satisfied by both the child and the person responsible for him.

---

1. S.I. 1976/961, Art. 2 provided that the appointed day was 4 April 1977.
2. In this respect the obligation does not appear to differ from that imposed with regard to social security benefits by SSA 1975, s.125(1): ante, p. 433.
3. 895 HC Deb., col. 233.
4. See ante, p. 449, for the gradual introduction of the new scheme.

A. The child

Section 2(1) of the Act provides that:

> 'a person shall be treated as a child for any week in which –
> (a) he is under the age of sixteen; or
> (b) he is under the age of nineteen and receiving full-time education by attendance at a recognised educational establishment'.

There is, therefore, a normal age limit of sixteen, with an upper age limit in some circumstances of nineteen.

i) The normal age limit

The normal age limit of sixteen provoked comparatively little discussion during the passage of the Bill. It seems that the government chose this age, because after a person is sixteen, he may be entitled to supplementary benefit.[5] Under the previous family allowances scheme, the normal limit was defined by reference to the school leaving age;[6] but as that has now been raised to sixteen, it is practicable to frame the general rule in terms of that age. This normal age limit is quite common in other countries: it is sixteen in New Zealand, Australia, Canada, Belgium, Holland and France. But in some countries, it is higher: eighteen in Germany, Italy and Denmark, and nineteen in Luxembourg.[7]

ii) The further age limit of nineteen

Under the new legislation benefit may be paid for a child under nineteen only if he is receiving full-time education at a recognised educational establishment. This is a more restrictive provision than its equivalent in the Family Allowances Act 1965, which also awarded allowances for children under nineteen in apprenticeships.[8] The failure to cover this group in the 1975 Act attracted some criticism, but it was pointed out that there were only thirty-eight families who were in receipt of allowances because of the 'apprenticeship' provision.[9] There was also some discussion of the failure to extend benefit to children over sixteen suffering from a physical handicap. This is a common provision in other European countries,[10] but, as was mentioned in the Committee proceedings,[11] in Britain a handicapped child over 16 is eligible for the new non-contributory invalidity pension, and to award child benefit would create an unnecessary overlap.[12]

The upper limit of nineteen is low in comparison with other European countries; in France it is twenty, while in Germany, Belgium and Luxem-

---

5. Standing Committee A Debates, col. 10. See chap. 12 for entitlement to supplementary benefits.
6. FAA 1965, s.2(1) and (2)(a).
7. See *Kaim-Caudle*, chap. VIII, and the figures given in Standing Committee A Debates, col. 39.
8. FAA 1965, s.2(1)(b).

9. B. O'Malley, Minister of State, DHSS, in Standing Committee A Debates, cols. 25–26.
10. *Kaim-Caudle*, chap. VIII, *passim*.
11. Standing Committee A Debates, cols. 39–40.
12. For non-contributory invalidity benefit, see chap. 4, ante, pp. 167–171.

bourg it is twenty-five, and in the Netherlands, twenty-seven.[13] Tax
allowances, to be phased out under the scheme, are without an upper age
limit at all for dependent children, and there was, therefore, some anxiety
on the opposition benches that parents with children at college or university would suffer financial hardship as a result of the change to child
benefit. But an assurance was given that CTA for children over nineteen
would not be abolished until changes were made in the system of educational grants; consequently, an amendment to provide benefit in respect of
such children was withdrawn.[14] There does not appear to be any particular
justification for nineteen being chosen as the upper age limit, apart from
the rather weak argument that this was the rule in the family allowances
system.[15] On the other hand, it might be thought odd that child benefit
may be paid at all in respect of someone who is legally an adult at the age of
eighteen![16] It would appear that the divergent rules of child benefit and tax
allowances with regard to age limits afford yet another example of the
inconsistency of approach which British law often adopts to young people
who have just become legally adult.[17]

iii) 'Receiving full-time education . . . at a recognised educational establishment.'

The Act provides that an educational establishment is one 'recognised by
the Secretary of State'[18] Under the Regulations a person may be treated as
receiving full-time education if he is in receipt of primary or secondary
education, otherwise than at a school by special arrangements made
under the Education Act;[19] moreover, in determining whether this condition is satisfied, no account is to be taken of a reasonable interruption of up
to six months, or even longer where the interruption is attributable to
illness or disability.[20] From the decisions of the Commissioner, interpreting the equivalent provision in the family allowances regulations,[1] it would
seem that school holidays, and leaving one school for the purpose of
removal to another, would both be treated as reasonable interruptions in
full-time education.[2] It was also decided that a child, unable to find a
school for several months because of his mental disability, was to be
treated as undergoing full-time instruction for that period;[3] but in another
case it was held that if education was continued beyond the child's sixteenth birthday *because of* his disability, any delay in finding a suitable
school could not be treated as a reasonable period of interruption.[4] This
distinction would appear applicable in interpreting the child benefit

13. *Kaim-Caudle*, p. 284; Standing
    Committee A Debates, cols. 13–14.
    Comparisons may be misleading unless
    account is also taken of the various
    systems of educational grants.
14. 895 HC Deb., cols. 202–208.
15. B. O'Malley, Minister of State, ibid.,
    col. 208.
16. Family Law Reform Act 1969, s.1.
17. See the various age limits governing
    maintenance of children in family
    proceedings: Cretney *Principles of*

Family Law (2nd edn) pp. 335, 338,
349 and 358.
18. CBA 1975, s.24(1).
19. S.I. 1976/965, Reg. 5: there is a
    comparable provision in Reg. 5(6) for
    Scotland.
20. Ibid., Reg. 6(1).
 1. S.I. 1969/212, Reg. 15.
 2. *R(F) 4/60*; *R(F) 1/68*.
 3. *R(F) 3/60*; cp., *R(F) 4/61*.
 4. *R(F) 1/68*.

Regulation. Another decision of the Commissioner which may afford guidance in determining whether the child is receiving full-time education is *R(F) 4/62*: there it was held that a person attending a secretarial college for thirteen and a half hours a week, with no homework outside this period, was not in receipt of *full-time* instruction.

Regulations in 1977 provide that benefit is not to be payable in respect of a child under nineteen who is receiving 'advanced education'.[5] This term is defined as courses in preparation for a degree, diploma or a teaching qualification, and any other courses certified by the Secretary of State as above GCE 'A' level standard.[6] Presumably the purpose of this rule is to prevent overlap between the benefit and the student grant.[7]

Under the family allowances rules it was sometimes difficult to determine whether a person receiving instruction at a technical college in connection with his work was to be regarded as receiving full-time instruction at an institution comparable to a school, or was alternatively to be treated as an apprentice.[8] Now that there is no entitlement in respect of apprentices, it is obviously crucial to know when vocational training will satisfy the requirements of section 2(1)(b) of the Act. The Act provides that education received by a child 'by virtue of his employment or of any office held by him' is not to qualify for this purpose[9] unless it is part of a course for at least six months and during that period he receives no financial support from his employment.[10] Reimbursement of the cost of books, equipment, tuition and other fees, and travelling expenses are not to be regarded as financial support.[11]

iv) Married children

There has been some discussion whether child benefit could ever be obtained in respect of a married child:[12] this would, of course, generally be applicable to a child over 16 with regard to whom it is payable under section 2(1)(b).[13] The government's intention was that benefit should be awarded in respect of a married child if he has left the other spouse and is in receipt of full-time education. This is covered by the General Regulations:[14]

> A person may be entitled to benefit in respect of a married child, provided that person is not the child's spouse,[15] *and* that either the

5. S.I. 1977/543, Reg. 2(3), inserting new Reg. 7A to the CB (General) Regulations, S.I. 1976/965.
6. Ibid., Reg. 2(1): the definition is inserted in Reg. 1(2) of S.I. 1976/965.
7. For the changes in supplementary benefits, see post, p. 551. Also see Finance Act 1979, s.26.
8. See the conflicting approaches in *R(F) 4/64* and *R(F) 1/70*. The difference could be important because an apprentice was only eligible for benefit if his earnings did not exceed a specified limit: FAA 1965, s.19.
9. CBA 1975, Sch. 1, para. 2.
10. S.I. 1976/965, Reg. 8(1).
11. Ibid., Reg. 8(2).
12. Standing Committee A Debates, cols. 19–22.
13. In a few cases a child under sixteen will lawfully be married under a foreign legal system and the marriage will be recognised in England if neither spouse is domiciled there: Morris *The Conflict of Laws* (1971), pp. 104–105.
14. S.I. 1976/965, Reg. 10.
15. Ibid., Reg. 11 prescribes the circumstances in which persons are not to be treated as having ceased to reside together: post, p. 463.

child is not residing with his spouse or that, if he is, the latter is receiving full-time education.

Interesting possibilities occur if the married child is a mother. She will herself be entitled to benefit in respect of her infant merely on the ground that it is living with her.[16] Further, her own mother (or other person with whom she is living) will also be entitled to benefit in respect of her. This odd situation could have occurred under the family allowances scheme, though the young mother under nineteen would have to have had two children in order to receive family allowances![17] It does seem, however, that one local tribunal was persuaded that a schoolgirl could not be both a mother and child for family allowances purposes.[18]

v) Disqualified children

Benefit is not payable in respect of certain children under Schedule 1 to the Act. Broadly the disqualifications apply if the child in the particular week is 'undergoing imprisonment or detention in legal custody', or is in the care of a local authority in various prescribed circumstances. These are set out in the General Regulations,[19] and are not discussed further here, though it is important to point out that the disqualification only applies if the child has been in detention, care, etc., for more than eight weeks.[20]

B. 'Person responsible for the child'

Under section 1, it is the person responsible for a child who is entitled to the benefit in respect of him. This term is primarily defined in section 3(1):

'a person shall be treated as responsible for a child in any week if –

(a) he has the child living with him in that week; *or*
(b) he is contributing to the cost of providing for the child at a weekly rate which is not less than the weekly rate of child benefit payable in respect of the child for that week.'

The claimant must, therefore, comply with one of these two conditions in order to establish entitlement. In many cases more than one person will satisfy them, and there are, therefore, rules in the Second Schedule to the Act determining which claimant has priority of title to the benefit. These rules are discussed in detail later, but it is perhaps useful to indicate at the outset that generally a person claiming it as 'responsible for a child' under section 3(1)(a) will have priority over a person claiming under section 3(1)(b); in other words, normally the person with whom the child is actually living will be entitled to benefit.[1]

16. CBA 1975, s.3(1)(a).
17. This, of course, was because family allowances were not payable in respect of the first child of a family.
18. *Poverty* (1975) No. 31, p. 50.
19. S.I. 1976/965, Reg. 16.

20. Ibid., Reg. 16(6): for the similar disqualifications for contributory benefits, see ante, pp. 421–424.
1. CBA 1975, Sch. 2, para. 2: post, pp. 461–465 for discussion of the priority rules.

These rules contrast sharply with the equivalent conditions for entitlement to family allowances.[2] As has been mentioned previously, they were paid for every family with two or more children, 'and for the benefit of the family as a whole'.[3] In the typical case eligibility was dependent on proof that the child was 'issue'[4] of the claimant and, therefore, a member of his family. Another person might apply in respect of a child whom he was maintaining, but that claim would always rank lower in priority to one made by the parent(s). It was difficult to defend these rules, as their effect was that the person primarily responsible in fact for keeping the child might not receive the allowance.[5] The provisions in the Child Benefit Act are in contrast designed to secure that benefit is paid to the person who prima facie most needs it.[6] No special privileges are conferred on a parent as such, though, of course, in normal circumstances it will be he who will receive it.

i) 'Child living with him in that week'

a) GENERAL. The Act does not define 'living with', but it would seem generally to mean living in the same place, under the same roof or in the same residence. The term was used in the family allowances legislation,[7] and the case-law interpreting it may provide some guidance with regard to this provision in the Child Benefit Act. In *R(F) 1/74*, it was argued that a child was not living with her mother, because the latter was not supporting her. The Commissioner rejected this contention:

' "Living with" implies no more than that mother and child are living together. The latter part of subsection (2) [of section 3 of the Family Allowances Act 1965] contrasts contributing to the cost of providing for the child as a separate consideration.'[8]

It is suggested that this view should prevail in the interpretation of section 3(1) of the 1975 legislation; here also, there is a separate provision in paragraph (b) to enable a person providing for the child to qualify for child benefit.

In certain circumstances the connection between the claimant and the child living in the same building with him may be so tenuous that it would be wrong to hold that he 'has the child living with him in that week'. This situation arose under the family allowances legislation. In *R(F) 1/71*,

the claimant lived with her daughter and the latter's illegitimate child. The child was provided for entirely by the grandmother, and had virtually no contact with her mother. The grandmother could only be awarded the allowance if it were shown that the child was

2. See Calvert *Social Security Law* (1st edn), pp. 259–270.
3. FAA 1965, s.1 (see ante p. 446).
4. Under FAA 1965, s.19, 'issue' meant issue of the first generation, and also see s.17 of that Act for other relevant rules.
5. See *Calvert*, ante n.2, at pp. 269–270.

6. Mrs B. Castle, Secretary of State, 892 HC Deb., col. 337.
7. FAA 1965, s.3: it was also used in the National Insurance legislation for the purposes of dependants' allowances: ante, pp. 390–391.
8. Para. 6, per J. S. Watson, Comr.

not living with her mother; otherwise the child would have been treated as a member of the mother's family, and the grandmother's claim would fail.[9] The Commissioner, R. J. A. Temple, held that the fact that mother and child were living under the same roof was not conclusive and that, as there was a complete absence of any normal parent-child relationship, it could not be said that they were living together. The grandmother's claim, therefore, succeeded.

Under the Child Benefit Act, it would on these facts be possible for the mother and grandmother each to contend that the child was living with her; if the mother's argument succeeded, she would receive the benefit under the priority rules to be discussed later.[10] It will, therefore, be important in these cases to decide whether a parent (or other claimant) does have a sufficiently close relationship with the child to justify the inference that they are living together. The fact that they are physically living under the same roof will raise a strong presumption that this is the case, but it is submitted that, as under the previous law, this should be rebuttable.

b) TEMPORARY ABSENCE[11]. Entirely different problems occur when a child and the person responsible for him (usually his mother) are temporarily apart, perhaps because the former is away at school or is in hospital, or because for some reason he is staying with other relatives. An absence of fifty-six days or less during the sixteen weeks preceding the claim is to be disregarded.[12] Thus, where a mother boards her child out with a relative for up to eight weeks, she continues to be entitled to benefit as she is to be treated as having her child living with her for that time. Only then (or after cumulative periods totalling fifty-six days within sixteen weeks) would she lose her entitlement on the basis of section 3(1)(a), so that the relative with whom the child is physically living would, if he made a claim, become entitled to benefit in priority to the mother.[13]

In some cases, a longer absence is disregarded in determining whether a person is to be treated as having a child living with him in the particular week. A separation which is attributable solely to the child's 'receiving full-time education by attendance at a recognised educational establishment' is wholly disregarded.[14] If, however, the child is away from the claimant's home for reasons additional to attendance at a school, the latter will not be entitled on a 'living with' basis.[15] Secondly, absence attributable to the child's 'undergoing medical or other treatment as an in-patient

9. The priority rules under the FAA 1965 were set out in the Schedule to the Act, para. 2.
10. See post, pp. 461–465.
11. See ante, pp. 391–392 for equivalent rules for the contributory benefits.
12. CBA 1975, s.3(2).
13. Before this period, the relative might claim under s.3(1)(a), but the parent would have the prior entitlement: Sch. 2, para. 4: post, p. 463.
14. CBA 1975, s.3(3)(a): see ante p. 454, for a discussion of 'full time education at a recognised educational establishment'.
15. See *Hill v Minister of Pensions and NI* [1955] 2 All ER 890 [1955] 1 WLR 899 DC, where a mother was refused family allowances in respect of children taken into care under the Children Act 1948, s.1 and put by the authority into a residential school.

in a hospital or similar institution', or being in residential accommodation under the Health Services and Public Health Act 1968 (or the National Health Service (Scotland) Act 1947) is to be disregarded for up to eighty-four consecutive days.[16] In these circumstances an unlimited period of absence (beyond the eighty-four days) may be ignored if 'the person claiming to be responsible for the child regularly incurs expenditure in respect of the child'.[17] Regulations may be made prescribing the circumstances in which this condition is satisfied[18] but at the moment of writing, none has been issued.

The purpose of these provisions is clearly to enable a person (generally, though not necessarily, a parent) to receive benefit for a child *normally* living with him. This is reasonable as a parent will often spend money on clothes and other articles for a child, even when the latter is away at school or in hospital. In the second situation there may also be the expense of paying frequent hospital visits. But where the child is in hospital for longer than eighty-four days, it is justifiable to require the claimant to show that he is regularly incurring expenditure.

c) THE RIGHT TO BENEFIT OF A VOLUNTARY ORGANISATION. A voluntary organisation may be regarded as a person with whom the child is living for any week when he is living in premises managed by the organisation or is boarded out by it.[19] Very similar provisions to those described in the previous section cover the temporary absence of the child from the voluntary organisation, so that the latter may continue to be entitled to receive benefit, even though the child is not in fact living in its premises.[20] The eligibility of an organisation for benefit here seems to be unique in the social security system;[1] there is no clear reason why it was decided to depart from the general rule that only natural persons are entitled. It should be noted, however, that an organisation is not entitled to child benefit on the alternative basis that it is contributing to the cost of providing for him.

ii) 'Contributing to the cost of providing for the child'
The second way in which a person may be treated as 'responsible for a child' is when

> 'he is contributing to the cost of providing for the child at a weekly rate which is not less than the weekly rate of child benefit payable in respect of the child for that week'.[2]

An application on this alternative basis will not succeed, because of the priority rules, if a claim has also been made by a person who has the child living with him. The main purpose, therefore, of this second head of

16. CBA 1975, ss.3(3)(b)–(c), and 3(4); S.I. 1975/965, Reg. 4.
17. CBA 1975, s.3(4).
18. Ibid., s.3(5).
19. S.I. 1976/965, Reg. 17(1).
20. Ibid., Reg. 17(2).

1. Cp., the refusal by the Commissioner to allow Dr Barnardo's to claim attendance allowance: *R(A) 3/75*, ante, p. 177.
2. CBA 1975, s.3(1)(b).

eligibility is to cover the case where the parent of a child arranges for it to be boarded with a relative or friend, and it is agreed that the parent should receive the benefit to cover the costs of the child's maintenance to which he is contributing.[3] If, however, the relative or friend himself claims in this situation, then he, and not the parent, would be entitled to the benefit.

Neither the Child Benefit Act nor the Regulations made under it define 'providing for' the child. This might seem odd because the family allowances legislation had defined this phrase.[4] It is, however, also used in the Social Security Act 1975 for the purposes of entitlement to an increase of benefit for a dependent child,[5] and there are a number of Commissioners' decisions interpreting it in this context. In some respects it seems that this legislation was the model for the concepts used in the Child Benefit Act and, therefore, the discussion in chapter 10 would appear to be relevant here.[6]

A problem which occurred under the family allowances legislation, and which may be of some importance under the new Act, is how periodic, but not weekly, payments made by the claimant to the person actually maintaining the child are to be treated for the purpose of determining the former's entitlement. The point is important because the claimant must contribute at a weekly rate not less than the weekly rate of benefit payable in respect of the child. The principles of 'spreading', as it is known, were set out in *R(F) 8/61*.[7] The period the payments relate to is a question of fact, the determination of which should take into account the payer's intentions. Regular periodic payments may be intended to cover a future period, and then they will be averaged over the number of weeks in this period. But if he has fallen behind with his payments, and then makes a large payment, this may be attributed to arrears.

The only Regulations made under the Child Benefit Act in this context provide that where two or more persons make weekly contributions, which individually do not, but together do, equal the amount of the benefit, the aggregate amount is to be treated as paid by one of them or, if they cannot agree on this, by that person nominated by the Secretary of State.[8] But after the week in which benefit is first paid under this arrangement, the recipient must contribute the full amount to retain his entitlement. It is further provided that where two spouses are residing together, a contribution made by one of them by their agreement, or (in default of that) at the discretion of the Secretary of State, be treated as contributed by the other.[9] It is not entirely clear what is the purpose of this provision, which applies whether the spouses concerned are parents of the child or not. Their ability to 'transfer' benefit to the non-contributing spouse may give a sensible measure of flexibility in some cases. But it less easy to see the justification for the power of the Secretary of State to treat the non-

3. Standing Committee A Debates, cols. 44–45.
4. FAA 1965, s.18.
5. SSA 1975, s.43(1)(b).
6. Ante, pp. 393–397.
7. See also *R(F) 1/73*.
8. S.I. 1976/965, Reg. 2(1), (2).
9. Ibid., Reg. 2(3).

contributing spouse as the contributor.[10] It appears to enable him in this situation to vary the provision which gives priority, as between a husband and a wife residing together, to the latter.[11] Fortunately, the situation will rarely arise, as the claim of either spouse will have lower priority than a claim by the person with whom the child is living.

iii) Priority between persons entitled

It has already been mentioned that one of the principal changes effected by the new scheme is the priority given to a claimant with whom the child is living, over other claimants, who might include the child's parents.[12] The Child Benefit Act sets out the relevant rules in Schedule 2. The exposition in this section follows the order of priority laid down there – with some examples to make it clearer. Two important preliminary points should be made. First, entitlement to child benefit is dependent on the making of a claim in the prescribed manner,[13] so if a person with a prior right under these rules has not in fact made a valid claim, they do not come into operation. Secondly, the right conferred by any of the priority rules (except, of course, the first one) only vests if nobody is entitled under one of the previous provisions.

a) PERSON WITH PRIOR AWARD. A person with an existing award of child benefit for a certain week is entitled to priority over anyone else who claims benefit in respect of the same child for that period. But this rule does not apply where the claim is made *for* a week later than the third week after that *in* which it is made.[14] The effect of these provisions is that, whatever the circumstances, a person with an existing award is entitled to priority over all other claimants for up to four weeks.[15] Thus,

> A is paying contributions to the cost of providing for the child and has been awarded benefit in respect of him. B, with whom the child is living, claims benefit. A is entitled under the prior award rule for at least the week in which B claims, and may be entitled for the next three weeks.

10. Under the family allowances legislation (FAA 1965, Schedule, para. 3) the Secretary of State had power to determine whether a child was to be included in his father's or his mother's family, in the absence of agreement between them. But this conflict could only arise if the child was provided for by *both* parents, was living with *both* of them, or was living with one and provided for by the other (see Calvert *Social Security Law* (1st edn), p. 267). The power under the 1975 Act seems wider in that the Secretary of State is able to award benefit in effect to a spouse who does not live with the child or even provide for him.

11. CBA 1975, Sch. 2, para. 3 (see post, p. 462).
12. See ante, p. 456.
13. CBA 1975, s.6(1): post, pp. 468–470 (claims and payments).
14. Ibid., Sch. 2, para. 1. Claims may be made fifty-six days before the claimant is entitled to benefit: S.I. 1976/964, Reg. 4.
15. If it is subsequently decided that the person with the existing award was not entitled to benefit and he has been required to repay it, then the second claimant may be awarded it for that week: S.I. 1976/964, Reg. 9, modifying CBA 1975, s.6(3).

This rule allows payments to continue, while the authorities investigate the facts to determine whether the new claimant should be awarded benefit.

b) PERSON HAVING THE CHILD LIVING WITH HIM. Any person entitled to benefit by virtue of having the child living with him is entitled to priority over anyone entitled on the alternative basis that he is contributing to the cost of maintenance.[16] This important departure from the rules applicable under the family allowances system represents one of the main advantages of the child benefit scheme. The reason for the change is that generally it is the person with whom the child is living who is primarily responsible for its care, and he should be entitled to priority.

c) HUSBAND AND WIFE. Subject to the application of the previous rules, if a husband and wife, who are residing together, both claim child benefit, the wife is entitled in priority to her husband.[17] Thus,

> where A and Mrs. A live with their children (and nobody has a prior award under the first rule), Mrs. A is entitled to the benefit; on the other hand, where they live together, but the child lives with B, it is B who has the prior entitlement and Mrs. A will only secure payment if B does not claim or waives his priority.

Family allowances had 'belonged to' the wife, where she and her husband were living together.[18] This was regarded as important, and the government was clear that she should also be entitled to the new benefit. An amendment was moved during the Committee stage of the Bill to provide that where the spouses agree, both should be equally entitled.[19] It was pointed out that there was little evidence that payment of allowances to the mother had alleviated family poverty and that in a number of other countries, e.g., France, the Netherlands, Italy, West Germany and Ireland, they are paid to the father. The government resisted the amendment, contending that in principle it was right for the mother to receive the benefit as she was primarily responsible for feeding and clothing the children. This conclusion had also been reached by the Select Committee of the House of Commons which had investigated the proposals for a tax-credit scheme.[20] There seems little doubt that it is right for the mother to have priority: the benefit may well be her only source of income. In this context it may be pointed out that a wife living with her husband cannot enforce a maintenance order against her husband, at least in the magistrates' courts.[1]

However, if the husband does claim he may be awarded the benefit, provided he submits a written statement signed by his wife that she does not wish to claim it.[2] As with family allowances, the husband may receive

---

16. CBA 1975, Sch. 2, para. 2.
17. Ibid., para. 3.
18. FAA 1965, s.4.
19. Sir G. Young, Standing Committee A Debates, cols. 57 ff.

20. Ante, p. 448.
1. Cretney *Principles of Family Law* (2nd edn), pp. 221–222.
2. S.I. 1976/964, Reg. 6(2).

payment of the benefit on behalf of his wife;[3] this will often be appropriate where, for example, the wife is too ill or handicapped to visit the post office to collect the weekly benefit.[4]

These provisions only apply when the husband and wife are residing together. If they are residing apart, the spouse with whom the child is living has priority under the rule described above.[5] Under the General Regulations, the spouses are not to be treated as having ceased to reside together by reason of an absence unlikely to be permanent, and, if in the week when benefit is claimed, they are not separated under a court order or a deed *or* have not been absent from each other for ninety-one consecutive days, this must be treated as unlikely.[6] (Nor are they to be treated as having ceased to reside together if one, or both, of them is receiving treatment in hospital.[7]) The consequences of these provisions may be illustrated by the following example:

> Mrs. A leaves her husband and her child, in respect of whom she is in receipt of benefit. Unless there has been a formal separation, the spouses are not to be treated under the Regulations as having ceased to reside together until they have been apart for ninety-one days and, therefore (subject to the other priority rules), Mrs. A retains her prior entitlement to benefit. It does not seem that A can claim priority over his wife under the previous priority rule for fifty-six days. This is because under section 3(2) of the Act, Mrs. A is still to be treated as living with her child, despite their absence from one another for fifty-six days. Until that period is over, A cannot claim to be entitled on the ground that he is living with the child, and his wife is not.[8]

This result seems difficult to defend, as for a considerable period Mrs. A has 'abandoned' her child, and Mr. A has been looking after it without any support. Under the family allowances legislation,[9] spouses were treated as living apart if one had deserted the other, so this result could not have occurred. It is submitted that the Regulation concerning 'residing together' may need reconsideration in the light of this difficulty.

d) PARENTS. The fourth priority rule is that, as between a parent and someone who is not a parent, the former is to have priority.[10] 'Parent' for this purpose includes natural parents, step-parents and adoptive parents.[11] The priority is, of course, subject to the previous rules: this can be illustrated by the following two examples.

3. Ibid., Reg. 13(2): see Mr B. O'Malley, Minister of State, Standing Committee A Debates, col. 71.
4. For the payment of child benefit, see post, pp. 469–470.
5. Ante, p. 462.
6. S.I. 1976/965, Reg. 11(1). Also see ante, p. 391.
7. S.I. 1976/965, Reg. 11(2).
8. It is possible that before then payment could be made to the husband on the wife's behalf under the power to divert payments conferred on the Secretary of State by S.I. 1976/964, Reg. 13(1): post, p. 470.
9. FAA 1965, s.17(1).
10. CBA 1975, Sch. 1, para. 4(1).
11. Ibid., s.24(3).

1. Miss A lives with her young child and B, not his father. Each is equally entitled as a person who has the child living with him. Miss A is awarded the benefit because she is a parent, and B is not.

2. Miss A does not live with her young child; he lives with her brother, B, though Miss A sends B a weekly sum towards the cost of providing for her child. Miss A does not have priority as a parent because B has priority under the earlier rule, which accords entitlement to the person with whom the child is living.[12]

Where two unmarried parents are residing together, the mother enjoys priority;[13] this is comparable to the priority a wife has under the previous rule. The General Regulations provide that two unmarried parents are not to be treated as having ceased to reside together by reason of 'any temporary absence',[14] but there is no specific rule (as there is for husband and wife) explaining the meaning of this phrase. The consequences of the Regulations may be illustrated by the following example, similar to that discussed on page 463 concerning a married couple.

Miss A who has been residing with B and is in receipt of benefit in respect of their illegitimate child, leaves that child with B. Under section 3(2) she is to be treated as having the child living with her for fifty-six days of absence. During this period, she will continue to have priority over B, provided it is held that she is still residing with B, notwithstanding her departure. But if it is decided that the absence is permanent, the rule conferring priority on her as the mother does not apply. It seems in that event that for the period of fifty-six days priority is to be determined under the rule discussed below, covering priority in other cases, where no previous rule applies. Under this *either* Miss A and B elect which of them is to be entitled *or* priority is decided by the Secretary of State. After fifty-six days B enjoys priority because he has the child living with him, and Miss A does not.

e) OTHER CASES. Finally, if none of the other priority rules determines entitlement, benefit is awarded to the person elected jointly by those eligible to claim it, or in default of election, the person chosen by the Secretary of State.[15] Under the Regulations an election must be made in writing on the appropriate form; it is not permanently binding, and may subsequently be changed.[16] An example of the possible application of this provision was given in the case discussed in the previous paragraph, but a more typical case would be the following:

---

12. Under the family allowances rules (FAA 1965, Sch., para. 2) Miss A would have been entitled in this example, as the child would have been her 'issue', and the issue link took priority over the maintenance link: see Calvert *Social Security Law* (1st edn), p. 268.

13. CBA 1975, Sch. 2, para. 4(2).

14. S.I. 1976/965, Reg. 11(3).

15. CBA 1975, Sch. 2, para. 5.

16. S.I. 1976/965, Reg. 13.

A and Miss B (a brother and sister living together) look after the young child of Mrs. C (their deceased sister). Neither has priority under any of the earlier rules, so they may elect which of them is to receive child benefit. If it subsequently becomes more appropriate for the other to receive it (Miss B who has been in receipt of it may become infirm), another election may be made and entitlement varied.

f) WAIVER OF PRIOR ENTITLEMENT. A person with a prior entitlement under these provisions may waive it.[17] The procedure for this step is set out in the General Regulations.[18]

> Thus, when a claim is made by A, a person (B) with prior entitlement, who is in receipt of the benefit,[19] may give the Secretary of State notice in writing at a Department office that he does not wish to have priority. In that case the provisions are ousted, and the claimant A is awarded the benefit (provided, of course, that he is otherwise entitled to it).

But the person who has waived his prior entitlement may subsequently make a further claim, and then the priority provisions in the Schedule take effect to give him title to the benefit.[20]

C. Residence qualifications

The Child Benefit Act 1975, as modified by Regulations made under it,[1] sets out a number of detailed provisions concerning residence qualifications. They concern both the residence, or more accurately, the presence in Great Britain of the child, in respect of whom benefit is claimed and the presence there of the claimant.[2] The law is extremely complex, largely because the government attempted to formulate rules which would combine the presence requirements for family allowances with the more generous conditions for tax allowances. Modifications applying to certain classes of persons were introduced by Regulations[3], but they do not cover immigrants to Britain who are supporting children overseas. (However, the Finance Act 1977 provides that tax allowances will not be reduced in 1977–78 for parents unable to claim benefit because their children do not satisfy the residence conditions.[4]).

This section first discusses the general requirements concerning the presence of the child, secondly, those concerning the presence of the

---

17. CBA 1975, Sch. 2, para. 6.
18. S.I. 1976/965, Reg. 14.
19. The problem only arises when the person with the prior entitlement is actually in receipt of the benefit, since under Section 6(1) of the Act, no person is entitled to the benefit unless he has claimed it.
20. S.I. 1976/965, Reg. 14(2).

1. S.I. 1976/963.
2. The usual requirements in social security law of 'residence' and/or 'ordinary residence' for which, see ante, pp. 214–216, are not exacted in this area.
3. S.I. 1976/963, Part II.
4. S. 25.

claimant and thirdly, the special relaxing provisions, applicable to certain categories of persons, in the Residence and Persons Abroad Regulations 1976.

i) Requirements with regard to the presence in Great Britain of the child

Section 13(2) provides that:

> 'Subject to any regulations . . . no child benefit shall be payable in respect of a child for any week unless –
> (a) he is in Great Britain in that week; *and*
> (b) either he or at least one of his parents has been in Great Britain for more than one hundred and eighty-two days in the fifty-two weeks preceding that week.'

Both these requirements have been modified by Regulations made under section 13(1).

(a) The absence of a child from Great Britain for a particular week will not be material if three conditions are satisfied.[5]

1. A person must be entitled to benefit for the week immediately before the first week of the child's absence from GB.

2. The child's absence is both initially and throughout intended to be temporary.[6]

3. The child must not be absent from GB for more than twenty-six weeks, *or* more than 156 weeks if the absence is solely attributable to receiving full-time education, *or* for more than such extended period as the Secretary of State allows if the absence is for the purpose of treatment for an illness, etc., which began before the period of absence.

(b) The purpose of the general requirement that either the child or one of his parents must have been present for more than half the year preceding the week for which benefit is claimed is to ensure that it is payable only for those children who have more than a transitory connection with Great Britain. This requirement is modified in certain ways by the Regulations,[7] the principal relaxation being that benefit may be payable if the child is in fact in Britain and (though not residing with his parent(s)) is living with another person with whom he is likely to continue to live permanently, and that person satisfies the requirements exacted by section 13(3)(b) of the Act, i.e., has been in Britain for more than 182 days in the year preceding the relevant week. The result is that benefit is payable for a child who has recently been left in Britain with a person who has been resident there for at least half the year preceding the week for which he claims.

---

5. S.I. 1976/963, Reg. 2(2).
6. For the meaning of 'temporary absence', see ante, p. 410.

7. S.I. 1976/963, Reg. 3.

ii) Requirements with regard to the presence in Great Britain of the person claiming benefit

As under the family allowances legislation,[8] there is a general requirement that the claimant is present in Britain, and has been present there for some time. Subject to Regulations, the claimant must be in Great Britain for the week for which he claims benefit, and must have been there for more than 182 days in the fifty-two preceding weeks.[9] Both these requirements have been modified to cover the cases where the claimant is, or has been, temporarily absent from the country, but still has sufficient connection with it to justify entitlement to benefit.

(a) The absence of the claimant from Britain for the relevant week is not material if three conditions are satisfied.[10]

1. That person must have been entitled to benefit for the week immediately before the first week of his absence from GB.

2. The claimant's absence is both initially and throughout intended to be temporary.[11]

3. The absence must not be longer than twenty-six weeks.

A person's absence for a week is also immaterial with regard to a child born to a mother within twenty-six weeks of her departure for a temporary absence – so that the claimant (not necessarily the mother) may be entitled to benefit for the twenty-six weeks following the *mother's* departure from Britain.[12] This enables a claimant to be entitled in respect of a child born abroad, perhaps because its mother wished to join her husband for the birth, even though he has been outside Great Britain for more than twenty-six weeks, so that he could not take advantage of the modifications in the Regulations.

(b) The general requirement that the claimant must have been present for the six months preceding the week for which benefit is claimed has been modified substantially.[13] In particular, the general condition is not to apply if the person is in fact in Great Britain and is responsible for a child who satisfies the presence requirements of section 13(2). This appreciably reduces the significance of the six months' presence requirement.

iii) Special relaxing provisions applicable to certain categories of persons

The general requirements, together with these modifications in the Regulations, may be further relaxed with regard to certain categories of persons by the rules in Part II of the Residence and Persons Abroad Regulations. These additional provisions were a response to the opposition anxiety that the presence requirements for child benefit appeared from the

---

8. FAA 1965, s.20.
9. CBA 1975, s.13(3).
10. S.I. 1976/963, Reg. 4(2).
11. Ante, p. 410.

12. S.I. 1976/963, Reg. 4(3).
13. Ibid., Reg. 5, as amended by S.I. 1976/1758, Reg. 4(2).

draft Bill to be more onerous than those applicable to the child tax allowances.[14]

> Part II applies to civil servants (other than those recruited outside the United Kingdom for service abroad), serving members of the forces,[15] and people temporarily absent from Britain, by reason only of employment abroad, for an income tax year in which at least half the earnings are liable to United Kingdom income tax.[16] It also applies to spouses of such people.[17]

Any week in which a person to whom Part II applies is away from Britain in connection with his employment is to be treated for the purposes of the presence requirements as one in which he is present there; moreover, a child's absence is to be disregarded entirely if he is living with a person to whom Part II applies, and that person is either a parent or someone who before the week in question was entitled to benefit in respect of him.[18] Days of separation of a child and such a person, which are attributable to the latter being abroad, are to be wholly disregarded under the 1975 Act for the purposes of determining whether he has the child living with him. Thus, a civil servant serving in a foreign embassy may be entitled to child benefit in respect of a child for whom he is responsible, even if the child spends the whole year in Britain, both school-terms and holidays. It seems that he would also be entitled if the child is being educated in and spends his holidays in another country, not the one in which the civil servant is working.[19]

Part three. Claims and Payments

A. Claims

It is provided by section 6(1) that no person is entitled to child benefit unless he makes a claim in the prescribed manner. Thus, as with almost all other benefits, the making of a claim is a necessary condition for entitlement.[20] The particular significance of this point with regard to the priority rules has already been mentioned:[1] these provisions will only operate to defeat a claim if a person with prior entitlement has in fact claimed benefit.

There are one or two special rules concerning the making of claims to child benefit which should be mentioned here.[2] First, a husband who resides with his wife and applies for benefit, may be required to provide a statement by her that she does not wish to make a claim.[3] This ensures that

14. For the residence requirements for tax see Whiteman & Wheatcroft *Income Tax* (2nd edn), chap. 2; see now Finance Act 1977, s.25.
15. Defined by S.I. 1975/492, Reg. 1(2).
16. S.I. 1976/963, Reg. 6(1)(a)–(c).
17. Ibid., Reg. 6(1)(d).
18. Ibid., Reg. 7(1), (2).
19. Ibid., Reg. 7(3). The Secretary of State, however, may refuse in his discretion to apply this disregard of days of absence in any case.
20. For the cases when a claim is not required, see post, p. 587.
1. Ante, p. 461.
2. For the general requirements of a valid claim, see post, pp. 587–593.
3. S.I. 1976/964, Reg. 3(2).

the wife's prior entitlement is protected. There is, however, no similar requirement when the father of a child living with its mother (though not a married couple) applies for benefit. Secondly, a claim may be made in advance by a person who does not at that time satisfy the requirements for entitlement, but expects to do so within fifty-six days.[4] Benefit may then be awarded, subject to the condition that the claimant does satisfy them when the award takes effect. It may be reviewed if the requirements are not met.[5] Finally, a claim may be made for up to one year after the week in respect of which it is made – an exceptionally generous time-limit.[6]

B. Payments

The procedure for making payments follows closely that established for family allowances. The Department sends the claimant notice that benefit may be collected weekly at a post office by means of an order book obtainable there. The benefit is payable on Monday or Tuesday.[7] This procedure was criticised by some opposition members as being too inflexible. They argued that there should be power to pay benefit quarterly or monthly in arrears, to pay by bankers' order into the claimant's bank account, or on request to provide lump sums periodically instead of regular weekly payments.[8] It is certainly arguable that the administration costs would be reduced if payments were made less often than weekly, as in Germany where they are made monthly, or by banker's order. But the government contended that most people were used to, and liked, weekly payments; for some families, there are obvious budgetary advantages in this method. The Regulations do, however, allow the Secretary of State to make other arrangements for payment, including payment in arrears, and this does give some measure of flexibility.

There is something to be said for enabling lump sums to be paid either in addition to, or in lieu of, weekly payments at certain stages when the parent is likely to have high capital expenses. New Zealand has enabled a year's benefit to be paid in advance as a lump sum on the occasion of the birth of a first child or when any child starts secondary education.[9] Even more unusually, parents may apply to the Social Security Commission to have benefits capitalised up to a certain sum to enable them to purchase or improve a house.[10] The introduction of such a procedure in this country would clearly be controversial; there is something to be said for this flexibility, but there is, of course, a danger that the children might suffer through the loss of a regular source of family support.

Section 6(3) of the Act provides that generally no person is entitled to receive benefit when another person has already received it in respect of that same child for the same week, whether or not the latter was entitled to

---

4. Ibid., Reg. 4(1).
5. Ibid., Reg. 4(2).
6. CBA 1975, s.6(2): for time limits generally, see post, pp. 592–600.
7. S.I. 1976/964, Reg. 6.

8. Standing Committee A Debates, cols. 181–192.
9. New Zealand Social Security Act 1964, s.36.
10. See *Kaim-Caudle*, pp. 251–252.

it. But this is modified in the Claims and Payments Regulations to allow payment in this circumstance when it has been decided that the benefit already paid should be repaid or it has been voluntarily repaid to the Department.[11] In this case there would be no duplication of payments. Another Regulation provides for payment in certain circumstances to a third party on behalf of the person entitled to benefit.[12] This may permit the Department in effect to vary the priority rules by diverting the payment to someone other than the person who is strictly entitled under the rules.[13]

11. S.I. 1976/964, Reg. 9.
12. Ibid., Reg. 13(1)(a).

13. Ante, p. 463, n.8.

12 Supplementary Benefits

Part one. Introduction

A. General

i) The role of supplementary benefits

Most social security systems provide some form of public assistance for people in need who are not for one reason or another able to maintain themselves out of other resources. In the British system supplementary benefits now provide this 'safety-net'. With some exceptions, in principle anyone in need is entitled to have it met by an award of supplementary benefit. (The main proviso, fully discussed in Part Two of this chapter,[1] is that normally benefit is not payable to someone with low earnings; he may instead be eligible for family income supplement.[2]) This general principle has been reflected in the law since the National Assistance Act 1948, the last of the measures which implemented the Beveridge proposals. National assistance was replaced by the present system of supplementary benefits in 1966, though the changes made then were relatively minor.[3] The basic conditions of entitlement to assistance, now governed by the Supplementary Benefits Act 1976, have remained unchanged in the last twenty years. Indeed, since the 1948 reforms public assistance has not been the subject of a major inquiry to consider its role in the context of social security provisions. Recently, however, the Supplementary Benefits Commission (SBC),[4] responsible for the administration of the benefit, has initiated a review of some of the policy issues, and it may be that important changes will be made in the next few years.[5]

Certainly, supplementary benefit has played a more significant role than that envisaged for national assistance by Beveridge. His Report argued that this would decline in importance. It added:

> 'Assistance will be available to meet all needs which are not covered by insurance. It must meet those needs adequately up to subsistence level, but it must be felt to be something less desirable than insurance benefit; otherwise the insured persons get nothing for their contributions.'[6]

1. Post, pp. 482–483.
2. Chap. 13.
3. Post, pp. 478–479, for a short discussion of the principal changes made by the Ministry of Social Security Act 1966, later renamed the Supplementary Benefit Act 1966, and now consolidated with other legislation in the Supplementary Benefits Act 1976.
4. See post, pp. 576–579, for a discussion of the Commission.
5. See the Annual Report of the SBC 1975, Cmnd. 6615, chap. 2, and Annual Report 1976, Cmnd. 6910, chap. 1.
6. Para. 369.

However, from the beginning of the post-Beveridge regime, the level of insurance benefits has never amounted to more than the standard weekly rate of assistance, and indeed has been less generous than the assistance receivable by a claimant also awarded the further rent allowance.[7] The predictable result has been that those unable to supplement contributory benefits, e.g., unemployment benefit or retirement pensions, with other income have come to rely on public assistance.[8] In practice, therefore, it is the means-tested benefit, rather than (as Beveridge had hoped) the contributory benefits, which now provides the minimum level of income for the poorest section of the community.

This is shown by the number of people in receipt of supplementary benefit. In 1948 there were 1 million recipients; at the end of 1976 benefit was paid to nearly 3 million people.[9] Over half the number are over retirement age, the overwhelming majority of whom (95%) are also in receipt of a retirement pension.[10] The next largest group is the unemployed, whose dependence on this benefit has risen dramatically in the last few years;[11] it is followed by single-parent families.[12] Recently governments have extended non-means tested provisions for certain groups, particularly the disabled,[13] which may have diminished their reliance on assistance. On the other hand, there has been no move to implement the Finer Committee's proposals to confer a benefit as of right on single-parent families,[14] and the number of unemployed claimants is still rising. Thus, there is every reason to think that supplementary benefits will continue to play a vital role in providing support for the very poor. The Commission has concluded:

> 'There are few countries in the world where those who might otherwise be destitute get help which is as prompt, as assured, or as generous in relation to social insurance benefits. But ... there are few urban industrial societies in which old age pensioners, the unemployed, the disabled, one-parent families and other large and predictably vulnerable groups are so likely to have to seek the help of a means-tested service originally devised as a last-resort safety net for the poor.'[15]

ii) Benefits and poverty
In view of the benefit's significance, there has been astonishingly little discussion concerning the principles on which the amount of weekly payments is assessed. It seems that in 1948 the assistance rates were fixed at a level just above the subsistence standard set by Beveridge for single adults and married couples, but a little below it for a family with chil-

7. Atkinson *Poverty in Britain and the Reform of Social Security* (1969), p. 24; Fiegehen, Lansley and Smith *Poverty and Progress in Britain 1953–1973* (1977), p. 134.
8. *George*, p. 210.
9. SBC Annual Report 1976, ante n.5, at paras. 2.6–2.8.
10. Ibid., paras. 2.9–2.12.
11. Ibid., paras. 2.13–2.14.
12. Ibid., paras. 2.15–2.16.
13. See chap. 4.
14. Post, p. 546.
15. Annual Report 1975, ante n.5, at para. 2.12.

dren.[16] This standard itself was lower than that arrived at by Rowntree in his studies shortly before the Second World War.[17] Both calculations had proceeded on the assumption that it was possible to measure 'poverty' by reference to absolute standards: a certain amount of money is needed for food, housing and clothing, and then a margin may be added for other expenditure and to allow for inefficiency.[18] There is no reason why weekly payments of public assistance could not be calculated in this way; it is very likely that initially such assessments played some part in the determination of the weekly benefit rates. But on this 'absolute standards' approach, it would be plausible to expect poverty to disappear over the years with continuing economic growth, and that correspondingly the numbers of people relying on assistance would decline.[19] In fact, as has been mentioned, the opposite has occurred.[20]

It is now more fashionable to measure poverty not by the absolute approach of a minimum acceptable living standard, but as relative to the general or average standard of living in the country.[1] On this approach those with an income below, say, 40% of the average industrial wage may be categorised as poor, even though they may have sufficient resources to feed and house themselves. To some extent the level of the supplementary benefit scale rates may now reflect this approach. From 1959 governments have explicitly acknowledged that those on assistance should have 'a share in increasing national prosperity'.[2] The scale rates have risen appreciably more than the increase in the Retail Prices Index, and have improved relative to the average net earnings of manual workers.[3] Thus, in November 1976 the ordinary weekly rate of benefit for a married couple was 49·8% of average net earnings for manual workers, compared with 36·1% in 1948.[4]

Supplementary benefit rates may be said, therefore, to reflect a combination of the old absolute and the relative concepts of poverty.[5] The standards of eligibility for benefit are also now commonly used to measure the extent of poverty in British society.[6] It is obviously outside the scope of this book to pursue these questions in detail, but some reservations to this test should be stated. First, as supplementary benefit rates are increased, so more people are defined as having a standard of living below the official 'poverty line'. This odd consequence – the more the government attempts to help the poor, the more 'poor' there are – is perhaps inevitable if this relative (and perhaps also tautologous) concept of poverty is adopted.

16. *Fiegehen et al.*, ante n.7, at p. 13.
17. Ante, pp. 21–22.
18. It is this further margin which identified people living in what Rowntree described as 'secondary poverty': 'primary poverty' refers to the situation where the people, however carefully they marshal their resources, cannot afford the necessities of life. See *Harris*, pp. 393–394.
19. *Fiegehen et al.*, ante n.7, at pp. 13–14.
20. Ante, p. 472.
  1. See Townsend, 13. Brit. J. of Sociology, 210; *Fiegehen et al.*, ante n.7, at pp. 14–15. See also ante, pp. 21–22.
  2. White Paper, Improvements in National Assistance (1959), Cmnd. 782, para. 3.
  3. Annual Report 1976, ante n.5, at 9.14–9.20.
  4. Ibid., Table 9.6.
  5. *Fiegehen et al.*, ante n.7, at pp. 15–17.
  6. See *Atkinson*, ante n.7 *passim*, and in ed. Wedderburn *Poverty, Inequality and Class Structure* (1974), p. 48.

Secondly, the number of recipients of benefit is an unreliable guide to the extent of poverty insofar as otherwise eligible people are disqualified from receiving assistance by the legislation. Persons in full-time work, however low their earnings, are not entitled to benefit, though if living in a family with at least one child, they may be entitled to FIS.[7] Claimants may also be disqualified because of their participation in a trade dispute, or because they are not genuinely looking for work.[8] Finally, an important group, living below the official poverty line but not receiving benefit, are those who for one reason or another do not claim it. The Commission estimates that only three-quarters of eligible pensioners, and a slightly lower proportion of persons under pensionable age, claim the benefit to which they are entitled.[9] This means that a large number of poor people, perhaps 900,000, do not receive any financial assistance. Moreover, an unknown number may not claim the additional discretionary payments which the Commission is empowered to make to supplement the weekly scale rate benefit.

iii) Entitlement and discretion

Since 1966 there has been an entitlement, or right, expressly stated in the legislation to the receipt of supplementary benefit.[10] But the Commission has a discretionary power to pay both additions to the weekly benefit and lump sums, and conversely to reduce or withhold benefit in some cases. The justifications given for according discretion a substantial role in the administration of the benefit are discussed later in the chapter.[11] It is sufficient here to point out that its existence is a prominent characteristic of supplementary benefits, unparalleled in any of the other benefits discussed in this book.[12] The growing reliance of claimants on additional discretionary payments is a problem which has increasingly concerned the Commission, and is one of the main reasons for its decision to review the scheme.[13]

iv) Sources of supplementary benefits law and policy

Because of the substantial part played by the exercise of discretionary power in the award of benefits, it is often not enough to analyse the Supplementary Benefits Act 1976 and regulations in order to see whether a payment will be made. An account of the Commission's policies with regard to the areas of discretion is published in the Supplementary Benefits Handbook, most recently revised in 1977. The officers of the

---

7. The problems of low wage-earners were first raised by Abel-Smith and Townsend *The Poor and the Poorest* (1965). Also see *Fiegehen et al.*, ante n.7, at p. 67.

8. Post, pp. 526, 533 respectively.

9. Annual Report 1976, Cmnd. 6910, chap. 10. For the problem of low take-up generally, see ante p. 13.

10. See now SBA 1976, s.1: post, p.479. The SBC Handbook is sub-titled, 'A guide to claimants' rights'.

11. Post, pp. 513–514.

12. Discretion is, of course, common in the administration of social services by local authorities: see Hill *The State, Administration and the Individual* (1976), *passim*.

13. SBC Annual Report 1975, Cmnd. 6615, at paras. 2.16–2.22; Annual Report 1976, ante n.9, at paras. 1.37–1.47.

DHSS[14] who implement them when they determine whether a claimant should receive benefit are further assisted by guidance issued in unpublished volumes of instructions prepared by the Commission. The government's refusal to permit the publication of the 'A' Code, as the principal volume is known, has frequently been criticised.[15] In fact the Commission claims, probably rightly, that no government department is as forthcoming in explaining how it works and on what principles it takes decisions.[16]

An unsuccessful claimant has a right of appeal to a supplementary benefits appeal tribunal, and from 1978 there is a further appeal on a point of law to the High Court.[17] Tribunal decisions are, of course, not reported officially, but a number of them are noted in the *LAG Bulletin* and *Poverty*; it is not clear how representative these 'reported' decisions are, but reference is made to them throughout this chapter, as at the very least they indicate the range of interpretations which may be given to the legislation and Commission policy.

B. The history of public assistance

Public assistance in Britain has a long history stretching back to the sixteenth century. To some extent the poor law provisions, and the modern reaction to them, have influenced the content of the supplementary benefits scheme.

i) The early history of the Poor Laws[18]

The first statutes encouraging parishes to assist the deserving poor (the old, sick and infirm) were passed in 1531 and 1536. These Acts, and other subsequent legislation, were consolidated in the famous Poor Relief Act of 1601. Under this overseers, to be appointed in each parish to act under the general supervision of the Justices of the Peace, were to give relief to the deserving poor and to raise local taxes for this purpose. The able-bodied were to be given work. Section 6 imposed a duty on a person's father, grandfather, mother, grandmother and child to maintain him. This assertion of family responsibility was not repealed until the 1948 Act.[19] Until then the primary obligation to maintain rested on the family, and though the parish might give relief to someone neglected by his relatives, it could

14. For administration of benefits at local offices, see post, pp. 575–576.
15. E.g., see the debate in the House of Commons, 827 HC Deb., cols. 1259ff.
16. See the Foreword by the chairman of the SBC, D. Donnison, to the Handbook, p. 9. It is fair to the Commission's critics to point out that it has only gradually disclosed more information about its policies – perhaps in response to their protests!
17. For supplementary benefit appeal tribunals and the appeal to the High

Court, see post, pp. 649–659.
18. There are many useful accounts of the early history of the poor laws: see de Schweinetz *England's Road to Social Security* (1949), chap. 1; Bruce *The Coming of the Welfare State* (4th ed.), chap. 2; the editors' introduction to *The Poor Law Report of 1834* (ed. by S.G. & E.O.A. Checkland, 1974). A more legal analysis is provided by Jennings *The Poor Law Code* (2nd edn, 1936).
19. See post, p. 540.

recover this from the defaulters. Thus, two important features of the poor law regime were established from the outset: first, its local administration which led to inconsistent provision in different areas of the country, and secondly, the emphasis on family responsibility.

Inevitably the administration of the poor law went through many changes in the two centuries before the reforms of 1834. The most important development was the 1662 Act of Settlement. Its object was to prevent poor people wandering round the country, imposing themselves as charges on other parishes. Any person, without property or other means of support, could be removed to his parish of 'settlement', that is generally, where he was born. In effect a pauper had to look to this parish for relief, a restriction which naturally hindered freedom of movement.[20]

The eighteenth century saw the first workhouses, which the able-bodied were required to enter as a condition of securing relief.[1] But the experiment was halted towards the end of the century. The poverty of agricultural workers at this time led to the use of poor law relief to supplement wages in the famous 'Speenhamland system'.[2] This in its turn became one of the reasons for the disquiet responsible for the institution of the Poor Law Commission in 1832. Many felt that relief for the employed merely subsidised low wages, an argument now deployed against the family income supplement.[3]

ii) Poor law reform: 1834–1930[4]

The Poor Law Commission found that provision for those able to work was corrupting for the recipients; in future they were only to be given relief in the workhouses. Under the notorious principle of 'less eligibility', conditions there were to be less attractive than those of the poorest worker outside.[5] Thus, the familiar distinction was drawn between the deserving poor, who might benefit from allowances paid outside the workhouse ('outdoor relief') and the less deserving who would only in practice be able to secure relief in conditions of extreme destitution. The objective of more efficient administration was achieved first, by the merging of parishes for poor law purposes into unions, with elected Boards of Guardians, and secondly, by the institution of a central Board of three Commissioners, responsible for the making of regulations and the national administration of the poor laws.

Though well intentioned the remedy was perhaps worse than the disease. The horrors of the workhouses, with their degrading treatment of the inmates and the enforced separation of husband and wife, are well-known from the novels of Dickens.[6] The sick and the old were often for reasons of

20. A reaction to this harsh law may be the present liberal 'residence' qualifications for public assistance: post, p. 480.
1. *Bruce*, ante, n.18, at pp. 54–55.
2. Ibid., pp. 55–56; *The Poor Law Report of 1834*, ante, n.18, at pp. 18–20.
3. Post, p. 555.

4. See the collection of materials in ed. Rose *The English Poor Law 1780–1930* (1971); Rose *The Relief of Poverty 1834–1914* (1972); *Bruce*, ante n.18, at chaps. 4 and 5.
5. Ibid., at pp. 96–97.
6. In particular, *Oliver Twist* and *Little Dorrit*.

economy housed together with the unemployed. However, there was no official reaction to the criticism until a Royal Commission was appointed in 1905. All its members were agreed that the 1834 reforms were misconceived, that the workhouses should be abolished and the administrative structure changed. But it was divided in its proposals for specific solutions; partly because of this and partly because other events dominated political discussion, there was no immediate attempt at reform.[7]

During the 1920s unemployment increased, exposing the weaknesses of the poor laws. Many unions, with the workhouses quite inadequate to cope, used their power to afford outdoor relief for the able-bodied in cases of 'urgent necessity'.[8] But they were not all so generous, with the result that provision varied widely from area to area. Naturally those with the heaviest unemployment were the least able to afford the costs of relief. The inherent weakness of local administration and financing became widely recognised. But even then, the solution of national administration was not immediately adopted. Instead by the Local Government Act 1929, the functions of the poor law guardians and unions were transferred to the local authorities to be discharged largely by their public assistance committees.[9] In the following year the last Poor Law Act, a consolidation measure, was passed.[10] A more significant event was the repeal of the Regulation which had made entry into the workhouse a condition of relief to the able-bodied.[11]

iii) Unemployment assistance and the end of the poor law 1930–1948

Governments in this period were troubled by the problems of those unemployed who were unable to claim the contributory benefit.[12] In October 1931 the National Government replaced the costly transitional benefits with means-tested transitional allowances for people out of work for more than twenty-six weeks.[13] These were funded nationally, but administered by the local authority public assistance committees. When it became clear that they were inconsistent in their administration of the allowances, the demand for a national scheme could no longer be resisted. The Unemployment Assistance Act 1934 instituted a Board to administer public assistance for the unemployed.[14] Thus an important group was taken out of the poor law system, and a precedent set for the 1948 reform.

In a number of respects the 1934 scheme is interesting as a forerunner of the modern law of supplementary benefits. Assistance was calculated by reference to the applicant's requirements, based on weekly scale rates, with a deduction for his resources. Extra lump sum payments could be made for exceptional needs, and the regular weekly payments could be increased

---

7. The Minority Report, largely the work of Beatrice Webb, was influential in that it proposed the transfer of administering assistance to local authorities.
8. *Bruce*, ante n.18, at p. 255.
9. Ibid., at pp. 258–259.
10. The Act is exhaustively analysed by *Jennings*, ante n.18.
11. S.R. & O. 1930, No. 186, Art. 6.
12. For unemployment benefit, see chap. 3.
13. *Bruce*, ante n.18, at p. 269.
14. For a further discussion of the Board, see chap. 14, post, p. 577.

in special circumstances.[15] An adjustment could be made for particularly high or low rents.[16] An important feature of the scheme was the 'household means' test: the resources of all members of the claimant's household were taken into account before determining that he was in need of assistance.[17] This imposition, in effect, of primary responsibility for maintenance on members of an applicant's household has been a feature of some social security systems,[18] but it nevertheless attracted strong criticism and did not survive long.

During the war years, the Unemployment Assistance Board's functions were increased to embrace the administration of the pensions payable under the Old Age and Widows' Pensions Act 1940.[19] It was then renamed the Assistance Board to denote its more general responsibilities. Another important group of people was thus taken out of the poor law. A further significant development was the virtual abolition of the 'household means' test by the Determination of Needs Act 1941. In future where the applicant was a householder, only his own resources and those of his wife and dependants were to be taken into account in assessing his need.[20]

It was the Beveridge Report which heralded the final demise of the poor law. It pointed out the anomalies necessarily entailed by the existence of a number of tests and authorities for giving assistance to different groups of the needy.[1] The Assistance Board's reputation had steadily improved during the war years, and this influenced the scheme of reform eventually made by the National Assistance Act 1948. Section 1 repealed the 'existing poor law' – without any trace of Parliamentary regret.[2] The provision of financial assistance became exclusively the function of central government acting through the National Assistance Board (NAB), as it was now called. Many features of the old poor law went: there was no law of settlement, so that it no longer mattered where the applicant was resident when he claimed assistance;[3] the requirement that applicants for assistance be set to work was replaced by a discretionary requirement to register for employment;[4] relief by way of loan, a common provision under the poor law, was abolished as a normal form of assistance.

iv) The reform of 1966[5]

In 1948, it was thought right to keep the administration of means-tested assistance entirely separate from that of the insurance benefits, as an aspect

15. Post, pp. 490 and 511–519, for further discussion of 'exceptional circumstances' payments.
16. See further, post, p. 494.
17. Unemployment Assistance Act 1934, s.38.
18. For the position in the USA, see La France, Schroeder, Bennett and Boyd *Law of the Poor* (1973), pp. 299ff.
19. For the history of pensions, see chap. 5, ante, pp. 190–195.
20. The 'household means' test survived in vestigial form for non-householders until 1948: see Determination of Needs

Act 1941, Sch. 1, para. 3(a).
1. Para. 372.
2. See 444 HC Deb., col. 1667, where Miss A. Bacon said: 'Today we are burying the Poor Law, and I do not think that many tears will be shed at its passing'.
3. See ante, p. 476, for the law of settlement, and post, p. 480, for the modern 'presence' requirement.
4. Post, pp. 483–485.
5. See the discussion in SBC Annual Report 1976, Cmnd. 6910, Appendix A.

of their distinct functions in the social security system.[6] The NAB was, therefore, an independent government department.[7] However, it gradually became apparent that national assistance was playing a more important role than had been foreseen at the end of the war,[8] and that potential applicants were discouraged from applying for it, partly because of the wide area of discretion accorded to officials under the 1948 legislation.

The Labour government decided, therefore, in 1966 to make some changes in the rules for awarding assistance, from that time to be known as supplementary benefit.[9] The major alteration was that the 1966 Act provided for a *right* to benefit in the circumstances set out in the legislation – a change designed to reduce the amount of discretion in the system. This was further reduced by the automatic provision of higher benefit rates for pensioners and also recipients who had been on benefit for two years. Under the 1948 legislation the special needs of these groups had been met by discretionary allowances. The principal administrative change was that the NAB was dissolved, and its functions transferred to the Ministry of Social Security[10] and to the Supplementary Benefits Commission, though the latter is not a separate department.[11] The primary object of these changes was to merge the administration of contributory and means-tested benefits, and thereby remove the stigma associated with claiming the latter.[12] It is arguable, however, that the reforms were relatively minor, and did not justify the claims made for them.[13]

Part two. Entitlement to Supplementary Benefit

A. General conditions

Section 1 of the Supplementary Benefits Act 1976 provides that:

'Every person in Great Britain of or over the age of 16 whose resources are insufficient to meet his requirements shall be entitled to benefit as follows –

(a) a supplementary pension if he has attained pensionable age, that is to say, in the case of a man, the age of 65 and, in the case of a woman, the age of 60; or

(b) a supplementary allowance if he has not attained pensionable age;

6. See Titmuss *Social Security in International Perspective*; *Essays in honor of Eveline M. Burns* (1969), p. 151.
7. See chap. 14, post, pp. 576–577.
8. Ante, p. 472.
9. The change was made by the Ministry of Social Security Act 1966, later renamed the Supplementary Benefit Act 1966 by SSA 1973, s.99(18).
10. His functions were later transferred to the Secretary of State for Social Services: post, p. 574.
11. Post, pp. 576–579.
12. Miss M. Herbison, Minister of Pensions and National Insurance, 729 HC Deb., col. 335 ff.
13. Miss M. Pike, ibid., at cols. 352ff.

and to such benefit by way of a single payment to meet an exceptional need as may be determined under section 3 of this Act.'

In some circumstances a person who satisfies these general conditions will be disqualified from benefit; they are discussed at pages 482–483. Entitlement[14] to a supplementary *allowance* (though not a pension) will also usually be conditional on the claimant registering for employment.[15] The final introductory point is that in many cases, principally where a husband and wife are living together, the requirements and resources of one person are aggregated with and treated as those of another, so that only the latter (e.g., the husband) is entitled to benefit.[16]

i) Age

The claimant must be at least sixteen. The needs of a child of fifteen or under may be met by his requirements being included in those of the person in the household who has to provide for him;[17] the availability of benefit will depend on that person's entitlement. The one situation where the minimum age condition may occasion hardship is where a young girl has a child, although she may be able to obtain some benefits in kind, e.g., welfare milk.[18]

The second respect in which the claimant's age is material concerns the difference between a supplementary *allowance* and a supplementary *pension*. If the claimant has reached pensionable age, he (or she) will be entitled to a supplementary pension. This automatically attracts the long-term scale rate,[19] and unlike an allowance is not subject to a reduction in 'exceptional circumstances'.[20] Since a wife's requirements and resources fall to be aggregated with, and treated as, those of her husband, and only he may claim benefit, it is his age which determines whether a pension or an allowance is payable.[1] Thus, if a husband is sixty-four and his wife sixty-three, an allowance is payable, while if he is sixty-six and she is forty, a pension may be paid.[2]

ii) Presence in Great Britain

There is no condition that only a British national or resident may be entitled to benefit.[3] Mere presence of the claimant in Britain is sufficient. This is an exceptionally generous provision, in marked contrast to the poor law which made the pauper look to his native parish for assistance.[4]

14. The significance of this term is discussed, ante, p. 474.
15. Post, pp. 483–485.
16. The aggregation provisions are discussed, post, pp. 485–488. Also see ante, pp. 404–408, for 'living together as husband and wife.'
17. Post, p. 488.
18. *Lynes*, pp. 137–138.
19. Post, pp. 492–494.
20. For reductions in exceptional circumstances, see post, pp. 500, 536,

and 551.
1. SBA 1976, Sch. 1, para 3(1)(a): post, pp. 485–488.
2. However, the further age addition of 25p is payable if *either* husband or wife is over eighty: SBA 1976, Sch. 1, para. 6.
3. For 'residence' and 'presence' requirements under the Social Security Act 1975, see chap. 10, ante, pp. 408–416.
4. Ante, p. 476.

A claimant may be awarded benefit either at his usual place of residence or at a place where he is staying temporarily. A foreign visitor is required by the immigration authorities to have enough resources to cover his own needs, but if for some reason he becomes short of money he would appear to be entitled under section 1 of the Act.[5] Unlike the British Supplementary Benefits Act, the Northern Ireland legislation does impose a requirement of five years' residence in the United Kingdom before benefit is payable, presumably to discourage people crossing the border from the Republic of Ireland to make claims.[6]

Benefit will not be paid in advance of a holiday to cover obligations that accrue during the period of absence,[7] though in one unusual case it appears that an appeal tribunal was persuaded to make an award which covered inter alia, travelling expenses for a conference in Geneva.[8] It seems unnecessarily restrictive for the Commission generally to refuse the award of a lump sum to cover continuing obligations, e.g., to pay rent, while the claimant is abroad.[9]

iii) Resources insufficient to meet requirements

This condition of financial need is clearly the crucial one in most cases. The methods for calculating the applicant's requirements and resources, and thus determining the level of supplementary pensions and allowances, are discussed in Part Three. Part Four deals with the circumstances in which a single payment for exceptional needs may be made. Section 1(3) of the 1976 Act provides that no account may be taken of 'medical, surgical, optical, aural or dental requirements' for the purposes of supplementary benefits. This is an overlap provision presumably designed to prevent payment for needs which are already met by the Health Service.[10] In *R v Peterborough Supplementary Benefits Appeal Tribunal, ex parte Department of Health and Social Security*,[11] the Divisional Court ruled that the section prohibited payment of benefit to cover the costs of private osteopathic treatment when this was recommended by a consultant. The cost of this treatment would not be borne by the Health Service, and, therefore, it is arguable that, in the light of its probable purpose, section 1(3) is drafted too widely.

---

5. But see the Handbook, paras. 165–166, which suggests that the Commission will only pay benefit to visitors in unusual cases. The general refusal to award benefit is (perhaps questionably) justified by reference to the Commission's discretionary power to withhold benefit in 'exceptional circumstances': SBA 1976, Sch. 1, para. 4(1)(b). See SBC Annual Report 1975, Cmnd. 6615, para. 8.14.
6. SB Act (Northern Ireland) 1966, s.7. This provision might be held unconstitutional in the United States: see *Shapiro v Thompson*, 89 S.Ct. 1322 (1969) and *Graham v Richardson*, 91 S.Ct. 1848 (1971). These cases are discussed in La France, Schroeder, Bennett and Boyd *Law of the Poor* (1973), pp. 343ff: see also Harvich 54 Calif. L.R. 567.
7. *Lynes*, pp. 163–164; see Handbook, para. 8.
8. *Poverty* (1975), No. 31, p. 48.
9. The Commission may make an exceptional needs payment in arrears in these cases: Handbook, para. 8.
10. For overlapping benefits generally, see chap. 10, at pp. 437–443.
11. (1977) 121 Sol Jo 202.

B. Exclusions from benefit

In three cases a claimant, otherwise eligible, will be excluded from entitlement to supplementary benefit.

i) Persons in full-time employment

A person 'engaged in remunerative full-time work' is not generally entitled.[12] With the major exception of the 'Speenhamland system' introduced in 1795,[13] public assistance was not used to supplement low wages until the introduction of family income supplement (FIS) in 1970.[14] The result is that supplementary benefits are of no assistance to one major group of people living below the official poverty line.[15]

Rather oddly neither the Act nor the regulations made under it defines 'remunerative full-time work'. The Family Income Supplement General Regulations do, however, define this term for FIS purposes as meaning at least thirty hours work a week.[16] As the purpose of FIS is to provide help for families ineligible for supplementary benefit, it might be thought that anyone working more than that amount would be excluded from benefit under the 1976 Act.[17] However, the Commission sometimes regards 'full-time work' as work for 'the recognised week in his trade or employment',[18] which may amount to more than thirty hours. The result is that a claimant working less than that recognised week may be able to apply for supplementary benefit and FIS, and indeed could legally be awarded both.[19] It is certainly possible for a person to be in receipt of the two benefits: a FIS award subsists for a year and during that period the recipient may become unemployed and, therefore, eligible for supplementary benefit.[20]

There are two cases where the full-time work exclusion does not apply. First, a person becoming engaged in full-time work after a period of unemployment is entitled to receive benefit for the first fifteen days following his return to work[1] The reason for this exception is that often a worker does not receive his first wage packet until after two weeks' work, and it is, therefore, reasonable to continue to pay benefit for this period.[2] Any wages actually received in these two weeks may be totally or partially deducted under the rules regarding assessment of resources.[3] The second exception is that a self-employed claimant, whose earning power is substantially reduced by reason of a disability, is entitled to benefit even though he is working full-time.[4] One effect of this provision is to enable a

12. SBA 1976, s.6(1).
13. Ante, pp. 476.
14. See chap. 13.
15. Ante, pp. 472–474, for the 'poverty line' concept.
16. S.I. 1971/226, Reg. 5.
17. For a fuller discussion of this point, see post, pp. 563–564.
18. Handbook, para. 4.
19. FIS is deducted in full as a resource of the recipient of supplementary benefit: post, p. 510.

20. Post, pp. 569–570, for the duration of FIS payments.
1. S.I. 1977/1141, Reg. 3.
2. *Lynes*, pp. 169–170.
3. Normally there is a disregard of £4, but this does not apply if the claimant returns to work after a trade dispute: post, p. 531. See also post, p. 532, for recovery of benefit in this case.
4. SBA 1976, s.6(3).

disabled person in receipt of benefit to supplement this with earnings from work which might be done at home.

Even if neither of these two exceptions applies, it is always open to a person in full-time work to apply under section 4(1) of the 1976 Act for an 'urgent need' payment.[5] This may be made to anyone otherwise disqualified from benefit under any of the grounds considered in this section, e.g., to a person in need who is not paid until a month after his return to work, or to someone who has lost his wages.[6] The Commission may decide that the whole or part of an urgent need payment should be recoverable from a recipient in full-time work.[7]

ii) Persons completing secondary education

In the absence of exceptional circumstances, 'a person attending a school, or receiving full-time instruction of a kind given in schools' is not entitled to benefit.[8] It has not always been clear what constitutes 'instruction of a kind given in schools'.[9] The Commission's policy, it now seems, is to treat non-advanced courses, that is, GCE 'A' level standard or below, as covered by the provision, while students taking advanced courses may be eligible in their own right.[10] The complex benefits position of students in further education is considered later in this chapter.[11]

The Commission will pay benefit to a person receiving secondary education in 'exceptional circumstances'. The Handbook gives as examples of such circumstances cases where the child is severely handicapped,[12] or where he is the 'head of the household'.[13] In one case benefit was paid to a sixteen year old schoolgirl who had left her parents' home on a social worker's recommendation.[14]

iii) Persons affected by trade disputes

Section 8 of the Supplementary Benefits Act 1976 provides that a person out of work owing to a trade dispute at his place of employment is not entitled for *his own* requirements, though he may be awarded benefit for his dependants: this controversial rule is discussed later in the chapter in the context of the provisions enabling benefit to be paid below the standard rate.[15]

C. The condition of registration for employment

Under section 5 the Commission may make the entitlement of any person to a supplementary *allowance* (but not a pension) dependent on the

5. Jordan, *LAG Bulletin*, Dec. 1974, p. 300.
6. Handbook, para. 9.
7. SBA 1976, s.4(3). An appeal may be brought against this decision: ibid., s.15(1)(c).
8. Ibid., s.7(1). If his parent is entitled, he will be treated as a dependant for the purpose of assessing that person's requirements: post, p. 488.
9. See *LAG Bulletin*, Nov. 1974, p. 271.
10. Ibid., and see *Lynes*, pp. 158–159.
11. Post, pp. 550–552.
12. See the case noted in *Poverty* (1973), No. 27, p. 23.
13. Para. 6.
14. *LAG Bulletin*, Aug. 1973, p. 177.
15. Post, pp. 526–533.

condition that he register for employment. This is satisfied by the claimant registering with the Employment Service Agency or a local education authority, and attending at an unemployment benefit office as if unemployment benefit were being claimed.[16] The requirement is reinforced by other provisions under which the SBC may withhold or reduce benefit payable to the 'voluntarily unemployed': these are considered later, together with some of the relevant policy questions.[17]

Clearly the power to require registration for work, or alternatively to exempt certain groups of claimants or particular individuals, is a significant one; it is arguably unfortunate that it is wholly unlimited by the Act and regulations. The Commission's policy is not to require registration of the following groups of claimants:[18]

(a) people incapable of work – subject to medical evidence;[19]
(b) men and women solely responsible for the care[20] of dependent children under sixteen living with them;
(c) blind people unaccustomed to working outside the home;
(d) people who, although not incapable of work, are so disabled as to be virtually unemployable.

For other people the requirement may be waived depending on the particular circumstances of the case. They include:[1]

(a) persons needed at home to look after sick relatives;
(b) women widowed in late middle age with no experience of employment and where there is evidence of poor health;
(c) certain people undergoing approved training or education courses.

The selection of these people is presumably the result of decisions by the Commission that it is right to require them not to work in view of their disabilities or their commitments. The general absence of discussion concerning the basis of these decisions is surprising and regrettable.[2]

The application of the Commission's policies could lead to difficulties. For example how are local officers to construe 'late middle age' ((b) in the second group) or to determine who qualifies as a 'sick relative' ((a) in the second group)? It may be that more detailed guidance is given them in the unpublished 'A' Code.[3] The Handbook gives some indication how the policies will be applied, particularly with regard to people looking after sick relatives and students on training and education courses.[4] Even this

---

16. S.I. 1977/1141, Reg. 4.
17. Post, pp. 533–539.
18. Handbook, para. 11.
19. For a case in which the requirement was waived for a man with personality problems, see *Poverty* (1969), No. 11, p. 17.
20. The exemption was extended to men responsible for children as a result of the recommendation of the Finer Committee, paras. 5.262–5.265.
1. Handbook, para. 12.

2. There is, for example, no discussion of this subject in the SBC Annual Reports 1975, Cmnd. 6615, or 1976, Cmnd. 6910.
3. Ante, p. 475.
4. Paras. 154–159. For a case in which a SBAT waived the requirement to register imposed on a student on the ground that the imposition of the condition had the effect of discriminating against men, see *LAG Bulletin*, Apr. 1977, p. 89.

information is not always clear. For example, in paragraph 12 it is stated that *people* required to care for *sick* relatives will not be required to register, while from paragraph 157 it would appear that only a *woman* looking after a sick *or aged* relative may benefit from the exemption!

Payment of benefit to a person required to register for work is made through the Department of Employment unemployment benefit offices, which he must usually attend weekly.[5] However, in some cases this requirement is relaxed: men of fifty-five and women of fifty who have been unemployed for two years, and claimants who have been out of work for a year and whose prospects of obtaining work are limited because of some disability, are only required to attend quarterly.[6] Neither of these 'concessions' applies if the claimant has a record of fraudulent claims or voluntary unemployment. The arrangement is humane, and may also reduce administrative costs, but it reveals the extent of the discretionary power the Commission enjoys in this area.[7]

Two further points may be made. First, a claimant subject to the registration condition, or who has been subject to it during the qualifying period, is not eligible for the higher long-term rate of allowance payable after two years' continuous receipt of supplementary benefit.[8] Secondly, where the claimant is required to register, there is a lower disregard of part-time earnings (£2) instead of the normal £4.[9]

D. The 'family unit' for supplementary benefits

The supplementary benefits scheme recognises that it is generally realistic to treat a married couple and their children as one unit for benefit purposes.[10] A married man, unable to work, will need assistance for his wife and children, though his financial position will improve if she has earnings or other resources to contribute to the family fund. There are also considerable economies of scale where a couple lives together. The Supplementary Benefits Act 1976, therefore, provides that it in some cases the requirements and resources of one person will be aggregated with, and treated as, those of another person, and then only the latter will be entitled to benefit.[11] The aggregation provision is Schedule 1, paragraph 3:[12]

'(1) Where –
    (a) a husband and wife are members of the same household, their requirements and resources shall be aggregated and treated as the husband's;
    (b) two persons who are not married to each other are living together as husband and wife, their requirements and

5. Handbook, para. 224; *Fisher*, para. 245.
6. Handbook, para. 192; Stevenson, *Claimant or Client?* (1973), pp. 104–106.
7. Ibid., at p. 106.
8. SBA 1976, Sch. 1, para. 6(1)(b)(ii): post, pp. 493–494.
9. Ibid., Sch. 1, para. 22(1)(a): post, p. 509.
10. See SBC Annual Report 1976, ante n.2, at paras. 6.12–6.15.
11. SBA 1976, s.1(2).
12. Amended by SS(MP)A 1977, s.14(7): ante, pp. 404–408.

resources shall, unless there are exceptional circumstances, be aggregated and treated as the man's.

(2) Where a person has to provide for the requirements of another person who is a member of the same household, not being a person falling within sub-paragraph (1) above –

  (a) the requirements of that other person may, and if he has not attained the age of 16 shall, be aggregated with, and treated as, those of the first mentioned person; and

  (b) where their requirements are so aggregated, their resources shall be similarly aggregated.'

The effect of this provision is that if a husband is out of work and entitled to claim benefit, his wife's and children's requirements will be aggregated with his, and he will be able to obtain benefit for the family's needs. On the other hand, a woman living with a husband, who is in work, is not entitled to benefit, even though she is short of housekeeping money, and she and her children live below subsistence level: the point is that their requirements are aggregated with the husband's, and he may not claim, as he is in full-time work.[13]

The aggregation rule is in a sense a relic of the notorious 'household means' test, which was not finally abolished till 1948.[14] The primary responsibility for relief of poverty was under this test placed on the other persons living in the household. Now the resources of the claimant's household, apart from those members covered by the aggregation provision, are entirely irrelevant, a position recently affirmed by the Divisional Court in *R v West London Supplementary Benefits Appeal Tribunal, ex parte Clarke*.[15]

The present provision is open to attack in that it discriminates between men and women by providing that only the husband (or a man with whom a woman is living as his wife) may claim benefit. This may be particularly inconvenient where the traditional roles are reversed, and the woman is the sole breadwinner: if she becomes unemployed, benefit will not be awarded unless the husband, as the person entitled, registers for work – although, of course, he may not want to find employment.[16] The Commission has, therefore, decided as part of its general review to investigate whether it is practicable to allow couples a choice as to which of them should be able to claim benefit in appropriate circumstances. There are a number of difficulties in this proposal, but the SBC takes the view that the goal of equal treatment is important and that it should be possible to surmount them.[17] The terms of the aggregation rule can now be examined.

i) Husband and wife who are members of the same household

The aggregation provision will only apply if the husband and wife are 'members of the same household', and not if they are living apart from

13. Ante, pp. 482–483, for disqualification from benefit of persons in full-time work.
14. Ante, p. 478.
15. [1975] 3 All ER 513, [1975] 1 WLR 1396: post, p. 504.
16. SBC Annual Report 1976, ante n.2, at paras. 6.8–6.11.
17. Ibid., at paras. 6.25–6.37.

each other.[18] In other words, the wife's resources are only relevant if the spouses form a 'family' or household unit. Entitlement to benefit is not affected under some wider notion of family responsibility if they are living entirely separate lives. The phrase, 'members of the same household', is not defined in the legislation.[19] In divorce and maintenance law, where it is commonly an issue whether the spouses are living separately, the test seems to be whether all cohabitation and forms of common life have ceased. If they have not, the courts will generally rule, at least if the parties are under the same roof, that they are still living in the same household and not separately.[20] The Commission seems to adopt this approach. The fact that a husband is not giving his wife any financial support does not in itself prevent them from being regarded as 'members of the same household', any more than the absence of financial support compels a finding that two persons are not living together as husband and wife.

ii) Two persons living together as husband and wife

The circumstances in which two persons, not married to each other, are regarded as living together as husband and wife have already been discussed in chapter 10.[1] Their requirements and resources will, however, not be aggregated for supplementary benefit purposes in 'exceptional circumstances'.[2] This provision in effect gives the Commission wide discretionary power not to apply the 'living together' rule. It appears that it is exercised in two situations.[3] First, where the woman has children whose father is not the man with whom she is living, the Commission may pay the woman benefit for a short period. Initially these payments would only be made for four weeks, but after its recent review of the cohabitation rule (as it was known), the Commission may be prepared to pay it for longer.[4] Secondly, if the man's income is so low (even including rent rebates and FIS) that the family would be living below supplementary benefit standards, the woman's requirements will not be aggregated with his, and she will be able to claim benefit.[5]

In this reconsideration of the cohabitation rule, the SBC also reviewed some aspects of its administration. Now when a visiting officer thinks that a claimant is living together with a man, the case is referred to a special interviewing officer. He explains the provision to her, and then submits a report together with her statement to a senior officer. This officer then decides whether the claimant is living together with a man as his wife.[6] A special investigation is only ordered at a Regional office of the DHSS when the facts cannot be discovered by interviewing the woman.[7] The Com-

18. A wife here may be a wife in a polygamous marriage: see *Imam Din v NAB* [1967] 2 QB 213, [1967] 1 All ER 750, DC, and ante, p. 403.
19. Nor is it in the Family Income Supplements Act 1970: post, p. 562.
20. E.g., *Hopes v Hopes* [1949] P. 227, [1948] 2 All ER 920, CA: see Cretney *Principles of Family Law* (2nd edn), pp. 135–136. For 'residing together' in the SSA 1975, see ante, pp. 390–393.

1. Ante, pp. 404–408.
2. SBA 1976, Sch. 1, para. 3(1)(b).
3. Handbook, paras. 24–25. See the criticism by *Lynes*, pp. 143–145, of the narrow view taken by the SBC of its powers.
4. SBC Report *Living together as Husband and Wife* (1976), para. 66.
5. Ibid., at para. 68.
6. Ibid., at paras. 81–87.
7. Ibid., at para. 90.

mission regrets the need to continue with these inquiries, which may involve putting questions to neighbours and watching the claimant's house, but considers there is no alternative in view of the number of cases where fraud is detected.[8] It also rejected the recommendation of the Finer Committee,[9] that where the facts are disputed, every cohabitation case should be referred to the appeal tribunal for decision and in the meantime benefit should be paid. This proposal would encourage frivolous appeals.[10]

iii) Children and other members of the household

Aggregation of requirements and resources is permitted where one person 'has to provide for the requirements of another' member of the household, and is mandatory where the latter is under sixteen.[11] The clear object is to aggregate children's requirements and resources with (normally) those of their father: this must be done if the child is under sixteen and living in the claimant's household, and may be done when he is over sixteen and unable to claim in his own right, e.g. because he is still attending school.[12] Nevertheless, the drafting of the provision 'has to provide for the requirements of another person' does give rise to difficulties and has led to some remarks in the Court of Appeal which cast some doubt on the proposition in the previous sentence. It seems right for the Commission not to construe the provision as meaning that there may only be aggregation if one person is under a *legal* obligation to provide for another; thus the requirements of a young grandchild living with the claimant may be aggregated.[13] However, it is clear that though legally it may aggregate the requirements of adult dependants (e.g. an aged relative), in practice it does not do so.[14] What is less clear is whether a parent or other person 'has to provide for the requirements of another person', usually a child, if the latter has adequate means to support himself. Two members of the Court of Appeal in *K v J.M.P. Co., Ltd.* held that a mother would not have to provide for her children after an award of damages to them and, therefore, that the aggregation provision would not apply.[15] It is submitted that this ruling, made in the context of a damages case, is unsound. The correct approach would have been to apply the aggregation provision, since the persons concerned were members of the same household, and to treat the children's income (subject to the normal disregards) as the mother's resources for benefit purposes – otherwise the object of treating such a family living together as one unit is defeated.

8. SBC Report Living together as Husband and Wife (1976), paras. 88–96. See the debate on special investigators, 837 HC Deb., cols. 1885ff., which contains some useful information on their work in this area.
9. Paras. 5.271–5.
10. Ante n.4, at paras. 75–77.
11. SBA 1976, Sch. 1, para. 3(2).
12. Handbook, para. 16.
13. Ibid.: under the old poor law, a grandparent was under a legal duty to maintain his grandchild: ante, p. 475.
14. Ibid., at para. 17.
15. [1976] QB 85 at 94, 97, per Cairns and Stephenson LJJ; Graham J was less clear on this question. Also see post, p. 545.

Part three. The Assessment of Weekly Benefit

A. General

Section 1 of the Act provides that a person 'whose resources are insufficient to meet his requirements' is entitled to benefit.[16] The claimant's requirements could be met in three alternative ways. He might be provided with assistance in kind, at least where this was practicable. If he needed a new suit or toilet goods, he would be provided with them on proof that he was unable to afford these articles himself. This used to be the usual practice for public assistance in the United States and to some extent it still is in certain states.[17] Secondly, cash payments might be awarded for the purposes of purchasing the specific goods or services required by the applicant. This is a common method of meeting requirements in the United States, and is used in Great Britain to meet exceptional needs.[18] The third means is the one generally used in Britain: a cash payment is made to the applicant to cover his assumed needs, which are calculated according to a standard formula set out in the legislation. Thus, the claimant is entitled to the amount by which his resources fall short of his presumed weekly requirements.[19] To determine the amount of supplementary benefit payable weekly, it is first necessary to assess such requirements in accordance with the rules set out in Schedule 1 to the 1976 Act and then to deduct his resources, which are similarly calculated in accordance with the terms of the Schedule.

The advantage of paying benefit according to a standard scale rate is that it gives the recipient some discretion how to spend it. Thus, in one week he may pay a little more for food than he does usually, while in the next he may spend some money on the cinema or other recreation. Alternatively he may save some money for a television licence. Moreover, the claimant is not obliged to apply for a sum of money every time he needs an article or service which the general scale rates enable him to afford.[20] To that extent the British practice of paying weekly sums in cash has much to commend it. It does, however, impose some responsibility on the recipient which he may not be able to discharge – perhaps at eventual cost to the Supplementary Benefits Commission if an exceptional needs payment is made to a claimant who has been less than careful with his weekly payments.[1] Moreover, if benefit is inadequate to meet the applicant's needs, the element of choice given him is illusory. The Commission, however, takes the view that the weekly payments are high enough to cover some amenities as well as bare subsistence,[2] and, if this is the case, then clearly the claimant has some real choice how to spend his benefit.

---

16. See ante, p. 479.
17. See La France et al *Law of the Poor* (1973), pp. 258–261, 266. For the rare use of payments in kind in Britain, see post, p. 609.
18. See post, pp. 519–525.
19. SBA 1976, Sch. 1, para. 1.

20. This point is emphasised by Titmuss, 42 Political Quarterly, 113. For a general discussion of benefits in kind or in cash, see ante, pp. 32–34.
1. See post, p. 523 for further discussion.
2. Handbook, para. 43: see post, p. 490.

Sometimes the standard weekly benefit is admittedly not adequate to meet an applicant's needs. This is particularly likely to be so where he is ill or infirm, and requires additional money for heating or a special diet. To meet these and other such cases the Commission may award in 'exceptional circumstances' an appropriate sum in addition to the normal weekly payment.[3] This is discussed after the general rules for assessing requirements and resources have been analysed. An applicant may also apply for a lump sum 'exceptional needs payment' under section 3 of the Supplementary Benefits Act 1976: these payments are considered in Part Four.

The last introductory point is that the SBC has discretionary power to reduce an *allowance* (though not a *pension*), or to withhold it altogether, 'in exceptional circumstances'.[4] It may be used in a variety of circumstances, to which reference is made at the appropriate points in the chapter.[5]

B. The assessment of requirements

There are two separate elements in the assessment of a claimant's weekly requirements for supplementary benefit. First, there are the weekly scale rates set out in Schedule 1 to the 1976 Act to cover the claimant's normal needs, apart from his housing costs. There is a special higher scale rate for blind people, and there is a long-term rate for all supplementary pensioners and for some of those who have been receiving an allowance for at least two years. The second element is a separate allowance for housing costs. A householder receives a sum to cover his rent or mortgage interest repayments, while a non-householder also receives a sum as a rent allowance. The requirements of those classified as 'boarders' are assessed in a different way.

i) The scale rates

a) GENERAL. The ordinary scale rates are regarded as covering all normal foreseeable necessities, such as food, fuel and lighting, clothes, and household goods, though not the replacement of more expensive items such as bedding and furniture.[6] As has been mentioned, the SBC envisages that the sums provided will be adequate to give the recipient some real choice as to how they are spent: 'what the scale rates provide is an amount for people to meet all ordinary living expenses in the way that suits them best.'[7]

The provision of a uniform scale was introduced by the National Assistance Act 1948, replacing the varying rates which had existed under the different schemes of assistance before this reform.[8] The rates provided in

3. SBA 1976, Sch. 1, para. 4(1)(a).
4. Ibid., Sch. 1, para. 4(1)(b). For the distinction between an allowance and a pension, see ante, p. 480.
5. E.g., post, pp. 500, 536 and 551.
6. Handbook, para. 43; see also the SBC

Paper *Exceptional Needs Payments* (1973), para. 16; SBC Annual Report 1976, Cmnd. 6910, para. 2.27.
7. Handbook, para. 43.
8. Ante, p. 478.

the 1948 legislation were criticised as ungenerous,[9] but their real value compared to prices has risen dramatically since then, and is now over 100% higher than in 1948.[10] In the last three years in particular, the ordinary rates have been frequently reviewed in order to keep pace with price rises.[11] From November 1977, this level of benefit for husband and wife (or man and woman living together[12]) is £23·55;[13] that for a single householder[14] is £14·50, and for any other person (non-householder) eighteen or older, is £11·60. There are other rates for persons between sixteen and eighteen, and for children according to their age.[15] The sums for children are aggregated with the sums representing their father's (or mother's) requirements to assess the benefit payable.[16]

Two elementary examples illustrate this:

1. Mr and Mrs A live with their children, aged fourteen, six and four. Mr A's requirements are £23·55 for his wife and himself (plus rent or mortgage allowance – see page 494), and £7·40, £4·95 and £4·10 for the three children respectively. This comes to a total of £40·00.

2. Mrs B, a widow and householder, lives with her two children aged twelve and ten. She has requirements of £14·50 for herself to which are aggregated the requirements of £7·40 and £6·10 for her two children respectively. This totals £28·00. (Her requirements will also include a sum for rent or mortgage payments.)

b) SPECIAL RATES (OTHER THAN THE LONG-TERM RATE). In the National Assistance Act 1948 there were only two special rates: blind persons and those who suffered a loss of income to undergo treatment for tuberculosis.[17] The power to make provision for other classes was never exercised, as it was thought it would be discriminatory.

The legislation now makes special provision for blind people. In the Committee stage of the Ministry of Social Security Bill 1966, it was argued that all disabled people should be entitled to a higher rate, but this was rejected on the ground that the Commission's discretionary powers were adequate to cope with their needs.[18] It is, indeed, difficult to justify the special treatment of blind claimants, though it is easy to explain

9. See *George*, pp. 208ff.
10. SBC Annual Report 1976, ante n.6, at para. 9.14.
11. The Secretary of State is under an obligation to review short-term contributory benefits in the light of price rises (ante, pp. 433–436), and in practice supplementary benefit ordinary rates are increased in line with these benefits: see SBC Annual Report 1975, Cmnd. 6615, chap. 4.
12. See ante, pp. 404–408, for a discussion of the 'living together' rule.
13. S.I. 1977/1326. The rates may be increased by regulations: SBA 1976,

s.2(3). Cp., the level of the disregarded resources, post, p. 507.
14. The distinction between a householder and non-householder is discussed, post, p. 495.
15. There are four such age rates for children up to sixteen: this feature of the scheme is now being considered as part of the review of the supplementary benefits scheme: SBC Annual Report 1976, ante n.6, at paras. 3.25–3.28.
16. Ante, p. 488.
17. NAA 1948, s.5(3).
18. 729 HC Deb., col. 1923.

historically,[19] and there are parallel examples in tax legislation.[20] At present the weekly scale rate for a husband and wife of whom one is blind is £24·80, and it is £25·60 if both are blind.[1]

The other departure from the ordinary scale rates occurs where an attendance allowance is payable in respect of the claimant's own severe disablement or that of one of his dependants.[2] A sum equivalent to the allowance (at either the higher or lower rate, whichever is appropriate)[3] is added to the usual weekly requirements. The effect of this provision is the same as if the attendance allowance were paid and then entirely disregarded in assessing the claimant's resources (as e.g., with mobility allowance).[4]

In a number of countries, notably West Germany, Holland and Denmark, more generous assistance is given to single-parent families by payments above the normal scale rates.[5] This impressed the Finer Committee on One-Parent Families which recommended that there should be a special addition to the ordinary and the long-term rates for these families.[6] The proposal has not been implemented.[7]

c) THE LONG-TERM RATES. The automatic payment of a higher rate to pensioners and those who have been on benefit for a considerable period was an innovation of the 1966 legislation.[8] Under the 1948 Act the special needs of those who required help over a long period, in particular the elderly, could only be catered for by a discretionary supplement to the ordinary weekly rate. The necessary inquiries into personal circumstances were often distressing, and to avoid this it was decided to make some extra payment automatic.[9] This at first took the form of a 'long-term addition' to the scale rates, but the arrangement caused confusion.[10] It was, therefore, decided in 1973 to incorporate the addition in the scale rates for those eligible. The difference between the standard scale rates and the long-term rates has grown appreciably over the last few years. This is because supplementary benefits are up-rated commensurately with contributory benefits; long-term benefits are increased in line with the rise in earnings or prices, whichever is the more favourable, and the same policy has been

19. Special provision could be made for the blind by local authorities under the Blind Persons Acts, 1920 and 1938.
20. See post, p. 497, for another example of special treatment for blind persons in the supplementary benefits scheme. Blind people receive special tax allowances: see Income and Corporation Taxes Act 1970, s.18. In its Annual Report for 1975, ante n.11, at para. 4.2, the SBC makes it clear that it regards the special rates for the blind as an anomaly.
1. S.I. 1977/1326, which sets out the other special rates for blind persons.
2. SBA 1976, Sch. 1, para. 10.
3. See chap. 4, ante, pp. 172-173, for the rates of the attendance allowance.
4. See post, pp. 507-511, for the disregards.
5. See Appendix 3 to Finer, paras. 101-106.
6. Ibid., at 5.254-5.255.
7. Though there is now a higher disregard of part-time earnings for one-parent families; see post, p. 509.
8. See Miss M. Herbison, Minister of Pensions and National Insurance, 729 HC Deb., cols. 335ff.
9. Ibid., col. 341: and see the Explanatory Memorandum to the Ministry of Social Security Bill (1966), Cmnd. 2997, para. 7.
10. See the 1973 Review of Social Security Benefits Cmnd. 5288, para. 19. The change was implemented by NISBA 1973, s.6.

adopted with regard to the long-term scale rates for supplementary benefit.[11]

The persons eligible for the long-term rates are virtually all those entitled to a supplementary *pension*, and those who have been continuously in receipt of a supplementary *allowance* for two years and who during that period have not been required to register for work.[12] There is no difficulty about the former. If the husband[13] has reached pensionable age and is entitled to benefit, the requirements of his wife and himself are assessed at the higher long-term rate of £28·35. A pensioner householder claiming only for himself is entitled to £17·90 as distinct from the ordinary rate of £14·50, and a non-householder is entitled to £14·35 on the long-term rate, as distinct from £11·60. A further 25p a week is payable if either the pensioner *or his wife* is over eighty years old. This has been paid since 1971 when the age addition was introduced for retirement pensions.[14] However, the long-term rates are not paid to pensioners resident in local authority accommodation.[15]

The second category of claimants eligible for the long-term rates creates more difficulties. They must have been continually in receipt of benefit for two years, and during that period they must not at any time have been required to register for employment. These conditions ensure first, that the higher scale is applicable only to people whose needs are greater because of the duration of their dependency on benefit,[16] and secondly, that it is not available to those expected to find work. The justification for this second condition is presumably that otherwise there would be an incentive to avoid work for two years.

Whether the conditions are generally reasonable or not, their inflexible application might cause injustice, and the SBC in the exercise of its discretionary powers to increase benefit in 'exceptional circumstances' has relaxed them in three types of case. First, a temporary interruption in the two year period of thirteen weeks or less, e.g, where the recipient takes a job and loses his entitlement to benefit for that time, is ignored. The same policy is applied where the person enters hospital during the two year period, whether his stay is for more or less than thirteen weeks.[17] The second modification has been made where a widow, not of pensionable age, claims benefit after the death of her husband who was in receipt of the long-term scale rate. Strictly, her claim is a new one, and, therefore, she could be required to wait for two years before receiving the higher rate in her own right. But the Commission's policy is to pay it immediately, unless she is required to register for work.[18] An appeal tribunal extended this principle and awarded the long-term rate to a woman *separated* from her

11. There is a full discussion of this in the SBC Annual Report 1975, ante n.11, at para. 4.3; see ante, pp. 433–436.

12. SBA 1976, Sch. 1, para. 6(1)(b).

13. It is the husband's age which is relevant: see ante, p. 480.

14. NIA 1971, s.5(2). See ante, p. 229, for the age addition.

15. See Handbook, para. 38: post, p. 548.

16. Miss M. Herbison, Minister of Pensions and National Insurance, 729 HC Deb., col. 1959.

17. Handbook, para. 40. There is a more generous relaxation where a break of entitlement occurs after the long-term rate has been paid: ibid. at para. 41.

18. See ibid., para. 40.

husband, who was himself in receipt of it.[19] The Commission has accepted this decision, and now pays the long-term rate in these circumstances.[20]

Thirdly, it seems that the SBC, again in the exercise of its discretion, pays this rate to those out of work for two years, but who are required to register only quarterly.[1] An appeal tribunal has awarded the long-term rate to someone who had been asked to register weekly, but whose chances of obtaining work were slight because of his disablement.[2] Frequent attendance at the employment office might have been required to boost the claimant's morale, and it would have been unfair not to pay the higher rate because the usual practice of requiring only quarterly registration was not followed here.

ii) Payments for rent

a) INTRODUCTION. Under the 1934 unemployment assistance scheme the scale benefit was initially designed to cover rent, but if that was more than one quarter of the total assistance paid, then a further amount could be added if the Board's officer thought this reasonable in the circumstances.[3] However, from 1943 the Assistance Board paid separate allowances for rent.[4] This has remained the case under the later legislation.

The payment of a rent allowance is very unusual in British social security law.[5] A number of arguments can be put forward to justify it in the context of means-tested benefits, the primary object of which is to meet the specific requirements of the claimant. First, there are significant regional and local variations in the rent payable for comparable properties. This would not appear to be the case for any other goods or services covered by an award of supplementary benefit. Secondly, the individual often does not have very much choice as to the amount of his rent. A third reason is that while an applicant can adjust his expenditure on, say, food or clothing to meet his reduced circumstances, this is not possible with rent. It must be paid regularly and it is unreasonable to expect a claimant to move to cheaper accommodation every time he is unemployed or ill. These arguments constitute a powerful case for the payment of a separate allowance.[6]

Apart from boarders who form an independent category,[7] the amount payable differs according to whether the claimant is a householder or non-householder. This distinction between householders and non-householders, as we have seen,[8] is also relevant for the weekly scale rates. Because of the more generous provision in both respects for householders, the difference is an important one.

19. *LAG Bulletin*, Nov. 1975, p. 292: *Poverty* (1975), No. 31, p. 41.
20. Handbook, para. 40.
 1. *LAG Bulletin*, Nov. 1975, p. 292. See ante, p. 483, for the registration requirement.
 2. Ibid.
 3. S.R. & O. 1936, No. 776, Sch. 1, para. 2.

 4. S.R. & O. 1943, No. 1759, Sch. 1, para. 1(2).
 5. See the supplementary rent allowance which may be paid to a widow under the war pensions scheme, ante, p. 377.
 6. *George*, pp. 214ff.
 7. Post, p. 502.
 8. See ante, p. 491.

b) THE DISTINCTION BETWEEN HOUSEHOLDERS AND NON-HOUSE-HOLDERS. Rather oddly the legislation is unhelpful on this crucial question. The only assistance is to be found in Schedule 1, paragraph 7, which sets out the ordinary scale rates for the weekly requirements of a 'person living alone or householder . . . who is directly responsible for household necessities and rent (if any)'. The Handbook states that the most common example of a claimant being treated as a non-householder is where he is living in a relative's house, the inference being that someone in that situation will rarely, if ever, be treated as a householder. This does indeed appear to represent the Commission's practice, as the following case shows:[9]

> A claimant lived with his stepbrother in the latter's council house. Although the claimant paid half the rent and contributed substantially to the household bills, he was classified both by the SBC, and the appeal tribunal, as a non-householder. However, when the local authority recognised the claimant as a joint tenant of the house, he was accorded householder status.

In this case it seems that the landlord's recognition was decisive as regards the claimant's status, although the latter's financial responsibilities had not changed after this.

In most situations, of course, it is not difficult to determine who is a householder. Clearly the owner occupier who has a legal interest in the property is a householder, as is one with an equitable interest by virtue of contributions to the purchase-money, mortgage instalments or improvements.[10] A tenant who pays rent directly to the landlord and whose name is on the rent book also clearly qualifies. Acute difficulties arise, however, where two or more people (not living together as man and wife) are sharing a house or flat. What criteria are to be used in this common situation to determine which of the persons concerned should be treated as householders? Is the fact that a person pays rent *directly* to the landlord a necessary or sufficient condition for him to be so treated? The Commission gives considerable weight to this factor.[11] It is suggested, however, that too great an emphasis on the rent arrangements, rather than on the extent to which the general household expenses are pooled, may lead to injustice. If three or four people are sharing some property, but to all intents and purposes are living entirely separately and meeting their own household expenses, (including a share of the total rent paid to the landlord), then they should all be treated as householders.

The classification of flat-sharers has been considered by the Court of Appeal in *R v Sheffield Supplementary Benefits Appeal Tribunal, ex parte Shine.*[12]

9. See Weir, *LAG Bulletin*, April 1974, p. 81; *Poverty* (1973), No. 26, p. 23, and No. 27, p. 22.
10. The rules regarding the ownership of a family home are set out in Bromley *Family Law* (5th edn), pp. 461–475;

and Cretney *Principles of Family Law* (2nd edn), pp. 260–279.
11. See Weir, ante n.9. cp., the case noted in *LAG Bulletin*, Apr. 1975, p. 99.
12. [1975] 1 WLR 624.

Shine shared a flat with three other students. They all separately paid their share of the total rent to the landlord each month, but only one of them, Fairbairn, received and paid the gas and electricity bills, the others each contributing a quarter share. The Commission paid Shine benefit as a non-householder, and this was upheld by the appeal tribunal on the ground that Fairbairn was the householder, and the other students were properly to be regarded as non-dependants contributing to his expenses.

The Court of Appeal, in a judgment delivered by Lord Denning MR, said that as a matter of law Shine's contention that he was a householder was probably correct:

'and these four students, being *jointly* responsible for household necessities and rent, are all four householders. It makes no difference in law that gas and electricity bills were sent in the name of one of them only.'[13]

Nevertheless the court declined to grant the applicant certiorari, on the ground that the error of law, if there were one, was minor and did not lead to a wholly unreasonable result.[14] Lord Denning's argument appears to be this: in a case where three or four people share a flat and pool household expenses, it would be unreasonable for them all to be awarded the full householder's allowance. They should all be treated as non-householders, with the grant of an exceptional circumstances payment as an addition to their rent allowance. This approach may lead to a reasonable result (and appears to have been accepted by the SBC),[15] and avoid the excessive payments which the technical reading of the Act might lead to. But it is difficult to defend it as a matter of statutory interpretation, and it places perhaps excessive reliance on the benevolent exercise of the Commission's discretion. The conclusion seems to be that the Act does not cater satisfactorily for flat-sharing arrangements.

Another problem which has given rise to controversy has been the treatment of squatters. The Commission's policy reflected in its decisions is that they are to be paid benefit as non-householders.[16] The reasons for this view are first, that they do not pay rent and secondly, their occupation is illegal. Against this approach it can be argued that the definition in Schedule 1, paragraph 7 only refers to a person responsible for household necessities and rent (*if any*); the implication might be that rent is irrelevant if it is not payable at all. On the second point, it seems dubious without statutory authority to refuse benefit, or pay reduced benefit, on the ground of the claimant's illegal act.

c) THE TREATMENT OF A HOUSEHOLDER PAYING RENT. Where the claimant is a householder, his requirements will include the net rent

13. Ibid., at p. 631.
14. See Street, *LAG Bulletin*, May 1975, p. 118; see chap. 15 post, p. 657, for a general discussion of the principles of judicial review of SBAT decisions.
15. Handbook, para. 42.
16. *LAG Bulletin*, June 1974, p. 133; *Poverty* (1974), No. 29, p. 36.

payable weekly, 'or such part of that amount as is reasonable in the circumstances.'[17] In the case of recipients of benefit who own their property, the term 'rent' refers to the allowance for 'necessary expenditure on repairs or insurance,' and interest payments on the mortgage.[18]

1. *The calculation of a tenant's rent.* In assessing rent, deductions are made for the proceeds of sub-letting the property, though the Commission makes an allowance for expenses in connection with this, e.g., on heating and lighting, which may appreciably reduce the deduction.[19] Where the rent paid to the landlord includes sums payable for lighting and heating and other services which are covered by the ordinary scale rate of benefit,[20] a reduction is made in the 'net rent' payable to the claimant in order to prevent overlap. Either the sum earmarked in the rent for the services in question is deducted, or the Commission makes an assessment of what the claimant is likely to pay for them.[1]

The most important deduction concerns the share of the rent attributable to non-dependants living with the claimant. The Schedule empowers the Commission to reduce the amount paid for rent, 'by an amount not exceeding such part of the net rent as is reasonably attributable' to the person concerned.[2] Deduction is, therefore, not mandatory, and it may not be made at all if either the claimant or his wife (or woman living with him) is blind – an interesting concession for this group of claimants. The Commission's general policy is set out in the Handbook.[3] The non-dependant's share is calculated by adding up the number of people in the household, children under sixteen counting as half-units, and then apportioning the rent accordingly. This policy may be illustrated by a simple example:

> Mr and Mrs A live with their adult child, George, eighteen, who is working, and two younger children, aged fourteen and twelve. There are, therefore, three adults in the household and two children under sixteen, totalling four units. If the net rent is £16·00 a week, George's share is one quarter, i.e., £4·00 a week, and this would be deducted from the sum payable for rent to his father.

This policy could work hardship, e.g., where the non-dependant has very low earnings and is unable to contribute much towards the rent. The rule applied by the Commission then is that the non-dependant's rent share should be so calculated as to leave him with a reasonable sum after the notional deduction of his contribution: in 1977 the figures were that a single non-dependent person was to be left with £14·00 net earnings, and a married man £23·00 with £6·00 in addition for each child.

In the example given above, if George's net earnings were only

17. SBA 1976, Sch. 1, para. 11(1).
18. Ibid., Sch. 1, para. 11(2)–(3): post, pp. 500–502, for home-owners.
19. Handbook, para. 52.
20. See ante, pp. 490–491.

1. Handbook, para. 51. For further details of this deduction, see *Lynes*, pp. 44–45.
2. SBA 1976, Sch. 1, para. 11(2).
3. Para. 53.

£17·00 a week, £3·00 would be the share of the rent attributed to him, and not the £4·00 assessed under the 'units rule'.[4]

Although this practice may substantially reduce the problems caused to poorer families by the 'rent-share' provision, it is arguable that the Commission should adopt a more discriminating policy. Where, for example, the non-dependant only occupies a small part of the property concerned, the share of the rent attributable to him should be proportionately small. But these calculations would necessarily be difficult.

If the non-dependent person is himself in receipt of benefit, he will receive a rent allowance as a non-householder,[5] and this sum will be deducted from the rent payable to the claimant, in whose house he is living.

The only other complication concerning the calculation of the rent concerns the relationship of supplementary benefits to the rent allowances and rebates, and rate rebates, payable by local authorities under the Housing Finance Act 1972. If a claimant is already in receipt of one of these payments at the time he claims supplementary benefit, he will continue to receive the rent rebate or allowance for eight weeks (and the rate rebate for the period specified in the award); during those periods the amounts payable by the Commission will reflect the fact that the tenant is paying a reduced rent.[6] But after the period is over, the Commission should pay the full rent, as otherwise the claimant will be worse off.[7]

2. *Unreasonable rents.* In certain cases the SBC will not pay the full rent actually paid by the tenant on the ground that it is unreasonable. The operation of this 'rent stop' provision used to cause great controversy, but the practice of the Commission has changed considerably in the last few years, in most cases with the express object of reducing the hardship which may result from withholding the full rent. It is now unusual for rent not to be met in full.[8]

In principle a rent may be considered unreasonable either if it is too high for the property, or if the property is not suitable for the claimant, ie, it is too luxurious, or situated in an expensive area.[9] The Commission's policy varies according to the type of property concerned, so a number of

4. This policy came into general operation in April 1975: see *LAG Bulletin*, June 1975, p. 159. It has replaced earlier policies designed to alleviate the rigours of the 'units rule': see Elks, *LAG Bulletin*, July 1974, p. 164.

5. For the householder/non-householder distinction and the reason why the non-dependant would be classified as the latter, see ante, p. 495.

6. SBA 1976, Sch. 1, para. 11(4).

7. Handbook, para. 63; *Lynes*, pp. 44–45; the SBC Annual Report 1975, Cmnd. 6615, para. 7.3 explains that in some circumstances claimants will do better

to receive housing allowances than claim supplementary benefit and that local offices are instructed to advise such people not to claim benefit. Also see SBC Annual Report 1976, Cmnd. 6910, paras. 11.2–11.5.

8. In 1975, only 0·6% of all rents were not met in full: SBC Annual Report 1975, para. 7.4 No figures are available for 1976.

9. The principle is most clearly set out in the S.B. Handbook of November, 1972, para. 44. Despite the modifications made since then, it is still relevant as the basic principle governing what is a 'reasonable rent'.

possibilities must be considered. First, it will always accept that a local authority rent is reasonable for council houses,[10] though it might conceivably take the view that the accommodation was not reasonable for the particular claimant. With regard to privately rented property, the Commission since October 1975 has made it clear that a rent will not be considered unreasonable if the local authority accepts it as fair for rent rebate or allowance purposes.[11]

In other cases, where the local authority's assessment for rebate purposes is irrelevant, the full rent will always be accepted as reasonable if it has been registered as fair by the rent officer, assessment committee, or rent tribunal. If no rent has been registered[12] the Commission will pay what it estimates would be registered as a fair rent, and under the policy pursued since October 1975, will advise the tenant to register where there is security of tenure; if the fair rent which is registered is higher than the estimate, then the excess will be paid by the Commission.[13] Where there is no security of tenure, it will consult the local authority as to the level of fair rents in the area, but the latter's opinion may be based on inadequate information and the Commission does not necessarily follow it.

Cases of great hardship may arise if the person on benefit is rent-stopped and so is induced to move to cheaper accommodation at what may well be a time of stress.[14] A number of changes in the Commission's policy were made in 1975 to improve the position of such a claimant. First, following the recommendation of the Finer Committee[15], the Commission has said that it will give special weight to the difficulties of single-parent families in finding cheaper accommodation[16] Secondly, it has decided normally to meet in full the rent of a claimant who does not enjoy security of tenure,[17] and who for reasons of age, health, difficulty of finding employment, etc., has to stay where he is. Most importantly, the full rent of a claimant who is too luxuriously housed *will* be met for a reasonable period to help him adjust to the new situation, unless there are very exceptional circumstances.[18]

3. *Method of payment for rent.* 'Net rent' means the rent payable for one week,[19] and, therefore, in the normal course of events the tenant on supplementary benefit is paid a sum equivalent to a week's rent. There may be difficulties where a claimant is required by his landlord to pay a month's rent in advance.[20] It would seem that the appropriate course is for the SBC to make an exceptional needs payment to cover the month's rent.[1]

10. Handbook 1977, para. 55.
11. The changes were announced in SBC Notes and news, No. 3 (October 1975): see *LAG Bulletin*, Dec. 1975, p. 319.
12. These cases will now be less common since the Rent Act 1974 has extended security of tenure to furnished property, and there is generally now no risk of eviction when the tenant applies to the rent officer to register a fair rent.
13. Handbook, para. 56.

14. See the cases mentioned in *LAG Bulletin*, June 1974, p. 136.
15. Paras. 6.97–6.102.
16. See Handbook, para. 56.
17. Such a tenant is clearly in a vulnerable position if he defaults in payment of his full rent.
18. Handbook, paras. 59–60.
19. SBA 1976, Sch. 1, para. 11(3).
20. *LAG Bulletin*, July 1973, p. 154.
1. See post, pp. 519–525, for exceptional needs payments.

The Commission is now willing to do this, 'where a claimant . . . can only secure accommodation (in the private sector) by paying rent in advance'.[2]

An even more troublesome problem arises where a person on supplementary benefit falls into arrears with his rent payments. The Commission may adopt a variety of courses of action in this event.[3] The rent may instead be paid to a social worker who is dealing with the family on benefit. Secondly, it may use its powers under section 14(3) of the Supplementary Benefits Act 1976 to make payment directly to the landlord; the Commission may do this either for the protection of the claimant or at his request. Until recently it has been reluctant to take this step partly out of anxiety that the claimant will lose the ability to budget for himself if this is in effect done for him.[4] But after the recommendation of the Finer Committee that direct payments should be made more often, the Commission's policy has been changed.[5]

Rent arrears may be paid by the Commission in exercise of its power to make exceptional needs payments. It is understandably reluctant to do this, since it will probably have already paid a rent allowance, but it does so if there is no other way to prevent eviction and to keep the claimant's family together.[6] Payment of the lump sum may be accompanied by the steps discussed in the previous paragraph to prevent the tenant getting into debt with his landlord again. The Commission may also, in the exercise of its discretionary power to reduce payment in 'exceptional circumstances',[7] withhold in future up to 50p of the claimant's weekly allowance.[8]

d) THE TREATMENT OF HOUSEOWNERS. For a houseowner the additional allowance payable for rent covers 'rates, a reasonable allowance towards any necessary expenditure on repairs or insurance, and such proportion as is for the time being attributable to interest of any sum payable in respect of a mortgage debt . . . charged on the house in which the householder resides . . .'.[9]

1. *Allowance for repairs and insurance.* The Commission assesses an annual allowance for repairs and insurance,[10] which is currently £39·80. This is clearly not enough to meet the more extensive repairs which are often needed even to the best-preserved properties, but the view is taken that a claimant should finance these through a second mortgage or local authority loan; the Commission may meet the interest on such a loan.

2. Handbook, para. 61. This appears to be a recent change in practice, since there was nothing in the 1974 Handbook to suggest that the SBC would pay rent in advance in this situation.

3. Ibid., para. 62.

4. The Commission's former policy on direct payments is fully stated in the Finer Report, para. 6.104.

5. There is a full discussion of this practice in the SBC Annual Report 1975, ante n.7, at para. 7.5. In 1974 there were 26,000 direct payments of rent; in 1975 there were 51,000. No figures are available for 1976.

6. Handbook, paras. 62 and 100. See also the Commission's report, *Exceptional Needs Payments* (1973), paras. 20–24.

7. SBA 1976, Sch. 1, para. 4(1)(7).

8. Handbook, para. 62.

9. SBA 1976, Sch. 1, para. 11(3)(b).

10. Handbook, para. 47. The allowance may also be paid to tenants responsible for repairs.

Only if this is not possible and the claimant has insufficient savings with which to finance the repairs, will the granting of an exceptional needs payment be considered.[11] In certain cases, however, the Commission has been persuaded to take a more generous attitude.[12]

2. *Mortgage payments.*[13] Under the Act's definition of 'rent' the Commission is obliged to pay mortgage interest to a claimant who owns his house.[14] There is nothing to prevent the Commission assisting the claimant with the capital element in repayments under its general discretionary powers, but it is not its policy to help those on supplementary benefits acquire capital assets. This is perhaps questionable in the light of other forms of assistance for home ownership, notably improvement grants, though income tax relief is only allowed on the interest part of mortgage repayments.[15] Whatever its overall merits, the Commission's policy may lead to hardship for those claimants, the bulk of whose repayments may consist of capital payments. For this reason there are a number of ways in which the Commission will assist claimants to avoid the effects of the policy, without derogating from its principle.

First, in assessing the regular weekly benefit, the Commission disregards income from relatives and friends which has been allocated for capital repayments.[16] Secondly, it generally allows the claimant to set-off the repayments against the proceeds of sub-letting the property, which would otherwise be deducted in full.[17] Thirdly, the Commission encourages claimants to persuade building societies to accept interest payments only for a period and defer the repayment of capital.

As with rents payable to a landlord, the Commission has power to withhold unreasonable mortgage repayments.[18] This will be exercised if they were unreasonable at the time they were incurred, usually when the claimant was in employment and was presumably able to meet the commitments.[19] However, the Commission may still apply the 'mortgage stop', if the accommodation is too large or expansive.[20]

e) SPECIAL CASES. There are a number of people who do not live in rented accommodation or own their own home. Two examples are members of a co-operative housing association and persons living in a caravan which they are buying on hire-purchase. The problem here is to separate the payments which represent rent, or interest, from those which represent a contribution to a share in the capital or part of the purchase

11. Ibid., at para. 96. Strangely, there is no mention of this power in the *Exceptional Needs Payments* report.
12. See Tunnard, *LAG Bulletin*, July 1975, pp. 184, 185, and ibid., Nov. 1975, p. 292.
13. See Tunnard, ibid., Feb. 1977, p. 36.
14. SBA 1976, Sch. 1, para. 11(3)(b).
15. Pinson *Revenue law*, (11th edn), para. 8–60.
16. For disregards of resources, see post, pp. 507–511.
17. Tunnard, ante, n.12, at p. 186.
18. SBA 1976, Sch. 1., para. 11(1).
19. Handbook, para. 57.
20. Ibid., at paras. 59–60. The figures suggest that the 'mortgage-stop' is applied very rarely, and then generally to the long-term unemployed: see SBC Annual Report 1975, Cmnd. 6615, at Table 16.

price. Only the former payments are added to the requirements of the claimant.[1]

f) THE TREATMENT OF NON-HOUSEHOLDERS. The distinction between a householder and a non-householder has already been discussed.[2] If a claimant is living in someone else's household and paying a regular sum for the accommodation, food, etc., it is probable that his requirements will be assessed on the basis that he is a boarder. The treatment of other non-householders, generally those living in a relative's household, is less generous than that of either a householder or a boarder, on the reasonable assumption that their commitments are less. The ordinary weekly scale rate for single non-householders is less than that for householders[3]: from November 1977 it is £11.60 for those eighteen and older, compared with £14.50 for householders.[4] In addition a non-householder's weekly requirements include a sum for rent, from November 1977 £1.20. The total of these sums is designed to cover the contribution which he or she is assumed to make to the costs of running the household. The Commission may increase these sums in exceptional circumstances to meet the situation where the non-householder has special needs. Following the Finer Committee Report,[5] it pays single parents under eighteen the full adult non-householder rate of £11.60 plus the appropriate addition for the child and the sum of £1.20 for rent.[6]

iii) Boarders

The weekly requirements of a 'person paying inclusive charge for board and lodging' are assessed at an appropriate sum, which is to be not less than the ordinary scale rates, or the long-term rates where relevant, but without the rent addition.[7] The Commission, therefore, has considerable discretion how to assess benefit for boarders; in fact, it pays the board and lodging charge, where this is reasonable, with an addition for the claimant's personal expenses such as clothing. From November 1977 this personal allowance is £4·70 for a single person and £7·70 for a married couple, with an extra 55p and £1·25 respectively for claimants entitled to the long-term rates.[8]

a) WHEN IS A CLAIMANT TREATED AS A BOARDER? The distinction between boarders and non-householders is an important one which has caused some difficulty. As the latters' requirements are assessed less generously, it is clearly advantageous for a claimant to establish that he is a boarder. The Commission's policy is to regard persons paying for board and lodging 'on a commercial basis' as boarders, while those living in a relative's household and paying a contribution for their food and room are

1. *Lynes*, pp. 54–57.
2. See ante, pp. 495–496.
3. Ante, p. 490.
4. S.I. 1977/1326. There is no difference for married couples, except with regards to the rent addition. A married couple, therefore, living in a relative's house is very well treated compared with a single person in the same position.
5. Para. 5.255.
6. Handbook, para. 42.
7. SBA 1976, Sch. 1, para. 15.
8. There are also allowances for a boarder's dependants. The full figures may be found in the leaflet, SB1.

normally treated as non-householders.[9] So are those 'just paying their way' in the household.[10] On occasion, the Commission seems to apply the 'commercial basis' test very strictly, so that if there is any personal relationship between lodger and landlord, the former will be classified as a non-householder. Thus in one case,

> C lived in a friend's house in Leeds, paying a weekly sum for board and lodging. At first when unemployed he was treated as a boarder, but his benefit was then reduced as the SBC decided he was a non-householder. C and his friend had shared accommodation at previous addresses, and for that reason it was decided by both the Commission and the appeal tribunal that the relationship was not a commercial one. Certiorari was refused by the vacation judge.[11]

In other cases, however, the existence of a personal relationship between the claimant and houseowner has not prevented the former from successfully contending that he should be regarded as a boarder. Thus, in a case where a prisoner released on parole lived with his fiancée's parents, the appeal tribunal, reversing the Commission's decision, held that he was a boarder.[12] A similar result was reached where a claimant and his two children lived with his sister and brother-in-law, paying them £7·00 a week.[13] It is difficult to suggest any single criterion which could be decisive in determining whether a claimant is to be treated as a boarder: clearly, the amount and regularity of payment are important factors, and another is the closeness of the relationship between the persons concerned. There is obviously a danger that a claimant might agree to pay his parents, or a brother with whom he is living, a high weekly sum in order to obtain the rate of benefit payable to boarders.

b) THE DISALLOWANCE OF AN UNREASONABLE BOARDING CHARGE. The Commission will not pay the whole of a board and lodging charge if it considers it unreasonable, either for the accommodation itself or because it is too luxurious for the claimant.[14] The charge is compared with others in the locality, though more will be paid to a claimant who receives extra care in his lodgings because of his health or general condition. In a number of cases the Commission reaches agreement concerning the level of lodging charges with an organisation running a home, e.g., the Abbeyfield Society.[15]

C. The assessment of resources

i) General

In order to calculate the supplementary benefit payable to the claimant, his resources are deducted from his requirements,[16] as assessed according

9. Handbook, para. 119.
10. Ibid.
11. LAG Bulletin, Apr. 1974, p. 82. See also Poverty (1975), No. 29, p. 36.
12. Poverty (1972), No. 24, p. 29.
13. Poverty (1973), No. 26, p. 23.
14. Handbook, paras. 119–121.
15. See LAG Bulletin, Apr. 1974, p. 83, for further details of these arrangements.
16. SBA 1976, s.I.

to the rules analysed in the previous section. This section is concerned with the rules used to assess his resources. Frequently, of course, the claimant will be completely destitute and have no resources at all, either in terms of capital or weekly income: in that case, benefit is simply assessed in terms of the applicant's weekly requirements. In many cases, however, he will have some savings and will also, or alternatively, be in receipt of other social security benefits or part-time earnings, some or all of which may be deducted from the sum representing his or her weekly requirements to arrive at the correct amount of benefit.

In principle, it might seem logical to deduct all the applicant's resources to estimate the needs to be met by an award. But under both the National Assistance Act 1948 and the supplementary benefits legislation[17] certain resources are wholly or partially ignored, or disregarded, in estimating the applicant's resources. Moreover, the Commission in its discretion also disregards other resources. The effect of these 'disregards' (as they are called) is to raise the poverty line, for those people with some capital or income, above the weekly scale rates of benefit.[18]

ii) The Applicant's 'resources'

Since the National Assistance Act 1948, only the resources of the applicant himself, and those of his wife (or woman living with him) and dependants, have been taken into account.[19] The ability of any other relatives to maintain the applicant is wholly irrelevant to the computation of his resources and, therefore, to his entitlement. Yet this seems to have been challenged by the Commission in *R v West London Supplementary Benefits Appeal Tribunal, ex parte Clarke*,[20] at least until the case came before the Divisional Court:

> The applicant, a widow and Indian citizen, was allowed to enter the UK after her son-in-law had given the immigration authorities an undertaking to support her. She lived with him for about two and a half years before there was a dispute which led to her moving to her son's house. She then claimed supplementary benefit. This was refused on the ground that she had weekly resources of £11.50, calculated by reference, it seems, to the son-in-law's undertaking. The decision was upheld by the appeal tribunal.

The Divisional Court granted certiorari, deciding that neither the son-in-law nor the son had an obligation to look after the applicant, and that, therefore, the family's resources as such were irrelevant. Neither the Commission nor the tribunal had considered whether the applicant was *in fact* being fully maintained.[1]

---

17. The rules are now set out in SBA 1976, Sch. 1, paras. 17–30.
18. See Kincaid *Poverty and Equality in Great Britain* (1973), pp. 175–177. See post, pp. 507–511, for the detailed rules.
19. SBA 1976, Sch. 1, para. 3: ante, pp.

485–488.
20. [1975] 1 WLR 1396.
1. A regular contribution from a relative is treated as a resource of the claimant, though there is a partial disregard of this: see post, p. 510.

The Act does not, rather surprisingly, define what an applicant's resources may be in positive terms. Schedule 1 does define the disregards, discussed later at pages 507–511, and it also makes clear which payments are *not* to be disregarded, but it does not spell out what 'resources' means.

The meaning of 'resources' was at issue in one of the three cases so far decided by the Court of Appeal on the supplementary benefits legislation, *R v Preston Supplementary Benefits Appeal Tribunal, ex parte Moore* :[2]

> Moore, a student with a wife and two children, received an education grant for the academic year 1971–72, that is from 1 September 1971 to 31 August 1972. In fact he left college at the end of June 1972, by which time he had spent all the grant. He claimed supplementary benefit for the first week of July. The SBC included in his resources 1/22 of that part of the grant allocated for the vacation and 1/52 of the dependant's allowance which he had been given for the whole year. The appeal tribunal upheld the Commission's decision.

The applicant's argument was that the 'resources' meant his *actual* resources in hand: since he had spent all his grant, under the impression that it was only intended to cover the period he was attending college, no portion of it could be deducted from his weekly requirements. However, in a judgment given by Lord Denning MR, the Court of Appeal upheld the Commission's view that 'resources' refer to the applicant's *notional* resources, and that the fact that part of the grant was earmarked for the vacation entitled the SBC to deduct an appropriate sum for the purpose of assessing weekly benefit. Lord Denning's reasons were first, that capital is treated in the Act as equivalent to a notional weekly income, irrespective of the actual income it produces,[3] and secondly, that earnings paid in advance are treated as resources for the whole of the relevant period, even if the applicant spends his wages completely in the first two or three days.[4] But generally this second case will not be one where benefit is claimable at all, since it may not be paid to a person in full-time work.[5] This argument does not, therefore, seem conclusive. It is also doubtful whether the treatment of capital affords any useful general guidance on the meaning of 'resources.' There is a further point which induces some doubt with regard to Lord Denning's argument. Under paragraph 28 of the Schedule, resources *deliberately* abandoned by a claimant for the purpose of claiming benefit are to be considered as if they are still his resources. The inference might be that money spent carelessly, as in *Moore's* case where the claimant did not appreciate that the grant was intended to cover the whole year, is not to be treated as a resource.

In *Moore's* case the claimant had at one time possessed the money treated as a resource. Another difficult question is whether it is ever permissible for a payment not received by the claimant to be so treated; if,

2. [1975] 1 WLR 624.
3. See post, p. 506, for further discussion of this provision: SBA 1976, Sch. 1, para. 20.
4. Earnings paid in arrears are not treated as resources for the week in which they are earned, but for the following week: *Lynes*, pp. 71–72.
5. Ante, pp. 482–483.

for example, the claimant is usually in receipt of a weekly allowance from a relative, may that be regarded as part of his resources for a week when it is in fact not paid? This is one of the issues which arose in *R v Barnsley Supplementary Benefits Appeal Tribunal, ex parte Atkinson.*[6] The Court of Appeal there held that it was legitimate to treat a regular cash grant from a parent to a student as part of the latter's resources, but that it must be open for him to show that the payment was not made. The Commission was, therefore, wrong to treat an assumed parental contribution to the student as part of his resources, when no contribution was actually made.[7] In this context resources does mean 'actual' and not 'notional' resources.

Some nice questions may arise with regard to the Commission's power to treat resources deliberately abandoned by the claimant as if they are still his. Suppose a claimant buys a house, (the value of which is entirely disregarded in assessing his resources[8]) shortly before he applies for benefit: can he be said to '*deprive* himself of any resources' as distinct from. redeploying them? What is to happen if the applicant makes a transfer out of mixed motives, partly to enhance his chance of securing benefit and partly out of generosity to a friend? The payment of debts or the purchase of necessities with capital resources would probably not be held to be an abandonment.[9]

iii) Income and capital resources[10]

It is often crucial to distinguish between the applicant's income and capital resources because of the more generous treatment of the latter. Some capital assets, such as an owner-occupied house, are disregarded altogether.[11] The value of all other capital assets, savings and investments is then aggregated and treated as producing a weekly income according to a statutory tariff.[12] Capital up to £1,200 is completely disregarded,[13] and after that each complete £50 is assumed to produce a notional weekly income of 25p which is taken into account in determining the claimant's resources. Thus, capital of £1,700 would be treated as producing an income of £2·50 per week. The actual income is ignored, even though it might be less than the tariff income which is fixed at a high level on the reasonable assumption that it is right for a person with substantial capital to support himself rather than rely on supplementary benefit.[14] The Act provides no definition of capital, in this reflecting income tax law where the distinction between capital and income is similarly obscure.[15] The Handbook states that capital 'normally includes all savings, investments, the net sale value of property not occupied by the claimant and other lump-sums such as redundancy payments and bequests.'[16]

6. [1977] 3 All ER 1031, [1977] 1 WLR 917. See post, pp. 514 and 551 for further discussion of the case.
7. See now S.I. 1977/619, Reg. 3: post, p. 552.
8. See post, p. 508.
9. See *LAG Bulletin*, Aug. 1974, p. 195. See also Handbook, para. 32.
10. Hodge, *LAG Bulletin*, March 1975, p. 70.
11. Capital disregards are treated, post, p. 508.
12. SBA 1976, Sch. 1, para. 20.
13. Ibid., para. 19.
14. Handbook, para. 31.
15. See Whiteman & Wheatcroft *Income Tax*, (2nd edn), 1.18–1.20.
16. Para. 29.

It is clear that tax refunds are generally treated as capital, though this is not the case for a claimant without employment or laid off because of a trade dispute: it is specifically provided that then tax refunds paid, or available to the applicant if he claimed them, are to be treated as income.[17] Difficulties arise with regard to the treatment of such payments as commission, and bonuses given for productivity or at particular times of year. If these are regarded as income, should they be treated as payments for the week in which they were received or averaged over a relevant period? It seems that the Commission's approach is to treat commission and bonuses as income for the particular week or month in which they were received.[18]

The distinction between income and capital resources was at issue in the Divisional Court in *R v West London Supplementary Benefits Appeal Tribunal, ex parte Taylor.*[19]

> The applicant was a mother who, with her illegitimate child, had been deserted by the father. A court order requiring the latter to pay her £2·50 a week was not enforced for about seven years, at the end of which period she was awarded supplementary benefit. The SBC then secured the payment of the maintenance arrears into court. It further decided that this sum of £704·75 should be regarded as income and that it should be spread over forty-four weeks in the future, during which period the mother's resources would meet her requirements, and she would not receive benefit. The appeal tribunal upheld the Commission's decision that the sum was income, but expressed no view as to how further it should be handled.

The Divisional Court was clearly sympathetic to the mother's contention that the sum should be treated as capital, but held that this was a decision for the Commission, and that a court should only intervene if it was grossly unreasonable.[20] But May J, who gave the court's judgment, held that the Commission was wrong to treat the arrears as *future* income for an arbitrary period of forty-four weeks; they were payments which had been in arrears for nearly seven years, and which should therefore be treated as *past* income, and not as present resources. It was also suggested that the position should be clarified by defining 'resources' in the Act and stating there whether particular types of payment should be treated as capital or income.[1]

iv) The disregards[2]
An interesting point is that the amount of the disregards can only be altered by statute. An attempt was made during the Committee stage of the 1966 Bill to give the Minister power to vary the disregards by regulation, but it was resisted on the ground that, as they conferred advantages on

17. SBA 1976, Sch. 1, para. 26: see post, p. 531, for further discussion.
18. *Lynes*, pp. 71–72.
19. [1975] 1 WLR 1048.
20. Ibid., at p. 1052. For the general principles of judicial review, see chap.

15, post, pp. 657–658.
1. Ibid., at p. 1051, per May J.
2. See post, pp. 551–552, for the modification of the disregard provisions applied to students.

those with certain kinds of income and capital, any change would be controversial and should not, therefore, be made by delegated legislation.[3]

The difficulty of amendment may have been partly responsible for the fact that the disregards were not increased from 1966 until 1975, a stagnation which was frequently criticised.[4] They were eventually raised by the Social Security Benefits Act 1975. The following paragraphs set out first, those items of capital and income which are entirely disregarded, secondly, those which are partially disregarded, and lastly those items which under the Act are taken fully into account in assessing resources. The difference between these three categories may be illustrated by the following example:

> C is in receipt of (i) part-time earnings of £10 net a week, (ii) mobility allowance, and (iii) child benefit for her two children. (ii) is wholly ignored, or disregarded, in computing her resources for supplementary benefit purposes, while (iii) is fully taken into account. There is a disregard of £6 (she is the parent in a one-parent family) of her earnings, so that only £4 of this is taken into account. Thus, her supplementary benefit will be assessed as her requirements less her resources (£4 + £5·60 child benefit – see chap. 11 for the assessment of child benefit).

Most of the disregards are set out in Schedule 1 to the 1976 Act, but some of them are discretionary and are allowed, therefore, only as a matter of Commission policy.[5]

a) RESÓURCES WHOLLY DISREGARDED

1. THE CAPITAL VALUE OF CLAIMANT'S DWELLING. The capital value of the claimant's 'interest in the dwelling in which he resides' is disregarded.[6] It is clear that the claimant must live in the house, but it is a moot point whether a person who divides his time between two properties is entitled to have the value of both disregarded. The Commission's policy is to disregard the value of the principal residence, a justifiable course which reflects the terms of the exemption from capital gains tax of dispositions of the taxpayer's residence.[7]

2. FURNITURE AND PERSONAL POSSESSIONS. These are disregarded at the Commission's discretion.[8] This is obviously desirable; it would be hard on a claimant to be required in effect to sell household goods, work equipment, etc., before he became eligible to receive benefit during a temporary period of illness or unemployment. But presumably it would not apply this policy to a claimant who possessed, for example, rare works of art of some value, which he might reasonably be expected to sell before claiming supplementary benefit.

3. 729 HC Deb., cols. 1128–1136.
4. See in particular, Finer, paras. 5.260–5.261.
5. SBA 1976, Sch. 1, para. 27.
6. Ibid., Sch. 1, para. 17.
7. Pinson, *Revenue Law* (11th edn), para. 16–41.
8. Handbook, para. 28.

3. BUSINESS ASSETS OF THE CLAIMANT'S LIVELIHOOD. The assets of the business conducted by the claimant may also be disregarded at the Commission's discretion.[9]

4. MISCELLANEOUS RESOURCES DISREGARDED UNDER THE ACT. By paragraph 18 of the Schedule, death grants,[10] maternity grants[11] and sums payable to holders of the Victoria or George Cross are wholly disregarded; as is mobility allowance.[12]

5. MISCELLANEOUS DISCRETIONARY DISREGARDS. The Commission in its discretion normally ignores *occasional* payments to the claimant by friends, relatives or charities for purposes assumed not to be covered by supplementary benefit. Examples are: payments for holidays, redecoration of the house or for repayment of the mortgage capital.[13] Occasional payments of this kind should be carefully distinguished from *regular* payments from relatives or charities which are *partially* disregarded: see page 510 below.

6. EARNINGS OF CHILDREN. Part-time earnings of children at school or otherwise completing secondary education are entirely disregarded.[14] This modifies in an important way the principle that the resources of dependent children are to be aggregated with those of their father (or mother, if she claims benefit).[15]

7. OTHER CAPITAL. The value of the claimant's savings, investments and other capital assets is ignored up to £1,200. Beyond that figure, the notional tariff income is included in the applicant's resources.

b) RESOURCES PARTIALLY DISREGARDED

1. *Earnings.* If the claimant is required to register for employment under section 5 of the 1976 Act,[16] then £2·00 of *his* net part-time earnings are disregarded. In most other cases, e.g., a wife's earnings or where he is not required to register, the earnings disregard is £4·00.[17] The lower disregard for those required to register is presumably designed to encourage them to secure full-time employment, and not rely on benefit plus part-time earnings.[18] There is a higher disregard of £6·00 a week for the part-time earnings of a parent of a one-parent family.[19] This was a response to the criticisms of the Finer Committee, though its Report had not suggested more favourable treatment in this respect of these parents compared with

9. Ibid.
10. See chap. 6, ante, pp. 243–247.
11. See chap. 7, ante, pp. 249–252.
12. SSA 1975, s.37A(8), inserted by SSPA 1975, s.22(1).
13. Handbook, para. 27; mortgage capital repayments are not payable by the Commission as part of the 'rent' addition: see ante, p. 501.
14. SBA 1976, Sch. 1, para. 22(2). For the similar provisions in the United States, see La France, et al. *Law of the Poor*

(1973), p. 306.
15. The general aggregation provisions are discussed in Part Two of this chapter: ante, pp. 485–488.
16. See ante, p. 483.
17. SBA 1976, Sch. 1, para. 22(1).
18. The provision of the part-time earnings disregard for those required to register for employment has been criticised: see *George*, p. 205.
19. SBA 1976, Sch. 1, para. 22(1)(b).

others.[20] Regulations provide that net earnings means the claimant's gross wages or salary less authorised deductions, such as income tax and social security contributions, and reasonable expenses, such as fares and trades union dues.[1] Where there is no regular weekly income, perhaps because the claimant is self-employed, the Commission must assess it in the way it judges appropriate.[2]

Two further points should be made. First, the claimant's right to have part of his earnings disregarded is not affected by the fact that he may have other income which is partially disregarded; he is entitled to have both the appropriate part of his earnings *and* £4·00 of his other income ignored in assessing his resources. Secondly, there is a more limited disregard of earnings where a person claims benefit for the first fifteen days after a return to work at the end of a trade dispute.[3]

2. *Other partial disregards.* £4·00 of all income, apart from part-time earnings (disregarded under the provisions discussed above), and the notional income from capital, is to be disregarded with the exception of certain further items listed in the Schedule.[4] (These are mostly social security benefits mentioned in the next sub-section). The £4·00 disregard does, however, cover industrial and war disablement pensions, and the excess of an industrial or war widow's pension over the standard widow's pension:[5] these benefits, in contrast to those fully taken into account, to a certain extent include elements of 'compensation', independently of the recipients' needs.

Other payments which may be included in the £4·00 to be disregarded include annuities or donations by friends, relatives or charities. There is, however, only a limited disregard (within the £4·00) of £1·00 with regard to occupational pensions.[6] Finally, it should be emphasised that the applicant may have only £4·00 of the total income from these sources disregarded. Thus, a claimant may have £4·00 of his part-time earnings *and* £4·00 of his war pension disregarded, but he cannot have both £4·00 of his war pension and £4·00 of any additional sums given him by relatives, etc., ignored in assessing his resources.

c) RESOURCES WHICH ARE TAKEN FULLY INTO ACCOUNT. There are a number of payments which must be taken fully into account when assessing the claimant's resources.[7] These are principally the benefits payable under the Social Security Act 1975 (except those wholly or partially disregarded), child benefit and family income supplement.[8] Maintenance payments for a spouse or children, whether made voluntarily or under a court order, are also included in the claimant's resources. The object of

20. In Germany more flexibility is achieved by the use of a percentage disregard of earned income instead of the British flat-rate disregard: see Müller-Fembeck and Ogus, 25 ICLQ 382, 396–397.
1. S.I. 1977/1141, Reg. 5.
2. Ibid., Reg. 5(2).
3. SBA 1976, Sch. 1, para. 22(3). See also post, p. 531.
4. SBA 1976, Sch. 1, para. 23(1).
5. Ibid., Sch. 1, para. 23(4)–(7).
6. Ibid., Sch. 1, para. 25.
7. SBA 1976, Sch. 1, para. 23(2)–(3).
8. For the circumstances in which supplementary benefit and FIS may be payable to the same claimant, see ante, p. 482.

these provisions is clearly to exclude duplication of benefit payments, and in the case of maintenance payments, the meeting by the Commission of a need which is already satisfied by a person legally liable to support the claimant.

d) CRITIQUE. It is arguable that the disregards are incompatible with a means-tested benefit, designed to cover cases of need.[9] This may be true, but they may nevertheless be justifiable on various grounds, which show that the rules of supplementary benefits cannot entirely be related to a single policy goal.[10] Thus the partial disregard of the applicant's capital, and the total disregard of the value of an owner-occupied house encourages savings and rewards thrift. The fact that to some extent donations from friends and charitable institutions are ignored may encourage private generosity to those in need. The partial disregard of part-time earnings enables some people to boost their morale and their resources by working; this is a common feature of public assistance programmes.[11]

D. Exceptional circumstances additions

i) General

Schedule 1, paragraph 4(1)(a) of the Supplementary Benefits Act 1976 provides that in exceptional circumstances, benefit may be awarded above the weekly scale rates. 'Exceptional circumstances additions' (ECAs as they are generally known) are, therefore, weekly payments made over and above the general supplementary benefit awards in order to meet special and recurrent needs. Exceptional needs which arise only once, or periodically, are met by lump sum exceptional needs payments, discussed in Part Four of the chapter.

There is very little law, either in the legislation or in statutory instruments, regulating the award of these exceptional circumstances additions. The Supplementary Benefits Act lays down no maximum awards for ECAs and does not itemise the particular requirements for which an additional payment may be made.[12] Some guidance is afforded by the policies of the Commission set out in the Supplementary Benefits Handbook. They are, however, not in law binding on the officers of the Commission or on appeal tribunals.[13]

Special circumstances payments, as they were then called, were introduced in 1934 as an aspect of the unemployment assistance scheme.[14]

9. *Walley*, pp. 122ff.
10. *George*, pp. 202ff.
11. For the American position, see *La France et al.*, ante n.14 at p. 303. Earned income disregards are incorporated in all the poverty schemes regulated by the federal Social Security Act 1935.
12. The SBC in its Annual Report 1976,

Cmnd. 6910, paras. 7.49–7.50, points out that the imposition of these restrictions would run contrary to the purpose of the discretionary powers.
13. See post, pp. 514–515, for further discussion.
14. See the historical survey in SBC Annual Report 1976, ante n.12, at Appendix C.

They became increasingly important under the national assistance legislation, particularly to help with the extra heating and fuel requirements of old people. At the end of 1948 only 26% of those in receipt of assistance were also obtaining a special circumstances addition, but by 1966 the corresponding figure was 58%.[15] A large number of these claimants were old or handicapped, and others had been out of work for a considerable period. This led in 1966 to the introduction of the long-term addition, now the long-term rates, for supplementary pensioners and people who have been continuously in receipt of an allowance for two years; these groups are assumed to have special requirements. The change reduced the need for the exercise of discretion on the part of Commission officers.[16] Thus, perhaps not surprisingly, the number of recipients of exceptional circumstances additions (as they were known from 1966) at first dropped; in 1971 only 15% of those on benefit received ECAs.[17] But since then the number of claimants relying on these discretionary additions has steadily risen, and in 1975 the relevant figure was 39%.[18]

The general problems raised by the existence of discretionary powers are discussed before the Commission's policies with regard to particular kinds of need are examined. Much of the discussion which follows is also relevant to the award of exceptional needs payments discussed in Part Four.

ii) The exercise of discretionary powers

a) IN WHAT SENSE DOES THE COMMISSION HAVE DISCRETION? The phrase in paragraph 4(1)(a) of Schedule 1, 'benefit *may* be awarded', certainly suggests that the Commission has unlimited discretion whether or not to pay an exceptional circumstances addition. Yet the Act makes it clear that a person in need is *entitled* to benefit, only the calculation of which is left to the provisions in the Schedule. It would, therefore, be difficult for the Commission to argue that, where there is a clear case of an exceptional need, e.g., the need of a bed-ridden person suffering from pneumonia for an addition to cover heating costs, it was legally free to refuse to meet it. The true position, it is submitted, is that the Commission must exercise judgment in assessing whether a claimant has exceptional needs, and if it finds that he has, it has some discretion to add the sum it thinks appropriate to cover them. But an applicant refused any further payment because the Commission obviously assessed the facts incorrectly, or arbitrarily decided that a particular requirement should never be met by an ECA, could obtain mandamus to require the Commission to exercise its powers legally.[19]

15. Ibid., para. 7.3.
16. The long-term rates are discussed ante, pp. 492–494. Stevenson *Claimant or Client?* (1973), pp. 41ff. contains a good discussion of the merits of the change.
17. SBC Annual Report 1975, Cmnd. 6615, para. 2.16.
18. Ibid., at Table 18. No figures are yet available for 1976.
19. The principle of *Padfield v Minister of Agriculture, Fisheries and Food* [1968] AC 997, [1968] 1 All ER 694, HL would seem to be applicable here.

To some extent the question whether a claimant is entitled to an ECA or may only be awarded one at the discretion of the Commission raises controversial problems now frequently discussed by legal philosophers.[20] On one view, as no precise legal rules bind the Commission as to what it regards as exceptional circumstances or what sum it may allow to cover them, it can be said to have a wide discretion whether to make an additional payment and to determine its amount. On another approach, however, it may be said to be under an obligation to grant an additional payment in appropriate cases in the light of its statutory duty to meet the needs of those persons whose resources do not meet their requirements, and its further duty to promote the welfare of claimants.[1] This latter approach does not deny that there is room for judgment and discretion in the determination of those cases which should be met by an award of an ECA, but does emphasise that the discretion is not absolute.[2]

b) IS IT NECESSARY FOR THERE TO BE SO MUCH DISCRETION? The significant practical question is whether it is necessary for the Commission to have so much discretion, even assuming that it is legally limited, as suggested in the previous paragraphs. This is most controversial where the SBC exercises its power to reduce or withhold a supplementary *allowance* altogether,[3] primarily to control claims by some unemployed applicants. There is a discussion of the justifications given for this use of the power in Part Five.[4] But the Commission's powers to award an ECA, or a lump sum exceptional needs payment,[5] have also given rise to disquiet.

Recently the Commission itself has expressed concern at the rapid increase in the last few years in the number of discretionary payments.[6] Reliance on these awards may show an inadequacy in the level of the ordinary weekly rates. Discretionary decisions are less predictable and consistent, and may lead to conflict between the claimant and officials.

'It leaves claimants uncertain about what they are entitled to and how to make a case for getting it; they may feel they depend increasingly on the discretion of increasingly overworked men and women, rather than on clearly defined rights.'[7]

Further, the administrative costs of a discretionary system are high.[8] For these reasons, the Commission has decided that this aspect of the supplementary benefits scheme should be carefully investigated as part of the overall review. In the Annual Report of 1976, it contemplates that the needs at present covered by ECAs might be listed in regulations 'so that

20. See in particular Dworkin *Taking Rights Seriously* (1977), esp. pp. 31–39.
1. SBA 1976, s.27(1).
2. This view is consonant with the general principles of English administrative law: see de Smith *Judicial Review of Administrative Action* (3rd edn), chap. 6.
3. SBA 1976, Sch. 1, para. 4(1)(b).
4. See post, p. 536.

5. See further, post, pp. 519–525.
6. SBC Annual Report 1975, ante n.17, at paras. 2.16–2.18; Annual Report 1976, ante n.12, at paras. 1.37–1.47, and chap. 7 *passim*.
7. SBC Annual Report 1975, ante n.17, at para. 2.17.
8. SBC Annual Report 1976, ante n.12, at paras. 7.31–7.32.

there was no ambiguity about rights to such payments'.[9] Another possibility would be the automatic award of a periodic lump sum, perhaps every six months, to all benefit recipients to cover those requirements at present met by ECAs or the lump sum payments discussed in Part Four.[10] These changes would reduce the discretionary element substantially, but the Commission recognises that they will lead to more expenditure.[11]

In addition to the economic arguments against replacing the discretionary payments, it may be contended that questions relating to an individual's needs are inherently incapable of being regulated by rules, and that, therefore, a large element of discretion is inevitable in any assistance scheme.[12] Certainly, any attempt to list exhaustively the exceptional needs for which weekly or lump sum payments could be made would lead to an intolerable lack of flexibility. There must, therefore, remain some element of discretion to cover urgent or genuinely 'exceptional' circumstances,[13] and in these cases the Commission's policies will continue to be relevant.

c) THE COMMISSION'S POLICIES AND THE EXERCISE OF DISCRETION. The SBC has formulated various general policies, and fixed 'tariff' payments for the particular needs which may be met by an ECA, or by a lump sum exceptional needs payment. Many of these policies are published in the Handbook, and some of them are discussed later in this section of the chapter.[14] For example, there is a standard ECA for those who need a special diet, with a higher payment for those claimants suffering from one of five specified conditions.[15] In practice this means that a claimant's circumstances are treated as 'exceptional' for the purposes of an ECA if he is a member of a group or class which has exceptional requirements, e.g., those with dietary problems. This approach was ruled illegal by the Court of Appeal in *R v Barnsley Supplementary Benefits Appeal Tribunal, ex parte Atkinson*.[16] There the Commission had deducted £1 from a student's benefit under what was then paragraph 4(1)(b) of Schedule 2 to the 1966 Act,[17] on the ground that students as a whole constituted a special class from whose benefit it was appropriate to make a deduction.[18] The Court of Appeal held that the 'exceptional circumstances' provision must be applied to the particular circumstances of an individual case, and that it was wrong to treat a group of claimants as a whole. This ruling has in effect been reversed by section 14(8) of the Social Security (Miscellaneous Provisions) Act 1977 which provides that,

9. SBC Annual Report 1976, ante n.12, at para. 7.54.
10. Ibid., at para. 7.56.
11. Ibid., at para. 1.46: and see Annual Report 1975, ante n.17 at para. 2.35.
12. See Jowell, [1973] P.L. 178; Titmuss, 42 Political Quarterly 113; Stevenson *Claimant or Client?* (1973), chap. 2, which summarises the arguments for and against the use of discretion. An account of the exercise of discretion by the National Assistance Board which illustrates many of these arguments is given by Hill, 47 Pub. Admin. 75.
13. SBC Annual Report 1976, Cmnd. 6910, paras. 7.56–7.57.
14. Post, pp. 516–519.
15. Post, p. 517.
16. [1977] 3 All ER 1031, [1977] 1 WLR 917.
17. Now SBA 1976, Sch. 1, para. 4(1)(b).
18. This point is considered more fully, post, p. 551.

'the circumstances of a case may be treated as exceptional if it falls within a class of case the circumstances of which are exceptional'.[19]

The Commission's practice has, therefore, been legitimated: it is permissible for an ECA to be awarded (or a reduction from an allowance made) on the ground that the claimant belongs to a group which requires special treatment.

However, it is important to realise that the Commission's policies with regard to the award of ECAs and other discretionary payments are not binding either on its officers or the appeal tribunals. There is, however, evidence that they are reluctant to depart from these policies, even where their application might be thought to lead to hardship.[20] If the Commission or an appeal tribunal decides an application, believing it is bound by the relevant policy or without considering whether it should be departed from, then it has failed to decide the case properly, and the decision may be quashed.[1] In this respect the legal position has not been affected by the 1977 Act. Unfortunately, one or two remarks in the Parliamentary discussion of the provision suggested it is permissible for the Commission to ignore the individual circumstances of the case.[2]

In practical terms there can be little doubt that the use of policies to 'govern' cases where the applicant claims an ECA (or an exceptional needs payment) is reasonable. They ensure equity between different claimants with comparable problems; they save the time of the deciding officials who do not have to devise a new solution to each case; and to some extent they reduce the chance of personal prejudice entering into the official's decision, as he merely applies the rule to the case, unless it presents unusual features. What is important is that a policy is not applied so mechanically as to preclude consideration of any special factors, or indeed its reconsideration in the light of the hardship its application may cause.[3]

d) GENERAL FACTORS AFFECTING THE AWARD OF ECAs. The Commission is empowered to make a further weekly payment in 'exceptional circumstances'. It would seem that these may arise either because of circumstances external to the claimant—for example, unusually cold weather or expensive central heating—or more usually because of the applicant's exceptional requirements, attributable to his characteristics, such as

19. The provision was inserted in the Bill at a late stage after the decision in the *Atkinson* case: see 380 HL Deb., col. 1310.
20. See, for example, the case reported in *LAG Bulletin*, Apr. 1975, p. 98.
1. See the principles of administrative law stated in *de Smith*, ante n.2 at pp. 274–277. The leading case is *British Oxygen Co. v Board of Trade* [1971] AC 610, [1970] 3 All ER 165, HL. The principles have been applied in the supplementary benefits field by the

Divisional Court in *R v Greater Birmingham Appeal Tribunal, ex parte Simper* [1974] QB 543, [1973] 2 All ER 461; post, p. 518.
2. See the remarks of Mr E. Deakins, Under-Secretary of State, 928 HC Deb., cols. 1516–1517.
3. Reconsiderations of policy may only take place at the Commission's head office: see Stevenson, ante n.12, at pp. 66–68, for a discussion of policy formation.

age, infirmity or illness. At times, the Commission seems reluctant to treat seasonal conditions which affect a large number of claimants as exceptional circumstances,[4] perhaps fearing that this might leave the door open to a very large number of claims. It is doubtful, for example, whether a freak increase in the price of food would constitute exceptional circumstances.

Nothing is specifically said in the legislation concerning the account to be taken of the applicant's resources in determining whether an ECA should be made. It would seem logically that, since it represents in effect a payment for further weekly requirements, no more account should be taken of the applicant's resources than that already taken in calculating the standard rate of benefit, and this has since 1972 been the Commission's position.[5]

iii) The Commission's policies with regard to particular ECAs[6]

a) EXTRA HEATING. Normal heating costs are covered by the ordinary weekly scale rates, but the Commission will grant an addition if there are extra heating costs because of the claimant's infirmity or illness, or because the accommodation is particularly damp and cold.[7] Six criteria for the award of an ECA relate to the health of the applicant or a dependant, and two to the quality of the accommodation.[8] Payment is made generally according to a tariff, its level depending on the seriousness of the case.

> For example, if the claimant requires extra heating because of chronic ill health, he will be awarded 70p a week. If, moreover, his property is difficult to heat adequately, he may receive a further 70p, while if it is exceptionally difficult to heat properly, he may be awarded an additional £1·40. There cannot, however, normally be a total award of more than £2·10 a week. The Commission will also pay an ECA where the claimant pays more than £2·80 a week for central heating.[9] The Handbook states that the excess over a fixed charge will be met by the addition, but there is some doubt whether this is always true in practice.[10] Where there is no fixed charge the ECA is calculated according to the number of rooms, e.g., 35p for a house with two rooms.

Payments for extra heating now constitute over two-thirds of the total number of ECAs awarded.[11]

b) SPECIAL DIET. Special diets are the second principal category of case in which an ECA is payable by the Commission.[12] Again there is a tariff to

4. See Lynes, p. 82.
5. SBC Annual Report 1976, ante n.13, at para. 7.7. Cp., the account taken of capital in determining whether to award an exceptional needs payment, post, p. 522.
6. See Lynes, pp. 75–83 for a full discussion of these policies.
7. Handbook, para. 72.
8. See LAG Bulletin, June 1975, p. 159.
9. Handbook, para. 74.
10. Hodge, in ed. Alder and Bradley Justice, Discretion and Poverty, (1976), p. 69.
11. SBC Annual Report 1976, ante n.13, at para. 7.14, and Table 7.1.
12. About one-quarter of all ECAs: see ibid.

obviate the task of working out the appropriate sum in each individual case:

> 75p is allowed for all cases, except five conditions listed in the Handbook (of which diabetes is the most important), where a special addition of £1·75 is given.[13] In the case of claimants on artificial kidney machines the Commission is normally prepared to pay £5 a week. The standard additions have been calculated on the basis of expert medical opinion, but the Commission is prepared to award a higher sum where it is clear that the dietary problem of the claimant is particularly acute.[14] In one case, an appeal tribunal departed from the tariff figure where a boy was suffering from a rare form of anaemia and the dietary costs were about £5·00 a week.[15]

c) LAUNDRY COSTS. 10p of the ordinary scale rates are notionally allocated to cover weekly laundry costs. If, because of his infirmity or lack of facilities, it is difficult or impossible for a claimant to do the washing at home, then an additional sum may be paid.[16] Here is a case, therefore, where the exceptional circumstances may result from facts external to the claimant – lack of facilities – or from his own disabilities. It seems that the Commission is more prepared to make an additional payment in the latter situation.[17]

d) HIRE-PURCHASE COMMITMENTS. Hire-purchase instalments on items which are 'absolutely essential' may be met.[18] These include bedding, basic cooking equipment and furniture, but not generally more expensive articles such as washing machines and television sets. This area shows very clearly the difficulty of determining what are fundamental needs in a means-tested system; for some disabled people, a washing machine is a necessity, and the same could be argued of a television set where the applicant is housebound.[19]

e) MISCELLANEOUS CASES. The Handbook lists a number of cases where an ECA may be paid: telephone rental for a person living alone in an isolated area, furniture storage charges, fares to visit a relative in hospital, etc.[20] The list is not exhaustive, and ECAs have been paid in other circumstances.

> Thus, a weekly sum of £3·20 was awarded to cover the bus fares of a mother, where the exceptional circumstances were that after her eldest child had been assaulted on a bus, she had been advised to accompany the others to school.[1] A tribunal has awarded an addition to cover the transport fares of a claimant attending a non-NHS treatment centre for drug addicts, despite the fact that the Act

13. Handbook, para. 71.
14. Ibid., para. 70.
15. *LAG Bulletin*, Apr. 1975, p. 98.
16. Handbook, para. 75.
17. *Lynes*, p. 79.

18. Handbook, para. 76(4).
19. See Jowell, [1973] P.L. 178, 207–213.
20. Para. 76; also see SBC Annual Report 1976, Cmnd. 6910, para. 7.15.
1. *LAG Bulletin*, Apr. 1975, p. 98.

excludes provision of medical requirements.[2] An ECA has also been paid to a mother to cover the cost of an 'au pair' girl looking after the children, while the former attended college.[3]

iv) The relationship between the long-term rates and ECAs

The long-term addition (now the long-term rates) was introduced in 1966 to save inquiries into the special needs of particular categories of persons on benefit.[4] The intention was that the automatic increase would replace the small discretionary supplements for extra heating costs, dietary requirements, etc. Therefore, the Commission, as a matter of policy, used always to deduct the value of the long-term addition from the ECA it would otherwise have paid. Only that part of the ECA not already covered by the long-term addition would, therefore, be paid. The policy was justified by reference to the provision that in assessing an ECA 'regard *shall* be had' to other additional payments.[5]

However, in *R v Greater Birmingham Appeal Tribunal, ex parte Simper*,[6] it was held by the Divisional Court that this policy was wrong, and that its implementation in every case amounted to an abuse of the discretion conferred on the Commission. The provision did not authorise an automatic deduction of the long-term addition in assessing what should be paid as an ECA. As a matter of law this decision was probably correct, but it required the SBC's officer to make a delicate judgment in each case where a person on the long-term rates claimed an ECA; he would have to decide to what extent the special need was already being covered by the long-term scale rate.

The law was altered by the National Insurance and Supplementary Benefit Act 1973;[7] this substantially restored the position which existed before the *Simper* decision. Now, whenever an ECA is claimed, 50p (or 75p if the claimant *or* his wife is over eighty) is deducted where the long-term rate is being paid.[8] This deduction is not, however, made in three cases: where extra heating expenses are claimed; where an additional sum is payable to cover the housing expenses of a non-householder; and where such a sum is payable to cover special expenses of children.[9]

Thus,

> a supplementary pensioner, seventy-five, claims a special allowance for his diet. This is estimated on the tariff basis to be 75p. Under the above rules, 50p is deducted as he receives the long-term rate, and he is paid 25p only. If he were eighty, he would not receive an ECA. However, if he claimed instead an extra heating allowance, this would be paid in full.

2. Ibid., June 1974, p. 133. See also the case in *Poverty* (1972), No. 23, p. 25, where an applicant received an addition of 70p a week to enable him to buy petrol for his car to travel to the local reference library!
3. *LAG Bulletin*, Nov. 1974, p. 273; also noted, *Poverty* (1974), No. 30, p. 33.
4. See ante, pp. 492–494.
5. SBA 1966, Sch. 2, para. 4(2)(a).
6. [1974] QB 543, [1973] 2 All ER 461.
7. S.6, and Sch. 4, para. 2.
8. SBA 1976, Sch. 1., para. 6(2).
9. Ibid., para 6(3).

At the present moment, the long-term rate for a husband and wife is £4·80 more than the ordinary scale rate, and for a single householder £3·40 more.[10] The mandatory deduction of 50p (or 75p) does not, therefore, substantially reduce the additional benefit payable to a person on the long-term rates.[11] Assuming that they exist to meet the extra requirements of their recipients, there would now seem to be a risk of duplication when an ECA is also awarded.

Part four. Exceptional Needs Payments

A. General

Under section 3 of the Supplementary Benefits Act 1976, the Commission is empowered to make single lump-sum payments for exceptional needs:

> 'Where it appears to the Commission reasonable in all the circumstances they may determine that supplementary benefit shall be paid to a person by way of a single payment to meet an exceptional need.'

Unlike ECAs these exceptional needs payments (ENPs) do not constitute supplements to the weekly benefit. They are isolated grants to meet special cases of need, designed to be 'the exception rather than the rule'.[12] Like ECAs they are discretionary, at least in the sense that the Commission must form a judgment on the facts whether a special need exists, and then must decide how much it is appropriate to pay to meet it.[13] The SBC has formulated general policies as to the types of case in which it will be prepared to award an ENP and the other factors which it will take into account. These are set out in the *Exceptional Needs Payments* Administration Paper published in 1973, as well as in a chapter of the general Handbook.

Lump-sum payments for exceptional needs existed under the 1934 unemployment assistance scheme, and then under the National Assistance Act 1948.[14] Since the latter date, the number of ENPs awarded has increased considerably; in 1949 the number was 102,000, 8·8% of the total number of claimants on national assistance,[15] while the number awarded in 1976 was 1,114,000, well over a third of those in receipt of benefit at the end of the year.[16] However, the total expenditure on ENPs remains comparatively small – in 1976, £24 million, about 2% of total expenditure on supplementary benefits.[17] The increase in the number of ENPs is possibly attributable to greater 'claims-consciousness' on the part of those

10. Ante, pp. 492–494.
11. See SBC Annual Report 1976, ante n.20, at para. 7.10.
12. See Handbook, para. 81.
13. See ante, p. 512, for a discussion of the nature of the Commission's discretion.
14. See SBC Annual Report 1976, ante

n.20, Appendix C, and paras. 7.2–7.10.
15. The figure is taken from the 1973 paper, *Exceptional Needs Payments*, para. 4.
16. SBC Annual Report 1976, ante n.20, at paras. 7.17 and 7.23–7.25.
17. Ibid., at para. 7.17.

eligible and the fact that more recipients of benefit are now advised to claim them by welfare rights agencies.[18]

The Commission is disturbed at the number of ENPs which are now awarded, particularly as the evidence suggests that with more awareness of their existence, even more payments might be claimed and made.[19] In addition to the arguments against discretion already discussed in the context of ECAs,[20] there is some suggestion that local offices vary in their willingness to make awards.[1] For these reasons the SBC is anxious to remove unnecessary discretion in this area, and has recently suggested that automatic lump sums might be paid every six months to all recipients of benefit.[2] It is difficult to believe, however, that there will not remain a residuary discretion to make a special lump sum payment in really exceptional cases.

B. Eligibility for an ENP

The Commission's view is clearly that ENPs are to be awarded only to persons who are entitled to receive weekly benefit. It regards itself as authorised 'to make single lump sum payments to people within the scope of the supplementary benefits scheme, over and above the weekly payments of benefit provided for in the other parts of the Act'.[3] It further claims that it is imperative to preserve equity between those eligible for an ENP and those 'who have retired on an income which may be only just above the supplementary benefit level',[4] the implication being that the latter are ineligible for an ENP. But it is not obvious that there is any legal justification for this attitude. Section 3 of the Act[5] is in general terms, empowering the SBC to award an ENP where it is reasonable in the circumstances. Admittedly under the terms of Section 1,[6] a person is only entitled to an ENP under section 3 'if his resources are insufficient to meet his requirements', but there is nothing here to indicate that 'requirements' means '*weekly* requirements', so that entitlement to a weekly allowance is a necessary condition for the award of an ENP. Moreover, any restrictive interpretation of these words would be impossible to reconcile with the clear meaning of section 3, and it is submitted, therefore, that the later provision in the Act should prevail.[7]

There must be many cases where people are just above the income limits for an award of weekly supplementary benefit, and yet occasionally have a need for, say, bedding or clothing, which cannot be met out of their

---

18. See the research discussed in the SBC Annual Report 1976, ante n.20, at paras. 7.43–7.48.
19. Ibid., at para. 7.49.
20. Ante, p. 513.
 1. SBC Annual Report 1976, Cmnd. 6910, paras. 7.33–7.35.
 2. Ante, p. 514.
 3. *Exceptional Needs Payments*, para. 3.

4. Ibid., at para. 7. See also the Handbook, para. 81.
5. Set out ante, p. 519.
6. Set out in full ante, p. 479.
7. On general principles of statutory interpretation, if a later provision in an Act conflicts with an earlier one, it is the later which prevails: see Maxwell *The Interpretation of Statutes* (12th edn), p. 187.

income.[8] This is particularly likely to be the case with pensioners, who may have an adequate income from their retirement pension and an annuity to meet their weekly requirements, but do not have enough money to purchase such essential goods. On both legal and social grounds, therefore, the argument for a change in the Commission's attitude on this question is very strong. It is interesting to note, incidentally, that the Commission does seem prepared to grant ENPs for hospital visits or for funeral expenses to a person whose income is just above the supplementary benefit limit.[9]

It is clear, however, that a person in full-time employment cannot receive an ENP.[10] Cases of need of those in work can only be met under section 4 of the 1976 Act by an urgent needs payment.[11] The aggregation provisions of the 1976 legislation apply to applications for ENPs as they do to claims for weekly benefit so that only the husband (or man with whom a woman is living) is entitled.[12]

C. Factors taken into account

i) What is an exceptional need?

A number of factors influence the Commission to take what may perhaps be characterised as a cautious approach to the award of ENPs. The first is the requirement of equity between those people on benefit who might be awarded an ENP, and those whose income is above the weekly supplementary benefit level and who, in the Commission's view, cannot claim one.[13] If awards were made for the purchase of, say, washing machines or television sets or top quality clothing, the position of those in receipt of such payments would be better than that of those who have bought these items for themselves only by a careful and judicious marshalling of their resources. The equity principle is certainly comprehensible when a comparison is drawn between people in full-time work and those claiming an ENP; it would not be right to make a grant for an asset which could not be afforded by most people in full-time employment.

Another argument used by the Commission to justify its overall policy is that a number of essential needs are covered by the ordinary weekly scale rates, e.g., to cover the replacement of clothing and footwear.[14] The Commission is, therefore, reluctant to grant an ENP to meet such needs, but it will do so where hardship would otherwise result.[15] In fact it frequently uses its powers in this kind of case, as is evidenced by the fact that over 50% of ENPs are for clothing and footwear.[16] The second category of exceptional need where payment will be made are cases where

8. See Drabble, *LAG Bulletin*, Nov. 1973, p. 246.
9. *Exceptional Needs Payments*, Appendix 1, paras. 2 and 27.
10. For the full-time work exclusion, see ante, pp. 482–483.
11. See ante, p. 483.
12. See *R v Supplementary Benefits*

Commission, ex parte Mainwaring, LAG Bulletin, Feb. 1975, p. 50.
13. *Exceptional Needs Payments*, para. 7.
14. Ibid., at para. 16.
15. Ibid., at para. 15; Handbook, para. 85.
16. SBC Annual Report 1976, ante n.1, at Table 7.4.

the expense is not covered at all by the weekly rates of benefit. These are either periodic major expenses which occur in most people's lives, such as bedding and furniture, or alternatively items such as telephone installation costs and fares for job interviews and hospital visits, where the need arises from less common, individual circumstances.

The Commission recognises, however, that it is not possible to give an exhaustive list of the needs which it may be prepared to meet by the award of an ENP.[17] Pressing needs are a matter largely of individual circumstances and preferences. It is this which makes it difficult to list exceptional needs in a Schedule. Commission officers are not legally bound by the terms of the policies issued by the SBC; they may depart from them and indeed should be prepared to do so in a suitable case and grant an ENP for an item not even mentioned in the Handbook or other guidelines.[18]

ii) The account taken of the applicant's resources

Section 3(2) of the 1976 Act provides:

> 'In determining whether supplementary benefit shall be paid under this section, and the amount of any such benefit, the Commission may have regard to any resources which would otherwise fall to be disregarded under Part III of Schedule 1 to this Act (calculation of resources)'.

Since November 1972, however, the Commission has decided not to take into account any disregarded income for the purpose of deciding whether to make an ENP.[19] The Commission's policy as regards capital is not to grant an ENP if the applicant has sufficient savings, in a realisable form, to leave him with £200 if he pays for the item himself.[20]

This may seem rather rigorous compared with the treatment by the Act of capital in assessing weekly benefit.[1] But it is arguable that, while someone should not be obliged to have resort to his savings in order to tide himself over a period of illness or unemployment, this is not the case with regard to capital purchases. All the Commission's rules in this area are discretionary, and can, therefore, be challenged on appeal in a case where their application causes hardship to the claimant.[2]

iii) Repeated applications by the same applicant

ENPs 'are not made at frequent intervals to the same claimant, unless there is no other way of dealing with the situation'.[3] The Commission is

---

17. Handbook, para. 84, and see SBC Annual Report 1976, ante n.1, at para. 7.18.
18. See ante, pp. 514–515, for a discussion of the effect of policies on the exercise of discretionary powers.
19. See DHSS Annual Report 1972, Cmnd. 5352, para. 12.13.
20. See Lynes, pp. 86–87, and Handbook, para. 80.

1. See ante, p. 506.
2. See the case noted in *LAG Bulletin*, Nov. 1975, p. 292, where a tribunal disregarded savings of £300, on the argument that the claimants (pensioners) were saving to pay for their own burial, and see *New Society*, 17 July 1975, p. 154.
3. Handbook, para. 83.

naturally anxious that claimants should not dissipate their weekly benefit, and then expect it to make regular lump-sum payments. On the other hand, the SBC itself has recognised that the number of such cases is relatively few, and that 'the existence of a debt is by no means evidence always of mismanagement'.[4]

It has evolved a number of policies to protect its funds against excessive claims when it has reason to believe that the applicant has mismanaged his weekly benefit payments. The first is to make deductions from future weekly payments to offset, or to put it more bluntly, recover a lump-sum payment which has been made.[5] This course is of dubious legality, though it might be justified under the power conferred by paragraph 4(1)(b) of Schedule 1 to the 1976 Act to withhold payments in 'exceptional circumstances'.[6] The second procedure is more easily justified under this provision: the Commission makes deductions from future weekly payments, and then pays these over in the form of lump sums either when required or at appropriate intervals.[7] It has been suggested that the claimant would have no entitlement to receive his 'savings'.[8] But this is not clear; it is arguable that their payment could be regarded as a delayed payment of his weekly benefit instead of a discretionary ENP. These practices are followed by the Commission when they award ENPs for clothing, footwear, and for the discharge of fuel debt arrears, all expenses which should be met by the claimant out of his weekly benefit.

iv) The Commission's particular policies[9]

a) CLOTHING AND FOOTWEAR. As has been mentioned,[10] although the weekly rates are intended to cover their replacement, over half the number of ENPs awarded are for clothing and footwear. The Commission has directed that special attention should be paid to the clothing needs of those without capital who have been on benefit for a long time, and those who have recently left hospital.[11]

The Commission has published a standard clothing and bedding list (with prices) as a guide to its officers in determining whether the applicant has an exceptional need.[12] It emphasises, however, that this is not a 'kit-list', showing the mandatory complement of clothing which every person should possess. It is a general guide to be applied flexibly from case to case.[13] Further, the amounts specified on the list are not binding if prices are particularly high in the relevant area.

There are some complex problems about the relationship between the responsibilities of the Commission and local education authorities for the

4. *Exceptional Needs Payments*, para. 21.
5. Handbook, para. 83.
6. See SBC Annual Report 1975, Cmnd. 6615, para. 8.15, though there is no attempt to justify the course legally.
7. Handbook, para. 83.
8. *Lynes*, p. 89.
9. See Handbook, paras. 84–111; *Exceptional Needs Payments*, paras. 14–

28 and Appendix I; and *Lynes*, pp. 89–109.
10. See ante, p. 521.
11. *Exceptional Needs Payments*, para. 25.
12. It is published as Appendix I to the Handbook.
13. *Exceptional Needs Payments*, para. 26; Handbook, para. 86.

provision of school uniform and other children's clothing.[14] It regards the local authority as primarily responsible for these items, but it may be persuaded to help where the authority is reluctant to exercise its powers. In one case, a tribunal awarded the applicant £14 for his child's sportskit, even though the local authority had power to make loans of these items.[15]

b) FUEL DEBTS AND RENT ARREARS. Although utility bills and rent should be met out of the weekly scale rates and rent allowance, the Commission is prepared to award an ENP where there is no other course available and the claimant is in real hardship, e.g., where he is faced with eviction for non-payment of rent, or threatened with immediate discontinuance of gas or electricity supplies.[16] Where there are children in the family, the Commission should consult the local authority social services department which may help in this situation.

c) HOUSE REPAIRS. The Commission includes a notional sum for house repairs in the rent supplement to the weekly benefit of a householder.[17] If this sum is inadequate, it expects the claimant to take out a second mortgage on the property, or secure a local authority loan, to finance such repairs, but in some cases it seems possible to persuade it, or an appeal tribunal, to grant an ENP.[18]

d) BEDDING, FURNITURE AND HOUSEHOLD EQUIPMENT. These expenses total about 26% of all ENPs.[19] The Commission's policy is cautious, having arguably become stricter in the last few years.[20] An ENP will be awarded to enable the claimant to buy new items in the case of beds, sheets, blankets, curtains and floor coverings (generally linoleum).[1] But where the need is for furniture (apart from beds) or household appliances, the claimant is first shown the furniture store of the local authority or a voluntary organisation which may be able to meet his requirements from their stock of second-hand furniture. If the essential items, which include an easy chair or a sofa,[2] are not available from the store or the claimant reasonably refuses those offered, he will be given an ENP to cover the cost of second-hand furniture from a local shop.[3] Only in the last resort will he be awarded a payment to cover the cost of new items.

e) TRAVELLING EXPENSES. Assistance will be given to enable someone to travel for an employment interview, at least if it is out of the locality.[4] In some cases an ENP will also be given to enable the claimant to visit relatives in hospital, even, it seems, if he is not in receipt of weekly supplementary benefit.[5] The position is different if a husband on benefit

14. The complexities are fully discussed in Lynes, pp. 91–94.
15. LAG Bulletin, Jan. 1975, p. 18.
16. Exceptional Needs Payments, para. 20.
17. Ante, p. 500.
18. LAG Bulletin, Nov. 1975, p. 292.
19. See the figures in SBC Annual Report 1976, Cmnd. 6910, Table 7.4.
20. See Lynes, pp. 95–97.
1. Handbook, para. 89; Exceptional Needs Payments, Appendix 1, para. 11.
2 Ibid., para. 10.
3. Handbook, para. 89.
4. Exceptional Needs Payments, Appendix, 1, para. 2.
5. Ibid. See ante, p. 520.

visits his wife in hospital; then for a period the ordinary weekly rates for a married couple are deemed sufficient to cover these expenses.[6] After some controversy, the cost of visiting a relative serving a prison sentence of more than three months is now borne by the Home Office, and payment is administered by the Commission.[7] The Act itself specifically enables the payment of travelling expenses in connection with the benefit claim itself.[8] The travelling costs of a mother attending her son's trial,[9] and of a claimant attending a bankruptcy examination, have also been covered by ENPs.[10]

f) MISCELLANEOUS. There are a number of other cases when the SBC may make an ENP.[11]

> Payments may be made for removal expenses, for the cost of materials for redecoration work, for expectant mothers who do not receive a lump-sum maternity grant because of inadequate contributions,[12] for funeral expenses,[13] and for the installation costs of a telephone where the claimant lives alone and is dangerously isolated.[14]

The fact that the Commission's list is not exhaustive is illustrated by a case noted in the *LAG Bulletin*.[15]

> An appeal tribunal in Bristol awarded the applicant £150 to take a course to teach him to drive a heavy goods vehicle – his employment before a serious accident put him out of work, and for which a special licence in the interim period had become necessary.

Part five. The Withholding and Reduction of Benefit

There are now two principal circumstances in which benefit may be paid below the standard scale rates or may be withheld altogether. The first involves strikers and other persons affected by trade disputes. The second concerns claims by the 'voluntarily unemployed', e.g., people who do not make any real attempt to find employment. A third category, recently abolished by legislation, was that of 'wage stopped' claimants; this is briefly discussed before the other two situations.

---

6. See the special rules for hospital patients on benefit: post, pp. 547–548.
7. See *Poverty* (1968), No. 8, p. 13, and No. 9, p. 5.
8. SBA, 1976, s.14(4).
9. *LAG Bulletin*, Nov. 1974, p. 272.
10. Ibid., Nov. 1975, p. 292.
11. *Exceptional Needs Payments*, Appendix 1; Handbook, paras. 90–98, 102–111; SBC Annual Report 1976, ante n.19, at para. 7.18.

12. For the law concerning maternity grants, see chap. 7, ante, pp. 249–252.
13. This is another case where the SBC seems prepared to make an ENP in favour of a claimant not in receipt of weekly benefit, notwithstanding that burials are provided free of charge by local authorities.
14. See the similar rules with regard to an award of an ECA, see ante, p. 517.
15. Jan. 1975, pp. 18–19.

A. The wage stop[16]

Prior to 1975 where a claimant was obliged to register for employment, his benefit could not 'exceed what would be his net weekly earnings if he were engaged in full-time work in his normal occupation'.[17] The purpose of the wage stop was not, as was often alleged, to induce people on benefit to secure work, but 'to ensure that an unemployed man's income is no greater than it would be if he were in full-time employment'.[18] The intention, in other words, was to secure equity between low wage-earners and unemployed persons, whose earnings in work would be no higher than those of the former.

The number of claimants affected by the wage stop steadily declined in the early 1970s, because the economic position of low earners gradually improved partly as a result of the introduction of FIS. Thus, in November 1970, about 34,000 families were affected by it, but four years later the corresponding number was only 8,000.[19] It began to seem ungenerous to retain the provision for this small number, and it was abolished by section 19 of the Child Benefit Act 1975.[20]

B. Persons affected by trade disputes

i) Introduction

With the possible exception of the cohabitation rule,[1] there is no area of the supplementary benefits scheme which has been more controversial than that governing the award of benefit to strikers and their families. The merits of the present law and its administration raise political issues on which views sharply differ. Nevertheless, the legal position has remained remarkably consistent for the last seventy five years or so. Under the poor law, the striker himself could not lawfully be maintained out of the rates, unless he was completely destitute, though his wife and children could be so supported.[2] Under the present law, a 'striker'[3] can only claim benefit for himself if there is an urgent need, which the Commission has a discretionary power to meet, though his wife and children are legally entitled to benefit.

16. For a full treatment of the wage stop, see *Lynes*, (2nd edn), pp. 110–126; Weir, *LAG Bulletin*, July 1973, p. 145. The rules and Commission policy are outlined in the Handbook of November 1974, paras. 77–84. Also see Stevenson *Claimant or Client?* (1973) pp. 84–86. For the comparable position in Germany, see Müller-Fembeck and Ogus, 25 ICLQ 382, 395.

17. SBA 1966, Sch. 2, para. 5(2).

18. *Administration of the wage stop*: Report by the SBC (1967), para. 4.

19. See *LAG Bulletin*, Feb. 1975, p. 33.

20. This is virtually ten years after the retention of the wage stop was criticised during the Second Reading

of the Ministry of Social Security Bill in 1966 by a Conservative MP, Mr M. Macmillan, 729 HC Deb., col. 406. But the Conservative government 1970–74. of which Mr Macmillan was a member, did nothing about the provision.

1. See ante, pp. 404–408.

2. *A-G v Guardians of the Poor of the Merthyr Tydfil Union* [1900] 1 Ch. 516.

3. This term is used for convenience in this section, though the definition of a person disqualified from claiming benefit for his own requirements goes well beyond the conventional definition of a 'striker': see post, p. 527.

The arguments against supporting strikers and their dependants with supplementary benefit are first, that it is wrong for people withholding their labour, for the purpose of 'inducing' their employers to pay them higher wages, to be supported by the general taxpaying public; and secondly, that the existence of welfare payments encourages a larger number and the longer duration of strikes.[4] The first argument is easy to formulate with regard to the strikers themselves: they are not the deserving poor and should not expect militancy to be subsidised.[5] It is less attractive when applied to their dependants; the proposition must then be that the primary responsibility for their welfare rests with the strikers themselves and their unions. The second argument has been frequently voiced, particularly by some Conservatives, since the increase in strikes which took place in the late 1960s and early 1970s. But the view that the availability of supplementary benefits encourages industrial unrest has been strongly challenged.[6]

It is sometimes contended that Britain is unusually generous in the benefits it affords strikers and their families.[7] In the United States, however, both the general assistance provided by the states and the federally financed AFDC (Aid for Families with Dependent Children) are available for strikers, or in the latter case, for the benefit of their children.[8] Further, the position of the striker claiming assistance there is generally not sharply distinguished from that of any person voluntarily unemployed. The question in the case of a striker, as for a person who has left his work for some other reason, is whether he is available for employment.[9]

Since the National Assistance Act 1948, the British system has made special provision for persons involved in trade disputes independently of voluntary unemployment.[10] The fundamental provision is now section 8(1) of the Supplementary Benefits Act 1976:

'Subject to subsection (2) below, where a person –
(a) is, by reason of a stoppage of work which is due to a trade dispute at his place of employment, without employment for any period during the stoppage; and
(b) has not during that stoppage become bona fide employed elsewhere in the occupation which he usually follows, or become regularly engaged in some other occupation;

4. See the discussion of the analogous arguments used for the 'trade disputes disqualification' in unemployment benefit: ante, pp. 122–123.
5. For a particularly robust assertion of this view, see Page in ed. Boyson *Down with the Poor* (1971).
6. Durcan & McCarthy [1974] British Journal of Industrial Relations, 26. A more cautious view is expressed by Hunter, ibid., at p. 438. See 39 U.Chi.L.Rev. 79, 101–106.
7. Sir K. Joseph, Secretary of State, 838 HC Deb., cols. 1231–1233.
8. See La France et al., *Law of the Poor* (1973), pp. 367–368; 67 North West L.
Rev. 245. In an important New York decision, it was ruled that the provision of general assistance to strikers did not violate the state's policy of neutrality in labour disputes: *Lascaris v Wyman*, 340 NYS 2d. 397 (1972).
9. *La France, et al.*, loc. cit.
10. The concept also appears in SBA 1976, s. 25(2), under which a person is not liable for the offence of a failure to maintain himself or any other persons by reason of anything done or not done in the course of a trade dispute – a rare example of exempting an individual from the general provisions of the criminal law.

his requirements for that period shall be disregarded for the purposes of supplementary benefit except so far as those requirements include the requirement to provide for any other person'.

Subsection (2) provides that this does not apply where a person proves 'that he is not participating in or directly interested in the trade dispute which caused the stoppage of work'. The provision mirrors that in section 19 of the Social Security Act 1975 (as amended), which disqualifies a person involved in a trade dispute from claiming unemployment benefit.[11] There is a considerable body of case-law concerning this disqualification, and the Commission regards this as binding when determining whether a claimant is disqualified on this ground from supplementary benefit.[12] On appeal, the supplementary benefits tribunal must refer the case to a local insurance tribunal for determination;[13] there is a further appeal to the National Insurance Commissioner.[14]

The effect of section 8(1) is to disqualify a single striker, without wife or children, from receiving supplementary benefit at all. Where a husband and wife are both involved in a trade dispute, the same total disqualification applies. But otherwise, the weekly requirements of a striker's wife and dependent children will be met.

ii) The single striker

The only recourse open to a single striker, who faces destitution, is to apply for an urgent needs payment, which the Commission may decide to award under section 4 of the 1976 Act.[15] Before 1973 there was no national policy on the criteria for making such a payment, the regard (if any) which should be paid to the claimant's resources, and the amount of any award. In February 1973, partly as a reponse to the increasing number of claims, particularly during the post office workers' and miners' strikes in 1971 and 1972 respectively, general rules were formulated by the Commission.[16] In determining whether there is an urgent need, all the claimant's income will be taken into account, including any strike pay, tax rebates and his last payment of wages. This payment will be assumed to cover his requirements at the rate of £11·00 a week.[17] Thus,

> if the last wage packet was £55·00, he will be ineligible for an urgent needs payment for the following five weeks. Indeed, it will often be at least six weeks before a single striker will be able to benefit from public funds; owing to the practice in manufacturing industry of working a 'week in hand', a striker will frequently receive his last

11. For the disqualification from unemployment benefit, see chap. 3, ante, pp. 122–130, where the legal difficulties of the provisions in the Social Security Act are fully discussed.
12. Handbook, para. 161.
13. SBA 1976, s.15(2).
14. See post, p. 650, for adjudication of these cases.
15. For a general article on urgent needs payments, see Jordan, *LAG Bulletin*, Dec. 1974, p. 300.
16. Gennard and Lasko British Journal of Industrial Relations (1974) 1, 3–4.
17. Handbook, para. 162.

wages a week after the dispute has begun, and this will be presumed to cover his requirements for the next five weeks.

It seems, moreover, that the Commission will generally not help unless either the claimant is in danger of being evicted from lodgings, or he lives alone and has no relatives to turn to for assistance.[18] If these onerous conditions are satisfied, the SBC will bring his income up to £8·50 a week, but this may be increased in exceptional circumstances.

The number of payments rose quite dramatically in the 1960s and early 1970s, presumably as a result of greater claims-consciousness on the part of strikers and their unions. In 1950 and 1951, no money at all was spent by the NAB in assisting single strikers; in 1964 the sum was only £602, but in 1972, the year of the first miners' strike under that Conservative government, £181,000 was paid to single strikers.[19] In 1975, the corresponding figure was only £2,080.[20]

iii) Strikers with dependants

The wife and children of a person affected by a trade dispute are entitled to have their requirements met by the Commission. Naturally there is nothing to prevent the striker from sharing in the benefit paid to them. In practice the wife's requirements are assessed as those of an adult non-householder,[1] those of the children at the standard scale rates, and the rent is usually met in full. In cases of hardship, where this sum is not enough to meet the family's needs, the Commission will be prepared to entertain an application for an ECA,[2] and it might also award the striker himself an urgent needs payment.

Although the striker's own requirements are not met, there is no reason why the normal rules about resources should not be applied, so that his capital and income are taken into account in assessing the benefit payable to his family. Such resources would include tax rebates and strike pay. However, the Supplementary Benefits Commission, following the practice of the NAB, used in its discretion to disregard this income up to the amount the striker himself would have received in benefit if he had not been disqualified. The effect of this practice was that while the state supported the striker's family, the unions could substantially help the striker himself without adversely affecting the level of benefit.[3]

During the late 1960s and early 1970s the amount of money paid by the Commission to strikers' dependants increased dramatically, doubling virtually every year.[4] During the first four months of 1971, more money was paid out in benefits to strikers' families by the Commission than during all the years to 1970 since the end of the war! The first Wilson

18. See *Lynes*, p. 112; Handbook, para. 162.
19. The figures taken from the Annual Reports of the DHSS are given in Gennard and Lasko, ante n.16, at p. 11.
20. See the figures given in the SBC Annual Report 1975 Cmnd. 6615,

Table 12.
1. *Lynes*, p. 112; it is not clear why the wife's requirements are not assessed as those of a householder.
2. Ante, pp. 511–519.
3. Gennard and Lasko, ante n.16, at p. 5.
4. Ibid., at pp. 9–20.

government introduced a measure, the National Superannuation and Social Insurance- Bill, which would have tightened up the law in some respects, but it lapsed when the 1970 General Election was called. When the Conservatives were returned, they passed the Social Security Act 1971 to stem the flow of funds, and presumably, though this was rarely stated by government spokesmen, to deter strikes. In the last few years the amount of money awarded to strikers' families has fluctuated largely according to the number of strikes; in 1975 only £776,441 was paid, less than 0·06% of all supplementary benefit payments,[5] and there was a further decline in 1976.[6]

iv) The reforms of 1971

a) THE TREATMENT OF RESOURCES. The first change brought about by the Social Security Act 1971 was to provide that tax refunds and strike pay were to be taken into account as resources of the family claiming benefit,[7] subject now to the disregard of £4·00.[8] The reform put an end to the generous policy of the Commission described in the previous subsection. Clearly the intention was that more of the burden of supporting a striker and his family should pass to the union, as supplementary benefit is in effect 'reduced' after the first £4·00 of strike pay has been disregarded. In fact it seems probable that the reform has not succeeded in its objective. First, strike pay is almost always only given when the dispute is official, so the change does not affect a large number of strikes. Secondly and more importantly, it has apparently led to a reduction in the strike benefits paid by many trades unions, and a diversion of funds to other purposes.[9] Moreover, only payments which the person concerned 'receives or is entitled to obtain . . . ' are to be treated as income;[10] as most strike benefits are payable at the discretion of the union, the provision in practice only covers payments actually received.

Normally tax refunds are treated as capital resources of a claimant.[11] From 1971 it has been provided that any sum which

'(i) becomes available to him; or
(ii) would become available to him on application being duly made;
by way of repayment of income tax . . . ' [is to be treated as income]
'except so far as the repayment in question is attributable to any period of absence from work through sickness or other similar cause or to any period of unemployment . . . '[12]

5. SBC Annual Report 1975, ante n.20, at Table 12.
6. SBC Annual Report 1976, Cmnd. 6910, para. 2.21.
7. SBA 1976, Sch. 1, para. 26.
8. Ibid., at para. 23: ante, pp. 507–511, for disregards.
9. Gennard and Lasko, ante n.16, at p. 7; Lasko, 38 MLR 31, 34.
10. SBA 1976, Sch. 1, para. 26(1)(b).
11. See ante, p. 507.
12. Now SBA 1976, Sch. 1, para. 26(1)(a).

The first point is that this provision does not only apply to those affected by the trade dispute disqualification in section 8 of that Act.[13] It covers all those temporarily laid off work as a result of any trade dispute, whether they are involved in it or not. Secondly, tax refunds are to be treated as income if they *could be claimed* by the worker from the employer or the local tax office. The provision was designed to penalise those who hitherto had not claimed tax rebates during the period of the strike and who had been able to rely on supplementary benefit for their family needs.[14] It is arguably reasonable, as the usual treatment of tax refunds as capital rather than income is perhaps generous.

b) EARNINGS DURING THE FIRST FIFTEEN DAYS AFTER RETURN TO WORK. Although generally a person in full-time employment cannot receive supplementary benefit, this disqualification does not apply to the first fifteen days after his return to work following, say, a period of sickness or unemployment.[15] He is then entitled to receive benefit, calculated according to the normal rules. In assessing his resources, the £4·00 (or £6·00) earnings disregard is applied.[16] However, special rules apply with regard to claimants returning to employment after a trade dispute, whether they are disqualified under section 8(1) of the Act or not.[17] First, any advance of earnings made or *offered* to a person returning to work is to be included in his resources; secondly, the normal £4·00 (or £6·00) disregard is not given.[18] The disregard in this situation is only to be applied to the amount by which his actual earnings (from all sources) exceed his earnings from full-time work – thus, if he has no other earnings, there is no disregard at all.

The purpose of this provision, introduced by section 1(3) of the Social Security Act 1971, in conjunction with that discussed in the next paragraph concerning the repayment of benefit paid during this fifteen day period, was to reduce reliance by these workers on supplementary benefits rather than on the advance of wages offered by their employers, generally called the 'sub'.[19] Throughout the late 1960s union members had become increasingly unwilling to take an advance on wages, repayable to the employer, preferring instead to receive unrepayable and untaxable supplementary benefit.[20] In this context, the reform is certainly understandable. On the other hand, it affected all persons returning to work after a trade dispute at their place of employment, whether the stoppage was attributable to a strike or lock-out, and whether they were participating in the dispute or not.[1]

13. See ante, p. 527.
14. Standing Committee F Debates on Social Security Bill 1971, cols. 159–160 (Mr Alison, Under-Secretary of State).
15. See ante, p. 482.
16. For these disregards, see ante, pp. 507–509.
17. See ante, p. 527.
18. SBA 1976, Sch. 1, para. 22(3).
19. An advance of wages may be offered because of the common practice of working a 'week in hand', so that wages are not paid till the end of the second week of work. Sometimes two weeks or even a month may be worked in hand.
20. See the figures given by Sir K. Joseph, Standing Committee F Debates on the Social Security Bill 1971, col. 197.
1. Mr R. Prentice, ibid., at cols. 192–193.

c) RECOVERY OF BENEFIT PAID DURING FIRST 15 DAYS AFTER RETURN TO WORK. The third reform made by the Conservative government only applies to persons affected by the disqualification now contained in section 8 of the 1976 Act. Any benefit paid to such a person for the first fifteen days after his return to work is recoverable by the SBC.[2] When an award is made, the Commission sends the Secretary of State and the claimant a notice to the effect that recoverable benefit has been paid, and stating the amount and the claimant's 'protected earnings'. These are the level of earnings below which no deduction may be made: they are now the applicant's weekly requirements plus £3·00, less any child benefit which forms part of his resources.[3] The Secretary of State must then serve a deduction notice on the claimant's employer, requiring him to deduct from the weekly wages up to one tenth of the total sum to be recovered, subject to the protected earnings figure. With the employee's consent more than one tenth may be deducted in a week. A notice will usually operate for a maximum of fourteen weeks, though if the full amount has not been recovered by then, the Secretary of State may serve a fresh notice on the claimant's employer. It seems that in practice the DHSS waives recovery if little has been recovered under the first deduction notice.[4]

Although the procedure under which an employer is responsible for discharging his employee's debts by making deductions from his wages is familiar in English law,[5] its use in this area was criticised by the opposition during the Committee debates. A number of employers feel it endangers labour relations, and it seems that some of them are prepared to make the repayments to the DHSS themselves.[6]

v) Further reform proposals

Dissatisfied with the apparent lack of results of the 1971 changes in reducing strikes or the level of benefits for strikers' families, some Conservative politicians and lawyers have made further proposals to tighten the law. It has been suggested that every striker should be deemed to receive a certain sum from his union; the effect would be to reduce benefits for strikers' families by that amount and pass the burden of maintaining them to the union.[7]

A more radical proposal was introduced in 1973 by Mr. Ralph Howell. Under this Bill, which never proceeded further than a formal introduction, the right of strikers' families to benefit would have been withdrawn, and the power to make urgent needs payments to strikers themselves would have been abrogated. The wife would have been able to claim an urgent needs payment for herself and her children, though it would, of course, be difficult to quantify this without indirectly benefiting the striker, e.g., by giving the wife a payment for rent. The practical difficulties of such a

---

2. See now SBA 1976, s.9, and Sch. 3.
3. Ibid., s.9(5).
4. Gennard and Lasko, British Journal of Industrial Relations (1974), p. 9.
5. See the Attachment of Earnings Act 1971, under which employers are

required to deduct maintenance payments from their employee's wages. There is a full discussion in *Finer*, paras. 4.140–4.149.
6. Gennard and Lasko, ante n.4.
7. Mr J. Page, 852 HC Deb., col. 1696.

radical change are clearly immense.[8] Nevertheless, proposals along these
lines have been recommended by the Society of Conservative Lawyers,[9]
and they appeared in an unspecific form, in the Conservative Manifesto at
the General Elections in 1974. Hostility to state aid for strikers is acknowledged to be widespread, as is the feeling that they and their unions should
assume primary responsibility for the welfare of their families. But radical
reform on these lines still seems relatively unlikely.

c. The voluntarily unemployed

i) Introduction

In any society where the 'work ethic' is important, it is inevitable that there
will be reluctance to extend assistance to those who are capable of
supporting themselves in employment, but refuse to obtain work.[10] Such
people, the 'work-shy' or 'scroungers' as they are often called, understandably arouse the resentment of the taxpaying public. Nevertheless, it
is important to understand the real nature of the problems involved.[11]
There is considerable argument about the part played by medical, psychological and social factors in bringing about unresponsive attitudes to
work: is, for example, a person with a history of mental illness, partly
attributable to frequent redundancies, to be dismissed as 'work-shy'
merely because he has difficulties in obtaining or staying in a job?[12] There
are almost certainly some cases where the system is exploited by those who
are perfectly capable of obtaining employment, but prefer to live off
welfare payments;[13] the difficulty is in distinguishing them from those who
have a genuine medical or psychological problem.

Not only is there uncertainty about the precise nature of the 'voluntary
unemployment' problem, there is also, as might be expected, doubt about
its scale. Statistics relating to the number and duration of claims for
supplementary benefit by the unemployed are given in the Commission's
Annual Report for 1976.[14] But there is no detailed breakdown of these
figures which would enable any reliable estimate to be made of the
numbers of the 'voluntarily unemployed'. The Fisher Committee
concluded that it is,

> 'fair to assume that a proportion of the younger men, and a far
> greater proportion of the older men, who are unemployed and in
> receipt of benefit for long periods are unemployed because of
> economic conditions or because of some physical or mental
> disability'.[15]

8. Gennard and Lasko, ante n.4, at pp. 22–25.
9. *Financing Strikers*, July 1974, discussed by Lasko, 38 MLR 31.
10. See ante, pp. 10–11.
11. See in particular Stevenson *Claimant or Client?*, chaps. 4 and 5; Hill, Harrison, Sargeant and Talbot *Men out of Work* (1973); Hill *Policies for the*
Unemployed: Help or Coercion? (1974), CPAG pamphlet 15.
12. *Stevenson*, ante n.11, at pp. 86–102.
13. See in particular the evidence of the SBC to the Fisher Committee, para. 266.
14. SBC Annual Report 1976, Cmnd. 6910, ch. 4.
15. Para. 246.

This observation would appear to be even more true today when unemployment has risen – so that in some areas there are 100 unskilled workers available for every vacancy.[16]

When introducing the Second Reading of the Social Security Bill 1971 (which made provision for a reduced benefit for the voluntarily unemployed)[17] Sir Keith Joseph remarked that about 10,000 people would be affected by the measure at any one time, of whom between one half and two thirds were single men.[18] The fact that the number is probably quite small is, of course, no argument one way or the other as to the merits of any proposal to reduce the benefit payable to this group of the unemployed. But it does show that the significance of the problem in terms of the total amount of payments should not be exaggerated.

Some of the rules and practices now considered in detail are specifically authorised by the Supplementary Benefits Act 1976; others are applied under the general discretionary power of the Commission to reduce or withhold a supplementary allowance in 'exceptional circumstances'.[19]

ii) Reductions in benefit: the 40% rule[20]

In certain circumstances the amount of benefit payable to an unemployed claimant may be reduced for a maximum of six weeks by an amount up to 40% of the single householder's ordinary scale rate.[1] The circumstances are broadly that he has been disqualified from receiving unemployment benefit as a result of being dismissed for misconduct, leaving his work voluntarily, or refusing suitable employment without good cause, or that he would be disqualified (in the Commission's view) on one of these grounds if he were to apply for that benefit.[2] Before the introduction of this provision by the Social Security Act 1971, the discretionary practice of the Commission had been to deduct 75p a week from the benefit payable to those voluntarily unemployed; but the government did not consider this enough to prevent someone leaving his employment frivolously, knowing that supplementary benefit would be payable at almost the full rate.

> 'We are seeking to do something relatively delicate to increase the deduction to a level which will enter into motivation without damaging severely the household concerned'.[3]

As might be expected, there was some criticism of the provision, but it was somewhat muted by the fact that a similar proposal had been part of the previous Labour government's National Superannuation and Social Insurance Bill!

16. See SBC Annual Report 1976, ante n.14, at paras. 4.8–4.10.
17. Post, p. 535.
18. 816 HC Deb., col. 51.
19. SBA 1976, Sch. 1, para. 4(1)(b).
20. Moore, *LAG Bulletin*, Aug. 1974, p. 183. This article is useful with regard to a number of the voluntary unemployment rules. See also SBC Annual Report 1975, Cmnd. 6615, paras. 8, 17–18.

1. SBA 1976, Sch. 1, para. 9.
2. For these grounds of disqualification from unemployment benefit, see ante, pp. 108–115.
3. Sir K. Joseph, Secretary of State, Standing Committee F Debates on the Social Security Bill 1971, col. 48.

It should be noted that the deduction may only be made for the six weeks or less during which unemployment benefit is not payable. The deduction is of 40% of the single householder's ordinary scale rate of benefit, or of the lower non-householder's rate if that is appropriate. It may not be more than 40% of the former figure but it may be less in certain circumstances. This power to reduce it is not specifically conferred by the Schedule to the Act itself, but presumably exists under the Commission's general power to pay more than the scale rates in 'exceptional circumstances'.[4] The Commission has instructed its officers that a lower deduction should be made in five sets of circumstances. Among these are cases where there is sickness in the family, where the claimant's wife is pregnant or there are very young children in the family, or where the claimant's last employment was of short duration or produced low wages.[5] But unless the circumstances are quite exceptional, a 75p deduction at least will be made to preserve the principle that the disallowance or suspension of unemployment benefit for industrial misconduct, etc., should not be a matter of indifference to a claimant 'who knows he can obtain supplementary benefit instead'.[6]

The question whether a claimant should be disqualified from receiving unemployment benefit on one of the relevant grounds is often an extremely difficult one on which there is a considerable number of decisions of the National Insurance Commissioners.[7] Where the insurance officer has already taken a decision to disallow benefit, then there is no difficulty for the Commission: the 40% deduction is made automatically. But where the officer is still making inquiries, it will be for the Commission itself to arrive at a judgment on the basis of the unemployment benefit case-law. In certain situations the Commission has instructed its officers not to make any deduction before the decision on entitlement to unemployment benefit; this, for example, is typically done where the claimant was dismissed from his previous employment because he had absented himself to look after a sick wife, or where he refused employment because of physical defects.[8] It was argued by the Labour opposition during the Committee stage of the 1971 Bill that the deduction should never be made until after the insurance officer had decided the unemployment benefit question, but the amendment to this effect was defeated.[9] Now if the unemployment benefit question is eventually decided, contrary to the Commission's view, in the applicant's favour, the amount of the deductions wrongly made will be paid to the claimant,[10] but this does not compensate for the loss of the particular sums at the time.

In view of the discretionary power to reduce the deduction, there is perhaps nothing particularly obnoxious in the 40% rule. It certainly has not encountered the objections which have been made to the practice of the Commission in withholding benefit altogether, or the former 'four-week

4. SBA 1976, Sch. 1, para. 4(1)(a): ante, pp. 511–519.
5. Handbook, para. 197.
6. Ibid., para. 196.
7. See chap. 3, ante, pp. 108–115.
8. *LAG Bulletin*, Aug. 1974, p. 183; *Fisher*, para. 256.
9. Standing Committee F Debates on Social Security Bill 1971, cols. 26ff.
10. Handbook, para. 195.

rule'.[11] The one unfortunate aspect is that the scope of 'industrial misconduct', etc., is so broad in unemployment benefit law that the deduction may well be made in a case where the applicant cannot really be said to be voluntarily unemployed.[12]

iii) The refusal and discontinuance of supplementary benefit

The second means which the Commission may employ to limit claims by the voluntarily unemployed is simply to refuse, or discontinue, the payment of all benefit. This draconian practice is adopted only exceptionally, *either* where it has been decided that the claimant has left his work without good reason or has been dismissed for misconduct, and there is a particular job immediately open to and suitable for him, *or* alternatively it is found that there have been several incidents of voluntary unemployment and there are abundant job opportunities for the claimant.[13] In other words, benefit is only denied to work-avoiders or 'shirkers'. This occurred in 15,000 cases during 1971, so the power is clearly significant.[14] In view of this, the doubts as to the legality of the Commission's practice are particularly important.

It takes the view that paragraph 4(1)(b) of Schedule 1 to the 1976 Act (power to reduce or withhold benefit 'in exceptional circumstances') gives it power to deny benefit to voluntarily unemployed claimants in suitable cases. The Fisher Committee expressed doubt whether the range of cases where an award is refused can really be said to constitute 'exceptional circumstances', and, therefore, whether the exercise of the power was lawful.[15] Though clearly the point is arguable, it is suggested that this scepticism is unfounded. The number of 'exceptional circumstances' in which the Commission exercises its power to *increase* benefit is, as has been seen,[16] infinitely various, and there seems no logical reason why the phrase should have a narrower meaning for the purpose of the power to *reduce*. In any case, the previous paragraph makes it clear that the Commission exercises its discretion within a relatively narrow range of circumstances.[17] But the Fisher Committee was on surer ground when it criticised the failure of the legislation to spell out more clearly the circumstances in which benefit could be refused.

Since the Committee in principle approved of the Commission's practice of denying benefit in certain cases and its legality has not been challenged, the continued use of the power to discontinue or withhold benefit in these circumstances seems reasonable.[18] There is, however, a powerful argument for amending the legislation so that the circumstances

---

11. Post, pp. 537–538.
12. For the meaning of 'industrial misconduct' in unemployment benefit law, see chap. 3, ante, pp. 109–111.
13. See Handbook, para. 189. A fuller statement of the Commission's policy, of which this is only a summary, appears in para. 259 of the Fisher Committee's Report.
14. *Fisher*, para. 233. In 1975 the power was used in 4,000 cases: SBC Annual

Report 1975, ante n.20, at para. 8.10.
15. *Fisher*, para. 257.
16. Ante, pp. 516–519.
17. The amendment to the Schedule made by SS(MP)A 1977, s.14(8) to the effect that 'exceptional circumstances' includes classes of case where there are exceptional circumstances would appear to reinforce the Commission's view.
18. Cp., *Lynes*, p. 126.

in which the Commission has power to deny benefit, and the factors it may take into account in exercising its discretion, are clearly spelt out.[19]

iv) The four-week warning

The present policy is largely a modification of the notorious four-week rule, which it superseded in 1974.[20] Under this the SBC in certain cases made an award limited to four weeks. If the claimant did not then reapply for its renewal, he received no further benefit.[1] The rule was applied to any single, unskilled workman under forty-five in areas where there were good employment opportunities, on the assumption that he ought to have found work within a month.[2]

Its legality was doubted on the ground that there was no specific power in the Act or regulations to make awards of benefit limited in duration.[3] But the doubt was not shared by the Fisher Committee which in principle supported the four-week rule: it saved the Commission a great deal of expenditure and time in investigating the circumstances of individual claimants, and also induced them to seek work quickly.[4]

Despite this support, the four-week rule continued to attract criticism.[5] It was suspended nationally during the three-day week at the end of 1973, and has now been replaced by the present procedure. Under this, in areas where the Employment Service Agency advises that there are good employment opportunities, a single, unskilled claimant under forty-five may be warned that if he does not find employment within four weeks, he may be asked to attend for an interview with a specialist unemployment review officer to discuss why he has not found work and his general employment problems.[6] If he can show that he has made serious efforts to find work or that his difficulty is attributable to some handicap or impediment, then benefit will continue to be paid. Only if it is found that the claimant is 'work-shy', or if he fails without good excuse to attend for the interview, will it be withdrawn. A similar four-week warning may be given to skilled or married claimants under forty-five if they have been in receipt of benefit for three months.[7] At the moment of writing, the four-week warning procedure is not generally in force because of the high level of unemployment. It is applied in a few areas, mostly seaside resorts, where there is plenty of work available.[8]

19. The Commission has defended the existence of its broad discretionary powers on the ground that it would be difficult to be more precise in the legislation: see SBC Annual Report 1975, ante n.20, at para. 8.11.
20. For criticism of the four-week rule, see Stevenson *Claimant or Client?* (1973), pp. 110–111; *LAG Bulletin*, Aug. 1974, p. 185; Lynes *New Society*, 20 Jan. 1972.
1. From 1971 the claimant was told, when the award was made, that it was for four weeks, and that after that he would have to reapply for benefit. This at least gave him in effect the chance of a hearing before benefit was 'denied'. In the United States, a fair hearing is constitutionally required before a welfare benefit may be terminated: see *Goldberg v Kelly* 397 US 254 (1970).
2. The rule was frequently suspended, nationally or in particular regions, if unemployment was particularly high.
3. *Fisher*, para. 263. (The sceptic was Lynes.)
4. Ibid., at paras. 265–266.
5. See esp. *Lynes* (2nd edn), pp. 141–146.
6. For these officers, see post, p. 579.
7. Handbook, paras. 199–200.
8. SBC Annual Report 1976, Cmnd. 6910, paras. 8.12–8.13.

It may be argued that the change in policy is one of form rather than substance. The difference seems principally to be that now benefit is payable until it is withdrawn (presumably under the powers conferred on the Commission by paragraph 4(1)(b)),[9] whereas previously it was only payable for a month unless specifically renewed. But this difference may be important; the claimant now has a continuing right unless found to be unwilling to secure employment, and this decision is only to be taken by a specialist officer.

v) Re-establishment centres and training courses[10]

In some cases the Commission may take positive steps to help voluntarily unemployed claimants acquire a responsive attitude to work. Under section 10 of the Supplementary Benefits Act 1976, it may apply to a supplementary benefits appeal tribunal for a direction that it may use the various powers conferred by that section in respect of a person claiming benefit who is refusing to maintain himself or his wife and children.[11] (A direction, however, cannot be made in respect of a claimant in receipt of unemployment benefit.) If the tribunal makes a direction, the Commission may determine that benefit be paid conditionally on the claimant's attendance at an approved course of training or instruction. Alternatively the Commission may decide that he should attend a re-establishment centre. A third possibility is that he might be required to attend a place similar to a re-establishment centre, organised by a government department or a voluntary organisation, though apparently this alternative is never used.[12] In practice, too, it is unusual for a claimant to be required to attend an approved course of training,[13] so the discussion here is concentrated on the re-establishment centres.

First established on an experimental basis under the 1948 legislation, there are now seventeen such centres, three of which have residential facilities.[14] The vast majority attending them do so voluntarily rather than in pursuance of a direction under section 10.[15] Their purpose is to provide 'the occupation, instruction or training requisite to fit' those attending them 'for entry into, or return to, regular employment'.[16] It seems they are relatively successful in reviving enthusiasm for work,[17] an achievement which is particularly creditable in light of the fact they are only used by the long-term unemployed for whom employment is difficult to find.

The Commission has a broad discretion to pay benefit to a person attending a re-establishment centre.[18] In practice the ordinary weekly benefit is paid where he is attending daily, with an addition to cover travelling expenses; a claimant at a residential centre receives an allowance

9. See ante, p. 536.
10. See generally, *Stevenson*, ante n.20, at pp. 116–121.
11. See SBA 1976, s.17, for liability to maintain.
12. *Fisher*, para. 279.
13. Ibid., at para. 278.
14. Handbook, Appendix 3.

15. In 1976, 2,444 attended voluntarily and only thirty-nine following a tribunal direction: SBC Annual Report 1976, ante n.8, at para. 14.6.
16. SBA 1976, Sch. 5, para. 1. Also see S.I. 1970/1765.
17. *Fisher*, para. 281; SBC Annual Report 1976, ante n.8, at paras. 14.6–14.8.
18. SBA 1976, s.10(4)(b).

for personal expenses, while his family is paid the normal benefit less that sum.[19]

vi) Criminal prosecution

Section 25(1) of the 1976 Act (as amended)[20] provides that,

> where a 'person persistently refuses or neglects to maintain himself or any person whom ... he is liable to maintain', and as a result of this, benefit is payable or free board and lodging are provided for him or the dependant at a reception centre,[1] he shall be liable summarily to imprisonment for 3 months, a fine of £400 or both.[2]

Prosecution is very rare, and only used as a last resort when all else has failed. The number brought against unemployed claimants has declined: in the late 1960s the average number a year was about 100, but in 1971 it had dropped to sixty-four.[3] In 1975 there were only twenty-three prosecutions.[4]

It does seem that about half of those concerned work considerably longer in the year following the prosecution, but overall the success of this method of control of the voluntarily unemployed is open to doubt.[5] The Fisher Committee concluded that there was no reason for thinking that insufficient use was made of prosecutions under this section:

> 'We agree that it is a measure which should be used only when all other methods of getting a man back to work have failed, and that care should be taken not to prosecute people who are seriously hampered by some physical, mental, or social disability'.[6]

Part six. Supplementary Benefits and Maintenance

A. Introduction

This Part is concerned with the award of benefit to separated and divorced wives and to unmarried mothers, and its relationship to maintenance and affiliation payments. Problems arise because the Supplementary Benefits Act 1976 imposes a duty on a husband and wife to maintain each other and

19. *Lynes*, p. 120; *LAG Bulletin*, Aug. 1974, p. 184.
20. SS(MP)A 1977, s.14(6).
 1. Reception centres, of which there are twenty-two, provide temporary board and lodging, generally for men without a family and 'without a settled way of living': see SBA 1976, Sch. 5, para. 2; and Handbook, paras. 250–253. Also see SBC Annual Report 1976, ante n.8, at paras. 14.9–14.13.
 2. SBA 1976, s.25(2) provides that a person shall not be deemed to refuse to maintain himself or any other person,

'by reason only of anything done or omitted in furtherance of a trade dispute'.
 3. *Fisher*, para. 442.
 4. SBA Annual Report 1975, Cmnd. 6615, at Table 25. These figures are for the prosecutions of the unemployed. Prosecutions are also sometimes brought where a man refuses to maintain his wife and children: this is discussed, post p. 544.
 5. See Stevenson *Claimant or Client?* (1973), pp. 121–124.
 6. *Fisher*, para. 445.

their children, and similarly a duty on a mother and a putative father to maintain illegitimate children.[7] Thus, a separated wife is entitled to look to her husband as well as the Commission for support if she and her children are in need. This raises a number of questions: in particular should the wife be expected to exhaust her maintenance remedies against her husband before turning to the Commission?

The SBC, in general following the practice of its predecessor, the NAB, has evolved a number of policies in this area, some of which are set out in the Handbook.[8] A particularly valuable source of information is the Report of the Finer Committee on One-Parent Families, making a number of recommendations for reform.[9]

B. Evolution of the present law[10]

The position of deserted wives and widows with children was not specifically covered by the Poor Law Amendment Act 1834. The practice of the poor law guardians varied widely; some refused relief on the ground that payment of assistance might encourage collusive desertion and fraudulent claims.[11] Those guardians who did provide outdoor relief could, after the Poor Law Amendment Act 1868, apply to a summary court for an order requiring the woman's husband to reimburse them.

The antecedents of the present law with regard to unmarried mothers can be seen even earlier in the nineteenth century.[12] The Poor Law Amendment Act 1834 enabled parishes to recover from the putative father any money spent on relief for an illegitimate child. An Amendment Act in 1844 temporarily took the matter out of the hands of the poor law guardians, and introduced a direct civil action by the mother against the putative father – the precursor of the modern affiliation proceedings. But legislation in 1868 restored the power of the poor law authorities to recover from him when the mother and her child became a charge on the parish.

These principles were substantially reflected in the National Assistance Act 1948. This removed the obligation of grandparents and children to maintain destitute relatives, which had existed since the Poor Relief Act 1601;[13] but the husband and wife were under a duty to maintain each other, and parents (including the putative father) owed the same obligation to their children.[14] These 'liable relative' provisions, as they are known, have been re-enacted in the present legislation.[15] The Supplementary Benefits Commission now has a right to recover sums paid by way of benefit from these liable relatives.[16]

7. S.17.
8. Also see Cretney *Principles of Family Law* (2nd edn), pp. 238–247: *Stevenson*, ante n.5, chap. 6; Marsden *Mothers Alone* (1973); McGregor, Blom-Cooper and Gibson *Separated Spouses* (1970), chap. 10; Brown, 18 MLR 113.
9. See post, pp. 546–547.
10. See *Finer*, Appendix 5, Section 5; Brown, 18 MLR 113, and the

judgment of Lord Goddard CJ, in *National Assistance Board v Wilkinson* [1952] 2 QB 648, [1952] 2 All ER 255, DC.
11. *Finer*, Appendix 5, para. 69.
12. Ibid., at paras. 55–65.
13. See ante, p. 475.
14. NAA 1948, s.42.
15. Now SBA 1976, s.17.
16. Ibid., ss. 18, 19: see post, pp. 544 and 546.

C. Separated wives[17]

i) General

A separated wife is clearly entitled to supplementary benefit in her own right: the aggregation provisions of the 1976 Act do not apply, as the husband and wife *ex hypothesi* are not members of the same household.[18] Her husband's income and capital are irrelevant when the amount of her benefit is determined, but, of course, any maintenance actually paid to her is fully taken into account when assessing her resources.[19] If the wife is not receiving maintenance from her husband and has taken no action in this respect, it is the Commission's policy to try to contact him as soon as possible and to persuade him to pay maintenance.[20] If the amount offered by him equals or exceeds the benefit paid to the wife, it is accepted, and provided payments are continued, that is the end of the matter.

However, much more often than not, the husband will have taken on other commitments since he left the wife, e.g. by living with another woman, and will not be able, or prepared, to pay very much. The Finer Committee found that in the vast majority of cases the liable relative was unable to afford as much as the supplementary benefit scale rates,[1] and concluded that:

> 'The overwhelming majority of one-parent families on supplementary benefits are better off with the scale rates of benefit which they receive than they would be on maintenance orders paid regularly and in full'.[2]

It is in these cases that the Commission's policy is in several respects controversial.[3]

Of course, the Commission may suspect, when an application for benefit is made by a deserted wife, that the case is one of collusive or fictitious desertion, that is, the husband is still supporting his wife. The Fisher Committee found that about 2,000 cases of suspected fictitious desertion were investigated each year, and concluded that they were less deserving of sympathy than the more frequent cohabitation cases.[4] This is perhaps a reasonable conclusion, but in some instances it may be that an apparent attempt to abuse the social security system masks a welfare problem which requires sympathetic treatment.[5]

ii) The liable relative's contribution

The Commission has evolved some guidelines for its officers to determine whether an offer made by the husband for the wife's maintenance should be accepted as reasonable, even though it does not equal the supplemen-

17. The position of divorced wives is considered at the end of this section: post, p. 545. For a comparision of the position in Britain and Germany, see Müller-Fembeck and Ogus, 25 ICLQ 382, 400–402.
18. The aggregation provision, SBA 1976, Sch. 1, para. 3, is discussed ante, pp. 485–488.

19. See ante, p. 510.
20. Handbook, para. 174.
 1. See Appendix 7, Table 60.
 2. Para. 4.185.
 3. See post, pp. 543–544.
 4. Paras. 346–347.
 5. *Stevenson*, ante n.5, at p. 138.

tary benefit she is entitled to receive. These guidelines are not published in the Handbook,[6] but are set out in broad terms in the Finer Report.[7] The principle is that the liable relative (generally, though not necessarily, the husband) should be left with enough money to meet his own requirements on the supplementary benefit scale rates including rent payments, and to meet the requirements of his new dependants, perhaps a mistress and her children; in addition to this, he is to be left with a margin of £5·00 or, if higher, one quarter of his *net* earnings, that is, his pay after deduction of tax and social security contributions. The sum left, after deducting all these amounts from his net earnings, is regarded as available for meeting the wife's needs. The Commission thus recognises that priority will be given to the family actually living with and dependent on the husband.

What is particularly interesting is that the Commission's policy is more generous to the husband and his 'second family' than that of the courts when they are confronted with a maintenance application by his wife (or former wife). The latter will not take any account of the fact that the wife is receiving supplementary benefit when deciding whether to award any maintenance or the amount of any such award.[8] The fact that the award will only lead to a decrease in the benefit payments and that, therefore, it will benefit the taxpayer rather than the wife is quite immaterial.[9] But an award will not be made so as to reduce the husband's resources below the weekly scale rate of benefit to which he would be entitled, if he were eligible to claim it.[10] If the husband is actually in receipt of benefit, the court is not, of course, bound by the Commission's determination of his resources, and consequently of his capacity to pay maintenance. But it must take the decision to pay supplementary benefit into account and it will rarely be appropriate in this case to award maintenance.[11]

The Commission's policy is more generous in that, in determining a reasonable contribution, it allows the husband a margin of £5 or a quarter of his net earnings, whichever is the higher amount, above the supplementary benefit scale rate and rent allowance. There is obviously room for two views on whether the Commission's approach or that of the courts is to be preferred. But it is difficult to disagree with the observation of Finer J, made in the course of his judgment in *L.A. Williams v E.M. Williams*,[12] that

> 'there is something radically unsatisfactory in a state of the law . . . which allows two authorities, the courts and the Supplementary Benefits Commission, when dealing with precisely

6. There does not appear to be any good reason for this omission.
7. Paras. 4.188–4.189.
8. *R.M. Barnes v G.W. Barnes* [1972] 3 All ER 872, [1972] 1 WLR 1381, CA. See *Cretney*, ante n.8, at pp. 178–179.
9. But, of course, the award will continue if the wife ceases to be in receipt of benefit, perhaps because she takes full-time employment: this was one of the Commission's justifications for its former policy of encouraging wives to take maintenance proceedings.
10. *Ashley v Ashley* [1968] P. 582, [1965] 3 All ER 554, DC.
11. *L.A. Williams v E.M. Williams* [1974] Fam. 55, [1974] 3 All ER 377, DC, distinguishing *McEwan v McEwan*, [1972] 2 All ER 708, [1972] 1 WLR 1217, DC. See Cretney *Principles of Family Law* (2nd edn), pp. 176–177.
12. Ante n.11, at p. 61.

the same people in the identical human predicament to make different determinations, each acting in ignorance of what the other is doing and applying rules which only tangentially meet each other'.

It was in the hope that publication would lead to reform that the Finer Committee disclosed the criteria applied by the Commission in assessing a reasonable contribution by the liable relative.[13] The Committee's own proposals for removing these inconsistencies are discussed later.[14]

iii) The Commission's policy with regard to maintenance applications

If the husband is not paying any maintenance for the wife when she claims benefit and is not persuaded to make a contribution when contacted by the Commission, the question arises whether the wife should be encouraged in any way to make a maintenance application, the effect of which (if successful) would be to transfer part of the burden of supporting her from the state to the husband. On this controversial question, the policy of the Commission has altered over the last few years. The 1972 Handbook stated that '... the Commission assists and encourages a woman to obtain her own Court order wherever it is practicable for her to do so'.[15] Three reasons were given for this policy.[16]

1. a direct action by the wife brings her into contact with court officials and, therefore, makes possible a reconciliation with her husband.
2. the sum awarded on the maintenance application may be greater than the supplementary benefit.
3. the maintenance award will not lapse when benefit is no longer payable, for example, if the wife secures full-time work.

The Finer Committee found the first two contentions unconvincing, but admitted there was some force in the third.[17] It also considered the allegation that Commission officers put undue pressure on separated wives to take proceedings.[18] It accepted that actual pressure was rare, but suspected that women in this situation felt that they were under some compulsion to apply for maintenance.[19] The Committee concluded that on balance the SBC policy was unjustifiable:

'... we consider that this policy causes pain and anxiety, for no tangible advantage, to far more claimants than those upon whom it may confer some advantage'.[20]

Since the Finer Report, the Supplementary Benefits Commission has revised its policy. It now only discusses with the woman the possible

13. Para. 4.190.
14. Post, pp. 546–547.
15. SBC Handbook (1972), para. 168. There is a good discussion of the old policy by Moore, *LAG Bulletin* Jan. 1974, p. 14.
16. 1972 Handbook, para. 174.
17. Paras. 4.199–4.201.
18. Stevenson *Claimant or Client?* (1973), pp. 137–138.
19. *Finer*, para. 4.197.
20. Ibid., at para. 4.202.

advantages of taking maintenance proceedings.[1] There is no encouragement to take them, and it is made plain that the decision is entirely hers.
An explanatory leaflet is given to her to ensure that she understands the
situation.[2] If she opts not to make an application, or is undecided, then the
Commission will determine whether to take proceedings itself.[3]

iv) The 'diversion' procedure

Under an administrative arrangement made with the co-operation of the
Home Office and justices' clerks, maintenance payments may be 'diverted'
to the DHSS, while the full supplementary benefit is paid weekly to the
woman.[4] This procedure saves her the anxiety occasioned by irregular
maintenance payments and the resulting necessity to visit the DHSS
offices to obtain benefit to meet the deficit. It may always be used where
the amount of maintenance is less than the full supplementary benefit to
which she is entitled; in the very rare case where the maintenance award is
equal to or higher than her benefit, the diversion procedure is only used if
it becomes apparent that the husband repeatedly fails to comply with the
court order. It may be employed for the benefit of divorced women,
though the court order must be registered in the magistrates' court, so that
periodic payments are made to the justices' clerk.[5]

This procedure is very frequently used; in 1970, 74% of court orders
were diverted.[6] It would, however, no longer be necessary if the proposals
of the Finer Committee mentioned later are eventually implemented.[7]

v) Enforcement by the Commission

The Commission may take *criminal* proceedings under section 25 of the
1976 Act, 'where all other efforts to obtain maintenance from a liable
relative have failed'.[8] The Finer Committee considered that use of prosecution in this situation should be discontinued.[9] However, it would, it is
submitted, be surprising if there were no circumstances in which the
threat of prosecution did not induce a recalcitrant husband to fulfil his
obligations.

Much more important would appear to be the power of the Commission
to take *civil* proceedings against the husband (or wife) under section 18 of
the Act. But in practice this power is used relatively infrequently. Thus, in
1976 there were only 200 applications by the Commission.[10] The magistrates' court considering the Commission's application, 'shall have regard
to all the circumstances', and the liable relative's resources.[11] Apart from
this, there is nothing in the legislation which limits the circumstances in
which the SBC may recover a contribution from the husband (or wife).

1. Handbook, para. 177.
2. This is set out in Appendix IV to the
   Handbook.
3. For proceedings by the SBC, see post,
   pp. 545–546.
4. See *Finer*, paras. 4.206–4.207;
   Handbook, para. 182; *LAG Bulletin*,
   Jan. 1974, p. 15.
5. See *Cretney*, ante n.11, at p. 230.

6. *Finer*, Table 4.12.
7. See post, pp. 546–547.
8. Handbook, para. 186. For prosecutions
   under s.25 in cases of voluntary
   unemployment, see ante, p. 539.
9. *Finer*, para. 4.211.
10. See SBA Annual Report 1976, Cmnd.
    6910, para. 15.11.
11. SBA 1976, s.18(3).

But the Divisional Court in *National Assistance Board v Wilkinson*[12] held that the wife's adultery or desertion might provide the husband with a defence to the proceedings. Later cases, however, explained that the wife's matrimonial offence, or conduct falling just short of such an offence, is only a consideration to be taken into account together with other relevant circumstances.[13] It is clear that a husband may be liable to make payments to the Commission, even though he has separated from his wife on condition that she would not claim maintenance at any time.[14]

vi) Divorced wives

For supplementary benefit purposes, the position of a divorced wife is very similar to that of a woman separated from her husband. Thus, she may claim benefit in her own right, and only the amount of maintenance actually paid by her former husband is included in her resources.[15] The only significant difference is that a former husband (or wife) is not a 'liable relative' under section 17 of the 1976 Act, and so the Commission has no power to recover payments from him (or her) in respect of benefit paid to the divorced spouse. However, as a parent, he (or she) is liable under the section to maintain the children.

D. Unmarried mothers

Some of the one-parent families in receipt of supplementary benefit are single women with illegitimate children, though they are a smaller group than either divorced or separated wives.[16] In many respects the entitlement of an unmarried mother is the same as that of a separated wife. Thus, she is entitled to claim benefit for her own and her children's requirements, though, of course, any money actually paid for her needs by the natural father must be taken into account as part of her resources.

A difficult question may arise with regard to the impact on the mother's benefit of a payment made by the natural father *for the benefit of the child*, whether under voluntary agreement or under an affiliation order. The usual view is that, if this payment exceeds the amount of benefit paid for that child's requirements, the excess becomes part of the mother's resources and should, therefore, be deducted in assessing her own benefit.[17] But the position would appear less certain in view of the remarks of the Court of Appeal in *K v J.M.P. Co Ltd.*[18] It was argued that under the aggregation rule, damages paid to the mother's children consequent on their natural father's fatal accident would have to be treated as part of her

12. [1952] 2 QB 648, [1952] 2 All ER 255 DC.
13. See *National Assistance Board v Prisk* [1954] 1 All ER 400, [1954] 1 WLR 443, DC; *National Assistance Board v Parkes* [1955] 2 QB 506, [1955] 3 All ER 1, CA.
14. Ibid.
15. There is no disregard of maintenance payments: ante, p. 511.
16. SBC Annual Report 1976, Cmnd. 6910, para. 2.15.
17. See *Lynes*, p. 136.
18. [1976] QB 85, [1975] 1 All ER 1030, see ante, p. 488.

resources.[19] However, this was rejected on the ground that after the receipt of the damages, the mother would not in fact have to provide for the children's requirements, and, therefore, the rule did not apply. The same conclusion might be reached in respect of affiliation payments or any other periodic payments made for the children.[20] In this case the mother would be entitled to benefit, no matter what the amount of the payments made by the father. But affiliation payments are legally a resource of the mother, and it seems, therefore, that the SBC takes them into account in assessing her benefit.[1] This does not apply to a voluntary payment made by the father for the child himself.[2]

As with separated wives, if no voluntary arrangement has been made, the Commission discusses with the woman the possibility of taking affiliation proceedings. This represents a relaxation of the earlier policy of encouraging the taking of such proceedings.[3] Any pressure on single women is particularly unfortunate, as many of them are reluctant to name the father of their child.[4]

The Commission may itself take proceedings under section 19 of the Supplementary Benefits Act 1976. Their effect may be to vary an existing affiliation order so as to direct payments to the DHSS, a variation which may be made even after the mother's death.[5] If, on the other hand, no affiliation order is in force,[6] the SBC may, within three years from the time benefit was last paid, apply for an independent order against the putative father.[7] This is entirely separate from the woman's affiliation proceedings: it does not matter, therefore, that she would be out of time if she were to apply herself,[8] or that she is not a 'single woman' for the purposes of an affiliation order,[9] or even that her own proceedings have been dismissed on the evidence.[10]

E. Reform of the law

The Finer Committee recommended a new scheme to regulate the relationship between benefit payments and contributions from liable rela-

19. SBA 1976, Sch. 1, para. 3.
20. Hodge, *LAG Bulletin*, Aug. 1975, p. 213, and ibid., Sept. 1975, p. 242.
1. Private communication from SBC. (For affiliation proceedings, see Cretney *Principles of Family Law* (2nd edn), pp. 422–429.)
2. Private communication from SBC. On this principle it would seem that such payments made by a divorced or separated husband for his children would not be included in the mother's resources.
3. Compare Handbook 1972, para. 177 with the 1977 Handbook, para. 180.
4. *Stevenson Claimant or Client?* (1973), pp. 137–138; Marsden *Mothers Alone*

(1973), pp. 190–194.
5. SBA 1976, s.19(5).
6. The order must actually provide for payments to be an 'affiliation order': *Oldfield v National Assistance Board* [1960] 1 QB 635, [1960] 1 All ER 524, DC.
7. SBA 1976, s.19(2).
8. *National Assistance Board v Mitchell* [1956] 1 QB 56, [1955] 3 All ER 291, DC.
9. *National Assistance Board v Tugby* [1957] 1 QB 507, [1957] 1 All ER 509, DC.
10. *Clapham v National Assistance Board* [1961] 2 QB 77, [1961] 2 All ER 50, DC.

tives.[11] A lone mother would apply for and receive benefit in the normal way.[12] She would not then be advised about, let alone encouraged to take, proceedings against the liable relative. Instead, the SBC would assess his means and determine what he should pay as a contribution. This would be enforced by the issue of an 'administrative order'. The liable relative would be able to appeal to a supplementary benefits appeal tribunal on questions of quantum, while on legal issues, e.g., non-paternity of a child or the wife's serious misconduct, he could appeal to a court. Only if the mother believed she could obtain more from a maintenance or affiliation order than she receives in benefit, would there be any point in her taking proceedings.

These proposals are entirely separate from the principal recommendation in the Report for a new non-contributory benefit for one-parent families, the guaranteed maintenance allowance.[13] Even if this new benefit were introduced, there would still be a role for supplementary benefits, particularly during the first three months of separation when according to the recommendation the allowance would not be payable. The Finer Committee's proposals would avoid many of the difficulties of the present system so far as the claimant is concerned, but it may be argued that it is in principle objectionable to require a liable relative to contribute without a court hearing.

Part seven. Special Cases

In this Part there is a brief discussion of some special cases, where the general principles for assessing benefit are not applied. In the first three cases the exception is covered in Schedule 1 to the 1976 Supplementary Benefits Act, but generally the provisions are in such broad terms that there is a substantial element of discretion in assessing benefit.[14]

A. Hospital patients[15]

The requirements of a person residing as a patient in hospital are 'such amount, if any, as may be appropriate, having regard to all the circumstances'.[16] The Commission's overall policy is to ensure that the patient has enough to provide for continuing commitments while he is in hospital, with a further sum to cover his personal expenses.[17]

Thus, in the case of married patients, full supplementary benefit is paid for the first eight weeks of one spouse's stay in hospital. After that a deduction of £3·05 a week is made from the sum which would be payable

11. *Finer*, Part 4, Sections 11 and 12 (noted by Reid, 38 MLR 52).
12. *Finer*, paras. 4.262–4.272 for the scope of the proposals.
13. Ibid., Part 5, Sections 5–7. See Eekelaar, [1976] P.L. 64.
14. For a full statement of the relevant

SBC policies, see Handbook, paras. 113–156, and also see *Lynes*, chap. 7.
15. There are very similar rules for contributory social security benefits: see chap. 10, ante, pp. 416–421.
16. SBA 1976, Sch. 1, para. 14.
17. Handbook, para. 134.

to a married couple. This is justifiable because of the 'savings' made with one spouse in hospital; on the other hand, it is right to pay the other more than a single person because he (or she) will have the expenses of hospital visits, and have financial commitments incurred on the assumption of the imminent return of the spouse.[18] After two years, if there is no likelihood of an early discharge from hospital, the patient will no longer be treated as married for benefit purposes, and his requirements will be assessed as if he were single.[19] The requirements of the other spouse will also then be assessed separately; fares and other expenses incurred for hospital visits may then be covered by an award of an ECA, or, where they are particularly onerous, by an ENP.[20]

The Commission's policy with regard to a single patient is to meet outside commitments, e.g., of rent, for three months, and pay a personal allowance of £3·05; if after that period there is no immediate possibility of his discharge, the Commission will review whether it should continue making the former payment.[1] An allowance may be made for his children if they are not taken into the care of the local authority.[2] When a child is in hospital, his requirements are met in full for the first twelve weeks. Subsequently £3·05 is paid instead of the normal scale rate.[3]

The personal needs of mental patients are now generally met by the Commission; before November 1975 responsibility for payments rested with the Area Health Authorities, but this distinction in the treatment of ordinary and mental patients was regarded as invidious.[4] Finally, it may be noted that the weekly allowance paid to an ordinary long-term patient may be stopped on the recommendation of a medical officer, if his general condition has so deteriorated that it cannot usefully be spent on his comfort.[5]

B. Persons in old people's homes and other residential institutions

The payments made to people living in old people's homes or other residential institutions vary according to whether the claimant is a person for whom a local authority has accepted responsibility under Part III of the National Assistance Act 1948, or whether he has made private arrangements with the home or other institution.

i) Persons accommodated under Part III of the National Assistance Act

Under section 21 of the National Assistance Act 1948,[6] local authorities are empowered, and may be directed by the Secretary of State for Social

---

18. Ibid., at para. 135.
19. Ibid., at para. 136.
20. Handbook, paras. 76 and 99(d).
 1. Ibid., at para. 139.
 2. For further details, see *Lynes*, p. 149.
 3. Handbook, para. 137.
 4. Ibid., at para. 140. See *Lynes*, p. 150.

5. Handbook, para. 141.
6. As amended by the Local Government Act 1972, Sch. 23, para. 2(1). The corresponding provision in Scotland is the Social Work (Scotland) Act 1968, s.87.

Services, to provide –

> 'residential accommodation for persons who by reason of age, infirmity or any other circumstances are in need of care and attention which is not otherwise available to them'.

This responsibility may be discharged either by local authorities providing their own home or by arrangements with private hostels and old people's homes. The requirements of persons in 'Part III accommodation' are to be assessed as the aggregate of the sums prescribed by the Secretary of State as the minimum charge for this accommodation (£12·25), and prescribed as the sum to be allowed by the local authority for the person's personal requirements (£3·05).[7] The total (£15·30) is doubled for a married couple living in 'Part III accommodation'. Any excess over this amount which is charged by a voluntary body or private home is paid by the local authority.

ii) Persons living in residential institutions for whom the local authority has not accepted responsibility

If a claimant is living in a private old people's home or other residential institution out of choice, and the local authority does not accept responsibility, probably because it takes the view that he is not in need of special care and attention, the Commission will make payments on the basis that he is a boarder.[8] This means that it will meet the board and lodging charge (subject to a maximum of £2.75 above the 'reasonable' board and lodging charge for the area) and pay in addition £5.25 for personal expenses.[9] An additional sum up to £3.50 may be paid if the applicant receives special care and attention in the home. These sums are more generous than those payable to a person in Part III accommodation, because the claimant here will have to meet various costs, such as bedding and toilet articles, which are usually provided in a local authority supported institution.[10]

iii) Homeless families[11]

Under section 21 of the National Assistance Act 1948 as amended,[12] local authorities may provide 'temporary accommodation for persons who are in urgent need thereof. . . . ' If homeless people living temporarily in a local authority home are provided with meals, their requirements are assessed in the same way as old people in this type of accommodation. If, on the other hand, they are not provided with meals their requirements are assessed as ordinary householders, with the charge made by the local authority counting as rent. In some cases, local authorities may board out homeless people in guest houses or a bed and breakfast establishment; then the Commission usually pays a reasonable board and lodging charge, any excess being met by the authority.[13]

---

7. SBA 1976, Sch. 1, para. 13, and see Handbook, paras, 113–114.
8. Ante, pp. 508–509.
9. Handbook, para. 116. £5·25 is the sum paid for the personal expenses of long-term claimants, and all pensioners fall into this category.
10. Handbook, para. 116.
11. See Yates, *LAG Bulletin*, Nov. 1973, p. 249.
12. Local Government Act 1972, Sch. 23, para. 2(1).
13. Handbook, para. 133.

iv) Persons suffering from mental disorder

Local authorities are under a duty imposed by the Health Services and Public Health Act 1968 to provide care, including where necessary residential accommodation, for people suffering or recovering from mental disorder.[14] In practice this responsibility is often discharged in the same way as that imposed by the National Assistance Act 1948, and supplementary benefit is paid as in that case.[15] In other circumstances, the authority may board the person out privately and then benefit is paid on the basis that he is a boarder, with the additional margin of £3·50 (for extra care and attention) allowed over the normal charge.[16]

C. Prisoners[17]

A prisoner, or other person 'detained in legal custody', has no requirements for benefit purposes, except for his wife and children.[18] Thus, a single prisoner without dependent children is not entitled to receive any benefit, though in some cases an urgent needs payment might possibly be made to pay the rent of a person who is only in custody for a very short time.[19] A prisoner's wife is treated as if she were a single person;[20] she is now entitled to payments for monthly prison visits under a Home Office scheme administered by local DHSS offices.[1]

On release a prisoner usually receives a discharge grant, which covers his requirements for the first week. No supplementary benefit is, therefore, payable unless it is clearly insufficient for his needs. After then, benefit may be payable in the normal way, and an application for ENP will be considered if he needs money to buy ordinary working clothes.[2]

D. Students

A young person at school or receiving non-advanced education ('A' level or below) at a technical college is ineligible for benefit under section 7 of the 1976 Act.[3] There is no statutory disqualification, however, for students taking degree or other further courses. But they cannot generally obtain benefit during term-time, because of their inability to meet the condition of registration for employment.[4] The Commission is rarely prepared to waive this, since it takes the view that it is the responsibility of other

14. In Scotland, the duty is imposed by the Social Work (Scotland) Act 1968.
15. Handbook, paras. 129–130.
16. Ibid. And see ante, p. 549, for the margin of £3·50 allowed for old people in boarding homes.
17. For the disqualification from contributory benefits of prisoners and other persons detained in legal custody, see chap. 10, ante, pp. 421–424.
18. SBA 1976, Sch. 1, para. 16. The term 'legal custody' is not defined in the

Act, but presumably its interpretation follows the regulations made under SSA 1975: ante, p. 422.
19. Lynes, p. 157.
20. Handbook, para. 144.
 1. See ante, p. 525, for discussion of this payment in the context of exceptional needs payments. See Handbook, para. 146.
 2. Ibid., paras. 150–153.
 3. Ante, p. 483.
 4. SBA 1976, s.5: ante, pp. 483–485.

bodies to finance people receiving higher education.[5] The Handbook sets out certain circumstances in which the requirement may be waived:

1. where the claimant is receiving training after a long spell of unemployment, and would be unlikely to obtain work without this training;

2. where he is receiving certain courses for which the training allowance is insufficient by supplementary benefit standards;

3. where he is in receipt of a maintenance grant for himself, but is ineligible for a dependant's allowance under the Student Hardship Allowance scheme because he is not married; he may then receive benefit for a dependant, in certain circumstances, of an amount equivalent to that available under the scheme.[6]

However, students may easily satisfy the registration condition during the vacations, though during the two short vacations (at Christmas and Easter) they are not able to take on work for more than a few weeks. In the 1970s, largely as a result of the publicity campaign organised by the National Union of Students, more students registered as unemployed and successfully claimed supplementary benefit.[7] This disturbed the Commission because of the additional burden put on local offices, particularly during the short vacations when it may often be difficult to determine whether the claimant is genuinely anxious to find work.[8] The SBC did not regard 'student support as a proper function of the supplementary benefit scheme'.[9] This attitude was exemplified by its policy of reducing the benefit by £1 on the basis that there were 'exceptional circumstances' justifying such a reduction under paragraph 4(1)(b) of the Schedule to the Act.[10] The Court of Appeal in *R v Barnsley Supplementary Benefits Appeal Tribunal, ex parte Atkinson*,[11] held that this was illegal; neither the fact that students were in receipt of maintenance grants from local authorities nor their inability to register for part of the year could constitute 'exceptional circumstances'.

The effect of the *Atkinson* decision has been nullified by Regulations made under the Social Security (Miscellaneous Provisions) Act 1977[12]. As a result of these recent changes, it will be difficult for a student to claim supplementary benefit at all in the short vacations, at least if he lives at

5. Handbook, para. 154; see SBC Annual Report 1975, Cmnd. 6615, para. 5.11.
6. Handbook, para. 155. Also see the case reported in *LAG Bulletin*, Apr. 1977, p. 89, where a tribunal was persuaded to waive the registration condition imposed on a student, whose wife was ill and unable to support him.
7. In August 1975 there were 121,000 successful claims by students: SBC Annual Report 1975, ante n.5, at para. 5.10.
8. Ibid.
9. Ibid., at para. 5.11.
10. For other examples of the reduction or withholding of benefit under this paragraph, see ante, pp. 500 and 536.
11. [1977] 3 All ER 1031, [1977] 1 WLR 917, allowing the appeal from the Divisional Court, [1976] 1 WLR 1047. Earlier challenges to the Commission's policy are discussed in *LAG Bulletin*, Dec. 1973, p. 272, and March 1974, p. 62.
12. S.14(1), (2). The legislative history of these controversial provisions is summarised in 928 HC Deb., cols. 1518–1523.

home. The student maintenance grant now includes a sum for the weeks of the short vacations equivalent to the non-householder benefit rate.[13] Under the Regulations this is taken into account in full without any disregard.[14] Moreover, where the student is not entitled to the maximum maintenance grant, the parental contribution is treated as part of his resources, whether it is actually paid or not, and there is no disregard of this income.[15] These changes do not apply to disabled students,[16] those who are parents in a one-parent family, or women students who are subject to the aggregation provisions.[17] They enjoy a disregard of £2 of their grant, and the parental contribution is not taken into account in assessing their income, unless it is actually paid.[18]

The student maintenance grant does not cover the summer vacation, so provided the student registers for work, he may be entitled to benefit for that period. The recent changes do not affect this entitlement.

13. SBC Annual Report 1975, ante n.5, at para. 5.11.
14. S.I. 1977/619, Reg. 3.
15. Ibid., Reg. 2.
16. 'Disabled students' are defined as students unlikely because of their disability to obtain – in comparison with others – employment within a reasonable time: ibid., Reg. 1(2).
17. For the aggregation provisions, see ante, pp. 485–488.
18. S.I. 1977/619, Regs. 3(2) and 4(2).

13 Family Income Supplement

Part one. Introduction

A. General

Family Income Supplement (generally known as 'FIS', and often referred to as such in this chapter) was introduced by the Conservative government in 1970. In broad terms, it is designed to provide some assistance for families with children where the wage-earner is on a very low salary. Like supplementary benefit it is, therefore, means-tested and financed by general taxation. It complements that benefit which, with rare exceptions, is not payable to a person engaged in full-time employment.[1] FIS, on the other hand, is *only* payable for a family where a man (or a single woman) is in full-time work and the income is less than the level prescribed under the Family Income Supplements Act 1970. In many respects, as will be seen, FIS differs substantially from supplementary benefit. In particular, there is relatively very little discretion in the administration of the scheme, though claims are determined by the same body – the Supplementary Benefits Commission. Moreover, FIS is administered by post, and not on the basis of interviews.[2]

Supplementary benefits play a crucial role in the British social security system, providing assistance now for nearly 3,000,000 people. In contrast, family income supplements are only paid to about 77,000 families, and their total cost is about £19 million.[3] The figures show a gradual decline from 1972–75 in the number of claimants and recipients.[4] This is perhaps attributable to a general improvement in the earnings of lower paid workers in these years. However, it has also been argued that the pre-scribed income level has not kept pace with the rise in average earnings.[5]

When FIS was introduced in 1970, it was strongly opposed on the Labour benches. This was largely because the Labour party has tradition-ally disliked means-tested benefits, which, it is argued, potential recipients are reluctant to claim.[6] But it was also generally contended that the new benefit was inadequate to cope with problems of family poverty, that it was wrong for the state to subsidise low wages, and that the withdrawal of FIS as the recipient's earnings were raised constituted a disincentive to self-

---

1. See chap. 12, ante, at p. 482.
2. See post, pp. 568–569.
3. SBC Annual Report 1976, Cmnd. 6910, paras. 16.5–16.6.
4. Ibid., Table 16.3.
5. *Poverty* (1975), No. 31, p. 17.
6. For the arguments against means-tested benefits, see ante, pp. 12–15.

improvement. These policy considerations are examined later.[7] But despite these reservations, there has been no sustained attempt to replace the benefit with some other provision. The present Labour government seems prepared to continue with it. Indeed, the only significant suggestion by a government for its replacement came in the Conservative Green Paper on Tax Credits in 1972.[8] The introduction of tax credits would absorb family income supplements: the lower paid would automatically receive an addition to their salary, if their tax credit exceeded any income tax deductible from their weekly wage.[9] It is, however, improbable that this scheme will be introduced in the next few years, whatever the composition of the next government. So it appears likely that the family income supplement, conceived by its sponsors as only the first stage in a continuing programme of reform,[10] will remain a feature of the social security system for some time.

B. Policy

In 1970 the Conservative party promised to attempt to ameliorate the problems of family poverty by raising family allowances. But after its return to office, this commitment was reconsidered and the family income supplement scheme introduced instead. Sir Keith Joseph explained that the extension of family allowances to cover families with only one child would have been both too costly and time-consuming.[11] Moreover, the lowering of the tax threshold in the previous few years made the raising of allowances with their 'claw-back' through the reduction in child tax allowances, a less efficient way of helping the poor.[12] The merit of the family income supplement, it was claimed, was that it directed help where it was most needed; for the first time a family with a wage-earner and only *one* child was eligible for assistance.[13] An interesting feature is that entitlement to FIS also enables its recipient to obtain a number of other welfare benefits, e.g. help with optical and dental charges, exemption from prescription charges and charges for school meals, free legal aid.[14] In the words often used, entitlement to FIS provides a 'passport' for a number of benefits.

The government did not see the new benefit as a final solution to the problems of family poverty but viewed it as an important ameliorating measure which should be introduced as quickly as possible. This consideration influenced the structure of the Act and the content of the

7. Post, pp. 555–558.
8. Cmnd. 5116, paras, 5 and 113.
9. For a discussion of the tax credit system, see ante, p. 37.
10. Sir K. Joseph, Secretary of State, 806 HC Deb., cols. 229–230.
11. Ibid., cols. 217ff. Though, N.B., this has now been accomplished by the introduction of child benefits, ante, chap. 11.

12. But it can be argued that a better course would have been to increase family allowances and raise the tax threshold: see Barker in ed. Bull *Family Poverty* (2nd edn), chap. 6. For 'claw-back', see ante, p. 447.
13. Family allowances were not payable for the first child of a family: see chap. 11, ante, p. 446.
14. SBC Handbook, para. 259.

benefit. First, a substantial amount of detail was left to be covered by regulations,[15] a feature which understandably attracted a large amount of suspicion and criticism in the House of Commons. Thus, while the disregards in the supplementary benefits scheme are covered by the Supplementary Benefits Act itself (and, indeed, their level may not be varied by regulations), the very few disregards allowed in assessing a claimant's income for FIS purposes are provided in regulations.[16] Secondly, the new benefit was designed to be as simple as possible. In particular, the discretionary element was to be kept to a minimum. For these reasons, there was no provision for varying the amount of supplement according to the *age* (as distinct from the *number*) of the claimant's children,[17] nor was there any separate provision for rent, as there is in the supplementary benefits scheme.[18] The opposition, therefore, stigmatised the Bill as crude and inflexible in its attempt to deal with poverty among the lower paid. Moreover, the level of the supplement – 50% of the difference between the claimant's gross income (subject to a few disregards), *and* the amounts prescribed in the Act was widely considered inadequate.[19]

Sir Keith Joseph indeed conceded that the measure would only assist between one-half and two-thirds of those working households living on an income below the supplementary benefit level.[20] The particular difficulties of those paying high rents were to be dealt with in the government's forthcoming Housing Finance Act 1972, which introduced rent allowances and rebates. The government was, however, unwilling to make more generous provision in the family income supplement scheme, because of its fear that this would remove the incentive to earn more, and encourage employers to pay artificially low wages to their employees, knowing that any shortfall below the market rate for the work would be met in full by the government.[1] For this reason it resisted amendments to pay more than 50% of the difference between the claimant's earnings and the prescribed amount, and to remove the limit on the maximum amount payable by way of FIS.

There are four broad lines of attack which have been directed against the use of FIS to help the lower paid. The first is the fundamental criticism expressed by Mr. Enoch Powell and one or two other Conservatives in the Second Reading Debate, that it is undesirable in principle for the state to supplement wages, as the relief provides a disincentive for employer and employee to negotiate a true market wage.[2] The objectors pointed out that in this respect the benefit marked a departure from the previous refusal of the social security system to help the low-paid. The

15. FISA 1970, s.10(2) enables regulations to be made for ten different purposes. This is not the only section in the Act empowering regulations to be made.
16. S.I. 1971/226, Reg. 2(5), as amended by S.I. 1972/1282, Reg. 2 and S.I. 1977/324, Reg. 2.
17. See the criticism by Mrs S. Williams, 806 HC Deb., col. 236.

18. Ibid., col. 236 and col. 1177.
19. Mr M. Meacher, ibid., col. 306, and Mr B. O'Malley. ibid., col. 318. And see *Barker*, ante, n.12, at pp. 76–80.
20. 806 HC Deb., col. 227.
1. Mr P. Dean, Under-Secretary of State, ibid., col. 1265.
2. Ibid., cols. 260–265.

only precedent was the 'Speenhamland system', under which, from 1795 till the reforms of 1834, poor law authorities supplemented low wages with relief calculated according to the price of bread.[3] This objection has, however, not been voiced recently. Whatever the argument's theoretical merits, it is doubtful whether FIS has had any serious effect on the wage rates of the lower paid.[4]

The second line of attack comes from the opposite end of the political spectrum. The left has argued that the introduction of FIS can at best be regarded as a palliative for the problems of the lower paid; in reality it should be seen as merely providing an excuse for the failure substantially to improve their economic position.[5] A more worthwhile step, it can be argued, would be the institution of a national minimum wage, though this might have significant and unwelcome economic consequences – almost certainly, for example, an immediate rise in unemployment – which militate against its adoption.[6] But the radicals contend further that it is impossible to divorce the problems of the low paid from the wider questions posed by economic and social inequality; only in a more equal society would it be possible for these problems to be removed.[7] Certainly it must be conceded that the use of a means-tested benefit to supplement low earnings contrasts markedly with much of the social security system which aims to provide compensation for the loss of earnings; it does not feature regularly in other welfare programmes. Whether it is desirable or practicable for the social security system to aim for a much more extensive redistribution of income, as proposed by critics of FIS, is a fundamental question, outside the scope of this chapter.[8]

The third objection to the scheme is the more detailed one that the lower paid are required themselves to claim the supplement. The government estimated that the 'take-up' would be as high as 85%, but the opposition was understandably sceptical, and it seems that at least in the first years of its operation, only about 50% of those eligible claimed the supplement. In 1973 take-up of FIS was officially estimated to have been about 66·6%, and in 1974, it is thought to have reached 75%.[9] Any increase may be attributable to the considerable sums spent by the government in advertising the availability of FIS.[10] To some extent, the

3. Bruce *The Coming of the Welfare State* (4th edn), pp. 55–56, 91–92; Fraser *The Evolution of the British Welfare State* (1975), pp. 33–34. And see ante, p. 476.
4. There is no study available on the effect of FIS, but for a comparable discussion on the effects of negative income tax, see Green, *Negative Taxes and the Poverty Problem* (1967), pp. 125–126.
5. See esp., George *Social Security and Society* (1973), pp. 67–69.
6. Hughes in ed. Bull *Family Poverty* (2nd edn), p. 93. Other alternative

strategies, such as a negative income tax, are considered ante, pp. 36–39.
7. *George*, ante n. 5, at pp. 73–79; Field, Meacher and Pond *To Him Who Hath* (1977), *passim*.
8. The question is discussed in chap. 1, ante, pp. 5–7.
9. 894 HC Deb., col. 273. See also SBC Annual Report for 1975, Cmnd. 6615, para. 12.8. The government figures are viewed with scepticism in *Poverty* (1976) No. 34, p. 3.
10. About £920,000 was spent in advertising FIS: 886 HC Deb., cols. 1–2.

problem of low 'take-up' is inevitable with a selective, means-tested benefit,[11] as opposed to, for example, a tax credit scheme.

The fourth criticism made by spokesmen of both parties during the debates on the 1970 Bill, concerns what is known as the 'poverty trap'.[12] This problem has become more acute in the last few years, and its existence must now probably be regarded as the principal weakness of the family income supplement. The poverty trap refers to the situation where a recipient of one (or more usually, a variety of) means-tested welfare benefits finds it difficult to improve his financial position by increasing his wages, because he then loses his entitlement to those benefits. Unless he receives an enormous wage increase, the person is in effect 'trapped' by his dependence on the state provisions. The result is a disincentive for the victims of the poverty trap to improve their position, or a feeling of despair and bitterness when the only result of wage increase or a bonus is that it is 'taxed away' by the withdrawal of welfare benefits. The problem arises in the context of family income supplement in this way. When a recipient of FIS increases his wages, his entitlement is then calculated by reference to the difference between his new wage and the prescribed amount in the Act.[13] Before the increase he used to receive 50% of the difference between his wage and the prescribed amount, so that in effect he loses half his wage increase through the reduction in his FIS entitlement. For example,

> C may receive £5 FIS weekly, calculated as half the difference between the prescribed amount, say, £45[14] and his earnings, £35. If he receives a salary increase of £5, his entitlement to FIS will be reduced to £2·50 (half the difference between £45 and £40).

The position may be even worse than that, since entitlement to FIS also carries with it eligibility for other welfare benefits. The result is that an increase in wages may be virtually cancelled out by the loss of, or a reduction in, FIS and other means-tested benefits.[15]

The phenomenon has become much more serious recently as the tax threshold has fallen, so that now many recipients of FIS are also paying income tax.[16] 34% of any wage increase may be payable to the Inland Revenue, so with the 50% or more taxed through loss of the supplement and perhaps other benefits, it is possible for someone to become worse off as a result of a wage increase. As is the case with the problem of take-up, it appears that a tax credit system, integrating income tax and some social security benefits, including FIS, would mitigate the severity of this problem.[17]

11. See ante, p. 13, and also the discussion in the National Consumer Council's *Means-Tested Benefits* (1977), chap. 3.

12. E.g., Sir B. Rhys-Williams, 806 HC Deb., col. 284 and Mr M. Meacher, ibid., cols 306 and 1277.

13. But he will continue to receive the amount awarded on the first assessment for twelve months from the date of the award: see post, p. 569.

14. For the actual prescribed amount in force for 1977–78, see post, p. 565.

15. See the examples given in the pamphlet, Howell *Why Work?*, Conservative Political Centre, 1976.

16. The relationship of income tax and social security benefits is fully considered, ante, pp. 36–39. Also see *Field et al.*, ante n.7, at pp. 52–57.

17. Ante, p. 37.

Hitherto, governments of both parties have resisted criticism, based on the poverty-trap implications of FIS, by pointing out that the benefit is now awarded for a period of twelve months;[18] it cannot then be withdrawn whether or not the family's circumstances change during that time. This by itself would, of course, merely postpone the effects of the poverty trap; but in conjunction with annual upratings of the FIS limits, it can successfully disguise the problem. By the time an award comes up for renewal, the prescribed amount for FIS will have been increased, and the recipient will be eligible for another award of a similar amount. The cost, however, of this 'solution' is that some families will remain more or less perpetually dependent on the state. This fact will make it more difficult to replace FIS than was originally supposed, and probably explains why the Labour government has made no move to do so.

To some extent the new child benefit,[19] making provision for the first child of a family, should reduce dependence on the supplement. But it is unlikely that the levels of this benefit are sufficiently high to make a marked difference in the numbers eligible for FIS. The introduction of the Guaranteed Maintenance Allowance (GMA) for single-parent families, recommended by the Finer Committee, would make more difference.[20] In 1974 and 1975 these families formed the majority among FIS recipients;[1] they would no longer be dependent on FIS if GMA was introduced at the levels recommended in the Finer Report.

Part two. Entitlement to Family Income Supplement

There are five requirements under the Family Income Supplements Act 1970 for entitlement, including the condition that a valid claim is made. This procedural requirement is discussed in Part Three. The claimant must show that (i) there is a family with at least one child, (ii) with one man or single woman engaged in remunerative full-time work, (iii) in Great Britain, (iv) whose weekly amount of resources falls short of the prescribed amount. These rules are fully analysed in this Part. As with supplementary benefits, questions as to entitlement to FIS are decided by the Supplementary Benefits Commission, with a right of appeal to the SBAT and, since 1977, to the courts.[2] But applications are made by post, and granted or refused at the central office in Blackpool.[3] There has not hitherto been any reported case in the courts on the meaning of the provisions in the 1970 Act, so inevitably many of the points made in the analysis must be rather tentative.

18. See post, pp. 569–570 for duration of FIS payments.
19. Chap. 11.
20. The recommendations are briefly discussed, ante, pp. 546-547.
 1. Social Security Statistics 1975, Title 31.10. But this was no longer true in 1976: see SBC Annual Report 1976, Cmnd. 6910, at Table 16.3.
 2. S.I. 1977/1735: post, p. 650 for adjudication of claims to FIS.
 3. Post, p. 569.

A. The 'family' for the purposes of FIS

Section 1(1) of the 1970 Act provides:

'a family shall consist of the following members of a household –

(a) one man or single woman engaged, and normally engaged, in remunerative full-time work; and

(b) if the person mentioned in paragraph (a) above is a man and the household includes a woman to whom he is married or who lives with him as his wife, that woman; and

(c) the child or children whose requirements are provided for, in whole or in part, by the person or either of the persons mentioned in the preceding paragraphs.'

Before analysing this section in detail, two preliminary points should be made. First, the intention of the Act, made plain by section 1(1)(c), was to benefit lower paid families *with a child or children*, and not childless couples. One Conservative did suggest that the measure should be expanded to cover the latter, but the proposal met with no support.[4] Secondly, the drafting of the section must be seen in the context of the law on supplementary benefits. FIS, as mentioned in the first paragraph of this chapter, was designed to complement supplementary benefit by providing assistance for families with a low income from work. In framing the legislation, therefore, the possible alternative availability of that benefit was taken into account.

In the case of supplementary benefit, where spouses, or a man and woman living together as husband and wife, are members of the same household, it is the man who is entitled, though the wife's, or woman's, needs are taken into account if he is so entitled.[5] The provisions in section 1 of the 1970 Act mirror this pattern: where a man and woman are living together in the same household (again, it does not matter whether they are husband and wife), entitlement to FIS depends on whether *he* is engaged in remunerative full-time work. Where he is unemployed and the woman is working full-time, he may claim supplementary benefit, and no member of the family is entitled to FIS. The opposition did indeed move an amendment to delete the word 'single' from section 1(1)(a), which would have had the effect of enabling a family, where the wife was the wage-earner, to receive FIS, instead of relying on the husband's entitlement to supplementary benefit.[6] This might in some circumstances be an advantageous alternative, in particular where a husband, though not in full-time work, is for some reason, e.g., because he is a student, not entitled to receive supplementary benefit. But the amendment was successfully resisted, and the symmetry of the relationship between

4. Mr P. Fry, 806 HC Deb., col. 299. The opposition was, it seems, in agreement with the government that the problem to be solved was that of family poverty affecting children, although it wished to do this by an extension of family allowances.

5. See chap. 12, ante, pp. 485–488.

6. 806 HC Deb., cols. 1118ff.

supplementary benefit and FIS – in both cases it is the man's position which is important – was preserved.

The best way of exploring the difficulties of section 1 is perhaps to list the various types of family which may be entitled to FIS.

i) Man with wife, or with woman living with him as his wife, and child or children

This was envisaged as the most typical type of family which might benefit from FIS, though, as has been mentioned earlier, from 1974–75 single-parent families outnumbered two-parent families as recipients of the supplement.[7] In two-parent families, it is the man who must satisfy the full-time work requirement, the content of which is discussed in the next section.[8] Under section 1(1)(b), his wife, or a woman living with him as his wife, is to be included in the 'family' for the purposes of the Act, though clearly there may be other people, e.g., grandparents, living in the particular household who are not so treated. The significance of such a woman's status as a member of the family is primarily that her gross income is included in its resources for the purposes of determining entitlement to, or the amount of, FIS.[9] In contrast, the income of other persons living in the household – even if they are contributing to the support of the children – is wholly disregarded.[10]

For the purposes of FIS, a woman living with the man as his wife is treated in the same way as a woman legally his wife. The 1970 Act, it may be noted, has always used the term 'lives with him as his wife' rather than the apparently more offensive 'cohabits', now deleted from the supplementary benefits and social security legislation.[11] The meaning of 'living together as man and wife' has been fully discussed in chapter 10,[12] and there is no need for a further treatment here.

Section 1(1)(c) states that a 'family' must include a child or children, 'whose requirements are provided for, in whole or in part, by the person or either of the persons mentioned in the preceding paragraphs'. Under the Act,[13] a 'child' must be under sixteen, but Regulations provide that someone over sixteen is to be treated as a child if he is continuing 'to receive full-time instruction of a kind given in a school'.[14]

The children need not be the natural children of the man or the woman providing for them.[15] The sole requirement in section 1(1)(c) is that he

7. See, ante, p. 558.
8. Post, p. 563.
9. FISA 1970, s. 4, discussed post, at pp. 566–567.
10. The point was emphasised repeatedly in the debates in the House of Commons, e.g., Sir K. Joseph, 806 HC Deb., cols. 1124 and 1153. It is the same position as that which applies in supplementary benefits, ante, p. 504.
11. SS(MP)A 1977, ss.14(7), 22(2)(4).
12. Ante, pp. 404–408.

13. FISA 1970, s.17(1).
14. S.I. 1971/226, Reg. 9. A child over sixteen who does not fall within this description will either be working or perhaps entitled to supplementary benefit on his own account.
15. Originally the Bill was not so widely drafted, but under opposition pressure, an amendment was introduced to enable *anyone* providing for a child in his or her household to claim FIS: 806 HC Deb., col. 1154.

(or she) is at least partly *providing for* the children.[16] It might have been thought that the children do at least have to live with the man and the woman in order to be included in the 'family', as any other view would be incompatible with the opening words of section 1, '. . . a family shall consist of the following members of a household'. However, the Commission has accepted the argument that a 'family' may include children boarded at a local authority school at the time of the claim, even though it is difficult to see how they could then be regarded as members of their parents' 'household'.[17] The fact that the children's absence from the household was temporary makes the result in this case reasonable, but it is submitted it would be wrong to allow a parent to claim FIS, when his (or her) children were away from home for very substantial periods.

Because a child may be provided for by two people living together in the same household (though not as man and wife), e.g., a brother and sister, or grandparents, it is possible for a child to be a member of two 'families' for the purposes of the legislation. The General Regulations state that in this case, in default of agreement between the persons concerned as to which family includes the child, the Commission or the appeal tribunal may determine this question in its discretion.[18] Rather oddly, it is not provided, as it was in the Family Allowances Act and is in the Child Benefit legislation, that in this situation the natural parent is to have priority.[19]

Finally, it is clear that where the 'family' consists of a man and a woman married to him, or living with him as his wife, only the man *or* the woman need be providing for the child for the latter to be included in the 'family'. This will be important in the situation where a man and woman are cohabiting, but the former (in full-time work with low earnings) refuses to look after her children. She will not generally be able to claim supplementary benefit,[20] but FIS may be paid for the family. Normally, a claim must be made jointly by the man and the woman, but the Secretary of State under the Regulations has power to accept a claim by one party, where, as here, it would be unreasonable to expect them both to apply.[1]

ii) Woman, not in the same household as husband, or man with whom living as wife, and child or children

The second type of 'family' is one where there is a 'single woman, engaged, and normally engaged, in remunerative full-time work', and a child or children for whom she is totally or partly providing.[2] A 'single woman' is defined by the Act to mean 'any woman other than one who is a member of

16. 'Providing for' is not defined in the 1970 Act, though S.I. 1971/226, Reg. 6 states that foster-parents are to be treated as not providing for children boarded with them. Cp FAA 1965, s.18, and see the Commissioners' decisions on the equivalent provision for dependants' allowances: ante, pp. 393–397.
17. *Poverty* (1974), No. 28, p. 32 and No.

29, p. 34. The meaning of 'household' is discussed in a different context, post, p. 562.
18. S.I. 1971/226, Reg. 7.
19. FAA 1965, Sch.; CBA 1975, Sch. 2, para. 4, ante, p. 463.
20. See chap. 12, ante, p. 486.
1. FISA 1970, s.5 and S.I. 1971/227, Reg. 2(6).
2. FISA 1970, s.1(1)(a) and (c).

the same household as a man to whom she is married or with whom she is living as his wife'.[3] Thus, a married woman living in a different household from her husband is a 'single woman' for the purposes of the legislation, and may be entitled to claim FIS, if she is in full-time work.[4]

There is nothing in the Act which affords any guidance on what it means to be a 'member of the same household' as someone else. This seems surprising; an identical omission also occurs in the supplementary benefits legislation.[5] The Supplementary Benefits Commission apparently adopts the view that a temporary physical separation does not mean that the spouses are not members of the same household,[6] but this may in some circumstances be too restrictive an approach. It is submitted that the Commission should place great weight on the financial arrangements between the woman and man concerned. If the woman is to all intents and purposes managing her own affairs, then it should be assumed that she, and the relevant children, form a separate family for FIS purposes.

The fact that a woman shares the household with, e.g., her brother or father, does not preclude her from being a 'single woman', as she is not then living with the man as his wife. If both she and her relative are contributing towards the maintenance of her children, then either could claim the supplement, assuming the applicant is engaged in remunerative full-time work. As Sir Keith Joseph pointed out, there may be two 'families' for FIS purposes in the same household.[7] The procedure for determining which of them is entitled to FIS has already been mentioned.[8]

iii) Man and child or children

The last category of family is the most straightforward, and numerically the least important.[9] A man, unmarried and not living with a woman as her husband, together with a child or children for whom he is wholly or partly providing, constitutes a 'family' for FIS purposes. In 1976 there were about 1,000 such families in receipt of the supplement.[10] It is, of course, irrelevant that the man's sister, or a housekeeper, is also living in the same household, though if she is also providing for the children concerned, then again there are two families for FIS purposes.

iv) Critique

The exposition of this section of the Family Income Supplements Act 1970 has been complicated. It may be, as one Labour lawyer suggested,[11] that it would have been better, certainly clearer, to have established a *'household income supplement'*, rather than have attempted to tie eligibility to the notion of a 'family'. It seems that the laudable extension of the notion of a 'family' to include, e.g., grandparents and grandchildren, has

---

3. Ibid., s.17.
4. Compare the similar rule for entitlement to affiliation payments: Cretney *Principles of Family Law* (2nd edn), pp. 422–423.
5. Ante, p. 487.
6. Handbook, para. 15.

7. 807 HC Deb., col. 1171.
8. Ante, p. 561.
9. See SBC Annual Report 1976, Cmnd. 6910, Appendix 5.
10. Ibid., Table 16.3.
11. Mr R. King Murray, 806 HC Deb., col. 1157.

led inevitably to complexity, and the oddity that children may be members of two, or possibly more, families. (Though it must be added that this has been a familiar source of difficulty in the law of family allowances, and there are comparable problems in the child benefit scheme[12]). A household income supplement might have been easier to understand; it might also be argued that it would have made more financial sense in the light of the aims of the legislation. Under the 1970 Act, a single woman, for example, will be entitled to FIS, as long as she makes some minimal contribution to providing for her children (and, of course, satisfies the other conditions). It is irrelevant that the major provision is made by, say, her parents with whom she shares a house. On the other hand, the alternative suggestion, necessitating the consideration of the resources of all members of that household, would have revived memories of the infamous 'household means test', abolished for national assistance purposes in 1940.[13] Moreover, it would still have been necessary to devise rules determining whose salary in the household was relevant and who was entitled to claim the benefit. In defence of the present law, it can also be stated that there is no evidence that it causes any practical problems.

B. Engaged in remunerative full-time work

The second condition is that the man, or single woman, must be 'engaged, and normally engaged, in remunerative full-time work'.[14] This requirement shows how FIS complements supplementary benefit, which is not payable to those in full-time work, with the exception of disabled self-employed people.[15] The government was clearly anxious to draw a sharp line between full-time and part-time employment, so that there would be no doubt which benefit a claimant might be entitled to.[16] The General Regulations, therefore, provide that thirty hours work a week is both a necessary and sufficient condition for being treated as 'engaged in full-time work'.[17] The implication of this might appear to be that a person working for more than thirty hours a week is ineligible for supplementary benefit; this view was put forward during the Committee Stage of the Bill.[18] But Sir Keith Joseph, rather contradicting his wish for a precise line, took the view that the SBC might in appropriate circumstances continue to make awards of supplementary benefit to someone working more than thirty hours a week, though less than the usual number of hours in his employ-

12. See chap. 11, *passim*.
13. See chap. 12, ante, p. 478. The present law on supplementary benefits does, however, treat householders and non-householders significantly differently, making much more generous provision for the former. This distinction is entirely absent in the family income supplements scheme, and may mean that some of those entitled are treated very

generously. But, conversely, there is no extra payment for those families paying an exceptionally high rent: post, p. 565.
14. FISA 1970, s.1(1)(a).
15. SBA 1976, s.6(1): ante, p. 482.
16. 806 HC Deb., col. 1135.
17. S.I. 1971/226 Reg. 5.
18. Mr C. Loughlin, 806 HC Deb., cols. 1138–1139.

ment.[19] This still seems to be the approach of the Commission, which states in the Handbook that, 'a person is considered to be in remunerative full-time work if he works the recognised week in his trade or employment'.[20] This may well be more than thirty hours. The borderline between eligibility for the two benefits is, therefore, not as precise as at times the government in 1970 wanted it to be. It appears extraordinary that this confusion still exists.

It seems that the thirty hours rule may be applied with some flexibility. In one case, an appeal tribunal upheld a submission that lunch hours should be included in addition to the twenty-eight and three-quarter hours actually worked in order to enable the claimant to be awarded FIS.[1]

The claimant must be in work at the time of the application; it is not enough that he has been at work and is temporarily sick or unemployed. The further requirement that the claimant is *normally* engaged' in full-time work prevents a person, usually employed, taking a casual short-term job, and supplementing his earnings for a full year by FIS.[2] On the other hand, the mere fact that the claimant has just ended a long period of unemployment before applying for FIS is irrelevant. In the ordinary course of events, FIS is assessed by reference to the claimant's gross earnings over the previous five weeks (or two months, if he is paid monthly), but the Regulations enable the Commission to assess his earnings on some other appropriate basis if he, inter alia, 'has commenced working in a gainful occupation shortly before the claim is made'.[3] The clear implication is that there is no minimum period for which the applicant must work before he claims the supplement.

Finally, the work must be *remunerative*. This has caused some difficulty in cases where the claimant is attending a course for which he is awarded some allowance. Can this be considered 'remunerative full-time work' for FIS purposes? In one case, an appeal tribunal in Coventry held that the claimant attending a government training centre for which he received a weekly allowance was entitled to FIS.[4] But more recently, a tribunal in Shoreditch took the opposite view, concluding that a trainee was neither employed nor self-employed, and an allowance was not the equivalent of wages for the purposes of the formula, 'remunerative work'.[5]

C. A family in 'Great Britain'

The 1970 Act[6] stipulates that the benefit shall be paid only to a 'family in Great Britain'. The General Regulations provide that a family is to be so

19. Ibid., col. 1139.
20. Para. 4.
 1. *LAG Bulletin*, Nov. 1974, p. 273.
 2. See EIRS, *LAG Bulletin*, May 1975, p. 124, to which the account in this paragraph is indebted; cf., on casual work, ante, p. 89.
 3. S.I. 1971/226, Reg. 2.

 4. *LAG Bulletin*, Jan. 1974, p. 16.
 5. Ibid., July 1976, p. 153. Handbook, para. 155 takes the view that in some cases a trainee will be eligible for supplementary benefit: ante, p. 551. This is consonant with the law under Social Security Act 1975: ante, p. 121.
 6. S.1(2).

treated if, and only if, at the date the claim is made, it is ordinarily resident in the United Kingdom and at least one adult member of it is resident in Great Britain.[7] It is ordinary residence and residence *when the claim is made* which are important; it does not seem to matter if, shortly after the award is made, the 'family' leaves the country. The requirement that one adult member only, and not the children, be actually resident in Britain at the relevant time appears generous. But, if the requirement that the 'family' must consist of 'members of a household' has any significance[8] then it is submitted that it would be rare in practice for one member of a family entitled to FIS to be resident without the others also satisfying the condition.

D. The weekly amount of resources falls short of the prescribed amount

The final condition relates naturally enough to the family's financial circumstances. The formula is that its resources (defined in section 4 of the Act and Regulations made under it) must fall short of the 'prescribed amount';[9] this amount, varying according to the number of children in the family, is set out in Regulations made under section 2.[10] The rate of FIS is half the difference between the prescribed amount and the family's resources, subject to a 'ceiling' or maximum award.[11]

i) The 'prescribed amount'

From November 1977 it is £43·80 for a family with one child, with a further £4·40 for each additional child.[12] It is not clear on what basis these amounts are calculated, though the impression was given in the Parliamentary debates that allowances were made for average weekly food, clothing and housing costs. The Liberal spokesman on social security matters, Mr. John Pardoe, moved an amendment to substitute for the figure given as the prescribed amount (then £15) a formula which would relate FIS to half the current national average wage, with 30% of this fraction for each additional child.[13] The suggestion was resisted. It is interesting that the prescribed amount has broadly kept pace with price increases, though not with the movement in average gross earnings.[14]

The most striking feature of the prescribed amount for FIS is, of course, its lack of flexibility, compared to supplementary benefit. In particular, despite a Labour attempt to make a provision for it,[15] there is no special rent allowance. The government wished the FIS scheme to be simple, and

7. S.I. 1971/226, Reg. 8. The concepts of 'residence' and 'ordinary residence' are discussed in chap. 10, ante, pp. 408–416.
8. For the meaning of 'household', see ante, p. 562.
9. FISA 1970, s.1(2).
10. As amended by CBA 1975, Sch. 4, para. 3.
11. FISA 1970, s.3.

12. S.I. 1977/1324. Recently increases have taken place twice yearly, partly, it would seem, to disguise the poverty trap; see ante, p. 558.
13. 806 HC Deb., col. 1159.
14. SBC Annual Report 1976, Cmnd. 6910, Table 16.2.
15. 806 HC Deb., col. 1177: see Barker in ed. Bull *Family Poverty* (2nd edn), pp. 77–79.

anticipated that the allowances and rebates introduced by the Housing Finance Act 1972 would deal with the difficulties arising from high rent payments. Nor does the amount of FIS vary with the age of the children, a factor which has been strongly criticised on the ground that older children are more expensive to feed and clothe.[16]

ii) The family's resources

Section 4(1) of the 1970 Act provides that the family's resources 'shall be the aggregate of the normal gross income of its members, including, except where regulations otherwise provide, the income of any child'.[17] Before discussing the assessment of resources, the preliminary point should be made that the income of all members of the family (except the children) must be aggregated; it is primarily for this reason that it is important to determine whether a woman is living with a man as his wife and, therefore, is a member of the 'family' for FIS purposes.[18]

a) THE CALCULATION OF EARNINGS. It is gross income which is relevant, not the person's net income after deduction of income tax, insurance contributions and expenses. The General Regulations provide that the weekly amount of the person's earnings is to be calculated by reference to his average earnings for the five weeks, or the two months (if paid monthly) preceding the date of the claim. But the Commission, or the appeal tribunal, may take some other appropriate period if this method is not suitable, e.g., because the claimant's earnings have fluctuated considerably during that time, or he has just started work.[19] This flexibility is particularly valuable for seasonal workers.[20] In the case of the self-employed, net profit is to be taken into account in assessing their income.[1]

b) THE CALCULATION OF OTHER INCOME, AND CAPITAL. Income, apart from earnings, is to be calculated or estimated on the basis the Commission, or appeal tribunal, thinks appropriate.[2] This is one of the few cases where the administering bodies have a wide discretion. The fact that under the legislation the income must be 'normal' precludes account being taken of occasional gifts. Some difficulty has arisen with regard to maintenance payments which a woman only receives occasionally or irregularly. It seems that the Commission has now accepted that the total amount of such irregular payments should not be averaged over the year in order to assess the woman's 'normal' gross income, but that a

16. Wynn *Poverty* (1970), No. 16–17, p. 24.
17. No regulations have, in fact, been made to aggregate children's income. The existence of the regulatory power was justified as a safeguard against possible abuse by parents in transferring income to their children: Sir K. Joseph, 807 HC Deb., col. 1292.
18. See ante, p. 560.

19. S.I. 1971/226, Reg. 2(2).
20. 807 HC Deb., cols. 1215–1220.
1. S.I. 1971/226, Reg. 2(3). The provision that *net* profits are to be taken into account is clearly sensible, and contrasts sharply with the refusal to allow any expenses in calculating earnings from employment.
2. Ibid., Reg. 2(4).

short-term award of FIS should be made for a few weeks, taking into
account only the maintenance received in the week of the claim.[3]

Under section 4(2) of the Act regulations may provide for treating
capital resources as equivalent to a gross income of the amount specified in
them.[4] But none has been issued, and it seems that the Commission in
practice ignores capital assets and investments in assessing entitlement to,
or the amount of, FIS.[5]

c) DISREGARDS. One of the most controversial aspects of the 1970 Act was
that it did not specify any disregards in assessing the family's income for
FIS purposes. Under considerable pressure from the opposition and some
of its own backbenchers, the government did promise that a few would be
allowed in regulations, but the eventual provision is very restrictive
compared with that in the supplementary benefits legislation.[6] There are,
however, some good reasons for thinking that the government was right in
its cautious attitude to this question. First, the existence of a large number
of disregards would have complicated the scheme, which was designed to
be simple and easy to administer. A more generous provision of disregards
would have necessitated the appointment of officials to check that they
were rightly claimed and not being abused. Secondly, it is not entirely
clear that their provision leads to equitable results. The point was well
made by Sir Keith Joseph, when he said that it was difficult to distinguish
'a family whose income is above the prescribed amount because of an
ingredient which is disregarded and is still helped by the supplement, and
another family whose income solely from earnings is the same but which
will not get a supplement'.[7]

The disregards which are allowed by the Regulations include the whole
of any attendance allowance,[8] the first £4 of a war disablement pension,
child benefit, boarding-out allowances paid by local authorities and the
rent allowances under the Housing Finance legislation.[9] A proposal to
allow a partial disregard of a wife's earnings, comparable to that available
for calculating supplementary benefit, was sternly resisted, on the ground
that this would be unfair to the family where the man's earnings were only
a little above the prescribed amount.[10] Other suggested disregards such as
that of sums paid by a man in maintenance to his separated wife, were
rejected because claims to them would require considerable scrutiny by
officials.

3. *LAG Bulletin*, April 1975, p. 99;
   Poverty (1976), No. 35, p. 50. For the
   power to make short-term awards of
   FIS, see post, p. 570.
4. This is done in the supplementary
   benefits legislation: SBA 1976, Sch. 1,
   para. 20: ante, p. 506.
5. *LAG Bulletin*, May 1975, p. 125.
6. For disregards in supplementary
   benefits, see chap. 12, ante, pp. 507–
   511.

7. 806 HC Deb., col. 1322.
8. A person entitled to an attendance
   allowance is paid supplementary
   benefit at a higher rate: see SBA 1976,
   Sch. 1, para. 10.
9. S.I. 1971/226, Reg. 2(5), as amended
   by S.I. 1972/1282 and S.I. 1977/324.
10. See Sir K. Joseph, 807 HC Deb., col.
    1191: see ante, p. 509 for this
    disregard in supplementary benefits.

iii) **The amount of family income supplement**

Under section 3 of the 1970 Act, the amount of FIS is to be one half the difference between the prescribed amount and the family's resources, but this is not to exceed (from November 1977) £9·50 with a further £1·00 for each additional child.[11] The assessment can be illustrated by a simple example:

A family with two children has a normal gross income of £35.80

The prescribed amount	£47·80 (£43·80 + £4·00 for the extra child)
Normal gross income	£35·80
The deficiency is	£12·00 and the amount of
FIS awarded is therefore	6·00

If the family's income were only £23·80, then the deficit would be £24·00, but the amount of FIS awarded would be only £10·50 because of the 'ceiling' imposed by section 3.

It seems that the object of paying only half the difference between the prescribed amount and the family's resources was to preserve some incentive on the part of the wage-earner to improve his position through salary rises, overtime, etc.[12] But, as has been mentioned in the discussion of the poverty trap,[13] it is arguable that the 50% 'marginal tax rate', consequent on the withdrawal of FIS after a wage rise, is itself enough to constitute a disincentive.

The imposition of the 'ceiling', or maximum award, has attracted some criticism.[14] Another justification was apparently the desire to avoid any collusion between employer and employee, which might occur if there were no limit on the amount which could be obtained.[15] The government even resisted a move at the Report stage to give the Supplementary Benefits Commission discretion to remove the 'ceiling' in cases of real hardship.[16] It is suggested that the government's case is hard to support, though it may be said that, because of the regular increases to the maximum permitted awards, the 'ceiling' now does not affect very many families.[17]

Part three. Claims to, and the Duration of, FIS

In this final Part the procedure for the making of claims and payments is briefly discussed. Inevitably the discussion here overlaps with the more general treatment of administration of benefits in chapter 14;[18] but it is important to mention the procedure here, because it reinforces the points

11. S.I. 1977/1324, Reg. 3.
12. See Sir K. Joseph, 806 HC Deb., col. 226.
13. Ante, p. 557.
14. George *Social Security and Society* (1973), p. 68.
15. Mr P. Dean, Under-Secretary of State, 806 HC Deb., col. 1265.
16. 807 HC Deb., cols. 1173–1178.
17. See the SBC Annual Report for 1976, Cmnd. 6910, para. No. 8.
18. Post, p. 587.

made earlier in this chapter concerning the scheme's alleged simplicity. Secondly, this Part is concerned with the duration of awards.

A. Claims to, and payment of, FIS

All claims must be made in writing on the prescribed form and sent to the offices of the DHSS in Blackpool where the scheme is administered. In contrast, therefore, to supplementary benefits, there are no interviews or applications across the counter in local offices.[19] The written claims procedure is consonant with the scheme's simplicity and the government's desire to reduce both the element of discretion in the making of awards and the administrative expenses. Pay-slips or other documentary evidence of income must be submitted with the claim form. Officials then check that the Act's requirements have been satisfied (e.g., the claimant is in remunerative full-time work and has a child or children) before making the award.

Usually a joint claim by the man and woman members of the family is required,[20] but the Secretary of State may accept as valid a claim by one of them if satisfied it would be unreasonable to exact this requirement.[1] Payment may be made to either person. The supplement does not 'belong' to one parent or the other.[2] This is perhaps a little surprising, as it might be thought that a measure directed largely to relieve child poverty would ensure that the supplement was the property of the mother. On the other hand, the point might be made that, as FIS supplements low *earnings* it would cause unnecessary conflict to pay it to the mother who is unlikely to be the family's principal earner.

B. Duration of FIS payments

The Family Income Supplements Act 1970 originally provided that payments of FIS should be made for twenty-six weeks, irrespective of any change in the family's circumstances subsequent to the making of the award. This period has since been extended to fifty-two weeks by the Pensioners and Family Income Supplement Payments Act 1972. The purpose is to reduce the number of claims, and thereby simplify the administration of the scheme. For this reason, the government successfully resisted a suggestion that a family should be able to reapply for FIS after a month, if its circumstances had changed for the worse in the meantime.[3] In effect, therefore, the family takes the original award 'for better or for worse' for the year: it is not entitled to a higher award, if its income drops or its requirements increase owing to the inclusion of another child within the family; but neither can the award be reduced if its earnings increase.

19. Post, p. 576.
20. FISA 1970, s.5(2).
 1. S.I. 1971/227, Reg. 2(6): see ante, p. 561.
 2. Compare the position under the family

allowances scheme and the priority of entitlement to the child benefit now enjoyed by the wife: ante, pp. 462–463.
 3. 807 HC Deb., col. 1203.

Although a change in the family's own circumstances will not affect the amount of FIS for the year following the award, it will benefit from any up-rating of the FIS levels during that period.[4] An additional reason for the twelve months duration of awards is that it postpones the operation of the poverty trap: a family with increased earnings keeps FIS for some time after this rise, and further if the FIS rates increase, as they now do at least annually, it will continue to receive the supplement (despite the higher earnings) and the effect of the poverty trap can be disguised for a very long time.[5]

When the applicant's earnings fluctuate considerably, it will be difficult for the Commission (or the appeal tribunal) to determine the appropriate rate of FIS, and the fact that an award subsists for a year may mean excessive payments will be made for a long time. The Commission, therefore, has power under the Regulations to make awards for a period of less than fifty-two weeks, though not less than four weeks, when the evidence leaves it in doubt as to the appropriate rate.[6]

4. S.I. 1971/226, Reg. 3(4).
5. See ante, p. 557, for a fuller discussion of the poverty trap.
6. S.I. 1971/226, Reg. 3(1).

14 Administration of Benefits

This chapter deals with a number of aspects of the administration of social security benefits, both contributory and non-contributory. Part One is concerned with the Department of Health and Social Security, the government department responsible now for all benefits, and Part Two with the Supplementary Benefits Commission, which superintends the administration of the two means-tested benefits. In Part Three the composition and functions of various advisory bodies are explored. The largest section of the chapter is Part Four, which analyses the rules regarding the making of claims to and payment of benefits. Lastly, Part Five discusses some of the various methods by which overpayments and mistaken payments of benefit are controlled – principally the procedure for recovery and criminal prosecutions.

Part one. The Department of Health and Social Security

Since 1968 the administration of social security benefits has been the responsibility of the Secretary of State for Social Services, who presides over the Department of Health and Social Security.[1] The survey of the Department's history and organisation here is necessarily brief; a fuller treatment will be found in books on the machinery of government and social administration.[2]

A. History

Before the reforms of 1946 heralded by the Beveridge Report, the administration of social security benefits was undertaken in a number of

1. As is usual in British government, the legal powers are vested in the Secretary of State, rather than in the department for which he is responsible: see S.I. 1968/1699. For general comment, see de Smith *Constitutional and Administrative Law* (3rd edn), pp 180–181.
2. See e.g., Willson *The Organisation of British Central Government, 1914–1964* (1967), pp. 143–174; Brown *The Management of Welfare* (1975), esp., chaps. 3–5.

different departments. The only Ministry with sole responsibility for a benefit was the Ministry of Pensions. This had been set up in 1916, and was responsible for the award of war pensions for death or disability suffered in the Great War and the Second World War.[3] Administration of health insurance, (the precursor of sickness benefit), and contributory pensions was shared by the Ministry of Health and the Approved Societies.[4] The Ministry of Labour was responsible for contributory unemployment insurance, which was paid at its labour exchanges. Unemployment assistance had since 1934 been the responsibility of the Unemployment Assistance Board; in 1940 this was renamed as the Assistance Board, when it was given the additional task of organising the payment of supplementary pensions.[5] The administration of non-contributory old age pensions paid under the 1908 Act was rather anomalously in the hands of the Commissioners of Customs and Excise.[6]

Beveridge proposed the creation of a Ministry of Social Security under a Minister with a seat in the Cabinet. It would be responsible for both social insurance and means-tested national assistance. The Report also urged consideration of an eventual merger of the new Ministry and the Ministry of Pensions.[7] The war-time government accepted these proposals only in part. The suggestion of a Ministry of Social Security, responsible for *all* welfare benefits, was rejected. Insurance and other universal benefits, such as family allowances, were to be the responsibility of a new Ministry, but public assistance was to be separately administered by the National Assistance Board.[8] The new Ministry of National Insurance was instituted by an Act of 1944. Originally, the measure had been entitled 'the Ministry of Social Insurance' Bill, but the term 'National Insurance' was preferred during the Committee stage. It seems that the desire for continuity with the pre-war national insurance legislation and the fact that the phrase 'social insurance' was used in Germany were largely responsible for this change.[9]

The Ministry of National Insurance became responsible for the administration of family allowances, benefits payable under the National Insurance Act 1946,[10] and industrial injuries benefits.[11] However, unemployment benefit was paid at offices of the Ministry of Labour, and,

3. See chap. 9 for the history of war pensions.
4. See chap. 4, ante, pp. 138–140, for the history of sickness benefit. The role of the Approved Societies in the administration of health insurance is discussed by Gilbert *The Evolution of National Insurance in Great Britain* (1966), *passim*, esp., pp 423–428.
5. Chap. 12 (history of supplementary benefits).
6. Chap. 5 (history of retirement pensions).
7. Paras. 385–387. See *Harris*, pp. 395–396.
8. Post, pp. 576–577.

9. It does not seem that the change was influenced by a dislike of the similarity between 'social insurance' and 'socialism'; cp., Bruce *The Coming of the Welfare State* (4th edn), p. 315. Both Attlee and Bevan voted for the change, though Beveridge himself resisted it.
10. Non-contributory pensions under the 1908 Act were administered by the National Assistance Board.
11. Workmen's compensation had been subject to the general control of the Home Office: see *Willson*, ante n.2, at p. 145.

since 1970, of the Department of Employment.[12] A new central office was set up in Newcastle to keep insurance records and superintend the administration and payment of long-term benefits and family allowances.[13] In line with the Beveridge proposals, the Ministry worked through regional and local offices.[14]

There was no move at this time to take further Beveridge's suggestion that there might be a merger of the new Ministry of National Insurance and the older Ministry of Pensions. Such a step would have been bitterly resented by the servicemen's organisations and would have run counter to the popular sentiment that war pensioners should have separate and privileged treatment. However, by the early 1950s there was a steady decline of war pensions awarded, and consequently of the staff and special hospitals required to deal with pensioners' problems.[15] In February 1953, the Prime Minister, Mr. W. Churchill, announced the government's intention to merge the two Ministries.[16] The change was made later that year despite fierce opposition in the House of Commons.[17] In one respect the position of war pensioners was much improved as a result of the merger. They had access to the 900 local offices of the Ministry of National Insurance, instead of the eighty to ninety local Pensions offices. War pensions continued to be administered (as they are now) under a central office at Blackpool.[18] Since 1953, a separate annual Report has been published on War Pensioners.

For the next twelve years there were relatively few changes in the structure of the new Ministry.[19] The next fundamental reform came in 1966, when at last Beveridge's wish for an integrated Ministry of Social Security was fulfilled.[20] The Ministry of Social Security Act of that year had the effect of merging the administration of insurance and means-tested benefits and hence abolished the National Assistance Board. Miss Herbison, then Minister of Pensions and National Insurance, gave four principal reasons for the decision.[1] First, it was desirable to co-ordinate policy for all social security benefits by vesting responsibility in one Ministry. Secondly, the merger would make it easier for those eligible to claim supplementary benefit in addition to contributory benefits. Thirdly, it would be possible to combine facilities to provide a comprehensive service. Fourthly, the reform would help to remove the suspicion that non-contributory benefits were inferior and the stigma associated with claiming them. Within the integrated Ministry, a separate body, the

12. For the special arrangements for claiming unemployment benefit, see post, p. 593.
13. 1st Report of the Ministry of National Insurance (1949), Cmd. 7955, paras. 19 and 64–80.
14. Ibid., at paras. 81–96.
15. 28th Report of the Ministry of Pensions, 1952–53 HC 271, paras. 116–120.
16. 511 HC Deb., col. 2314.
17. 517 HC Deb., col. 267: the Address

was only carried by 226–212 votes.
18. Report of the Ministry of Pensions and National Insurance for 1953, Cmd. 9159, paras. 242–244.
19. For the definitive account of the structure and work of the Ministry, see King *The Ministry of Pensions and National Insurance* (1958). (Sir Geoffrey King had been a Permanent Secretary at the Ministry.)
20. Ante, p. 572.
1. 729 HC Deb., cols 337 ff.

Supplementary Benefits Commission, was to be responsible for formulating policy on means-tested benefits.[2]

The main criticism voiced by the Conservative opposition was that this measure did not go far enough in bringing together the organisation of welfare benefits and social services. In particular, it was argued that the new Ministry should be combined with the Ministry of Health, and take over the children's department of the Home Office.[3] Two years later the Labour government accepted this. The Ministries of Health and of Social Security were abolished, and were replaced by the Department of Health and Social Security.[4] The Ministers' functions were transferred to the Secretary of State for Social Services. His title emphasises that he is not only responsible for the Department (DHSS), but also for the co-ordination of the whole range of social services.[5] The opposition naturally welcomed the change, though some anxieties were expressed that the reform might lead to the remoteness of the Department from the public.

B. The structure and organisation of DHSS

i) Department headquarters[6]

The Secretary of State for Social Services, who is always a Cabinet Minister, is assisted at the political level by a Minister for Social Security (since 1976 also in the Cabinet), and a Parliamentary Under-Secretary. At the top of the civil service structure is the Permanent Secretary responsible for all social security matters. Under him the social security branch of the Department is divided into two 'commands', each headed by a deputy secretary. One is responsible for contributory benefits policy, the other for the administration of all social security benefits[7] and overall control of regional and local offices. A Regional Directorate was set up in 1972 in the headquarters as a separate division under this second deputy secretary to form a link with the organisation of the Department outside London.[8]

Most of the social security work at headquarters is concerned with research into, and policy formulation on, benefits. All this is done by only 2,500 staff, a tiny fraction of the total employees of the DHSS (in 1976, about 85,000).[9]

ii) Regional offices

There are ten regional offices in England, and one in both Scotland and Wales.[10] All these offices have been integrated since the reforms of 1966, in that they are concerned with the administration of both contributory and means-tested benefits. The head of such an office, known as the regional

2. Post, pp. 576–577.
3. 729 HC Deb., cols. 1073–1078.
4. S.I. 1968/1699.
5. Mr R. Crossman, Secretary of State, 770 HC Deb., cols. 1609 ff.
6. This section is, of course, only concerned with the social security branch and not the health work of the DHSS.

7. This 'command' is subject to the policy directions of the SBC.
8. DHSS Annual Report 1972, Cmnd. 5352, para. 17.10.
9. DHSS Annual Report 1976, Cmnd. 6931, Table 29.
10. SBC Report 1976, Cmnd. 6910, para. 19.23 and Table 19.5.

controller, is responsible to the Regional Directorate at London headquarters. Assistant controllers superintend the various aspects of the work done by local offices in the particular region – e.g., the award of benefits, staffing and personnel, fraud and contributions matters.[11]

Control over local offices is exercised in a number of ways.[12] For example, finance officers control local office accounts, and check payment forms to see that the correct benefit is being paid.[13] A number of decisions, for example, to prosecute for abuse, must be taken at regional office level.[14]

iii) Local offices

The aim of the 1966 reform was to integrate as many offices as possible so that the public could claim and obtain advice at the same place on all benefits. At the end of 1976 there were 560 local offices of the Department, of which 365 were integrated.[15] In addition there are about 335 inquiry offices, (some of them only open part-time), where claims may be accepted and advice given. These offices, generally manned by one officer, are being closed down as the need for them declines.

At the head of a local office is the manager, with a senior executive officer as his deputy. Below them are the higher executive officers, responsible in a typical integrated office for sections dealing with contributory benefits, supplementary benefits, and contributions and fraud.[16] There are three further grades of staff: local officers I (formerly executive officers), local officers II (formerly clerical officers) and clerical assistants. The insurance officers who take decisions on entitlement to the contributory benefits are all local officers I.[17] Other officials of this grade superintend the actual payment of these benefits which is handled by local officers II. On the supplementary benefits side, it is the local officers I who take decisions on entitlement. Local officers II interview claimants and make a preliminary assessment of the award, but payment may only be authorised by a member of the higher grade. Clerical assistants perform routine tasks such as filing.

Mr. J. Griffiths, then Minister of National Insurance, said when introducing the 1946 Bill, that local offices should be 'centres where people will not be afraid to go, where they will be welcome, and where they will not only get benefits, but advice'.[18] In recent years there has been some anxiety about the difficulties caused by rapid staff turnover; this particularly affects the administration of supplementary benefits where there is so much personal contact between applicant and the Department's staff.[19]

11. See *Brown*, ante p. 572 n.2, at pp. 98–100.
12. See ibid., at p. 100, and *Fisher*, paras. 53–54.
13. Ibid., at para. 55.
14. Ibid., at para. 58 (decisions to prosecute); para. 338 (decisions to use special investigators in cohabitation cases where fraud is suspected).
15. SBC Report 1976, ante n.10, at para. 19.23.
16. See Brown *The Management of Welfare*
(1975), pp. 86–93; Stevenson *Claimant or Client?* (1973), chap. 3 contains some useful information on the structure of the Department so far as it is concerned with supplementary benefit administration. The text here owes much to these two books.
17. See post, pp. 624–625 for the insurance officer's adjudicatory role.
18. 418 HC Deb., col. 1754.
19. SBC Report 1975, Cmnd. 6615, para. 15.5.

A safeguard against incompetence is that a sample of awards is checked by senior executive officers or the office manager to ensure that the correct payments are made.[20] An important development has been the greater emphasis on staff training which is given at various regional centres.[1]

iv) The central office at Newcastle

In addition to policy headquarters in London, there are two central offices. The first, at Newcastle upon Tyne, was set up in 1946, and now employs over 12,000 staff.[2] The contribution records are kept there, so every claim for benefit, where entitlement depends on a contributions' record, is referred to Newcastle. It is also from there that books are issued and renewed for the long-term benefits, such as retirement and widows' pensions. A new office nearby at Washington in County Durham has been set up to administer the child benefit scheme.

v) The central offices at Blackpool

The Blackpool central offices process claims for war pensions, attendance allowance, mobility allowance and FIS.[3] The office at Norcross has been responsible for the central administration of war pensions since the 1920s. FIS is administered at an office at Poulton-le-Fylde, Blackpool, which employs about 100 staff to deal with postal claims.[4]

Part two. The Supplementary Benefits Commission

A. General

The origins of the SBC can be traced to the creation in 1934 of the Unemployment Assistance Board which administered assistance for unemployed people. Its institution to some extent represented a middle course between the two more obvious alternatives of entrusting the administration to central government or, as under the poor law from 1930, to the committees of local authorities.[5] The latter was rejected, because it was thought that public assistance committees were too generous with their awards. On the other hand, to have made the Ministry of Labour responsible would have been to expose the Minister to criticism in Parliament for particular decisions,[6] and generally to have made the details of the scheme a matter of party politics. This was avoided by the institution

20. *Fisher*, paras. 49–52.
 1. See DHSS Annual Report 1972, ante n.8, at para. 17.16, and SBC Report 1975, ante n.19, at para. 15.6.
 2. DHSS Annual Report 1976, Table 29. For a general treatment and description of the work at the Newcastle office, see *Brown*, ante n.16, at pp. 81–86.
 3. See DHSS Annual Report 1975, Cmnd. 6565, paras. 2.21 and 8.33.

 4. SBC Report 1976, ante n.10, at para. 16.5 (see chap. 13 for claims for FIS).
 5. See chap. 12, ante, pp.475–479, for the history of public assistance and the poor laws.
 6. The constant barrage of Parliamentary Questions to which the Ministers of Pensions have been subject during both world wars on the award of war pensions shows the extent of this problem!

of an independent Board which took responsibility for both policy and the making of individual decisions, subject to general control by the Minister of Labour. Another factor may have been the contemporary enthusiasm for semi-independent public boards aroused by the success of the BBC and the Central Electricity Board.[7]

The Unemployment Assistance Board was given additional functions in 1940 when it was made responsible for the payment and administration of supplementary pensions.[8] When the government at the end of the war decided not to implement the Beveridge proposal for a Ministry of Social Security responsible for all forms of welfare benefit,[9] it was natural that public assistance should be administered by the Assistance Board, now renamed as the National Assistance Board. Its membership remained unchanged, but it is clear from the drafting of the 1948 Act that it was to be regarded as an independent government department.[10] The most important regulations concerning the requirements and resources of applicants were made by the Minister of National Insurance on the basis of drafts submitted by the NAB, but the latter had substantial power to make regulations for the general administration of the scheme.[11]

The Board's abolition in 1966 was really an inevitable consequence of the integration of the administration of insurance and means-tested benefits.[12] At first, the Minister, Miss Margaret Herbison, was even opposed to the institution of a separate body within the Ministry for superintending the award of supplementary benefits; but eventually she appreciated the advantage of creating the Commission, particularly to take controversial discretionary decisions – otherwise the Ministry would be exposed to constant criticism.[13] Thus, the SBC is responsible for adjudicating on claims, and subject to the Act and regulations, for formulating general policies to guide officers in exercising the Commission's discretionary powers. It, however, has no regulatory power.

It is clear that the SBC is not a separate government department.[14] Thus, the Parliamentary Commissioner for Administration deals with suspected cases of maladministration concerning supplementary benefits, because the DHSS is listed in Schedule 2 to the 1967 Parliamentary Commissioner Act as a department which may be subject to investigation. The Commission is a body corporate,[15] and, therefore, may enter into contracts, etc., and be sued in its own name. The members of the Commission itself, (unlike its staff)[16] are not civil servants, and their tenure is regulated by their terms of appointment.[17] It is difficult, therefore, to improve on de Smith's description of the Commission as 'a semi-autonomous public corporation'.[18]

7. See Willson *The Organisation of British Central Government, 1914–1964* (1957), pp. 157–159.
8. See the history of public assistance in chap. 12, ante, p. 478.
9. Ante, p. 572.
10. See NAA 1948, ss. 2(3) and 10(4). (For a legal analysis of the position of the NAB, see Steele *The National Assistance Act 1948* (1949)).
11. NAA 1948, s.15(1).
12. See ante, p. 573.
13. 729 HC Deb., col. 339.
14. See de Smith *Constitutional and Administrative Law* (3rd edn), pp. 177–178, 603.
15. SBA 1976, Sch. 3, para. 1(1).
16. See post, pp. 578–579.
17. SBA. 1976, Sch. 3, para. 2.
18. *de Smith*, ante n.14, at p. 183.

The formal powers and legal status of the Commission, however, do not necessarily give an accurate impression of its influence.[19] The expertise and experience of its members may make the Commission influential in the development of social security policy. In this context, it is perhaps important that Mrs. Barbara Castle, the Secretary of State in 1975, asked the Commission to submit a separate Annual Report in which it could indicate what it saw as the priorities in the development of policies.[20] This marks a return to the practice of the NAB. The Commission's first two reports have been long documents, which contain many valuable ideas concerning the future of means-tested benefits and show clearly that the SBC is prepared to take an independent approach.[1]

The Commission consists of a chairman, deputy chairman and up to six other members, all appointed by the Secretary of State for Social Services.[2] At least two members must be women.[3] Otherwise there is no restriction on those eligible for appointment. The chairman from October 1975 has been David Donnison, formerly a Professor of Social Administration. Most of the other members have some social services experience. Two are trade unionists.[4] In practice, the Commission meets once a month to consider policies with its advisers from the DHSS. Working parties of three or four members are set up to examine particular questions, such as the operation of the cohabitation rule.[5] The Commission does not employ its own staff, but works through DHSS officials at all levels from policy advisers down to the officers who handle claims in the Department's local offices.

B. Officers of the Commission

This Part concludes with some brief remarks on various officers of the Commission who perform special tasks, often of a general welfare nature. Their existence emphasises the peculiar character of the SBC, which seems to some extent to assume a welfare role in addition to performing the functions of a cash providing agency.[6] There often is some resulting confusion between the responsibilities of the Commission and of local authority social services departments.[7]

i) The social work adviser and the social work service
The adviser's function is to give the SBC assistance in the performance of

19. On this subject, see Stevenson *Claimant or Client?* (1973), pp. 69–70; Donnison, 5 Jnl. Soc. Pol., 337.
20. 891 HC Deb., col. 262.
 1. For a critical review of the first Report by Field, and a reply by the Chairman of the SBC, see *New Society*, 23 Sept. 1976, p. 658, and 30 Sept. 1976, p. 704.
 2. SBA 1976, Sch. 3, para. 1.
 3. Ibid., para. 1(3). Under the NAA 1948, only one member of the NAB had to be a woman, and it consisted of a chairman, deputy chairman and up

to four other members.
 4. For the present composition of the Commission, see its Annual Report 1976, Cmnd. 6910, p. xvi.
 5. SBC Annual Report 1975, Cmnd. 6615, para. 1.5. The results of this study are discussed, ante, p. 405.
 6. Some mild scepticism about the value of this welfare role is expressed in the SBC Report 1975, ante n.5, at paras. 2.23–2.29.
 7. Hill *The State, Administration and the Individual* (1976), pp. 178–180.

its welfare roles, and help in the provision of suitable training for the specialised officers. He is now at the head of the social work service, established within the Department when the children's service was transferred from the Home Office in 1971.[8] Social work service officers are now attached to the regional offices of the Department.[9]

ii) Special welfare officers[10]

There are about fifty special welfare officers attached to the DHSS regional offices. Cases of particular difficulty, e.g., where the claimant is completely unable to look after his financial arrangements, are referred to them by local offices.

iii) Unemployment review officers[11]

Their function is to interview and help those who are out of work and have been in receipt of supplementary benefit for a substantial time.[12] There are about 110 executive officers working full-time in this capacity at regional offices; others work full or part-time at local offices.

iv) Special investigators[13]

Special investigators are based in regional offices of the Department. Their function is to investigate cases of suspected abuse or fraud in obtaining social security benefits. Cases are referred by local offices, when they present particularly intractable problems. The investigators are recruited from the ranks of executive officers and receive a month's training for their work which obviously requires tact and patience. It is particularly sensitive in cohabitation cases; the use of investigators in this area has been reviewed earlier.[14]

v) Liable relative officers[15]

Unlike the other specialist officers, they are based in local offices. Their task is to interview women, separated from their husbands, and single women with illegitimate children, and discuss the possibility of taking maintenance or affiliation proceedings against the man liable to maintain them and their children.[16]

Part three. Standing Advisory Bodies[17]

Government departments have often made use of advisory bodies in the administration of the various social security schemes, the first of these

8. See Brown *The Management of Welfare* (1975), pp. 74–75.
9. *Stevenson*, ante n.19, at p. 68.
10. Ibid., at pp. 72–73.
11. Ibid., at pp. 76–78, and see SBC Report 1975, ante n.5, chap. 9.
12. See ante, pp. 537–538, for a detailed account of their work.
13. *Stevenson*, ante n.19, at pp. 74–76, and see *Fisher*, paras. 408–417.
14. Ante, p. 487.
15. *Stevenson*, ante n.19, at pp. 73–74.
16. Ante, pp. 543–546, for further discussion of this work.
17. This discussion does not cover the work of the Royal Commissions and ad hoc Departmental Committees, which have also obviously played an important part in the development of social security law and policy.

committees being set up soon after the end of the First World War for war pensions.[18] Advisory bodies may either be national organisations or local committees. To a large extent their functions will differ according to this categorisation. Central advisory bodies will tend to be employed to give advice on matters of general policy, and to comment on the drafting of regulations made by the Secretary of State in the exercise of his delegated legislative powers. They are not suited to handling complaints from claimants, or dealing with detailed questions concerning the administration of benefits in the regions. On the other hand, local bodies are able to perform these functions, though, of course, they may also be competent to give advice on broader questions.

A second general point concerns the attitude to be adopted by the advisory committees to the government Department on the one hand, and to social security claimants on the other. The question is whether these committees regard themselves primarily as experts consulted to give disinterested advice on the formation of policy, or whether they see themselves as mainly concerned to 'represent' the public as consumers of welfare benefits. In this second case, there will inevitably be some tensions between the Department and its advisory committee. Unfortunately, there has been no full study of the role of these committees which would enable a coherent answer to be given to this question. The probability is that the committees' attitudes reveal both approaches at different times, depending on the issues and the composition of the particular body.

A. The National Insurance Advisory Committee[19]

i) Composition and powers

Under the Unemployment Insurance Act 1934 there had been an Unemployment Insurance Statutory Committee, the principal duty of which was to report on the financing of the scheme. It also scrutinised the draft regulations made under the Act, and made recommendations to the Minister of Labour for improvements in the law.[20] The Committee's chairman was Beveridge. His report in 1942 recommended the institution of a general social insurance statutory committee to take over all the functions performed in a narrower context by the Unemployment Statutory Committee, and in addition to make recommendations for changes in the level of benefits and contributions.[1] The Labour government did not support this proposal, but instead set up the National Insurance Advisory Committee (NIAC).

It is interesting that the Minister of National Insurance had contemplated a much larger committee, consisting of up to fifty people and representative of all types of contributors under the new scheme.[2] But it

---

18. War Pensions Act 1921: see post, pp. 585–586.
19. See *George*, p. 92. See also Harrison, [1952] Public Administration, 149; Griffith, 12 MLR, pp. 311 ff.

20. Bruce *The Coming of the Welfare State* (4th edn), p. 271; *Harris*, pp. 357–361.
1. Para. 390.
2. 418 HC Deb., cols. 1736–1737.

was decided that such a body would be too large, and a smaller committee on the lines of the Unemployment Statutory Committee was preferred. NIAC consisted then of a chairman, and between four and eight other members.[3] Its functions were, and still are, first, to prepare reports on general matters referred to it by the Minister (now the Secretary of State), and secondly, to consider regulations submitted to it in draft. Under the National Insurance Act 1946 *all* regulations made by the Minister had to be submitted to NIAC, though in cases of extreme urgency, he could issue regulations without waiting for the Committee to report; they would, however, only be in force until three months after he received its report.[4] The Comittee was under a duty imposed by the 1946 legislation to publish the draft regulations and receive comments from the public; this is no longer mandatory.[5] However, the requirements that NIAC report on the regulations submitted to it, and that he lays this report before Parliament, are still exacted under the Social Security Act 1975.[6] He must provide reasons for any failure to follow the committee's recommendations.

In its initial years the Committee was extremely busy. By July 1949 it had reported on twenty-seven sets of regulations, and all its recommendations with one exception had been adopted.[7] In the eighteen months before the end of 1950 it met twenty-six times and submitted a further eighteen reports on regulations, in addition to a major review of the position of seasonal workers.[8] Though its work-load became less heavy during the 1950s, largely because fewer regulations were made, the Committee continued to make a substantial contribution by producing some major reports on general matters – e.g., maternity benefits,[9] the death grant,[10] widows' benefits[11] and contribution conditions.[12] These reports often contain the best published discussion of the policies underlying the law, and the reasons for the formulation of the rules in the statutes and regulations. Their usefulness has been recognised by the Commissioners who are willing to look at them as an aid to the interpretation of regulations.[13] The NIAC reports are generally unanimous, but there have been one or two influential minority reports.[14]

There was no legal change in the composition or powers of the Committee until 1973. In the Schedule to the Social Security Act of that year the composition of the Committee was increased to a chairman and six to ten other members.[15] All members hold appointment for three to five years as determined by the Secretary of State, and are eligible for re-appointment. Apart from the chairman, four members are to be appointed after

---

3. NIA 1946, Sch. 5, para. 1.
4. Ibid., s.77(4).
5. Post, p. 582.
6. S.139(3), (4).
7. 1st Report of the Ministry of National Insurance (1949), Cmd. 7955, para. 61.
8. 2nd Report of Ministry of National Insurance (1951), Cmd. 8412, para. 112.
9. (1951), Cmd. 8466, ante, p. 248.
10. (1956), Cmnd. 33, ante, p. 244.
11. (1956), Cmnd. 9684, ante, p. 236.

12. (1956), Cmd. 9854, ante, p. 71.
13. R(G) 3/58; R(U) 7/73 (Tribunal decision).
14. See, in particular, the dissenting opinion of Lord Collison to the effect that persons with occupational pensions should retain their full entitlement to unemployment benefit, a view still represented by the law: NIAC Report (1968), Cmnd. 3545: see ante, p. 442.
15. See now SSA 1975, Sch. 15, para. 1.

consultation with respectively employers' representatives, workers' organisations, friendly societies and the head of the Northern Ireland Department.[16] These provisions have not been changed since the 1946 Act. In addition, the Committee must now include 'one person with experience of work among, and of the needs of, the chronically sick and disabled', and in selecting a member regard is to be had to the desirability of having a chronically sick or disabled person on the Committee.[17] NIAC's composition was discussed at some length by the Standing Committee on the 1973 Bill. The opposition argued that there should be two members chosen after consultation with organisations representative of persons claiming benefit, e.g., the Child Poverty Action Group, Age Concern and the National Council of Women.[18] The amendment was resisted by the government on the ground that, even with the increase in the size of the Committee to ten members (in addition to the chairman), it was difficult enough to secure a balanced body; moreover, consideration had to be given to securing a geographical balance and ensuring that there were women members.[19]

It is perhaps unfortunate that MPs did not debate two more serious changes made by the 1973 Act. First, it is provided that the Secretary of State is to refer proposals for regulations to NIAC, 'unless it appears to him that by reason of the urgency of the matter it is inexpedient to do so'.[20] This appears to give him a very wide discretion not to submit draft regulations to the Committee. There is no apparent reason for this change; it may be that it was thought right to give the Secretary of State the broad discretion not to refer which he has always enjoyed in regard to the Industrial Injuries Advisory Council.[1] It is also true that referral entails delay of a few months. The result, however, is that now comparatively few regulations are submitted to NIAC.[2] The second change made by the Social Security Act 1973 is that it is no longer *mandatory* for NIAC to publish notice of the fact that draft regulations have been submitted to it, allowing objections by interested groups. In practice it seems that the Committee does still usually follow this procedure, leaving four weeks for representations to be made by the public.[3]

It is difficult not to conclude that to some extent the importance of the National Insurance Advisory Committee has been in decline over the last few years. More disturbingly, the DHSS seems to have connived in this process. Not only are fewer regulations referred to it, but the work of the Committee is not now given the emphasis in the DHSS Annual Reports that

---

16. SSA 1975, Sch. 15, para. 3.
17. See the Chronically Sick and Disabled Persons Act 1970, s. 11.
18. Standing Committee E Debates on the Social Security Bill 1973, col. 800.
19. Ibid., at cols. 803–804.
20. See now SSA 1975, s.139(1), consolidating SSA 1973, s.48(1).
 1. See post, p. 584.
 2. In 1975 NIAC did not make any reports, while in 1976 it reported on

five sets of regulations. Of these, HC 271 on S.I. 1976/409 (Invalid Care Allowance Regulations) and HC 349 on S.I. 1976/615 (Medical Evidence Regulations) are important reports, which critically examine the policy behind the Regulations.
 3. It does not appear that NIAC always gives an opportunity for the public to submit comments on draft regulations, particularly of a technical nature.

it used to be in the 1940s and 50s.[4] In its comments on draft regulations, it should reinforce Parliamentary scrutiny of delegated legislation, though there is some doubt whether this aspect of its work was ever very effective.[5] In the Standing Committee debates on the 1973 Social Security Bill, Sir Brandon Rhys-Williams urged the Secretary of State to give NIAC more important work to do. He concluded: 'Potentially it is a standing Royal Commission'.[6] This opportunity has certainly been missed.

ii) The effect of a failure to consult NIAC

There is no direct authority on the legal consequences of a failure by the Secretary of State to refer draft regulations to NIAC, in those cases where he is under a duty to do this. The broad discretion not to refer, where it is inexpedient because of urgency,[7] makes this question now less important, perhaps even academic. In those cases where he did not refer a regulation to the Committee, it might be open to the Secretary of State to argue that it was inexpedient – though it is the practice to state that this view was taken in the preface to the statutory instrument. The consequence of a failure to consult a particular body, where there is a duty to do so imposed by statute, is a general problem in administrative law. A recent case suggests that this requirement will be treated as mandatory, and, therefore, that non-compliance will render a regulation void.[8] This is also the view of writers on administrative law.[9] In the absence, therefore, of the deliberate and valid exercise of a discretion not to refer a regulation to NIAC, it is submitted that failure would entail the nullity of the regulation.[10]

B. The Industrial Injuries Advisory Council[11]

The Industrial Injuries Advisory Council (IIAC) was set up by the 1946 legislation to act as an advisory body to the Minister of National Insurance

4. Indeed in the Annual Reports of the DHSS 1973–76, there is no mention of NIAC, except in Appendices where its composition is given!
5. See Harrison, [1952] Public Administration, 149, 158.
6. Standing Committee E Debates on the Social Security Bill 1973, col. 806.
7. See ante, p. 582.
8. *Agricultural, Horticultural and Forestry Industry Training Board v Aylesbury Mushrooms Ltd* [1972] 1 All ER 280, [1972] 1 WLR 190.
9. See Griffith and Street *Principles of Administrative Law* (5th edn), pp. 101–102; Garner *Administrative Law* (4th edn), pp. 76–77; de Smith *Judicial Review of Administrative Action* (3rd edn), p. 125.
10. This also applies to a failure to refer

industrial injuries regulations to the Industrial Injuries Advisory Council, where the mandatory requirement, subject to the discretion not to refer, has existed since 1946: see post, p. 584. On general principles, a ministerial decision not to refer to NIAC or IIAC could be challenged in the courts, e.g., if it was taken in bad faith or was grossly unreasonable, but it is doubtful whether in practice such a challenge would succeed.
11. See King *The Ministry of Pensions and National Insurance* (1958), pp. 119–120; *George*, p. 92. A Workmen's Compensation (Supplementation) Board exercised certain administrative functions with regard to pre-1948 industrial injuries cases: see chap. 8, ante, p. 340.

on industrial injuries matters. It has always been a larger body than NIAC, and its procedure less formal. It consists of a chairman and an unspecified number of other members to be determined, and appointed by, the Secretary of State.[12] At the end of 1975, it consisted of sixteen members in addition to the chairman, Professor D. S. Lees.[13] After consultation with various outside organisations four of the members must be appointed to represent employers, and four to represent employed earners.[14] The Council must also include at least one person experienced in the needs of the chronically sick and disabled, and as with NIAC, in choosing this person the desirability of having a disabled person as a member should be taken into account.[15] The difficult medical questions involved in determining whether there is a case for prescribing a disease as an 'industrial disease' under section 76 of the Social Security Act 1975 are normally referred for examination to an Industrial Diseases Sub-Committee.[16] Its views are considered by the full Council, and then embodied in a report to the Secretary of State. The Dale Committee in 1948 recommended that a separate body should be instituted to advise on industrial diseases;[17] but the idea was rejected because IIAC would in any case have to look at the industrial diseases regulations, so the setting up of a second body would entail unnecessary duplication.[18]

The Council has two functions under the legislation.[19] First, it considers draft regulations relating to industrial injuries referred to it by the Secretary of State. He is under a duty to refer all such regulations unless it appears inexpedient to do this because of urgency. This discretion not to refer has existed since the National Insurance (Industrial Injuries) Act 1946.[20] IIAC has never been under any procedural requirements with regard to publication of regulations and the consideration of objections from the public. The Secretary of State does not have to lay before Parliament the Council's report, or state why he does not propose to follow its conclusions. In practice the Council does not often publish its reports on regulations. This would seem to make the work of IIAC in this repect less effective than that of NIAC; it reflects the fact that, in comparison with the latter, IIAC does not generally deal with matters of policy.

The second function of the Council is to advise on general questions relating to industrial injuries benefits and administration referred to it by the Secretary of State. Like the National Insurance Advisory Committee, IIAC is not entitled to choose its own subjects for review, though in June 1956, it seems that arrangements were agreed which enable the Council to select for inquiry those diseases which it wishes to consider for prescription as an 'industrial disease'.[1] Several valuable reports on various aspects of industrial injuries benefits have been submitted: time-limits for claim-

12. SSA 1975, Sch. 16, para. 1.
13. Professor Lees is also chairman of NIAC: see DHSS Annual Report 1975, Cmnd. 6565.
14. SSA 1975, Sch. 15, para. 1(2).
15. Chronically Sick and Disabled Persons Act 1970, s.12.

16. See Chap. 8 on industrial injuries, ante, pp. 293–297.
17. Cmd. 7557.
18. See King, ante n.11, at p. 120.
19. SSA 1975, s.141.
20. S.61(2)(a).
 1. Report of Ministry of Pensions and N.I. 1956, Cmnd. 229, para. 259.

ing benefit,[2] recovery for pneumoconiosis,[3] 'paired organs',[4] and on a number of occasions whether a disease should be prescribed as an 'industrial disease'.[5] Dissents to the reports have been submitted quite frequently; for example, one member dissented from one of the recommendations in the 'paired organs' report, and five signed a separate minority report.

C. The Attendance Allowance Board

The Attendance Allowance Board was set up by the National Insurance (Old persons' and widows' Pensions and attendance allowance) Act 1970.[6] It consists of a chairman and between four and nine other members, appointed by the Secretary of State. All except two of them must be medical practitioners, and of the other two, one or both may be a medical practitioner.[7] At the end of 1975, the Board had nine members, two of whom were not medically qualified.

In addition to its primary function to adjudicate on claims to an attendance allowance,[8] the Board also has an advisory role, now imposed by section 140 of the Social Security Act 1975. It advises the Secretary of State on matters which he refers to it, and may recommend changes in the attendance allowance provisions.[9] It may also be asked to give advice to him on the exercise of his powers in relation to the scheme.[10] For the purpose of exercising these advisory functions only, additional members (not necessarily medical practitioners) may be appointed to the Board.[11] These powers are certainly as broad as those of NIAC and IIAC, though at the moment of writing, there does not appear to have been any published report of the Board in the exercise of these functions, notwithstanding that regulations have been referred to it under section 140.[12] What is particularly interesting is the combination in one body of adjudicatory and advisory roles. Perhaps it would be useful to repeat this in other areas: might not, for example, social security law be improved if general matters were on occasion referred to the National Insurance Commissioners for their comment?

D. The Central Advisory Committee on War Pensions[13]

The Central Advisory Committee was set up by the War Pensions Act 1921.[14] It is a large body consisting of about thirty members, with the

2. (1952), Cmd. 8511. See post, pp. 594–599.
3. (1953), Cmd. 8866.
4. (1956), Cmd. 9827.
5. E.g., the Reports on Brucellosis, (1972), Cmnd. 4971, and on Occupational Deafness (1973), Cmnd. 5461.
6. Renamed as NIA 1970, by NIA 1972, s.8(4).
7. SSA 1975, Sch. 11, para. 1(1).

8. Ibid., s. 105: see chap. 15, post, pp. 641–642.
9. Ibid., s.140(1)(a).
10. Ibid., s.140(1)(b).
11. Ibid., Sch. 11, para. 1(2).
12. E.g., S.I. 1975/598.
13. See King The Ministry of Pensions and National Insurance (1958), pp. 33–34; George, p. 92.
14. S.3.

Secretary of State as chairman. Under the Chronically Sick and Disabled Persons Act 1970, it must include in its composition at least twelve local war pensions committee chairmen and one war disabled pensioner.[15] It is required to meet at least once a year; in practice it does not meet more frequently. Its role is essentially to give advice to the Secretary of State on questions concerning entitlement to, and the administration of, war pensions. The membership of the Committee and some details of its work are given in the annual Reports on War Pensioners.

E. War Pensions Committees

These committees, often known as local war pensions committees, were set up by the War Pensions Act 1921[16] to give advice to pensioners on the various benefits they might be entitled to and to give general welfare assistance. With the decline in the number of pensioners in the last few years, several committees have been disbanded or amalgamated with others, and now the number is eighty-one.[17] Although one of their functions is to advise the Secretary of State on the local administration of war pensions, it seems that the committees' principal role is to help the pensioners themselves. This general 'welfare' role is now unique in the social security system, and shows the particularly favourable treatment which has often been accorded to war pensioners.[18]

F. Local Social Security Advisory Committees[19]

The continued existence of the war pensions committees contrasts sharply with the fate of the local social security advisory committees: they were abolished by the Social Security Act 1971.[20] They had been formed in 1966 on the merger of the administration of national insurance and national assistance by the Ministry of Social Security Act.[1] Previously there had been area advisory committees, which assisted officers of the NAB on local matters, e.g., as to the prevailing rents in the area, and gave advice in individual cases.[2] There had also been local national insurance committees which were more concerned with such matters as the location of and facilities at local insurance offices, and how publicity for the benefits might be improved.[3]

The social security advisory committees elected panels of members whom managers of local offices could consult on the particular problems of people in receipt of supplementary benefit,[4] as well as discharging the

15. S.9(1).
16. S.2.
17. Report for 1976, HC 472, p. 13.
18. See chapter 9, where this point is made at p. 355.
19. See *George*, p. 93; *King*, ante n.13, at p. 121.
20. S.9.
  1. Ante, pp. 573–574.

2. See the last Report of the NAB (1965), Cmnd. 3042, p. 2.
3. There is a full description of the composition and functions of these committees in the 2nd Report of the Ministry of National Insurance (1951), Cmd. 8412, paras. 115–117.
4. Report of Ministry of Social Security (1967), Cmnd. 3693, para. 86.

general advisory rules of their predecessors. The principal reason for their abolition, given by Sir Keith Joseph during the Standing Committee debates on the 1971 Bill, was that in view of the greater expertise of office managers and their staff, the committees were no longer needed.[5] To some extent this raises the general issues discussed in the introductory paragraphs of this Part. If the primary role of these committees had been to advise the government Department, then the facts that local managers were more familiar with the area's problems, and employed expert staff would be relevant. On that assumption there is much to be said for Sir Keith Joseph's argument. But, as a number of opposition members stressed, the committees could also be useful in representing the views of people who were or had been in receipt of welfare benefits.[6] If emphasis is put on that role of the local advisory committees, their abolition seems much less justifiable.

Against this background it is interesting to note the recent recommendation by the National Consumer Council that a User Consultative Committee should be set up to monitor the work of the SBC.[7] This body should, the Council suggested, be composed of social workers, representatives of welfare rights organisations and the recipients themselves, and local office managers of the DHSS. It should review such matters as the general policy with regard to discretionary payments, the information and assistance given by staff to 'customers', and any reasons for delays in processing claims.[8] Some of these matters were within the functions of the disbanded advisory committees, and others might usefully have been referred to them. It might be concluded, therefore, that in the context of the trend towards greater citizen involvement, the step taken by the Social Security Act 1971 was unfortunate.

Part four. Claims and Payments

A. Claims: General rules

i) When a claim is necessary

It is almost always a necessary condition for entitlement to benefit that a claim is made in the manner prescribed under the legislation. Thus, a claim is necessary for almost all contributory and other benefits payable under the Social Security Act 1975,[9] for child benefit,[10] for supplementary benefits[11] and for FIS.[12] There are a few exceptions under the Social Security Act 1975:[13]

5. See Sir K. Joseph in Standing Committee E Debates on the Social Security Bill 1971, cols. 461–464.
6. Ibid., at cols. 452–458.
7. National Consumer Council discussion paper, *Means-Tested Benefits* (1976).
8. Ibid., at pp. 61–62.
9. SSA 1975, s.79(1).
10. CBA 1975, s.6(1): see chap. 11, ante, p. 468.
11. There is no express provision that entitlement is to depend on the making of a valid claim, but it is a reasonable implication from SBA 1976, s.14(2)(a).
12. FISA 1970, s.1(2).
13. S.79(2).

a Category A or B retirement pension to a woman over 65 on her ceasing to be entitled to a widow's benefit; in some circumstances a Category C or D retirement pension; an age addition.[14]

An increase of benefit, *either* in respect of a child or adult dependant *or* for a supplement to disablement benefit, e.g., for unemployability or special hardship, must be the subject of a separate claim.[15]

The desirability of the condition that a claim must be made was emphasised by a majority of a Tribunal of Commissioners in *R(1) 6/62*. It was argued there by the claimant that there was no need for him to make a further claim for a special hardship allowance at the end of the period for which it had previously been awarded, since he continued throughout to be entitled and could, therefore, rely on his original claim.[16] This contention was rejected by the majority. They said that if it were correct,

> 'a claimant could compel the statutory authorities to leave a claim in abeyance and could then revive it many years afterwards, when owing to the lapse of time there would be the utmost difficulty in investigating it'.[17]

It is submitted that this approach is right. Although the requirement of a valid claim may on occasion work hardship for someone who has omitted to claim (or claim in time[18]), a system of automatic entitlement to welfare benefits would *generally* be unworkable. There are, however, important exceptions such as child benefit and FIS, where it would be possible to integrate payment with the tax system, and thereby avoid the necessity of making an application for benefit.[19]

ii) The claim must be made in writing on an appropriate form

There is a general requirement that a claim must be submitted in writing to the Secretary of State on the form approved by him for the particular benefit, 'or in such other manner, being in writing, as he may accept as sufficient in the circumstances...'.[20] In the relevant Supplementary Benefit, FIS and Child Benefit Regulations, the detail is added that the form must be delivered or sent to an office of the DHSS.[1] Claim forms are to be supplied without charge.[2] In practice almost all claims, except those for unemployment benefit and sometimes supplementary benefit, are made by post.

If the claim is defective when received by the Secretary of State, e.g., because the wrong form has been used, he may refer it to the claimant; provided the form is then returned correctly completed within a month, the application may be treated as if it had been properly made in the first place.[3] Under the Social Security and the Child Benefit Regulations, a

---

14. The conditions in which a claim need not be made are set out in S.I. 1975/560, Reg. 3, amended by S.I. 1977/1509, Reg. 4.
15. S.I. 1975/560, Reg. 2(4), now replaced by S.I. 1976/1736, Reg. 5(2).
16. For special hardship allowance, see chap. 8, ante, pp. 318–332.
17. *R(I) 6/62*, para. 15; and see *R(F)*

18. See post, pp. 593–600, for time-limits.
19. See ante, pp. 36–39.
20. S.I. 1975/569, Reg. 4. Also see S.I. 1976/964, Reg. 2 (Child Benefit Regs.).
1. S.I. 1977/1142, Reg. 3; S.I. 1971/227, Reg. 2; S.I. 1976/964, Reg. 2.
2. E.g., S.I. 1975/560, Reg. 5.
3. E.g., S.I. 1975/560, Reg. 8(1); S.I. 1976/964, Reg. 2(4).

claim may be amended by notice in writing sent to the Department, and then the amended claim may also be treated as if it had been made in the first instance.[4]

These requirements have been considered by the Commissioner. The most important ruling is that, while it is for the Secretary of State to decide whether to accept a document as an alternative to the approved form, it is for the statutory authorities to determine whether the documents constitute a valid claim. Therefore, the fact that the Secretary of State had accepted letters from the claimant's father, instead of the appropriate form, did not preclude the Commissioner from ruling that they did not amount to a good claim for unemployment benefit.[5] The intention to claim must appear on the face of the relevant documents. It is not enough if it can only be inferred from other papers.[6]

iii) Information to be given when making a claim for benefit

It is a standard rule that the claimant shall furnish those certificates, documents, information and evidence for the purpose of determining his claim, which are required by the Secretary of State, and if reasonably so required, shall attend an office of the DHSS.[7] These provisions appear to enable the Secretary of State to impose requirements as to the evidence, etc., to be adduced by a *particular claimant*. The Chief Commissioner in Northern Ireland has doubted whether such rules are intra vires.[8] The Social Security Act 1975 empowers the making of regulations,

> 'for requiring claimants to furnish to the prescribed person any information required for the determination of the claim or of any question arising in connection with it'.[9]

As the Chief Commissioner suggested, this provision would only seem to authorise the making of regulations imposing requirements to supply information (the exact character of which must be specified in the regulation) in various types of case (e.g., a medical certificate in a sickness benefit claim), but not regulations giving the Secretary of State power to require the production of unspecified documents. Moreover, it is difficult to reconcile the power, which appears to be conferred by the regulations, with the fact that under the legislation it is for *the insurance officer* to determine whether a claim should succeed or fail on the evidence.[10] Certainly there does not appear to be any warrant for a conclusion that a failure to produce the required evidence necessarily entails the failure of the claim. It is clearly for the statutory authorities to decide whether it should succeed.[11]

4. S.I. 1975/560, Reg. 8(2), and S.I. 1976/964, Reg. 2(5).
5. *R(U) 9/60.*
6. *R(S) 1/63.*
7. See, e.g., S.I. 1975/560, Reg. 7(1), and S.I. 1976/964, Reg. 3(1).
8. *R 1/75 (P)*, T.A. Blair, Chief Comr.
9. SSA 1975, s. 79(5).
10. Ibid., s.98; post, pp. 624–625, for adjudication by insurance officers.
11. See *R 1/75 (P)*, where the Commissioner took this view. It is perhaps possible that a claim submitted without the required information is not made *in the prescribed manner*, and, therefore, fails to meet the condition for entitlement imposed by section 79(1) of the Act. But this would seem to be reading too much into the emphasised words.

A more acceptable use of the regulatory power is made in the provisions requiring, inter alia, the production of a birth certificate in a claim for widowed mother's allowance or child's special allowance or an increase of benefit in respect of a child, and a death certificate where the death grant is claimed.[12] Even in these cases, it seems clear that the omission to produce the required evidence will not entail the claim's failure.[13] A certificate (now a doctor's statement) is normally required by the Medical Evidence Regulations made under section 115(1) of the Social Security Act 1975, when a claim is made for sickness, injury or maternity benefit.[14]

The power of the SBC, under the Supplementary Benefit Regulations, to require a person to attend at an office or place[15] is understood by the Commission to authorise the requirement of a medical examination. This view has been approved, it seems, by the Parliamentary Commissioner for the Administration; he, therefore, rejected a charge of maladministration by a person refused benefit after failing to attend an examination.[16] This seems an unfortunately wide interpretation of the scope of the Regulation. In other areas of social security law, the legislation itself specifically empowers the making of regulations which either expressly require the claimant to submit himself for a medical examination, or alternatively disqualify him from benefit if he fails to attend.[17] It is submitted that such an obligation should only be imposed under precise powers.

iv) Interchange with claims for other benefits

In certain circumstances it has been provided that a claim for one benefit may be treated alternatively or additionally as a claim for another benefit to which the person is entitled.[18] This provision assists a person who has made a claim for one allowance, and then discovers that he is really entitled to another. If his application for this second allowance were regarded as made only at this later stage (and not when the original claim was made), he might be disqualified from receiving it because of the time-limits.[19] Regulations providing for the interchangeability of claims have been made under both the Social Security and the Child Benefit Acts.[20]

> The Social Security Regulations provide, inter alia, that where a person has claimed a benefit listed in one column of Schedule 3 to the Regulations, the claim may be treated as a claim in the alternative for any benefit listed in the second column of the Schedule.[1]

12. S.I. 1975/560, Regs. 7(2)–(4).
13. The failure to produce a death certificate will not defeat a claim for widow's benefit: see ante, p. 232.
14. S.I. 1976/615, Reg. 2 (for details on the medical certification procedure, see chap. 4, ante, pp. 152–155).
15. S.I. 1977/1142, Reg. 4.
16. 3rd Report of the PCA for 1974–75, HC 241, Case No. C 156/J.
17. See e.g., SSA 1975, s. 20(2)(b)

(sickness benefit); s.22(9)(b) (maternity allowance); s. 89(2)(a) (industrial injury benefits).
18. Ibid., s.80(1), as amended by SS(MP)A 1977, s.17(2).
19. See post, pp. 593–600, for time-limits.
20. S.I. 1975/560, Reg. 9 and S.I. 1976/964, Reg. 5.
1. S.I. 1975/560, Reg. 9(1). Schedule 3 has been amended by S.I. 1975/1058, Sch. 2 & S.I. 1976/409, Reg. 17(6).

Thus, a claim for sickness benefit may be treated as a claim for invalidity benefit, injury benefit or non-contributory invalidity pension,[2] a claim for maternity allowance may be treated as a claim for sickness, invalidity benefit, or non-contributory invalidity pension, and a claim for a retirement pension of one category may be treated as a claim for such a pension of any category. Other regulations provide that where one person has made a claim for a dependant's increase to which he is not entitled, the claim may be treated as made by some other person who may be entitled to an increase in respect of this dependant.[3]

It was at one time unclear whether the decision to treat a claim as one in the alternative for another benefit was to be made by the Secretary of State or the statutory authorities. The British Commissioner decided that the matter was one for the Secretary of State,[4] but a Northern Ireland Tribunal held that it was for the statutory authorities to determine this question.[5] As it is the authorities who determine whether the documents submitted constitute a valid claim,[6] there was much to be said in principle for allowing them to decide whether to treat a claim as one for another benefit. However, it is now clearly provided that the question is one for the Secretary of State.[7] This is also made plain in the Child Benefit Regulations, under which the Secretary of State may in his discretion accept a claim for child benefit as a claim for –

child's special allowance, guardian's allowance, maternity benefit claimed after confinement, industrial death benefit for children, and increases for child dependants.[8]

Correspondingly, a claim for one of these benefits may be treated as a claim for child benefit, where it appears that the claimant may be entitled alternatively, or in addition to, that benefit.[9]

Finally, it may be mentioned that the Claims and Payments Regulations provide that, where a certificate of expected confinement has been issued and the woman has claimed sickness benefit (or her claim for maternity allowance is treated as one for sickness benefit), her claim may be treated as one for sickness benefit for the *whole maternity allowance period*.[10] She is, of course, only entitled to sickness benefit if she satisfies the relevant conditions; the Regulation merely provides that her claim may be treated as a claim for it.[11]

v) When a claim is made
The date on which a claim is made may be important for determining the

---

2. A claim for any of these four benefits may be interchangeable with a claim for one of the others.
3. S.I. 1975/560, Reg. 9(3).
4. R(I) 79/54.
5. R 2/69 (II).
6. Ante, p. 589.
7. SSA 1975, s. 95(1)(e): for Secretary of State's questions, see chap. 15, post, pp. 621–624.
8. S.I. 1976/964, Reg. 5(1).
9. Ibid., Reg. 5(2).
10. S.I. 1975/560, Reg. 10. For the maternity allowance period, see chap. 7, ante, p. 253.
11. See R(S) 1/74, H. Magnus, Comr.

relevant time-limit.[12] The Social Security Act 1975 now provides that when a claim or notice is sent by post, it

> 'shall be deemed to have been made or given on the day on which it was posted'.[13]

This confirms a decision of the Chief Commissioner interpreting earlier regulations.[14] Provided the claimant can show that he has posted the claim, the 'risk' of non-delivery is placed on the DHSS. In other areas, however, the rules are not so generous to the claimant:

> The Child Benefit (Claims and Payments) Regulations provide that the date of claim is the date on which it is received in a department office, though if the Secretary of State knows that a claim sent by post has not been delivered in the ordinary course of post, he *may* treat the claim as made on an earlier date: the date on which it would have been delivered in the ordinary course of post or the date thirteen weeks before it was delivered, whichever is the later.[15] There is a similar rule in the FIS Regulations.[16]

There is no obvious reason why these Regulations should differ from the general social security rule; one possible explanation is that, as both FIS and child benefit must be claimed from a central office,[17] and not locally, it is less reasonable for the DHSS automatically to run the risk of the post going astray.

vi) Time-limits: general principles

The most important aspect of the Claims and Payments Regulations is the imposition of time-limits for claiming the various benefits. If the claim is not made within the time prescribed for the particular benefit, then the claimant is disqualified from receiving it, either absolutely or in respect of the period specified in the Regulations.[18] The reasons which may justify the imposition of time-limits are largely those which support limitation periods in all civil proceedings: the desire to achieve certainty and avoid adjudicating claims on stale evidence. The absence of time-limits would, moreover, make administration more costly and the financing of the National Insurance Fund less predictable. These arguments are persuasive with regard to certain benefits, such as those for sickness and unemployment, where it may well be difficult to decide a late claim because of the unreliability of the evidence. On the other hand, it seems difficult to defend the existence of a time-limit for claiming a retirement pension, when the applicant would probably have little trouble in substantiating a claim brought months or years after he attained pensionable age and became entitled. The National Insurance Advisory Committee and the

12. Post, pp. 593–600.
13. S.79(6).
14. *R(I)* 2/71.
15. S.I. 1976/964, Reg. 2(2).
16. S.I. 1971/227, Reg. 2 (1A), inserted by S.I. 1972/1282, Reg. 3: see post, p.

599, for mobility allowance.
17. From the central offices at Blackpool, and Washington, Co. Durham, respectively: ante, p. 576.
18. S.I. 1975/560, Reg. 13.

Industrial Injuries Advisory Council have both emphasised that a balance should be struck between the desire to protect the administration against an abundance of stale claims, and the need of the individual to have a reasonable time within which to bring his claim.[19] In particular, the claimant 'should not be precluded from drawing the appropriate benefit by any act or default on his part, for which the ordinary man would hold that he had a good excuse'.[20]

These ends are achieved, first, by the imposition of time-limits which vary from one benefit to another. Thus, benefits which an ordinary man may claim frequently in his life, (e.g., sickness benefit), have shorter time-limits than those which are less often applied for, where it is understandable that the applicant may take longer to appreciate that he has a claim, (e.g., the death grant). The details of the various time-limits are mentioned in the next section. Secondly, for most of the benefits available under the Social Security Act 1975, the prescribed time-limit may be extended if the claimant shows that there is 'good cause' for his failure to apply within the specified period.[1]

B. The time-limits and other rules for particular benefits

i) Unemployment benefit

In addition to submitting a written claim, a person applying for unemployment benefit is usually required to attend in person at an unemployment benefit office of the Department of Employment.[2] Unemployment benefit is thus the only contributory benefit for which an application is not normally made by post. At the benefit office, the claimant is interviewed and told to register for work at the separate employment office. The latter office registers him and calls him in for interview if he finds difficulty in finding work. The former office processes the claim for benefit, and the practice is that the applicant is told to come back weekly, at a particular time on a particular day, to claim benefit for the previous week.[3]

Under Schedule 1 to the Claims and Payments Regulations,

> the claim for unemployment benefit must be made on the day in respect of which the claim is made, and the claimant loses benefit if it is not claimed then.

But this is modified so that the applicant is not disqualified provided he claims on the day of the week specified in the notice given him by the

---

19. Report of NIAC on Time-Limits, (1952), Cmd. 8483; Report of IIAC on Time-Limits for claiming industrial injury benefits, (1952), Cmd. 8511; Report of NIAC on Time-Limits (1968), Cmnd. 3597, paras. 6–7.
20. Cmd. 8483, para. 15.
1. See post, pp. 601–606.

2. S.I. 1975/560, Reg. 4.
   Unemployment benefit is administered by the Department of Employment, subject to the policy directions of the DHSS.
3. See *Fisher*, paras. 80 and 244–245. But see post, p. 608, n.20 for the experimental system of fortnightly payments.

unemployment benefit office.[4] This qualification now provides the legal basis for the practice discussed in the previous paragraph. The rule is illustrated by *R(U) 6/75* :

> The claimant was required to attend the benefit office on Wednesday of each week. He failed to attend on Wednesday, 18 December 1974, but called the following day to claim benefit from 12 December 1974 to 19 December 1974, explaining that his failure to attend on the Wednesday was due to his presence at his old firm's Christmas lunch. The Commissioner, H. A. Shewan, held that the claimant had failed to show good cause for his delay in claiming benefit, and was disqualified from receiving it for the period 12 to 18 December 1974.

The Commissioner said that unemployment benefit was a day-to-day benefit, and that the effect of the modification was only to remove the disqualification for a late claim, where such claim was made *on the day specified by the office*. A failure to claim on this specified day inevitably entailed the claimant's disqualification from benefit for all the days for which the claim was late.

A certain amount of additional flexibility is provided by Regulation 12. This empowers the Secretary of State to certify that there are or will be circumstances making it difficult to apply the normal rules and practices concerning claims to unemployment benefit. This certificate may have effect either generally, or in relation to a case or class of cases or an area.[5] When it does have effect, the insurance officer may treat a claim for benefit as one for up to thirteen weeks, and then benefit may be awarded for the whole or part of that period.[6] The award only subsists as long as the claimant satisfies the conditions of entitlement.[7] This power is useful for times and in areas where long-term unemployment may be anticipated, or where, perhaps because of geographical remoteness, it is difficult for the claimant to attend weekly at a benefit office.

ii) Sickness, invalidity and industrial injury benefit, and non-contributory invalidity pension

In all these cases the time-limit varies according to whether the claim is an original claim, the first claim in a period of illness or a continuation claim.[8]

a) ORIGINAL CLAIM. This is a claim 'where the claimant has at no time made a claim for sickness or injury benefit or non-contributory invalidity pension under the Act or a claim which has been treated as a claim for sickness or injury benefit or non-contributory invalidity pension.'[9] It does not matter if the previous application was ineffective; it was still a claim and any subsequent one cannot be regarded as original.[10]

---

4. S.I. 1975/560, Sch. 2, para. 1.
5. Ibid., Reg. 12(1)(a).
6. Ibid., Reg. 12(2). Also see S.I. 1977/1288, Reg. 3.
7. S.I. 1975/560, Reg. 12(3).

8. Ibid., Sch. 1.
9. Ibid., as amended by S.I. 1975/1058, Reg. 21(5)(b).
10. *R(S) 8/52.*

The prescribed time for making an original claim is twenty-one days from the earliest day for which the claim is made; if it is made after that time (in the absence of good cause for the delay), the person concerned is disqualified from receiving benefit for any day more than 21 days before the date on which it is made.

This time-limit is generous in comparison with the six and ten day limitation periods for first and continuation claims respectively.

This twenty-one day period for initial claims was introduced in 1951 following a recommendation of the National Insurance Advisory Committee, and was designed to give a more generous period for applicants who, it might reasonably be presumed, were unfamiliar with the requirements for making a claim.[11] In 1964 NIAC questioned whether this 'concession', as it was termed, was necessary in view of the existence of the benefit for nearly twenty years. But it thought it should be retained for young claimants making their first claim soon after leaving school and starting work.[12]

b) FIRST CLAIM IN A SPELL OF ILLNESS OR INJURY. Unless the claim is an original one, the first claim for benefit in a spell of illness or injury must be made within a period of six days from the earliest day in respect of which the claim is made. If a claim is submitted after this period, no benefit is payable in respect of any day more than six days before the actual date of claim. Before 1964, the applicant was required to submit a notice of incapacity for work within three days,[13] but upon the recommendation of NIAC this requirement was abolished and the general time-limit of six days imposed.[14]

c) CONTINUATION CLAIM. Any other claim is known as a continuation claim and must be made within ten days of the start of the period for which it is made. NIAC in 1964 rejected suggestions to extend this period to fourteen days.[15] Generally there will be no difficulty in determining whether a claim is a first or a continuation claim, but problems did arise in R(S) 1/68;

> On 15 September 1966 C submitted three medical certificates, claiming benefit from 29 August 1966 to 12 September 1966. On these three forms his doctor had certified (on three different days in this period) that C was incapable of work for a particular period. The question was whether these forms constituted one claim or three. The Chief Commissioner, R. G. Micklethwait, ruled that there were three claims and that the last two certificates constituted continuation claims. On that basis, C was not disqualified from receiving sickness benefit after 3 September 1966.[16]

11. 1951, HC 240.
12. Cmnd. 2400, paras. 22–23.
13. The notice could be accompanied by the claim for benefit or be followed by a claim within the next seven days.
14. Ante n.12, at paras. 16–21.

15. Ibid., at para. 24.
16. The 4.9.66 was ten days before the date of the claim (15.9.66), as Sundays are not counted in estimating the limitation period: see R(S) 3/56.

It is provided that a claim for sickness, invalidity or industrial injury benefit or for non-contributory invalidity pension is to be treated (unless the Secretary of State otherwise directs) as if made for the period specified in the medical certificate.[17] Benefit may be awarded on that claim for the whole or part of that period up to thirteen weeks. The usual requirement that a medical certificate in the form of a doctor's statement be submitted with a claim for sickness, invalidity and injury benefit is discussed elsewhere in this book.[18]

iii) Increase, in respect of any dependant, of the benefits in i) and ii) and of invalid care allowance

As has been mentioned previously,[19] an increase in benefit for a dependant must be separately claimed, and there are separate claim forms.[20]

> The increase must be claimed within the longer of two periods: one month from the day in respect of which the claim is submitted *or* the period from that day until one month after the date of a timeous claim in respect of that day for the relevant personal benefit.[1]

In other words, the claimant has at least one month from the time that the personal benefit is payable for himself, within which to claim for dependants.[2] NIAC has expressed satisfaction with this limitation period.[3] If an applicant is out of time for claiming a dependant's increase, he is disqualified from receiving it. (He may, of course, claim an increase for a later period in respect of which he does satisfy the time-limit).

iv) Maternity benefit

a) MATERNITY GRANT

> A maternity grant claimed on the ground of actual confinement must be claimed within three months of the confinement.[4] When it is claimed on the alternative basis of an 'expectation of confinement', it may be applied for within the period beginning fourteen weeks before the expected week of confinement and ending immediately before the date of confinement. The grant is entirely forfeited if it is not claimed within these periods.

b) MATERNITY ALLOWANCE

> A maternity allowance in respect of an expectation of confinement may be claimed during the three week period beginning with the fourteenth week before the expected week of confinement. If, however, it is claimed on the basis of actual confinement, then it

---

17. S.I. 1975/560, Reg. 11(1).
18. Ante, pp. 152–155.
19. Ante, p. 588.
20. *Fisher*, para. 86.
1. S.I. 1975/560, Sch. 1 para. 3, as amended by S.I. 1976/409. See Appendix.

2. See *R(S) 38/52*, para. 7.
3. Cmd. 8483, para. 30.
4. For the alternative bases for claiming a maternity grant or allowance, see chap. 7, ante, pp. 249–254.

must be applied for within three weeks of that date. A late claim leads to disqualification for receipt of benefit in respect of any week before the claim is actually made. Benefit is, however, payable for the remainder of the maternity allowance period.

c) INCREASE OF MATERNITY ALLOWANCE IN RESPECT OF A DEPENDANT

The limitation period for claims for dependant's increases to awards of sickness benefit, etc., applies here.[5] In effect, the applicant may claim in the period between the first day in respect of which the claim is made and one month after the maternity allowance itself was timeously claimed. If she claims late, she is disqualified for receipt of benefit for any period more than one month before the date of claim.

Under Schedule 2 it seems that a claim for an increase may alternatively be made in advance of the period for which it is claimed, provided it is made within fourteen weeks of the expected week of confinement, when the claimant becomes entitled to the allowance itself.[6]

v) Retirement pension, widow's benefit and other benefits

The prescribed time-limit for claiming a retirement pension of any category, widow's benefit, child's special allowance, guardian's allowance and invalid care allowance is three months from the date on which the claimant became entitled to the benefit in question.[7] If the claim is made after that period, benefit is forfeited for the period more than three months before it was made.

Under Schedule 2 a retirement pension may be claimed in advance up to four months before the date on which the applicant becomes entitled.[8] In practice what normally happens is that about four months before someone reaches pensionable age, he is informed by the DHSS that he may claim a pension and an application form is sent to him. On its return pension is assessed in the central office at Newcastle,[9] where the documents go for incorporation in the records.[10]

A request for a claim form for widow's benefit (and the death grant) is found on the back of the death certificate issued by the Registrar.[11] The claim is generally made at the local office. A claim for guardian's or child's special allowance is usually sent to the local office, from where it is forwarded to the child benefits central office at Washington, Co. Durham where a decision is given.[12]

5. See Appendix.
6. S.I. 1975/560, Sch. 2, para. 3.
7. Ibid., Sch. 1, para. 5. (The list here is not exhaustive.) For invalid care allowance, see S.I. 1976/409, Reg. 17(5).
8. S.I. 1975/560, Sch. 2, para. 4(1). See ante, p. 211 for the separate requirement of notice of retirement.
9. For the central office at Newcastle, see ante, p. 576.
10. *Fisher*, para. 85. It is not maladministration if the DHSS neglects to operate the 'reminder system'. See 5th Report of PCA for 1975–76, HC 496, Case No. C.644/V.
11. *Fisher*, para. 84.
12. For this new office, see ante p. 576.

vi) Death grant

Every person claiming a death grant may be required by the Secretary of State to provide a death certificate, and in some cases of a child's death a birth certificate.[13]

> The grant must be claimed within six months of the death, or a longer period to be determined by the Secretary of State.[14] The grant is forfeited entirely if not claimed in time.

The period for claiming used to be only one month, but NIAC in its report of 1952 recommended an extension – as that period was too short in view of the emotional distress often suffered.[15]

vii) Disablement benefit (including increases) and industrial death benefit

> In all these cases the prescribed time for claiming is the period of three months from the first day on which the conditions of entitlement to the benefit, or additions to benefit such as unemployability supplement or the special hardship allowance, are satisfied.[16] A late claim leads to disqualification from receipt of the benefit for the period more than three months before it was made.

But this does not apply to a disablement gratuity; in effect there is no penalty at all for making a late claim for this benefit. This was decided by the Commissioner in two cases in the early 1950s,[17] and they were followed with reluctance by R. S. Lazarus in *R(I) 14/74*:

> 'The regulation perpetuates in the law governing the industrial injuries insurance scheme an anomaly which cannot have been intended when the scheme came into force in 1948, and for which I am unable to perceive any justification'.[18]

The point does not appear to have been discussed in the IIAC report of 1952, though that body did recommend on a related matter that the *payment* of lump sum gratuities should not be extinguished within the (then) period of three months.[19]

There are a variety of special procedural rules relating to claims for disablement benefit, including the requirement with regard to giving notice of accidents, and the obligation to submit to medical examination or treatment.[20] A claimant may withdraw an application for disablement benefit (for the purpose of continuing his entitlement to injury benefit) by delivering a notice to that effect at the office of the DHSS dealing with his

---

13. S.I. 1975/560, Reg. 7(4).
14. Ibid., Sch. 1, para. 6. This appears to be the only case where the Secretary of State has discretionary power to extend the normal time-limit.
15. Ante n.3, at paras. 45–46.
16. These periods were harmonised after the Report of IIAC on Time-Limits in 1952, Cmd. 8511, at paras. 17–21. See Appendix.

17. *R(I) 27/52*; *R(I) 51/53*.
18. Para. 6. The regulation referred to is now S.I. 1975/560, Sch. 1, para. 7, col. 3, which clearly excludes the gratuity from the disqualification provision.
19. Ante n.16, at para. 25: see post, p. 610.
20. Chap. 8, ante, pp. 337–338.

claim.[1] This will be effective if it is received before the application for disablement benefit has been 'finally determined'.[2]

An increase of disablement benefit in respect of a child or adult dependant must be separately claimed.

> The prescribed time is the longer of two periods: three months from the first day on which the claimant is entitled to that increase *or* the period from that day to one month after the date of a claim for the unemployability supplement.[3]

viii) Attendance allowance
Attendance allowance cannot be paid for any period before the claim is made.[4] There is also no question of extending the period in which a claim may be made by showing 'good cause' for the failure to make the claim earlier.[5]

ix) Mobility allowance
A person is not entitled to a mobility allowance for any week before that in which the claim is *received by* the Secretary of State.[6] If the claimant satisfies the Secretary of State that a claim has been posted earlier but it has not been received in the ordinary course of post, entitlement may begin in an earlier week, though not more than three months before the date on which the claim is received.[1] This rule is similar to those for child benefit and FIS, and less generous than the normal rule that a claim is made when it is posted.[8] A claim for a further period, made within three months after the end of a period for which the allowance has been awarded, may be treated as if it had been made immediately after the end of the latter period, and entitlement determined on that basis.[9]

A forward claim for the allowance may be made for a period beginning not more than three months after the claim has been received, and an award made for that period.[10] There is the usual provision in this situation that, if the person does not suffer from the anticipated disability, the award will be reviewed.[11]

x) Supplementary benefit[12]
There are two claim forms for supplementary benefit. The general form used, SB1, is available at any post office or local office of the Department. Unemployed claimants are required to submit their claims on the form B1, obtainable at the unemployment benefit offices of the Department of

1. S.I. 1975/560, Reg. 25.
2. For the meaning of this, see ante, p. 301.
3. S.I. 1975/560, Sch. 1, para. 10. The increase is only payable to persons entitled to the supplement: cf., ante, p. 385.
4. SSA 1975, s.35(4). See 1st Report of the PCA for 1975–76, HC 37, Case No. C.347/V.
5. This extension only applies to the benefits specified in Sch. 1 of S.I. 1975/560, as amended: see post, p. 601, n.9.
6. SSA 1975, s.37A(5)(b), inserted in that Act by SSPA 1975, s. 22.
7. S.I. 1975/1573, Reg. 4(1).
8. Ante, p. 592.
9. S.I. 1975/1573, Regs. 4(2) and 6.
10. Ibid., Reg. 5(1).
11. Ibid., Reg. 5(3).
12. See *Lynes*, pp. 33–35 and 37–38.

Employment.[13] On receipt of the form, the manager of the local office may arrange for a home visit to be paid when details of the claimant's resources and requirements will be taken. This visit is normally made within a week, though it may be expedited if the applicant has indicated that his needs are pressing.[14]

Alternatively the applicant may decide to claim in person at the local office. Normally appointments are arranged to save time. The applicant is advised to arrive with as much supporting information as possible, e.g., rent book, child benefit order book, wage-slips, and any evidence of other income or expenditure.[15] If all the relevant information is forthcoming at this interview, then the officer may make a full award of benefit. On the other hand, when the information is not complete, an interim award may be made and a final decision postponed until a home visit is made.[16]

The claim for supplementary benefit must be made at the start of the period to which it relates.[17] But in 'exceptional circumstances' the SBC may treat a claim as made earlier and award benefit from that date.[18] 'This may be done, for example, if a person was wrongly advised that he was not entitled to benefit'.[19] An appeal tribunal has backdated a claim, when the applicant had wrongly claimed unemployment benefit, thinking that she was claiming supplementary benefit.[20]

xi) FIS

Many of the particular rules for claiming FIS have been discussed in chapter 13.[1] Awards run from the date on which the claim is received by the Department, though the Secretary of State may treat an application as made earlier (up to three months before it was received) if this is requested, or he is aware that the claim has not been delivered in the ordinary course of post *and* the claimant has not been at fault.[2] A renewal claim for FIS to be continued may be made from four weeks before until four weeks after the period of initial entitlement.[3]

xii) Child benefit[4]

A claim may be made up to fifty-two weeks after the week for which it is claimed:[5] this would appear to be much the longest period for social security benefits which impose a time-limit.

xiii) War pensions

There is no time-limit on claiming a war pension, though the burden of proof shifts to the applicant if he makes a claim more than seven years after leaving service.[6]

13. Handbook, paras. 208–210.
14. Ibid., para. 211.
15. Ibid., paras. 214–215.
16. Ibid., paras. 215–217.
17. S.I. 1977/1142, Reg. 5(1).
18. Ibid., Reg. 5(2): for payment of supplementary benefits, see post, p. 608.
19. Handbook, para. 219.
20. Moore, *LAG Bulletin*, July 1974, p. 165.
1. Ante, p. 569.
2. S.I. 1971/227, Reg. 2(1A), inserted by S.I. 1972/1282, Reg. 3.
3. S.I. 1971/226, Reg. 3(2).
4. See ante, p. 468, for detailed rules concerning this benefit.
5. CBA 1975, s.6(2).
6. Ante, pp. 365–369.

C. Extension of time-limits for 'good cause'

i) The law on 'good cause'

The Claims and Payments Regulations made under the Social Security Act 1975[7] provide that:

> 'If in any case the claimant proves that there was good cause for the failure to make the claim before the date on which it was made, the prescribed time for making that claim shall (subject to the provisions of section 82(2)) be extended to the date on which the claim is made: . . .'[8]

Section 82(2) provides that for most benefits there is an absolute bar on payment for a period more than twelve months before the claim is made. Subject then to this limitation, the prescribed time for claiming most of the various benefits discussed in the previous section will be extended if the claimant shows that there was good cause fot the delay in presenting his claim.[9] (The analogous extension in 'exceptional circumstances' applicable to a supplementary benefits claim has already been mentioned[10]). It is also provided that if the claimant (apart from the claim condition) was entitled to the benefit on an earlier date to that on which the claim was made, and there was good cause for the delay in claiming between these two dates, then he is not to be disqualified for receiving any benefit to which he would have been entitled if it had been made on that earlier date.[11] In other words, a claimant will not be wholly disqualified if there was good cause for the later part of the period of delay immediately before the claim was made. But the fact that there was good cause for the failure to claim in an earlier part will not lead to an extension of the prescribed time-limit.[12]

a) GENERAL PRINCIPLES IN DETERMINING 'GOOD CAUSE'. Before the National Insurance &c. Act 1964,[13] the industrial injuries scheme used the concept of 'reasonable cause' for the failure to make the claim within the prescribed time; the principles for determining whether this existed were the same as those for deciding whether there was 'good cause'.[14] These were stated in *CS 371/49:*

> 'It will be observed that the expression used is "good cause", not "a good excuse". "Good cause" means, in my opinion, some fact which, having regard to all the circumstances (including the claimant's state of health and the information which he had received and that which he might have obtained) would probably

7. SSA 1975, s.82(1).
8. S.I. 1975/560, Reg. 13.
9. These are the benefits, (i) to (vii), specified in S.I. 1975/560, Sch. 1, col. 1.
10. Ante, p. 600.
11. S.I. 1975/560, Reg. 13(3). This will not necessarily be the whole of the benefit claimed, but that benefit from which the person would not have been disqualified (if he had claimed on the earlier date) under the rules described in the previous section.
12. *CS 34/49.*
13. Sch. 6, para. 15.
14. *CSI 10/50*; *R(U) 6/52*. The principles are the same for all benefits: see T.A. Blair, Chief Comr., in *R 1/70 (MB)*.

have caused a reasonable person of his age and experience to act (or fail to act) as the claimant did'.

It was also emphasised that the burden of proof is on the claimant. These principles have been approved by both NIAC and IIAC,[15] and followed in later decisions of the Commissioner.[16] NIAC had, however, contemplated the formulation of a provision which would allow extension in cases of 'excusable ignorance', though it was persuaded that this was neither necessary nor practicable.[17] In its more recent report on time-limits for claiming sickness benefit, it concluded that there had been a continual trend towards a more liberal interpretation of the 'good cause' provision, and did not see any case for a change in its formulation.[18]

Two cases show the generous approach now often taken by the Commissioner. A familiar source of difficulty is whether a claimant, who has not claimed benefit because he did not realise he was entitled to it, has good cause for his failure to claim within the prescribed time. A number of old decisions had held that it was the duty of such a claimant to find out his rights from the authorities.[19] However, in *R(S) 2/63*, this approach was not taken by a Tribunal of Commissioners:

> C did not claim sickness benefit while he had reasonable grounds for believing, and did believe, that he would be paid wages in full during his period of sickness, and that this would preclude him from claiming benefit. Both beliefs were wrong. The Tribunal held that he had good cause for his failure to claim, while he suffered from this misapprehension.

It was emphasised that 'over the years there has been a gradual, but appreciable relaxation of the strictness with which problems of good and reasonable cause have been approached'; this was particularly true of sickness benefit claims where the applicant might not act promptly because of his ill-health. In determining how a reasonable person should behave, it is permissible to take account of the conduct of other claimants, as revealed in the cases which come before the Commissioners.[20]

Similar problems occur when a new benefit is introduced, or the rules of entitlement to an old one are changed. Generally ignorance of a new entitlement has not been held to afford good cause for delay in claiming the particular benefit within the permitted time.[1] But in *R(G) 2/74*, the Commissioner, H. Magnus, seems to have taken an extremely generous view:

> From 5 April 1971 C became entitled to a widow's pension after the change in the conditions of entitlement introduced by NIA 1970.

15. Supra, n.19, ante p. 593.
16. See esp., *R(S) 2/63* (Tribunal decision).
17. Cmd. 8483, paras. 19–22.
18. Cmnd. 2400, para. 27.
19. E.g., *CWS 3/48*; *CWG 2/49*; *R(U) 35/56*.
20. See the statement of general principle in *CS 371/49*, and by the Chief Comr., in Northern Ireland, T.A. Blair, in *R 1/70 (MB)*.

1. See *CG 125/50* (failure to claim death grant six months after it had first become available), and *R(I) 82/53* (no good cause when a dock worker did not appreciate that his rash was a prescribed disease).

(She had become a widow in 1961 when forty-eight, and under the law then was not entitled to a pension).[2] C then claimed a retirement pension on 14 November 1972 when she became sixty, and it was only then that she appreciated her previous entitlement to a widow's pension. She argued that the DHSS publicity campaign in 1970–71 concerning the change in the widow's pension rules had 'passed her by'. This was accepted by the Commissioner, who held that C had good cause for her failure to claim and was entitled to the widow's pension from 16 November 1971.[3]

It was not appropriate here to apply the principle that a claimant ignorant of his rights has a duty to take reasonable steps to find out what they are, and the Commissioner emphasised that all the facts must be considered in determining whether there is good cause.

In contrast two other cases show a more cautious attitude. In the first, a self-employed travel agent did not claim sickness benefit as he did not think the self-employed were eligible for it.[4] H. A. Shewan held that he should have checked this with the Department's office, and that there was no good cause for the delay.[5] In *R(I) 10/74*:

> Following an industrial accident and a short spell of injury C returned to his regular employment as a colliery overman on 1 February 1956. On that date he claimed disablement benefit, and the local office told him correctly that in the circumstances he could not claim special hardship allowance (SHA). In May 1958 C abandoned his job and took up lighter work. At the end of 1961, and again in 1962, he made further visits to the local office applying successfully for a renewal of his disablement benefit. On both occasions he inquired whether he might be eligible for other benefits, and was told he was not. Eventually in March 1970 he claimed SHA. It was agreed that if he had claimed it, he would have been entitled to the allowance since 1958.

The Commissioner, D. Neligan, held that in view of the advice given him in February 1956, the claimant should have sought further guidance when he left his regular job in May 1958. There was no good cause, therefore, for the failure to claim between then and 1961. But the inquiries made in 1961 and 1962 should have made it clear to the Ministry that the claimant was entitled to SHA and he should have been invited to claim it. So there was good cause from the end of 1961 until the claim was eventually made in March 1970.[6]

It may be appreciated first, that the determination whether there is good cause is a complex matter, requiring examination of all the facts, and

2. See chap. 6, ante, p. 236.
3. The claimant was not entitled to a pension for more than twelve months before her claim: see post, p. 606.
4. *R(S) 1/73*.
5. The Commissioner refused to apply the dictum of McKenna J in *Ely v Bedford* [1972] QB 155, 158, [1971] 3 All ER

285, 288 (a mitigation of damages case) that: 'A plaintiff who does not know that he has a right does not act unreasonably in failing to exercise it'.
6. The Commissioner's decision was upheld by the Divisional Court: *R v Industrial Injuries Comr, ex parte Parkin* (1972) 13 KIR 213.

secondly, that the Commissioners' decisions do not always appear consistent. To state this is not, however, to deny the proposition that *generally* a more generous approach is now adopted towards the claimant than used to be the case. The main heads under which the question of good cause has arisen are now briefly discussed.[7]

b) RELYING ON OTHER PEOPLE'S OPINION AS TO ENTITLEMENT. Good cause is not generally shown if the claimant has relied on another person's view that he is not entitled to claim.[8] This is true even if the advice has come from a doctor in a sickness benefit case.[9] It is otherwise if it has come from a solicitor, since it is reasonable for an applicant to rely on his opinion.[10]

> In a recent unemployment benefit case, J. S. Watson, Commissioner, ruled that there was good cause when the claimant had been incorrectly advised by the local Citizen's Advice Bureau that he should take his insurance card to the unemployment benefit office, and he had, therefore, waited until it was returned by his former employer.[11]

c) ACTING ON INADEQUATE INFORMATION GIVEN BY THE DEPARTMENT OFFICE. Perhaps the most frequent type of case where good cause is shown by the claimant is where he has delayed in reliance on inadequate or misleading information given at a local office or in a DHSS leaflet.[12] This may occur even if the leaflet refers to another one where accurate information is obtainable.[13] *R(I) 10/74* shows that in some circumstances there may be good cause if the officials culpably fail to tell the applicant that he has a claim.[14]

d) CLAIMANTS OUTSIDE THE COUNTRY. In *R(G) 3/53*, a maternity benefit case, the Commissioner ruled that a liberal view should be taken of any delay attributable to the fact that the claimant was abroad at the time she made inquiries concerning her rights. A similar approach was taken where a claimant had emigrated to the United States of America before the present system of retirement pensions was introduced, and only claimed eighteen months after her entitlement arose, when she read an article about pensions in an American weekly paper.[15]

e) THE CLAIMANT'S STATE OF HEALTH. The fact that the claimant has been under some physical pain or emotional distress may persuade the Commissioner to find good cause.

---

7. To some extent the headings follow those in the Digest of Commissioners' Decisions.
8. *CSG 9/49*; *R(U) 35/56*.
9. *R(S) 5/56*; cp., *R(I) 40/59*.
10. *CS 50/50*; *CSI 10/50*. Contrast the position where there is a general delegation of affairs to a solicitor: post, p. 605.
11. *R(U) 9/74*.

12. *R(S) 14/54*; *CP 30/50*; *R(U) 3/70*; cp., *R(G) 15/56*, where the claimant's failure to understand the leaflets was her fault. This is also a frequent ground of complaint to the Parliamentary Commissioner.
13. *R(G) 4/68*; *R(I) 25/61*.
14. See ante, p. 603; see also *R(U) 3/60*.
15. *R(P) 5/58*.

Thus, a young girl under nervous strain on her confinement,[16] a war veteran who developed a phobia of seeing doctors,[17] and an employee who developed a neurotic condition as a result of explosions at work[18] all benefited from an extension of time.

f) EDUCATIONAL LIMITATIONS. Allowance may be made for the fact that the claimant is of limited intelligence.[19] In a recent maternity benefit case,[20] J. S. Watson, Commissioner, decided that lack of familiarity with the English language or illiteracy is not in itself likely to constitute good cause, though it might be an element in reaching the conclusion that there was such a failure of communication between the officer and the claimant that the latter had good cause for the delay.

g) DELEGATION BY THE CLAIMANT TO ANOTHER PERSON. Particularly fine distinctions have arisen when the making of a claim has been entrusted by one person to another, and the latter delays: does the former have good cause for failure to claim within the prescribed period? It seems that the Commissioner draws a distinction between a specific delegation to make a particular claim, and a general agency under which one person's affairs are handled by a representative. In the first case, a delay by the agent will not prevent the principal from contending that there was good cause.[1] But in the second, the agent's delay will be imputed to the principal.

> Thus in *R(S) 2/51*, C was a member of a religious order and had wholly abandoned the management of her own affairs. The convent's prioress was late in making a claim on her behalf for sickness benefit and this was imputed to C.

> The same result was reached where an estate was administered by a solicitor on behalf of the executor, and the former was late in claiming the death grant.[2]

h) DELIBERATE DECISION NOT TO CLAIM BENEFIT. In a variety of circumstances the claimant may decide not to claim because of some view as to his entitlement, or some expectation as to the future, which turns out to be untrue. Some cases involving the former error have already been discussed.[3] In *R(U) 34/51*, the claimant did not claim unemployment benefit for a Monday, because he thought he would only be unemployed for that one day; this mistake was held not to constitute good cause. However, in another case good cause was found when the claimant had not claimed one day because he was attending a meeting at the request of his union in the hope of being reinstated.[4] A rare case, where ignorance of the legal position did constitute good cause, was *R(S) 18/52*: the claimant in

---

16. *R 1/73 (MB)*.
17. *R(S) 7/61*.
18. *R(I) 43/55*.
19. *R(P) 10/59*.
20. *R(G) 1/75*.
1. See *CG 1/50*; *CU 78/49*; *R(S) 25/52*; *CSI 5/64*.

2. *R(G) 9/52* (Tribunal decision); cp., *R(G) 17/52*.
3. Ante, pp. 602–603.
4. *R(U) 20/56*; also see *R(U) 33/58* – a Rabbi who did not claim benefit on two days of the Passover was held to have good cause.

perfect health was excluded from work because he had been in contact with an infectious disease, and understandably he did not at first appreciate his entitlement.

j) HOSPITAL IN-PATIENTS. Under Schedule 2 to the 1975 Regulations, there is deemed to be 'good cause' for certain late claims by hospital in-patients for sickness, invalidity and industrial injury benefit, and for non-contributory invalidity pension.[5]

ii) The absolute bar on extension for 'good cause'

Section 82(2) of the Social Security Act 1975 provides that for most benefits there is an absolute time-limit of twelve months in which the claim must be made. Beyond this there can be no extension, no matter how good the reason or explanation for the delay. The justification for this overriding limit is that, 'nonsense is not to be made of the initial time-limits and a strain placed on the good cause condition that it was never intended to carry'.[6]

> The first rule is that no sum is to be paid by way of maternity grant for a confinement which has occurred more than twelve months before the claim.[7] Secondly, a death grant is not to be paid outside the prescribed time, plus twelve months extension for good cause.[8] Finally, no other benefit '(except a death grant, or disablement benefit or industrial death benefit)', is to be paid 'in respect of any period more than twelve months before the date on which the claim is made'.[9]

The result is that the only benefits which do not have an absolute time-limit imposed on their claim are industrial disablement and death benefits.

Before 1966 there was no absolute time-bar on the recovery of any industrial injuries benefit.[10] The reason given for this distinction from other benefits was that industrial benefits involved some element of 'compensation' for injury as well as of maintenance of living standards during a spell of incapacity for work.[11] However, the National Insurance Act of that year has reduced the scope of this principle to disablement and death benefits to which it is clearly more applicable than injury benefit.

D. Payments

i) Short-term and other benefits payable under SSA 1975

Regulation 14 of the Claims and Payments Regulations applies to the following benefits:

5. S.I. 1975/560, Sch. 2, para. 2.
6. NIAC Report (1968), Cmnd. 3591, para. 8.
7. SSA 1975, s.82(2)(a).
8. Ibid., s.82(2)(b).
9. Ibid., s.82(2)(c).
10. See *R(I) 9/68*, where the

Commissioner, H.A. Shewan, reviewed the history of the time-limits in industrial injuries cases.
11. See the Reports of NIAC in 1952, Cmd. 8483, para. 7, and of IIAC in the same year, Cmd. 8511, para. 22.

unemployment, sickness, invalidity, maternity and industrial injury benefits, death grant, hospital treatment increase and non-contributory invalidity pension.

These benefits are to be paid by means of an instrument of payment or other appropriate means as soon as reasonably practicable after the award has been made by the determining authority.[12] In practice, they are generally paid by means of a Girocheque.

ii) Long-term benefits payable under SSA 1975
Regulation 15 applies to the following benefits:

> widow's benefit, retirement pension of any category, child's special, guardian's and attendance allowances, disablement pension (including any increase, with the exception of that for hospital treatment), any allowance for industrial injuries (not being injury benefit), and invalid care allowance.

These benefits are to be paid weekly in advance by means of benefit orders cashable at such place as the Secretary of State determines (in effect, a post office) after inquiry of the beneficiary as to which office is most convenient for him. The successful claimant obtains a book of benefit orders, renewable when it has expired;[13] each order can then be cashed on the appropriate day.

Under the Regulations the appropriate days are:[14]

child's special, guardian's allowance and (generally) widow's pension	– Tuesday
retirement pensions	– Thursday
(but where woman previously entitled to widow's benefit)	– Tuesday
attendance allowance and invalid care allowance	– Monday[15]
industrial injuries benefits covered by this Regulation	– Wednesday

The effect of the rule that benefit is to be payable on one of these particular days (in advance for the following week) is that, even though under other provisions of the Act entitlement begins on some other day, the right to the benefit only commences on the particular day of the week allocated for payment.[16] In two retirement pensions cases it was decided that the pension commenced from the appropriate date of payment, i.e., the first Thursday after entitlement otherwise arose.[17] The decisive point is that the Regulation states that benefit is to *commence* from the appropriate day

---

12. S.I. 1975/560, Reg. 14(2).
13. Ibid., Reg. 15(2)–(4).
14. Ibid., Reg. 15(5)–(8): A number of details and exceptions are omitted.
15. The Secretary of State may arrange for payment of attendance allowance to be made on other days; an invalid care

allowance for a severely disabled person is payable on Wednesdays: S.I. 1976/409, Reg. 17(3)(b).
16. S.I. 1975/560, Reg. 15(9).
17. *R(P) 16/52* ; *R(P) 2/73* ; see ante, p. 199.

for payment, not merely that it is to be payable from this date. Conversely where a benefit ceases to be payable on a day which does not immediately precede the appropriate day of payment, it is nevertheless payable for the *whole of the week up to the appropriate day*;[18] this may have the result that two benefits are payable for the same day, although the recipient is not otherwise entitled to both.[19]

One difference between the payment of benefits under Regulations 14 and 15 is that the latter (long-term) are always *weekly* payments, whereas the former may be for a day or a few days, or of single lump sums.[20] However, Regulation 15(14) enables the Secretary of State to make other arrangements for the payment of long-term benefits; under this power, retirement pensions may be, and frequently are, paid by monthly cheque.

iii) Mobility allowance

This allowance is payable on Wednesdays, at various intervals of time, not longer than four weeks, to be determined by the Secretary of State.[1] There are provisions which make it clear that payment is only to *commence* from the appropriate Wednesday, and is to continue to the Tuesday of the payment week in which entitlement ceases.[2] There is discretion to pay the allowance in a different way.

iv) Other benefits under SSA 1975

There are a number of other minor provisions in the Claims and Payments Regulations.[3] Two merit a short mention:

(a) *age addition*: this is payable weekly in advance, either on the day of the week on which the retirement pension is paid if the person is actually in receipt of a pension, or otherwise on the day determined by the Secretary of State.

(b) *industrial injuries gratuities*: normally a gratuity is to be paid in one sum, but it may be paid in instalments in certain circumstances.[4]

v) Supplementary benefits

In a recent case arising under the 1966 Supplementary Benefit Claims and Payments Regulations,[5] the Divisional Court ruled that a person's entitlement began on the day of the claim and not on the day on which the first payment of benefit was made to him.[6] The position has now been

---

18. S.I. 1975/560, Reg. 15(10).
19. *R(I) 13/57* (disablement benefit and injury benefit both payable in full for a few days, despite the overlapping provision): see chap. 8, ante, p. 301.
20. In the summer of 1977, fortnightly payments of unemployment benefit were introduced on an experimental basis in an attempt to reduce administrative costs: S.I. 1977/1289. See NIAC Report, (1977) Cmnd.,

6897, pp. 4–7. See Appendix.
1. S.I. 1975/1573, Reg. 9(1), (2) and (4).
2. Ibid., Reg. 9(3) and (5).
3. S.I. 1975/560, Regs. 16–19.
4. These are discussed, ante, p. 316, in the chapter on industrial injuries.
5. S.I. 1966/1067.
6. *R v Bristol Supplementary Benefits Appeal Tribunal, ex parte Southwell*, *Times*, 21 July, 1977.

altered by new Regulations made under the Social Security (Miscellaneous Provisions) Act 1977.[7] Entitlement to a weekly pension or allowance[8] is not to begin until the first day of the 'benefit week' following the day of the successful claim:[9] for unemployed claimants, this means the week beginning with the day on which unemployment benefit is payable (or would be, if the claimant were entitled to it); for beneficiaries in receipt of a retirement or widow's pension, the week beginning with the day when that benefit is payable; and for others, the week beginning on a Monday.[10] Payment is to be made on, or as soon as practicable after, the first day of the benefit week.[11] The effect of these changes is to bring the rules regarding payment of supplementary benefits substantially into line with those concerning long-term payments under the Social Security Act 1975: in both cases the right to benefit only *commences* on the day of the week allocated for payment.[12]

In practice, payment is by means of an order book, cashable weekly at the recipient's post office – in the same way as retirement pensions.[13] For claimants also in receipt of other benefits, one order book is normally issued for both. Unemployed claimants receive a Girocheque for their allowance (and unemployment benefit when this is also payable) from the local unemployment benefit office, which acts as agent for the local social security office for this purpose.[14] It is rare for a cheque to be handed over the counter, but this may be done in cases of urgent need.[15]

It was pointed out in the chapter on supplementary benefits that generally the provision of means-tested assistance takes the form of a cash payment, which is not earmarked for a particular item, but leaves the recipient with considerable choice.[16] However, the Commission does have power in exceptional circumstances to make payment in kind.[17] This power is exercised in three types of case:

> First, where there is urgent need after some disaster, such as fire or flood; secondly, where the claimant has no fixed address to which payment can be sent, when it is a usual course to provide a voucher for board and lodging at a local hostel; and thirdly, when the claimant has repeatedly misspent his benefit or has spent an ENP on articles other than that for which it was granted.[18]

There is a right of appeal against the exercise of this power.[19]

vi) FIS

Payment of benefit by order-book cashable at a post office, commences on Tuesday, and even if entitlement would end on a day other than Monday, benefit is to be paid for the days of the week up to and including the

---

7. S.14(4).
8. For these terms, see ante, p. 480.
9. S.I. 1977/1141, Reg. 11(1).
10. Ibid., Reg. 11(2).
11. S.I. 1977/1142, Reg. 6. An exceptional needs payment is to be made as soon as practicable after its award: ibid., Reg. 7.
12. See ante, p. 608.
13. Handbook, paras. 221–223.
14. Ibid., para. 224.
15. Ibid., para. 225.
16. See chap. 12 ante, p. 489.
17. SBA 1976, s.11(1).
18. Handbook, para. 233.
19. SBA 1976, s.15(1)(e).

Monday:[20] this provision is similar to the one obtaining for social security benefits payable under Regulation 15.[1]

vii) Extinguishment of right to sums payable by way of benefit

It is a common provision that if payment is not obtained within twelve months from the date on which the right is treated as having arisen, then the right is extinguished.[2] The reason for this time-limit on encashment of benefits is said to be that the administrative costs (e.g., of storing copies of instruments of payment and cash instruments) necessary to check late requests for payment, and so prevent abuse, could be very heavy.[3] The right to payment under the Social Security Claims and Payments Regulations is to be treated as having arisen in the following circumstances:[4]

1. in relation to a sum contained in an instrument of payment sent to the beneficiary, or to an approved place for collection by him, whether or not he has received or collected it – ON THE DATE OF THE INSTRUMENT;

2. where notice has been given or sent that the sum contained in it is available for collection, and the notice has been sent by post – ON THE DATE ON WHICH IT WOULD BE DELIVERED IN THE ORDINARY COURSE OF POST –

   or if not sent by post – ON THE DATE OF NOTICE;

3. in relation to sums to which the preceding sub-paragraphs do not apply – ON THE DATE DETERMINED BY THE SECRETARY OF STATE.

It seems that, with the exception of cases under (3), the relevant date is now to be determined by the statutory authorities.[5] It may be noted that here it is the recipient who takes the risk of the notification not being delivered in the ordinary course of post,[6] though the consequences of this may be mitigated by an extension of the time allowed.

There will be an extension of the twelve months period if the statutory authorities are satisfied first, that after the twelve months the Secretary has received a notice requesting payment and secondly, that throughout a period, starting within the twelve months and continuing till the notice was given, there was good cause for not giving it earlier.[7]

The extinguishment provisions do not apply to the payment of death grants, industrial injuries gratuities (if paid as a single sum and not by

---

20. S.I. 1971/227, Reg. 4(3).
1. See ante, p. 608.
2. S.I. 1975/560, Reg. 20; S.I. 1976/964, Reg. 8 (child benefit); S.I. 1977/1142, Reg. 12 (supp. benefit); S.I. 1971/227, Reg. 5 (FIS).
3. NIAC Report (1968), Cmnd. 3591, paras. 18–26.
4. Some details are omitted.

5. This follows recommendations of NIAC in 1952, Cmd. 8483, para. 54 and of IIAC in the same year, Cmd. 8511, para. 28.
6. SSA, 1975, s.79(6).
7. See S.I. 1975/560, Reg. 20(2). It would seem that good cause has the same meaning here, as it does in the context of late claims.

instalments)[8] or a sum paid in satisfaction of a right to graduated retirement pension.[9]

E. Miscellaneous

i) Persons unable to act

Regulations cover the case where the person alleged to be entitled to a benefit, or to whom a benefit is payable, is unable for the time being to act for himself.[10] The basic rule is:

> unless a receiver has been appointed by the Court of Protection with power to claim benefit, etc.,[11] the Secretary of State may, on written application to him by a person over eighteen, appoint that person to exercise, on behalf of the person unable to act, all his rights and to receive benefit to which he is entitled. There are provisions for the revocation of, or resignation from, this appointment.

ii) Payments on death

When a claimant dies, the Secretary of State may appoint a person of his choice to proceed with the claim.[12] If written application is then made for the sums payable by way of benefit within twelve months (or such longer period as the Secretary of State may determine) the following consequences ensue:

> any sum payable may be paid or distributed among persons over sixteen claiming as personal representatives, legatees, next of kin or creditors of the deceased, at the discretion of the Secretary of State; he may pay this to some person on behalf of another under sixteen. The same rules apply to a sum payable to the deceased before his death, but not obtained by him. (There are some special provisions with regard to the death grant in this context.)[13]

The Family Income Supplement Regulations provide that a claim will lapse:

> where a man and a woman are included in the family for whom the claim is made, and both have died before the claim is determined, *or* in any other case, the man or the single woman has died before the claim is determined.[14]

Where, however, one or both of these persons die after the claim has been decided, benefit is payable on behalf of the family to a person over the age of eighteen, who applies to receive the benefit and whom the Secretary of State considers suitable.[15]

8. See ante, p. 316.
9. S.I. 1975/560, Reg. 20(5).
10. S.I. 1975/560, Reg. 26; S.I. 1976/964, Reg. 10; S.I. 1977/1142, Reg. 13; S.I. 1971/227, Reg. 6.
11. There is a similar rule for Scotland: S.I. 1975/560, Reg. 26(1)(d).
12. Ibid., Reg. 27; S.I. 1976/964, Reg. 12; S.I. 1977/1142, Reg. 15.
13. Ante, p. 246.
14. S.I. 1971/227, Reg. 7(1).
15. Ibid., Reg. 7(2).

iii) Payment to a third party

Under both the Social Security and Child Benefit Claims and Payments Regulations, payment may be made to a third party in certain circumstances.

> Under the former,[16] the power may be exercised by the Secretary of State where a beneficiary is receiving benefit in respect of another person whom he is maintaining at not less than the prescribed weekly rate.[17] The power to direct payments to another person may be exercised in the interests of the beneficiary, or the other person, or on the former's request.

> There is a similar broad power for the Secretary of State to 'divert' payments of child benefit to a third party in the interests either of the child or of the person entitled to the benefit.[18] The importance of this power has been discussed in the Child Benefit chapter.[19]

In some cases supplementary benefit may be paid to a third party, e.g., a landlord; these have been discussed in the chapter dealing with this benefit.[20]

iv) Benefit to the inalienable

It is a standard provision that any assignment or charge on, or agreement to assign or charge, the benefit is void.[1] The benefit does not pass to the trustee, or any other person acting on the creditors' behalf, on the bankruptcy of the person entitled. There are obvious policy reasons why it is undesirable to allow a beneficiary to give up or put at risk benefits designed to ensure a minimum standard of living for himself and his family.

Part five. Overpayments and Criminal Offences

A. Recovery of overpaid benefit

i) Recovery of benefits paid under the SSA 1975, etc.

Section 119(1) of the Social Security Act 1975 provides that where benefit has been paid under a decision, subsequently reversed on appeal or revised on review, 'the decision given on the appeal or review *shall* require repayment to the Secretary of State' of any benefit which has been wrongly paid. This provision, with a modification mentioned later, applies to child benefit overpayments.[2]

The terms of section 119 require the statutory authorities to order repayment of the sum overpaid, unless due care and diligence is shown;

16. S.I. 1975/560, Reg. 28.
17. For the circumstances in which this benefit may be paid, see ante, pp. 393–397.
18. S.I. 1976/964, Reg. 13.
19. Chap. 11, ante, p. 470.
20. See chap. 12, ante, p. 500.
1. SSA 1975, s.87; CBA 1975, s.12; SBA 1976, s.16; FISA 1970, s. 9.
2. CBA 1975, s.8: see post, p. 614.

they do not have any discretion on this question.[3] The requirement to repay must be contained in the decision itself, and not left to a subsequent letter.[4] Otherwise, the beneficiary's right of appeal against the decision to order repayment may be prejudiced. In *R(S) 2/70*, the Chief Commissioner, R. G. Micklethwait, ruled that section 119 only allows recovery from a 'beneficiary', that is, a person who has made a claim which has been wrongly accepted. It does not permit recovery from someone who has obtained payment by forging the claimant's signature to the relevant documents; in that case, recovery would presumably be obtainable under the general law of restitution.[5] The authorities have no jurisdiction to direct that repayment should be made by instalments; it is for the Secretary of State to decide whether this is acceptable.[6]

Regulations provide that overpaid benefit (either that paid under the Social Security Act, or child benefit) is not to be recovered where it is certified by the SBC that additional supplementary benefit would have been payable.[7] Nor will there be recovery if on the appeal or review the beneficiary is awarded some other benefit to which he has been entitled; the sums already paid will be treated as having been paid on account of this benefit.[8]

Repayment will not be ordered if 'the beneficiary, and any person acting for him, has throughout used *due care and diligence* to avoid overpayment'.[9] This test was introduced by section 9 of the National Insurance Act 1961. Previously repayment was not ordered if the beneficiary had acted in '*good faith*'. The editor of the Digest of Commissioners' Decisions states that the two phrases are intended to have substantially the same effect.[10] But, if this is so, it is difficult to see why the 'good faith' test was replaced; moreover, the Commissioner in *R(G) 9/62* said that the tests are different – though he did not specify in what respect. It seems clear that the new formula imposes on the claimant the duty to be careful, and not merely the duty of honesty.[11]

The onus of proof is generally on the claimant to show that he has acted with due care and diligence,[12] and he must show this for the whole of the period from the time when the benefit was claimed.[13] He is under a duty to tell the Department all the facts which he should appreciate are relevant.[14] But due care and diligence may be shown if the beneficiary has relied on information given by his employer in deciding not to withdraw his claim.[15]

3. *R(U) 5/63*.
4. *R(P) 1/73*, and also see CSP 11/50.
5. See Goff and Jones, *The Law of Restitution* (1966), p. 70.
6. *R(G) 7/51*.
7. S.I. 1975/558, Reg. 38; S.I. 1976/962, Reg. 22.
8. S.I. 1975/558, Regs. 33, 34.
9. SSA 1975, s.119(2).
10. Digest, Volume 1, p. 465.
11. See esp., *R(S) 2/74*; *R(U) 7/75*; *CU 5/77*.
12. *R(G) 2/72*; cp., the rule in S.I. 1976/963, Reg. 8(2)(b).
13. *CF 1/65*. The proposition in the text was doubted very cautiously by the Chief Commissioner, T.A. Blair in *R 2/73 (FA)*. Also see *CS 11/76*, where the Commissioner, V.G.H. Hallett, only permitted recovery of that part of a weekly overpayment in respect of which the claimant did not show due care and diligence.
14. *R(P) 1/70*; *R(S) 2/74*; *R 3/73 (IVB)*.
15. *R(U) 1/73*. The same result was reached on the 'good faith' test: see *R(P) 13/53*.

The fact that he is illiterate would appear to be a relevant factor. This was so for the 'good faith' test,[16] and in *R(U) 7/64* the Commissioner said, obiter, that the local tribunal was right to take this into account here. But the beneficiary was required to repay in this case because his wife, who had filled in the claim forms on his behalf, had not used due care and diligence.

The relationship between the requirement to repay overpaid benefit and a criminal prosecution for fraudulently obtaining it was considered in *R(U) 7/75*.[17]

> C claimed and was awarded an increase of unemployment benefit for his wife from whom he was living apart. When it was discovered that she was earning more than the prescribed limit, the award was revised and C was required to repay the benefit he had received for her. He appealed on the ground that he had been acquitted on a charge of fraudulently obtaining benefit. The Commissioner, H. A. Shewan, held that his acquittal was irrelevant and did not establish that he had exercised due care and diligence.

The point is that in the criminal case, the burden of proof is on the prosecution to show beyond reasonable doubt that the accused has acted fraudulently, while in the proceedings before the statutory authorities it is for the beneficiary to show that he has used due care and diligence. In some cases the proceedings before the statutory authorities will be adjourned if a criminal prosecution is brought, so that the claimant does not run the risk of giving evidence in the former proceedings which might be used against him in the criminal court.[18]

The 'due care and diligence' provision applies to child benefit, though where payment has been 'diverted' to a spouse other than the one entitled, or to someone other than the person entitled, under the Claims and Payments Regulations,[19] repayment will be required from the actual recipient (rather than the person entitled) if he has not, and the person entitled has, used due care and diligence.[20]

ii) Recovery of supplementary benefit and FIS[1]

Section 20 of the Supplementary Benefits Act 1976 provides for recovery of any expenditure incurred by the Secretary of State from a person if he, fraudulently or otherwise, 'misrepresents, or fails to disclose, any material fact'. A question whether, or what amount of, benefit is recoverable, must be referred to the SBAT. Its decision is final, subject, of course, to judicial review.[2] In three respects this section would appear to confer a wider right of recovery than its equivalent in the Social Security Act 1975:

16. *R(G) 6/53*.
17. See the analogous question for unemployment benefit of the relationship between criminal proceedings and the misconduct disqualification: ante, p. 111.
18. *R(S) 2/70*.
19. S.I. 1976/964, Reg. 13: see ante, p. 470.

20. S.I. 1976/962, Reg. 21; also see S.I. 1975/1573, Reg. 23 (mobility allowance regulations).
1. For a discussion of some investigations by the Parliamentary Commissioner in this area, see Partington *LAG Bulletin*, Oct. 1975, p. 269.
2. Post, pp. 657–659.

1. It seems that not only overpaid benefit is recoverable, but also any expenditure incurred as a result of the misrepresentation or failure to disclose the material fact. This might enable the Secretary of State to recover the expenses involved in taking recovery proceedings.[3]

2. There is no exception that benefit cannot be recovered where the claimant has acted with due care and diligence. It is not obvious why there is this difference.

3. Unlike the Social Security Act,[4] recovery can be secured from anyone, and not only the beneficiary. In *Secretary of State for Social Services v Solly* the Court of Appeal held that overpaid supplementary benefit could be recovered from the deceased claimant's executor.[5]

Recovery may be made by deduction from any social security benefits paid under the Social Security Act 1975.[6] Alternatively, it may be effected by ordinary civil action for restitution. More doubtfully, the Commission might reduce or withhold any future payments of supplementary allowance (not pension) under the discretionary power conferred by Schedule 1, paragraph 4(1)(b); the legality of this would depend on whether the past overpayment constitutes 'exceptional circumstances', justifying this course.[7]

FIS overpayments may be recovered if the Commission or the SBAT finds that the sums were not due, and 'the persons by whom the sums were receivable cannot satisfy the Commission or the Appeal Tribunal that they had disclosed all material facts'.[8] This seems in one respect the most onerous of the recovery provisions: it is for the recipient to show that he has disclosed all the relevant facts.

B. Offences

A variety of specific offences are created by the social security legislation, though a person who obtains benefit by deliberate deception may also be prosecuted under the general law, e.g., for obtaining property by deception under the Theft Act 1968.[9]

i) Obtaining benefit by false statements, etc.

Section 146(3)(c) of the Social Security Act 1975 provides that it is an offence punishable on summary conviction by a fine of £400 or imprisonment for three months, or both, if a person

---

3. The Legal Action Group *A Lawyer's Guide to Supplementary Benefit* (1976), p. 58.
4. See ante, p. 612.
5. [1974] 3 All ER 922.
6. SBA 1976, s.20(4).

7. See ante, pp. 511–516 for a general discussion of this provision.
8. S.I. 1971/226, Reg. 10.
9. S.15. See Smith and Hogan *Criminal Law* (3rd edn), pp. 437–446.

'for the purpose of obtaining any benefit or other payment under this Act, whether for himself or some other person, or for any other purpose connected with this Act –

(i) knowingly makes any false statement or false representation, or

(ii) produces or furnishes, or causes or knowingly allows to be produced or furnished, any document or information which he knows to be false in a material particular'.

There is an identical provision in the Child Benefit Act,[10] and very similar provisions in the Supplementary Benefits Act[11] and Family Income Supplements Act.[12] In *Moore v Branton*[13] the Divisional Court ruled that the supplementary benefits offence necessarily involved mens rea, a dishonest intention to obtain benefit by fraud. A person who makes an untrue statement, believing that it does not affect his entitlement to benefit does not commit the offence. This ruling would clearly apply to the other provisions.

An important question arose in *Tolfree v Florence* :[14]

On 20 January 1969 D applied for sickness benefit for 18 January 1969 to 27 January 1969. The DHSS duly sent him a postal draft for £12 17s 10d for this period, though D worked on 23 and 24 January, and so was not entitled to the whole of this sum. On 25 January 1969 he presented the draft at a post office, and signed below the words: 'Received the above sum to which I am entitled'. The Divisional Court held that making this representation constituted the offence under the Act, since it was made for the purpose of obtaining *payment* of the benefit. It did not matter that the decision to pay benefit had already been made before the false representation.

This decision seems right. It is not clear what offence under the legislation the defendant would have committed if he had honestly presented the draft for payment on the 25th January and subsequently decided to work on the 26th and 27th. It is possible that he would only have been guilty of the offence under the Claims and Payments Regulations, consisting of a failure to inform the authorities of a relevant change in circumstances.[15]

ii) Other offences
The other offences under the social security legislation are less important.

1. It is an offence under the Social Security Act, the Supplementary Benefits Act and the Family Income Supplements Act to delay or obstruct wilfully an inspector in the exercise of his powers, or to refuse either to answer questions or to provide documents and information.[16]

10. S.11.
11. S.21, as substituted by SS(MP)A 1977, s.14(5).
12. S.11, as amended by SS(MP)A 1977, s.22(16).
13. [1974] Crim. LR 439. Also see *Department of Health and Social*

Security v *Ashley*, *LAG Bulletin*, Oct. 1977, p. 240.
14. [1971] 1 WLR 141.
15. See S.I. 1975/560, Regs. 21 and 29.
16. See SSA 1975, s. 145(3); SS(MP)A 1977, s.19. For the powers of inspectors, see SSA 1975, ss. 144, 145.

2. There are some offences with regard to non-payment of contributions and misuse of contribution cards under Section 146 of the Social Security Act 1975. (Failure to pay Class 4 contributions, recoverable by the Inland Revenue, may be prosecuted under the Taxes Management Act 1970[17]).

3. Under the Supplementary Benefits Act 1976[18] it is an offence –
   (i) to impersonate officers of the DHSS and the Commission;
   (ii) to be in illegal possession of documents issued on behalf of the Secretary of State in connection with the payment of any benefit;
   (iii) to fail to comply with an obligation to notify cessation of employment or re-employment in connection with the administration of deduction notices.[19]

iii) General rules

Proceedings for these offences must be brought within three months from the date when evidence, sufficient to justify a prosecution in the view of the Secretary of State, is available, or if later, within twelve months of the commission of the offence.[20] This is a longer limitation period than the normal six months for bringing proceedings for summary offences.[1] A prosecution under the Social Security and Child Benefits Acts is not to be brought except with the consent of the Secretary of State or of an authorised officer;[2] this precludes private prosecutions.

C. The recommendations of the Fisher Committee

In the course of this book frequent references have been made to the Report of the Fisher Committee on *Abuse of Social Security Benefits*. This Committee was set up early in 1971 to review the adequacy of the measures taken by government departments to control abuse through wrongful claims to social security benefits and to recommend changes in these procedures. Its principal conclusion was that while it was clear that abuse was a serious problem, there was not enough information to show its overall extent or its frequency in claims for particular benefits.[3]

Therefore, although in general the measures taken to check abuse were approved, the departments were criticised for not having made more thorough attempts to find out its extent. Two principal recommendations were made in this respect. First, the Committee suggested that detailed surveys should be made on sample claims, chosen at random. Various checks and tests were recommended in chapter 22 of the Report to ascertain the abuse in claims for particular benefits. If this suggestion had been adopted, it would have marked a departure from the usual depart-

---

17. Ss. 93–107.
18. Ss. 22–24, as amended by SS(MP)A 1977, s.14(6).
19. See chap. 12, ante p. 532 and these notices.
20. SSA 1975, s.147(3); CBA 1975,

s.11(5); SBA 1976, s.26(3)(b); FISA 1970, s.12.
1. Magistrates' Courts Act 1952, s.104.
2. SSA 1975, s. 147(1); CBA 1975, s.11(3).
3. Paras. 487–490.

mental practice, which is to make checks only on suspicious claims, and would inevitably have led to some intrusion into the lives of wholly innocent claimants; the government, therefore, rejected it. Intensive local campaigns against already identified areas of abuse – particularly, failure to disclose earnings while drawing unemployment benefit or supplementary benefit – were preferred.

The second general recommendation was that there should be a new Standing Committee to oversee the control of abuse and to suggest new methods for tackling the problem. The majority of the Fisher Committee recommended that it should contain some members from outside the DHSS and the Department of Employment. All agreed that it should have responsibility for both contributory and supplementary benefits, and that it should have a staff of its own.[4] The government took the view, however, that it was unnecessary to institute such a general body.[5]

Since the report of the Fisher Committee there have continued to be allegations of widespread fraud and abuse. Whatever truth there is in these rumours, there is little doubt that it will remain a matter of general controversy, as will the analogous phenomenon of tax evasion.[6] The Labour government in 1976 made a special study of the techniques used to gain benefits by fraud, and on the basis of its findings new instructions have been given to local offices to guide them in handling suspicious claims.[7] A specialist 'fraud' unit has been set up in the Department headquarters, and the number of special investigators has been increased.[8]

4. Chap. 23 of the Report.
5. See Sir K. Joseph, Written Answer, 853 HC Deb., cols. 363–364.
6. For a comparison of the extent of abuse of taxation and social security, see Field, Meacher and Pond *To Him Who Hath* (1977), chap. 8.
7. 926 HC Deb., cols. 303–306.
8. Mr S. Orme, Minister of Social Security, Written Answer, 915 HC Deb., cols. 294–296.

15 Adjudication

Part One of this chapter is concerned with the methods for determining questions under the Social Security Act 1975 and the Child Benefit Act 1975. Part Two discusses judicial review of decisions under this legislation. Part Three deals with the tribunals which hear appeals from decisions of the Supplementary Benefits Commission on entitlement to supplementary benefit and family income supplement. Part Four contains a short discussion of the tribunals which adjudicate appeals on war pensions claims. Part Five is concerned with the circumstances in which a reference should be made to the European Court of Justice.

Part one. Adjudication under Social Security Act 1975

A. General

From the beginning of the modern social security system before the First World War, powers of adjudication have been vested in special tribunals or other bodies.[1] The decision not to confer jurisdiction on the courts was largely attributable to an understandable fear that their procedure would be too formal and expensive. The 1906 Liberal government was also influenced by the successful use in Germany of special tribunals in this area. Thus, claims for the unemployment benefit introduced by the National Insurance Act 1911 were decided in the first instance by Board of Trade insurance officers. Appeal then lay to a court of referees, a three member tribunal, with a chairman, one member drawn from an 'employer's panel' and the other drawn from a 'workmen's panel'. A further appeal could be made to an Umpire, a lawyer of standing appointed by the Crown.[2] This became the model for the present system introduced by the National Insurance Act 1946.

---

1. See Wraith and Hutchesson *Administrative Tribunals* (1973), pp. 33–38; Robson *Justice and Administrative Law* (3rd edn), pp. 188–198.
2. For a full discussion of this system, see the Committee on Procedure and Evidence for the Determination of Claims for Unemployment Insurance Benefit (the Morris Committee) (1929), Cmd. 3415.

Another pattern of adjudication was established when contributory pensions were introduced in 1925.[3] A claim for an old age or widow's pension would be made in the first place to the Minister; if he rejected it, an appeal lay to an independent Referee, a senior lawyer. His decisions, unlike those of the Umpire under the unemployment insurance legislation, were not publicly reported.[4] This system was adopted in 1945 for the adjudication of disputed claims to family allowances. Under the Family Allowances Act 1945 the Referee could state a case on a point of law for the High Court, though it seems that this was done very rarely.[5]

The Beveridge Report recommended a right of appeal to a local tribunal, analogous to the court of referees, and then to the Umpire, whose decisions would be final.[6] This was accepted in principle by the government. The National Insurance Act 1946 provided that claims should initially be determined by the insurance officer,[7] with a right of appeal to a national insurance local tribunal, and then to the National Insurance Commissioner or one of the Deputy Commissioners. Certain questions, however, particularly on contributions, were reserved for the Minister, with an appeal only on a point of law to the High Court. A similar system was instituted under the industrial injuries legislation. An appeal lay to a local appeal tribunal, and from it to the Industrial Injuries Commissioner or a Deputy Commissioner. But certain questions concerning entitlement to, and the assessment of, disablement benefit were entrusted to medical boards, with an appeal to medical appeal tribunals. The ordinary courts had decided claims for workmen's compensation, now replaced by the state benefit; there was some anxiety that the new authorities would not be competent to determine the difficult questions of law arising under the industrial injuries scheme.[8]

Some of the major developments in the last thirty years should be mentioned before the present system is discussed in detail.[9] First, following a recommendation of the Franks Committee on Tribunals and Enquiries,[10] the adjudication of claims to family allowances was transferred in 1959 to the insurance officers and on appeal the local tribunal and the National Insurance Commissioner.[11] This change has not been affected by the Child Benefit Act 1975.[12] Secondly, the 1959 legislation also conferred a right of appeal on a point of law from the medical appeal tribunals to the Commissioner. This interesting development reflected the general confidence in the Commissioners and enhanced their position at

3. For the history of pensions, see chap. 5, ante, pp. 190–195.
4. Safford, 17 MLR 197, 201 (the author was a Deputy Insurance Commissioner).
5. In 596 HC Deb., col. 713, Mr D. Freeth, introducing the 2nd Reading of the Family Allowances and National Insurance Bill 1959, said that only four references to the High Court had been made by the Referee.
6. Paras. 394–395.

7. Post, pp. 624–625.
8. See 414 HC Deb., cols. 311–312 (Mr H. Raikes) and cols. 324–325 (Mr B. Nield).
9. For a full discussion, see Sir R. Micklethwait *The National Insurance Commissioners*, (Hamlyn Lectures, 1976), chap. 2.
10. (1957), Cmnd. 218, para. 184.
11. FANIA 1959, s.1.
12. S.7.

the apex of the tribunal system.[13] Thirdly, the National Insurance Act 1966 merged the systems of adjudication under the national insurance and the industrial injuries legislation, so that industrial injury cases (apart from those referred to the medical authorities) are now determined by the national insurance statutory authorities.[14] Another change made by this Act was that the National Insurance Commissioner was renamed the Chief National Insurance Commissioner, and the Deputy Commissioners became National Insurance Commissioners; this removed the dissatisfaction previously voiced by appellants when they had heard that their cases were to be decided by a *Deputy* Commissioner![15] Finally, a new body, the Attendance Allowance Board, was set up in 1970 to adjudicate claims to attendance allowance.[16] There is an appeal from its decisions on a point of law to the Commissioner.[17]

B. Questions for the Secretary of State

i) General

Under the Social Security Act 1975[18] certain matters are reserved for decision by the Secretary of State. These include the following:

(a) whether a person is an earner and, if so, in which category of earners (employed or self-employed) he is to be included;

(b) whether the contribution conditions for the benefit in issue have been satisfied and any question 'relating to a person's contributions or his earnings factor';[19]

(c) whether a person is, or was, employed in employed earner's employment for the purposes of industrial injuries benefits;

(d) whether a person was under the relevant regulations precluded from regular employment by home responsibilities;[20]

(e) whether a constant attendance allowance or an exceptionally severe disablement allowance should be awarded or renewed and, if so, how it is to be assessed;[1]

(f) whether to accept a claim for one benefit as a claim in the alternative, or as a claim also, for another benefit.[2]

These questions are entirely outside the jurisdiction of the statutory authorities, i.e., the insurance officer, tribunal and Commissioner.[3] It is

13. FANIA 1959, s.2: see 596 HC Deb., cols. 714–715.
14. S.8. The term 'statutory authorities' is frequently used to refer to the insurance officer, local tribunal and the Commissioner, though its origin is shrouded in mystery: see *Micklethwait*, p. 18, n.4.
15. Miss M. Herbison, Minister of Pensions and National Insurance 724 HC Deb., col. 50.
16. See chap. 4, ante, pp. 171–178.
17. See post, pp. 641–642.
18. Ss. 93 and 95, as amended by CBA 1975, Sch. 4, paras. 30 and 31, SSPA 1975, s.60, and SS(MP)A 1977, s.22(5).
19. SSA 1975 s.93(1)(b): see ante, pp. 69–76, for contributions requirements.
20. See Appendix.
1. See ante, pp. 333–335.
2. Ante, p. 591.
3. *R(G) 1/61.*

not enough for them to rely on an informal opinion from an official of the DHSS; there should be a formal referral to the Secretary of State for the matter to be decided by him.[4]

It would appear that a question for the decision of the Secretary of State will only arise if a claimant has formally applied to him,[5] or if it is raised before the statutory authorities. If, however, the issue is not disputed by the claimant, it seems that the authorities may determine a matter which, if disputed, would have to be referred to the Secretary of State. This seems to be the implication of the Social Security (Determination of Claims and Questions) Regulations which provide that an insurance officer may issue a decision where he –

> 'has decided any claim or question on an assumption of facts as to which there appeared to him to be no dispute, but concerning which, had a question arisen, that question would have fallen for determination by the Secretary of State . . .'[6]

Thus, if a self-employed person claims industrial injury benefit and does not even contend that he is an employed earner, it would appear permissible for the insurance officer to refuse the claim without referring the matter to the Secretary of State. This view is supported by the remarks of the Commissioner, J. G. Monroe, in the recent case, *Re Retirement to Ireland*.[7]

ii) Procedure on determination by the Secretary of State

When a question is to be determined by the Secretary of State under section 93 (e.g., questions (a)–(d) referred to above), he may appoint a person to hold an inquiry into and report on it.[8] The inquiry is generally held by a member of the DHSS Solicitor's Office; the procedure is oral and all interested persons have the right to attend and be heard.[9] The Secretary of State must notify them of his decision and, if requested, give reasons.[10] Decisions have not been published since 1960.[11] This procedure is frequently invoked in cases concerning liability to pay contributions, where the correct categorisation of the person concerned may raise difficult questions of law and fact.[12]

In contrast there are no procedural rules at all for the determination by the Secretary of State of questions under section 95 (e.g., questions (e) and (f) referred to above). It seems that in practice decisions are made at regional offices, or in some cases at headquarters in London. Advice on medical matters relevant to a determination of entitlement to, and

4. *R(I) 2/75*, J.S. Watson, Comr.
5. S.I. 1975/558, Reg. 6(1).
6. Ibid., Reg. 9(1), and see S.I. 1976/962, Reg. 5(3) (Child Benefit Regulations). These regulations so closely follow the pattern of S.I. 1975/558 that they are not referred to unless there is a material difference from the regulations under the Social Security Act.
7. [1977] CMLR 1, 3. See the similar principle applied in cases under the

Rent Acts: *R v Westminster (City) London Borough Council Rent Officer, ex parte Rendall*, [1973] QB 959, [1973] 3 All ER 119, CA.
8. SSA 1975, s.93(3); see S.I. 1975/558, Reg. 6(3).
9. See DHSS Annual Report 1975, Cmnd. 6565, para. 9.12.
10. S.I. 1975/558, Regs. 6(5), and 7.
11. See chap. 2, ante, p. 47.
12. Ante, pp. 48–53.

assessment of, constant attendance allowance is given by medical boards.[13]

iii) Reference and appeal to the High Court

A question of law arising in connection with the determination by the Secretary of State of any question under section 93 may be referred by him to the High Court (or in Scotland, the Court of Session).[14] Alternatively, there may be an appeal on a point of law by 'any person aggrieved' with his decision.[15] The appeal is heard by a judge sitting alone, and there is (unusually) no further appeal.[16] Most appeals are brought on the question whether a person is properly to be regarded as employed or self-employed for the purpose of liability to pay contributions, and judicial decisions have substantially shaped the development of this area of law.[17]

The precise grounds on which the judge will entertain an appeal were fully considered by Lord Widgery CJ in *Global Plant Ltd v Secretary of State for Social Services*.[18] He concluded that the court would only allow an appeal –

1. if the decision contained a false proposition of law ex facie;

2. if the decision was one supported by no evidence; or

3. if the decision reached was one which no person acting judicially and properly instructed as to the relevant law could have come to.

It is an open question whether these grounds might be widened in view of recent developments in the scope of judicial review, in particular to allow an appeal if the facts found leave out of account relevant evidence.[19] As will be seen, the approach of Lord Widgery has been followed by the Commissioner in determining the grounds of appeal to him from decisions of medical appeal tribunals and of the Attendance Allowance Board.[20]

iv) Critique

There has never been any substantial argument for allocating these decisions to the Secretary of State, rather than the statutory authorities. It may be that there are some practical reasons as regards decisions on whether a claimant has satisfied the relevant contribution conditions. But it is not clear why the statutory authorities should not decide the related question whether a claimant should contribute as an employed or self-employed person. This involves difficult issues of law and fact which are suitable for a tribunal. Broader policy decisions in this area can, of course, be taken by the Secretary of State under his power to make regulations

---

13. Carson, 126 NLJ, p. 59: see ante, p. 334, for criticism of the absence of a formal procedure in these cases.
14. SSA 1975, s.94.
15. Ibid., s.94(3). 'Person aggrieved' here means any person with a financial interest in the decision, e.g., an employer in a case concerning the classification of a contributor.
16. Ibid., s.94(6), (7).

17. See the discussion in chap. 2, ante, pp. 48–53.
18. [1972] 1 QB 139, [1971] 3 All ER 385.
19. See in particular Scarman LJ, and Lord Wilberforce in *Secretary of State for Education v Tameside Metropolitan Borough Council* [1977] AC 1014, 1030, and 1047.
20. See post, pp. 641–642.

concerning the categorisation of earners.[1] Nor is there any obvious reason why entitlement to the constant attendance and exceptionally severe disablement allowances should be decided by him, while for the other additional allowances this is determined by the statutory authorities.

The Labour government in 1969–70 did indeed propose that 'Minister's questions' should be determined by a new 'special tribunal' with a right of appeal to the High Court on a point of law.[2] The Council on Tribunals argued that they should be decided by the existing statutory authorities with a final appeal to the Commissioner, but this was rejected, apparently on the ground that the matters were too complicated for local tribunals.[3] The Bill lapsed when the 1970 General Election was called.

c. Insurance officers

i) General

All claims under the Social Security Act 1975 are initially submitted to an insurance officer for determination, unless they are for disablement benefit or for an attendance allowance.[4] Insurance officers are appointed by the Secretary of State for Social Services, or in the case of unemployment benefit, the Secretary of State for Employment. They are civil servants, working in local offices – not necessarily full-time as an insurance officer.[5] They may refer difficult cases to a Regional Insurance Officer. It is the responsibility of the Chief Insurance Officer, now based in Southampton, to issue general guidance as to the discharge of their duties.

ii) Procedure for determining claims[6]

The insurance officer decides the application entirely on the documents sent to him by the claimant and branches of the Department. He does not interview the claimant or witnesses, though on rare occasions he may obtain statements through a Department inspector.[7] His duties have been characterised as 'administrative' in that he is not adjudicating between the contentions of the claimant and those of the Department or any other party.[8] When he finds it impossible to determine a complex case, he may refer it to the local insurance tribunal for initial decision.

The insurance officer should decide the application so far as practicable within fourteen days after its submission to him.[9] This is often impossible, particularly where, in an unemployment benefit case, written evidence has to be obtained from the claimant's employer. The case must be decided in

1. See ante, pp. 53–55.
2. National Superannuation and Social Insurance Bill 1969, cl. 78.
3. See the Annual Report of the Council on Tribunals for 1969–1970, para. 47 and Appendix B.
4. S.98. Any question for the determination of the Secretary of State must be referred to him by the insurance officer: s.98(2)(a).
5. *Micklethwait*, p. 66. See ante, p. 575,

for the civil service grade of insurance officers.
6. For a full discussion, see Farmer *Tribunals and Government*, (1974), pp. 102–105.
7. Street *Justice in the Welfare State* (2nd edn), p. 13.
8. See Diplock LJ in *R v Deputy Industrial Injuries Comr, ex parte Moore* [1965] 1 QB 456 at 486.
9. SSA 1975, s.99(1).

accordance with Commissioners' decisions, but the officer is not bound to follow his own previous decision on a prior claim.[10] The claimant must be told in writing of the decision with its reasons, and also of his right to appeal to the local tribunal.[11] However, where the claim has been decided by the officer on an assumption of facts, which if challenged would have raised a question for the Secretary of State, it is enough for the claimant to be told that, if he is dissatisfied with the decision, he can reply to that effect.[12] The claimant is only to be told of his right of appeal if he remains dissatisfied after the appropriate investigations have been made, or the Secretary of State has decided the relevant question.[13]

iii) Local referees
One power of the insurance officer and also of the local tribunal chairman requires brief mention: both may refer any question of fact concerning the claimant's right to benefit for 'examination and report to two persons ... residents in the neighbourhood' where the claimant lives.[14] One must be drawn from each panel from which the members of the local tribunal are chosen.[15] Referees are occasionally used by local tribunals to obtain evidence from a claimant who is unable to attend the hearing.[16]

D. National insurance local tribunals

i) Organisation and membership
National insurance local tribunals entertain appeals from insurance officers' decisions, and they also decide cases referred to them by insurance officers.[17] There were 182 local tribunals at the end of 1975,[18] each of which had a chairman and two members, one drawn from a panel of persons representing employers and self-employed earners, and the other drawn from a panel of persons representing employed earners.[19] The chairman is appointed for the particular tribunal area by the Secretary of State, but is chosen from a panel drawn up by the Lord Chancellor.[20] Despite the recommendations of the Franks Committee in 1957,[1] the other members continue to be chosen by the Secretary of State, and he may end their appointment at any time.[2]

Though there is no requirement that the chairman must be a lawyer, in practice he almost always is. Legal qualifications are clearly desirable in view of the complex law applied by the tribunals, and the need for the procedure to be in accordance with the standards of fairness imposed by

10. *CI 440/50.* The subject of precedent in social security law is considered post, pp. 634–635.
11. SSA 1975, s.100(2).
12. S.I. 1975/558, Reg. 9(1): see ante, p. 622.
13. Ibid., Reg. 9(3), (5).
14. Ibid., Reg. 14(1).
15. Ibid.
16. See *Farmer*, ante n.6, at p. 108.
17. Referrals are relatively infrequent:

thus, in 1976, while tribunals heard 37,425 cases, only about 1,200 were referrals by insurance officers – DHSS Annual Report 1976, Cmnd. 6931, paras. 58–59.
18. DHSS Annual Report 1975, Cmnd. 6565 para. 9.3.
19. SSA 1975, s.97(2).
20. Tribunals and Inquiries Act 1971, s.7.
1. (1957), Cmnd. 218, paras. 45–49.
2. SSA 1975, Sch. 10.

the courts.[3] In this context it is worth pointing out that the chairman has a number of specific powers, which include the following:

1. to determine the tribunal's procedure (subject, of course, to the requirements imposed under the legislation);[4]

2. to allow a hearing in private in certain circumstances;[5] and

3. to secure the assistance of a medical assessor.[6]

It is the chairman who explains the procedure to the appellant, and in practice it is he who asks most of the questions. Recent studies of local tribunals in the North of England and Scotland show general satisfaction by claimants with the part played by chairmen in the proceedings.[7]

On the other hand, there is rather more uncertainty, and some dissatisfaction expressed, about the role of the other (lay) members. It seems clear that, despite the method of selection, they are not expected to represent the interests of either the employee or the employer, but are required to exercise the same impartiality as the chairman.[8] It is not certain whether this is always understood by claimants. The remarkably high incidence of unanimous decisions (about 95%) found in the recent studies suggests that it is rare for a tribunal member to adopt a biased approach to the case. Indeed, the chairman dissents more often than the lay members:[9] this perhaps occurs when the majority think the claim should succeed on the 'merits', while the chairman takes the correct legal view that it must fail. What sometimes seems to be less satisfactory is the degree of participation by the lay members in the hearing.[10] There are often complaints that they leave all the questioning to the chairman. To some extent the lesser involvement of the lay members is understandable: they do not sit as often, and they have less formal responsibility than the chairman. Moreover, the holding of regional conferences for tribunal chairmen, where legal points are discussed, enables them to develop an expertise which lay members could not be expected to have.[11]

The administrative arrangements are made by a clerk, an officer of the DHSS who may combine these duties with other work.[12] He is generally responsible for convening tribunal sittings, choosing members from the panel, and arranging for the papers to be sent to the tribunal members. The tribunal is under no obligation to require him to leave when it is

3. For the rules of natural justice, see post, p. 648.
4. S.I. 1975/558, Reg. 3(1).
5. Ibid., Reg. 11(1).
6. Ibid., Reg. 11(4).
7. See Bell, Collison, Turner and Webber (1974) 3 Jnl. Soc. Pol. 289, and (1975) 4 Jnl. Soc. Pol. 1, esp. pp. 8–9.
8. See the speech of Lord Gardiner, then Lord Chancellor, quoted in Cavanagh and Newton, [1971] Public Administration 197, 210.
9. Bell et al., (1974) ante n.7, at pp. 303–304.

10. Bell et al., (1975) ante n.7, at p. 9; cp., the more favourable impression given by Street Justice in the Welfare State (2nd edn), p. 16.
11. Regional conferences of tribunal chairmen have been held since 1973 under the encouragement of the Council on Tribunals: see Annual Report for 1973–74, para. 20, and Wraith & Hutchesson Administrative Tribunals (1973), p. 168.
12. Wraith and Hutchesson, ante n.11, at pp. 121–122.

considering its decision,[13] though in practice the clerk does withdraw. This is also the position for medical boards and appeal tribunals.[14]

Some tribunals have their own premises, while others meet in Town Halls. Many sit in DHSS premises, but every attempt is then made to emphasise the independence of the tribunal by segregating its rooms from other parts of the building.[15] It is rarely suggested that these tribunals are subject to departmental pressure.[16]

ii) The selection of a particular tribunal

As far as possible, each member of a panel takes his turn to sit.[17] Schedule 10 to the Social Security Act 1975 lists a number of disqualifications. No member may sit in a case:[18]

1. in which he appears as the claimant's representative;

2. by which he is or may be directly affected; or

3. in which he has taken any part as an official of an association, as an employer, witness, local referee or otherwise.

Further, a member must stand down if his presence on the tribunal would infringe the rule against bias.[19] This has been a ground of appeal to the Commissioner in a few cases, though usually the contention that the constitution of the tribunal infringed the rule has failed. In *R(I) 51/56*,

it was held that there was nothing wrong in an area labour officer of the National Coal Board sitting as a member, when the claimant was an employee of the Board and worked in the officer's area.[20] It would have been different if the officer had given information concerning the case, or in any other way taken part.[1]

Where the claimant is female, at least one of the members, if possible, should be a woman.[2] The Commissioner has ruled that it would be helpful for the tribunal to indicate if this was not practicable; this will avoid later inquiries if the claimant alleges that there was no attempt to secure the participation of a woman.[3]

iii) Notice of appeal and of the hearing

A notice, stating the grounds of appeal,[4] must be given at a local office within twenty-one days of the insurance officer's decision.[5] The *chairman* of the tribunal may allow an extension where good cause is shown;[6] there

13. S.I. 1975/558, Reg. 3(2).
14. See post pp. 635–641, for medical authorities.
15. *Wraith and Hutchesson*, ante n.11, at p. 122.
16. Cp., supplementary benefit tribunals, post, pp. 649–659.
17. SSA 1975, Sch. 10, para. 1(4).
18. Ibid., para. 1(4), proviso (a).
19. For this principle of administrative law, see de Smith *Judicial Review of Administration Action* (3rd edn), chap. 5.

20. *R(U) 8/53*.
1. *R(I) 26/54*.
2. SSA 1975, Sch. 10, para. 1(4), proviso (c).
3. *R(G) 6/62*.
4. SSA 1975, s.100(5).
5. Ibid., s.100(4).
6. Ibid. The case-law on the meaning of this phrase for the purpose of late claims may be of assistance in interpreting the provision here: see ante, pp. 601–606.

is no appeal to the Commissioner, however, if he refuses to extend the time-limit.[7]

The clerk then arranges the date and time of the hearing, and sends the claimant all the relevant papers, including the insurance officer's submissions, and any documentary evidence. Also enclosed is a notice that the claimant may attend, alone or with a representative. In order to encourage his attendance, experiments have been conducted in which he has been notified of the names and addresses of people and organisations willing to help him.[8] Reasonable notice of the time and place of the hearing must be given; the Commissioner has held that five days' notice is adequate in view of the tribunal's power to adjourn proceedings.[9]

There is, in fact, no express general power to adjourn, but its existence is a reasonable implication from the proviso to Regulation 10(2). This precludes a tribunal from determining a case in the absence of the claimant without his consent, if he has given a reasonable explanation for his absence, 'unless the hearing has at first been adjourned for at least one month and reasonable notice of the time and place of the adjourned hearing has been given to him'. The resumed hearing in this situation cannot be taken earlier even if the applicant consents.[10] A Tribunal of Commissioners has ruled that the same tribunal must sit when the case is resumed, unless the claimant consents to a different membership.[11]

iv) The conduct of the hearing

There are relatively few rules with regard to tribunal procedure. Every hearing must be in public unless the *chairman* takes the view that 'intimate personal or financial circumstances may have to be disclosed or that considerations of public security are involved'.[12] If a claimant wishes to make a private statement, the chairman should explain that it may have to be disclosed in outline to other witnesses.[13] The only persons entitled to be *heard* are the claimant, the insurance officer, the Secretary of State, any one whose right to benefit may be affected by the tribunal's decision,[14] and the representative of all such persons. The representative need not have professional or legal qualifications. Any person entitled to be heard *may* also call witnesses, and has a right to put questions to any other witnesses.[15]

Apart from these rules, it is for the chairman to determine the procedure. But this is subject to the control of the Commissioner, who will

7. *R(I) 44/59*: see post, p. 632, for appeals to the Commissioner.
8. See the Report of the Council on Tribunals for 1972–73, para. 67.
9. *R(S) 13/52*, interpreting what is now S.I. 1975/588, Reg. 10(1). Cp., S.I. 1976/962, Reg. 13(1), which provides that ten days' notice must be given for the hearing of a child benefit appeal.
10. *R(U) 5/70*, J.S. Watson, Comr. This does not apply to child benefit appeals:

see S.I. 1976/962, Reg. 10.
11. *R(I) 3/51*, and see also *R(I) 31/57*; *R(S) 3/64*. But see *R(I) 40/61* where it was held that a differently constituted tribunal may hear the case provided it starts the hearing afresh.
12. S.I. 1975/558, Reg. 11(1).
13. *R(U) 2/56*.
14. S.I. 1975/558, Reg. 11(2).
15. Ibid., Reg. 3(1)(b) and 3(3).

allow an appeal if it has been irregular, contrary to the rules of natural justice or in any way unfair.[16] Clearly, in the absence of detailed rules, procedure will vary a little from one tribunal to another, though there is a standard order of proceeding. When the claimant attends, he is asked to outline his case and, if he wishes, to call witnesses. The chairman, and sometimes the other members, intervene to clarify the argument. Then the insurance officer (not necessarily the same person who decided the case[17]) is invited to ask the claimant (and his witnesses) any questions. In the second stage of the proceeding, the insurance officer makes his submissions. Often he brings out points favourable to the claimant.[18] Diplock LJ has emphasised that the role of the insurance officer is not that of a party adverse to the claimant, but resembles that of an *amicus curiae*.[19] The claimant may put questions to him. Finally, the chairman asks the appellant whether he wishes to add anything, and then the tribunal considers its decision.[20]

The recent study of insurance tribunals has shown that, despite the fact that their expenses are paid,[1] only about 50% of appellants attend the hearing, and that just over 20% are represented. Much the highest levels of attendance and representation occur in industrial injury cases where trades unions almost always provide assistance.[2] It was also discovered that appellants who attend, and still more those who are represented, have a higher rate of success than those who do not come to the tribunal.[3] The significance of these findings can be challenged. On one view many claimants automatically appeal, but only those with an arguable case trouble to attend or seek representation. But there is some evidence that the reasons for failure to attend are more complex – inability to get to the hearing, unwarranted pessimism about the chances of success and fear of involvement in unfamiliar proceedings.[4] The comparative lack of available assistance for preparing a case or presenting it to the tribunal appears disturbing, particularly as the high success rate of claimants represented by trades union officials in industrial injury cases shows its value.[5] It is more contentious whether representation by lawyers should be encouraged. Clearly in some cases their skills are invaluable in presenting an argument to the tribunal; on the other hand, it has been argued that

16. See *R(I) 3/51*; *R(U) 2/71*; *R(U) 44/52* for rare cases where a tribunal's procedure was successfully challenged, and see the cases mentioned in *R(U) 3/63*, para. 12.
17. See Street *Justice in the Welfare State* (2nd edn), p. 15.
18. Ibid., at p. 16.
19. *R v Deputy Industrial Injuries Comr, ex parte Moore* [1965] 1 QB 456 at 486.
20. See post, p. 630.
1. See *Micklethwait*, pp. 65–66; *Wraith and Hutchesson Administrative Tribunals* (1973), pp. 181–185.

2. Bell, Collison, Turner and Webber (1974) 3 Jnl. Soc. Pol., pp. 300–301. Thus, there was an attendance rate of 83% in industrial disablement cases, and a similarly high rate of representation in these cases.
3. Bell *et al.*, (1975) 4 Jnl. Soc. Pol. 1, at pp. 11–21.
4. Ibid., at pp. 5–6.
5. The *Bell* study shows that appellants represented by trades union officials have a success rate of 43%, compared with 39% for those assisted by lawyers and 16% for unrepresented appellants: ibid., at p. 15.

their participation often leads to delay and undue formality.[6] Obviously lawyers would be employed more often if legal aid were extended to cover representation before administrative tribunals.[7]

v) The tribunal's decision

The tribunal may take into account issues which were not considered by the insurance officer,[8] provided it has given the parties an opportunity to comment on them.[9] When considering its decision it must order all persons, other than the clerk, to withdraw.[10] Decisions have been set aside because the insurance officer had remained in the room when the tribunal was considering its verdict, even though there was no suggestion that he had influenced the result.[11]

The local tribunal may decide by a majority; if it has only two members, the chairman has a second or casting vote.[12] It must record its decision in writing, including its findings of fact and reasons. The grounds for a dissenting opinion must also be stated.[13] There is no duty to record which member is dissenting, though the general practice is to indicate whether it is the chairman or a lay member. The Commissioner has consistently emphasised the importance of a full statement of the findings of fact and the grounds for decision.[14] A failure to do this will often make an oral hearing before the Commissioner necessary where otherwise it could be dispensed with.[15] A copy of the decision must be sent to the parties as soon as is practicable.[16] The claimant must also be told of his right to appeal to the Commissioner, when he has been unsuccessful before the tribunal.

vi) Medical assessors

The chairman of the tribunal may decide that a medical practitioner should sit with the tribunal as an assessor.[17] He is not to take any part in its determinations 'except in an advisory capacity'.[18] It seems that he is usually a general practitioner, rather than a specialist.[19] The Commissioners have further defined his role: it is undesirable for the assessor to put questions to the claimant or witnesses, and the tribunal should summarise his advice and give the parties a chance to comment on it.[20] He

6. For some of the extensive literature on this difficult question, see Whitmore, 33 MLR 481; Society of Labour Lawyers *Justice for All* (1968) Fabian Research series No. 273; Society of Conservative Lawyers *Rough Justice* (1968), Conservative Political Centre; LAG *Representation before Tribunals*: Memorandum to the Lord Chancellor's Legal Aid Advisory Committee *LAG Bulletin*, Feb. 1974, p. 27.

7. Extension was recommended by the 24th Report of the Lord Chancellor's Advisory Committee on Legal Aid, 1973–74 HC 20, but its proposal has not been implemented by the government.

8. SSA 1975, s.102.

9. *R(U) 2/71*; *R(F) 1/72*; *R(I) 4/75*.

10. S.I. 1975/558, Reg. 3(2). A member of the Council on Tribunals may stay for the deliberations if no member of the tribunal or party objects.

11. *CSS 87/49*; *CU 331/49*; *CP 127/49*.

12. S.I. 1975/558, Reg. 12(1).

13. Ibid., Reg. 12(2).

14. *R(I) 81/51*; *R(I) 42/59*; *R(U) 16/60*; *R(I) 14/59*.

15. *R(G) 1/63*.

16. S.I. 1975/558, Reg. 12(3).

17. S.I. 1975/558, Reg. 11(4).

18. Ibid., Reg. 11(5).

19. Street *Justice in the Welfare State* (2nd edn), p. 20.

20. *R(I) 14/51*.

should not be cross-examined by them or in any way treated as a witness.[1] Finally, it is generally no function of the assessor to examine the claimant medically, unless he consents and this course is necessary to save delay.[2]

In effect, the assessor's sole duty is to assist the tribunal evaluate the medical evidence. The Commissioner may also have the assistance of assessors where there is 'a question of fact of special difficulty'.[3] Here the power to call for assistance is not limited to *medical* assessors. There are no regulations governing their role at this level but the limits on their functions with regard to tribunals would appear also to apply to their role in assisting Commissioners. In *R v Deputy Industrial Injuries Comr, ex parte Jones*, the Divisional Court made it clear that the assessor's role was to help the Commissioner *weigh* the evidence given by the parties, and not to *give* evidence or an opinion on the case.[4] Further, where there is an oral hearing the assessor must be present at least to hear the medical evidence. These restrictions have been criticised by the former Chief Commissioner, Sir Robert Micklethwait.[5]

E. National Insurance Commissioners

i) The Commissioners and their jurisdiction

Appeals from local insurance tribunals lie to one of the National Insurance Commissioners,[6] who must be barristers (or in Scotland, advocates) of ten years' standing.[7] There is a Chief National Insurance Commissioner, and others may be appointed by the Crown to meet current needs: there are now nine, apart from the Chief Commissioner, R. J. A. Temple. The status of decisions of the Chief and other Commissioners is the same,[8] but the former is statutorily responsible for convening a Tribunal of three Commissioners to sit where an appeal 'involves a question of law of special difficulty'.[9] He also has general administrative responsibilities, the most important of which is selecting the decisions to be reported.[10]

The Commissioners are appointed to hear appeals in Great Britain, and not for particular areas. In practice two of them sit in Edinburgh and decide appeals largely from Scottish tribunals, while another sits in Cardiff and takes cases from Wales and the West country. The others sit in London. In addition to their appellate jurisdiction from insurance tribunals, from 1959 the Commissioners have heard appeals on points of law from medical

1. *R(I) 23/57.*
2. *R(I) 14/51.*
3. SSA 1975, s.101(6).
4. [1962] 2 QB 677, [1972] 2 All ER 430.
5. See *Micklethwait*, pp. 60–61. He points out that SSA 1975, Sch. 13, para. 9 confers a power, by regulations, to expand the assessor's functions and that this has not been exercised.
6. SSA 1975, s.101(1).
7. Ibid., s.97(3). For a discussion of the Commissioners, their jurisdiction and

terms of service, see Micklethwait, chap. 5.
8. This was true of the decisions of the Commissioner and the Deputy Commissioners before the reform of 1966, though it was not always appreciated: see ante p. 621.
9. SSA 1975, s.116: see post p. 634 for a further discussion of Tribunals of Commissioners.
10. *Micklethwait*, p. 43: see post, p. 634, for a further discussion of this.

appeal tribunals, and since 1970 from the Attendance Allowance Board.[11]

ii) Notice of appeal and the request for a hearing

An appeal may be brought from a decision of a local tribunal by –

> the claimant, the insurance officer, a trade union in certain cases (in particular, where the claimant is a member of that union both at the time the case arose and at the time of the appeal) or a person whose right to industrial death benefit may be affected by the decision.[12]

It must be brought within three months, though this period may be extended at the discretion of the Commissioner.[13] An insurance officer must give notice on an approved form to the claimant, and the claimant or trade union must give notice in writing at a local office. In practice appeals by insurance officers are brought only when it is considered that a point of principle is in issue, after consultation with the Regional Insurance Officer.[14] The grounds of appeal must be stated, though these need not be particularised in great detail.[15] But it is not enough merely to send the Commissioner the documents and leave it to him to ascertain the ground of appeal.[16]

When the insurance officer's submissions have been obtained, the claimant is invited to make further observations and is asked whether he wishes to request an oral hearing.[17] The Commissioner must grant this,

> 'unless, after considering the record of the case and the reasons put forward in the request for the hearing, he is satisfied that the appeal can properly be determined without a hearing...'[18]

An oral hearing will be granted unless it is clear that the appeal must be upheld, or alternatively it is a hopeless case.[19] In practice it appears that many appeals are decided on written submissions, though this may be because the claimant does not generally request an oral hearing.[20] (There may be an oral hearing even if one has not been requested, if the Commissioner thinks this is desirable[1]).

When a hearing is held, reasonable notice of its time and place must be given to the parties.[2] If the claimant does not attend, the Commissioner has power to proceed with the case, but it would also be open to him to adjourn.[3] There has been some concern expressed by the Council on Tribunals about the long time taken to dispose of a case.[4] This now seems to be about twenty-two weeks – considerably longer than the three or four weeks taken by local tribunals.[5]

11. See post, pp. 640 and 641.
12. SSA 1975, s.101(2)–(3); for child benefit appeals, see S.I. 1976/962, Reg. 6(2).
13. SSA 1975, s. 101(5).
14. Street, ante n.17, at p. 24.
15. R(I) 15/53.
16. R(F) 1/70.
17. Micklethwait, p. 48.
18. S.I. 1975/558, Reg. 13(1).

19. R(I) 4/75, at para. 9, R.G. Micklethwait, Chief Comr.
20. Micklethwait, p. 49.
1. S.I. 1975/558, Reg. 13(2).
2. Ibid. In practice, three to four weeks' notice is given.
3. Ibid. Reg. 13(4).
4. Annual Report for 1969-70, para. 29.
5. Wraith and Hutchesson Administrative Tribunals (1973), pp. 185–186.

iii) The hearing[6]

The only procedural rules are those already discussed in the context of local tribunals – providing a right to representation and governing the calling and cross-examination of witnesses.[7] Subject to them, the Commissioner is empowered to decide the procedure. This is in practice very similar to that at local tribunals; in particular, the appellant, usually the claimant, has the last word.[8] The rules of natural justice apply to ensure fairness.[9]

The hearing before the Commissioner is not confined to the issues discussed before the local tribunal or those raised by the parties; the tribunal's findings of fact are not binding on him.[10] He may adjourn proceedings while further inquiries are made.[11] The Act specifically empowers him to refer questions to a medical practitioner for the latter to prepare a report,[12] which must be given to the parties for their comments.[13] Also, as has been mentioned, a medical or other expert assessor may perform the limited function of helping the Commissioner evaluate the evidence.[14]

iv) The Commissioner's decision

The Commissioner's decision with reasons must be sent to the parties as soon as possible.[15] In practice the claimant is often told the result immediately after the hearing, and the reasons are given later.[16] The various alternatives open to the Commissioner when a local tribunal's decision is challenged for jurisdictional error were fully considered by a Tribunal in *R(U) 3/63*. It held that where the local tribunal has acted outside its jurisdiction, the appropriate course is simply to set the decision aside. However, where there has been a procedural irregularity, the Commissioner has discretion to decide the case himself or to remit it to the tribunal. If there are sufficient materials on which to give a decision and the claimant does not wish a rehearing, the Commissioner should generally adopt the former course.[17]

A decision of the Commissioner is final, and there is no appeal to a further tribunal or the High Court.[18] This statement, however, must be qualified in four ways:

1. there may be judicial review in the Divisional Court by the prerogative orders;[19]

2. the fact that the decision is final does not mean that a finding of fact necessary for this decision is conclusive for other proceedings;[20]

6. See generally, *Micklethwait*, pp. 48–53.
7. See ante p. 628.
8. *Micklethwait*, p. 52.
9. See post, p. 648, for a discussion of the rules of natural justice.
10. *R(P) 1/55*; *R(I) 42/56*; *R(I) 4/75*.
11. *R(G) 2/63*.
12. SSA 1975, s.101(7).
13. *R v Deputy Industrial Injuries Comr, ex parte Jones* [1962] 2 QB 677, [1962] 2 All ER 430, DC.
14. See ante, p. 631.
15. S.I. 1973/558, Reg. 13(6).
16. *Micklethwait*, p. 71.
17. However, see *R(U) 5/70*, where J.S. Watson, Comr., referred the case back to a differently constituted tribunal.
18. SSA 1975, s.117(1).
19. See post, pp. 644–648.
20. See post p. 636, for a short discussion of the relationship between the jurisdiction of the statutory and medical authorities, and see chap. 8, ante, pp. 306–308.

3. the decision may be reviewed by an insurance officer in certain circumstances, e.g., if it is clear on fresh evidence that the decision was based on a mistake as to a material fact;[1]

4. the Commissioner himself may set aside the decision if it is clear there was some accident or mistake in the procedure, e.g., a letter requesting an oral hearing never reached him.[2]

v) A Tribunal of commissioners

The Chief Commissioner may direct that a Tribunal of three Commissioners hear an appeal involving a point of law of special difficulty.[3] It may decide by a majority. In fact both dissents and separate concurring opinion are relatively uncommon.[4] It seems that a Tribunal may be ordered to resolve a conflict of views between the Commissioners in two previous cases,[5] but they are now convened very rarely.[6]

vi) Precedent and the reporting of decisions[7]

There have been about 60,000 decisions of the National Insurance Commissioners since 1948,[8] the annual number of cases, therefore, averaging about 2,000. It would be quite pointless to report all, or even a majority of these decisions, as a very large number simply involve the application of familiar principles to the facts. The vast majority are, therefore, kept unnumbered on the Commissioner's file.[9] But if a case is of some importance, either because of its particular facts or because a legal principle is developed, he may decide that it should be included in the numbered series of Commissioners' decisions. It can then be read at one of their offices, and copies can be supplied. Finally, the Chief Commissioner selects for reporting the most important numbered decisions, provided this course is assented to by a majority of the Commissioners. About 2,000 cases have been reported since 1948.[10]

It hardly needs stating that the purpose of publishing these decisions is to enable claimants to know their legal rights, and to ensure the uniform application of social security law by tribunals and insurance officers. These objectives will not be fully attained if, as sometimes appears to be the case, important decisions of the Commissioner are not reported. Often it seems surprising that a numbered decision, fully discussed in a later case, has not itself been reported.[11]

1. See post p. 642.
2. S.I. 1975/572, Regs. 2, 3, (and see *CU* 248/49; *R(I) 39/51*).
3. SSA 1975, s.116.
4. But see, e.g., *R(I) 7/64* (dissent); *R(U) 8/73* and *R(U) 9/73* (separate concurring opinions).
5. *R(U) 1/66*, para. 8.
6. See the Annual Reports of the DHSS for 1974, Cmnd. 6150, para. 10.8; 1975, Cmnd. 6565, para. 9.8, and 1976 Cmnd. 6931, para. 64.
7. The citation of Commissioners' Decisions is treated at the beginning of this book.
8. See *R(I) 12/75*, from which many of the observations in this paragraph are taken.
9. See *Micklethwait*, pp. 75–76.
10. Reported decisions are published by HMSO, and are bound in volumes every four years.
11. See, e.g. *R(U) 4/72*, considering *CU 14/65*; *R(U) 4/75*, where a Tribunal discussed 5 numbered decisions; and *R(S) 2/69*, where a numbered case is reported four years after it was decided.

The reporting of decisions assumes particular importance because of the system of precedent which has been developed by the Commissioners.[12] The rules were recently set out at length by a Tribunal in *R(I) 12/75*:

(1) All statutory authorities are bound to follow decisions of the High Court and other superior courts.

(2) A decision of a Commissioner must be followed by local tribunals and insurance officers, unless it can be distinguished.[13]

(3) If two Commissioners' decisions conflict, a local tribunal and insurance officer *must* –
(a) prefer a decision of a Tribunal of Commissioners to that of a single Commissioner;
(b) give more weight to a reported decision than to an unreported one; and
(c) if (a) and (b) do not apply, choose between the conflicting decisions.[14]

(4) A single Commissioner –
(a) should follow a decision of a Tribunal of Commissioners unless there are compelling reasons why he should not; and
(b) should normally follow the decision of another single Commissioner.[15]

The Tribunal did not comment on the circumstances in which one Tribunal might depart from the previous decision of another, but it seems that it may do so when satisfied the former decision was wrong.[16] The strict doctrine of *stare decisis* followed by the British courts has, therefore, never been adopted by the National Insurance Commissioners.[17]

Finally, it may be noted that decisions of the Northern Ireland Commissioners are not binding in Great Britain. But they may be of persuasive authority, and at least in one case a Northern Ireland Tribunal decision was followed in preference to an unreported decision of the British Commissioner.[18]

F. Medical authorities

i) General

Under section 108 of the Social Security Act 1975 some questions of entitlement to disablement benefit ('disablement questions') are referred to

12. See *Micklethwait*, pp. 73–75. An opinion on a medical question expressed in a previous case is, of course, not binding on the statutory authorities: see *R(I) 16/56*; *R(I) 9/67*; *R(I) 12/68*.

13. This proposition was already well established: see *CS 25/48*; *R(U) 23/59*; *R(G) 3/62*.

14. No preference is to be given to the earlier or the later decision as such.

15. This proposition is in line with *R(G) 3/62* and *R(I) 23/63*, and see Roskill LJ in *R v National Insurance Comr, ex parte Michael* [1977] 1 WLR 109 at 115, CA.

16. *R(U) 7/68*.

17. See *Micklethwait*, pp. 74 and 129. See the similar liberal view of precedent in war pensions cases, discussed at post, p. 662.

18. *R(I) 14/63*.

separate medical authorities, viz., medical boards and medical appeal tribunals.[19] It is not entirely clear why this course has been taken. On one view, in claims for industrial injury benefit, the statutory authorities have to decide medical questions as difficult as those reserved for the medical authorities.[20] From this premise it might be reasonable to argue that the existence of the special medical tribunals is unnecessary. On the other hand, it may be more persuasively contended that, as disablement benefit may be awarded for a long period (in some cases, for the rest of the claimant's life) and its assessment depends on the degree of disablement, questions concerning its award should be reserved for an expert medical tribunal. This view was expressed by Lord Diplock in *Jones v Secretary of State for Social Services*:

> 'One would, therefore, expect that Parliament would provide machinery for a more thorough and expert diagnosis and prognosis of the claimant's medical condition resulting from the injury where a claim was for disablement benefit, than whatever diagnostic material happened to be available to an insurance officer at an earlier date when he was called upon to deal with a claim for injury benefit.'[1]

Whatever its merits in terms of principle, the division of function between the statutory and the medical authorities has led to complex legal problems which have twice been before the House of Lords.[2] Its decisions and the subsequent change in the law made by Parliament[3] have been described fully in the chapter on industrial injuries.[4]

The general character of the medical authorities' jurisdiction has been frequently discussed by the courts.[5] The remarks of Diplock J (as he then was) in *R v Medical Appeal Tribunal, ex parte Hubble*, are still apposite:

> 'As an expert investigating body it is the right and duty of the medical board to use their own expertise in deciding the medical questions referred to them. They may, if they think fit, make their own examination of the claimant and consider any other facts and material to enable them to reach their expert conclusion as doctors do in diagnosis and prognosis of the case of an ordinary patient.'[6]

He added that these observations were also applicable to medical appeal

---

19. See ante, pp. 303–314, for disablement benefit.
20. Lord Reid in *Jones v Secretary of State for Social Services* [1972] AC 944, 967–968, HL.
1. Ibid., at p. 1007.
2. *Minister of Social Security v Amalgamated Engineering Union* [1967] 1 AC 725, [1967] 1 All ER 210, HL and *Jones v Secretary of State for Social Services*, ante n.20.

3. See now SSA 1975, s.117(1), (3).
4. Chap. 8, ante p. 306–308. See also p. 328 for the relationship between medical authorities' determinations on disablement questions and the statutory authorities' jurisdiction on entitlement to special hardship allowance.
5. For judicial review by the courts, see post, pp. 644–648.
6. [1958] 2 QB 228, 240–241, DC.

tribunals. In a more recent case, the Court of Appeal has emphasised the inquisitorial nature of proceedings before these tribunals.[7]

ii) Medical boards

They sit at 105 centres, and consist of two medical practitioners, one of whom acts as chairman.[8] If they are unable to agree, the disablement question is referred to a three-member board, which may decide by majority.[9] The claimant does not have a *right* to be represented at its sitting, though the presence of anyone likely to assist in the determination of the medical question may be permitted.[10] Otherwise the proceedings are in private; in fact, they consist of a medical examination of the claimant who may also be asked a few questions.[11]

With the claimant's consent a disablement question may be referred for initial decision to a single medical practitioner.[12] However, he may not make an assessment for more than six months.[13] The medical board (or single medical practitioner) is required to state the facts material to the decision but there is no obligation to state its reasons.[14] It is hard to see the justification for this, particularly as when there is a dissent (in a three-member board), the reasons for the minority view must be given.[15]

Medical boards also exercise appellate jurisdiction from decisions by insurance officers (taken consequent to a medical report) on the diagnosis of a prescribed disease.[16] Further, they hear appeals from insurance officers on the medical questions involved in determining entitlement to mobility allowances.[17]

iii) Medical appeal tribunals

a) COMPOSITION. There is a right of appeal from a medical board (or medical practitioner) to a medical appeal tribunal.[18] Alternatively, the Secretary of State may require a decision to be referred to the tribunal, which may then confirm, vary or reverse it as on an appeal.[19] The tribunals consist of three members, a legally-qualified chairman and two doctors, both of consultant status.[20] Under the Determination of Claims and Questions Regulations a person directly affected by the case or who has taken any part in it as a medical assessor, the claimant's doctor, a member of a medical board or an employer or witness, may not sit on a tribunal.[1] A doctor who has examined a person in connection with his common law suit for damages may not sit as a member of a tribunal deciding a claim for benefit arising from the same accident.[2] But it has also been held, perhaps

7. *R v National Insurance Comr, ex parte Viscusi* [1974] 2 All ER 724, [1974] 1 WLR 646.
8. S.I. 1975/558, Reg. 16.
9. Ibid., Reg. 16(4).
10. Ibid., Reg. 18(2).
11. Hodge *LAG Bulletin*, Jan. 1974, p. 13.
12. SSA 1975, s.111(1).
13. Ibid., s.111(1), proviso.
14. S.I. 1975/558, Reg. 19.

15. Ibid., Reg. 19(1)(b).
16. SSA 1975, s.113, and see S.I. 1975/1537, Regs. 22–29.
17. S.I. 1975/1573, Regs. 12–19.
18. SSA 1975, s.109(2).
19. Ibid., s.109(3).
20. See Wraith and Hutchesson *Administrative Tribunals* (1973), p. 94.
1. S.I. 1975/558, Reg. 20.
2. *R(I) 28/61* (Tribunal decision).

surprisingly, that it is not a breach of the rule against bias for a medical practitioner to sit and *review* a decision of another tribunal of which he was a member.[3] This practice has been criticised by the Council on Tribunals and the Department now ensures that it does not happen.[4]

b) PROCEDURE BEFORE THE TRIBUNAL. An appeal, or a Secretary of State's reference, must be brought within three months of notification of the board's decision, though the chairman of the tribunal may grant an extension. Notice of the appeal with its grounds must be given at a local office.[5] In most respects the rules governing the conduct of the hearing are identical to those for local tribunals. There is, however, one important aspect of the medical appeal tribunal's procedure which distinguishes it from the usual form of proceedings before a local tribunal: it is the general rule for the claimant to be examined by the two medical members of the tribunal *after* the hearing,[6] though this need not be done in all cases.[7]

c) NATURAL JUSTICE IN TRIBUNAL PROCEEDINGS. There have been numerous decisions concerning the application of the natural justice rules to medical appeal tribunal proceedings, first, by the courts on application for certiorari,[8] and secondly, by the Commissioner after 1959 when the right of appeal on a point of law was created.[9] The cases can be discussed under the following heads:

1. A NEW POINT TAKEN BY THE TRIBUNAL MUST BE PUT TO THE CLAIMANT. This requirement was first stated, obiter, by Lord Denning MR, in *R v Industrial Injuries Comr, ex parte Howarth*.[10] The Commissioner has repeatedly emphasised that if the tribunal considers an issue of real significance, which has not been discussed at the medical board, it must invite the claimant to comment.[11] In some circumstances he should be asked to comment on the points arising from the medical examination,[12] though this is not an absolute rule.[13]

2. THE GENERAL DUTY OF THE TRIBUNAL TO HELP THE CLAIMANT. The Commissioner has stressed that the tribunal may be in breach of the rules of natural justice if it does not invite the claimant to address it.[14] In one case, the Commissioner suggested that the duty of the tribunal is to assist the claimant in making his case.[15]

3. THE USE BY THE TRIBUNAL OF SPECIALISTS' REPORTS. It is open to the tribunal to ask for a specialist's report, but a copy must be

3. *R(I) 28/61* (Tribunal decision).
4. See the Annual Report for 1965, paras. 58–61, and the Report for 1967, para. 70.
7. S.I. 1975/558, Reg. 21.
6. See *Wraith and Hutchesson*, ante, n.20, at p. 147; Hodge, ante n.11.
7. *R(I) 35/61*.

8. See post, p. 645, for judicial review.
9. See post, p. 640.
10. (1968) 4 KIR 621.
11. *R(I) 4/71*; *R(I) 29/61*; *R(I) 2/74*.
12. *R(I) 29/61* (Tribunal decision).
13. *R(I) 2/64*.
14. *R(I) 10/62*.
15. *R(I) 6/69*, H. Magnus, comr.

given to the claimant.[16] The same is true of hospital case notes.[17] If the claimant then wishes to call his own expert evidence, the tribunal should adjourn to allow him to do this.[18]

4. EVIDENCE ACQUIRED AFTER THE PROCEEDINGS. In *R(I) 2/72*, the Commissioner, D. Neligan, ruled that it was contrary to natural justice for the clerk to ask the claimant questions subsequent to the hearing, and communicate the answers to the tribunal.[19]

In view of this wealth of authority, it is suprising to find in a recent decision of the Court of Appeal a suggestion that the rules of natural justice do not apply to hearings before medical appeal tribunals.[20] It was emphasised that within the limits of fairness they were masters of their own procedure and were entitled to use their own expertise. But in an earlier case the Divisional Court had concluded that this feature of medical tribunals did not justify the exclusion of the rules of natural justice.[1] This latter approach is consistent with the leading authorities on the proper use by specialist tribunals of their expertise and should, it is suggested, be followed.[2]

d) THE DECISION OF THE TRIBUNAL. The appeal tribunal has jurisdiction to determine the questions arising before it de novo, and is not limited to the issues considered by the board.[3] The courses open to the tribunal when an appeal is brought on jurisdictional or technical grounds were considered by the Commissioner, D. Reith, in *R(I) 7/75*. He held that the tribunal has a discretion to deal with the case itself or to remit the case to another medical board.[14] Where the board's decision is a complete nullity because it was improperly constituted, it is generally more appropriate to adopt the latter course, but a tribunal might properly decide the case itself when there has been only a minor irregularity in the proceedings.

The decision must contain a statement of reasons with findings on the material facts and a summary of this must be sent to the claimant as soon as practicable.[5] (Rather oddly, though the tribunal may decide by a majority, there is no provision for recording a dissenting opinion.)[6] The record should state whether the claimant has been medically examined,

16. *R(I) 35/61*.
17. *R(I) 6/67*; *R(I) 13/74*.
18. *R v Medical Appeal Tribunal, ex parte Carrarini* [1966] 1 WLR 883, DC.
19. The Commissioner is not entitled to receive evidence after the oral hearing without allowing the parties an opportunity to comment on it: see *R v Deputy Industrial Injuries Comr, ex parte Jones* [1962] 2 QB 677 [1962] 2All ER 430.
20. See Buckley LJ in *R v National Insurance Comr, ex parte Viscusi* [1974] 1 WLR 646, [1974] 2 All ER 724.
 1. See *R v Medical Appeal Tribunal, ex parte Carrarini*, ante n.18.

 2. See de Smith *Judicial Review of Administrative Action* (3rd edn), pp. 180–182.
 3. Diplock J in *R v Medical Appeal Tribunal, ex parte Hubble*, [1958] 2 QB 228, 241, DC. Also see ante, p. 314, for the tribunal's powers to revise provisional assessments.
 4. The Commissioner followed the Tribunal decision in *R(U) 3/63*, see ante, p. 633.
 5. S.I. 1975/558, Reg. 23.
 6. Cp., the provision for local tribunals and medical boards, ante, pp. 630 and 637.

and make it clear why his contentions were accepted or rejected.[7] It is not enough merely to state that the tribunal considers the board's decision 'just and reasonable'.[8] On the other hand, there is no need for every step in the reasoning to be set out.[9]

iv) Appeal to the Commissioner

Since 1959 there has been a right of appeal on a point of law from a medical appeal tribunal to the National Insurance Commissioner – though either the tribunal or the Commissioner must give leave.[10] This was introduced because in the previous years there had been a number of successful applications for certiorari from the tribunals, and it became clear that they were not always applying the law consistently.[11] The appeal to the Commissioner now obviates the need to apply to the Divisional Court.[12]

An application for leave must first be made to the tribunal, either orally at the conclusion of its hearing or in writing within three months of its decision.[13] If it refuses leave, the applicant has twenty-one days to apply to a Commissioner – though this period may be extended at his discretion.[14] Both the appeal tribunal and the Commissioner may refuse consent where the point of law is without substance.[15]

If leave is granted, the appeal itself must then be brought within three months from this grant.[16] In the most recent case to consider the question, *R(I) 14/75*, the Commissioner, J. S. Watson, stated that an appeal will be allowed on a point of law if –

1. there has been a breach of the rules of natural justice;

2. the tribunal has not stated its reasons and findings of fact adequately;

3. the decision contains a false proposition of law ex facie;

4. the decision is not supported by any evidence;

5. the tribunal's findings of fact were such that no reasonable body acting judicially and properly instructed on the law could have reached the conclusion it arrived at.

A copy of the Commissioner's decision is sent to the chairman of the medical appeal tribunal, the Secretary of State and the claimant (or his trade union).[17] It is then the duty of the tribunal to confirm or revise its

7. *R(I) 18/61*; *R(I) 30/61*; *R(I) 8/63*.
8. *R(I) 7/65*.
9. *R(I) 3/68*; *R(I) 1/73*.
10. SSA 1975, s.112.
11. E.g. see *R v Medical Appeal Tribunal, ex parte Gilmore*, [1957] 1 QB 574, [1957] 1 All ER 796, CA; *R v Medical Appeal Tribunal, ex parte Burpitt* [1957] 2 QB 584, [1957] 2 All ER 704, DC; *R v Medical Appeal Tribunal, ex parte Griffiths* [1958] 2 All ER 227 [1958] 1 WLR 517, DC; *R v Medical Appeal*

Tribunal, ex parte Hubble [1958] 2 QB 228, [1958] 2 All ER 374, DC, [1959] 2 QB 408, [1959] 2 All ER 40, CA.
12. *Micklethwait*, pp. 132–133.
13. S.I. 1975/558, Reg. 26(1).
14. Ibid., Reg. 26(2).
15. *R(I) 3/61*.
16. S.I. 1975/558, Reg. 27(1): on other points the procedure resembles that for an appeal from a local tribunal: ante, p. 632.
17. S.I. 1975/558, Reg. 29(9), (10).

decision.[18] Where the Commissioner has upheld the original decision, this may simply be confirmed, but in other cases there must be a further hearing by the same or a differently constituted tribunal.[19]

G. The Attendance Allowance Board

i) General

The Attendance Allowance Board was set up in 1970 to determine claims for attendance allowance.[20] Its composition and advisory functions have been discussed in chapter 14.[1] In practice it seems that initial decisions whether the conditions for an award have been satisfied are usually made by medical practitioners to whom the Board has power to delegate its adjudicatory functions.[2] There are no procedural rules governing this initial determination. The Board, or more usually its delegate, receives written evidence from the claimant's doctor and a departmental medical officer, and the application is decided on this basis.[3]

Either the claimant or the Secretary of State may apply within three months for a review of this decision on any ground, or at any time on the limited grounds set out in section 106(1)(a) of the Social Security Act 1975: that there has been a change in the circumstances since the decision, or that it was reached in ignorance of, or on a mistake as to, a material fact. (A further application for review with the leave of the Board may be made within twelve months of the first request.)[4] The application for review is generally determined by a medical practitioner acting under delegated powers, though the Board itself sometimes decides the more difficult cases. Again there are no procedural rules for these determinations. The DHSS takes the view that there is no reason why the Board should not hold an oral hearing at this stage, though this is not the normal practice.[5] The claimant is sent a copy of the departmental doctor's report and given an opportunity to comment.[6] The Commissioner has also indicated that if the Board at some point forms a provisional view, it should be put to the claimant so that he can adduce evidence to contradict it.[7] A decision on review must be notified to the parties with reasons, and the claimant told that he has a right of appeal to the Commissioner.[8]

ii) Appeal to the Commissioner

There is a right of appeal on a point of law to the Commissioner from a decision of the Board (or its delegate) on review, or refusing a review.[9]

18. SSA 1975, s.112(5).
19. S.I. 1975/558, Reg. 30.
20. National Insurance (Old Persons' and Widows' Pensions and Attendance Allowance) Act 1970, renamed NIA 1970, by NIA 1972, s.8(4).
1. Ante, p. 585.
2. SSA 1975, Sch. 11, para. 5: see Carson LAG Bulletin, March 1975, p. 67.
3. Micklethwait, pp. 134-137.
4. S.I. 1975/598, Reg. 8.
5. R(A) 1/73, para. 31. It seems that in some areas, as an experiment, oral hearings have been held in the claimant's home: see Carson, ante n.2
6. Carson ibid., at p. 68.
7. R(A) 1/73, at para. 31, R.G. Micklethwait, Chief Comr.
8. S.I. 1975/598, Reg. 9(2).
9. SSA 1975, s.106(2); S.I. 1975/598, Reg. 10(1).

Leave must first be obtained from a Commissioner – within three months of the review or the refusal of a review.[10] The grounds on which a decision of the Board may be held to be wrong in law are the same as those which apply to medical appeal tribunals.[11] In *R(A) 1/72* the Commissioner, R. J. A. Temple, emphasised the importance of the Board's obligation to give reasons. It must make it clear to the claimant why his contentions were rejected.[12]

The Chief Commissioner in *R(A) 1/73* pointed out that it was not for him to reverse the Board's decision on the facts or on the inferences to be drawn from them. Moreover, it is for the Board to use its own expertise in applying the legislative standards (e.g., 'severely disabled', 'requires . . . continual supervision').[13] The Commissioner is empowered to entertain an appeal on the construction of the statutory provisions, as this is a matter of law, but not on the meaning of ordinary words, as this is a question of fact.[14] This distinction is often hard to draw in practice. Thus, in *R v National Insurance Comr, ex parte Secretary of State for Social Services*,[15] the Divisional Court held that the Commissioner had exceeded his jurisdiction in ruling that assistance given the claimant in undressing and going to bed was necessarily relevant to the question whether 'repeated attention' was needed during the *night*, rather than (as the Board had found) to the question whether attention was required during the *day*. The Commissioner was wrong to treat the issue as a question of law, rather than one of fact and, therefore, his decision was quashed.

iii) Critique

In its first years the Attendance Allowance Board attracted a considerable amount of criticism, partly because of its procedures.[16] The absence of procedural rules may suggest that it is more properly to be regarded as an informal administrative body rather than as a tribunal exercising adjudicative functions.[17] However, its duty to give reasons and the existence of the appeal to the Commissioner point to the opposite conclusion. It remains an open question whether its functions could more appropriately be given to the medical authorities.[18]

H. Review of decisions under Social Security Act 1975

Decisions taken by the statutory and other authorities under the Social

10. S.I. 1975/598, Reg. 10(2); the procedure governing the appeal is similar to that for appeals from local and medical appeal tribunals.

11. See ante, p. 640: see Carson, 26 NILQ 291, 319–320.

12. *R(A) 1/72*, para. 8, and see *R(A) 1/73*, paras. 13, 14.

13. *R(A) 1/73* para. 21, R.G. Micklethwait, Chief Comr.

14. See Lord Reid in *Cozens v Brutus* [1973] AC 854, 861, HL.

15. [1974] 3 All ER 522, [1974] 1 WLR 1290: see chap. 4, ante, p. 174, for a discussion of the issues in this case.

16. Carson, ante n.11, *passim.*

17. See Annual Report of the Council on Tribunals for 1969–70, Appendix B, (letter to the Lord Chancellor concerning the role of the Attendance Allowance Board); and see Wraith and Hutchesson *Administrative Tribunals* (1973), pp. 64–65.

18. This was suggested by the Council on Tribunals: ante n.17.

Security Act 1975 may be reviewed if they were based on a mistake as to the facts or there has been a change of circumstances since the decision was taken. This affords a simple method of revising determinations which were either at the time, or have since become, wrong, without requiring the applicant to resort to a formal appeal or to make a fresh claim. Review by the medical boards has been discussed in the chapter on industrial injuries;[19] reviews by the Attendance Allowance Board and by the Supplementary Benefits Commission are treated elsewhere in this chapter.[20] The grounds on which these authorities review previous determinations are for the most part the same as those available for review by the insurance officer and, therefore, the case-law discussed here is relevant to their powers. The principal provision is Section 104(1):[1]

> 'Any decision under this Act of an insurance officer, a local
> tribunal or a Commissioner may be reviewed at any time by an
> insurance officer or, on a reference from an insurance officer, by a
> local tribunal, if –
> (a) the officer or tribunal is satisfied and, in the case of a decision
> of a Commissioner, satisfied by fresh evidence, that the
> decision was given in ignorance of, or was based on a mistake
> as to, some material fact; or
> (b) there has been any relevant change of circumstances since the
> decision was given; . . .'

i) General

A review may be requested by written application to the insurance officer,[2] though the Commissioner has ruled that there is no need for a formal application and that in certain circumstances a claim for benefit should be treated as an application for review.[3] It is for the person seeking revision of the decision to show that this should be done.[4] The Commissioner has emphasised that a revision is not to be made merely because the conditions set out in section 104(1)(a) or (b) are satisfied: the insurance officer (or tribunal) must decide that in the light of the facts now found to exist it is right to revise the original determination.[5]

ii) Ignorance of, or mistake as to, a material fact

Review will not be permitted if the mistake was as to law,[6] or as to an inference drawn from the primary facts.[7] The determining authority must have been in ignorance of, or been mistaken as to, some specific fact. Thus,

19. Ante, pp. 314–316.
20. Ante, p. 641 (Attendance Allowance Board); post, p. 653 (SBC).
1. See SSA 1975, ss.95(2), 96, for the review of Secretary of State's decisions.
2. Ibid., s.104(2) (and see S.I. 1976/962, Reg. 9 for the review of child benefit decisions: Reg. 9(2) permits review of an insurance officer's decision on the ground that it was wrong in law).

3. *R(I) 50/56*; cp., *R(I) 11/62*. This may enable the applicant to surmount the time-limits for making claims: ante, pp. 592–600.
4. *R(I) 1/71.*
5. *R(I) 18/62*, *R(I) 1/71*.
6. *R(G) 18/52*, Tribunal Decision; cp., ante n.2, for review of child benefit decisions.
7. See H. Magnus, Comr., in *R(I) 3/75*, para. 9.

an award of maternity allowance may be revised if it was made on the basis of a mistake concerning the expected week of confinement.[8] In the case of Commissioners' decisions, review can only take place if there is *fresh evidence* to show that the determination was wrong. The meaning of 'fresh evidence' has given rise to some difficulty, particularly in cases concerning the review of medical authorities' decisions.[9] Clearly it covers evidence which came to light after the decision. The Commissioner has held in a number of cases that it also includes evidence which the claimant could not reasonably have been expected in the circumstances to have adduced at the hearing.[10] The fact that the claimant is a person of relatively low intelligence or is illiterate is relevant.[11] It seems that the Department is prepared to adopt a wide view of 'fresh evidence'.[12] What, however, is clearly excluded is evidence which the claimant could have produced without difficulty at the hearing.[13]

iii) Relevant change of circumstances

A change in the claimant's condition may justify revision of the award,[14] as may a change in the law,[15] or a later decision of the Commissioner which undermines the basis of the previous determination.[16] A Tribunal has held, perhaps surprisingly, that a court decision in a damages case which cast doubt on an earlier award of industrial injuries benefit was not a 'relevant change of circumstances'.[17]

Part two. Control by the Courts of Decisions under Social Security Act 1975

A. General

As has been said, the general intention from the first decade of this century has been to keep disputes concerning state benefits away from the ordinary courts.[18] That initial prejudice was reinforced by experience of their interpretation of the workmen's compensation legislation, which was often considered to be unduly technical and restrictive from the claimant's point of view.[19] The 1946 legislation, therefore, conferred exclusive jurisdiction on the statutory and medical authorities and made no provision for appeal

8. *R(G) 8/55*: see ante, p. 253.
9. See chap. 8, ante, p. 315.
10. *R(I) 27/61*; *R(I) 17/66*; *R(P) 3/73*. See also Lord Denning MR, in *R v National Insurance Comr, ex parte Viscusi*, [1974] 1 WLR 646, 652. The proposition in the text was doubted because of the restrictive terms of Diplock J's judgment in *R v Medical Appeal Tribunal, ex parte Hubble* [1958] 2 QB 228, 242–243.
11. *R(P) 3/73*, R.J.A. Temple, Comr. (Illiterate immigrant did not produce birth certificate as·evidence of his age).
12. See Roskill LJ in *R v National Insurance Comr, ex parte Viscusi*, ante n.10, at p. 657.
13. *R(I) 47/59* (evidence in solicitor's hands before the Commissioner gave his decision), and see *R(S) 25/51*.
14. *R(I) 11/59*.
15. *R(G) 3/58*, Tribunal Decision.
16. *R(I) 25/63*, distinguishing *R(I) 11/59*.
17. *R(I) 11/59*.
18. See ante, p. 619.
19. See 414 HC, col. 281ff (2nd Reading of National Insurance (Industrial Injuries) Bill 1946).

to the courts. Decisions of the authorities were 'final' (though, of course, there has always been an appeal from the Secretary of State).[20] The Franks Committee on Administrative Tribunals and Enquiries thought it right that there should be no appeal from their decisions: there was little demand for such a right; the Commissioners were experienced lawyers, expert in their field; and it was important that a final decision should be reached quickly.[1] As a result, there is no right of appeal on a point of law to the courts under the Tribunals and Inquiries Act.[2]

Initially the availability of judicial review by way of the prerogative order of certiorari was contested by the Minister of National Insurance. In the first case under the 1946 legislation in which the remedy was sought, it was argued that the Divisional Court had no power to grant it as the statute provided that the Commissioner's decision was 'final'.[3] The court did not have to decide the point, as the application was dismissed on the merits.[4] The question next arose in *R v Medical Appeal Tribunal, ex parte Gilmore*.[5] At this time there was no appeal on a point of law from a medical appeal tribunal to the Commissioners, so the tribunal's decision also was 'final'. Counsel for the Ministry conceded that certiorari should be granted in this case, but reserved his position on whether it should be available to control Commissioners' decision. All the members of the Court of Appeal indicated that the 'finality' clause did not preclude judicial review, and only meant that there could be no *appeal* against the tribunals' decision.[6] In an important statement of principle, Romer LJ said:[7]

'I therefore think . . . that it is not in the public interest that inferior tribunals of any kind should be ultimate arbiters on questions of law.'

After this decision the availability of the prerogative order does not seem to have been challenged.

On balance the arguments in favour of access to the courts by the prerogative orders[8] are to be preferred. Quite apart from the general principle that it is usually desirable for the courts to have the last word on questions of law, it is important that they should occasionally be able to resolve a disagreement between the Commissioners. A Tribunal may be used for this purpose, but now that there are nine or ten Commissioners the approach of three of them may not always represent the majority view.[9] If there were no judicial review, it probably would be necessary to treat

---

20. NIA 1946, s.43(1): for the appeal from the Secretary of State's decisions, see ante, p. 623.
1. Cmnd. 218, para. 108.
2. See now Tribunals and Inquiries Act 1971, s.13.
3. *R v National Insurance Comr, ex parte Timmis* [1955] 1 QB 139, 147, DC.
4. See chap. 10, ante p. 422.
5. [1957] 1 QB 574, [1957] 1 All ER 796, CA.
6. See de Smith *Judicial Review of Administrative Action* (3rd edn), pp.

321–323, for a discussion of this general principle of interpretation by the courts.
7. Ante n.5, at p. 587.
8. In principle the prerogative orders of *prohibition* and *mandamus* are obtainable, though there is no case where either has been granted in respect of the proceedings or decision or statutory authorities. For declarations, see post, p. 648.
9. *Micklethwait*, p. 123.

decisions of a Tribunal as absolutely binding on a single Commissioner.[10] Otherwise there would be no means for securing certainty in the law.

Although the right to apply for certiorari is no longer in doubt, the courts have generally been reluctant to intervene. They take into account the expertise of the Commissioners, and the deliberate omission to provide an appeal to the courts from their decisions.[11] In one leading case, Lord Denning MR observed that the courts should only intervene if there is a 'real error of law'.[12] This cautious approach has recently been followed by the Court of Appeal in *R v National Insurance Commissioner, ex parte Michael*.[13] Roskill LJ said, in a passage which seems to represent the general attitude of the judges:[14]

> 'The fact that special provision is made for some hearings to take place before a tribunal of three commissioners reinforces the view that it was the intention of the legislature to avoid appeals from the commissioners to the courts, even on questions of law . . . .
> The courts must not be astute to convert questions of fact or of mixed fact and law into questions of law so as to justify interference by prerogative order in cases where no right of appeal has been given by statute. There must be a clear error of law appearing on the face of the decision before the courts will interfere . . .'

In the same case Lord Denning MR said that the courts should only interfere when there is a general principle of law involved, or where Commissioners were divided in their views.[15] The implication is that the court should not issue certiorari merely because it has concluded that there is some minor error of law in the challenged decision.[16] This approach may lead occasionally to judicial tolerance of an incorrect decision; on the other hand, it probably accords with the intention of the legislature that for the most part it is the Commissioners who should adjudicate points of law.

Now that there is a right of appeal to the Commissioner,[17] certiorari will not be granted to quash a medical tribunal's decision.[18] Nor will the prerogative order lie to control a decision of a local insurance tribunal, as the right of appeal to the Commissioner is an equally appropriate

10. For precedent, see ante, p. 634.
11. See *R v Industrial Injuries Comr, ex parte Amalgamated Engineering Union (No. 2)* [1966] 2 QB 31, [1966] 1 All ER 97, CA; *R v Industrial Injuries Comr, ex parte Ward* [1965] 2 QB 112, 121, per Lord Parker CJ, DC; *R v Industrial Injuries Comr, ex parte Fieldhouse* (1974) 17 KIR 63, 67, per Lord Widgery CJ, DC.
12. *R v Industrial Injuries Comr, ex parte Amalgamated Engineering Union (No. 2)*, ante n.11, at p. 49.
13. [1976] 1 All ER 566, [1977] 1 WLR 109.
14. Ibid., at p. 116.
15. Ibid., at p. 112.
16. The Court of Appeal has adopted a similar approach, with perhaps less justification, to review of supplementary benefit appeal tribunal decisions: see post p. 657.
17. See ante, p. 640.
18. *R v Medical Appeal Tribunal, ex parte Carrarini* [1966] 1 WLR 883, DC.

remedy.[19] In both cases, the courts require that the applicant exhaust his statutory remedies before applying to them.

B. The grounds of review

i) Error of law on the face of the record

Much the most common ground of judicial review is that there has been an error of law on the face of the record – that is, an error apparent from a scrutiny of the Commissioner's decision.[20] The Commissioner must give the reasons for his conclusions,[1] and these form part of the record,[2] as will a document, such as a medical report, referred to in the decision.[3] If no reasons are given, or if they are wholly inadequate or unintelligible, mandamus might be obtained to compel the Commissioner to comply with his statutory duty.[4]

It has been pointed out that the courts will intervene only if the record discloses a real error of law.[5] They will certainly not grant certiorari if the mistake is merely one of fact.[6] But a wholly mistaken inference from the primary facts,[7] or the wrongful exclusion of relevant evidence by the Commissioner[8] may be categorised as errors of law. In one leading case, it was argued that the Commissioner had erred in law because he had wrongly admitted evidence in breach of the rules of natural justice.[9] On the general principles of administrative law, a breach of these rules is more appropriately classified as a species of jurisdictional error, and the case is discussed under this head.[10]

Because a Commissioner's decision is fully reasoned, error of law on the face is the usual ground of judicial review. There is no need then for the applicant for certiorari to show that he has exceeded his jurisdiction; the decision can simply be quashed for an intra vires error.[11] Two important qualifications must be made to this account. First, there is now some doubt whether the courts in Scotland may quash by a decree of reduction a

19. *R v Hoxton Local Tribunal, ex parte Sinnott* (1976) 126 NL Jo 413, DC; Appendix to *R(F) 1/74*. It is not clear that it would be right to refuse certiorari if the ground on which it was sought was either a jurisdictional error of law or breach of the natural justice rules: see *de Smith*, ante n.6, at pp. 374–376 for a full discussion of these difficult points. It may be that certiorari would be a quicker remedy than an appeal to the Commissioner and then perhaps it should be granted.

20. For error of law on the face of the record, see de Smith *Judicial Review of Administrative Action* (3rd edn) pp. 353–361.

1. S.I. 1975/558, Reg. 13(6): ante, p. 633.

2. Tribunals and Inquiries Act 1971, s.12(5).

3. See Denning LJ in *R v Medical Appeal Tribunal, ex parte Gilmore* [1957] 1 QB 574, 582, CA.

4. *de Smith*, ante n.20, at pp. 129–130.

5. See ante, p. 646.

6. *R v National Insurance (Industrial Injuries) Comr, ex parte Richardson* [1958] 1 WLR 851, DC.

7. See *ex parte Gilmore*, ante n.3.

8. *R. v Industrial Injuries Comr, ex parte Ward* [1965] 2 QB 112, [1964] 3 All ER 907.

9. *R. v Deputy Industrial Injuries Comr, ex parte Moore* [1965] 1 QB 456, [1965] 1 All ER 81, CA.

10. See post, p. 648.

11. For a discussion of the close resemblance between an appeal and review for error of law on the face, see *de Smith*, ante n.20, at p. 119.

decision challenged for an intra vires error of law.[12] It might, however, be possible to apply to the Divisional Court for certiorari to quash the decision of a Commissioner sitting in Edinburgh, on the ground that he is a British 'tribunal' and is, therefore, amenable to control by any superior court in Great Britain.[13] Secondly, a declaration cannot be granted to state that there is an error of law in the Commissioner's decision.[14] The reason is that this remedy, unlike certiorari, does not quash the voidable decision; it still stands and, therefore, the grant of a declaratory judgment would be pointless.[15]

ii) Jurisdictional error: breach of the rules of natural justice

A Commissioner's decision taken outside his statutory jurisdiction could be quashed by certiorari or declared void.[16] However, the relative ease with which a decision may be challenged for error of law within jurisdiction has rendered this ground of judicial review of little practical importance. Indeed, the only case where the Divisional court might be said to have granted the prerogative order because of an error going to jurisdiction is *R v National Insurance Comr, ex parte Secretary of State for Social Services*, where appellate jurisdiction was wrongly exercised by the Commissioner on a question of fact.[17]

A failure to comply with the rules of natural justice means that a decision is (procedurally) ultra vires and void.[18] The application of the rules to Commissioners' decisions has been discussed in two leading cases.[19] In *R v Deputy Industrial Injuries Comr, ex parte Jones*,[20] Lord Parker CJ, giving the Divisional Court's judgment, held that the Commissioner, as a quasi-judicial tribunal, must observe the rules of natural justice. The rule requiring a fair hearing was broken when he received further medical evidence after the oral proceedings were over, and he did not put this to the parties for their comments.[1] The Court of Appeal in the second case, *R v Deputy Industrial Injuries Comr, ex parte Moore*,[2] said that the rules required the Commissioner to base his decision on the evidence, and where a hearing is held, to listen fairly to the contentions of the parties and to afford them an opportunity to comment on all the evidence received. But it was no requirement of natural justice that the strict rules of evidence be complied with and, therefore, it was permissible for him to take into account medical opinions given in previous cases.[3]

12. *Watt v Lord Advocate* 1977 SLT 130.
13. This point is made in the Franks Committee Report, Cmnd. 218, para. 110.
14. *Punton v Ministry of Pensions and National Insurance (No. 2)* [1964] 1 All ER 448, [1964] 1 WLR 226, CA.
15. *de Smith*, ante n.20, at pp. 462–464.
16. Ibid. There is no objection to the grant of a declaration that a tribunal's decision is void, as distinct from voidable for error of law on the face.
17. [1974] 3 All ER 522, [1974] 1 WLR 1290, and see ante, p. 642.
18. *de Smith*, ante n.20, at pp. 209–212.

19. For the rules of natural justice applied to medical appeal tribunal decisions, see ante, p. 638. In theory it would seem that the same rules would apply to the conduct of local tribunal hearings, though there is little case-law on this: see ante, p. 629.
20. [1962] 2 QB 677, [1962] 2 All ER 430.
1. See ante, p. 631, for the argument that the Commissioner was taking the advice of a medical assessor.
2. Ante, n.9.
3. For Commissioners' rulings that hearsay evidence is admissible, though of little weight, see e.g., *R(G) 1/51*;

Part three. Supplementary Benefit Appeal Tribunals

A. General

The origins of supplementary benefit appeal tribunals (SBATs) can be traced to the tribunals set up in 1934 to hear appeals from the Unemployment Assistance Board.[4] At this time there was relatively little suggestion that it was right in principle to provide an appeal; the real reason for the tribunals' institution was to insulate the Ministry from political pressure arising from decisions on assistance.[5] The administrative character of these tribunals was emphasised by the fact that one of the three members was appointed to represent the Board, and could sometimes be its district officer.[6] The national assistance tribunals set up by the 1948 legislature were closely modelled on them, though for the future no member was to be appointed by the National Assistance Board to represent its interests.[7] Other changes were those dispensing with the requirement of the chairman's leave before an appeal was brought, and allowing non-legal representation.[8] The government, however, successfully resisted an amendment to provide a further appeal from the tribunal to an umpire, on the ground that this would lead to the development of 'case-law' and consequent rigidity.[9]

The Franks Committee took the view that in two respects assistance tribunals were different from insurance tribunals. First, as their hearings might often involve disclosure of personal details, it was right for them to be in private.[10] Secondly, there was no need to provide a further right of appeal from their decisions. The justification for this lay partly in the need to arrive at a final decision quickly, but the argument was also supported by a famous passage in the Report which seemed to cast doubt on the judicial (or quasi-judicial) character of assistance tribunal proceedings:

> 'Although in form these Tribunals hear and determine appeals against decisions of local officers of the National Assistance Board and therefore exercise adjudicating functions, in practice their task much resembles that of an assessment or case committee, taking a further look at the facts and in some cases arriving at a fresh decision on the extent of need.'[11]

The uncertainty whether these tribunals, and their successors, should be regarded primarily as *judicial* bodies set up to resolve conflicts, or as *administrative* bodies, as the Franks Committee appeared to suggest,

R(U) 12/56; R(U) 10/63; R(U) 2/74. In the last case, the Chief Commissioner, R.G. Micklethwait ruled that the findings of fact by an industrial tribunal may be admitted as evidence in proceedings of the statutory authorities: see ante, p. 112.

4. For the Unemployment Assistance Board, see ante, pp. 576–577.

5. Lynes, in ed. Adler and Bradley *Justice, Discretion and Poverty* (1976), pp. 5–8.

6. Ibid., at pp. 8–12.

7. Bradley, ante n.5, at p. 37.

8. Ibid.

9. Mr J. Griffiths, Minister of National Insurance, Standing Committee C Debates on the National Assistance Bill 1947, col. 2465.

10. Report of the Committee on Administrative Tribunals and Enquiries (1957), Cmnd. 218, paras. 64, 79, and 180.

11. Ibid., at para. 182.

has been partly responsible for the controversy surrounding them[12]

When national assistance was replaced by supplementary benefits in 1966, the tribunals' structure was unaffected, though they were renamed supplementary benefit appeal tribunals. There was no suggestion that the change to a system based on 'entitlement' (though with elements of discretion) had any implications for the tribunal system.[13] What is perhaps more surprising is that in 1970 these tribunals were given appellate jurisdiction over questions of entitlement to family income supplement, in which there is virtually no element of discretion.[14] It might have been more appropriate to confer it on the local insurance tribunals.[15] As it happens, FIS appeals are relatively few compared with supplementary benefit appeals: in 1976 1,147 as against 101,112.[16]

In addition to their appellage jurisdiction under the Family Income Supplements Act 1970,[17] SBATs have power under the Supplementary Benefits Act 1976 to entertain an appeal against a Commission decision (or a refusal by the SBC to review a decision) on the following matters:[18]

1. the right to, or amount of, benefit;

2. the issuing of benefit to a person other than the claimant;

3. the recovery of sums paid by way of urgent needs payments;

4. the imposition of a condition that the claimant register for employment;

5. the payment of benefit in kind rather than in cash;

6. the determination of the excess supplementary benefit paid for a period in which the beneficiary was also entitled to other social security benefits.[19]

The tribunal also has *original* jurisdiction to determine:

1. whether to issue a direction that a person may be subject to a requirement to attend a place of instruction or training as a condition of receiving benefit;[20]

2. whether overpaid benefit is recoverable under section 20 of the Act.[1]

Finally, it should be noted that the question whether a person's own requirements are to be disregarded for benefit purposes, because of his

12. The distinction is well drawn by Bradley, 27 NILQ 96, 99–101, and see post, pp. 658–659.
13. Bradley, ante n.7 at p. 49.
14. See chap. 13, ante, at p. 553.
15. An amendment at the Committee stage of the Family Income Supplements Bill to this effect was withdrawn: see 806 HC Deb., cols. 1355ff. The Council on Tribunals unsuccessfully pressed for a change in the name of the SBATs to reflect their further jursidiction: see
Annual Report for 1970–71, paras. 49–50.
16. The figures are taken from the Supplementary Benefits Commission Annual Report 1976, Cmnd. 6910, Tables 16.9 and 18.1.
17. S.7.
18. S.15.
19. Ibid., s.12.
20. Ibid., s.10.
1. See chap. 14, ante, pp. 614–615.

participation in a trade dispute, must be referred by a SBAT to a local insurance tribunal for the latter to decide.[2] This question will often raise issues of legal complexity, familiar to local insurance tribunals in the context of unemployment benefit which may be claimed at the same time as the supplementary benefit;[3] the procedure may, however, be thought to show a relative lack of confidence in the ability of SBATs to determine difficult points of law.[4]

B. Composition and structure

Each SBAT has jurisdiction over the area assigned to it by the Secretary of State.[5] It consists of a chairman and two other members, the former being appointed by the Secretary of State from a panel drawn up by the Lord Chancellor (or in Scotland, the Lord President of the Court of Session).[6] In practice, he has usually served on the tribunal for some years as an 'other' member.[7] This 'other' member is appointed by the Secretary of State, after interview at a regional office of the Department, from people suggested by various local organisations. The third member, still rather quaintly described in the Act as being 'appointed from among persons appearing to the Secretary of State to represent work-people',[8] is chosen in effect by local Trades Council Federations.[9] It seems that few of them are subsequently appointed chairmen.[10]

In contrast to the chairmen of insurance tribunals, relatively few SBAT chairmen are lawyers.[11] The recent study undertaken for the DHSS by Bell indicates that they were more proficient in their handling of cases than lay chairmen and more knowledgeable about supplementary benefits law.[12] Recently, the government has decided to appoint more lawyers to preside in SBATs.[13] It is highly controversial whether the further step should be taken of making legal qualifications necessary.[14]

The *Bell* study showed the same widespread dissatisfaction with the role played by the lay members of SBATs which has been found in insurance tribunals.[15] Their reluctance to participate might be overcome by arranging courses and conferences so that they could sharpen their awareness of

2. SBA 1976, s.15(2). An appeal lies to the National Insurance Commissioner in the normal way: *R(U) 3/71*, J.S. Watson, Comr.
3. See chap. 3, ante, pp. 122–131.
4. The same course was adopted with regard to the tribunals under the 1934 and 1948 Acts: see Bradley, ante, n.12, at pp. 115–116.
5. SBA 1976, Sch. 4, para. 2.
6. Tribunals and Inquiries Act 1971, s.7.
7. Herman *Administrative Justice and Supplementary Benefits* (1972), pp. 20–22.
8. SBA 1976, Sch. 4, para. 3(1).
9. *Herman*, ante n.7, at p. 20.
10. Ibid., at p. 21.
11. The general estimate is that under

10% of chairmen are legally qualified: see LAG, *A lawyer's guide to supplementary benefit* (1976), p. 55.
12. Bell *Research Study on Supplementary Benefit Appeal Tribunals, Review of Main Findings: Conclusions: Recommendations*, published by DHSS (1975).
13. See Mr S. Orme, Minister of Social Security, Written Answer 923 HC Deb., cols. 164–165.
14. In favour of mandatory legal qualifications are *Bell*, ante n.12, at p. 23, and Lewis [1973] P.L. 257, 280–281.
Against are Lister and Bradley: see Bradley, 27 NILQ 96, p. 116.
15. *Bell*, ante n.12, at pp. 6–7 and 17–18.

supplementary benefits law, and of the problems faced by claimants.[16] Perhaps it would be an improvement if tribunals were composed of a wider range of people, including social workers.[17]

In a weak tribunal too much reliance is often placed on the clerk. He is an executive officer in one of the Department's regional offices, seconded to work for the tribunals for about three years.[18] In 1971 the DHSS, after encouragement from the Council on Tribunals, issued instructions which emphasise his subordinate role: he is not to raise issues of law or policy, or to take part in the tribunal's deliberations, but is merely to assist it by taking notes of evidence and verifying law already referred to by the parties. The *Bell* study found that in practice clerks sometimes played a more active role, though not always to the claimant's disadvantage.[19]

Discussion recently has focussed on possible changes to the structure of these tribunals as a means of strengthening them. Although there are occasional regional conferences of chairmen,[20] there is no regular method by which either they or other members can obtain advice with regard to the discharge of their duties – except, unfortunately, from the DHSS itself. If SBATs were organised nationally or regionally with a President at the head of the structure, it would be possible for him to give independent advice on general policy and procedural questions.[1] A move in this direction has been recommended by Bell.[2] Other, more radical changes are discussed later.[3]

c. Procedure before the hearing

i) The SBC decision

The Supplementary Benefit General Regulations provide that notice of a decision by the Commission must be given in writing, though a determination relating to a cash payment of a supplementary *allowance* (not pension) may be communicated orally, unless a written decision is requested.[4] However, the SBC Handbook states that administratively it is not possible to issue all decisions in writing.[5] In any event, there is no legal obligation on the Commission to give reasons though it generally does so whenever the decision requires explanation.[6] In contrast, under the Family Income Supplement General Regulations, the Commission must give a reasoned decision in writing and notify the applicant of his right of appeal.[7] It would clearly be desirable for this rule to govern supplementary benefit applications, though doubtless there are administrative objections.

16. Ibid., at p. 21.
17. See Bradley, ante n.14, at p. 116.
18. *Bell*, ante n.12, at pp. 8–9; Wraith and Hutchesson *Administrative Tribunals* (1973), pp. 121 and 302. See Appendix.
19. *Bell*, loc. cit.
20. These conferences have been encouraged by the Council on Tribunals: see the Annual Report for 1969–70, paras. 27–28.
1. There is a 'presidential system', as it is generally known, for pensions appeal tribunals (see post, p. 660) and industrial tribunals.
2. *Bell*, ante n.12, at pp. 8 and 20: see also Lister, in ed. Adler and Bradley *Justice, Discretion and Poverty* (1976), p. 179.
3. See post, pp. 658–659.
4. S.I. 1977/1141, Reg. 12.
5. Para. 239. See *LAG Bulletin*, Aug. 1975, p. 213.
6. Handbook, para. 220.
7. S.I. 1971/226, Reg. 12.

ii) Notice of appeal

An appeal concerning either supplementary benefits or FIS must be brought within twenty-one days of the decision by a notice in writing given at a local office.[8] The chairman of the SBAT, however, may extend this time if there is good cause.[9] The appeal need not be made on the official form, or state the grounds, though it is helpful for them to be given in outline.[10]

iii) Review by the Commission

On receipt of an appeal the Commission automatically reviews its decision.[11] It will be revised if it was made in ignorance of, or based on a mistake as to, some material fact or the law, or there has been a relevant change in the circumstances since the initial determination.[12] There is then a new decision, and so strictly the appeal – brought against the first decision – lapses. However well intentioned this procedure may be, its existence has always caused acute controversy.[13] The danger is that the Commission may exploit the fact that some applicants will not pursue their case to the appeal tribunal after a revised decision has been given – even though the second decision only partially satisfies the claimant's needs. On the other hand, the Commission's practice does enable bad decisions to be corrected more speedily than would be the case if all appeals went to the tribunals.[14]

In the light of the criticisms, the Commission decided in 1975 to make some important changes in the review procedure.[15] The claimant is now given full details of how the original and the revised decisions have been reached, and he is invited to make an appeal (against the latter) if he is still dissatisfied. Where, however, the claim is for a specific need and the second determination does not fully meet it, the appeal automatically goes forward, unless the claimant decides to withdraw it.[16]

iv) Notice of the hearing

The clerk must give the appellant reasonable notice of the time and place of the hearing and send him copies of the documents supplied to the

8. S.I. 1971/680, Rule 5 (SB Appeal Tribunal Rules); S.I. 1971/622 (FIS Appeal Tribunal Rules). The procedural rules are so similar that it is surprising that the DHSS did not accept the suggestion of the Council on Tribunals that they should be merged: Annual Report for 1970–71, paras. 49–50. The FIS rules are not referred to subsequently, unless they differ materially from the supplementary benefit rules.
9. See ante, p. 627, for the similar power of chairmen of local insurance tribunals.
10. Handbook, para. 239.
11. Handbook, para. 240.
12. S.I. 1977/1141, Reg. 9. See ante, pp. 642–644, for the interpretation by the Commissioner of these concepts, also used in the SSA 1975.
13. For the power of review exercised by the Unemployment Assistance Board, see Lynes in ed. Adler and Bradley, *Justice, Discretion and Poverty* (1976), pp. 23–28; for more recent experience, see Herman *Administrative Justice and Supplementary Benefits* (1972), pp. 31–32; Coleman *Supplementary Benefits and the administrative review of administrative action*, Child Poverty Action Group pamphlet (1970).
14. Of 101,112 appeals brought in 1976, 23,856 led to a revision by the Commission and did not reach the tribunal for this reason: see Annual Report 1976, Cmnd. 6910, Table 18.1.
15. Annual Report 1975, Cmnd. 6615, para. 14.2.
16. Handbook, paras. 240–242.

SBAT.[17] It is said in the Handbook that normally at least seven days' notice is given,[18] though it has been suggested that sometimes applicants have been notified only two or three days before the hearing.[19] This might not be 'reasonable notice', particularly where the tribunal is situated some distance from the appellant's residence.[20] The documents consist of the written notice of appeal, the decision against which the appeal is brought, and the observations of a Commission officer explaining the reasons for it. A leaflet is also enclosed, giving information about the tribunal's procedure and emphasising the appellant's right to attend with representatives.[1]

D. Procedure at the hearing

i) The role of the presenting officer

The Commission's argument is put forward by the presenting officer, a specialist official of Higher Executive Officer status.[2] There is a suggestion that on occasion he may feel under pressure to win the case, no matter what its merits, and this may lead to its inaccurate presentation.[3] However, the *Bell* study found that there was no evidence of unfairness in the manner in which cases were presented, and like insurance officers, presenting officers often raised points favourable to the appellant.[4]

ii) Attendance and representation of the appellant

The presenting officer's impartial discharge of his role is naturally more important when the appellant does not attend. In the *Bell* study only about 40% of appellants attended tribunal hearings, and less than 20% were represented.[5] The majority of representatives in the study were friends and relatives and not, as in insurance tribunals, trades union officials.[6] Legal assistance at the hearing is very rare indeed.[7] There is no doubt that an appellant who attends has a higher chance of success before the tribunal than one who does not.[8] The reasons for the relatively low attendance rate have been discussed already in the context of insurance tribunal hearings.[9]

If the appellant does not attend, the tribunal has power to adjourn, and may in the meantime send him a letter impressing on him the importance of his presence.[10] When an appellant has given advance notice that the

17. S.I. 1971/680, Rule 9(1).
18. Para. 243.
19. *Herman*, ante n.13, at p. 33.
20. See ante, p. 628, for the notice required for insurance tribunal hearings.
1. Bell *Research Study on Supplementary Benefit Appeal Tribunals, Review of Main Findings: Conclusions: Recommendations*, published by DHSS 1975, p. 22.
2. *Herman*, ante n.13, at p. 25.
3. Ibid., at pp. 26–28.
4. *Bell*, ante n.1, at pp. 10–11; see ante,

p. 629 for insurance officers.
5. Ibid., at p. 12: see also SBC Annual Report 1976, ante n.14, Table 18.2.
6. *Bell*, ante n.1, at pp. 15–16.
7. In 1976 there were only 233 cases where the appellant was represented by a solicitor: Annual Report 1976, ante n.14, at Table 18.2.
8. Flockhart in ed. Adler and Bradley *Justice, Discretion and Poverty* (1976), pp. 106–107.
9. Ante, pp. 629–630.
10. S.I. 1971/680, Rule 9(2).

specified time is inconvenient for him, this course is invariably adopted.[11] But it is rarely practicable when no explanation for non-attendance has been given. The tribunal will not know whether the appeal is serious, and it would be unfortunate to induce an appellant to attend and then dismiss his appeal.

iii) The conduct of the hearing

A major difference between hearings at insurance and supplementary benefit appeal tribunals is that the latter are conducted in private. The following may attend:[12]

1. the parties themselves, that is, the appellant and the Commission;

2. two representatives for each party;

3. two bona fide researchers into the work of SBATs, with the chairman's consent and provided the parties do not object.

Experience suggests that most appellants are willing for observers to attend the hearings, and it may be questioned whether the provision for national insurance tribunals – a private hearing when the chairman thinks that there is a good reason for it – would not be adequate.[13]

The parties (or their representatives) are entitled to be heard, to call witnesses and to put questions to any other party and his witnesses.[14] Apart from this, the procedure is for the chairman to determine.[15] It is usual in practice for the presenting officer to start by reading out the appeal documents, and then the claimant and the officer put forward their arguments.[16] There has been much criticism concerning the conduct of SBAT hearings, particularly with regard to the lack of clarity with which issues are presented to the claimant and the reliance sometimes placed on documents not disclosed to all the parties.[17]

E. The powers and decisions of SBATs

i) The powers of the SBATs

The supplementary benefit appeal tribunal may confirm the decision (or the Commission's refusal to review a decision), or may

> 'substitute for any determination appealed against any determination which the Commission could have made'; . . .[18]

There seems little doubt in the light of this provision that the tribunal is

11. It may be a breach of the rules of natural justice if the tribunal does not adjourn: *R v South West London Supplementary Benefits Appeal Tribunal, ex parte Bullen* (1976) 120 Sol Jo 437, DC.

12. S.I. 1971/680, Rule 11. The list is not exhaustive.

13. Adler, Burns and Johnson, n.8, at pp. 113–114.

14. S.I. 1971/680, Rule 11(2) and (4).

15. Ibid., Rule 11(10).

16. *Lynes*, pp. 197–199; and see the Handbook, paras. 246–247.

17. Adler, Burns and Johnson, ante n.8, at pp. 114–116; Herman *Administrative Justice and Supplementary Benefits* (1972) at pp. 39–40; *Bell*, ante n.1, at pp. 21–22.

18. SBA 1976, s.15(3)(c).

not limited to correcting errors of law or fact made by the Commission, but may take a different view of the merits of the case. Therefore, although it is normally bound by the Act, regulations and any court decision, the tribunal is free to depart from SBC policy or hold that it is not applicable to the case.[19] This freedom may not always be appreciated. Moreover, many SBATs apparently take the view that they are bound only to consider the issues raised by the notice of appeal; they do not, for example, consider it appropriate to discuss whether the appellant is entitled to some further payment which he has not previously claimed.[20] This seems a narrower approach than that adopted by insurance tribunals and the Commissioner.[1] The *Bell* study has called for clarification of the tribunals' powers in these respects.[2]

ii) Deliberation in private

The tribunal *may* order any person to withdraw while it is considering its decision.[3] Three points call for comment. First, unlike insurance and medical appeal tribunals, there is no duty here to order the parties to leave.[4] Secondly, it is not clear whether the clerk may ever be asked to leave during the deliberation of a SBAT; the Regulation provides that 'the clerk shall be present at all sittings of the Appeal Tribunal'.[5] Thirdly, it seems that presenting officers often remain with the tribunal while it considers its decision in a case where the appellant does not attend.[6] This practice constitutes, it is submitted, a breach of the rules of natural justice.[7]

iii) Reasons for the decision

The tribunal's decision with its reasons must be recorded in writing, and the clerk must send it to the parties as soon as possible.[8] The duty to give reasons in every case was imposed in 1971; previously they had only been supplied on request.[9] Unlike insurance tribunals, SBATs are not obliged to record their findings of fact or indicate whether and, if so, why one of their members dissents.[10] In response to a number of complaints about the adequacy of statement of reasons, the Council on Tribunals in 1973 took the unusual step of setting out, in a letter sent to all tribunal chairmen, what the statement should contain.[11] They should set out the findings of fact, and the reasons for the tribunal's conclusions. Despite this, there is still evidence that reasons are cursory.[12]

19. See Lewis, [1973] P.L. 257, pp. 280–281.
20. *Herman*, ante n.17, at p. 38; *Bell*, ante n.1, at p. 13.
1. See ante, pp. 630 and 633, for local tribunals and the Commissioner respectively.
2. Bell *Research Study on Supplementary Benefit Appeal Tribunals, Review of Main Findings: Conclusions: Recommendations*, published by DHSS (1975), pp. 21–22.
3. S.I. 1971/680, Rule 11(8).
4. See ante, pp. 630 and 638.
5. S.I. 1971/680, Rule 11(1).
6. *Bell*, ante n.2, at p. 21.
7. See de Smith *Judicial Review of Administrative Action* (3rd edn), pp. 227–229.
8. S.I. 1971/680, Rule 12.
9. Under the requirement imposed by the Tribunal and Inquiries Act, 1958, s.12.
10. See ante, p. 630.
11. Annual Report for 1972–73, paras. 70–72, and Appendix B.
12. Adler, Burns and Johnson in ed. Adler and Bradley *Justice, Discretion and Poverty* (1976), p. 113; *Bell*, ante n.2, at p. 6.

The general practice is for the clerk to record the tribunal's decision, a task which the chairman of an insurance tribunal discharges himself.[13] It is difficult to resist the conclusion that a lawyer chairman would be more likely to articulate a fully reasoned decision than lay chairmen or tribunal clerks.

F. Review of tribunal decisions

i) Review by the Supplementary Benefits Commission

Although the Act provides that a tribunal decision is 'conclusive for all purposes', it may subsequently be reviewed by the SBC.[14] It will be revised if it was based on mistaken facts, or in the case of supplementary benefit decisions (but not FIS decisions)[15] there has since been a change of circumstances.[16] This power has been criticised on the ground that it removes the significance of the right of appeal to an independent tribunal if its decisions can be revised by one of the parties, i.e., the Commission.[17] On the other hand, there is no evidence to suggest that the power is abused and, of course, it may be exercised for the benefit of a claimant whose appeal has been dismissed or only partly allowed.[18]

ii) Control by the courts

From January 1978 there has been a right of appeal on a point of law from a SBAT to the High Court (in Scotland, the Court of Sessions).[19] This development was largely attributable to the increasing dissatisfaction with the tribunals and also with the limitations of judicial review – discussed in the following paragraphs. The step is not, however, to preclude further consideration of a right of appeal to a second-tier tribunal.[20] The significance of the appeal to the High Court will only become apparent when it is seen how broadly the judges interpret the notion of an appeal on *a point of law*. There are many issues arising under the Supplementary Benefits Act 1976 which could be categorised as questions of law – the meaning of 'resources",[1] the distinctions between a 'householder', 'boarder' and other persons,[2] and the interpretation of the new 'living with' test for the purposes of the aggregation provision.[3]

It is hoped that the judges will adopt a less cautious approach than that generally followed by the courts on an application for judicial review by the prerogative orders. The claimant (or the Commission)[4] could apply to

13. *Bell*, ante n.2, at pp. 9–10.
14. SBA 1976, s.15(3).
15. S.I. 1971/226, Reg. 11.
16. S.I. 1977/1141, Reg. 9(1); see ante pp. 642–644, for the interpretation by the Commissioner of the very similar grounds of review in contributory benefit cases.
17. *Herman*, ante n.17, at p. 29.
18. As in the example given in the Handbook, para. 229.
19. S.I. 1977/1735.
20. See Mr S. Orme, Minister of Social Security, Written Answer 923 HC

Deb., cols. 164–165. See post, p. 659, for further discussion.
1. See ante, pp. 504–507.
2. Ante, pp. 495–496 and 502–503.
3. Ante, pp. 404–408.
4. Eg, *R v Peterborough Supplementary Benefits Appeal Tribunal, ex parte Department of Health and Social Security* (1977) 121 Sol Jo 202 DC. (It is odd that the application was brought by the Department and not the SBC – an aspect of the uncertain relationship between the two bodies.)

the Divisional court for an order to quash a tribunal's decision on the same grounds as those available to secure review of a Commissioner's decision:[5] jurisdictional error, including a breach of the rules of natural justice,[6] and error of law on the face of the record. (It is still open for an applicant to ask for the prerogative orders, but this course will almost always be less convenient than the appeal to the High Court.) In the leading case on review of tribunal decisions, *R v Preston Supplementary Benefits Appeal Tribunal, ex parte Moore*,[7] Lord Denning MR said the courts should only intervene when the tribunal's decision was wholly unreasonable, though they should be ready to lay down guidelines to assist tribunals interpret the Act and quash the decision if there was an excess of jursidiction or breach of the natural justice rules.

This approach was hard to defend. Its justification lay in the courts' fear that they might become flooded with applications for certiorari.[8] This was understandable, but the implication that errors of law committed by SBATs would not always be corrected was disturbing. The tribunals are not expert bodies, similar to the Commissioners, to whose decisions it may be appropriate to adopt a respectful attitude.[9] In other cases subsequent to *ex parte Moore* the courts were willing to intervene,[10] but sometimes Lord Denning's approach was used to justify what seemed an excessively tolerant attitude to the tribunal's reasoning.[11] On an appeal, it would not be open to the judges to draw a distinction between substantial and technical errors of law and it, therefore, seems likely that the courts will now play a more active role in the development of supplementary benefits law.

G. Radical reform proposals

Prompted by the recommendations in the *Bell* study, the DHSS, in consultation with the Commission and the Council on Tribunals, is reviewing every aspect of the tribunal system.[12] There has also recently been a wealth of literature, stressing the need for reform and proposing fundamental changes in the tribunal structure.[13] Two of the principal proposals should be briefly discussed here.

5. Ante, pp. 647–648.
6. *R v South West London Supplementary Benefits Appeal Tribunal, ex parte Bullen*, (1976) 120 Sol Jo 437, DC.
7. [1975] 2 All ER 807, [1975] 1 WLR 624, CA: see ante, p. 505.
8. Ibid., at p. 631. See Street *LAG Bulletin*, May 1975, p. 118.
9. Ante, p. 646.
10. E.g. *R v West London Supplementary Benefits Appeal Tribunal, ex parte Taylor* [1975] 2 All ER 790, [1975] 1 WLR 1048, DC; *R v West London Supplementary Benefits Appeal Tribunal, ex parte Clarke* [1975] 3 All ER 513, [1974] 1 WLR 1396, DC.

11. See in particular the Divisional Court's judgment in *R v Barnsley Supplementary Benefits Appeal Tribunal, ex parte Atkinson* [1976] 2 All ER 686, [1976] 1 WLR 1047, rev'd on grounds not material to the discussion, [1977] 3 All ER 1031, [1977] 1 WLR 917, CA.
12. SBC Annual Report 1976, Cmnd. 6910, para. 18.10.
13. See in particular Calvert and the conclusion by Adler and Bradley in *Justice, Discretion and Poverty* (1976), pp. 183 and 207 respectively; Bradley, 27 NILQ 96, pp. 111–119.

The first is that there should be an appeal from a SBAT to a second-tier tribunal, almost certainly the National Insurance Commissioner. The Commissioners' rulings on points of law would then be binding on tribunals and on the SBC. This has been suggested for cohabitation appeals by the Fisher Committee, which was concerned to secure uniformity of approach between widow's and supplementary benefits cases.[14] It was recommended generally in the *Bell* study.[15] The result of this change would be greater legalisation of the supplementary benefits scheme – more predictability and certainty of decision at the cost of some flexibility.[16] The Commissioners would have to be sensitive to the distinction between questions of law and questions of discretion; they would presumably have no jurisdiction over the latter, provided the SBC had exercised its powers within reasonable bounds.[17]

A more radical solution, canvassed as an ultimate objective by Bell, would be the integration of insurance tribunals and SBATs into one system, perhaps presided over by a Chief Social Security Commissioner.[18] This ambitious proposal had been rejected by the Franks Committee, largely on the ground that the issues before the two types of tribunal were different.[19] It is not clear that this is now as true as it was then, and it can be argued that an amalgamated social security tribunal would still be dealing with a narrower range of questions than an inferior court.[20]

Part four. Pensions Appeal Tribunals

A. Composition and structure

Pensions appeal tribunals (PATs) were first set up in 1919; they did not, however, have jurisdiction over claims in respect of service after 1921.[1] Two different types of tribunal were established by the Pensions Appeal Tribunals Act 1943. The first deals with appeals on *entitlement*, where the issue is whether the Secretary of State was right to reject the claim. The hearing is de novo and there is no onus on the appellant to show that the decision was wrong.[2] Both medical and legal issues come before these tribunals, and this is reflected in their composition. The chairman is a

14. Para. 341.
15. Bell *Research Study on Supplementary Benefit Appeal Tribunals, Review of Main Findings: Conclusions: Recommendations*, published by DHSS (1975), pp. 24–25.
16. For this reason, it would undoubtedly have been resisted by Titmuss: see 42 Political Quarterly 113.
17. The Commissioner's jurisdiction would thus be similar to that of courts controlling the legality of discretionary powers, though it might be appropriate for him to intimate the correct approach to the exercise of discretion, the factors to be taken into account, etc.

18. *Bell*, ante n.15, at p. 25; Calvert, ante n.13, at pp. 197–205.
19. (1957), Cmnd. 218, para. 138.
20. See Wraith and Hutchesson *Administrative Tribunals* (1973), pp. 289–292 for a general discussion of the relevant arguments. A full amalgamation would also involve the Attendance Allowance Board and Pensions appeal tribunals.
1. Chap. 9, ante, pp. 351–354, for the history of war pensions.
2. *Barratt v Minister of Pensions* (1946) 1 WPAR 1225. The rules concerning the burden of proof discussed, ante, pp. 365–369, therefore, apply.

lawyer, and one of the other two members is a doctor. Both these persons must be of seven years' standing in their profession. The third member is a retired or demobilised officer or serviceman of the same sex and rank as the person in respect of whose disability the claim is made.[3] The second type of tribunal entertains appeals from the *assessment* of disabilities.[4] It has two medical members, both doctors of more than seven years' standing, one of whom is appointed to act as chairman of the tribunal.[5] The third member is an ex-serviceman or officer of the same status and rank as the claimant.

Members and chairmen are appointed by the Lord Chancellor. Further, it is the Lord Chancellor's Office which is responsible for providing the tribunals' staff. Another significant aspect is that they are organised on the presidential system.[6] The President of the Pensions Appeal Tribunals is responsible for their administration, as well as sitting himself as a chairman. The Tribunal Rules confer on him various specific powers, e.g., to order the disclosure to the claimant of official documents,[7] to direct that a case be placed on the deferred list,[8] and to make arrangements where an infirm appellant is unable to attend a hearing.[9] The value of the presidential system is that chairmen have available an independent source of advice; moreover, the President is a person of sufficient authority to ensure that the tribunals are, and are seen to be, independent of the government.[10] The tribunals are national, both in terms of their administration and jurisdiction.[11] In practice they sit in regional centres (as well as in London) for reasons of convenience to the claimant.[12]

B. Procedure

The procedural rules governing appeals to PATs, for the most part contained in the Rules,[13] are detailed, and compared with the provisions concerning other social security tribunals, are favourable to the appellant.

1. The appellant has a year within which to appeal against a decision on entitlement or a final assessment, or three months in the case of an interim assessment.[14]

---

3. Pensions Appeal Tribunals Act 1943, Sch., para 3.
4. Ante, pp. 370–372, for the rules regarding assessment.
5. Pensions Appeal Tribunals Act 1943, Sch., para. 3.
6. See *Wraith and Hutchesson*, ante n.20 at pp. 85–86.
7. S.I. 1971/769, Rule 6, and also see Rule 22. (These Rules govern PATs in England and Wales: there are comparable Scottish tribunal rules: S.I. 1971/2124).
8. S.I. 1971/769, Rule 10.
9. Ibid., Rule 21.

10. See the intervention by the President concerning the departmental practice of reviewing cases after an assessment appeal: Annual Report of the Council on Tribunals for 1969–70, paras. 62–63.
11. *Wraith and Hutchesson*, ante n.20, at pp. 74, 174.
12. They sit at twelve centres in the UK: Report on War Pensioners for 1976, HC 472, p. 4.
13. S.I. 1971/769.
14. Pensions Appeal Tribunals Act 1943, s.8.

2. On receipt of the notice of appeal (which need not state its grounds), it is for the Secretary of State to prepare a Statement of Case, containing the relevant facts and the reasons for the decision. This is sent to the claimant for him to submit, if he wishes, an answer; the Statement of Case, the claimant's answer and the Secretary's comments on this (if any) are sent to the Pensions Appeal Office.[15]

3. The appellant may apply to the President of the PATs for disclosure of official documents which are likely to be relevant to his case.[16]

4. The parties are given ten clear days notice of the hearing.[17]

5. It is the duty of the tribunal to assist any appellant who appears unable to make the best of his case, and further the chairman may examine an unrepresented appellant's witnesses, if he requests.[18]

6. Though the tribunal may obtain the opinion of a medical specialist or other technical expert, it must be sent to the parties for them to comment on, and either may request a further hearing.[19]

The appellant's interests are particularly safeguarded by the provision that the appeal is not to be heard in his absence, unless he has requested this; even then the tribunal has discretion not to hear the case.[20] The President may make arrangements, inter alia, for the appellant to be interviewed at home by one or more members of the tribunal, if he is too infirm to attend, and the incapacity is likely to be of a long duration.[1] If for some reason an appeal is not prosecuted, e.g., the appellant simply fails to attend without explanation, it may be put on the deferred list.[2] An application may then be made within the next year for the case to be heard,[3] and this will be granted unless the President is satisfied 'that the appellant's failure to prosecute the appeal was due to his wilful default'.[4]

There are other interesting provisions which do not necessarily benefit the claimant. The PAT may itself summon expert or other witnesses,[5] as well as taking into account the evidence produced by the parties; evidence is not to be refused merely on the ground that it would be inadmissible in a court of law.[6] Rule 18 specifically provides that the tribunal's decision may be announced immediately after the hearing, or within seven days; but only a short indication of reasons need be given. It is surprising that there is no requirement to state them more fully.[7] It is even more surprising that there is no provision at all concerning majority decisions of a PAT.

15. S.I. 1971/769, Rule 5.
16. Ibid., Rule 6.
17. Ibid., Rule 8(1); cp., the provisions for 'reasonable notice' of insurance tribunal and SBAT hearings, ante, pp. 628, 654.
18. Ibid., Rules 11(3), 13(1).
19. Ibid., Rule 15.
20. Ibid., Rule 20.
 1. Ibid., Rule 21.

2. Ibid., Rule 10.
3. Ibid., Rule 26(1), (2).
4. Ibid., Rule 26(3).
5. Ibid., Rule 12(4).
6. Ibid., Rule 12(5): this is also the practice of insurance tribunals and the Commissioners: ante, pp. 633, 648.
7. See ante, pp. 630, 656 for local tribunals and SBATs respectively.

The nominated judge on appeal has, therefore, ruled that the decision of a tribunal must be unanimous and, if the members cannot agree, the case must be referred to another tribunal.[8]

Like medical appeal tribunals, PATs may use the expertise of their medical member (or in assessment cases, members) in assessing the claimant's condition.[9] The medical member may conduct an examination of the appellant with his consent.[10] But the member's views are not to be taken as evidence which is itself capable of rebutting the presumption that the injury was attributable to service.[11] If the medical member is inclined to doubt the appellant's case, an independent medical specialist should be consulted and his advice given to the claimant for comment.[12]

c. Appeal to the nominated judge

From decisions on entitlement there is a further right of appeal on a point of law to a High Court judge nominated by the Lord Chancellor to hear such appeals (hence the phrase, 'the nominated judge').[13] Leave of either the tribunal or the judge himself must first be obtained; this should be granted whenever there is any reasonable doubt as to the correctness of the tribunal decision.[14] The grounds on which an appeal may be made were fully considered by Denning J (as he then was) in *Armstrong v Minister of Pensions*:[15] they include a wrong direction on law, incorrect admission or exclusion of evidence and breach of the procedural rules or the rules of natural justice. Unless all the facts are before the judge, the correct course is for him to remit the case for the PAT to reconsider.

There is no further appeal to the Court of Appeal.[16] This may afford some justification for the view expressed in two cases by Denning J, that the doctrine of *stare decisis* does not apply in its full rigour in war pension cases.[17] Decisions of the judge are binding on PATs, but need not be followed by the judge in another case if there is a strong reason for taking a different view. There are now very few cases taken to the nominated

---

8. *Brain v Minister of Pensions* [1947] KB 625, [1947] 1 All ER 892 (PAT disallow claimant's appeal by a majority); *Minister of Pensions v Horsey* [1949] 2 KB 526 (majority allow appeal by claimant).

9. For medical appeal tribunals, see ante, pp. 636–637.

10. S.I. 1971/769, Rule 17.

11. *Moxon v Minister of Pensions* [1945] KB 490: for the presumption, see ante, pp. 365–368.

12. *Diamond v Minister of Pensions* (1947) 1 WPAR 313, 317. For the correct procedure when an independent medical specialist's advice is sought, see *Harris v Minister of Pensions* (1948) 4 WPAR 82.

13. Pensions Appeal Tribunals Act 1943,

s.6(2): for the distinction between an appeal to the High Court and to a nominated judge, see Wraith and Hutchesson *Administrative Tribunals*, (1973) p. 160. In Scotland appeal lies to the Court of Session.

14. *Atkinson v Minister of Pensions* (1947) 1 WPAR 981.

15. (1948) 3 WPAR 1449.

16. Pensions Appeal Tribunals Act, s.6(2). There is also no right of appeal to the Court of Appeal from a decision of the nominated judge refusing leave to appeal: see *ex parte Aronsohn* [1946] 2 All ER 544, CA.

17. *James v Minister of Pensions*, [1947] KB 867, [1947] 2 All ER 432; *Minister of Pensions v Higham*, [1948] 2 KB 153, 155.

judge.[18] Part of the explanation for this may be the availability since 1970 of an alternative procedure: the claimant and the Secretary of State may present a joint application to the President of the PATs for him to direct that the tribunal's decision be treated as set aside, either on the ground that additional evidence is available or because of some error of law, and that the appeal be heard again by the tribunal.[19]

There is no appeal at all from the decision of an assessment tribunal. The reason given for this is that there are no questions of law involved in such decisions.[20] Nor is the alternative procedure discussed in the last paragraph available.

Part five. Reference to the European Court of Justice

The significance of European Economic Community law for particular social security benefits is fully discussed in the next chapter. The 1971 EEC Social Security Regulation[1] (as amended) is directly applicable; it must, therefore, be implemented by the British courts and the statutory authorities.[2] In most cases it will be for the national courts to interpret Community regulations but, in order that there may be uniformity of interpretation in the member states, there is a procedure under which a point of difficulty may be referred to the European Court of Justice in Luxembourg (ECJ) for it to give a preliminary ruling.[3] Article 177 of the Treaty of Rome provides that the Court of Justice has jurisdiction to give preliminary rulings on the interpretation of the Treaty and the validity and interpretation of Community legal acts, e.g., regulations and directives. It further provides in paragraphs 2 and 3:

> 'Where such a question is raised before any court or tribunal of a Member State, that court or tribunal may, if it considers that a decision on the question is necessary to enable it to give judgment, request the Court of Justice to give a ruling thereon.

18. In 1976, there were fourteen applications for leave, of which four were granted: Annual Report on War Pensioners for 1976, HC 472, p. 4.
19. Pensions Appeal Tribunals Act 1943, s.6(2A), added by the Chronically Sick and Disabled Persons Act 1970, s.23. For a case in which it was unsuccessfully argued that there was maladministration in the Department's decision not to agree to a joint application to the President, see Fourth Report of the PCA 1970–71, HC 490, Case No. C. 214/73.
20. *Morris v Minister of Pensions* [1948] 1 All ER 748.
 1. Regulation 1408/71: see post, pp. 670–683.

2. For the direct applicability of EEC law, see Lasok and Bridge *An Introduction to the Law and Institutions of the European Communities* (2nd end), pp. 199ff. and Collins *European Community Law in the United Kingdom*, (1975), chap. 2. The directly applicable effect of the EEC Social Security Regulation was recognised by the Commissioner, J. G. Monroe, in *Re a Holiday in Italy*, [1975] 1 CMLR 184 (*R(S) 4/74*, para. 7).
3. *Lasok and Bridge*, ante n.2, at pp. 209–216; *Collins*, ante n.2, at pp. 110–127; Jacobs and Durand *References to the European Court: Practice and Procedure* (1975), *passim*.

Where any such question is raised in a case pending before a court or a tribunal of a Member State, against whose decisions there is no judicial remedy under national law, that court or tribunal shall bring the matter before the Court of Justice.'

A. The discretion to refer

i) 'Court or tribunal'
Under the second paragraph of Article 177, a question may be referred for a preliminary ruling by a 'court or tribunal'. This enables any part of the Supreme Court of Judicature to ask for a preliminary ruling in a suitable case.[4] The National Insurance Commissioner clearly is entitled to refer, and it seems that a local insurance tribunal could do so.[5] It is possible that the statutory authorities could refer a contributions question to the European Court;[6] this step might not contravene the requirement in the Social Security Act 1975 that a contributions question must be determined by the Secretary of State.[7] In any event it is not clear that the Secretary of State himself could make a reference, since he may not constitute a 'tribunal' for the purpose of Article 177.[8]

ii) The decision must be 'necessary'
A question may only be referred to the European Court if a decision on it is 'necessary' for the national court or tribunal to give judgment. In the leading English case, *H. P. Bulmer Ltd. v J. Bollinger SA*, Lord Denning MR, took the narrow view that a court should only refer a point, if a decision on it would be *conclusive* of the case.[9] The Commissioner, however, has followed the broader approach of Stephenson LJ in the *Buler* case,[10] and ruled that a reference is permissible if a case cannot be determined without a decision on the point referred to the European court.[11] This seems the better view, and is consistent with that adopted by English judges in other cases.[12]

iii) Factors relevant to the exercise of the discretion
The factors to be taken into account in deciding whether to refer were discussed at length by the Court of Appeal in the *Bulmer* case.[13] The

4. The Divisional Court asked for a preliminary ruling in *R v National Insurance Comr, ex parte Warry*, [1977] 2 CMLR 783. So far no other court has done so in a social security case.
5. It is believed that only one tribunal has made a reference to the ECJ, and this was subsequently withdrawn.
6. This course is not ruled out by the Commissioner's decision in *Re Retirement to Ireland* [1977] 1 CMLR 1.
7. S.93: ante, p. 621.
8. The ECJ which may give a preliminary ruling on the interpretation of Art. 177 itself has

interpreted 'tribunal' broadly: see *Collins*, ante n.2 at 72–75; *Jacobs and Durand*, ante n.3, at pp. 156–157.
9. [1974] Ch. 401, [1974] 2 All ER 1226, CA.
10. Ibid., at p. 428.
11. *Re an Illness in France* [1976] 1 CMLR 243; *Kenny v Insurance Officer* [1978] 1 CMLR 181.
12. See Graham J in *Lowenbrau München v Grünhalle Lager International* [1974] 1 CMLR 1, 9; Pennycuick VC in *Van Duyn v Home Office* [1974] 1 WLR 1107, 1115–1116.
13. Ante, n.9, at pp. 423–425, 429–430.

desirability of ensuring uniform interpretation of Community law must be balanced against the costs and delay entailed by a reference. The more important and difficult the point of law, the more inclined the judge should be to refer it to the Luxembourg Court.[14] The Commissioner has generally decided questions of European law himself, and in only two reported cases so far has he discussed at length whether to request a preliminary ruling. In the first, *Re an Illness in France*,[15] the Commissioner decided to refer a question on the invitation of the DHSS. It was emphasised that the claimant welcomed this step. The issue – the meaning of 'worker' for the purposes of the EEC Regulation[16] – was one which had been previously ruled on by the Commissioner, and it was clear that an authoritative interpretation from the European Court was now desirable.[17] In *Re a Visit to Italy*,[18] however, the Commissioner refused to refer, largely because of the delay involved and the fact that the claimant might not be paid benefit for the interim period.

B. The duty to refer

In the circumstances covered by its third paragraph quoted above,[19] Article 177 imposes a duty to refer. Which British courts or tribunals deciding issues of social security law are under this duty, because 'there is no judicial remedy' against their decision? In *Re a Holiday in Italy*,[20] the Commissioner, J. G. Monroe, decided that he was not bound to refer, as the prerogative order of certiorari was available to quash his decision for an error of law, including a wrong interpretation of the EEC Regulation; it did not matter that leave had to be obtained from the Divisional Court before the order could be applied for. This decision has been criticised on the ground that it assumed that leave to apply for certiorari is granted as a matter of course, where a point of Community law is involved.[1] As has been said earlier in this chapter,[2] the courts will not intervene to control every error of law, so it is difficult to be confident that there will always be an available judicial remedy against Commissioners' decisions.

It is clear that a High Court judge entertaining an appeal on a contributions question would be under a duty to request a preliminary ruling since there is no appeal from his decision.[3] It is arguable that the Court of Appeal is bound to refer under Article 177(3) on the ground that leave is required for an appeal to the House of Lords, but the point was left open by Stephenson LJ in the *Bulmer* case.[4]

14. Ibid., at p. 430, per Stephenson LJ.
15. Ante n.11.
16. Post, p. 672, for the decision of the ECJ on this point.
17. The earlier decision of the Commissioner in *Re an Ex-Civil Servant* [1976] 1 CMLR 257 did not satisfy the DHSS.
18. [1976] 1 CMLR 506, *(R(I) 1/75)*.
19. Ante, p. 664.
20. [1975] 1 CMLR 184 *(R(S) 4/74*, para. 8).

1. See Bridge, 1 European L. Rev. 13, 19; Jacobs, 2 European L. Rev. 119; cp., Collins, ante n.2, at p. 105. In view of the doubts as to the availability of a remedy for error of law on the face in Scotland, it may be that the Commissioner in a Scottish case is bound to refer: ante, p. 647.
2. At p. 646.
3. Ante, p. 623.
4. Ante n.9, at p. 430.

16 International and European Law

Part one. General

International collaboration and coordination in the social security field has been a widespread phenomenon in the second half of the twentieth century. In part it is associated with the general movement on human rights;[1] in part it results from an increase in the mobility of labour,[2] a consequence not only of individual initiative but also of governmental stimulus, notably within the European Communities.[3] The legal instruments directed towards these ends may be divided into three groups.

A. Minimum standards

In the first place, there are multilateral instruments imposing obligations on those states which ratify them to conform to certain minimum standards. At a comprehensive, but necessarily vague, level there is the Universal Declaration of Human Rights conferring on an individual the right to 'security in the event of unemployment, sickness, disability, widowhood, old age or other lack of livelihood in circumstances beyond his control'.[4] More specifically there is the work of the International Labour Organisation (ILO) established after the First World War,[5] but reconstituted as an agency of the United Nations in 1946.[6] Among its manifold activities, this body through its assembly, comprising not only governments but also representatives of employers and employees, enacts conventions which once ratified by individual states are binding on them as norms of international law.[7] There have been a a number of such

1. See e.g., Jenks *Human Rights and International Labour Standards* (1960), chap. 7; Watson, 6 Jnl. Soc. Pol. 31.
2. See generally Lyon-Caen *Droit Social International et Européen* (4th edn), pp. 1–17; Bohning *The Migration of Workers in the United Kingdom and the European Community* (1972); International Labour Organisation *Social Security for Migrant Workers* (1977).
3. Treaty of Rome, arts. 48–51, on which see: Lipstein *Law of the European Communities* (1974), chap. 5; Lyon-Caen, ante n.2, at pp. 185–228; Collins *The European Communities* (1975), vol. 2, chap 4.
4. (1948) UN Doc. A/811, art. 25. See also, Jenks *Social Justice in the Law of Nations* (1970), pp. 69–79.
5. By Part XIII of the Treaty of Versailles 1914. See on the early history, Lowe *International Protection of Labour* (1921).
6. By the International Labour Conference, Montreal.
7. See generally: Jenks, ante n.4; Lawly *The Effectiveness of International Supervision* (1966).

conventions in the field of social security but the most important is that which lays down minimum standards to deal with the social hazards of illness, invalidity, unemployment, old age, maternity, death and industrial accidents.[8] The original plan was to prescribe both minimum and maximum standards, but the latter was abandoned in 1952 and even the former appears in a muted form: a state ratifying the convention need only conform to the standard of three of the nine risks specifically dealt with.[9] The standards under the ILO Convention had to be of a nature that would be feasible for states of widely differing economic development. Moreover, it applied only for the protection of employed workers. Within the ambit of Western European industrialised states, it was hoped to improve on the standards, and work to this end has been undertaken by the Council of Europe.[10] What eventually emerged in 1964 was the European Code of Social Security.[11] This was in fact not so much a code in the conventional sense of the term but a convention like that of the ILO, open to ratification by member states. Similar in scope to the ILO Convention, it nevertheless was more exacting as regards both the standards to be achieved for individual social hazards and the extent of commitment vis-à-vis the range of those hazards – the Code contains twelve points[12] and the ratifying state is to conform to at least six of these.[13] Despite the fact that the majority of member states has been slow to ratify the Code (though the United Kingdom has already done so), steps were taken to reach even higher standards in a Protocol which was annexed to the Code.[14]

B. Equality of treatment and aggregation of entitlement

It is obvious that with the growth of migrant labour, the multinational enterprises and increased foreign travel possibilities, problems would be caused for individuals subjected to social security systems based entirely on residence and/or contribution conditions. While the need of a state to protect its own workers temporarily employed abroad has always been recognised and to a large extent catered for by its own internal rules, there was naturally a reluctance to extend the provisions of a system to foreigners, at the cost to national contributors or taxpayers, without there being a reciprocal arrangement in the foreigner's own system. Until recently, therefore, the typical solution to the problem was found in bilateral reciprocal treaties. Most obviously this occurred at an early stage in the history of national insurance in relation to the Republic of Ireland.[15] The

8. Convention no. 102, 210 UNTS 131: *Jenks*, ante n.4, at pp. 107–111; *Lyon-Caen*, ante n.2, at pp. 62–67.
9. Art. 2(a).
10. *Lyon-Caen*, ante n.2, at pp. 68–87.
11. European Treaty Series, No. 48. See also Explanatory Reports on the Code (1961), Council of Europe.
12. In fact provision for old age covers three points, and that of medical care two points: art. 241.

13. Art. 2(2).
14. The Protocol forms part of the same Treaty as the Code. At the time of writing it has still not been ratified by the UK.
15. The power to give effect to reciprocal arrangements on unemployment income was conferred by the Irish Free State (Consequential Provisions) Act 1922, s. 6(1)(c).

Social Security Act 1975[16] explicitly provides that to give effect to any such agreement the Crown may by Order in Council modify or alter the Act, and there are over thirty such Orders currently in force.[17] Within the Western European context, the Council of Europe has introduced a convention based on a principle of multilateral reciprocity.[18] If and when ratified, this will replace bilateral agreements between member states.

By far and away the most important international coordination in this field has been that achieved by the European Economic Communities. One of the pillars of the Treaty of Rome, as expressed in Article 3(c), was the 'abolition . . . of obstacles to freedom of movement or persons'. The implications of this objective for social security legislation were spelled out in Article 51:

> 'the Council shall . . . adopt such measures in the field of social security as are necessary to provide freedom of movement for workers; to this end, it shall make arrangements to secure for migrant workers and their dependants:
> (a) aggregation, for the purpose of acquiring and retaining the right to benefit and of calculating the amount of benefit, of all periods taken into account under the laws of the several countries;
> (b) payment of benefits to persons resident in the territories of Member States'.

The direction was quickly implemented by a Council Regulation of 1958,[19] borrowed substantially from the Coal and Steel Community.[20] While the principles underlying the 1958 Regulation were clear – equal treatment for all workers of member states, aggregation of insurance periods served while working in different member states, exporting of benefits from one state to another – the rules themselves posed grave difficulties of interpretation, not least because the frequent rulings of the European Court of Justice (ECJ) produced a body of law not always anticipated by the draftsmen of the Regulation. In the light of these difficulties, the 1958 Regulation was replaced by a new set of provisions in 1971.[1] This new Regulation was formulated without any regard to the social security systems of the new members (including the United Kingdom) admitted in 1972.[2] While essential modifications have been made to accommodate their peculiarities, substantial problems in the adjustment of

---

16. S.143. Agreements previously in force are preserved by the Social Security (Consequential Provisions) Act 1975, Sch. 3, para. 10.
17. They are listed in a note to SSA 1975, s.143 in Halsbury Statutes, vol. 43, p. 1241. The DHSS publishes leaflets summarising the provisions of the most important of such Orders in the SA series.
18. European Convention on Social Security 1972, European Treaty Series No. 78 At the time of writing this has

been ratified only by Austria and Luxembourg. See also the Explanatory Reports on the Convention (1973), Council of Europe.
19. Reg. 3/58, OJ 1958, 561.
20. European Convention on Social Security for Migrant Workers 1957.
1. Reg. 1408/71, OJ 1971, L 149/2, supplemented by the implementing Reg. 574/72, OJ 1972, L 74.
2. See the observations of the ECJ in *Brack v Insurance Officer*, [1976] 2 CMLR 592.

the British system to its European counterparts still remain.[3] Be that as it may, the 1971 Regulation, as modified, is now incorporated into British law, and forms an important part of the social security system.[4] As such, it is the subject matter of the bulk of this chapter; its effect on the adjudication of claims was discussed in chapter 15.[5]

C. Harmonisation

None of these measures affected the huge differences between the systems of the member states as regards their structure, their range of benefits, the rates payable and the mode of financing them.[6] An economic argument for harmonisation, based on the theory that different rates and systems of contributions for firms distort competition, has been doubted: contributions may be seen as part of the employer's total labour cost and this will vary according to the level of productivity rather than to any varying rates of contributions.[7] More compelling are the arguments based on reducing the complexity and administrative costs involved in resolving conflicts of rules and of achieving greater social justice for workers who have been employed in different states.[8] Whatever the merits of the policy, it was envisaged as a goal by the draftsmen of the Rome Treaty:

> 'Member States agree upon the need to promote improved working conditions and an improved standard of living for workers, so as to make possible their harmonisation while the improvement is being maintained.'[9]

In fact, progress in this field has been almost non-existent. The obstacles were fully expressed at a Conference convened by the Commission in 1962: the goal of harmonisation was a very vague one; the enormous differences between the systems of member states in terms both of structure and of level of support posed political as well as technical difficulties; the Commission lacked the power to achieve the goal; and national governments were unwilling to commit themselves.[10] The single, and not very important, achievement has been some standardisation in the area of industrial diseases.[11]

3. Perhaps the most important difference lies in the British coverage of the self-employed: post, p. 672.
4. Constitutionally by the European Communities Act 1972, s. 2(1).
5. Ante, pp. 663–665.
6. For accounts of the major differences between the national systems see: Lawson and Reed *Social Security in the European Community* (1975); van Langendonck, 2 ILJ 17; Kaim-Caudle *Comparative Social Policy and Social Security* (1973); Dupeyroux *Évolution et tendances des systèmes de sécurité des pays membres des Communautés Européenes et de la Grande Bretagne* (1966); and the EEC Commission Comparative Tables of the Social Security Systems in the Member States, published periodically.
7. See, EEC Study Serie Politique Sociale No. 21, *Les Incidences Économiques de la Sécurité Sociale* (1970), esp. chap. 6; Wedel 102 Int. Lab. Rev. 591, 592–605; van Langendonck, ante, n.6, at p. 24.
8. Collins, *The European Communities* (1975), vol. 2, chap. 6; van Langendonck, ante n.6, at pp. 24–27.
9. Art. 117.
10. See EEC, *Conférence Européene sur la Sécurité Sociale* (1964).
11. Resulting from the Commission Recommendation 66/462/CEE. OJ 2696/66.

Part two. Scope of EEC Regulation

A. Legislation

Regulation 1408/71 governs national legislation concerned with benefits[12] for unemployment, sickness, invalidity,[13] old age, industrial injuries and diseases, and survivors, as well as death grant and family benefits.[14] The legislation referred to includes regulations and other implementing instruments and even private law agreements provided that they serve to establish a scheme under such legislation and are the subject of a declaration by a member state.[15] All instruments so governed by Regulation 1408/71 are to be specified by the member states.[16] However, a failure to do this may not, it seems, exclude a law, for in a case under the 1958 Regulation the ECJ held that it applied both to present and future legislation, irrespective of notification.[17] Apart from war pension and civil service schemes,[18] all social security, whether contributory or non-contributory,[19] dealing with the hazards listed above are included. But 'social security' must be distinguished from 'social assistance' which is outside the scope of the Regulation.[20] No definitions of these two concepts are provided; and the ECJ faced with the problem of classifying schemes has understandably been reluctant to offer any. It is, however, clear from its various judgments on the point[1] that it regards as characteristic of social assistance schemes those based on 'individual assessment of need', as opposed to the 'conferring of . . . a statutory defined status'.[2] This criterion is an unreliable one – as noted in connection with the British supplementary benefits scheme (clearly and rightly regarded by the United Kingdom government as a 'social assistance' scheme[3]), the relationship between 'discretion' and 'right', between 'individual assessment' and 'statutory entitlement' is a very fluid one.[4] More persuasive, it is submitted, are the guidelines suggested by Mayras, Advocate-General, in his opinion in *Frilli v The State*:[5] whether or not, vis-à-vis other social security benefits, the scheme in question has a supplementary or subsidiary quality. In deciding this, regard should be had, for example, to the extent to which in assessing

---

12. I.e., payments in cash or in kind, including up-rating increases and supplementary allowances: Reg. 1408/71, art. 1(f). Lump sums granted in lieu of a pension (e.g., to a widow on remarriage: *Vandeweghe v Berufsgenossenschaft für die Chemische Industrie*, [1974] 1 CMLR 499) are also included, but not payments intended for purposes unconnected with the hazard, e.g., to finance contributions: *Dekker v Bundesversicherungsanstalt für Angestellte* [1966] CMLR 503.

13. This is deemed to include the British attendance allowance: Reg. 1209/76, and see *Re a Road Accident in Ireland* [1976] 1 CMLR 512 (*R(A) 4/75*).

14. Reg. 1408/71, art. 1(1).

15. Ibid., art. 1(j); and see *Vaassen-Göbbels v Beambtenfonds voor het Mijnbedrijf*

[1966] CMLR 508.

16. Reg. 1408/71, art. 5. See OJ. 1973, C43 for the UK legislation so specified.

17. *Dingemans v Sociale Verzekeringsbank* [1965] CMLR 144.

18. Reg. 1408/71, art. 4(4).

19. Ibid., art. 4(2).

20. Ibid., art. 4(4).

1. *Frilli v The State* [1973] CMLR 386; *Costa v Belgian State* [1974] ECR 1251; *Caisse Régionale d'Assurance Maladie de Paris v Biason* [1975] 1 CMLR 59.

2. *Biason* case, ibid., at p. 70.

3. Neither the SBA 1976 nor the FISA 1970 have been specified as being governed by the Regulation: cf., ante n.16.

4. Cf., ante, pp. 512–515.

5. Ante n.1, at pp. 393–397.

entitlement account is taken of the receipt of other benefits, of the fulfilment of maintenance obligations, and whether or not the fund concerned is subrogated to the rights of the beneficiary against third parties.

B. Persons

The 1971 Regulation applies

> 'to workers who are or have been subject to the legislation of one or more Member States and who are nationals of one of the Member States or who are stateless persons or refugees residing[6] within the territory of one of the Member States, as also to the members of their families[7] and their survivors[8]

Most significantly this excludes the nationals of non-member states. Legally, a major problem has been the meaning of 'worker'. The cases soon established that the protection conferred by the Regulation was to extend to a group wider than migrant workers stricto sensu. Provided they are 'workers', their residence or presence in another member state need not be in pursuance of employment there.[9] But are those not engaged under a contract of employment[10] so included? The 1958 Regulation had employed the notion of 'wage-earners or assimilated workers'.[11] While the intention was clearly to exclude in general self-employed and non-employed persons, such persons might be covered if under their national law they were assimilated to the position of persons working under a contract of employment. According to the ECJ, this condition would be satisfied if, and to the extent that, a scheme designed for employed workers generally was extended to other workers.[12] The principle was incorporated in the 1971 Regulation: in particular a 'worker' includes

6. 'Residence' means 'habitual residence': Reg. 1408/71, art. 1(h); see further, *Angenieux v Hakenberg* [1973] ECR 935; *Di Paolo v Office National de l'Emploi* [1977] ECR 315.

7. In general, the members of the family included are determined by the law under which the benefit is provided; but if that law regards as members only persons living under the same roof as the worker, this condition is regarded as satisfied if such persons are 'mainly dependent' on the worker: Reg. 1408/71, art. 1(f).

8. Ibid., art. 2(1). 'Survivors' are determined in a way similar to 'members of the family' (ante n.7) but survivors who are themselves nationals of a member state or are resident stateless persons or refugees are included irrespective of the nationality

of the deceased worker; Reg. 1408/71, art. 2(2).

9. *Unger v Bestuur der Bedrijfsvereniging voor Detailhandel en Ambachten* [1964] CMLR 319; *Hessische Knappschaft v Maison Singer* [1966] CMLR 82; *Gemeenschappelijke Verzekeringskas 'De Sociale Voorzorg' v Bertholet* [1966] CMLR 191.

10. Cf. ante, pp. 47–53.

11. Reg. 3/58, art 4(1).

12. *De Cicco v Landesversicherungsanstalt Schwaben* [1969] CMLR 67; *Janssen v Landsbond der Christelijke Mutualiteiten* [1972] 1 CMLR 13. The word 'worker' does not imply that the individual must be engaged on work at the time of the claim; it includes those who are attached to the labour market in the sense of being readily available for work: *Unger* case, ante n.9..

'a person who is compulsorily insured[13] ... under a social security scheme for all residents or for the whole working population if such a person ... can be identified as an employed person by virtue of the manner in which such scheme is administered or financed.'[14]

Whether the definitions cover a given individual is a question of Community Law,[15] and though a member state may in an Annexe to the Regulation indicate the categories of person whom it regards as 'workers' for the purpose of these rules, such a declaration may not restrict or conflict with the definitions provided by that law.[16] The matter is well illustrated by *Brack v Insurance Officer*.[17]

> C, a British national resident in the UK, had from 1948 until 1957 paid contributions as an employed person (Class 1). Since then he had contributed as a self-employed person (Class 2). In 1974 he was on holiday in France when he fell ill. His claim for sickness benefit was rejected on the ground of absence,[18] and the question was whether title was revived by Reg. 1408/71. The UK government had inserted in Annexe V to the Regulation a declaration to the effect that 'all persons required to pay contributions as employed workers shall be regarded as workers'.[19] On a reference from the Commissioner, the ECJ held that C was a 'worker', notwithstanding the annexed provision. The latter, it was judged,[20] was intended to deal with the practice peculiar to the British system, of classifying as employed persons some subject to no contract of service[1]. It made clear that any person who was bound to pay contributions as an employed person, though in labour law he was not regarded as such, could be identified as a 'worker' for the purpose of the Regulation. It therefore had no restrictive operation.[2] C was 'compulsorily insured'[3] and his previous contributions as an employed person, which continued to be taken into account for the purpose of his claim meant that he could be 'identified as an employed person by virtue of the manner in which such scheme is administered or financed'.

The decision does not extend the status of 'worker' to a large number of self-employed persons: it is confined to those who have paid Class 1 contributions for a period which is regarded as relevant for the purposes of

---

13. In *Brack v Insurance Officer (No. 2)* [1977] 1 CMLR 277 the Commissioner held that a person who, under British law, postpones retirement and thereby continues to pay contributions is 'compulsorily insured'.

14. Reg. 1408/71, art. 1(a).

15. *Unger* case, ante n.9, as adopted in *Brack v Insurance Officer*, [1976] 2 CMLR 592.

16. *Brack* case ibid., and *Re an Ex-Civil Servant* [1976] 1 CMLR 257.

17. Ante n.15.

18. Cf. ante, pp. 408–410.

19. Part I, para. 1.

20. Ante n.15, at p. 615, and see the exposition by Mayras, A-G, at pp. 600–602.

1. Cf., ante, p. 54.

2. Thus making it unnecessary to declare as invalid a provision which to that extent conflicted with Community Law: see Mayras, A-G, at pp. 607–608.

3. Cf., ante, n.13.

entitlement to benefit. The Commission has now made proposals to extend the Regulation to cover a wider group.[4]

Part three. Choice of Competent Legislation

The first substantive issue determined by Community Law is the resolution of the conflict of legislative systems which might potentially govern a migrant worker. Article 13(1) of the 1971 Regulation prescribes that 'a worker . . . shall be subject to the legislation of a single Member State only'. The meaning of this provision, which had no exact equivalent in the 1958 Regulation, is somewhat uncertain.[5] The generally accepted view, and that which is consistent with the rulings of the ECJ,[6] holds that the reference to the exclusive jurisdiction of one member state applies for the purpose only of imposing on the worker *liabilities* which arise under one social security system, most importantly that of paying contributions.[7] Subject to certain principles governing overlaps (discussed in a later paragraph[8]), it does not prevent him acquiring rights to benefits under the legislation of other states.

Article 13(2) then lays down rules determining the member state to whose legislation a worker is subject. In general this is the state where his place of work is situated even if he is normally resident in another member state or the enterprise employing him has its place of business in another state.[9] But the general rule is subject to the following exceptions.

1. The first and most important exception is that of 'posting' abroad. Where the worker employed in one member state by an undertaking to which he is normally attached is posted by the employer to work in another member state, he remains subject to the legislation of the first state if the anticipated duration of the work in the second state does not exceed twelve months, and even for longer if the prolongation of the period was due to unforeseen circumstances and the authority of the second state

---

4. See OJ 1978, C14.
5. See the discussions in Lipstein *Law of the European Communities* (1974), pp. 96–99 and in ed. Jacobs *European Law and the Individual* (1974), chap. 4; Tantaroudas, 8 Rev. Trim. Dr. Eur. 36.
6. See, the decisions cited post n.3, on p. 677.
7. See, esp. *Moebs v Bestuur der Sociale Verzekeringsbank* [1964] CMLR 338.
8. Post, pp. 678–679.
9. Art. 13(2)(a). For this purpose, mariners are regarded as employed in the state whose flag is flown by the vessel in which they serve: art.

13(2)(b). Civil servants and members of the armed forces are regarded as employed in the state to whose administration or force they belong: art. 13(2)(c)–(d). In *Sociale Verzekeringsbank v Van der Vecht* [1968] CMLR 151 it was held that the whole of a journey (in transport provided by the employer) from the place of the worker's residence across the frontier to the place of work was subject to the law of the place of work. The 'employment' involved in the journey was regarded as inseparable from the employment on the site.

has given its consent.[10] The policy is to avoid the administrative inconvenience of changes in insurability for short periods. The rule applies to cases where the 'undertaking' is merely an employment agency,[11] and less obviously it was held in *Angenieux v Hakenberg*[12] to apply to an agent on commission from his employers who worked for nine months every year in another member state.

2. An employee of an international transport undertaking whose work takes him to more than one member state is subject to the law of the place where the undertaking has its registered office or place of business.[13] But if the undertaking has a branch in another member state, an employee working for that branch is governed by the law of that state.[14] Finally, if the worker is employed principally in the territory of the member state in which he resides, the law of that state will prevail, notwithstanding that the undertaking has no place of business or branch there.[15]

3. A worker, other than (2), who normally[16] pursues his employment in two or more member states is governed by the law of the state where he resides if it is one of those where he works;[17] if it is not, then by the law of the state where his employer has his registered office or place of business.[18]

4. There are special rules for frontier workers, mariners, those in the diplomatic service and auxiliary staff of the EEC.[19]

Part four.　General Principles

The rules described in Part Three determine the legislation applicable to a given individual – they indicate what will be referred to in the remainder of this chapter as the 'competent legislation', or, where more appropriate, the 'competent state'. It remains to consider the principles of Community Law to which that legislation is subject.

A.　Non-discrimination

It is enunciated in the Regulation that subject to special provisions

10. Reg. 1408/71, art. 14(1)(a).
11. *Manpower SARL, Strasbourg Regional Office v Caisse Primaire d'Assurance Maladie de Strasbourg* [1971] CMLR 222.
12. [1973] ECR 935.
13. Reg. 1408/71, art. 14(1)(b).
14. Ibid., art. 14(1)(b)(i).
15. Ibid., art. 14(1)(b)(ii).
16. 'Normally' apparently covers cases where the worker is 'occasionally' so employed: see *Caisse Primaire d'Assurance Maladie Sélestat v Association du Football Club Andlau* [1975] 2 CMLR 383.
17. Reg. 1408/71, art. 14(1)(c)(i).
18. Ibid., art. 14(1)(c)(ii).
19. Ibid., arts. 14(1)–(2), and 16.

'Persons resident in the territory of one of the Member States ... shall be subject to the same obligations and enjoy the same benefits under the legislation of any Member State as the nationals of that State'.[20]

The principle of equality of treatment for nationals of member states is the least original: it has been a regular feature of international instruments.[1] The assimilation governs both obligations of the individual, most importantly the payment of contributions, and rights to benefit. It also applies as regards periods of residence in another territory. Thus, in *Sécurité Sociale Nancy v Hirardin*,[2]

A Belgian national, working in France, and affiliated to the insurance scheme there, sought to have taken into account in the computation of his benefit periods of employment in Algeria. The ECJ held that the French authorities could not rely on a *loi* of 1964 which purported to restrict the aggregation of such periods to French citizens.

B. Aggregation of periods of insurance

The principle of aggregation of periods of insurance, employment or residence abroad for the purposes of satisfying the contribution conditions of the competent legislation is referred to in the Preamble of the Regulation, but not in its General Part. This is because it does not apply to all benefits or allowances, particularly those resulting from an industrial accident or disease[3] where entitlement is based on the employment alone. For each of the benefits for which the principle is relevant (sickness and maternity,[4] invalidity,[5] old age and death,[6] unemployment,[7] family[8] and orphans'[9] benefits) the rule is stated explicitly in the Special Provisions in substantially the same form:

'the competent institution of a Member State whose legislation makes the acquisition, retention or recovery of the right to benefits conditional upon the completion of insurance periods or periods of employment or residence shall, to the extent necessary, take account of insurance periods or periods of employment or residence completed under the legislation of any other Member State as if they were periods completed under the legislation which it administers'.[10]

20. Ibid., art. 3.
 1. E.g. European Code on Social Security, European Treaty Series, No. 48, art. 73. ILO Convention No. 102, 210 UNTS, art. 68.
 2. [1976] ECR 553.
 3. Though in this latter case there is partial recognition of the principle with regard to pneumoconiosis where periods of activity in a prescribed occupation in another member state

may be aggregated: Reg. 1408/71, art. 57(3). For some reason, the provision does not extend to other industrial diseases.
 4. Ibid., art. 18(1).
 5. Ibid., art. 38(1).
 6. Ibid., art. 45(1).
 7. Ibid., art. 67(1)–(2).
 8. Ibid., art. 72.
 9. Ibid., art. 79(1).
10. Ibid., art. 18(1).

What constitutes the appropriate 'insurance periods or periods of employment or residence' is determined by the legislation under which they were completed or treated as completed.[11] So in *Murru v Caisse Régionale d'Assurance Maladie de Paris*,[12] an Italian worker claiming a disability pension in France was unable to rely on a period of unemployment in Italy, for while the period might have counted if it had been completed in France, in Italy it was not treated as equivalent to a 'period of employment'.[13] For the purposes of British law, a woman claiming retirement pension on the basis of her husband's contributions may rely on periods of insurance completed by him in another member state.[14] In *Re Invalidity Benefit in Germany*,[15] however, the Commissioner was faced with a situation for which there was no explicit provision.

> C, a British national, was employed and insured in Germany when he became incapable of work; he received there sickness benefit for a year, and then claimed a British invalidity benefit. Entitlement to this depends, it will be recalled,[16] not on completion of contribution conditions per se, but on previous entitlement to sickness benefit combined with a continuous period of incapacity for work. The Commissioner held that the claim succeeded on the ground that C would have been entitled to sickness benefit (and hence also to invalidity benefit) in Britain if he had paid contributions there for the insurance periods in fact completed in Germany. Under the aggregation principle he was entitled to treat the latter as if they were periods completed in Britain.

C. Calculation and apportionment

Subject to the deterritoriality principle described below, it is for the member state under whose legislation benefit is claimed to assess the amount payable, but in so doing it is bound to apply certain rules of Community Law. If, as under the British legislation, the amount of benefit varies according to the number of dependants, those residing in the territory of another member state are to be treated as if residing in the territory of the determining member state.[17] As regards the short-term benefits for sickness, maternity, unemployment and industrial injury,

11. Ibid., art. 1(r), 1(s) and 1(s)(a). Where for the purpose of invalidity or old age pension the competent legislation requires the completion of insurance periods in an occupation subject to a special scheme or in a special employment, periods completed in another member state may only be taken into account if they are involved in the same occupation or employment: arts 38(2) and 45(2).
12. [1972] CMLR 888.
13. Cp. *Direction Régionale de la Sécurité Sociale de la Région Parisienne v* *Mancuso* [1973] ECR 1449, where, for an old age pension under German law, periods of unemployment and periods of completed insurance were *separate* conditions: reference to the law of the state where the period of unemployment had been spent was therefore unnecessary.
14. Reg. 1408/71, Annex V, Part I, para. 3.
15. [1976] 1 CMLR 494; cf., Appendix.
16. Ante, p. 165.
17. Reg. 1408/71, arts. 23(3), 39(4), 58(3), 68(2).

where reference is made to the average earnings of the claimant, account is to be taken only of earnings received in the determining member state.[18] In the case of unemployment benefit, this will be based on the worker's last employment there, but if such employment did not exceed four weeks, reference is made instead to the normal earnings in the territory where the claimant is residing for an employment which is equivalent or similar to his last employment in another member state.[19] Any up-rating of benefits under national legislation must of course be applied to those workers claiming under the Regulation.[20]

The difficult question now arises as to the extent to which a benefit may be reduced on the ground of overlap with benefit payable for a similar risk for a similar period by another member state. The matter is governed by two principles elaborated in the Regulation, but these may be ousted by a third principle enshrined in the decisions of the ECJ.

i) Accumulation independently of Community Law

This 'ousting' principle has been the subject of a number of the leading decisions on the scope of Community Law and has given rise to considerable debate.[1] In interpreting the overlapping provisions of the 1958 Regulation (the predecessor to that made in 1971) the ECJ drew inspiration from the wording of Article 51 of the Treaty of Rome (quoted on page 668) which the Regulation was designed to implement. That Article was concerned to *extend* the rights of migrant workers, not to reduce them.[2] The Regulation, in furtherance of this aim, contained principles whereby rights acquired under different legislative systems might be aggregated and co-ordinated. The overlapping rules were complementary to these aggregation and co-ordination principles but had no force independently of them. If, without recourse to the Regulation, an individual had acquired rights under the legislation of different states, these could not be overriden by the Regulation:[3] any other interpretation would conflict with Article 51 as reducing rather than extending the facilities of migrant workers.[4] Any limitation on the ability to accumulate had thus to be provided for in the national laws of the systems in question.[5]

---

18. Ibid., arts. 23(1), 58(1), 68(1). Mutatis mutandis the same applies to awards based on 'standard' earnings. For the UK calculations of earnings-related supplements see ibid., Annex V, Part I, para. 10, as inserted by Reg. 1392/74.
19. Reg. 1408/71, art. 68(1).
20. Ibid., art. 11.
1. See the authorities cited ante n.5 on p. 673.
2. *Moebs v Bestuur der Sociale Verzekeringsbank* [1964] CMLR 347; *Guissart v Belgian State* [1967] ECR 425, 433; *Niemann v Bundesversicherungsanstalt für Angestellte* [1974] ECR 571, 579.

3. *Ciechelski v Caisse Régionale de Sécurité Sociale Orleans du Centre* [1967] CMLR 192, 205; *Guissart* case, ante n.2, at p. 433; *Caisse d'Assurance Vieillesse des Travailleurs Salariés de Paris v Duffy* [1971] CMLR 391, 400; *Mancuso* case, ante n.13, at p. 1455.
4. *Duffy* case, ante n.3, at pp. 399–400; *Bestuur van de Nieuwe Algemene Bedrijfsvereniging v Kaufmann* [1974] ECR 517, 525; *Niemann* case ante n.2, at p. 578; *Caisse de Pensions des Employés Privés v Massonet* [1975] ECR 1473, 1481–1482.
5. *Guissart* case, ante n.2 at p. 434; *Mancuso* case, ante n.13, at p. 1456; *Massonet* case, ante n.4, at p. 1484.

The 1971 Regulation reformulated some of the rules and also introduced the provision in Article 13(1) that workers governed by the Regulation were to be subject to the legislation of a single member state only.[6] It
was at one time conjectured that the intention was to alter the position
resulting from the cases under the 1958 Regulation.[7] But, as has already
been suggested, the object of Article 13(1) was to avoid the overlapping of
liability under two systems rather than interfere with *rights*.[8] The ECJ has
now confirmed that the principle whereby a worker may accummulate
benefits independently of Community Law has not been abrogated by the
1971 Regulation. In *Petroni v Office National des Pensions Pour Travailleurs
Salariés*,[9]

> The Belgian Social Security institution, in calculating an old age
> pension payable to a worker who also had acquired title to benefit in
> Italy, sought to invoke an article of the 1971 Regulation[10] purporting
> to limit the maximum payable when a worker had been subject to
> the legislation of two or more member states in respect of the same
> risk. It was categorically held by the ECJ that to the extent that the
> article in question imposed a limitation on the accumulation of two
> benefits acquired in different member states by reference to the
> legislation of those member states, it was void as being inconsistent
> with the fundamental objective of Article 51 of the Treaty of Rome:
> the aim of Community Law was to extend the protection of social
> security systems to cover migrant workers, and unless there were
> compensating advantages for a worker under Community Law, it was
> not to be interpreted as limiting his rights.

It follows that the two other principles now to be discussed apply only
where a claimant invokes the Regulation for the purposes of benefiting
from the aggregation or deterritoriality principles.

ii) No overlap of short-term or family benefits
Article 12(1) of the 1971 Regulation provides that

> 'This Regulation can neither confer nor maintain the right to
> several benefits of the same kind for one and the same period of
> compulsory insurance. However, this provision shall not apply to
> benefits in respect of invalidity, old age, death (pensions) or
> occupational disease which are awarded by institutions of two or
> more Member States . . .'

If, then, as a result of the aggregation or deterritoriality provisions, a
claimant acquires title for the same period under more than one system for
a sickness, maternity, unemployment, industrial injury, family benefit, or
death grant, he can receive no more than is payable under any one such
system. The rule does not, however, apply to benefits payable under

6. Ante, p. 673.
7. Cf. *Tantaroudas*, 8 Rev. Trim. Dr.
   Eur. 56–57.
8. Ante, p. 673.

9. [1975] ECR 1149. See to the same
   effect, *Strehl v Nationaal Pensioenfonds
   voor Mijnwerkers* [1977] 2 CMLR 743.
10. Art. 46(3), post, p. 680.

voluntary schemes,[11] nor, of course, if the aggregation arises independently of the Regulation.

iii) Apportionment of long-term benefits

The Regulation contains detailed and complicated rules for apportioning the amount payable where entitlement to the long-term benefits is based on an aggregation of periods completed in different member states. These rules therefore apply to all old-age and survivors' pensions, but as regards invalidity benefit an important distinction is made. If a claimant to such a benefit has completed periods of insurance *exclusively* under legislation of member states all of which calculate the amount of benefit independently of the duration of such insurance periods[12] (as e.g., the present UK invalidity pension), there is no need of apportionment and the ordinary rule in Article 12(1) against overlap applies.[13] If, however, one or more of the legislations under which periods of insurance have been completed determine the amount according to the duration of such periods (as will be the case in Britain when the earnings component introduced by the 1975 Pensions Act comes into effect[14]), then the apportionment rules on old age pensions are applied by way of analogy.[15] These may be summarised as follows.

1. Each state in which the claimant has completed periods of insurance of at least twelve months must make two calculations of the pension payable.[16]

2. The first assessment is that payable under the legislation of that state without regard being had to periods completed in other member states.[17]

3. The second assessment is based on the theoretical amount that would have been payable if all periods (including those of less than twelve months)[18] completed in other member states had been completed in the member state making the calculation – often referred to as the 'highest theoretical amount'. This amount is then reduced according to the proportion of the periods completed in the individual state to the total of periods completed in all member states.[19] (E.g. C has completed 300

11. The meaning of 'voluntary', however, remains obscure, cf., Reg. 1408/71, art. 1(a).
12. The legislation referred to is listed in Annexe III of Reg. 1408/71.
13. Ibid., art. 37.
14. Ante, p. 224.
15. Reg. 1408/71, art. 40(1). Classification of invalidity benefit into these two categories is a question for the national law concerned, not for Community Law: *Dingemans v Sociale Verzekeringsbank* [1965] CMLR 144.
16. Reg. 1408/71, arts. 46(1) and 48(1).
17. Ibid.

18. Ibid., art. 48(2).
19. Ibid., art. 46(2). For examples of the calculation see: *Ciechelski* case, ante n.3; *Niemann* case, ante n.2; *Petroni* case, *supra* n.9; and *Plaquevent v Caisse Primarie d'Assurance Maladie du Havre* [1975] ECR 1581. If the total number of periods exceeds the maximum required by the legislation of one of the member states in question that state calculates the proportion according to such maximum rather than the total number of periods actually completed: Reg. 1408/71, art. 46(2)(c).

months in state X and 100 months in state Y. If state X pays a pension of £30 a week on 300 months' contributions and £40 on 400 months', the second assessment will be £40 (highest theoretical amount) multiplied by $\frac{3}{4} = £30$ a week.)

4. The claimant is entitled from each state to either (2) or (3) whichever is the higher.[20] But if and insofar as the total thereby acquired exceeds the highest theoretical amount, each state is to reduce the benefit payable on a proportionate basis.[1] (It was this rule which was the subject of the *Petroni* decision:[2] the highest theoretical amount can therefore be exceeded if the beneficiary is entitled under the respective legislations independently of the Regulation.)

5. The amount payable under (4) may, however, be exceeded where a claimant is permanently resident in a member state under whose legislation he is entitled to a pension. If that state would have granted a pension greater than (4) had all the periods of insurance aggregated under the Regulation been completed there, it must pay the claimant a supplement to raise the pension to that greater amount.[3]

D. Deterritoriality

The deterritoriality principle necessary for a proper co-ordination of the systems is that the right to benefit acquired under the legislation of one member state should continue notwithstanding any change either in the legal system applicable or in the transfer of residence or presence to another member state. For long-term benefits, the need to maintain links between the claimant, wherever he is residing or staying, with the state under whose legislation the benefit accrues is of less importance. The 1971 Regulation thus provides that:

> 'invalidity, old age or survivors' cash benefits, pensions for accidents at work or occupational diseases and death grants acquired under the legislation of one or more Member States shall not be subject to any reduction, modification, suspension, withdrawal or confiscation by reason of the fact that the recipient resides in a territory of a Member State other than that in which the institution responsible for payment is situated'.[4]

---

20. Ibid., art. 46(1).
1. Ibid., art. 46(3).
2. Ante n.10.

3. Reg. 1408/71, art. 50(1).
4. Ibid., art. 10(1).
5. *Re an Absence in Ireland* [1977] CMLR 5.

quoted above therefore does not apply; instead there are special rules for the various categories of benefit.

i) Sickness and maternity benefit

The availability of benefit in kind (medical services) is the reason for special provision here. Three situations are envisaged by the Regulation. In the first, the worker resides in a member state other than the competent state. If he satisfies the conditions of entitlement under the legislation of the latter, he is entitled to cash benefits and benefits in kind as provided by the state of residence.[6] The rule applies by analogy to benefits claimed by members of the worker's family in the member state where they are permanently resident.[7] The second situation is that in which workers and/or members of their family, while resident in another member state, return to the competent state for a visit. The obvious solution applies that they receive the benefit (cash or kind) from the competent state as if they were resident there, but it is rather surprisingly provided that this holds true even if they had already received benefit for the same sickness or maternity before their stay.[8] The third and final situation is that in which the claimant (or a member of his family) is resident in the competent state but visits another member state. To claim the benefits from the latter state he must show that he satisfied the conditions of entitlement under the legislation of the competent state and

> *either* (1) his condition necessitated immediate benefits during the stay in the other state, *or* (2) he was authorised by the competent state to transfer his residence to the other state,[9] *or* (3) he was authorised by the competent state to go to the territory of the other state to receive there treatment appropriate for his condition.[10]

Where, under these rules, cash benefits are payable under the legislation of the state of residence or presence, the rate and conditions for receipt (e.g., medical certification and examination) are governed by that legislation.[11] As regards benefits in kind, their cost is reimbursed by the institution of the competent state.[12]

ii) Industrial injury benefits

As applied to the industrial injury benefits, the deterritoriality principle has two dimensions:[13] on the one hand, it enables benefit to be paid for accidents happening, or industrial diseases incurred, during work in a

6. Reg. 1408/71, art. 19(1).
7. Ibid., art. 19(2).
8. Ibid., art. 21.
9. The authorisation can be refused only if such a movement would be prejudicial to the claimant's state of health or his receipt of medical treatment: ibid., art. 22(2).
10. Ibid., art. 22(1). The authorisation cannot be refused if the benefit in question cannot be provided in the

territory of the competent State: ibid. The condition appears to be, for practical purposes, the same as that applied generally under the British legislation (ante, p. 411): see *Re a Visit to Holland* [1977] 1 CMLR 502.
11. Reg. 1408/71. art. 19(1)(b).
12. Ibid., art. 36.
13. See *Re a Visit to Italy* [1976] 1 CMLR 506 (*R(I) 1/76*).

member state other than the competent member state;[14] on the other hand, in whichever member state the accident took place or disease was incurred, it provides for the receipt of benefit in kind or money in states other than the competent member state.[15] For this latter purpose, the rules described above for sickness and maternity apply.[16]

iii) Unemployment

The special considerations of unemployment requiring separate treatment are the problem of controlling the claimant's genuine availability for work, and the sometimes conflicting objective of encouraging him to transfer his search for employment to another member state where more vacancies exist.[17] The first is responsible for what at first sight may seem to be a serious limitation of the deterritoriality principle: an unemployed person must normally have been last employed (or insured) in the state under whose legislation he claims benefit.[18] There are, however, two exceptions to assist those seeking work in another member state.

1. A worker returning to the member state in which he resides, and who registers with the employment services there, may receive benefit as if he had last been employed there.[19]

2. A worker who satisfies the conditions for entitlement to benefit in one member state and who travels to another member state to seek employment there may be paid benefit in the second state if (A) he had been registered with the employment services of the first state for at least four weeks prior to his departure and (B) he registers with the equivalent services of the second state and subjects himself to the control procedures there.[20] Under this arrangement benefit is payable by the second state only for a maximum of three months (or less if the maximum period of entitlement under the legislation of the first state is exceeded).[1]

The limitations on the right to benefit in other member states do not affect a worker whose entitlement arises independently of the Regulation[2] –

---

14. Reg. 1408/71, arts. 52, 57. See, e.g., *Gemeenschappelijke Verzekeringskas 'De Sociale Voorzorg' v Bertholet* [1966] CMLR 191, and *Manpower SARL, Strasbourg Regional Office v Caisse Primaire d'Assurance Maladie de Strasbourg* [1971] CMLR 222. Some industrial injury schemes cover journeys to work, others do not. In order that the position taken in the competent legislation should prevail, it is provided that 'an accident while travelling which occurs in the territory of a Member State other than the competent State shall be deemed to have occurred in the territory of the competent State': Reg. 1408/71, art. 56.

15. Ibid., arts. 52, 54 and 55.
16. Ante, p. 681.
17. Collins *The European Communities* (1975), vol. 2, pp. 63–77.
18. Reg. 1408/71, art. 67(3).
19. Reg. 1408/71, art. 71(b)(ii), on which see *Di Paolo v Office National de l'Emploi* [1977] ECR 315. There is also an exception for frontier workers: Reg. 1408/71, art. 71(a)(ii).
20. Ibid., art. 69(I).
1. Ibid., art. 69(1)(c). The cost of benefit is reimbursed by the state where the worker was last insured: ibid., art. 70(1).
2. *Bonaffini v Istitutio Nazionale della Previdenza Sociale* [1975] ECR 971.

another example of the principle, developed by the ECJ, allowing accumulation of rights not derived from Community legislation.[3]

iv) Family benefits

The Regulation distinguishes between 'family allowances', i.e., periodical cash payments determined exclusively by reference to the number and age of the members of the family (e.g., the British child benefit); and 'family benefits' i.e., benefits in cash or kind, including 'family allowances', intended to meet 'family expenses' (other than childbirth) and coming within the scope of the Regulation.[4] If the competent state for the worker's claim is not France, he is entitled to claim family benefits for members of his family[5] residing in another member state as if they were residing in the competent state.[6] If the competent state is France, for members of his family residing in another member state the worker is entitled to such allowances as are provided for by the legislation of such state.[7] The reason for this special provision for France is the peculiarly high level of family support prevailing there.[8] Benefits are payable by the appropriate institution of the competent member state normally to the worker himself, but if it is established that the benefit is not being applied for the members of the family there is power to pay it instead to another person actually maintaining the members of the family, and if that person (and the family) is resident abroad, this will be expedited by the social security institution in that country.[9]

3. Ante, p. 677.
4. Reg. 1408/71, art. 1(u).
5. For the meaning of 'members of family' see ante n.7 on p. 671.
6. Reg. 1408/71, art. 73(1). See, e.g., *Re Family Allowances for Irish Children* [1976] 1 CMLR 515.

7. Reg. 1408/71, art. 73(2).
8. Cf. *Dupeyroux*, chap. 4, and Rodgers, Greve and Morgan *Comparative Social Administration* (1971), pp. 314–318.
9. Reg. 1408/71, art. 75(1).

Appendix

CHAPTER 2. CONTRIBUTIONS

p. 58 *Class 1 Contributions*: *Amount* Since 6 April 1978 employed earners over pensionable age have not been liable to contribute (see p. 57). To avoid undue discrimination, new Regulations (S.I. 1978/410) have prescribed a special annual maximum of Class 1 contributions (on employment not contracted-out) for earners reaching pensionable age in the year ending 5 April 1979. It is $\frac{23}{26}$ of the liability which would otherwise be imposed.

p. 66 *Married Women and Widows.* For the definition of 'precluded from regular employment by responsibilities at home', see the Regulation summarised under chap. 5, post.

p. 70 *Earnings Factors.* A revised version of the technical rules for calculating earnings factors from Class 1 contributions has been issued (S.I. 1977/1706).

p. 75 *Credits*: *Termination of Marriage.* The facility of crediting a widow with Class 3 contributions (described in para. 3) will not be available for any contribution year after that ending on 5 April 1978 (S.I. 1977/1484).

CHAPTER 3. UNEMPLOYMENT BENEFIT

p. 107 *Students and the Condition of Availability.* Contemporaneously with the announcement of new rules governing the entitlement of students to supplementary benefit during the short Christmas and Easter vacations (ante, p. 555), the Department sought to introduce regulations excluding for such periods also entitlement to unemployment benefit. The new system of starting credits (ante, p. 73) would greatly increase the number of those eligible who had never been wholly in the employment field, and it argued that (i) it was not realistic to regard students as 'genuinely in the field of employment during the short vacation' and (ii) it was wrong to pay unemployment benefit on top of the vacation support grant for students (which has recently been increased). The National Insurance Advisory Comittee in its Report on the Draft Regulations (Cmnd. 6976) recommended that they should not be made. A majority was not prepared to see undermined the general principle of national insurance in this way and did not feel it incumbent on them to pronounce on the adequacy of the grant system. The difficulty of differentiating between those who were genuinely available for work and those who were not was conceded, but it was felt that the proposed regulations were too blunt an instrument to achieve that objective.

pp. 132–136   *Seasonal Workers.* The report of the National Insurance Advisory Committee on the eligibility conditions for seasonal workers (ante, p. 132) has been published (Cmnd. 6991). The Committee, with one dissentient, found that there was a continued need for special conditions as the 'availability' test could not be effectively applied during a seasonal worker's off-season. It was conceded that the current Regulations were cumbersome, might sometimes operate harshly, were difficult to operate, and might have a disincentive effect, but it was doubtful whether a more satisfactory way of dealing with the problem of seasonal workers could be found. The recommendations were therefore confined to advocating minor improvements to the detailed rules. These were as follows. First, the definition of seasonal worker (ante, p. 133) should be amended to include only those following an occupation which was itself fundamentally seasonal in character in the particular locality. Secondly, the 'seven-weeks' rule (ante, p. 133) should be extended to thirteen weeks. Thirdly, the registration condition (ante. p. 135) should be abolished.

CHAPTER 4. BENEFITS FOR SICKNESS AND DISABILITY

pp. 137–145   *General.* The Report of the Royal Commission on Civil Liability and Compensation for Personal Injury (The Pearson Commission) (Cmnd. 7054) contains matters of interest on provision for the disabled generally, quite independently of its specific proposals on handicapped children, industrial injury and the overlap of social security and the common law (post). Notwithstanding that the Commission construed its terms of reference as precluding consideration of all forms of accident and sickness (thus inhibiting comprehensive proposals which would include, e.g. sickness and home accidents), it did affirm the primacy of social security in the compensation of personal injury, with tort law playing only a subordinate role (see e.g., para. 1732). Secondly, while impeded from any general review of social security provision, it did allow itself to reflect both on the undue complexity of that provision (though *quaere* whether its own proposals would not substantially exacerbate that problem) and on the need to spend more on serious, as opposed to minor, injuries (paras. 264–267). It also found anomalies in the relationship between benefits and taxation, and recommended that the government rationalise the arrangements (para. 267). Our criticism (ante, p. 145) on the lack of compensation for the partially disabled finds some echo in the Report (paras.

814–821). The Commission did not make specific proposals but urged the government to study European systems for compensating partial incapacity for work.

Arguably the most important proposal is the suggested creation of a new area of social security provisions, viz. for victims of road accidents (chap. 18). This would confer benefits similar to those available under the industrial injury scheme, which themselves would be significantly improved (post). It would be administered by the DHSS but would be financed by a levy on petrol. Special provision would be made for children and non-earners (e.g. housewives and retirement pensioners).

p. 144 *Children.* Exceptionally, the Pearson Commission deliberately exceeded its terms of reference in order to suggest a major improvement in the financial provision for disabled children (chap. 27). It recommended the introduction of a new non-taxable allowance of £4 per week for all 'severely handicapped children' payable from the age of two as an addition to the child benefit, and financed by the Exchequer.

pp. 155–6 *Deemed Incapable.* The grounds on which a claimant should be certified under Regulation 3(1)(a)(ii) have been made more explicit. An amending Regulation (S.I. 1978/394) requires the doctor to certify that 'for precautionary or convalescent reasons consequential on such a disease or disablement he should abstain from work'.

p. 168 *Entitlement to Non-contributory Invalidity Pension.* In *R v National Insurance Comr., ex parte Fleetwood* (1978) 122 Sol. Jo. 146, the Divisional Court quashed a decision of the Commissioner (to be reported as *R(S) 3/78*), holding ultra vires Regulation 4(2), which discounts as days of incapacity for the purposes of the '196 consecutive days' test days when the claimant was absent from Great Britain (see p. 168, n. 4). Kenneth Jones J, with the concurrence of the other members of the Court, did not agree with the Commissioner that the power granted under SSA 1975, s. 36(7) to prescribe 'circumstances in which a person is or is not to be treated . . . as "incapable of work"' was confined to the process of defining that term. In any event, he felt that the Regulation could quite properly be made under the wider power conferred under section 131, which deals with persons absent from Great Britain. Finally, he rejected the 'extreme submission' that the Regulation was 'so capricious in its effect that it must be unreasonable'. In the case in question, the claimant had been absent in a warm climate for the purpose of trying a breathing jacket as a possible substitute for the iron lung on which he was dependent. Following the decision, the Department is reviewing the possibility of extending to the NCIP the disregard of temporary absences which currently applies to the contributory sickness and invalidity benefits (see pp. 410–412).

pp. 172–176 *Attendance Allowance: degree of disability.* Difficulties have been caused by the application of the criteria to patients dependent on kidney machines. A private member has been given leave to introduce a Bill to confer greater discretion on the determining authorities to cover such cases (944 HC Deb., cols. 446–449).

p. 185   *Mobility Allowance*: *inability to walk.* In a case which received some considerable publicity, the Chief Commissioner held that a medical appeal tribunal had not erred in law in granting the allowance to a mongol child (*R*(*M*) 2/78). The tribunal had attributed the virtual inability to walk to a 'reaction' which was directly due to his physical condition, rather than resulting from a mental disability independently of that condition. The Chief Commissioner did not purport to lay down a general principle to govern these cases: the weight to be attached to physical and mental disablement in cases where both factors may be present he held to be for the medical authorities to decide.

pp. 186–187   *Mobility Allowance*: *age.* The government has announced its plans to extend the age limits: from 6 September 1978 it will be payable to those born on or after 14 January 1921, and from 20 December 1978 to those born on or after 21 December 1919 (Written Answer, 944 HC Deb., col. 729).

Meanwhile, a private member was given leave to introduce a Bill making the allowance payable to those over pensionable age (945 HC Deb., cols. 1230–1234) and the Pearson Commission has recommended that entitlement should be extended to children aged two or more, and that the conditions of eligibility should be reviewed so as to help those children who are technically mobile but whose mobility is subject to special difficulties (paras. 1533–1534).

CHAPTER 5. RETIREMENT PENSIONS

p. 212   *Contributions*: *Home Responsibilities Regulation.* The Regulation (S.I. 1978/508, Reg. 2) has been issued, defining the circumstances in which a person will be treated as 'precluded from regular employment by responsibilities at home' for the purposes of the contribution conditions. A person will be so treated if throughout any year after April 1978:

(a) he receives child benefit for any child under sixteen, or
(b) he is regularly engaged for at least thirty-five hours a week in caring for a person in receipt of the attendance allowance, or a constant attendance allowance in either the war pensions or the industrial injuries scheme; or
(c) he is in receipt of supplementary benefit under the SBA 1976, the Supplementary Benefits Commission having waived, on the ground that he is caring for an elderly or incapacitated person, the condition that he register for employment.

CHAPTER 6. BENEFITS ON DEATH

pp. 230–232   *Widow's Benefit – General.* Though the matter did not come within its terms of reference the Pearson Commission (see note to chap. 4) has advocated the more equal treatment of women widowed by industrial and non-industrial causes respectively. It suggested, as a first step, that the government should consider removing the contribution conditions for the flat-rate benefit under the non-industrial scheme (para. 844).

CHAPTER 8. INDUSTRIAL INJURIES

pp. 264-265 *Industrial Preference.* The Report of the Pearson Commission (see generally under chap. 4) is curiously Janus-like in its attitude to the industrial preference. On the one hand, it could find no reason for endorsing the argument which Beveridge had deployed for favouring those whose injuries were work-caused ('it seemed to us that his arguments carry a good deal less weight now' – para. 290). On the other hand, the effect of its proposals if implemented would be clearly to boost by a significant degree the differentials which, since 1946, inflation has been allowed to erode. The key to understanding this apparent contradiction (which is not rendered less anomalous by the proposal to extend the preference to victims of road accidents) may be found in political considerations. The Commission presumably did not wish to render its proposals unattractive to the trade union movement. This is hinted at in para. 284 where the Commission observes that elimination of the overlap between common law and social security 'without anything to balance it, would have implied a drop in entitlement for those injured through the fault of their employer'.

pp. 267-268 *Risk-Related Finance.* Subject to a powerful dissent from Prest, (paras. 940–948), the Pearson Commission has recommended that the industrial injuries scheme should continue to be financed as at present, except that the increased cost resulting from the improved benefits should be borne by the employers' contributions only. It felt that risk-relating contributions for each employer would involve substantial administrative costs which would outweigh any benefits in terms of increased safety. An argument to relate contributions according to the *industry* concerned was rejected on similar grounds (paras. 898–904).

pp. 296-270 *Overlap.* If implemented, the proposals of the Pearson Commission would considerably reduce the anomaly referred to. Its recommendations are mentioned under chap. 10, post.

pp. 270-272 *Persons Covered.* The Pearson Commission (paras. 851–857) has proposed that the industrial scheme should be extended to cover the self-employed, notwithstanding the difficulties that would be created in applying the 'out of and in the course of employment' test. However, because of the anomalies which would be created in other parts of the social security system if benefits for this group were earnings-related, it recommended that 'for the time being' benefits should be flat-rate.

pp. 272-276 *Requirement of 'accident'.* The Pearson Commission (paras. 880–887) has now urged on the government the adoption of the mixed system of compensating occupational diseases as incorporated in the EEC Recommendation of 1962 (see p. 276).

pp. 276–293   *Employment Risks.* The claim to benefit of an employee forced to leave his employer's premises during a bomb scare and injured before he regained access to them was rejected by R. S. Lazarus, Commissioner, in *R(I) 6/76*. The facts were regarded as analogous to 'lunch-hour' accidents off the premises (cf., p. 285) and at the time the claimant was not fulfilling any purposes of the employment. The Pearson Commission (paras. 893–897) remained unconvinced by the arguments of the TUC that the 'out of and in the course of employment' definition should be extended. However, by a majority of one, it recommended that injuries occurring on the way to and from work (see pp. 283–284) should be covered by the scheme (paras. 858–868).

pp. 293–297   *Industrial Diseases.* The Pearson Commission has recommended adoption of the EEC mixed system allowing for proof of causal connection between disease and employment in individual cases, where not covered by the prescribed list (paras. 880–887). In accordance with another EEC Recommendation (20 July 1966) it also proposed that the special restrictive conditions on occupational deafness and byssinosis (see p. 297) should be removed (paras. 867–874). Finally it expressed concern about the time taken under the current procedure for scheduling diseases and has urged the government to examine the case for a speedier procedure (paras. 869–876).

p. 302   *Injury Benefit: amount payable.* The Pearson Commission was of the opinion that the calculation of the earnings-related element in the short-term injury and long-term disablement benefits should gradually be brought into line (paras. 806–808). As a first step, it therefore recommended that in the former case the proportion of earnings to be paid between £30 and the upper limit should be increased from 15% to 25% (see pp. 425–426, for the current method of calculation). It also proposed (para. 809) that the supplement be paid to all those receiving injury benefit, and not merely those who satisfy the contribution conditions for sickness or maternity benefit (see p. 425).

pp. 303–317   *Disablement benefit.* The form and method of assessing the basic element in the disablement benefit (pension or gratuity) were approved by the Pearson Commission (paras. 822–823). However, for those rendered totally incapable of work, it was thought that some more overt form of earnings-related compensation should be payable (paras. 800–805). An appropriate model was to be found in the earnings-related invalidity pension which forms a part of the new pensions programme (ante, pp. 165–166). Of course, under that scheme, maximum benefits will not be payable until 1998 and the Commission thus proposes that for those injured at work the provisions be accelerated so that claimants be treated as if they had been in the scheme for twenty years. It is recognised that if account is also taken of dependants' and other increases, the amount payable would be substantially higher than at present, and there might be problems of work incentives (paras. 825–826).

pp. 318–332 *Special hardship allowance. In R v National Insurance Commissioners, ex parte Steel,* (*The Times,* 17 February 1978), the Divisional Court upheld a decision of a Tribunal of Commissioners (*R(I)* 4/76) that there was nothing to prevent post-accident work under approved dust-free conditions in the claimant's regular occupation from being regarded as employment 'of an equivalent standard' (see p. 323).

In *R(I)* 4/77, H. G. Shewan, Commissioner, held that it was wrong to use for the purposes of the comparisons under both section 60(1) and section 60(6) (see pp. 324 and 329) the claimant's hypothetical ability to earn in sheltered employment. This was not indicative of her potential earning capacity in the open market (though for the purposes of *quantification* under section 60(6) the case might have been different if the claimant had actually been working there).

As was mentioned in the note to chap. 4, the Pearson Commission recommended the government to study European experience in the compensation of those rendered only partially incapable of work. In this connection, it recognised the unsatisfactory nature of the current method of assessing special hardship allowance for members of this group within the industrial injury scheme (paras. 810–821). The DHSS had itself submitted a critical account of the problems encountered with the allowance (helpfully republished in Annex 6 to the Report). Pending the recommended study, the Commission felt itself unable to offer any specific alternative.

pp. 333–335 *Constant attendance and exceptionally severe disablement allowances.* The Pearson Commission considered that the case for distinguishing between industrial and non-industrial cases was less strong at these extremes of disablement. It therefore recommended that the CAA and ESDA should eventually be abolished, leaving those within that category to rely on non-industrial attendance allowance (ante, pp 171–178). However, rather than withdrawing them immediately it suggested that the government continue to pay the increases both to existing beneficaries and for new work injuries, but that with payment to be frozen at present rates, so that the differential will eventually be eroded (paras. 827–834).

pp. 344–345 *Death benefit – widows.* The Pearson Commission was also unconvinced of the need to maintain differentials between industrial and non-industrial widows (paras. 835–842). It recommended that the long-term benefits should be payable at the same rates and under the same conditions as the non-industrial benefits (see pp. 234–237), except that the earnings-related component under the new pensions scheme (ante, p. 237) should, as with personal benefit, be calculated as if the former husband had been contributing for twenty years. As regards the short-term benefit, the earnings-related supplement should fall in line with that proposed for industrial injury benefit (ante).

p. 346 *Widowers.* Conversely, the Pearson Commission felt that the different treatment of widowers by the industrial and non-industrial schemes should be taken further (paras. 845–847). It proposed that industrial widowers should be treated, for benefit purposes, as if they were widows.

pp. 347–349 *Parents and other relatives.* The almost token quality of
the compensation payable to this group has been recognised by the
Pearson Commission (paras. 849–850). Persons covered are often the
subject of other forms of social security provision, and the abolition of
these forms of industrial death benefit has therefore been recommended.

CHAPTER 9. WAR PENSIONS

pp. 374 *Allowance for lowered standard of occupation.* A new Regulation (S.I. 1978/278, Reg. 4) provides in effect that the allowance may be
awarded to a member of the forces who had no 'regular occupation'
before his period of service. In this respect the allowance might be
awarded in circumstances not covered by the comparable 'special hardship allowance' in the industrial injuries scheme (ante, pp. 319–321).

pp. 380–1 *Commencing date of awards.* These dates have been altered
by S.I. 1978/278, Reg. 7, substituting a new Article 65 in the Royal
Warrant 1964. A pension may (from April 1978) be awarded from a)
the day after the termination of service where this was due to invaliding
and the claim was brought within six months of that event, *or* b) the
day after the end of service if the claim was brought within three
months, *or* c) the date of the claim.

In a widely publicised report (4th Report of the PCA for 1977–78,
HC 312), the Parliamentary Commissioner has criticised the DHSS for
its reluctance to pay arrears of war pensions to a number of ex-officers,
unless these back payments were specifically requested.

CHAPTER 10. GENERAL PROVISION

p. 418 *Hospital In-patients.* The adjustement to increases for dependants has been modified (S.I. 1977/1693). If the *beneficiary* has been an
in-patient for a period of fifty-two weeks, the increase is payable either
to the dependant (if an adult) or to someone undertaking to apply it for
the benefit of the dependant or child of the beneficiary.

pp. 422–424 *Imprisonment and detention in legal custody.* In *Kenny v
Insurance Officer* [1978] 1 CMLR 181, J. G. Monroe, Commissioner,
expressed the view that the disqualification should be construed as
applying only to imprisonment or detention within Great Britain. He
referred to the European Court of Justice the question whether under
EEC law the British authorities were entitled to treat imprisonment in
another member state as if it had occurred in Great Britain.

pp. 433–436 *Up-rating.* The decision of Megarry VC in *Metzger v
Department of Health and Social Security* has been upheld by the Court
of Appeal (10 February 1978 – copy of transcript received by courtesy
of DHSS). Giving the judgment of the court, Stamp LJ agreed with
the Vice-Chancellor that the Secretary of State's duty to review (SSA

1975, s.125) did not extend to the end of the period of the last review (see p. 435). The Court of Appeal appears to have expressed no opinion on Megarry VC's obiter dictum (ibid.) that a revision of benefit rates should be intended to restore the value when the order comes into effect (rather than some earlier date), but it did expressly reject the plaintiff's contention that the up-rating duty includes an obligation to make good any underestimates of rises in earnings and prices reflected in orders of previous years.

pp. 437-433 *Overlapping benefits.* The Overlapping Benefits Regulations have been amended to take account of benefits payable under the Social Security Pensions Act 1975 (S.I. 1978/524). The principal features of the new provisions are as follows.

1. The earnings-based 'additional component' in a retirement, invalidity or widow's pension as well as a graduated retirement benefit will be treated, for the purposes of the rules, as part of the principal benefit which they supplement (cf. ante p. 438).
2. A widow is entitled to accumulate an invalidity pension with her pension or widowed mother's allowance, but not so as to exceed the maxima prescribed under the Pensions Act for the basic and additional components respectively (cf. ante, p. 224).
3. An adjustment to the personal income-replacement benefits (listed on p. 437) is not required on receipt of the additional component in a retirement pension or a graduated retirement benefit.

As regards overlap with common law actions (p. 443), the Pearson Commission (see note to chap. 4) had much to contribute. One of the major features of the Report is the desire to achieve a much closer co-ordination of the common law action and social security provisions (see, especially, paras. 277–280 and 467–476). The Commission's recommendations include not only the general principle (paras. 481–482) that the full value of social security benefits payable to an injured person or his dependants should be deducted in the assessment of damages, but also detailed proposals on how this should be achieved (paras. 484–496).

CHAPTER 11. CHILD BENEFIT

p. 465 *Residence qualifications.* A report published by the Joint Council for the Welfare of Immigrants and the Child Poverty Action Group ('Divide and Deprive' by John Plummer) has urged the government to extend child benefit to parents with children overseas; the gradual withdrawal of income tax allowances (ante, p. 449) from such parents, who at the moment are not entitled to child benefit, might lead to hardship for many immigrants.

CHAPTER 12. SUPPLEMENTARY BENEFITS

p. 481 *Resources insufficient to meet requirements.* The exclusion of 'medical . . . requirements' for supplementary benefits purposes was in issue in *R v West London Supplementary Benefits Appeal Tribunal, ex parte Wyatt* [1978] 1 RWL 240. The claimant applied for benefit to assist him meet the running costs of electrical equipment provided for his wife who suffered from multiple sclerosis. The Divisional Court ruled that the Commission was wrong simply to refuse to pay benefit on the ground that the claim was for 'medical requirements'; it should look at each item of equipment separately and take into account its purpose, and by whom it had been provided, before deciding whether or not to grant benefit.

In an interesting passage, May J giving the court's judgement, added that the claimant's requirements might alternatively be met by an exercise of the SBC's discretionary power to make payments in 'exceptional circumstances', (ante, pp. 511–519), and that this discretion was not limited by the terms of section 1(3) of the Act. The implication of these remarks could be wide: might it be argued, for example, that the Commission's discretionary powers under paragraph 4 of Schedule 1 could also be exercised to make payments to a person in full-time work or otherwise disqualified from receiving benefit?

pp. 541–543   *The liable relative's contribution.* The different approaches of the courts and the SBC to the assessment of maintenance contributions have been considered in two recent cases. In *Smethurst v Smethurst* [1977] 3 RWL 472, Sir George Baker, President of the Family Division, implied that the courts might adopt the Commission's guidelines when they determine how much maintenance a husband (or former husband) should pay. But this suggestion was firmly repudiated by the Court of Appeal in *Swallow v Swallow* [1978] 3 RWL 583. Ormrod LJ pointed out that application of the Commission's formula would leave the former husband with an income considerably above subsistence level, while the wife and children would have to resort to supplementary benefit. The courts will, it seems, adhere generally to their one-third rule in maintenance cases, but Ormrod LJ admitted that the SBC formula might be an acceptable alternative guideline in low income cases.

CHAPTER 14. ADMINISTRATION OF BENEFITS

pp. 596–8   *Time-Limits for dependants' increases.* A new Regulation (S.I. 1978/433, Reg. 4(3)) has changed the time-limit for claiming a dependant's increase to any short-term benefit and to the unemployability supplement under the industrial injuries scheme: after April 1978 the increase must be claimed within the period of one month (or three months in the case of the unemployability supplement) from the day for which the increase is claimed. The previous alternative time-limit, that the claim must be brought within one month of the day when the relevant main benefit was claimed, was found difficult to apply (see NIAC Report, 1977–78 HC 314) and has been revoked.

p. 608   *Payment of unemployment benefit.* After the favourable report of a Department of Employment committee on the local experiments in 1977, the government is contemplating the introduction of fortnightly payments of unemployment benefit throughout the country (Written Answer 945 HC Deb., cols. 294–295).

pp. 649–659 *Supplementary Benefit Appeal Tribunals.* An independent advisory group has produced a guide to the procedure of these tribunals, primarily for the benefit of tribunal chairmen and members. In addition to setting out the procedural requirements imposed by the legislation and regulations, it explains the responsibilities and powers of the tribunals in the light of relevant court decisions and the guidance offered by the Council on Tribunals. If the advice contained in the booklet (HMSO, 1977), is generally followed, most of the complaints made against SBATs should be satisfied. The following are among the more important points made in the report.

  (i) The participation of the other members is to be encouraged (paras. 42, 53 and 65: see ante, pp. 651–2).
 (ii) The clerk is a servant of the tribunal, and it is not his duty to act as spokesman for the DHSS or SBC (paras. 7 and 28). In particular, he is not to volunteer advice concerning Commission policy (para. 66: see ante, p. 652).
(iii) Where a party has given reasonable explanation for his inability to attend the hearing, it is right to adjourn. Where no explanation has been given, it will usually be right to proceed, unless there are questions of fact which cannot easily be decided in his absence (para. 38: see ante, p. 655).
 (iv) Caution should be exercised in accepting hearsay evidence; relevant documents should be made available to all parties before the hearing (paras. 55–59: see ante, p. 655).
  (v) The tribunal is not bound by SBC policy (para. 16: see ante, p. 656). But it should confine its decision to the issue raised by the appeal – if the tribunal thinks that another asspect of the case requires consideration, it should refer it to the SBC (para. 17; compare the opposite view tentatively expressed, ante, p. 656).
 (vi) The chairman of the tribunal must ensure that a full finding of the facts is recorded and adequate reasons given for the decision (paras. 69–73: see ante, pp. 656–657).

pp. 663–5 *Reference to the European Court of Justice.* The National Insurance Commissioner, J. G. Monroe, has recently rejected the argument – based on the decision of the Employment Appeal Tribunal in *Snoxell v Vauxhall Motors Ltd* [1978] QB 11 – that he has no jurisdiction to decide questions of EEC law, or by implication refer a question to the European Court. In *Re Medical Expenses incurred in France* [1977] 2 CMLR 317, he ruled that section 2(1) of the European Communities Act 1972 gives direct effect to the EEC Social Security Regulation (ante, pp. 670–683) and therefore the statutory authorities must implement it insofar as it affects title to the social security benefits over which they have jurisdiction.

CHAPTER 16. INTERNATIONAL AND EUROPEAN LAW

pp. 671–672 *Persons.* In *Re Medical Expenses incurred in France* [1977] 2 CMLR 317 (*CS 2/77*), J. G. Monroe, Commissioner, held that it was not necessary, under the principle of *Brack v Insurance Officer* (p. 672), for the contributions as an employed person, which are regarded as indicative of his status as a 'worker', to have covered the contingency in respect of which his claim is made. It was sufficient if 'it can be shown that at the time he was insured against *any* contingency . . . in respect of which the contributions paid by him as an employed person affected the rate of benefit payable'. In the instant case, his claim was for sickness benefit but his employed earner's contributions were relevant only to a retirement pension. A parallel decision of the Parliamentary Commissioner for Administration (reported also at [1977] 2 CMLR 317), arising from the same case, indicates that the Department applies the same principle for the reimbursement of medical expenses incurred in other member states.

p. 675 *Non-discrimination.* In *Kenny v Insurance Officer* [1978] 1 CMLR 181 the Commissioner, J. G. Monroe, referred to the ECJ the question whether, as a result of the Regulation, the British authorities were entitled to treat imprisonment in another member state as if it had occurred in Great Britain, for the purposes of disqualification from benefit (see also note to chap. 10 ante).

p. 676 *Aggregation of Periods of Insurance.* the insurance officer applied to the Divisional Court for an order of certiorari to quash the decision in *Re Invalidity Benefit in Germany*. The Divisional Court referred the question to the European Court. The latter in its decision, reported *sub nom. Rv National Insurance Comr., ex parte Warry* [1977] 2 CMLR 783, confirmed the Commissioner's view (reported on p. 676) that since the 1971 Regulation had the effect of treating the insurance periods completed in Germany as though completed under the British legislation, those periods must be taken into account for entitlement to sickness benefit, insofar as that was necessary to ground entitlement to the invalidity benefit. This interpretation has now been confirmed by an amendment to the 1971 Regulation which provides that where the legislation of one member state makes entitlement to invalidity benefit dependent on previous entitlement to sickness benefit, that state may treat receipt of invalidity benefit in another member state as a period during which sickness benefit was received under its own law: Regulation 2595/77, OJ 1977, L302/1.

p. 682 *Unemployment.* The exception referred to in para. 2 does not cover a person entitled to benefit in the first member state only by virtue of an agreement between that state and a non-member state: *Re Unemployment Benefit in France* [1977] 2 CMLR 451 – Report of the Parliamentary Commissioner for Administration, criticising the DHSS for having given incorrect advice on the point.

Index

Absence,
  Great Britain, from, meaning, 413,
    414
Accident,
  causal link between injury and, 275
  conduct at time of, 337
    post-accident, 338
  meaning, 273–275
  successive accidents, disablement
    resulting from, 336, 337
Administration of benefits,
  Attendance Allowance Board, 585
  Central Advisory Committee on
    War Pensions, 585, 586
  claims, 587 et seq.
  Department of Health and Social
    Security, 571–576
  Industrial Injuries Advisory
    Council, 583–585
  Local Social Security Committees,
    586, 587
  National Insurance Advisory
    Committee, 580–583
  payments, 606 et seq.
  Supplementary Benefits
    Commission, 576–579
  War Pensions Committees, 586
Advisory bodies,
  generally, 579 et seq.
Aggregation,
  supplementary benefits, of, for
    families, 485 et seq.
Airman,
  contributions by, 69
  treatment as employed worker, 271
Adopted child,
  guardian's allowance for, 262
Apprentice,
  employed earner, treated as, 271
Armed forces,
  contributions by, 68
  unemployment benefit, whether
    claimable by member of, 131

Attendance allowance,
  claim for, generally, 599
  constant attention, allowance for,
    333–335
  degree of disability—
    attention and supervision, 174–
      176
    criteria to be applied, 173, 687
    nature of tests, 173
    night and day, 173, 174
    severely disabled, 173
  exclusions, 177, 178
  generally, 171, 172
  payment of, 607 et seq.
  period, 176
  residence, 176, 177
  time-limit for claiming, 599
Attendance Allowance Board,
  appeal from, 641, 642
  constitution and function, 585
  criticism of, 642
  generally, 641
Availability,
  work, for—
    adverse industrial conditions, 107
    generally, 104
    physical condition of applicant,
      107
    reasonable restrictions test, 106–
      108
    reasonableness, 108
    stated terms of, prospects of
      employment on, 105
    statutory test, 105–108
    willingness and ability to accept,
      105, 106

Bedding,
  exceptional needs payment, 524
Benefits,
  administration of, generally, 571 et
    seq.

Industrial diseases,
  byssinosis, 297
  causal link between occupation
    and disease, 296, 297
  claimant's occupation, disease
    prescribed for, 295, 296
  deafness, 297
  generally, 293–295, 690
  pneumoconiosis, 297
  proof of prescribed disease, 295
  recrudescence and fresh attacks,
    297
  "schedule approach", 294
  suffering from prescribed disease,
    295
  tuberculosis, 296
Industrial injury,
  accident—
    causal link between injury and,
      275
    meaning, 273–275
    personal injury must be caused
      by, 272, 273
    requirement of, generally, 275,
      276, 689
  Advisory Council, constitution and
    functions, 583–585
  characteristics of, 264
  conduct of claimant—
    at time of accident, 337
    post-accident, 338
  constant attendance allowance, 333–
    335, 691
  death—
    children, claims on behalf of, 346,
      347
    generally, 341, 342
    instantaneous, 342, 343
    non-instantaneous, 343, 344
    parents, claims on behalf of, 347–
      349
    relatives, claims on behalf of,
      347–349
    widow's benefits—
      entitlement, 344, 345, 691
      form and duration, 345
    widower's benefit, 346
    women having care of children,
      claims on behalf of, 349
  disablement benefit—
    amount, 316, 317
    assessment of disablement—
      extraneous causes, disability
        resulting from, 311–314
      generally, 308–310
      non-prescribed conditions, 311
      prescribed conditions, 310, 311

Industrial injury—*continued*
  disablement benefit—*continued*
    causal link with relevant accident,
      306–308—
    generally, 303–305
    loss of faculty, 305, 306
    review, 314–316
  diseases. *See* INDUSTRIAL
    DISEASE
  employment risk—
    course of employment. *See*
      EMPLOYMENT
    generally, 276, 277, 690
    statutory test, 278
  exceptionally severe disablement
    allowance, 335, 691
  generally, 264–270, 689–692
  history of, 266–270
  hospital treatment allowance, 332,
    333
  increases and additions, 317 *et seq.*
  injury benefit—
    amount, 302, 690
    benefit period—
      days of incapacity, 300, 301
      duration of benefit, 301
      unavailability of benefit, 301,
        302
    causal link between injury and
      incapacity, 299, 300
    claim for. *See* CLAIMS
    deterritoriality, effect of, 681
    generally, 298, 299
      incapacity for work, 299
      payment of, 606 *et seq.*
      time limit for claiming, 594–
        596
  personal injury must be suffered,
    272
  persons covered, 270–272, 689
  special hardship allowance—
    amount and duration, 328–331
    "continuing" condition, 325–327
    generally, 318, 319, 691
    incapacity, 327, 328
    "permanent" condition, 322–325
    regular occupation to be
      regarded, 319–322
  successive accidents, 336, 337
  unemployability supplement, 317,
    318
  workmen's compensation cases,
    338–340
Injury,
  industrial. *See* INDUSTRIAL
    INJURY
  meaning, 359
  personal, meaning, 272

Secretary of State—*continued*
  procedure on determination by,
    622, 623
Self-employed,
  age limits, 60
  Class 2 contributions—
    amount, 61
    exceptions from liability, 60
    persons liable, 58–60
    contract for services distinguished
        from contract for service, 48
        et seq.
  contributions, amount of, 61
  definition, 58
  duration of occupation, 85
  earnings-related contributions, 62–
    64
  exceptions from liability to
      contribute, 60
  gainful occupation, difficulty of
      ascertaining, 81, 82
  general position of, 84
  insurance schemes affecting,
      generally, 43
  residence of earner, 60
Service,
  contract of. *See* CONTRACT
Share fishermen,
  position of, 131
  unemployment benefit, claim for,
    131
Short-time,
  "full extent normal" rule, 94, 95
  guarantee agreements, 93, 102–104
  meaning, 93
  "normal idle day" rule, 95–99
  unemployment benefit during, 92 *et
    seq.*
Sick pay,
  agreements as to, 442
Sickness,
  crediting of contributions during, 72
Sickness benefit,
  claim for. *See* CLAIMS
  contribution conditions, 149
  deterritioriality, effect of, 681
  disqualification—
    behaviour, failure to observe rules
        of, 161–163
    examination, failure to submit to,
      159, 160
    misconduct, 159
    period of, 163
    treatment, refusal to submit to,
      160
  generally, 137, 147–149, 686
  history of, 138–145

Sickness benefit—*continued*
  incapacity for work—
    disease or bodily disablement,
      150
    evidence of incapacity, 152–155
    exclusion of certain days, 156–158
    "incapable of work", meaning,
      151, 152
    mental disablement, 150, 151
    payment in respect of, generally,
      149, 150
    persons deemed incapable, 155,
      156
  payment of, 606 *et seq.*
  temporary absence, effect of, 410–
    412
  time-limit for claiming, 594–596
Social Security,
  benefits in cash or kind, 32–34
  financing of, 26–32
  cash benefit, levels of, 19–26
  contribution, types of, 28–30
  demographic aims, 7
  family relationships, effect on, 8
  generally, 1 *et seq.*
  ideologies, 1–7
  illicit relationships, 8
  insurance concept behind, 26–28
  means-tested benefits, 12–15
  needs, assumed, criterion of, 15–19
  objectives of, 1 *et seq.*
  selection and classificatioan of need,
    12–19
  sexual equality, considerations of, 9
  strategies, 12 *et seq.*
  taxation, general, contributions
      from, 30–32
  systems, relationship with, 34–39
  welfare provision, other forms, 32–
    39
  work and productivity, values
      connected with, 10
Social work service,
  generally, 578, 579
Spouse,
  excluded from treatment as
      employed earner, 271
Standing advisory bodies,
  generally, 579 *et seq.*
Strikes. *See* TRADE DISPUTES
Students,
  benefits for, 550–552, 685
Subsidiary occupations,
  exclusion of, where unemployment
      benefit claimed, 89, 90
Sunday,
  claim for sickness benefit, 157

Sunday—*continued*
claim for unemployment benefit on, 91
rest day, as, 91
Supplementary benefit,
appeals. *See* SUPPLEMENTARY
  BENEFIT APPEAL
  TRIBUNALS
assessment of—
  borders, 502, 503
  exceptional circumstances
    additions, 511–519
  generally, 489 *et seq.*
  rent, payments for, 494 *et seq.*
  resources, 503 *et seq.*
  scale rates, 490–494
attendance at benefit offices,
  necessity for, 485
blind claimants, 491, 492
caravan dwellers, 501
claim for—
  forms, 599
  home visit following, 600
  information to be supplied, 600
  time limit, 600
Commission. *See*
  SUPPLEMENTARY
  BENEFIT COMMISSION
disabled persons, 492
discretionary powers acts, 474, 509,
  572–576
entitlement to—
  age, condition as to, 480
  allowance and pension
    distinguished, 480
  foreign visitors, 481
  generally, 479, 480
  Northern Ireland, 481
  presence in Great Britain, 480,
    481
  resources, insufficient to meet
    requirements, 481
exceptional circumstances
  additions—
  discretionary powers, exercise of,
    512–516
  generally, 511, 512
  policy of Commission, 516–518
exclusions from benefit—
  full-time work, meaning, 482
  persons affected by trade
    disputes, 483
  persons completing secondary
    education, 483
  persons in full-time employment,
    482, 483
  aggregation rule, 485 *et seq.*

Supplementary benefit—*continued*
"family unit" for—
  children and other members of
    household, 488
  generally, 485, 486
  husband and wife members of
    same household, 486, 487
  persons living together, 487, 488
generally, 471–475, 693, 694
handicapped child, payment to, 483
homeless families, 549
hospital patients, 547, 548
housewives, treatment of, 500–502
insurance, allowance for, 500, 501
maintenance—
  generally, 539, 540
  separated wives, 541–545
  unmarried mothers, 545, 546
mental disorder, persons suffering
  from, 550
methods of payment, 489
mortgage payments, 501
non-householders, treatment of, 502
old people's homes, persons in,
  548–550
payment of, 608, 609
persons in full-time work not
  entitled to, 474
poor laws, history of, 475–477
poverty and, relationship, 472, 473
prisoners, 550
public assistance, history of, 475–
  479
registration for employment,
  condition of, 483–485
rent, payment for—
  calculation of rent, 497, 498
  flat sharers, 495, 496
  generally, 494
  hardship cases, 499
  householders and non-
    householders distinguished,
    495, 496
  method of payment, 499, 500
  treatment of householder paying
    rent, 496–500
  unreasonable rent, 498, 499
repairs, allowance for, 500, 501
resources, assessment of—
  applicant's resources, 504–506
  disregards, 507–511
  generally, 503, 504
  income and capital resources,
    506, 507
  partially disregarded, 509, 510
  taken fully into account, 510, 511
  wholly disregarded, 508, 509